COSTA RICA

CHRISTOPHER P. BAKER

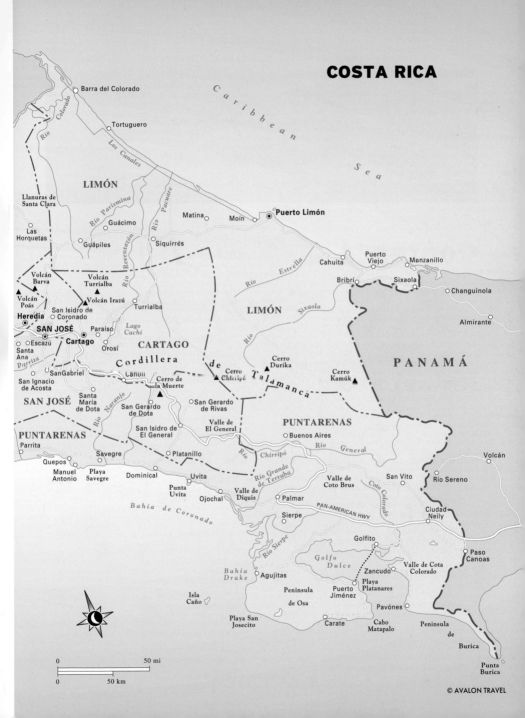

Contents

Discover Costa Rica

On my first visit to Costa Rica in 1985 I performed yoga in a crisply cool cloud forest, with accommodation in a Swiss-style hotel amid the pines. The next day I participated in dawn calisthenics on a Pacific beach within sight of marine turtles and monkeys. Therein lies its beauty.

Despite its diminutive size, Costa Rica is a kind of microcontinent unto itself – one sculpted to show off the full potential of the tropics. The diversity of terrain is remarkable. You can journey from the Amazon to a Swiss alpine forest simply by starting on the coastal plains and walking uphill. The tableau changes from dense rainforest, dry deciduous forests, open savanna, and lush wetlands to montane cloud forest swathing the upper slopes of volcanoes. Along the Pacific and Atlantic Oceans, dozens of inviting beaches run the gamut from frost-white to chocolate, and islands and offshore coral reefs open up a world more beautiful than a casket of gems.

The nation's 12 distinct ecological zones are home to an astonishing array of flora and fauna – approximately 5 percent of all known species on earth – and include more butterfly species than in the whole of Africa, and more than twice the number of bird species in the whole of the United States. Stay here long enough and you'll begin to think that with luck you might, like Noah, see examples of all the creatures on earth.

Unlike many destinations, where humans have driven the animals into the deepest seclusion, Costa Rica's wildlife loves to put on a song-and-dance. Animals and birds are prolific and relatively easy to spot. Sleek jaguars on the prowl. Sloths moving languidly among the high branches. Scarlet macaws that launch from their perches and go squalling away. The whistle of a quetzal is the tropical birder's Holy Grail.

Since my first visit, the country has also exploded as a world-class venue for active adventures – scuba diving, sportfishing, white-water rafting, surfing, and horseback riding. The adrenaline rush never stops, be it ATV tours or zipline adventures.

Plus, the nation boasts a huge choice of fantastic resorts, boutique hotels, rustic lodges, surfer camps, and budget cabinas. And while its neighbors have been racked by turmoil, Costa Rica has been blessed with a remarkable normalcy – few extremes of wealth and poverty, no standing army, a proud history as Central America's most stable democracy, and a quality of life among the highest in the Western Hemisphere.

Planning Your Trip

▶ WHERE TO GO

San José

The bustling capital city is a handy hub for forays farther afield. Pre-Columbian artifacts are exhibited at three small yet excellent museums; a handful of galleries satisfy art enthusiasts; and souvenir shoppers are well served by quality crafts stores. The city boasts superb restaurants, a thriving nightlife, and great hotels.

Central Highlands

Wrapped by volcanoes and rugged mountains, the densely populated highlands are tremendously scenic, with a springlike climate. The scenery is best enjoyed by ascending Poás or Irazú Volcano, with stops at Café Britt or Doka Estate, or to explore the nation's major pre-Columbian site at Guayabo National Monument. Two of the nation's premier white-water runs cascade from these mountains.

IF YOU HAVE . . .

- **ONE WEEK:** Visit Poás Volcano National Park, Arenal Volcano National Park, and Monteverde.
- **TWO WEEKS:** Add Rincón de la Vieja National Park, Playa Grande, Tamarindo, and Nosara.
- **THREE WEEKS:** Add Manuel Antonio and Osa Peninsula.
- **FOUR WEEKS:** Add Tortuguero National Park, Cahuita, and Puerto Viejo.

peering into the main crater at Poás Volcano

The Northern Zone

Guanacaste and the Northwest

The Caribbean Coast

Central Highlands

San José

The Nicoya Peninsula

Central Pacific

South-Central Costa Rica

Golfo Dulce and the Osa Peninsula

© AVALON TRAVEL

the coast. Anglers are gung-ho about Barra del Colorado.

The Northern Zone

The lowland is a center for active adventures focused around Arenal Volcano National Park. Hiking, hot springs, horseback riding, and zipline adventures are popular. Lake Arenal draws windsurfers and freshwater anglers, while Caño Negro National Wildlife Refuge is a nirvana for anglers and birders. Nature lodges grant access to rugged Braulio Carrillo National Park, and the Tenorio volcano region is evolving as a new frontier for active adventures.

The Caribbean Coast

This humid zone is notable for its Afro-Caribbean culture. Offbeat Cahuita and Puerto Viejo draw surfers and backpackers and serve as departure points for treks into indigenous reserves. Wildlife-rich Cahuita and Tortuguero National Parks are easily accessed—the latter by canal from waterfront nature lodges. Marine turtles lay eggs up and down

Guanacaste and the Northwest

The northwest is distinct for its climate and dry tropical forests: Birding is superb at Palo Verde National Park and Santa Rosa National Park, which boasts historical sites. This is also cowboy country; numerous ranches double as eco-centers at the base

lovers walking on Playa Guiones, Nosara

sunset off Corcovado National Park from the *Sea Voyager*

of volcanoes. The big draw is Monteverde, boasting attractions and activities that will hold your attention for days.

The Nicoya Peninsula

This region is known for its white-sand beaches linked by dirt roads that may require fordings. Scuba diving, surfing, and sportfishing are key draws. Playa Grande and Ostional are important nesting sites for marine turtles. Inland, Guaitíl preserves its indigenous pottery tradition and nearby Barra Honda is the nation's major speleological site. Accommodations range from surf camps to sublime large-scale resorts, concentrated at Playa Tamarindo and Bahía Culebra.

Central Pacific

Forest-clad mountains hem a narrow coastal plain fringed by beaches washed by waves beloved by surfers. Jacó, Costa Rica's most developed resort, is popular with the party crowd. Tárcoles is great for crocodile safaris; Carara National Park offers world-class birding; and Manuel Antonio combines all manner of wildlife encounters with a huge selection of fine lodging and dining. Nearby Quepos is a center for sportfishing. Whale-watching is a draw to the Costa Ballena.

Golfo Dulce and the Osa Peninsula

Soaking rains nurture the rainforests of Corcovado National Park. The humble port of Golfito is a base for sportfishing and forays to remote rainforest lodges. Kilometer-long waves wash up to Pavones. Tucked-away Drake Bay is good for whale-watching excursions and trips to Caño Island, an erstwhile indigenous ceremonial site. Some 500 kilometers southwest of Costa Rica, Cocos Island is off-limits to all but experienced divers.

South-Central Costa Rica

The nation's Cinderella region has relatively few sites of interest to tourists, excepting Las Cusingas (great for birding) and Wilson Botanical Gardens. Hale and hearty adventure seekers can follow the trail up Chirripó, the nation's highest mountain; the trailhead is accessed by one of several Shangri-la valleys that lead into the rugged La Amistad International Peace Park. Indigenous communities exist in isolation.

▶ WHEN TO GO

Costa Rica has two distinct seasons: dry season (December–April) and wet season (May–November). Although regional distinctions exist, rainy season is typified by brief afternoon showers or downpours. As the season progresses, more sustained rains occur, often lasting for days. Prices are usually lower in rainy season, and it is easier to find vacant rooms in popular destinations. The Caribbean and Osa Peninsula can be rainy year-round. Dry season is usually sunny.

Peak season rates usually apply for Christmas, New Year's, and Easter, when many accommodations and car rentals are booked months in advance.

My favorite time to visit is May through early June, when crowds have departed and the first rains have greened up the scenery.

▶ BEFORE YOU GO

Passports and Visas

Citizens of the United States, Canada, the United Kingdom, and most European nations traveling to Costa Rica need a passport valid for at least six months beyond their intended length of stay, plus a ticket for onward travel. Stays of up to 90 days are permitted without a visa.

Vaccinations

Officially, no vaccinations are required for entry into Costa Rica, but it's a good idea to be up to date on tetanus, typhoid, and hepatitis shots. If you plan on taking preventive medications against malaria, start taking them a few weeks before potential exposure.

Transportation

Most international visitors fly into San José's Juan Santamaría International Airport. Visitors planning on visiting only Nicoya and Guanacaste might consider flying in and out of Liberia's Daniel Oduber International Airport. Many people choose to travel around Costa Rica on inexpensive domestic flights. It's also easy to get between popular tourist destinations on cheap public buses and tourist shuttle vans. Car rental agencies are located in every major tourist destination, but it's wise to book ahead. A four-wheel-drive is essential; most main roads are paved, but many popular tourist spots are accessed by rutted dirt roads.

What to Take

Bright clothing tends to scare off wildlife; pack khakis and subdued greens, plus binoculars, for nature viewing. Pack a warm sweater or jacket for San José and the highlands. The lowlands are humid and hot; you'll want light, loose-fitting clothing. Everything should be drip-dry, cotton-polyester blends— denim jeans take forever to dry when wet. In wet season, eschew raincoats for a breathable, waterproof jacket (such as Gore-Tex) or a hooded poncho, plus a small umbrella.

A comfortable pair of sneakers will work for most occasions. Wear lightweight canvas hiking boots with ankle protection for hiking.

Knee-length shorts for men are acceptable almost anywhere, except in nicer restaurants; save your running shorts for the beach.

Space on buses and planes is limited. Limit yourself to one bag plus a small day pack or camera bag.

Explore Costa Rica

▶ THE 21-DAY BEST OF COSTA RICA

Few visitors have time to explore Costa Rica from tip to toe, but the following three-week itinerary takes in half a dozen of the best national parks, a potpourri of active adventures, and many of the best sights.

Day 1

Arrive at Juan Santamaría International Airport; transfer to the Hotel Grano de Oro or other hotel in San José. Take the afternoon to visit the Jade Museum and Pre-Columbian Gold Museum.

Day 2

An early-morning visit to Poás Volcano National Park is followed by a visit to the La Paz Waterfall Gardens. In late afternoon, get a feel for Costa Rica's coffee culture with a tour at Café Britt.

Day 3

The next day, head to Zoo Ave and the Botanical Orchid Garden, then continue to the La Fortuna area for two nights.

Day 4

Fill your first day with hiking at Arenal Volcano National Park; a ride on the Arenal Aerial Tram, including the zipline; and a soak at Tabacón Hot Springs. A traditional meal at La Choza is a good way to end the day.

Costa Rica's national orchid, at the Botanical Orchid Garden

THE BEACHCOMBER

Costa Rica boasts glorious beaches. Only a few, however, are of the frost-white variety, restricted to sections of Nicoya, plus Manuel Antonio National Park. Virtually all are backed by jungly forest; on remote beaches, it's not unusual to discover paw prints of jaguars drawn by the arrival of marine turtles. Swimming requires caution, however, as many beaches are known for riptides.

THE CARIBBEAN
Tortuguero: Stretching into the hazy horizon, this silvery beach backed by lush rainforest is the most important nesting site in the Caribbean for the green turtle.

Playa Blanca, Cahuita National Park: With several beautiful golden-sand beaches broken by rocky headlands, Cahuita is a great place to sunbathe or snorkel amid the offshore coral reef. Playa Blanca adjoins Cahuita village.

THE NICOYA PENINSULA
Playa Conchal: Although always crowded, this beach of tiny seashells changes from bleach white to gray, depending on tidal and weather conditions. The calm turquoise waters host a coral reef.

Playa Flamingo: Perhaps the most magnificent white-sand beach in the nation, this gently curving scimitar is cusped by rugged headlands.

Playa Grande: A miles-long beach with vast views across the bay toward Tamarindo. It's also the nation's prime nesting site for leatherback turtles.

Playa Montezuma: Stretching east from the eponymous village, this palm-shaded coral-colored beach is washed by crashing surf.

Playa Naranjo: Surrounded on two sides by swampy estuaries good for spotting crocodiles, this lovely golden sand beach provides access to trails that wind through Santa Rosa National Park. Big cats, tamanduas, and scarlet macaws are among the creatures to be seen.

Playa Ostional: Time your visit for an *arribada* (mass arrival) of olive ridley turtles and you'll be rewarded with the unique sight of thousands of turtles crawling ashore to lay their eggs.

Playa Pelada, Nosara: Studded with rocky islets and tidepools, this ruler-straight expanse can be 200 meters deep with the tide out.

Playa Santa Teresa: Rugged headlands and isles, tropical moist forest leaning over the beach, and fearsome surf combine to make this one of the most visually dramatic of the nation's beaches.

CENTRAL PACIFIC
Playa Manuel Antonio: Curling around a sheltered bay like a shepherd's crook, this beach has it all: calm turquoise waters, rocky headlands, rainforest behind, and views toward distant mountains.

Playas Esterillos: Four beaches in one running along some 20 kilometers of shoreline, these gray sands are palm-fringed for their entire length.

GOLFO DULCE AND THE OSA PENINSULA
Playa Platanares: A short distance east of Puerto Jiménez, Platanares abuts both rainforest and mangrove, is an important nesting site for marine turtles, and offers the potential of viewing whales and dolphins offshore.

Playa Zancudo: Washed by surf and littered with tree trunks, this beach has stupendous views across the Golfo Dulce.

Playa Flamingo, Nicoya Peninsula

Day 5

On day 5, opt for a horseback ride to La Catarata and an ATV tour or other activity such as white-water rafting.

Day 6

Transfer via Lake Arenal and Tilarán to Monteverde, where the Monteverde Lodge makes a fine base. After lunch, head to Selvatura for a canopy adventure and the Jewels of the Rainforest Bio-Art Exhibition.

Day 7

The next day rise early for a guided hike in Monteverde Cloud Forest Biological Reserve or Santa Elena Cloud Forest Reserve. In the afternoon, visit the Serpentarium and Ranarium. This evening, take a guided twilight walk at Bajo del Tigre.

Days 8-9

Transfer to Rincón de la Vieja National Park. After settling in at one of the nature lodges that double as activity centers, you'll want to visit the bubbling mud pools and fumaroles and partake of canopy tours, horseback riding, and hikes. If you are feeling adventurous, you can hike to the summit of the volcano with an early start.

Day 10

Continue north to Santa Rosa National Park for a hike offering great wildlife viewing.

Day 11

On day 11, head to the Nicoya Peninsula and Tamarindo, arriving in time for lunch at a beachfront restaurant. This evening, head to Playa Grande to witness marine turtles laying eggs (in season)—you'll need to make reservations.

Day 12

The next day, active travelers might take a surfing lesson or head out to sea on a half-day sportfishing excursion. Spend the rest of the day sunning on the beach or by the pool, or follow the beach trail to Playa

Arenal is one of the world's most active volcanoes.

L'Acqua Viva resort, Nosara

Ventanas, with tidepools for snorkeling and bathing.

Day 13

Transfer to Nosara via Ostional Wildlife Refuge. If you're driving, the coast road will prove an adventure! With good timing and prior planning, you can visit the turtle *arribada* at Ostional.

Day 14

Spend the rest of your time surfing or relaxing at Nosara, where the beaches are good for tidepooling. Playa Guiones is popular with surfers while Playa Nosara sees the occasional turtle *arribada*.

Day 15

On the morning of day 15, depart Nicoya for the Central Pacific and a crocodile safari on the Río Tárcoles.

Days 16-17

Continue to Manuel Antonio for wildlife viewing, snorkeling, and relaxing in and around Manuel Antonio National Park. The resort hotels here offer superb accommodations, and there are plenty of excellent restaurants and a lively night scene.

Day 18

Transfer to San José and fly from Pavas airport to Carate, on the Osa Peninsula. Overnight at a nearby nature lodge. Alternately, fly to Tortuguero where you can enjoy two days exploring Tortuguero National Park by canoe or boat.

Day 19

A guided hike along coastal and rainforest trails in Corcovado National Park leads to waterfalls and offers phenomenal wildlife sightings.

Days 20-21

Return to San José for your last night in Costa Rica. Relax on your final afternoon or spend time shopping for souvenirs downtown, treating yourself to a meal at either Restaurante Grano de Oro or Esquina de Buenos Aires. Depart on day 21.

▶ OFFBEAT COSTA RICA

If you want to escape the madding crowds and experience the *real* off-the-beaten-path Costa Rica, the following itinerary will help you see and experience some truly fascinating places that most visitors miss.

Days 1-3

After arriving at Juan Santamaría International Airport, transfer to the Terminal Caribe for a bus to Cahuita for two days of relaxing at this lazy Caribbean village. While here, consider a horseback ride along Playa Negra, and snorkeling at Cahuita National Park, which you'll also want to explore on foot for marvelous wildlife encounters. Make the most of regional cuisine with dinner at the down-home Miss Edith's.

yellow eyelash viper

Days 4-5

Head south the short distance to Puerto Viejo, a great base for simply hanging out; the motto here is sunning by day and kicking it at night at Puerto Viejo's hip and funky barefoot and carefree bars. Surfers will want to tackle Salsa Brava, the local wave. Others might want to explore Gandoca-Manzanillo Wildlife Refuge, and even sign up for a

tannin-stained lagoon at Gandoca-Manzanillo

TOP WILDLIFE SPOTS

National parks, wildlife refuges, and biological reserves are found throughout the country. They range from swampy wetlands to dry forest environments, and from lowland rainforests to high-mountain cloud forests. There's enough diversity of terrain and wildlife to keep nature lovers enthralled for weeks. Plan to visit three or four diverse reserves to get the full range. Many of the best reserves are privately owned, including breeding centers and zoos. Unless you're hugely experienced in tropical environments, I recommend that you sign up for guided natural history excursions; at the least, you should hire a local naturalist guide. You'll see many times more critters in the company of an eagle-eyed guide.

THE BEST OF THE BEST

- **Tortuguero National Park:** This is my favorite place for wildlife viewing, not least because it's like shooting fish in a barrel as you glide by boat through the canals and lagoons, with the forest open to view. River otters, caimans, and even manatees are some creatures you might spot. Turtle-viewing at night is icing on the cake (page 174).

- **Manuel Antonio National Park:** This popular park offers easy wildlife viewing from wide-open trails (page 459).

- **Santa Rosa National Park:** Wildlife-rich, this is a great venue to visit in the dry season when deciduous trees drop their leaves (page 318).

- **Corcovado National Park:** Remote and with a dense rainforest, it is worth the effort to get here; it's one place you may be able to spot tapirs and jaguars, and scarlet macaws are a dime a dozen (page 501).

- **Monteverde Cloud Forest Biological Reserve:** Monteverde draws birders keen to spot a quetzal (page 285).

- **Quetzals National Park:** Your chances of seeing quetzals are vastly improved at this new national park (page 148).

- **Jungle Safari** on the **Tárcoles River:** You are guaranteed close-up sightings of giant crocodiles (page 426).

- **Palo Verde National Park:** This national park is known for its vast flocks of waterfowl and migratory birds (page 306).

- **Zoo Ave:** The nation's largest zoo, it provides a great intro to all the creatures you might see in the wild (page 117).

- **La Paz Waterfall Gardens:** This splendid park has a fabulous aviary plus snake, butterfly, hummingbird, and frog exhibits (page 104).

red-eyed tree frog

Cerro Chirripó and Los Crestones from Talamanca Reserve

kayak trip or dolphin safari. And trips into remote indigenous reserves are a great way to learn from and about the nation's earth-grounded cultures.

Days 6-7

Return to San José and take a bus to the surfers' village of Dominical. The travel could take the better part of a day. Once settled in, surfers will no doubt want to check out the wave action while novices can take lessons. Nearby Hacienda Barú offers the thrill of a canopy tour and kayaking, and you can even sleep atop a tree! An excursion to Don Lulo's Nauyaca Waterfall will satisfy the urge for an invigorating hike.

Days 8-9

On day 8, head to Reserva Biológica La Danta, an organic fruit farm in the Escaleras hills. Here, take a two-day hike into the mountains to spend a night with a *campesino* (peasant) family.

Days 10-12

Return to Dominical and take a bus to San Isidro and onward to San Gerardo de Rivas,

at the upper reaches of a Shangri-la valley good for spotting quetzals. Be sure to pack some warm clothes. Having previously made a reservation through the national parks service, begin your hike in Chirripó National Park, accompanied by a local guide. You'll overnight near the mountain summit. The next day you'll be on the trail well before dawn for the final hike to the summit of Costa Rica's highest mountain. Congratulations! After time to enjoy the thrill, return to San Gerardo de Rivas, where you can overnight in charmingly rustic accommodations.

Days 13-15

Take a bus to Buenos Aires, from there a Jeep-taxi can deliver you to Durika Biological Reserve, a well-run commune deep in the mountains on the edge of La Amistad International Park. The rugged drive is not for the faint-hearted, but once there you can participate in a reforestation project, and even help milk the goats.

Day 16

Take a public bus to San Isidro and from there to San José for your flight home.

► FAMILY ADVENTURE

Catering to kids takes some forethought. Here I offer a suggested itinerary that combines educational and fun options sure to keep children (and parents) enthralled.

Day 1

Arrive at Juan Santamaría International Airport; transfer to a hotel in or near San José. On your first full day, take a fun-filled tour of Café Britt, where actors in period costume educate about coffee production.

Day 2

Today it's uphill to visit La Paz Waterfall Gardens, with time to hike to the waterfalls (it's a stiff climb, so be prepared) as well as viewing the snake, frog, butterfly, and bird exhibits. You may want to overnight at the Peace Lodge, with its charming ambience straight out of J. R. R. Tolkien's *Lord of the Rings*.

La Paz Waterfall Gardens

cocoa Woodcreeper at Selva Verde

Days 3-4

This morning, continue downhill to Selva Verde for guided hikes in the rainforest, including a nocturnal nature hike. The lodge makes a good base for a white-water raft trip on the Río Sarapiquí on day 4 before transferring to the Rainforest Aerial Tram for an educational ride through the forest canopy. The tram facility also includes a snake exhibit, plus frog and butterfly gardens. Continue to San José for overnight.

Day 5

Today, take the children to Zoo Ave, where they'll get to see animals and birds typical of Costa Rica, and to the World of Snakes, where the kids can hold snakes. Continue to El Silencio de Los Angeles Cloud Forest Reserve for an overnight stay at Villablanca Cloud Forest Hotel & Spa.

Day 6

The next morning, take a guided hike in the cloud forest before continuing to Manuel Antonio via the Río Tárcoles for an afternoon crocodile safari.

VIEWING AND SAVING MARINE TURTLES

Turtles nest at beaches all along the Caribbean and Pacific shores. Here are the major venues worth planning a trip around:

CARIBBEAN COAST

- **Barra de Matina/Parismina:** Leatherbacks, greens, and hawksbills come ashore at this private sanctuary north of Puerto Limón (page 173).

- **Gandoca-Manzanillo National Wildlife Refuge:** April and May are the best months to spot leatherbacks. By July, they are gone, replaced by greens, which can be seen in large numbers through September. Hawksbills also come ashore year-round, mostly March–August (page 216).

- **Tortuguero:** Loggerheads and hawksbills come ashore year-round but especially in August. Green turtles nest here June–November (page 176).

PACIFIC COAST

- **Curú National Wildlife Refuge:** Three species of turtles come ashore at this private refuge, on the eastern coast of the Nicoya Peninsula (page 403).

- **Marino Las Baulas National Park:** Playa Grande is Costa Rica's preeminent nesting site for leatherback turtles. Leatherbacks come ashore October–April. Olive ridley and green turtles can be seen here in small numbers May–August (page 361).

- **Ostional National Wildlife Refuge:** This 248-hectare refuge, north of Playa Nosara, protects the major nesting site of olive ridleys (locally called *lora*). It is one of three sites in Costa Rica where synchronized mass nestings (*arribadas*) of the olive ridley occur, at two- to four-week intervals (generally between the third quarter and full moon) April–December, peaking July–September. During each *arribada* (which may last four to eight days), up to 120,000 turtles may nest at Ostional. Solitary nesters can be seen on most nights. Leatherbacks and Pacific greens also nest here (page 381).

- **Playa Camaronal:** Located in south-central Nicoya, this beach experienced an *arribada* for the first time in 2006, although ridleys nest year-round, and leatherbacks nest March and April (page 395).

VOLUNTEER PROGRAMS TO SAVE THE TURTLES

If you're interested in helping save endangered marine turtles, consider volunteering with the following organizations:

- **Caribbean Conservation Corps** (CCC, 4424 NW 13th St. Suite #A1, Gainesville, FL 32609, U.S. tel. 352/373-6441 or 800/678-7853, www.cccturtle.org)

- **Earthwatch Institute** (3 Clock Tower Place, Suite 100, Box 75, Maynard, MA 01754, U.S. tel. 978/461-0081 or 800/776-0188, www.earthwatch.org)

- **Save the Turtles of Parismina** (P.O. Box 738, Occidental, CA 94565, tel. 707/538-8084, www.costaricaturtles.com)

ridley turtles nesting during an *arribada* at Playa Camaronal

the beach at Manuel Antonio National Park

Days 7-8

Enjoy two days of relaxing on the beach, hikes in Manuel Antonio National Park, plus options for canopy tours, white-water rafting, surfing lessons, inflatable sea-kayak trips, and even a boat trip to spot whales and dolphins on the Pink Panther Boat.

Days 9-10

On day 9, transfer back to San José with a stop at Panaca, where a horse-drawn carriage ride delivers you to a fascinating farm facility with trained dog exhibitions, a petting zoo, and dozens of farm animals from around the world. On your final day, transfer to the airport for your departure flight.

▶ ADRENALINE RUSH

The vast majority of visitors come to Costa Rica to *do* something fun. In fact, the chance to partake of bicycling, golfing, surfing, white-water rafting, and zipline canopy tours is one of the great appeals of Costa Rica. Wherever you are in the country, there are dozens of options to choose from. Here I guide you to some of the best of countless experiences.

Day 1

Following arrival at Juan Santamaría International Airport, transfer to Villablanca Cloud Forest Hotel & Spa.

Day 2

The next morning, take a guided hike in the

aerial tram

SURF'S UP

Dedicated surfers are constantly in search of the perfect wave. For many, the search has ended in Costa Rica, the "Hawaii of Latin American surf." You're spoiled for choice, with dozens of world-class venues and no shortage of surf camps, surf schools, and rental outlets.

THE CARIBBEAN COAST

The Caribbean has fewer breaks than the Pacific but still offers great surfing. Waves are short yet powerful rides, sometimes with Hawaiian-style radical waves. The best time is late May through early September and December-March (when Atlantic storms push through the Caribbean, creating three-meter swells).

A 20-minute boat ride from Puerto Limón is **Isla Uvita,** with a strong and dangerous left. Farther south there are innumerable short breaks at **Cahuita.** Still farther south, **Puerto Viejo** has the biggest rideable waves in Costa Rica. Immediately south, **Playa Cocles** is good for beginners.

GUANACASTE AND THE NORTHWEST

Surfing is centered on **Santa Rosa National Park.** The best time is during the rainy season (May–November). Hot spots such as Witch's Rock at **Playa Naranjo** (one of the best beach breaks in the country) require four-wheel drive for access, but surf excursions operate from Nicoya beach resorts.

THE NICOYA PENINSULA

Nicoya offers more than 50 prime surf spots, more than anywhere else in the nation. **Tamarindo** is the surfing capital and is an excellent jumping-off place for a surf safari south to more isolated beaches. Just north of Tamarindo is **Playa Grande,** with a five-kilometer-long beach break acclaimed as Costa Rica's most accessible consistent break. There's fine surfing the whole way south from Tamarindo, including at **Playa Avellanas** and **Playa**

Negra, a narrow beach with fast waves breaking over a coral shelf – definitely for experts only when the waves are big. Continuing south you'll find **Nosara** and **Playas Sámara, Coyote, Manzanillo,** and **Malpaís,** all with good surf, lively action, and several surf camps.

CENTRAL PACIFIC

The best time is July to December. Central Pacific surfing centers on **Jacó,** though the waves there really appeal to beginners and intermediates. Farther south lie **Playa Hermosa,** which has expert beach breaks and an international contest every August, and **Playas Esterillos Este and Oeste.** Farther south, what **Manuel Antonio** lacks in consistency it more than makes up for in natural beauty. **Dominical** has "militant" sandbars and long point waves in an equally beautiful tropical setting.

GOLFO DULCE AND THE OSA PENINSULA

The cognoscenti head to **Pavones,** on the southern shore of the Golfo Dulce. On a decent day, the fast, nearly one-kilometer left break is one of the longest in the world. The waves are at their grandest in rainy season, when the long left point can offer a three-minute ride. **Cabo Matapalo,** on the Osa Peninsula, is another top spot.

surf lessons at Tamarindo

ziplining through the cloud forest

Day 3

Plan an ATV tour, go mountain biking, or go kayaking on the Peñas Blancas River. You'll want at least half a day for hiking Arenal Volcano National Park, followed by an invigorating soak at Tabacón Hot Springs or one of the other hot spring facilities.

Days 4-6

Transfer to Tamarindo, the Pacific beach resort where your activity options include sportfishing, scuba diving, and surfing. Tamarindo is a great place to learn to surf, and the rides at Playa Grande and Playa Avellanas will challenge experienced surfers. You can fill in any spare hours with ATV tours or other off-road adventures, and the Tamarindo Tennis Club will put you in the swing.

cloud forest before continuing to La Fortuna, the country's premier activity center. Fill the days with a horseback ride to La Catarata waterfall; a zipline ride at the Arenal Aerial Tram or another of the many options for canopy tours.

Day 7

Enjoy a relaxing day as you transfer via San José to Turrialba, arriving mid-afternoon

the towns and beaches of Langosta, Tamarindo, and Playa Grande

Tamarindo beach is family friendly.

Day 8

On the morning of day 8, be prepared for an exhilarating white-water rafting trip on the Pacuare River, the nation's most exciting run. Return to San José in the late afternoon for your final overnight.

Day 9

Transfer to San José airport for your departure flight.

SAN JOSÉ

San José, the nation's capital, squats on the floor of the Meseta Central, a fertile upland basin 1,150 meters (3,773 feet) above sea level in the heart of Costa Rica. Surrounded by mountains, it's a magnificent setting. The city's central position makes it an ideal base for forays into the countryside, applying the hub-and-spoke system of travel—almost every part of the country is within a four-hour drive.

San José—or "Chepe," as Ticos call it—dominates national life. Two-thirds of the nation's urban population lives in greater (or metropolitan) San José, whose population of 1.3 million represents 30 percent of the nation's total. San José is congested, bustling, and noisy. Its commercial center is dominated by hotels, offices, ugly modern high-rises, and shops. Though the city is not without its share of homeless people and beggars, there are few of the ghoulish *tugurios* (slums) that scar the hillsides of so many other Latin American cities. The modest working-class *barrios* (neighborhoods) are mostly clean and well ordered, while the tranquil residential districts such as Sabana Sur, San Pedro, and Rohrmoser are blessed with gracious houses with green lawns and high metal fences.

The city's chaos of architectural styles is part Spanish, part Moorish, and many streets in the older neighborhoods are still lined with one- or two-story houses made of wood or even adobe, with ornamental grillwork. What few older structures remain are of modest interest, however: The city is almost wholly lacking the grand colonial structures of, say, Havana or Mexico City. If it's colonial quaintness you're seeking, skip San José.

© CHRISTOPHER P. BAKER

HIGHLIGHTS

◖ Museo del Oro Precolumbino: The highlight of the Museos Banco Central de Costa Rica, this splendid collection of pre-Columbian gold and jade displays a cornucopia of indigenous ornaments and artifacts. Also here is an excellent numismatic museum (page 31).

◖ Teatro Nacional: San José's architectural pride and joy gleams after a recent restoration. View by day, then don your duds for a evening classical performance in season (page 31).

◖ Museo de Jade: The world's largest col-

lection of pre-Columbian jade ornamentation is exhibited in creative displays in a recently opened new facility (page 41).

◖ Parque Nacional: A breath of fresh air in the crowded city, this leafy park is the setting for the Monumento Nacional (page 42).

◖ Mercado Central: Tuck your wallet safely away to explore this tight-packed warren of stalls and stores selling everything from pig's heads to saddles. This is a great place to eat for pennies in true Tico fashion (page 44).

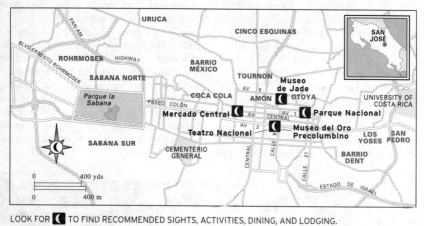

LOOK FOR ◖ TO FIND RECOMMENDED SIGHTS, ACTIVITIES, DINING, AND LODGING.

Nonetheless, the city offers several first-rate museums and galleries. Despite its working-class tenor, the city is large enough and its middle-class component cosmopolitan enough in outlook to support a vital cultural milieu. And the city has scores of accommodations for every budget, including backpackers' hostels and one of the world's preeminent boutique hotels. The restaurant scene is impressive, with dozens of globe-spanning eateries, including some exciting nouvelle options. And night owls will appreciate San José's vivacious nightlife, from modest casinos to raging discos with Latin music hot enough to cook the pork.

PLANNING YOUR TIME

The vast majority of visitors to the country spend one or two days in the capital city, whose bona fide tourist attractions can be counted on two hands. After a day or two, it is time to move on.

You'll appreciate basing yourself in a leafy residential district to escape the noise and bustle of downtown, where the major sights of interest are located. Your checklist of must-sees downtown should include **Teatro Nacional,** San José'slate 19th-century belle-epoque theater, and the modest **Catedral Metropólitana,** as well as the **Fidel Tristan Museo de Jade** and **Museo de Oro Precolumbino,** which honor the nation's pre-Columbian legacy with fine displays. The **Centro Nacional de Cultura,** also downtown, pays tribute to the works of contemporary artists, as does the **Contemporary Art Museum,** near Sabana Parque. If you enjoy walking, the historic **Barrio Amón** district makes for a pleasant stroll. By night, **El Pueblo,** a shopping and entertainment complex north of downtown, will prove fulfilling.

San José's outer-perimeter sights are few. An exception is **Pueblo Antiguo,** where the nation's almost extinct traditional lifestyle is honored in yesteryear re-creations.

SAFETY CONCERNS

Avoid driving in San José. Despite the city's grid system of one-way streets, finding your way around can be immensely frustrating. San José is ideal for walking: Downtown is compact, with everything of interest within a few blocks of the center. Watch out for potholes, tilted flagstones, and gaping sewer holes. And be wary when crossing streets—Tico drivers give no mercy to those still in the road when the light turns to green. Don't take your eyes off the traffic for a moment. Stand well away from the curb, especially on corners, where buses often mount the curb.

San José has a high crime rate. Be especially wary in and around the "Coca-Cola" bus terminal (avoid the area altogether at night) and the red-light district south of Avenida 2 (especially between Calles Central and 10) and the sleazy zone northwest of the Mercado Central. Be cautious in parks. And give a wide berth to Barrio Lomas, in the extreme west of Pavas; this is the city's desperately poor slum area and the domain of violent gangs. Also avoid Parque Nacional at night. Don't use buses at night, and be alert if you use them by day.

HISTORY

Until little more than 200 years ago, San José was no more than a few muddy lanes around which clustered a bevy of ramshackle hovels. The village first gained stature in 1737 when a thatched hermitage was built to draw together the residents then scattered throughout the valley. The new settlement was christened Villa Nueva de la Boca del Monte del Valle de Abra, later shortened to San José in honor of the local patron saint.

San José quickly grew to equal Cartago (the colonial capital city founded in 1564 by Juan Vásquez de Coronado) in size and developed a lucrative monopoly on the tobacco and nascent coffee trades, whose profits funded civic buildings. By the close of the 18th century, San José had a cathedral, a mint, a town council building, and military quarters.

When the surprise news of independence from Spain arrived by mail in October 1821, the councils of the four cities (Alajuela, Cartago, Heredia, and San José) met to determine their fate, and a constitution—the Pacto de Concordia—was signed. Alas, says historian Carlos Monge Alfaro, early Costa Rica was not a unified province but a "group of villages separated by narrow regionalisms." A bloody struggle for regional control soon ensued.

On April 5, 1823, the two sides clashed in the Ochomogo Hills. The victorious republican forces stormed and captured Cartago. San José thus became the nation's capital city. Its growing prominence, however, soon engendered resentment and discontent. In March 1835, in a conciliatory gesture, San José's city fathers offered to rotate the national capital among the four cities every four years. Unfortunately, the other cities had a bee in their collective bonnet. In September 1835, they formed a league, chose a president, and on September 26 attacked San José in an effort to topple the government. The Josefinos won what came to be known as La Guerra de la Liga (The War of the League), and the city has remained the nation's capital ever since.

By the mid-1800s the coffee boom was bringing prosperity, culture, and refinement to the once-humble backwater. San José developed a substantial middle class eager to spend its newfound wealth for the social good. Mud roads were bricked over and the streets illuminated by kerosene lamps. Tramways were built.

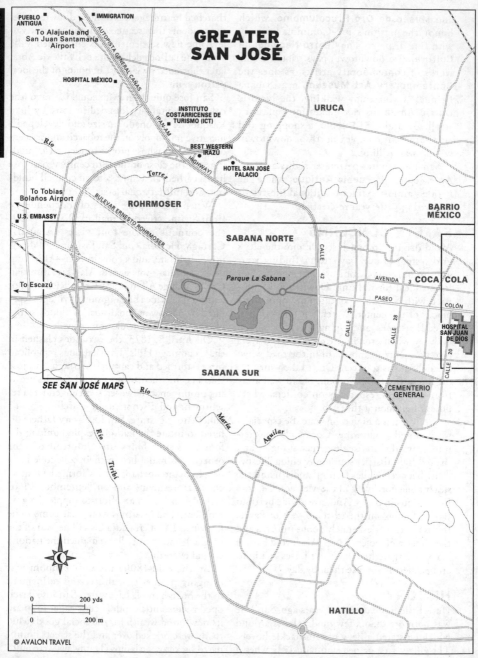

GREATER SAN JOSÉ

PUEBLO ANTIGUA

IMMIGRATION

To Alajuela and San Juan Santamaría Airport

AUTOPISTA GENERAL CAÑAS

HOSPITAL MÉXICO

PAN-AM

INSTITUTO COSTARRICENSE DE TURISMO (ICT)

URUCA

Río

Torres

BEST WESTERN IRAZÚ

HIGHWAY

HOTEL SAN JOSÉ PALACIO

To Tobias Bolaños Airport

BULEVAR ERNESTO ROHRMOSER

ROHRMOSER

U.S. EMBASSY

BARRIO MÉXICO

SABANA NORTE

CALLE 42

To Escazú

Parque La Sabana

AVENIDA 3

COCA COLA

PASEO

COLÓN

CALLE 36

CALLE 28

HOSPITAL SAN JUAN DE DIOS

CALLE 20

SABANA SUR

SEE SAN JOSÉ MAPS

Río

María

Aguilar

CEMENTERIO GENERAL

Río Tiribí

HATILLO

0   200 yds

0   200 m

© AVALON TRAVEL

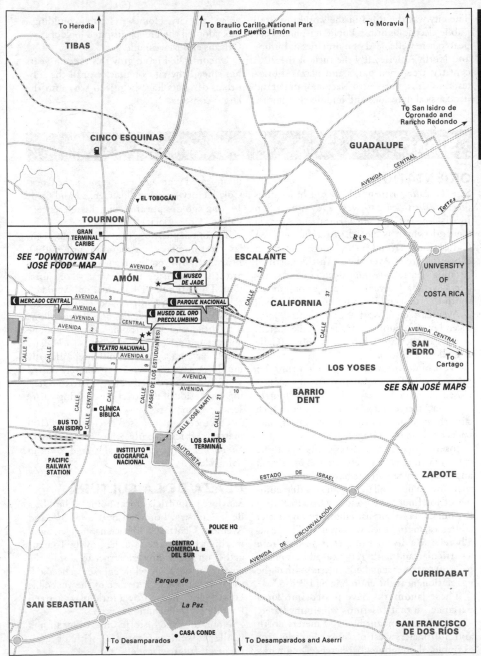

To Heredia

To Braulio Carillo National Park and Puerto Limón

To Moravia

TIBAS

To San Isidro de Coronado and Rancho Redondo

CINCO ESQUINAS

GUADALUPE

AVENIDA CENTRAL

Torres

▼ EL TOBOGÁN

TOURNON

GRAN TERMINAL CARIBE

Río

SEE "DOWNTOWN SAN JOSÉ FOOD" MAP

OTOYA

ESCALANTE

AVENIDA 9

AMÓN

★ MUSEO DE JADE

CALLE 23

CALLE 37

UNIVERSITY OF COSTA RICA

MERCADO CENTRAL

AVENIDA 3

AVENIDA 1

PARQUE NACIONAL

CALIFORNIA

AVENIDA CENTRAL

AVENIDA CENTRAL

AVENIDA 2

MUSEO DEL ORO PRECOLUMBINO

SAN PEDRO

To Cartago

CALLE 14

CALLE 8

TEATRO NACIONAL

AVENIDA 6

LOS YOSES

AVENIDA 9

CALLE 2

(PASEO DE LOS ESTUDIANTES)

AVENIDA

AVENIDA 8

SEE SAN JOSÉ MAPS

AVENIDA

BARRIO DENT

CALLE CENTRAL

CALLE

CALLE

CALLE 21

10

CLÍNICA BÍBLICA

CALLE JOSÉ MARTÍ

BUS TO SAN ISIDRO

LOS SANTOS TERMINAL

ZAPOTE

PACIFIC RAILWAY STATION

INSTITUTO GEOGRÁFICA NACIONAL

AUTOPISTA

ESTADO DE ISRAEL

POLICE HQ

AVENIDA DE CIRCUNVALACIÓN

CURRIDABAT

CENTRO COMERCIAL DEL SUR

Parque de

La Paz

SAN SEBASTIAN

SAN FRANCISCO DE DOS RÍOS

• CASA CONDE

To Desamparados

To Desamparados and Aserrí

The city was the third in the world to install public electric lighting. Public telephones appeared here well ahead of most cities in Europe and North America. By the turn of the 20th century, tree-lined parks and plazas, libraries, museums, the Teatro Nacional, and grand neoclassical mansions and middle-class homes graced the city. Homes and public buildings, too, adopted the French-inspired look of New Orleans and Martinique.

Uncontrolled rapid growth in recent years has spread the city's tentacles until the suburban districts have begun to blur into the larger complex.

Sights

ORIENTATION

Streets *(calles)* run north to south; avenues *(avenidas)* run east to west. Downtown San José is centered on Calle Central and Avenida Central (which is closed to traffic between Calles Central and 11), though the main thoroughfare is Avenida 2. To the north of Avenida Central, *avenidas* ascend in odd numbers (Avenida 1, Avenida 3, and so on); to the south they descend in even numbers (Avenida 2, Avenida 4, etc.). West of Calle Central, *calles* ascend in even numbers (Calle 2, Calle 4, etc.); to the east they ascend in odd numbers (Calle 1, Calle 3, and so on).

West of downtown, Paseo Colón runs 2.5 kilometers to Parque Sabana (Paseo Colón is closed to traffic Sundays). East of downtown, Avenida 2 merges into Avenida Central, which runs through the Los Yoses and San Pedro districts en route to Cartago.

Josefinos (as San José residents like to be called) rarely refer to street addresses by *avenida* and *calle*. Very few streets have street numbers, there are no post codes, and an amazing number of Josefinos have no idea what street they live on! Costa Ricans use landmarks, not street addresses, to find their way around. They usually refer to a distance in meters *(metros)* from a particular landmark. A typical address might be "200 meters east and 425 meters south of the gas station, near the church in San Pedro."

These landmarks have passed into local parlance, so that Josefinos will immediately know where is meant by "100 meters north and 300 meters west of Auto Mercado," for example, although many reference landmarks disappeared years ago. For example, the Coca-Cola factory near Avenida Central and Calle 14 long ago disappeared, but the reference is still to "Coca-Cola."

The initial phase of a plan to introduce regular street numbers was begun in spring 2000. Progress, however, has been slow. Addresses are still written by the nearest street junction. Thus, the Bar Esmeralda, on Avenida 2 midway between Calles 5 and 7, gives its address as "Avenida 2, Calles 5/7." In telephone directories and advertisements, *calle* may be abbreviated as "c," and *avenida* as "a." Many streets have no signs. And although officially buildings have numbers, they're rarely posted and almost never used. Thus, there's no telling which side of the street the building you're seeking is on.

Distances are expressed in *cien metros* (100 meters), which usually refers to one block. *Cinquenta metros* (50 meters) is used to mean half a block.

PLAZA DE LA CULTURA

San José's unofficial focal point is the Plaza de la Cultura, bordered by Calles 3/5 and Avenidas Central/2. Musicians, jugglers, and marimba bands entertain the crowds. Tourists gather on the southwest corner to absorb the colorful atmosphere while enjoying a beer and food on the open-air terrace of the venerable Gran Hotel, fronted by a little plaza named **Parque Mora Fernández**.

Note, too, the historic **Cine Diversiones** (Calle 5, Avenidas Central/2), with a beautiful metal-filigree facade.

© CHRISTOPHER P. BAKER

entrance to Museo del Oro Precolumbino

⟨ Museo del Oro Precolumbino

The world-class Pre-Columbian Gold Museum (tel. 506/2243-4202, 2243-4216 for tickets, www.museosdelbancocentral .org, 9:30 A.M.–5 P.M. daily, $7), in the triple-tiered former bank vaults beneath the plaza (the entrance is on Calle 5), is the highlight of the Museos Banco Central de Costa Rica, run by the state-owned Banco Central. The more than 2,000 glittering pre-Columbian gold artifacts displayed weigh in at over 22,000 troy ounces. Highlights include displays on early metallurgy and a gold-adorned, life-size *cacique* (chieftain), plus there's a large collection of pre-Columbian metates and more. A collection of old coins is displayed in the adjoining **Museo Numismática** (Numismatic Museum), while a small exhibit hall features works from the bank's art collection.

A self-guided audiotape tour costs $2. Guided tours are given with one week's notice ($35, 1–15 people). Bring identification for entry.

⟨ Teatro Nacional

The nation's architectural showpiece, the National Theater (Avenida 2, Calles 3/5, tel. 506/2221-9417, www.teatronacional.go.cr, 9 A.M.–4 P.M. Mon.–Sat., $5), on the south side of Plaza de la Cultura, is justifiably a source of national pride. The theater was conceived in 1890, when a European opera company featuring the prima donna Adelina Patti toured Central America but was unable to perform in Costa Rica because there was no suitable theater. Jilted, the ruling *cafeteleros* (coffee barons) voted a tax on coffee exports to fund construction of a theater, and craftsmen from all over Europe were imported. It was inaugurated on October 21, 1897, to a performance of *Faust* by the Paris Opera.

Outside, the classical Renaissance facade is topped by statues (they're replicas; the originals are inside) symbolizing Dance, Music, and Fame; note the figures of Beethoven and Spanish dramatist Calderón de la Barca to each side of the entrance. Inside, the vestibule, done in pink marble, rivals the best of ancient Rome,

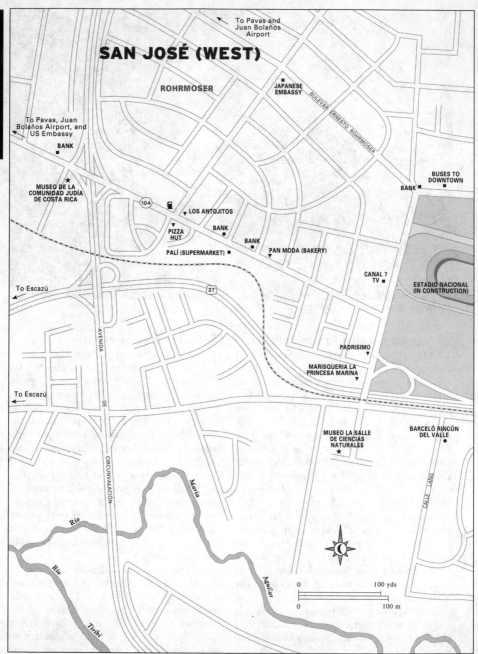

SAN JOSÉ (WEST)

ROHRMOSER

To Pavas and
Juan Bolaños
Airport

JAPANESE
EMBASSY

BULEVAR ERNESTO ROHRMOSER

To Pavas, Juan
Bolaños Airport, and
US Embassy

BANK

BUSES TO
DOWNTOWN

BANK

MUSEO DE LA
COMUNIDAD JUDÍA
DE COSTA RICA

104

LOS ANTOJITOS

PIZZA
HUT

BANK

BANK

PALÍ (SUPERMARKET)

PAN MODA (BAKERY)

CANAL 7
TV

ESTADIO NACIONAL
(IN CONSTRUCTION)

To Escazú

27

AVENIDA DE CIRCUNVALACIÓN

To Escazú

PADRISIMO

MARISQUERIA LA
PRINCESA MARINA

MUSEO LA SALLE
DE CIENCIAS
NATURALES

BARCELÓ RINCÓN
DEL VALLE

CALLE LANG

María

Río

Río

Aguilar

Tiribí

0   100 yds

0   100 m

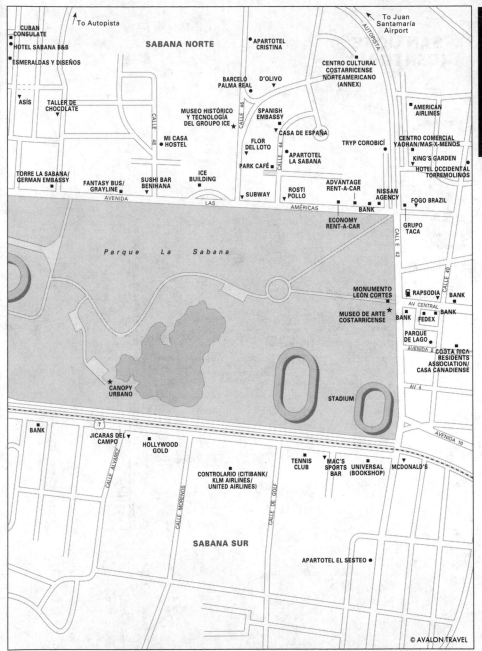

To Autopista

To Juan
Santamaría
Airport

CUBAN
CONSULATE

HOTEL SABANA B&B

ESMERALDAS Y DISEÑOS

SABANA NORTE

APARTOTEL
CRISTINA

CENTRO CULTURAL
COSTARRICENSE
NORTEAMERICANO
(ANNEX)

BARCELÓ
PALMA REAL

D'OLIVO

ASÍS

TALLER DE
CHOCOLATE

MUSEO HISTÓRICO
Y TECNOLOGÍA
DEL GROUPO ICE

SPANISH
EMBASSY

AMERICAN
AIRLINES

CALLE 46

MI CASA
HOSTEL

CASA DE ESPAÑA

CENTRO COMERCIAL
YAOHAN/MAS-X-MENOS

CALLE 48

FLOR
DEL LOTO

TRYP COROBICÍ

CALLE 44

KING'S GARDEN

PARK CAFÉ

APARTOTEL
LA SABANA

HOTEL OCCIDENTAL
TORREMOLINOS

TORRE LA SABANA/
GERMAN EMBASSY

FANTASY BUS/
GRAYLINE

SUSHI BAR
BENIHANA

ICE
BUILDING

ADVANTAGE
RENT-A-CAR

NISSAN
AGENCY

FOGO BRAZIL

AVENIDA

SUBWAY

ROSTI
POLLO

BANK

LAS

AMÉRICAS

ECONOMY
RENT-A-CAR

GRUPO
TACA

CALLE 42

Parque   La   Sabana

MONUMENTO
LEÓN CORTES

CALLE 40

RAPSODIA

BANK

AV CENTRAL

MUSEO DE ARTE
COSTARRICENSE

BANK

BANK

FEDEX

PARQUE
DE LAGO

AVENIDA 2

COSTA RICA
RESIDENTS
ASSOCIATION/
CASA CANADIENSE

CANOPY
URBANO

AV 4

STADIUM

AVENIDA 10

BANK

JICARAS DEL
CAMPO

HOLLYWOOD
GOLD

CALLE ALVAREZ

CALLE MORENOS

TENNIS
CLUB

MAC'S
SPORTS
BAR

UNIVERSAL
(BOOKSHOP)

MCDONALD'S

CONTROLARIO (CITIBANK/
KLM AIRLINES/
UNITED AIRLINES)

CALLE DE GOLF

SABANA SUR

APARTOTEL EL SESTEO

© AVALON TRAVEL

SAN JOSÉ

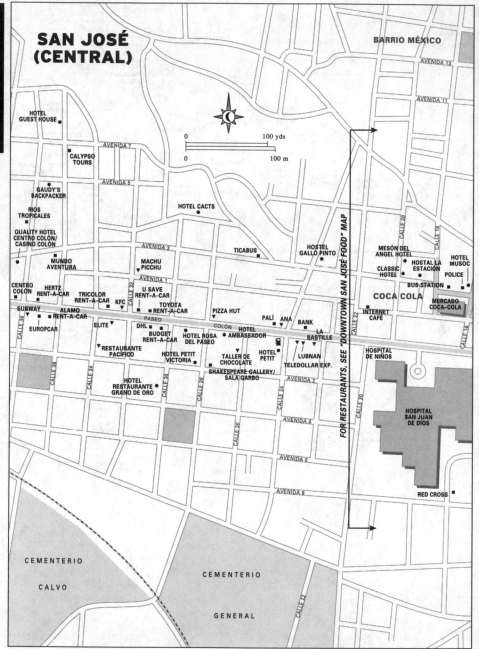

SAN JOSÉ (CENTRAL)

BARRIO MÉXICO

AVENIDA 13

AVENIDA 11

HOTEL GUEST HOUSE

AVENIDA 7

CALYPSO TOURS

AVENIDA 5

GAUDY'S BACKPACKER

RIOS TROPICALES

QUALITY HOTEL CENTRO COLÓN/ CASINO COLÓN

AVENIDA 3

HOTEL CACTS

TICABUS

HOSTEL GALLO PINTO

MESÓN DEL ANGEL HOTEL

HOTEL MUSOC

MUNDO AVENTURA

MACHU PICCHU

CLASSIC HOTEL

HOSTAL LA ESTACIÓN

POLICE

AVENIDA 1

CENTRO COLÓN

HERTZ RENT-A-CAR

TRICOLOR RENT-A-CAR

KFC

U SAVE RENT-A-CAR

BUS STATION

COCA COLA

MERCADO COCA-COLA

SUBWAY

ALAMO RENT-A-CAR

TOYOTA RENT-A-CAR

PIZZA HUT

PALÍ

ANA

BANK

INTERNET CAFÉ

EUROPCAR

ELITE

DHL

PASEO

COLÓN

HOTEL AMBASSADOR

LA BASTILLE

BUDGET RENT-A-CAR

HOTEL ROSA DEL PASEO

HOSPITAL DE NIÑOS

RESTAURANTE PACÍFICO

HOTEL PETIT VICTORIA

TALLER DE CHOCOLATE

HOTEL PETIT

LUBNAN

TELEDOLLAR EXP.

HOTEL RESTAURANTE GRANO DE ORO

SHAKESPEARE GALLERY/ SALA GARBO

AVENIDA 2

AVENIDA 4

HOSPITAL SAN JUAN DE DÍOS

AVENIDA 6

AVENIDA 8

RED CROSS

FOR RESTAURANTS, SEE "DOWNTOWN SAN JOSÉ FOOD" MAP

CEMENTERIO CALVO

CEMENTERIO GENERAL

CALLE 38 · CALLE 36 · CALLE 34 · CALLE 32 · CALLE 30 · CALLE 28 · CALLE 26 · CALLE 24 · CALLE 22 · CALLE 20 · CALLE 18 · CALLE 16

0   100 yds

0   100 m

SAN JOSÉ

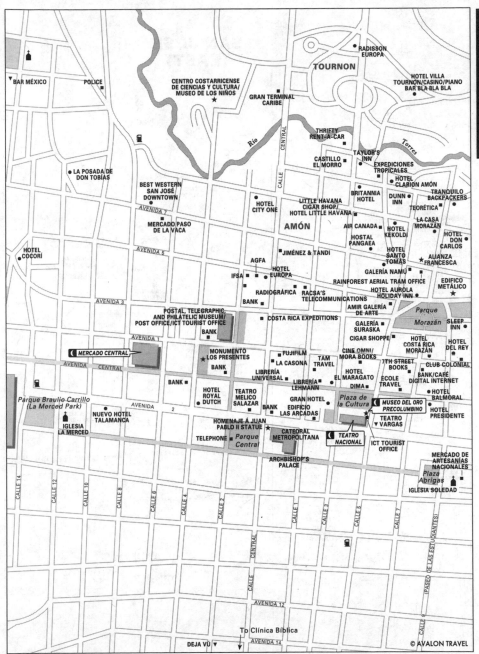

BAR MÉXICO

POLICE

CENTRO COSTARRICENSE
DE CIENCIAS Y CULTURA/
MUSEO DE LOS NIÑOS

TOURNON

RADISSON
EUROPA

GRAN TERMINAL
CARIBE

HOTEL VILLA
TOURNON/CASINO/PIANO
BAR BLA-BLA BLA

Río

Torres

THRIFTY
RENT-A-CAR

TAYLOR'S
INN

CASTILLO
EL MORRO

EXPEDICIONES
TROPICALES

LA POSADA DE
DON TOBÍAS

HOTEL
CLARION AMÓN

BEST WESTERN
SAN JOSÉ
DOWNTOWN

BRITANNIA
HOTEL

DUNN
INN

TRANQUILO
BACKPACKERS

AVENIDA 7

HOTEL
CITY ONE

LITTLE HAVANA
CIGAR SHOP/
HOTEL LITTLE HAVANA

TEORÉTICA

MERCADO PASO
DE LA VACA

AMÓN

AIR CANADA

LA CASA
MORAZÁN

AVENIDA 6

HOSTAL
PANGEA

HOTEL
KEKOLDI

HOTEL
DON
CARLOS

HOTEL
COCORÍ

JIMÉNEZ & TANDI

HOTEL
SANTO
TOMÁS

ALIANZA
FRANCESCA

AGFA

HOTEL
EUROPA

GALERÍA NAMÚ

AVENIDA 3

IFSA

RAINFOREST AERIAL TRAM OFFICE

EDIFICO
METÁLICO

RADIOGRÁFICA

RACSA'S
TELECOMMUNICATIONS

HOTEL AURÓLA
HOLIDAY INN

BANK

Parque
Morazán

POSTAL, TELEGRAPHIC,
AND PHILATELIC MUSEUM/
POST OFFICE/ICT TOURIST OFFICE

COSTA RICA EXPEDITIONS

AMIR GALERÍA
DE ARTE

SLEEP
INN

AVENIDA 1

BANK

GALERÍA
SURASKA

HOTEL
DEL REY

MERCADO CENTRAL

MONUMENTO
LOS PRESENTES

CIGAR SHOPPE

HOTEL
COSTA RICA
MORAZÁN

AVENIDA CENTRAL

FUJIFILM

BANK

LA CASONA

CINE OMNI/
MORA BOOKS

TAM
TRAVEL

7TH STREET
BOOKS

CLUB COLONIAL

Parque Braulio Carrillo
(La Merced Park)

BANK

LIBRERÍA
UNIVERSAL

LIBRERÍA
LEHMANN

HOTEL
EL MARAGATO

ECOLE
TRAVEL

BANK/CAFÉ
DIGITAL INTERNET

HOTEL
ROYAL
DUTCH

TEATRO
MELICO
SALAZAR

DIMA

HOTEL
BALMORAL

AVENIDA 2

GRAN HOTEL

Plaza de
la Cultura

MUSEO DEL ORO
PRECOLUMBINO

HOTEL
PRESIDENTE

NUEVO HOTEL
TALAMANCA

BANK

EDIFICIO
LAS ARCADAS

TEATRO
VARGAS

IGLESIA
LA MERCED

HOMENAJE Á JUAN
PABLO II STATUE

TELEPHONE

Parque
Central

CATEDRAL
METROPOLITANA

TEATRO
NACIONAL

ICT TOURIST
OFFICE

ARCHBISHOP'S
PALACE

MERCADO DE
ARTESANÍAS
NACIONALES

Plaza
Abrigas

IGLESIA SOLEDAD

CALLE 14

CALLE 12

CALLE 10

CALLE 8

CALLE 6

CALLE 4

CALLE 2

CENTRAL

CALLE 1

CALLE 3

CALLE 5

CALLE 7

PASEO DE LAS ESTUDIANTES

CALLE 9

AVENIDA 12

To Clínica Bíblica

DEJA VÙ

AVENIDA 14

© AVALON TRAVEL

SAN JOSÉ

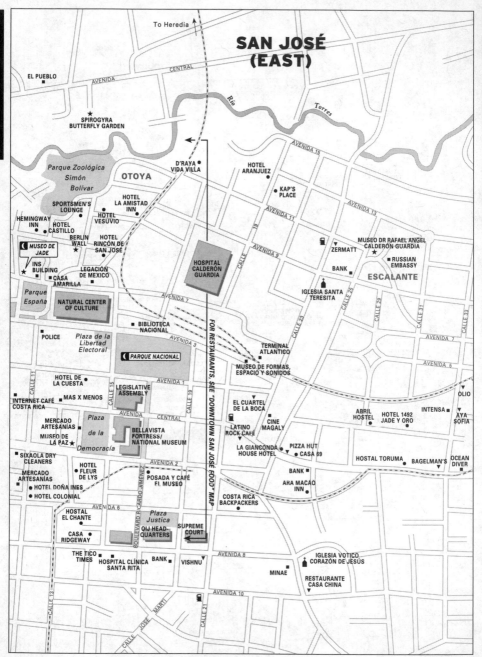

SAN JOSÉ (EAST)

To Heredia

EL PUEBLO

AVENIDA CENTRAL

Río

Torres

SPIROGYRA BUTTERFLY GARDEN

AVENIDA 15

HOTEL ARANJUEZ

D'RAYA VIDA VILLA

Parque Zoológica Simón Bolívar

OTOYA

KAP'S PLACE

AVENIDA 13

AVENIDA 11

HOTEL LA AMISTAD INN

SPORTSMEN'S LOUNGE

HOTEL VESUVIO

ZERMATT

MUSEO DR RAFAEL ANGEL CALDERÓN GUARDIA

HEMINGWAY INN

HOTEL CASTILLO

BERLIN WALL

HOTEL RINCÓN DE SAN JOSÉ

AVENIDA 9

RUSSIAN EMBASSY

MUSEO DE JADE

INS BUILDING

CASA AMARILLA

LEGACIÓN DE MEXICO

HOSPITAL CALDERÓN GUARDIA

BANK

ESCALANTE

IGLESIA SANTA TERESITA

Parque España

NATURAL CENTER OF CULTURE

AVENIDA 7

POLICE

BIBLIOTECA NACIONAL

Plaza de la Libertad Electoral

AVENIDA 3

TERMINAL ATLANTICO

AVENIDA 7

PARQUE NACIONAL

AVENIDA 5

HOTEL DE LA CUESTA

AVENIDA 1

MUSEO DE FORMAS, ESPACIO Y SONIDOS

INTERNET CAFÉ COSTA RICA

MAS X MENOS

LEGISLATIVE ASSEMBLY

EL CUARTEL DE LA BOCA

OLIO

MERCADO ARTESANÍAS

AVENIDA CENTRAL

CINE MAGALY

ABRIL HOSTEL

HOTEL 1492 JADE Y ORO

INTENSA

AYA SOFIA

Plaza de la Democracia

BELLAVISTA FORTRESS/ NATIONAL MUSEUM

LATINO ROCK CAFÉ

PIZZA HUT

MUSEO DE LA PAZ

LA GIANCONDA HOUSE HOTEL

CASA 69

HOSTAL TORUMA

BAGELMAN'S

OCEAN DIVER

SIXAOLA DRY CLEANERS

AVENIDA 2

BANK

MERCADO ARTESANÍAS

HOTEL FLEUR DE LYS

POSADA Y CAFÉ EL MUSEO

ARA MACAO INN

HOTEL DOÑA INES

HOTEL COLONIAL

AVENIDA 6

COSTA RICA BACKPACKERS

HOSTAL EL CHANTE

Plaza Justicia

CASA RIDGEWAY

OIJ HEAD-QUARTERS

SUPREME COURT

THE TICO TIMES

AVENIDA 8

IGLESIA VOTICO CORAZÓN DE JESÚS

HOSPITAL CLÍNICA SANTA RITA

BANK

VISHNU

MINAE

RESTAURANTE CASA CHINA

AVENIDA 10

CALLE 13

CALLE JOSÉ MARTI

CALLE 21

BOULEVARD RICARDO JIMENEZ

CALLE 15

CALLE 19

CALLE 23

CALLE 25

CALLE 27

CALLE 29

CALLE 31

CALLE 33

CALLE 11

FOR RESTAURANTS, SEE "DOWNTOWN SAN JOSÉ" MAP

FOR RESTAURANTS, SEE "DOWNTOWN SAN JOSÉ FOOD" MAP

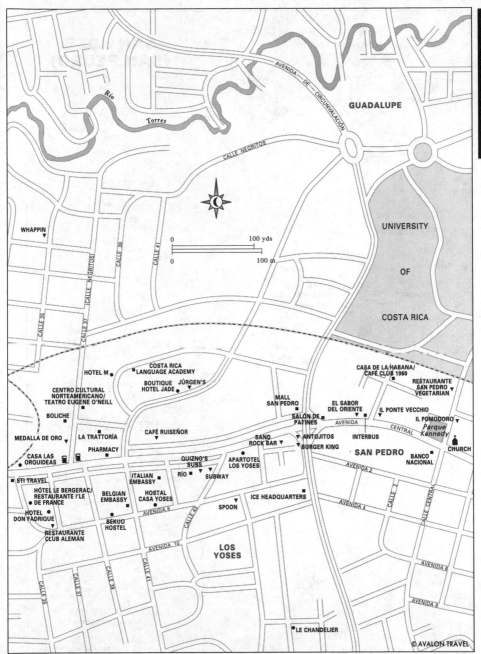

GUADALUPE

UNIVERSITY

OF

COSTA RICA

Río Torres

AVENIDA — DE — CIRCUNVALACIÓN

CALLE NEGRITOS

WHAPPIN ▼

CALLE 39

CALLE NEGRITOS

CALLE 41

CALLE 35

CALLE 37

0 ____ 100 yds
0 ____ 100 m

HOTEL M ■

COSTA RICA
LANGUAGE ACADEMY ■

CASA DE LA HABANA/
CAFÉ CLUB 1960 ▼

BOUTIQUE
HOTEL JADE ▼   JÜRGEN'S ▼

RESTAURANTE
SAN PEDRO
VEGETARIAN ▼

CENTRO CULTURAL
NORTEAMERICANO/
TEATRO EUGENE O'NEILL ■

MALL
SAN PEDRO ■

EL SABOR
DEL ORIENTE ▼

IL PONTE VECCHIO ▼

IL POMODORO ▼

BOLICHE ■

SALON DE
PATINES ▼

AVENIDA   CENTRAL

Parque
Kennedy

MEDALLA DE ORO ●

LA TRATTORÍA ■

CAFÉ RUISEÑOR ▼

SAND
ROCK BAR ▼

ANTOJITOS ▼

INTERBUS ▼

CHURCH ♠

PHARMACY ■

BURGER KING ▼

SAN PEDRO

BANCO
NACIONAL ■

CASA LAS
ORQUIDEAS ●

QUIZNO'S
SUBS ■

APARTOTEL
LOS YOSES ■

STI TRAVEL ■

ITALIAN
EMBASSY ■

RÍO ■

SUBWAY ▼

AVENIDA 2

CALLE 2

CALLE CENTRAL

HÔTEL LE BERGERAC/
RESTAURANTE I'LE
DE FRANCE ■

BELGIAN
EMBASSY ■

HOSTAL
CASA YOSES ■

ICE HEADQUARTERS ■

AVENIDA 4

HOTEL
DON FADRIQUE ■

SPOON ■

AVENIDA 8

CALLE 43

BEKUO
HOSTEL ■

RESTAURANTE
CLUB ALEMÁN ●

AVENIDA 10

LOS
YOSES

AVENIDA 6

AVENIDA 8

CALLE 35

CALLE 37

CALLE 39

CALLE 41

● LE CHANDELIER

© AVALON TRAVEL

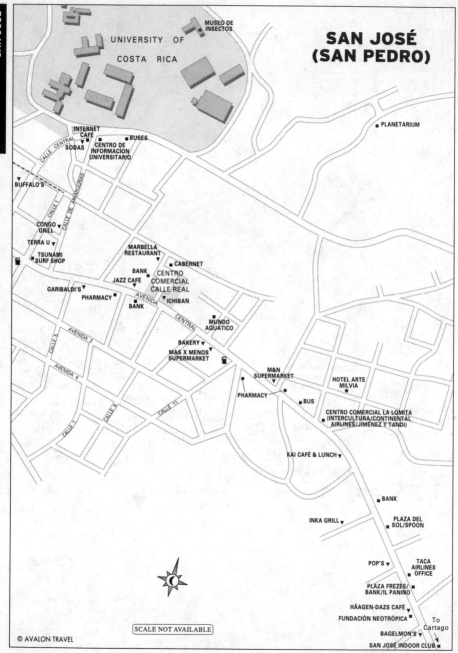

SAN JOSÉ
(SAN PEDRO)

UNIVERSITY OF
COSTA RICA

MUSEO DE
INSECTOS

■ PLANETARIUM

INTERNET
CAFÉ
CALLE CENTRAL
SODAS   ■ BUSES
              ■ CENTRO DE
              INFORMACIÓN
              UNIVERSITARIO

BUFFALO'S

CALLE 1

CALLE DE AMARGURA

CONGO
GRILL

TERRA U

TSUNAMI
SURF SHOP

MARBELLA
RESTAURANT
              ■ CABERNET
       BANK   ■ CENTRO
JAZZ CAFÉ   COMERCIAL
              CALLE REAL
GARIBALDI'S
    PHARMACY ■   ▼ ICHIBAN
         ■ BANK   AVENIDA
AVENIDA 2   CENTRAL

CALLE 5

AVENIDA 4   ■ MUNDO
                  AQUÁTICO

CALLE 7

CALLE 9

CALLE 11

BAKERY
MAS X MENOS
SUPERMARKET

              M&N
              SUPERMARKET

PHARMACY   HOTEL ARTE
                    MILVIA
              ■ BUS
              ■ CENTRO COMERCIAL LA LOMITA
                (INTERCULTURA/CONTINENTAL
                AIRLINES/JIMÉNEZ Y TANDI)

KAI CAFÉ & LUNCH ▼

              ■ BANK

INKA GRILL ▼   ■ PLAZA DEL
                   SOL/SPOON

              POP'S ▼   TACA
                          AIRLINES
                          OFFICE

              PLAZA FREZES/ ■
              BANK/IL PANINO

              HÄAGEN-DAZS CAFÉ
              FUNDACIÓN NEOTRÓPICA ■   To
                                         Cartago
              BAGELMON'S ■
              SAN JOSÉ INDOOR CLUB ■

SCALE NOT AVAILABLE

© AVALON TRAVEL

© CHRISTOPHER P. BAKER

Plaza de la Cultura and Teatro Nacional

with allegorical figures of Comedy and Tragedy, stunning murals depicting themes in Costa Rican life and commerce, and a triptych ceiling supported by six-meter-tall marble columns topped with bronze capitals; a ceiling mural to the rear by Italian artist Milanés Villa shows an allegorical coffee and banana harvest.

Art and good taste are lavishly displayed on the marble staircase, with its gold-laminated ornaments sparkling beneath bronze chandeliers and in the upstairs foyer. A grandiose rotunda painted in Milan in 1897 by Arturo Fontana highlights the three-story auditorium, designed in a perfect horseshoe and seating 1,040 in divine splendor. The auditorium floor was designed to be raised to stage level by a manual winch so the theater could be used as a ballroom.

Guided tours are offered.

PARQUE CENTRAL

This small, palm-shaded park, laid out in 1880 between Calles Central/2 and Avenidas 2/4, is San José's main plaza. The unassuming park has a fountain, a bronze statue, hardwood sculptures, and a large domed structure where the municipal band plays concerts on Sunday. The bandstand rests over the **Carmen Lyra Children's Library,** named for a Costa Rican writer famous for her children's stories.

Across Avenida 2, the **Teatro Melico Salazar** (tel. 506/2233-1500 or 2222-5424, open by appointment, free), dating to the 1920s and named for a famous Costa Rican tenor, is a study in understated period detail.

The area immediately southwest of the square is best avoided for safety reasons.

Catedral Metropólitana

Dominating the east side of Parque Central is the city's modest, Corinthian-columned Metropolitan Cathedral (tel. 506/2221-3826, 6 A.M.–noon and 3–6 P.M. Mon.–Sat., and 6 A.M.–9 P.M. Sun.), with a Greek Orthodox–style blue domed roof. The original cathedral was toppled by an earthquake in 1821; the current structure dates from 1871. The interior is unremarkable, barring its lofty barrel-arched ceiling supported by fluted columns. Outside, at the corner of Avenida Central, is

© CHRISTOPHER P. BAKER

facade of Catedral Metropólitana

the **Homenaje a Juan Pablo II,** the Homage to Pope John Paul II statue inaugurated in September 2006.

Tucked in the cathedral's shadow to the south is the **Curía** or Archbishop's Palace, dating from 1887.

PARQUES ESPAÑA AND MORAZÁN

Parque Morazán is tucked between Calles 5/9 and Avenidas 3/5. The park's four quadrants surround the domed **Temple of Music,** supposedly inspired by Le Trianon in Paris. The park has busts of various South American heroes.

Parque Morazán merges east into diminutive Parque España, a secluded place to rest your feet. Its tall and densely packed trees have been adopted by birds, and their chorus is particularly pleasing just before sunrise and sunset. Note the busts that form a pantheon of national figures. A life-size statue of a conquistador stands on the southwest corner. On the north side of the park you will see an old, ornately stuccoed, ocher-colored colonial building (dating from 1917), **Casa Amarilla,** which

once housed the Court of Justice and today is the Chancellery, or State Department (no entry). Alas, a giant ceiba tree planted out front in 1963 by President John F. Kennedy during his state visit was cut down in 2008. A huge chunk of the Berlin Wall is displayed in the northeast corner of the grounds.

The **Edificio Metálico,** between Parque Morazán and Parque España, is one of San José's more intriguing edifices. This ocher-colored prefabricated building is made entirely of metal. Designed by the French architect Victor Baltard, the structure was shipped piece by piece from Belgium in 1892 and welded together in situ. The facade is dressed with a bust of Minerva, the goddess of wisdom. The building is now a school.

The gleaming white **Legación de México** (Avenida 7, Calles 11/15), one block east of the park, is adorned with ceramic tiles.

Centro Nacional de Cultura

On the east side of Parque España is the erstwhile Fábrica Nacional de Licores (Liquor Factory), now housing the multifaceted

homage to Pope John Paul II outside the
Catedral Metrópolitana

National Center of Culture (CENAC, tel. 506/2221-2022, www.mcjdcr.go.cr/ministerio/cenac.html, 10:30 A.M.–5:30 P.M. Tues.–Sat., free admission). The building dates to 1887, and though it's drained of alcohol, relics of the distilling days linger. The ho-hum **Museo de Arte y Diseño Contemporáneo** (Museum of Contemporary Art and Design, tel. 506/2257-7202, www.madc.ac.cr) shows revolving displays by leading Costa Rican artists. Note the old sun clock and decorative stonework on the southeast side. The National Dance Company, National Theater Company, and Museum of Iberoamerican Culture are housed here.

◖ Museo de Jade

The fabulous Fidel Tristan Jade Museum (Calle 9 and Avenida 7, tel. 506/2287-6034, http://portal.ins-cr.com/Social/MuseoJade, 8 A.M.–3:30 P.M. Mon.–Fri., 9 A.M.–1 P.M. Sat., $7), adjoining the Instituto Nacional de Seguro (INS), displays the largest collection of jade in the Americas, including pre-Columbian

carved adzes and pendants, backlit to show off the beautiful translucence. The museum also displays pre-Columbian ceramics and gold miniatures organized by culture and region. It has excellent signage in English.

PLAZA DE LA DEMOCRACÍA

This square, between Avenidas Central/2 and Calles 13/15, was built in 1989 to receive visiting presidents attending the Hemispheric Summit. Dominating the plaza is the crenellated 1870 **Bellavista Fortress,** which today houses the National Museum. On the west side is a bronze statue of Don "Pepe" Figueres. The formerly unkempt, dreary plaza was being remodeled in early 2009. Two blocks south are the buildings of the "Judicial Circuit," including the Supreme Court and criminal investigation (OIJ) buildings. The National Museum and modernist **Supreme Court,** on Plaza Justicia, are linked by a pedestrian precinct, **Boulevard Ricardo Jiménez,** known colloquially as Camino de la Corte, with shade trees, wrought-iron lampposts, and benches.

Museo de la Paz

The tiny Museum for Peace (Avenida 2, Calle 13, tel. 506/2223-4664, www.arias.or.cr, 8 A.M.–noon and 1:30–4:30 P.M. Mon.–Fri., free) is 50 meters west of the plaza. Run by the Arias Foundation, it displays the Costa Rican president's Nobel Peace Prize and other awards.

Asamblea Legislativa

The Legislative Assembly (tel. 506/2243-2547, www.asamblea.go.cr) occupies three buildings on the north side of the plaza on Calle 15. The blue building—the **Castillo Azul**—to the east, was originally the Presidential Palace, built in 1911 by presidential candidate Máximo Fernández in anticipation of victory in the 1914 elections. He lost, then lent his home to president-elect Alfredo González Flores as his official residence. Later it served as the U.S. Diplomatic Mission. Behind it, the **Casa Rosada** (Pink House), dating from 1833, has two rooms with galleries of paintings and photographs of past Costa Rican presidents. The **Edificio Central**

© CHRISTOPHER P. BAKER

Asamblea Legislativa building

(main building), built in 1937, houses the Congress, or legislative assembly.

Guided visits are offered 8 A.M.–4 P.M. Monday–Friday (tel. 506/2243-2545, ext. 2546, rruiz@congreso.aleg.go.cr). A dress code applies: no sandals or shorts (for men), nor miniskirts for women. Cameras are permitted, without flash.

Museo Nacional

A superb collection of pre-Columbian art (pottery, stone, and gold) and an eclectic mix of colonial-era art, furniture, costumes, and documents highlight the National Museum (Calle 17 and Avenidas Central/2, tel. 506/2257-1433, www.museocostarica.go.cr, 8:30 A.M.–4:30 P.M. Tues.–Sun., $4, $2 students), in the old Bellavista Fortress on the east side of Plaza de la Democracía. Separate exhibition halls deal with history, archaeology, geology, religion, and colonial life. Only a few exhibits are translated into English. The towers and walls of the fortress are pitted with bullet holes from the 1948 civil war. The museum surrounds a landscaped courtyard featuring colonial-era cannons and ancient stone spheres.

Steps lead down to a netted butterfly garden, and in May 2008 it opened a passion flower garden.

◖ PARQUE NACIONAL

Recently renovated Parque Nacional, the largest and most impressive of the city's central parks, graces a hill that rises eastward between Calles 15/19 and Avenidas 1/3. At the park's center is the massive **Monumento Nacional** (National Monument), one of several statues commemorating the War of 1856. The statue depicts the spirits of the Central American nations defeating the American adventurer William Walker. The monument was made in the Rodin studios, in Paris. Avoid the park at night.

On the north side of the square, note the impressive Modernist **Biblioteca Nacional** (tel. 506/2257-4814), built in 1971.

The **Museo de Formas, Espacios y Sonidos** (Museum of Forms, Space and Sounds, Avenida 3, Calles 21/23), dedicated to plastic arts, architecture, and sounds and housed in the ornate former Atlantic Railway Station (built in 1907) immediately northeast of the park, closed in 2008 and its future is uncertain. To the rear are vintage rolling stock and an old steam locomotive, Locomotora 59 (or *Locomotora Negra*), imported from Philadelphia in 1939 for the Northern Railway Company. Ostensibly, the museum will move to an as-yet-unspecified location and the former station will become a reception hall for a new **Casa Presidencial** (www.casapres.go.cr) to house the president's office.

BARRIO AMÓN AND BARRIO OTOYA

Barrio Amón and Barrio Otoya, north of Parques Morazán and España, form an aristocratic residential neighborhood founded at the end of the 19th century by a French immigrant, Amón Fasileau Duplantier, who arrived in 1884 to work for a coffee enterprise owned by the Tournón family. The area, full of grand historic homes, is worth an exploratory walk. Of particular note is the **Castillo el Morro** (Avenida 11, Calle 3), an ornate, Moorish-style, turreted former home of Archbishop Don Carlos Humberto Rodriguez Quirós.

Avenida 9, between Calles 7 and 3, is lined with beautiful ceramic wall murals depicting traditional Costa Rican scenes. Check out the home with life-size figure of a *campesino* at Calle 11 #980.

TeoréTica (Calle 7, Avenidas 9/11, tel./ fax 506/2233-4881, www.teoretica.org, 9 A.M.–6 P.M.Mon.–Fri., 10 A.M.–4 P.M. Sat.) is a local artists' foundation and gallery displaying revolving avant-garde exhibitions. It offers workshops.

Centro Costarricense de Ciencias y Cultura

The castle-like hilltop structure on the west side of Barrio Amón, at the north end of Calle 4, served as the city penitentiary from 1910 until 1979. Today it houses the Costa Rican Science and Cultural Center (tel. 506/2238-4929, www.museocr.com, 8 A.M.–4:30 P.M. Tues.–Fri., 9:30 A.M.–5 P.M. Sat.–Sun., $2

adults, $1.30 children), comprising a library and auditorium (note the fantastic sculptures outside), plus the **National Gallery** (not to be confused with the National Gallery of Contemporary Art), dedicated to contemporary art displayed in airy exhibition halls conjured from former jail cells. Also here is the **Museo de los Niños** (closed Mon., $1.50 adults, $1 children). The Children's Museum lets children reach out and touch science and technology, with exhibits that include a planetarium and rooms dedicated to astronomy, planet earth, Costa Rica, ecology, science, human beings, and communications.

Parque Zoológico

The 14-acre Simón Bolívar Zoo (Calle 7 and Avenida 11, tel. 506/2256-0012, www.funda zoo.org, 8 A.M.–3:30 P.M. Mon.–Fri., 9 A.M.–4:30 P.M. weekends and holidays, $3.50 adults, $2.50 children) has steadily improved, although conditions for many animals still fall short. The native species on display include spider and capuchin monkeys, amphibians and reptiles, most of the indigenous cats, and a small variety of birds, including toucans and tame macaws. A Nature Center has a video room, library, and work area for schoolchildren.

BARRIO TOURNÓN

This *barrio* (district) lies north of Barrio Amón, north of the Río Torres, and a hilly, 20-minute walk from the city center. Its main tourist draw is **Centro Comercial El Pueblo** (Avenida 0, tel. 506/2221-9434, info@ccelpueblocr.com, 11 A.M.–2 A.M. daily), an entertainment and shopping complex designed to resemble a Spanish colonial village. El Pueblo's warren of alleys harbors art galleries, craft stores, restaurants, and nightclubs. The Calle Blancos bus departs from Calles 1/3 and Avenida 5. Use a taxi by night. Taxis to and from El Pueblo often overcharge, so settle on a fee before getting into your cab. There's free parking and 24-hour security.

Worth a browse, too, is the **Spirogyra Butterfly Garden** (Avenida 0, tel./fax 506/2222-2937, www.infocostarica.com/

butterfly, 8 A.M.–4 P.M. daily, $6 adults, $5 students, $3 children), a small butterfly farm and botanical garden 50 meters east and 150 meters south of El Pueblo. More than 30 species flutter about in the netted garden. Hummingbirds abound! Bilingual tours are offered every half hour, or you can opt for a 30-minute self-guided tour; an educational video is shown.

WEST-CENTRAL DOWNTOWN
◖ Mercado Central
The Central Market (6 A.M.–8 P.M. Mon.–Sat.) between Avenidas Central/1 and Calles 6/8, is San José's most colorful market and heady on atmosphere. There are booths selling octopus, dorado, and shrimp; butchers' booths with oxtails and pigs' heads; flower stalls; saddle shops; and booths selling medicinal herbs guaranteed to cure everything from sterility to common colds. Pickpockets thrive in crowded places like this—watch your valuables.

Two nearby statues worth noting are the **Monumento Los Presentes** (Calle 4, Avenida Central), seven patinated statues of Costa Rican folk; and the bronze statue dedicated to Guanacastecan women, one block farther east.

Museo Postal, Telegráfico y Filatélico
Overlooking a grassy plaza, the exquisite **Edificio Postal** (Calle 2, Avenidas 1/3), the main post office, dates from 1911 in a dramatic eclectic style with Corinthian pilasters adorning the facade. The Postal, Telegraphic, and Philatelic Museum (tel. 506/2223-9766, ext. 205, 8 A.M.–5 P.M. Mon.–Fri., 150 colones; buy your ticket—a prepaid postcard—in the philately office downstairs), on the second floor, features old telephones, philatelic history displays, and postage stamps including Costa Rica's oldest stamp—dating from 1863. It hosts a stamp exchange the first Saturday of every month.

Parque Braulio Carrillo
Tiny Parque Braulio Carrillo, between Avenidas 2/4 and Calles 12/14, is also known as La Merced Park, because it faces **Iglesia La Merced,** completed in 1907 and gleaming

afresh after a lengthy restoration. The park is pinned by a monument honoring the astronomer Copernicus.

WEST OF DOWNTOWN
Cementerio General
When you've seen everything else, and before heading out of town, check out the Cementerio General (Avenida 10, Calles 20/36), the final resting place of Josefinos, with its many fanciful marble mausoleums of neoclassical design. The cemetery is particularly worth seeing on November 1 and 2, when vast numbers of people leave flowers at the tombs of their relatives.

Parque la Sabana
This huge park, one mile west of the city center, at the west end of Paseo Colón, used to be the national airfield. Today it's a focus for sports and recreation. A small lake on the south side is stocked with fish, and fishing is permitted. the park contains the **Canopy Urbano** (tel. 506/2215-2544, 9 A.M.–5 P.M., $20), a 10-platform zipline between treetops and over the lake! And a new **Estadio Nacional** soccer stadium, funded by the Chinese government, is to be built on the west side.

The Sabana-Cementerio bus, which leaves from Calle 7 and Avenida Central, will take you there.

The old terminal now houses the **Museo de Arte Costarricense** (Contemporary Art Museum, tel. 506/2222-7155, www.musarco.go.cr, 9 A.M.–5 P.M. Tues.–Fri., 10 A.M.–4 P.M. Sat.–Sun., $5 adults, $3 students, free Sun.), which faces Paseo Colón on the east side. The museum houses a permanent collection of important works by Costa Rica's leading artists, including a diverse collection of woodcuts, wooden sculptures, and 19th- and 20th-century paintings. Revolving exhibitions of contemporary artists are also shown. The Golden Hall (Salón Dorado), on the second floor, depicts the nation's history from pre-Columbian times through the 1940s; done in stucco and bronze patina, the resplendent mural was constructed by French sculptor Louis Feron. A highlight is the sculpture garden to the rear, combining magnificent contemporary and pre-Columbian pieces.

Museo La Salle de Ciencias Naturales (La Salle Museum of Natural Sciences, tel. 506/2232-1306, www.lasalle.edu.co/museo, 8 A.M.–4 P.M. Mon.–Sat., 9 A.M.–5 P.M. Sun., $2 adults, $1 children), in the Colegio La Salle on the southwest corner of Sabana Park, displays a comprehensive collection of Central American flora and fauna (mostly stuffed animals and mounted insects), plus geological specimens and other exhibits covering zoology, paleontology, archaeology, and entomology. Some of the stuffed beasts are a bit moth-eaten (others are so comic, you wonder if the taxidermist was drunk), but the overall collection is impressive. The foyer contains life-size dinosaurs (well, fascimiles). The Sabana-Estadio bus, which departs from the Catedral Metropólitana on Avenida 2, passes Colegio La Salle.

Towering over the north side of the park is the headquarters of **ICE** (Instituto Costarricense de Electricidad). Technicians on a busman's holiday might visit the **Museo Histórico y Tecnológico del Grupo ICE** (200 m north of ICE, tel. 506/2220-7656, 8 A.M.–4 P.M. Mon.–Fri., free), with various exhibits relating to electricity and telephones.

A short distance west, in Rohrmoser, the **Museo de la Comunidad Judía de Costa Rica** (tel. 506/2520-1013, ext. 129, www.geocities .com/museojudiodecostarica, 10 A.M.–2 P.M. by appointment) opened in 2007 and tells of the Jewish community in Costa Rica. It also has a Holocaust exhibit. It's inside the synagogue, behind huge metal gates. Entry is by prior application only; you will need to supply your passport details.

Pueblo Antiguo and Parque de Diversiones

This splendid 12-acre Disney-style attraction (tel. 506/2290-3035, www.parque diversiones.com/pueblo.htm, 9 A.M.–7 P.M. Fri.–Sun., free), 200 meters northeast of Hospital México, in La Uruca, is the Colonial Williamsburg of Costa Rica. It re-creates the

locales and dramatizes the events of Costa Rica history. Buildings in traditional architectural styles include a replica of the National Liquor Factory, Congressional Building, a church, a market, a fire station, and the Costa Rican Bank. The place comes alive with oxcarts, horse-drawn carriages, live music, folkloric dances, and actors dramatizing the past. The park has three sections: the capital city, coast, and country (with original adobe structures, including a sugar mill, coffee mill, and milking barn). There are crafts shops, and a restaurant serves typical Costa Rican cuisine. It hosts "Costa Rican Nights" with traditional entertainment 6:30–9:30 P.M. Friday and Saturday ($34 including historic show, $40 with transfers and dinner).

Pueblo Antiguo is part of a theme park *(parque de diversions)* that features roller coasters, bumper cars, and water slides.

SOUTH OF DOWNTOWN

Iglesia Soledad is a pretty, ocher-colored church fronting a tiny plaza at Avenida 4 and Calle 9, Paseo de los Estudiantes. Paseo runs south two kilometers to the **Parque de la Paz** (Peace Park), which is a favorite of Josefinos on weekends. It has a lake with boats, plus horseback rides, kite-flying, sports fields, and even horse-drawn carriage rides.

Desamparados, a working-class suburb on the southern outskirts of San José, has an impressive church that is a smaller copy of London's St. Paul's cathedral; and, on its north side, the **Museo de la Carreta** (Oxcart Museum, tel. 506/2259-7042, 8 A.M.–noon and 2–6 P.M. Tues.–Sun., $1) is in a venerable home displaying artifacts profiling the traditional peasant lifestyle, notably rustic oxcarts spanning the decades.

At **Fossil Land** (tel. 506/2276-6060, www.fossillandcr.com), two kilometers east of Patarrá, about three kilometers southeast of Desamparados, visitors can witness a fossil dig in the midst of mountains, although the place is more geared to activities such as rappelling, spelunking, ATV tours, and mountain biking.

EAST OF DOWNTOWN

The relatively upscale *barrios* of Los Yoses and San Pedro sprawl eastward for several kilometers but offer few attractions.

Immediately northeast of downtown, the suburb of Barrio Escalante hosts the **Museo Dr. Rafael Angel Calderón Guardia** (Avenida 11, Calles 25/27, tel. 506/2221-1239, www.mcjdcr.go.cr/patrimonio, 9 A.M.–5 P.M. Mon.–Sat., $0.50), celebrating the life of the former president (whose term was 1940–1944).

Iglesia Votico Corazón de Jesú (tel. 506/2222-6486), on Avenida 8 three blocks east of the Tribunales de Justicias, is a stunning contemporary Catholic church worth the visit to admire its stained glass.

University of Costa Rica

The university campus (tel. 506/2207-4000, www.ucr.ac.cr), in San Pedro, about two kilometers east of downtown, is a fine place to take in Costa Rica's youthful bohemianism. The School of Music (Facultad de Artes Musicales) basement houses the **Museo de Insectos** (tel. 506/2207-5647, www.miucr.ucr.ac.cr, 1–5 P.M. Mon.–Fri., $2 adults, $0.50 children), one of the largest collections of insects in the world. The Insect Museum features an immense variety of Costa Rican and Central American insects, including a spectacular display of butterflies. Knowledgeable guides are available, but call ahead. It was slated to move to a new location in the Centro de Investigación para la Protección de Cultivos (CIPROC), in the Escuela de Agronomía (Agronomy School).

The university **planetarium** (tel. 506/2202-6302, http://planetario.ucr.ac.cr) has three daily presentations on astronomy (in Spanish only, $3 adults, $2.50 students). English-language presentations can be requested in advance.

Entertainment and Recreation

Whatever your nocturnal craving, San José has something to please. The *Tico Times* and the "Viva" section of *La Nación* have listings of what's on in San José.

BARS

Tourist bars are concentrated in "Gringo Gulch" (Calles 5/9, Avenidas Central/3) but many are salacious, and muggings on the street are frequent. Bars in San Pedro are more bohemian, catering to the university crowd and upscale Ticos. Most of the other class acts are in the suburb **Escazú**, about seven kilometers west of town. Avoid the spit-and-sawdust workingmen's bars, with their many drunkards seeking a fight.

Downtown

Bar Morazán (Avenida 3, Calle 9, tel. 506/2221-9527, 11 A.M.–2:30 A.M. Mon.–Fri., 5 P.M.–3 A.M. Saturday) draws an eclectic crowd for its warm ambience—redbrick walls adorned with traffic signs. It has a jukebox and serves meals.

Catercorner, the slightly salacious **Key Largo** (Calle 7, Avenidas 1/3, tel. 506/2221-0277, 11 A.M.–3 A.M. daily) draws a Latin clientele with live music (Tuesday, Wednesday, and Friday is pop, Thursday is tropical music, and Saturday has the 1960s' greatest hits) and dancing. Local prostitutes have always been part of Key Largo and are still there since the owners of Hotel Del Rey took over.

Local bohemians prefer the laid-back **El Cuartel de la Boca del Monte** (Avenida 1, Calles 21/23, tel. 506/2221-0327, 11:30 A.M.–2 P.M. and 6 P.M.–2 A.M. Mon.–Fri. and 4 P.M.–2 A.M. Sat.–Sun., $4 men, free to women), a popular hangout for young Josefinos and the late-night, post-theater set. The brick-walled bar is famous for its 152 inventive cocktails, often served to wild ceremony and applause. It has live music on Monday, Wednesday, and Friday. It doesn't get in the groove until around 10 P.M.

The liveliest spot among gringos is the 24-hour **Blue Marlin Bar** (Calle 9, Avenida 1), in the Hotel Del Rey. Fishermen gather here to trawl for a good time while soliciting skippers' mates. It screens U.S. sports, as does the more upscale yet similarly inclined **Sportsmens Lodge** (Calle 13, Avenidas 9/11, tel. 506/2221-2533, www.sportsmenscr.com).

West of Downtown

The venerable and lively **Bar México** (Avenida 13, Calle 16, tel. 506/2221-8461, 10 A.M.–2 A.M. daily) serves excellent *bocas* and margaritas and has mariachi music. Music videos light up a giant screen, and there's live music on Friday and Saturday nights.

The **Shakespeare Bar** (Avenida 2, Calle 28, tel. 506/2258-6787, noon–midnight daily) brings a more intellectual crowd, drawn to the adjoining Teatro Laurence Olivier and Sala Garbo cinema. It has a piano bar and sometimes hosts live jazz. On Sabana Sur, **Mac's** (tel. 506/2231-3145, 9 A.M.–2 A.M. daily) is a TV bar popular with gringos. There's a pool table upstairs.

Rapsodia (Paseo Colón, Calle 40, tel. 506/2248-1720, www.rapsodialounge.com, 6 P.M.–1 A.M. Tues.–Thurs., until 2 A.M. Fri.–Sat.) is one of the chicest lounge bars in the city with its minimalist decor and retro lava lamp videos, although the dining here disappoints.

East of Downtown

Río (tel. 506/2225-8371, 5 P.M. until the last guest leaves, daily), on Avenida Central in Los Yoses, is a lively place with TVs showing music videos. A hip young crowd gathers, especially for occasional all-day musical events when the street outside is closed and the party spills out onto the road. It's often open until the last guest goes home. A short distance east, several club-bars congregate on the southwest side of the San Pedro traffic circle. Calles Central, 3 (also known as Calle de Amargura), and 5, north of Avenida Central in San Pedro, are lined with student bars. All get crowded, but otherwise offer nothing in decor.

Fancy a pint of Guinness? Then head to **Stan's Irish Pub** (tel. 506/2253-4360),

125 meters west of the Casa Presidencial, in the southeasterly district of Zapote. Owner Stanley Salas sells more than 60 beers from around the world.

Cigar Rooms

The classy **Casa del Habano** (Calle 4, Avenida 1, tel. 506/2253-4629, www.habanoscr.net, noon–2 A.M. Tues.–Sun.), in San Pedro, offers a VIP room with pool table, a café, mini-museum of cigars, plus a large collection of premium smokes. Nearby, **Jürgen's** (tel. 506/2283-2239, noon–2 P.M. and 6–10 P.M. Mon.–Fri., 6–11 P.M. Sat.) has a tasteful cigar lounge with leather seats.

Downtown at the risqué Hotel Little Havana is **The Cigar Bar** (tel. 506/2257-8624, www.hotellittlehavana.com, 24 hours), which aims for an upscale clientele. It offers female accompaniment, as the website makes plain.

Gentlemen's Nightclubs

San José has no shortage of gentlemen's strip clubs. Many are sleazy. Even the most respectable clubs are prone to ripping off patrons with exorbitant charges and strong arm tactics. *Caveat emptor!*

DISCOS AND NIGHTCLUBS

The in-vogue spot at last visit was **El Tobogán** (tel. 506/2223-8920, 8 P.M.–2 A.M. Fri.–Sat., 4–9 P.M. Sun., $5), 200 meters north of *La República* office, off the Guápiles highway, where patrons dance beneath a huge *palenque* (thatched roof).

El Pueblo (9 P.M.–2 A.M. daily), in Barrio Tournón, boasts about a dozen bars and discos, featuring everything from salsa to Bolivian folk music. The most sophisticated disco is **Ebony 56** (tel. 506/2223-2195, 8 P.M.–4 A.M. Thurs.–Sun.), which revs things up with two dance floors and live bands on weekdays. Next door is **Twister** (tel. 506/2222-5749, 7 P.M.–4 A.M. Tues.–Sat.), with a choice of three dance floors playing salsa, rock, and Latin sounds. **Bongo's** (tel. 506/2222-5746, 5 P.M.–4 A.M. nightly) has Latin dancers on Tuesday and Wednesday.

East of downtown, multitiered **Planet Mall**

GAY SAN JOSÉ

ACCOMMODATIONS

A U.S. travel agency, Colours Destinations, operates **Colours Oasis Hotel** (tel. 506/2296-1880, toll-free from North America tel. 866/517-4390, www.coloursoasis.com, $59–169 low season, $79–219 high season), a small gay-owned colonial-style property in the quiet residential Rohrmoser district. It has exquisite contemporary decor. There's a pool, whirlpool tub, TV room, plus a café, restaurant, and bar.

In Barrio Amón is the gay-run and gay-friendly **Joluva Guesthouse** (Calle 3 bis, Avenidas 9/11, tel. 506/2223-7961, www.joluva.com). Other gay-friendly hotels include **Hotel Fleur de Lys, Hotel Kekoldi,** and **Hotel Santo Tomás.**

MEETING PLACES

Gay-friendly spots include **Café Mundo** (Avenida 9, Calle 15, tel. 506/2222-6190) and **Café La Esquina,** in Colours Oasis Hotel. The latter has gay theme parties monthly.

Joseph Itiel, author of *iPura Vida!: A Travel Guide to Gay & Lesbian Costa Rica,* strongly advises against "cruising" the parks, where "you can get yourself into real trouble." Transvestites hang out at night around Parque Morazán.

Gay saunas are particularly popular rendezvous, notably at **Hispalis** (Avenida 2, Calles 17/19, tel. 506/2256-9540, www.clubhispalis.com) and **Paris** (Calle 7, Avenida 7, tel. 506/2257-5272).

ENTERTAINMENT AND EVENTS

El Bochinche (Calle 11, Avenidas 10/12, tel. 506/2221-0500, www.bochinchesanjose.com), a two-story bar and restaurant with an art deco interior, is popular, as is **Puchos** (Avenida 8, Calle 11, tel. 506/2256-1147, www.puchosnightclub.com), with nude dancers nightly. The elegant **Deja Vu Disco** (Calle 2, Avenidas 14/16, tel. 506/2248-1500, www.clubohcr.com) caters to both men and women; don't go wandering alone around the run-down neighborhood. And **La Avispa** (Calle 1, Avenidas 8/10, tel. 506/2223-5343, www.laavispa.co.cr) caters to both gays and lesbians with a disco playing mostly techno and Latin music, plus a pool room, a bar, and a big-screen TV upstairs. Drag queens flock on show night.

(tel. 506/280-4693, 8 P.M.–2 A.M. Thurs.–Sat., $5–10) claims to be the largest disco in Central America, on the fifth and sixth floors of the Mall San Pedro.

Stylish **Club Tragaldabas** (tel. 506/8825-9611, www.clubtrabaldabas.com, 8 P.M.–4 A.M. Thurs.–Sat., $5), upstairs in Plaza Rohrmoser, packs in young sophisticates for sexy dancing into the wee hours. For rave-style partying, hit **Vértigo** (tel. 506/2257-8424, 8 P.M.–4 A.M. Mon.–Sat.), in Edificio Colón on Paseo Colón.

CINEMAS

More than a dozen movie houses show American and other foreign movies. (Movies with Spanish soundtracks are advertised as *hablado en Español.*) *La Nación* and the *Tico Times* list current movies. Most movie houses charge $2–6.

Sala Garbo (Calle 28 and Avenida 2, tel. 506/2222-1034) shows avant-garde international movies. Other venues include **Cine Magaly** (Calle 23, Avenidas Central/1, tel. 506/2223-0085); **Cine Omni** (Calle 3, Avenidas Central/1 tel. 506/2221-7903); and the eight-cinema **Cineopolis** (tel. 506/2278-3631), in TerraMall, off the Cartago highway east of town.

THEATER

Theatergoing here is still light-years from Broadway, but San José has a score of professional theaters (many are tiny venues), including a viable fringe; many serve up burlesque. Book early. Tickets rarely cost more than $2. Performances normally run Thursday–Sunday and begin at 7:30 or 8 P.M. Most performances are in Spanish.

The **Little Theater Group** (tel. 506/8355-1623, www.littletheatregroup.org) presents

English-language musicals and comedies throughout the year at the Teatro Laurence Olivier (Avenida 2, Calle 28).

La Nación and the *Tico Times* list current productions.

LIVE MUSIC, DANCE, AND ART

Visiting big-time artists hit Costa Rica occasionally and typically perform at the Teatro Nacional, Teatro Melico Salazar, or Auditorio Nacional. Look for advertisements in the local newspapers.

Folklórica

The most colorful cabaret in town is the **Fantasía Folklórica,** which depicts the traditions, legends, and history of Costa Rica's seven provinces. The program blends traditional Costa Rican dances with avant-garde choreography and stunning stage backdrops. Shows are held at 8 P.M. every Tuesday at the Melico Salazar Theater (tel. 506/2222-5424).

Pueblo Antiguo (tel. 506/2231-2001, www.parquediversiones.com) hosts "Costa Rican Nights" with traditional entertainment at 7–10 P.M. Wednesday, Friday, and Saturday, with folkloric dancing ($40 with dinner).

Classical

The **National Symphony Orchestra** (tel. 506/2221-9417, www.osn.go.cr) performs at the Teatro Nacional (tickets tel. 506/2221-5341, www.teatronacional.go.cr) on Thursday and Friday (8 P.M.) and Sunday mornings (10:30 A.M.), April–December.

The **North American-Costa Rican Cultural Center** (tel. 506/2225-9433 or 800-2077-7500, www.cccncr.com) presents the "U.S. University Musicians Series," with concerts each month. The **National Lyric Opera Company** (tel. 506/2222-8571) presents operas June–mid-August in the Teatro Melico Salazar.

Jazz

The nascent jazz scene is now fairly robust. Venues include the **Shakespeare Gallery** (Calle 28, Avenida 2, tel. 506/2258-6787, 7 P.M.–midnight daily), but the big enchilada is the **Jazz Café** (Avenida Central, tel. 506/2253-8933, www.jazzcafecostarica.com, 6 P.M.–midnight daily, $5 pp cover) in a venerable redbrick building in San Pedro. It hosts big names from around the globe and has all the ambience one could hope for in a classic jazz club.

A pianist tickles the ivories nightly in the **Piano Bar Bla, Bla, Bla** in the Hotel Villa Tournon.

Dance Classes

Merecumbé (tel. 506/2224-3531, www.merecumbe.net) offers dance classes that include salsa and merengue. It has schools throughout San José and the highlands. **Prodanza** (tel. 506/2290-7969, http://katabamibudokan.tripod.com/prodanza) offers classes spanning ballet to flamenco. And **Taller Nacional de Danza** (tel. 506/2227-3017, www.crtallernacionaldedanza.com) offers classes from belly dance to hip-hop!

Peñas

TeoréTica (Calle 7, Avenidas 9/11, tel./fax 506/2233-4881, www.teoretica.org), a local artists' foundation and gallery, hosts *tertulias* (get-togethers) every second Tuesday at 7 P.M.

CASINOS

Many major tourist hotels have a casino where the familiar sounds of roulette, craps, and blackjack continue until dawn. Rummy (a form of blackjack), canasta (a form of roulette, but with a basket containing balls replacing the roulette wheel), craps, and *tute* (a local variant of poker) are the casino games of choice. House rules and payoffs are stacked far more heavily in the house's favor than they are in the United States. As of 2008, hotel casinos are restricted to operating 6 P.M.–2 A.M.

The most upscale are **Club Colonial** (Avenida 1, Calles 9/11, tel. 506/2258-2807); **Horseshoe Casino** (Avenida 1, Calle 9, tel. 506/2233-4383); and the casinos in Aurola Holiday Inn, Hotel Clarion Amón Plaza, Barceló San José Palacio, Best Western Hotel Irazú, Centro Colón, and Radisson Europa Hotel.

SAN JOSÉ

Motorcyclists parade down Avenida 2.

© CHRISTOPHER P. BAKER

FESTIVALS

The **International Arts Festival** in November is launched with a street parade.

The **Oxcart Festival** (Festival de las Carretas), along Paseo Colón, in November, celebrates traditional rural life with a parade of dozens of oxcarts *(carretas)*.

The **Festival of Light** (Festival de la Luz; mid-December) is a Christmas parade along Calle 42 highlighted by floats trimmed with colorful Christmas lights (6–10 P.M.).

The annual running of the bulls occurs during Christmas and New Year's at the fairground in Zapote with a *tope* (horse parade) and bull riding and taunting. There's a special tourist-only section, with fireworks. It coincides with a massive *tope* each December 26, when as many as 3,000 men and women ride down Paseo Colón and downtown.

SPORTS AND RECREATION

Sabana Park has baseball diamonds, basketball courts, jogging and walking trails, soccer fields, tennis and volleyball courts, plus an Olympic-size swimming pool (open noon–2 P.M. daily, $3) and showers. Sabana's trails provide a peaceful environment for running.

The members-only **San José Indoor Club** (tel. 506/2225-9344, www.indoorclub.com), in Curridabat, has the best all-around facilities in the city.

Bowling

At **Boliche** (Calle 37, tel. 506/2253-5745, 11 A.M.–midnight daily), in Los Yoses, 10-pin bowling costs $10 per hour. And the **Costa Rica Tennis Club** (tel. 506/2232-1266, www.costaricatennisclub.com), in Sabana Sur, has eight lanes.

Gyms and Health Clubs

Most upscale hotels have spa facilities: the **Crowne Plaza Corobicí** (tel. 506/2232-8122) and **Hotel Palma Reál** (tel. 506/2290-5060) are noteworthy.

Skating

The **Salón Los Patines** (Avenida Central,

tel. 506/2224-6821, 7–10 P.M. Mon.–Fri., 1–3:30 P.M., 4–6:30 P.M., and 7–10 Sat.–Sun., $3), just east of the San Pedro roundabout, offers roller-skating.

Soccer

You can ask to join in a soccer game in Sabana Park. The San José team, Saprissa, plays at

Estadio Ricardo Saprissa (tel. 506/2235-3591 or 800-2727-7477), in Tibas.

Tennis

You'll find public courts in Sabana Park. Close by, members and guests can play at the **Tennis Club** (tel. 506/2232-1266, www.costaricatennisclub.com), on Sabana Sur.

Shopping

Shop hours are usually 8 A.M.–6 P.M. Monday–Saturday. Many places close at noon for a siesta; a few stay open until late evening.

BOOKS

American-owned **7th Street Books** (Calle 7 and Avenidas Central/1, tel. 506/2256-8251, marroca@racsa.co.cr) has the widest variety of books in English, emphasizing travel and nature, but also offering novels and nonfiction.
Librería Internacional (www.libreriainternacional.com), Costa Rica's answer to Barnes & Noble, has stores on Avenida Central (tel. 506/2257-2563), in Rohrmoser (tel. 506/2290-3331) and San Pedro (tel. 506/2253-9553), and outside town in Escazú (tel. 506/2201-8320). Arch-rival **LibroMax** (tel. 800/542-7662, www.libromax.com) has outlets in Mall San Pedro and Multiplaza (in Escazú); and **Librería Universal** has outlets at Avenida Central and Calles Central/1 (tel. 506/2222-2222) and on Sabana Sur at Calle 42 (tel. 506/2296-1010).
Mora Books (Avenida 1, Calles 3/5, tel./fax 506/2255-4135, www.morabooks.com, 11 A.M.–7 P.M. Mon.–Sat.), in the Omni Building, sells used books, plus magazines and maps.

COFFEE

Every souvenir store sells premium packaged coffee. Make sure the package is marked *puro*, otherwise the coffee may be laced with enough sugar to make even the most ardent sugar-lover turn green. You can also buy whole beans—albeit not the finest export quality—roasted

before your eyes at the Mercado Central. Ask for whole beans *(granos)*, or you'll end up with superfine grounds. One pound of beans costs about $1.
The airport departure lounge has several well-stocked coffee stores.

ART, HANDICRAFTS, AND SOUVENIRS

San José is replete with arts and crafts, such as reproduction pre-Columbian gold jewelry, hammocks, wood carvings, Panamanian *molas*, and miniature oxcarts. **Mercado de Artesanías Nacionales** (Calle 11, Avenidas 4/6, closed Sun.), in Plaza Artigas, teems with colorful stalls. The plaza hosts an open-air art exhibition *(Pintura al aire libre)* every Saturday (10 A.M.–4 P.M.), March–July. And the **Mercado Central,** on Avenida 1, has a panoply of leather work and other artisans' stalls.
Specialty handicraft stores concentrate on Calle 5 between Avenida 1/5 and include **Suraska Gallery** (tel. 506/2222-0129), selling top-quality woodcarvings and furniture. And a handful of handicrafts stores cluster together on two levels at **La Casona** (Calle Central, Avenidas Central/1, 9:30 A.M.–6:30 P.M. Mon.–Sat. and 9 A.M.–5 P.M. Sun.). **Centro Comercial El Pueblo** also has many high-quality art galleries and crafts stores.
My favorite store is **Galería Namú** (Avenida 7, Calles 5/7, tel. 506/2256-3412, www.galerianamu.com), where the superb indigenous art and crafts include Boruca masks and weavings and jewelry from Panamá and elsewhere.

SHOPPING WITH A CONSCIENCE

Think twice before buying something exotic: The item may be banned by U.S. Customs and, if so, you could be fined. Even if legal to import, consider whether your purchase is an ecological sin. In short, shop with a conscience. Don't buy:

• Combs, jewelry, or other items made from tortoise shells.

• Coral or coral items. Costa Rica's coral reefs are being gradually destroyed. And every

shell taken from a beach is one less for the next person to enjoy.

• Jewelry, artwork, or decorated clothes made of feathers.

• Furs from jaguars, ocelots, and other animals in danger of extinction. Such furs are illegal.

• Tropical hardwood products, unless denoted as made from fallen timber.

East of downtown, the new **Fine Art Cellar Gallery** (tel. 506/2384-3544, www.fineartcellar.com) sells works by the nation's finest contemporary artists. Another excellent gallery is **Arte Contemporáneo Andrómeda** (Avenida 9, Calle 9, tel. 506/2223-3529).

CLOTHING

If you admire the traditional Tico look, check out the **Mercado Central** (Avenida 1, Calle 6), where you'll find embroidered *guayabero* shirts and blouses and cotton *campesino* hats. **La Choza Folklórica** (Avenida 3, Calle 1) specializes in replicas of national costumes. Shoemakers abound, many selling cowboy boots, including dandy two-tones; a bevy of high-quality shoemakers can be found on Avenida 3 between Calles 24 and 26.

The best place for upscale brand-name boutiques is **Mall San Pedro** (Avenida Central and *circunvalación,* San Pedro, tel. 506/2283-7540).

You can buy hiking gear, from fanny-packs to safari vests, at **Mundo Aventura** (Avenida 3, Calle 36, tel. 506/2221-6934, www.maventura.com).

JEWELRY

Artisan markets sell attractive ethnic-style earrings and bracelets. Much of what you'll see on

the street is actually gold-washed, not solid gold. Most upscale hotel gift stores sell Colombian emeralds and semiprecious stones, 14-karat-gold earrings and brooches, and fabulous pre-Columbian re-creations: try **Esmeraldas y Diseños** (tel. 506/2231-4808) in Sabana Norte and **Esmeraldas y Creaciones** (tel. 506/2280-0808) in Los Yoses.

Galerías Metallo (tel. 506/2225-1570, www.studiometallo.com), in Barrio Escalante, has both a jewelry academy and showroom.

The **Gold Museum Shop** (tel. 506/2256-9125), beneath the Plaza de la Cultura, sells quality gold reproductions.

CIGARS

Costa Rica is a prime spot to buy Cuban cigars. (U.S. citizens should note that it is illegal to buy Cuban cigars, and even non–U.S. citizens can have them confiscated in transit home via the United States.) Costa Rica's own selections run the gamut from mediocre to superb, including some brands made of leaves aged with aromatic coffee beans.

Good bets are the **Tobacco Shop** (tel. 506/2223-0873) in Centro Comercial El Pueblo and, best of all, the **Casa del Habano** (Calle 4, Avenida 1, tel. 506/2253-4629, www.habanoscr.net) in San Pedro.

Accommodations

San José's accommodations run the gamut from budget hovels to charming boutique hotels and large name-brand options. San José is a noisy city; it is always wise to ask for a room away from the street. Hotels are arranged by price category, then by area.

UNDER $25
Downtown

Among budget dorm options, number one choice is (**Costa Rica Backpackers** (Avenida 6, Calles 21/23, tel. 506/2221-6191, www.costaricabackpackers.com, $12 pp dorms, $26–28 private rooms), run by two friendly and savvy French guys, Stefan and Vincent. This splendid, spotless, secure backpackers' pad is in a large house with a small kidney-shaped swimming pool and garden with hammocks and swing chairs. It offers clean male, female, and mixed dorms with shared bathrooms, plus private rooms (one a lovely space with king-size bed), all with heaps of hot water. A huge TV lounge has leather sofas. It has cooking facilities, laundry, storage, and tour-planning room, as well as free 24-hour Internet and coffee. Movies are shown nightly. All dorms have lockers.

The same owners recently opened the more upscale **Costa Rica Guesthouse** (tel./fax 506/2223-7034, www.costa-rica-guesthouse.com) across the road, with 23 rooms perfect for couples.

Readers also rave about **Pangea Hostel** (Avenida 7, Calles 3/5, tel. 506/2221-1992, www.hostelpangea.com, $12 pp dorm, $28–35 private rooms), in a converted old home in Barrio Amón. And no wonder! Splashed with colorful murals throughout, this thoughtfully prepared hostel offers splendid services, from a kitchen, TV lounge, and pool table to a lovely pool with whirlpool tub and wet bar. Eden here has its own shuttle, and the open-air restaurant upstairs has a licensed bar with views. There are six clean dorms and 26 basically furnished private rooms, all with shared bathrooms with hot water. It offers free storage, free Internet access, free international calls, and free breakfast.

Nearby, the no-frills, German-run **Tranquilo Backpackers** (Calle 7, Avenida 11, tel. 506/2222-2493, www.tranquilobackpackers.com, $10 pp dorms, $28 s/d private rooms) is another good option, although here furnishings are more bare-bones.

The best of several new hostels near the Coca-Cola bus terminal is (**Hostel Gallo Pinto** (Calle 24, Avenida 3/5, tel. 506/2257-1618, www.gallopintocr.com, $12 pp dorm, $25 s/d room). This exquisite conversion of a gracious old home has four dorms with shared bath, and five private rooms with private bath, all delightfully furnished with art pieces and lovely color schemes. Rates include breakfast and free Internet, plus kitchen use. *Nice!*

Nearby, **La Posada de Don Tobías** (Calle 12, Avenidas 7/9, tel. 506/2258-3162, $12–20 s, $22–30 d), adjoining Terminal Atlántico Norte, is a clean, safe, well-run budget option with clean private rooms.

If you prefer a conventional hotel near the bus stations, the best bet is the **Hotel Cocorí** (Avenida 3, Calle 16, tel. 506/2233-0081, fax 506/2255-1058, $15 s, $25 d), with 26 rooms with simple but adequate furnishings, a TV lounge, restaurant, and laundry.

Backpacker alternatives include **Casa Ridgeway** (tel. 506/2233-6168, www.amigosparalapaz.org) and, across the street, the well-run **Abril Hostel** (Calle 29 #124, esq. Avenida 1, tel. 506/2233-6397, www.abrilhostel.com).

West of Downtown

A shining star among San José's hostels is (**Mi Casa Hostel** (Calle 48, tel. 506/2231-470, www.micasahostel.com, $12 pp dorm, $26–30 s/d room including breakfast), a beautiful 1950s modernist home with a pool table and Internet in the exquisite stone-faced TV lounge, opening through a wall of glass to a stone patio and quaint garden. It has a communal kitchen and laundry. A superb mixed dorm upstairs gets heaps of light; a women's dorm is simpler. Four private rooms have foam mattresses and vary in size. It's 150 meters north and 50 meters west of ICE, in Sabana Norte.

I also recommend **Gaudy's Backpackers** (Avenida 5, Calle 36/38, tel. 506/2258-2937, www.backpacker.co.cr, from $10 pp dorm, $25 shared room, $28–30 private room), in a beautiful and spotless home in a peaceful residential area. You enter to a lofty-ceilinged TV lounge with sofas and pool table. It opens to a courtyard with hammocks. There are two co-ed dorms (one with eight bunk beds, another with 12 bunk beds) and 13 small private rooms. Guests get use of a full kitchen, and there's laundry service, plus free Internet.

The new, super-clean **Hostel Guest Home** (Calle 36, Avenidas 7/9, tel./fax 506/2223-6302, www.hostelguesthomecr.com, $7–23 s, $24–35 d) is another great option for backpackers.

East of Downtown

The **Hostal Toruma** (Avenida Central, Calles 29/31, tel. 506/2234-8186, www.hostel toruma.com, $12 pp dorm; $30 s/d shared bath; $35 s, $55 d private bath) is a beautiful old colonial-style structure with segregated dormitories accommodating 95 beds in 17 well-kept rooms, plus seven private rooms with shared baths. There are laundry facilities and a restaurant, plus Internet, cable TV, and parking. Rates include breakfast.

I Hostel Bekuo (Avenida 8, Calles 39/41, tel. 506/2234-1091, www.hostelbekuo.com, $12 pp dorm, $30 s/d shared bath, $35–40 s/d private bath) is a conversion of a beautiful 1950s home with shiny hardwood floors, clean modern bathrooms, a breeze-swept lounge with pool table, and an Internet and TV lounge. Walls of glass open to a garden. It has male, female, and mixed dorms, plus private rooms.

One block east, and also a winner, **Hostal Casa Yoses** (Avenida 8, Calles 41/43, tel. 506/2234-5486, www.casayoses.com, $12 pp dorm, $18 s or $28 d shared bath, $32 s/d private bath) occupies a colonial mansion and has dorms and private rooms, plus heaps of services including games and Wi-Fi.

$25-50
Downtown

The **Hotel Talamanca** (Avenida 2, Calles 8/10, tel. 506/2233-5033, hoteltalamanca@ racsa.co.cr, $45 s/d, $50 suite) is an elegant option on the city's main drag. The 50 air-conditioned rooms and four junior suites (with hot tubs and minibars) are tastefully appointed and have TVs and telephones.

For something more eccentric, try **Hotel La Cuesta** (Avenida 1, Calles 11/13, tel. 506/2256-7946, www.pensiondelacuesta.com, $20 s, $28 d), a cozy charmer for those who like offbeat hotels. This 1930s house, full of antiques and potted plants, is owned by local artists Dierdre Hyde and Otto Apuy, whose artworks adorn the walls. There are nine rooms, plus a furnished apartment for up to six people. The shared baths are clean. There's a TV room and self-service laundry. Guests get use of the kitchen and Wi-Fi.

I like the **Hotel Colonial** (Calle 11, Avenidas 2/4, tel. 506/2223-0109, www.hotelcolonial cr.com, $42 s, $52 d low season; $50 s, $60 d high season), a lovely conversion of an old three-story mansion with high ceilings and carved hardwood beams. Rooms boast spacious bathrooms and picture windows opening to a courtyard with a pool.

Others to consider in this price range include the **Hotel Costa Rica Morazán** (Calle 7, Avenida 1, tel. 506/2222-4622, www.costa ricamorazan.com); the **Hotel Vesuvio** (Avenida 11, Calles 13/15, tel. 506/2221-7586, www.hotel vesuvio.com); the **Hotel & Casino Royal Dutch** (Avenida 2, Calle 4, tel. 506/2222-1414, www.hotelroyaldutchcr.com); the **Hemingway Inn** (Calle 9, Avenida 9, tel./fax 506/2221-1804, www.hemingwayinn.com); and the **Hotel El Maragato** (tel. 506/2222-7737, www.hotelel maragato.com), formerly the Hotel Gran Vía.

West of Downtown

The **Hotel Petit** (Calle 24, Paseo Colón, tel. 506/2233-0766, fax 506/2233-4794, $25 s, $35 d including full breakfast) has 15 simple rooms, all with hot showers. Rooms vary. Some are light and airy, others dingy; some have electric stoves. There's a kitchen, laundry service, secure parking, and a cable TV in the lounge, plus a bar and café.

Mesón del Ángel Hotel (Calle 20, Avenidas 3/5, tel. 506/2222-3405, www.hotelmesondel angel.com, $49 s, $59 d) is a restored two-story, mid-20th-century home with natural stone highlights. The huge lounge with mirrored wall is graced by a hardwood floor and opens to a pleasing dining room and garden courtyard with outside lounging areas. The 21 rooms (some spacious and with floor-to-ceiling windows onto the courtyard) feature tall ceilings, modest but pleasing furnishings, cable TV, security box, and private bathroom. Rooms facing the street get traffic noise. It offers parking and Internet. Rates include breakfast and tax.

The rambling **Hotel Cacts** (Avenida 3 bis, Calles 28/30, tel. 506/2221-2928, www.hotel cacts.com, $40 s or $45 d standard, $50 s or $60 d superior including breakfast and tax) offers 33 nonsmoking rooms, all with telephone and cable TV, plus private bath with hot water. Some rooms in the new extension are a bit dark and have small bathrooms, although all are kept sparklingly clean. Meals are served refectory-style in a rooftop bar-restaurant. It offers a tour agency, airport pick-up, secure parking, and a swimming pool.

The high-rise **Hotel Ambassador** (Paseo Colón, Calles 26/28, tel. 506/2221-8155, www.hotelambassador.co.cr, $45 s or $50 d standard, $55 s or $60 d junior suite, $85 s or $90 d suite) offers a good location within a 20-minute walk of both the city center and Sabana Park. The 74 air-conditioned rooms are clean and spacious and have minibars, safes, and cable TVs. Amenities include a restaurant, a coffee shop, and a bar with dance floor. Rates include continental breakfast.

Also to consider in this category is the ho-hum **Hotel Petit Victoria** (Calle 28, Avenida 2, tel. 506/2255-8488, fax 506/2221-6372).

East of Downtown

Bamboo and rattan abounds in the **Ara Macao Inn** (Calle 27, Avenidas Central/2, tel. 506/2233-2742, www.aramacaoinn.com, $45 s, $55 d), a restored early-20th-century house in Barrio La California. The four sun-filled standards and seven triples have polished hardwood floors, ceiling fans, cable TV, and radios. Some are compact, pleasantly furnished apartments; triples have coffeemakers, refrigerators, and microwaves. Rates include tax and breakfast, served in a breeze-swept patio corridor.

Readers rave about 【 **Kap's Place** (Calle 19, Avenidas 11/13, tel. 506/2221-1169, www.kapsplace.com, $25–80 s, $35–95 d), a clean, charming guesthouse with 23 rooms (including six hostel-type rooms; three with shared bathrooms) in various adjoining buildings, on a tranquil street in Barrio Aranjuez, a 20-minute walk from downtown. All rooms are decorated in lively colors and have cable TV and telephones, and there's free Internet and Wi-Fi access. Twelve rooms have full kitchens. Two small rooms are for one person only. A lovely covered patio garners sunlight and has hammocks. No meals are served, but guests have kitchen privileges, and there's a kids' playroom. Karla Arias, the erudite Tica owner, speaks fluent English and French. No unregistered guests are permitted.

Across the street, the rambling **Hotel Aranjuez** (Calle 19, Avenidas 11/13, tel. 506/2256-1825, www.hotelaranjuez.com, $23 s or $26 d with shared bath, $30 s or $40 d standard, $36 s or $47 d superior) has 23 eclectically decorated rooms rich with hardwoods and all with cable TV, phones, and hair dryers. It's formed of four contiguous houses, each with its own personality. Together, they operate like a hostel. It has Internet, and an airy garden lounge.

Of similar standard, **Boutique Hotel Casa Las Orquídeas** (tel. 506/2283-0095, www.las orquideashotel.com, $12 pp dorm, $50 s, $60 d), on Avenida Central in Los Yoses, is an attractive option done up in pea-green and tropical murals. The 11 rooms have tile floors and New Mexico–style bedspreads. Upstairs rooms have more light plus king-size beds. There's a small yet elegant restaurant, plus secure parking.

$50-100
Downtown

The adorable **Hotel Kekoldi** (Avenida 9, Calles 5/7, tel. 506/2240-0804, www.kekoldi.com, $51 s, $62 d standard, $73 s, $83 d superior low season; $57 s, $69 d standard, $79 s, $89 d superior high season), in a two-story 1950s house in Barrio Amón, offers 10 spacious rooms with hardwood floors, heaps of light, and lovely albeit modest furnishings in tropical pastels, plus cable TV, fans, and security box. Breakfasts are served in a beautiful garden in Japanese style.

Also worth considering is the small and homey **Hotel Doña Inés** (Calle 11, Avenidas 2/6, tel. 506/2222-7443, www.donaines.com, $40 s or $55 d low season, $45 s or $60 d high season), behind the Iglesia la Soledad. It's a good bet for its luxury bathrooms with full-size tubs, plus TVs, phones, and reproduction antique furnishings in the 20 carpeted bedrooms. It has a small and pleasant restaurant for breakfasts and dinner. Rates include breakfast and tax.

The **Gran Hotel** (Avenida 2, Calle 3, tel. 506/2221-4000, www.grandhotelcostarica .com, $85 s/d standard, $97 s/d superior, $135–179 suites), dating from 1899 and named a national landmark, recently emerged from a total remake that has reinvigorated this once-dowdy dowager. It has a basement casino, plus an elegant open-air restaurant merging into the hotel's 24-hour Café 1830. However, the 102 air-conditioned, modestly furnished rooms are still unexciting; all have telephones and cable TVs, plus bright art, and older tiled baths. Rooms facing the plaza can be noisy. The five junior suites are elegant.

Hotel Europa (Calle Central, Avenidas 3/5, tel. 506/2222-1222, www.hoteleuropacr.com, $50 s, $60 d) has 72 spacious, paneled, air-conditioned rooms, and two suites with more elegant tones. All have cable TVs, direct-dial telephones, and safes, although the hotel remains frumpy. Four larger "deluxe" rooms have wide balconies at no extra cost. Avoid lower-floor rooms facing onto the noisy street (quieter, inner-facing rooms are more expensive).

It has a small plunge pool, a reasonable restaurant, and efficient service. Rates include breakfast and tax.

The **Hotel Balmoral** (Avenida Central, Calles 7/9, tel. 506/2222-5022, www.balmoral .co.cr; $75 s, $95 d standard, $109 s/d premier, $139–155 s/d suites), a steps-to-everything option one block east of Plaza de la Cultura, offers 112 small, air-conditioned, carpeted rooms, plus four junior suites and four suites, all with cable TVs and safe-deposit boxes. A sauna and mini-gym, a restaurant and pleasing outdoor café, a casino, and tour desk and car rental agencies are on the ground floor. It has secure parking. Rates include breakfast. Opposite the Balmoral, and preferable following a snazzy makeover, the **Hotel Presidente** (tel. 506/2222-3022, www.hotel-presidente.com, $89 s/d, $131 s/d "spa" rooms, $125 s/d junior suites, $145 s/d suites) has also upgraded its 110 air-conditioned bedrooms, each with a direct-dial telephone, cable TV, and safe-deposit box. The spacious rooms now boast a lovely contemporary elegance and travertine-clad bathrooms. The hotel has a rooftop whirlpool and sauna, a casino, and bar, plus a wonderful street-front restaurant and café. Rates include breakfast and free Wi-Fi. Nice!

For old-world charm, consider the **Britannia Hotel** (Calle 3, Avenida 11, tel. 506/2223-6667, www.hotelbritanniacostarica.com, $65 s or $76 d standard, $80 s or $93 d deluxe, $93 s or $105 d junior suite low season; $77 s or $89 d standard, $93 s or $105 d deluxe, $106 s or $117 d junior suite high season), in a neoclassical Victorian-style mansion built in 1910 in Barrio Amón. The five deluxe rooms and four junior suites in the old house boast high ceilings, stained glass, arches, ceiling fans, mosaic tile floors, and English-style furniture. A new block has 14 standard rooms, all with cable TVs, telephones, safe-deposit boxes, a king-size or two twin beds, plus a private bathroom with tub. The boutique hotel features "tropical courtyards," a restaurant converted from the old cellar, a coffee shop, and room service.

Another historic charmer is the U.S.–run **Hotel Santo Tomás** (Avenida 7, Calles 3/5, tel.

506/2255-0448, www.hotelsantotomas.com, $80 s/d standard, $90 s/d superior, $110 s/d deluxe), an intimate bed-and-breakfast with 19 nonsmoking rooms in an elegant turn-of-the-20th-century plantation home with high vaulted ceiling and original hardwood and colonial tile floors. Rooms vary (some are huge), but all have cable TV and direct-dial phones, queen-size beds with orthopedic mattresses, antique reproduction furniture, throw rugs, and watercolors. There are three separate TV lounges and a full-service tour planning service, library, gift store, and Internet access. The hotel features the delightful Restaurant El Oasis, a solar-heated swimming pool, whirlpool tub, and water slide. Rates include breakfast.

Nearby, the homey, well-run **Hotel Don Carlos** (Calle 9 bis, Avenidas 7/9, tel. 506/2221-6707, www.doncarloshotel.com, $65 s or $75 d standard, $75 s or $85 d superior, $95 family room) occupies an aged colonial-style mansion replete with Sarchí oxcarts, magnificent wrought-iron work, stained-glass windows, stunning art, and bronze sculptures. It has 36 rooms and suites, including colonial-era rooms reached by a rambling courtyard. All rooms have cable TVs, safes, and hair dryers. It has a gift shop, free Internet service, a tour service, small gym, sundeck with water cascade and plunge pool, plus an espresso bar and a restaurant lit by an atrium skylight. Rates include continental breakfast.

Somewhat more dowdy, **La Casa Morazán** (Calle 7, Avenidas 7/9, tel. 506/2257-4187, www.casamorazan.com, $45 s or $55 d low season, $55 s or $65 d high season) is also set in a colonial mansion boasting antique furnishings and modern art, plus original (rather stained) tile floors. The 11 air-conditioned rooms all have cable TV, old-style telephones, large bathrooms, and 1950s furniture. Breakfast (included in rates) and lunch are served on a small patio.

Similarly gracious, the Swiss-owned **Hotel Fleur de Lys** (Calle 13, Avenidas 2/4, tel. 506/2223-1206, www.hotelfleurdelys.com, $79 s or $89 d standard, $104 s/d junior suite, $119–135 suite low season; $84 s or $94 d standard, $109 s/d junior suite, $124–139 suite high season). This restored mansion offers 31 individually styled rooms, each named for a species of flower. All have sponge-washed pastel walls, tasteful artwork, phones, cable TVs, hair dryers, and wrought-iron or wicker beds with crisp linens. A wood-paneled restaurant serves Italian cuisine, and live music is offered twice weekly in the bar. There's a tour desk and on-site parking. Rates include breakfast.

For more contemporary styling, try the modern **Hotel Villa Tournon** (tel. 506/2233-6622, www.costarica-hotelvillatournon.com, $75 s or $80 d standard, $90 s or $97 d superior), in Barrio Tournón, 200 meters from El Pueblo, and brimful of contemporary art and sculpture. The 80 mammoth air-conditioned rooms are graciously appointed in autumnal colors with wood furnishings and leather chairs. The restaurant, centered on a massive brick hearth, offers fireside dining, and there's a piano bar. Ask for rooms off the street. It has free Internet, secure parking, and a swimming pool.

City slickers might appreciate the hip Austrian-run **Hotel City One** (Avenida 9, Calles Central/2, tel. 506/2248-1778, www.hotelcityone.com, $60 s/d low season, $70 s/d high season), with its white, orange, and chocolate brown color schemes, modernist decor, and contemporary art. The lobby makes a good impression, but many of the 50 rooms furnished in simple 1950s retro vogue are dowdy and dark and somewhat spartan. The upstairs Caribbean restaurant and all-white lounge-bar have volcano views.

A complete opposite in decor, the **Raya Vida Villa** (tel. 506/2223-4168, www.rayavida.com, $80 s, $95 d) bed-and-breakfast is a lovely two-story antebellum-style mansion tucked in a cul-de-sac in Barrio Otoya, at the end of Avenida 11 and Calle 17. The live-in owner, Michael Long, rents four rooms, each delightfully done up in individual decor: the Pineapple Room, ideal for honeymooners, has a four-poster bed; the Mask Room features masks from around the world; another room has a king-size bed and limestone floor and opens to a shaded patio with fountain. There's an exquisite TV lounge and reading room with fireplace and chandeliers, although all rooms have cable TV plus fans. The place is secluded and peaceful and festooned with original artwork, including Toulouse-Lautrec and Salvador Dalí. Rates include full breakfast and airport pickup.

Sportsmens Lodge (Calle 13, Avenida 11, tel. 506/2221-2533 or 800/291-2798, www.sportsmenscr.com, $119–159 s/d), in the historic Barrio Otoya district, offers a tranquil setting a stone's throw from downtown. Centered on a colonial building, it has 22 rooms; most have classy antique furnishings and silent air-conditioning, including 10 elegant rooms in a new wing, while a Penthouse Suite ($250) is super-contemporary. It advertises adult TV channels, and draws heavily from the sportfishing crowd trawling for the girls who flock to the bar. Likewise, bed-and-bawd is the theme at the five-story, 104-room **Hotel Del Rey** (Avenida 1, Calle 9, tel. 506/2258-4880, www.hoteldelrey.com), appealing mainly to a male clientele making out with the professional gals in the bar. Hustlers outside the door are an annoyance. *Caveat emptor!*

If you don't mind institutional-style hotels, the centrally located **Sleep Inn** (Avenida 3, Calles 9/11, tel. 506/2222-0101, www.sleep innsanjose.com, $90–100 s/d) offers good value for the money. It's done up in earth tones, with charming contemporary furnishings and Internet connections, plus marble tops and king-size beds in junior suites; my mattress gave me a backache! It adjoins the Club Colonial Casino, but the restaurant (also in the casino) is gloomy and affected by the casino's smokers. Rates include local calls.

The 27-room, Dutch-run **Hotel Rincón de San José** (Avenida 9, Calles 13/15, tel. 506/2221-9702, www.hotelrincondesanjose .com, $52 s, $66 d), in a quiet part of Barrio Otoya, offers a pleasing ambience combining antique furnishings and a subdued elegance. It has a lovely skylit restaurant.

And the new-in-2007 **Hotel Inca Real** (Ave. 11, Calles 3/5, tel. 506/2223-8883, http://gruporealinternacional.com, $45 s, $55 d)

offers a combination of gracious yesteryear-themed intimacy and comfort in its 33 rooms. Nothing outstanding here, but it's a perfectly adequate option.

Also-rans to consider include the **Hotel Posada de Museo** (Avenida 2, Calle 17, tel. 506/2258-1027, www.hotelposadadelmuseo .com), catercorner to the Museo Nacional; **Hotel Castillo B&B** (Avenida 9, Calle 9, tel. 506/2221-5141, www.hotelcastillo.biz), a cheap conversion of a 1900-era three-story colonial home; **Taylor's Inn** (Avenida 13, Calles 13/15, tel. 506/2257-4333, taylor@catours.co.cr), with nine nonsmoking rooms in a 1908 property; and **Dunn Inn** (Calle 5, Avenida 11, tel. 506/2222-3232, www.hoteldunninn.com), in a restored 19th-century home and operated by Texan Patrick Dunn.

West of Downtown

The slightly jaded **Hotel Rosa del Paseo** (Paseo Colón, Calles 28/30, tel. 506/2257-3213, http://rosadelpaseo.com, $70 s or $80 d standard low season; $75 s or $85 d high season; $90 s or $100 d junior suite, $120 s or $140 d suite year-round) has 18 nicely decorated rooms plus one suite in a century-old residence on Paseo Colón. Architectural details combine parquet and tile floors, original artwork, and art-nouveau flourishes with "Victorian Caribbean." All rooms have cable TV, safes, and ceiling fans, plus white-tiled private bathrooms with hot water. A master suite has a large whirlpool tub, and there's a garden courtyard and secure parking. Rates include breakfast.

Focusing on a business clientele, the **Quality Hotel Centro Colón** (Avenida 3, Calle 38, tel. 506/2257-2580, www.hotelcentrocolon.com, $75–95 s/d standard, $85 s/d superior and business room, $90 junior suite) is in the Centro Colón complex. The 126 carpeted, air-conditioned rooms (including 42 suites) are "extra-large" and have king-size beds as well as cable TVs, safe-deposit boxes, hair dryers, and telephones. Some rooms have volcano views. An executive floor has a business center and business rooms have Wi-Fi, plus there's a restaurant, casino, and a nightclub/bar.

The delightful **Hotel Occidental Torremolinos** (Avenida 5, Calle 40, tel. 506/2222-5266, www.occidental-hoteles.com, $72 s/d standard, $85 s/d suite) is entered via a classically elegant lounge and bar opening to a lush garden with shade umbrellas and a pool. Its 80 rooms and 12 suites in contemporary style are modest in size but handsomely furnished, with lots of hardwoods. All have cable TVs, carpeting, clock radios, direct-dial telephones, and hair dryers. Suites have glassed-in balconies. It offers a pool and a whirlpool tub, plus a courtesy bus, car rental service, and a beautiful restaurant. Rates include breakfast.

In a similar vein is the stylish **(Barceló Palma Real** (tel. 506/2290-5060, www.hotel palmareal.com, $105 s/d standard, $166 s/d executive, $182 s/d junior suite), in a quiet residential area 200 meters north of the ICE in Sabana Norte. This upscale, contemporary boutique hotel, full of marble and autumnal colors, draws a business clientele. It features 65 carpeted, tastefully decorated, air-conditioned rooms, with handsome wooden floors, orthopedic mattresses, and spacious travertine-lined bathrooms. Two suites have king-size beds and whirlpool bathtubs. There's a state-of-the-art gym, whirlpool tub, business center, bar, and elegant restaurant.

Looking for something more intimate? The small, family-run **Hotel Sabana B&B** (tel. 506/2296-3751, www.costaricabb.com, $65 s or $75 d low season, $70 s or $90 d high season), on the north side of Sabana, offers five simple yet cozy upstairs rooms with parquet floors, fans, cable TVs, and private baths with hot water. It also has one downstairs room for handicapped travelers, plus Internet and Wi-Fi, a tour desk, kitchenette, free tea and coffee, and a terrace and garden. Rates include airport pickup, breakfast, and tax.

The **Costa Rica Tennis Club & Hotel** (tel. 506/2232-1266, www.costaricatennis club.com) offers a reasonable alternative, as does the nearby and contemporary themed **Barceló Rincón del Valle** (tel. 506/2231-4927, www.barcelo.com). Both are on the south side of Sabana Park.

For self-catering, the best options are **Apartotel La Sabana** (tel. 506/2220-2422, www.apartotel-lasabana.com), on the north side of Sabana Park; **Apartotel Cristina** (tel. 506/2220-0453, www.apartotelcristina .com) nearby, 300 meters north of ICE; and the **Apartotel El Sesteo** (tel. 506/2296-1805, www.sesteo.com), 200 meters south of McDonald's on Sabana Sur.

East of Downtown

The **Hotel Don Fadrique** (Calle 37, Avenida 8, tel. 506/2225-8186, www.hoteldon fadrique.com, $65 s, $75 d) claims 20 "luxuriously furnished rooms" and "lush tropical gardens." The rooms are decorated in tropical pastels (some have Guatemalan bedspreads), with original modern art on the walls. Each has parquet wood or tile floor, telephone, cable TV, safe-deposit box, and fan. Take an upstairs room, with heaps of light. There's a lounge with lush sofas, and a charming patio where you can enjoy breakfast, included in rates.

Nearby, **L'Hôtel Le Bergerac** (Calle 35, Avenida Central, tel. 506/2234-7850, www.bergerachotel.com, $80 s or $90 d standard, $105 s or $115 d superior, $125 s or $135 d deluxe) is a pretty colonial home in Los Yoses, with views south toward the Cordillera Talamanca. Exuding French influence, Le Bergerac is a full-service hotel with a deep maroon and gray color scheme and the feel of a bed-and-breakfast. Service is discreet. The hotel has 19 rooms in three buildings (five in the original home, reached via a sweeping spiral staircase), all with cable TVs, direct-dial telephones, Internet access, and safes, plus hardwood floors and classical furniture. Rooms vary in size, and some have bidets and their own patio gardens. It boasts a gourmet restaurant and has secure parking, a travel agency, and a conference room. Rates include full breakfast. It was for sale at last visit.

In a similar vein, the Italian-run **La Giaconda House Hotel** (tel. 506/2248-9422, www.costa ricahousehotel.com) offers a viable alternative at similar rates. A stone's throw away, the **Casa 69** (tel. 506/2256-8879, www.casa69.com,

$40–65 s/d) is a graceful conversion of a centenary mansion and now offers tasteful furnishings and king-size beds in some rooms. It has a rooftop terrace. Both hotels opened in 2008. Traffic noise is an issue here!

In San Pedro, the modestly appealing **Hotel Arte Milvia** (tel. 506/2225-4543, www.hotel milvia.com, $59 s, $69 d) has three spacious, individually styled rooms in the restored turn-of-the-20th-century wooden home, plus six downstairs rooms in a contemporary add-on built around a tiny garden courtyard (noise from adjoining rooms can be a problem). All have king-size beds and tiny TVs; bathrooms feature hand-painted decorative tiles. There's a dining room, lounge with TV and VCR, and boutique. Lively pop-art works by owner Florencia Urbia, a well-known artist, adorn the walls. Rates include taxes and continental breakfast.

A more appealing option, the **Hotel 1492 Jade y Oro** (Avenida 1 #2985, Calles 31/33, tel. 506/2225-3752, www.hotel1492.com, $60 s or $70 d standard, $80 s/d deluxe, $90 s/d junior suite), in the quiet residential neighborhood of Barrio Escalante, is a beautiful colonial-style residence boasting 10 handsomely appointed rooms (three are junior suites) with hardwood floors, private bath, hot water, ceiling fan, telephone, and cable TV. Most rooms have windows that open to small gardens, and there's a patio garden done up in Tico fashion where a happy hour of wine and cheese is hosted nightly. The handsome lounge has a soaring ceiling and fireplace. Rates include Tico breakfast.

$100-150
Downtown

Dominating the downtown skyline is the sophisticated **Hotel Aurola Holiday Inn** (Avenida 5, Calle 5, tel. 506/2523-1000, www.aurola-holidayinn.com, $104 s/d standard, $140 executive, $200 s/d suite). The modern high-rise overlooking Parque Morazán offers 201 hermetically sealed, air-conditioned rooms featuring regal furnishings. The 11th floor is smoke-free, an executive floor caters to

business travelers, and one room is wheelchair accessible. Topping off the hotel's attractions is the *mirador* restaurant on the 17th floor, adjacent to the casino. The hotel contains a gym, sauna, and indoor pool.

For purely functional comfort, try the handsome albeit overpriced **Clarion Hotel Amón Plaza** (Avenida 11, Calle 3 bis, tel. 506/2523-4600, www.choicehotels.com, $120–165 s/d, $185–295 suites), in the historic Barrio Amón area. This modern, four-story, "neo-Victorian" hotel has 90 air-conditioned rooms, including 24 junior and six deluxe suites, all with subdued decor and the expected appointments. Facilities include a spa and solarium, casino, disco, and underground parking, plus elegant restaurant.

The business-oriented **Radisson Europa Hotel & Conference Center** (Calle 3, Avenida 15, tel. 506/2257-3257, www.radisson.com/san josecr, from $135 s/d) is a contemporary five-star hotel with 107 "superior" rooms, six executive suites, and one presidential suite, all with air-conditioning, 24-hour room service, direct-dial telephones, cable TVs, minibars, and safes.

If you're considering **Best Western San José Downtown** (tel. 506/2255-4766, www.bestwesterncostarica.com), note that it has an awful location on the edge of the city's roughest neighborhood.

West of Downtown

The ◖ **Hotel Restaurante Grano de Oro** (Calle 30, Avenida 2, tel. 506/2255-3322, www.hotelgranodeoro.com, $105–140 s/d rooms, $160–275 suite low season; $115–165 s/d rooms, $175–305 suite high season) is indisputably the city's finest hotel (and a great bargain). It's my hotel of preference whenever I stay in San José. The guestbook is a compendium of compliments. "What charm! What comfort!" "The best hotel we've stayed in—ever!" "We would love to keep it a secret, but we promise we won't." A member of the Small Distinctive Hotels of Costa Rica, the gracious turn-of-the-20th-century mansion, in a quiet residential neighborhood off Paseo Colón, proves that a fine house, like a jewel, is made complete by its setting. Congenial hosts Eldon

© CHRISTOPHER P. BAKER

Executive room at Hotel Restaurante Grano de Oro

and Lori Cooke have overseen the creation of a real home away from home that combines traditional old-world Costa Rican style with sophisticated elegance. A recent expansion has graced the hotel with a 21st-century staircase entry, a contemporary lobby, and a superlative restaurant that is now indisputably San José's finest. Orthopedic mattresses guarantee contented slumber in the 41 faultlessly decorated guest rooms (including five more stately rooms in a new wing). Upgraded in 2008, they're done up in a tasteful combination of regal greens and maroons or deep blues; black rattan and handcrafted iron furniture; and king-size canopied beds in some rooms. Gleaming hardwood floors add to the sense of refinement. Flat-screen cable TV and direct-dial telephones are standard. Extravagant bathrooms have also been modernized and boast torrents of piping-hot water. The sumptuous rooftop wood-paneled Vista de Oro suite has a plate-glass wall providing views of three volcanoes. There's a well-stocked gift shop and a rooftop solarium with two whirlpool tubs. No request is too much for the ever-smiling staff.

Nearby, and a total contrast, is the **Crowne Plaza Corobicí** (tel. 506/2232-8122, www.crowneplaza.com, $110 s/d standard, $140 junior suite, $331–501 suite), on the northeastern corner of Sabana Park. Its angled exterior is ungainly, but its soaring atrium with a surfeit of marble and tier upon tier of balconies festooned with ferns is impressive. The 200 spacious rooms and eight suites boast handsome furnishings and modern accoutrements. Suites have kitchenettes. It has a business center, nightclub, casino, 24-hour cafeteria, Internet café, plus Italian and Japanese restaurants.

Nearby, and bringing San José squarely into the 21st century, **Parque del Lago** (Paseo Colón, Calles 40/42, tel. 506/2257-8787, www.parquedellago.com, $130 s/d studio, $149 s/d superior, $160 s/d executive, $175 s/d junior suite) is a modern four-story hotel with 33 exquisitely decorated, air-conditioned rooms, plus six suites with kitchenettes, all with a hip contemporary vogue (and to-die-for mattresses) and white, orange, and dark hardwood color schemes. Cable TV, direct-dial phone with fax, minibar, coffeemaker, and hair dryer are standard. Suites have kitchenettes. There's a fabulous café/restaurant and bar, plus a spa, Internet room, and meeting rooms. Still, I consider it overpriced.

Dominating the advertising pages of local publications, the **Hotel Casa Roland** (tel. 506/2231-6571, www.casa-roland.com, $85 s or $95 d rooms, $145 s/d executive, $200 s/d suite) is off Rohrmoser Boulevard, in Pavas. Crammed full of original paintings and oversize murals, plus potted plants, this rambling entity is claustrophobic (many rooms have no windows). An adjoining restaurant, however, impresses.

The overpriced **Barceló San José Palacio** (tel. 506/2220-2034, www.barcelo.com, $177 s/d standard, $223 junior suite, $235 executive, $270 suites) has 254 carpeted, air-conditioned rooms, plus all the expected facilities for a hotel of its size. However, the hotel's location on the Autopista General Cañas two kilometers northwest of the city necessitates a taxi, and it charges for its three-times-a-day shuttle to San José.

Other good options in this range, including the Ramada Plaza Herradura and the Costa Rica Marriott Hotel and Resort, can be found in Ciudad Cariari, just outside town and close to the airport.

East of Downtown

A standout hotel is the members-only (yet walk-ins allowed) **Hotel M** (tel. 506/2253-8345 or U.S. tel. 800/304-1625, www.hotelmcosta rica.com, $150–250 s/d), 100 meters north and 200 meters west of Mall San Pedro, in Barrio Dent. A tasteful restoration of a huge modernist 1950s home has produced a luxury hotel with 10 individually styled rooms. It has a "Sports Viewing Room," bar, gym, 12-person whirlpool tub, and solarium. However, it aims

for an uninhibited mature adult crowd and can get very risqué!

Around the corner, and also offering a classy contemporary theme, the low-rise **Boutique Hotel Jade** (tel. 506/2224-2445, www.hotel boutiquejade.com, $107 s or $117 d standard, $142 s or $152 d suite) has 30 spacious, air-conditioned, carpeted, executive-style rooms with rich and lively decor, handsome fittings, cable TVs, desks, phones, modems, minibars, vanity chairs and sofa, and spacious showers. Six are handicapped equipped, and there are some nonsmoking rooms. Junior suites are truly classy. Murals adorn the corridor walls. There's a small lounge, a rear garden with a beautiful swimming pool and fountain, and a café. The highlight, however, is the sophisticated Jürgen's Restaurant, and there's a cafeteria and a gift store.

Casa Conde Apartotel & Suites (tel. 506/2274-2326, www.grupocasaconde.com, $165 s/d standard to $320 s/d suites), just south of the Autopista, is handy for exploring south of the city.

Farther Afield

To the northwest, in Uruca, the **Best Western Irazú** (Autopista General Cañas, tel. 506/2290-9300, www.bestwestern.com, $132 s/d) has 350 rooms, including a nonsmoking floor. Most rooms have a balcony overlooking the pool or gardens, plus direct-dial telephones, cable TVs, irons and ironing boards, and air-conditioning. The hotel is popular with tour groups and features all the amenities of a deluxe property: tennis courts, sauna, swimming pool, restaurant, casino, plus shops. It's overpriced, and its out-of-the-way location has little to recommend it, although there's an hourly shuttle bus to downtown.

Food

Recommended restaurants are listed according to type and location. Many of the best restaurants can be found in the suburb of Escazú, within a 15-minute drive of San José.

BREAKFAST
Downtown

I always enjoy **La Criollita** (Avenida 7, Calles 7/9, tel. 506/2256-6511, 7 A.M.–8 P.M. Mon.–Fri., 7–11 A.M. Sat.), a clean and atmospheric favorite of the business crowd. It serves full American breakfasts ($5) plus Tico breakfasts ($4), as well as soups, salads, sandwiches, tempting entrées such as garlic shrimp ($8) and roast chicken ($5), plus natural juices. You can choose an airy, skylit indoor setting with contemporary decor, or a shaded patio.

West of Downtown

The ◖ **Restaurante Grano de Oro** (Calle 30, Avenidas 2/4, tel. 506/2255-3322, 7 A.M.–10 P.M. daily) is justifiably popular with both tourists and Tico families and businesspeople for intimate breakfasts on the outdoor patio. Try the superb gringo or Tico breakfasts. The Gringo—a large bowl of granola with bananas, and thick slices of freshly baked whole-wheat toast—should see you through the day.

East of Downtown

One of the best spots is **Bagelmen's** (Avenida 2, Calle 33, tel. 800/2212-1314, 7 A.M.–9 P.M. daily), in Barrio La California; it also has an outlet in eastern San Pedro. The ambience is pleasing, with dark wood paneling and wrought-iron chairs. It serves Reuben, tuna, smoked ham, and other sandwiches ($2–5), as well as bagels (onion, pumpernickel, etc.), muffins, brownies, and cinnamon rolls, plus breakfast specials, from *gallo pinto* to scrambled eggs.

© CHRISTOPHER P. BAKER

Restaurante Grano de Oro

DOWNTOWN SAN JOSÉ FOOD

© AVALON TRAVEL

SODAS

Sodas—cheap snack bars serving typical Costa Rican fare—are a dime a dozen. They serve "working-class" fare, such as tripe soup, and chicken with rice-and-bean dishes. You can usually fill up for $2–4.

Downtown

The **Mercado Central** (Avenidas Central/1 and Calles 6/8) has dozens of inexpensive *sodas*, as does **Mercado La Coca Cola** (Avenidas 1/3, Calles 16/18), at the Coca-Cola bus station.

Manolo's (Avenida Central, Calles Central/2, tel. 506/2221-2041) is a lively 24-hour bistro with a menu that runs from salads to filet mignon. Try the *churros,* greasy Mexican doughnuts, best enjoyed at the patio open to the pedestrian street. Upstairs you can fill up on sandwiches, seafood, meat dishes, and other fare; the third story is a bit more elegant and double the price. It has a daily special for $2.50.

Another of my favorites is **Mama's Place** (Avenida 1, Calles Central/2, tel. 506/2223-2270, 7 A.M.–7 P.M. Mon.–Fri., 7 A.M.–4 P.M. Sat.), a mom-and-pop restaurant run by an Italian couple and serving huge portions heavy on the spaghetti. It serves *casados* ($4.50).

West of Downtown

I like **Sabor Nicaragüense** (Calle 20, Avenidas Central/1, tel. 506/2248-2547, and at Calle 1, Avenida 7, tel. 506/2223-1956, 7 A.M.–9 P.M. daily), a clean family diner with heaps of light and both inside and outside dining. It serves *gallo pinto,* enchiladas, and Nicaraguan specialties.

COSTA RICAN
Downtown

The Centro Comercial El Pueblo, in Barrio Tournón, has several restaurants known for traditional Costa Rican fare. **La Cocina de Leña** (tel. 506/2555-1360, 11:30 A.M.–10 P.M. Sun.–Thurs., 11 A.M.–11:30 P.M. Fri.–Sat., entrées $10) is touted as one of the best (although food and service don't always live up to expectations). Here, you'll dine by candlelight, surrounded by the warm ambience of a cozy rural

farmhouse. Dishes include creole chicken; *olla de carne* soup; and square tamales made with white cornmeal, mashed potatoes, and beef, pork, or chicken, wrapped tightly in a plantain leaf. The open-air **Lukas** (tel. 506/2257-7124), also in El Pueblo, is a steakhouse with a pleasing aesthetic that stays open until dawn. It serves an executive lunch (noon–3 P.M.) plus such dishes as mixed tacos and *picadillos* (small chopped-vegetable platter), fried pork, mixed meats, and grilled corvina in garlic butter prepared al dente over a large grill.

Budget hounds should head to **La Casona Típica** (Avenida 2, Calle 10, tel. 506/2248-0701, 6 A.M.–10 P.M. daily), done up like a traditional farmhouse. It serves great *casados* (from $4) and traditional Costa Rican fare.

The 24-hour **Café 1930** (tel. 506/2221-4000), the terrace café fronting the Gran Hotel, serves simple but filling Costa Rican fare—*arroz con pollo* (rice with chicken; $4) plus an excellent buffet (until 10 A.M.) and more—at a reasonable price. The hustle and bustle of the *plazuela* out front provides good theater. A pianist entertains.

West of Downtown

Jicaros del Campo (tel. 506/2520-1757, 11 A.M.–10 P.M. daily), on Sabana Sur, recreates a country farmhouse and serves *típico* cuisine, include a lunch buffet ($5). Try the tongue in tomato sauce ($12).

East of Downtown

Whappin' (Calle 35, Avenida 13, tel. 506/2283-1480, 11:30 A.M.–3 P.M. and 6–10 P.M. Mon.–Sat.), in Barrio Escalante, serves up delicious Caribbean cooking in no-frills surrounds. Many dishes are cooked in coconut milk, such as *rondon* stew, and even classic chicken, rice, and beans.

NOUVELLE
Downtown

Also on a Caribbean theme, **Caribbean Loft** (Avenida 9, Calles Central/2, tel. 506/2248-1778, 6–10 P.M. daily), in the Hotel City One, serves Caribbean fusion cuisine such as plantain ceviche, shrimp soup with rum and coconut ($5), and chicken in coconut sauce ($10). It has a huge cocktail list, and the magnesium-white decor transports you to a groovy Soho nightspot.

Alas, the world-class **Bakéa** closed in 2008.

West of Downtown

Don't leave town without eating at least once at the **(Restaurante Grano de Oro** (Calle 30, Avenidas 2/4, tel. 506/2255-3322, 7 A.M.–10 P.M. daily), where chef Francis Canal has successfully merged Costa Rican ingredients into an exciting fusion menu. Opened in 2007, this supremely elegant twin-level, wood-paneled restaurant has elevated dining in San José to new levels. The menu features such dishes as poached mahi mahi with leeks, tenderloin in green peppercorn sauce, a superb salmon soufflé, and sweet curry chicken sprinkled with coconut. Prices are exceedingly fair. So, too, the specialty cocktails and an array of desserts (you *must* try the sublime Pie Grano de Oro). The gracious interior has huge windows open to the shady dining patio surrounded by lush palms and stained-glass windows. And you can even dine at the island bar, with high chairs on the patio side. Upstairs, elegant banquet rooms accommodate groups.

Nearby, the **Iconos Café Bar** (tel. 506/2257-8787, 5 A.M.–10 P.M. daily) at Hotel Parque del Lago, is a chic option where the sophisticated decor is matched by superlative dishes that include ceviche, tilapia in olive oil with white wine and herb sauce ($15), and cheesecake.

(Park Café (Calle 44, tel. 506/2290-6324, noon A.M.–3 P.M. and 7–9:30 P.M. daily), off Sabana Norte, ranks among the finest restaurants in the country. Set in an antique store with courtyard garden, its contemporary styling (not to mention the setting) is bold and exciting. Michelin-starred English chef Richard Neat (with his wife Louise) conjures up divine tapas and globe-spanning dishes. Lunch might include a roasted tuna filet with ginger chutney and artichoke salad under the shade of the flowering orchid tree, while candlelit dinner might be ballotine of foie gras with grilled sweet corn.

East of Downtown

I like the marvelous aesthetic at **Jürgen's** (tel. 506/2283-2239, noon–2 P.M. and 6–10 P.M. Mon.–Fri., 6–10 P.M. Sat., $5–25), in the Boutique Hotel Jade in San Pedro. It serves such nouvelle treats as gazpacho, mussels Rockefeller, toast Winston (beef with white wine sauce, mushrooms, and cheese with salad), shrimp gratin with camembert and jelly, and tilapia with mustard. A bar and cigar lounge offer postprandial pleasure. It has a dress code and exemplary service.

CONTINENTAL
Downtown

The streetfront **News Café** (tel. 506/2222-3022, 6 A.M.–11 P.M. daily) of the Hotel Presidente has lost much of its cozy charm following a recent remodel, but is an airy place to watch the street life. Its wide-ranging menu runs from soups, salads, and sandwiches to calamari rings ($4), fajitas ($6), burgers (from $5), and even rib eye steak ($13) and garlic tilapia ($8.50). It has lunch specials and scrumptious desserts. Across the street, the **El Patio del Balmoral,** in the Hotel Balmoral, is a carbon copy.

East of Downtown

Restaurante Club Alemán (Avenida 8, Calles 35/37, tel. 506/2225-0366, fax 506/2225-2016, www.clubaleman.org, 11 A.M.–3 P.M. and 5–11 P.M. Tues.–Sat., 11 A.M.–6 P.M. Sun., $6.50–9) is a clean and elegant place with a typical German menu: Bismarck herring, sauerkraut and sauerbraten, pork Cordon Bleu, and peach melba.

SPANISH AND SOUTH AMERICAN
Downtown

The atmospheric **Goya** (Avenida 1, Calles 5/7, tel. 506/2221-3887, 11:30 A.M.–11 P.M. Mon.–Fri., noon–9 P.M. Sat.) provides generous *bocas* as well as excellent Spanish cuisine, including a splendid paella plus rabbit in wine, at moderate prices (entrées begin at about $6). It has live entertainment nightly.

One of my favorite gems is **(La Esquina**

de Buenos Aires (Calle 11, Avenida 4, tel. 506/2223-1909, laesquina@ice.co.cr, 11:30 A.M.–3 P.M. and 6–10:30 P.M. Mon.–Fri., 12:30–11 P.M. Sat., noon–10 P.M. Sun., $5–20), a genuine Argentinian restaurant with tremendous atmosphere. The wide-ranging menu of gourmet dishes is supported by a vast wine list heavy with malbecs. The onion soup is excellent, and I enjoyed a filet of sole in blue cheese with boiled potatoes ($9).

Meat eaters will salivate at **Fogo do Brasil** (Avenida las Amémericas, Calles 40/42, tel. 506/2248-2526, venast@fogobrasi.co.cr, 11:30 A.M.–10:30 P.M. daily, $6–25), a classy Brazilian steakhouse where waiters dressed as Argentinian *gauchos* serve charcoal roasted meats. It also has a pasta bar and excellent buffet and the wide-ranging menu even has sushi. And the caipirinhas are great! It offers free hotel shuttles.

West of Downtown

The **Café España** (Calle 44, tel. 506/2290-8526, noon–8 P.M. Mon.–Sat.), in Edificio Casa de España, on Sabana Norte, offers tapas in an elegant bar setting. Prices are fair at $2–9.

Another of my favorite restaurants is ◖ **Machu Picchu** (Calle 32, Avenidas 1/3, tel. 506/2222-7384, 11 A.M.–3 P.M. and 6–10 P.M. Mon.–Sat.), with delicious authentic Peruvian seafood and *spicy* sauces! Try the superb ceviches ($2.50–5) or the *picante de mariscos* (seafood casserole with onions, garlic, olives, and cheese), enjoyed in a suitably nautical ambience. The menu is moderately priced (some potato entrées are less than $4; garlic octopus is $6). The pisco sours are powerful.

East of Downtown

Chef Emilio Machado works wonders at **Marbella Restaurant** (Centro Comercial de la Calle Real, tel. 506/2224-9452, 11:30 A.M.–3 P.M. and 6:30–10:30 P.M. Tues.–Thurs., until 11 P.M. Fri., noon–3:30 P.M. and 6:30–11:30 P.M. Sat., noon–5 P.M. Sun., $5–15), in San Pedro. The large selection of seafood dishes includes paella Marbella (shellfish and sea bass) and paella Valenciana (chicken and seafood). The paella Madrilena (rabbit, chicken, and pork) is particularly good.

FRENCH AND MEDITERRANEAN
Downtown

The Italianate **Gourmet Restaurant** (Avenida 2, Calle 3, tel. 506/2221-4000, noon–3 A.M. daily, $11–28), on the ground floor of the Gran Hotel, is a lovely space for enjoying Mediterranean seafood.

West of Downtown

The elegant **La Bastille** (Paseo Colón, Calle 22, tel. 506/2255-4994, www.la-bastille-restaurante.com, noon–2 P.M. and 6–10 P.M. Mon.–Fri., 6–10 P.M. Sat., $6–30) is the oldest French restaurant in San José. Chef Hans Pulfer produces superb French cuisine.

East of Downtown

Cognoscenti craving classical French head to the **L'Ile de France** (tel. 506/2234-7850, 6 A.M.–10 P.M. Mon.–Sat.), at L'Hôtel Le Bergerac, serving entrées such as *pâté de lapin au poivre* (rabbit with green peppercorns and cognac), vichysoisse, salon in cream of watercress, and sea bass in thyme sauce. Desserts include profiteroles, and there's a large wine collection.

Nearby is **Le Chandelier** (tel. 506/2225-3980, www.lechandeliercr.com, 11:30 A.M.–2:30 P.M. and 6:30–11 P.M. Mon.–Fri., and 6:30–11 P.M. Sat., $5–25), in a restored Mediterranean-style mansion 400 meters south of the ICE building in San Pedro. It has 10 separate dining areas, including a sculpture garden. Chef Claude Dubuis conjures up imaginative cuisine, stunning sauces, and his own version of typical Costa Rican fare: roasted heart of palm, cream of *pejivalle* soup, gratin of corvina with avocado. The restaurant is adorned with murals and the owner's art.

Exuding romantic ambience with its dark wainscoting and soft lighting, the bistro-style **Olio** (Calle 33, Avenida 3/5, tel. 506/2281-0541, 11:30 A.M.–1 A.M. Mon., 4 P.M.–midnight Sat., $5–12), 200 meters north of Bagelmon's in Barrio Escalante, specializes in

Spanish tapas and Mediterranean fare, such as a Greek *mezza* plate. Meat lovers should try the *arrollado siciliano*—a filet of steak stuffed with sun-dried tomatoes, spinach, and mozzarella. It has a large wine list.

ITALIAN
Downtown

The **Balcón de Europa** (Calle 9, Avenidas Central/1, tel. 506/2221-4841, 11:30 A.M.–10 P.M. Sun.–Fri., below $10) is a revered culinary shrine where the late chef Franco Piatti was a local institution who presented moderately priced cuisine from central Italy in an appropriately warm, welcoming setting with wood-paneled walls festooned with historic photos and framed proverbs. New chef Jean Pierre has tilted the menu towards French-Italian.

West of Downtown

The elegant **L'Olivo** (tel. 506/2220-9440, noon–3 P.M. and 6:30–10:30 P.M. Mon.–Sat., $4–15), next to Hotel Palma Real on Sabana Norte, serves pastas and seafood.

East of Downtown

Il Ponte Vecchio (tel. 506/2283-1810, noon–2 P.M. and 6–10:30 P.M. Mon.–Sat., $5–15), 200 meters west of San Pedro church, serves moderately priced, tasty cuisine cooked with imported Italian ingredients such as sun-dried tomatoes, porcini mushrooms, and basil. Pastas are homemade by chef Antonio D'Alaimo.

A more down-home ambience can be enjoyed at **Il Pomodoro** (Calle Central, tel. 506/2224-0966, 11:30 A.M.–11 P.M. Sun.–Mon. and Thurs., 11 A.M.–midnight Fri.–Sat.), 100 meters north of San Pedro church; it's a popular hangout for university types who favor the pizzas ($4–8).

MIDDLE EASTERN

For a taste of the Levantine, head to **Lubnan** (Paseo Colón, Calles 22/24, tel. 506/2257-6071, 11 A.M.–3 P.M. and 6–11 P.M. Tues.–Sat., 11 A.M.–4 P.M. Sun.), serving noteworthy Middle Eastern specialties such as shish kebob, falafel, *michi malfuf* (stuffed cabbage), and *kafta naie* (marinated ground beef); most entrées cost less than $10. Middle Eastern music plays, waiters wear fezzes, and a hookah is passed around!

East of downtown, **Aya Sofia** (Calle 31, tel. 506/2224-5050, 7 A.M.–7 P.M. Mon.–Sat.), in Barrio Escalante, is a Turkish bistro serving hummus, goat cheese marinated with olives and herbs ($3), and sandwiches. It has belly dancing.

MEXICAN

One of the best options is **Los Antojitos** (11:30 A.M.–11 P.M. Mon.–Thurs., 11 A.M.–midnight Fri.–Sat., 11 A.M.–10 P.M. Sun.), inexpensive yet classy, and popular with Ticos. Meals start at $4 and a grilled tenderloin costs $10. It has four outlets in San José: west of Sabana Park, in Rohrmoser (tel. 506/2231-5564); east of downtown in Los Yoses (tel. 506/2225-9525); in Centro Comerciál del Sur, in San Pedro (tel. 506/2227-4160); and north of town on the road to Tibas (tel. 506/2235-3961).

ASIAN
Downtown

My favorite Asian restaurant is **Tin Jo** (Calle 11, Avenidas 6/8, tel. 506/2221-7605, 11:30 A.M.–3 P.M. and 5:30–10 P.M. Mon.–Thurs. and Sun., 11:30 A.M.–11 P.M. Fri.–Sat.). The decor is quaintly colonial Costa Rican, but the food is distinctly Asian: tasty Mandarin and Szechuan specialties, plus Thai, Indian, Indonesian, and Japanese food at moderate prices. It even has sushi, satay ($4), samosas ($3), and curries ($6).

Next door, **Don Wang** (tel. 506/2223-6484, 10:30 A.M.–3:30 P.M. and 5:30–10:30 P.M. Mon.–Thurs., until 11 P.M. Fri., 10:30 A.M.–11 P.M. Sat., 10 A.M.–10 P.M. Sun.) serves generous, reasonably priced portions, although the quality isn't up to par with Tin Jo. It offers Taiwanese dishes and dim sum. Seafood dishes are a particular bargain ($4–6); it also has *platos fuertes* (set meals) for $3.

West of Downtown

The **Flor del Loto** (Calle 46, tel. 506/2232-4652, 11 A.M.–3 P.M., 6–11 P.M. Mon.–Fri.,

11 A.M.–11 P.M. Sat., 11 A.M.–9:30 P.M. Sun., $7), in Sabana Norte, is the place if you like your Chinese food hot and spicy. Mouth-searing specialties include *mo-shu-yock* (Shi Chuen–style pork) and *ma po tofu* (vegetables, bamboo shoots, and tofu stir-fried in sizzling hot-pepper oil).

Another acclaimed option is **King's Garden** (tel. 506/2255-3838, 11 A.M.–1 A.M. daily), adjoining the Centro Comercial Yaohan. The head chef is from Hong Kong; the menu features many favorites from the city, as well as Cantonese and Szechuan dishes. A set dinner for two costs about $14.

Restaurante Pacífico (Calle 24, Paseo Colón/Avenida 2, tel. 506/2257-9523, 11:30 A.M.–3 P.M. and 5:30–10:30 P.M. Mon.–Sat., 5–9 P.M. Sun.) is a small family-run Japanese restaurant with a sushi bar. It has a homey atmosphere.

East of Downtown

The **Restaurante Casa China** (Calle 25, Avenidas 8/10, tel. 506/2257-8392, 9 A.M.–11 P.M. daily) is the real McCoy and the head-quarters for the Asociación China de Costa Rica. This no-frills, refectory-style eatery serves real Chinese dishes for $4–12. You could be in Shanghai! It even has ping-pong and theatrical performances.

For sushi, head to **Ichiban** (tel. 506/2291-5220, noon–3 P.M. and 6:30–11 P.M. Mon.–Fri., noon–10 P.M. Sat.–Sun., $5–15), in Centro Comercial Calle Real, on Avenida Central, in San Pedro. Try the Ichiban roll: fried noodles with crab, eel, avocado, and cream cheese.

SEAFOOD AND STEAKS
Downtown

I recommend **Restaurant El Oasis** (Avenida 7, Calles 3/5, tel. 506/2255-0448, 4–11 P.M. Tues.–Sat., noon–7 P.M. Sun., $5–20), in the Hotel Santo Tomás, a real charmer with a co-lonial tiled bar, elegant place settings, ceiling fans, and a courtyard garden with waterfall. It serves shrimp cocktails, salads, filet mignon, sea bass with garlic and white wine, pastas, and desserts such as banana flambé.

West of Downtown

For a cheap meal, check out **Marisquería La Princesa Marina** (tel. 506/2296-7667, 11 A.M.–10:30 P.M. Mon.–Sat., 11 A.M.–9 P.M. Sun., $1–9), on Sabana Oeste. This canteen-like seafood spot is a favorite of Ticos at lunch. It serves from a wide menu and wins no gour-met prizes, but at least you fill up.

Another great spot is **La Fuente de Los Mariscos** (tel. 506/2231-0631, 11:15 A.M.–10:30 P.M. daily, $4–12), in Centro Comercial San José adjacent to the Hotel Irazú in La Uruca, with seafood at moderate prices.

VEGETARIAN
Downtown

The superb **(** **Restaurante Vishnu** (Avenida 1, Calles 1/3, tel. 506/2250-6063, vishnu@racsa.co.cr, 7 A.M.–9 P.M. Mon.–Sat., 9 A.M.–7 P.M. Sun.) serves health-food break-fasts, lunches, and dinners. Meals are generous in size and low in price (a *casado* costs $4); the menu includes veggie lasagna, veggie burgers, and fruit salads. Vishnu has 10 other outlets around town, including at Calle 14, Avenida Central/2, and at Calle 1, Avenida 4.

Restaurant Eco-Shakti (Avenida 8, Calles 11/13, tel. 2222-4475, 7:30 A.M.–7 P.M. Mon.–Fri., 8 A.M.–6 P.M. Sat.) serves veggies dishes, from black bean soup to soy burgers and yo-gurt shakes.

East of Downtown

The small, simple, inexpensive **Restaurante Vegetariano San Pedro** (tel. 506/2224-1163, 10 A.M.–6 P.M. Mon.–Fri.), on Calle Central 200 meters north of San Pedro church, has a *casado* with juice ($2), plus soy burgers, salads, and pastas.

CAFÉS AND PASTRY SHOPS
Downtown

One of the best coffee shops in town is the **Café Teatro** (tel. 506/2221-1329 ext. 250, 9 A.M.–5 P.M. Mon.–Fri., 9 A.M.–4 P.M. Sat.) inside the foyer of Teatro Nacional. A lovely neoclassical Parisian ambience is comple-mented by tempting sandwiches, snacks, and desserts. Across the plaza, the **Café Teándo** (tel. 506/2221-4000, 24 hours) in the foyer of the Gran Hotel competes with hip contemporary decor.

The **Café del Correo** (tel. 506/2257-3670, 9 A.M.–7 P.M. Mon.–Fri., 10 A.M.–5 P.M. Sat.), in the post office overlooking Avenida Central, is another little gem. Soft lighting and jazz provide a romantic background for enjoying lattes, espressos, mochas, and pastries such as cheesecakes and strawberry tarts.

The artsy, Argentinian-run **Café de la Posada** (Avenida 2, Calle 17, tel. 506/2258-1027, 9 A.M.–7 P.M. Mon.–Thurs., 9 A.M.–11 P.M. Fri.–Sun.) appeals to a bohemian crowd. It offers jazz and classical music and serves espressos and cappuccinos, plus quiches, omelettes, sandwiches (all from $1.50), Argentinian *empanadas,* and tempting desserts.

The bohemian **Café Mundo** (Avenida 9, Calle 15, tel. 506/2222-6190, 11 A.M.–11 P.M. Mon.–Fri., noon–2:30 P.M. and 5 P.M.–midnight Sat.) is popular with businessfolk. This handsome remake of a colonial mansion has open patios and several indoor rooms. Its eclectic menu spans tempura veggies ($5.50), chicken satay ($5.50), Caesar salad (from $3.50), pastas, pizzas, surf and turf (from $8), desserts such as tiramisu, plus cappuccino ($1.75). Portions are generous.

◖ **Spoon** (www.spooncr.com) has burgeoned over the past decade from a small takeout bakery into a chain with outlets throughout the city, including Avenida Central, Calle 5/7 (tel. 506/2255-2480) and Mall Pedro in Los Yoses (tel. 506/2283-4538). In addition to desserts, Spoon serves sandwiches, salads, lasagna, soups, *empanadas* (pastries stuffed with chicken and other meats), and *lapices,* the Costa Rican equivalent of submarine sandwiches, all at bargain prices. **Musmanni** (tel. 506/2296-5750, www.musmanni.net) is a national *pastelería* chain selling pastries and fresh breads.

West of Downtown

Chocoholics should sniff out the **Taller de Chocolate** (Calle 26, Paseo Colón/Avenida 2, tel. 506/2231-4840, and 100 meters north of Torre La Sabana, on Sabana Norte, 10 A.M.–6 P.M. Mon.–Fri., 10 A.M.–3 P.M. Sat.). It sells delicious homemade chocolates, plus cappuccinos and espressos.

One block west, a gorgeous 1950s modernist home hosts **Asís** (tel. 506/2232-2657, noon–6 P.M. Mon.–Fri.), a marvelously upscale venue for pastries, teas, and coffees, plus pastas, pizzas, and *casado* lunches ($4).

East of Downtown

In Los Yoses I like **Café Ruiseñor** (Avenida Central, Calles 41/43, tel. 506/2225-2562, 7 A.M.–7:30 P.M. Mon.–Fri., 10 A.M.–6 P.M. Sat.), a classy, trendy spot serving a range of coffee drinks including lattes ($1.75), plus soups, salads, sandwiches, and entrées such as curried chicken, sea bass with herbs and white wine, pepper steak, as well as desserts such as banana splits, German apple tart, and parfaits.

Ice cream fans should head to **Häagen-Dazs Café** (Avenida Central, tel. 506/2280-5245, 10 A.M.–10 P.M. Sun.–Thurs., 10 A.M.–11 P.M. Fri.–Sat.), in San Pedro. This clean, contemporary parlor serves everyone's favorite ice cream, from cones to special sundaes. It also has espressos and cappuccinos. Nearby, and new in 2008, the **Kai Café and Lunch** (Avenida Central, tel. 506/2281-0955, 9 A.M.–9 P.M. Mon.–Sat., 10 A.M.–8 P.M. Sun.) offers a beautiful contemporary elegance, with leather sofas and walls of glass. It serves sandwiches, paninis, salads, and scrumptious desserts.

MARKETS

Within the warren of the **Mercado Central** (Calles 6/8, Avenidas Central/1, closed Sun.) and adjoining **Mercado Borbón** (Calle 8, Avenidas 3/5) are stands selling poultry, flowers, meat, fish, medicinal herbs, fresh produce, and coffee. The **Mercado Paso de la Vaca** (Avenida 7, Calle 6) is a clean produce market selling everything from fresh herbs to meats; take a taxi and be careful walking around this area.

Cabernet (in the Centro Comercial Real #16, tel. 506/2281-2481, mseaward@racsa.co.cr), off Avenida Central in San Pedro, sells all things wine-related and is well stocked with wines.

Information and Services

TOURIST INFORMATION

ICT operates a tourist information office booth at the airport (tel. 506/2443-2883). Its main tourist information office (tel. 506/2222-1090, ictplazacultura@icc.co.cr), beneath the Plaza de la Cultura on Calle 5, is open 9 A.M.–1 P.M. and 2–5 P.M. Mon.–Sat.; its outlet in the post office (Calle 2, Avenidas 1/3) was temporarily closed at last visit.

TRAVEL AGENCIES

There are dozens of English-speaking travel agencies in San José. They can arrange city tours, one- and multi-day excursions, beach resort vacations, air transportation, and more. Above all I recommend U.S.–run **Costa Rica Expeditions** (Avenida 3, Calle Central, tel. 506/2257-0766, www.costarica expeditions.com). **STI Travel** (Avenida Central, Calle 35, tel. 506/2283-8200, www.stitravel.com), in Los Yoses, specializes in cheap airfares.

NEWSPAPERS AND MAGAZINES

Most major hotel gift stores sell popular international newspapers and periodicals, as does **7th Street Books** (Calle 7, Avenidas Central/1). **La Casa de las Revistas** has outlets at Calle Central, Avenidas 4/6 (tel. 506/2222-0987), and Calle 7, Avenidas 1/3 (tel. 506/2256-5092), selling a wide range of Spanish- and English-language magazines.

LIBRARIES

The **Biblioteca Nacional** (National Library, Avenida 3, Calles 15/17, tel. 506/2257-4814, 8 A.M.–4 P.M. Mon.–Fri.) has more than 100,000 volumes.

You may be able to access the **Biblioteca Universidad de Costa Rica** (tel. 506/2253-6152), at the university in San Pedro; and the **Mark Twain Library** (Calle Negritos, tel. 506/2225-9433 or 800/2077-7500, www.cccncr.com/biblioteca.html, 9 A.M.–7 P.M.

Mon.–Fri., 9 A.M.–noon Sat.), in the Centro Cultural Norteamericano in Los Yoses.

MONEY

San José has dozens of banks. Most have a separate foreign exchange counter, will give cash advances against your Visa card (and in some cases, your MasterCard), and have ATM machines that issue cash advances against credit cards. Outside banking hours, head to **Teledolar Casa de Cambio** (Paseo Colón, Calle 24, tel. 506/2248-1718, 8:30 A.M.–4 P.M. Mon.–Sat., 8:30 A.M.–2 P.M. Sun.), which changes foreign currency.

Credomatic (Calle Central, Avenidas 3/5, tel. 506/2295-9000, www.credomatic.com) will assist you with card replacement for Visa and MasterCard.

POST AND COMMUNICATIONS
Mail

The main post office, or **Correo Central** (Calle 2, Avenidas 1/3, tel. 506/2223-9766, www.correos.go.cr, 8 A.M.–5 P.M. Mon.–Fri. 7:30 A.M.–noon Sat.), has a 24-hour stamp machine. You can also buy stamps and post your mail at the front desks of upscale hotels.

To collect incoming mail at the Correo Central, go to window 17 through the entrance nearest Avenida 1. You'll need to show your passport. There's a small charge (about $0.25) per letter.

FedEx (Paseo Colón, Calle 40, tel. 506/2255-4567) and **DHL** (Paseo Colón, Calles 30/32, tel. 506/2209-6000) offer courier service.

Telephones

There are public telephones throughout the city. **KitCom** (Calle 3, Avenidas 1/3, tel. 506/2258-0303, www.kitcom.net), on the second floor of the OTEC Building, 175 meters north of the Plaza de la Cultura, has a complete telecommunications office.

Alternately, use the **ICE** offices on Sabana

Casa Amarilla and INS building

© CHRISTOPHER P. BAKER

Norte or south of the San Pedro roundabout; or RACSA's **Telecommunications Center** (Avenida 5, Calle Central/1, tel. 506/2287-0515, 7:30 A.M.–4:30 P.M. Mon.–Fri., and 9 A.M.–1 P.M. Sat.).

Internet Access

Most hotels have Internet access for guests, and there are Internet cafés throughout the city.

Downtown, one of the best Internet cafés is the **CyberCafé** (Avenida 2, Calles 1/3, tel. 506/2233-3310, 7 A.M.–9 P.M. daily), in the basement of Las Arcadas, 50 meters west of the Teatro Nacional. It also has a pleasant outdoor dining area and a travel desk.

Internet Café Costa Rica has outlets at Avenida Central, Calle 2 (tel. 506/2255-0540, 9 A.M.–10 P.M. daily); at Avenida Central, Calle 3 (tel. 506/2255-1154, 9 A.M.–10 P.M. daily); west of downtown in Centro Colón (tel. 506/2233-3179, 8 A.M.–9 P.M. Mon.–Sat.); and east of downtown at Avenida Central, Calle Central (tel. 506/2224-7382, 24 hours), in San Pedro.

LAUNDRIES

Most laundries *(lavanderías)* offer a wash-and-dry service (about $4 per load). Downtown, try **Sixaola** (Avenida 2, Calles 7/9, tel. 506/2240-7667), which has outlets throughout San José. The **CyberCafé** (Avenida 2, Calles 1/3, tel. 506/2233-3310, 7 A.M.–9 P.M. daily) has a self-service laundry ($5 wash and dry per tub).

PHOTOGRAPHY

The major photographic outlet is **Dima** (Avenida Central, Calles 3/5, tel. 506/2222-3969), which also offers repair service.

MEDICAL SERVICES

The privately run **Hospital Clínica Bíblica** (tel. 506/2522-1000 or 2257-5252) is the best hospital in town and accepts U.S. Medicare.

The public **Hospital Dr. Calderón Guardia** (tel. 506/2257-7922) and **Hospital México** (tel. 506/2242-6700) are alternatives, as is the public **Hospital San Juan de Díos** (Paseo Colón, Calle 16, tel. 506/2257-6282), the most centrally located medical facility. They provide free emergency health care on the Social Security system. The **Children's Hospital** (Hospital Nacional de Niños, Paseo Colón, tel. 506/2222-0122) cares for children. Women are served by the **Hospital** **de la Mujer** (Calle Central, Avenida 22, tel. 506/2257-9111).

TOILETS

There are clean public toilets beneath the Plaza de la Cultura.

Getting There and Around

GETTING THERE
By Air
Juan Santamaría International Airport (tel. 506/2437-2626, www.alterra.co.cr) is on the outskirts of Alajuela, 17 kilometers west of San José.

A tourist information booth (tel. 506/2443-2883, 9 A.M.–5 P.M. Mon.–Fri.) is in the baggage claim area, and another immediately beyond Customs. There's a bank in the departure terminal. Taxis accept dollars, but you'll need local currency for public transport into San José. (At press time, the **departure tax** for travelers leaving Costa Rica was $26, payable in dollars or colones equivalent. You pay at the booth to the right inside the departure lounge prior to checking in. To avoid long lines, pay your departure tax when you arrive in Costa Rica.)

Pavas Airport (Tobías Bolaños, tel. 506/2232-2820), about four kilometers west of town, is used for domestic flights, including small charter planes and air-taxis. Bus 14B runs from Avenida 1, Calles 16/18, and stops in Pavas, a short walk from the airport.

By Train
Train service runs between San Pedro and Pavas, five times daily Monday–Friday and three times daily Saturday and Sunday, departing the **Pacific Railway Station** (Avenida 20, Calle Central/7, tel. 506/2257-6161).

By Car
Westbound from downtown San José, Paseo Colón feeds right onto the Pan-American Highway (Hwy. 1, or Autopista General Cañas), which leads to the Pacific coast, Guanacaste, and Nicaragua. A tollbooth just east of the airport charges 60 colones ($0.25) per vehicle for westbound traffic only.

Calle 3 leads north from downtown and becomes the Guápiles Highway (Hwy. 32) for Puerto Limón and the Caribbean and Northern Zone. Avenida 2 leads east via San Pedro to Cartago and the southern section of the Pan-American Highway (Hwy. 2), bound for Panamá; there's a tollbooth (60 colones) about three kilometers east of the suburb of San Pedro.

By Bus
San José has no central terminal. Buses for Puerto Limón and the Caribbean depart from the **Gran Terminál Caribe** on Calle Central, Avenidas 15/17. Most buses to other destinations leave from the area referred to as **Coca-Cola** (the zone is centered on Avenida 3, Calles 16/18, but encompasses many surrounding streets; there's a 24-hour **police station,** tel. 506/2257-3096). Other buses leave from the bus company office or a streetside bus stop (*parada*). Many street departure points are unmarked, so ask locals.

A Safe Passage/Viaje Seguro (tel. 506/8365-9678, www.costaricabustickets.com) will make your bus reservations and buy your tickets for you in advance. Tickets cost $15 single, $25 a pair to anywhere in the nation. It also offers airport transfers.

The ICT publishes a listing of current bus schedules, including the bus company and telephone numbers.

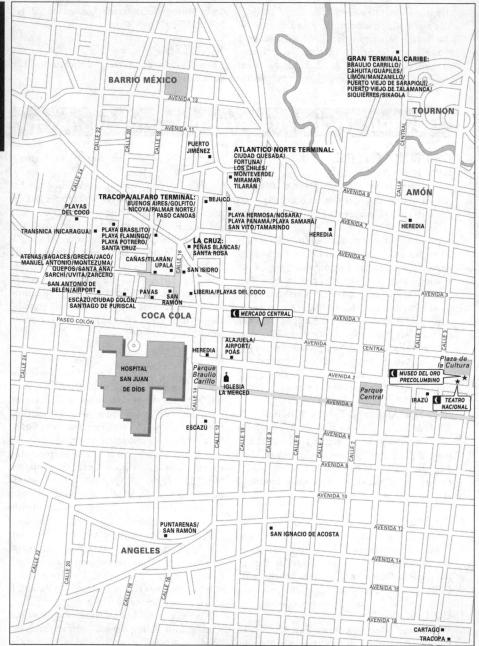

BARRIO MÉXICO

AVENIDA 13

AVENIDA 11

CALLE 22
CALLE 20
CALLE 18

PUERTO JIMÉNEZ

GRAN TERMINAL CARIBE:
BRAULIO CARRILLO/
CAHUITA/GUAPILES/
LIMÓN/MANZANILLO/
PUERTO VIEJO DE SARAPIQUI/
PUERTO VIEJO DE TALAMANCA/
SIQUIERRES/SIXAOLA

TOURNÓN

CALLE CENTRAL

ATLANTICO NORTE TERMINAL:
CIUDAD QUESADA/
FORTUNA/
LOS CHILES/
MONTEVERDE/
MIRAMAR
TILARÁN/

AVENIDA 9

AMÓN

CALLE 24

PLAYAS DEL COCO

TRACOPA/ALFARO TERMINAL:
BUENOS AIRES/GOLFITO/
NICOYA/PALMAR NORTE/
PASO CANOAS

BEJUCO

PLAYA HERMOSA/NOSARA/
PLAYA PANAMÁ/PLAYA SAMARÁ/
SAN VITO/TAMARINDO

AVENIDA 7

HEREDIA

AVENIDA 5

TRANSNICA (NICARAGUA)

PLAYA BRASILITO/
PLAYA FLAMINGO/
PLAYA POTRERO/
SANTA CRUZ

HEREDIA

LA CRUZ:
PEÑAS BLANCAS/
SANTA ROSA

ATENAS/BAGACES/GRECIA/JACÓ/
MANUEL ANTONIO/MONTEZUMA/
QUEPOS/SANTA ANA/
SARCHI/UVITA/ZARCERO

CAÑAS/TILARÁN/
UPALA

CALLE 16

SAN ISIDRO

SAN ANTONIO DE
BELÉN/AIRPORT

PAVAS

SAN
RAMÓN

LIBERIA/PLAYAS DEL COCO

AVENIDA 3

ESCAZÚ/CIUDAD COLÓN/
SANTIAGO DE PURISCAL

COCA COLA

PASEO COLÓN

CALLE 24

**HOSPITAL
SAN JUAN
DE DÍOS**

(**MERCADO CENTRAL**

*Parque
Braulio
Carillo*

HEREDIA

IGLESIA
LA MERCED

CALLE 14

ALAJUELA/
AIRPORT/
POÁS

AVENIDA 1

AVENIDA

CENTRAL

CALLE 1
CALLE 3

*Plaza de
la Cultura*

(**MUSEO DEL ORO
PRECOLUMBINO**

★ ★

AVENIDA 2

*Parque
Central*

IRAZÚ

(**TEATRO
NACIONAL**

ESCAZÚ

CALLE 12

CALLE 10

CALLE 8

AVENIDA 6

CALLE 6

CALLE 4

CALLE 2

AVENIDA 8

AVENIDA 10

PUNTARENAS/
SAN RAMÓN

SAN IGNACIO DE ACOSTA

AVENIDA 12

ANGELES

CALLE 22

CALLE 20

CALLE 18

CALLE 16

AVENIDA 14

AVENIDA 16

AVENIDA 18

CARTAGO

TRACOPA

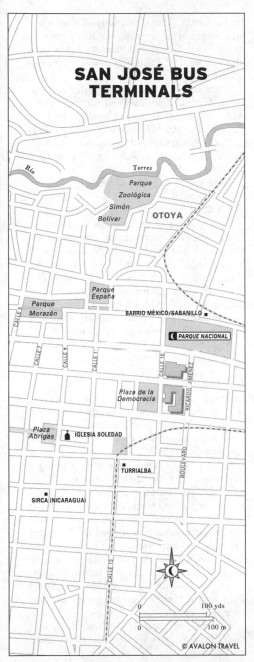

SAN JOSÉ BUS TERMINALS

GETTING AROUND
Getting to and from the Airport
TAXIS
Taxi Aeropuerto (tel. 506/2222-6865, www.taxiaeropuerto.com) operates taxis between the airport and downtown and accepts 24-hour reservations; they're orange (local San José taxis are red). The legally sanctioned fare into downtown San José adjusts according to gasoline prices and at press time was $23 by day and night ($5 to Alajuela); you pay in advance at an official booth immediately outside the arrivals lounge and are given a ticket.

BUSES
Public buses run by **Tuasa** (tel. 506/2222-5325) operate between downtown San José (Avenida 2, Calles 12/14) and Alajuela every five minutes via the airport, 5 A.M.–10 P.M., and then every 30 minutes 10 P.M.–5 A.M. The fare is 250 colones ($0.50). The driver will make change, but you'll need small bills or coins. The journey takes about 30 minutes. Luggage space is limited.

SHUTTLES
Interbus (tel. 506/2283-5573, www.interbus online.com) offers a 24-hour airport shuttle for $6 per person by reservation. **Grayline** (tel. 506/2220-2126, www.graylinecosta rica.com) operates an "Airline Express" linking the airport and downtown San José every 30 minutes ($10). Some hotels offer free shuttles.

   Costa Rica Van Go (tel. 506/2441-7837, www.costaricavango.com) offers private airport transfers.

CAR RENTAL
Several car-rental companies have offices immediately beyond Customs; additional offices are within one kilometer east of the airport, in Río Segundo de Alajuela. If you plan on spending a few days in San José before heading off to explore the country, you'll be better off using taxis and local buses. Make your reservations *before* departing home.

Park & Fly (tel. 506/2441-3134, www.park andflycr.com) offers 24/7 shuttle service between its parking facility and the airport.

By Car

There are about 50 car-rental agencies in San José, concentrated along Paseo Colón. However, don't even think about using a rental car for travel *within* San José. Too many headaches! Most places are quickly and easily reached by taxi, by bus, or on foot. Note that Paseo Colón (normally with two-way traffic) is one-way only—eastbound—weekdays 6:30–8:30 A.M.

A peripheral highway *(circunvalación)* passes around the south and east sides of San José.

Private parking lots offer secure 24-hour parking; you must leave your ignition key with the attendant. Never park in a no-parking zone, marked Control por Grúa (Controlled by tow truck). Regulations are efficiently enforced.

Break-ins and theft are common (rental cars are especially vulnerable). Never leave anything of value in your car, even in the trunk.

By Bus

San José has an excellent network of privately owned local bus services. Most buses operate 5 A.M.–10 P.M., with frequency of service determined by demand. Downtown and suburban San José buses operate every few minutes. Buses to suburbs often fill up, so it's best to board at their principal downtown *parada,* designated by a sign, Parada de Autobuses, showing the route name and number.

A sign in the windshield tells the route number and destination. Fares are marked by the doors and are collected when you board. Drivers provide change and tend to be honest. Buses cost 75 colones ($0.15) downtown and under 100 colones elsewhere within the metropolitan area.

From the west, the most convenient bus into town is the Sabana-Cementerio service (route 2), which runs counterclockwise between Sabana Sur and downtown along Avenida 10, then back along Avenida 3 (past the "Coca-Cola" bus station) and Paseo Colón. The Cementerio-Estadio service (route 7) runs in the opposite direction along Paseo Colón and Avenida 2 and back along Avenida 12. Both take about 40 minutes to complete the circle.

Buses to Los Yoses and San Pedro run east along Avenida 2 and, beyond Calle 29, along Avenida Central. Buses to Coronado begin at Calle 3, Avenidas 5/7; to Guadalupe at Avenida 3, Calles Central/1; to Moravia from Avenida 3, Calles 3/5; and to Pavas from Avenida 1, Calle 18.

Be wary of pickpockets on buses.

By Train

A great way to beat the cross-town traffic is to hop on the **Tren Interurbano** commuter train that links Pavas (on the west side of town) with San Pedro (on the east side). Trains operate five times daily in each direction (5 A.M.–6 P.M. Mon.–Fri., 150 colones, or $0.25 cents), stopping at or near the U.S. Embassy, La Salle (south side of Parque La Sabana), and Universidad de Costa Rica (University of Costa Rica).

As of May 2009, San José is also linked by train to the nearby town of Heredia.

By Taxi

Licensed taxis are red (taxis exclusively serving the airport are orange); if it's any other color, it's a "pirate" taxi operating illegally. You can travel anywhere within the city for less than $6 (the base fare is $0.85).

By law taxi drivers (who must display a business card with name, license plate, and other details) must use their meters *(marias)* for journeys of less than 12 kilometers. Always demand that the taxi driver use his meter, otherwise you're going to get ripped off. Some taxi drivers get commissions from certain hotels: They may tell you that the place you're seeking is closed or full and will try to persuade you to go to a hotel they recommend. Don't fall for this! If the cabbie insists, get out and take another cab.

You do not normally tip taxi drivers in Costa Rica, but give your taxi driver any small change.

Finding a taxi is usually not a problem, except during rush hour and when it's raining. One of the best places is Parque Central, where they line up on Avenida 2, and in front of the Gran Hotel and Teatro Nacional two blocks east. Otherwise, call **Coopetaxi** (tel. 506/2235-9966) or **Coopetico** (tel. 506/2224-7979).

There are reports of taxi drivers making sexual advances toward single women; this is more likely to happen with pirate taxis, which you should always avoid. Few taxis have seat belts! The belts are usually there; it's the connecting latches that are missing. And if an on-call taxi draws up to your hotel against the flow of traffic, as often happens, you'd be wise to seek another taxi.

By Tour

Californian Kevin Wilks's **Tico Walks** (tel. 506/2234-8575, www.ticowalks.com, $10 per person) offers 2.5-hour educational tours of downtown San José, beginning at the Teatro Nacional on Tuesday, Thursday, Saturday, and Sunday at 10 P.M.

A fun way to explore is with **Segway Costa Rica** (tel. 506/2232-4822, www.segwaycosta rica.com), which currently has a two-hour tour of Parque Sabana ($69). Expect more options to be added.

CENTRAL HIGHLANDS

The beauty of the Central Highlands region owes much to the juxtaposition of valley and mountain. The large, fertile central valley—sometimes called the Meseta Central (Central Plateau)—is a tectonic depression some 20 kilometers wide and 70 kilometers long. The basin is held in the cusp of verdant mountains that rise on all sides, their slopes quilted with dark green coffee and pastures as bright as fresh limes. Volcanoes of the Cordillera Central frame the valley to the north, forming a smooth-sloped meniscus. To the south lies the massive, blunt-nosed bulk of the Cordillera Talamanca. The high peaks are generally obscured by clouds for much of the "winter" months (May–November). When clear, both mountain zones offer spectacularly scenic drives, including the chance to drive to the very crest of two active volcanoes: Poás and Irazú.

The Meseta Central is really two valleys in one, divided by a low mountain ridge—the Fila de Bustamente (or Cerro de la Carpintera)—which rises immediately east of San José. West of the ridge is the larger valley of the Poás and Virilla rivers, with flanks gradually rising from a level floor. East of the ridge the smaller Valle de Guarco (containing Cartago) is more tightly hemmed in and falls away to the east, drained by the Río Reventazón.

Almost 70 percent of the nation's populace lives here, concentrated in the four colonial cities of San José, Alajuela, Cartago, and Heredia, plus lesser urban centers that derive their livelihood from farming. Sugarcane, tobacco, and corn smother the valley floor, according to

HIGHLIGHTS

◖ **Rancho San Miguel:** This stable comes into its own on Saturday night when it hosts an Andalusian horse show offering a dramatic display of fine horsemanship (page 97).

◖ **Flor de Mayo:** Visits are strictly by appointment at this private breeding center for endangered macaws. Serious birders and nature lovers will be enthralled (page 98).

◖ **La Paz Waterfall Gardens:** The world's largest butterfly enclosure, an aviary, snake and frog exhibits, hiking trails, and spectacular waterfalls highlight a visit to this nature theme park. It also has a fine restaurant and luxurious accommodations (page 104).

◖ **Poás Volcano National Park:** Imagine a drive-in volcano! You can park near the summit, then walk to the crater rim of this steaming volcano. As a bonus, you're blessed with stupendous views (page 108).

◖ **Taller Eloy Alfaro:** An astonishing workshop where traditional *carretas* (oxcarts) are still made in traditional fashion, with power supplied by a waterwheel (page 112).

◖ **Bajos del Toro:** This remote, seldom-visited Shangri-la offers prime birding and wildlife-viewing, plus superb lodging in a rain-soaked mountain setting (page 113).

◖ **Zoo Ave:** A Noah's Ark-ful of critters are displayed at this well-run zoo offering close-up encounters with animals and birds you may not wish to meet in the wild. All the favorites are here, from monkeys to the big cats (page 117).

◖ **Los Angeles Cloud Forest Reserve:** There are no quetzals here, but sloths, monkeys galore, and countless bird species inhabit this mountain-crest, mist-shrouded forest with nature trails and a short zipline canopy tour (page 120).

◖ **Café Britt:** Workers in *campesino* outfits provide an entertaining entrée to the world of coffee, including theatrical skits and ending with your favorite beverage (page 128).

◖ **Irazú Volcano National Park:** The drive up Volcán Irazú is a scenic switchback made more fun by the anticipation of magnificent views from the summit (page 140).

◖ **San Gerardo de Dota:** Here you'll find a paradisiacal valley with a magnificent climate, a choice of delightful accommodations, and birding – including quetzal-viewing – as good as anywhere in the nation (page 148).

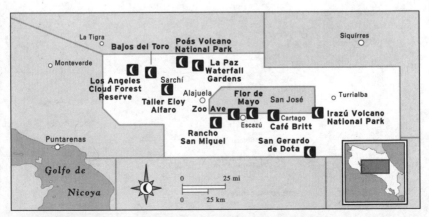

LOOK FOR ◖ TO FIND RECOMMENDED SIGHTS, ACTIVITIES, DINING, AND LODGING.

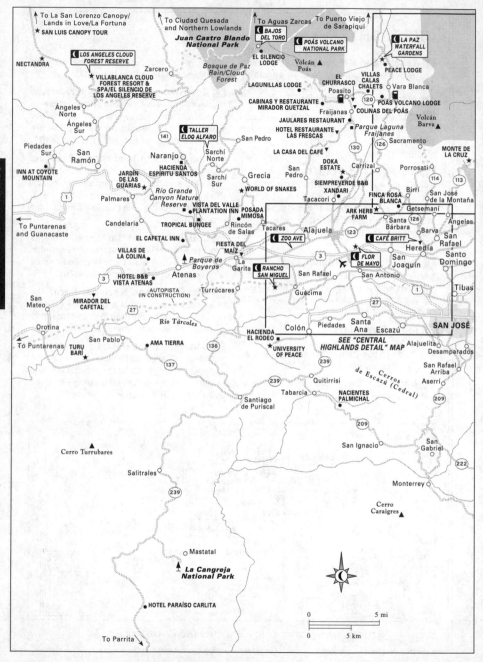

To La San Lorenzo Canopy/
Lands in Love/La Fortuna
★ SAN LUIS CANOPY TOUR

To Ciudad Quesada
and Northern Lowlands

To Aguas Zarcas

To Puerto Viejo
de Sarapiquí

BAJOS
DEL TORO

POÁS VOLCANO
NATIONAL PARK

LA PAZ
WATERFALL
GARDENS

**Juan Castro Blando
National Park**

LOS ANGELES CLOUD
FOREST RESERVE

EL SILENCIO
LODGE

PEACE LODGE

NECTANDRA

VILLABLANCA CLOUD
FOREST RESORT &
SPA/EL SILENCIO DE
LOS ANGELES RESERVE

Zarcero

Bosque de Paz
Rain/Cloud
Forest

Volcán ▲
Poás

EL
CHURRASCO

VILLAS
CALAS
CHALETS

Vara Blanca

LAGUNILLAS LODGE

Poasito

120

POÁS VOLCANO LODGE

Ángeles
Norte

CABINAS Y RESTAURANTE
MIRADOR QUETZAL

Fraijanas

COLINAS DEL POÁS

Volcán
Barva ▲

Ángeles
Sur

JAULARES RESTAURANT

Parque Laguna
Fraijanes

Piedades
Sur

TALLER
ELOQ ALFARO

HOTEL RESTAURANTE
LAS FRESCAS

Sacramento

MONTE DE
LA CRUZ

San
Ramón

141

San Pedro

130

126

INN AT COYOTE
MOUNTAIN

Naranjo

Sarchí
Norte

LA CASA DEL CAFÉ

San
Pedro

DOKA
ESTATE

Carrizal

Porrosatí

114

113

JARDÍN
DE LAS
GUARIAS

HACIENDA
ESPÍRITU SANTOS

Sarchí
Sur

Grecia

SIEMPREVERDE B&B
XANDARI

Birrí

San José
de la Montaña

Palmares

Río Grande
Canyon Nature
Reserve

WORLD OF SNAKES

Tacacori

FINCA ROSA
BLANCA

Getsemaní

Candelaria

VISTA DEL VALLE
PLANTATION INN

POSADA
MIMOSA

ARK HERB
FARM

Santa
Bárbara

126

Angeles

TROPICAL BUNGEE

Rincón
de Salas

Tacares

Alajuela

123

Barva

San
Rafael

EL CAFETAL INN

FIESTA DEL
MAÍZ

ZOO AVE

CAFÉ BRITT

Heredia

Santo
Domingo

VILLAS DE
LA COLINA

La
Garita

FLOR
DE MAYO

San
Joaquín

Atenas

Parque de
Boyeros

RANCHO
SAN MIGUEL

San Rafael

San
Antonio

1

Tibas

HOTEL B&B
VISTA ATENAS

3

Guácima

27

SAN JOSÉ

San
Mateo

MIRADOR DEL
CAFETAL

AUTOPISTA
(IN CONSTRUCTION)

Turrúcares

27

Orotina

Río Tárcoles

Colón

Piedades

Santa
Ana

Escazú

To Puntarenas

San Pablo

AMA TIERRA

HACIENDA
EL RODEO

SEE "CENTRAL
HIGHLANDS DETAIL" MAP

Alajuelita

Desamparados

TURU
BARÍ

136

UNIVERSITY
OF PEACE

239

San Rafael
Arriba

Aserrí

137

Quitirrisí

Cerros
de Escazú (Cedral)

209

239

Tabarcia

NACIENTES
PALMICHAL

Santiago
de Puriscal

209

Cerro Turrubares ▲

San Ignacio

San
Gabriel

Salitrales

222

Monterrey

239

Cerro
Caraigres ▲

Mastatal

**La Cangreja
National Park**

HOTEL PARAÍSO CARLITA

To Parrita

0   5 mi

0   5 km

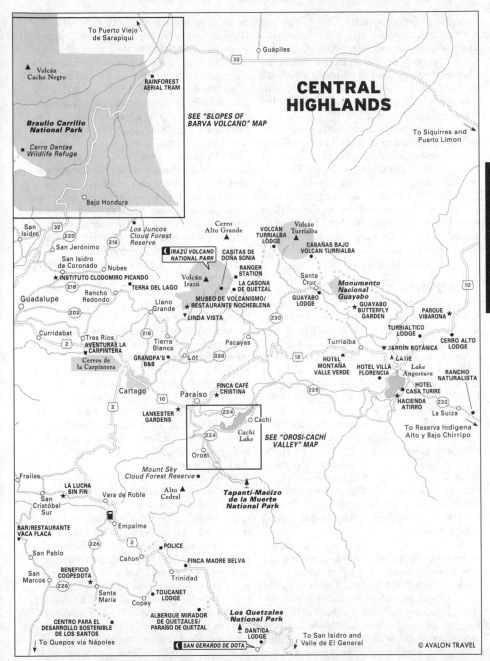

CENTRAL HIGHLANDS

CENTRAL HIGHLANDS

To Puerto Viejo de Sarapiquí

○ Guápiles

▲ Volcán Cacho Negro

■ RAINFOREST AERIAL TRAM

Braulio Carrillo National Park

■ *Cerro Dantas Wildlife Refuge*

SEE "SLOPES OF BARVA VOLCANO" MAP

To Siquirres and Puerto Límon

■ Bajo Hondura

San Isidro

■ *Los Juncos Cloud Forest Reserve*

○ San Jerónimo

San Isidro de Coronado ○ Nubes

★ INSTITUTO CLODOMIRO PICANDO

Guadalupe

Rancho Redondo

○ TERRA DEL LAGO

Llano Grande

Cerro Alto Grande

VOLCÁN TURRIALBA LODGE

Volcán Turrialba ▲

CABAÑAS BAJO VOLCÁN TURRIALBA

IRAZÚ VOLCANO NATIONAL PARK

CASITAS DE DOÑA SONIA

RANGER STATION

Volcán Irazú ▲

LA CASONA DE QUETZAL

Santa Cruz

Monumento Nacional Guayabo

MUSEO DE VOLCANISMO/ RESTAURANTE NOCHEBLENA

GUAYABO LODGE

★ GUAYABO BUTTERFLY GARDEN

PARQUE VIBARONA ★

★ LINDA VISTA

Curridabat

Tres Ríos

AVENTURAS LA CARPINTERA

Tierra Blanca

Pacayas

Turrialba

TURRIALTICO LODGE

CERRO ALTO LODGE

★ JARDÍN BOTÁNICA

Cerros de la Carpintera

GRANDPA'S B&B

Lot

HOTEL MONTAÑA VALLE VERDE

HOTEL VILLA FLORENCIA

★ CATIE

Lake Angostura

RANCHO NATURALISTA

Cartago

Paraíso

FINCA CAFÉ CRISTINA

HOTEL CASA TURIRE

HACIENDA ATIRRO

La Suiza

LANKESTER GARDENS

Cachí

Cachí Lake

SEE "OROSI-CACHÍ VALLEY" MAP

To Reserva Indígena Alto y Bajo Chirripo

Orosi

Mount Sky Cloud Forest Reserve ■

Frailes

LA LUCHA SIN FIN

San Cristóbal Sur

Vara de Roble

Alto Cedral ▲

Tapantí-Macizo de la Muerte National Park

BAR/RESTAURANTE VACA FLACA ▼

Empalme

San Pablo

POLICE

Cañon

FINCA MADRE SELVA

San Marcos

BENEFICIO COOPEDOTA ★

Trinidad

Santa María

Copey

TOUCANET LODGE

CENTRO PARA EL DESARROLLO SOSTENIBLE DE LOS SANTOS

ALBERGUE MIRADOR DE QUETZALES/ PARAÍSO DE QUETZAL

Los Quetzales National Park

DANTICA LODGE

To Quepos vía Nápoles

SAN GERARDO DE DOTA

To San Isidro and Valle de El General

© AVALON TRAVEL

elevation and microclimate. Dairy farms rise up the slopes to more than 2,500 meters. Small coffee *fincas*, too, are everywhere on vale and slope. Pockets of natural vegetation remain farther up the slopes and in protected areas such as Braulio Carrillo National Park, Tapantí-Macizo de la Muerte National Park, and other havens of untamed wildlife.

Though variations exist, an invigorating and salubrious climate is universal. In the dry season, mornings are clear and the valley basks under brilliant sunshine. In the wet ("green") season, clouds typically form over the mountains in early afternoon, bringing brief downpours. Temperatures average in the mid-20s Celsius (mid- to high 70s Fahrenheit) year-round in the valley and cool steadily as one moves into the mountains, where coniferous trees lend a distinctly alpine feel.

PLANNING YOUR TIME

You could well spend two weeks touring the highlands, but for most folks three or four days should prove sufficient. Ideally you'll want your own car, although tour operators in San José offer excursions. Don't underestimate the time it can take to move between destinations: Roads are convoluted and signage is poor. Touring the highlands en route to another region makes sense; choose your destinations accordingly.

West of San José, the town of **Escazú** melds quaint historical charm with a cosmopolitan vibe and offers some of the nation's finest dining, plus nightspots that draw the youth from San José. Nearby, and long a staple of the tourist circuit, the **Butterfly Farm** will teach you all about butterfly lore, while the Andalusian horse show at **Rancho San Miguel** is breathtaking.

Northwest of San José, two must-sees are **Poás Volcano National Park,** where you can peer into the bowels of a living volcano, and **La Paz Waterfall Gardens.** The drive up the mountain slopes is tremendously scenic, although the same can be said for any journey into the mountains *(note that this area was devastated by an earthquake on January 8, 2009, and at press time many of the tourism facilities*

in the area remained closed). If heading for Ciudad Quesada, Highway 141 will deliver you via the **World of Snakes,** the crafts town of **Sarchí** (to be avoided on weekends, when tour buses crowd in), and the delightful village of **Zarcero,** renowned for the topiary in the church plaza. From here, nature lovers might make the side trip to **Bajos del Toro** and its Bosque de Paz Rain/Cloud Forest Biological Reserve. Alternately, the fast (perhaps too fast) Highway 1 speeds you westward via La Garita for the **Botanical Orchid Garden** and a few hours at **Zoo Ave,** the nation's finest zoo. Travelers heading to La Fortuna might consider hiking in **Los Angeles Cloud Forest Reserve** and, if active adventure is your bag, an adrenaline-packed ride through the forest at the **San Lorenzo Canopy Tour.**

Heredia, north of San José, is appealing for its colonial-era cathedral and fortress. To learn about Costa Rica's *grano de oro* (coffee), stop in at **Café Britt** near Heredia. Nearby, **INBioparque** is a worthy place to learn about the nation's diverse ecosystems, while the montane rainforests of **Braulio Carrillo National Park** offer tremendous hiking opportunities for the hale and hearty. The **Rainforest Aerial Tram** (tel. 506/2257-5961 or North America tel. 305/704-3350, www.rainforesttram.com, 6:30 A.M.–4 P.M. Tues.–Sun., 9 A.M.–4 P.M. Mon., $55 adults, $27.50 students/children) on the eastern side of Braulio Carrillo, is popular and fun; you might stop in while en route to the Caribbean.

A less daunting, albeit longer, route to the Caribbean is via **Cartago,** worth a stop only for its Cathedral of Our Lady of the Angels. If you're planning on driving from San José to the summit of **Irazú Volcano National Park,** I recommend the scenic route via Rancho Redondo. **Guayabo National Monument,** east of Cartago, is a great birding spot and of interest for anyone keen on pre-Columbian culture, while the colorful and varied **Lankester Gardens** thrills everyone fond of gardens. A sojourn in the **Orosi-Cachí Valley** makes a thrilling scenic excursion, as do the rugged journey to the off-the-beaten-track hamlet of

Moravia del Chirripó; a drive along the **Route of the Saints,** which begins due south of San José; and the daunting drive to **Cerro de la Muerte,** from which you might descend to **San Gerardo de Dota** to view quetzals.

Lastly, white-water enthusiasts can get their kicks on the **Ríos Reventazón** or **Pacuare,** offering tremendous opportunities for viewing wildlife, as does the easily accessed **Tapantí-Macizo de la Muerte National Park.**

Escazú and Vicinity

ESCAZÚ

Beginning only four kilometers west of San José's Parque Sabana, Escazú is officially part of metropolitan San José. However, it is divided from the capital by a hill range and river canyon and is so individualistic that it functions virtually as a sister city. The town, one of the oldest settlements in the country (and also among its most modern), is accessed by the Carretera Prospero Fernández (Hwy. 27), an expressway that passes north of Escazú and continues via Ciudad Colón to the Pacific lowlands.

There are actually three Escazús, each with

its own church, patron saint, and character. **San Rafael de Escazú** is the ultramodern, congested lower town, nearest the freeway. Its once sleepy *campesino*-town ambience has been pushed aside by a wave of modern development, including chic restaurants, nightclubs, and shopping plazas, plus condominium towers that have drawn scores of English-speaking expatriates. A beautiful old church stands here in colonial counterpoint.

San Rafael merges south to **San Miguel de Escazú,** about one kilometer uphill. San Miguel, the heart of old Escazú, was originally a crossroads on trails between indigenous

© CHRISTOPHER P. BAKER

San Rafael de Escazú

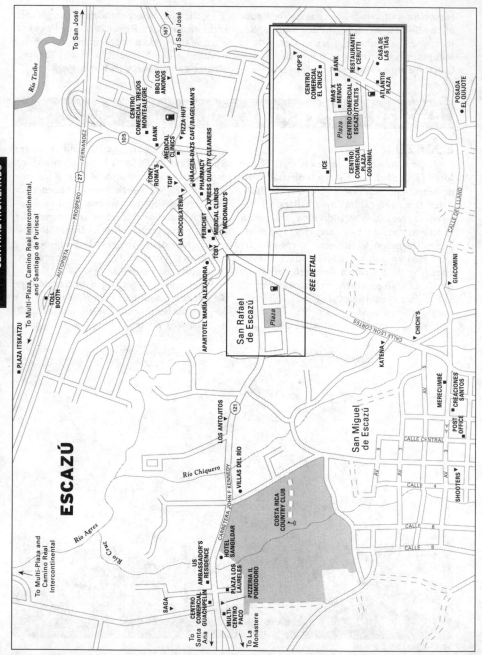

ESCAZÚ

To San José

Río Tribe

To San José

167

Río Agres

Río Cruz

To Multi-Plaza and Camino Real Intercontinental

SAGA

CENTRO COMERCIAL GUACHIPELIN

MULTI-CENTRO PACO

To Santa Ana

To La Monastere

US AMBASSADOR'S RESIDENCE

PLAZA LOS LAURELES

PIZZERIA IL POMODORO

HOTEL SANGILDAR

CARRETERA JOHN F KENNEDY

Río Chiquero

COSTA RICA COUNTRY CLUB

VILLAS DEL RÍO

LOS ANTOJITOS

121

San Miguel de Escazú

PLAZA ITSKATZU

To Multi-Plaza, Camino Real Intercontinental, and Santiago de Puriscal

TOLL BOOTH

PROSPERO

27

FERNANDEZ

105

AUTOPISTA

APARTOTEL MARÍA ALEXANDRA

LA CHOCOLATERÍA

TONY ROMA'S

TGIF

TOBY

CENTRO COMERCIAL TREJOS MONTEALEGRE

BANK

MEDICAL CLINICS

BBQ LOS ANONOS

PIZZA HUT

HÄAGEN-DAZS CAFÉ/BAGELMAN'S

PERICHET

PHARMACY

XPRESS QUALITY CLEANERS

MEDICAL CLINICS

MCDONALD'S

San Rafael de Escazú

Plaza

SEE DETAIL

CALLE LEÓN CORTES

CHICHI'S

KATENA

MERECUMBÉ

CREACIONES SANTOS

POST OFFICE

SHOOTERS

CALLE CENTRAL

CALLE 4

CALLE 6

CALLE 8

AV 9

AV 7

AV 5

AV 3

AV 1

CALLE DEL LLANO

GIACOMINI

POSADA EL QUIJOTE

Detail

POP'S

CENTRO COMERCIAL EL CRUCE

MAS X MENOS

BANK

RESTAURANTE CERUTTI

CASA DE LAS TIAS

Plaza

CENTRO COMERCIAL ESCAZÚ/TOILETS

ATLANTIS PLAZA

ICE

CENTRO COMERCIAL PLAZA COLONIAL

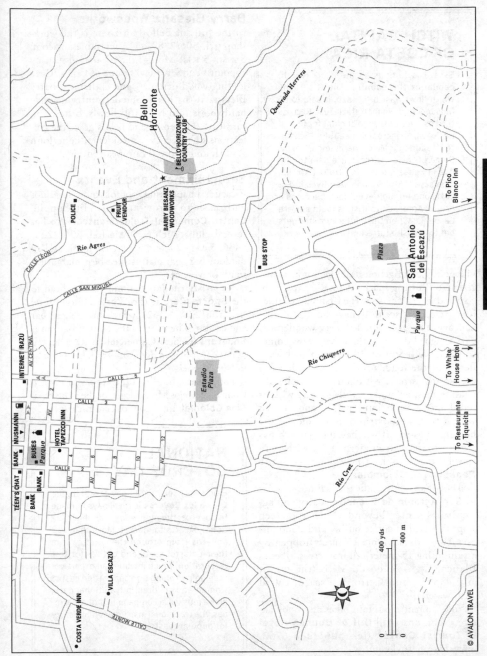

© AVALON TRAVEL

WITCH CAPITAL OF COSTA RICA

Escazú is famous as the *bruja* (witch) capital of the country. The Río Tiribi, which flows east of Escazú, is said to be haunted, and old men still refuse to cross the Los Anonos Bridge at night for fear of La Zegua, an incredibly beautiful enchantress, and Mico Malo, the magic monkey. Some 60 or so witches are said to still live in Escazú, including Doña Estrella, who says, "Any woman who lives in Escazú long enough eventually becomes a *bruja*." Amorous tourists should beware La Zegua: When the (un)lucky suitor gets her to bed, she turns into a horse.

villages. The indigenous folks gave it its name, Itzkatzu (Resting Place). A small chapel constructed in 1711 became the first public building. Here, time seems to have stood still for a century. The occasional rickety wooden oxcart weighed down with coffee beans comes to town, pulled by stately oxen. Cows wander along the road. And there are still a few cobblestone streets with houses of adobe, including those around the village plaza with its red-domed church, built in 1799 and painted with a traditional strip of blue color at the bottom to ward off witches. The church has a new frontage in modern style, with twin towers. It overlooks a new plaza—**Parque República de Colombia.**

Above San Miguel, the road climbs steadily to **San Antonio de Escazú,** a dairy and agricultural center beyond which the steep slopes are clad in coffee bushes and cloud forest. Above rises Monte La Cruz (topped by an imposing 15-meter-tall iron cross), Piedra Blanca, Cerro Rabo de Mico (the tallest at 2,455 m), and Cerro de Escazú, fluted with waterfalls.

You can rent mountain bikes and book active excursions with **Out of Bounds Hotel & Tourist Center** (tel. 506/2288-6762, www.bikeandsurf.com).

Barry Biesanz Woodworks

In the hills of Bello Horizonte is the workshop (tel. 506/2289-4337, www.biesanz.com, 8 A.M.–5 P.M. Mon.–Fri., 10 A.M.–4 P.M. by appointment Saturday) of one of Costa Rica's leading wood designers and craftsmen. Barry Biesanz turns his adopted country's native hardwoods into beautiful bowls, boxes, and furniture. His boxes and bowls grace the collections of three U.S. presidents, Pope John Paul II, and assorted European royalty.

Entertainment and Events

Escazú is a happening spot for young Josefinos with cash to throw around. Hip-hoppin' **Centro Comercial Trejos Montealegro** has several clubs, such as **Órale** (tel. 506/2228-6436, 5 P.M.–2 A.M.), with lively music and an outdoor bar that claims the "best margaritas south of Mexico."

To satisfy the James Bond within, head to the **Sports Bar,** at the White House Hotel (tel. 506/2288-6362), which has a cigar bar and casino. The yang to the Sport's Bar yin is **Shooters** (Centro Comercial La Rambla, tel. 506/2228-6619), a down-to-earth bar popular in San Miguel.

For movies, head to **Cine Rock,** in Centro Comercial Trejos Montealegre; or the two-screen **Cine Colonial,** in Plaza Colonial Escazú.

NATIONAL BOYEROS DAY

Held every second Sunday of March, the **Día de los Boyeros** festival pays homage to *boyeros,* the men who guide the traditional oxcarts to market. More than 100 *boyeros* from around the country trim their colorful carts and gather for this celebration, which includes an oxcart parade helped along by a supporting cast of women and children in traditional garb, plus a musical accompaniment of *cimarronas,* the traditional instrument mandatory for popular feasts.

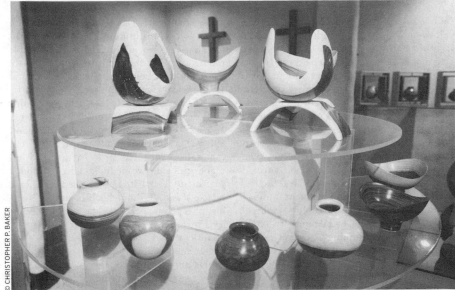

© CHRISTOPHER P. BAKER

wooden bowls at Barry Biesanz Woodworks

On Christmas Day, a hydraulic engine is employed to move singular figures —including a headless priest, the devil spinning a Ferris wheel, the corpse who opens his coffin, and a carousel, all elements of a Nativity celebration—in front of Iglesia San Antonio.

The new hotspot in 2008 was **Jazz Café** (tel. 506/2288-4740, www.jazzcafecostarica .com), in Plaza Itzkazú, on the Autopista, and where the lineup features everyone from hot locals to Cuban superstar Chucho Váldez. Shows typically begin at 10 P.M. ($5).

Accommodations
$25-50
The only option in this price category is the unremarkable **Hotel Tapezco Inn** (tel. 506/2228-1084, www.tapezco-inn.co.cr, $35 s, $45 d), one block south of the main square in San Miguel de Escazú.

$50-100
The lofty-ceilinged **Costa Verde Inn Bed and Breakfast** (off Calle Monte, tel. 506/2228-4080, www.costaverdeinn.com, $45 s or $50 d low season, $55 s or $65 d high season) is a beautiful, atmospheric, and peaceful bed-and-breakfast long on creature comforts Hardwoods abound; walls are adorned with hand-colored historic photos; decor is slightly outdated yet tasteful. The lounge with plump leather sofas has an open fireplace and a large-screen TV. Twelve individually styled bedrooms come with king-size beds, built-in hardwood furniture, and huge, beautifully tiled bathrooms. Room 8 has a bathroom in natural stone with open pit shower. Outside, a shaded terrace has an open fireplace, swimming pool, and sundeck with whirlpool, plus there's tennis. Rates include breakfast.

Hotel Relax Bed and Breakfast (tel. 506/2289-3981, www.hotelrelaxbandb.com, $50–70 low season, $60–80 high season), a modern three-story structure in Bello Horizonte, has large picture windows offering views. It has eight rooms, a junior suite, and loft apartment, all modestly furnished, plus a Jacuzzi and pool.

My favorite bed-and-breakfast is the **Casa de Las Tías** (200 m south and 200 m east of El

Cruce, tel. 506/2289-5517, www.hotels.co.cr/casatias.html; $72 s, $82–92 d). This exquisite yellow-and-turquoise, Southern plantation–style wooden home has five airy, wood-paneled rooms, all with polished hardwood floors, wooden ceilings, wicker and antique furniture, ceiling fans, and Latin American art and other tasteful decor. The beautiful suite boasts a king-size bed and heaps of light. A hearty breakfast is served on the garden patio full of birdsong. Delightful live-in hosts oversee the property, which is just a short stroll to downtown. Airport pickups are available with advance notice. Rates include full breakfast.

Villa Escazú Bed and Breakfast (off Calle Monte, tel./fax 506/2289-7971, www.hotels.co.cr/villaescazu, $49–65 s/d rooms, two-night minimum) boasts stunning hardwood interiors mixed with rustic and tasteful modern decor in a pretty Swiss-style chalet. A "minstrel's gallery" overhangs the lounge, with its stone fireplace. Two bedrooms on both the main and third floors share three bathrooms. A deluxe room has a private bath. A studio apartment has cable TV, a sofa, kitchenette, and modern bathroom with large walk-in shower ($225, five-night minimum). There's also a two-bedroom apartment ($250, five-night minimum). The lovely house boasts a wraparound veranda with wicker chairs for enjoying the view. Breakfast is served on a terrace overlooking landscaped lawns that cascade downhill to a fruit orchard full of birds. Villa Escazú is run by friendly Floridian Inez Chapman, who prepares full breakfasts. Guest-friendly dogs abound. Rates include breakfast and tax.

And a lovely newcomer, **Tierra Mágica B&B** (tel. 506/2289-9154, www.tierramagica-costa rica.com, $70 s, $75 d), on Calle San Miguel, offers two cozy rooms with charming decor, acid-stain floors, and either two queens or a king-size bed. Full breakfast is served on a delightful garden terrace.

High in the hills above San Antonio de Escazú, the **Hotel Mirador Pico Blanco Inn** (tel. 506/2228-1908, www.hotelpicoblanco.com, $35 or $45 d standard, $50 s or $55 d mini-suite, $65 s/d cottage low season; $45 s or $50 d standard, $55 s or $60 d mini-suite, $70 s/d cottage high season) is a bed-and-breakfast with lots of wicker furniture and a cozy Georgian-style bar-cum-restaurant. The 20 comfortable rooms are a bit drab and the bathrooms are small, but the fabulous views make amends and are the sole reason to bunk here.

Self-catering? **Apartotel María Alexandra** (200 m north and 100 west of El Cruce, tel. 506/2228-1507, www.mariaalexandra.com, $90 s/d), a quiet and comfy retreat away from the main road, offers 14 fully furnished, elegant one- and two-bedroom air-conditioned apartments, each with king-size bed, telephone, cable TV and VCR, full kitchen, air-conditioning, plus private parking. There are also twin-level townhouses that sleep up to five people. Facilities include a lounge and restaurant, pool, sauna, and mini-golf. A reader praises the attentive and superlative service. There's a tour and travel operation on-site.

Apartotel Villas del Río (tel. 506/2208-2400, www.villasdelrio.com), nearby, offers an excellent alternative.

$100-150

The **Hotel Sangildar** (tel. 506/2289-8843, www.hotelsangildar.com, $110 s/d), set in lush grounds adjoining the Costa Rica Country Club on the western outskirts of Escazú, is a handsome contemporary Spanish-style building. Hardwoods and stonework abound, and the 27 luxurious rooms reflect tasteful albeit conservative decor. Amenities include a swimming pool, a bar, and the elegant Terraza del Sol restaurant. Airport transfers are provided. Rates include continental breakfast.

Also recommended is the American-run **Posada El Quijote** (off Calle del Llano, tel. 506/2289-8401, www.quijote.co.cr, $85–105 s, $95–115 d), in the Bello Horizonte hills. This beautiful Spanish colonial home is exquisitely decorated and stocked with modern art. The eight tastefully appointed rooms look out over beautiful gardens and have queen- or king-size beds, telephones, and cable TVs; room 25 has a bathroom to die for. Two superior rooms have patios, and there are also two studio apartments. Breakfast is served under an arbor on the intimate patio, also good for cocktails from the bar.

If steadfast U.S.-style hospitality is your thing, opt for the 125-room **Courtyard Marriott San José** (tel. 506/2208-3000 or U.S. tel. 800/321-2211, www.courtyard.com, $162–197 s/d), in Plaza Itskatzu.

Adventure-minded folks should check into **Out of Bounds Hotel & Tourist Center** (tel. 506/2288-6762, www.bedandbreakfast cr.com, $70–110 s/d low season, $80–120 s/d high season), on Carretera John F. Kennedy, on the old road to Santa Ana. New in 2007, this lovely modern hotel combines handsome, almost Zen-like, contemporary decor and hardwood floors in its five air-conditioned rooms and junior suites, all with quality bedding plus ceiling fans, coffeemakers, cable TV, and Wi-Fi access. Rates include full breakfast. It has bike and kayak rentals and offers tours.

$150-250

Large-scale and deluxe, the **Intercontinental Real Hotel & Club Tower** (tel. 506/2208-2100, www.ichotelsgroup.com/Intercont inental, $225–330 s/d rooms, $655–1,100 s/d suites), off the Prospero Fernandez Highway at Boulevard Camino Real, two kilometers west of Escazú, exudes contemporary opulence. Each of the 261 luxuriously carpeted, air-conditioned rooms has a king-size bed with orthopedic mattress. Marbled bathrooms are magnificent. It has a concierge floor with junior suites and a presidential suite. The hotel—centered on a five-story atrium lobby—has a clover-shaped pool with swim-up bar, a business center, conference center, two restaurants, a fitness center, spa, stores, and car rental and travel agencies. A shuttle runs to San José. Rates include breakfast.

The **Alta** (tel. 506/2282-4160 or U.S. tel. 888/388-2582, www.thealtahotel.com, $175 s/d standard, $197 junior suite, $390 master suite, $820 penthouse) sits on a hillside three kilometers west of Escazú on the "old road" to Santa Ana. The contemporary-style five-story hotel is lent a monastic feel by its hand-forged ironwork, whitewashed narrow corridors, and cathedral ceilings. The 23 deluxe rooms (including four suites and a three-bedroom penthouse suite) display a fine aesthetic and all have Internet access and splendid bathrooms. Some rooms hug the oval, glass-tiled swimming pool in the shade of a spreading *Guanacaste* tree. The acclaimed La Luz restaurant serves creole-fusion cuisine. There's a full-service spa, plus executive services. All said, however, I consider it overpriced.

Rhett and Scarlett would feel at home at the **White House** (tel. 506/2288-6362, www.whitehousecostarica.com, $200 s/d room, $225 junior suite, $250–1,000 suite), in the hills above Escazú, with staggering views. Who said the South's plantation lifestyle has gone with the wind? The Greek Revival plantation mansion offers 15 bedrooms with antique rosewood tester beds and private verandas, plus 26 two-bedroom villas in classical style, all with fax, printer, and computers with Internet access. A penthouse suite offers a 360-degree view. There's a gym, pool, whirlpool, cigar bar, casino, and restaurant. Health nuts will love The Garden Spa, and there's a tennis court and croquet lawn.

Food

Escazú is a center for fine-dining, with dozens of great options. The scene is ever-changing.

A splendid breakfast or lunch option is **Bagelmen's** (tel. 506/2228-4460, 7 A.M.–9 P.M. daily), 100 meters north of El Cruce, resembling Starbucks but also serving bagels (onion, pumpernickel, etc.), muffins, brownies, and cinnamon rolls, plus breakfast specials from *gallo pinto* to scrambled eggs. You can sit in the air-conditioned café or outside on a shady patio.

Plaza Colonial, at El Cruce, has several inexpensive cafés.

Popular with U.S. football fans, the no-frills **Chichi's** (Calle León Cortes, tel. 506/2228-1173, 11 A.M.–midnight daily, entrées $8–20), serves steaks, baby back ribs, the house specialty ($11), grilled pork chops, and the like. It has live music Thursday and Friday. Giving

Chichi's a run for its money, **Hooters** (tel. 506/2289-3498, noon–1 A.M. daily), in Plaza Itzkazú, is good for chili, curly fries, and burgers, and has the eye-candy that Chichi's lacks. Head there on Wednesday for all-you-can-eat wings (7–10 P.M.).

¢ Cerutti (tel. 506/2228-4511, noon–3:30 P.M. and 6:30–11 P.M. Wed.–Mon.), at El Cruce, is acclaimed as one of the finest Italian restaurants in the country. Society figures frequent this atmospheric eatery in a centenary home, with antique prints adorning the whitewashed walls. Sublime dishes run from New Zealand lamb to fresh pasta dishes. Expect to pay $25 or more per head.

At **La Luz** (tel. 506/2282-4160, 6:30 A.M.–3 P.M. and 6–10 P.M. daily, $7–25), in the Hotel Alta, Chef Carlos Zuñiga's quality fusion cuisine melds Costa Rican ingredients with spicy creole influences. The setting—a contemporary remake on a Tudor theme—is classy, the views splendid, and the service exemplary. Try the macadamia nut–crusted chicken in *guaro*-chipotle cream, or fiery garlic prawns in tequila-lime-butter sauce, followed by a chocolate macadamia tart. Sunday brunch (9 A.M.–4 P.M.) is a special treat. And there's live jazz on Saturday night. A dress code applies.

The **White House** (tel. 506/2288-6362, noon–5 P.M. and 6–11 P.M. daily, $5–25) offers grand elegance and spectacular views. It specializes in steaks, plus such dishes as grilled beef with shrimp and béarnaise sauce and lobster bisque.

Le Monastère (tel. 506/2289-4404, www.monastere-restaurant.com, 5 P.M.–midnight Mon.–Sat.) has been called a "religious dining experience," not for the cuisine but for the venue—a restored chapel amid gardens in the hills west of town (it's signed on the Santa Ana). The waiters dress like monks and Gregorian chants provide background music. The French menu includes grilled lamb chops and *vol au vent* of asparagus. Expect to pay $30 per person. The restaurant's more casual **La Cava Grill,** in an intimate cellar below Le Monastère, offers the same views and a better bargain.

For a far less pretentious hillside option, head up the mountain to **Restaurante City Lights Tiquicia** (tel. 506/2289-5839, tiquiciacr@costarricense.cr, 5 P.M.–midnight Tues.–Fri., noon–midnight Sat., and noon A.M.–6 P.M. Sun.), which entertains diners with folkloric dances at noon Tuesday and Sunday, and live music on Friday and Saturday nights. Food here is traditional Costa Rican.

Saga (tel. 506/2289-6615, www.sagarestaurant.com, 11 A.M.–11 P.M. Mon.–Sat., 11 A.M.–6 P.M. Sun.), 400 meters north of Plaza de la Paco, is a hip fusion restaurant for a monied clientele. I like its minimalist, contemporary decor and walls of glass. The dishes are works of art. Try the ravioli stuffed with shrimp and heart of palm ($10), followed by salmon in carrot ginger broth with sautéed spinach ($15) or the seafood risotto with coconut ($18). The addition of a jazz lounge was in the works.

Nearby, **Il Panino** (tel. 506/2228-8606, ilpanino@racsa.co.cr, 8 A.M.–midnight daily), in Plaza de la Paco, is equally stylish, with its walls of glass opening to an airy patio. It serves more than 60 paninis ($4–10), plus *bocas* and salads ($10–16). It's a hot spot for the young and beautiful.

Many of the best restaurants in town can be found at Plaza Itzkazú, on the *autopista*. These include **La Fogueira** (tel. 506/2289-3216, noon–3 P.M. and 6–11 P.M. Tues.–Sat.), an elegant Brazilian *churrascaría* with waiters in gaucho costume; **La Guagua** (tel. 506/2288-5112, noon–3 P.M. and 6–11 P.M. Mon.–Sat., noon–11 P.M. Sun.), a Cuban restaurant with a lovely ambience and a succulent *ropa vieja* with yucca and rice and beans; and **Samurai** (tel. 506/2289-3456, noon–3 P.M. and 6–11 P.M. Mon.–Fri., and noon–10 P.M. Sat.–Sun.), a sushi and Pacific fusion restaurant with classy contemporary decor.

There are two chocolate specialty shops: **La Chocolatería** (tel. 506/2289-9637, 8 A.M.–7 P.M. Mon.–Fri. and 10 A.M.–7 P.M. Sat.), above El Cruce; and **Giacomini** (tel. 506/2288-3381, 10 A.M.–7 P.M. Mon.–Sat.), on Calle de Llano. The latter is a coffee shop with a classy contemporary decor and a patio open to a garden with waterfalls. It serves panini (from $5), croissants, salads, pastries, cappuccinos, and espresso, in addition to chocolate delights. **Häagen-Dazs Café** (tel. 506/2228-4260, 10 A.M.–10 P.M. Mon.–Thurs. and Sun., 10 A.M.–11 P.M. Fri.–Sat.), beside Bagelmen's, 100 meters north of El Cruce, serves excellent ice cream sundaes. And **Pops** (9 A.M.–10 P.M. daily), at El Cruce, sells ice cream.

The classiest café is **ℂ Fitzgeralds' Coffee** (tel. 506/2288-1633, 6:30 A.M.–10 P.M. Mon.–Sat., 8 A.M.–8 P.M. Sun.), in Plaza Itzkazú. Super-chic decor (including lush leather sofas), breakfasts such as granola with yogurt and fruit, plus bagels with smoked salmon, fabulous sandwiches, and desserts from carrot cake to chocolate Fitzgerald make this a winner! Oh, and it has intelligent reading, such as *The Economist,* free for patrons.

Services

There are plenty of banks, which are clearly marked on the Escazú map. The **post office** (Calle Central, Avenida 1) is in San Miguel.

For Internet service, try **Internet Irazú** (Calle 5, Avenida Central, tel. 506/2288-5086), in San Miguel, or **Café Internet** (tel. 506/2289-9169), in Plaza Colonial.

X-Press Quality Cleaners (tel. 506/2289-9878, 11 A.M.–8 P.M. Mon.–Fri., 7 A.M.–7 P.M. Sat.) has laundry service costing $2 per kilo for wash, dry, and fold.

Getting There

Buses depart San José for Escazú from Avenida 1, Calle 18, every 15 minutes. The "Bebedero" bus departs San José from Calle 14, Avenida 6, for San Antonio de Escazú. A bus for San Rafael de Escazú departs Calle 16, Avenidas Central/1.

SANTA ANA TO CIUDAD COLÓN

Santa Ana, about five kilometers west of Escazú, is a sleepy town set in a sunny mountain valley. The church dates from 1870, and there are still many old adobe and wooden houses clad in bougainvillea. Today it is famous for ceramics; there are some 30 independent pottery shops in the area, many still using old-fashioned kick-wheels to fashion the pots. However, the area all around the town itself (especially north toward San Antonio de Belén) is the fastest-growing area in the nation and a center for high-tech service industries, new malls, and traffic jams!

Worth a quick stop is the **Museo Histórico Agrícola de Santa Ana** (tel. 506/2282-8434, www.fundazoo.org/museo.php, 8 A.M.–4 P.M. Mon.–Fri., 9 A.M.–4 P.M. Sat.–Sun., $2), housed in an antique *casona* (farmstead) and exhibiting machinery relating to coffee and sugar production.

Continuing west you reach **Piedades,** about five kilometers west of Santa Ana. This peaceful village has a beautiful church. The road gradually rises to **Ciudad Colón,** a neat little town about eight kilometers west of Santa Ana. The **Julia and David White Artists' Colony** (tel. 506/2249-1414, www.forjuliaanddavid.org) offers residential artists' courses, May–November.

Reserva Forestal el Rodeo

This reserve—in the hills about five kilometers southwest of Ciudad Colón and part of a cattle estate called **Hacienda el Rodeo** (tel. 506/2249-1013, 10 A.M.–6 P.M. Sat., Sun., and holidays)—protects the largest remaining tract of virgin forest in the Meseta Central. A rustic restaurant serves Tico fare.

One kilometer beyond Hacienda el Rodeo is the **University for Peace** (tel. 506/2205-9000, www.upeace.org, 8 A.M.–4:30 P.M. Mon.–Fri.), charged with the mission of global education and research in support of the peace and security goals of the United Nations and contributing to building a culture of peace. The 303-hectare facility includes botanical gardens containing busts of famous figures, such as Gandhi and Henry Dunant (founder of the Red Cross). Visitors are welcome; follow the road that passes the entrance gate and you'll arrive at the **Monument for Disarmament, Work, and Peace,** set around a lake full of geese (open 8 A.M.–4 P.M. daily, $0.75).

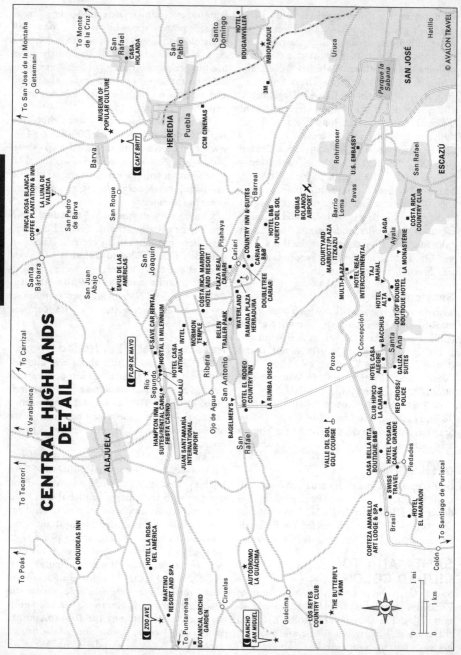

CENTRAL HIGHLANDS DETAIL

SAN JOSÉ

ESCAZÚ

ALAJUELA

HEREDIA

© AVALON TRAVEL

To Monte de la Cruz
To San José de la Montaña
To Poás
To Tacarori
To Carrizal
To Varablanca
To Puntarenas
To Santiago de Puriscal
To Colón

Getsemani
Santo Domingo
Hatillo
San Rafael
San Pablo
Uruca
CASA HOLANDA
HOTEL BOUGAINVILLEA
INBIOPARQUE
3M
Parque la Sabana
Puebla
Barva
San Pedro de Barva
San Roque
Santa Bárbara
MUSEUM OF POPULAR CULTURE
CAFÉ BRITT
CCM CINEMAS
Rohrmoser
San Rafael
FINCA ROSA BLANCA COFFEE PLANTATION & INN
LA LUNA DE VALENCIA
U.S. EMBASSY
Barreal
HOTEL B&B PUERTO DEL SOL
COUNTRY INN & SUITES
Pitahaya
EJVUS DE LAS AMERICAS
San Juan Abajo
San Joaquin
Cariari
CARIARI B&B
TOBIAS BOLAÑOS AIRPORT
Barrio Loma
Pavas
COSTA RICA COUNTRY CLUB
SAGA
Ayala
LA MONASTÈRE
COURTYARD MARRIOTT/PLAZA ITZKAZU
HOTEL REAL INTERCONTINENTAL
TAJ MAHAL
HOTEL ALTA
OUT OF BOUNDS BOUTIQUE HOTEL
COSTA RICA MARRIOTT HOTEL AND RESORT
PLAZA REAL CARIARI
DOUBLETREE CARIARI
WATERLAND
RAMADA PLAZA HERRADURA
BELEN TRAILER PARK
MULTI-PLAZA
MORMON TEMPLE
INTEL
U-SAVE CAR RENTAL
HOSTAL II MILLENNIUM
HOTEL CASA CALALÚ ANTIGUA
FLOR DE MAYO
Río Segundo
Ribera
San Antonio
Concepción
Pozos
BACCHUS
Santa Ana
HOTEL CASA ALEGRE
GALIZA SUITES
CLUB HIPICO LA CARAÑA
HOTEL EL RODEO COUNTRY INN
LA RUMBA DISCO
BAGELMEN'S
Ojo de Agua
HAMPTON INN & SUITES/RENTAL CARS/FIESTA CASINO
JUAN SANTAMARIA INTERNATIONAL AIRPORT
San Rafael
RED CROSS/POLICE
VALLE DEL SOL GOLF COURSE
CASA BELLA RITA BOUTIQUE B&B
HOTEL POSADA CANAL GRANDE
Piedades
SWISS TRAVEL
HOTEL EL MARAÑÓN
Brasil
CORTEZA AMARILLO ART LODGE & SPA
ORQUIDEAS INN
HOTEL LA ROSA DEL AMÉRICA
MARTINO RESORT AND SPA
BOTANICAL ORCHID GARDEN
ZOO AVE
Ciruelas
Guácima
AUTÓDROMO LA GUÁCIMA
THE BUTTERFLY FARM
LOS REYES COUNTRY CLUB
RANCHO SAN MIGUEL
Guácima

1 mi
1 km

0
0

Entertainment

The **Rock n Roll Pollo** (tel. 506/2282-9613), on the east side of Santa Ana, speaks for itself. It's a hot spot on weekends.

Sports and Recreation

Golf at **Parque Valle del Sol** (tel. 506/2282-9222, www.vallesol.com) costs $85 for 18 holes. It has a golf academy.

Club Hípico La Caraña (tel. 506/2282-6754, www.lacarana.com) offers classes in dressage and jumping, as well as guided horseback tours in the mountains south of Santa Ana. You can also rent horses at **Hacienda el Rodeo** (tel. 506/2249-1013, 10 A.M.–6 P.M. Sat., Sun., and holidays).

Accommodations

In the heart of Santa Ana, the **Hotel Casa Alegre** (tel. 506/2235-5485, www.hotelcasa alegre.com, $61 s/d standard, $76 superior low season; $71 s/d standard, $87 s/d superior high season) has charming decor and a friendly, homey feel. Rooms have cable TV, fans, and wireless Internet service.

Aiming for executives, and making a splash with its sensational minimalist decor, the **Galiza Suites** (tel. 506/2205-2222, www.galiza suites.com, $150–375 s/d), on the southwest side of town, opened in 2008 with stylishly contemporary nonsmoking suites with state-of-the-art amenities. The sumptuous apartments have flat-screen TVs and Wi-Fi, plus full kitchen, and divinely comfortable king-size beds. Request a rear-facing unit to minimize traffic noise.

A few kilometers west of Piedades, in the hillside hamlet of La Trinidad, is the simple yet tasteful and reclusive **Hotel El Marañon** (tel. 506/2249-1271, www.cultourica.com, $35 s, $50 d), surrounded by an orchard and with views toward Poás enjoyed from a terrace. It has 14 lovely rooms done up in lively tropical pastels. Hammocks are slung beneath ranchitas in the garden. There's also a three-room apartment with kitchen for $70. Children are welcome. A restaurant offers creative dishes and occasionally hosts live music. It hosts two-week

Spanish-language courses and offers three- to 20-day excursions. Rates include breakfast.

"Splendid" is the word for **Hotel Posada Canal Grande** (tel. 506/2282-4089, www.hotel canalgrande.com, $58 s, $78 d), on an old coffee *finca* 800 meters north of the church in Piedades. The two-story villa-hotel is operated by a Florentine art collector and boasts an old terra-cotta tile floor, rustic antique furnishings, plump leather chairs, and a fireplace. The 12 bedrooms have parquet wood floors, exquisite rattan-framed queen-size beds with Guatemalan bedspreads, cable TV, and wide windows offering views toward the Gulf of Nicoya. Italian taste is everywhere, from the ultra-chic furniture and halogen lamps to the classical vases overflowing with flowers. There's a large pool in grounds mantled in coffee and fruit trees. It has a restaurant, sauna, and tour agency, and massage and horseback rides are offered. Airport transfers are provided, and rates include breakfast.

The **Corteza Amarilla Art Lodge & Spa** (tel. 506/2203-7350, www.cortezaamarilla lodge.com, $145 s/d junior suite, $175 s/d suite), five kilometers west of Santa Ana, on the main San José–Colón road, is a unique, rambling offbeat charmer—almost Haight-Ashbury bohemian in tone—that you may or may not love. The 12 spacious, delightful, air-conditioned rooms and suites are set amid a tropical *Fantasia* and feature ceiling fans, TVs, wireless Internet, mini-bar, hair-dryers, and coffeemakers, plus stone-walled showers. However, some rooms get hot!

The most exquisite place around is **Casa Bella Rita Boutique B&B** (tel. 506/2249-3722, www.casabellarita.com, $119–139 s/d low season, $129–159 s/d high season), at Brasil de Santa Ana. New owners (it was formerly a gay hotel) Steve and Rita bring 50 years of restaurant experience to their intimate bed-and-breakfast. It has a gorgeous aesthetic to its six individually styled rooms and public lounges, and Steve and Rita give you all the fancy touches, such as bathrobes. There's a well-equipped gym and a lovely patio garden where scrumptious breakfasts are served. Beauty treatments are also offered.

Food

The elegant **Restaurante Canal Grande** (7 A.M.–10 P.M. daily) at the Hotel Posada Canal Grande serves ambitious Italian fare, such as scallops al vino and pastas. Even better is **Essentia** (7 A.M.–10 P.M. daily), at the Corteza Amarilla Art Lodge & Spa, where artfully presented gourmet fusion cuisine is a hit, such as gravlax of salmon ($6), Mediterranean octopus carpaccio ($10), and penne pasta with shrimp and scallops in a brandy sauce ($20). The menu displays a Hindu influence. Meals are delicious and artfully presented.

However, *the* en-vogue place to dine is **Bacchus** (tel. 506/2282-5441, www.bacchus restaurante.com, noon–3 P.M. and 6–11 P.M. Tues.–Sat., noon–9 P.M. Sun.), a Mediterranean-themed, Italian-run restaurant and *pizzería* considered one of the best restaurants in the country. Housed in a converted colonial home furnished in contemporary vogue, this classy eatery delivers consistently excellent nouvelle dishes. I enjoyed a tuna tartare appetizer ($11.50), three-mushroom soup ($10), and gnocchi *de espinaca* (spinach, $13). Sophisticated dining at its best!

Getting There

Empresa Cotrasuli (tel. 506/2248-1703) buses to Ciudad Colón depart San José from Calle 20, Avenidas 3/5, every 30 minutes 5 A.M.–10:30 P.M. Driving, take the Santa Ana exit off the Carretera Prospero Fernandez freeway. From Escazú, take the road west from El Cruce in San Rafael.

SANTIAGO DE PURISCAL

Santiago de Puriscal, 20 kilometers west of Ciudad Colón, is an important agricultural town. Santiago's main plaza is overlooked by a pretty church.

Midway between Ciudad Colón and Santiago, at Kilometer 30, is the entrance for the **Reserva Indígena Quitirrisí** (Indigenous Reserve), protecting the land of the Quitirrisí on the slopes of Cerro Turrubares. This remnant indigenous community lives a relatively marginalized life, though members sell their fine baskets at roadside stalls.

From Santiago you can follow a paved road southwest to **Salitrales,** 18 kilometers west of Santiago. Due west from Santiago, another road snakes through the mountains and descends to Orotina via San Pablo de Turrubares. By continuing south 11 kilometers beyond Salitrales and turning east, you arrive at **Rancho Mastatal Environmental Learning Center and Lodge** (tel. 506/2416-6263, www.ranchomastatal.com), a 219-acre farm and private wildlife refuge. Rancho Mastatal has seven kilometers of wilderness trails leading through pristine forest replete with wildlife. It offers environmental workshops and languages courses, and it welcomes volunteers. Horses can be rented ($10 with guide).

Rancho Mastatal adjoins **La Cangreja National Park** (tel. 506/2416-6359, www .lacangreja.com, 8 A.M.–4 P.M. daily, $6), protecting 2,240 hectares of virgin tropical montane forest. It has three short trails. Camping is permitted ($2 pp).

Accommodations

Rancho Mastatal Environmental Learning Center and Lodge (tel. 506/2416-6263, www.ranchomastatal.com, $15 homestay, $20 camping, $35–40 s or $60–65 d The Hooch, $30 s or $55 d main house, $30 s or $50 d Jeanne's House, $40 s or $75 d Leo's House) has three rooms in the main century-old farmhouse with shared bathrooms. A porch has hammocks. Jeanne's House has six bamboo bunks and two double beds, a stove, and electricity, indoor and outdoor showers, and shared toilets. Leo's House is a finely built wooden cabin sleeping up to six people. The Hooch is an A-frame structure made of bamboo. You can camp if you bring your own tent, or choose to stay with local *campesino* families. Rates include all meals.

The **Hotel Paraíso Carlisa** (tel. 506/2778-1112, www.hotelparaisocarlisa.com, $89 s/d standard, $109 s/d suite low season; $99 s/d standard, $119 s/d suite high season) nestles in the forested mountains at Alto Gloria, 16 kilometers south of La Cangreja National Park; a four-wheel-drive vehicle is required. It has 20 rooms and an apartment with lovely decor, plus a rustic-themed but elegant bar, a film room where movies are shown, and an international restaurant. Horseback riding to a huge waterfall is a thrilling specialty.

Seeking a healthful retreat? Head to the family-run **Ama Tierra** (tel. 506/2419-0110 or U.S. tel. 866/659-3805, www.amatierra.com, $110 s or $129 d low season, $127 s or $149 d high season), two kilometers east of San Pablo de Turrubares, 19 kilometers west of Santiago de Puriscal, and set in an eight-acre estate with trails. It has 10 endearingly (albeit sparsely) furnished duplex *casita* "junior suites" with satellite TV, DVD player, mini-fridge, coffeemaker, telephone, terrace, and private bathrooms with

Jacuzzi tubs. Health-conscious meals are served on a veranda with magnificent views. There's a lounge, game room, Internet access, and infinity-edge swimming pool inset in a wooden deck. It specializes in yoga retreats and has an open-air dojo, plus a full-service spa. Twelve more cabins are to be added.

Getting There and Around
The Ciudad Colón bus from San José continues to Santiago de Puriscal. The **Empresa Cotrasuli** (tel. 506/2248-1703) buses to Ciudad Colón depart San José from Calle 20, Avenidas 3/5, every 30 minutes 5 A.M.–10:30 P.M. Jeep-taxis line the square in Santiago.

Cariari to La Guácima

CIUDAD CARIARI AND SAN ANTONIO DE BELÉN
Ciudad Cariari is centered on an important junction on the Autopista General Cañas, 12 kilometers west of San José and about five minutes' drive from Juan Santamaría Airport. Here are San José's leading conference center, a major shopping mall, a golf course, and two of the nation's longest-standing premium hotels.

From Ciudad Cariari, the road west leads five kilometers to San Antonio de Belén, a small, unassuming town that has taken on new importance since the recent opening of Intel's microprocessor assembly plant. The road system hereabouts is convoluted.

Entertainment
One of Costa Rica's hottest discos, **La Rumba** (tel. 506/2239-8686, 9 P.M.–4 A.M. Tues.–Sun., $10), is tucked off the Santa Ana-San Antonio de Belén road. This salsa and meringue hot spot has a small dance floor and gets hot and smoky, but it packs in the crowds.

Sports and Recreation
The 18-hole championship **Cariari Country Club** (tel. 506/2293-3211, www.clubcariari.com,

6 A.M.–5 P.M. daily) golf course was designed by George Fazio; it charges $60 to guests.

Waterland (tel. 506/2293-2891, 9 A.M.–5 P.M. Tues.–Sun., $10 adults, $5 children), 500 meters west of the Autopista General Cañas, is a 12-hectare, open-air aquatic amusement complex centered on a massive 1,300-square-meter pool with volleyball, water slides, and rope swing, plus underwater cave. There's also an artificial river, a wave pool, miniature golf, and horseback riding, plus a Jungle Park with iguanas, turtles, and crocodiles. A tree-to-tree cable-and-pulley ride, go-karts, and ATVs cost extra.

Autódromo La Guácima (tel. 506/2293-6359, www.laguacima.com) is the nation's main auto race track and has an active annual calendar.

Accommodations
$25-50
The gringo-owned **Belén Trailer Park** (tel. 506/2239-0421, www.belentrailerpark.com, $14–16 RV nightly, $12 s/d tent), about one kilometer east of Belén Plaza, is Costa Rica's only fully equipped RV and camper site. It has hookups with electricity and water, plus laundry, hot showers, and secure parking.

Hotel B&B Puerta del Sol (tel. 506/2293-8109, www.bbpuertadelsol.com, $50 s, $65 d, including breakfast and tax), outside Cariari, is run by a friendly Tico family and offers 20 modestly furnished rooms in a two-story modern home. All have fans, TVs, telephones, refrigerators. Second-floor rooms get hot but have air-conditioning. Two are wheelchair accessible, and an apartment has a large lounge and king-size bed. Breakfast is served on a patio facing the pool. It offers free Internet. No smoking is permitted.

$50-75

Nearby, **Cariari B&B** (Avenida La Marina #12, tel. 506/2239-2585, www.cariaribb.com, $75–90 s/d), tucked behind the Cariari resort, is a lovely Spanish-style house offering family hospitality. A wrought-iron staircase curls up to three bedrooms in an eclectic yesteryear style.

$100-150

The **Ramada Plaza Herradura** (tel. 506/2209-9800, www.ramadaherradura.com, from $125 s/d standard, from $195 s/d suite), at Ciudad Cariari, is renowned as a convention hotel. It offers 234 spacious, elegantly furnished, air-conditioned rooms (including 28 suites) accented with dark hardwoods. Some have a patio or a balcony. The Herradura has several restaurants, a spa, a large outdoor swimming pool with swim-up bar and mammoth whirlpool, 10 night-lit tennis courts, and impressive entertainment facilities, including a casino and a 51,000-square-foot conference center. A shuttle runs to downtown.

The upscale **Hotel El Rodeo Country Inn** (tel. 506/2293-3909, www.elrodeohotel.com, $105 s or $115 d standard, $155 s or $175 d junior suite), two kilometers south of San Antonio de Belén on the road to Santa Ana, is a contemporary-style hacienda with 29 rooms, all with air-conditioning, cable TV, telephone, safety box, and elegant contemporary furnishings. The spacious junior suites are fabulous, with beautiful hardwood floors, two queen beds, and huge bathrooms with marble tile floors and sinks. Facilities include a swimming pool, whirlpool

tub, tennis courts, and a splendid restaurant (noon–10:30 P.M. Mon.–Sat., 11:30 A.M.–5 P.M. Sun.). Rates include breakfast and dinner.

$150-250

The colonial-style **Costa Rica Marriott Hotel & Resort** (tel. 506/2298-0000 or U.S. tel. 888/236-2427, www.marriotthotels.com, from $208 s/d), at Ribera de Belén, one kilometer northeast of San Antonio, occupies a 30-acre coffee plantation with panoramic views over lush landscaped grounds to distant mountains. This jewel has 252 rooms and seven suites, all exquisitely decorated and with French doors opening to a patio or balcony. The decor fits the bill: Public areas feature evocative antiques, distressed timbers, and stone floors, while the large bedrooms boast regal furnishings and fabrics and a full complement of modern amenities. It features a ballroom, golf practice range, horizon swimming pool, three restaurants, three tennis courts, a gym, shops, and a business center.

Immediately south of the Herradura is the **Doubletree Cariari by Hilton** (tel. 506/2239-0022, http://doubletree1.hilton.com, from $152 s/d), offering deluxe resort facilities, including access to the Cariari Country Club and its championship golf course, 10 tennis courts, and Olympic-size pool. The 220 spacious, handsomely appointed, carpeted, air-conditioned rooms and 24 suites are arrayed around an outdoor swimming pool with swim-up bar. The hotel also has a kiddie pool, health club, whirlpool, massage service, beauty salon, and playground. Plus, there are two restaurants and a casino.

Food

For traditional Costa Rican fare, head to **El Rodeo** (tel. 506/2293-3909, www.elrodeo hotel.com, noon–10:30 P.M. Mon.–Sat., 11:30 A.M.–5 P.M. Sun.), decorated in traditional hacienda style and adorned with saddles and other rodeo-themed miscellany. It serves a wide-ranging menu that includes sliced tongue on corn tortilla ($1), ceviche, and hot jalapeño cream tenderloin ($9).

Antonio Ristorante Italiano & Cigar Room (tel. 506/2293-0622, 11:30 A.M.–11 P.M.

The Butterfly Farm, La Guácima

Mon.–Fri., 4–11 P.M. Sat.–Sun.), 100 meters east of the Ramada Herradura, serves exquisite cuisine. Try the *melazane* (baked eggplant topped with marinara sauce; $10), gnocchi ($10), or calamari with spaghetti ($13). There's an "executive lunch" special ($5).

Sakura (tel. 506/2239-0033, ext. 33, 11:30 A.M.–3 P.M. and 6–11 P.M. Mon.–Sat., 11 A.M.–10 P.M. Sun.), in the Herradura, is expensive but offers superb Teppan-style Japanese cooking and an excellent sushi bar.

Getting There

Buses depart San José from Avenida 1, Calles 20/22, hourly on the half hour, every quarter hour on weekends. Buses also depart Alajuela from Calle 10, Avenida Central.

LA GUÁCIMA

The road west from San Antonio de Belén continues to La Guácima, known for the members-only Los Reyes Country Club.

Local residents have recently painted buildings throughout the village with butterfly murals. It's art in the streets at its best!

◖ Rancho San Miguel

This stable and stud farm (tel. 506/2439-0909, ranchosanmiguel@gmail.com), about three kilometers north of La Guácima, raises Andalusian horses and has a tiny museum relating to horsemanship. The highlight is the *Fantasia Ecuestre*, a nocturnal one-hour dressage and horsemanship show to the accompaniment of classical Spanish music. It's a fabulous experience. The show is offered at 8 P.M. Saturday November–July (and by arrangement for groups). The show costs $26, $37 with dinner, or $42 including hotel transfers, cocktail, performance, and dinner. The stable offers horse-riding lessons.

The Butterfly Farm

The Butterfly Farm (tel. 506/2438-0400, www.butterflyfarm.co.cr, 8:45 A.M.–4:30 P.M. daily, $15 adults, $10 students, $7.50 children), established in 1983 as the first commercial butterfly farm in Latin America, has grown to be the second-largest exporter of living pupae in the world. A two-hour visit begins with a video documentary followed by a guided tour through the netted gardens and laboratory, where you witness and learn all about each stage of the butterfly life cycle. Hundreds of butterflies representing 60 native species flit about in an endless ballet.

The guides will show you the tiny eggs and larvae that are coded to "eat and grow, eat and grow." If a newborn human baby ate at the same rate, it would grow to the size of a double-decker bus in two months. Although butterfly activity is greatly reduced in late afternoon, that's the time to enjoy the spectacular show of the *Caligo memnon* (giant owl butterfly). The insects are most active on sunny days.

Guided tours are offered at 8:45 A.M., 11 A.M., 1 P.M., and 3 P.M. daily. Hotel transfers are offered ($30 adults, $15 children) from San José at 7:30 A.M., 10 A.M., and 2 P.M. daily.

Getting There
Public buses depart hourly (except Sun.) from Avenida 4, Calles 10/12, behind the Merced church in San José. Take the bus until the last stop (about 60 minutes), from where you walk—follow the signs—about 400 meters.

From Alajuela, buses marked La Guácima Abajo depart from Calle 10, Avenida 2, seven times daily. Ask the driver to stop at La Finca de Mariposas.

Alajuela and Vicinity

ALAJUELA
Alajuela (pop. 35,000) sits at the base of Volcán Poás, 20 kilometers northwest of San José and two kilometers north of Juan Santamaría Airport and the Pan-American Highway. First named La Lajuela in 1657, the town is known locally as "La Ciudad de los Mangos" for the mango trees around the main square. Today, Costa Rica's "second city" is a modestly cosmopolitan town with strong links to the coffee industry. Saturday is market day.

Sights
At the heart of town is **Parque Central,** officially called Plaza del General Tomás Guardia, with various busts of important locals from decades past. Twice weekly, music is played in the domed bandstand. Pretty 19th-century structures with fancy iron grilles surround the park. The square is backed by a red-domed colonial-era **cathedral,** where ex-presidents Tomás Guardia and León Cortés Castro are buried. It has some impressive religious statuary, including a glass cabinet brimful of eclectic and macabre offerings to La Negrita. **Iglesia de Agonía** church, in Greek-Orthodox-meets-baroque style, is five blocks east.

Memories of Juan Santamaría—or "Erizo"

(Hedgehog, referring to Santamaría's bristly hair)—the homegrown drummer-boy hero of the Battle of 1856, figure prominently in Alajuela, notably in the **Museo Histórico Cultural Juan Santamaría** (Avenida 3, Calles Central/2, tel. 506/2441-4775, 10 A.M.–5:30 P.M. Tues.–Sun., free), housed in the former colonial city jail on the northwest corner of the Parque Central. This small museum tells the story of the War of 1856 against the no-good American adventurer William Walker. Call ahead to arrange a screening of an English-language film. Guided tours are given 9 A.M.–4:30 P.M. Tuesday–Friday.

Two blocks south of Parque Central is **Parque Juan Santamaría** (Calle 2, Avenidas 2/4), a tiny concrete plaza with a statue of the national hero rushing forward with flaming torch and rifle to defend the country against William Walker's ragtag army. It was recently relaid. Opposite, the **Teatro Municipal** (tel. 506/2435-2362) was also restored and re-opened in 2007.

◖ Flor de Mayo
At Río Segundo de Alajuela, three kilometers southeast of Alajuela, Richard Frisius breeds green and scarlet macaws for eventual release

statue of Juan Santamaría in Parque Juan
Santamaría

into the wild. The home and breeding center, Flor de Mayo (tel./fax 506/2441-2658,
www.hatchedtoflyfree.org, $20 donation),
features three huge aviaries where pairs of
breeding macaws are housed, plus a flyway
where they can fly and learn to flock. Dozens
of other birds have been welcomed into the
beautiful home, surrounding a lush botanical
garden. *Visitation is strictly by appointment!* Flor
de Mayo is 600 meters east of the Hampton
Inn and 100 meters east of the Hostal II
Millennium, where you turn north at the traffic light; go 400 meters to a Y-fork, then 200
meters uphill; Flor de Mayo is on the left.

Entertainment and Events

The **Fiesta Casino** (tel. 506/2431-1455,
www.fiesta.cr), by the Hampton Inn, 400
meters east of the airport, has slots and roulette, plus U.S. sports on the big screen and
Las Vegas–style cabarets nightly. Happy hour
lasts 4–7 P.M.

For roller-skating, head to **Patines
Internacional** (tel. 506/2443-8087, 7–10 P.M.

Mon.–Sat., 5–10 P.M. Sun., $2.50), behind
Mall Internacional on the airport boulevard.

Every April 11, **Juan Santamaría Day** is
cause for celebration, with parades, bands,
dancing, and arts-and-crafts fairs. The town
also hosts the annual nine-day **Mango Festival**
in July.

Accommodations

UNDER $25

Backpackers have several options downtown,
not least the **Hostel Trotamundos** (Avenida
5, Calles 2/4, tel. 506/2430-5832, www.hostel
trotamundos.com, $10 dorm, $25–35 s/d private room), with clean and comfy dorms, plus
private rooms, and hot water showers. There's
a community kitchen and TV lounge. Several
similarly priced newcomers recently opened
within shouting distance to compete for budget traffic, including the comfortable **Hostel
5ta Avenida** (Avenida 5, Calles Central/1, tel.
506/2441-1563), and the **Hotel Green Day
Inn** (Avenida 3, Calle 5, tel. 506/2242-6326,
www.greendayinn.com).

Another great backpackers' option is **Maleku
Hostel** (tel. 506/2430-4304, www.maleku
hostel.com, $10 dorms, $25 s, $35 d private
room), opposite the new hospital. **Mango
Verde Hostel** (Avenida 3, Calles 2/4, tel.
506/2441-6330, fax 506/2443-5074, mira
flores@hotmail.com, $10 s or $20 d shared
bath, $15 s or $25 d private bath) is also popular. It has 10 rooms with fans, some private
baths with hot water, and a shared kitchen
and TV lounge. The old house has terra-cotta
tile and wood floors, and a large rear courtyard with hammocks and a basic kitchenette.
Internet service is offered.

$25-50

Upgraded under new owners who've added
colorful touches, the **Pensión Alajuela**
(Calle Central, Avenida 9, tel. 506/2443-
1717, www.pensionalajuela.com, $25 s or $30
d shared bath, $35 s or $45 d private bath,
$45 s or $55 d "deluxe") is simple yet appealing, with 12 clean rooms with small, private
bathrooms with hot water (eight rooms have

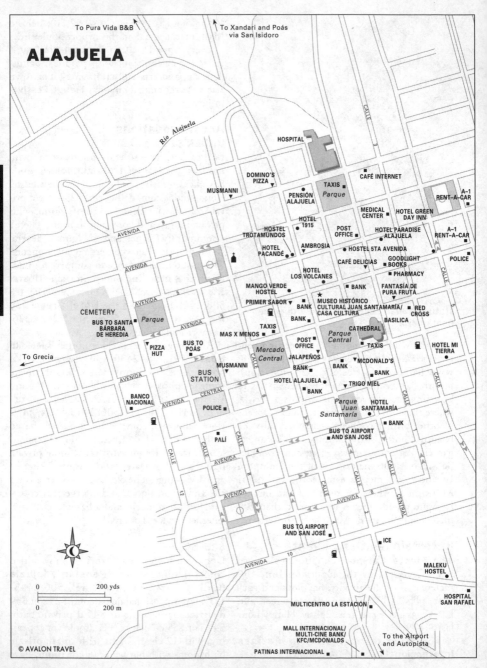

ALAJUELA

To Pura Vida B&B

To Xandari and Poás
via San Isidoro

Rio Alajuela

HOSPITAL

DOMINO'S
PIZZA

CAFÉ INTERNET

MUSMANNI

TAXIS
Parque

PENSIÓN
ALAJUELA

A-1
RENT-A-CAR

MEDICAL
CENTER

HOTEL GREEN
DAY INN

HOTEL
1915

POST
OFFICE

HOTEL PARADISE
ALAJUELA

A-1
RENT-A-CAR

HOSTEL
TROTAMUNDOS

AMBROSIA

HOSTEL 5TA AVENIDA

POLICE

HOTEL
PACANDÉ

CAFÉ DELICIAS

GOODLIGHT
BOOKS

HOTEL
LOS VOLCANES

PHARMACY

MANGO VERDE
HOSTEL

BANK

FANTASÍA DE
PURA FRUTA

PRIMER SABOR

MUSEO HISTÓRICO
CULTURAL JUAN SANTAMARÍA/
CASA CULTURA

BANK

RED
CROSS

CEMETERY

Parque

BANK

CATHEDRAL

BASILICA

BUS TO SANTA
BÁRBARA
DE HEREDIA

AVENIDA

TAXIS

MAS X MENOS

Parque
Central

To Grecia

PIZZA
HUT

BUS TO
POAS

POST
OFFICE

TAXIS

HOTEL MI
TIERRA

Mercado
Central

JALAPEÑOS

BUS
STATION

MUSMANNI

MCDONALD'S

BANK

BANK

BANK

HOTEL ALAJUELA

BANK

TRIGO MIEL

BANCO
NACIONAL

Parque
Juan
Santamaría

HOTEL
SANTAMARÍA

BANK

POLICE

PALÍ

BUS TO AIRPORT
AND SAN JOSÉ

BUS TO AIRPORT
AND SAN JOSÉ

ICE

MALEKU
HOSTEL

0   200 yds

0   200 m

MULTICENTRO LA ESTACIÓN

HOSPITAL
SAN RAFAEL

MALL INTERNACIONAL/
MULTI-CINE BANK/
KFC/MCDONALDS

To the Airport
and Autopista

PATINAS INTERNACIONAL

© AVALON TRAVEL

To Yara Blanca

Soccer Stadium

AVENIDA

Plaza

CALLE

CALLE

AVENIDA

MERECUMBÉ

IGLESIA DE AGONÍA

MUSMANNI

Parque

PAPA JOHN'S

CALLE

AVENIDA

CALLE

BUSES TO HEREDIA

AVENIDA

DELICIAS

AVENIDA

CALLE

HOTEL VILLA BONITA B&B

TACO BELL

BANK

MCDONALD'S

MAS X MENOS

BANK

Río Ciruelas

To **FLOR DE MAYO** and Hampton Inn

cable TV). There's a snack bar, laundry service, and Internet.

Offering excellent conditions and value, **Hotel Paradise Alajuela** (Avenida 5, Calles 1/3, tel. 506/2431-2541, www.hotelparadise alajuela.com, $15 pp shared room, $25 s, $25/35 d) is an impeccably clean hotel with simply but nicely furnished dorms and rooms.

Hotel Alajuela (Calle 2, Avenidas Central/2, tel. 506/2441-1241, fax 506/2441-7912, $20 s or $30 d shared bath, $35 s or $40 d private bath), catercorner to Parque Central, has 50 clean and nicely furnished rooms, most with private baths with hot water. Apartment rooms with kitchens in the old section are dark. It has laundry service but no restaurant. Competing is the **Hotel Santamaría** (Avenida 4, Calle Central, tel. 506/2442-8388, www.santamariacr.com, $35 s, $40 d), a lovely yet simple hotel kept impeccably clean. Guest rooms have colorful spreads, cable TV, and private bathrooms.

I like the family-run **Hotel Pacandé B&B** (Avenida 5, Calles 2/4, tel. 506/2443-8481, www.hotelpacande.com, $27–50 s/d), 200 meters north and 50 meters west of the park. This handsome 1950s home has eight modestly furnished rooms: Five share three bathrooms; others have private bathrooms, all with hot water. Upstairs rooms get lots of light; cheaper rooms downstairs are ill-lit. There's laundry and secure parking, plus airport shuttle, Internet, and kitchen privileges. Rates include breakfast.

My favorite in this category is **Hotel Los Volcanes** (Avenida 3, Calles Central/2, tel. 506/2441-0525, www.hotellosvolcanes.com, $30 s or $40 d shared bath, $40 s or $52 d private bath), facing the museum. Housed in a charming, fully restored 1920s home with lofty paneled ceilings and polished hardwoods, it offers six large, well-lit bedrooms with ceiling fans and pleasing furnishings (wrought-iron and hardwood beds), wooden floors, lofty wooden ceilings, cable TV, and handsome bathrooms. Two more elegant rooms are to the rear, where there's a patio with hammocks. It has a small TV lounge, plus laundry and secure parking. Rates include full breakfast and airport transfers.

CENTRAL HIGHLANDS

An equally pleasant recommendation is the **Hotel Villa Bonita Bed and Breakfast** (Avenida 8, Calle 9, tel. 506/2441-0239, www.hotelvillabonita.com, $47 s, $57 d), a gracious home with inviting, impeccably kept rooms and a welcoming homey charm.

$50-100

Close to the airport, the **Hostal II Millenium B&B** (tel. 506/2430-5050, www.bbmilleniumcr.com, $61 s, $67 d) is a charming and popular bed-and-breakfast in a middle-class home at Río Segundo de Alajuela. The former dorms have been turned into private rooms, all with small cable TVs, fans, and private bath with hot water. It has a TV lounge with leather sofas and rattan furniture, plus a shaded dining area. Guests get kitchen access. There's parking and 24-hour airport pick-up service. Rates include breakfast and tax.

Half a dozen newcomers have opened nearby to take advantage of Millenium's success.

In town, I like the family-run **Hotel 1915** (Calle 2, Avenidas 5/7, tel./fax 506/2440-7163, http://1915hotel.com, $45–75 s/d), three blocks north of the central plaza. It has 18 clean and homey rooms (some air-conditioned) whose modern bathrooms have large walk-in hot-water showers with little gardens attached. It has a huge lounge with fabulous antique hardwood furnishings and earth tones, plus stone and stucco walls, creating a delightful, upscale ambience. Breakfast is served on a shaded patio with a grill and wood-fired oven.

Up the price chart, in the northern suburbs, **Pura Vida Hotel** (tel. 506/2430-2929, www.puravidahotel.com, $85–140 s/d), off the road to Tuetal, is an intimate place set in a beautiful one-acre garden and run by Californians Nhi and Bernie. The handsome old timber-beamed home has been restored with an exciting contemporary aesthetic, with hints of Santa Fe in the lounge. Its seven rooms and self-contained bungalows are all themed. The Orchid Room, for example, is done up in whites and reds with a black four-poster metal bed. All have

splendid bathrooms. It offers baggage storage, Internet access, a small library with TV and stereo system, plus a garden restaurant serving gourmet dishes by reservation. There are lots of guest-friendly dogs, plus secure parking. Excursions are offered. Rates include breakfast.

$100-150

A mere 400 meters from the airport, the **Hampton Inn and Suites** (tel. 506/2436-0000 or 800/426-7866, www.hampton-inn.com, $140–179 s/d) is perfect if you have tight flight transfers and don't mind charmless motel-style Americana. It's somewhat soulless, but it's clean and has all the amenities you'll need for a one-night stay, and the Fiesta Casino is a stone's throw away. Rates include continental breakfast and airport transfers but are vastly overpriced.

Food

Alajuela is curiously devoid of noteworthy restaurants.

Jalapeños Comida Tex-Mex (Calle 1, Avenida Central/1, tel. 506/2430-4027, 11:30 A.M.–9 P.M. Mon.–Fri., 11:30 A.M.–10 P.M. Sat.), on the west side of Parque Central, is a cheerful place offering great bargains on eggs ranchero, omelettes, and nachos (made with fresh corn *flautas*). I recommend the spicy *sopa Azteca* ($2). The hosts, Norman and Isabel, are delightful.

Ambrosia (tel. 506/2440-3440, 10 A.M.–6:30 P.M. Mon.–Sat.) offers a pleasantly airy ambience for enjoying Costa Rican fare and Italian dishes.

In Río Segundo de Alajuela, the **Calalú Typical & Caribbean Food Restaurant** (tel. 506/2441-2121, 7 A.M.–8 P.M. daily) is a great place for shrimp in Caribbean sauce ($$10), grilled chicken breast ($7), and coconut flan. It also serves *casados* ($5).

Seeking a delightful little coffee spot? Then head to the clean and airy **Trigo Miel** (Avenida 2, Calles Central/2, tel. 506/2442-2263, 7 A.M.–8 P.M. Mon.–Sat., 8 A.M.–6 P.M. Sun.), which has Wi-Fi. And you can buy baked goods at **Musmanni** (Calle 8, Avenidas Central/1, and Calle 9, Avenidas 1/3).

Information and Services

goodlight books (Avenida 3, Calles 1/3, tel. 506/2430-4083, www.goodlightbooks.com, 9 A.M.–6 P.M. daily) has more than 10,000 books and serves espressos and pastries on the patio.

Hospital San Rafael (Avenida 12, tel. 506/2436-1000) is full service. The **police station** (tel. 506/2440-8889) is at Avenida 3, Calle 7 (for the local traffic police, call tel. 506/441-7411; for criminal investigation, call the OIJ, tel. 506/437-0442).

The many Internet cafés include **Café Net** (Avenida 9, Calles 1/3, tel. 506/2441-1210).

Getting There

TUASA (tel. 506/2222-5325) buses depart San José from Avenida 2, Calle 10/12, every 10 minutes, 4 A.M.–10 P.M. daily. Return buses (tel. 506/2442-6900) depart from Calle 8, Avenidas Central/1, in Alajuela. The buses run past the airport.

Major car rental companies have offices in Río Segundo de Alajuela. **A-1 Rentacar** (tel. 506/2443-8109, www.a1cr.com) is at Avenida 3, Calle 7.

THE SLOPES OF POÁS VOLCANO

Above Alajuela, the scenic drive up Poás Volcano takes you through quintessential coffee country, with rows of shiny dark-green bushes creating artistic patterns on the sensuous slopes. Farther up, coffee gives way to fern gardens and fields of strawberries grown under black shade netting, then dairy pastures separated by forests of cedar and pine.

There are three routes to Poás Volcano National Park. All lead via **Poasito,** the uppermost village on the mountain and a popular way station for hungry sightseers.

Alajuela to Vara Blanca via Carrizal: From Alajuela, Avenida 7 exits town and turns uphill via Carrizal and Cinco Esquinas to **Vara Blanca,** a village nestled just beyond the saddle

between Barva and Poás Volcanoes on the edge of the Continental Divide about 25 kilometers north of Alajuela. At Vara Blanca, you can turn west for Poás Volcano National Park, or descend northward via Cinchona and the marvelously scenic valley of the Río Sarapiquí to the Northern Zone.

Alajuela to Poasito via San Isidro: From downtown Alajuela, Calle 2 leads north through the heart of coffee country. At **San Isidro de Alajuela,** about seven kilometers above Alajuela, a turn leads four kilometers west to **Doka Estate** (tel. 506/2449-5152, www.dokaestate.com, 9:30 A.M.–1:30 P.M. Mon.–Sat., by reservation on Sun.), at Sabanilla de Alajuela, a great place to learn about coffee production and processing. This privately owned coffee plantation and century-old mill that still operates entirely by hydraulic power offers the Doka Coffee Tour ($18; an optional breakfast costs $4, and lunch costs $7), where visitors are taught the age-old techniques of coffee growing, milling, and roasting. There's a coffee-tasting room and gift store, and an open-air restaurant with magnificent views. A butterfly farm was added in 2008. Also here: a **Bonsairetum,** or bonsai farm! The same family, which sells its coffee under the Café Tres Generaciones label, also runs **La Casa del Café La Luisa** (tel. 506/2449-6035, 7 A.M.–5 P.M. Mon.–Thurs., 7 A.M.–7 P.M. Fri.–Sun.), a lovely café perched above the coffee fields three kilometers north of San Isidro de Alajuela.

Colinas del Poás (tel. 506/2430-4113, www.colinasdelpoas.com), at Fraijanes, has a canopy tour (9 A.M., 11 A.M., and 2 P.M., $50) plus trout fishing.

Alajuela to Poasita via San Pedro: A more common route to Poás is via San José de Alajuela, San Pedro, and Sabana Redondo. **San José de Alajuela,** about three kilometers west of Alajuela, is a village at a major junction: west (Hwy. 3) for La Garita and northwest to Grecia, Sarchí, and San Ramón. The road to Poás begins at **Cruce de Grecia y Poas,** one kilometer along the road to Grecia. From here it's uphill all the way via the pretty hamlet of

© CHRISTOPHER P. BAKER

coffee tour at Doka Estate

San Pedro. The road merges with the road via San Isidro at Fraijanes and continues two kilometers uphill to Poasito.

La Casa del Café La Hilda (tel. 506/2448-6632, 7 A.M.–5 P.M. daily), a coffee shop overlooking the coffee fields, makes for a pleasant stop.

Shortly after my research trip, Vara Blanca was the epicenter for the 6.1 earthquake that struck on January 8, 2009, devastating this area with landslides that claimed as many as 40 lives. The village of Cinchona was completely destroyed, as were large sections of the road to Sarapiquí. The area around Fraijanes also suffered devastating landslides, and Poasito was badly damaged. At press time, some businesses in this area remained closed for repairs. Call ahead.

❰ La Paz Waterfall Gardens

This splendid nature and wildlife park (tel. 506/2482-2720, www.waterfallgardens.com, 8 A.M.–5:30 P.M. daily, $35 adults, $26 students and children; $35 guided tour), at Montaña Azul, about four kilometers north of Vara Blanca, features trails through a soaring hangar-size aviary with separate climate-controlled butterfly cage. There's also a hummingbird garden, a serpentarium (snakes), a marvelous walk-in ranarium (frogs), a monkey exhibit, plus a trout lake and orchid houses. The highlight is the vast walk-in aviary, with everything from macaws and toucans to guans. Don't wear earrings, which the macaws like to swoop down and seize. A Jungle Cat exhibit ($5 extra) offers a rare chance to see ocelots, margays, jaguarundis, and puma. The various exhibits are accessed by concrete trails that eventually lead steeply along the river to four waterfalls. Standing on the viewing platform at the Templo Fall, you're pummeled by spray blasted from the base of the fall. Continuing downriver, a metal staircase that clings to the cliffside descends to the Magía Blanca (the largest cascade), Encantada, and the La Paz falls—a pencil-thin, roadside fall that attracts Ticos en masse on weekends. It's a daunting climb back, but shuttles back to the hotel are offered from the roadside trail exit. The Casita de la Paz re-creates a traditional farmhouse. The restaurant has a superb

CENTRAL HIGHLANDS

recreated farmstead, La Paz Waterfall Gardens

buffet plus marvelous views. Birding tours are offered. Last admission is 4 P.M. Damage by the 2009 earthquake was relatively minor and the property reopened in June 2009.

Accommodations
ON THE VARA BLANCA ROAD
The **Pura Vida Health Spa** (tel. 888/767-7375, U.S. tel. 770/403-0238, www.pura vidaspa.com, contact the resort for rates), at Pavas de Carrizal, seven kilometers northeast of Alajuela, offers 50 villas, cabanas, and luxury carpeted chalet tents ("tentalows") with shared bath, amid enchanting gardens with pools, plus two suites with king-size beds in the main house. The deluxe Japanese Pagoda has a sunken living room, king-size bed, whirlpool tub, deck, and outdoor shower. It offers various health-themed packages. (When driving from Alajuela, turn sharp left at Salon Apolo 15, and Pura Vida is one kilometer up the dirt road.)

I adore (**Poás Volcano Lodge** (tel. 506/2482-2194, www.poasvolcanolodge.com, $50 s or $60 d shared bath, $65 s or $90 d standard, $75 s or $110 d junior suite, $90 s

or $150 d suite), on a dairy farm about one kilometer west of Vara Blanca. The magnificent rough-stone mountain lodge, stunningly situated amid emerald-green pastures betwixt Poás and Barva volcanoes, might have been conceived by Frank Lloyd Wright. Actually, it was built as a farmhouse by an English family. The unusual design lends immense atmosphere to the lodge, which was severely damaged by the January 2009 earthquake (at press time it planned to reopen after repairs). Centerpiece is a timber-beamed lounge with sumptuous sofas and chairs in front of a massive open fireplace. French doors open onto a patio with fabulous views. The nine bedrooms are rustic yet comfortable, with thick down comforters; some rooms have shared but voluminous baths. The large suite has a stunning bathroom with a fathoms-deep, freeform stone bathtub designed to resemble a natural pool; the skylit bedroom has its own fireplace, plus a magnificent contemporary four-poster king-size bed. Eight rooms are in an adjacent block. Horseback rides and mountain bikes are offered, and there's a game room with billiards. Trails lead into the forest, good for spotting quetzals. The lodge serves filling breakfasts, and dinners by request. Rates include breakfast.

For a Tolkien-meets-Disney treat, check into the (**Peace Lodge** at the La Paz Waterfall Gardens (tel. 506/2482-2720, www.waterfall gardens.com, $235–295 s/d standard, $295–365 deluxe, $375–475 suite, depending on time of year). Imagine natural stone, huge hemispheric stone fireplaces, rough-hewn four-poster king-size beds with canopy netting, tables hewn of diced timbers, hardwood floors, lofty ceilings, and stone balconies with stone whirlpool tubs and awesome views toward Poás. The mammoth skylit bathrooms resemble natural caverns and have natural stone whirlpool tubs and separate all-stone waterfall showers. The two-story, 1,200-square-foot Monarch Villa "honeymoon suite" is the ultimate in romantic indulgence. Every need is catered to, from umbrellas for rainy days and flashlights for electricity black-outs to a well-stocked mini-bar, plus CDs for the CD player standard in every room. Excellent buffet meals are served by day, and the elegant, guests-only upstairs restaurant offers three-course dinners ($28).

Nearby, and new in 2007, the **Rainbow Valley Cabins & Restaurant** (tel./fax 506/2482-1053, www.rainbowvalleytrails.com, $60 s/d low season, $75 high season) offers an alternative with its lovely cabins with glossy hardwood floors and heaps of glass, although bathrooms are simple. It, too, was damaged in the 2009 earthquake but was under repair at press time.

ON THE SAN ISIDRO ROAD

The **Siempre Verde B&B** (tel. 506/2449-5562, http://siempreverdebandb.com, $75 s/d low season, $85 s/d high season), two kilometers west of the Alajuela–San Isidro road, is a charming albeit simple bed-and-breakfast in an old wooden home set amid the coffee fields of the Doka Estate. The setting is sublime. It offers three upstairs rooms, plus a triple downstairs, all entirely of wood. They are drenched in sunlight and have modest but delightful decor, and deep, tiled shower tubs. There's a large TV lounge, a huge airy patio, and a garden with

caged birds. It has a café open to the public 1–6 P.M. Saturday and Sunday. Rates include breakfast and tax.

I absolutely love (**Xandari** (tel. 506/2443-2020 or U.S. tel. 866/363-3212, www.xandari .com, $160–235 s, $185–260 d low season; $215–290 s, $230–315 d high season), a contempo stunner perched amid the hotel's own coffee fields in the hills above Tacacori, five kilometers north of Alajuela. The 22 villas (each slightly different) are furnished with dark hardwoods and explosively colorful works of art, poured-concrete sofas with heaps of cushions, plus sponge-washed walls, Guatemalan bedspreads, and plump down pillows; rippling hardwood ceilings and voluptuously curving walls balanced by warm tropical pastels and stained-glass windows echo the theme in the public lounge. Each room has a kitchenette, its own expansive terrace with shady *ranchita,* and a voluminous bathroom with heaps of fluffy towels, bathrobes, and a cavernous walk-in shower with a wall of glass facing onto a private courtyard garden. Take your pick of one king-size or two full-size beds. The restaurant serves superbly executed, health-conscious meals supported by a full wine list. There are two lap pools with whirlpool tubs; a handsome bar and lounge; a soundproofed TV lounge with VCR, well-stocked video library, and plump leather sofas; a crafts store; a studio for artists and yoga practitioners; a gym; and an electric car to transport guests to and from the full-service **Xandari Spa Village** (spa@ xandari.com). Rates include airport transfers and breakfast.

ON THE SAN PEDRO ROAD

The **Jaulares** (tel. 506/2482-2600, www.jaulares .com, $25 s/d), in addition to serving wonderful food, rents five basic and rustic wooden *cabinas* overlooking a river accessible by trails; each features a fireplace. A larger cabin costs $70 for up to seven people.

Above Poasito, **Lagunillas Lodge** (tel. 506/2448-5506, $20 s, $25 d), two kilometers below the park entrance, has eight simple cabins with shared bathroom and splendid views down

room at Xandari, Alajuela

the mountainside. They're lit by kerosene lamps, but the owners recently added electricity. There are trails for horseback rides, plus trout fishing and a basic albeit homey Hansel and Gretel–type restaurant. Access is by four-wheel drive only, along a steep and rugged track.

The colorfully decorated **Hotel Orquídeas Inn** (tel. 506/2433-7178, www.orquideas inn.com, $69–84 s or $79–94 d rooms, $109–140 s or $119–150 d suite), at Cruce de Grecia y Poás, has become a kind of home away from home for local expat gringos who pop in and out to sup and shoot the breeze at the hotel's famous Marilyn Monroe Bar. The hacienda-style home is set amid five acres of landscaped grounds and fruit orchards. There are 10 types of rooms, and even a skylit geodesic dome with a kitchenette, sunken tub, and spiral staircase that leads to a loft with a king-size bed and twin beds. Rooms in the old house are preferred to the spacious but meagerly furnished 'Superior Rooms' in the newer block, where the individually styled suites are appealing standouts. There's a marvelous floodlit swimming pool with fountains and wooden sundeck, plus a reclusive whirlpool spa garden; a souvenir store stocks fine national artisan work.

Food

ON THE VARA BLANCA ROAD

The **Restaurante Colbert** (tel. 506/2482-2776, jsuirer@racsa.co.cr, 7 A.M.–9 P.M. daily), at Vara Blanca, is a French-run bakery and café with an airy, well-lit hillside restaurant with magnificent views. It offers set breakfasts, plus croissants, crepes Suzette, sandwiches, plus French-Tico fusion cuisine such as tilapia in tomato sauce ($7).

La Paz Waterfall Gardens has a magnificent buffet restaurant (8 A.M.–4 P.M. daily, $10). And **Rainbow Valley Cabins & Restaurant** (7 A.M.–9:30 P.M. daily) serves buffet meals, plus breakfasts such as Belgian crepes and granola, around a huge fireplace.

A suitably Bavarian ambience pervades the German-run **Casa Bavaria** (tel. 506/2483-0716, www.casabavaria.net, noon A.M.–11:30 P.M. Fri.–Sat., 11 A.M.–5 P.M. Sun.), with a huge and impressive international menu.

ON THE SAN ISIDRO ROAD

You owe it to yourself to dine at **Xandari** (tel. 506/2443-2020 or U.S. tel. 866/363-3212, www.xandari.com, 7–10 A.M., 11:30 A.M.–4 P.M., and 6–9 P.M. daily, $5–25) for its superb health-oriented dishes, such as Greek Island sea bass with feta cheese, olives, and tomato.

ON THE SAN PEDRO ROAD

I love the atmospheric and rustic ❿ **Jaulares** (tel. 506/2482-2600, 10 A.M.–10 P.M. Mon.–Sat., 8 A.M.–6 P.M. Sun.), serving meals cooked on an open wood-burning stove. The black bean soup ($2) is superb, as is the jalapeño steak ($10). It also serves lunch specials (*casados,* $5), plus an open buffet on Sunday noon–5 P.M. ($12). It's favored by locals on Friday and Saturday night, when it has live music.

Colinas del Poás (tel. 506/2430-4113), one kilometer farther north, has a beautiful restaurant specializing in trout dishes.

At Poasito, the **Steak House El Churrasco** (tel. 506/2482-2135, http://elchurrascocr.com, 9 A.M.–5 P.M. Tues.–Sun.) is a popular spot for tenderloins, *lengua en salsa,* and other meat dishes ($4 and up). Try the bean dip with tortillas and jalapeños, followed by tiramisu.

Getting There

Buses (tel. 506/2449-5141) for Poasito depart Alajuela from Avenida Central, Calle 10, at 9 A.M., 1 P.M., 4:15 P.M., and 6:15 P.M. Return buses depart at 6 A.M., 10 A.M., 2 P.M., and 5 P.M. Buses operate hourly 9 A.M.–5 P.M. weekends.

❿ POÁS VOLCANO NATIONAL PARK

Few volcanoes allow you to drive all the way to the rim. Poás does—well, at least to within 300 meters, where a short stroll puts you at the very edge of one of the world's largest active craters (1.5 km wide). The viewing terrace gives a bird's-eye view not only 320 meters down into the hellish bowels of the volcano, but also down over the northern lowlands.

Poás (2,708 m) is a restless giant with a 40-year active cycle. It erupted moderately in the early 1950s and has been intermittently active ever since. The park is frequently closed to visitors because of sulfur gas emissions. Over the millennia it has vented its anger through three craters. Two now slumber under a blanket of vegetation; one even cradles a lake. But the main crater bubbles persistently with active fumaroles and a simmering sulfuric pool that frequently changes hues and emits a geyser up to 200 meters into the steam-laden air. The water level of the lake has gone down about 15 meters during the past decade, one of several indications of a possible impending eruption (after laying silent for 12 years, in March 2006 a series of explosions caused the park to temporarily close). In the 1950s a small eruption pushed up a new cone on the crater floor; the cone is now 220 feet high and still puffing.

The **Botos Trail,** just before the viewing platform, leads to an extinct crater filled with a cold-water lake—Botos. The recently opened **El Canto de los Aves Trail** explores the lake region. This and the **Escalonia Trail,** which begins at the picnic area, provide for pleasant hikes. The park protects the headwaters of several important rivers, and the dense forests are home to emerald toucanets, coyotes, resplendent quetzals, sooty robins, hummingbirds, frogs, and the Poás squirrel, which is endemic to the volcano.

Oft as not it is foggy up here, and mist floats like an apparition through the dwarf cloud forest draped with bromeliads and mosses. Clouds usually form mid-morning. Plan an early-morning arrival to enhance your chances of a cloud-free visit. On a sunny day it can be 21°C (70°F). On a cloudy day, it is normally bitterly cold and windy at the crater rim. Dress accordingly. Poás is popular on weekends with local Ticos who arrive by the busload with their blaring radios. Visit midweek if possible.

Information and Services

Poás Volcano National Park (tel./fax 506/2482-2165, www.sinac.go.cr, $11.80 adults) offers parking, toilets, a souvenir store, and café, plus an exhibit hall and an auditorium where audiovisual presentations are given on Sunday. There's wheelchair access to the exhibits and trails. The park has no accommodations, and camping is not permitted. It's open 8 A.M.–3:30 P.M. daily May–November; 8 A.M.–5 P.M. Monday–Thursday and 8 A.M.–4:30 P.M. Friday–Sunday December–April.

Getting There

TUASA (tel. 506/2222-5325) buses depart San José daily at 8 A.M. from Avenida 2, Calles 12/14 ($5). The journey takes 90 minutes. Return buses depart at 2:30 P.M. TUASA buses (tel. 506/2442-6900) also leave from the plaza in Alajuela at 8:30 A.M.

Tour operators in San José offer day trips to Poás (average $35 half day, $55 full day).

Grecia to Zarcero

Highway 141 leads west from Alajuela, snaking through scenic coffee country and then climbing into an alpine setting—a marvelous drive!

GRECIA

Grecia, on Highway 141, some 18 kilometers northwest of Alajuela, is an important market town famous for its rust-red, twin-spired **metal church** made of steel plates imported from Belgium in 1897. An all-marble altar rises fancifully like one of Emperor Ludwig's fairy-tale castles. The church is fronted by a pretty park with tall palms, an obelisk erected to commemorate the foundation of Grecia in July 1864, fountains, and a domed music temple.

The **Centro de la Museo de Cultura** (tel. 506/2444-6767), on the park's northwest corner, houses a regional museum.

World of Snakes

Just east of Grecia, on the main Sarchí road, the Austrian-run World of Snakes (tel./fax 506/2494-3700, www.theworldofsnakes.com, 8 A.M.–4 P.M. daily, $11 adults, $6 children and students) displays a collection of more than 150 snakes from around the world, including many of Costa Rica's most beautiful critters. The facility breeds 70 different species for sale and for reintroduction to the wild. It educates visitors to dispel the negative image with a clear message—don't harm snakes! The critters live behind glass windows in re-creations of their natural habitats. You can handle non-

venomous snakes. And there are caimans, snapping turtles, and poison-dart frogs.

Accommodations

For budget travelers, **B&B Backpackers Grecia** (tel. 506/2494-2573, www.bandbgrecia.com, $40–55 s, $55–75 d) is 150 meters south of the park. This two-story, German-run modern house has simply appointed yet comfy rooms, plus Internet (including Wi-Fi),

rattlesnake at the World of Snakes

© CHRISTOPHER P. BAKER

© CHRISTOPHER P. BAKER

metal church, Grecia

kitchen access, a reading room, and a garden with hammocks.

Posada Mimosa (tel. 506/2494-5868, www.mimosa.co.cr, $50 s or $65 d rooms, $100 s/d guesthouse, $60 s or $70 d small cabin, $110 s/d family cabin), in the hamlet of Rincón de Salas, is an exquisite bed-and-breakfast run by Canadians Tessa and Martin Borner. Set amid seven hectares of lush landscaped gardens and forest, the hillside home offers dramatic views; the grounds are fantastic for birding. It has four no-frills rooms in the house, all with private baths, as well as a charming studio *casita* and two modestly furnished self-catering *casitas*. Traditional Costa Rican motifs adorn the walls. There's a small horizon swimming pool and a poolside grill where breakfasts are served. Rates include breakfast.

Services

Café Internet (tel. 506/2444-3640, 2–9 P.M. Mon.–Sat., 9 A.M.–9 P.M. Sun.) is 50 meters southeast of the plaza.

Hospital San Francisco de Asis (tel. 506/2444-5045) and the **Red Cross** (tel. 506/2444-5292) provide medical care.

Getting There

Buses (tel. 506/2258-2004) depart San José every 25 minutes 5:30 A.M.–10:10 P.M. from Avenida 3, Calles 18/20 ($1.30). The bus station in Grecia is at Avenida 2, Calles 4/6, two blocks west of the plaza, where taxis congregate on the north side.

SARCHÍ

Sarchí, set amid coffee fields 29 kilometers northwest of Alajuela, is Costa Rica's crossroads of crafts—famous for the intricately detailed, hand-painted oxcarts that originated here in the middle of the 19th century. (The town celebrates them on the first week of February with bull-riding, amusement rides, and, of course, a parade of oxcarts.) Handcrafted souvenirs—from chess sets and salad bowls, leather sandals and rockers to miniature oxcarts decorated in traditional geometric designs—are sold at shops all along the road of Sarchí Sur, which sits atop a steep hill about one kilometer east

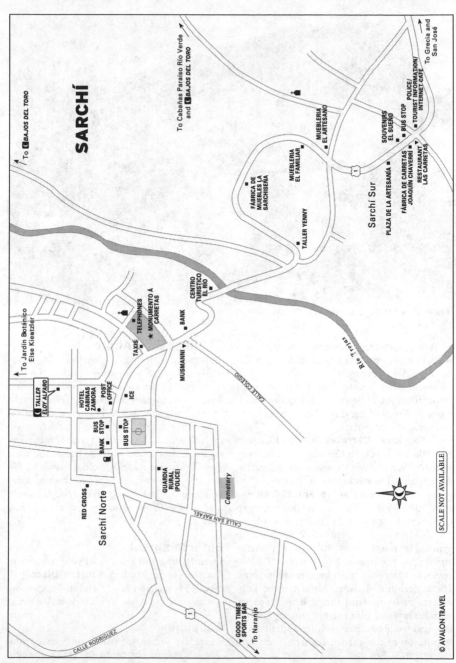

CENTRAL HIGHLANDS

SARCHÍ

To ◗ BAJOS DEL TORO

To Cabañas Paraíso Río Verde
and ◗ BAJOS DEL TORO

To Grecia and
San José

MUEBLERÍA
EL ARTESANO ■

MUEBLERÍA
EL FAMILIAR ■

SOUVENIRS
EL SUEÑO ■

BUS STOP ■

TOURIST INFORMATION/
INTERNET CAFÉ ■

FÁBRICA DE
MUEBLES LA
SARCHISENA ■

RESTAURANT
LAS CARRETAS ■

TALLER YENNY ▼

FÁBRICA DE CARRETAS
JOAQUÍN CHAVERRI ■

Sarchí Sur

PLAZA DE LA ARTESANÍA ■

BUS STOP/
POLICE ■

① To ◗ BAJOS DEL TORO

CENTRO
TURÍSTICO
EL RÍO ■

BANK ■

★ MONUMENTO A
CARRETAS

TELEPHONES ✝

TAXIS ■

MUSMANNI ▼

Río Trojas

CALLE COLEGIO

To Jardín Botánico
Else Kientzler

TALLER
◗ ELOY ALFARO ■

HOTEL
CABINAS ■
ZAMORA ●

POST
■ OFFICE

ICE ■

BANK ■

BUS STOP ■

BUS
■ STOP

RED CROSS ■

Sarchí Norte

GUARDIA
RURAL
(POLICE) ■

Cemetery

CALLE SAN RAFAEL

SCALE NOT AVAILABLE

CALLE RODRÍGUEZ

① GOOD TIMES
SPORTS BAR ■

To Naranjo

© AVALON TRAVEL

Taller Eloy Alfaro, Sarchí

of Sarchí Norte, the town center. Many white-washed buildings are painted with the town's own floral motif trim.

Sarchí Norte's **church** is one of the most beautiful in the nation and has a vaulted hard-wood ceiling and carvings. Note the humongous oxcart in the plaza!

At **Fábrica de Carretas Joaquín Chaverrí** (tel. 506/2454-4411, http://sarchicostarica.net), in Sarchí Sur, you can see souvenirs and oxcarts being painted in workshops at the rear.

The **Else Kientzler Botanical Gardens** (tel. 506/2454-2070, www.elsekientzlergarden.com, 8 A.M.–4 P.M. daily, $14 adults, $8 children and students; $12 per hour for guides, by reservation), 800 meters north of the stadium in Sarchí Norte, displays 2,000 species of flora on seven hectares of gardens. It's superb for birding. Almost three kilometers of trails wind through the gardens, which represent plants from throughout the tropical world and even feature a small maze. A portion of the garden features a trail for the blind.

Taller Eloy Alfaro

This piece of living history (tel. 506/2454-4131, 6 A.M.–6 P.M. Mon.–Fri.) is the *only* workshop in the country still making Costa Rica's famous *carretas* (oxcarts) featuring the 16-pie-wedge-piece wheel bound with a metal belt. Señor Alfaro's family can be seen making yokes and 11 different types of oxcarts in traditional manner, with the lathes and tools all still powered by an age-old waterwheel. Go just after dawn to see the red-hot metal frames being put on the wheels. *You're free to wander around at will, but be careful of all the whizzing belts and pulleys!*

Entertainment

Overnighting and want to let your hair down? On weekends, head to **Scratch Disco** (tel. 506/2454-4580, 8 P.M.–2 A.M. Fri.–Sun.), above Restaurante Helechos, in Plaza de la Artesanía.

Shopping

There are dozens of places to choose from. The largest is **Fábrica de Carretas Joaquín**

Chaverrí (tel. 506/2454-4411, http://sarchi-costarica.net). One hundred meters west is the **Plaza de la Artesanía** (tel. 506/2454-3430), a modern complex with 34 showrooms, souvenir stores, and restaurants. You can order custom-made furniture from any of dozens of work-shops *(talleres)*.

Accommodations
Pickings are slim. In Sarchí Sur, the overpriced **Hotel Cabinas Zamora** (tel. 506/2454-4596, hotelvilla@racsa.co.cr, $35 s/d) has seven simple, clean, air-conditioned rooms with small cable TVs, fans, and private baths with hot water.

The otherwise so-so **Cabinas Paraíso Río Verde** (tel./fax 506/2454-3003, paraisorio verde@racsa.co.cr, $20 s or $25 d budget rooms, $30 s or $40 d rooms, $40 s or $50 d cabins), at San Pedro, about five kilometers north of Sarchí Sur on the road to Bosque del Paz, has the advantage of a peaceful hillside setting, and a kidney-shaped pool and sundeck with spectacular views of four volcanoes.

Food
In Sarchí Sur there are several eateries in the Plaza de la Artesanía, including the small, homey **Restaurant Helechos** (tel. 506/2454-4560, 10 A.M.–6 P.M. daily), which serves tacos, burgers, and such tantalizing dishes as tongue in salsa, garlic shrimp, and desserts, natural juices, and cappuccinos. On the east side of the plaza, **La Troja del Abuelo** (tel. 506/2454-4973, 11 A.M.–6 P.M. Mon.–Thurs., 11 A.M.–midnight Fri.–Sun.) offers a large menu of *típico* dishes (try the sea bass in mushroom sauce).

Restaurant Las Carretas (tel. 506/2454-1633, 9 A.M.–6 P.M., $5), adjoining Fábrica de Carretas Joaquín Chaverrí, has a shaded patio out back; it serves *típico* dishes plus chicken parmigiana, pastas, salads, and burgers.

Services
The **post office** (7 A.M.–5 P.M. Mon.–Fri.) is 50 meters west of the square.

Getting There and Around
Buses (tel. 506/2258-2004) depart San José from Calle 18, Avenidas 5/7 every 30 minutes 5 A.M.–10 P.M. daily. Buses (tel. 506/494-2139) depart Alajuela from Calle 8, Avenidas Central/1 every 30 minutes daily.

Taxis wait on the west side of the square in Sarchí Norte, or call **Sarchí Taxi Service** (tel. 506/2454-4028).

◖ BAJOS DEL TORO
From Sarchí, at a turnoff 100 meters east of the Río Trojas, a road climbs north up the mountain slopes via Luisa and Angeles to the saddle between Poás and Platanar Volcanoes before dropping sharply to Bajos del Toro, a tranquil Shangri-la hamlet at the head of the valley of the Río Toro. The route is incredibly scenic, and at times daunting, as you weave along a road that clings precariously to the face of the often cloud-shrouded mountains. An alternative route is the road that begins by the church in Zarcero; it's a 30-minute, often-foggy drive with a dauntingly steep switchback.

The 400-hectare **Bosque de Paz Rain/Cloud Forest Biological Reserve** (tel. 506/2234-6676, www.bosquedepaz.com), accessed via a reclusive valley west of Bajos del Toro, boasts 22 kilometers of hiking trails leading to waterfalls, a botanical garden, hummingbird gardens, and lookout points. The forests are replete with exotic wildlife, including howler, capuchin, and spider monkeys, as well as cats and—according to the owner—more bird species than anywhere else in the nation.

Bajos del Toro is also gateway to **Parque Nacional Juan Castro Blanco** (tel. 506/2460-7800, www.sinac.go.cr). Part of the Arenal Conservation Area, the 14,453-hectare park protects forested slopes of the Cordillera de Tilarán extending from 700 meters elevation to 2,267 meters. At its heart is still-active Volcán Platanar (2,183 m). It is replete with wildlife, including Baird's tapir, and the resplendent quetzal at upper elevations. At last visit it had no tourist facilities. The entrance is two kilometers north of the plaza in Bajas del Toro.

If butterflies excite you, visit **El Remanso de las Mariposas** (tel. 506/2241-5840), a butterfly garden at the north end of the hamlet.

© CHRISTOPHER P. BAKER

El Silencio Lodge & Spa

About seven kilometers north of Bajos del Toro is a 200-meter waterfall—**Catarata del Toro.** There are trails; the bottom of the falls is reached by a 500-step staircase! There's also a restaurant. Entrance costs $35, including lunch ($79 with transportation).

Accommodations and Food

There are several simple *cabinas* in the hamlet, including **Bajos del Toro Hotel** (tel. 506/2761-0284), with rooms in a modern two-story block.

Bosque de Paz (tel. 506/2234-6676, www.bosquedepaz.com, $147 s or $228 d standard, $125 pp superior, $150 pp junior suite, all-inclusive) has a rustic stone and log lodge with a handsome restaurant serving *típico* food, plus 12 cozy rooms with wrought-iron beds, terra-cotta floors, and private baths with hot water. A one-day excursion from San José for an additional fee includes lunch. Reservations are required.

The supremely relaxing ☾ **El Silencio Lodge & Spa** (tel. 506/2291-3044, fax 506/2232-2183, www.elsilenciolodge.com, $365 s or $420 d low season, $385 s or $480 d high season) is a

stunning newcomer with a gorgeous 21st-century aesthetic. Combining eco-sensitivity with world-class accommodations, this first-rate hotel operates on an all-inclusive principle and has spacious bungalows perched on the forested slopes: all have gleaming hardwood floors, peaked rattan ceilings, soothing white and beige color schemes, cast-iron hearths, divinely comfortable king-size beds with down duvets, and a wall of glass that slides open to put you closer to Mother Nature. Travertine-clad bathrooms have huge walk-in showers, and there are whirlpool tubs on the wooden decks, which lack privacy, alas. Thoughtful extras range from fluffy robes and slippers to umbrellas and a fully stocked fridge on the house. A gas-stove kicks on automatically at night to keep things cozy. Classy! The luxurious, domed Zen-like spa in the forest is like something out of *Star Trek* and has an open-air yoga dojo, while the elegant restaurant (open to nonguests at the management's discretion), serving healthy gourmet meals, has walls of glass on three sides. I was served by the fireplace in a comfy leather chair while listening to Andrea Bocelli, Sibeliuss *Finlandia,* and jazz. My

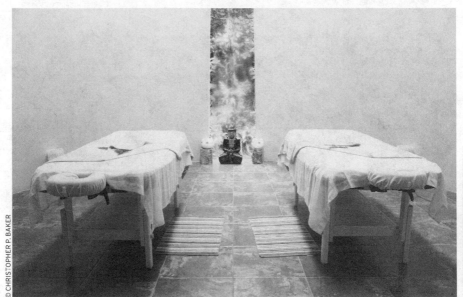

spa at El Silencio

CHRISTOPHER P. BAKER

dinner of choice: cream of pumpkin soup and pan-grilled trout with green rice, almonds, and orange-rum sauce. All this comes at a price!

Getting There

Buses and Jeep-taxis run from Sarchí and Zarcero.

NARANJO TO ZARCERO

Naranjo, five kilometers west of Sarchí and three kilometers north of the Pan-American Highway, is an important agricultural center with a pretty, twin-towered, cream-colored, red-roofed baroque church worth a stop. **Coopronaranjo** (tel. 506/2450-0138, http://web.coopronaranjorl.com) has tours of its coffee *beneficio* (well signed in town) during the October–February harvest season ($30).

North of Naranjo, the main road leads to Ciudad Quesada and the northern lowlands. It is one of the most scenic drives in the country. Beyond **San Juanillo,** the scenery becomes distinctly alpine, with dairy cattle munching contentedly on the emerald slopes. Higher up, beyond the hamlet of **Llano Bonito,** the road

twists and coils as you ascend to Zarcero, a pleasant mountain town with an impressive setting beneath green mountains. Dominating the town is the whitewashed church fronted by **Parque Francisco Alvarado**—a veritable "open-air museum" of fantastic topiary. The work is that of Evangelisto Blanco, who has unleashed his wildest ideas in leafy splendor: a cat riding a motorcycle along the top of a hedge, an elephant with light bulbs for eyes, corkscrews whose spiral foliage coils up and around the trunks like serpents around Eden's tree, even a bullring complete with matador, charging bull, and spectators.

At **Zapote,** eight kilometers north of Zarcero, you reach the Continental Divide, with sweeping vistas of the northern lowlands far below. **Rancho Amalia** (tel. 506/2463-3335, www.ranchoamalia.com, 9 A.M.–4 P.M. daily), one kilometer south of Zarcero, offers horseback rides on a coffee *finca* with forest ($10–20).

Accommodations and Food

Hotel Don Beto (tel. 506/2463-3137, www.hotel donbeto.com, $30 s/d shared bath, $35–45

© CHRISTOPHER P. BAKER

Zarcero

s/d private bath), facing the north side of the church in Zarcero, is a handsome hostelry with eight clean, modestly furnished rooms with TVs and hot water. It offers airport transfers ($20 each way) plus tours.

The **Restaurante El Mirador** (tel. 506/2451-1959, 6 A.M.–5 P.M.), near San Juanillo, has telescopes for better enjoying views over the valley and good *típico* food *a la leña* (grilled over coffee wood) that'll fill you up on a dime.

Getting There

Buses (tel. 506/2255-4318) for Zarcero depart San José every 30 minutes 5 A.M.–7:30 P.M. daily from Calle 12, Avenidas 7/9; and from San Ramón at 5:45 A.M., 8:30 A.M., noon, 2:30 P.M., and 5 P.M. daily. Buses depart from the southwest corner of the park in Zarcero; the bus stop for San José faces the church.

La Garita to San Ramón

LA GARITA

La Garita, spanning the Pan-American Highway (Hwy. 1) about 12 kilometers west of Alajuela, is important for its location at the junction of Highway 3, which leads west for Atenas, Orotina, and Puntarenas (and east for Alajuela). The area boasts a salubrious climate, and La Garita is famed for ornamental-plant farms known as *viveros*.

The **Botanical Orchid Garden** (tel. 506/2487-8095, www.orchidgardencr.com, 8:30 A.M.–4:30 P.M. Tues.–Sun., $12 adults, $6 children), abut two km west of the Autopista, opened in 2007 after 30 years in the making. This lovely garden displays 75 native orchid species, and about 75 exotics. Educational tours are fascinating; not least, I was surprised to learn about how global warming is affecting orchid flowering patterns. And did you know that vanilla comes from a Mexican

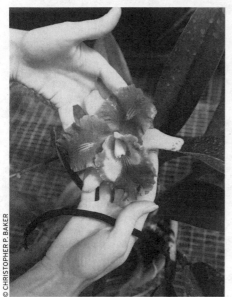

© CHRISTOPHER P. BAKER

Botanical Orchid Garden, La Garita

orchid? It also displays palms, heliconias, and bamboos, and there is an orchid reforestation program, plus it breeds macaws and parrots. A lovely airy café serves salads and quesadillas and the like.

⚫ Zoo Ave

This splendid zoo (tel. 506/2433-8989, www.zooave.org, 9 A.M.–5 P.M. daily, $15 adults, $3 children), at Dulce Nombre, on Highway 3, about 3.5 kilometers east of the Pan-American Highway, is a *must-see*. It covers 59 hectares of landscaped grounds and is a wildlife rescue center for injured and confiscated wildlife. The fantastic bird collection (the largest in Central America) includes dozens of toucans, cranes, curassows, parrots, and more than 100 other Costa Rican species. Zoo Ave is one of only two zoos in the world to display resplendent quetzals. Macaws fly free. You'll also see crocodile, deer, turtles, ostrich, tapirs, peccaries, pumas, and all four species of indigenous monkeys in large enclosures. The zoo has successfully bred the scarlet macaw, green macaw, curassow, guan,

and about 50 other native bird species with the help of a human-infant incubator. The breeding center is off-limits. A visitors center shows video presentations and offers educational events.

The Atenas and La Garita buses from Alajuela pass by the zoo.

Accommodations

The Canadian-run **Hotel La Rosa de América** (tel./fax 506/2433-2741, www.larosa deamerica.com, $52 s or $63 d low season, $63 s or $75 d high season), in Barrio San José de Alajuela, is a charming, mid-priced, country-style option 100 meters south of La Mandarina on the main Alajuela–La Garita road. Set amid a lushly landscaped garden, its 12 modestly appointed but recently upgraded cabins have fans, cable TVs, tile floors, security boxes, and balconies with rocking chairs. Tropical breakfasts are served in a homey restaurant. There's a small swimming pool, a day spa, a TV lounge with VCR/DVD player, and free Wi-Fi throughout. Rates include breakfast and tax.

A similar option, **Jardín Tropical B&B** (tel. 506/2433-5055, www.jardintropical bandb.com, $30–40 s, $40–50 d), 800 meters west of Zoo Ave, is a lovely homestay run by Cynthia, a delightful Costa Rican woman.

At the top end of the scale is the gracious **Martino Resort and Spa** (tel. 506/2433-8382, www.hotelmartino.com, $130 s or $145 d low season, $140 s or $160 d high season), in six acres of lushly manicured grounds with classical statuary. The motif melds a Romanesque theme with abundant lacquered hardwoods, as in the majestic columned lounge boasting plump sofas with exquisite Italian fabrics. It has 34 air-conditioned suites with hardwood ceilings, tile floors, double doors for soundproofing, terraces (some facing a lake), spacious bathrooms with monogrammed towels, cable TVs, phones, mini-bars, and king-size beds with fine linens. Facilities include a huge swimming pool, an Italian restaurant, a bar, casino, tennis court, and a state-of-the-art gym and spa. Trails access a bird sanctuary.

CENTRAL HIGHLANDS

Food

For a genuine local experience, I recommend **Fiesta del Maíz** (tel. 506/2487-5757, 10 A.M.–8 P.M. Tues.–Thurs., 7 A.M.–9 P.M. Fri.–Sun.), on Highway 3, about one kilometer west of the Pan-American Highway. This large, cafeteria-style restaurant is famous for tasty corn meals that include *chorreadas* (corn fritters), tamales (corn pudding), corn on the grill, and tasty rice with corn and chicken. No plate costs more than $3.

The restaurant at **Martino Resort and Spa** (7 A.M.–10 P.M. daily, $5–20) serves Italian fare.

Getting There

Buses for La Garita depart Alajuela every 30 minutes (6 A.M.–9 P.M.) daily from Avenida 2, Calle 10.

ATENAS AND VICINITY

Balmy Atenas, on Highway 3, five kilometers west of La Garita, is an agricultural town renowned for its quality fruits and perpetually springlike climate. (In 1994, *National Geographic* declared it the best climate in the world.) A beautiful church built in 1908 stands over the plaza, two blocks south of Highway 3. The old *camino de carretas* (oxcart trail) ran through Atenas, and during the peak of coffee harvest, trains of 800-plus carts would pass by, carrying beans to Puntarenas. The **Monument to the Boyeros** (oxcart driver) stands at the eastern entrance to town. The **Museum of Popular Culture** (tel. 506/446-0091, 8 A.M.–6 P.M. Sun.) recalls those days, while the **Museo Ferroviario** (Railway Museum, tel. 506/8810-0660, 7 A.M.–6 P.M. Sunday only, by donation), four kilometers north of town at Río Grande, displays a German locomotive.

The **Central American School of Animal Husbandry** (Escuela Centroamericana de Ganadería, tel. 506/2455-1000), one kilometer east of Atenas, welcomes visitors for a firsthand look at dairy operations, reforestry programs, and iguana farming. Half-day tours ($40 with lunch at an old hacienda) and full-day tours ($60 including lunch and a horseback ride into

the mountain forests) are offered; reservations must be made a week in advance.

Bungee Jumping

Thrill seekers can leap off the 83-meter Puente Negro bridge over the Río Colorado, one kilometer east of Rosario, just west of the Pan-American Highway, eight kilometers northeast of Atenas. **Tropical Bungee** (tel./fax 506/2248-2212, www.bungee.co.cr) offers bungee jumps under the guidance of "jump masters" using an 11-meter bungee. The company charges $65 for the first jump, $95 for two jumps. Anyone with back, neck, or heart problems is advised not to jump. Jumps are offered 9 A.M.–3 P.M. Saturday and Sunday, and weekdays by reservation in low season; and 9 A.M.–3 P.M. daily in high season. The San José–Puntarenas bus from Calle 12, Avenida 7, or the San José–Naranjo bus from Calle 16, Avenida 1, will drop you off at Salon Los Alfaro, a short walk north to the bridge.

Shopping

One of the best-stocked souvenir stores in the country is here: **Molas y Cafe Gift Shop** (Molas and Coffee, tel. 506/2446-5155, molasy cafe@racsa.co.cr), on the main highway on the east side of Atenas.

Accommodations

I like the Belgian-run **Hotel B&B Vista Atenas** (tel. 506/2446-4272, www.vista atenas.com, $65 s or $75 d room, $70–80 s/d cabins), a pleasing modern property high in the hills about three kilometers west of Atenas. The six rooms are airy and have heaps of light through floor-to-ceiling windows. Two cabins have kitchenettes and hammocks on verandas. All are clean and modestly furnished and have fans. There's a small pool and sundeck offering one of the most spectacular views in the country. The host is friendly, and the restaurant is a choice option.

Finca Huetares (tel./fax 506/446-4147, brownie@racsa.co.cr, $35 s/d room, $50 apartment, $55 house low season; $45 room, $60 apartment, $70 house high season), two kilometers east of Atenas and two kilometers northeast via Barrio Los Angeles, is an eight-hectare fruit farm with fantastic vistas and trails. It's a peaceful place and offers four rooms, four apartments, and two houses, all with cable TV and hot water. One is wheelchair accessible. Its well-named Restaurant Bella Vista features floor-to-ceiling windows with awesome views (open to the public noon–9 P.M. Sat.–Sun.). There's a large swimming pool and a kids' pool, and camping is permitted.

El Cafetal Inn (tel. 506/2446-5785, www.cafetal.com, $70 s or $85 d standard, $95 s/d suites, $105 s/d bungalow) is an elegant bed-and-breakfast on a small coffee and fruit *finca* in Santa Eulalia, about five kilometers north of Atenas. Lee and Romy Rodríquez (he's Salvadoran, she's Colombian), the superfriendly owners, run their 10-bedroom hostelry like a true home away from home. The lounge has marble floors and a cascade, and bay windows proffer valley and mountain vistas. The upstairs rooms (some quite small) are modestly appointed, with thin panel walls. A romantic Hansel-and-Gretel cottage has a king-size bed, sofa, cable TV, Persian rug on terra-cotta tile floor, kitchenette, and patio with volcano views. There's a large, clover-shaped swimming pool; a thatched coffee bar where hearty meals are served; and a pergola offering views over a canyon accessed by trails. Howler monkeys hang out in the trees nearby. Wedding packages and tours are offered.

The best bet is **Vista del Valle Plantation Inn** (tel./fax 506/2451-1165, www.vistadelvalle.com, $100 s/d rooms, $150–175 s/d cottages), a serene bed-and-breakfast on a working citrus and coffee *finca* on the edge of the Río Grande Canyon Preserve. Lush lawns fall away into tall bamboo forest. The main lodge is a Frank Lloyd Wright–style architectural marvel in wood; floor-to-ceiling plateglass windows flood Vista del Valle with light. Twelve cottages are reached by stone trails; some have their own kitchens. All boast tasteful yet minimalist decor and furnishings plus private balcony or wraparound veranda, and lavish Oriental-style bathrooms with granite tilework. New condo-villas have been added, but they're far less appealing. Facilities include a beautiful pool and whirlpool tub fed by a water cascade, plus mountain bikes and a stable. It has Wi-Fi throughout. Gourmet meals are served in a new restaurant with a bar. Rates include breakfast.

Food

On the northeast side of the village square, **Rick's Café** (tel. 506/2446-0810, 8 A.M.–8 P.M. Mon.–Sat., 10 A.M.–6 P.M. Sun.) offers an intimate atmosphere and tasty budget treats such as sandwiches, plus calzones, pizzas, and spaghettis for under $8, while $10 buys a dinner special on Thursday night.

◀ **Mirador del Cafetal** (tel. 506/2446-7361, 6:30 A.M.–5 P.M. daily), on the main highway about eight kilometers west of Atenas, offers awesome vistas down through a coffee-clad valley toward the Pacific. The 23-page menu (!) includes granola, omelettes, or *gallo pinto* breakfasts; soups and salads; creative lunches, from chicken fajitas ($5) to garlic sea bass with veggies and baked potato ($9), smoked chicken or fish cooked in banana leaves, and indigenous dishes (such as tamal wrapped in banana leaf); and fruit smoothies.

The modestly elegant restaurant at **Hotel B&B Vista Atenas** (tel./fax 506/2446-4272, 6:30–10 P.M. Thurs.–Sat., $5–15) serves French-Belgian cuisine.

Information and Services

Rick's Café (tel. 506/2446-0810, www.ricks internetcafe.com), on the plaza, charges $1 per hour. It's a good source for information.

Getting There

Buses (tel. 506/2446-5767) for Atenas depart San José more or less every hour 5:50 A.M.–10 P.M. from Calle 16, Avenidas 1/3 ($1.10); and from Alajuela every 30 minutes 6 A.M.–10 P.M. from Avenida 2, Calles 8/10.

An exciting option is a unique cycling tour with **Railbike Tours** (tel. 506/2233-3300, www.railbike.com, $85 including lunch), which offers a 15-kilometer-long tour by a "cycle-train" that follows disused railroad tracks to Atenas, beginning in Ciruelas, south of Alajuela.

PALMARES

Palmares, 1.5 kilometers south from the Pan-American Highway, 10 kilometers west of Naranjo, is renowned for its lively weeklong agricultural and civic fiesta held mid-January each year. The impressive stone **church,** built in 1894, is attractive in its ornamental setting and is fronted by a peaceful plaza.

At Cocaleca, one kilometer south of Palmares, is **Jardín de las Guarias** (tel. 506/2452-0091, 7 A.M.–6 P.M., $4, May–June by donation), a private orchid collection. Owner Javier Solórzano Murillo has more than 180 orchid species on display, but it is Costa Rica's national flower, the violet *guaria morada* orchid, that blossoms most profusely—more than 40,000 of them. The best time to visit is February–April, when the place explodes into color.

Accommodations and Food

In town, the lovely **Casa Marta Boutique Hotel** (tel. 506/2453-1010, www.hotel-casamarta.com, $50 s/d), a former mansion that makes fine use of lava stone and hardwoods, has 12 spacious and endearing rooms in a garden setting with secure parking. It has a plunge pool and hot tub.

SAN RAMÓN AND VICINITY

San Ramón, about 12 kilometers due west of Naranjo and one kilometer north of Highway 1, is an agricultural and university town known for its Saturday *feria del agricultor* (farmers market). The impressive **church** on the main square is built of steel manufactured by the Krups armament factory in Germany. It has a beautiful colonial tile floor and stained-glass windows. The **San Ramón Museum** (tel. 506/2437-9851, 8 A.M.–5 P.M. Mon.–Fri., free) on the north side of the plaza, focuses on local history and has a motley collection; it features a re-created turn-of-the-20th-century *campesino* home. One block east, the **José Figueres Ferrer Historic Museum and Cultural Center** (tel. 506/2447-2178, www.centrojosefigueres.org, 10 A.M.–7 P.M. Mon.–Sat., by donation) has

an exposition on the life of Figueres and the 1948 civil war.

In town, the **Hacienda Espíritu Santo** (tel. 506/2450-3838, www.espiritusantocoffeetour .com, 8 A.M.–5 P.M. daily, $10) coffee estate and mill offers one-hour tours that teach about coffee production.

North of San Ramón

San Ramón is a gateway to the northern lowlands via a mountain road that crests the cordillera, then begins a long sinuous descent to La Tigra.

Nectandra Cloud Forest Garden (tel./fax 506/2445-4642, www.nectandra.org, 7 A.M.–5 P.M. Tues.–Sun., $60 including guided tour), 15 kilometers north of San Ramón, is a botanical garden surrounded by 104 hectares of forest reserve where quetzals can be seen while hiking miles of trails.

About 18 kilometers north of San Ramón, a dirt road leads west to the 7,800-hectare **Alberto Manuel Brenes Biological Reserve** (tel. 506/2437-9906, www.so.ucr.ac.cr/Enlaces/RBAMB), created in 1993 to protect watershed forest on the Atlantic slope of the Cordillera de Tilarán. It's administered by the University of Costa Rica. It has trails, plus cabins available by reservation.

About 32 kilometers north of San Ramón is the **San Lorenzo Canopy Tour** (tel. 506/2447-9332, www.landsinlove.com/Canopy.htm) with two options. The first features 13 platforms, eight cables, and two hanging bridges spanning two guided trails; or you can take the "Adventure Cable Tour" by zipline using six cables (the longest is 850 meters). The latter has two parallel cables, so you can race your best friend. Each costs $35 for 90 minutes, or $55 for both. There's also a "canyoning" option involving a waterfall rappel ($50).

The nearby **San Luis Canopy Tour** (www .sanluiscanopytour.com) competes.

◖ Los Angeles Cloud Forest Reserve

The 800-hectare Los Angeles Cloud Private Biological Forest Reserve & Adventure Park (tel. 506/2461-0643, 8 A.M.–4 P.M. daily) begins at 700 meters' elevation and tops out at 1,800 meters (when the clouds clear you can see Volcán Arenal). The hills are covered with thick cloud forest, with the calls of howler monkeys emanating from its shrouded interior. Bird species include bellbirds, trogons, and aracaris. Laureles trees have been planted to lure quetzals. Three species of monkeys abound, and other mammals such as ocelots, jaguars, and jaguarundis are present. Two short trails (1.5 km and 2 km) have wooden walkways with non-slip surfaces. A third, hard-hiking trail (plan on 6–9 hours) descends past waterfalls and natural swimming pools.

A **zipline canopy tour** ($42) features 10 treetop platforms; guided horseback rides ($15 per hour) and birding and nature hikes ($24–55) are offered.

The reserve adjoins the superb Villablanca Cloud Forest Hotel & Spa (tel. 506/2461-0300, www.villablanca-costarica.com), which has its own manicured, well-signed trails into its **El Silencio de los Angeles** reserve. Various guided hikes ($24–55) are offered, as are self-guided hikes. INBio has a research center here specializing in butterflies; hotel guests can assist.

Accommodations and Food

Budgeting backpackers can try the **Nuevo Hotel Jardín** (tel. 506/2445-5620, $10–15), on the west side of the bus station. There's a Chinese restaurant to one side and a bakery to the other.

La Posada Bed and Breakfast (tel. 506/2445-7359, www.posadahotel.com, $35 s or $50 d standard, $40 s or $60 d with a/c and hot tub, $100 s/d suites), 50 meters east of the hospital, is a conversion of a home furnished with antique reproductions, albeit a bit gauche for some tastes. The 15 rooms in the original home have hardwood walls and ceilings, 37-inch cable TVs (eight also have stereo systems), and huge bathrooms; some have magnificent Louis XIV–style beds. Some downstairs rooms get little light; upstairs rooms are preferred and open to a balcony. Avoid the cramped and carpeted rooms in the annex. It has laundry, Internet, and secure parking.

Run by a charming North American couple, **Angel Valley Farm Bed & Breakfast** (tel. 506/2447-4084, www.angelvalleyfarm bandb.com, $35 s or $50 d low season, $40 s or $60 d high season), at Los Angeles del Sur, has a picture-perfect setting with gorgeous views. Individually styled rooms have delightful handmade components. Horseback riding and hiking are among the many activities available, and it has two vehicles for rent.

The mountaintop **Inn at Coyote Mountain** (tel. 506/8383-0544, www.cerrocoyote.com, $153–219 s/d), near San Francisco de Piedades Sur, about 12 miles west of San Ramón, is set in its own nature reserve. Designed on a Mujedar-meets-monastery theme, this upscale hotel has four individually themed guest rooms, all with unbeatable views and soaring hardwood ceilings. Four-poster beds sport high-thread-count cotton sheets, and Oriental wall rugs enliven whitewashed walls. The Tamarindo Room boasts a circular mosaic tub. The Observatory suite, atop a tower and accessed by a spiral staircase, has wraparound walls of glass and the most stupendous views. The hotel hosts the Creole Cooking School. The restaurant is open to the public and serves gourmet Latin-creole meals. Four-course candlelit dinners with daily menus might include wild mushroom soup, tomato and feta salad with sherry dressing, macadamia nut–crusted marlin filet, and fresh mango tart. It's not signed and is hard to find; at Piedades Sur, follow the paved road around the plaza to San Francisco; its about two kilometer by 4WD from there.

The **Hotel Ecocolonia Resort** (tel./fax 506/2222-2333, www.ecocolonia.com, $25–55) is an ecolodge that stands amid 102 hectares of rainforest, nine kilometers by dirt road from the main road; the turnoff is 24 kilometers northwest of San Ramón. Four-wheel drive is recommended. It has eight rooms and two cabins, which vary widely. All have decks and private, tiled bathrooms with hot water; some have outdoor whirlpool tubs. There's a restaurant, bar, and game room. Trails lead into the forest, and there's a stable.

A perfectly adequate alternative is the **Lands**

in Love (tel. 506/2231-0906, fax 506/2232-9591, www.landsinlove.com, $60 s, $80 d), on the northern slopes en route to La Tigra, 32 kilometers north of San Ramón. While the public arenas appeal, the accommodations are uninspired, although most have lovely valley views. It operates as a pet hotel. Dogs abound!

Glowing after a total remake, the superb ◖ **Villablanca Cloud Forest Hotel & Spa** (tel. 506/2461-0300, www.villablanca-costa rica.com, $155 s/d superior, $175 s/d deluxe low season; $170 s/d superior, $192 s/d deluxe high season) sits atop the Continental Divide on the edge of the Los Angeles reserve. The main lodge reflects its former life as a colonial farmhouse, albeit with a hip contemporary face-lift melding perfectly into the original structure. The 35 cozy chalets (sleeping 2–6 people; some are handicapped equipped) are appointed with handmade hardwood pieces and tasteful decor. A small fireplace decorates one corner and the bathrooms are a testament to 21st-century good taste: They include huge walk-in showers and (in suites) separate whirlpool tubs big enough for a *Playboy* party. The full-service spa is welcome after a day of hiking or horseback riding, and the El Sendero restaurant serves gourmet nouvelle Latin American fare. The bar-lounge with two huge hearths, flat-screen TVs, and plump leather sofas is inviting, and there's even a surround-sound movie theater (a nature documentary is shown at 6 P.M. nightly, followed by a top movie at 8 P.M.)! While here, be sure to visit **La Mariana Wedding Chapel,** with a ceiling inlaid with painted ceramic tiles on the theme of Latin American religious virgins. This hotel is one of only four "five leaf" Certified Sustainable Tourism hotels in the country.

Getting There and Around

Buses (tel. 506/2222-0064) depart San José every 30 minutes from Calle 16, Avenidas 10/12, 6 A.M.–9 P.M. daily ($1.60). Taxis operate from the main plaza, or call **Taxis San Ramón** (tel. 506/2445-5966 or 506/2445-5110).

Heredia and Vicinity

HEREDIA

Heredia (pop. 32,000), 11 kilometers north of San José, and colloquially known as La Ciudad de las Flores (City of the Flowers), is surrounded by coffee fields. A pleasant atmosphere pervades the grid-patterned town despite its jostling traffic. The **National University** is here.

Heredia is centered around a weathered colonial cathedral—the **Basílica de la Imaculada Concepción**—containing beautiful stained-glass windows as well as bells delivered from Cuzco, Peru. The church was built in 1797. It is squat and thick-walled and has withstood many earthquakes. The church faces west onto lively **Parque Central,** shaded by large mango trees and with various busts and monuments. On the north side of the cathedral, across the street, is the bronze **Monumento Nacional á la Madre** (National Monument to the Mother), by contemporary artist Francisco Zuúiga.

El Fortín, a circular fortress tower, borders the north side of the plaza. The gun slits widen to the outside, a curious piece of military ineptitude—they allow bullets in easily but made it difficult for defenders to shoot out.

The **Casa de la Cultura** (tel. 506/2261-4485, 9 A.M.–9 P.M. daily, free), next to El Fortín, contains a small art gallery and historic exhibits. It was once the residence of president Alfredo González Flores (1914–1917), who was exiled in 1917 after a coup d'état. He was later welcomed back and ran much of his presidency from his home, where he lived until his death in 1962. Refurbished, it is today a National Historic Monument.

INBioparque

INBioparque (tel. 506/2507-8107, www.in bioparque.com, 8 A.M.–4 P.M. Tues.–Fri., 8 A.M.–5 P.M. Sat.–Sun., $23 adults, $17

© CHRISTOPHER P. BAKER

Basílica de la Imaculada Concepción

students, $12 children) is an educational park two kilometers southwest of Santo Domingo, a historic village three kilometers southeast of Heredia and three kilometers north of San José. It's run by the Instituto Nacional de Biodiversidad, a nongovernmental organization devoted to cataloging Costa Rica's biodiversity. One exhibition hall focuses on the planet's biodiversity. The second hall lets you observe how Costa Rica was formed and inhabited, including humans' degradation of the environment. Interpretive trails lead through native habitats, with sheltered wildlife exhibits scattered along the trails. Botanists will have a field day, and there are caimans, frogs, iguanas, and a butterfly garden. Visitors can opt for guided tours ($3 for two hours). Last admission is one hour before closing. Transfers cost $10.

Entertainment

Bars popular with students include **La Choza** (Avenida Central, Calles 7/9, tel. 506/2237-1553, www.lachozabar.com, 4 P.M.–1 A.M. Mon.–Fri., 3 P.M.–1 A.M. Sat.–Sun.), which

packs 'em in nightly for music from salsa to rock, and for football games on the big-screen TV. **Caramba** (tel. 506/2261-2200, 11 A.M.–1 A.M. Mon.–Sat.), 50 meters away, has reggae and two-for-one beers all day Tuesday.

Champs (tel. 506/8391-8181, 7 P.M.–2:30 A.M. Thurs.–Sun.), in Plaza Heredia, has discos on two levels drawing the university crowd; Tuesday is ladies' night and Friday is reggae night. **Bar Speed 7** (tel. 506/8849-9871, 7 P.M.–2 A.M. Fri.–Sun., $3), adjacent, is similar and has a shaded deck; Thursday is ladies' night with a Chippendales-style show.

For something more highbrow, head to **Teatro Dionisio** at Café Britt (tel. 506/2277-1600, www.coffeetour.com), in Barva, which hosts shows on Saturday and Sunday nights ($12).

Spanish-Language Courses

Heredia is known for its language schools, which include **Centro Panamericano de Idiomas** (tel. 506/2265-6306, www.cpi-edu.com), in San Joaquín de Heredia; and **Instituto de Lenguaje Pura Vida** (Avenidas 1, Calle 6/8, tel. 506/2237-0387).

CENTRAL HIGHLANDS

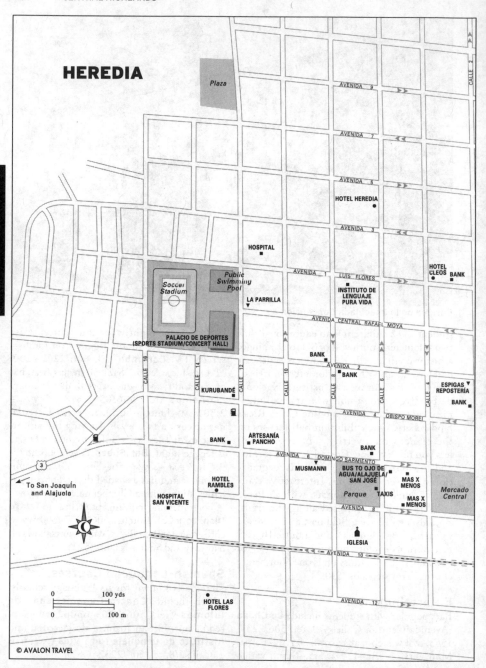

HEREDIA

Plaza

AVENIDA 9

AVENIDA 7

AVENIDA 5

HOTEL HEREDIA

AVENIDA 3

HOSPITAL

HOTEL
CLEOS   BANK

Public
Swimming
Pool

AVENIDA 1   LUIS FLORES

Soccer
Stadium

INSTITUTO DE
LENGUAJE
PURA VIDA

LA PARRILLA

AVENIDA CENTRAL RAFAEL MOYA

PALACIO DE DEPORTES
(SPORTS STADIUM/CONCERT HALL)

CALLE 16

CALLE 14

CALLE 12

CALLE 10

CALLE 8

CALLE 6

CALLE 4

CALLE 2

BANK

AVENIDA 2   BANK

KURUBANDÉ

ESPIGAS
REPOSTERÍA

BANK

AVENIDA 4   OBISPO MOREI

3

To San Joaquín
and Alajuela

BANK

ARTESANÍA
PANCHO

AVENIDA 6   DOMINGO SARMIENTO

MUSMANNI

BANK

BUS TO OJO DE
AGUA/ALAJUELA/
SAN JOSÉ

MAS X
MENOS

HOTEL
RAMBLES

Parque   TAXIS

MAS X
MENOS

Mercado
Central

HOSPITAL
SAN VICENTE

AVENIDA 8

IGLESIA

AVENIDA 10

0   100 yds

0   100 m

HOTEL LAS
FLORES

AVENIDA 12

© AVALON TRAVEL

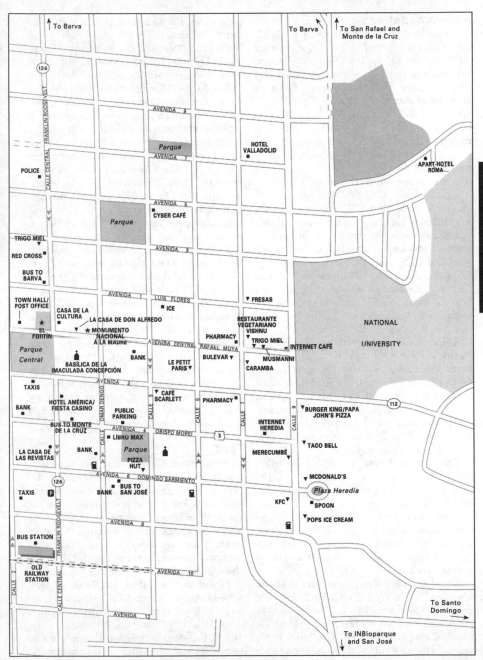

Accommodations

The twin-level **Hotel Las Flores** (Avenida 12, Calles 12/14, tel. 506/2261-8147, www.hotel-lasflores.com, $14 pp) has 12 simply furnished yet clean and comfy rooms with private baths and hot water. Two blocks north, **Casa de Huéspedes Ramble** (Avenida 8, Calles 10/12, tel. 506/2238-3829, $20 s, $35 d) has 10 small but clean, well-kept wood-paneled rooms with minimal furnishings; it also has an entrance gate with an electronic lock—a potential safety hazard in a fire.

A similar option, **Hotel Heredia** (Calle 6, Avenidas 3/5, tel. 506/2238-0880, www.enheredia.com/america, $16 s, $22 d) also has 12 rooms in a charming old house and offers perfectly adequate digs for budget travelers. A carbon copy nearby, **Hotel Ceos** (Avenida 1, Calles 2/4, tel. 506/2262-2628, www.enheredia.com/america, $20 s, $30 d) is a colonial home with 10 simply furnished, carpeted rooms with balconies. One large room has cable TV. The interior fails to live up to its splendid exterior, but it is fine for budget travelers. It has a seafood restaurant.

The modern **Hotel América** (Calle Central, Avenidas 2/4, tel. 506/2260-9292, www.enheredia.com/america, $40 s, $50 d), 50 meters south of Parque Central, is a good mid-priced bargain. It features 50 air-conditioned rooms and suites, all with pleasing decor, telephones, and private baths with hot water. It has a steakhouse and offers 24-hour room service, plus tours. Rates include breakfast.

Apart-Hotel Roma (tel. 506/2260-0127, www.apart-hotelroma.com, $24–39 pp), 150 meters east of the University Nacional, has small, individually decorated one- and two-bedroom suites with kitchenettes with microwave ovens, cable TVs, direct-dial telephones, and hot water. Some are cramped, others surprisingly elegant, and a suite has views. There's a restaurant and bar.

The class act in town is the **Hotel Valladolid** (Avenida 7, Calle 7, tel. 506/2260-2905, www.hotelvalladolid.net, $81 s, $94 d), with 11 air-conditioned rooms featuring cable TVs, phones, and kitchenettes. The hotel has a sauna, whirlpool tub, rooftop solarium with great views, bar and restaurant, as well as its own travel agency.

Outside town, the superbly run, Dutch-owned **Hotel Bougainvillea** (tel. 506/2244-1414, www.bougainvillea.co.cr, $103–120 s/d rooms, $128–140 junior suite), about 800 meters east of Santo Domingo, is a splendid bargain. This contemporary three-story hotel is set in vast landscaped grounds (with a hedge maze) surrounded by a sea of coffee plants, with a beautiful view of the mountain ranges and San José. The 82 spacious rooms each have two double beds, TV, and balcony, plus luxurious bathrooms in newer rooms. Modern artwork decorates public areas. There's a gift shop, swimming pool, tennis court, and an elegant restaurant. A shuttle runs to San José.

For a serene bed-and-breakfast experience, check into **Casa Holanda** (tel. 506/2238-3241, www.casaholanda.com, $60 s or $75 d rooms, $125 s or $150 d suite), at San Pablo de Heredia, about 4 kilometers north of Santo Domingo. It's run by accomplished musician James Holland. His beautiful, two-story, three-bedroom modernist home in the heart of coffee country offers stylish comfort. Elegance is a watchword throughout. The vast Honeymoon Suite has a whirlpool tub and large balcony. Meals are served family style (the garden is a peaceful place to enjoy breakfast), and there's a cozy lounge where James plays piano.

Food

Le Petit Paris (Calle 5, Avenidas Central/2, tel./fax 506/2262-2564, noon–10 P.M. Mon.–Sat.), a French restaurant under new owners since 2008, has spruced up its interior and has a patio. It features such dishes as crepes ($2–5), quiche, tripe with tomato sauce, and nougat ice cream. It has live music on Friday night and Sunday afternoon. I'm not too thrilled about the chef with a cigarette in his mouth, however!

Facing the cathedral, **La Casa de Don Alfredo** (Avenida Central, Calles Central/1, tel. 506/2262-4804, lacasadedonalfredo@gmail.com, 11 A.M.–10 P.M. Sun.–Thurs., 11 A.M.–11 P.M. Fri.–Sat.) is the most elegant place in town and has a superb menu of continental and

TREN INTERURBANO

After several years of speculation and anticipation, a commuter train finally began service in May 2009, connecting San José and Heredia. Operated by TUASA (Transportes Unidos Alajuelenses), which also operates local bus service, the route is served by four air-conditioned, two-carriage, diesel-powered trains along a 10-kilometer route between San José's Terminal Pacífico and the Terminal Heredia (Avenida 10, Calle Central).

The trains make two stops along the route: Santa Rosa de Santo Domingo, and Cuatro Reinas and Cinco Esquinas in Tibás. A total of 42 trips per day are scheduled.

The trip takes 30 minutes and costs a bargain 355 colones ($0.70 cents). Not bad for a service that has cost Costa Rica's INCOFER rail agency $3.5 million to purchase and install. And the trains make the commute oh-so-much easier — those commuting by car are often stuck for up to one hour in traffic on the congested roads linking the capital with the country's third largest city.

On May 25 the Costa Rican government announced plans to introduce a high-speed electric train (dubbed TREM, for Electric Metropolitan Train) on the route. Way to go!

Costa Rican nouvelle dishes, such as carpaccio de pescado (fish, $5), garlic shrimp ($7), and filet mignon ($15).

Fresas (Calle 7, Avenida 1, tel. 506/2262-5555, 8 A.M.–midnight daily), a clean, airy eatery, serves meals for less than $5, as well as all things strawberry, including ice cream.

Outside town, at Santo Domingo, the **Hotel Bougainvillea** (tel. 506/2244-1414, www.bougainvillea.co.cr) is known for its excellent cuisine. It offers a *plato fuerte* (entrée, dessert, and coffee) for $12—a good value. On Sundays, don't miss the buffet brunch. Also in Santo Domingo, **Ceviche del Rey** (tel. 506/2244-2985, 11:30 A.M.–3 P.M. and 6–11 P.M. Mon.–Thurs., 11:30 A.M.–11 P.M. Fri.–Sun.) serves superb Peruvian dishes.

Good for filling up for pennies is **Spoon** (tel. 506/2260-1333, 8 A.M.–9 P.M. daily), in Plaza Heredia; this clean, well-run, air-conditioned café serves a wide range of value-priced set meals, salads, pastries, and desserts.

For vegetarian dishes, head to **Restaurante Vegetariano Vishnu** (Calle 7, Avenidas Central/1, tel. 506/2237-2526, 8 A.M.–8 P.M. Mon.–Thurs., 8 A.M.–7 P.M. Fri.–Sat., 9 A.M.–6 P.M. Sun.), serving sandwiches (from $2), veggie burgers ($2), and *batidos* ($1) in several cubicle-like rooms.

You can buy baked goods at **Musmanni,** 50 meters south of the plaza. The two classiest cafés in town are **Café Scarlett** (Avenida 2, Calle 3, tel. 506/260-1921), with a warm and romantic ambience; and **Trigo Miel** (tel. 506/2237-9696, 7 A.M.–8 P.M. Mon.–Sat., 8 A.M.–6 P.M. Sun.), which has a pleasant Wi-Fi lounge. I also like **Espigas Repostería** (Avenida 2, Calle 2, tel. 506/2237-3275, 7 A.M.–9:30 P.M. daily), a well-run café and bakery with a pleasing ambience. It serves pastries, patties, and a value-priced lunchtime buffet ($4).

Information and Services

Hospital San Vicente (Calle 14, Avenida 8, tel. 506/2261-0091) and the **Red Cross** (Avenida 3, Calle Central) provide medical service. There's a **pharmacy** at Avenida 2, Calle 7. The **police station** is on Calle Central, Avenidas 5/7. Criminal investigation is handled by the OIJ (tel. 506/2262-1011).

The **post office** is on the northwest corner of the plaza.

Internet cafés are many.

Getting There

Microbuses Rápido (tel. 506/2233-8392) offers bus service from San José every 10 minutes, 5 A.M.–midnight daily (and every 30 minutes midnight–5 A.M.), from Calle 1, Avenidas 7/9 ($0.55); and on the same schedule from Avenida 2, Calles 12/14 (tel. 506/2222-8966).

In Heredia, minibuses depart for San José

Basílica de Barva

from Calle 1, Avenidas 7/9, and buses from Avenida 2, Calles 10/12.

Taxis wait on the south side of Parque Central, or call 506/2260-3300.

BARVA

Barva, about two kilometers north of Heredia amid coffee fields, is one of the oldest settlements in the country. The **Basílica de Barva,** which dates back to 1767, features a grotto (on its northeast corner) dedicated to the Virgin of Lourdes. The exquisite church faces a square full of contemporary sculptures and surrounded by red-tiled, colonial-era adobe houses.

The **Museum of Popular Culture** (tel. 506/2260-1619, 8 A.M.–4 P.M. Mon.–Fri. and Sunday, Saturday by appointment, $1), signed 1.5 kilometers southeast of Barva, at Santa Lucía de Barva, presents a picture of rural life at the turn of the 20rh century. It is housed in a renovated, adobe home dating from 1885 and once owned by former president Alfredo González Flores; the house has been kept as it was when he died. It has exhibits on traditional Costa Rican architecture through the ages. Guided tours are

offered for groups only. Sunday is family day, with clowns and shows for children.

Worth a visit, too, is the mask-making studio of **Francisco Montero** (tel. 506/2237-5426, by appointment). Barva is famous as a center for masks and huge *mascaras*.

◖ CAFÉ BRITT

Midway between Heredia and Barva is the *finca* and *beneficio* of Café Britt (tel. 506/2277-1600, www.coffeetour.com), where you can learn the story of Costa Rican coffee from the plantation to the cup. The company, which roasts, packs, and exports to specialty stores around the world, welcomes visitors to its coffee fields and garden. Vastly entertaining tours are offered, led by staff in traditional country costumes and highlighted by a "Flavors of Costa Rica" multimedia presentation telling the history of coffee.

The three-hour Classic Coffee Tour (9 A.M., 11 A.M., and 3 P.M. mid-December–April, and 9 A.M. and 3 P.M. daily May–mid-December, $25 pp or $35 with transportation) concludes in the tasting room, where you are shown how

© CHRISTOPHER P. BAKER

coffee tour at Finca Rosa Blanca Coffee Plantation & Inn

experts taste coffee. The four-hour Coffee Lover's Tour ($40 pp, or $50 with transportation) includes a visit to the company's historic **Beneficio Tierra Madre**, at San Rafael de Heredia; it is also open to individual visits by prior arrangement (tel. 506/2277-1600, www.beneficiotierramadre.com). Here you can witness firsthand the processing of coffee in a facility adorned with exquisite murals by the nation's leading artists.

There's a cinema for private events, and more in-depth private tours are offered by reservation. The factory store offers mail-order delivery to the United States. It has an elegant gourmet restaurant.

SANTA BARBARA DE HEREDIA

This lively and compact town with colonial-era adobe houses sits in the heart of coffee country, about five kilometers northwest of Heredia and three kilometers west of Barva.

Who would have thought that you could find a house full of emus in Costa Rica? Well, not a house, but an entire garden! **Emús de las Américas** (tel. 506/2265-5441, info@colegiosaintjohn.com, free), in San Juan de Santa Barbara, is about two kilometers southwest of Santa Barbara. Here, Rodrigo Salazar Villalobos welcomes visitors by appointment. He breeds emus for shipment abroad. His house is hard to find; it's behind a high blue wall (#23) on the main road 400 meters southwest of the village plaza.

The Ark Herb Farm (tel. 506/2239-2111, www.arkherbfarm.com, 8 A.M.–4 P.M. Mon.–Sat. by appointment, $12), 2.5 kilometers above Santa Barbara de Heredia, covers 20 acres of tranquil gardens on the lower slopes of Barva. More than 400 varieties of medicinal herbs, shrubs, and trees from around the world are grown here, mostly for export to North America. Another 600 species are grown in the garden. Owners "Tommy" and Patricia Thomas offer fascinating one-hour tours (by appointment) that will leave you enthralled.

A perfect complement, or alternative, to Café Britt is the **Finca Rosa Blanca Organic Coffee Tour,** at Finca Rosa Blanca Coffee

Plantation & Inn (tel. 506/2269-9392, www.fincarosablanca.com), a 14-hectare sustainable organic coffee estate that produces solely for use at the eponymous hotel. Tours are led by acclaimed *barista* Leo Vergnani, one of Costa Rica's most knowledgeable coffee experts. Leo is also a tremendous orator who infuses his presentations with vitality and fascinating lore. You can even participate in the coffee harvest, October–January. And the *finca* has a stable for horseback rides.

Accommodations

The modern **La Catalina Hotel & Suites** (tel. 506/2269-7445, www.lacatalinasuites.com, call for rates) is set in beautiful landscaped grounds with ponds. It offers rooms, studios, and one- and two-bedroom suites, all elegantly furnished in Edwardian style. The dining room doubles as a bar and library, and there's a gym, spa and swimming pool.

Imagine if Gaudí and Frank Lloyd Wright had combined their talents and visions; the result might be an architectural stunner as eclectic and electrifying as **C Finca Rosa Blanca Coffee Plantation & Inn** (tel. 506/2269-9392, www.fincarosablanca.com, $290–450 s/d). Inspired by Gaudí's architectonics and the Santa Fe style, the family-run Rosa Blanca is one of Costa Rica's preeminent boutique hotels. Its hillside position amid six hectares of coffee and orchards one kilometer northeast of Santa Barbara de Heredia offers romantic vistas. The focal point is a circular atrium lounge with wraparound sofas and an open-hearth fireplace that resembles a mushroom. The whole is contrived by the genius of architect Francisco Rojas in a flurry of voluptuous curves and finely crafted hardwoods. The place is like a museum, with imaginative and tasteful statuettes, prints, and New Mexican artifacts in every delightful nook and cranny. Fresh from a remake completed in 2007, it now has 13 rooms, 11 gorgeous junior suites, two master suites, and two villas, all individually themed and with luxurious pillow-top mattresses, down duvets, and whirlpool tubs; most are named for their trompe l'oeil landscapes. The honeymoon suite has a bathroom

Finca Rosa Blanca Coffee Plantation & Inn

© CHRISTOPHER P. BAKER

with walls painted to resemble a tropical rainforest, with water that tumbles down a rocky cascade into the fathoms-deep tub shaped liked a natural pool. A hardwood spiral staircase—each step shaped like a petal—twists up to a rotunda bedroom with a canopied bed and wraparound windows. The ecologically sensitive hotel—it scored highest in the nation in recent sustainable tourism awards—has a horizon swimming pool fed by a cascade, plus a hot tub, Internet access, a library, and a stable for guided horseback rides ($45 pp, two-hour minimum). A gourmet restaurant and full-service spa (11 A.M.–7 P.M. Mon.–Sat. or by reservation) have been added. The coffee-estate tour is a must. Rates include full American breakfast.

Food

(El Tigre Vestido Restaurant (6 –10 P.M. daily by reservation only), set above coffee fields at Finca Rosa Blanca Coffee Plantation & Inn, serves superb fare, including gourmet four-course dinners using organic, estate-grown produce. Lunches such as Central

© CHRISTOPHER P. BAKER

Vicente Aguilar with paella, La Luna de Valencia

American *pupusas* are served on a huge banana leaf. Leave room for the homemade ice cream. Dinners, prepared by local chef Pedro Alas, are consistently of Michelin-rated quality. Choose the cozy indoors or a lovely shaded deck. It has a small yet sophisticated lounge-bar with leather seats and flat-screen TV.

It could be the most fun you've had at a restaurant in eons, so *do* plan on dining at **(La Luna de Valencia** (tel. 506/2269-6665, www.lallunadevalencia.com, 7–10 P.M. Thurs., noon–10 P.M. Fri.–Sat., and noon –5 P.M. Sun.), an informal Spanish restaurant at San Pedro de Barva, between Barva and Santa Barbara de Heredia. It boasts heaps of colorful flavor, much thanks to the ebullient and eccentric Catalan owner, Vicente Aguilar. The setting is a charming centenary building with a rustic thatched extension out back. They serve a killer sangría to accompany flavorful Spanish dishes. For appetizers, try the gazpacho ($6) or octopus in wine ($7.50). For main course, you simply *must* try a paella, especially the seafood paella ($9.50). End with a *carajillo* house café with various liqueurs. Go for the flamenco and live music every Thursday night. And, boy, can Vicente sing!

The **Oky Delishop** (tel. 506/2263-6633, 10 A.M.–6 P.M. Mon.–Sat.), in Barva, is a delightful deli, whose owner, Oky María Numez, also sells delicious homemade chocolates.

Getting There

Buses depart Heredia for Barva from Calle Central, Avenidas 1/3. A bus for Santa Barbara de Heredia departs Heredia from Avenida 1, Calles 1/3, every 15 minutes Monday–Friday.

If driving from Heredia, Calles Central and 2 lead north to Barva, where you turn left at the plaza and head straight, westward, for Santa Barbara de Heredia.

THE SLOPES OF BARVA VOLCANO
Porrosatí

Half a kilometer north of Barva, the road forks. The left fork leads via the village of **Birrí** to Vara Blanca on the ridge of the Continental Divide.

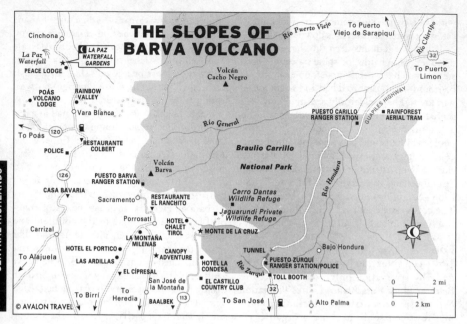

THE SLOPES OF BARVA VOLCANO

In Birrí, a road to the right at Restaurante Las Delicias leads east steeply uphill to the hamlet of Porrosatí (also known as Paso Llano), a true alpine setting where the air is decidedly chilly. The area below Porrosatí is known for its mountain resorts in the midst of pine forests. (The right fork at the Y-junction north of Barva also leads uphill to Porrosatí via San José de la Montaña.)

At Porrosatí, a turnoff to the left leads via the hamlet of Sacramento to the **Braulio Carrillo National Park** ranger station. The **Canopy Adventure** (tel. 506/2266-0782, www.canopycr.com), one kilometer below Porrosatí, has 13 platforms with ziplines ($40 adults, $30 children). The longest run is 200 meters! Prefer to keep your feet on the ground? It has trails, and two- to eight-hour guided hikes.

Monte de la Cruz Reserve

Two kilometers northeast of Heredia, and two east of Barva, lies **San Rafael,** on the lower slopes of Volcán Barva. A medieval stonemason would be proud of the town's Gothic church,

with its buttresses and magnificent stained-glass windows.

North of San Rafael, the road begins a progressive ascent, the temperatures begin to drop, and hints of the Swiss Tyrol begin to appear, with pine and cedar forests and emerald-green pastures grazed by dairy cattle. Remnants of ancient oaks and other primary forests carpet the higher reaches.

Ticos flock on weekends and holidays to a series of recreation areas, the largest and most popular being the upscale **Club Campestre El Castillo** (El Castillo Country Club, tel. 506/2267-7111, www.castillocountryclub.com, $15 admission). You need a passport.

At a Y-fork two kilometers north of El Castillo, head right to Monte de la Cruz Reserve (Centro Turístico Monte de la Cruz, 8 A.M.–4 P.M. Mon.–Fri., 8 A.M.–5 P.M. weekends). This 15-hectare private forest reserve, eight kilometers north of San Rafael, offers trails through pine forest and cloud forest great for spotting quetzals. It is often cloudy and usually crisp, if not cold and wet.

The road—climbing steeply and deteriorating steadily—continues seven kilometers to the 69-hectare **Cerro Dantas Wildlife Refuge** (Refugio de Vida Silvestre Cerro Dantas, tel. 506/2274-1997, www.cerrodantas.co.cr), part of Braulio Carrillo National Park, and known for its tapirs. Here, the Cerro Dantas Ecological Center offers environmental study and education programs. The rugged track is daunting and a four-wheel-drive vehicle is essential.

The fork to the left north of El Castillo leads to the Parque Residencial del Monte, an exclusive residential area with the **Hotel Chalet Tirol** within the 15-hectare private **Tirol Cloud Forest** on the upper reaches of Barva. Horseback rides cost $50, by reservation.

Events

The **International Music Festival** is hosted at Hotel Chalet Tirol each July and August in the Salzburg Café Concert Dinner Theater, looking like a set for *The Sound of Music*. The hotel offers other events throughout the year.

Accommodations

BIRRÍ TO PORROSATÍ

The **Hotel El Portico** (tel. 506/2266-1000, www.elporticohotel.com, $50 s/d) is set in a six-hectare farm with forest trails. The atmospheric lodge has 19 rooms plus three exquisite cabins with rough-stone tiled floors and private bathrooms; some have romantic canopied beds perfect for rainy days with your lover. There's a beautiful and spacious lounge with leather sofas, a large stone fireplace, and vast windows offering views down the mountainside. It also has a sauna and whirlpool tub, plus an atmospheric Swiss-style restaurant with bar. Beautiful artwork abounds. Landscaped grounds contain a small swimming pool and lake. Rates include tax.

Las Ardillas Spa Resort (tel. 506/2266-0015, www.grupoardillas.com, $70 s/d) has eight rustic log-and-brick cabins, each with fireplace, kitchenette, and private bathroom. There's a game room, bar and restaurant, children's play area, and simple spa with whirlpool and sauna. Hiking is offered. Meals are

prepared on a wood-burning stove using organic, homegrown produce. Rates include breakfast and tax, plus spa treatment on weekends. Associated with Las Ardillas, and farther uphill, is **Cabañas La Montaña Milenas** ($70 s/d), a stone and timber lodge with 10 romantic, rustic log cabins in the woods to the rear; each has double and single bed, TV, and fireplace. The main lodge has sumptuous sofas in front of the hearth; upstairs is a Colorado-style bar with live music.

SAN RAFAEL TO MONTE DE LA CRUZ RESERVE

The **Cerro Dantas Ecological Center** ($50 pp) has simple dorm accommodations and a communal dining area. Rates include meals.

The resort-style **Hotel La Condesa Monte de la Cruz** (tel. 506/2267-6000, www.hotel lacondesa.com, $146 s/d standard, $192 s/d junior suite, $256–872 s/d suite), immediately above El Castillo Country Club at San Rafael de Heredia, is a classy option with 60 spacious, beautifully furnished rooms and 37 suites, the latter with king-size beds. Facilities include two restaurants, a heated indoor pool, children's pool, sauna, jogging track, squash court, gym, and free shuttles to San José. Rates include breakfast and dinner.

For charm, check into **Hotel Chalet Tirol** (tel. 506/2267-6222, www.eltirol.net, $80 s/d year-round), a delightful Tyrolean-style place with a superb restaurant. Ten rustic yet charming twin-level alpine cabins—hand-painted in Swiss fashion—surround a small lawn. There are also 13 modern hotel rooms, each with a TV, fireplace, spacious bathroom, and furnishings from a Hansel-and-Gretel story. One suite has a spiral staircase to a mezzanine bedroom. There's a pool, sauna, and massage/fitness room, plus two tennis courts.

A similar alternative is the **Quality Hotel Monte Campaña** (tel. 506/2269-8724, www .qualitycostarica.com), at Birrí. And new in 2008, the **Hotel Cibeles Resort** (tel. 506/2260-3176, www.hotelcibelesresort.com), at San Rafael de Heredia, offers a cozy familial feel.

Food

BIRRÍ TO PORROSATÍ

At Porrosati, the rustic **Restaurante El Ranchito** (11:30 A.M.–7:30 P.M. Thurs.–Sun.) offers plenty of warming charm around a log fire. Meals are simple and cheap.

For a wonderful rustic mountain ambience, try **Las Ardillas** (tel. 506/2266-0015, www.grupoardillas.com, 7 A.M.–8 P.M. Mon.–Thurs., 7 A.M.–9 P.M. Fri., 7 A.M.–11 P.M. Sat., 7 A.M.–9 P.M. Sun., $4–10), centered on a stone hearth and serving steak in red wine, filet mignon, almond sea bass, and the like.

SAN RAFAEL TO MONTE DE LA CRUZ RESERVE

The **Bistro Chamonix** (noon–7 P.M. Mon., until 8:30 P.M. Tues.–Wed., until 10 P.M. Thurs., until midnight Fri.–Sat., and until 6 P.M. Sun.) French restaurant at Hotel Chalet Tirol (tel. 506/2267-6222, www.eltirol.net) is twinned, incongruously, with a Scottish pub called the **Green Dragon**. Think escargots ($8) and chateaubriand with béarnaise and mushroom sauce ($18).

I love ❰ **Baalbek Bar and Grill** (tel. 506/2267-6683, www.baalbekbaryrestaurante .com, noon–midnight Tues.–Sun.), at Los Angeles de San Rafael. This upscale Lebanese restaurant boasts sublime views as well as splendid Mediterranean food such as *mehshe* (chicken and rice rolled in cabbage leaves, with hummus and salad, $12) and *baba ghanoush* (grilled eggplant with tahini, $6.50). Choose from the elegant downstairs restaurant, or more intimate booths with hookahs upstairs. It has live music, from blues to Arabian, plus belly dancers on Saturday night.

Getting There

Buses depart Heredia for San José de la Montaña, Porrosatí, and Sacramento from Calle 1, Avenidas Central/2 at 5:25 A.M., 6:25 A.M., noon A.M., and 4 P.M. Mon.–Fri. (6:30 A.M., 11 A.M. and 4 P.M. Sat.–Sun.). Buses from Porrosatí depart at 7:30 A.M., 1 P.M. and 5 P.M. daily.

Buses for San Rafael depart Heredia from the Mercado Central hourly 8 A.M.–8 P.M. daily. Buses to El Castillo and Bosque de la Hoja depart Heredia from the Mercado Central hourly 8 A.M.–8 P.M. daily. For Monte de la Cruz, take a bus departing at 9 A.M., noon, or 4 P.M. daily.

Braulio Carrillo National Park and Vicinity

BRAULIO CARRILLO NATIONAL PARK

Northeast from San José, the Guápiles Highway (Hwy. 32) climbs up the saddle between Barva and Irazú Volcanoes and enters Braulio Carrillo National Park before descending to the Caribbean lowlands. Rugged mountains, dormant volcanoes, deep canyons, swollen rivers, and seemingly interminable clouds, torrential rains, and persistent drizzle characterize Parque Nacional Braulio Carrillo, 20 kilometers northeast of San José. The 47,699-hectare park (84 percent of which is primary forest) was established in 1978 and named in honor of the president who promoted the cultivation of coffee. It extends from 2,906 meters above sea level atop Volcán Barva down to 36 meters at La Selva, in Sarapiquí in the Caribbean lowlands. This represents the greatest altitudinal range of any Costa Rican park. Temperature and rainfall vary greatly and are extremely unpredictable. Annual rainfall is between 400 and 800 centimeters. Rains tend to diminish in March and April.

Encompassing five life zones ranging from tropical wet to cloud forest, Braulio Carrillo provides a home for 600 identified species of trees, more than 500 species of birds, and 135 species of mammals, including howler and capuchin monkeys, tapirs, jaguars, pumas, ocelots, peccaries, and the tepezcuintle, the park's mascot. The park provides excellent birding. Quetzals are common at higher elevations, and toucans, parrots, and hummingbirds are ubiquitous. Those elephant-ear-size leaves common in Braulio Carrillo are *sombrilla del pobre* (poor man's umbrella).

Entrances

The main entrance ($10) is the **Puesto Quebrada González** (tel. 506/2233-4533, ext. 125, or 506/2257-0922) ranger station, on Highway 32 approximately 42 kilometers northeast of San José on the lower northern slopes, 15 kilometers north of the Zurquí tunnel; ironically you pass *through* the park to get there! Northbound from San José, you first enter the park at Zurquí just west of the tunnel; there's a tollbooth (250 colones—$0.50). Zurquí (tel. 506/2268-1039) is the administrative headquarters and the trails here are closed to the public.

You can also enter the park at **Puesto Barva** ranger station (tel. 506/2261-2619, 8 A.M.–4 P.M. Tues.–Sun.), three kilometers northeast of Sacramento and just three kilometers from the summit of Volcán Barva (2,906 meters); access is via a very steep, deeply rutted rock road; four-wheel drive is essential (and you'll be in first gear).

Two other stations—**Puesto El Ceibo** and **Puesto Magsasay**—lie on the remote western fringes of the park, reached by rough trails from just south of La Virgen, on the main road to Puerto Viejo de Sarapiquí.

Trails and Facilities

Three short and moderately easy trails lead from Quebrada González: **Sendero El Ceibo** is one kilometer; **Sendero Las Palmas** is two kilometers; and **Sendero Los Botarramas** is approximately three kilometers. South of the ranger station is a parking area on the left (when heading north) with a lookout point and a trail to the Río Patria, where you can camp (no facilities). Another parking area beside the bridge over the Río Sucio (Dirty River) has picnic tables and a short loop trail.

The one-kilometer **Sendero Capulin** trail from south of the Zurquí Tunnel was closed at last visit, as was the **Sendero Histórico,** which follows the Río Hondura all the way from Bajo Hondura to the Guápiles Highway at a point near the Río Sucio.

Four trails are accessed from Puesto Barva. A loop trail leads to the summit from Porrosatí (the trail is marked as BCNP Sector Barva) and circles back to the ranger station (four or five hours of hiking, round-trip). The trail leads through cloud forest—good for spotting resplendent quetzals—to the crater and a lookout point. Fog, however, is usually the order of the day. From the summit, you can continue all the way downhill to La Selva in the northern lowlands. It's a lengthy and arduous hike that may take several days and is recommended only for experienced hikers with suitable equipment. Take an Instituto Geográfica map and a compass, plus high-quality waterproof gear and warm clothing, and—of course—sufficient food and water. You can camp beside the crater lake, behind the ranger station, or at two picnic areas with barbecue grills on the trail (no facilities). You can join this trail from Puesto El Ceibo and Puesto Magsasay; you can also drive in a short distance along a four-wheel-drive trail from Puesto Magsasay.

Bring sturdy raingear, and preferably hiking boots. The trails will most likely be muddy. Several hikers have been lost for days in the fog and torrential rains. If you intend to do serious hiking, let rangers know in advance, and check in with them when you return.

There have been armed robberies in the park. Hike with a park ranger if possible. Theft from cars parked near trailheads has also been a problem.

Getting There

Buses for Guápiles and Puerto Limón depart several times per hour from San José's Gran Terminal Caribe, at Calle Central, Avenidas 15/17; they drop off and pick up at the Zurquí and Puesto Carrillo ranger stations.

Most tour operators in San José offer tours to Braulio Carrillo.

SAN ISIDRO DE CORONADO

San Isidro de Coronado is a somnolent country town six kilometers northeast of the San José suburb of Guadalupe, and about four kilometers east of Highway 32. The Gothic **Parroquia de San Isidro** church is impressive. A fiesta is held here each February 15.

The **Instituto Clodomiro Picado** (tel. 506/2229-0344, 8 A.M.–noon and 1–4 P.M. Mon.–Fri.), the "snake farm" of the University of Costa Rica, about one kilometer southwest of Coronado, is dedicated to snake research. Although a museum and serpentarium have been planned, at last visit no progress had been made.

A turnoff from the Guadalupe–San Isidro road leads east, uphill to **Rancho Redondo,** scenically hoisted on the lower western flanks of Volcán Irazú, northwest of Cartago. The dramatic views are some of the best in the highlands, and very quickly you find yourself amid cattle and pasture.

El Tronco Adventures (tel. 506/2245-1340,

© CHRISTOPHER P. BAKER

Parroquia de San Isidro church, San Isidro de Coronado

www.eltroncoadventures.com) specializes in guided hikes and horseback rides in a private cloud forest reserve on the northwest slopes of Irazú; trips include transfers from/to San José. And similar day trips are offered by **Los Juncos Cloud Forest** (www .costaricacloudforest.com), a 200-hectare reserve 14 kilometers north of Los Juncos and where trails connect with Braulio Carrillo National Park.

Accommodations and Food

Terraza del Lago (tel. 506/2229-5058, www .terrazadellago.com, $50 "deluxe," $70–78 s/d junior suites) is a rustic yet atmospheric stone-and-timber lodge on a working dairy farm 0.5 kilometer east of Rancho Redondo. It has eight simply furnished, carpeted rooms with stone and wood walls and stone bathrooms with spacious hot water showers; electric blankets are provided for chilly nights. "Deluxe" rooms are more spacious and have cable TV and king-size beds. Junior Suites are more spacious and have cable TV and king-size beds. The homey lounge boasts a fireplace, plump sofas, and a TV/VCR. There's also a whirlpool tub, a game room, and a restaurant. Horseback rides ($5 for two hours) and guided hikes are offered.

Hotel Zurquí (tel. 506/2268-8856, http:// hotelvillazurqui.com, $60 s/d rooms, $70 s/d cabins), set in lush gardens off Highway 32 just 500 meters south of the tollbooth, makes a great base from which to explore Braulio Carrillo National Park. It has 35 standard rooms plus cabins with fireplaces, all with cable TV. The setting is marvelous and the accommodations are charming.

The U.S.–run, Texan themed **Lone Star Grill** (tel. 506/2229-7597), one kilometer east of the church in San Isidro de Coronado, offers "A Taste of Texas"—including "the best fajitas south of the Río Grande"—with Texan-size margaritas. Choose from charbroiled meats, salads, burgers, soups, and delectable desserts.

Getting There

Buses marked Dulce Nombre de Coronado depart for San Isidro de Coronado from Calle 3, Avenidas 5/7, in San José.

Cartago and Vicinity

East of San José, the Autopista Florencio del Castillo freeway passes through the suburb of Curridabat, climbs over the ridge known as Cerros de la Carpintera, then drops steeply to the colonial capital, Cartago, about 21 kilometers southeast of San José.

The **Parque Ecológico Aventuras La Carpintera** (tel. 506/2225-5829, www.aventuras lacarpintera.com), at Hacienda Chirraca, in San Diego de Tres Rios, has a zipline tour in premontane forest ($69) with 19 platforms and 13 cables. It also offers horseback riding.

CARTAGO

The city of Cartago (pop. 120,000) was founded in 1563 by Juan Vásquez de Coronado, the Spanish governor, as the nation's first city. Cartago—a Spanish word for Carthage, the ancient North African trading center—reigned as the colonial capital until losing its status to San José in the violent internecine squabbles of 1823. In 1841 and again in 1910 earthquakes toppled much of the city. Though the remains of the ruined cathedral testify to Mother Nature's destructive powers, many old buildings still stand. Volcán Irazú looms over Cartago.

Cartago's central landmark is the ruins of the **Iglesia de la Parroquia** (Avenida 2, Calle 2), colloquially called "Las Ruinas." Completed in 1575 to honor Saint James the Apostle, the church was destroyed by earthquakes and rebuilt a number of times before its final destruction in the earthquake of 1910. Today, only the walls remain.

Other sights of tourist interest are few but include the **Museo Etnográfico** (Elias Leiva Museum of Ethnography, Calle 3, Avenidas 3/5, tel. 506/2551-0895 ext.106, 7 A.M.–2 P.M. Mon.–Fri.), which displays pre-Columbian and colonial artifacts such as religious icons and suits of armor. It's in the neoclassical Colegio San Luis Gonsaga.

Basílica de Nuestra Señora de los Angeles

Cartago's imposing, cupola-topped Cathedral of Our Lady of the Angels (Avenidas 2/4, Calles 14/16, tel. 506/2551-0465, basilicalosangeles@racsa.co.cr), 10 blocks east of the main plaza, faces onto Plaza de Sanctuario Nacional. There's a unique beauty to the soaring, all-wood interior, with its marvelous stained-glass windows, ornate altar, various shrines, and columns and walls painted in floral motifs. The cathedral is home to Costa Rica's patron saint, La Negrita, or Virgen de los Angeles, and the goal of thousands of Costa Ricans during the annual *La Romería* pilgrimage. The eight-inch-high black statue of La Negrita is embedded in a gold- and jewel-encrusted shrine above the main altar. According to the legend, in 1635 a mulatto peasant girl named Juana Pereira found a small stone statue of the Virgin holding the Christ child. Twice Juana took the statue home and placed it in a box, and twice it mysteriously reappeared at the spot where it was discovered. The cathedral is said to mark the spot (the first cathedral was toppled by an earthquake in 1926).

Beneath the basilica (and entered from the northeast corner) is the **Cripta de la Piedra de**

CENTRAL HIGHLANDS

LA NEGRITA PILGRIMAGE

Every August 2, hundreds of Costa Ricans walk from towns far and wide to pay homage to the country's patron saint, La Negrita, at Cartago's Basílica de Nuestra Señora de los Angeles. The event attracts pilgrims from throughout Central America. Many *crawl* all the way from San José on their knees, starting at dawn. Others carry large wooden crosses. On any day, you can see the devout crawling down the aisle, muttering their invocations, repeating the sacred names, oblivious to the pain.

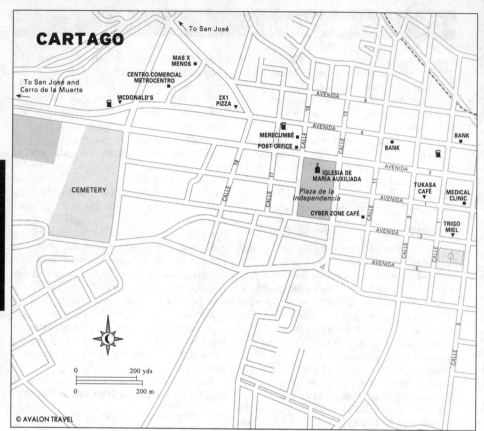

CARTAGO

Hellaza—a crypt with the rock where Juana found La Negrita, plus fascinating displays of ex-votos or *promesas:* gold and silver charms and other offerings for prayers answered, games won, etc. On the southeast corner, a spring *(el fuente)* that emanates from the ground is said to have curative powers.

North out of town, the village of **San Rafael de Cartago** has a beautiful contemporary church with a bas relief facade.

Accommodations

The **Hotel San Francisco Lodge** (Calle 3, Avenida 6, tel. 506/2574-2359, $18 s, $25 d) has eight spacious and spartan but clean rooms with kitchenettes, TV, and private bathroom with hot water. The surrounding area is a bit dicey by night. It has secure parking. The **B&B Los Angeles Lodge** (Avenida 4, Calles 14/16, tel. 506/2551-0957), on the north side of the cathedral, offers a near identical option.

Hotel Las Brumas (tel. 506/2553-3535, www. hotelasbrumas.com. $36 s or $53 d low season, $39 s or $61 d high season), above San Rafael de Cartago, offers a modern alternative with delightfully furnished rooms. Its **Restaurante Mi Tierra** serves Costa Rica fare.

New in 2007, and the best option by far, is **Casa Mora B&B** (tel. 506/2551-0324, www. casamoracr.com, call for rates), the city's only boutique hotel. This converted wooden mansion, built in 1972 in traditional style, boasts

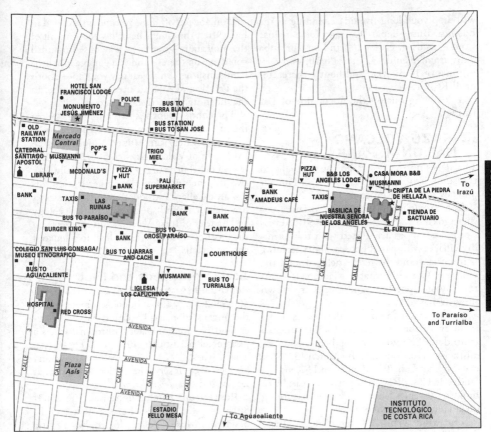

five junior suites and suites furnished in antique fashion. It has free Wi-Fi.

Food
Cartago Grill (Avenida 1, Calles 8/10, tel. 506/2551-5342, 11 A.M.–2:30 P.M. daily) specializes in meats and Argentinian-style grills and serves a *casado* (set lunch, $3), or *almuerzo ejecutivo*, as does **Amadeus Café** (Calle 10, Avenidas 2/4, tel. 506/2552-6262, 11 A.M.–7 P.M. Mon.–Sat., $2–12), a small, pleasant conversion of a colonial home, now filled with contemporary art.

For a clean, pleasant coffee shop with Wi-Fi, head to **Trigo Miel** (Avenida 4, Calles 4/6, tel. 506/2552-2260; and Avenida 5, Calles 3/5,

tel. 506/2552-6303; 7 A.M.–8 P.M. Mon.–Sat., 8 A.M.–6 P.M. Sun.).

Information and Services
There are banks downtown. Medical clinics cluster around **Hospital Dr. Max Peralta** (Avenida 5, Calles 3/5, tel. 506/2550-1999, www.hmp.sa.cr). There are more pharmacies, and dentists than you would care to count.

The **police station** is at Avenida 6, Calle 2.

Getting There
Empresa Lumaca (tel. 506/2537-0347) buses depart San José daily from Avenida 4, Calle 3, every seven minutes, 4:45 A.M.–11 P.M. ($0.70), and Fri.–Sat. 11:30–3 A.M. Buses

will drop you along Avenida 2, ending at the Basílica. Buses depart Cartago for San José from Avenida 4, Calles 2/4; and for Turrialba daily from Avenida 3, Calles 8/10, every 30 minutes 6–10:30 A.M. and hourly thereafter until 10:30 P.M.

Taxis hang out on the north side of Las Ruinas.

◖ IRAZÚ VOLCANO NATIONAL PARK

The slopes north of Cartago rise gradually to the summit of Volcán Irazú, a 21-kilometer journey to the entrance to Parque Nacional Volcán Irazú (tel. 506/2200-5025, volcanirazu@sinac.go.cr, 8 A.M.–3:30 P.M. daily, $10 admission). The slopes are dotted with tidy farming villages with pastel houses. Dairy farming is important and the fertile fields around the village of Cot are veritable salad bowls—carrots, onions, potatoes, and greens are grown intensively.

Volcán Irazú (3,432 m) derives its name from two tribal words: *ara* (point) and *tzu* (thunder). The volcano has been ephemerally active, most famously on March 13, 1963, the day that U.S. President John F. Kennedy landed in Costa Rica on an official visit; Irazú broke a 20-year silence and began disgorging great columns of smoke and ash.

The windswept, 100-meter-deep Diego de la Haya crater contains a sometimes-pea-green, sometimes-rust-red, mineral-tinted lake. A larger crater is 300 meters deep. Two separate trails lead from the parking lot to the craters. Follow those signed with blue-and-white symbols (*don't* follow other trails made by irresponsible folks whose feet destroy the fragile ecosystems). The crater rims are dangerously unstable. Keep your distance.

A sense of bleak desolation pervades the summit, like the surface of the moon. It is often foggy. Even on a sunny day expect a cold, dry, biting wind. Dress warmly. Little vegetation lives at the summit, though stunted dwarf oaks, ferns, lichens, and other species are making a comeback. The best time to visit is March or April.

Don't be put off if the volcano is shrouded in fog. Often the clouds lie below the summit of the mountain—there's no way of telling until you drive up there—and you emerge into brilliant sunshine. On a clear day you can see both the Pacific and Atlantic oceans. The earlier in the morning you arrive, the better.

The **ranger booth** is two kilometers below the summit, where there's a café and toilets.

The privately run **Museo Vulcanológico** (Museum of Vulcanicity, tel. 506/2503-8013, www.nochebuena.org, 9 A.M.–4 P.M. daily, $4), two kilometers below the ranger station, offers an excellent introduction to the processes of vulcanicity and specifically to the geology and history of Irazú Volcano and its effects on the local community. Trails lead to a lookout and waterfalls.

Accommodations and Food

Restaurante y Cabañas El Volcán (tel. 506/8352-5129, $30 s/d), one kilometer below the ranger station, has 12 rustic cabins with heaters and private hot-water bathrooms. It has a pleasant albeit rustic restaurant (8:30 A.M.–4 P.M. Thurs.–Tues., $1–8) with counter seating around an open oven. It serves hearty local fare, such as *ceviche* and *sopa de modongo*.

Restaurant Nochebuena (tel. 506/2503-8013, www.nochebuena.org, $30 s, $50 d), beside the Museo Vulcanológico, has a rustic three-room cabin with fireplace and kitchen. The restaurant (9 A.M.–4 P.M. daily) is modestly elegant; the menu ranges from *pozole* (thick corn soup with pork, onions, and oregano, $4) to grilled sirloin steak ($8).

Farther uphill, **Bar/Restaurante Linda Vista** (tel. 506/8386-9097, $20 s, $25 d) has a simple A-frame cabin for five people, with hot water and fabulous views. It claims to be the highest restaurant in Central America (2,693 meters). Take your business card to pin to the walls. It serves *típico* dishes (average $6) and sandwiches 7 A.M.–6 P.M. daily.

Enjoying a lovely location on the lower slopes, **Grandpa's B&B** (tel. 506/2536-7418, www.grandpasbedandbreakfast.com, $35 s, $55 d) is an old house on a working farm 400 meters above the Christ statue near Cot. It has five simply appointed bedrooms with terracotta floors and nice hardwood beds. The huge main bedroom has its own fireplace.

Getting There

Buses (tel. 506/2530-1064) depart San José from Avenida 2, Calles 1/3, at 8 A.M. daily, returning at 12:30 P.M. daily ($3). You can also hop aboard this bus in Cartago on Avenida 2, by Las Ruinas.

A taxi will cost upward of $25 from Cartago.

If you drive from Cartago, take the road leading northeast from the Basílica. At a Y-junction just below Cot, seven kilometers northeast of Cartago, is a **statue of Jesus,** his arms outstretched as if to embrace the whole valley. The road to the right leads to Pacayas, Santa Cruz, and Guayabo National Monument. That to the left leads to Irazú Volcano National Park (turn right before Tierra Blanca; Irazú is signed).

PARAÍSO

Paraíso, a small town seven kilometers east of Cartago on Highway 10, is gateway to the Orosi-Cachí Valley, to the southeast. The **Museo Histórico Religioso de Ujarrás** (tel. 506/2574-7376, 8 A.M.–noon and 2–5 P.M. Mon.–Fri., 8 A.M.–noon Sat., free), on the northeast corner of the church, is dedicated to the region's religious history.

Linda Mayher and Ernesto Carman run **Finca Cristina** (tel./fax 506/2574-6426 or 800/355-8826, www.cafecristina.com), a 12-hectare, environmentally sound organic coffee farm about six kilometers east of Paraíso, at Birrisito de Paraíso. They welcome visitors by appointment only for fascinating educational tours ($10 adults, $5 children) that give a total immersion in understanding the ecology of an organic coffee farm. Bring insect repellent. The sign on the highway is easy to miss; look for a white arch, then take the next dirt road to the east and go 500 meters to the unsigned red gate.

Lankester Gardens

Covering 10.7 hectares of exuberant forest and gardens, Lankester Gardens (tel. 506/2552-3247, www.jardinbotanicolankester.org, 8:30 A.M.–4:30 P.M., $7.50 adults, $5.50 students and children), one kilometer west of Paraíso, is one of the most valuable botanical centers in the Americas, with about 700 native and exotic orchid species, plus bromeliads, heliconias, bamboos, cacti, and palms, all laid out in gardens that span 11 hectares. Peak blooming is February through April. In all, the garden displays about 3,000 species, including 1,000 kinds of orchid. A Japanese garden and a fern garden were being completed in 2009.

The gardens were conceived by an Englishman, Charles Lankester West, who arrived in Costa Rica in 1898 and established the garden in 1917 as an adjunct to his coffee plantation. After his death, the garden was donated to the University of Costa Rica in 1973.

Buses (tel. 506/2574-6127) depart Cartago for Paraíso from the southeast side of Las Ruinas on Avenida 1 every 10 minutes 5 A.M.–11 P.M. daily ($0.30). Get off at the Camp Ayala electricity installation and walk approximately 600 meters to the south.

OROSI-CACHÍ VALLEY

South of Paraíso, Highway 224 drops steeply into the Orosi Valley, a self-contained world dedicated to raising coffee and centered on a huge man-made lake drained by the Río Reventazón. Highway 224 divides below Paraíso and loops around Lake Cachí: one way drops to Orosi, the other to Ujarrás; thus the valley makes a fine full-day circular tour.

For a fabulous view over the valley, call in at **Mirador Orosi** (tel. 506/2574-4688, 7 A.M.–5 P.M. daily, free), two kilometers south of Paraíso. This park has lawns, topiary, and picnic tables.

Orosi

The village of Orosi, eight kilometers south of Paraíso, is the center of the coffee-growing region. Its main claim to fame is its charming **Iglesia San José de Orosi,** built by the Franciscans in 1735 of solid adobe with a rustic timbered roof, terra-cotta tiled floor, and gilt altar. The recently restored church, adorned

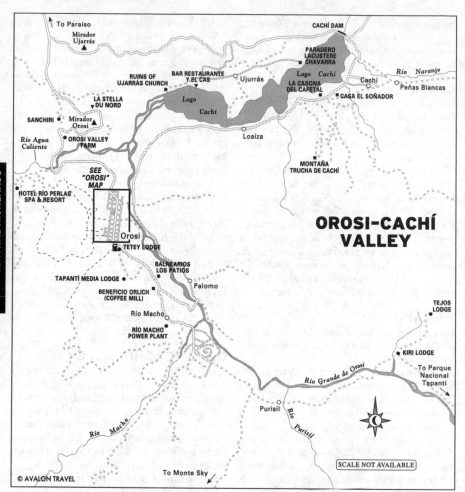

OROSI-CACHÍ VALLEY

SCALE NOT AVAILABLE

© AVALON TRAVEL

with gilt icons, has withstood earth tremors with barely a mark for almost three centuries. The church adjoins a small **religious art museum** (tel. 506/2533-3051, 1–5 P.M. Tues.–Fri, 9 A.M.–5 P.M. Sat.–Sun., $0.75) displaying furniture, religious statuary, paintings, and silver. Photography is not allowed.

Balnearios Termales Orosi (tel. 506/2533-2156, 7:30 A.M.–4 P.M. Wed.–Mon., $2), two blocks west of the plaza, has thermal mineral pools (30°C). It's clean and well run. Another hot springs, **Balnearios Los Patios** (tel.

506/2533-3009, 8 A.M.–4 P.M. daily, $2.50), about one kilometer south of Orosi, at Río Macho, has more simple pools but packs in the locals on weekends. Across the road, the **Beneficio Orlich** (tel. 506/2533-3535, fax 506/2533-3735, lballestero@econtrading.com, 9 A.M.–noon and 1:30–4 P.M. Mon.–Fri.) offers one-hour tours of the coffee-processing plant by appointment ($5 pp). Afternoon is best.

Vivero Anita (tel. 506/2533-3307, www.viveroanita.com, 8 A.M.–5 P.M., $1), next to Orosi Lodge, raises orchids and welcomes visitors.

OROSI

PANDERÍA ARCE BAKERY
BAR/RESTAURANTE EL NIDO
MEDICAL CLINIC
POLICE
ROSSMON INTERNET CAFÉ
BAR/RESTAURANTE COTO
IGLESIA SAN JOSÉ DE OROSI/ RELIGIOUS ART MUSEUM
JEEP TAXIS
HELADERÍA
SCHOOL
MONTAÑA LINDA B&B
ICE
BANK
DENTAL CLINIC
MUSMANNI
BALNEARIOS TERMALES OROSI
OTIAS
HOTEL REVENTAZÓN
HORSE RENTAL
OROSI LODGE
VIVERO ANITA
ANTONIO'S PIZZA
COSTA RICA MOTO
SCALE NOT AVAILABLE
© AVALON TRAVEL

South of town, the road divides at Río Macho: the main road crosses the river (a small toll is collected on Sun.) and turns north to continue around the lake's southern shore via the village of Cachí; a side road continues south nine kilometers to Tapantí National

Park via the Río Grande Valley, where just west of **Purisil,** four kilometers southeast of Orosi, a dirt road clambers uphill two kilometers to **Monte Sky Mountain Retreat** (tel. 506/2231-3536, www.intnet.co.cr/montesky), a 56-hectare private cloud forest reserve with trails and waterfalls, and camping ($10 per tent) with shared cold-water bathrooms. It's great for birding. A four-wheel-drive vehicle is recommended for the rocky uphill clamber; you have to hike in from an unguarded parking lot, so don't leave any valuables.

Around Lake Cachí

Lake Cachí (Lago Cachí) was created when the Instituto Costariccense de Electricidad built the Cachí Dam across the Río Reventazón to supply San José with hydroelectric power.

On the southern shore, just east of Cachí village, **Casa El Soñador** (Dreamer's House, tel. 506/2577-1983, 9 A.M.–6 P.M. daily) is the unusual home of brothers Hermes and Miguel Quesada, who carry on their father Macedonio's tradition of carving crude figurines from coffee

© CHRISTOPHER P. BAKER

Iglesia San José de Orosi

plant roots. The house—with carved figures leaning over the windows—is made entirely of rough-cut wood. Check out the *Last Supper* on one of the walls.

Ujarrás, on the north shore of the lake, seven kilometers southeast of Paraíso, is the site of **Las Ruinas de Ujarrás** (open 6 A.M.–6 P.M. daily, free), the ruins of the Church of Nuestra Señora de la Limpia Concepción, built out of limestone between 1681 and 1693 to honor the Virgen del Rescate de Ujarrás. The church owes its existence to an imagined miracle. In 1666, the pirate Henry Morgan led a raiding party into the Turrialba Valley to sack the highland cities. They were routed after the defenders prayed at Ujarrás. The ruins are set in a walled garden. Thousands of pilgrims from Paraíso flock each Easter Sunday to honor the imagined intercession of the Virgin Mary in the pirate attack.

Sports and Recreation
Orosi Lodge (tel./fax 506/2533-3578, www.orosilodge.com) offers excursions and rents mountain bikes ($3 per hour; $10 per day) and canoes ($30 per day, including transport to the lake). Montaña Linda (tel. 506/2533-3640, www.montanalinda.com) also rents bikes ($4 per day).

Santos Tours (tel. 506/8855-9386) has a highlands fruit tour and biocoffee adventure, among others. **Hotel Reventazón** (tel. 506/2533-3838, fax 506/2533-3737) rents ATVs ($25 per hour with guide). And locally based **Costarica-Moto** (tel. 506/2533-1564. www.costarica-moto.com) offers motorcycle tours.

Each April, the **Fundación para el Desarrollo, la Conservación y la Protección del Reventazón** (tel. 506/2258-2178, www.fundecopro.org) organizes a horseback ride to the annual **Festival Ranchero** rodeo in Pejibaye, about 20 kilometers northeast of Cachí, on the rough dirt road to Turrialba.

Paradero Lacustre Chavarra (tel. 506/574-7557, 8:30 A.M.–4:30 P.M. daily, $2 entrance), one kilometer east of Ujarrás, is an ICT recreational complex on the north shore of the lake.

You can fish for trout at **Montaña Trucha de Cachí** (tel. 506/2577-1457), 1.5 kilometers south of Highway 224, near the village of Cachí.

Accommodations
You can camp at **Paradero Lacustre Chavarra** (tel. 506/2574-7557, $3) and at **Montaña Linda** (tel. 506/2533-3640, www.montanalinda.com, $3 pp camping, $4 with tent rental, $7.50 pp dorm, $12.50 s or $20 d private room), one block north of Balnearios Termales. It's a rustic yet welcoming place primarily catering to backpackers. It has three dorms and eight private rooms with hot water, plus a separate building three blocks away has three upstairs rooms (two with double beds, one with a double and a bunk, $25 s, $30 d). Meals are provided, but guests get kitchen privileges ($1).

Pensión Doña Mayela (tel. 506/2533-1848), with rooms for around $10, has been recommended for budget travelers. It's 100 meters north and 75 meters east of Restaurante Coto.

I recommend the delightful **Orosi Lodge Cabinas y Cafetería** (tel./fax 506/2533-3578, www.orosilodge.com, $45 s/d low season, $58 s/d high season), next to Balneario Martínez. Inspired by local architecture, with clay lamps and locally crafted hardwoods, it has six simply furnished rooms in a charming, two-story, whitewashed structure. All have bamboo furnishings, firm mattresses, ceiling fans, tile or wooden (upstairs) floors, minibar, coffeemaker, colorful little bathrooms with hot water, and a balcony with views. You can also choose a two-bedroom chalet ($70 s/d, $5 each extra person). Its coffee shop is a delight on rainy days.

One block east, the modern **Hotel Reventazón** (tel. 506/2533-3838, fax 506/2533-3737, $45 s/d) has seven clean, simply furnished rooms with black tile floors, flouncy bedspreads, color TVs, telephones, fans, and hot water. It has a restaurant. Rates include breakfast.

Sanchiri Mirador and Lodge (tel. 506/2574-5454, www.sanchiri.com, $48 s or $60 d low season, $56 s or $72 d high season) has five basic cabins plus 12 sophisticated hillside rooms with walls of glass. Spectacular views combine with a delightful contemporary aesthetic and spacious modern bathrooms in the newer rooms. Noise from barking dogs and trucks negotiating the hill can be a problem. Three rooms are wheelchair accessible. It has a kids' playground. Rates include tax and breakfast.

Set in lush hillside gardens below Sanchiri, **Orosi Valley Farm** (tel. 506/2533-3001, in North America tel. 866/369-7871, www.orosi valleyfarm.com, $40 s/d low season, $45 s/d high season including breakfast), one kilometer east of Mirador de Orosi, offers two rooms, a casita, and a two-story guesthouse for rent, all modestly appointed and with patios to enjoy the grounds full of ornamentals and orchids. The lovely lounge doubles as a library and is filled with eclectic art, from wooden carvings to Carnival masks.

The most upscale place is **Hotel Río Perlas Spa & Resort** (tel. 506/2533-3341 or 800/286-2922, www.rioperlasspaandresort.com, $80–94 s, $88–100 d standard low season; $88–104 s, $96–112 d standard high season; $114 s or $140 d junior suites, $140–184 s, $159–202 d suites year-round), on the south side of the Rio Agua Caliente in a lush mountainside setting. Red-tiled villas stair-step the hillside and include six tastefully decorated standard rooms, 26 superiors, 15 junior suites, and two suites. It has two restaurants, a swimming pool fed by thermal waters, ponds for fishing, and a spa offering a full range of treatments.

The neo-colonial style **Tetey Lodge** (tel. 506/2533-1335, www.teteylodge.com, $33–39 s, $43–52 d low season; $41–49 s, $53–63 d high season), on the south side of Orosi, offers nine large, nicely furnished rooms around a courtyard. Two have full kitchens, and there's a delightful restaurant. The only drawback is the small bathrooms. Competing, and a stone's throw south, is the **Tapantí Media Lodge** (tel. 506/2533-9090, www.hoteltapanti.com), also with nine rooms and a lofty restaurant overlooking coffee fields.

El Copal Biological Reserve & Lodge (tel. 506/2535-0047), near Pejibaye, has five rooms with bunks and shared bathrooms. It has horseback riding, and tours of the farming

community are a highlight. **Costa Rican Association of Community-based Rural Tourism** (ACTUAR, tel. 506/2248-9470, www.actuarcostarica.com) handles reservations and arranges tours.

Food

The open-air **Bar/Restaurant Mirador Sanchiri** (tel. 506/2574-5454, www.sanchiri .com, 7 A.M.–9 P.M. daily) serves *comida típica* ($6–10), enjoyed to stunning vistas through plate-glass windows. Nearby, and recommended for pizzas and pastas, is **La Stella del Nord** (tel. 506/2573-0103, 1–10 P.M. Tues., noon–10 P.M. Wed.–Thurs., noon–11 P.M. Fri.–Sat., 11:30 A.M.–8 P.M. Sun., $2–14). Leave room for strawberries in chantilly cream. In Orosi, **Antonio's Pizza** (tel. 506/2533-2127, 4–9 P.M. Mon.–Thurs., 1–10 P.M. Fri. & Sat., noon–9 P.M. Sun.) is the place for pizza.

In Orosi, **Orosi Lodge** (tel./fax 506/2533-3578, www.orosilodge.com, 7 A.M.–7 P.M. Mon.–Sat.) serves an excellent continental breakfast ($4), pizza ($3.50), sandwiches, croissants, bagels with salami and cheese, natural juices, and ice cream sundaes. On Sunday its open to guests only. Nearby, the open-air, rustic **Restaurant Hotel Reventazón** (tel. 506/2533-3838, fax 506/2533-3737, 7 A.M.–9 P.M. daily) serves American breakfasts ($4), salads, ceviche, sandwiches, jalapeño chicken ($7), and beef Stroganoff with mashed potatoes ($10).

Restaurant Coto (tel. 506/2533-3032, 8 A.M.–midnight daily) on the north side of the soccer field, serves oven-roasted fare baked over coffee wood, plus *casados* (set lunches, $4) and dishes from burgers to trout.

Within a stone's throw of Ujarras ruins, the rustic **Bar y Restaurante El Cas** (tel. 506/2574-7984, 7 A.M.–7 P.M. daily) is set on a traditional farmstead with geese and goats. It serves typical Costa Rican dishes.

On the south side of the lake, **La Casona del Cafetal** (tel. 506/2533-3280, 11 A.M.–6 P.M.) serves crepes, soups, salads, and dishes such as tilapia with mushrooms, garlic tilapia, trout, or jumbo shrimp. It's set in pleasing surroundings on a coffee *finca* with horseback riding).

The **Panadería Arce** (tel. 506/2533-3244, 4 A.M.–6 P.M. Mon.–Sat., 5 A.M.–noon Sun.) bakery is three blocks north of the soccer field in Orosi.

Information and Services

The **Orosi Tourist Info & Art Café** (tel. 506/2533-3640) is a good resource. It has a Spanish-language school (OTIAC).

A **medical clinic** (tel. 506/2374-8225 or 2552-0851) is 50 meters northeast of the soccer field. The **police station** is on the northwest corner of the soccer field.

Orosi Lodge (tel./fax 506/2533-3578, www .orosilodge.com, 7 A.M.–7 P.M. daily) offers Internet access, as does **Rossmon** (tel. 506/2566-1301, 10 A.M.–8 P.M. Mon.–Fri., 9 A.M.–5 P.M. Sat.), one block northeast of the soccer field.

Getting There and Around

Buses (tel. 506/2533-1916) depart Cartago for Orosi from Calle 4, Avenida 1, every 30 minutes 5:30 A.M.–10:35 P.M. ($0.65). Return buses depart from the soccer field in Orosi. Buses do not complete a circuit of Lake Cachí; you'll have to backtrack to Paraíso to visit Ujarrás and the Cachí dam by public bus. Buses depart Cartago for Cachí via Ujarrás from one block east and one block south of Las Ruinas.

Taxis El Rescate (tel. 506/2574-4442) is in Paraíso. Jeep-taxis (tel. 506/2533-3087 or 506/8378-0357) await customers on the north side of the soccer field in Orosi. A tour around the lake will cost about $20.

TAPANTÍ-MACIZO DE LA MUERTE NATIONAL PARK

Parque Nacional Tapantí–Macizo de la Muerte (tel. 506/2200-0090 or 506/2551-2970, fax 506/771-3297, www.sinaccr.net, 8 A.M.–4 P.M. daily, $10), 27 kilometers southeast of Cartago, sits astride the northern slopes of the Cordillera Talamanca, which boasts more rain and cloud cover than any other region in the country. February, March, and April are the driest months. The many fast-flowing rivers and streams are excellent for fishing, permitted in designated areas April–October.

The 58,328-hectare park, at the headwaters of the Río Reventazón, climbs from 1,200 to 2,560 meters above sea level (it extends all the way up to Cerro de la Muerte) and forms a habitat for resplendent quetzals (often seen near the ranger station) and more than 260 other bird species, plus mammals such as river otters, tapirs, jaguars, ocelots, jaguarundis, howler monkeys, silky anteaters, and multitudinous snakes, frogs, and toads.

The park possesses several life zones, from lower montane rainforest to montane dwarf forest. Terrain is steep and rugged. Well-marked trails begin near the park entrance ranger station, which has a small nature display. Sendero Oropendola leads to a deep pool by the Río Macho. There's a vista point—a short trail, Sendero La Catarata, leads from here to a waterfall viewpoint—about four kilometers along. A trailhead opposite the beginning of the Oropendola Trail leads into the mountains.

Accommodations and Food

The ranger station no longer offers accommodation, and camping is no longer allowed.

Kirí Lodge (tel. 506/2533-2272, www.kiri lodge.net, $35 s, $45 d including breakfast and tax), two kilometers west of the park, has six cabins with handsome stone-walled showers. Some rooms have bunk beds. The restaurant (7 A.M.–8 P.M. daily, $4–15) specializes in trout culled from its own ponds. If it's full, the **Albergue Montaña Tejos Lodge** (tel. 506/2533-2147, www.tejoslodge.net, $30 s, $40 d including breakfast) is two kilometers farther uphill and offers spectacular views. The five basic rooms are cozy and have private bathrooms with hot water. Trout is a specialty at the rustic restaurant, and guided horseback rides are offered ($6 per hour).

Finca Los Maestros (tel. 505/2533-3312, $2 pp), one kilometer before the park entrance, has camping. If driving, you'll need a four-wheel drive for the muddy uphill clamber.

Getting There

A bus departs Cartago at 6:30 A.M., 11 A.M.,

1 P.M., and 4 P.M. and travels via Orosi as far as Purisil, five kilometers from the park entrance (later buses go only as far as Río Macho, nine kilometers from Tapantí). You can hike or take a Jeep-taxi from Orosi ($10 each way) or Purisil ($5 each way).

CARTAGO TO CERRO DE LA MUERTE

South of Cartago, the Pan-American Highway (Hwy. 2) begins a daunting ascent over the Talamanca Mountains, cresting the range at Cerro de la Muerte (Mountain of Death) at 3,491 meters before dropping down into the Valle de El General and the Pacific southwest. The vistas are staggering, and opportunities abound for hiking, trout fishing, and birding—notably for resplendent quetzals, which are common hereabouts (especially Nov.–March). The region is clad in native oak and cloud forest. The climate is brisk.

Drive carefully! The road is often fog-bound (early to mid-morning is best, before the clouds roll in). It also zigzags with sudden hairpin turns, is washed out in places, and is used by buses and trailer rigs driven by madmen. Kilometer distance markers line the route.

Cartago to Cañon

At **Enpalme,** 30 kilometers south of Cartago, a side road descends in a series of spectacular switchbacks to Santa María de Dota; while at **Vara de Roble** (2 km north of Enpalme), another road—known as *The Route of the Saints*—leads west to San Cristóbal via La Lucha Sin Fin. You can also reach Santa María de Dota from **Cañon,** five kilometers south of Enpalme at Kilometer 58 via a dirt road that descends steeply to **Copey.** Copey is a small agricultural village at about 2,121 meters, eight kilometers southwest of Cañon and five kilometers east of Santa María de Dota.

Cañon to Cerro de la Muerte

At Trinidad, five kilometers south of Cañon, you pass through the **Tapantí-Macizo de la Muerte National Park.** The Cuenca Queberi Trail, which begins at Kilometer 61, leads into the reserve.

At Kilometer 70, a side road leads to **Paraíso de Quetzal** (tel. 506/2390-7894, 8 A.M.–5 P.M. daily, $6 for trail access), a.k.a. Finca Eddie Serrano, the perfect spot for viewing quetzals. Up to 20 pairs of quetzals have been seen feeding in treetops near the *finca.* Serrano leads guided quetzal hikes ($15 pp), 6:30 A.M.–4 P.M. daily, and the Robledal Oak Forest Trail is open to self-guided hikes with a map and illustrated booklet.

Finally, at Kilometer 89 you crest **Cerro de la Muerte.** (The name derives not from the dozens who have lost their lives through auto accidents, but from the many poor *campesinos* who froze to death in days of yore while carrying sacks of produce to trade in San José.) The summit is marked by a forest of radio antennae. A dirt road leads up to the antenna, from where you'll have miraculous views, weather permitting. At 3,000 meters the stunted vegetation is Andean *páramo,* complete with wind-sculpted shrubs, peat bogs, and marshy grasses. Be prepared for high winds.

Accommodations and Food

At Kilometer 70 on the Pan-American Highway, is **Albergue Mirador de Quetzales** (tel. 506/2381-8456, $50 pp), at Finca Eddie Serano. This rustic yet cozy lodge is set amid cloud forest at 2,600 meters where quetzals congregate to nest. There are 11 A-frame log cabins boasting marvelous views, all with one double and one single bed and a private bath with hot water. You can camp for $6 per person under thatch with tables and barbecue grills. Rates include three meals daily and quetzal tour. The same family runs the adjoining **Paraíso de Quetzal** (tel. 506/2390-7894, 7 A.M.–8:30 P.M. daily, $2–10), serving *comida típica.*

Getting There

The San Isidro bus departs San José from Calle Central, Avenidas 22, and will drop you or pick you up anywhere along Highway 2. Most hotel owners will pick you up with advance notice.

There's a gas station at Enpalme.

◖ SAN GERARDO DE DOTA

San Gerardo de Dota, nine kilometers west and sharply downhill from the Pan-American Highway at Kilometer 80, is an exquisite hamlet tucked at the base of a narrow wooded valley at 1,900 meters—a true Shangri-la cut off from the rest of the world. It's a magnificent setting. The road is snaking, steep, and breathtakingly beautiful.

The Río Savegre valley is a center for apples and peaches; it also attracts resplendent quetzals, especially during the April and May nesting season. The Savegre Mountain Hotel hosts the **Quetzal Education Research Complex,** a Creationist entity operated in association with the Southern Nazarene University of Oklahoma. Also here, the **Savegre Biological Reserve** (www.savegre.co.cr), with trails.

The **Trogon Lodge Canopy Tour** offers a zipline ride between five treetop platforms ($35), plus a waterfall hike and horseback ride ($35).

After hiking, you can relax with a massage at **Las Cumbres de Altamira** (tel. 506/2740-1042), at the top of the mountainside.

Quetzals National Park

San Gerardo is a gateway to the Parque Nacional Los Quetzales (tel. 506/2200-5354, 8 A.M.–4 P.M., $10), created in 2005 and covering 5,000 hectares of cloud forest on the upper reaches of the Río Savegre. The park borders the Pan-American Highway between Kilometer 70 and Kilometer 80; the main entrance is opposite Restaurante Los Chesperitos, at Kilometer 76.5. It currently has three trails. The park opens at 6 A.M. by appointment for birders; guides can be hired with 24 hours' notice ($10 pp). The San José–San Isidro bus (hourly from Calle Central, Avenida 22, tel. 506/2222-2422) will drop you at the entrance.

Accommodations and Food

Rodolfo Chacón and his wife, Maribel, have four *cabinas*—**Cabinas El Quetzal** (tel./fax 506/2740-1036, www.cabinaselquetzal.com, $45 pp including meals), on the banks of the river. All have hot water. There's a children's playground. "We slept so well there with the woodstove going," reports one reader.

Trogon Lodge (tel. 506/2293-8181, www.grupomawamba.com, $59 s or $79 d standard, $110 s or $130 d junior suite) enjoys a beautiful and secluded setting at the head of the San Gerardo Valley, beside the burbling river tumbling through exquisitely landscaped grounds. There are 10 simply appointed, two-bedroom hardwood cabins with tasteful fabrics, heater, private bathroom with hot water, and veranda. Meals are served in a rustic lodge overlooking a trout pond. Fishing is available. Trails lead to waterfalls. Guided horseback rides, quetzal tours, a canopy tour, and mountain bike rentals are offered.

Savegre Mountain Hotel (tel. 506/2740-1028, www.savegre.co.cr, $90 s/d standard, $123 s/d junior suite), in the midst of the tiny little community, has 20 handsome yet basic all-wood cabins with heaters. There are also 10 newer, more spacious, wood-paneled cabins. Readers report that upkeep may be a problem. There are trails, plus bird-watching trips, cloud-forest hiking, guided horseback riding, and trout fishing.

Suria Lodge (tel. 506/2740-1004, www.suria-lodge.com, $60 pp including all meals), at the end of the road, also offers lovely Colorado-style cabins.

On the upper levels of the valley, **Las Cataratas Lodge** (tel. 506/2740-1065, www.cataratas.guiapz.com, call for rates) offers a forest hideaway. Its three cozy cabins offer no frills, but offer comfort nonetheless, not least thanks to red velvet bedspreads plus a wood-burning fireplace in one cabin. Trout dishes are a specialty. Trails lead to waterfalls.

One of my favorite hotels in Costa Rica, ◖ **Dantica Cloud Forest Lodge & Gallery** (tel. 506/2740-1067, www.dantica.com, $110 s/d superior, $135 s/d deluxe low season; $135 superior, $165 deluxe high season), midway between the highway and valley bottom, is a dramatic modernist creation with walls of glass throughout. Run by a Danish-Colombian couple, it has seven one- and two-bedroom villas plus a suite (with its own private garden)

© CHRISTOPHER P. BAKER

Dantica Cloud Forest Lodge & Gallery

tastefully furnished Ikea-style, with cozy down duvets and thermal blankets. Lovely details include teak and gray stone floors, space heaters, halogen ceiling lights, tasteful art pieces, genuine antique doors, window rails, and even roof tiles imported from Colombia. There are lots of thoughtful extras, such as flashlights, ponchos, and walking sticks in every room. These details, and hip contemporary bathrooms with whirlpool tubs, gracefully combine old and new into a delightful aesthetic. The two-bedroom villas have fully equipped kitchens. Some rooms are a hilly 200-meter hike from reception. A highlight is the exhibition of ethnic art, and a gift store sells quality indigenous pieces. Massages are offered, and trails lead into a private 20-hectare forest adjoining Parque Nacional Los Quetzales. A restaurant (7 A.M.–6 P.M. daily, $2–18) with walls of glass serves such treats as European-style pancakes, bagel with smoked salmon, cream cheese, capers, and pepper; and steak sandwiches with onions, mushrooms, and paprika. After dining you can relax in a sumptuous leather sofa and watch nature documentaries on the flat-screen TV. As yet, no dinner is served, but a 400-meter uphill hike brings you to **Comida Típica Miriam** (tel. 560/2740-1049, 6 A.M.–8 P.M., $5–10), a local farmstead and *soda* where the charming Serrano family serves delicious, filling meals in a simple room heated by an old cast-iron stove. Miriam also rents out basic cabins with heaters ($35) and has trails good for spotting quetzals.

Restaurant Los Lagos (tel. 506/2740-1009, 6 A.M.–7 P.M. Mon.–Thurs., until 9 P.M. Fri.–Sun., $5–12) in the valley bottom specializes in trout dishes.

Getting There

A minibus (tel. 506/8367-8141) connects the Pan-American Highway with San Gerardo and meets the bus at Kilometer 80 at 7:40 A.M. daily, and departing San Gerardo for the highway at 6:50 A.M. daily.

The Route of the Saints

South of San José lies a little-touristed region of hidden valleys perfect for a full-day drive along the scenic "Route of the Saints," so-called because most of the villages are named after saints. These saintly villages can also be accessed by driving south from Cartago along the Pan-American Highway (Highway 2) and turning west at Enpalme or Cañon.

SAN JOSÉ TO SAN GABRIEL

From San José's southern suburb of Desamparados, Highway 209 climbs into the Fila de Bustamante mountains via **Aserrí**, a pretty hillside town famed for its handsome church and for La Piedra de Aserrí—a massive boulder with a cave at its base that was once inhabited, apparently, by a witch. The gradient increases markedly to the crest of the mountains just north of **Tarbaca**. En route you gain a breathtaking view of Volcán Irazú.

Three kilometers south of Tarbaca is a Y-junction. The road to the right (Hwy. 209) drops westward to **San Ignacio de Acosta,** a charming little town nestled on a hillside. You can see its whitewashed houses for miles around. The sun sets dramatically on its steep west-facing slopes. (For a wildly scenic drive, continue west from Acosta to the **Balneario Valle Cantado** (Fri.–Sun.), with swimming pools fed by hot springs. Beyond, the unpaved road switchbacks to **Tabarcia** (not to be confused with Tarbaca). Turn right in Tabarcia and you will climb to Highway 239, which runs along the ridge of the Cerros Escazú mountains; turn right to return to San José via Colón and Santa Ana.

The road to the left (Hwy. 222) at the Y-junction south of Tarbaca drops to **San Gabriel,** gateway to the "Route of the Saints" proper.

Accommodations

The modern and rather institutional **Colinas Altavista Resort & Conference Center** (tel. 506/2230-5008, www.colinasaltavista.com,

$55 s/d cabins, $85–95 villas), outside Aserrí, has six deluxe rooms, 10 apartment units, and a three-bedroom master suite, all modestly furnished and with broad verandas with magnificent views. It has a restaurant and offers horseback riding.

The Costa Rican Association of Community-Based Rural Tourism (ACTUAR, tel. 506/2248-9470, www.actuarcostarica.com) arranges accommodation at **Nacientes Palmichal** (tel. 506/2418-4328, www.nacientespalmichal.com), at Palmichal de Acosta, between San Ignacio and Tabarcia. This delightful alpine lodge has eight rooms with private bathrooms; musicians perform after dinner.

SAN GABRIEL TO SANTA MARÍA DE DOTA

Highway 222 leads southeast from San Gabriel, dropping and rising via Frailes to **San Cristóbal Sur,** a market town better known to Ticos for **La Lucha Sin Fin** (The Endless Struggle), the *finca* of former president and national hero Don "Pepe" Figueres, who led the 1948 revolution from here, two kilometers east of San Cristóbal. There's a **museum** in the high school (open weekends only, free).

East of La Lucha, the road clambers precipitously through pine forests three kilometers to the Pan-American Highway. Instead, turn south from San Cristóbal and follow a scenic route via **San Pablo de León Cortes** to **San Marcos de Tarrazú,** dramatically situated over coffee fields and dominated by a handsome white church with a domed roof. You can visit the local coffee mill, **Beneficio Coopetarrazú** (tel. 506/2546-6098, http://cafetarrazu.com) by prior arrangement.

From San Marcos, the main road climbs southeast to **Santa María de Dota,** a tranquil village whose main plaza has a small but dramatic granite monument—the **Monumento Liberación Nacional**—honoring those who died in the 1948 revolution. It's a major coffee-producing area; indigenous people from as far away as Boca del Toro, in Panamá, provide the field labor. You can visit the **Beneficio Coopedota** (tel. 506/2541-2828, www.dotacoffee.com, 9 A.M.–5 P.M. Mon.–Fri.), which handles the beans for 700 local producers and accepts visitors by reservation, in season; the visit includes a plantation tour, video, and tasting ($10).

The wonderful coffee of the region is available for purchase through **Down to Earth** (tel. 866/653-2784, www.godowntoearth.org).

From Santa María, the roads east snake steeply to the Pan-American Highway, with dramatic views en route. Alternately, you can head south five kilometers into the mountains to the **Centro Para el Desarrollo Sostenible de Los Santos** (Center For Sustainable Development of Los Santos), with cabins, trails, and spectacular vistas.

Accommodations

Cabinas Cecilia (tel./fax 506/2541-1233, from $20 pp), 400 meters south of the plaza in Santa María de Dota, is set in a lovely garden surrounded by coffee fields. It has nine simple cabins of rough-hewn timbers and stone floors around a farmhouse-style open-air dining area serving food from a wood-fired stove.

The exquisite **El Toucanet Lodge** (tel. 506/2541-3045, www.eltoucanet.com, $55 s or $71 d standard, $120 s/d suite, including breakfast and tax), on a 40-hectare fruit farm one kilometer east of Copey, is perfect for birders—more than 170 species have been seen at the lodge; quetzals are virtually a daily occurrence (the property adjoins Parque Nacional Los Quetzales). Made of stone and polished timbers, it has a wide veranda with valley views, a lounge with fireplace, and six hardwood *cabinas* plus a family cabin for six people with a fireplace, kitchenette, and hot water. Rooms are spacious and have simple furnishings and clean tiled bathrooms with hot water. Two suites each feature a wall of glass and whirlpool tub. It has a charming pinewood restaurant, plus a wood-fired, stone-lined hot tub. It offers hiking trails, plus horseback tours, a coffee tour, and a free quetzal tour for guests.

If the Toucanet Lodge is full, then the simpler but charming **Cabinas Las Manzanas** (tel. 506/2541-3084), in Copey, might accommodate you.

Food

The place to eat is **La Casona de Sara** (tel. 506/2541-2258, 7 A.M.–7 P.M. daily), in Santa María (take the first left after the bridge into town when approaching from Enpalme). This clean family restaurant serves filling meals. Take a peek in the kitchen to choose from the simmering pots. A filling lunch costs about $3. It typically stays open until the last guest leaves.

I love **Restaurante Bar Vaca Flaca** (tel. 506/2274-1868, 11 A.M. until the last guest leaves, daily), at Alto de Abajonal, near San Antonio. This rustic Colorado-style place is very country, very cowboy (think cowhide seats and rifles on the walls), and serves a house special: chicken breast with mushrooms and broccoli ($3).

Getting There

Buses (tel. 506/2410-0330) from San José depart for Aserrí from Calle 2, Avenidas 6/8, and for San Ignacio from Calle 8, Avenidas 12/14, hourly 5:30 A.M.–10:30 P.M. daily ($0.75). Buses (tel. 506/2410-0015) to San Ignacio de Acosta depart from Calle 8, Avenidas 12/14 every 30 minutes 5:20 A.M.–10:30 P.M. daily.

Empresa Los Santos buses (tel. 506/2546-7248) to San Marcos and Santa María depart San José from Avenida 16, Calles 19/21, at 6 A.M., 7:15 A.M., 9 A.M., 12:30 P.M., 3 P.M., 5 P.M., and 7:30 P.M. daily ($2.15). Return buses to San José depart Santa María at 5:15 A.M., 7:15 A.M., 9:15 A.M., 12:40 P.M., 3 P.M., and 6:15 P.M. daily.

CENTRAL HIGHLANDS

Turrialba and Vicinity

East of Cartago, Highway 230 falls eastward through the valley of the Río Reventazón before a final steep descent to the regional center of Turrialba. The route leads via **Cervantes**. An alternate, less-traveled mountain route from Cartago leads via **Pacayas**.

TURRIALBA

Turrialba, a small town 65 kilometers east of San José, was until recently an important stop on the old highway between San José and the Caribbean. The opening of the Guápiles Highway via Braulio Carrillo National Park stole much of its thunder, and the town was further insulated when train service to the Caribbean was ended in 1991. The now-rusted tracks still dominate the town, which squats in a valley bottom on the banks of the Río Turrialba at 650 meters above sea level.

Turrialba is a base for white-water adventures on the Ríos Reventazón and Pacuare. However, there's little to see in town, which is centered on the undistinguished **Parque la Dominica,** other than the small **Museo Regional Omar Salazar** (tel. 506/2558-3615, 9 A.M.–noon and 1–4 P.M. Tues.–Sun., $1), with archaeological exhibits; it's on the campus of the University of Costa Rica.

Biological Reserve Espino Blanco (c/o Hotel Wagelia, tel. 506/2556-1566, www.hotel wageliaturrialba.com), at La Verbana, eight kilometers north of Turrialba, has forest trails good for birding.

CATIE

The **Centro Agronómico Tropical de Investigación y Enseñanza** (Center for Tropical Agriculture Investigation and Learning, tel. 506/2556-2700, www.catie .ac.cr), four kilometers east of Turrialba, is one of the world's leading tropical agricultural research stations. It covers 1,036 hectares devoted to experimentation and research on livestock and tropical plants and crops, including more than 2,500 coffee varieties. Trails provide superb bird-watching, and the orchards, herbarium, and husbandry facilities are fascinating. CATIE also contains the largest library on tropical agriculture in the world. The grounds include the **Jardín Botánico** (Botanic Garden, 7 A.M.–4 P.M. Mon.–Fri., $5), with a lake full of waterfowl; guided five-hour tours are given ($20 per person). It has a café and reception area with exhibition. Weekend visits are offered by appointment.

Buses depart for CATIE from Avenida Central, Calle 2, in Turrialba. You can also catch the bus to Siquirres from Avenida 4, Calle 2, and ask to be dropped off.

Sports and Recreation

The U.S.–run **Serendipity Adventures** (tel. 506/2558-1000, in North America tel. 877/507-1358, www.serendipityadventures .com) offers hot-air ballooning, rafting, hiking, kayaking, and other adventures.

Costa Rica Rios (tel. 506/2556-9617, in North America tel. 888/434-0776, www.costa ricarios.com) specializes in canoeing and kayaking. **Rainforest World** (tel. 506/2556-0014, www.rforestw.com) also offers white-water trips.

Accommodations

The American-run **Hotel Interamericano** (Avenida 1, Calle 1, tel. 506/2556-0142, www .hotelinteramericano.com, $12 s or $22 d shared bath, $25 s or $30–35 d private bath), beloved of budget travelers, offers 22 clean rooms in several categories with cable TV and hot water. It offers Internet access and laundry, plus a small bar and cafeteria.

The rambling **Hotel Kardey** (Calle 4, tel. 506/2556-0050, $20 pp) offers two dorms plus 13 simply furnished, carpeted rooms with cable TV and fans. Rooms to the fore are airy and get heaps of light (as well as street noise); interior rooms are somewhat gloomy but have natural stone walls and are clean. No two rooms are the same. It has a pool table. Rates include

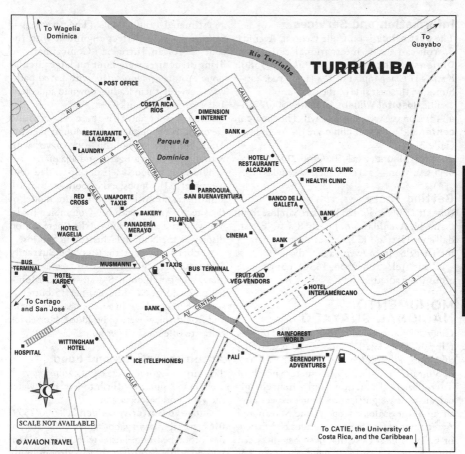

breakfast. Similar no-frills alternatives include the **Wittingham Hotel** (tel. 506/2556-8822), opposite La Roche, and **Hotel Alcazar** (Calle 3, Avenidas 2/4, tel. 506/2556-7397).

Hotel Wagelia (tel. 506/2556-1566, www .hotelwageliaturrialba.com, $55 s, $69 d), on Avenida 4, is the only class act in town. It has 18 well-lit, modestly decorated rooms with air-conditioning, TVs, telephones, and private baths. They surround a lush courtyard. The hotel offers tours locally. The restaurant is one of Turrialba's best. Rates include breakfast and tax. The sibling **Hotel Wagelia Dominica** (tel. 506/2556-1029, www.hotelwageliadominica .com, $55 s, $69 d), 800 meters north of town, offers a similar standard.

Food

You can fill up for less than $3 at **Restaurante La Garza** (tel. 506/2556-1073, 10 A.M.–11 P.M. daily), on the plaza's northwest corner; it has set lunches, plus pastas and even Chinese fare.

You can buy baked goods at **Musmanni,** at Calle 2, Avenida 2, or at **Panadería Merayo** (5:30 A.M.–7 P.M. daily), 50 meters north.

Banco de la Galleta (Calle 3, Avenidas Central/1, 8 A.M.–7 P.M. Mon.–Sat.) sells all kinds of nuts, biscuits, and candies.

Information and Services

The **post office** is on Calle Central, Avenida 8. You can make international calls from **Dimension Internet** (tel. 506/2556-1586, 8 A.M.–11 P.M. Mon.–Fri., 9 A.M.–10 P.M. Sat.–Sun.), on the east side of the square.

The **Hospital William Allen** (tel. 506/2556-4343) is on the west side of town. The **medical center** and a **dental clinic** are on Avenida 2, Calle 3.

There's a **laundry** (tel. 506/2556-2194, 8 A.M.–4:45 P.M. Mon.–Sat.) on Calle 2, Avenidas 6/8.

Getting There

Buses (tel. 506/2556-4233) depart San José from Calle 13, Avenidas 6/8, hourly 8 A.M.–8 P.M. daily via Cartago ($2). Buses depart Cartago for Turrialba from Avenida 3, Calle 8.

Taxis (tel. 506/2556-3434) congregate around the square.

MONUMENTO NACIONAL GUAYABO

Guayabo National Monument (public phone, tel. 506/2559-1220, 8 A.M.–3:30 P.M. daily, $6 adults, $1 children), on the southern flank of Volcán Turrialba, 19 kilometers north of Turrialba, is the nation's only archaeological site of any significance. Don't expect anything of the scale or scope of the Mayan and Aztec ruins of Guatemala, Honduras, Mexico, or Belize. The society that lived here between 1000 B.C. and A.D. 1400, when the town was mysteriously abandoned, was far less culturally advanced than its northern neighbors. No record exists of the Spanish having known of Guayabo. In fact, the site lay uncharted until rediscovered in the late 19th century. Systematic excavations—still under way—were begun in 1968.

The 218-hectare monument encompasses tropical wet forest on valley slopes surrounding the archaeological site. Trails lead to a lookout point, where you can surmise the layout of the pre-Columbian village. To the south, a wide cobbled pavement leads past ancient stone entrance gates and up a slight gradient to the village center, which at its peak housed

an estimated 1,000 people. (The pavement—*(calzada)*—is in perfect alignment with the cone of Volcán Turrialba.) Conical bamboo living structures were built on large circular stone mounds *(montúculos)*, with paved pathways between them leading down to aqueducts and a large water tank.

About four hectares have been excavated and are open to the public via the Mound Viewing Trail. Note the monolithic rock carved with petroglyphs of an alligator and a jaguar.

The ranger booth sells a self-guided tour pamphlet ($1). Opposite the booth are the park administration office, a miniature model of the site, and a hut with pre-Columbian finds. Many of the artifacts unearthed here are on display at the National Museum in San José.

Just below the park, the **Guayabo Butterfly Garden** (tel. 506/2559-0162, mariposas guayabo@gmail.com, 8 A.M.–4 P.M. Mon.–Sat., $2 adults, $1 children) has 15 butterfly species flitting about in a netted garden. Snake and frog displays were to be added. Horseback rides are offered ($10 per hour).

Accommodations and Food

The ranger station offers eight campsites with shelters ($2 pp), plus flush toilets, cold-water showers, and barbecue pits.

Guayabo Butterfly Garden (tel. 506/2559-0162, mariposasguayabo@gmail.com, $15 pp) has a four-bedroom hostel with basic kitchen; plus a simply furnished three-bedroom house ($50). A-frame cabins and a restaurant were being added.

The delightful, eco-sensitive **Guayabo Lodge** (tel./fax 506/2556-1628, www.guayabo lodge.com, $65 s, $85 d year-round), 400 meters west of Santa Cruz, enjoys a hillside setting. This modern two-story structure has 23 uniquely decorated rooms with parquet floors and delightful decor that includes wrought-iron beds, gaily painted armoires, and charming sculptures and other artwork depicting various indigenous gods of the Americas. A six-bedroom villa was to be added ($400 per night). When not exploring the 80-hectare *finca,* settle yourself in a hammock and enjoy the superb views. The *finca* has its own dairy and cheese factory (tours are given), and it hosts a cooking school. There is a hiking trail.

You can catch a filling meal at **La Calzada** (tel. 506/2559-0437, 8 P.M.–5 P.M. Tues.–Thurs.), 400 meters below the park entrance. It serves local fare, plus trout fresh from its own pond.

Getting There

Buses depart Turrialba for Guayabo village from Avenida 4, Calle 2, at 11:15 A.M., 3:15 P.M. and 5:15 P.M. Monday–Saturday and at 9 A.M. and 3 P.M. Sunday. Return buses depart Guayabo at 5:30 A.M., 7 A.M., 12:45 P.M., and 3 P.M. Monday–Saturday (12:45 P.M. and 4:15 P.M. Sun.). A taxi from Turrialba will cost about $30 round-trip.

The paved road from Turrialba deteriorates to a rough dirt and rock path about four kilometers below Guayabo. You can approach Guayabo from the northwest, via Santa Cruz; it's about 10 kilometers by rough dirt road and is signed.

TURRIALBA VOLCANO NATIONAL PARK

Volcán Turrialba (3,329 meters), the country's most easterly volcano, was very active during the 19th century but has slumbered peacefully since. In 2001, it showed signs of activity after 135 years of dormancy. It can be very cold and rainy up here—bring sweaters and raingear. There are no ranger stations at Parque Nacional Volcán Turrialba; hence access is free.

A paved (but badly eroded) road winds steeply north from **Santa Cruz,** about 12 kilometers north of the town of Turrialba, to Finca Central; it's a rugged three-kilometer drive by four-wheel drive from there. An alternate route for 4WD vehicles only is via the Irazú Volcano National Park road; turn off (signed for Volcán Turrialba Lodge) two kilometers below the park ranger station.

You can also hike from the hamlet of **Santa Teresa,** reached by direct bus or car from Cartago via Pacayas, on the southwestern slope. The trail climbs through cloud forest

to the summit, which features three craters, a *mirador* (lookout point), and guardhouse topped by an antenna. A trail at the summit leads to the crater floor; another circumnavigates the crater (there are active fumaroles on the western side).

Accommodations and Food

Perfect for birders and hikers, **Volcán Turrialba Lodge** (tel. 506/273-4335, www.volcan turrialbalodge.com, $50 pp including breakfast and tax) is set magnificently in the saddle between Irazú and Turrialba Volcanoes at 2,800 meters elevation, about three kilometers north of Esperanza and eight kilometers northwest of Santa Cruz. The rustic lodge—on a working farm—has 18 simple yet comfy rooms with private baths. Meals are cooked over a wood fire and served in a cozy lounge heated by a woodstove. Guided hikes and horseback rides are offered.

A simpler alternative is **Cabañas Bajo Volcán Turrialba** (tel. 506/2538-8513), a rugged, 20-kilometer-long, 4WD clamber from Santa Cruz. Be sure to call ahead, as it is usually closed in wet season.

Getting There

Buses depart Cartago for Pacayas and Santa Cruz from south of Las Ruinas, and from the bus center at Calle 2, Avenidas 2/4, in Turrialba. You can take a Jeep-taxi from Santa Cruz or Pacayas.

LAGO ANGOSTURA AND VICINITY

East of Turrialba, Highway 10 continues past CATIE two kilometers to a Y-junction: the main highway descends to Siquirres and the Caribbean after switchbacking steeply uphill to tiny **Turrialtico,** eight kilometers east of Turrialba. The branch road off Highway 10 leads southeast to the valleys of the Río Atirro and, to the east, Río Tuis.

One kilometer east of CATIE you cross the **Río Reventazón** (Exploding River). The river, which begins its life at the Lake Cachí dam, was recently dammed about two kilometers upstream of the bridge to create the 256-hectare (450,000-cubic-meter) **Lake Angostura.** The **Proyecto Hidroeléctrico Angostura** (Angostura Hydroelectric Project), the largest hydroelectricity-generating plant in the country, began humming in July 2000. Below Lake Angostura, the river cascades down the eastern slopes of the Cordillera Central to the Caribbean plains. On a good day it serves up Class III–IV rapids.

Hacienda Atirro dominates the flatlands of the Reventazón and Atirro Rivers south of the lake. The sugarcane-processing factory can be visited in harvest season as part of a plantation tour; you can book through Hotel Casa Turire (tel. 506/2531-1111, www.hotelcasaturire.com). And the **Beneficio Grano de Oro** (tel. 506/2531-2008, www.goldenbean.net) also welcomes visitors for the Golden Bean Coffee Tour.

Parque Viborana (tel. 506/2538-1510 or 506/8882-5406, viborana@racsa.co.cr, 9 A.M.–5 P.M. daily, $10 one hour, $15 two hours) is a serpentarium near Pavones, beyond Turrialtico. About 100 snakes are displayed in cages, including a large boa pit. Your visit begins in the open-air lecture room. Trails lead into the forest.

At **Tayutic: The Hacienda Experience** (tel. 506/2280-8686, www.haciendatayutic.com) you can witness rural traditions being kept alive. This faux colonial village has coffee, macadamia, and sugarcane plantation to each side, with demonstrations of the production and processing of each crop. It's a fun learning experience, especially for kids. The turnoff from the Siquirres road is at Boveda, about two miles west of Pavones.

Sports and Recreation

Hotel Casa Turire (tel. 506/2531-1111, www.hotelcasaturire.com) offers horseback tours, mountain biking, and other activities.

Accommodations and Food

Turrialtico Mountain Lodge & Restaurant (tel. 506/2538-1111, www.turrialtico.com, $46 s or $56 d low season, $52 s or $62 d high season), amid landscaped grounds with views over the Reventazón Valley, has 14 rustic and basically furnished rooms ("yucky" beds, reports one reader) with private baths with hot water. The rustic restaurant (7 A.M.–10 P.M. daily) offers seafood (like sea bass in garlic, $12), tenderloin ($10), and local fare, enjoyed at tables made from Sarchí oxcart wheels. Rates include breakfast and taxes.

Nearby, the deluxe **Hotel Hacienda Tayutic** (tel. 506/2280-8686, www.haciendatayutic.com, call for rates) opened in 2008. It combines cozy rusticity with sumptuous furnishings, as well as spectacular views. Your lovely digs here come with terra-cotta floors, Wi-Fi, satellite TV, and coffeemaker, plus spacious bathrooms. It has a spa, plus tours.

Also new in 2008, the **Hotel Villa Florencia** (tel. 506/2557-3536, www.villaflorencia.com, $107 s/d standard, $159 superior, $170 family rooms, $226 suite) occupies a hilltop overlooking cane fields on the west side of Lago Angostura. The former deluxe mansion offers 11 nicely furnished rooms (one for handicapped travelers, one a suite) and boasts lots of redbrick and terra-cotta tile, plus river stones and gleaming hardwoods. The lovely suite has a king bed, flat-screen TV, and a gorgeous half-moon bathroom with whirlpool tub and separate shower. It's a good base for birders. The restaurant and swimming pool were being completed during my visit.

The most outstanding hotel for miles is **Hotel Casa Turire** (tel. 506/2531-1111, www.hotelcasaturire.com, $120 s/d standard, $140 junior superior, $150 junior suite, $290 master suite low season; $135 standard, $155 junior superior, $165 junior suite, $330 master suite high season), on the south shore of Lake Angostura, about 15 kilometers southeast of Turrialba. Relaxing and romantic, this hotel is infused with a Georgian England motif and is justifiably a member of the Small Distinctive Hotels of Costa Rica. You sense the sublime the moment you arrive via a long palm-lined driveway and enter the atrium lobby of the plantation property, with its colonial-tiled floors, Roman pillars, and sumptuous leather sofas and chairs. The 12 spacious, lofty-ceilinged rooms have direct-dial telephones, Wi-Fi, and TVs (alas with only a handful of channels), and comfortable mattresses, although the bathrooms call out for renovation. Four suites have French doors opening onto private verandas, and the master suite has a whirlpool tub. A wide wraparound veranda opens onto manicured lawns and a small figure-eight pool and sunning deck. There's an eco-farm (with water buffalo) and a stable, plus a spa, and a fitness trail is planned. This is also the place to treat yourself to a meal: Culinary treats include curried banana soup ($6), dorado with orange sauce and almonds and mashed potatoes ($12), and hot chocolate cake with flambéed bananas ($5).

Getting There

Buses (tel. 506/2556-4233) for Siquirres depart Turrialba from Avenida 4, Calle 2, hourly 5:30 A.M.–6:30 P.M. daily; ask to be let off at Turrialtico.

TURRIALBA TO CHIRRIPÓ INDIAN RESERVE

Heading east from Atirro through the valley of the Río Tuis via the tiny communities of Tuis, Bajo Pacuare, and Hacienda Grano de Oro, you find yourself in an alpine plateau not unlike parts of Colorado—fabulous! You'll need four-wheel drive. A few kilometers beyond, about 30 kilometers east of Highway 10, the dirt road passes through the off-the-beaten-track-hamlet of **Moravia del Chirripó** and peters out at **Hacienda Moravia,** from where trails filter into the foothills of the Cordillera Talamanca. Moravia is the gateway to the **Reserva Indígena Chirripó,** a remote reserve that receives few visitors. The indigenous presence is strong, in local faces and in bright traditional garb.

You may be able to hire guides in Moravia for excursions into the Talamancas and **La Amistad International Peace Park.**

Evangelical Christians have made a serious dent in this region, eroding indigenous culture; many tourist businesses are evangelical focused.

Sports and Recreation

Bajo Pacuare is a traditional starting point for white-water rafting trips on the **Río Pacuare,** a thrilling river that plunges through remote canyons and rates as a classic white-water run. A reader wrote rave reviews of her experience with **Tico's River Adventures** (tel. 506/8394-4479, www.ticoriver.com), based in Turrialba; **Pacuare River Tours** (tel. 506/2291-6844 or 888/472-3827, www.pacuarerivertours.com) is also recommended.

Accommodations and Food

Rancho Naturalista (tel. 506/2554-8101 or U.S. tel. 888/246-8513, www.ranchonaturalista .net, $145 pp low season, $190 pp high season, including meals), one kilometer beyond Tuís, is a rustically elegant hilltop hacienda-lodge run by American evangelists. It sits on a 50-hectare ranch surrounded by premontane rainforest at 900 meters' elevation at the end of a steep dirt-and-rock road. The mountain retreat is popular with nature and bird-watching groups (more than 410 bird species have been recorded by guests). It has 15 rooms, which vary. All are pleasant and feature hardwood beams and down comforters. The upstairs also has a lounge with library. Rates include three meals, guided hikes, and horseback riding.

Albergue Hacienda Moravia de Chirripó (tel. 506/2225-5128, www.haciendamoravia .com, $60 pp including all meals) is a rustic Colorado-style lodge in a Shangri-la setting, with fantastic views across a green vale. It has 10 dorms with rough-hewn bunks: six downstairs rooms have private baths; four upstairs rooms share baths with hot water. Local indigenous people put on traditional shows for groups. The hacienda is a working cattle farm and offers horseback rides and mountain biking. You can camp here ($30 pp).

Several rafting companies have lodges in the Pacuare Canyon. You have to be a participant on the companies' river trips to stay here. You'll need a rugged four-wheel-drive vehicle to reach **Pacuare Jungle Lodge** (tel. 800/963-1195, www.pacuarelodge.com, from $421 s, $632 d for a two-day package inclusive of transport, meals), set high on a lush jungle hilltop, overlooking the Pacuare River. This thatched, jungly retreat (owned by the Ríos Tropicales white-water rafting company), has a cozy lounge bar and gourmet restaurant. The gorgeous, exquisitely appointed, palm-thatched bungalows each boast a wall of glass, teak floors, handcrafted rattan wicker chairs, and king-size canopy bed with 300-thread-count Egyptian cotton linens and a vast canyon view. There's even a huge "honeymoon" suite with a private infinity pool fed by a natural waterfall; heck, it even has its own suspension bridge linked to a private treetop canopy! Most guests are white-water rafters partaking of fun on the river. You have to hike the last 300 meters to get here. The company offers packages that include transport.

Getting There

Buses (tel. 506/2556-5155) for Tuís and Moravia depart from the bus center at Calle 2, Avenidas 2/4, in Turrialba.

THE CARIBBEAN COAST

Costa Rica's Caribbean coast extends some 200 kilometers—from Nicaragua to Panamá. The zone—wholly within Limón Province—is divided into two distinct regions.

North of Puerto Limón, the port city midway down the coast, is a long, straight coastal strip backed by a broad alluvial plain cut through by the Tortuguero Canals, an inland waterway that parallels the coast all the way to the Nicaraguan border. Crocodiles, caimans, monkeys, sloths, and exotic birds can be seen from the tour boats that carry passengers through the jungle-lined canals and freshwater lagoons culminating in Tortuguero National Park and Barra del Colorado National Wildlife Refuge. A few roads have penetrated to the northern frontier far inland of the coast, but they are often impassable except for brief periods in the dry season. For

locals, motorized canoes *(cayucos* or *canoas)* and water-taxis are the main means of getting about the swampy waterways.

South of Puerto Limón is the Talamanca coast, a narrow coastal plain broken by occasional headlands and coral reefs and backed by the looming Cordillera Talamanca. A succession of sandy shores leads the eye toward Panamá. The beaches are popular with surfers.

The coast is sparsely settled, with tiny villages spaced far apart. Except for the coastal town of Puerto Limón, what few villages lie along the coast are ramshackle, browbeaten by tropical storms and the curse of an ailing economy recently given a boost by the tourism boom. Life along the Caribbean coast of Costa Rica is fundamentally different than in the rest of the country. Life is lived at an easy

HIGHLIGHTS

(Rainforest Aerial Tram: A ride through the rainforest canopy on this "ski lift"-style tram provides a fabulous introduction to tropical ecology, while a serpentarium and other wildlife exhibits display some of the creatures you may be lucky enough to see on the ride (page 164).

(Veragua Rainforest Research & Adventure Park: Combining superb exhibits on local flora and fauna with an exhilarating tram ride, plus hiking trails, this nature facility has it all (page 167).

(Tortuguero National Park: Wildlife galore awaits in this watery world where everyone gets around by boat. The beach is a prime nesting site for marine turtles, the national park is absolute tops for birding and animal viewing, and the village is a funky charmer (page 174).

(Barra del Colorado National Wildlife Refuge: The big one that didn't get away

awaits you at this prime sportfishing spot near the Nicaraguan border. Several sportfishing lodges cater to anglers keen to tackle prize tarpon and snook (page 185).

(Cahuita: Popular with the offbeat crowd, this small village has heaps of character. Several eateries serve spicy local cuisine, and Cahuita National Park offers great beaches, diverse wildlife, and a small coral reef (page 190).

(Puerto Viejo: Drawing surfers and latter-day hippies, this somnolent village has tremendous budget accommodations. Activities include horseback riding and hikes to indigenous villages, and beautiful beaches ease south for miles (page 198).

(Gandoca-Manzanillo National Wildlife Refuge: This reserve spans several ecosystems teeming with animal life, from crocodiles to monkeys to manatees. Turtles also come ashore to lay eggs (page 214).

LOOK FOR **(** TO FIND RECOMMENDED SIGHTS, ACTIVITIES, DINING, AND LODGING.

pace. It may take you a few days to get in the groove. Don't expect things to happen at the snap of your fingers.

The black *costeños* (coast dwellers), who form approximately one-third of Limón Province's population of 220,000, have little in common with the *sponyamon*—the "Spaniard man," or highland mestizo, who represents the conservative Latin American culture. More than anywhere else in Costa Rica, the peoples of the Caribbean coast reflect a mingling of races and cultures. There are Creoles of mixed African and European descent; black Caribs, whose ancestors were African and Caribbean Indian; mestizos, of mixed Spanish and Amerindian blood; more Chinese than one might expect; and, living in the foothills of the Talamancas, approximately 5,000 Bribrí and Cabecar indigenous peoples.

The early settlers of the coast were British pirates, smugglers, log-cutters, and their slaves, who brought their own Caribbean dialects with words that are still used today. During the late 19th century, increasing numbers of English-speaking Afro-Caribbean families—predominantly from Jamaica—came to build and work the Atlantic Railroad and banana plantations, eventually settling and infusing the local dialect with lilting parochial patois phrases familiar to travelers in the West Indies. Afro-Caribbean influences are also notable in the regional cuisine.

West Indian life might be typified by the Rastafarians one meets in Cahuita and Puerto Viejo. Some of the young black males here appear sullen and lackadaisical, even antagonistic (some seem to harbor a resentment of white tourists). But most locals have hearts of gold, and there's a strong, mutually supportive community that tourists may not easily see: When a local has a need, such as medical care, locals often band together to pay the bills. (Paula Palmer's *What Happen: A Folk History of Costa Rica's Talamanca Coast* and *Wa'apin Man* provide insight into the traditional Creole culture of the area.)

The Caribbean coast is generally hot and exceedingly wet (averaging 300–500 cm of rain annually). Fortunately, light breezes blow consistently year-round. The region has no real dry season and endures a "wet season" in which the rainfall can exceed 100 centimeters per month. Rains peak May–August and again in December and January, when sudden storms blow in, bowing down the coconut palms and deluging the Talamancas.

PLANNING YOUR TIME

There are many visitors who arrive with no schedule, intent on kicking it until the money runs out or they otherwise get an urge to move on. This is particularly so of the funky, laid-back hamlets of **Cahuita** and **Puerto Viejo,** budget havens popular with surfers, the tie-dyed backpack set, and those seeking immersion in Creole culture. Most people stay at least a week to get in the groove and make the most of the southern Caribbean zone's many offbeat offerings, including **Cahuita National Park,** protecting a rainforest full of monkeys, as well as one of Costa Rica's few coral reefs. Surfers head to Puerto Viejo and the beaches that run south in a paternoster to the hamlet of **Manzanillo** and **Gandoca-Manzanillo National Wildlife Refuge.** You'll want to take horseback rides along the beach and/or a "dolphin safari" into Gandoca-Manzanillo, while experienced surfers might want to check out the Hawaiian-size waves two miles off Punta Cocles. And if you don't mind roughing it, consider an excursion into the Talamancas for an overnight at **Reserva Indígena Yorkín.**

Farther north, most travelers head to **Tortuguero National Park** for 1–3 days of viewing wildlife by rented canoe or on guided boat tours offered by nature lodges. Tortuguero is famous as the most important nesting site in the western Caribbean for the Pacific green turtle, one of four species that come ashore predictably at numerous beaches up and down this shore. Anglers favor **Barra del Colorado,** acknowledged for the best tarpon- and snook-fishing in the world; two or three days is sufficient. Tour operators and specialist lodges can make all arrangements.

You'll need to fly to Tortuguero or Barra, or take a boat. Buses serve Cahuita and Puerto

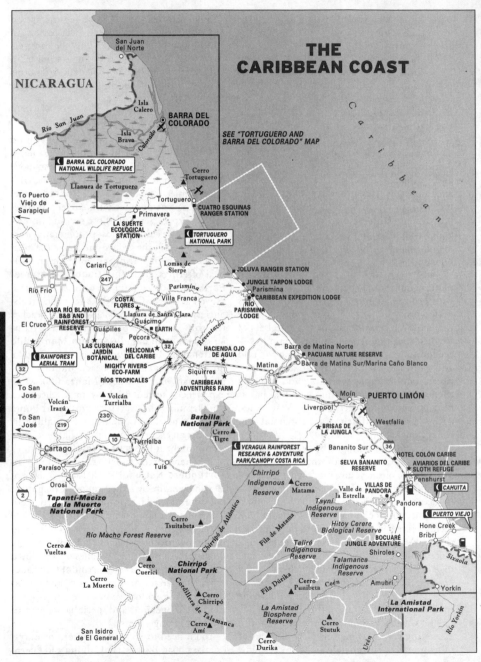

THE
CARIBBEAN COAST

NICARAGUA

San Juan
del Norte

Isla
Calero

Río San Juan

Isla
Brava

BARRA DEL
COLORADO

Colorado

SEE "TORTUGUERO AND
BARRA DEL COLORADO" MAP

Caribbean

BARRA DEL COLORADO
NATIONAL WILDLIFE REFUGE

Cerro
Tortuguero

Llanura de Tortuguero

To Puerto
Viejo de
Sarapiquí

Tortuguero

CUATRO ESQUINAS
RANGER STATION

Primavera

LA SUERTE
ECOLOGICAL
STATION

TORTUGUERO
NATIONAL PARK

4

Cariari

Lomas de
Sierpe

JOLUVA RANGER STATION

247

Parismina

JUNGLE TARPON LODGE

Río Frío

Villa Franca

Parismina

COSTA
FLORES

Llanura de Santa Clara

RÍO
PARISMINA
LODGE

CARIBBEAN EXPEDITION LODGE

CASA RÍO BLANCO
B&B AND
RAINFOREST
RESERVE

Guácimo

El Cruce

Guápiles

EARTH

Pocora

Reventazón

HACIENDA OJO
DE AGUA

32

Barra de Matina Norte

LAS CUSINGAS
JARDÍN
BOTÁNICAL

HELICONIA
DEL CARIBE

PACUARE NATURE RESERVE

RAINFOREST
AERIAL TRAM

MIGHTY RIVERS
ECO-FARM

Siquirres

Matina

Barra de Matina Sur/Marina Caño Blanco

32

RÍOS TROPICALES

CARIBBEAN
ADVENTURES FARM

Moín

PUERTO LIMÓN

To San
José

Volcán
Turrialba

Liverpool

To San
José

Volcán
Irazú

Barbilla
National Park

BRISAS DE
LA JUNGLA

Westfalia

219

230

Cerro
Tigre

VERAGUA RAINFOREST
RESEARCH & ADVENTURE
PARK/CANOPY COSTA RICA

36

10

Turrialba

Bananito Sur

HOTEL COLÓN CARIBE

Cartago

Tuis

SELVA BANANITO
RESERVE

AVIARIOS DEL CARIBE
SLOTH REFUGE

Paraíso

Chirripó
Indigenous
Reserve

Cerro
Matama

Valle de
la Estrella

VILLAS DE
PANDORA

Penshurst

Orosi

Tapantí-Macizo
de la Muerte
National Park

Tayní
Indigenous
Reserve

Pandora

CAHUITA

Cerro
Tsuitabeta

Fila de Matama

Hitoy Cerere
Biological Reserve

PUERTO VIEJO

Río Macho Forest Reserve

Cerro
Vueltas

Chirripó de Atlántico

Teliré
Indigenous
Reserve

BOCUARÉ
JUNGLE ADVENTURE

Hone Creek

Bribrí

Cerro
Cuerici

Chirripó
National Park

Fila Dúrika

Cerro
Punibeta

Talamanca
Indigenous
Reserve

Shiroles

Sixaola

Cerro
La Muerte

Coén

Amubri

Yorkín

Cordillera de Talamanca

Cerro
Chirripó

La Amistad
Biosphere
Reserve

La Amistad
International Park

Cerro
Amí

Cerro
Stutuk

Río Yorkín

San Isidro
de El General

Cerro
Durika

Urén

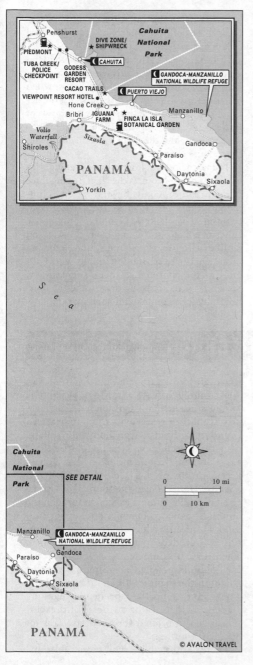

Viejo, from where tour excursions to sites of interest are offered. If you're driving along Highway 32, which connects San José to Puerto Limón, the **Rainforest Aerial Tram** makes for a rewarding stop while en route from San José to the Caribbean. And the exciting must-see **Veragua Rainforest Research & Adventure Park** opened in 2008 a short distance west of Limón.

SAFETY CONCERNS

Despite new opportunities from the tourism boom (or perhaps because of it), the region has witnessed a burgeoning drug trade, and in recent years Limón has been consumed by murderous gang wars. The southern Caribbean has also developed a reputation for crime against tourists.

On both scores, things have improved markedly in recent years, although drugs are still prevalent. (You may be pestered by young Rastas or Rasta-wannabes trying to sell you drugs.) Many undercover policemen operate locally. Hoteliers in the region claim that the bad reputation is all a sad misrepresentation, but I keep getting letters from readers who've been victims; 2005 brought reports of machete-wielding robbers around Cahuita! Don't let this put you off visiting, however—the negativity is more than counterbalanced by the scores of wonderful, welcoming souls. And local residents' associations formed by expatriate business owners have done much to eradicate crime.

Some local Afro-Caribbean men are very forward with their advances toward women, and judging from the number of young foreign women on the arms of local men, their approaches are sometimes warmly received. The "rent-a-Rasta" syndrome engendered by these foreign women with gigolos in tow has inspired a reputation for "free love" that other female travelers must contend with. Be prepared for subtle to persistent overtures.

HISTORY

In 1502, Columbus became the first European to set foot on this coast when he anchored at Isla Uvita on his fourth and last voyage to the

New World. Twenty-two years later, Hernán Cortés mapped the coast. The records the early Spaniards left tell of contact with indigenous tribes: subsistence hunters and farmers, and skilled seamen who plied the coastal waters and interior rivers in carved longboats (Cortés even mentioned Aztec traders from Mexico visiting northern Costa Rica in search of gold). The indigenous culture was quickly destroyed, however, by conquistadors. Later it was also the haunt of rumrunners, gunrunners, mahogany cutters, and pirates, mostly British, attracted by the vast riches flowing through colonial Central America. Between raids, buccaneers anchored along the wild shorelines, where they allied themselves with local native peoples. Because of them, the Caribbean coast was never effectively settled or developed by the Spanish.

Cacao was grown here in the late 17th century and was Costa Rica's first major export. Despite this, the region remained virtually uninhabited by Europeans until the Atlantic Railroad was built in the 1880s and a port at Limón was opened for coffee export. Significant numbers of Jamaican laborers were brought in.

In 1882, the government began to offer land grants to encourage cultivation of bananas. Plantations prospered until the 1930s, when banana crops were hit by disease. With the demise of the banana industry, the region went into decline. During the 1960s, plantations were revived, and the industry again dominates the region's economy.

Today, the port of Puerto Limón, along with its sister port of Moín, is the chief driving force of the urban economy. Beyond the city's hinterland, most people make their living from farming or as plantation laborers. Small-scale fishermen eke out a living from the sea, and families cling to a precarious living growing cacao (in 1979 the *Monilia* fungus wiped out most of the commercial crop). Increasingly, however, locals are being drawn into the tourism industry as guides and hotel workers.

Highway 32 to Puerto Limón

Highway 32 (the Guápiles Highway) connects San José with the Caribbean and runs east–west 104 kilometers from the foot of the Cordillera Central to Puerto Limón. Drive carefully: The heavily trafficked Highway 32 coils steeply down the mountains and is often fog-bound, landslides are frequent, and Costa Rican drivers can be exceedingly reckless—all of which makes for a white-knuckle drive. The road is frequently closed due to landslides; call the *tránsitos* (tel. 506/2268-2157) in Zurquí before setting out.

The road spills onto the northern lowlands at **El Cruce,** at the junction with Highway 4, with a gas station and **Rancho Roberto's** (tel. 506/2711-0050), a huge, modestly elegant thatched restaurant.

◖ RAINFOREST AERIAL TRAM

The Rainforest Aerial Tram (tel. 506/2257-5961 or North America tel. 305/704-3350, www.rainforesttram.com, 6:30 A.M.–4 P.M. Tues.–Sun., 9 A.M.–4 P.M. Mon., $55 adults, $27.50 students/children), on a 475-hectare private nature reserve on the northeastern boundary of Braulio Carrillo National Park, is an unforgettable experience. Constructed at a cost of more than $2 million by Dr. Donald Perry, author of the fascinating book *Life Above the Jungle Floor,* the tram takes visitors on a guided 90-minute excursion through the rainforest canopy. The mysteries of the lush canopy unfold with each passing tree. Your ride is preceded by an instructional video. Then it's 2.6 kilometers via cable car (each car holds six people, including a naturalist guide) in the manner of a ski-lift, giving you a new vantage on the "spectacular hanging gardens of the rainforest roof." Bird excursions are also offered (bring a flashlight for nocturnal outings).

There's also a zipline with seven cables and

BANANAS . . . TURNING GREEN OR NOT?

Banana production is a monoculture that causes ecological damage. Banana plants deplete ground nutrients quickly, requiring heavy doses of fertilizer to maintain productivity. Eventually, the land is rendered useless for other agricultural activities. Fertilizers washed down by streams have been blamed for the profuse growth of water hyacinth and reed grasses that now clog the canals and wildfowl habitats, such as the estuary of the Río Estrella. And silt washing down from the plantations is acknowledged as the principal cause of the death of the coral reef within Cahuita National Park and, more recently, of Gandoca-Manzanillo.

Bananas are also prone to disease and insect assault. Pesticides such as the nematocide DBCP (banned in the United States but widely used in Costa Rica) are blamed for poisoning and sterilizing plantation workers, and for major fish kills in the Tortuguero canals.

Campaigns by local pressure groups and the threat of international boycotts have sparked a new awareness among the banana companies. A project called Banana Amigo recommends management guidelines. Companies that follow the guidelines are awarded an Eco-OK seal of approval to help them export bananas; companies continuing to clear forests are not.

Banana producers assert that the industry provides badly needed jobs. Environmentalists claim that devastating environmental effects are not worth the trade-off for a product for which demand is so fickle. The multinational corporations, too, are hardly known for philanthropy. Workers' unions, for example, have historically been pushed out of the banana fields. Some banana companies have been accused of operating plantations under virtual slave-labor conditions. The Limón government and environmentalists have also denounced British company Geest's clearcutting of forests separating Barra del Colorado and Tortuguero National Parks.

In recent years, the banana companies have scaled back due to overcapacity, and the first people to lose out have been the independent small-scale producers, many of them poor *campesinos* who had been induced to clear their forests and raise bananas for sale to the big banana companies, who are no longer buying.

six platforms ($45); several trails; an open-air serpentarium with some 20 species of snakes ($10); plus a butterfly and frog garden ($10). The fee includes all the facilities, plus as many tram rides as you wish. Expect a wait of up to one hour, as the lines are long (coffee, fruit drinks, and cookies are served). It has a restaurant and accommodations.

The tram is on Highway 32, four kilometers past the Braulio Carrillo ranger station and 15 km west of Guápiles). The parking lot is on a dangerously fast bend! The bus between San José and Guápiles will drop you off at Chichorronera la Reserva or "El Teleférico" ($1.50), but be sure to tell the driver to drop you at the entrance to the tram. Many unfortunate guests have had to trek back uphill after the driver passed the entrance and kept going!

GUÁPILES

Guápiles, 14 kilometers east of Santa Clara, is a center for the Río Frío banana region that spreads for miles to the north. It's the largest town in the Caribbean lowlands (larger by far than Limón) but there is no reason to visit.

Artist Patricia Erickson (tel./fax 506/2711-0823, patricia_erickson@amerisol.com, by appointment only) welcomes visitors to her **Gallery at Home** studio on the west bank of the Río Blanco, south of the highway, six kilometers west of town. Her vibrant paintings dance with brilliant Caribbean colors, many of them portraying her trademark faceless Limonense women of color with floating limbs. Her husband, Brian, makes fabulously creative bamboo furniture at nearby **Muebles de Bamboo** (tel. 506/2710-1958, brieri99@yahoo.com, 8 A.M.–4 P.M. Mon.–Fri., 8 A.M.–noon Sat.). He offers tours of his bamboo and sculpture garden by appointment ($25 for 1–2 people). **Las Cusingas Jardín Botánico** (Las Cusingas Botanical Garden, tel. 506/2382-5805, $5 admission), two kilometers east of Guápiles and four kilometers south by dirt road (the turn is at Soda Buenos Aires; 4WD recommended), undertakes research; raises ornamentals, medicinal plants, and fruit trees; and serves to educate visitors about tropical ecology. Trails lead into tropical forest. Horseback rides are offered. Birding is excellent. Guided two-hour tours ($5) are given.

La Suerte Biological Field Station Lodge (tel. 506/2710-8005, in North America tel. 305/666-9932, www.lasuerte.org), at La Primavera, on the banks of the Río Suerte, near the southwestern border of Barra del Colorado and 20 kilometers inland from Tortuguero National Park, has 10 kilometers of rainforest trails open to ecotourists ($8 pp day visit, including lunch). It teaches workshops in tropical ecology, from primate behavior to herpetology. It has rustic accommodations. A bus leaves Cariari, 15 kilometers north of Guápiles, at 6:30 A.M. and 10:30 A.M. daily.

Accommodations and Food

West of Guápiles, the **Hotel y Cabinas Lomas del Toro** (tel./fax 506/2710-2934, $12 s/d cold water, from $20 s/d with a/c), overlooking the Río Toro Amarillo, about two kilometers west of Guápiles, has 48 rooms with private bath. Twenty-two have cold water only and are sparsely furnished, albeit clean. Air-conditioned rooms contain modest furnishings. All rooms have a fan and cable TV. There's a swimming pool and restaurant.

I highly recommend **Casa Río Blanco Ecolodge** (tel./fax 506/2710-4124, www.casarioblanco.com, $45 s, $65 d including breakfast), on the banks of the Río Blanco, seven kilometers west of Guápiles and one kilometer south of the bridge (and only 12 kilometers from the Rainforest Aerial Tram). It has two pleasant rooms in the main lodge, plus four charming wooden cabins, all with private baths with hot water, plus orthopedic mattresses. The cabins

have one screened wall open to a spacious porch so that you can look directly into the rainforest canopy and see the river bubbling away below. They're warmly decorated with colorful spreads and pre-Colombian pottery. The delightful owners, Annette and Herbie, lead birding and nature hikes. The lodge is popular with birders and offers fantastic wildlife viewing. Vegetarian meals are served.

Continuing past Casa Río Blanco Ecolodge, David and Dalia Vaughan offer four-day, three-night rainforest adventures at **La Danta Salvaje** (tel./fax 506/2750-0012, www.ladantasalvaje.com; 4-day packages cost $210), a 410-hectare private reserve bordering Braulio Carrillo. Accommodations are in a rustic yet cozy wooden lodge. It's a tough slog by 4WD, then a stiff hike to the mountainside property (helicopter transfers are also offered). It charges $210 including lodging, meals, and guided hikes.

In Guápiles, the lively **Hotel & Country Club Suerre** (tel. 506/2710-7551, www.suerre .com, $60 s, $75 d, $120 s/d junior suite), at the east end of town, is an elegant, modern hacienda-style property with 55 spacious air-conditioned rooms appointed with hardwoods. Each has satellite TV. The hotel features an Olympic-size pool, a restaurant, two bars and a disco, and a whirlpool tub and sauna. Day guests can use the facilities for $2.50.

Alternately, the **Hotel Talamanca Pococí** (tel. 560/2710-3030), beside the gas station at the entrance to town, is an option, but traffic noise might be an issue here.

The handsome **Restaurante Río Danta** (tel. 506/2710-2626, 11 A.M.–1 P.M.), five kilometers west of Guápiles, serves *típico* lunches and has short trails leading into the adjacent private forest reserve (good for spotting poison-dart frogs).

Getting There

Empresario Guápileños (tel. 506/2222-2727) buses from San José depart the Gran Terminal del Caribe on Calle Central, Avenidas 13/15, every hour 5:30 A.M.–7 P.M. daily ($2.50). And Transportes Caribeños (tel. 506/2221-

2596) buses depart the same terminal hourly 5:30 A.M.–7 P.M., bound for Limón.

Buses depart Guápiles for Puerto Viejo de Sarapiquí seven times daily.

GUÁCIMO

Guácimo is a small town and important truck stop about 12 kilometers east of Guápiles and about 400 meters north of Highway 32. Signs point the way north to **Costa Flores** (tel. 506/2716-7645 or 506/2716-6430, costaflo@ sol.racsa.co.cr, 8 A.M.–4 P.M. $15), a tropical flower farm with more than 600 varieties of plants blossoming gloriously across 120 blazingly colorful hectares. Call ahead, as it has always been closed when I've passed by.

EARTH (Escuela de Agricultura de la Región Tropical Húmeda, tel. 506/2713-0000, www.earth.ac.cr), School of Tropical Humid Agriculture, one kilometer east of town, is a university that teaches agricultural techniques to students from Latin America. It specializes in researching ecologically sound, or sustainable, agriculture. EARTH has its own banana plantation and 400-hectare forest reserve with nature trails. Visitors are welcome. Costa Rica Expeditions (tel. 506/2257-0766, www.costarica expeditions.com) offers a full-day tour.

Getting There

Buses (tel. 506/2222-0610 and 506/2716-6037) for Guácimo leave San José from Gran Terminal del Caribe on Calle Central, Avenidas 13/15 ($2.75), at 5:30 A.M., 7 A.M., 11:30 A.M., 2 P.M., and 7 P.M. daily.

SIQUIRRES

Siquirres, 25 kilometers east of Guácimo and 49 kilometers west of Limón, is a major railroad junction, echoing to the clanging of locomotives working freight for the banana companies. One reader states, "Yuck! Don't bother" (with Siquirres). However, on Sunday at 4 P.M., head to **Finca Las Tilapias** (tel. 506/8398-1517, $12), where owner Gilberto "Chito" Sheedan swims, wrestles, and does tricks with Poncho, his one-eyed, five-meterlong crocodile.

The Standard Fruit Co. offers a tour of its **Esperanzas banana plantation** (tel. 506/2768-8683, www.bananatourcostarica.com) and packing plant. **Agritours** (tel. 506/2282-1349, www.agritourscr.com) offers 90-minute tours of Del Monte's Hacienda Ojo de Agua pineapple plantation (8 A.M.–5 P.M. Mon.–Fri., $19 adult, $8 children), 10 kilometers east of Siquirres. **Hacienda Milla 25** (tel. 506/2241-3233, www.milla25.com), at Batáan, about 10 km east of Siquirres, has horseback and wagon rides on the cattle farm, including a round-up. And **Mighty Rivers Eco-Farm** (tel. 506/2765-1116, http://mightyrivers.net) offers tours of this sustainable dairy farm, where a medley of world-spanning cattle, from Norwegian Fjord to African Watusi, are bred and milked to produce milk and yogurt.

The town is two kilometers east of the Río Reventazón and one kilometer west of the Río Pacuare. White-water rafters traditionally take out at Siquirres.

About five kilometers east of Siquirres and 100 meters west of the Río Pacuarito, a dirt road leads south 17 kilometers to the remote 12,000-hectare **Barbilla National Park** (Parque Nacional Barbilla), on the northeast flank of the Talamanca Mountains. Its creation in the face of heavy logging is a testament to the efforts of the Fundación Nairi, which has a small field station: Estación Biológica Barbilla. The park ($6 admission) is administered by SINAC's Amistad Caribe Conservation Area office (tel. 506/2768-5341, fax 506/2768-8603, aclac@minae.go.cr) in Siquirres. The ranger station at Las Brisas del Pacuarito (10 km from the highway) has restrooms and potable water. A four-wheel-drive vehicle is required to get there.

◖ Veragua Rainforest Research & Adventure Park

This superb facility (tel. 506/2296-5056, www.veraguarainforest.com, $65 adults, $45 children half-day, $99/70 full-day), which opened in summer 2008, is the keystone of a private reserve protecting 1,300 hectares of primary and secondary rainforest at Las Brisas

© CHRISTOPHER P. BAKER

the aerial tram at Veragua Rainforest Research & Adventure Park

del Veragua; the turnoff is at Liverpool, about 12 kilometers west of Limón (4WD required). Highlights include butterfly, snake, and frog exhibits (including a walk-through nocturnal frog garden with misters) linked by elevated boardwalks over the forest. An open-air tram through the canopy whisks you steeply down to the "Trail of the Giants" riverside trail (good for spotting poison-dart frogs), which leads to a fabulous waterfall. Thoughtful education signage is a bonus. This is an active research facility also, run in collaboration with INBio; you can watch biologists at work. Even the stylishly modern yet old-fashioned urinals offer forest views! The entrance fee includes a guided tour and lunch in a lovely open-air restaurant.

Sports and Recreation

The **Original Canopy Tour** (tel. 506/2291-4465, www.canopytour.com, $45 adult, $35 student, $25 child), at Veragua Rainforest Research & Adventure Park, offers a thrilling zipline adventure through the rainforest canopy. On the access road to Veragua, **Brisas de la Jungla** (tel. 506/2797-1291,

© CHRISTOPHER P. BAKER

Veragua Rainforest Research & Adventure Park

www.junglebreeze.com) competes with a 13-platform zipline tour ($45 adults, $35 children), plus horseback rides, and a trail.

Caribbean Adventures Farm (tel. 506/2765-9912, www.caribbeanadventuresfarm.com), eight kilometers east of Siquirres, offers horseback riding, waterfall rappelling, river floats, and hikes.

Accommodations and Food

In Siquirres, the **Hotel Alcema** (tel. 506/2768-6004, $10 pp shared bath, $20 s/d private bath), two blocks north and two east of the plaza, has 23 small and simply furnished but clean rooms with fans and shared bath with cold water. Six newer cabins to the rear have TV and private bath. There's a TV lounge and a small restaurant.

Of the several simple hotels along the main highway, **Cabinas Don Quito** (tel. 506/2765-8076), five kilometers east of town, is one of the better options.

Getting There

Buses (tel. 506/2222-0610 or 506/2768-9484) for Siquirres leave San José from Gran Terminal del Caribe on Calle Central, Avenidas 13/15, at 6:30 A.M. and 9:30 A.M., then hourly 10 A.M.–6 P.M. daily ($2.75). Buses from Siquirres depart hourly for Guápiles, Puerto Limón, and San José from the bus terminal on the main street, 50 meters north of the plaza.

Puerto Limón and Vicinity

PUERTO LIMÓN

Puerto Limón (pop. 65,000) is an important maritime port and gateway to all other points on the Caribbean. The harbor handles most of the sea trade for Costa Rica. Trucks hauling containers rumble along the main road day and night. A new cruise port (tel. 506/2799-0215) draws cruise ships. However, except for Carnival, when it gets in the groove, Puerto Limón is merely a jumping-off point for most travelers as there is little of interest to see.

The earthquake of April 22, 1991, dealt Puerto Limón a serious blow. The city has come a long way since, as reflected in the razing of decrepit buildings and a sense of new-found prosperity.

The city has a bad reputation among Ticos and is often referred to as Piedropolis (Crack City). You should beware of pickpockets by day and muggings at night, and gang violence has recently consumed the city.

Orientation

Highway 32 from San José enters town from the west and becomes Avenida 1, paralleling the railway track that runs to the cruise port. The *avenidas* (east–west) are aligned north of Avenida 1 in sequential order. The *calles* (north–south) are numbered sequentially and run westward from the waterfront. The street signs are not to be trusted. Most addresses and directions are given in direction and distance from the market or Parque Vargas.

The road leading south from the junction of Avenida 1 and Calle 9 leads to Cahuita and Puerto Viejo. Avenida 6 leads out of town to Moín and the JAPDEVA dock, where boats can be hired for the trip to Tortuguero.

Sights

There's not much to hold you in town, although the **Mercado Central** (Avenidas Central/2, Calles 3/4), at the heart of town, is worth a browse. The unremarkable **Parque Vargas,** at the east end of Avenidas 1 and 2, is literally an urban jungle, with palm promenades and a crumbling bandstand amid a tangle of vines. On the north side, a fading mural shows life in Limón since pre-Columbian days. A bronze bust of Christopher Columbus, erected in 1990 for the 500th anniversary of his party's landing, faces the sea. On the west side of the park is the stucco **Town Hall** (Alcadía), a fine example of tropical architecture.

THE CARIBBEAN COAST

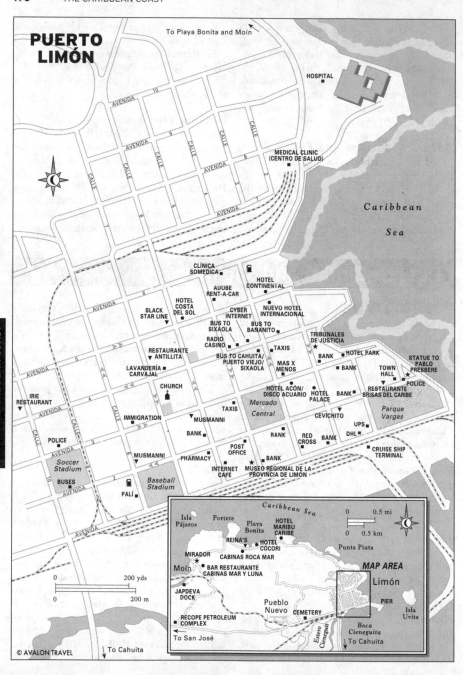

PUERTO LIMÓN

To Playa Bonita and Moín

HOSPITAL

MEDICAL CLINIC
(CENTRO DE SALUD)

Caribbean Sea

CLÍNICA SOMEDICA

ADOBE RENT-A-CAR

HOTEL CONTINENTAL

BLACK STAR LINE

HOTEL COSTA DEL SOL

CYBER INTERNET

NUEVO HOTEL INTERNACIONAL

BUS TO SIXAOLA

BUS TO BANANITO

RADIO CASINO

TRIBUNALES DE JUSTICIA

RESTAURANTE ANTILLITA

BUS TO CAHUITA/ PUERTO VIEJO/ SIXAOLA

TAXIS

BANK

HOTEL PARK

LAVANDERÍA CARVAJAL

MAS X MENOS

BANK

TOWN HALL

STATUE TO PABLO PRESBERE

CHURCH

HOTEL ACÓN/ DISCO ACUARIO

HOTEL PALACE

BANK

POLICE

IRIE RESTAURANT

TAXIS

Mercado Central

RESTAURANTE BRISAS DEL CARIBE

IMMIGRATION

MUSMANNI

CEVICHITO

Parque Vargas

UPS

POLICE

BANK

BANK

RED CROSS

BANK

DHL

MUSMANNI

PHARMACY

POST OFFICE

BANK

CRUISE SHIP TERMINAL

Soccer Stadium

BUSES

PALÍ

Baseball Stadium

INTERNET CAFÉ

MUSEO REGIONAL DE LA PROVINCIA DE LIMÓN

0   200 yds
0   200 m

To Cahuita

© AVALON TRAVEL

Caribbean Sea

Isla Pájaros

Portete

Playa Bonita

HOTEL MARIBU CARIBE

REINA'S

HOTEL COCORI

MIRADOR

CABINAS ROCA MAR

Moín

BAR RESTAURANTE CABINAS MAR Y LUNA

JAPDEVA DOCK

Pueblo Nuevo

CEMETERY

RECOPE PETROLEUM COMPLEX

To San José

To Cahuita

0   0.5 mi
0   0.5 km

Punta Piuta

MAP AREA

Limón

PIER

Isla Uvita

Boca Cieneguita

To Cahuita

Estero Cieneguita

The oldest building in town, the **Black Star Line** (Avenida 5, Calle 6, tel. 506/2798-1948), was built in 1922 as Liberty Hall, former headquarters of Jamaican black activist Marcus Garvey's Black Star Line Steamship Company. The **Museo Regional de la Provincia de Puerto Limón** (Calle 4, Avenidas 1/2, tel. 506/2758-2130, 9 A.M.–noon and 1–4 P.M. Mon.–Fri., free) displays artifacts, photography, and exhibits tracing the culture and history of the region.

Craggy **Isla Uvita** lies one kilometer offshore. Columbus supposedly landed on the islet in 1502; it is now a national landmark park.

Playa Bonita, four kilometers north of Puerto Limón, boasts a golden beach popular with Limonenses. Swimming is safe only at the northern end. The surf is good, but unreliable.

The port of **Moín,** six kilometers north of Puerto Limón, is where Costa Rica's crude oil is received for processing (RECOPE has its main refinery here) and bananas are loaded for shipment to Europe and North America. The only reason to visit Moín is to catch a boat to Tortuguero from the dock north of the railway tracks. However, boat captains here offer one-hour tours of the local mangroves ($10 pp), good for spotting sloths and other wildlife.

Entertainment and Events

The **Black Culture Festival** is hosted in late August and early September, with domino and oratory contests, music, and art. Contact the Black Star Line (Avenida 5, Calle 6, tel. 506/2798-1948), which has a legendary social club upstairs and also hosts an annual "Lady Black Beauty" contest for women over 35.

Each October 12, Puerto Limón explodes in a bacchanal. The annual Columbus Day **Carnival** is celebrated with a fervor akin to the bump-and-grind style of Trinidad, with street bands, floats, and every ounce of Mardi Gras passion, though in a more makeshift fashion. The weeklong event attracts people from all over the country, and getting a hotel room is virtually impossible. The celebrations include a Dance Festival—a rare opportunity to see dances from indigenous tribes, Afro-Caribbeans, and the Chinese communities—plus bands from throughout the Caribbean and Latin America, as well as beauty contests, crafts stalls, fireworks, theater, and calypso contests.

Most bars have a raffish quality. An exception is **Cevichito** (Avenida 2, Calles 2/3, tel. 506/2758-4976, from 10 A.M. daily). This tremendous bar, decorated with flags of the world, has a large-screen TV and one-armed bandits, plus groovy music.

The weekend **Disco Acuario** in the Hotel Acón is jam-packed and sweaty, with a pulsing Latin beat ($5, including a beer; free to hotel guests).

Accommodations

IN LIMÓN

It's not safe to park outside anywhere in Puerto Limón at night; your car will probably be broken into. The Hotel Acón, Hotel Park, and Hotel International have secure parking.

A stand-out among the budget options is **Hotel Continental** (Avenida 5, Calles 2/3, tel. 506/2798-0532, $10 s, $15 d), with 12 simple but spacious rooms with fans and private baths with hot water. It's spotlessly clean and offers secure parking. The same owners run the **Nuevo Hotel Internacional** (tel. 506/2758-0434, $10 s or $15 d with fans, $12 s or $18 d with a/c) across the road; it has 22 tiled rooms of a similar standard to the Continental.

Likewise, the **Hotel Costa del Sol** (Avenida 5, Calle 5, tel. 506/2798-0808, grupodelso@ racsa.co.cr, $12 s, $20 d), offers clean rooms with modest, modern furnishings, fans, and private baths with hot water. It has secure parking.

The best bet in town is the **Hotel Park** (Avenida 3, Calle 1, tel. 506/2758-3476, fax 506/2758-4364, parkhotellimon@ice.co.cr, $38 s or $50 d standard, $40 s or $55 d ocean view with balcony), with 32 air-conditioned rooms featuring TVs and private baths with hot water. Prices vary according to room standard and view. It has a nice restaurant, plus secure parking.

Slightly less appealing is the four-story **Hotel Acón** (Avenida 3, Calles 2/3, tel. 506/2758-1010, fax 506/2758-2924, hotel acon@racsa.co.cr, $32 s, $38 d), with 39 air-conditioned rooms. The hotel has a reasonable restaurant. Take a top-floor room away from the noise of the second-floor disco.

OUTSIDE LIMÓN

At Playa Bonita, **Hotel Cocori** (tel. 506/2798-1670, fax 506/2758-2930, $40 s, $50 d) is a modern clifftop complex with a pleasing oceanview terrace restaurant open to the breezes. It fills with Ticos on weekends, when the disco could wake the dead. It has 25 simple but pleasing air-conditioned rooms with cable TV and private bathrooms with hot water. Rates include breakfast.

Hotel Maribu Caribe (tel. 506/2795-2543, fax 506/2795-3541, maribucaribe@hotmail.com, $70 s or $82 d standard, $120 family suite), at the south end of Playa Bonita, has a scenic setting above the ocean. The simple, uninspired resort, which caters mostly to Ticos, is centered on a swimming pool. It has two restaurants and offers 17 round, thatched, African-style bungalows and 50 rooms, each with air-conditioning, telephone, and private bath. Rooms have narrow beds and unappealing decor. Roomy showers make amends with piping hot water.

At Moín, **Hotel Mar y Luna** (tel. 506/2795-1132, fax 506/2795-4828, $20 pp) sits atop the hill above the dock to Tortuguero. It has 14 modestly appointed air-conditioned rooms with TV and hot water. There's secure parking and a clean restaurant that has karaoke.

Food

You can sample local Caribbean dishes at the open-air *sodas* around the Mercado Central, good for filling *casados* (set lunches, $2).

I also recommend the modestly upscale, air-conditioned **Restaurante Brisas del Caribe** (Avenida 2, tel. 506/2758-0138, 9 A.M.–11 P.M. Mon.–Fri., 11 A.M.–11 P.M. Sat.–Sun.), on the north side of Park Vargas, serving an excellent, bargain-priced set buffet of *típico* dishes.

The clean, air-conditioned restaurant in the **Hotel Park** (6:30 A.M.–midnight daily) is also recommended; it serves soups, salads, shrimp cocktail ($8), lobster ($16), sea bass in garlic ($8), pastas, and cheesecake.

For Caribbean dishes, head to the **Black Star Line** (Calle 5, Avenida 5, tel. 506/2798-1948, 7:30 A.M.–10 P.M. Mon.–Sat., 11 A.M.–5 P.M. Sun., *casado* $3), in an old wooden structure where locals gather to play dominoes and socialize; or the simple **Irie Restaurant** (Calle 9, Avenidas 4/5, tel. 506/2798-3668, $2–12), serving I-tal (Rastafarian) health foods and Jamaican fare, with seating on a small balcony.

At Playa Bonita, the open-air beachfront **Reina's** (tel. 506/2795-0879, 10 A.M.–11 P.M. Mon.–Thurs., 8 A.M.–1 A.M. Fri.–Sun.) is the hip spot hereabouts and draws the party crowd on weekends. It's a good place to hang and watch the surf pump ashore while savoring a shrimp cocktail ($9), ceviche ($6), snapper ($10), or rice and beans Caribbean-style ($6).

Information and Services

The **Hospital Tony Facio** (tel. 506/2758-2222; for emergencies, tel. 506/2758-0580) is on the seafront *malecón,* reached via Avenida 6. For private service, head to **Clínica Somedica** (Avenida 6, Calle 4, tel. 506/2798-4004, www.somedicacr.com). The **Red Cross** (tel. 506/2758-0125) is at Avenida 1, Calle 4.

The **police station** is on the northwest corner of Avenida 3, Calle 8. Criminal investigation is handled by the OIJ (tel. 506/2799-1437).

The **post office** is at Calle 4, Avenida 2. The best Internet café is **Cyber Internet** (Avenida 4, Calle 4, tel. 506/2758-5061).

Immigration (Dirección de Migración y Extranjerá) is on Avenida 3, Calles 6/7.

Getting There and Away

Nature Air and **SANSA** offer regular service to the airport (tel. 506/2758-1379) two kilometers south of Limón.

Transportes Caribeños (tel. 506/2221-2596) double-decker buses depart the Gran Terminal del Caribe, on Calle Central, Avenidas 13/15 in San José hourly 5 A.M.–7 P.M. daily. The buses continue to Cahuita, Puerto Viejo, Bribrí, and Sixaola. Buses to San José depart Puerto Limón from Calle 2, Avenida 2 ($4).

Local buses depart Limón for Cahuita ($1.25), Puerto Viejo ($2), and Sixaola ($3.50) from opposite Radio Casino on Avenida 4 eight times daily (5 A.M.–6 P.M.). Buses for Manzanillo ($2) leave at 6 A.M., 2:30 P.M., and 6 P.M. daily. Buy tickets in advance at the *soda* beside the bus stop, as buses get crowded. Around the corner on Calle 4 to the north is the bus stop for Playa Bonita and Moín.

Getting Around

From Puerto Limón, the bus to Playa Bonita, Portrete, and Moín operates hourly from Calle 4, Avenida 4, opposite Radio Casino.

Taxis await customers on the south side of the market.

PUERTO LIMÓN TO TORTUGUERO

Lagoons and swamps dominate the coastal plains north of Limón. Many rivers meander through this region, carrying silt that the coastal tides conjure into long, straight, brown-sand beaches. The only community along the canals is **Parismina**, on the Oceanside spit at the mouth of the Río Parismina, 45 kilometers north of Moín. It is popular year-round with anglers.

Sea turtles come ashore to nest all along the shore, notably at **Barra de Matina,** midway between Moín and Parismina (see www.costaricaturtles.com). Here, the **Pacuare Nature Reserve** (tel. 506/2719-7702, www.parisminaturtles.org) exists primarily to protect the eggs of leatherback turtles from poachers during the nesting season. The reserve is run in conjunction with Rainforest Concern (in the U.K., 8 Glanricarde Gardens, London W2 4NA, tel. 020/7229-2093, www.rainforestconcern.org) and is open to visitors March 25–August 15. Volunteers are needed to join biologists and hired guards to patrol the beach, tag and measure turtles, and relocate nests; contact c.fernandez@turtleprotection.org. There is a one-week minimum stay. Conselvatur (tel./fax 506/2253-8118, www.conselvatur.com) offers an eight-day Sea Turtle Research and Rainforest Exploration trip that features Reserva Pacuare.

The reserves can be accessed by road via **Matina,** a banana town on the banks of the Río Matina four kilometers north of Highway 32 (the turnoff is at Bristol, about 28 kilometers east of Siquirres); and by boat from Moín ($20 pp) or **Caño Blanco Marina** (tel. 506/2710-1299, or tel. 506/2206-5138 in San José), near Barra de Matina Sur.

Accommodations and Food

In Parismina, **Carefree Ranch** (tel. 506/2798-0839, $10 pp including breakfast), set in a landscaped garden, has nine rooms along a porch

---

COSTA RICA'S AQUATIC COASTAL HIGHWAY

During the Trejos administration (1966–1970) four canals were dug from solid ground to link the natural channels and lagoons stretching north of Moín to Tortuguero and the Río Colorado. Today these canals form a connected "highway" – virtually the only means of getting around along the coast. One can now travel from Siquirres eastward along the Río Pacuare, then northward to Tortuguero, and from there to the Río Colorado, which in turn connects with the Río San Juan, which will take you westward to Puerto Viejo de Sarapiquí.

The waterway is lined with rainforest vegetation in a thousand shades of green, making for a fascinating journey. Noisy flocks of parrots speed by doing barrel rolls in tight formation. Several species of kingfishers patrol the banks. In places the canopy arches over the canal, and howler monkeys sounding like rowdy teenagers may protest your passing. Keep a sharp eye out, too, for mud turtles and caimans absorbing the sun's rays on logs.

with decorative *carretas* (oxcarts). They're simply appointed, cross-lit, and have fans and somewhat basic private bathrooms. The restaurant appeals. And it rents kayaks.

Nearby, and also set in a lovely garden, is **Iguana Verde** (tel. 506/2710-1528, $10 pp with fan, $20 pp with a/c), with three clean rooms with private bath. It has a café and grocery. The neighboring **Carablanco Lodge** (tel. 506/2710-1161, $8 pp with fan, $12 pp with a/c) has 10 clean rooms with private baths, plus an open-air restaurant (9 A.M.–9 P.M.)

serving Caribbean fare; its bar draws locals for dancing.

Sportfishing enthusiasts are catered to at three dedicated sportfishing lodges at Parismina: **Caribbean Expedition Lodge** (tel./fax 506/2232-8118, www.costarica sportfishing.com); **Río Parismina Lodge** (tel. 506/2229-7597, in North America tel. 800/338-5688, www.riop.com); and **Jungle Tarpon Lodge** (U.S. tel. 800/544-2261, www.jungle tarpon.com). All offer fishing packages and take in guests on an ad-hoc basis.

Tortuguero and Barra del Colorado

◖ TORTUGUERO NATIONAL PARK

Parque Nacional Tortuguero extends north along the coast for 22 kilometers from Jaloba, six kilometers north of Parismina, to Tortuguero village. The 19,000-hectare park is a mosaic of deltas on an alluvial plain nestled between the Caribbean coast on the east and the low-lying volcanic hills. The park protects the nesting beach of the green turtle, the offshore waters to a distance of 30 kilometers, and the wetland forests extending inland for about 15 kilometers.

The park—one of the most varied within the park system—has 11 ecological habitats, from high rainforest to herbaceous marsh communities. Fronting the sea is the seemingly endless expanse of beach. Behind that is a narrow canal, connected to the sea at one end and fed by a river at the other; it parallels the beach for its full 35-kilometer length. Back of the canal (and the lagoon to its north) is a coastal rainforest and swamp complex threaded by an infinite maze of serpentine channels and streams.

Tortuguero shelters more than 300 bird species, among them toucans, aricaris, oropendolas, herons, kingfishers, anhingas, jacanas, and the great green macaw; 57 species of amphibians and 111 of reptiles, including three species of marine turtles; and 60 mammal species, including jaguars, tapirs, ocelots, cougars, river

otters, and manatees. Tortuguero's fragile manatee population was thought to be extinct until a population was found in remote lagoons. A decade ago a study indicated that about 100 manatees inhabited the area. The population seems to be growing, as indicated by an increase in the number of collisions with boats

VOLUNTEERS FOR CONSERVATION

The **Caribbean Conservation Corps** (CCC, tel. 506/2224-9215 or 506/2238-8069, fax 506/2225-7516, baulas@racsa.co.cr; in the U.S., 4424 NW 13th St. Suite #A1, Gainesville, FL 32609, tel. 352/373-6441 or 800/678-7853; www.cccturtle.org) needs volunteers to assist in research, including during its twice-yearly turtle tagging and monitoring programs.

The CCC also invites volunteers to join its fall and spring bird-research projects at Tortuguero. No experience is needed. The fieldwork is complemented by guided hikes, boat tours, and other activities.

The numerous other organizations that seek volunteers for environmental, social, and developmental work include **Planet Conservation** (UK tel. 7878-055265, www.planetconservation).

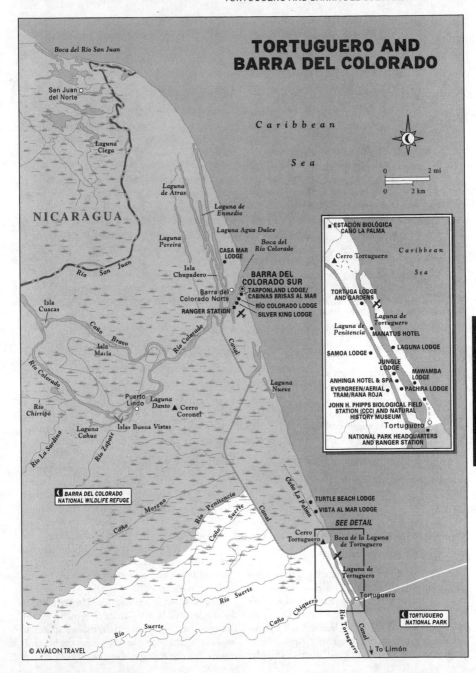

TORTUGUERO AND BARRA DEL COLORADO

Boca del Río San Juan

San Juan
del Norte

Laguna
Ciega

C a r i b b e a n

S e a

0   2 mi

0   2 km

Laguna
de Atras

Laguna de
Enmedio

Laguna Agua Dulce

Laguna
Pereira

NICARAGUA

Boca del
Río Colorado

**CASA MAR
LODGE**

Isla
Chupadero

**BARRA DEL
COLORADO SUR**

Barra del
Colorado Norte

Río   San   Juan

**TARPONLAND LODGE/
CABINAS BRISAS AL MAR**

RÍO COLORADO LODGE

RANGER STATION

SILVER KING LODGE

Isla
Cuacas

Caño   Bravo

Río Colorado

Río Colorado

Isla
Maíla

Laguna
Nueve

*Río
Chirripó*

Puerto
Lindo

Laguna
Danto

▲ Cerro
Coronel

Laguna
Cahue

Islas Buena Vistas

Río La Sardina

Río Zapote

**BARRA DEL COLORADO
NATIONAL WILDLIFE REFUGE**

Caño

Moreno

Río Penitencia

Caño   Suerte

Caño   La Palma

TURTLE BEACH LODGE

VISTA AL MAR LODGE

SEE DETAIL

Cerro
Tortuguero ▲

Boca de la Laguna
de Tortuguero

Laguna de
Tortuguero

Río Suerte

Caño Chiquero

*Río
Suerte*

**TORTUGUERO
NATIONAL PARK**

Río Tortuguero

Tortuguero

↓ To Limón

© AVALON TRAVEL

Detail inset

■ **ESTACIÓN BIOLÓGICA
CAÑO LA PALMA**

▲ Cerro Tortuguero

C a r i b b e a n

S e a

**TORTUGA LODGE
AND GARDENS**

Laguna de
Tortuguero

Laguna de
Penitencia

MANATUS HOTEL

SAMOA LODGE ●

● **LAGUNA LODGE**

**JUNGLE
LODGE**

**MAWAMBA
LODGE**

ANHINGA HOTEL & SPA ●

**EVERGREEN/AERIAL
TRAM/RANA ROJA** ●

● **PACHIRA LODGE**

**JOHN H. PHIPPS BIOLOGICAL FIELD
STATION (CCC) AND NATURAL
HISTORY MUSEUM**

Tortuguero

**NATIONAL PARK HEADQUARTERS
AND RANGER STATION**

© CHRISTOPHER P. BAKER

boat speeding on Laguna Penitencia

(in 2005, several "manatee sanctuaries" were created, where boats are prohibited or velocity is restricted, although boat captains still whiz through these zones at high speed).

The wide-open canals are superb for spotting crocodiles, giant iguanas, basilisk lizards, and caimans luxuriating on the fallen raffia palm branches. At night you might even spy bulldog bats skimming the water and scooping up fish right on cue. Amazing!

The western half of the park is under great stress from logging and hunting, which have increased in recent years as roads intrude. The local community is battling a proposed highway sponsored by banana and logging interests. Rubbish disposal is a problem: leave no trash.

Turtles

The park protects a vital nesting ground for green sea turtles, which find their way onto the brown-sand beaches every year June–October (the greatest numbers arrive in September). Mid-February–July, giant leatherback turtles arrive (with greatest frequency Apr.–May), followed by female hawksbill turtles in July.

Tortuguero is the most important green-turtle hatchery in the western Caribbean; annually as many as 30,000 greens swim from their feeding grounds as far away as the Gulf of Mexico and Venezuela to lay their eggs on the beach. Each female arrives 2–6 times, at 10- to 14-day intervals, and waits two or three years before nesting again. The number of green turtles nesting has quadrupled during the last 25 years; that of leatherbacks continues to decline.

During the 1950s, the Tortuguero nesting colony came to the attention of biologist-writer Archie Carr, a lifelong student of sea turtles. His lobby—originally called the Brotherhood of the Green Turtle—worked with the Costa Rican government to establish Tortuguero as a sanctuary where the endangered turtles could nest unmolested. The sanctuary was established in 1963 and the area was named a national park in 1970.

Local guides escort **Turtle Walks** at 8–10 P.M. and 10 P.M.–midnight each evening in turtle-nesting season ($10, including guide, who alone can buy tickets to access the beach at night). *No one is allowed on the 22-mile nesting*

© CHRISTOPHER P. BAKER

Don't Bother Turtles sign in Tortuguero

THE CARIBBEAN COAST

sector without a guide after 6 P.M. (10 people maximum per guide per night). Each of the five sectors has a guard post. No cameras or flashlights are permitted. Keep quiet, as the slightest noise can send the turtle hurrying back to sea, and keep a discreet distance. *You are asked to report any guide who digs up turtle hatchlings to show you—this is absolutely prohibited.*

Exploring Tortuguero

Trails into the forests—frequently waterlogged—also begin at the park stations at both ends of the park; the number of people permitted at any one time is limited. The two-kilometer-long **El Gavilán Trail** leads south from the Cuatro Esquinas ranger station south of Tortuguero village and takes in both beach and rainforest. Rubber boots are compulsory in wet season, when the trail is often closed due to flooding (you can rent boots at Ernesto Tours, tel. 506/2709-8070, $1). A two-kilometer section of **Sendero Jaguar** is accessible with a guide; the other 16 km is accessible at night for turtle viewing.

Outside the park, but within Barra del Colorado Wildlife Refuge, a trail (in terrible condition at last visit) that begins north of Tortuga Lodge leads two kilometers to **Cerro Tortuguero** (119 meters), the highest point for miles around, offering a superb perspective over the swamps and coastline. Officially, the trail is closed.

You can hire dugout canoes (*cayucas* or *botes*) in Tortuguero village ($6 pp the first hour, $3 each additional hour, without a guide). Check on local currents and directions, as the former can be quite strong and it's easy to lose your bearings amid the maze of waterways. Skippered *pangas* (flat-bottomed boats with outboard motors) and *lanchas* (with inboard motor) can also be rented; try to rent one with an electric or non-polluting four-stroke motor. And don't forget to pay your park entrance fee before entering Tortuguero National Park.

If you want to see wildlife you *absolutely* need a guide. The local guides—there are about 40 trained guides organized into a local cooperative—have binocular eyes; in even the darkest shadows, they can spot caimans, birds, crocodiles, and other animals you will most

caiman at Turtle Beach Lodge

likely miss. You can hire local guides in the village for about $10 per person per hour (go only with a certified guide, such as Daryl Loth at Tortuguero Safaris). The best guides are employed by the local lodges.

You can also book guided trips at any of the lodges or through tour companies in San José and Tortuguero village. **Costa Rica Expeditions** (tel. 506/2257-0766, www.costaricaexpeditions.com) is recommended.

When to Go

Rain falls year-round. The three wettest months are January, June, and July. The three driest are February, April, and November. Monsoon-type storms can lash the region at any time. The interior of the park is hot, humid, and windless. Bring good raingear, and it can be cool enough for a windbreaker or sweater while speeding upriver. Take insect repellent—the mosquitoes and no-see-ums can be fierce.

Information and Services

The park ($10 entrance) is open 6 A.M.–6 P.M. daily; last entry is at 5 P.M.; admission also includes access to Caúa de Palma, in Barra del Colorado Wildlife Refuge. The fee is payable at the **Cuatro Esquinas** ranger station (tel./fax 506/2709-8086), at the southern end of Tortuguero village, or at **Estación Jalova,** at the park's southern end (45 minutes by boat from Tortuguero village). No fee applies if you're in transit. The ranger station has an excellent information center. You can camp ($2 pp) at Jalova, with outside showers and toilets. (Crocodiles are often seen sunning on the mud banks immediately south of the Jalova station.)

TORTUGUERO VILLAGE AND LAGOON

Somnolent, funky Tortuguero Village (pop. 550), on the northern boundary of Tortuguero National Park, sprawls over a thin strip of land at the northern end of the **Canal de Tortuguero** and the southern end of **Laguna del Tortuguero,** at the junction with **Laguna Penitencia,** a canal that leads to Barra del Colorado. Laguna del Tortuguero extends north six kilometers to the ocean, where the

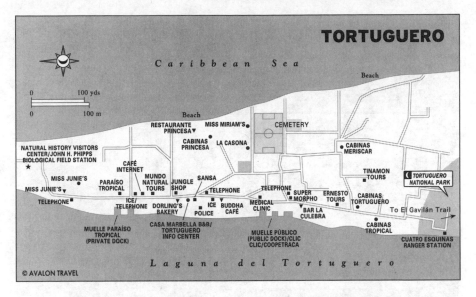

TORTUGUERO

© AVALON TRAVEL

tannin-stained freshwater pours into the Caribbean; it is lined with nature lodges.

It's an 80-kilometer, three-hour journey along the Canal de Tortuguero from Moín; by small plane from San José, it's a 30-minute flight that sets you down on a thin strip of land with the ocean crashing on one side and the lagoon and the jungle on the other (the ocean here is not safe for swimming because of rip currents and the large number of sharks).

The higgledy-piggledy village comprises a warren of narrow sandy trails (there are no roads) lined by rickety wooden houses and, increasingly, more substantial buildings spawned by the tourism boom. The south end of the village is best avoided after dark.

The **John H. Phipps Biological Field Station** (tel. 506/2709-8125, www.cccturtle.org), about 500 meters north of the village, can be accessed by boat or via a trail behind the beach. It features a must-see **Natural History Visitor's Center** (tel. 506/2709-8091, 10 A.M.–noon and 2–5 P.M. Mon.–Sat., 2– P.M. Sun., $1) with turtle exhibits and educational presentations on rainforest ecology, including a video about turtle ecology, and life-size models of turtles hatching and another of a female laying eggs.

Sports and Recreation

The most reputable tour operator in the village is **Tortuguero Wildlife Tours,** based out of Casa Marbella B&B (tel. 506/2709-8011, http://casamarbella.tripod.com), run by Daryl Loth, a multilingual Canadian naturalist, who offers canal trips ($15 pp for up to three hours), turtle-watching trips ($10), rainforest hikes ($15 two hours), and kayak rental ($10). Also recommended is multilingual German biologist and guide, Barbara Hartung. Her **Tinamon Tours** (tel. 506/2709-8004, www.tinamontours.de) offers canoe tours, turtle-watching, and medicinal plant tours. **Mundo Natural Tours** (tel. 506/2709-8159, mundonaturaltours@hotmail.com) and **Caiman Tours** (tel. 506/8814-7403) have similar programs.

Eddie Brown Sportfishing (c/o Costa Rica Expeditions, tel. 506/2257-0766, www.costaricaexpeditions.com) operates from Tortuga Lodge using 26- and 28-foot boats with Bimini tops. Rates of $320–395 per fishing day include lodging, all meals, and open bar. He also offers fishing by the hour ($50). **Caribbean Fishing** (tel. 506/2709-82113) and **Caribeño Fishing Tours** (tel. 506/2709-8026) also arrange fishing trips.

THE CARIBBEAN COAST

Tortuguero village map

© CHRISTOPHER P. BAKER

Yes, even Tortuguero has a zipline! **Aerial Trails Tortuguero Canopy** (tel. 506/2223-6200), at Evergreen, has eight platforms and 11 suspension bridges and offers zipline tours at 11:30 A.M. and 2:30 P.M. daily ($25, including transfers). You need to reserve 24 hours ahead.

You can rent hydrabikes (floating pedal-bikes) at Manatu Hotel ($10 for two hours).

Tortuguero Jungle Spa (tel. 506/2256-7080, info@pachiralodge.ca), at Pachira Lodge, offers massage and a delectable chocolate body treatment ($95).

Accommodations
IN THE VILLAGE

Tortuguero sometimes fills up; if you arrive without reservations, make it a priority to secure accommodations immediately. Many of the accommodations listed here are profiled at www.tortuguerovillage.com.

You have two dozen options in the budget bracket. The **John H. Phipps Biological Field Station** (tel. 506/2709-8125, www.ccc turtle.org) has dormitory accommodations with communal kitchen and bathroom for researchers, students, and volunteers only.

A good backpackers' option is **Cabinas Meriscar** (tel. 506/2709-8202, cabinas meriscar@rocketmail.com, $7 pp shared bath, $9 pp private bath), with 18 simply appointed rooms with fans and hot water. Owner (and local baker) Dorling plans to upgrade and turn it into a classic bed-and-breakfast. And **Mundo Natural Tours** ($20 s, $30 d) has two charming cabins with colorful decor, ceiling fans, heaps of light, and modern bathrooms.

Cabinas Tortuguero (tel. 506/2709-8114, $10 s, $16 d shared bath year-round; $15 s, $20 d private bath low season; $20 s, $25 d private bath high season), toward the southern end of the village, is run by friendly Italian Borghi Morena. It has 11 simple rooms, each with three single beds, ceiling fan, and baths with hot water.

Cabinas Miriam (tel. 506/2709-8002, $15 pp), on the north side of the soccer field, has six simple rooms with fans and private bathroom with hot water. You should stay here for Miss Miriam's restaurant.

CHRISTOPHER P. BAKER

Miss Junie's Hotel in Tortuguero village

I also like **La Casona** (tel. 506/2709-8092, $15 s, $20 d), on the west side of the soccer field. It has nice cabins with modern bathrooms in a garden; the rustic restaurant with sand floor is a charmer; there's an Internet café here; and Andres is a licensed tour guide. And the **Cabinas Tropical Lodge** (tel. 506/2709-8110, $10 pp) has charming, simple cabins that are a worthy alternative.

Miss Junie's (tel. 506/2709-8102, www .iguanaverdetours.com, $40 s/d downstairs, $60 s/d upstairs, including breakfast), at the north end of the village, has parlayed its international fame into exorbitant rates for what you get: 12 clean and simply furnished rooms in a two-story unit, each with tiled floor, ceiling fan, screened windows, and modern bathroom with hot water.

One of the nicest options is **Casa Marbella B&B** (tel. 506/2709-8011, http://casa marbella.tripod.com, $30 s or $35 d low season, $35 s or $40 d high season), a bed-and-breakfast with five airy, clean, delightfully simple bedrooms with terra-cotta floors, high ceilings with fans, and clinically clean and spacious bathrooms with tiled showers and hot water. You can settle down in a common room to watch TV or enjoy games when rain strikes, plus there's a communal kitchen and a dock with hammocks. Rates include a hearty Costa Rican breakfast.

For a beachfront locale, opt for **Cabinas Princesa** (tel. 506/2709-8131, $15 pp). This two-story wooden structure has 12 no-frills but clean rooms with private bathrooms; they open to a breeze-swept veranda. It has a restaurant serving seafood and Caribbean dishes.

ALONG THE LAGOONS

Most nature lodges offer multi-day packages, with meals, transfers, and tours included in the rates below.

The **Canadian Organization for Tropical Education and Rainforest Conservation** (COTERC, P.O. Box 335, Pickering, Ont. L1V 2R6, tel. 905/831-8809, www.coterc.org, $40 pp) has a research field station, Estación Biológica at Caño Palma, a dead-end channel about eight kilometers north of Tortuguero. A dorm has bunk beds. You may also camp or sleep in hammocks. Rates include all meals and a guided walk on trails into the rainforest and swamps.

I'm fond of **Turtle Beach Lodge** (tel. 506/2248-0707, www.turtlebeachlodge.com, from $245 s, $410 d for one-night/two-day packages), also at Caño Palma. It has 25 spacious, simply furnished cabins raised on stilts, with fans, porches, and modern bathrooms. Meals are served in an airy thatched restaurant, and you can relax in the hammock hut or take a cooling dip in the turtle-shaped pool with sundeck. It has the advantage of both beach and lagoon location.

Nearby, the almost identical **Vista al Mar Lodge** (tel. 506/2709-8180, www.vistaalmar lodge.com) is also a pleasant option.

Mawamba Lodge (tel. 506/2293-8181, www.grupomawamba.com, from $240 s or $396 d low season, $289 s or $506 d high season, for one-night/two-day packages, including transport and meals), about 800 meters north of Tortuguero on the east side of Laguna del Tortuguero, has 36 attractive all-wood rooms reached by canopied walkways. There's an airy family-style restaurant and bar, a lovely swimming pool and sun deck, plus a whirlpool tub, game room, and nature trail. Nearby, almost identical and with identical pricing, the **Laguna Lodge** (tel. 506/2709-8082, www.laguna tortuguero.com), sprawls amid spacious landscaped grounds. It has 52 modestly elegant rooms in eight hardwood bungalows, plus a swimming pool, and a hip riverside *ranchito* restaurant and bar.

Set in lush grounds, **Pachira Lodge** (tel. 506/2256-7080, www.pachiralodge.com, from $249 s, $418 d for a two-day, one-night package), on the west side of the lagoon, has 34 attractively furnished thatched cabins. A handsome dining room serves buffet meals, and there's a gift store, bar, and turtle-shaped pool. The owners of Pachira Lodge also operate **Anhinga Hotel & Spa,** a more upscale option in the same style, using 32 A-frame stilt cabins connected by raised boardwalks; the aesthetic is lovely and they get heaps of light. It has a large turtle-shaped pool and whirlpool tub, and

an open-air, full-service spa with steam baths. Monkeys abound at this property, in the thick of the forest. And Pachira also has an annex—**Evergreen** (www.evergreentortuguero.com)—on the west bank of Laguna Penitencia. Actually, it's divided into **Evergreen I** and **Evergreen II.** Together they have 36 handsome stilt-legged A-frame cabins (some in a riverside clearing; some in the forest) and rooms with wrought-iron furniture. There's a pool in a raised sun-deck, plus a nice restaurant, and the Aerial Trails Canopy Tour.

Squeezed between the two Evergreens, and sharing its pool (yet independently owned), is **Rana Roja** (tel. 506/2709-8211, www .tortuguerocabinasranaroja.com), with identical units to Evergreen I.

Two similar options are the **Jungle Lodge** (tel. 506/2223-1200, www.grupopapagayo .com), 400 meters north of Pachira Lodge; and, on Laguna Penitencia, **Samoa Lodge** (tel. 506/2258-5790, www.samoalodge.com).

Manatus Hotel (tel. 506/2709-8197, www .manatuscostarica.com, from $300 s or $540 d low season, $355 s or $640 d high season for a one-night/two-day package) is the snazziest show in Tortuguero. The reception lobby has a pool table, a small gym, and Internet. The 12 air-conditioned rooms with glazed hardwood floors are beautifully appointed with canopy beds, cable TV, and spacious modern bathrooms with both indoor and outdoor showers (the latter in their own garden patios). Sheltered raised pathways connect the units. Kayaks and aquabikes are available for guests, and a nice pool and the finest restaurant for miles round out this winner. A potential downside: All the glass and the TVs potentially divorce you from the nature experience.

I still prefer ◖ **Tortuga Lodge and Gardens** (tel. 506/2257-0766, www.costarica expeditions.com, $118 s/d standard low season, $208 d penthouse low season; $128 s/d standard high season, $218 s/d penthouse high season; rates include guided tours and tax), operated by Costa Rica Expeditions and offering the best food, the best guides, and the best overall experience. The eco-sensitive lodge, facing the airstrip four kilometers north of town, upgraded in 2008 with a sophisticated lounge bar and gourmet nouvelle Costa Rican cuisine in its torch-lit waterfront restaurant. It has 24 spacious riverfront rooms (each with ceiling fans plus fully equipped bathrooms with heaps of solar-heated water; telephones were to be added) fronted by wide verandas with leather rockers. Each has queen-size beds, huge screened windows, ceiling fans, and modern bathrooms. The lovely two-bathroom penthouse suite has king-size *and* queen-size beds! A stone-lined, gradual-entry swimming pool shines beside the river, where a sun deck has lounge chairs. It's set amid 20 hectares of landscaped grounds and forest; a short (albeit muddy) nature trail offers good sightings of poison-dart frogs and other wildlife. Service is exemplary. It's also the only fishing lodge in Tortuguero and also offers hikes, turtle walks, plus multi-day packages. Guests arriving by boat are greeted with a gourmet picnic lunch mid-way, and staff gather to wave as guests arrive and depart. Nice!

Tortuga Lodge's gourmet lunch at Jalova ranger station

© CHRISTOPHER P. BAKER

Food

Not to be missed for local fare is (**Miss Junie's** (tel. 506/2709-8102, 7:30 A.M.–2:30 P.M. and 6:30–9:30 P.M. daily), where $10 will buy you a platter of fish, chicken, or steak, with rice and beans simmered in coconut milk, plus fruit juice and dessert. Reservations are needed. For better or worse, Miss Junie's has enclosed her restaurant in glass; the funky charm has been replaced with air-conditioned elegance. **Miss Miriam's** (7:30 A.M.–9 P.M. daily), on the north side of the soccer field, offers a similar experience and cuisine.

The colorful, thatched **Buddha Café** (tel. 506/2709-8084, 11 A.M.–10:30 P.M. daily, below $8), riverside in the village center, serves Italian cuisine that includes crepes and lasagna.

La Casona (tel. 506/2709-8092, 7:30–11:30 A.M. and 1–9 P.M. daily), on the north side of the soccer field, serves pancakes with bananas, plus omelettes, lasagna, and *casados*. I recommend the chicken in coconut ($6).

At **Dorling's Bakery** (tel. 506/2709-8132, 5 A.M.–9 P.M. daily), gracious Nicaraguan Dorling bakes delicious *empanadas,* cakes, apple pie, and cheesecakes. You've got to try the raspberry truffle brownie! Dorling also has hearty breakfasts (including omelettes and granola with fruit and yogurt), plus cappuccinos, milk shakes, and cheap lunches, including pizza.

To splurge, catch a ride to **Manatus Hotel** (7–9 A.M., noon–2 P.M. and 6:30–8:30 P.M. daily), offering romantic candlelit settings and a three-course prix fixe dinner ($25) for nonguests by reservation. The menu is gourmet—think hearts of palm sushi with avocado spinach appetizer, and vegetable penne pasta with herb pesto and stuffed roasted tomato, eggplant, and cheese.

Information and Services

Daryl Loth mans the **Tortuguero Information Center** at Casa Marbella B&B (tel. 506/2709-8011, http://casamarbella.tripod.com) and is by far the best source of information. **Jungle Shop** (tel. 506/2709-8072, jungle@racsa.co.cr), in the village center, and **Paraíso Tropical** (tel.

506/2709-8095), 50 meters farther north by the main dock, also offer tourist information services. Both sell souvenirs and telephone cards.

The **medical clinic,** facing the dock, is open 8 A.M.–4 P.M. Tuesday and Wednesday. There's a **pharmacy** 100 meters farther south, near the **police station** (public tel. 506/2709-8188). There's a **Café Internet** (tel. 506/2709-8058, 9 A.M.–9 P.M. daily) on the waterfront path. **Mundo National Tours** (tel. 506/2709-8159, 7 A.M.–7 P.M. Mon.–Sat.) also has Internet service.

Getting There
BY AIR
Both **Nature Air** and **SANSA** operate scheduled daily flights between San José and the landing strip four kilometers north of Tortuguero village. SANSA offers a boat transfer to the village.

Costa Rica Expeditions (tel. 506/2257-0766, www.costaricaexpeditions.com) and other tour operators with lodges in Tortuguero operate private charter service; tour members get priority, but you may be able to get a spare seat (about $75 one-way). You can arrange charter flights for about $500 per plane, one-way.

BY BOAT
Locals prefer to use public *lanchas* (tel./fax 506/2709-8005 in Tortuguero) that leave from **La Pavona marina.** To get there, take the 9 A.M. Empresario Guápileño (tel. 506/222-2727 or 2710-7780) bus to Cariari (15 km northeast of Guápiles) from San José's Gran Caribe bus terminal. Buses also depart at 6:30 P.M., 10:30 A.M., 1 P.M., 3 P.M., 4:30 P.M., 6 P.M., and 7 P.M.; buy your ticket in the Guápiles booth. A Coopetraca bus leaves Cariari for La Pavona from the local bus station, five blocks north of the San José terminal in Cariari at noon (and 6 A.M. and 3 P.M.), arriving at La Pavona (29 km from Cariari) in time for the early afternoon boat departures. Buy your boat ticket at La Pavona dock (which has secure parking, $10 nightly) rather than prepaid at the bus station. Several boat companies compete and touts are known to direct

you to specific businesses for commission; their information cannot be trusted! **Clic Clic** is the most trustworthy boat company: Its boats leave at 8 A.M., 1 P.M., and 4 P.M. daily ($10 pp each way for bus-and-boat); return boats depart Tortuguero for La Pavona at 6 A.M., 11:30 A.M., and 3 P.M. The route follows the Río Suerte through Tortuguero National Park and can be impassable in extreme high and low waters; you might even have to get out and help push the boat over sandbars—a good reason to choose the *least* full boat at La Pavona. The quickest way back to San José is to take the early boat, then a direct bus to Guápiles, then a bus to San José.

An alternative to La Pavona is to take a bus from Cariari to La Geest dock; the banana company requires passengers to get off the bus and walk through a mold poison. And private cars may not enter. Most locals avoid this route. *Lanchas* operated by Empresarios de Transportes Acuático Tortuguero (tel. 506/2709-8005, www.tortuguero-costa rica.com), the boatmen's cooperative, depart Geest for Tortuguero at 3 A.M. and 1:30 P.M.; return boats depart Tortuguero at 7 A.M. and 11 A.M. ($10 pp).

Private water-taxis also serve Tortuguero from the JAPDEVA dock in Moín (public tel. 506/2795-0066), including the **Riverboat Francesca** (tel. 506/2226-0986, www.tortu guerocanals.com). Prices are negotiable. Expect to pay $60–80 pp for four people round-trip ($220 for one or two people). *Warning:* Some boat captains work in union with touts in Tortuguero to steer you toward specific lodgings and guides. Most cannot be relied upon.

Private boats for package tour groups serve Tortuguero from **Caño Blanco Marina** (tel. 506/2710-1299, or tel. 506/2206-5138 in San José), near Barra de Matina Sur. Tour operators in San José will accept reservations for these boat transfers on a space-available basis. A private skipper willing to take individuals without pre-booked group boat transfers can usually also be found here; a private charter to Tortuguero costs about $100 one-way, $180

© CHRISTOPHER P. BAKER

children playing at Barra del Colorado

round-trip. To get to the marina from San José, take a 9 A.M. bus (buses run 5 A.M.–7 P.M.) from San José's Gran Caribe bus terminal and get off at Siquirres, from where buses depart for Caño Blanco Marina at 4:30 A.M. and 1 P.M. Monday–Friday and at 7:30 A.M. and 3 P.M. Saturday and Sunday (return buses depart Caño Blanco at 6 A.M. and 3 P.M. Mon.–Fri. and 9 A.M. and 5 P.M. Sat.–Sun.). Caño Blanco Marina has secure parking, 10 simple cabins with fans ($25 s/d with fan, $30 s/d with a/c), plus a restaurant.

◖ BARRA DEL COLORADO NATIONAL WILDLIFE REFUGE

Refugio Nacional de Vida Silvestre Barra del Colorado (91,200 hectares) protects the vast rainforests and wetlands extending north from the estuary of Lagunas del Tortuguero to the Río San Juan, the international border with Nicaragua. About 30 kilometers from the sea, the Río San Juan divides, with the San Juan flowing northeast and the main branch—the Río Colorado—flowing southeast to the sea

through the center of the reserve. Dozens of tributaries form a labyrinth of permanent sloughs and ephemeral waterways that have made the region inaccessible to all but boat traffic.

Barra del Colorado is a replica of Tortuguero National Park—to which it is linked by canal—on a larger scale, and it protects a similar panoply of wildlife. Great green macaws wing screeching over the canopy, mixed flocks of antbirds follow advancing columns of army ants, and jabiru storks with two-meter wingspans circle above. Large crocodiles inhabit the rivers and can be seen basking on mud banks. However, there are virtually no facilities for exploring, and no ranger station.

Unexciting and ramshackle Barra del Colorado village sits astride the mouth of the 600-meter-wide Río Colorado. **Barra del Norte,** on the north side of the river, has no roads (just dirt paths littered with trash and a broken concrete walkway down its center between cabins made of corrugated tin and wooden crates). The slightly more salubrious **Barra del Sur** has an airstrip and most of the hamlet's few services. The village once prospered as a lumber center but went into decline during two decades of Nicaraguan conflict, when the village became a haven for Nicaraguan refugees. Locals mainly rely on fishing or serve as guides for the half dozen sportfishing lodges, but drug trafficking is also entrenched.

Despite the end to the conflicts, tensions with Nicaragua run high. Nicaragua disputes Costa Rica's territorial rights to land north of the Río Colorado. The Río San Juan is entirely Nicaraguan territory (when you are on the water you are inside Nicaragua). Costa Ricans have right of use. Nicaraguan authorities charge foreigners for use of the Río San Juan ($5 pp, plus $7 per boat); you must carry your passport on the river.

Local expat resident Diana Graves at **CyD Souvenirs** (tel. 506/2794-0152, 8 A.M.–9 P.M. daily) is the best source of tourist information; she has an Internet café.

Sportfishing

The rivers are famous for their game fishing; all of the lodges specialize in sportfishing. Local tarpon are so abundant that a two-meter whopper might well jump into your boat. Gar—with an ancestry dating back 90 million years—is also common; growing up to two meters long, these bony-scaled fish have long, narrow, crocodile-like snouts full of vicious teeth.

Accommodations and Food

The sportfishing lodges rely on group business. When there are no groups, they can be lonely places. All offer multi-day packages.

Hardy budget travelers might try the dingy **Tarponland Lodge** (tel. 506/2710-2141, $15 pp), in Barra del Sur; at least it has reasonable local fare.

Far nicer is **Cabinas Brisas del Mar** (tel. 506/2794-116, $30 pp including three meals), on the east side of the airstrip and run by a pleasant Tico couple. It has two rooms upstairs (with carpets) and two below, all with screened windows, local TV, ceiling fans, and clean bathrooms with hot water. Seafood, Chinese, and local dishes are served in a simple thatched *soda*.

Casa Mar Fishing Lodge (tel. 506/8381-1380 or U.S. tels. 714/578-1881 or 800/543-0282, www.casamarlodge.com; fishing packages from $2,495 pp for five nights), on Laguna Agua Dulce, about two kilometers north of Barra, offers 12 rustic, comfortable, and spacious thatched duplex cabins set in attractive landscaped grounds. Each has shining hardwoods, screened windows, fans, clean bathrooms, and wooden canoes that serve as planters. There's a tackle shop, a handsome restaurant, and a bar with leather Sarchí rockers, a dartboard, and large-screen TV with VCR.

The venerable **Río Colorado Lodge** (tel. 506/2232-4063 or U.S. tels. 813/931-4849 or 800/243-9777, www.riocoloradolodge.com, $505 s, $950 d all-inclusive of meals and fishing, $120 for non-fishing guests) at Barra del Sur has 18 rather spartan air-conditioned rooms open to the breeze; all have no-frills baths, hot showers, and electric fans. The rooms and public areas are connected by covered walkways perched on stilts (when the river rises, the lodge extends only a few inches above the water). There's an open-air restaurant, TV and VCR room, bar, game room, whirlpool tub, and tackle shop. The lodge offers five-, six-, and seven-night packages.

More salubrious, **Silver King Lodge** (tel. 506/8381-1403, or U.S. tel. 800/847-3474, www.silverkinglodge.net, call for rates), 300 meters upriver, offers 10 spacious, modestly furnished duplexes linked by covered catwalks. All have queen-size beds with orthopedic mattresses, ceiling fans, coffeemakers, plus private baths with their own water heaters and large showers. Other features include a small swimming pool and sundeck with hammocks, a masseuse, a huge colonial-tiled indoor whirlpool tub, tackle shop, a restaurant serving all-you-can-eat buffets, and a bar with widescreen TV and VCR. A heavy-duty offshore craft permits deep-sea fishing. The lodge closes mid-June–August and in December. Rates include meals.

Food is available at all of the lodges listed in this section.

© CHRISTOPHER P. BAKER

Río Colorado Lodge, Barra del Colorado

Getting There

Both **SANSA** and **Nature Air** fly daily from San José if they get two or more passengers. You can also charter a light plane from San José.

A rough road leads from Puerto Viejo de Sarapiquí to Pavas (at the juncture of the Ríos Toro and Sarapiquí), where you can also charter a boat.

Water-taxis serve Barra del Colorado from the dock at La Pavona. Lodge boats will also pick you up by prior arrangement.

South of Puerto Limón

PUERTO LIMÓN TO CAHUITA

South of Puerto Limón, the shore is lined by brown-sand beaches fringed by palms. About 30 kilometers south of Limón the road crosses the Río Estrella a few kilometers north of the village of **Penshurst,** where a branch road leads into the Valle del Río Estrella.

The Valle del Río Estrella is blanketed by banana plantations of the Dole Standard Fruit Company, headquartered at **Pandora,** about six kilometers inland of Penshurst. The Río Estrella is spawned in the foothills of the steep-sided, heavily forested Talamanca massif, and it irrigates the banana plantations as it crosses the broad plains in search of the Caribbean. The river estuary forms a dense network of channels and lagoons that shelter birds, including great flocks of snow-white cattle egrets.

At **Piedmont** (tel. 506/2750-0789, orchid pierrre@yahoo.com, 9 A.M.–3 P.M. daily, $10), about 500 meters south of the gas station in Penshurst, Pierre Dubois welcomes visitors to his organic fruit farm. Here you can even cut banana stems and taste homemade chocolate.

Unfortunately, the **Aviarios del Caribe**

Sloth Refuge (tel. 506/2750-0775, www.sloth rescue.org, $30 by reservation only), one kilometer north of the Río Estrella, has become focused on cruise-ship business and less welcoming to individual visitors; complaints about owner Luis's cranky attitude continue to trickle in (be sure to visit when his amiable wife, Judy, is available). It has a "slothpital" where injured sloths are cared for, plus a learning center.

Bocuare Jungle Adventure (tel. 506/2759-0122, www.bocuarejungle.com), 14 km inland of Penshurst, is a lodge and ecological plantation on the edge of the rainforest. It has a frog garden and butterfly garden and offers horseback rides, river tubing, birding, and guided hikes to local indigenous communities. It didn't overly impress me.

Selva Bananito Reserve

This 950-hectare private reserve (Conselvatur, tel. 506/2253-8118, www.selvabananito.com), 15 kilometers inland from Bananito (five kilometers inland from the coast road), protects primary rainforest on the slopes of the Talamancas. Two-thirds is rainforest; the rest is devoted to low-impact agriculture and cattle management. Activities from birding and nature hikes to horseback riding and waterfall rappels are offered, as is a trip to a Dole banana packing plant.

The reserve is tough to get to; a high-clearance four-wheel-drive vehicle is absolutely essential for the muddy track churned into an assault course by logging trucks. Ask in the village of Bananito, where you cross the railway lines and keep going straight; take the right fork at the Y junction. Eventually you'll get to a metal gate with a sign reading "No entrance. Private Property." You've arrived. There are two more barbed wire gates to pass through, then you have to drive along a riverbed to cross to the lodge (or you can park at the farm facing the lodge).

Hitoy-Cerere Biological Reserve

Undeveloped and off the beaten track, the 9,050-hectare Reserva Biológica Hitoy-Cerere (tel. 506/2798-3170, www.sinac.go.cr, 8 a.m.–5 p.m. daily, $10), part of the Parque Internacional La Amistad, is one of the nation's least-visited parks. It is surrounded by three indigenous reservations—Talamanca, Telire, and Estrella. Dense evergreen forests are watered by innumerable rivers.

Take your pick of arduous trails or moderately easy walks from the ranger station along the deep valley of the Río Hitoy-Cerere to waterfalls with natural swimming holes. The park is a starting point for trans-Talamanca journeys to the Pacific via a trail that leads south to the village of San José Cabecar and up the valley of the Río Coén and across the saddle between Cerro Betsú (2,500 meters) and Cerro Arbolado (2,626 meters) to Ujarrás, in the Valle de El General. Large sections have not been explored, and trails into the interior are overgrown, unmarked, and challenging (indigenous guides are available for local hikes).

Rainfall is prodigious: seven meters a year is not unknown (March, September, and October are usually the driest months). The result: one of the best specimens of wet tropical forest in the country. Large cats are found throughout the reserve, as well as margays, tapirs, peccaries, agoutis, pacas, otters, monkeys, and harpy eagles.

You can reserve basic lodging at the ranger station; researchers get priority. Camping is permitted; there are basic showers and toilets.

The park is signed from Pandora. You'll need a four-wheel-drive vehicle if driving.

Accommodations and Food

Hotel Colón Caribe (tel. 506/2256-5520, www.coloncaribe.com, $78 pp low season, $87 pp high season), 22 kilometers south of Puerto Limón and 200 meters from a lonesome beach that seems to stretch to eternity, is an attractive resort. The lobby provides a touch of Tahiti with its soaring *palenque* roof and bamboo furnishings in bright floral prints. Choose from 32 air-conditioned *cabinas* or 11 standard rooms set amid shade trees and boasting cable TVs, and private bathrooms with hot water. There's a swimming pool, plus tennis court and volleyball. It also offers all-inclusive options with meals, well drinks, and entertainment. Rates include tax.

ranger station at Hitoy-Cerere Biological Reserve

© CHRISTOPHER P. BAKER

Selva Bananito Lodge (Conselvatur, tel. 506/2253-8118, www.selvabananito.com, $152 s, $260 d standard, $172 s, $280 d superior) is on a 950-hectare private reserve, 15 kilometers inland from Bananito (five kilometers inland from the coast road), and has 11 elegant wooden cabins on stilts on a ridge. Each has a queen- and full-size bed, tiled bathroom and solar-heated water (there's no electricity), and deck with hammocks for enjoying the splendid views. More spacious superior cabins have terra-cotta floors, fold-away doors opening to verandas with hammocks, plus bathrooms with high-tech fittings and picture windows. Dining is family style (I've received complaints about food quality). It offers various packages, with a two-night minimum.

Bocuare Jungle Adventure (tel. 506/2759-0122, www.bocuarejungle.com), 14 kilometers inland of Penshurst, offers rustic accommodations in cozy wooden cabins. More salubrious digs are available at **Villas de Pandora** (tel. 506/2759-0440, www.banana tourcostarica.com, $50 for up to five people), 10 km inland of Penshurst, at the Dole headquarters. Here, five former managers' duplex bungalows have metamorphosed into tourist villas pleasantly furnished with colorful fabrics, cable TV, and simple but full kitchens. Packages include a plantation tour, meals, and activities such as horseback riding. The huge employees' club has a game room and kids' playground, and there's tennis and a swimming pool.

Getting There

Cahuita-bound Transportes Mepe (tel. 506/2257-8129) buses depart the Gran Caribe terminal in San José at 6 A.M., 10 A.M., 1:30 P.M., and 3:30 P.M., all stopping in Estrella en route.

Local buses depart Puerto Limón (Calles 3/4, Avenida 4) for Pandora and the Dole banana plantation (10 kilometers from the Hitoy-Cerere park entrance) every two hours 5 A.M.–6 P.M. daily. Jeep-taxis from Finca 6 in the Estrella Valley cost about $15 one-way. Jeep-taxis from Cahuita cost about $50 each way (you will need to arrange your return trip in advance if you stay overnight in the park).

Cahuita and Vicinity

◖ CAHUITA

This offbeat village (pop. 3,000), 45 kilometers south of Puerto Limón and one kilometer east of Highway 36, is an in-vogue destination for the young backpacking crowd and others for whom an escapist vacation means back to basics. Cahuita is no more than two parallel dirt streets crossed by four rutted streets overgrown with grass, with ramshackle houses spread apart. The village is totally laid-back and not for those seeking luxuries. What you get is golden- and black-sand beaches backed by coconut palms, an offshore coral reef (now severely depleted), and an immersion in Creole culture, including Rastafarians, with their dreadlocks and a lifestyle that revolves around reggae, Rasta, and—discreetly—reefer. Bob Marley is God in Cahuita.

Cahuita has struggled to recover from a lingering negative perception fed by high crime (and the surly attitude displayed by many local Afro-Caribbeans). The bad publicity stuck; for several years, tourists and Ticos shunned Cahuita. The police force has been beefed up (there's even a police checkpoint on the main road north of Cahuita; every vehicle is searched). Cahuita has regained its popularity, and locals now run a committee to police the community, keep the beaches clean, and generally foster improvements. Crime is no more prevalent here than on the Pacific beaches.

In 2006, the first shopping mall and bank arrived, but Cahuita thus far seems immune to the boom in nearby Puerto Viejo and to the upscale boutique revolution sweeping the rest of the country.

North of Cahuita village is a black-sand beach, **Playa Negra,** which runs for several miles. Cahuita's more famous beach, **Playa Blanca,** is a two-kilometer-long scimitar of golden sand that stretches south from the village along the shore of the national park. Beware riptides! A second pale-sand beach lies farther along, beyond the rocky headland of Punta Cahuita; it is protected by an offshore coral reef and provides safer swimming in

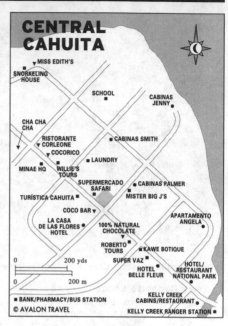

calmer waters. Theft is a problem on the beach; do not leave possessions unattended.

Entertainment and Events

Cahuita hosts a five-day mini-Carnival—Carnavalitos Cahuita—in early December, when theater comes to town, the calypso and reggae is cranked up, and everyone lets their hair down. At other times, there's plenty of night action in Cahuita, though it's an almost exclusively male affair (as far as locals go).

The class act is **Café Cocorico** (50 meters north of the plaza, tel. 506/2755-0324, 7 A.M.–2 P.M. and 5 P.M.–midnight Wed.–Mon.), which shows free movies nightly while you sip killer cocktails.

Coco's Bar (tel. 506/2755-0437), across the street from Cocorico, is the livelier spot. Formerly a laid-back reggae bar that drew dreadlocked Rastas (plus a few drug dealers and leeches hitting up the clientele for drinks),

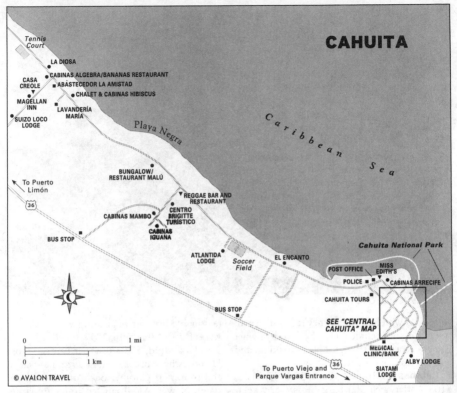

CAHUITA

Tennis Court
LA DIOSA
CASA CREOLE
CABINAS ALGEBRA/BANANAS RESTAURANT
ABASTECEDOR LA AMISTAD
CHALET & CABINAS HIBISCUS
MAGELLAN INN
LAVANDERÍA MARÍA
SUIZO LOCO LODGE
Playa Negra
Caribbean Sea
To Puerto Limón
36
BUNGALOW/ RESTAURANT MALÚ
REGGAE BAR AND RESTAURANT
CABINAS MAMBO
CENTRO BRIGITTE TURÍSTICO
CABINAS IGUANA
BUS STOP
ATLANTIDA LODGE
Soccer Field
EL ENCANTO
Cahuita National Park
POST OFFICE
MISS EDITH'S
POLICE
CABINAS ARRECIFE
CAHUITA TOURS
BUS STOP
SEE "CENTRAL CAHUITA" MAP
MEDICAL CLINIC/BANK
ALBY LODGE
0   1 mi
0   1 km
© AVALON TRAVEL
To Puerto Viejo and Parque Vargas Entrance
36
SIATAMI LODGE

it has cleaned up its act and is now preferred by the Latin set for salsa.

Sports and Recreation

Turística Cahuita (tel. 506/2755-0071, dltacb@racsa.co.cr), **Cahuita Tours** (tel. 506/2755-0000, www.cahuitatours.com), and **Willie's Tours** (tel. 506/2755-0267, www.willies -costarica-tours.com), in the village center, offer a panoply of tours and activities, including snorkeling trips, bird-watching, fishing, dolphin-watching, horseback rides, and trips farther afield. Cahuita Tours even has a full-day manatee-spotting tour to the San San Wetlands, in Panama ($95).

Mister Big J's (tel. 506/2755-0353) offers fishing and horseback rides. Cabinas Brigitte also offers guided horseback rides.

Hotel National Park specializes in snorkeling tours of the national park reefs ($25 pp), as does **Snorkeling House** (tel. 506/2755-0248, www.snorkelinghouse.com), with tours at 9 A.M. and 1 P.M.

Accommodations in Cahuita

Cahuita offers lots of options; most are in the budget category. Hustlers hang around the bus stop with the intent of guiding you to a hotel where they receive commission; they're not above lying (such as telling you that your preferred hotel has closed or is full). Many hoteliers are as laid back as their clientele, and don't expect Wi-Fi. There are many more options than listed here.

UNDER $25

In the village, **Cabinas Palmer** (tel. 506/2755-0046, fax 506/2755-0340, $15 s, $20 d) has 20

© CHRISTOPHER P. BAKER

Cabinas Jenny, Cahuita

rooms (13 with hot water); they're mainly small but clean, and include fans. The friendly owner Rene accepts credit cards. There's parking, and a sunny garden out back.

Cabinas Smith (tel. 506/2755-0157, $12 s, $16 d) offers a similar bargain, is nicely kept, and has secure parking. And **Cabinas Jenny** (tel. 506/2755-0256, www.cabinasjenny.com, $25 s/d downstairs, $35 s/d upstairs) has two simple downstairs cabins with ceiling fans and small, hot-water bathrooms; and four larger, nicer, cross-ventilated upstairs rooms with balconies with hammocks.

$25-50

A good option is the **Hotel National Park** (tel. 506/2755-0244, www.cahuitanational parkhotel.com, $40 s, $45 d), directly in front of the park entrance. The 20 pleasant air-conditioned rooms are clean and bright, with cable TV, safes, and private baths and hot water. Oceanview rooms have larger beds and more facilities. An Internet café was being added.

On the east side of the village are several reasonable options beginning with **Cabinas Arrecife** (tel./fax 506/2755-0081, $25 s or $30 d standard, $35 s/d larger units), whose 11 rooms have breezy verandas and are clean and roomy, if gloomy. Bathrooms have hot water. Newer wood-paneled units are larger and have shady verandas with swing chairs. There's a delightful open-air dining area and small pool.

The simple **Hotel Belle Fleur** (tel./fax 506/2755-0283, hotelbellefleur@hotmail.com, $15 s or $20 d rooms, $30 s/d cabins low season; $25 s or $35 d rooms, $45 s/d cabins high season) offers cross-ventilated, wood-paneled rooms with small modern bathrooms above Super Vaz, and colorful cabins in the garden. It also has two air-conditioned suites with cable TV. It has secure parking.

Seeking self-catering? **Apartmento Angela** (tel. 506/2755-0319, lizchacon42@ hotmail.com, $40 s/d) offers humongous octagonal units in a four-story tower beside the shore. All have wraparound glass walls with veranda and simple wooden furnishings. Two-week rentals are the norm.

© CHRISTOPHER P. BAKER

beach cruiser in Cahuita

$50-100

I like **Kelly Creek Cabins & Restaurant** (tel. 506/2755-0007, www.hotelkellycreek.com, $45 s/d low season, $55 s/d high season) for its location beside the park entrance. Run by a Spanish couple, it has four large, simply furnished rooms in a single, handsome, all-hardwood, Thai-style structure with heaps of light pouring in through tall louvered windows. Each has two double beds with cheap mattresses, and uninspired bathrooms and dribbling hot water. A restaurant serves Spanish cuisine. Past guests report that this hotel has a habit of not honoring reservations.

A romantic gem, the private and peaceful Austrian-run **Alby Lodge** (tel./fax 506/2755-0031, www.albylodge.com, $50 s/d) has four beautiful, thatched, Thai-style cabins sitting on stilts amid lawns and hibiscus. All have tons of character, with high-pitched roofs, screened and louvered windows, hardwood floors, bamboo furnishings, mosquito nets, nice bathrooms with hot water, safes, fans, Wi-Fi, and private patios with hammocks and marvelous tables hewn from logs. There's a common

kitchen, and a natural pond attracts frogs. Rates include tax.

Nearby, the "quaint" description fits Cahuita Tours' pastel-hued, gingerbread, air-conditioned cabins at **Ciudad Perdida Ecolodge** (tel. 506/2755-0303, www.ciudadperdida ecolodge.com, call for rates), 600 meters inland of Kelly Creek. Each has mod cons such as ceiling fans, safes, and cable TV.

In 2008, Cahuita acquired its first real two-story modern hotel, the Italian-owned **La Casa de las Flores Hotel** (tel. 506/2755-0326, www.lacasadelasfloreshotel.com, $70 s/d low season, $80 s/d high season). This handsome complex centered on a garden courtyard makes good use of hardwoods and ocher color schemes and is the class act in town. The lovely air-conditioned rooms have platform beds and contemporary bathrooms with small, hot-water showers. Flat-screen TVs were to be added. One room has a full kitchen.

Accommodations in Playa Negra

UNDER $25

On the shorefront road about three kilometers

north of the village is **Cabinas Algebra** (tel./ fax 506/2755-0057, www.cabinasalgebra.com, $18–30 s/d), run by a German named Alfred and his charming wife, Andrea; they offer three double cabins with hot water, and a four-person unit with kitchen. I enjoyed a tasty, wholesome meal in the offbeat restaurant.

$25-50

The **Chalet & Cabinas Hibiscus** (tel. 506/2755-0021, www.hotels.co.cr/hibiscus .html, from $40 s/d, $50–100 chalets low season; $50 s/d, $60–120 chalets high season) is one of the best places in Cahuita, with five pleasing *cabinas* plus four chalets for 3–10 people. There's no restaurant, but the units have kitchens, plus ceiling fans and hot water. Chalets have a spiral staircase up to the second floor, where rockers and hammocks allow a balcony siesta. There's a swimming pool, volleyball court, and game room.

The Swiss-run **Bungalow Malú** (tel. 506/2255-0114, bungalowmalu@gmail.com, $30 s or $35 d standard, $40 s or $45 d with a/c, $50 s or $55 d with kitchen) offers five exquisite, thatched octagonal cabins in landscaped grounds. They're spacious and have refrigerator, fans, Guatemalan bedspreads, and quaint stone-floored bathrooms with hot water, plus stone balconies. One unit has a kitchen. The restaurant offers fine Italian fare.

Farther south, a dirt road leads inland 50 meters to **Centro Turístico Brigitte** (tel. 506/2755-0053, www.brigittecahuita.com, $20 s or $25 d without kitchen, $30 s or $35 d with kitchen), run by Swiss-born Brigitte. She has two simple cabins with hot water. Meals are served in a charming little restaurant, and Brigitte offers horseback tours ($45, half-day). Brigitte also rents houses.

Cabinas Iguana (tel. 506/2755-0005, www.cabinas-iguana.com, $20 s/d rooms, $35–70 bungalows low season; $25 s/d rooms, $40–78 bungalows high season), still farther south, is also run by a Swiss couple. They offer a large wooden house with rooms for six people, a smaller house for three people, and a bungalow (without kitchen) with bunks and

a double bed. All have hot water, plus verandas with hammocks. There's a small, attractive pool and sundeck with cascade, and trails lead through the expansive grounds.

$50-100

I recommend **El Encanto Bed & Breakfast Inn** (tel. 506/2755-0113, www.elencantobed andbreakfast.com, $55 s or $60 d low season, $60 s or $70 d high season), a splendid and fully equipped two-story bed-and-breakfast run by French-Canadians. They offer three rooms in the main building, with queen-size orthopedic mattresses and Guatemalan bed covers, Oriental carvings, ceiling fans, and pleasant bathrooms. They also have cabins in the well-maintained garden, plus a small but exquisite patio restaurant and secure parking. It has a yoga center and oozes tranquility. Rates include breakfast (and taxes in low season).

The romantic **Magellan Inn** (tel./fax 506/2755-0035, www.magellaninn.com, $69 s/d standard, $89 s/d with a/c low season; $79 s/d standard, $99 s/d with a/c high season, including continental breakfast) is set in lush landscaped grounds. Six spacious, sparsely furnished rooms are done up in mauves, with plentiful hardwoods (and musty carpets), and bathrooms with piping hot water. French doors open onto private patios. All rooms have Wi-Fi. The lounge, with Oriental rugs and sofas, is an atmospheric place to relax. A sunken swimming pool is cut into a coral reef. Alas, its Casa Creole restaurant has closed.

Claiming its own little beach, **La Diosa** (tel. 506/2755-0055, www.hotelladiosa.net, $50– 75 s, $65–95 d low season; $55–85 s, $65–95 d high season) is one of the most inviting lodgings in Cahuita. Adorned with river stones, the four lovely rooms and six inviting bungalows are painted in lively canary yellow and tropical blues, with divinely comfortable double beds (with batik spreads) on poured concrete platforms, plus spacious modern bathrooms. Two cabins have whirlpool tubs in raised platforms. It has a small pool and a lovely yoga space adorned with Asian art. The owner was due to open the **Goddess Garden Eco-Resort**

© CHRISTOPHER P. BAKER

restaurant sign, Cahuita

& Spa (tel. 506/2755-0444, www.thegoddess garden.com) amid rainforest at Tuba Creek, one kilometer north of Playa Negra. Intended as a spiritual retreat, it will have 12 rooms, a restaurant, and conference center, plus a huge yoga center.

Suizo Loco Lodge & Resort (tel. 506/2755-0349, www.suizolocolodge.com, $55–95 s, $76–95 d low season; $63–99 s, $89–110 d high season), inland at the north end of Playa Negra, is a tropics-meets-Alps lodge with 10 cozy if meagerly appointed cabins in landscaped grounds. The highlight is the romantic thatched restaurant overlooking a figure-eight pool.

Competing in the same price range and with similar ambience and facilities is the French-Canadian–run **Atlantida Lodge** (tel. 506/2755-0115, fax 506/2755-0213), closer to the village.

Food

There's excellent eating in Cahuita, but the scene is ever-changing. Some places are only open in season (Dec.–May), and most accept cash only.

In Playa Negra, **Bananas Restaurant** (7 A.M.–10 P.M.), at Cabinas Algebra, is recommended for breakfasts, and at lunch and dinner serves salads, burgers, and a choice of fish, chicken, or steak with rice and beans and coconut sauce (from $5). It occasionally has live music at night. My preferred breakfast spot in the village is **100 percent Natural Chocolate** (tel. 506/2755-0311, 6:30 A.M.–4 P.M. daily), a delightful, airy café with split-tree-trunk tables. It serves omelettes, plus burritos, sandwiches, and veggie plates.

The renowned **Miss Edith's** (tel. 506/2755-0248, 11:30 A.M.–10 P.M. Mon.–Sat., noon–10 P.M. Sun., $6–10), 50 meters east of the police station, is a homey place that offers aromatic Caribbean specialties such as "rundown" (a spiced stew of fish, meat, and vegetables simmered in coconut milk), or lobster with curry and coconut milk ($15). Miss Edith also offers a vegetarian menu.

Otherwise the best dining in town is the open-air **Cha Cha Cha** (tel. 506/2755-0476, noon–10 P.M. daily, $5–15), an unpretentious place where Chef Bertrand Fleury serves

CARIBBEAN SPICY

One of the pleasures of the Caribbean coast is the uniquely spicy local cuisine, which owes much to the populace's Jamaican heritage. The seductive flavors are lent predominantly by coconut, ginger, chiles, and black pepper. Breadfruit, used throughout the Caribbean isles but relatively unknown elsewhere in Costa Rica, is a staple, as are various tropical roots.

You'll even find ackee and saltfish (one of my favorite breakfasts), made of ackee fruit and resembling scrambled eggs in texture and color. It is often served with johnnycakes, fried sponge dumplings that make great fillers to accompany escoveitched (pickled) fish, or "rundown," mackerel cooked in coconut milk. You must try highly spiced jerk chicken, fish, or pork, smoked at open-air grills and lent added flavor by tongue-searing pepper marinade.

Desserts include ginger cakes, puddin', *pan bon* (a kind of bread laced with caramelized sugar), banana brownies, and ice cream flavored with fresh fruits.

superb "cuisine of the world" with such appetizers as tapenade ($6) and grilled calamari salad ($7.50) and such entrées as curried chicken ($10), followed by banana flambé, all artfully presently on chic oversize plates. The rustic decor is romantic by candlelight, while world music adds just the right note. Kitchen service is excruciatingly slow and, alas, smoking is permitted.

Also for romantic atmosphere, head to **Café Cocorico** (50 meters north of the plaza, tel. 506/2755-0324, 7 A.M.–2 P.M. and 5 P.M.–midnight Wed.–Mon.) for its colorful decor and Arabian-style ceiling drapes. An Italian chef conjures gnocchi, pizzas, and homemade ice cream. All dishes are less than $10. Nearby, the lively **Ristorante Corleone** (tel. 506/2755-0341, noon–10 P.M. Sat.–Wed., 5–10 P.M. Fri.) competes with Italian fare such as carpaccio

($7) and pasta pomodoro ($6.50), plus two dozen types of pizza.

The **Kelly Creek Cabins & Restaurant** (6:30 P.M.–10 P.M. Mon.–Sat., $3–15) is a winner with its paella and sangria, to be enjoyed on an open deck facing the beach.

Information and Services

Cahuita Tours (tel. 506/2755-0000, www.cahuitatours.com) acts as an informal tourist information office. So, too, **Mister Big J's** (tel. 506/2755-0353, 8 A.M.–6 P.M. daily) which does laundry ($7 for a full basket) and has a book exchange in addition to fishing and horseback tours. **Centro Turístico Brigitte** also offers laundry ($8 a basket).

MINAE (tel. 506/2755-0060, 8 A.M.–4 P.M. Mon.–Fri.) has a National Parks Service office in the village.

There's a government **medical center** at the entrance to town, on the main road from Highway 36. There is a private clinic (tel. 506/2755-0345, cell 506/8352-6981) at Suizo Loco Lodge.

The **post office** (tel. 506/2755-0096, 8 A.M.–noon and 1:30–5:30 P.M. Mon.–Fri.) is three blocks north of the plaza. The **police station** (Guardia Rural, tel. 506/2755-0217 or 911) is next door.

The **bank** (tel. 506/2284-6600) is open 8 A.M.–4 P.M. Monday–Friday.

Centro Turístico Brigitte has Internet service (7 A.M.–7 P.M. daily) for $1 per 30 minutes, as does **Willie's Tours** (tel. 506/2755-0267, www.willies-costarica-tours.com, 8:30 A.M.–12:30 P.M. and 2–8 P.M. Mon.–Sat., 4–8 P.M. Sun.), in the village center.

Getting There

Transportes Mepe (tel. 506/2257-8129) buses depart the Gran Caribe terminal in San José for Cahuita ($8) at 6 A.M., 10 A.M., 1:30 P.M., and 3:30 P.M. They continue to Puerto Viejo and Sixaola. Local buses depart Puerto Limón (tel. 506/2758-1572) from Avenida 4, Calles 3/4, hourly 5 A.M.–6 P.M. daily (one hour, $1.25).

Buses depart Cahuita (from 50 meters southwest of Coco Bar) for San José at 8 A.M.,

9:30 A.M., 11:30 A.M., and 4:30 P.M.; and for Limón hourly 6:30 A.M.–8 P.M. The ticket office is open 7 A.M.–5 P.M. daily.

The nearest gas stations are at Penshurst and about 15 kilometers southeast of Bribrí. Several locals sell gas (petrol) from jerry cans.

Getting Around

For a taxi, call 506/2755-0435, or contact Cabinas Palmas (tel. 506/2755-0046) and Cahuita Tours (tel. 506/2755-0000, www .cahuitatours.com). Mister Big J's (tel. 506/2755-0353) arranges car rental.

Centro Turístico Brigitte also rents bicycles ($6 daily).

CAHUITA NATIONAL PARK

Cahuita's 14 kilometers of beaches are shaded by palm trees, lush forests, marshlands, and mangroves. Together they make up Cahuita National Park (1,067 hectares), created in 1970 to protect the 240 hectares of offshore coral reef that distinguish this park from its siblings. Animal life abounds in the diverse habitats— an ideal place to catch a glimpse of tamanduas, pacas, coatis, raccoons, sloths, agoutis, armadillos, iguanas, and troops of howler and capuchin monkeys, and to focus your binoculars on ibis, rufous kingfisher, toucans, and parrots (and even, Dec.–Feb., macaws). Cahuita's freshwater rivers and estuaries are also good places to spot caimans.

The offshore reef lies between Puerto Vargas and Punta Cahuita. Smooth water here provides good swimming; it's possible to wade out to the edge of the coral with the water only at knee level. At the southern end of the park, beyond the reef, huge waves lunge onto the beach—a nesting site for three species of turtles—where tidepools form at low tide. Check with rangers about currents and where you can walk or snorkel safely. Snorkelers can try their luck near Punta Cahuita or Punta Vargas (you must enter the water from the beach on the Punta Vargas side and swim out to the reef). *Snorkeling is only permitted with a guide or organized snorkeling tour.* Up to 500 species of fish gambol among the much-diminished reefs.

sign at entrance to Cahuita National Park

© CHRISTOPHER P. BAKER

Besides what remains of the coral, there are two old shipwrecks about seven meters below the surface, both with visible ballast and cannons; one wreck has two cannons, and the second, a more exposed site, has 13. The average depth is six meters. The best time for diving and snorkeling is during the dry season, February–April; water clarity during the rest of year is not good because of silt brought by rivers emptying from the Talamanca mountains.

Gangs of capuchin monkeys may beg for tidbits, often aggressively. Many folks have been bitten. Feeding wild monkeys with human foodstuffs alters their habits and can adversely affect their health. *Don't feed the monkeys!*

Information and Services

A footbridge leads into the park from the **Kelly Creek Ranger Station** (tel. 506/2755-0461, 6 A.M.–5 P.M. daily, entry by donation) at the southern end of Cahuita village. A shady seven-kilometer nature trail leads from the Kelly Creek Ranger Station to the **Puerto Vargas Ranger Station** (tel. 506/2755-0302, 8 A.M.–4 P.M. Mon.–Fri., 7 A.M.–5 P.M. Sun.,

THE CARIBBEAN COAST

THE DESTRUCTION OF CAHUITA'S CORAL REEFS

Corals are soft-bodied animals that secrete calcium carbonate to form an external skeleton that is built upon and multiplied over thousands of generations to form fabulous and massive reef structures. The secret to coral growth is the symbiotic relationship with single-celled algae – zooxanthellae – that grow inside the cells of coral polyps and photosynthetically produce oxygen and nutrients, which are released as a kind of rent directly into the coral tissues. Coral flourishes close to the surface in clear, well-circulated tropical seawater warmed to a temperature of between 21° and 27°C.

Twenty years ago, Cahuita had a superb fringing reef – an aquatic version of the Hanging Gardens of Babylon. Today, much of it is dead following uplift during the 1991 earthquake and silt washing down from mainland rivers. Coral growth is hampered by freshwater runoff and by turbidity from land-generated sediments, which clog their pores so that zooxanthellae can no longer breathe. Along almost the entire Talamanca coast and the interior, trees are being logged, exposing the topsoil to the gnawing effects of tropical rains. The rivers bring agricultural runoff, too – poisonous pesticides used in the banana plantations and fertilizers ideal for the proliferation of seabed grasses and algae that starve coral of vital oxygen. It is only a matter of time before the reef is completely gone.

Prospects for the reef at Gandoca-Manzanillo are equally grim.

entry costs $10), three kilometers south of Cahuita midway along the park; the trail takes about two hours with time to stop for a swim. You must wade the Perozoso (Sloth) River just west of Punta Cahuita.

The main park entrance is about 400 meters west of Highway 36, about three kilometers south of Cahuita (the Sixaola-bound bus will drop you off near the entrance). You can drive to Puerto Vargas from here; the entrance gate is locked after hours.

Camping is not permitted.

Puerto Viejo and Vicinity

◖ PUERTO VIEJO

About 13 kilometers south of Cahuita, the road forks just after Hone Creek (also spelled Home Creek). The main road turns east toward Bribrí; a spur leads three kilometers to Playa Negra, a black-sand beach that curls east to Puerto Viejo, enclosing a small bay with a capsized barge in its center. The tiny headland of Punta Pirikiki at its eastern end separates Puerto Viejo from the sweep of beaches—Playa Pirikiki, Playa Chiquita, and others—that run all the way to Manzanillo and Panamá. You can walk along the beach from Cahuita at low tide.

Puerto Viejo is one of the most happenin' spots in Costa Rica. The discos are hopping, and, on peak weekends, you can't find a room to save your soul. Nonetheless, it is low-key and funky. The surfer, backpacker, and counterculture crowds are firmly rooted here and dominate the scene, having settled and established bistros and restaurants alongside the locals. Drugs traded up the coast from Colombia find their way here, and the whiff of ganja (marijuana) drifts on the air. Violent crime has risen accordingly.

The first deluxe hotels, however, have opened. Malls have arrived. And a huge 398-slip marina was proposed but was killed in 2008 due to local opposition.

The overpriced **Caribe Butterfly Garden** (8 A.M.–4 P.M. daily, $5), at Cabinas Calalú east of town, has a netted garden with about

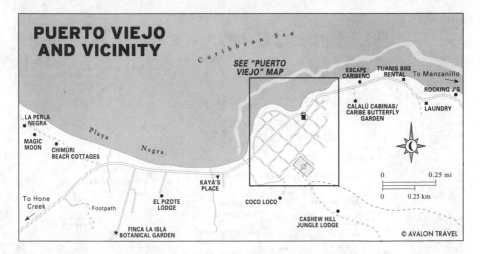

PUERTO VIEJO AND VICINITY

Caribbean Sea

SEE "PUERTO VIEJO" MAP

ESCAPE CARIBEÑO
TUANIS BIKE RENTAL
To Manzanillo

ROCKING J'S

CALALÚ CABINAS/ CARIBE BUTTERFLY GARDEN
LAUNDRY

LA PERLA NEGRA

MAGIC MOON
CHIMÚRI BEACH COTTAGES

Playa Negra

KAYA'S PLACE

To Hone Creek
Footpath
EL PIZOTE LODGE
COCO LOCO

FINCA LA ISLA BOTANICAL GARDEN
CASHEW HILL JUNGLE LODGE

0   0.25 mi
0   0.25 km

© AVALON TRAVEL

20 species of butterflies. Also overpriced is **Cacao Trails** (tel. 506/2756-8186, www .cacaotrails.com, $25), at Hone Creek. This cacao farm with a tiny "chocolate museum" also has crocodiles, a snake exhibit, a museum on indigenous culture, and a botanical garden, plus canoeing ($25) on canals through the cacao plantation. Stay a while and enjoy a meal at the thatched restaurant.

Viewpoint Resort Hotel (tel. 560/2750-8038, www.viewpoint-resorthotel.com), a private 30-acre nature park about four kilometers south of Cahuita, midway between Cahuita and Hone Creek, offers magnificent views up and down the coast from a hilltop *mirador* amid forest; it's a stiff hike uphill. Day guests get use of a small swimming pool and sundeck, an oversize chess game under a shade canopy, and hiking trails that lead into the forest. It has a shuttle service. Day use costs $3, or $5 including the swimming pool.

Finca la Isla Botanical Garden

This five-hectare botanical garden and farm (tel. 506/2750-0046, jardbot@racsa.co.cr, 10 A.M.–4 P.M. Fri.–Mon., $5 admission, $10 with guided tour for three people or more), one kilometer west of town, is a treat for anyone interested in nature. Here, Lindy and Peter Kring grow spices, exotic fruits, and ornamental

plants for sale. You can sample the fruits and even learn about chocolate production. There's also a self-guided booklet. Toucans and sloths are commonly seen, and poison-dart frogs make their homes in the bromeliads grown for sale. You're virtually guaranteed to see them hopping around underfoot even as you step from your car! The *finca* is 400 meters from the road (200 meters west of El Pizote Lodge) and is signed. Lunches are offered by arrangement.

Keköldi Indigenous Reserve

The 3,547-hectare Reserva Indígena Keköldi, in the hills immediately west of Puerto Viejo, extends south to the borders of the Gandoca-Manzanillo refuge. It is home to some 200 Bribrís and Cabecar people. Reforestation and other conservation projects are ongoing. Gloria Mayorga, coauthor of *Taking Care of Sibo's Gift,* educates tourists on indigenous history and ways.

You can visit the **Iguana Farm** ($1.50) where green iguanas are raised; the turnoff is 400 meters south of Hone Creek, beside Abastacedor El Cruce, then 200 meters along the dirt road.

The **Talamanca Association for Ecotourism and Conservation** (ATEC, tel./fax 506/2750-0191 www.ateccr.org, 8 A.M.–9 P.M. Mon.–Sat. and 10 A.M.–6 P.M. Sun.) arranges tours (from $20 half day, $35 full day). The

THE CARIBBEAN COAST

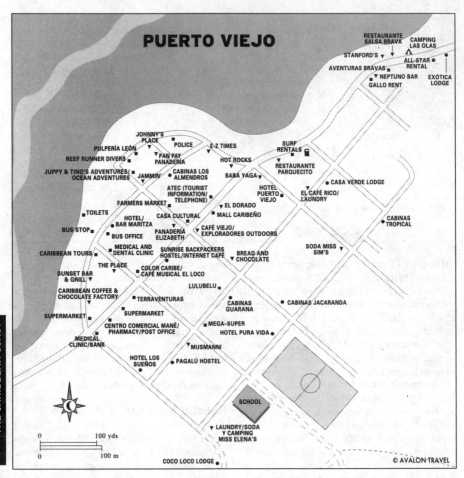

PUERTO VIEJO

RESTAURANTE SALSA BRAVA
CAMPING LAS OLAS
STANFORD'S
AVENTURAS BRAVAS
ALL-STAR RENTAL
NEPTUNO BAR
GALLO RENT
EXÓTICA LODGE

JOHNNY'S PLACE
PULPERÍA LEÓN
POLICE
E-Z TIMES
REEF RUNNER DIVERS
PAN PAY PANADERÍA
HOT ROCKS
SURF RENTALS
JUPPY & TINO'S ADVENTURES/ OCEAN ADVENTURES
JAMMIN'
CABINAS LOS ALMENDROS
BABA YAGA
RESTAURANTE PARQUECITO
ATEC (TOURIST INFORMATION/ TELEPHONE)
CASA VERDE LODGE
FARMERS MARKET
HOTEL PUERTO VIEJO
EL CAFÉ RICO/ LAUNDRY
TOILETS
EL DORADO
MALL CARIBEÑO
HOTEL/ BAR MARITZA
CASA CULTURAL
CABINAS TROPICAL
BUS STOP
CAFÉ VIEJO/ EXPLORADORES OUTDOORS
BUS OFFICE
PANADERÍA ELIZABETH
CARIBBEAN TOURS
MEDICAL AND DENTAL CLINIC
SUNRISE BACKPACKERS HOSTEL/INTERNET CAFÉ
BREAD AND CHOCOLATE
SODA MISS SIM'S
THE PLACE
COLOR CARIBE/ CAFÉ MUSICAL EL LOCO
SUNSET BAR & GRILL
LULUBELU
CARIBBEAN COFFEE & CHOCOLATE FACTORY
TERRAVENTURAS
CABINAS GUARANA
CABINAS JACARANDA
SUPERMARKET
SUPERMARKET
CENTRO COMERCIAL MANÉ/ PHARMACY/POST OFFICE
MEGA-SUPER
HOTEL PURA VIDA
MEDICAL CLINIC/BANK
MUSMANNI
HOTEL LOS SUEÑOS
PAGALÚ HOSTEL

SCHOOL

0   100 yds
0   100 m

LAUNDRY/SODA Y CAMPING MISS ELENA'S
COCO LOCO LODGE

© AVALON TRAVEL

Costa Rican Association of Community-Based Rural Tourism

(tel. 506/2248-9470, www.actuarcostarica.com) also offers tours.

The **Kéköldi Scientific Center** (tel. 506/2756-8136, www.kekoldi.org) works to safeguard the local environment through research projects. It welcomes volunteers and offers dorm accommodation ($20 per night including meals). Ad you can donate to **The Bridge** (tel. 506/2750-0524, www.elpuente -thebridge.org), a community assistance organization that works to help indigenous communities help themselves.

Entertainment and Events

Puerto Viejo is known for its lively bars and discos, and folks travel from as far afield as Limón to bop. The prize dance spots are **Stanford's** (tel. 506/2750-0016, 9 P.M.–2 A.M. Wed.–Sun.) for reggae! reggae! reggae!; and **Johnny's Place** (tel. 506/2750-0445, 6 P.M.–2:30 A.M. Mon., noon–2:30 A.M. Tues.–Sat.), where a bonfire draws patrons to dance in the sand.

The happenin' bar at last visit was the **Hot Rocks Bar** (6 P.M. until the last guest staggers home), which shows open-air movies nightly and epitomizes Puerto Viejo's laid-back

© CHRISTOPHER P. BAKER

girl with dog on the beach at Puerto Viejo

philosophy; its cocktail list runs from mojitos to *orgasmos*.

Baba Yaga (tel. 506/2750-0587) is the hot spot on Sunday and Monday nights, with reggae, while **Bar Maritza** (tel. 506/2750-0003), on the waterfront, also packs 'em in Fri.–Sun. nights. Also on Fridays, DJ Dodo spins at **Sunset Bar & Grill** (no tel.), 100 meters south of Maritza.

El Dorado (tel. 506/2750-0604, 8 A.M.–midnight daily), on the main drag, has a bar, pool table, board games, and movies on a TV.

The **ArteViva Festival** (www.arteviva-puertoviejo.com), each fall, features fireworks, live music, and art exhibits.

Sports and Recreation

The local community organization **ATEC** (tel./fax 506/2750-0191 www.ateccr.org, 8 A.M.–9 P.M. Mon.–Sat. and 10 A.M.–6 P.M. Sun.) offers hiking and nature excursions, including into the Keköldi reserve. Hiking and horseback trips into Keköldi are also offered by Mauricio Salazar from Beach Cottages Chimúri (seven hours, $25 pp, including box lunch and a contribution to the Indian

Association). Three-day trips cost $140, including overnight stays with the locals.

Caribbean Tours (tel. 506/2750-0306, www.ptoviejotours.com) offers a range of tours from local jungle hikes to tours to Boca del Toro, in Panamá. **Terraventuras** (tel. 506/2750-0750, www.terraventuras.com) offers similar trips.

Rolf, of **Bushmaster Expeditions** (tel./fax 506/2750-0283, www.cabinas-tropical.com), offers nature tours to Gandoca ($40).

All-Star Rental (tel. 506/2750-0511) rents snorkeling gear ($15 half day, $20 all day), sea kayaks ($25 half day, $40 full day), and Jet Skis.

Puerto Viejo is legendary among the surfing crowd. November through April, especially, the village is crowded with surfers, who come for a killer six-meter, storm-generated wave called La Salsa Brava. Beach Break, at Playa Cocles, about three kilometers south of Puerto Viejo, is good for novices and intermediates. Snorkelers should use extreme caution in these waters, and never snorkel during rough weather; at least two snorkelers drowned in 2008.

Salsa Brava beach, Puerto Viejo

Reef Runner Divers (tel. 506/2750-0480, www.reefrunnerdivers.com) offers guided dive tours ($50 one tank, $80 two tanks, $60 night dive), PADI certification ($325), and dolphin and snorkeling tours. **Juppy & Tino Adventures** (tel. 506/2750-0621) rents kayaks, boogie boards, and snorkeling and surfing gear; it also has kayak tours to Gandoca.

Aventuras Bravas (tel. 506/2750-2000, junglejamjohn@mail.com) also has kayak tours, shuttles to Boca del Toro (in Panamá), and a surf school that guarantees you'll get standing on a board.

Shopping

Color Caribe (tel. 506/2750-0075, 9 A.M.–8 P.M. daily), on the main drag, stocks a great selection of clothing, jewelry, and souvenirs, including hand-painted and silk-screened clothing, plus hammocks and colorful wind chimes. **LuluBelu** (tel. 506/2750-0394, 9 A.M.–9 P.M. daily), one block east of the main drag, sells an original range of ceramics, jewelry, and miscellany.

Accommodations

Demand is high; make your reservation in advance or secure a room as soon as you arrive. Beware touts who await as the bus arrives and try to entice you to specific lodgings—they're known to tell lies to dissuade you from any specific place you may already have in mind. The following are the best of dozens of options.

CAMPING

The beachfront **Camping Las Olas** (tel. 506/2750-0424, $5 pp low season, $8 pp high season), on the east side of town, is well run and has large tents under metal shade platforms. It has basic toilets and showers. **Soda y Camping Miss Elena** (tel. 506/2750-0580), on the southwest side of the village, charges $5 per person low season, $10 high season with your own tent ($2 pp extra for tent and cushion rental). Miss Elena is a charmer and offers storage, baths, hammocks, parking, and American breakfasts.

UNDER $25

Backpackers have two great options. The first is **Rocking J's** (tel. 506/2750-0665,

ATEC: GRASSROOTS ECOTOURISM

The grassroots **Asociación Talamanca de Ecoturismo y Conservación** (ATEC, tel./fax 506/2750-0191, www.ateccr.org, 8 A.M.-9 P.M. Mon.-Sat. and 10 A.M.-6 P.M. Sun.), in Puerto Viejo, trains locals as approved guides and sponsors environmental and cultural tours of the Talamanca coast (from $20 half day, $35 full day).

Options include "African-Caribbean Culture and Nature Walks," trips to the Keköldi and other indigenous reserves, rainforest hikes, snorkeling and fishing, bird and night walks, overnight "Adventure Treks" into the Gandoca-Manzanillo reserve, and an arduous eight-day trek over the Talamancas. Trips are limited to six people.

www.rockingjs.com, $5 hammocks, $6 tents, $7 pp dorm, $20 private room, $25 tree house, $50–60 suites, $350 house), a splendid and well-run backpackers' haven landscaped with ceramics and seats roughly hewn from tree trunks. You can pitch your tent at one of the sheltered campsites beneath shade eaves, or sleep outside at the "hammock hotel," with hammocks under shade canopies. It also has two dorm rooms, plus private rooms in varying configurations with lofty bunks and desks below; rooms share two solar-heated showers and five cold-water showers. Other accommodation options here include a tree house, suites, and a three-story house. Guests can use a community kitchen, plus there's laundry, grill, and secure parking, and an upstairs bar with live music midweek. Kayaks and bicycles are available for rent.

Opened in August 2008, the German-run **Pagalú Hostel** (tel. 506/2750-1930, www.pagalu.com, $9 pp dorm, $20 s or $22 d shared bathroom, $25 s or $28 d private bathroom) elevated the concept of hostel accommodation to a whole new level with its beautiful contemporary design. It makes great use of space, with a huge open-air lounge with kitchen. All rooms have ceiling fans, super clean and tasteful bathrooms with glass-brick walls and plenty of real hot water, plus thoughtful extras such as bedside halogen reading lights and shelving. One room is wheelchair equipped, and there's secure parking.

Sunrise Backpackers Hostel (tel. 506/2750-0028, sunrisebackpackers@hotmail.es, $14 s/d shared bathroom, $25 s/d private

bathroom) has an upstairs tent deck, plus a dorm and 13 private rooms (some are singles, others are doubles), all spartan and with particle-board walls. It has a pleasant café and Internet café.

Less appealing, but still popular with surfers is the venerable **Hotel Puerto Viejo** (tel. 506/2750-0620, $5–8 pp shared bath, $10 pp private). It has 72 small, spartan rooms with fans, mosquito nets, and shared, tiled bathrooms (upstairs rooms are preferable). Larger, more appealing cabins are at the rear. It has a community kitchen and surf school.

$25-50

The **Hotel Maritza** (tel. 506/2750-0003, fax 506/2750-0313, $35 s, $40 d *cabinas*), on the beachfront, has 14 clean rooms with ceiling fans, double and single beds, and private baths with hot water. On weekends, the bar and disco make the walls throb. There's parking.

I love **Cabinas Jacaranda** (tel./fax 506/2750-0069, www.cabinasjacaranda.net, from $20 s or $28 d low season, from $25 s or $32 d high season), with 14 cabins set in an exquisite garden, all with private bathroom and hot water. Furnishings are basic but delightful, with subdued tropical walls and colorful mosaic floors throughout. Japanese paper lanterns, mats, Guatemalan bedspreads, hammocks, and mosquito nets are nice touches. A garden massage is offered, and there's a communal kitchen.

For heartfelt hospitality and positive vibes, I recommend **Kaya's Place** (tel. 506/2750-0690, www.kayasplace.com, $14 s or $21 d

© CHRISTOPHER P. BAKER

Sunrise Backpackers Hostel

shared bath, $20–55 s, $30–65 d private low season; $19 s or $27 d shared bath, $25–60 s, $35–70 d private high season), a two-story stone-and-timber lodge supported by tree trunks washed up from the beach. It has 26 rooms of varying sizes and types, all charmingly if simply furnished with hardwood beds and furniture, screened windows, and walls in Caribbean pastels (however, dust from the road is a problem). Some rooms have huge double bunks. It has an Internet café and Wi-Fi. Parking, a swimming pool, and a sunset *mirador* (lookout) were planned.

For out-of-town seclusion I like **Chimúri Beach Cottages** (tel./fax 506/2750-0119, www.chimuribeach.com, $29–55 s/d), west of town, with three nice log-and-thatch cabins set on pleasant grounds. Each is a different size; one, in Caribbean style, has a colorful gingerbread motif and a loft bedroom plus kitchenette and hot water. A three-person unit also has a loft bedroom. Two have kitchens. Owner Mauricio Salazar, a generous, genteel host, offers guided day trips into the Keköldi Indigenous Reserve. Low-season rates are variable.

In the village, the delightful, bargain-priced, Italian-run **Cabinas Guarana** (tel. 506/2750-0244, www.hotelguarana.com, $25 s or $30 d low season, $30 s or $37 d high season) is entered by a charming lobby with bar. It has 12 simple but clean and tastefully decorated rooms with colorful sponge-washed walls and tasteful ethnic fabrics, plus fans, tile floors, mosquito nets, and private bath with hot water. Larger cabins have louvered windows and patios with hammocks. They're set in a lush garden with a tree house. Guests get use of a kitchen, and there's a laundry and secure parking.

One of the nicest options, and a superb bargain, is the clinically clean, Swiss-run **Casa Verde Lodge** (tel. 506/2750-0015, www.cabinascasaverde.com, $28–42 s, $30–48 d low season; $32–48 s, $34–62 d high season). It has six cabins, five double rooms, and two single rooms, each with ceiling fans, mosquito nets, and lots of light, plus hot water in spotlessly clean showers and bathrooms. Wide balconies have hammocks. There's also a small bungalow, romantic as all get out, plus Casa Topo. Features include a gift store, a laundry,

Pagalú Hostel

secure parking, a tour booth, a lovely café, and a beautiful landscaped swimming pool with raised whirlpool tub. The lush garden includes a poison-frog garden. At last visit, there were plans to open a dorm as well.

Nearby, the German-run **Cabinas Tropical** (tel. 506/2750-0645, www.cabinas-tropical .com, $30 s or $35 d low season, $35 s or $40 d high season) has eight pleasing rooms: clean and airy, with ceiling fans, huge showers with hot water, mosquito nets, and wide French doors opening onto little verandas. Smaller single rooms are dingy; three newer rooms are larger and have refrigerators and balconies. It's quiet and secure. There's also parking.

I always enjoy resting my head at **Coco Loco** (tel./fax 506/2750-0281, www.cocoloco lodge.com, $30–45 s/d low season, $35–50 s/d high season), where eight handsome Polynesian-style *cabinas* are raised on stilts amid lawns. The log-and-thatch huts are simply furnished but crafted with exquisite care. They have mosquito nets over the beds and hammocks on the porches. Simple breakfasts are served on a raised deck. Two two-room

bungalows with kitchen are also available. The Austrian owners offer tours.

East of the village, **Calalú Cabinas** (tel. 506/2750-0042, www.bungalowscalalu.com, $28–45 s, $36–45 d) has five handsome little A-frame thatch huts in a compact garden, each cross-ventilated through screened louvered windows, with large walk-in showers and porches with hammocks. Three units have kitchens; all have fans and hot water. It has a small pool. A surcharge applies for credit cards.

$50-100

The **Cabinas Los Almendros** (tel. 510/2750-0235, www.cabinaslosalmendros.com, $40 s or $60 d rooms, $70 up to six people for apartments) is a modern structure with 10 rooms, four cabins, and three apartments around a courtyard with secure parking. The clean, spacious rooms are cross-ventilated and have both front and back entrances, double and single beds, ceiling fans, tile floors, Wi-Fi, and private bathrooms with hot water.

El Pizote Lodge (tel. 506/2750-0088, www.pizotelodge.com, $55 s/d standard,

$66–93 s/d bungalow, $93–96 s/d cabin low season; $63 standard, $79–109 bungalow, $106–108 cabin high season), inland of Playa Negra, is set in nicely landscaped grounds complete with giant hardwoods and sweeping lawns—a fine setting for eight small but clean and atmospheric rooms with four shared bathrooms with huge screened windows. There are also six bungalows and two houses. Four luxury bungalows have air-conditioning, refrigerators, and hot water. The lodge even has a swimming pool, volleyball court, and a pool table. The breeze-swept restaurant gets good reviews.

About 400 meters east of town, the Italian-run **Escape Caribeño** (tel./fax 506/2750-0103, www.escapecaribeno.com, $65–75 s, $70–80 d) has 11 attractive hardwood cabins with double beds (some also have bunks) with mosquito nets, plus clean bathrooms with hot water, minibars, fans, and hammocks on the porch. They're widely spaced amid landscaped gardens and reached by raised wooden walkways. It also has brick-and-stucco bungalows with kitchenettes, plus a wood-paneled house for four people ($65 per day, one-week minimum).

In a similar vein, although less appealing, is the **La Perla Negra** (tel. 506/2750-0111, www.perlanegra-beachresort.com, $40 s or $45 d low season, $80 s or $100 d high season, $120 suites year-round), on Playa Negra. It has 24 spacious rooms in a two-story, all-hardwood structure cross-ventilated with glassless screened windows, charming albeit minimally appointed bathrooms with large walk-in showers, and bare-bones furnishings. There's a lap pool, sundeck, and bar, plus tennis court and basketball. Rates include breakfast and tax.

I like the secluded and vibrant **Cashew Hill Jungle Lodge** (tel. 506/2750-0256, www.cashewhilllodge.co.cr, $90–110 s/d), on a hill south of the soccer field. Six simple cottages have heaps of charm thanks to lively Caribbean color schemes and other endearing artistic touches. They vary from one- to three-bedroom units, but all have screens, mosquito nets, broad decks, and hammocks, plus Wi-Fi. This offbeat charmer is the creation of Erich and Wende Strube, your delightful hosts.

$100-150
Samasati Nature Retreat (tel. 506/2756-8015 or U.S. tel. 800/563-9643, www.samasati.com, $98 s or $190 d guesthouse, $185 s or $270 d bungalows, including meals and tax) is a holistic retreat hidden amid 100 hectares of private rainforest on the mountainside one kilometer inland of Hone Creek. It specializes in yoga and other meditative practices, but anyone is welcome. Accommodations are in 10 handsome yet ascetically furnished Japanese-style log cabins with ocean and jungle vistas, all with verandas, loft bedrooms, and tiled walk-in showers. Larger units have mezzanine bedrooms with wraparound windows. There are also five simpler rooms in a guesthouse with shared bathrooms, plus three two-bedroom *casas* with living rooms and kitchens. Vegetarian meals (and seafood) are served buffet-style in a handsome lodge open to the elements. It has a whirlpool tub. You'll need a four-wheel-drive vehicle for the rugged climb up the mountain.

In 2009, the region gained its first deluxe boutique hotel, **Le Caméléon** (tel. 506/2582-0140, www.fashionhotels.info or www.lecameleon.cr). This chic retro-contemporary pad promises to draw fashionistas to town with its all-white vogue decor.

Food
Puerto Viejo is blessed with a cosmopolitan range of eateries, even gourmet cuisine.

For breakfast, I head to **Café Rico** (tel. 506/2750-0510, 6 A.M.–2 P.M. Fri.–Wed.), a laid-back place serving on a palm-fringed veranda; Roger, the English owner, serves huevos rancheros ($4), omelettes ($4), granola with yogurt and fruit ($3.50), pancakes, and sandwiches. I recommend the Annarosa special: fried potatoes with cheddar cheese, fried eggs, and bacon ($4). Competing in style and substance, **Bread and Chocolate** (tel. 506/2750-0723, 6:30 A.M.–6:30 P.M. Wed.–Sat., and 6:30 A.M.–2:30 P.M. Sun.) has killer cinnamon oatmeal pancakes ($4), crispy sautéed potatoes with jerk barbecue sauce, sandwiches, brownie sundaes, and more.

Alternately, consider **Pan Pay Panadería**

(tel. 506/2750-0081, 7 A.M.–5 P.M. daily), which serves omelettes and scramble breakfasts (from $2.50) and has fruit salads ($2) and fruit-filled pastries, croissants, breads, tortillas, and coffees. The **Caribbean Coffee & Chocolate Factory** (tel. 506/2750-0850, 7 A.M.–10 P.M. Sun.–Wed. and 7 A.M.–midnight Thurs.–Sat.) is a cool spot to enjoy home-baked muffins, macadamia cookies, multigrain breads, and veggie dishes, plus organic coffee and chocolate drinks. It has free Wi-Fi. And the **Musmanni** bakery chain was due to open an outlet here in 2009.

Justifiably popular by night, **Chile Rojo** (tel. 506/2750-0025, 9 A.M.–10 P.M. daily) has a simple open-air setting. The Asian-inspired menu packs in diners who know a good thing. I recommend the veggie samosa with tamarind chutney ($3.50), Thai fish and coconut soup ($6), and the delicious green curry with coconut milk and veggies ($9).

Restaurante Tamara (tel. 506/2750-0148, 11:30 A.M.–10 P.M. Thurs.–Tues., $5–10) has a shaded patio done up in Rastafarian colors. The menu runs to burgers and *típico* dishes such as fried fish with *patacones* (plantain), plus great *batidos* (milk shakes). For genuine Caribbean fare, head to **Jammin'** (tel. 506/8826-4332, 9 A.M.–9 P.M. daily), a small Rasta-styled *soda* with tree-trunk stools. I recommend the jerk chicken ($5) and roast fish ($3.50). It has tremendous rootsy Jamaican atmosphere.

I like the open-air, offbeat, Spanish-run **Salsa Brava** (tel. 506/2750-0241, noon–11 P.M. Tues.–Sun., $4–15), with rainbow-hued furniture. The menu includes tuna ceviche salad, Caesar salad with chicken teriyaki, and grilled garlic fish, plus sangria and ice cream. Portions are huge and the fare is surprisingly good. Nearby, the beachfront **Restaurante Parquecito** (tel. 506/2750-0748, noon–midnight daily, $5–10) offers a fabulous ambience, with pendulous surfboards. It's good for cheap *casados* and specializes in simple seafood.

Café Viejo (tel. 506/2750-0817, 6–10 P.M. daily), the snazziest place in town, serves good Italian fare, including pizzas (from $3), pastas ($5), and a large dessert menu.

Stanford's (tel. 506/2750-0016, 9 P.M.–2 A.M. Wed.–Sun.), with a fine beachside perch, has cleaned up its act of late and is now a lovely place to dine on ceviche ($5), garlic shrimp ($7), and other seafoods.

At night, a delightful Jamaican lady named **Bou Bou** sells jerk chicken from her streetside stand outside Johnny's Place. And "Miss Sam" bakes tarts and bread and offers meals at **Soda Miss Sam's.**

For ice creams, sundaes, and shakes, head to **Lechería Las Lapas** (no tel., 10 A.M.–10 P.M. daily).

There's a *feria agrícola* (farmers market) every Saturday morning.

Information and Services

ATEC (tel./fax 506/2750-0191 www.ateccr.org, 8 A.M.–9 P.M. Mon.–Sat. and 10 A.M.–6 P.M. Sun.) is the informal node of local activity and acts as a tourist information bureau.

There's a **medical clinic** (tel. 506/2750-0079, or emergency tel. 506/8870-8029, 10 A.M.–7 P.M. Mon.–Fri. and weekends for emergencies). There are **dental clinics** 50 meters inland from the bus stop (tel. 506/2750-0303, or 506/2750-0389 for emergencies) and next to Bread & Chocolate café (tel. 506/8336-2339, 9 A.M.–noon and 1–6 P.M. Mon.–Fri., and 9 A.M.–2 P.M. Sat.).

The **police station** (tel. 506/2750-0230) is next to Johnny's Place. There's a **bank** with ATM, plus at **post office** (tel. 506/2750-0404) and pharmacy in Centro Comercial Mané, which also has a **laundry** (8 A.M.–7 P.M. daily). **Café Rico** also has laundry service using biodegradable products and offers free coffee while you wait.

The ATEC office has public telephones (tel. 506/2750-0188) and Internet access.

Getting There

The bus fare from San José to Puerto Viejo is $8, and from Limón $2. Transportes Mepe (tel. 506/2257-8129) buses depart the Gran Caribe terminal in San José for Cahuita ($8) at 6 A.M., 10 A.M., 1:30 P.M., and 3:30 P.M. They continue to Puerto Viejo.

Return buses depart Puerto Viejo (tel.

© CHRISTOPHER P. BAKER

chilling at Playa Cocles

506/2750-0023) for San José at 7:30 A.M., 9 A.M., 11 A.M., and 4 P.M.; and for Limón hourly 6:45 A.M.–7:30 P.M. The Puerto Limón–Puerto Viejo buses are usually crowded; get to the station early.

Interbus (tel. 506/283-5573, www.interbus online.com) operates minibus shuttles from San José.

Getting Around
ATEC can arrange taxis.

Surf Rentals (tel. 506/8375-7328, surf rentals@gmail.com) rents beach cruiser bikes ($1 per hour, $5 daily) and scooters ($15 one hour, $48 per day). Each scooter is sponsored, with a portion of the rental fee donated for charity; for example "Drummer Boy" is named for a local boy who wants a drum set.

Poás Rent-a-Car (tel. 506/2750-0400) has an outlet here.

PLAYA COCLES TO PUNTA UVA
South of Puerto Viejo, the paved road runs via Punta Cocles and Punta Uva to Manzanillo, a fishing village at the end of the road, 13 kilometers southeast of Puerto Viejo. Coral-colored Playa Cocles runs southeast for four kilometers from Puerto Viejo to the rocky point of Punta Cocles, beyond which **Playa Chiquita** runs south four kilometers to Punta Uva, where caimans can be seen in the swampy estuary of the Río Uva. From here, a five-kilometer-long gray sand beach curls gently southeast to Manzanillo. Coral reefs lie offshore, offering good snorkeling and diving.

There are no settlements (except the tiny hamlet of Punta Uva).

A Swiss couple offers tours and demos at their cocoa farm and chocolate "factory," **Chocoart** (tel. 506/2750-0075, chocoart@ racsa.co.cr, 8 A.M.–5 P.M. daily, $15 pp, by reservation only), at Playa Chiquita. You'll learn all about cacao production, from the bean to the chocolate bar, on their hilly farm.

Fascinated by butterflies? **Mariposario Punta Uva** (tel. 506/2750-0086, 7 A.M.–5 P.M. daily, $5 adults, children free), a netted butterfly garden and reproduction center in the hills above Punta Uva, has some 20 butterfly

© CHRISTOPHER P. BAKER

rastafarian relaxing at Punta Uva

species within its netted garden, and monkeys and other animals are easily seen on trails into the surrounding forest.

The dirt road to the butterfly garden ascends one kilometer to **La Ceiba Private Biological Reserve** (tel. 506/2750-0710, www.rp ceiba.com, open by appointment), an animal rescue center that works to rehabilitate wildlife for reintroduction into the forest. The delightful Spanish couple that runs it, Francisco and Angela, offer guided hikes ($30 pp four hours). The forest reserve and two-hectare garden are great for birding and animal sightings, and a lagoon is a poison-dart frog breeding ground good for a nocturnal "sex show" tour. La Ceiba rents three wooden cabins with kitchens, huge decks, and modern bathrooms; they're perfect for families.

Sports and Recreation

Seahorse Stables (tel. 506/2750-0468, www.horsebackridingincostarica.com, from $55), near Punta Cocles, offers horseback rides by reservation. Edwin Salem, the gracious Argentinian owner, arranges occasional polo matches on the beach. He also offers sailing lessons on his 18-foot Hobie Cat, as well as overnight turtle-watching tours ($150 including lodging), plus surfing trips.

Punta Uva Dive Center (tel. 506/2759-9191, www.puntauvadivecenter.com) has scuba trips to the reefs of Gandoca-Manzanillo, as does **Crocodive Caribe** (tel. 506/2750-2136), in La Terraza Cocles plaza.

Crazy Monkey Canopy Ride (tel. 800/317-4108, www.crazymonkeycanopytour.com), at Almonds & Corals Lodge Tent Camp (tel. 506/2271-3000, www.almondsandcorals.com), has zipline rides at 8 A.M. and 2 P.M. ($40).

Treat yourself to a decadent chocolate body rub and cacao butter massage at the **Pure Jungle Spa** (tel. 506/2750-0080), at La Costa de Papito.

Accommodations

UNDER $25

At **Cabinas El Tesoro** (tel. 506/2750-0128, www.puertoviejo.net/cabinaselteroro.htm, $11.50 pp dorm, $20–55 s/d private rooms) about one kilometer from Puerto Viejo, 11 simply furnished rooms have orthopedic mattresses, screened windows, fans, and private baths with hot water, plus hammocks on patios. There's also a his-and-hers surf dorm at the back, with a communal kitchen, toilets, and showers. Three more upscale rooms have earth-tone stucco, cross-ventilation, cable TV, refrigerators, and large walk-in showers; two have air-conditioning. It's well run by a friendly, in-the-know American, Charlie Wanger. There's free Internet, coffee, and parking, and free movies are shown nightly on a wide-screen television.

$25-50

La Casita (in Jamaica, tel. 876/974-2870, fax 876/974-2651, info@harmonyhall.com, $300/350 weekly low/high season) is a delightful albeit rustic log-and-thatch *casita* set in lush gardens, with forest all around. It's just you and the monkeys and geckos. A path leads to Playa Cocles, and a grocery store and restaurant are a short stroll.

In a similar vein, I like the German-run **El Tucán Lodge** (tel. 506/2750-0026, www.eltucanjunglelodge.com, $28 s, $40 d), a lovely spot to lay your head in the forest in stylishly simple wooden cabins on the edge of the Río Caño Negro, at Cocles.

$50-100

La Costa de Papito (tel. 506/2750-0704, www.lacostadepapito.com, $48–73 s/d low season, $54–78 s/d high season, including taxes), at Playa Cocles, is run by Eddie Ryan, a New York hotelier who has conjured 10 simple yet tastefully decorated bungalows at the jungle edge of a lush five-acre garden. Each has ceiling fan, leopard-skin sheets (!), exquisite tiled bathrooms, and shady porches with hammocks under thatch. Four smaller cabins have polished hardwoods and outside "rainforest" bathrooms. There's a laundry and massage, plus bicycle, surfboard, boogie board, and snorkel rentals. Hearty breakfasts are served on your porch and in a new restaurant. It has a full-service spa.

The Italian-run **Totem Hotel Resort &**

Restaurant (tel. 506/2750-0758, www.totemsite.com, $65 s or $80 d standard, $100 s/d suite) is a reasonable option on Playa Cocles. It has two types of accommodations in effusive gardens. Standards in a thatched, stone-and-timber two-story structure, although dark, have colorful decor and spacious gray-tile bathrooms. Suites boast huge lounges with terra-cotta floors and screened glassless walls opening to a walk-in landscaped pool with cascade. Two handicapped-accessible rooms were being added, along with six bungalows and six suites. There's an outdoor games room with Wi-Fi, a large thatched bar with TV, plus a surf shop. The Mediterranean restaurant doubles as an oyster bar by day.

I highly recommend 【 **Aguas Claras** (tel. 506/2750-0131, www.aguasclaras-cr.com, $70 s/d one-bedroom, $130–160 two-bedroom, $220 three-bedroom), nearby, with five adorable *casas* on well-groomed grounds. Each is a different size, accommodating 2–6 people. Of a delightful Victorian style, they have gingerbread trim, bright tropical color schemes, ceiling fans, modern tiled bathrooms with hot water, large full kitchens, and shady verandas with rattan furnishings. Miss Holly's Kitchen is here.

The **Jardín Miraflores Lodge** (tel./fax 506/2750-0038, www.mirafloreslodge.com, $25–60 s/d), at Punta Cocles, appeals to nature lovers. Choose from double rooms with shared bathroom or private bathroom and balcony with hammock, and suites with king-size beds, private bathrooms, and living areas. Downstairs rooms have kitchenettes and king-size beds plus two sofa beds. Mosquito nets hang above the beds. It also has a basic six-bed dormitory with outside bathrooms for groups only ($10 per person). The wood and bamboo hotel is adorned with Latin American fabrics, masks, and art, and vases full of fresh tropical blooms. Upstairs, cool breezes flow through the rooms. Health-conscious meals are served in a rustic *rancho*. Tours are offered. Rates include a hearty breakfast.

Playa Chiquita Lodge (tel. 506/2750-

0062, www.playachiquitalodge.com, $55 s/d low season, $70 s/d high season), three kilometers south of Punta Cocles, is appealing for its jungle ambience. Eleven colorful and spacious "bungalows" offer murals, sunken bathrooms (no hot water), fans, and leather rocking chairs on a wide veranda. You can dine alfresco under thatch in the restaurant. The lodge arranges diving and snorkeling, boat trips, and bike and horse rentals.

The Italian-run **Pachamama B&B** (tel. 506/2759-9196, www.pachamamacaribe.com, $45–75 s/d low season, $55–75 high season) enjoys a marvelous riverside forest setting amid trees festooned with epiphytes. It has two one-bedroom bungalows featuring pastel color schemes including sponge-washed floors, simple furnishings, mosquito nets, pleasing tiled bathrooms with hot water, and hardwood decks. A spacious wooden one-bedroom house is a charmer. And a two-bedroom *casa* ($100) has a lively color scheme. The overall mood is endearing.

I like **Cariblue Bungalows** (tel. 506/2750-0035, www.cariblue.com, $95–110 s/d bungalows, $220 s/d house year-round), one kilometer south of Puerto Viejo, with 15 handsome, spacious hardwood *cabinas* amid shaded lawns. Some have king-size beds. All have colorful sponge-washed decor, bamboo ceilings with fans, private bathrooms with mosaic tiles, and sliding doors opening to delightful porches with hammock. There's boogie board and bike rentals, plus a gift shop, TV lounge, and a freeform pool with whirlpool tub and wet bar. An Italian seafood restaurant serves meals under thatch. Rates include tax and buffet breakfast.

Almost identical, **Azánia Bungalows** (tel. 506/2750-0540, www.azania-costarica.com, $70 s/d low season, $85 s/d high season), next to Cariblue, is another beautiful property on lush grounds. Eight thatched, hardwood cottages with large decks with hammocks are delightfully simple and have batik blinds on all-around screened windows, queen beds plus singles in a loft, and handsome bathrooms with colorful tiles, drop-down walk-in

showers with sauna seating, and huge windows. It rents bikes. The restaurant specializes in Argentinian fare.

Of similar standard, **Casa Camarona** (tel. 506/2750-0151, www.casacamarona.co.cr, $61.50 s/d low season, $66 s/d high season) is well-run by a Tico couple and offers 18 modestly furnished, air-conditioned wooden rooms with tile floors and hot water. It has an intimate breeze-swept restaurant, La Palapa, decorated in Jamaican style. There's also a gift store, beach bar, laundry, safe parking, bicycle and kayak rental, and tours. The facilities are wheelchair accessible.

At Punta Cocles, the upscale **Villas del Caribe** (tel. 506/2750-0202, www.villasdelcaribe.com, $69 s/d standard, $79 s/d junior villa, $99 s/d villa low season; $79 s/d standard, $89 s/d junior villa, $109 s/d villa high season) has a superb location in the cusp of the bay. It has 12 colorfully furnished rooms in a two-story complex in landscaped gardens 50 meters from the beach. Fully equipped kitchen, hot water, and fans are standard. It has a restaurant and bar. The hotel is eco-conscious—even the soaps and toiletries are biodegradable. Rates include breakfast and tax.

Another Caribbean-cabin-style entity, **Hotel Kashá** (tel./fax 506/2750-0205, www.costarica-hotelkasha.com, $90 s, $110 d) offers all-inclusive packages in addition to rack rates. This place has 14 handsome hardwood bungalows set back from the road amid the forest. The units are spacious, with plenty of light, screened windows, ceiling fans, two double beds, and pleasant bathrooms with heated water and beautiful Italian ceramics. Some units are for two people; others are for four people. The hotel has a small *ranchito* restaurant and bar, plus a small pool with water cascade. Rates include tax and breakfast.

The relatively upscale **Hotel Punta Cocles** (tel. 506/2750-0337, www.hotelpuntacocles.com, $75 s/d low season, $80 s/d high season), about four kilometers south of Puerto Viejo, sprawls over covering 10 forested hectares well inland of the beach, accessed via a path. The hotel's 60 spacious, modern air-conditioned cabins (five with kitchenettes) appeal to Costa Rican families and have porches good for bird-watching. An open-air restaurant overlooks a swimming pool, and there's a whirlpool tub, game room, and TV lounge.

French-run **El Colibri Lodge** (tel. 506/2759-9036, www.elcolibrilodge.com, $50 s, $65 d), south of Punta Uva, has a lush jungle setting. Its four concrete cabins lack ventilation and get hot, but they boast hardwood floors, nice color schemes, and modern bathrooms with hot water. It has a gourmet restaurant, and trails lead to the beach. Monkeys hang out in the trees overhead, and an adjacent lagoon harbors caimans. The owners are a delight. Rates include breakfast.

OVER $100

The fanciest digs around are at the bargain-priced, French-owned **((Shawandha Lodge** (tel. 506/2750-0018, www.shawandhalodge.com, $95 s/d low season, $115 high season), one kilometer farther south at Playa Chiquita. It has 12 spacious, thatched, hardwood cabins, each marvelously furnished with simple yet beautiful modern decor, including four-poster beds, screened windows, and large verandas with hammocks. The bathrooms boast large walk-in showers with exquisite tile work. The restaurant is one of the best around, and there's a splendid open-air lounge with contempo decor. Rates include American breakfast.

Lovely, but overpriced, **Almonds & Corals Lodge Tent Camp** (tel. 506/2271-3000, www.almondsandcorals.com, $235 s or $300 d suite, $315 s or $400 d master suite), is three kilometers north of Manzanillo, with a lonesome forested setting a few leisurely steps from the beach. Each of 24 tent-huts is raised on a stilt platform and features two singles or one double bed, a locker, night lamps, table and chairs, plus mosquito nets and deck with hammock—a touch of Kenya come to the Caribbean. Very atmospheric! Separate junior suites and suites are even nicer and verge on luxe. Each cabin has its own shower and toilet in separate washhouses. Raised walkways lead to the beach, pool, snack bar, and restaurant serving Costa Rican food. You can rent kayaks, bicycles, and snorkeling gear. It has four leaves in the Certified Sustainable Tourism program but in 2008 was accused by authorities of illegally clear-cutting protected forest for an expansion.

Eclectic in the extreme, **((Tree House Lodge** (tel. 506/750-0706, www.costaricatreehouse.com, $150–390 s/d depending on the unit), at Punta Uva, is a rustic yet upscale place with a fabulous Middle Earth feel. Having recently expanded, it now offers four individual and irresistible units with forest or beach setting. The original all-wood two-story Tree House is built in and around a huge tree, with separate elements connected by a steel suspension bridge. Two bedrooms share a bathroom; a spiral staircase leads to a loft bedroom with king-size bed. The Beach Suite features a Tolkien-style dome bathroom (owners claim it's the largest in the country) with stained-glass windows and huge Jacuzzi. *Fantastic!*

Food

Totem Hotel Resort & Restaurant (tel. 506/2750-0758, noon–10 P.M. daily) has great ambience, the advantage of beach views, plus great pizza, risotto, and Italian seafood. By day it's an oyster bar.

Speaking of Italian, the finest cuisine east of San José is to be savored south of Punta Cocles at **((La Pecora Nera** (tel. 506/2750-0490, pecoranera@racsa.co.cr, 5:30 P.M.–11 P.M. Tues.–Sun. high season only, $5–20), a genuine fine-dining experience in unpretentious surrounds at fair prices. Ilario Giannono, the young Italian owner, offers delicious bruschetta, spaghetti, pizzas, calzones, and a large selection of daily specials—all exquisitely executed. I recommend the mixed starters plate, a meal in itself. A wine cellar has been added. Credit cards are not accepted. Ilario also runs the adjoining **Il Gato Ci Cora** (noon–10 P.M. daily), serving salads, pizzas, and panini.

At Punta Uva, I love the **Punta Uva Lounge** (tel. 506/2659-9048, 11 A.M.–5 P.M. daily), with simple thatched dining areas in lawns opening to the beach; it serves sandwiches and simple rice and fish dishes, plus ice cream and cocktails.

Miss Holly's Kitchen (tel. 506/2750-0131, 8 A.M.–6 P.M.) has a gourmet café with Wi-Fi. It's a great breakfast spot for omelettes and fruit salads, and for lunchtime salads and sandwiches. Nearby **La Casa del Pan** is a lovely roadside café that doubles as a French bakery and pizzeria.

At Punta Cocles, you can stock up on food at the **El Duende Gourmet** deli and grocery, or at the fully stocked **Super Pirripí.**

Services

Café Internet Río Negro (tel. 506/2750-0801, 8 A.M.–8 P.M. Mon.–Sat.) serves fruit shakes, sandwiches, and Argentinian *empanadas.*

La Terraza Cocles plaza has a bookstore and Internet café.

Manzanillo and Vicinity

MANZANILLO

This lonesome hamlet sits at the end of the road, 13 kilometers south of Puerto Viejo. The populace has lived for generations in what is now the wildlife refuge, living off the sea and using the land to farm cacao until 1979, when the *Monilia* fungus wiped out the crop. Electricity arrived in 1989, four years after the first dirt road linked it to the rest of the world. The hamlet has become a darling of the off-beat, alternative-travel set.

From Manzanillo, a five-kilometer coastal trail leads to the fishing hamlet of **Punta Mona** (Monkey Point) and the heart of Gandoca-Manzanillo National Park.

Sports and Recreation

A local cooperative, **Guías MANT** (tel. 506/2759-9064), offers birding, fishing, hiking, horseback riding, and snorkeling excursions.

Aquamor (tel. 506/2759-9012, www.green coast.com/aquamor.htm, 7 A.M.–6 P.M. daily) is a full-service dive shop offering dives ($35–95), PADI certification course ($350), snorkeling ($8–35), kayak trips (from $35), and a dolphin observation safari ($40).

Manzanillo Tarpon Expeditions (tel. 506/2759-9118 or U.S. tel. 406/586-5084, www.tarponville.com) has sportfishing packages.

Accommodations and Food

No camping on the beach is permitted. You can camp under palms at **Camping Manzanillo** (tel. 506/2759-9008, $5 pp).

Cabinas Maxi (tel. 506/2759-9086 or 2759-9042, $25 s/d standard, $35 s/d with refrigerator and TV), adjoining Restaurant/Bar Maxi, has six modern, clean, simple concrete *cabinas* with TV, fans, bamboo furnishings, and private bathrooms. Similar alternatives include **Cabinas Manzanillo** (tel. 506/2759-9033).

Pangaea (tel. 506/2759-9204, pangaea@racsa.co.cr, $25 s, $35 d including breakfast), 100 meters inland of the beach, has two simple yet pleasing, well-lit rooms with tin roofs, screened windows, fans, mosquito nets, hammocks on porches, and private bathrooms with hot water. It also has a beach house with kitchen for four people ($60).

By far the nicest digs are at the new, Dutch-run **Cabinas Faya Lobi** (tel. 506/2759-9167, www.cabyinasfayalobi.com, $25 s/d), a modern two-story building with black stone highlights. It has four cross-ventilated rooms with stone floors and quaint bathrooms with hot water and mosaics. They share a simple kitchen and an open-air lounge with hammocks.

For your own house rental, I recommend

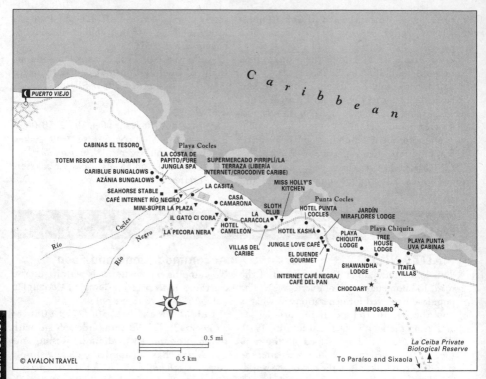

CABINAS EL TESORO
LA COSTA DE
PAPITO/PURE
JUNGLA SPA
TOTEM RESORT & RESTAURANT
CARIBLUE BUNGALOWS
AZÁNIA BUNGALOWS
SEAHORSE STABLE
CAFÉ INTERNET RÍO NEGRO
MINI-SÚPER LA PLAZA
IL GATO CI CORA
LA PECORA NERA

Playa Cocles
SUPERMERCADO PIRRIPLÍ/LA
TERRAZA (LIBERÍA
INTERNET/CROCODIVE CARIBE)
LA CASITA
CASA
CAMARONA
LA
CARACOLA
HOTEL
CAMELEÓN
VILLAS DEL
CARIBE
EL DUENDE
GOURMET
INTERNET CAFÉ NEGRA/
CAFÉ DEL PAN
CHOCOART

MISS HOLLY'S
KITCHEN
Punta Cocles
SLOTH
CLUB
HOTEL PUNTA
COCLES
JARDÍN
MIRAFLORES LODGE
Playa Chiquita
HOTEL KASHÁ
JUNGLE LOVE CAFÉ
PLAYA
CHIQUITA
LODGE
TREE
HOUSE
LODGE
PLAYA PUNTA
UVA CABINAS
SHAWANDHA
LODGE
ITAITÁ
VILLAS
MARIPOSARIO

Caribbean

PUERTO VIEJO

Río Cocles
Río Negro

0   0.5 mi
0   0.5 km

© AVALON TRAVEL

La Ceiba Private
Biological Reserve

To Paraíso and Sixaola

the all-wood, beachfront **Dolphin Lodge** (in North America tel. 406/586-5084, www.vrbo.com/18442, $175–200), east of the river outside Manzanillo and inside the reserve. It's a two-story, three-bedroom, three-bathroom beach house with kitchen. No smokers are permitted. A caretaker and his family prepare meals.

Restaurant/Bar Maxi (tel. 506/2759-9086, restmaxis@racsa.co.cr, 11:30 A.M.–10 P.M. daily, $5–15) serves *típico* dishes and seafood, such as *pargo rojo* (red snapper) and lobster. Bar Maxi is one of the liveliest spots on the Caribbean. The gloomy disco-bar downstairs is enlivened by the slap of dominoes and the blast of Jimmy Cliff and Bob Marley, and the dancing spills out onto the sandy road. The upstairs bar has a breezy terrace and gets packed to the gills on weekends and holidays, even in the middle of the day. Service can be slow and indifferent, alas.

Getting There

Buses depart Puerto Limón for Manzanillo (two hours) via Cahuita and Puerto Viejo on an irregular (but more or less hourly) basis 6 A.M.–8 P.M. daily.

☾ GANDOCA-MANZANILLO NATIONAL WILDLIFE REFUGE

The 9,446-hectare Refugio Nacional de Vida Silvestre Gandoca-Manzanillo protects a beautiful, brown-sand, palm-fringed, nine-kilometer-long, crescent-shaped beach where four species of turtles—most abundantly, leatherback turtles—come ashore to lay their eggs (Jan.–Apr. is best). Some 4,436 hectares of the park extend out to sea. The ocean has riptides and is not safe for swimming. The reserve—which is 65 percent tropical rainforest—also protects rare swamp habitats, including the only mangrove

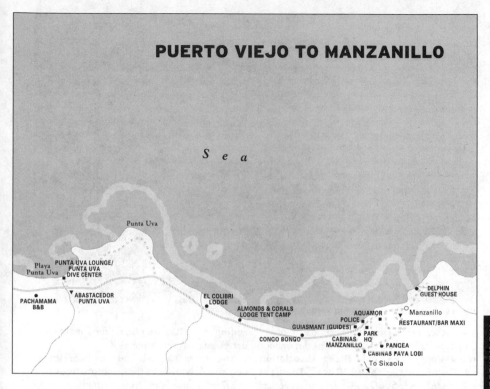

PUERTO VIEJO TO MANZANILLO

Sea

Punta Uva

Playa Punta Uva

PUNTA UVA LOUNGE/ PUNTA UVA DIVE CENTER

PACHAMAMA B&B

ABASTACEDOR PUNTA UVA

EL COLIBRI LODGE

ALMONDS & CORALS LODGE TENT CAMP

DELPHIN GUEST HOUSE

AQUAMOR
POLICE
GUIASMANT (GUIDES)

Manzanillo
RESTAURANT/BAR MAXI

CONGO BONGO

PARK HQ
CABINAS MANZANILLO

PANGEA
CABINAS FAYA LOBI

To Sixaola

forest on Costa Rica's Caribbean shores, two jolillo palm swamps, a 300-hectare cativo forest, and a live coral reef.

The large freshwater **Gandoca Lagoon,** one kilometer south of Gandoca village, has two openings into the sea. The estuary, full of red mangrove trees, is a complex world braided by small brackish streams and snakelike creeks. The mangroves shelter both a giant oyster bed and a nursery for lobster and the swift and powerful tarpon. Manatees and a rare estuarine dolphin—the *tucuxí*—swim and breed here, as do crocodiles and caimans. The park is home to at least 358 species of birds (including toucans, red-lored Amazon parakeets, and hawk-eagles) as well as margays, ocelots, pacas, and sloths.

The hamlets of Punta Uva, Manzanillo (the northern gateway), Punta Mona, and Gandoca (the southern gateway) form part of the refuge. Because local communities live within the park, it is a mixed-management reserve; the locals' needs are integrated into park-management policies. **Punta Mona Center for Sustainable Living and Education** (tel. 506/2614-5735 or 506/8391-2116, http://puntamona.org) is an organic farm and environmental center. It teaches traditional and sustainable farming techniques and other environmentally sound practices. It accepts volunteers, and internships are available. Kayaking, guided hikes, and yoga retreats are offered. It's open to day visits Tuesday, Thursday, and Saturday ($40 pp including boat transfers, guided tour, and kayaking).

ANAI (Asociación Nacional de Asuntos Indígenas, tel. 506/2224-3570, www.anai cr.org) works to protect the forest and to evolve a sustainable livelihood through reforestation

© CHRISTOPHER P. BAKER

hikers at Gandoca-Manzanillo Wildlife Refuge

and other earth-friendly methods; it offers "Talamanca Field Adventures" trips throughout the southeast. The **Costa Rican Association of Community-Based Rural Tourism** (ACTUAR, tel. 506/2248-9470, www.actuar costarica.com) offers eco-minded tours, plus homestay accommodation with locals.

Turtle Patrol

Volunteers are needed for the **Marine Turtle Conservation Project,** which conducts research and protects the turtles from predators and poachers. Contact **ANAI** (tel. 506/2224-3570, www.anaicr.org) or **ATEC** (tel./fax 506/2750-0191 www.ateccr.org) to see how you can help.

Exploring the Park

The park is easily explored simply by walking the beaches; trails also wind through the flat, lowland rainforest fringing the coast. A coastal track leads south from the east side of Manzanillo village to Gandoca village (two hours), where you can walk the beach one kilometer south to Gandoca Lagoon. Beyond the lagoon, a trail winds through the jungle,

ending at the Río Sixaola and the Panamá border. A guide is recommended.

You can hire a guide and boat in Sixaola to take you downriver to the mangrove swamps at the river mouth (dangerous currents and reefs prevent access from the ocean).

The **MINAE ranger station** (tel. 506/2759-9001, 8 A.M.–4 P.M. daily) is at the entrance to Manzanillo village; the MINAE headquarters (tel. 506/2759-9100), at Gandoca, is 0.5 kilometer inland from the beach. Entrance costs $6 but there is rarely anyone to collect the fee.

Accommodations and Food

Camping is permitted in the park, but there are no facilities.

The nearest accommodations are in the villages of Manzanillo and Gandoca, on the northern and southern entrances to the reserve, respectively.

The various accommodations at Gandoca are often closed in low season and include the breeze-swept **Cabinas Orquideas** (tel. 506/2754-2392), run by a friendly elderly couple. They have 18 rooms. Four upstairs

THE *TUCUXÍ* DOLPHIN

The *tucuxí* dolphin (*Sotalia fluviatilis*) is a rare species whose existence hereabouts, though known to local anglers for generations, only recently filtered out from the swamps of Manzanillo to the broader world. The little-known species is found in freshwater rivers, estuaries, and adjacent coastal areas of South America and has recently been found as far north as Laguna Leimus, in Nicaragua. Pods of *tucuxí* (pronounced "tooKOO-shee") interact with pods of bottle-nosed dolphins, and interspecies mating has been observed.

The **Talamanca Dolphin Foundation** (tel. 506/2759-9118; in the U.S., 3150 Graf St. #8, Bozeman, MT 59715, tel./fax 406/586-5084; www.dolphinlink.org) is a nonprofit organization that conducts research into the dolphins and offers guided boating tours.

Gandoca is **Cabinas Kaniki** (tel. 506/2754-1071, info@alberguekaniki.com, $17 pp), with three small dorm rooms with bunks and lots of light and cold-water bathrooms. You can also camp on lawns. Two cabins were to be added. Meals are served. It rents sea kayaks and has horseback rides, plus birding, hiking, and dolphin tours.

Sportfishers opt for **Tarponville** (tel. 506/2759-9118 or U.S. tel. 406/586-5084, www.tarponville.com, $100 pp including meals, or from $1,880 five-day angling package, $825 non-angler), a handsome, two-story wooden lodge inside the reserve. It offers sportfishing packages from five days. Simply furnished rooms have ceiling fans. Rates include meals.

Punta Mona Center for Sustainable Living and Education (tel. 506/2614-5735 or 506/8391-2116, http://puntamona.org, $40 pp including meals) has cabins.

Getting There

You can drive to Gandoca village via a 15-kilometer dirt road that leads north from the Bribrí–Sixaola road; the turnoff is signed about three kilometers west of Sixaola. Keep left at the crossroads 1.5 kilometers down the road. If you get caught short of money, there's a roadside 24-hour **ATM** at Finca Sixaola, midway to Gandoca.

rooms have bunks and shared bath with cold water only for $12 per person ($20 with meals). Others have private bathrooms ($25 pp, or $30 with meals). The best bet in

Río Sixaola Region

BRIBRÍ AND VICINITY

From Hone Creek, Highway 36 winds inland through the foothills of the Talamancas and descends to **Bribrí,** a small town 60 kilometers south of Puerto Limón, and the administrative center for the region. It is surrounded by banana plantations spread out in a flat valley backed by tiers of far-off mountain. The indigenous influence is noticeable.

The paved road ends in Bribrí, but a dirt road leads west through the gorge of the Río Sixaola and the village of **Bratsi,** where the vistas open up across the Valle de Talamanca surrounded by soaring mountains—a region

known as **Alta Talamanca.** The United Fruit Company once reigned supreme in the valley, and the history of the region is a sad tale (many of the tribes who opposed destruction of their forests at the turn of the 20th century were hunted and jailed). You'll need a four-wheel-drive vehicle.

Talamanca Indigenous Reserves

The **Reserva Indígena Talamanca-Bribrí** and **Reserva Indígena Talamanca-Cabecar** are incorporated into La Amistad International Peace Park, on the slopes of the Talamanca mountains. The parks were established to protect the traditional lifestyle of the indigenous people, though the communities and their land remain under constant threat from loggers and squatters.

The Cabecar native peoples have no villages, as they prefer to live apart. Though the people speak Spanish and wear Western clothing, their philosophy that all living things are the work of Sibo, their god of creation, has traditionally pitted the native peoples against pioneers. Government proposals to build a trans-Talamanca highway and a hydroelectric dam are being fought by the local tribes. The communities supplement their income by selling crafts, and organically grown cacao.

The "capital" of the Talamanca-Bribrí reserve is the hamlet of **Shiroles,** setting for **Finca Educativa Indígena** (tel. 506/8373-4181), an administrative center for the Bribrí people.

The Cabecar are now turning to ecotourism as a means of preserving their culture. **Amubri,** eight kilometers west of Bratsi, is the "capital" and gateway to the reserve. If you go, enter with a sense of humility and respect. Do not treat the community members as a tourist oddity: You have as much to learn from the indigenous communities as to share.

Beyond Bribrí, a moderate 30-minute hike off the Bratsi road leads to the 20-meter **Volio waterfall,** popular with local tour guides; it has a pool good for swimming.

The **Reserva Indígena Yorkin** (tel. 506/8375-3372, www.greencoast.com/yorkin.htm) welcomes tourists and leads hikes. Artisans of the **Estibrawpa Women's Group** display their traditional (rather crude) crafts. The reserve is accessed by canoe up the Río Yorkin from Bambú. The two-day, one-night trip includes lodging, transport, and meals ($50 pp, $25 extra day). However, it is extremely basic (no towels, nor even toilet paper) and reports of the experience are mixed. The **Costa Rican Association of Community-Based Rural Tourism** (ACTUAR, tel. 506/2248-9470, www.actuarcostarica.com) offers tours.

Accommodations and Food

In Shiroles, **Finca Educativa Indígena** ($10

pp) has a rustic 12-bedroom lodge. At Buena Vista, northeast of Shiroles, **ACODEFO** (Asociación de Conservación y Desarrollo Forestal de Talamanca, tel. 506/2751-0020, acodefo@hotmail.com, $40 pp) has a basic, two-story, A-frame wooden lodge with six rooms, private bathrooms, and solar-generated power. Rates include three meals and a guided excursion to the reserves. **Reserva Indígena Yorkin** has a lodge for 15 people.

Information and Services

Banco Nacional (10 A.M.–noon and 1–3:45 P.M. Mon.–Fri.) in Bribrí has a $100 limit. It gets crowded and can take half a day to get money changed.

There's a **Red Cross** (tel. 506/2758-0125) evacuation center for emergencies. The **police station** (tel. 506/2758-1865) is opposite the Red Cross.

Getting There

The San José–Limón bus passes through Bribrí en route to Sixaola ($3.50 to Sixaola). Buses depart Limón from opposite Radio Casino on Avenida 4 eight times daily (5 A.M.–6 P.M.).

Buses depart Bribrí for Shiroles at 8 A.M., noon, and 5:30 P.M. daily.

If driving from Puerto Viejo, you can take a dirt road that crosses the mountains, linking Punta Uva to Paraíso, about 10 kilometers west of Sixaola.

SIXAOLA: CROSSING INTO PANAMÁ

Sixaola, 34 kilometers southeast of Bribrí, is on the north bank of the 200-meter-wide, fast-flowing Río Sixaola. The only visitors to this dour border town (it's not a place to get stuck overnight) are typically crossing the river into Panamá en route to Boca del Toro (the equally dour Panamanian village of Guabito is on the south bank of the river). You can walk or drive across the border. Remember to advance your watch by one hour as you enter Panamá.

The Costa Rican Customs and Immigration offices (tel. 506/2754-2044; open 7 A.M.–5 P.M.)

are on the west end of the bridge that links the two towns. The Panamanian office (tel. 507/759-7952), on the east end of the bridge, is open 8 A.M.–6 P.M.

The basic **Hotel el Imperio** (tel. 506/2754-2289) is on the left as you come into Sixaola. Its sole room costs $8. There are a few other grim cabins, and a fistful of uninspired eateries.

Buses depart Sixaola for San José at 5 A.M., 7:30 A.M., 9:30 A.M., and 2:30 P.M. daily; and for Limón at 5 A.M., 8 A.M., 10 A.M., 1 P.M., 3 P.M., and 5 P.M. daily.

There's a Texaco **gas station** about 10 kilometers east of Bribrí. You'll be stopped and possibly searched at the *comando* (police checkpoint, tel. 506/2754-2160) as you enter Sixaola.

THE NORTHERN ZONE

The northern lowlands constitute a 40,000-square-kilometer watershed drained by the Ríos Frío, San Carlos, and Sarapiquí and their tributaries, which flow north to the Río San Juan, forming the border with Nicaragua. The rivers meander like restless snakes and flood in the wet season, when much of the landscape is transformed into swampy marshlands. The region is made up of two separate plains *(llanuras):* in the west, the Llanura de los Guatusos, and farther east the Llanura de San Carlos.

Today, tourists are flocking, thanks to new roads and the singular popularity of Arenal Volcano, the catalyst for a burgeoning adventure industry based in La Fortuna.

These plains were once rampant with tropical forest. During recent decades much has been felled as the lowlands have been transformed into farmland. Yet, there *is* still plenty of rainforest extending for miles across the plains and clambering up the north-facing slopes of the *cordilleras,* whose scarp face hems the lowlands.

Today, the region is a breadbasket for the nation, and most of the working population is employed in agriculture. The southern uplands area of San Carlos, centered on the regional capital of Ciudad Quesada, devotes almost 70 percent of its territory to dairy cattle. The lowlands proper are the realm of beef cattle and plantations of pineapples, bananas, and citrus.

The climate has much in common with the Caribbean coast: warm, humid, and consistently wet. Temperatures hover at 25–27°C year-round. The climatic periods are not as

HIGHLIGHTS

◖ Thermal Springs: At Tabacón Hot Springs, one of your enticing hot springs options, you can bathe in steaming waters that tumble from the bowels of Arenal Volcano to cascade through a landscaped garden (page 232).

◖ Arenal Volcano National Park: With a symmetrical volcano at its heart, this national park has hiking trails over still-warm lava flows, and the open spaces offer prime wildlife-viewing (page 241).

◖ Rancho Margot: This ecologically self-sustaining farm and wildlife rescue center has rustic but endearing accommodations, plus hiking, rappelling, and horseback riding (page 244).

◖ Arenal Rainforest Reserve: The aerial tram at this private reserve promises high-mountain rides and staggering vistas. Nature trails and canopy tours provide close-up encounters with wildlife (page 244).

◖ Caño Negro Wildlife Refuge: This croc-infested swamp and forest ecosystem is a dream for birders and wildlife lovers, and a

nirvana for anglers come to hook tarpon, garfish, and snook (page 253).

◖ Tenorio Volcano and Vicinity: Long off the tourist charts, this volcano is a new-found frontier for hiking, including to the jade-colored Río Celeste, and accommodations are coming on strong (page 256).

◖ Centro Neotrópico Sarapiquís: This educational center offers a museum of indigenous culture, an archaeological park, and nature trails through the Tirimbina Rainforest Reserve (page 259).

◖ Selva Verde: Enfolded by rainforest, this dedicated nature lodge offers instant access to wildlife-rich terrain. Options include guided hikes by day and night, plus canoeing on the Río Sarapiquí (page 260).

◖ Isla Las Heliconias: The Dutch owners will guide you on a tour of his beautifully landscaped Sarapiquí Botanical Garden near Horquetas. In addition to heliconias, it also displays hundreds of species of ginger, palms, orchids, bamboo, and other tropical flora (page 265).

LOOK FOR ◖ TO FIND RECOMMENDED SIGHTS, ACTIVITIES, DINING, AND LODGING.

THE NORTHERN ZONE

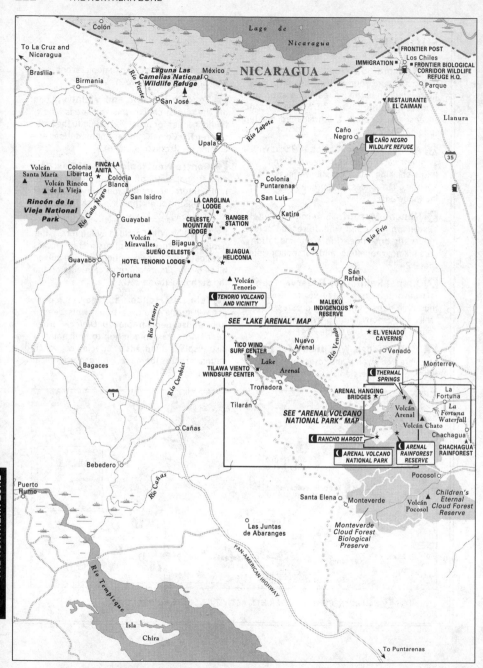

THE NORTHERN ZONE

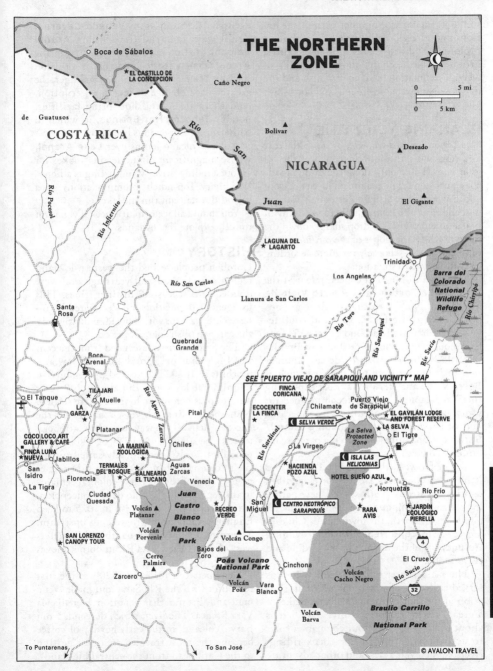

THE NORTHERN ZONE

Boca de Sábalos

★ EL CASTILLO DE
LA CONCEPCIÓN

▲ Caño Negro

de Guatusos

COSTA RICA

Río San

▲ Bolivar

▲ Deseado

Juan

NICARAGUA

▲ El Gigante

Río Infiernito

Río Pocosol

LAGUNA DEL
★ LAGARTO

Trinidad ○

Barra del
Colorado
National
Wildlife
Refuge

Río Chirripó

Río San Carlos

Los Angeles ○

Llanura de San Carlos

Río Toro

Río Sarapiquí

Río Sucio

Santa
Rosa ○

Quebrada
Grande ○

Boca
Arenal ○

Río Agua Zarcas

SEE "PUERTO VIEJO DE SARAPIQUÍ AND VICINITY" MAP

FINCA
CORICANA

TILAJARI ○
El Tanque ○ ★ ● Muelle
LA
GARZA

Pital ○

ECOCENTER
LA FINCA

Chilamate ○

Puerto Viejo
de Sarapiquí

EL GAVILÁN LODGE
AND FOREST RESERVE

Platanar ○

SELVA VERDE

LA SELVA

La Selva
Protected
Zone

○ El Tigre

COCO LOCO ART
GALLERY & CAFÉ
FINCA LUNA
★ NUEVA ○ Jabillos

LA MARINA
ZOOLÓGICA
★

Chiles ○

○ La Virgen

ISLA LAS
HELICONIAS

San
Isidro ○

TERMALES
DEL BOSQUE
★

Aguas
Zarcas

★ HACIENDA
POZO AZUL

La Tigra ○

Florencia ○

BALNEARIO
EL TUCANO
★

Venecia ○

HOTEL SUEÑO AZUL ●

Horquetas ○

Río Frío

Ciudad
Quesada ○

Juan
Castro
Blanco

San
Miguel ○

CENTRO NEOTRÓPICO
SARAPIQUÍS

RARA
AVIS

JARDÍN
ECOLÓGICO
PIERELLA

Volcán ▲
Platanar ★ RECREO
VERDE

National

SAN LORENZO
CANOPY TOUR ★

Volcán ▲
Porvenir

Park

Volcán Congo ▲

4

Cerro
Palmira ○

Bajos del
Toro ○

El Cruce ○

Zarcero ○

Poás Volcano
National Park

Cinchona ○

Volcán ▲
Cacho Negro

Río Sucio

32

Volcán ▲
Poás

Vara
Blanca ○

Braulio Carrillo

Volcán ▲
Barva

National Park

To Puntarenas ←

← To San José ↓

© AVALON TRAVEL

0   5 mi

0   5 km

well defined as those of other parts of the nation, and rarely does a week pass without a prolonged and heavy rain shower (it rains a little less from February to the beginning of May). Precipitation tends to diminish and the dry season grows more pronounced northward and westward.

PLANNING YOUR TIME
The region is a vast triangle, broad to the east and narrowing to the west. Much of the region is accessible only along rough dirt roads that turn to muddy quagmires in wet season; a four-wheel-drive vehicle is essential. You can descend from the central highlands via any of half a dozen routes that drop sharply down the steep north-facing slopes of the *cordilleras* and onto the plains. Choose your route according to your desired destination.

Most sights of interest concentrate near the towns of **La Fortuna** and **Puerto Viejo de Sarapiquí.** For the naturalist, there are opportunities galore for birding and wildlife-viewing, particularly around Puerto Viejo de Sarapiquí, where the lower slopes of Braulio Carrillo National Park provide easy immersion in rainforest from nature lodges such as **Selva Verde** and **Rara Avis.** Boat trips along the Río Sarapiquí are also recommended for spotting monkeys, crocodiles, green macaws, and other wildlife, and **Heliconia Island/ Sarapiquí Botanical Garden** is a paradise for birders and botanists.

To the far west, the slopes of Tenorio and Miravalles Volcanoes are less developed but coming on strong, with several new nature lodges around **Bijagua,** one of my favorite regions. To the north, the town of Los Chiles is a gateway to **Caño Negro National Wildlife Refuge,** one of the nation's prime birding and fishing sites.

The main center is La Fortuna, which is served by dozens of accommodations. Its situation at the foot of Arenal Volcano makes it a great base for exploring; three days here is about right. Numerous tour companies cater to active travelers with horseback riding, river trips, bicycle rides, and other adventure excursions, including to **Venado Caverns.** You'll want to spend time hiking **Arenal Volcano National Park,** perhaps from the **Arenal Observatory Lodge** or via a ride on the **Sky Tram.** The more time you linger, the greater your chance of seeing an eruption. And there are several hot spring facilities, notably **Tabacón Hot Springs,** in which to bathe with a stupendous backdrop.

Arenal Volcano looms over **Lake Arenal,** whose magnificent alpine setting makes for an outstanding drive. Windsurfing is a popular activity. Top-notch accommodations and a splendid restaurant rim the lake.

You should allocate up to a week if you want to fully explore the lowlands.

HISTORY
Corobicí people settled the western lowland region several thousand years ago and were divided into at least 12 distinct tribes. This indigenous population was decimated by internecine warfare with Nicaraguan tribes in the early Spanish colonial period.

The Spanish first descended from the central highlands on a foray into the lowland foothills in 1640. They called the region San Jerónimo de los Votos. But almost 200 years were to pass before the foothills were settled. Nonetheless, Spanish vessels navigated the Río San Juan all the way from the Caribbean to Lake Nicaragua, a journey of 195 kilometers. Pirates also periodically sailed up the river to loot and burn the lakeside settlements. One of the very few colonial remains in the region is El Castillo de la Concepción, a fort erected by the Spanish in 1675 to keep English pirates from progressing upstream. The ruins are in Nicaragua, three kilometers west of where the Costa Rican border moves south of the river.

Only between 1815 and 1820 was the first road link with the Río Sarapiquí made, via a mud-and-dirt trail that went from Heredia via Vara Blanca. The river, which descends from Barva Volcano, in the early heyday of coffee became the most traveled route for getting to the Caribbean from the central highlands.

Beginning in the 1950s the government helped finance small cattle farmers as part of its policy to promote new settlements outside the Meseta Central, and settlement began to edge slowly north. In recent decades, construction of paved highways has accelerated settlement and clearing of forest for cattle and fruit farms.

Ciudad Quesada and Vicinity

CIUDAD QUESADA

Ciudad Quesada (pop. 30,000), known locally as **San Carlos,** hovers above the plains at 650 meters elevation on the north-facing slope of the Cordillera de Tilarán, with the lowlands spread out at its feet. Despite its mountainside position, the bustling market town is the hierarchical center of (and gateway to) the entire northern region. It is surrounded by lush pasture grazed by prize-specimen dairy cattle.

Termales del Bosque (tel. 506/2460-4740, www.termalesdelbosque.com), about five kilometers east of Ciudad Quesada, is billed as an "ecological park" with hiking trails through botanical gardens, plus horseback rides ($15–45) and thermal mineral springs. It offers aromatherapy, mud applications, and massage. Entrance costs $12 adults, $6 children.

Entertainment and Events

There's a small **casino** in the Hotel La Central. The liveliest nightspot is **Bar la Yunta** (Avenida 4, Calles Central/2, 7 P.M.–2 A.M.), with live music most nights. The annual **Feria del Ganado** (Cattle Fair) in April is one of the largest in the country, with a horse parade (tope) and general merriment.

Accommodations

There's no shortage of budget accommodations in town, most offering a choice of shared or private bathrooms for around $10 per person. Try **Hotel del Norte** (Calle 1, Avenidas 1/3, tel. 506/2460-1959), though as is typical of these spartan hotels, the small rooms have thin partition walls. Somewhat nicer, **Hotel El Parqueo** (Avenida 7, Calles Central/2, tel. 506/2460-2573, $18 s, $25 d) has 10 clean rooms in a converted home. All have modern tiles and small bathrooms; some have refrigerator and cable TV.

Better yet, **Hotel Don Goyo** (Calle 2, Avenida 4, tel. 506/2460-1780, fax 506/2460-6383, $20 s, $30 d) offers 21 clean, modern rooms that stair-step down a hillside. Each has cable TV and private bath with hot water; most have heaps of light. It has a pleasant restaurant. The **Hotel y Casino La Central** (Calle 2, Avenidas Central/2, tel. 506/2460-0301, www.hotellacentral.net, $25 s, $32 d), on the west side of the plaza, has 48 clean, meagerly furnished rooms (some with balconies), with fans, TVs, and hot-water showers.

The best place in town is **Hotel Loma Verde** (tel. 506/2460-1976, www.hotellomaverde.net, $28 s or $32 d with fan, $40 s or $48 d with a/c), about two kilometers north of the town center and set in a pretty garden atop the scarp face overlooking the lowland plains. This well-kept, clinically clean, peaceful, modern facility has whitewashed walls. The 18 rooms vary in size, but all have nice fabrics, cable TV, and private bathrooms with hot water. Some rooms offer views. There's an ascetic open-air TV lounge with a pool table, and parking is available. Rates include breakfast.

Termales del Bosque (tel. 506/2460-4740, www.termalesdelbosque.com, $60 s, $75 d), an ecological park with hot springs, has 44 attractive, albeit small, modern cabins with private bathrooms with hot water, and balconies amid landscaped grounds. Rates include breakfast.

Hotel Occidental El Tucano (tel. 506/2460-6000, www.occidentalhotels.com, $93 s/d standard, $140 deluxe, $170 master suite low season; $105 s/d standard, $143 s/d deluxe, $176 s/d master suite high season), eight kilometers east of Ciudad Quesada, promises healing for those

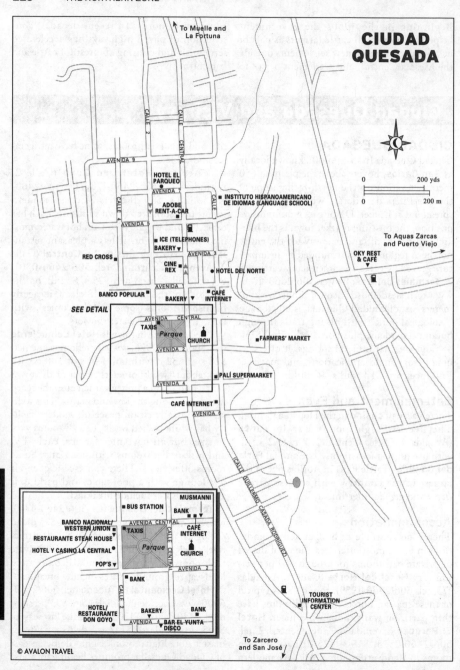

CIUDAD QUESADA

To Muelle and La Fortuna

0   200 yds
0   200 m

To Aquas Zarcas and Puerto Viejo

HOTEL EL PARQUEO

INSTITUTO HISPANOAMERICANO DE IDIOMAS (LANGUAGE SCHOOL)

ADOBE RENT-A-CAR

ICE (TELEPHONES)

BAKERY

RED CROSS

OKY REST & CAFÉ

CINE REX

HOTEL DEL NORTE

BANCO POPULAR

BAKERY

CAFÉ INTERNET

SEE DETAIL

AVENIDA   CENTRAL

TAXIS

Parque

CHURCH

FARMERS' MARKET

PALÍ SUPERMARKET

CAFÉ INTERNET

CALLE GUILLERMO CASADA RODRIGUEZ

MUSMANNI

BUS STATION

BANK

BANCO NACIONAL/ WESTERN UNION

AVENIDA CENTRAL

TAXIS

CAFÉ INTERNET

RESTAURANTE STEAK HOUSE

HOTEL Y CASINO LA CENTRAL

Parque

CHURCH

POP'S

AVENIDA 2

BANK

TOURIST INFORMATION CENTER

HOTEL/ RESTAURANTE DON GOYO

BAKERY

BANK

BAR EL YUNTA DISCO

To Zarcero and San José

© AVALON TRAVEL

dipping their toes into the hot springs that hiccup out of clefts in the rocks on which the hotel is built. The riverside hotel—built around a large open-air swimming pool—is styled loosely as a Swiss chalet complex, with wrought-iron lanterns and window boxes full of flowers. The 87 guest rooms are rather ho-hum in decor, despite beautiful hardwoods and king-size beds; master suites are wood-paneled. It has a restaurant, casino, full-service spa, forest trails, gym, tennis, miniature golf, and horseback riding.

Food

The clean and modern **Restaurante Steak House** (tel. 506/2460-3208, 11 A.M.–11 P.M. daily), on the west side of the plaza, specializes in *lomitos* (steaks) from $5.

The nicest place in town is **Oky Rest & Café** (tel. 506/2460-4335, 11 A.M.–10 P.M. Tues.–Sun.), on the east side of town. This converted mansion offers elegant indoor and outdoor dining. The eclectic menu runs from pizza to chicken curry and pepper tenderloin, plus a lunchtime *casado* ($6). It has Wi-Fi.

You can buy fresh bread and pastries at **Musmanni** (Avenida Central, Calles Central/1).

Information and Services

CATUZON, the Cámara de Turismo de la Zona Norte (Northern Zone Chamber of Tourism, tel. 506/2461-1112, 8 A.M.–4 P.M. Mon.–Sat.) has an ill-stocked tourist bureau two blocks south of the main square.

The **hospital** (tel. 506/2460-1080) is on Calle Central, about two kilometers north of the plaza. The **Red Cross** is at Avenida 3, Calle 4. There are banks in the center of town.

Getting There

Buses (tel. 506/2255-4318 or 506/460-5064) depart San José from Calle 12, Avenidas 7/9, every 45 minutes 5 A.M.–7:30 P.M. daily (three hours via Zarcero, $2.30).

In Ciudad Quesada, the bus terminal is one block northwest of the plaza. Buses (tel. 506/2460-5032) serve La Fortuna at 6 A.M., 10:30 A.M., 1 P.M., 3:30 P.M., and 5 P.M. daily; to Los Chiles every two hours 5 A.M.–5 P.M.

daily; and to Puerto Viejo at 6 A.M., 10 A.M., and 3 P.M. daily.

You can rent cars from **Alamo Rent-a-Car** (Avenida 5, Calle Central, tel. 506/2460-0650).

AGUAS ZARCAS

Aguas Zarcas (Blue Waters), an important agricultural town at the foot of the cordillera, 15 kilometers east of Ciudad Quesada, gets its name from the mineral hot springs that erupt from the base of the mountain. Juan Castro Blanco National Park flanks the slopes.

The road from Ciudad Quesada continues east via **Venecia** (7 km east of Aguas Zarcas) to a T-junction at **San Miguel,** 24 kilometers east of Aguas Zarcas. The road to the right leads south to Alajuela via Vara Blanca, nestled in the saddle of Poás and Barva Volcanoes; the road to the left leads to Puerto Viejo de Sarapiquí.

Two kilometers east of Venecia, a road leads two kilometers south to **Recreo Verde** (tel. 506/2472-2270, www.recreoverde.com, $12 adults, $6 children), a splendid *centro turístico* tucked riverside, deep in the thickly forested valley of the Río Toro Amarillo—a magnificent setting! Three thermal pools (and two cold-water pools) limn the river, a raging torrent to beware. There are lush lawns with volleyball, and you can explore the "Cave of Death" with a guide, marveling at the dripstone formations. Trails lead into the forest, where there's a canopy tour ($25 adults, $15 children).

La Marina Zoológica

This private zoo (tel./fax 506/2474-2202, www.zoocostarica.com, 8 A.M.–4 P.M. daily, $8 adults, $5 children), opposite the gas station three kilometers west of Aguas Zarcas, houses jaguars, tapirs, agoutis, peccaries, badgers, monkeys, and other mammal species, as well as birds from around the world. The Alfaro family has been taking in orphaned animals for three decades, and the zoo now has more than 450 species of animals and birds, many confiscated by the government from owners who lacked permits to keep them. The zoo even has two lions and successfully breeds tapirs. The zoo is nonprofit; donations are appreciated.

Accommodations and Food

You can camp at **Recreo Verde** ($15), which also has simple wooden cabins ($60 s, $70 d), each with a double bed and bunks, plus private bath with hot water.

In Venecia, **Hotel Torre Fuerte** (tel. 506/2472-2424, $20 s, $28 d) has 12 modern, clinically clean, spacious rooms in a two-story structure. Each has furnishings of thick bamboo, ceiling fan, local TV, tile floors, and modern private bathrooms with hot water. It has a pleasant restaurant open 5:30 A.M.–10 P.M. daily.

Getting There

Buses between Ciudad Quesada and Puerto Viejo de Sarapiquí stop along the route; or take the 3.5-hour bus ride from San José ($2.50).

PITAL

Pital, about six kilometers northeast of Aguas Zarcas (turn right just north of Los Chiles) is an agricultural town. A road leads due north from Pital to **Laguna del Lagarto,** a private reserve about 40 kilometers north of Pital via the hamlet of Boca Topada (seven kilometers southwest of Laguna del Lagarto). A four-wheel-drive vehicle is recommended. The reserve protects 500 hectares of virgin rainforest and bayou swamps harboring crocodiles, caimans, turtles, poison-dart frogs, as well as ocelots, sloths, and all kinds of colorful bird species, including the rare green macaw. There's a butterfly garden plus forest trails for hiking and horseback rides ($20 two hours). Four-hour boat trips on the San Carlos and San Juan Rivers cost $26 per person (minimum four people). It offers transfers from San José.

Accommodations and Food

Perfect for nature lovers, the delightfully rustic **Laguna del Lagarto Lodge** (tel. 506/2289-8163, www.lagarto-lodge-costa-rica.com, $33 s or $44 d low season, $44 s or $57 d high season) offers 20 comfortable rooms in two buildings (18 with private baths, two with shared bath; all with hot water). Each has a large terrace with a view overlooking the San Carlos River and forest.

A restaurant serves hearty Costa Rican buffet meals and arranges transfers.

Getting There

Buses (tel. 506/2258-8914) for Pital depart San José from Calle 12, Avenidas 7/9, at 7:40 A.M., 12:30 P.M., 3 P.M., and 7:30 P.M. daily; and from Ciudad Quesada hourly 5:30 A.M.–8:30 P.M. daily. From Pital, buses run to Boca Tapada at 9:30 A.M. and 4:30 P.M. daily. A taxi from Pital costs about $25 one-way.

MUELLE

This important crossroads village is 21 kilometers north of Ciudad Quesada, at the junction of Highway 4 (running east–west between Upala and Puerto Viejo de Sarapiquí) and Highway 35 (north–south between Ciudad Quesada and Los Chiles). There's a gas station. Muelle is worth a visit to view the iguanas that reliably congregate in the treetops, seen at eye-level from the bridge beside the Restaurante Iguana Azul.

The **Reserva Biológica La Garza** (tel. 506/2475-5222) at Platanar, four kilometers south of the Muelle crossroads, protects wildlife on a 600-hectare working cattle and stud farm with forest trails. Horseback rides (from $10 for 90 minutes) and hikes are offered, and it has rappelling. Day visitors are welcome to use the pool and facilities.

Accommodations

Hotel La Garza (tel. 506/2475-5222, www.hotel lagarza.com, $75 s/d low season, $85 s/d high season), at Reserva Biológica La Garza and reached by a suspension bridge over the Río Platanar, has 12 beautifully kept, air-conditioned cabins with polished wood floors, ceiling fans, telephones, Guatemalan fabrics, bamboo furnishings and paneling, heaps of potted plants, and verandas with tables and chairs overlooking the river. There's a pool with sundeck and a three-kilometer hiking/jogging trail. Meals are served in a charming old farmhouse restaurant. Delightful! Rates include breakfast.

I recommend **Tilajari Resort Hotel** (tel.

506/2462-1212, www.tilajari.com, $76–84 s/d standard, $90 s or $100 d junior suite low season; $89 s or $99 d standard, $108 s or $120 d junior suite high season), one kilometer west from the Muelle crossroads, which doubles as a social club for wealthy Ticos. Tilajari has 60 spacious, nicely furnished air-conditioned rooms and 16 newly remodeled junior suites, some with king-size beds. It offers three tennis courts, a swimming pool, a children's pool, racquetball courts, a sauna, gym, and a sensational whirlpool complex. There's an open-air bar and lounge, an elegant open-sided restaurant, a disco, and conference facilities. Ticos flock on weekends. Crocodiles sun themselves on the banks of the Río San Carlos in plain view of guests, iguanas roost in the treetops, and hummingbirds emblazon the 16-hectare garden.

Getting There
Buses to/from Los Chiles and San Rafael can drop you in Muelle.

CHACHAGUA
The village of Chachagua, 10 kilometers southeast of La Fortuna, is evolving as a center for ecotourism. About one kilometer east of Chachagua, a dirt road leads west and dead-ends at the **Chachagua Rainforest** (tel. 506/2468-1010, www.chachaguarainforesthotel.com), a 130-hectare private forest reserve, cattle ranch, and fruit farm nestled at the foot of the Tilarán mountain range. It has a lodge, plus a small butterfly garden and orchid garden, and the forest is a great place for birding and hiking.

Nearby, **Finca Luna Nueva Lodge** (tel. 506/2468-4006, http://fincalunanueva lodge.com) is a working organic herbal farm that welcomes visitors for hikes and horseback tours. It's unsigned; take the dirt track on the south side of the highway and 100 meters east of Restaurante Los Piruchos del Volcá, at San Isidro de Peñas Blancas.

La Tigra, 12 kilometers southeast of Chachagua, is a gateway to the Bosque Eterno de los Niños (Children's Eternal Forest) and Monteverde Cloud Forest Biological Reserve;

you'll see a sign about 800 meters south of La Tigra and an information office one kilometer north of town. At La Tigra, the highway begins to climb into the central highlands via San Ramón.

Accommodations and Food
Chachagua Rainforest Lodge (tel. 506/2468-1010, www.chachaguarainforesthotel.com, $66 s or $85 d low season, $87 s or $103 d high season) has 22 spacious, simply appointed wooden cabins, each with two double beds and a deck with a picnic table and benches for enjoying the natural surroundings. The atmospheric natural-log restaurant looks out upon a corral where *sabaneros* (cowboys) offer rodeo shows. There's a swimming pool, horseback riding, and nature and bird-watching hikes.

A similar and delightful alternative is **Tree Houses Hotel** (tel. 506/2475-6507, www.tree houseshotelcostarica.com, $95 s/d including breakfast), midway between San Pedro and Florencia. Yes, you'll sleep in actual tree houses within a private wildlife refuge great for wildlife viewing. The cozy, rustic, air-conditioned units have en-suite bathrooms, plus double beds and a loft with two singles perfect for kids.

And the eco-conscious **Finca Luna Nueva Lodge** (tel. 506/2468-4006, http://fincaluna nuevalodge.com, see the website for rates) has a lodge with seven spacious air-conditioned rooms in two raised wooden structures with wraparound balconies; plus three bungalows. It also has Wi-Fi, plus a spa and solar-heated tub, and serves organic meals.

A lovely alternative, **Jardines Arenal Hotel** (tel. 506/2479-9728, www.hoteljardinesarenal .com, $45 s or $57 d low season, $57 s or $66 d high season) offers modestly furnished rooms in a two-story lodge set in handsome gardens.

You *must* visit ◖ **Coco Loco Art Gallery & Café** (tel. 506/2468-0990, www.arenal byowner.com, 8 A.M.–5 P.M.), five kilometers east of Chachagua. This exquisite, German-run roadside bistro serves milk shakes, natural smoothies, and coffees and teas. It also has various art galleries displaying the very finest Costa

Rican crafts, including hammocks, exquisite marble carvings, and ceramics, plus owner Ruth Deiseroth-Kweton's own exotic indigenous-infused art and masks. It offers free shipping on purchases over $250. A fully equipped cabin with forest views is available for rent. It, too, is a sheer work of art, with bamboo ceiling, faux-forest wall, Guatemalan curtains, king-size bed with built-in sofa-bed, and a fantasy bathroom (at $65 s/d with breakfast, it's a bargain).

La Fortuna and Arenal

LA FORTUNA TO TABACÓN

The town of La Fortuna is the main gateway to Volcán Arenal, which looms to the southwest. A decade ago, La Fortuna was a dusty little agricultural town with potholed dirt streets. Today it thrives on tourist traffic. In town there's not much to see except the church on the west side of the landscaped plaza, anchored by a sculpture of a volcano, but outside town the range of activities impresses and grows by leaps and bounds every year.

West from La Fortuna, the road begins a gradual, winding ascent to Lake Arenal around the northern flank of Arenal Volcano, 15 kilometers from town. It's a stupendously scenic drive.

La Fortuna Waterfall Ecological Reserve

Reserva Ecológica Catarata La Fortuna (8 A.M.–5 P.M. daily, closed during heavy rains, $7), about four kilometers south of town, is in the care of a local community development group—the Asociación de Desarollo Integral de La Fortuna (tel. 506/2479-8078, www.arenal adifort.com). The turnoff for the falls is two kilometers southeast of town, where a rocky road leads uphill 2.5 kilometers to the entrance. From here you have to negotiate a slippery and precipitous trail (20 minutes' walk) that leads down a steep ravine to the base of the cascade; there are steps and handrails for the steepest sections. You can swim, but it's not advised, as any sudden surge could prove deadly. The **Americas Paradise Center** (tel. 506/2479-7777, www.americasparadise.net), adjoining, offers guided two-hour hikes up Cerro Chato volcano from here ($10 pp).

Other Nature Sites and Reserves

The **La Catarata Ecolodge** (tel. 508/2479-9522, www.cataratalodge.com, 7 A.M.–4 P.M. daily, $5), run by the local Association for the Environment & Sustainable Development (ASPROADES), has a **butterfly garden** and **Zoo Tepescuintle,** where tepescuintles (charming dog-sized rodents) are raised for release into the wild. Entrance is by donation.

And the **Ecocentro Danaus Butterfly Farm and Tropical Garden** (tel. 506/2479-7019, www.ecocentrodanaus.com, 8 A.M.–4 P.M. daily, $5 admission with tour), three kilometers east of town, has trails through a netted butterfly garden. A separate garden features red-eyed tree frogs and poison-dart frogs in re-creations of their natural environments; there are also eyelash vipers in cages. A small lake has caimans, turtles, and waterfowl. The night walk is recommended.

Los Lagos Jungle and Trails (tel. 506/2479-1000, www.hotelloslagos.com, $7 admission), six kilometers west of La Fortuna, is a quasi-theme park with 400 hectares of primary forest with trails and horseback riding, plus a ranarium (frog exhibit), butterfly garden, and lush gardens with water slides augering down to hot- and cold-water swimming pools.

Reserva Privada El Silencio (no tel., 7 A.M.–9 P.M. daily, $3), a half kilometer east of the turnoff for the national park, has a three-kilometer trail. You can even drive up to a lookout beneath the flow. The closest hiking to the lava flows, however, is at nearby **Arenal 1968** (no tel., 7 A.M.–10 P.M. daily, $7), near the entrance to Arenal Volcano National Park. Horseback tours are offered. Oropendolas and

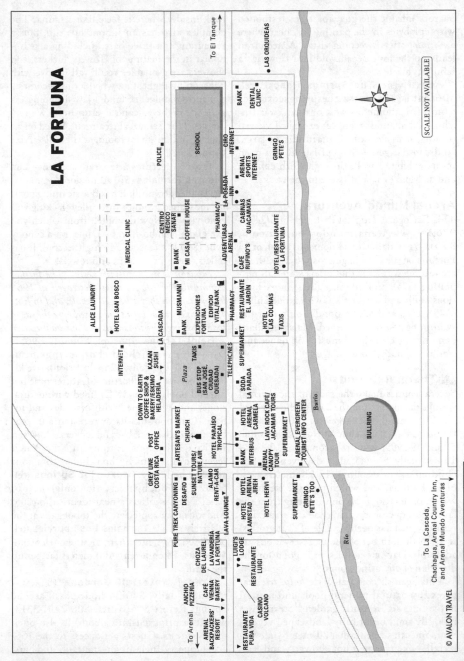

LA FORTUNA

To El Tanque →

SCALE NOT AVAILABLE

LAS ORQUIDEAS

BANK

DENTAL CLINIC

CIRO INTERNET

GRINGO PETE'S

ARENAL SPORTS INTERNET

LA POSADA INN

SCHOOL

POLICE

ADVENTURAS ARENAL

PHARMACY

CABINAS GUACAMAYA

CENTRO MEDICO SANAR

BANK

MI CASA COFFEE HOUSE

CAFÉ RUFINO'S

HOTEL/RESTAURANTE LA FORTUNA

MEDICAL CLINIC

ALICE LAUNDRY

HOTEL SAN BOSCO

LA CASCADA

MUSMANNI

EXPEDICIONES FORTUNA

EDIFICIO VITAL/BANK

PHARMACY

RESTAURANTE EL JARDIN

HOTEL LAS COLINAS

BANK

TAXIS

INTERNET

KAZAN SUSHI

TAXIS

Plaza

BUS STOP (SAN JOSÉ, CIUDAD QUESADA)

SODA LA PARADA

SUPERMARKET

TELEPHONES

DOWN TO EARTH COFFEE SHOP & BAKER ESKIMO HELADERIA

POST OFFICE

ARTESAN'S MARKET

CHURCH

HOTEL PARAISO TROPICAL

HOTEL ARENAL CARMELA

LAVA ROCK CAFE/ JACAMAR TOURS

SUPERMARKET

ARENAL EVERGREEN TOURIST INFO CENTER

Barrio

BULLRING

GREY LINE COSTA RICA

PURE TREK CANYONING

DESAFIO

SUNSET TOURS/ NATURE AIR

ALAMO RENT-A-CAR

LAVA-LOUNGE

HOTEL LA AMISTAD

HOTEL ARENAL JIREH

BANK INTERBUS

ARENAL CANOPY TOUR

HOTEL HERVI

SUPERMARKET

GRINGO PETE'S TOO

Río

THE NORTHERN ZONE

CHOZA DEL LAUREL

LAVANDERIA LA FORTUNA

LUIGI'S LODGE

RESTAURANTE LUIGI

ANCHO PIZZERIA

CAFÉ VIENNA BAKERY

CASINO VOLCANO

ARENAL BACKPACKERS' RESORT

RESTAURANTE PURA VIDA

To Arenal

To La Cascada, Chachagua, Arenal Country Inn, and Arenal Mundo Aventuras →

© AVALON TRAVEL

parrots inhabit the guayaba trees festooned with epiphytes in the parking lot, near where a *mirador* offers sweeping vistas. A steep trail leads up the four-decade-old lava flow. It's a fabulous hike!

At last visit, **The Springs Resort** (tel. 506/2401-3313, www.thespringscostarica.com), five kilometers west of town, was finishing off a fantastic big cat exhibit. I viewed ocelots, margays, and jaguarundis in large, landscaped cages. A "Jaguar Island," an open puma exhibit, a walk-through sloth exhibit, and a "Monkey Island" were in the works.

Arenal Mundo Aventura

This Ecological Tropical Park (tel. 506/2479-9762, www.arenalmundoaventura.com, 8 A.M.–5 P.M. daily), two kilometers south of La Fortuna on the Chachagua road, is a 552-hectare rainforest reserve that offers waterfall rappelling ($75), zipline tours ($65), horseback rides ($40), and nature trails with guided hikes ($25). Frog and snake ponds, plus thermal swimming pools, are planned. Malekú Indians demonstrate traditional music and dance in a traditional indigenous village.

◖ Thermal Springs

Several entities make the most of the thermal springs that pour from the base of the volcano.

Most famous and largest of the *balnearios* (bathing resorts) is **Tabacón Hot Springs** (tel. 506/2519-1999, www.tabacon.com, 10 A.M.–10 P.M. daily, $60/45 adult day/evening, $20 children day or evening), 13 kilometers west of La Fortuna, and which taps the steaming waters of the Río Tabacón tumbling from the lava fields to cascade alongside the road. The resort (which has been a staple of tour groups) restricts the number of guests; reservations are advisable. Day-rate admission is good for the duration of operating hours.

This Spanish colonial–style *balneario* features five natural mineral pools and natural hot springs set in exotic gardens. Steam rises moodily amid beautifully landscaped vegetation. You can sit beneath a 20-meter-wide waterfall—like taking a hot shower—and lean back inside, where it feels like a sauna. The complex also has an indoor hot tub, plus a restaurant and three bars, including a swim-up bar in the main pool. Towels, lockers, and showers are available. You'll fall in love with Tabacón by night, too, when a dip becomes a romantic indulgence (and a jaw-dropping experience if the volcano is erupting). We recommend the Temazcal treatment, based on an ancient Indian steam room, at the full-service Grand Spa.

Tabacón features a separate section—**Las Fuentes Termales** ($10 admission)—100 meters farther downhill. It has five steaming pools in landscaped grounds in a valley (lacking volcano views) below the hotel, from which you can glide, Rambo-like, by rappel on a canopy **tour** ($40 low season, $45 high season). It has toilets, changing rooms, and towels.

Tabacón is a "high-risk zone." The former community of Tabacón was destroyed in 1968 by an eruption that killed 78 people, and in June 1975, an eruptive lava flow passed over the site of today's springs. Visitors assume their own risk.

Baldi Termae Spa (tel. 506/2479-9651, www.arenal.net/baldi-hot-springs.htm, 10 A.M.–10 P.M. daily, $25 admission), five kilometers west of La Fortuna, features nine hot mineral pools (20.5–35°C) lined with natural stone, and landscaped with cascades and foliage. One pool has its own restaurant, plus there's a small snack bar and lockers. However, service quality appears to be an issue. You'll receive a discount by booking with a tour agent. The lovely **Titokú Hot Springs** (tel. 506/2579-1700, by reservation only), next to Baldi Termae, offers a near-identical option. And kids may appreciate the toboggans at the relatively simple **Termales Los Laureles** (tel. 506/8306-7674, http://termalesloslaureles.com, $6 adults, $4 children), 400 meters farther up the road.

Arenal Waterfall Gardens (8 A.M.–midnight daily, $40 24-hour pass), at The Springs Resort & Spa (tel. 506/2401-3313, www.thespringscostarica.com) is also open to day guests. Guests get access to the 165-acre property, including restaurants and bars, as well as the 18 thermal river pools and cascades, fed by natural thermal mineral water pumped up from 120 meters below ground. This facility uses state-of-the-art filtration and other technology to maintain water purity. Eventually, kayaking, tubing, and fishing will be added.

Entertainment

The huge **Volcán Look Disco** (tel. 506/2479-9691, 7 P.M.–12:30 A.M. Wed.–Sat.), four kilometers west of town, has a restaurant, pool tables, and ping-pong. It has happy hour 9–11 P.M. and gets packed on weekends.

The new **Lava Lounge Bar & Grill** (tel. 506/2479-7365, www.lavaloungecostarica .com, 11 A.M.–midnight daily) is an atmospheric place to enjoy a cocktail.

The Springs Resort Casino (tel. 506/2401-3313, www.thespringscostarica.com), five kilometers west of town, caters to sophisticates and has 50 slots, plus 11 blackjack, baccarat, craps, and roulette tables.

Sports and Recreation

More than a dozen tour agencies in town offer a similar menu that includes fishing at Lake Arenal; trips to Arenal Volcano and Tabacón (check that the entrance fee is included in the tour price), Catarata La Fortuna, Caño Negro, and Venado Caves; mountain biking; horseback trips; a safari float on the Río Peñas Blancas ($35); and white-water trips. You may be approached on the street by so-called guides. The local chamber of commerce warns tourists "not to take tours or information off the street."

The best all-around company is **Desafío Adventure Company** (tel. 506/2479-9464, www.desafiocostarica.com), a one-stop shop for adventure. It also operates "Lost Canyon Adventures," with waterfall rappelling (8 A.M., 10 A.M., and 1:30 P.M. daily, $75). **Pure Trek Canyoning** (tel. 506/2461-2110, www.pure trekcostarica.com) also has waterfall rappelling at 7 A.M. and noon daily.

For horseback rides, **Desafío** (tel. 506/2479-9464, www.desafiocostarica.com) and **Don**

Tobías Cabalgate (tel. 506/2479-1212, www.cabalgatadontobias.com), at Hotel Arenal Springs Resort, are recommended.

You can rents ATVs and take ATV tours with **Arenal ATV** (tel. 506/2479-9222, www.atvarenal.com), **ATV Arenal Tours** (tel. 506/2479-9883, www.lapraderadelarenal.com), and **Fourtrax ATV Tours** (tel. 506/2479-8444, www.fourtraxadventure.com).

Serendipity Adventures (tel. 506/2558-1000, www.serendipityadventures.com) offers hot-air balloon rides at dawn.

Mountain biking? Try **Bike Arenal** (tel. 506/2479-7150, www.bikearenal.com).

Arenal Bungee (tel. 506/2479-7440, www.arenalbungee.com, 9:30 A.M.–8:30 P.M.) offers bungee jumping ($50) from a metal tower right in La Fortuna! You can even touch down in a water pool, which you skim. And there's a high-speed oversized catapult for an added adrenalin boost.

For **canopy tours,** you're spoilt for choice! The **Costa Rica Arenal Canopy Tour** (tel. 506/2479-9769, www.crarenalcanopy.com, $45) offers a package that begins with a 40-minute horseback ride; you'll then whiz between five tree platforms using rappelling equipment. Trips are offered at 8 A.M., 11 A.M., and 1 P.M. daily.

New in 2008, **Ecoglide Tarzan Swing** (tel. 506/2479-7120, www.arenalecoglide.com, $45) also has a zipline, plus a Tarzan swing.

Arenal Canopy Tour (tel. 506/2460-5828, $45), at Miradas Arenal Hotel (tel. 506/2479-1944, www.miradasarenal.com), features ziplines between 12 platforms and takes two hours to traverse the circuit in harness. **Arenal Paraíso Canopy Tour** (tel. 506/2460-5333, $45), at the Arenal Paraíso Hotel, has two-hour tours at 8 A.M., 11 A.M., and 2:30 P.M. The Los Lagos Hotel (tel. 506/2479-1000, www.hotelloslagos.com) hosts the **Canopy Tour Los Cañones.**

Accommodations

Every year sees several new hotels open. There are too many accommodations to list in full; their omission here does not necessarily

LA FORTUNA TOUR COMPANIES

The following tour operators and wholesalers are recommended. **Aventuras Arenal** (tel. 506/2479-9133, www.arenaladventures.com). **Desafío Adventure Company** (tel. 506/2479-9464, www.desafiocostarica .com) specializes in rafting but offers a full range of tours. **Jacamar Naturalist Tours** (tel. 506/2479-9767, www.arenaltours.com). **Pura Vida Tours** (tel. 506/2479-9045, www.puravidatrips.com) offers a full range of local activities, plus excursions far and wide.

indicate that they are not to be considered. In high season, it pays to book ahead.

UNDER $25

In Town: Backpackers should head to ◖ **Gringo Pete's** (tel. 506/2479-8521, gringopetes2003@yahoo.com, $4–5 pp dorms, $5–7 pp private room), a rambling home-turned-hostel in lively color schemes with an open-air dorm with eight bunk beds. A second dorm has seven bunks and en-suite shower. Three private rooms share bathrooms. There's a lounge with sofas, a communal kitchen, lockers, and hammocks and a barbecue grill outside. Tours are offered. A solid bargain. Gringo Pete recently opened **Gringo Pete Too**, with six dorm rooms and 15 rooms with private bathrooms.

Arenal Backpackers' Resort (tel. 506/2479-7000, www.arenalbackpackers.com, $14 pp dorm, $26 pp room) is a worthy alternative and even boasts a lovely swimming pool and hammocks on spacious lawns. Orthopedic mattresses, silent air-conditioning, and flat-screen TVs are among the treats at this first-class budget option, three blocks west of the church.

The **Hotel Hervi** (tel. 506/2479-9430, fax 506/2479-9100, $20 s/d low season, $25 s/d high season), 50 meters southwest of the church, has eight clean, simply appointed

rooms in a modern two-story unit, all with cable TV, fans, and spacious showers with hot water. It also has two-bedroom apartments.

A recently opened alternative in this price range is **Las Orquideas** (tel. 506/2479-8136, horquideas@hotmail.com, $10–15 pp low season, $15–20 pp high season), a small boutique-style hotel with wrought-iron furnishings. It has four simply appointed upstairs rooms, one with whirlpool tub, and all with cable TV. Two rooms share a bathroom. The downstairs grill restaurant serves cheap *casados* (set lunches). Nonsmokers will not appreciate the staff smoking.

$25-50

In Town: About 400 meters east of town, **Villa Fortuna** (tel./fax 506/2479-9139, $40 s/d low season, $45 s/d high season) has 11 clinically clean, modestly furnished modern rooms with refrigerators, fans, tile floors, and private baths with hot water. Seven rooms have air-conditioning and TVs. The landscaped grounds include a small swimming pool and caged toucans.

Hotel La Amistad (tel. 506/2479-9364, www.hotellaamistadarenal.com, $15 s, $30 d) offers 13 air-conditioned rooms and four upstairs apartments, all with ceiling fans, cable TV, and private bath with hot water. The simply furnished downstairs rooms are a bit gloomy and open to the parking lot.

Cabinas Guacamaya (tel. 506/2479-9393, www.cabinasguacamaya.com, $35 s or $40 d low season, $40 s or $45 d high season) is a modern house with nine clean, spacious air-conditioned rooms with refrigerators, private baths with hot water, and patios with rockers. It has secure parking and earns positive reviews from readers.

Hotel Paraíso Tropical (tel. 506/2479-9222, paraisotropical@arenal.net, $40 s, $45 d), on the south side of the church, has 13 spacious, modestly elegant air-conditioned rooms with sponge-washed walls, fans, cable TV, microwave, coffeemaker, private bath, and hot water. Three rooms have king-size beds; four have refrigerators. Upstairs rooms are larger and have balconies with views. There's secure

© CHRISTOPHER P. BAKER

Arenal volcano is in an active phase.

parking, a restaurant, and a tour office, plus Internet access.

Several reasonable options are available on the road between Fortuna and El Tanque. They offer no advantages in location, however, being farther away from the volcano.

La Fortuna to Tabacón: The well-run **Hotel Arenal Rossi** (tel. 506/2479-9023, www.hotelarenalrossi.com, $36 s, $42–52 d low season; $40 s, $47–57 d high season, including tax and breakfast), about two kilometers west of Fortuna, offers 25 simple but pretty *cabinas* with refrigerators, TVs, and private baths with hot water. One has a full kitchen and skylit bathroom. Twelve have air-conditioning. Rooms vary in size. "Immaculate and comfortable," reports a reader, but walls are thin. There's a steakhouse, plus a kids' pool and swings, and a gift store.

$50-100

In Town: The **Hotel Arenal Jireh** (tel. 506/2479-9236, www.hotelarenaljireh.com, $65 s, $80 d), one block west of the church, has 12 pleasant and spacious air-conditioned rooms

with refrigerator, cable TV, tile floors, single and double bed, and hot water. Take an upper-story room in the three-story block for volcano views. There's a small swimming pool, laundry, gift store, tour desk, Internet, and secure parking.

The recently upgraded **Hotel Arenal Carmela** (tel./fax 506/2479-9010, www.hotel arenalcarmela.com, $62 s, $75 d), on the southwest corner of the plaza, has 13 clean air-conditioned rooms with hardwood walls, orthopedic mattresses, cable TVs, refrigerators, in-room safes, patios with hammocks and Sarchí rockers, plus private skylit bathrooms with hot water. There's secure parking. Rates include taxes.

Hotel San Bosco (tel. 506/2479-9050, www.arenal-volcano.com, $45–50 s, $55–60 d low season; $61–66 s, $72–77 d high season), 200 meters north of the plaza, has 34 air-conditioned rooms (11 are cabins) with private baths and hot water. Some of the rooms are small and overpriced; newer rooms are nicer. It has a souvenir shop, plus swimming pool and whirlpool tub. Rates include tax and breakfast.

Boasting a fine restaurant, **Luigi's Hotel &**

THE NORTHERN ZONE

© CHRISTOPHER P. BAKER

Arenal inspires pampering.

Restaurant (tel. 506/2479-9636, www.luigis hotel.com, $48 s/d low season, $60 s/d high season, including breakfast and tax) is a two-story wooden lodge with 20 simply furnished, air-conditioned rooms (as with many hotels, the TVs are in a neck-craning position). There's a pool, whirlpool tub, Internet, gym, casino, and bar.

High-rise has come to town in the form of the **Hotel Fortuna** (tel. 506/2479-9197, www.la fortunahotel.com, $50 s or $60 d standard, $60 s or $70 with view), with 44 clean, tidy, somewhat clinical air-conditioned rooms.

Also to consider in this price bracket are the **Arenal Country Inn** (tel. 506/2479-0101, www.arenalcountryinn.com), 600 meters southeast of town; the **Cataratas Resort** (tel. 506/2479-8181, www.cataratasresort.com); and **Arenal Oasis Ecolodge** (tel. 506/2479-9526, www.arenaloasis.com), both on the road to La Fortuna Waterfall.

La Fortuna to Tabacón: The **Miradas Arenal** (tel. 506/2479-1944, www.miradas arenal.com, $80 s/d), about nine kilometers west of La Fortuna, has fine views. It has three attractive wooden cabins amid broad lawns. Each has a tile floor, refrigerator, coffeemaker, bathrooms with views from the tub/shower and hot water, and French doors that open to verandas.

Erupciones B&B (tel. 506/2479-1400, www.erupcionesinn.com, $65–80 s/d low season, $80–95 s/d high season) is a delightful little place with three cabins in a meadow on a cattle farm. Gaily colored in tropical colors, they're spacious, cross-lit and ventilated through louvered glass windows. Rooms have tile floors, fans, clean modern bathrooms with hot water, and patios. Rates include breakfast.

The **Arenal Volcano Inn** (tel. 506/2479-1122, www.arenalvolcanoinn.com, $70 s or $75 d standard, $74 s or $84 d deluxe, $120 s or $130 d suite low season; $80 s or $90 d standard, $92 s or $106 d deluxe, $150 s or $176 d suite high season) offers an airy, glass-walled restaurant and gorgeous rooms, also with walls of glass plus river-stone walls, colorful decor, dark hardwood furnishings, and modern bathrooms.

$100-200

La Fortuna to Tabacón: I like the secluded **Lomas del Volcán** (tel. 506/2479-9000, www.lomasdelvolcan.com, $100 s, $110 d year-round), set amid dairy pasture about one kilometer off the main road, four kilometers west of town. It has 13 spacious wooden cabins raised on stilts, with king-size and double beds, fans, refrigerator, beautiful modern bathrooms, and volcano views from glass-enclosed porches. Nature trails lead into nearby forest. Horses can be rented.

The ever-improving **Los Lagos Hotel & Resort** (tel. 506/2479-1000, www.hotelloslagos.com, $110–120 s/d low season, $138–174 s/d high season, including taxes) has 105 attractive air-conditioned rooms and cabins of varying standards, all with wooden ceilings, cable TV, phones, safes, minibars, refrigerators, and private baths with hot water. It also has two-bedroom villas with kitchens. There are two restaurants and a spa.

Volcano Lodge (tel. 506/2479-1717, www.volcanolodge.com, $84 s/d low season, $125 s/d high season), about six kilometers west of town, offers 20 beautifully appointed two-bedroom cottages with large picture windows, and porches with rockers for enjoying the volcano views beyond the gardens with a lovely swimming pool with swim-up bar. Facilities include a pool and whirlpool tub. The restaurant is one of the finest around.

Almost identical options include **Arenal Paraíso Resort & Spa** (tel. 506/2479-1100, www.arenalparaiso.com, $75 s/d standard, $105 s/d superior low season; $80 standard, $110 superior high season), about seven kilometers west of town, with 21 all-hardwood standards and 55 air-conditioned superior rooms; and **Montaña de Fuego Resort & Spa** (tel. 506/2479-1220, www.montanadefuego.com, $110–169 s/d year-round), where 66 handsome hardwood air-conditioned *cabinas* and bungalow suites sit on a hillock with splendid volcano views through glass-enclosed verandas (many rooms face away from the volcano). The latter has a glass-enclosed restaurant, plus a swimming pool and the En-Gadi Spa.

I like the new **Hotel Arenal Springs** (tel. 506/2479-1212, www.hotelarenalsprings.com, $107 s/d) for its 65 graciously appointed, low-slung, peak-roofed bungalows dispersed amid lush gardens.

Competing, in a Spanish colonial theme, the **Mountain Paradise Hotel** (tel. 506/2479-1414, www.hotelmountainparadise.com, $105 s/d standard, $120 s/d suite low season; $140 standard, $160 suite high season) offers 40 rooms with river-stone walls and rustic decor. Another colonial-inspired newcomer is **Casa Luna Lodge** (tel. 506/2479-7368, www.casalunalodge.com, $90 s/d low season, $105 s/d high season), with a lovely aesthetic to its 35 rooms.

Also to consider is the less inspired **Hotel Restaurante Lavas Tacotal** (tel. 506/2479-1200, www.hoteltacotal.com).

OVER $200

La Fortuna to Tabacón: The contemporary, upscale, nonsmoking **Tabacón Lodge** (tel. 506/2479-2000, www.tabacon.com, $285–454 s/d year-round), 200 meters uphill of Balneario Tabacón, is set amid well-maintained verdant gardens. The property has 73 air-conditioned rooms, all with beautiful furnishings and a patio affording a volcano view. Nine rooms are junior suites with private garden whirlpool tubs, minibars, and cotton bathrobes. There's a small gym, gourmet restaurant, a bar, a swim-up bar in a thermal pool, and the Grand Spa at the *balneario*. Rates include breakfast and unlimited access to the *balneario*.

Taking the prize for locale is the all-suite **Arenal Kioro** (tel. 506/2479-1700, www.hotelarenalkioro.com, $275 s or $310 d low season, $310 s or $345 d high season), at the very base of the volcano. Its 53 spacious and graciously appointed air-conditioned suites have walls of glass, lush contemporary furnishings, minibars, safes, marble-clad bathrooms, and all modern conveniences. All rooms have an en-suite whirlpool tub with volcano views. There's a gorgeous full-service spa, an excellent gym, and two swimming pools with thermal waters, while the superb Restaurante Heliconias enjoys a grandstand volcano view.

© CHRISTOPHER P. BAKER

Arenal volcano viewed from The Springs Resort & Spa.

Hot on Arenal Kioro's heels, **Magic Mountain Hotel** (tel. 506/2479-7246, www.hotelmagicmountain.com, $235 s/d) opened in 2008 and offers a similarly luxurious experience in its 40 junior suites. It, too, has a conference room, spa, and landscaped swimming pool.

The **Hotel Royal Corin Resort & Loto Spa** (tel. 506/2479-1515, www.royalcorin.com, $195 s/d standard, $245 s/d suite) opened in 2008. Although this large-scale, four-story hotel has an ungainly exterior, the interiors feature sophisticated styling for those who appreciate a chic contemporary vogue. Plush linens and state-of-the-art amenities such as flat-screen TVs combine to make this a winner. It has a spa and hip lounge bar that will suit city-slickers. Nice!

One of the finest additions is **(Arenal Nayara Hotel & Gardens** (tel. 506/2479-1600, www.arenalnayara.com, $265 s/d), inspired by Balinese architecture and making tremendous use of Indonesian hardwood furnishings. The huge, gracious guest rooms have lively color schemes (lime green, tangerine, etc.) and a traditional feel melding with flat-screen TVs and other contemporary touches. Most rooms have king-size beds, many canopied, and all come with a full panoply of modern amenities, plus raised bamboo ceilings and large glass French doors on two sides opening to balconies with whirlpool tubs. The stylish bathrooms have indoor and outdoor showers. The restaurant is one of the best around. Lovely!

By far the most exciting and impressive newcomer is **(The Springs Resort & Spa** (tel. 506/2401-3313, www.thespringscostarica.com, $365–430 s/d low season, $375–440 s/d high season). This stupendous, all-suite property, which opened in October 2008, is one of the nation's most deluxe hotels. The six-story main building is built on a hillside, with tiered thermal springs landscaped into grottos, waterfalls, and pools. The architecture makes good use of gleaming travertine, black marble, lava-stone columns and walls, decorative stained glass, and masses of glossy hardwoods. The suites all have wall-of-glass views of the volcanoes from raised king-size beds. Huge flat-screen TVs above the windows are angled for perfect viewing. Luxurious furnishings include rattan chairs, top-quality linens and mattresses, and sumptuous marble-clad bathrooms with walk-in showers and separate his-and-hers whirlpool tubs. Golf carts are on hand to take guests to and from their villas. When complete, it will offer 200 rooms, plus a casino. *Wow!*

Food

In Town: The simple, clean 24-hour **Soda La Parada** (tel. 506/2479-9547, 24 hours), on the south side of the plaza, serves around the clock and offers lunchtime *casados* for $2, but it also serves a broad menu, from sandwiches to pizza. The thatch-roofed **Rancho La Cascada Restaurant** (tel. 506/2479-9145, 6 A.M.–11 P.M. daily), on the north side of the plaza, serves filling breakfasts plus *típico* and eclectic dishes, from burgers to pastas ($2–6).

For traditional local fare, head to **Choza de Laurel** (tel. 506/2479-7063, www.lachozade laurel.com, 6:30 A.M.–10 P.M. daily), a rustic Tican country inn with cloves of garlic hanging from the roof and an excellent *plato especial*—mixed plate of Costa Rican dishes. Grilled chicken ($2–6) and *casados* ($4) are other good bets.

For in-town elegance, I opt for **Restaurante Luigi** (tel. 506/2479-9636, 6 A.M.–11 P.M. daily), two blocks west of the plaza. This airy upscale option lists a large pasta and pizza menu, plus the likes of bruschetta ($5), cream of mushroom soup ($4), beef stroganoff ($10), and sea bass with shrimp ($15). It specializes in flambées and has a large cocktail list.

The best eats in town, however, are at **[Café Rufino** (tel. 506/2479-9997, 10 A.M.–10:30 P.M. daily), one block east of the plaza. Airy and elegant, it offers a wide menu that ranges from veggies on the grill ($6) and mushrooms à la Marseillaise ($10) to filet mignon ($15). It serves great *bocas* at the bar.

Craving steak? Make a beeline to **Steak House Arenal** (tel. 506/2479-9023, 6 A.M.–10 P.M. daily, $5–12), 800 meters west of town. This charming place is festooned with hanging plants and has traditional hardwood decor.

And sushi has come to town at the stylishly contemporary, open-air **Kazan** (tel. 506/2479-7561, noon–10 P.M. daily). Most dishes, such as mixed tempura, cost $12 or less.

Musmanni (6 A.M.–10 P.M. daily), two blocks east of the plaza, sells baked goods, as does the delightful **Mi Casa Coffee House** (tel. 506/2479-7115, 7 A.M.–6 P.M. daily), one block east of the plaza. For ice cream, head to **Eskimo Heladería**, on the plaza's north side.

La Fortuna to Tabacón: You don't have to pay the entrance fee to eat at the **Ave del Paraíso Restaurante** (506/2519-1999, noon–4:30 P.M. and 5–9:30 P.M. daily), at Balneario Tabacón. It serves splendid Tico and creative continental fare, such as French onion soup ($3) and sea bass in apple and chile pepper ($10). It also has salads and pastas ($3–5). The surroundings are unbeatable and the service professional. The **Los Tucanes Restaurant** (6:30–10 A.M. and 5–10 P.M. daily), also at Tabacón, is equally upscale and offers magnificent volcano views; its menu spans the globe.

Meat eaters should head to **Restaurante Mirador Arenal Steak House** (tel. 506/2479-9023, www.restaurantesteakhousemirador arenal.com, 10 A.M.–10 P.M. daily, $3.50–$11), a clean, modern restaurant featuring onion soup, gazpacho, tenderloin in jalapeño sauce, and tilapia in pimento sauce.

An upscale standout south of town, the elegant **[Restaurante Heliconias** (tel. 506/2479-1700, www.hotelarenalkioro.com, 6:30 A.M.–10 P.M. daily), in the Hotel Arenal Kioro, is right below the lava flows. Its position is spectacular, with a wall of glass that opens so you can even hear the lava while you dine! And the cuisine rates, too. Begin, perhaps, with the octopus cocktail ($12) or pejibaye cream ($6) followed by sea bass in caper sauce ($16), and perhaps the seafood salad made at your table with 12 ingredients.

Even classier is **[Las Ventanas Restaurant** (tel. 506/2401-3313, www.the springscostarica.com, 11 A.M.–10 P.M. daily), in The Springs Resort & Spa. It also has incredible wall-of-glass views of the volcano plus the northern lowlands. It serves gourmet Costa Rican fusion cuisine. And of the hotel restaurants recently opened,

Las Ventanas Restaurant

Altamira (6:30 –10 A.M., 11 A.M.–2 P.M., and 5:30 –10 P.M. daily) at the Hotel Arenal Nayara is the most stylish, blending a Balinese theme into a contemporary vogue; you dine beneath a huge palenque roof hung with Chinese lanterns. Gazpacho ($6), ceviche, mushroom gratin, beef jalapeño tenderloin ($16), and seafood Pernod ($18) exemplify the menu.

Information and Services
The **Clínica La Fortuna** (tel. 506/2479-9142, 7 A.M.–5 P.M. weekdays, 7 A.M.–noon Saturday) is two blocks northeast of the gas station. The private **Clínica Médico Sanar** (tel. 506/2479-9420), two blocks east of the plaza, has ambulance service. There's a **dental clinic** (tel. 506/2579-9696) on the southeast side of town.

The **police station** (tel. 506/2479-9689) is on the main drag, one block east of the plaza.

There are three banks in town, and more Internet cafés than you can shake a stick at, including **Arenal Evergreen Tourist Information Center** (tel. 506/2479-9511).

Dirty laundry? Head to **Lavandería La Fortuna** (tel. 506/2479-9547, 8 A.M.–9 P.M. Mon.–Sat.) or **Alice Laundry** (tel. 506/2479-7111, 7 A.M.–10 P.M. daily), two blocks west of and two blocks east of the plaza, respectively.

Getting There and Away
Autotransportes San Carlos (tel. 506/2256-8914) buses depart San José from Calle 12, Avenidas 7/9, at 6:15 A.M., 8:40 A.M., and 11:30 A.M. daily ($3). Return buses depart La Fortuna from the south side of the plaza at 12:45 P.M. and 2:45 P.M. Buses (tel. 506/8379-3153) depart Ciudad Quesada for La Fortuna 15 times daily (irregular hours, $1.05). Buses depart Tilarán for La Fortuna at 7 A.M. and 12:30 P.M. daily (four hours, $2), returning at 8 A.M. and 4:30 P.M.

Interbus (tel. 506/2283-5573 and 506/2479-9796, www.interbusonline.com) and **Grayline Costa Rica** (tel. 506/2220-2126, www.graylinecostarica.com) operate shuttles from San José ($35) and popular tourist destinations in Nicoya and Guanacaste.

Alamo (tel. 506/2479-9090, www.alamocostarica.com) has a car-rental office in town.

© CHRISTOPHER P. BAKER

Getting Around

Bike Rental Arenal (tel. 506/2479-7150, www.bikearenal.com) rents mountain bikes ($22 daily, $132 weekly).

◖ ARENAL VOLCANO NATIONAL PARK

The 12,016-hectare Parque Nacional Volcán Arenal (tel. 506/2461-8499, 8 A.M.–4 P.M. daily, last entrance at 3 P.M., $10 admission) lies within the 204,000-hectare Arenal Conservation Area, a polyglot assemblage protecting 16 reserves in the region between the Guanacaste and Tilarán mountain ranges, and including Lake Arenal. The park has two volcanoes: extinct Chato (1,140 meters), whose collapsed crater contains an emerald lagoon, and active Arenal (1,633 meters), a picture-perfect cone. Arenal is also Costa Rica's most active volcano and a must-see on any tourist's itinerary. Note, however, that it is most often covered in clouds, and getting to *see* an eruption is a matter of luck (the dawn hours are best, before the clouds roll in; seasonally, you stand a reasonable chance in dry season, and less than favorable odds in rainy season). Arenal slumbered peacefully throughout the colonial era. On July 29, 1968, it was awakened from its long sleep by a fateful earthquake. The massive explosion that resulted wiped out the villages of Tabacón and Pueblo Nuevo. The blast was felt as far away as Boulder, Colorado. Its lava flows and eruptions have since been constant, and on virtually any day you can see smoking cinder blocks tumbling down the steep slope from the horseshoe-shaped crater—or at night, watch a fiery cascade of lava spewing from the 140-meter-deep crater. Some days the volcano blows several times in an hour, spewing house-size rocks, sulfur dioxide and chloride gases, and red-hot lava. The volcano's active vent often shifts location; for the past decade it has been on the western side, but in 2008 a collapse at the crater rim shifted the predominant lava flows to the eastern side. Explosions and eruptions, however, occur on all sides.

MINAE's Comisión Nacional de Emergencías has set up four "safety zones" around the volcano and ostensibly regulates commercial development. It's highly arbitrary, however, and any cataclysmic eruption would devastate the entire area.

The turnoff to the entrance is 3.5 kilometers east of Lake Arenal dam and 2.5 kilometers west of Tabacón. The dirt access road leads 1.5 kilometers to the ranger station, which gives a small informational pamphlet and has restrooms. A dirt road leads north from here 1.5 kilometers to a parking lot and hiking trails. The Arenal Observatory Lodge (tel. 506/2479-1070, www.arenalobservatorylodge.com) has a small but interesting **Museum of Vulcanicity.**

Trails

The one-kilometer **Las Heliconias Trail** leads from the ranger station past an area where vegetation is recolonizing the 1968 lava flow. The trail intersects the **Look-Out Point Trail,** which leads 1.3 kilometers from the ranger station to a *mirador*—a viewing area—from which you can watch active lava flowing. **Las Coladas Trail** begins at the intersection and leads 2.8 kilometers to a lava flow from 1993. The **Los Miradores Trail** begins at park headquarters and leads southwest 1.2 kilometers to Lake Arenal.

You can also hike various trails at the **Arenal Observatory Lodge.** A guided hike is offered at 8:30 A.M. daily (complimentary to guests). The four-kilometer-long Lava Trail (a tough climb back to the lodge—don't believe your guide if he/she says it is easy) is free; it takes about three hours round-trip (it was temporarily closed in late 2008 due to eruptions). The Chato Trail (four hours) is longer and more difficult.

Hotels and tour companies in La Fortuna offer volcano tours and can arrange guides. And at the entrance to the lodge is the trailhead for the private **Los Tucanes Trail** (8 A.M.–8 P.M., $4 self-guided), which leads to the southernmost lava flows (one hour one-way).

Hiking too close to the volcano is not advisable. Heed warning signs. This isn't Disneyland! The volcano is totally unpredictable, and there is a strong possibility of losing your life if you venture into restricted zones.

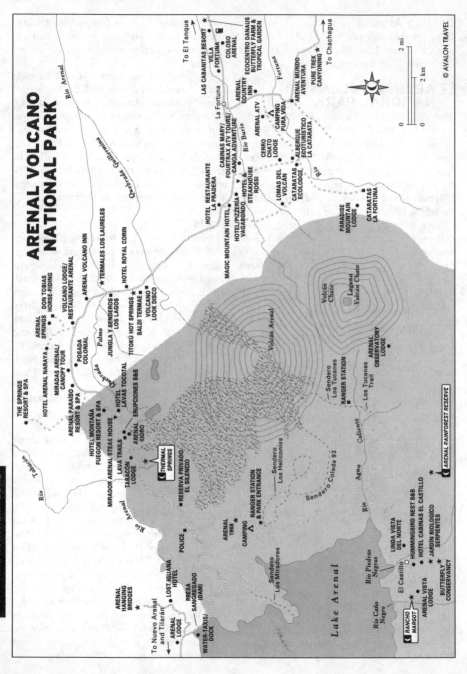

ARENAL VOLCANO NATIONAL PARK

© AVALON TRAVEL

© CHRISTOPHER P. BAKER

Arenal volcano viewed from Arenal Kioro

Accommodations and Food

No camping is allowed in the park. However, you can camp on land adjacent to the ranger station ($2.50 pp), with basic toilets and showers.

Enjoying an enviable setting at a higher elevation than any other hotel in the region, the (**Arenal Observatory Lodge** (tel. 506/2479-1070 or 506/2290-7011 for reservations, www.arenalobservatorylodge.com, $71 s or $83 d standard, $96 s or $108 d Smithsonian, $115 s or $120 d junior suite low season; $86 s or $98 d standard, $116 s or $128 d Smithsonian, $141 s or $148 d junior suite high season) is a ridge-top property offering immaculate views over the lake and volcano (you're viewing the east side, not the side with lava flows, however). The facility, built in 1987 as an observatory for the Smithsonian Institution and the University of Costa Rica, has 40 rooms of three types in four widely dispersed buildings. Recently remodeled standard rooms offer plenty of comfort, with twin beds and sliding glass doors opening to volcano-view balconies. Four observatory rooms have volcano views through vast picture windows, as do

nine modestly appointed but spacious superior rooms in the Smithsonian block, reached via a suspension bridge. Five luxury junior suites are more graciously furnished and have the best views. Five rooms are wheelchair accessible. A converted farmhouse—**La Casona**—half a kilometer away accommodates 14 more people in four rooms with shared bathrooms; only three rooms have volcano views. The **White Hawk Villa** accommodates 10 people. The lodge offers horseback rides, hikes, and free canoeing on Lake Chato. And there's a splendid walk-in horizon-edge swimming pool, plus whirlpool tub, kids' pool, and wet bar. A car is essential.

The Arenal Observatory Lodge restaurant is open to nonguests and serves breakfast 7–8:30 A.M., lunch 11:30 A.M.–4:30 P.M., and dinner 6–8:30 P.M. daily. It's worth it for its magnificent vantage. I've enjoyed cream of asparagus soup, chicken in curry sauce, and splendid tilapia dishes.

EL CASTILLO

The dirt road to Arenal Observatory Lodge splits about four kilometers east of the ranger

THE NORTHERN ZONE

station, with one branch leading south along the southern edge of Lake Arenal via the tiny community of El Castillo, beyond which it deteriorates rapidly and requires a four-wheel-drive vehicle. The arduous route eventually connects with Tronadora on the south shore. There are several rivers to cross, and only in the driest of dry seasons is it passable.

Butterfly Conservancy

The Butterfly Conservancy (tel. 506/2479-1149, www.butterflyconservatory.org, 8 A.M.–5 P.M. daily, $12 adults, $8 students and children under eight), about one kilometer above El Castillo, is a butterfly garden and insect museum with live scorpions, rhinoceros beetles, lizards, among other creatures. About 30 species of butterflies flit beneath seven netted arenas. It also has a poison-dart frog exhibit, a botanical garden with medicinal plants, and trails good for viewing monkeys.

Next door, the **Jardín Biológico y Serpientes del Arenal** (tel. 506/8358-6773, 8 A.M.–9 P.M. daily, $12 low season, $15 high season) has an excellent snake exhibit with about 35 species, including pit vipers and fer-de-lance, plus poison-dart frogs, lizards, turtles, and arachnids.

(Rancho Margot

Rancho Margot (tel. 506/2479-7259, www.ranchomargot.org), on the banks of the Río Caño Negro, at the end of the dirt road west of El Castillo, is a self-sufficient organic farm with stables. It has 152 hectares of forest bordering the Children's Eternal Rainforest Reserve. Pigs and cattle are raised; prosciutto, cheeses, and other products are made on-site; and visitors can participate in farm activities. It's based around an ivy-clad farmstead in traditional colonial style. *Comida típica* meals are served hot from the stove, and the Sunday buffet here draws locals from far and wide. A wildlife rehabilitation center housing deer and monkeys is evolving. Educational tours are offered (you'll even get to see the pig-waste compost heater), as are horseback rides ($30–65), kayaking ($35–70), waterfall rappelling ($45–80), and

hiking. Appealing to the Indiana Jones within, its **Raid Arenal** (www.raidarenal.com, $160 one-night, $300 two-night) tours are Army-style, overnight rainforest adventures that have you wading through rivers and hacking your way through the jungle with a machete.

(Arenal Rainforest Reserve

This private reserve (tel. 506/2479-9944, www.arenalreserve.com, 7:30 A.M.–5 P.M. daily), near El Castillo, on the north-facing slopes of the Cordillera de Tilarán offers phenomenal volcano views, to be enjoyed from an aerial **Sky Tram** ($55 adult, $28 children) that rises 236 meters, taking visitors up to a *mirador* (lookout point) and the **Sky Trek** ($66 adults, $42 children, including tram) zipline circuit, with 2.8 kilometers of ziplines stretching across canyons and between treetops. This is perhaps the most thrilling zipline in the country. There's also a **Butterfly Kids' Garden.**

Accommodations

Hotel Cabinitas El Castillo (tel./fax 506/8383-7196, $15 pp), above El Castillo, has 10 *cabinas* with large picture windows on three sides. There's a cozy restaurant with sweeping vistas.

Hotel Linda Vista del Norte (tel. 506/2479-1551 or U.S. tel. 866/546-4239, www.hotellinda vista.com, $58 s or $68 d standard, $85 s or $105 d junior suite, $140 s/d suite low season; $68 s or $78 d standard, $105 s or $115 d junior suite, $150 s/d suite high season), east of El Castillo, enjoys a splendid hilltop position with views of both lake and volcano. It adjoins a 210-hectare private forest reserve with trails. It has modestly furnished yet attractive cabins. The 11 standard rooms have two full-size beds and a bunk bed. Two junior suites have two queen beds, air-conditioning, and mini-refrigerator, plus there's a suite. The colorful restaurant has picture-perfect views. Guided horseback tours are offered. Rates include taxes and breakfast.

The **Arenal Vista Lodge** (tel. 506/2479-1802, www.arenalvistalodge.com, $75 s or $91 d low season, $87 s or $103 d high season),

© CHRISTOPHER P. BAKER

tour boats at the Lake Arenal dam

west of El Castillo, perches on a landscaped terraced hill with a private forest reserve behind. Decor in the 28 cabins is rather drab, despite vast picture windows with window boxes and small balconies with lake views. A dining room and terrace offer panoramas. It has a swimming pool and sundeck.

The lovely **Hummingbird Nest B&B** (tel. 506/8835-8711, www.hummingbird nestbb.com, $30 pp including breakfast), set in hilltop gardens, has fabulous volcano views through picture windows in its three lovely guest rooms; bathrooms are a bit small, though. All have ceiling fans and mini-fridges. It has a patio whirlpool tub. A solid bargain!

Rancho Margot (tel. 506/2479-7259, www.ranchomargot.org, $40 s, $70 d bunkhouse, $104 s, $140 d bungalows, including breakfast and tax), an organic farm, has bunks in basic yet super-clean and well-thought-out dorm rooms with shared bathrooms; plus 18 lovely bungalows at the forest edge. The latter are nicely furnished and boast terra-cotta floors, whitewashed walls, modern bathrooms, and spacious decks.

LAKE ARENAL

This picture-perfect lake might have been transplanted from the English Lake District, surrounded as it is by emerald-green mountains. The looming mass of Volcán Arenal rises over the lake to the east. About 2–3 million years ago, tectonic movements created a depression that filled with a small lagoon. In 1973, the Costa Rican Institute of Electricity (ICE) built an 88-meter-long, 56-meter-tall dam at the eastern end of the valley, creating a narrow 32-kilometer-long reservoir covering 12,400 hectares. The northern shores are backed by thick primary forest.

The only town along the entire perimeter is **Nuevo Arenal.** This small town on the north-central shore, 32 kilometers northeast of Tilarán, immediately west of the Guanacaste-Alajuela provincial boundary, was created in 1973 when the man-made lake flooded the original settlement.

The lake is easily reached from La Fortuna (20 kilometers east of the dam), or from the Pan-American Highway via Tilarán. The paved road swings around the north and west side of

THE NORTHERN ZONE

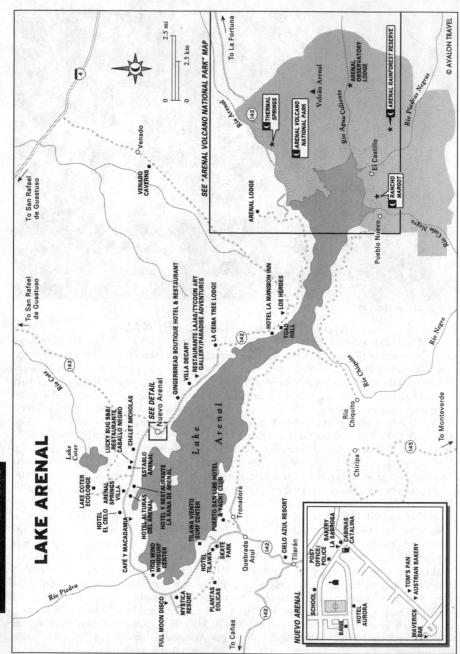

LAKE ARENAL

To San Rafael de Guastuso

To San Rafael de Guastuso

Río Cote

Río Piedra

Lake Coter

LAKE COTER ECOLODGE

HOTEL EL CIELO

ARENAL SPRINGS VILLA

LUCKY BUG B&B/ RESTAURANTE CABALLO NEGRO

CHALET NICHOLAS

CAFÉ Y MACADAMIA

HOTEL ALTURAS DEL ARENAL

ESTABLO ARENAL

HOTEL Y RESTAURANTE LA RANA DE ARENAL

TICO WIND WINDSURF CENTER

TILAWA VIENTO SURF CENTER

PUERTO SAN LUIS HOTEL & YACHT CLUB

HOTEL TILAWA

SKATE PARK

FULL MOON DISCO

MYSTICA RESORT

PLANTAS EÓLICAS

GINGERBREAD BOUTIQUE HOTEL & RESTAURANT

VILLA DECARY

RESTAURANTE LAJAS/TYCOON ART GALLERY/PARADISE ADVENTURES

LA CEIBA TREE LODGE

HOTEL LA MANSION INN

LOS HÉROES

TOAD HALL

SEE DETAIL Nuevo Arenal

Lake Arenal

Tronadora

Quebrada Azul

CIELO AZUL RESORT

Tilarán

CHALET NICHOLAS

To Cañas

Río Piedra

Río Chiquito

Río Chiquito

Chiripa

Río Negro

To Monteverde

Venado

VENADO CAVERNS

To La Fortuna

© AVALON TRAVEL

2.5 mi

2.5 km

SEE "ARENAL VOLCANO NATIONAL PARK" MAP

THERMAL SPRINGS

ARENAL VOLCANO NATIONAL PARK

Volcán Arenal

ARENAL OBSERVATORY LODGE

ARENAL RAINFOREST RESERVE

Río Arenal

Río Agua Caliente

Río Piedra Negra

El Castillo

ARENAL LODGE

RANCHO MARGOT

Pueblo Nuevo

Río Caño Negro

NUEVO ARENAL

SCHOOL

BANK

HOTEL AURORA

POST OFFICE/ POLICE

BAKERY LA SABROSA

CABINAS CATALINA

TOM'S PAN

AUSTRIAN BAKERY

MAVERICK BAR

M0 BANK

kite-surfing at Lake Arenal

© CHRISTOPHER P. BAKER

the lake, linking the two towns. Landslides are a frequent occurrence and often close the road for days at a time. A dirt road that begins opposite Toad Hall leads over the cordillera to Venado Caverns; another traverses the mountains, linking Lake Coter (a small lake, five kilometers northwest of Nuevo Arenal) with San Rafael de Guatuso.

On the south side, a road is paved as far as **Tronadora,** beyond which it turns to dirt and leads to El Castillo and Arenal Volcano National Park. Access is highly tenuous, and usually impossible in wet season.

Arenal Hanging Bridges

Arenal Hanging Bridges (tel. 506/2290-0469, www.hangingbridges.com, 8 A.M.–4:30 P.M. daily, $22 adult, $17 senior, $12 student), within a 250-hectare reserve immediately east of the dam, provides a marvelous entrée to forest ecology as you follow a three-kilometer self-guided interpretive trail with 15 sturdy bridges (some up to 100 meters long) suspended across ravines and treetops. Guided tours include an early-morning birding tour ($25). Last entrance is at 3:30 P.M.

Entertainment

Maverick's (tel. 506/2694-4282), at the Aurora Inn, in Nuevo Arenal, cranks it up on Saturday nights. Entry is $2 when live bands play.

Sports and Recreation

WINDSURFING AND WATER SPORTS

In the morning the lake can look like a mirror, but the calm is short-lived. More normal are nearly constant 30- to 80-kph winds, which whip up whitecaps and turn the lake into one of the world's top windsurfing spots. Swells can top one meter. Twenty-five mph is the *average* winter day's wind speed. November, December, and January are the best months for windsurfing, and June and October the worst.

The **Tilawa Viento Surf Center** (tel. 506/2695-5050, http://windsurfcostarica.com), on the southwest shore, focuses on beginners ($35 per two-hour lesson) and has kayaks. **Tico Wind Surf Center** (tel. 506/2692-2002 or U.S. tel. 800/433-2423, www.ticowind.com), on the western shore, is open 9 A.M.–6 P.M. daily November–April.

Paradise Adventures (tel. 506/8319-4625,

http://paradise-adventures-costa-rica.com), at Lajas, spices up the experience with "wakeboarding" behind speedboats—it's like snowboarding on water.

FISHING

The lake is stocked with game fish—guapote, machaca, and (for lighter tackle enthusiasts) mojarra. Most of the hotels hereabouts offer fishing tours, as does **Capt. Ron's Lake Arenal Fishing Tours** (tel. 506/2695-4678, www.arenalfishing.com), in Nuevo Arenal. The *Rain Goddess* (tel. 506/2231-4299 or U.S. tel. 866/593-3168, www.bluwing.com) is a deluxe 65-foot live-aboard vessel that caters to anglers with multi-day packages. It has two double and four triple wood-paneled cabins. Gourmet meals are served. And **Gabino Hidalgo** (tel. 506/2461-2108, gabinoaventurascr@hotmail.com) offers fishing, departing the water-taxi dock by the dam.

OTHER RECREATION

There's a **canopy tour** ($50) at the Lake Coter Ecolodge (tel. 560/2289-6060 or U.S. tel. 866/211-0956, www.ecolodgecostarica.com), which offers hiking ($15), horseback rides ($20), canoeing ($20) and kayaking ($20), and water sports.

The **Establo Arenal** (tel. 506/2694-4434, www.thestablearenal.com), about three kilometers west of Nuevo Arenal, rents horses ($30 half day).

Hotel Tilawa has a skateboard park.

Shopping

The **Lucky Bug Gallery** (tel. 506/2694-4515, www.luckybugcr.com) sells a fabulous array of quality custom crafts, from metal insects and naked fairy lamps to masks, exquisite hammered tin pieces, and ceramics. **Toad Hall** (tel. 506/2692-8001, www.toadhall-gallery.com, 8:30 A.M.–4:30 P.M. daily) has an impressive and eclectic range of art and crafts in addition to serving food.

Accommodations

Hotels are listed predominantly along the north shore. There are many more to choose from than those listed here.

$25-50

In Nuevo Arenal, **Cabinas Catalina** (tel. 506/8819-6793, $15 s, $20 d) has somewhat spartan rooms in a two-story block in the village center; it makes a pretense of hot water.

At Tronadora, on the south shore, the **Puerto San Luis Lodge & Yacht Club** (tel. 506/2695-5750, $40 up to four people) occupies a sheltered cove. Its 19 rooms remain almost ascetic, but the setting is lovely, there's a pool with water slide, and a restaurant takes advantage of the views.

Perfectly adequate, yet winning no prizes, are the modest **Hotel Alturas del Arenal** (tel. 506/2694-4039, fax 506/2694-4670, alturasarenal@hotmail.com, $25 s, $40 d), with 10 small, simply furnished rooms overlooking landscaped gardens with a whirlpool tub and a freshwater pool fed by natural springs; and the **Hotel y Restaurante La Rana de Arenal** (tel./fax 506/2694-4031, $30 s, $45 d), a modern, German-owned option with seven rustic cabins and an apartment on landscaped grounds with lake views.

$50-100

The Swiss-owned **Hotel & Restaurant Los Héroes** (tel. 506/2692-8012, www.hotellosheroes.com, $55–65 s/d, $115 s/d apartment, including breakfast) is a chalet-style hotel with hints of the Alps at every turn. Twelve nicely appointed rooms feature brass beds and balconies. International cuisine is served in the Tyrolean restaurant. Highlights include a pool and whirlpool tub, stables for horseback rides, and a boat for dinner and sunset cruises! Irrevocably Swiss, the hotel even has its own miniature diesel train that runs on a rail circuit through tunnels and over bridges. Credit cards not accepted.

I recommend the hillside **Mystica Resort** (tel. 506/2692-1001, www.mysticalodge.com, $85 s, $100 d), on the west shore, run by an Italian couple. It has a beautiful ambience and offers six large, simply furnished rooms in lovely pastel earth tones, and with odd, delightful touches. You can sit on your veranda festooned by an arbor and admire the landscaped grounds cascading to the lake below and the volcano in the distance. Gourmet dinners are served in a cozy, high-ceilinged restaurant. Rates include breakfast.

La Ceiba Tree Lodge (tel./fax 506/2692-8050, www.ceibatree-lodge.com, $55 s/d standard, $75 suite low season; $69 s/d standard, $90 suite high season), about six kilometers east of town, is a small German-run bed-and-breakfast amid a 16-hectare farm that swathes the hillside and is shaded by a mammoth ceiba tree. Five large and airy rooms have orthopedic mattresses, plus private baths with hot water. There's also a suite, plus a small apartment with kitchen. Breakfast is served on the patio of the owner's fabulous A-frame contemporary house with fine lake views. Trails lead into a forest reserve. Rates include breakfast.

Groups gravitate toward **Lake Coter Ecolodge** (tel. 560/2289-6060 or U.S. tel. 866/211-0956, www.ecolodgecostarica.com, $65 s or $75 d standard, $80 s or $90 d cabins), an elegant hardwood and brick structure in landscaped grounds backed by 300 hectares of forest reserve west of Lake Coter. A cozy lounge with deep-cushioned sofas is centered on a large open-hearth fireplace. The 23 recently remade garden-view rooms are fairly small and clinical, but pleasant enough. Preferable are the 14 four-person duplex cabins, with smashing views. The lodge has a game room, a lounge bar, a pleasing restaurant, and all manner of activities.

Two friendly Great Danes welcome guests to the American-run **◖ Chalet Nicholas** (tel./fax 506/2694-4041, www.chaletnicholas.com, $58 s/d low season, $68 s/d high season), a splendid three-bedroom Colorado-style guesthouse two kilometers west of Nuevo Arenal (at road marker Km 48). It exudes charm and all the comforts of home. Two bedrooms are downstairs. A spiral staircase winds up to a larger "semi-private" loft bedroom with cozy sitting room boasting a deck good for bird-watching. All rooms have volcano views, orthopedic mattresses, and intriguing wall hangings. The inn proffers a TV lounge,

a fruit orchard and orchid house, plus hiking and horseback riding along trails into an adjacent forest reserve. The organic meals get rave reviews. No smokers or credit cards. A splendid bargain. Rates include breakfast.

The charming **Villa Decary** (tel./fax 506/2694-4330, www.villadecary.com, $99 s/d rooms, $129–149 *casitas*) is a small country inn on a former fruit and coffee *finca* on three hilly hectares between Nuevo Arenal and the botanical gardens. The contemporary two-story structure glows with light. Hardwood furniture gleams. Five large bedrooms each have bright Guatemalan covers, plus a balcony with a handy rail that serves as bench and table. Three new *cabinas* are perched farther up the hill. The gardens and surrounding forest are great for birding. The American-run hotel is gay-friendly and has Wi-Fi. No credit cards are accepted. Rates include full breakfast.

The Israeli-owned **Gingerbread Boutique Hotel & Restaurant** (tel. 506/2694-0039, www.gingerbreadarenal.com, $85 s/d low season, $100 s/d high season) has three exquisitely decorated, air-conditioned rooms with cable TV, telephone, Wi-Fi, ceiling fans, plus colorful art and murals with themes of butterflies, jungle, and cupid (for honeymooners). The stone-clad restaurant with wrought-iron furniture is a delightfully shaded space for dining.

On the south shore, the **Hotel Tilawa** (tel. 506/2695-5050, www.hotel-tilawa.com, $48–78 s/d low season, $58–88 s/d high season) is inspired by the Palace of Knossos on Crete: Thick bulbous columns, walls painted with flowers and dolphins, and ocher pastels play on the Cretan theme. It has 24 spacious albeit simply furnished rooms and four junior suites with magnificent views over the lake, plus six more appealing apartments with thick columns and gorgeous bathrooms. Alas, in inclement weather the place is blasted by wind and rains and is drafty and damp. A bar and restaurant are somewhat shielded from the winds by floor-to-ceiling windows, and there's a brewpub! The hotel specializes in windsurfing and has a swimming pool and tennis court.

Lucky Bug B&B (tel. 506/2694-4515,

THE NORTHERN ZONE

© CHRISTOPHER P. BAKER

bedroom at Lucky Bug B&B, Lake Arenal

www.luckybugcr.com, $59 s/d, $89 suite low season; $79 s/d, $120 suite high season), two kilometers west of Nuevo Arenal, has five delightful, individually themed rooms (such as the Frog Room and the Lizard Room) with lively art, balconies, and quaint bathrooms. Being upstairs in a two-story building, they can get hot. Downstairs comprises a large family suite.

On the outskirts of Nuevo Arenal, the **Hotel Lago Arenal** (tel. 506/2694-4319, www.arenal lake.com, $80 s, $90 d), new in 2008, offers spacious, clinically clean rooms with lake views.

$100-150

Arenal Lodge (tel. 506/2460-1881, www.arenal lodge.com, $64–135 s, $72–139 d low season; $71–158 s, $78–164 d high season), at the extreme northeast of the lake, is a Spanish colonial-style lodge with an inviting atmosphere and an improved new look. The 50 spacious and attractive rooms—some with volcano view—come in seven types, from standards to chalets and suites. Most have wood-paneling, louvered windows, and colorful fabrics. Most have balconies with rockers for enjoying the grandstand volcano views; the modestly furnished hilltop junior suites have the best views. There's a library, kids' room, lounge bar, cable TV, and a lovely heated pool with sundeck. It has a butterfly garden plus trails into its own primary forest reserve. A weak link is the uninspired cuisine in the restaurant with view.

OVER $150

Lost Iguana Hotel (tel. 506/2479-1551, www.lostiguanaresort.com, $185 s/d standard, $255–460 s/d deluxe suites, $395 s/d villa), near Hanging Bridges, just east of the dam, has beautifully laid-out and classily furnished accommodations, including luxury villas with two-person tubs. A delightful thatched, open-air restaurant and bar overlooks the landscaped pool and grounds, with the volcano as a backdrop. Trails lead into a private reserve.

The **(Hotel La Mansion Inn** (tel. 506/2692-8018, www.lamansionarenal.com, $150–395 s/d low season, $225–495 s/d high season), eight kilometers east of Nuevo Arenal, is the most beautiful place for miles. Its hillside

THE NORTHERN ZONE

setting is complemented by bougainvillea clambering over 16 *cabinas* with lake views. Each beautifully decorated unit has a timbered ceiling, elegant antiques and wrought-iron furniture, and a mezzanine bedroom with king-size bed, with a small lounge below. French doors open onto a veranda with Sarchí rockers. Five luxury rooms take the decor to new heights. Each unit has its own sheltered carport. And the ultra-luxe Royal Honeymoon Suite and Royal Cottage sleep up to six people ($795 low season, $995 high season). The open-air bar (shaped like a ship's prow) and restaurant are decorated with nautical motifs. There's a spring-fed, horizon-edge swimming pool. Guests get use of horses, canoes, and rowboats, and tours are offered. Rates include breakfast and horseback riding.

Food
For breakfast, I head to ◖ **Tom's Pan** (tel./fax 506/2694-4547, 7:30 A.M.–4 P.M. daily low season, 7:30 A.M.–5:30 P.M. high season), in Nuevo Arenal. This delightfully rustic, German-run outdoor café is splendid for enjoying American breakfasts. It also has sandwiches; beef stew with veggies; dumplings with bacon; sauerkraut; chicken with rice; roast pork with homemade noodles; and Tom's pastries and other splendid baked goods. Competing next door, the **Austrian Bakery** (tel. 506/2694-4445, 8 A.M.–5 P.M. daily) is more contemporary and serves fabulous bread, croissants, and cappuccinos, among other treats. It also has a tremendous crafts store.

At **Los Héroes** (7 A.M.–3 P.M. and 6–8 P.M. Mon. and Wed., 7 A.M.–9 P.M. other days) the French-Swiss menu includes beef bouillon, smoked pork cutlet, and fondue, washed down with kirsch. The charming restaurant at **Mystica Resort** (noon–9 P.M. daily) has a splendid Italian menu: pasta al pomodoro, 16 types of pizza, and a large Italian wine list. And Levantine dishes feature on the menu at the Tuscan-style **Gingerbread** at the Gingerbread Boutique Hotel (tel. 506/2694-0039, www .gingerbreadarenal.com, 5–9 P.M. Tues.–Sat.), with a daily menu that can also include filet

mignon, jumbo shrimp with couscous and lentils, and tuna sashimi. Dishes top out at $20.

The drive along the north shore is worth it to dine at **Restaurante Caballo Negro** (tel. 506/2694-4515, www.luckybugcr.com, 7 A.M.–8 P.M. daily, $5–12), at Lucky Bug B&B. It has an eclectic menu ranging from schnitzel and chicken cordon bleu to eggplant parmigiana—plus cappuccinos. I enjoyed an avocado burger ($7.95). You dine overlooking a delightful garden and lake; you can even fish from a canoe and catch your own tilapia or bass. It has Wi-Fi. Likewise, near La Mansion, ◖ **Toad Hall** (tel. 506/2692-8001, www.toad hall-gallery.com, 8:30 A.M.–4:30 P.M. daily), equal parts deli, café, gallery, book shop, and general store, is a gem. Breakfasts include granola, waffles, and omelettes, and the lunch menu includes a fabulous herb-roasted chicken sandwich ($8).

A more contemporary-style alternative, **Gallery y Restaurante Lajas** (tel. 506/694-4385, 8 A.M.–5 P.M. daily), 300 meters east of Villa Decary, serves espressos and cappuccinos, sandwiches, salads, soups, seafood dishes, and tenderloin in mushroom sauce on an open-air veranda.

For superb lake views, I head to the endearingly rustic **Café y Macadamia** (tel. 506/2692-2000, 7:30 A.M.–5 P.M. daily), where the enthusiastic owners deliver tasty tilapia *campesina* ($10), beef *chalupa* ($9), and pasta tagliatelli ($9), plus macadamia muffins, blackberry cakes, and fruit shakes.

Information and Services
There's a bank and gas station in Nuevo Arenal. **Lucky Bug Gallery** (tel. 506/2694-4515, www.luckybugcr.com) and **Tom's Pan** (tel./ fax 506/2694-4547) have Internet access.

Getting There
Buses (Garaje Barquero, tel. 506/2232-5660) depart San José for Nuevo Arenal from Calle 16, Avenidas 1/3, at 6:15 A.M., 8:40 A.M., and 11:30 A.M. daily. Buses depart Cañas for Tilarán and Nuevo Arenal at 7:30 A.M. and 3 P.M. daily ($0.50); from Tilarán at 8 A.M.

© CHRISTOPHER P. BAKER

water-taxi on Lake Arenal

and 4:30 P.M. daily; and from La Fortuna to Tilarán via Nuevo Arenal at 7 A.M. and 12:30 P.M. daily.

An express bus departs Nuevo Arenal for San José via Ciudad Quesada at 2:45 P.M. daily; additional buses depart for Ciudad Quesada at 8 A.M. and 2 P.M. daily. A bus marked Guatuso

also departs Arenal at 1:30 P.M. daily for San Rafael, Caño Negro, and Upala in the northern lowlands.

Getting Around
Capt. Ron (tel. 506/2695-4678, www.arenal fishing.com) offers water-taxi service.

Los Chiles and Vicinity

LOS CHILES
Los Chiles, a small frontier town on the Río Frío, about 100 kilometers north of Ciudad Quesada and four kilometers south of the Nicaraguan border, is a gateway to Caño Negro Wildlife Refuge. The ruler-straight drive north from Muelle is modestly scenic, with the land rolling endlessly in a sea of lime-green pastures and citrus—those of the TicoFrut company, whose *fincas* stretch all the way to the Nicaraguan border. The colors are marvelous, the intense greens made more so by soils as red as bright lipstick. There are

two civil guard checkpoints on the road to Los Chiles.

Crossing into Nicaragua
In late 2008, plans were announced for a border crossing to be established at Tablillas, seven kilometers north of Los Chiles. Meanwhile, foreigners can cross into Nicaragua by a *colectivo* (shared water-taxi) that departs Los Chiles for San Carlos de Nicaragua at 11 A.M. (it departs when full, which often isn't until 1:30 P.M.) and 2:30 P.M. daily ($10 pp). A private boat costs $150 (for

five to seven passengers); call the public dock (tel. 506/2471-2277) or **Río Frío Tours** (tel. 506/2471-1090).

The **immigration office** (tel. 506/2471-1233, 8 A.M.–6 P.M. daily) is by the wharf.

Sports and Recreation
No Frills Sportfishing (tel. 506/2471-1200), one kilometer south of Los Chiles, and **Heliconia Tours** (tel. 506/2471-2096, $45 three hours Caño Negro, $150 pp full-day fishing), on the north side of the plaza, offer trips.

Accommodations and Food
The best of motley options for budget travelers is **Cabinas Jabirú** (tel./fax 506/2471-1496, $20 s/d with fan, $25 s/d with a/c).

The nicest place is **Hotel Tulipán** (tel./fax 506/2471-1414, cssibaja@racsa.co.cr, $30 s, $50 d), opposite the Immigration office, 50 meters from the dock. This clean, modern hotel features a pleasant, country-style bar and restaurant. The 10 spacious, simply furnished air-conditioned rooms have private baths with hot water. There's secure parking, plus Internet and a laundry, and Oscar Rojas, the owner, arranges trips to Caño Negro.

Soda Pamela (6 A.M.–8 P.M. daily), by the bus station at the north end of town, is a pleasant and cheap open-air place to eat. The nicest place, however, is **Heliconia Tours & Restaurant** (tel. 506/2471-2096, 8 A.M.–10 P.M. daily), a clean, modern restaurant serving seafood and *comida típica*, plus a Thursday-night barbecue.

Information and Services
There's a **hospital** 500 meters south of town and a **Red Cross** clinic on the northwest side of the plaza. The **police station** (tel. 506/2471-1183) is on the main road as you enter town, and there's another by the wharf.

There's a **bank** on the northeast side of the soccer field.

Getting There
You can charter flights to the small airstrip.

Autotransportes San Carlos (tel. 506/2255-4318) buses depart San José from Calle 12, Avenidas 7/9, at 5:30 A.M. and 3 P.M. daily (return buses depart at 5 A.M. and 3:30 P.M. daily; $3.50). Buses run between Ciudad Quesada and Los Chiles throughout the day.

There's a gas station one kilometer south of town, and another 22 kilometers south of Los Chiles at Pavón.

◖ CAÑO NEGRO WILDLIFE REFUGE
Refugio Nacional de Vida Silvestre Fauna Caño Negro is a remote tropical everglade teeming with wildlife. The 9,969-hectare reserve protects a lush lowland basin of knee-deep watery sloughs and marshes centered on **Lago Caño Negro,** a seasonal lake fed by the fresh waters of the Río Frío. The region floods in wet season. In February–April, the area is reduced to shrunken lagoons; wildlife congregate along the watercourses, where caimans gnash and slosh out pools in the muck.

Caño Negro is a bird-watcher's paradise. The reserve protects the largest colony of neotropic cormorants in Costa Rica and the only permanent colony of Nicaraguan grackle. Cattle egrets, wood storks, anhingas, roseate spoonbills, and other waterfowl gather in the thousands. The reserve is remarkable, too, for its large population of caiman. And looking down into waters as black as Costa Rican coffee, you may see the dim forms of big snook, silver-gold tarpon, and garish garfish.

Bring plenty of insect repellent.

The hamlet of **Caño Negro,** 23 kilometers southwest of Los Chiles, nestles on the northwest shore of Lago Caño Negro. Locals make their living from fishing and guiding. The **ranger station** (tel. 506/2471-1309, 8 A.M.–5 P.M. daily) is 400 meters inland from the dock and 200 meters west of the soccer field.

The village also has a butterfly garden: **Mariposario La Reinita** (tel. 506/2471-1301, 8 A.M.–4 P.M. daily, $4 pp), with 16 species flitting about within nets.

Sports and Recreation
Caño Negro's waters boil with tarpon, snook,

© CHRISTOPHER P. BAKER

Caño Negro Wildlife Refuge

drum, guapote, machaca, and mojarra. Fishing season is July–March (no fishing is allowed Apr.–June); licenses ($30) are required, obtainable from the ranger station in the village or through the various fishing lodges.

Hotel de Campo has fishing packages and lagoon tours, and you can rent canoes and kayaks. **Natural Lodge Caño Negro** follows suit.

You can hire guides and boats at the dock. Try Joel Sandoval (tel. 506/8823-4026), or Manuel Castro of **Pantanal Tours** (tel. 506/8825-0193, $50 up to four people for four hours).

Accommodations and Food

You can stay overnight in the Caño Negro ranger station if space is available ($6 pp). You'll need a sleeping bag and, ideally, a mosquito net. It has cold showers. Meals cost $5.

The **Hotel de Campo** (tel. 506/2471-1012, www.hoteldecampo.com, $75 s, $85 d), in Caño Negro village, stands lakeside amid landscaped grounds with a citrus orchard. Sixteen handsome, cross-ventilated, air-conditioned cabins have a choice of king- or queen-size bed and have terra-cotta floors, lofty wooden ceilings with fans, and large modern bathrooms with hot water. There's a bar and restaurant, gift store, and tackle shop, plus a new swimming pool.

About 500 meters south, **Natural Lodge Caño Negro** (tel. 506/2471-1000, www.canonegrolodge.com, $65 s or $75 d low season, $90 s or $100 d high season) has 22 spacious and comfortable air-conditioned bungalows with rich ochre color schemes, polished hardwoods, ceiling fan, security box, and handsome modern bathrooms with hot water. The restaurant, open to all sides, has a rustic elegance. There's a swimming pool (unsightly at last visit) with whirlpool and swim-up bar. It has 16-foot skiffs for fishing, plus mini-golf, volleyball, and indoor games.

The **Bar y Restaurante El Caimán** (tel. 506/2469-8200, 6:30 A.M.–7 P.M.), beside the bridge at San Emilio, is a most unlikely find. Fishing writer Jerry Ruhlow says it's "sort of a drive-in for boats, where you can get a cold beer or soda pop and plate of *gallo pinto*." It serves typical Tico fare. Canoe and boat trips are offered ($70 two hours).

Getting There

A road from El Parque, 10 kilometers south of Los Chiles, runs 10 kilometers west to a bridge at San Emilio, from where you can reach Caño Negro village via a dirt road that continues south to Colonia Puntarenas, on the main La Fortuna–Upala road (Hwy. 4). A four-wheel drive car is recommended.

Buses depart daily from Upala to Caño Negro village via Colonia Puntarenas at 11 A.M. and 3 P.M. daily.

You can rent a boat in Los Chiles ($70 for two people, or $15 pp for six people or more).

Highway 4 to Upala

Relatively few tourists drive the route between La Fortuna (or, more correctly, Tanque, eight kilometers east of La Fortuna) and Upala, in the extreme northwest of the Northern Zone. The region is fast evolving, however, as a tourist mecca focused on the natural delights of Tenorio Volcano National Park.

SAN RAFAEL AND VICINITY

From Tanque (a major crossroads town eight kilometers east of La Fortuna, paved Carretera 4 shoots northwest to **San Rafael de Guatuso,** an agricultural town on the Río Frío, 40 kilometers northwest of Tanque. There is little of interest in San Rafael (often called Guatuso), which subsists largely on cattle ranching and rice farming. You can rent boats and guides here for trips down the Río Frío to Caño Negro National Wildlife Refuge, reached via dirt road from **Colonia Puntarenas,** 25 kilometers northwest of San Rafael.

El Venado Caverns

At Jicarito, about 25 kilometers northwest of Tanque and 15 kilometers southeast of San Rafael de Guatuso, a paved road leads south seven kilometers to the mountain hamlet of **Venado,** nestled in a valley bottom and famous for the caverns (tel. 506/2478-9081, 7 A.M.–4 P.M. daily, $10), two kilometers farther west. The limestone chambers, which extend 2,700 meters and feature stalactites, stalagmites, and underground streams, weren't discovered until 1945, when the owner of the farm fell into the hole. A guide will lead you on a two-hour exploration of the caverns. The admission includes a flashlight, safety helmet, and rubber boots. Bats and tiny, colorless frogs and fish inhabit the caves, which also contain seashell fossils and a luminous "shrine." Expect to get soaked—you'll wade up to your chest!—and covered with ooze (bring a change of clothes). The farm has a rustic *soda,* a swimming pool, and changing rooms.

You can also reach Venado via a rough dirt road from the north shore of Lake Arenal. Tour operators in La Fortuna offer tours.

A bus departs Ciudad Quesada for Venado at 1 P.M. daily; it returns at 4 P.M.

Maleku Indigenous Reserve

Two kilometers east of San Rafael, a dirt road leads south to the 3,244-hectare Reserva Indígena Maleku, in the foothills of the *cordillera.* Here, the **Centro Ecológico Maleku Araraf** (tel. 506/8888-4250, 8 A.M.–4 P.M.) has trails and a cultural presentation. **Eco-Adventure Tafa Maleku** (tel. 506/2464-0443, 7 A.M.–4 P.M. daily, $1) competes with a museum on indigenous culture. And **Rancho Típico Maleku Araraf** (tel. 506/2839-0540) has a traditional music and dance performance ($35 pp, including a tour) by reservation only. The three indigenous communities are gracious in the extreme—these lovely people, who speak Maleku Jaica, helped me immensely when I seriously injured myself falling through a rotten bridge.

Accommodations and Food

Hospedaje Las Brisas (public tel. 506/2460-8107, $10 s, $15 d), in the hamlet of Venado,

THE MALEKÚ CULTURE

About 600 Malekú survive on the Tongibe reservation (palenque) on the plains at the foot of Volcán Tenorio, near San Rafael de Guatuso, on land ceded to them by the government in the 1960s. While struggling to preserve their cultural identity, today they are mostly farmers who grow corn and a type of root called tiquisqui.

Until a few generations ago, Malekú (also known as Guatusos) strolled through San Rafael wearing clothes made of cured tree bark, called tana. No one wears tana these days, but the Malekú take great pride in their heritage. Many continue to speak their native dialect. Radio Cultural Malekú (1580 AM, 88.3 FM) airs programs and announcements in Malekú, and Eliécer Velas Álvarez instructs the youngsters in Malekú at the elementary school in Tongibe.

The San Rafael area has many ancient tombs, and jade arrowheads and other age-old artifacts are constantly being dug up. Reconstructions of a typical Malekú village have been erected at Reserva Indígena Malekú, Lake Coter Ecolodge on Lake Arenal and Arenal Mundo Aventura, just south of La Fortuna.

has six basic but clean and appealing rooms, with pastel wooden walls and shared bathrooms with cold water. It is run by a delightful older woman, María Nuñoz, whom you may join on rockers on the patio.

There are several basic hostelries in San Rafael, including **Cabinas Tío Henry** (tel. 506/2464-0344, $9 pp with shared bath, $17 s or $20 d with a/c, cable TV, and private bath), two blocks southwest of the soccer field.

By far the nicest place is **Leaves and Lizards** (tel. 506/2478-0023 or U.S. tel. 888/828-9245, www.leavesandlizards.com, $150 s/d including breakfast), in the hills of Monterrey de Santo Domingo, 18 kilometers northwest of Tanque and three kilometers south of Highway 4. Run by Steve and Debbie Legg, an eco- and community-friendly couple from Florida, it has three simply furnished but delightful hillside cabins with decks for enjoying volcano views over 26 acres of property. Meals are provided at the main lodge, which has Wi-Fi.

Getting There

Buses (tel. 506/2255-4318) for San Rafael de Guatuso depart San José from Calle 12, Avenidas 7/9, at 8:30 A.M., 11 A.M., 1 P.M., 4 P.M. and 5:30 P.M. daily ($3.85). Buses also depart for San Rafael from Tilarán at noon daily.

ℂ TENORIO VOLCANO AND VICINITY

Upala, 40 kilometers northwest of San Rafael de Guatuso, is another agricultural town only 10 kilometers south of the Nicaraguan border. Dirt roads lead north to Lake Nicaragua. Beyond Upala, the road (unpaved) leads to Brasilia via Santa Cecilia and, from there, by paved road to La Cruz, on the Pan-American Highway in the extreme northwest of Costa Rica.

From Upala a paved road leads south via the saddle between Tenorio and Miravalles Volcanoes before descending to the Pan-American Highway in Guanacaste. The only town is **Bijagua,** a center for cheese-making 38 kilometers north of Cañas, on the northwest flank of Volcán Tenorio. (A quicker route to Bijagua begins at San Luis.)

Several private reserves abut Tenorio National Park and grant access via trials. For example, about 200 meters north of the park access road, another dirt road leads to the American-owned **La Carolina Lodge,** a ranch and stables with trails into the park. Horseback rides are offered. Another dirt road leads east from the Banco Nacional in Bijagua two kilometers to **Albergue Heliconia Lodge & Rainforest,** run by a local cooperative. The lodge sits at 700 meters elevation abutting the park. Three trails lead into prime rainforest and cloud forest.

Various nature lodges offer guided hikes and horseback rides, as do **Bijagua Adventure** (tel. 506/2455-6271, aventurasbijagua@gmail.com), roadside in town, and **Celeste Tours** (tel. 506/2402-1571), in Katira.

Refugio Nacional de Vida Silvestre Laguna Las Camelias (Las Camelias Lagoon National Wildlife Refuge), on the outskirts of the community of San José, 13 kilometers northwest of Upala, is a rare wetland system with abundant caimans and birdlife.

A partially paved highway leads south from San José and cuts between the saddle of Miravalles and Rincón de la Vieja volcanoes via the village of San Isidro and Agua Claras.

Tenorio Volcano National Park

Volcán Tenorio (1,916 meters), rising southeast of Upala, is blanketed in montane rainforest and protected within 18,402-hectare Parque Nacional Volcán Tenorio ($10 admission, $1 if entered via the private reserves). Local hiking is superb (albeit often hard going on higher slopes). Cougars and jaguars tread the forests, where birds and beasts abound.

A rugged dirt road (4WD required) that begins five kilometers north of Bijagua, on the west side of Tenorio, leads 11 kilometers to the main park entrance at the **Puesto El Pilón ranger station** (tel. 506/2200-0135). The park headquarters (tel. 506/2466-8610) is at Bijagua.

At press time only two trails were open to the public. The main trail—Sendero Misterio del Tenorio—leads to the Río Celeste and **Los Chorros** thermal springs (this is the only place where swimming is permitted). The second leads to the **Río Celeste Waterfall** (Catarata del Río Celeste) and the **Pozo Azúl** (a teal-blue lagoon). A third trail, accessible with a guide only, was being completed and will lead to three waterfalls. Contrary to reports, you cannot hike to the summit; access is permitted solely to biologists, who head to **Lago Las Dantas** (Tapir Lake), named for the tapirs that drink in the waters that fill the volcanic crater. Guided hikes are offered by the local guides association: try Jonathon Ramírez (tel. 506/2402-1330, from $20). The station has a small butterfly and

insect exhibit, plus horseback riding. And a Malekú cultural exhibit was planned.

No camping is permitted within the park.

In late 2008, a new road linking Bijagua directly with **Katira,** on Highway 4, was being carved.

Accommodations and Food

You can camp at **Posada La Amistad** (tel. 506/8356-0285, $4), near the ranger station on the north side of Tenorio. It also has simple cabins ($30 including three meals). Nearby, **Río Celeste Lodge** (tel. 506/8359-6235, rio-celeste2011@yahoo.com, $10 pp dorm, $50 s/d room) may satisfy budget travelers with its three simple rooms, including a dorm with bunks, and a toilet with no seat. It has a rustic roadside restaurant serving local fare.

In Upala, the best bet is **Cabinas Buena Vista** (tel. 560/2470-0186 $10 pp), a well-maintained wooden clapboard mansion with secure parking. Simple rooms have local TV and private hot water bathrooms. Alternatively, try **Hotel Upala** (tel./fax 506/2470-0169, $10 s, $15 d with a/c and TV), on the south side of the soccer field. It has 18 clean, modern rooms with fans, louvered windows, and private baths (some with cold water only).

At Bijagua, **Albergue Heliconias** (tel./fax 506/2466-8493, www.heliconiaslodge.com, $55 s or $67 d rooms, $79 s or $94 d cottages), on the mid-level flanks of Tenorio Volcano, has six rustic but well-kept cabins (two have a double bed and a bunk; four have two bunks) with small bathrooms and hot showers; plus there are four newer, more upscale octagonal cottages. The simple wooden lodge has a bar/restaurant. The setting is splendid, with magnificent views. Rates include breakfast.

The charming little Belgian-run **Sueño Celeste B&B** (tel. 506/2466-8221, www.sueno-celeste.com, $60 s, $65 d), on the south side of Bijagua, offers two cozy rooms, each with sponge-washed walls, glazed concrete floors, colorful fabrics, and quirkily lovely bathrooms. The European owners, Daniel and Dominique, are a delight, and you'll love breakfasting on the terrace with views.

Nearby, the similarly impressive **Tenorio Lodge** (tel. 506/2466-8282, www.tenorio.lodge.com, $115 s, $125 d), offering great valley views from a hillside, opened in 2007 on a huge property with heliconia garden and trails. Its eight peak-roofed, stylishly contemporary wooden bungalows also have walls of glass, sponge-washed walls and glazed concrete floors, plus king-size beds with romantic mosquito drapes, ceiling fans, and chic solar-powered designer bathrooms. The glass-walled volcano-view restaurant is a class act and features live *marimba* music. At night, you can soak in either of two cedar hot tubs. The café-restaurant is open to the public (7 A.M.–9 P.M. daily) for contintental fare.

La Carolina Lodge (tel. 506/8380-1656, www.lacarolinalodge.com, $$65–80 pp including three meals and guided tour) is a rustic but charming farmstead on the north flank of Tenorio. It has four double rooms with solar-powered electricity and shared bathrooms with hot water. There are also four private cabins with private bathrooms. A wooden deck hangs over a natural river-fed pool, and a porch has rockers and hammocks. Rates include meals, guided hikes, and horseback riding.

The French-run, eco-conscious 🅒 **Celeste Mountain Lodge** (tel. 506/2278-6628, www.celestemountainlodge.com, $120 s, $129 d including tax) opened in 2008 three kilometers northeast of Bijagua in a pristine and sensational location at the base of Tenorio with even better views toward Miravalles volcano. Innovative and stylishly contemporary with its open-plan design, stone tile floor, gum-metal framework, glistening hardwood ceiling, and halogen lighting, this dramatic two-tier lodge boasts vast angled walls of glass plus glass-less walls with panoramic volcano views from restaurant, public arenas, and the 18 rooms on two levels. The rooms, though small, are comfy, with king-size beds, lively fabrics, and stylish bathrooms. Dining is gourmet (dishes here are "Tico fusion") and family style atop bench seats stuffed with coconut fiber. There's a wood-heated hot tub. Trails guarantee thrills for hikers (handicapped visitors can opt for an innovative human-powered one-wheel rickshaw); packed lunches are prepared. And biking, horseback trips, and float trips are to be offered. I love this place, where everything is made of recycled materials, right down to bio-degradable soaps!

Information and Services

A good resource for updates on this fast-evolving region is the **Cámara de Turismo Tenorio-Miravalles** (tel. 506/2466-8221, tenorio-miravalles@hotmail.com, 9 A.M.–3 P.M. daily), the local Chamber of Tourism, on the south side of Bijagua.

There's a **hospital** (tel. 506/2470-0058) in Upala, plus a **bank** five blocks north of the bridge in Upala. The **police station** (Guardia Rural, tel. 506/2470-0134) is 100 meters north and west of the bridge.

Getting There

Buses (tel. 506/2221-3318 or 506/2470-0743) for Upala depart San José from Calle 12, Avenidas 3/5, at 10:15 A.M., 3 P.M., 5:15 P.M., and 7:30 P.M. daily. Return buses depart Upala at 4:30 A.M., 5:15 A.M., 9:30 A.M., and 9:30 A.M.

Buses also run between Cañas and Upala several times daily.

Puerto Viejo de Sarapiquí and Vicinity

The Llanura de San Carlos comprises the easternmost part of the northern lowlands. The Ríos San Carlos, Sarapiquí, and other rivers snake across the landscape, vast sections of which are waterlogged for much of the year. The region today is dependent on the banana industry that extends eastward almost the whole way to the Caribbean in a gridwork maze of dirt roads and rail tracks linking towns.

Fortunately, swaths of rainforest still stretch north to the Río San Juan, linking Braulio Carrillo National Park with the rainforests of the Nicaraguan lowlands, much of which is protected within private reserves. Fishing is good, and there are crocodiles and river turtles, plus sloths, monkeys, and superb birdlife to see while traveling on the rivers. Even manatees have been seen in the lagoons between the Río San Carlos and Río Sarapiquí.

The area is also one of the last refuges for the endangered green macaw, which is threatened by loss of habitat.

Routes to Puerto Viejo

There are two scenic routes to Puerto Viejo from San José, forming a loop ringing Braulio Carrillo National Park. The less trafficked western route is via Vara Blanca, between the saddle of Poás and Barva Volcanoes, then dropping down to San Miguel, La Virgen, and Chilamate. *On January 8, 2009, this route was rendered impassable by massive landslides caused by the earthquake; repairs were ongoing at press time.* The easterly route traverses the saddle between Barva and Irazú Volcanoes via Highway 32 (Guápiles Highway), dropping down through Braulio Carrillo National Park then north via Las Horquetas.

Buses from San José to Puerto Viejo make the circle in both directions.

SAN MIGUEL TO PUERTO VIEJO DE SARAPIQUÍ

The road that drops down from Vara Blanca falls northward through the valley of the Río Sarapiquí, which offers kayaking and white-water rafting. About 10 kilometers north of San Miguel, you drop onto the plains at the hamlet of **La Virgen.** Call in at **Rancho Leona** to visit the Internet Café and stained-glass studio where Ken Upcraft conjures fabulous windows and other master-quality glasswork using the copper foil technique. Ken also maintains a private forest reserve on the edge of Braulio Carrillo National Park, 14 kilometers east of La Virgen.

The **Snake Garden** (tel. 506/2761-1059, snakegarden1@costarricense.co.cr, 9 A.M.– 5 P.M. daily, $6 adults, $5 students and children), immediately north of La Virgen, exhibits some 70 species of snakes, plus iguanas, turtles, and other reptiles.

Hacienda Pozo Azul (tel. 506/2761-1360 or U.S. tel. 877/810-6903, www.hacienda pozoazul.com), at La Virgen, raises Holstein cattle and offers horseback rides (from $35), white-water trips (from $50), a canopy tour ($45), river-canyon rappelling (from $28), forest hikes (from $10), and mountain biking ($45).

Finca Corsicana (tel. 506/2761-1052, www.collinstreet.com/pages/finca_corsicana_ home, 8 A.M., 10 A.M., noon, and 2 P.M. daily, $15) offers two-hour tours of its organic pineapple farm, at Llano Grande, seven kilometers northwest of La Virgen.

◀ Centro Neotrópico Sarapiquís

This facility (tel. 506/2761-1004, www .sarapiquis.org, $5 garden only, $14 museum only, $20 entire facility), on the banks of Río Sarapiquí about one kilometer north of La Virgen, is sponsored by the Belgian nonprofit Landscape Foundation and serves as a scientific research and educational center.

The **Museum of Indigenous Culture** (9 A.M.–5 P.M. daily), with more than 400 pre-Columbian artifacts and a 60-seat movie theater, is a centerpiece of the center. There's an archaeological dig—**Alma Alta Archaeological**

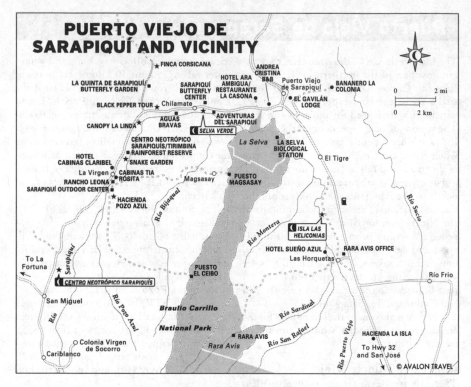

PUERTO VIEJO DE SARAPIQUÍ AND VICINITY

FINCA CORSICANA

Park—of four indigenous tombs dating 800 B.C.–A.D. 155, plus a reconstruction of an Indian village. A farm grows fruits and vegetables based on ecological farming practices. There's an astronomical observatory and the **Chester's Field Botanical Garden,** with about 500 native species.

A 250-meter-long canopied bridge leads across the river gorge and into the **Tirimbina Rainforest Reserve** (tel. 506/2761-1579, www.tirimbina.org, 7 A.M.–5 P.M. daily), which has eight kilometers of trails, with suspension bridges and a 110-meter canopy walkway. A museum portrays life in the forest. Nature walks cost $15 self-guided, $20 guided), and it has a "World of Bats" night walk ($17), a chocolate tour ($18), and birding ($22). Students and children get discounts. Tirimbina has its own entrance from the road, adjoining the Centro.

◖ Selva Verde

Selva Verde (tel. 506/2766-6800, www.selva verde.com, 7 A.M.–3 P.M. daily, $5 admission, free to hotel guests), on the banks of the Río Sarapiquí, about one kilometer east of Chilamate and eight kilometers west of Puerto Viejo, is a private reserve protecting some 192 hectares of primary rainforest adjacent to Braulio Carrillo National Park. At its heart is an internationally acclaimed nature lodge and the **Sarapiquí Conservation Learning Center** (Centro de Enseñanza), with a lecture room and library. The reserve is renowned for its birdlife, and it has a small butterfly garden. Poison-dart frogs are also easily spotted. Trails lead through the forests, and the lodge has naturalist guides. Guided hiking is available ($15 two hours, $35 four hours), plus the reserve offers a wildlife boat ride ($20), white-water rafting ($45), and horseback trips ($25).

SHARKS IN THE RÍO SAN JUAN

If you see a shark fin slicing the surface of the Río San Juan, you will be forgiven for thinking you've come down with heatstroke. In fact, there *are* sharks in this freshwater river. The creatures, along with other species normally associated with saltwater, migrate between the Atlantic Ocean and the murky waters of Lake Nicaragua, navigating 169 kilometers of river and rapids en route. The sharks are classified as euryhaline species – they can cross from saltwater to freshwater and back again with no ill effects.

For centuries, scientists were confounded by the sharks' presence in Lake Nicaragua. The lake is separated from the Pacific by a 17-kilometer chunk of land, and, since rapids on the Río San Juan seemingly prevent large fish from passing easily from the Caribbean, surely, the thinking went, the lake must have once been connected to one or the other ocean. Uplift of the Central American isthmus must have trapped the sharks in the lake.

Studies in the early 1960s, however, showed that there were no marine sediments on the lake bottom. Thus, the lake was never part of the Atlantic or the Pacific. (It was actually formed when a huge block of land dropped between two fault lines; the depression then filled with water.)

Then, ichthyologists decided to tag sharks with electronic tracking devices. It wasn't long before sharks tagged in the Caribbean turned up in Lake Nicaragua, and vice versa. Incredibly, the sharks are indeed able to negotiate the rapids and move between lake and sea.

Accommodations

For budget travelers, **Rancho Leona River Lodge** (tel. 506/2761-1019, www.rancho leona.com, $12 pp) is recommended for its family coziness and delightfully funky ambience. The seven rooms, in a rambling wooden lodge, are rustic but appealing, with fans, stained-glass skylights, and solar-heated showers. Some rooms have bunks. Ken Upcraft runs the place like an offbeat clubhouse and offers kayaking trips. When you return, hop into the stone and timber riverside sweat lodge or the cooling tub.

Next door, **Cabinas Tia Rosita** (tel. 506/2761-1032, $15 s, $22 d) is a clean, modern place with four rooms and four spacious cabins attached to a restaurant.

Tirimbina (tel. 506/2761-1579, www .tirimbina.org, $69 s/d room including breakfast and tax, $42 pp field station including meals) has 15 simple yet lovely little rooms with private bathrooms, phones, and Wi-Fi. Plus there are 10 simpler rooms with twin bunks and shared bathrooms at a remote field station with kitchen.

Cuculmeca Tent Camp (tel. 506/2761-1360, www.haciendapozoazul.com, $50 s, $80 d including all meals), at Hacienda Pozo Azúl, has 30 roomy four-person tent-suites under tarps on raised platforms in the forest. Clean, well-maintained shared bathrooms have hot water. Gosh, there's even Wi-Fi! The hacienda also has **Magasay Jungle Lodge** ($60 s, $96 d including all meals), bordering Parque Nacional Braulio Carrillo. This wooden lodge has 10 rooms with bunks, plus solar power and hot showers.

At **La Quinta de Sarapiquí Lodge** (tel. 506/2761-1300, www.quintasarapiqui.com, $80 s/d standard, $95 s/d superior), on the banks of the Río Sardinal, at Bajo de Chilamate, about three kilometers north of La Virgen and 10 kilometers west of Puerto Viejo, attractions include butterfly and frog gardens, a tree house for kids, and a botanical garden. It has 15 clinically clean, well-lit cabins with contemporary furnishings, ceiling fans, and private baths with hot water. A swimming pool and deck are suspended over the river. An open dining room and bar, a well-stocked gift store, plus a riverside trail for hikes and mountain bikes or horseback rides complete the picture.

Perfect for naturalists, **(Selva Verde** (tel. 506/2766-6800, www.selvaverde.com, $80 s or $95 d river lodge, $90 s or $115 d bungalow low season; $95 s or $110 d river lodge, $110 s or $135 d bungalow high season, including breakfast) has a 45-room lodge set in 20 acres of forest on the banks of the Río Sarapiquí. Thatched walkways lead between the spacious and airy hardwood cabins raised on stilts. Choose between cabins with private baths at the River Lodge and rooms with shared baths at the Creek Lodge; all units are simply furnished in pleasing pastels and have ceiling fans, two single beds, screened windows, large bathrooms with piping hot water, and verandas slung with hammocks and rockers. Five more upscale, cozy bungalow rooms have air-conditioning and coffeemakers, and a swimming pool has been added. Meals are served buffet-style. Selva Verde is popular with groups; book well in advance.

Sarapiquí Rainforest Lodge (tel. 506/2761-1004 or 866/581-0782, www.sarapiquis.org, $80 s/d standard, $90 deluxe low season; $95 s/d standard, $109 deluxe high season), at Centro Neotrópico Sarapiquís, is a marvelous upscale option centered on a thatched ecolodge in pleasing ochre yellow and sienna red. Each of three units has eight "deluxe" rooms shaped like pie slices arrayed in a circle around an atrium, plus there are 12 standard rooms in an adjunct. All feature ochre walls, lively fabrics, handmade furniture, natural stone floors, fans, large walk-in showers, and telephones, and all have Internet access. Eight rooms are air-conditioned. They're delightful but, alas, lack windows. In each, a glass door opens to a wraparound veranda overlooking the gardens or river. The main lodge features the lobby, bar, gift shop, and a splendid new fusion restaurant: El Sereno.

Food

The restaurant at **Selva Verde** (7 A.M.–8 P.M. daily, $10–15) is open to non-guests, so pop in for filling and tasty home-style Costa Rican cooking.

The elegant **El Sereno Restaurant** (7 A.M.–10 P.M. daily), at Centro Neotrópico Sarapiquís, offers gourmet dining.

Getting There

The Río Frío bus departs San José from Calle 12, Avenidas 7/9, at 6:30 A.M., noon, and 3 P.M. daily.

PUERTO VIEJO DE SARAPIQUÍ

This small landlocked town (not to be confused with Puerto Viejo de Talamanca, on the Caribbean coast), 34 kilometers north of Highway 32, at the confluence of the Ríos Puerto Viejo and Sarapiquí, was in colonial times Costa Rica's main shipping port. Today the local economy is dominated by banana plantations: you can take a tour of Dole's **Bananero La Colonia** (tel. 506/2768-8683, www.bananatourcostarica.com), five kilometers southeast of Puerto Viejo, at 1:30 P.M. Tuesday by appointment.

Sports and Recreation

Puerto Viejo is the base for waterborne nature-viewing or fishing trips on the Río Saripiquí, as well as white-water rafting and kayaking. This section of the Río Sarapiquí offers a prime white-water challenge, notably for kayaks. The most popular put-in point is at La Virgen, with Class II and III rapids below. A second put-in point is Chilamate, offering more gentle floats of Class I and II.

The following companies offer tours: **Kayak Jungle Tours** (tel. 506/2761-1019, www.rancholeona.com); **Aguas Bravas** (tel. 506/2296-2072 and 2766-6524, www.aguas-bravas.co.cr); **Aventuras del Sarapiquí** (tel./fax 506/2766-6768, www.sarapiqui.com); **Costa Rica Expeditions** (tel. 506/2257-0766, www.costaricaexpeditions.com); and **Ríos Tropicales** (tel. 506/2233-6455, www.riostropicales.com).

Aguas Bravas (tel. 506/2766-6727, www.aguas-bravas.co.cr), opposite Banco Nacional at the east end of town, specializes in white-water trips ($60) and has birding tours, horseback riding, and other adventures.

You can explore the rainforest canopy at the **Sarapiquí Canopy Tour** (tel. 506/2290-6015, www.crfunadventures.com), which has 15 platforms, a suspension bridge, and one kilometer of zipline. It has a full-day river trip and canopy tour ($88).

Accommodations and Food

Immediately west of the soccer field is the modern **Mi Lindo Sarapiquí** (tel. 506/2766-6281, fax 506/2766-6074, $15 s, $25 d), with 14 clean rooms with TVs, fans, and private baths with hot water. It has a pleasing open-air restaurant that gets lively at night.

In town, the ever-improving **Hotel Bambú** (tel. 506/2766-6005, www.elbambu.com, $55 s or $60 d standard, $65 s or $80 d superior, including breakfast), facing the soccer field, has 17 clean, modern rooms with ceiling fans and air-conditioning, TVs, and private baths with hot water. It also has two self-sufficient apartments for six people, plus a large modern restaurant and a delightful swimming pool in a thatch-fringed courtyard.

My preferred great bargain option is **Andrea Cristina Bed & Breakfast** (tel./fax 506/2766-6265, www.andreacristina.com, $25 s, $45 d including breakfast) half a kilometer west of town. It has four rooms with lofty wooden ceilings, tile floors, and private baths with hot water. Two additional, simple yet appealing A-frame bungalows share a bathroom. There's a restaurant with patio in the garden, which attracts sloths and kinkajous. It's run by friendly owners, Alexander and Floribell Martínez. English-speaking Alex is a leading local conservationist and arranges nature and bird-watching tours. Readers rave about the meals.

Hotel Ara Ambigua (tel. 506/2766-7101, www.hotelaraambigua.com, $50 s or $65 d standard, $65 s or $83 d superior), sitting on a hillside 400 meters north of La Guaíra, one kilometer west of Puerto Viejo, is a rustic and adorable farmhouse property in traditional Costa Rican style. It's named for the scientific name of the green parrot, which can sometimes be seen on the property. It has 19 simply furnished Hansel-and-Gretel-style *cabinas,* some with natural stone floors; all have hot water. It has a swimming pool and Wi-Fi. A small lake has waterfowl and caimans, and there's a frog garden *(ranario)* with poison-dart frogs. Hiking trails lead into the forest. And its delightful rustic farmhouse **Restaurant La Casona** (7 A.M.–10 P.M. daily) is adorned with saddles and farm implements hanging from the dark, wood-beamed ceiling; it serves *típico* dishes.

Information and Services

There are two banks near the soccer field. The post office is opposite Banco Nacional at the east end of town. The **Red Cross** (tel. 506/2766-6212) adjoins the **police station** (tel. 506/2766-6575) at the west end of town, near the **hospital** (tel. 506/2766-6212).

Cafenet de Sarapiquí (tel. 506/2766-6223, 8 A.M.–10 P.M. daily), at the west end of town, offers Internet access.

Getting There

Buses (tel. 506/2222-0610) depart San José Gran Terminal Caribe nine times daily 6 A.M.–6 P.M. via the Guápiles Highway and Horquetas (two hours, $2); and via Heredia and Vara Blanca at 6:30 A.M., 1 P.M., and 5:30 P.M. daily (3.5 hours).

Buses depart Puerto Viejo for San José 5:30 A.M.–5:30 P.M. daily via Horquetas; and 5 A.M., 7:30 A.M., 11:30 A.M., and 4:30 P.M. daily via Vara Blanca.

Taxis wait on the north side of the soccer field, next to the bus stop.

FRONTIER BIOLOGICAL CORRIDOR WILDLIFE REFUGE

The Refugio de Vida Silvestre Corredor Fronterizo extends for two kilometers south of and along the entire border with Nicaragua, coast to coast. Boats ply the Río San Juan, connecting Puerto Viejo de Sarapiquí with Barra del Colorado and Tortuguero (and west with San Carlos, in Nicaragua). The nature viewing is fantastic, with birds galore, monkeys and sloths in the trees along the riverbank, and crocodiles and caimans poking their nostrils and eyes above the waters.

You can even visit **El Castillo de la Inmaculada Concepción,** built by the Spanish in 1675 on a hill dominating the river and

THE NORTHERN ZONE

intended to repel pirates and English invaders. The ruins are in Nicaragua, three kilometers west of where the Costa Rican border moves south of the river (you'll need your passport).

The transboundary park was birthed in 1985, when Nicaraguan President Daniel Ortega seized on the idea as a way to demilitarize the area, at the time being used by anti-Sandinista rebels. Ortega proposed the region be declared an international park for peace and gave it the name Si-a-Paz—Yes to Peace. Efforts by the Arias administration to kick the rebels out of Costa Rica's northern zone led to demilitarization of the area, but lack of funding and political difficulties prevented the two countries from making much progress. The end of the Nicaraguan war in 1990 allowed the governments to dedicate more money to the project. In 2003, the efforts led to formalization of the boundaries of a new national park, the 30,000-hectare Maquenque National Park, a massive swath to encompass heavily logged and denuded terrain between the Sarapiquí and San Carlos Rivers and extending northward from Braulio Carrillo National Park to the Indio Maíz Biological Reserve, which protects nearly half a million hectares of rainforest in the southeast corner of Nicaragua. Maquenque will link the Frontier Corridor Wildlife Refuge with the San Juan–La Selva Biological Corridor, covering 340,000 hectares and 29 protected areas, including Tortuguero National Park and Barra del Colorado Wildlife Refuge.

The **Ministro de Ambiente y Energía** (Ministry of Environment and Energy, tel. 506/2471-2191, refugio.fronterizo@sinac.co.cr, 8 A.M.–4 P.M. Wed. and Fri. only), in Los Chiles, has responsibility.

Getting There

A regular water-taxi departs the dock in Puerto Viejo at 1:30 P.M. for Trinidad (on the east bank of the Río Sarapiquí at its junction with the Río San Juan, $5). Water-taxis are also for hire, from slender motorized canoes to canopied tour boats for 8–20 passengers. Trips cost about $10 per hour for up to five people. A full-day trip to the Río San Juan and back costs

from $100 per boat. Expect to pay $500 for a charter boat all the way down the Río San Juan to Barra del Colorado and Tortuguero National Parks.

SOUTH OF PUERTO VIEJO

Highway 4 runs due south from Puerto Viejo for 34 kilometers and connects with Highway 32, the main highway between San José and the Caribbean lowlands. The forested slopes of Braulio Carrillo rise to the west. The flatlands to the east are carpeted with banana plantations.

El Gavilán Lodge and Forest Reserve, a 180-hectare private forest reserve on the east bank of the Río Sarapiquí, is splendid for bird-watching, although readers report that the guides here aren't particularly knowledgeable. It offers horseback rides, guided hikes, and fishing trips. If driving, it is accessed by a dirt road about two kilometers south of town and one kilometer north of La Selva. The lodge is about two kilometers north from the junction.

The only community of note it the hamlet of **Las Horquetas** is located 17 kilometers north of the Guápiles Highway and 17 kilometers south of Puerto Viejo. Horquetas is a setting for the **Jardín Ecológico Pierella** (tel. 506/2764-7257, visits by appointment), a butterfly breeding center set in a manicured garden. Visitors also get to see animals such as peccaries, agoutis, and toucans.

La Selva Biological Station

La Selva (tel. 506/2766-6565, www.ots. ac.cr), four kilometers south of Puerto Viejo, is a biological research station run by the Organization of Tropical Studies (OTS). The station is centered on a 1,500-hectare reserve—mostly premontane rainforest but with varied habitats—linked to the northern extension of Braulio Carrillo National Park. More than 420 bird species have been identified here, as have more than 500 species of butterflies, 120 species of mammals, and 55 species of snakes. The arboretum displays more than 1,000 tree species.

Almost 60 kilometers of trails snake through the reserve. Some have boardwalks. Others are no more than muddy pathways. Rubber boots or waterproof hiking boots are essential, as is raingear. Guided nature walks are offered at 8 A.M. and 1:30 P.M. daily ($30 adults, $22 children half day; $38 adults, $28 children full day), and an early-bird birding tour departs at 5:30 A.M. You may not explore alone. Only 65 people at a time are allowed in the reserve, including scientists. It is often booked solid months in advance. Reservations are required.

The OTS operates a shuttle van from San José on Monday ($10), space permitting (researchers and students have priority); and between La Selva and Puerto Viejo, Monday–Saturday. Transporte Caribe (tel. 506/2221-7990) buses from San José will drop you off at the entrance, from where you'll need to walk to La Selva (2 km).

❰ Isla Las Heliconias

Heliconia Island (tel. 506/2764-5220, www.heliconiaisland.com, $10 self-guided tour, $15 guided tour), about five kilometers north of Horquetas, is indeed an island-turned-heliconia-garden created with an artist's eye and lovingly tended by naturalist Tim Ryan and now tended by Dutch owners, Henk and Carolien Peters-van Duijnhoven. Exquisite! The garden was started in 1992 and today boasts about 80 species of heliconia, plus ginger and other plants, shaded by almendro trees in which green macaws nest. The garden also includes palms, orchids, and bamboo from around the world. Needless to say, birds abound.

Rara Avis

This 1,280-hectare rainforest reserve (tel. 506/2764-1111, www.rara-avis.com) abutting Braulio Carrillo National Park, 15 kilometers west of Las Horquetas, contains a biological research station and a host of novel projects designed to show that a rainforest can be economically viable if left intact, not cut down. Projects include ecotourism and producing exportable orchids and philodendrons for wicker.

And there's a butterfly farm and orchid garden. More than 360 bird species inhabit the reserve, along with jaguars, tapirs, monkeys, anteaters, coatimundis, and butterflies galore.

Visitors can view the canopy from two platforms ($35, including two-hour guided hike), including one at the foot of a spectacular double waterfall. Rara Avis gets up to 5.5 meters of rain a year; it has no dry months. The trails range from easy to difficult. Rubber boots are recommended (the lodge has boots to lend for those with U.S. shoe sizes of 12 or smaller).

Some people I've spoken to consider the experience of getting to Rara Avis part of the fun; others have stated that no reward is worth three hours of bumping about on the back of a canopied trailer. Even the tractor sometimes gets stuck! Rara Avis is not a place for a day visit; plan on at least one overnight.

Rara Avis has three options ($80–90 s, $140–160 d low season; $85–95 s, $150–170 d high season). Waterfall Lodge features eight rooms, each with private bathtub and hot water, and a wraparound balcony with great views. Ten minutes' walk from the lodge, the two-room River Edge Cabin is ideal for bird-watchers and honeymooners and has hammocks on a balcony, solar lighting, and private bath with hot water. And there are four simple two-room cabins with bunks ($50 pp year-round). A two-night minimum stay is required. Reservations are essential. Rates include meals.

Accommodations

Isla Las Heliconias ($72 s/d with fan, $82 s/d with a/c) has four lovely cabins furnished with black-stone floors and bamboo pieces; one has a king-size bed, and all have spacious verandas and modern bathrooms. There's a restaurant on-site.

The peacefull, no-frills **El Gavilán Lodge and Forest Reserve** (tel. 506/2766-6743 or 506/2234-9507, www.gavilanlodge.com, $50 s or $60 d standard, $70 s or $75 d superior, including breakfast) has four rooms in the main two-story structure (with hardwood verandas and rockers), plus bungalows with 13 simply appointed rooms with private bathrooms and hot water. Simple meals are served in an open-air restaurant. It has an open-air whirlpool tub and playground. Boating, hiking, and excursions are offered. You can take a boat to El Gavilán from the wharf in Puerto Viejo.

La Selva has comfortable dormitory-style accommodations (reservations c/o OTS, tel. 506/2524-0627, www.ots.ac.cr, $89 s, $168 d, including meals, tax, and guided hike) with four bunks per room and communal bathrooms; some are wheelchair accessible. It also has private rooms, but researchers and students get priority. Tourists are allowed only on a space-available basis. Meals are served bang on time and latecomers get the crumbs. *Reservations are essential.*

Farm-style rusticity and elegant accommodations combine at **Hotel Sueño Azul** (tel. 506/2764-1000, www.suenoazulresort.com, $76 s or $92 d low season, $103 s or $125 d high season), near Horquetas. Rattan and bamboo features enhance the 55 graciously appointed rooms with rich earth-tone decor; suites have outdoor whirlpool tubs. The magnificent *rancho* restaurant (with limited menu) is converted from a cattle corral and overlooks a freeform pool with cascade. There's a lagoon and trails into adjacent forest, plus horseback riding, a canopy tour, a rodeo, a folkloric evening, a Museum of Local Legends, and even a full-service spa and yoga studio.

The owners of Sarapiquí Rainforest Lodge have opened a sensational 15-room boutique hotel, **☾ Hacienda La Isla** (tel. 506/2764-2576, www.haciendalaisla.com, $95 s/d standard, $116 s/d suite low season; $119 s/d standard, $145 s/d suite high season, including tax) near Rancho Roberto, three kilometers north of El Cruce. Themed to Costa Rica's colonial past, this former *hacienda* exudes the feel of yesteryear and is set in amid orchards and lush gardens. The 14 rooms are exquisitely furnished, with hardwood pieces and ochre color schemes. The restaurant delivers gourmet fusion cuisine. It has trails, and horseback riding is a specialty here. The rates are an absolute bargain compared to competing hotels.

Getting There

Empresario Guapileños (tel. 506/2222-2727, $2) buses from San José depart Terminal Caribe for Puerto Viejo de Sarapiquí at 6:30 A.M. and 11:30 A.M. via the Guápiles Highway (do *not* take the bus via Heredia; and do not take the Puerto Viejo de Talamanca bus). These two buses will drop you at Horquetas in time for the tractor-hauled transfer to Rara Avis from Las Horquetas at 9 A.M. and 2 P.M. If driving, you can leave your car in a parking lot at the Rara Avis office in Las Horquetas. Later arrivals can rent horses ($35, four hours), but not after noon.

GUANACASTE AND THE NORTHWEST

Guanacaste has been called Costa Rica's "Wild West." The name Guanacaste derives from *quahnacaztlan,* a native word meaning "place near the ear trees," for the tall and broad *guanacaste* (free ear or ear pod) tree which spreads its gnarled branches long and low to the ground; in the heat of summer, all that walks, crawls, or flies gathers in its cool shade in the heat of midday.

The lowlands, to the west, comprise a vast alluvial plain of seasonally parched rolling hills broadening to the north and dominated by giant cattle ranches interspersed with smaller pockets of cultivation. To the east rises a mountain meniscus—the Cordillera de Guanacaste and Cordillera de Tilarán—studded with symmetrical volcanic cones spiced with bubbling mud pits and steaming vents. These mountains are lushly forested on their higher slopes. Rivers cascade down the flanks, slow to a meandering pace, and pour into the Tempisque basin, an unusually arid region smothered by dry forest and cut through by watery sloughs. The coast is indented with bays, peninsulas, and warm sandy beaches that are some of the least visited, least accessible, and yet most beautiful in the country. Sea turtles use many as nurseries.

The country's first national park, Santa Rosa, was established here, the first of more than a dozen national parks, wildlife refuges, and biological reserves in the region. The array of ecosystems in the region ranges from pristine shores to volcanic heights, encompassing just about every imaginable ecosystem within Costa Rica.

No region of Costa Rica displays its cultural

© CHRISTOPHER P. BAKER

GUANACASTE

HIGHLIGHTS

(**Monteverde, Cerro Plano, and Santa Elena:** These popular mountain communities known for their cloud forest reserves have no end of attractions, not least stupendous opportunities for wildlife-viewing (page 280).

(**Monteverde Cloud Forest Biological Reserve:** The *sine qua non* of a visit to Monteverde, this world-famous biological reserve is laced by nature trails fabulous for viewing wildlife (page 285).

(**Selvatura:** An activity center in Santa Elena with a canopy tour and other attractions, highlighted by the Jewels of the Rainforest Bio-Art Exhibition, a private insect collection that is one of the nation's preeminent nature displays (page 288).

(**Centro de Rescate Las Pumas:** You're guaranteed eyeball-to-eyeball encounters with all the big cats you're not likely to see in the wild at this rescue center (page 300).

(**Río Corobicí:** A float trip on this relatively calm river is fun for all the family (page 300).

(**Las Hornillas Volcanic Activity Center:** This walk-through active crater with fumaroles also has therapeutic mud pools you can actually bathe in (page 305).

(**Palo Verde National Park:** Birding *par excellence* is the name of the game at this watery world best explored by boat (page 306).

(**Rincón de la Vieja National Park:** Magnificent scenery, bubbling mud pools, and trails to the volcano summit are highlights at this national park (page 313).

(**Santa Rosa National Park:** The finest of the dry-forest reserves offers unrivaled wildlife-viewing and top-notch surfing (page 318).

LOOK FOR (TO FIND RECOMMENDED SIGHTS, ACTIVITIES, DINING, AND LODGING.

heritage as overtly as Guanacaste, whose distinct flavor owes much to the blending of Spanish and indigenous Chorotega cultures. The people who today inhabit the province are tied to old bloodlines and live and work on the cusp between cultures. Today one can still see deeply bronzed wide-set faces and pockets of Chorotega life.

Costa Rica's national costume and music emanate from this region, as does the *punto guanacasteco,* the country's official dance. And the regional heritage can still be traced in the creation of clay pottery and figurines. The *campesino* life here revolves around the ranch, and dark-skinned *sabaneros* (cowboys) are the preeminent sight. Come fiesta time, nothing rouses so much cheer as the *corridas de toros* (bullfights) and *topes,* the region's colorful horse parades. Guanacastecans love a fiesta: the biggest occurs each July 25, when Guanacaste celebrates its independence from Nicaragua.

Guanacaste's climate is in total contrast to the rest of the country. The province averages less than 162 centimeters of rain a year, though regional variation is extreme. For half the year (Nov.–Apr.) the plains receive no rain, it is hotter than Hades, and the sun beats down hard as a nail, although cool winds bearing down from northern latitudes can lower temperatures pleasantly along the coast December–February. The dry season usually lingers slightly longer than elsewhere in Costa Rica. The Tempisque Basin is the country's driest region and receives less than 45 centimeters of rain in years of drought, mostly in a few torrential downpours during the six-month rainy season. The mountain slopes receive much more rain, noticeably so on the eastern slopes, which are cloud-draped and deluged for much of the year.

PLANNING YOUR TIME

Guanacaste is a large region; its numerous attractions are spread out and getting between any two major regions can eat up the better part of a day. The region is diverse enough to justify exploring in its entirety, for which you should budget no less than a week. Monteverde alone requires a minimum of two days, and ideally four to take advantage of all that it offers. Nor would you wish to rush exploring Rincón de la Vieja National Park, requiring two or three nights.

Recent years have seen a boost in regional tourism following expansion of the new international airport at Liberia, now served with direct flights by most key U.S. carriers. The airport is well served by car rental companies.

The Pan-American Highway (Highway 1) cuts through the heart of lowland Guanacaste, ruler-straight almost all the way between the Nicaraguan border in the north and Puntarenas in the south. Juggernaut trucks frequent the fast-paced and potholed road, which is one lane in either direction. *Drive cautiously!* North of Liberia the route is superbly scenic. Almost every sight of importance lies within a short reach of the highway, accessed by dirt side roads. If traveling by bus, sit on the east-facing side for the best views.

Touristy it might be, but **Monteverde,** the big draw, delivers in heaps. Its numerous attractions include canopy tours; horseback riding; art galleries; orchid, snake, frog, and butterfly exhibits; and, at **Selvatura,** the one-of-a-kind Jewels of the Rainforest Bio-Art Exhibition is worth the arduous uphill journey to Monteverde in its own right. Most visitors come to hike in the **Monteverde Cloud Forest Biological Reserve,** the most famous of several similar reserves that make up the Arenal-Monteverde Protection Zone.

Back in the lowlands, the town of **Cañas** offers **Las Pumas Rescue Center** and the **Río Corobicí,** the former a refuge for big-cat species; the latter good for relatively calm whitewater trips. To the north, few visitors bother with **Miravalles Volcano,** where several recreational facilities take advantage of thermal waters that also feed bubbling mud-pots and geysers. A side trip to **Palo Verde National Park,** with more than a dozen distinct habitats, is recommended for birders. Nearby, **Liberia** is worth a stop for its well-preserved colonial homesteads. The city is gateway to both the Nicoya Peninsula and **Rincón de la Vieja**

GUANACASTE AND THE NORTHWEST

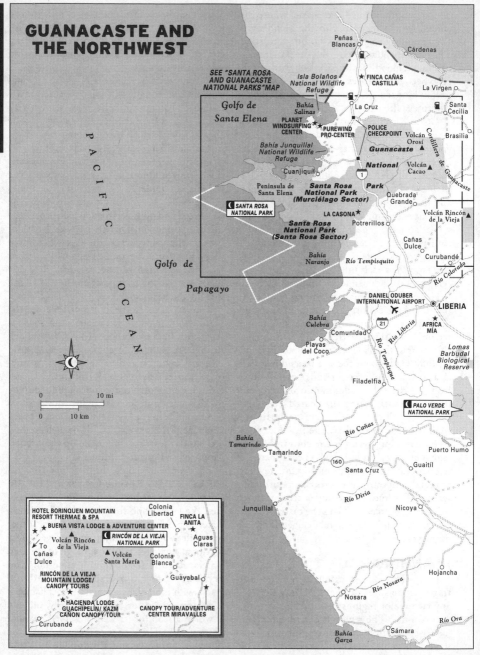

SEE "SANTA ROSA AND GUANACASTE NATIONAL PARKS" MAP

Peñas Blancas
Cárdenas
Isla Bolaños National Wildlife Refuge
FINCA CAÑAS CASTILLA
La Virgen

Golfo de Santa Elena
Bahía Salinas
PLANET WINDSURFING CENTER
PUREWIND PRO-CENTER
La Cruz
Santa Cecilia

POLICE CHECKPOINT
Volcán Orosí
Brasilia

Bahía Junquillal National Wildlife Refuge

Guanacaste
Volcán Cacao

Cuanjiquil

National

Peninsula de Santa Elena

Santa Rosa National Park (Murciélago Sector)

Park

Quebrada Grande

SANTA ROSA NATIONAL PARK

LA CASONA

Volcán Rincón de la Vieja

Santa Rosa National Park (Santa Rosa Sector)

Potrerillos

Cañas Dulce

Curubandé

Bahía Naranjo
Río Tempisquito
Río Colorado

Golfo de Papagayo

PACIFIC OCEAN

DANIEL ODUBER INTERNATIONAL AIRPORT
LIBERIA

Bahía Culebra
Comunidad
AFRICA MÍA

Playas del Coco
Lomas Barbudal Biological Reserve

Filadelfia

PALO VERDE NATIONAL PARK

0   10 mi

0   10 km

Bahía Tamarindo
Tamarindo
Puerto Humo

Santa Cruz
Guaitíl

Río Cañas

Río Diriá

Junquillal
Nicoya

Río Nosara

Río Ora

Bahía Garza
Sámara

Inset (lower left)

HOTEL BORINQUEN MOUNTAIN RESORT THERMAE & SPA
Colonia Libertad
BUENA VISTA LODGE & ADVENTURE CENTER
FINCA LA ANITA
Volcán Rincón de la Vieja
To Cañas Dulce
RINCÓN DE LA VIEJA NATIONAL PARK
Aguas Claras
Volcán Santa María
Colonia Blanca
RINCÓN DE LA VIEJA MOUNTAIN LODGE/ CANOPY TOURS
Guayabal
HACIENDA LODGE GUACHIPELÍN/ KAZM CAÑON CANOPY TOUR
CANOPY TOUR/ADVENTURE CENTER MIRAVALLES
Nosara
Cúrubandé

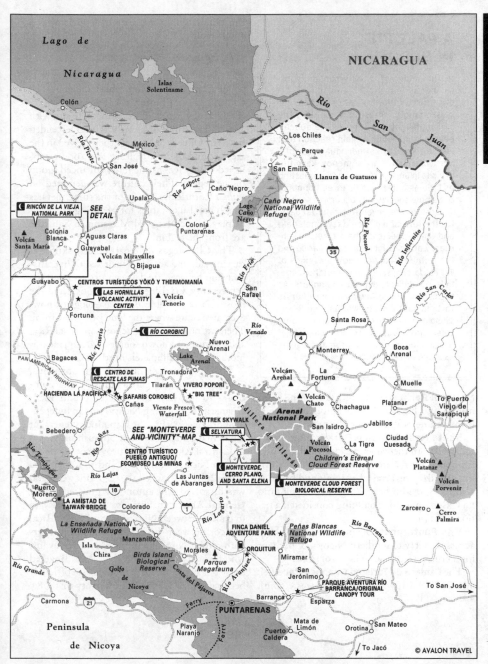

Lago de Nicaragua

Islas Solentiname

Colón

NICARAGUA

México

San José

Río Pizote

Los Chiles

Parque

Río San Juan

San Emilio

Llanura de Guatusos

Upala

Río Zapote

Caño Negro

Caño Negro National Wildlife Refuge

Lago Caño Negro

RINCÓN DE LA VIEJA NATIONAL PARK

SEE DETAIL

Colonia Blanca

Colonia Puntarenas

Volcán Santa María

Aguas Claras

Guayabal

Volcán Miravalles

Bijagua

Río Pacosol

Río Infiernito

Río San Carlos

35

Guayabo

CENTROS TURÍSTICOS YÖKÖ Y THERMOMANÍA

LAS HORNILLAS VOLCANIC ACTIVITY CENTER

Fortuna

Volcán Tenorio

San Rafael

Río Venado

Santa Rosa

Boca Arenal

RÍO COROBICÍ

Nuevo Arenal

Monterrey

Río Tenorio

PAN AMERICAN HIGHWAY

Bagaces

CENTRO DE RESCATE LAS PUMAS

Lake Arenal

Tronadora

Volcán Arenal

La Fortuna

Muelle

HACIENDA LA PACÍFICA

SAFARIS COROBICÍ

Tilarán

VIVERO POPORÍ "BIG TREE"

Volcán Chato

Chachagua

Platanar

To Puerto Viejo de Sarapiquí

Cañas

Viento Fresco Waterfall

SKYTREK SKYWALK

Volcán Arenal National Park

San Isidro

Jabillos

Ciudad Quesada

Bebedero

SEE "MONTEVERDE AND VICINITY"-MAP

SELVATURA

Volcán Pocosol

La Tigra

Volcán Platanar

Río Cañas

CENTRO TURÍSTICO PUEBLO ANTIGUO/ ECOMUSEO LAS MINAS

Las Juntas de Abaranges

MONTEVERDE, CERRO PLANO, AND SANTA ELENA

Children's Eternal Cloud Forest Reserve

Volcán Porvenir

Río Tempisque

Río Lajas

18

MONTEVERDE CLOUD FOREST BIOLOGICAL RESERVE

Zarcero

Cerro Palmira

Puerto Moreno

LA AMISTAD DE TAIWAN BRIDGE

Colorado

1

Río Lagarto

Río Barranca

La Ensenada National Wildlife Refuge

Manzanillo

FINCA DANIEL ADVENTURE PARK

Peñas Blancas National Wildlife Refuge

Isla Chira

Birds Island Biological Reserve

Morales

Parque Megafauna

ORQUITUR

Miramar

San Jerónimo

Río Grande

Golfo de Nicoya

21

Costa del Pájaros

Río Aranjuez

PARQUE AVENTURA RÍO BARRANCA/ORIGINAL CANOPY TOUR

To San José

Carmona

Ferry

Barranca

Esparza

Peninsula de Nicoya

Playa Naranjo

PUNTARENAS

Ferry

Mata de Limón

Puerto Caldera

Orotina

San Mateo

To Jacó

© AVALON TRAVEL

GUANACASTE

A PALETTE IN BLOOM

In the midst of dry-season drought, Guanacaste explodes in Monet colors – not wildflowers, but a Technicolor blossoming of trees. In November, the saffron-bright flowering of the guachipelín sets in motion a chain reaction that lasts for six months. Individual trees of a particular genus are somehow keyed to explode in unison, often in a climax lasting as little as a day. Two or three bouquets of a single species may occur in a season. The colors are never static. In January, it's the turn of pink *poui* (savannah oak) and yellow *poui* (black bark tree). By February, canary-bright *Corteza amarillo* and the trumpet-shaped yellow blossoms of *Tabebuia chrysanta* dot the landscape. In March delicate pink curao appears. As the curao wanes, *Tabebuia rosea* bursts forth in subtle pinks, whites, and lilacs. The *malinche* – royal poinciana or flame tree – closes out the six-month parade of blossoming trees with a dramatic display as bright as red lipstick.

National Park, popular for hikes to the summit and for horseback rides and canopy tours from nature lodges outside the park.

Santa Rosa National Park is more easily accessed from the Pan-American Highway and is popular for nature trails offering easy viewing of a dizzying array of animals and birds. It also has splendid beaches, great surfing, and La Casona, a historic building considered a national shrine.

Visit **Puntarenas,** the main town, solely to access the ferry to southern Nicoya, or perhaps for a cruise-excursion to **Isla Tortuga.**

The **Cámara de Turismo Guanacasteca** (tel. 506/2690-9501, www.letsgoguanacaste.com), the Guanacaste Chamber of Tourism, is a good resource.

HISTORY

The Guanacaste-Nicoya region was the center of a vibrant pre-Columbian culture: The Chorotegas celebrated the Fiesta del Maíz (Festival of Corn) and worshiped the sun with the public sacrifice of young virgins. Descended from the Olmecs of Mexico, they arrived in the area around the 8th century and soon established themselves as the most advanced group in the region. Their culture was centered on *milpas* (cornfields). Many of the stone metates (small stool-like tables for grinding corn) on display in the National Museum in San José are from the region.

The Chorotegas were particularly skilled at carving jade and achieved their zenith in craftsmanship between the last century B.C. and the 5th century A.D. Blue jade was considered the most precious of objects. Archaeologists, however, aren't sure where the blue jade came from. There are no known jade deposits in Costa Rica, and the nearest known source of green jade was more than 800 kilometers north in Guatemala.

The region was colonized early by Spaniards, who established the cattle industry that dominates to this day. Between 1570 and 1821, Guanacaste (including Nicoya) was an independent province within the Captaincy General of Guatemala, a federation of Spanish provinces in Central America. The province was delivered to Nicaragua in 1787, and to Costa Rica in 1812. In 1821, when the Captaincy General was dissolved and autonomy granted to the Central American nations, Guanacaste had to choose between Nicaragua and Costa Rica. Rancor between Liberians—cattle ranchers with strong Nicaraguan ties—and Nicoyans, who favored union with Costa Rica, lingered until a plebiscite in 1824. Guanacaste officially became part of Costa Rica by treaty in 1858.

The Southern Plains

The Pan-American Highway (Hwy. 1) descends from the central highlands to the Pacific plains via **Esparza,** at the foot of the mountains about 15 kilometers east of Puntarenas. The town has one of the most impressive churches in the country, with a neoclassical facade and a domed clock tower.

Want to whiz through the treetops on a zipline? You can do so at **Parque Aventura** (tel. 506/2635-5858, www.canopyparque aventura.com, $40 adults, $30 students and children), about three kilometers west of Esparza, with tours at 8 A.M., 11 A.M., and 2:30 P.M. Unlike most ziplines, this straps you in Superman style! It also has rappelling and ATV quad tours.

PUNTARENAS

Five kilometers long but only five blocks wide at its widest, this sultry port town, 120 kilometers west of San José, is built on a long narrow spit—Puntarenas means "Sandy Point"—running west from the suburb of **Cocal** and backed to the north by a mangrove estuary; to the south are the Gulf of Nicoya and a beach cluttered with driftwood.

Puntarenas has long been favored by Josefinos seeking R and R. The old wharves on the estuary side feature decrepit fishing boats leaning against ramshackle piers popular with pelicans.

The peninsula was colonized by the Spaniards as early as 1522. The early port grew to prominence and was declared a free port in 1847, a year after completion of an oxcart road from the Meseta Central. Oxcarts laden with coffee made the lumbering descent to Puntarenas in convoys; the beans were shipped from here via Cape Horn to Europe. It remained the country's main port until the Atlantic Railroad to Limón, on the Caribbean coast, was completed in 1890 (the railroad between San José and Puntarenas would not be completed for another 20 years). Earlier this century, Puntarenas also developed a large conch-pearl fleet. Some 80 percent of Porteños, as the inhabitants of Puntarenas are called, still make their living from the sea.

The town's main usefulness is as the departure point for day cruises to islands in the Gulf of Nicoya and for the ferries to Playa Naranjo and Paquera, on the Nicoya Peninsula.

Cruise ships berth at the terminal opposite Calle Central.

Sights

The tiny **Catedral de Puntarenas** (Avenida Central, Calles 5/7), built in 1902, abuts the recently renovated **Antigua Comandancia de la Plaza,** a fortress-style building complete with tiny battlements and bars on its windows. It once served as a barracks and city jail; today it houses the **Museo Histórico Marino** (tel. 506/2661-5036, 9:45 A.M.–noon and 1–5:15 P.M. Tues.–Sun., free), a marine history museum that also has exhibits on city life from the pre-Columbian and coffee eras.

Everything of import seems to happen along the **Paseo de las Turistas,** a boulevard paralleling the Gulf of Nicoya and abuzz with vendors, beachcombers, and locals flirting and trying to keep cool in the waters. The boulevard's beachfront park is studded with contemporary statues.

The **Parque Marino del Pacífico** (tel. 506/2661-5272, www.parquemarino.org, 9 A.M.–5 P.M. Tues.–Sun., $7 adults, $4 children) occupies the old railway station, 300 meters east of the cruise terminal. Its three hectares of aquariums display a wide spectrum of marinelife, including motley outdoor tanks with a few sharks, marine turtles, and crocodiles. The indoor aquarium is worth the money, however, if killing time.

On the north side of the peninsula, the sheltered gulf shore—the estuary—is lined with fishing vessels in various states of decrepitude. Roseate spoonbills, storks, and other birds pick among the shallows.

GUANACASTE

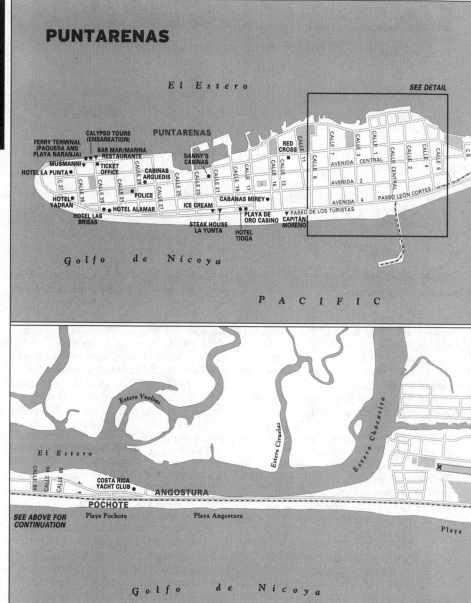

PUNTARENAS

El Estero

SEE DETAIL

PUNTARENAS

CALYPSO TOURS
(EMBARKATION)

FERRY TERMINAL
(PAQUERA AND
PLAYA NARANJA)

BAR MAR/MARINA
RESTAURANTE

MUSMANNI

HOTEL LA PUNTA

TICKET
OFFICE

CABINAS
ARGUEDIS

DANNY'S
CABINAS

RED
CROSS

CALLE 11

CALLE 9

CALLE 7

CALLE 5

CALLE 3

CALLE 1

CALLE CENTRAL

CALLE 2

CALLE 4

CALLE 6

CALLE 8

AVENIDA CENTRAL

AVENIDA 2

AVENIDA 4

PASEO LEÓN CORTES

POLICE

HOTEL
YADRÁN

HOTEL ALAMAR

HOTEL LAS
BRISAS

ICE CREAM

CABANAS MIREY

STEAK HOUSE
LA YUNTA

PLAYA DE
ORO CASINO

PASEO DE LOS TURISTAS

HOTEL
TIOGA

CAPITÁN
MORENO

CALLE 37

CALLE 35

CALLE 33

CALLE 31

CALLE 29

CALLE 27

CALLE 25

CALLE 23

CALLE 21

CALLE 19

CALLE 17

CALLE 15

CALLE 13

Golfo   de   Nicoya

PACIFIC

Estero Vueltas

Estero Ciruelas

Estero Chacarita

El Estero

CALLE 66

CALLE 64

CALLE 6B

COSTA RICA
YACHT CLUB

ANGOSTURA

POCHOTE

SEE ABOVE FOR
CONTINUATION

Playa Pochote

Playa Angostura

Playa

Golfo   de   Nicoya

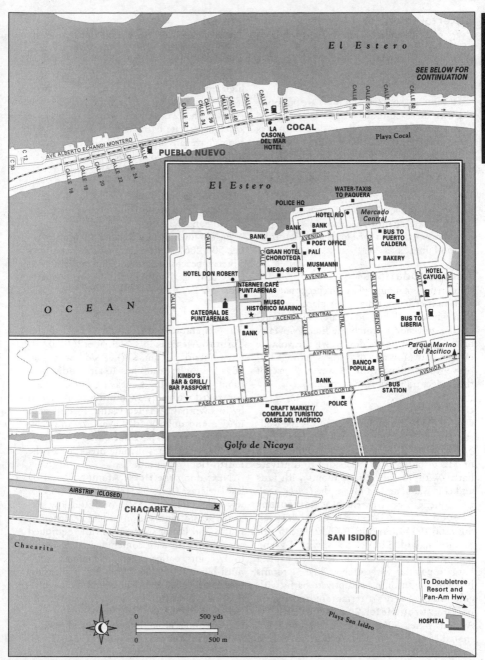

El Estero

SEE BELOW FOR
CONTINUATION

CALLE 32
CALLE 34
CALLE 36
CALLE 38
CALLE 40
CALLE 42
CALLE 44
CALLE 46
CALLE 48

CALLE 54
CALLE 56
CALLE 58
CALLE 80

COCAL

Playa Cocal

LA
CASONA
DEL MAR
HOTEL

C 12
C 30

AVE ALBERTO ECHANDI MONTERO

CALLE 16
CALLE 18
CALLE 20
CALLE 22
CALLE 24

PUEBLO NUEVO

El Estero

WATER-TAXIS
TO PAQUERA

POLICE HQ

HOTEL RÍO

Mercado
Central

BANK

BANK

AVENIDA 3

BUS TO
PUERTO
CALDERA

POST OFFICE

PALÍ

BAKERY

GRAN HOTEL
CHOROTEGA

MUSMANNI

HOTEL
CAYUGA

MEGA-SUPER

HOTEL DON ROBERT

AVENIDA

INTERNET CAFÉ
PUNTARENAS

CALLE 7

CALLE 9

CALLE CENTRAL

CALLE PBRO FLORENCIO DE CASTILLO

ICE

O C E A N

CATEDRAL DE
PUNTARENAS

MUSEO
HISTÓRICO MARINO

BUS TO
LIBERIA

ACENIDA

CENTRAL

CALLE 5

CALLE CENTRAL

BANK

Parque Marino
del Pacífico

AVENIDA 2

P. DE LAMADOR

BANCO
POPULAR

KIMBO'S
BAR & GRILL/
BAR PASSPORT

AVENIDA 4

BANK

BUS
STATION

PASEO LEÓN CORTÉS

PASEO DE LAS TURISTAS

POLICE

CRAFT MARKET/
COMPLEJO TURÍSTICO
OASIS DEL PACÍFICO

Golfo de Nicoya

AIRSTRIP (CLOSED)

CHACARITA

Chacarita

SAN ISIDRO

To Doubletree
Resort and
Pan-Am Hwy

0   500 yds

0   500 m

Playa San Isidro

HOSPITAL

Entertainment and Events

Every mid-July the city honors Carmen, Virgin of the Sea, in the annual **Sea Festival,** a boating regatta with boats decorated in colorful flags and banners. The local Chinese community contributes dragon boats.

In summer, concerts and plays are put on at the Casa de la Cultura.

A series of bars along Paseo de las Turistas cater to the locals. **Caribbean Breeze** (Calle 23) has karaoke on Friday and Saturday nights, and "nostalgia" music on Wednesdays at its colorful bar with TV. **Kimbo's** (Calles 7/9) has karaoke on Thursdays, plus a large-screen TV. Otherwise, the local bars are overwhelmingly raffish (guard against pickpockets).

There's a casino in the Doubletree Resort by Hilton Puntarenas.

Accommodations

Puntarenas is a muggy place, so check that ventilation is efficient (this is one place in Costa Rica where you'll be glad for a/c). Take a hotel on the gulf side to catch the breezes. Many of the low-end hotels downtown are volatile refuges of drunks and prostitutes. Things improve west of downtown. However, all except the budget properties are overpriced.

UNDER $25

One of the better budget bargains is the well-run **Hotel Río** (Calle Central, Avenida 3, tel. 506/2661-0331, fax 506/2661-0938, $8 s or $12 d shared bath, $12 s or $16 d private bath), with 90 clean, basic rooms with fans and cold water, and handy for the *lancha* dock to Paquera. Similarly, **Hotel y Restaurant Cayuga** (Calle 4, Avenidas Central/1, tel. 506/2661-0344, fax 506/2661-1280, $15 s or $22 d standard, $26 s or $37 d with TV and telephone) is simple, clean, and well kept, a bargain popular with gringos. The 31 rooms have air-conditioning and private baths with cold water. There's a restaurant and secure parking. **Gran Hotel Chorotega** (Calle 1, Avenida 3, tel. 506/661-0998, $12 s or $19 d shared bath, $20 s or $30 d private bath) is of similar standard.

$25-50

The American-run **Hotel La Punta** (Avenida 1, Calles 35/37, tel. 506/2661-0696, fax 506/2661-4470, lapunta@ice.co.cr, $15–25 s, $25–40 d low season; $25–35 s, $30–50 d high season) is a good place to rest your head if you want to catch the early-morning ferry to Nicoya. The 12 dowdy and spartan rooms have spacious private baths with hot water; some rooms have fans only, while others are air-conditioned. Upper rooms have balconies. It has a small pool and a restaurant, plus parking.

Downtown, **Hotel Don Robert** (tel. 506/2661-4610) is the same price as Hotel La Punta, with 10 no-frills rooms plus secure parking and Wi-Fi.

East of town, the **La Casona del Mar Hotel** (tel. 506/2661-4035, olgacabr@gmail.com) has a breezy beachside setting. This modern two-story unit has 17 air-conditioned rooms with cable TV.

$50-100

The venerable **Hotel Tioga** (Paseo de las Turistas, Avenidas 15/17, tel. 506/2661-0271, www.hoteltioga.com, $74–89 s/d low season, $89–114 high season) has 46 air-conditioned rooms surrounding a pleasing but compact courtyard with tiny swimming pool graced by its own palm-shaded island. Rooms vary in size and quality; all have TVs and telephones but not all have hot water. There's secure parking. Rates include breakfast in the fourth-floor restaurant.

Next door, the **Hotel Alamar** (Paseo de las Turistas, Calle 32, tel. 506/2661-4343, www.alamarcr.com, $50 s or $60 d low season, $90 s/d high-season) offers 28 spacious rooms and junior suites, plus fully equipped apartments, all with contemporary design in lively colors, coffeemakers, telephones, safes, mini-bars, and cable TV. It has a pleasant breeze-swept courtyard with pool and a whirlpool tub. If it's full, the adjoining **Hotel Las Brisas** (tel. 506/2661-4040, www.lasbrisas hotelcr.com) is of similar standard and price, as is the **Hotel Yadran** (Avenida 2, Calles 31/33, tel. 506/2661-2662, www.puntarenas.com/

© CHRISTOPHER P. BAKER

Doubletree Resort by Hilton Puntarenas

yadran), one block west at the breezy tip of the peninsula.

Perfect for families, **Doubletree Resort by Hilton Puntarenas** (tel. 506/2663-0808, http://doubletree1.hilton.com, $299–419 year-round) is an attractive all-inclusive beach resort with 230 spacious and modestly furnished air-conditioned rooms, including 87 junior suites, and an opulent presidential suite, all with contemporary furnishings, including 27-inch flat-screen TVs. Formerly Fiesta Caribbean Village, this hotel was recently taken over by Hilton and remade with a stylish new look, most notable in the modern annex, where new rooms are spacious and now have Neutrogena toiletries. It has heaps of facilities, including an immense free-form swimming pool, water sports, activities, a casino, and nightly entertainment. The resort is popular with Tico families and gets noisy and active on weekends and holidays.

Food

Cheap *sodas* abound near the Central Market and along the Paseo de las Turistas, between Calles Central and 3.

More substantial options along Paseo include **Matobe's** (Paseo, Calles 15/17, no tel., 11 A.M.–10 P.M. daily), which serves fresh-baked pastas (I recommend the chicken fettuccine alfredo, $5) plus wood-fired pizza; and the rustically elegant **Steak House La Yunta** (Calle 21, tel. 506/2661-3216, 10 A.M.–midnight, daily), where you dine on an open veranda of a historic two-story seafront house. It has a huge menu that includes shrimp, ceviche, tenderloins ($9–10), tongue in beet sauce ($7), and pork chops.

Capitán Moreno (Avenida 4, Calles 13/15, tel. 506/2661-0810, 11 A.M.–midnight daily) is the best option for seafood, enjoyed beside the beach. It's also one of the city's major live music venues.

Musmanni (Avenida Central, Calles Central/1) sells baked goods. The central market (Avenida 3, Calle Central) sells produce.

Information and Services

The city's **tourist information office** (tel. 506/2661-2980, camaraturismopuntarenas@gmail.com, 8 A.M.–5 P.M. Mon.–Fri.) is above Bancrédito, opposite the cruise ship pier.

The **Monseñor Sanabria Hospital** (tel. 506/2630-8000) is eight kilometers east of town. There's a branch hospital at Paseo de las Turistas and Calle 9.

The **police station** (tel. 506/2661-0740) is at Paseo and Calle Central. Criminal investigation is handled by the OIJ (tel. 506/2630-0377). The **post office** is on Avenida 3, Calles Central/1.

Puntarenas Cyber Café (tel. 506/2661-3927, 9 A.M.–9 P.M. daily) is tucked behind the Casa de la Cultura. The **Coonatramar** ferry terminal (Avenida 3, Calles 33/35, tel. 506/2661-1069, www.coonatramar.com, 8 A.M.–5 P.M. daily) also has Internet service.

Getting There

Empresarios Unidos (in San José tel. 506/2222-0064, in Puntarenas tel. 506/661-2158), buses depart San José from Calle 16, Avenidas 10/12, every hour 4 A.M.–7 P.M. daily ($3).

Return buses depart Puntarenas for San José from the bus station (Calle 2, Paseo de las Turistas, tel. 506/661-2158) at 4:15 A.M., then every 30 minutes 5:30 A.M.–8 P.M. ($2.50). Buses also depart Puntarenas for Cañas and Tilarán at 11:30 A.M. and 4:15 P.M.; Monteverde at 1:15 P.M. and 2:15 P.M.; Jacó six times daily; Liberia six times daily; and Quepos at 4:30 A.M., 7:30 A.M., 10:30 A.M., and 3 P.M.

Interbus (tel. 506/2283-5573, www.inter busonline.com) operates minibus shuttles from San José ($25) and popular tourist destinations in Nicoya and Guanacaste.

Car-and-passenger ferries for the Nicoya Peninsula leave the **Coonatramar ferry terminal** (Avenida 3, Calles 33/35, tel. 506/2661-9011, www.coonatramar.com); the office is open 8 A.M.–5 P.M. Monday–Saturday. A passengers-only *lancha* (water-taxi, tel. 506/2661-0515) departs Puntarenas for Paquera at 11:30 A.M. and 4 P.M. from Avenida 3, Calles 2/Central. Return ferries depart Paquera at 7:30 A.M. and 2 P.M. ($1.25 adults, $1 for bicycles and children). Buses marked Ferry operate along Avenida Central to the terminal ($2).

The **Costa Rica Yacht Club and Marina** (tel. 506/2661-0784, www.costaricayacht club.com) has facilities for yachters.

Getting Around

Buses ply up and down Avenidas Central and 2. Coopepuntarenas (tel. 506/2663-1635) offers taxi service.

MIRAMAR AND VICINITY

Eleven kilometers north of Esparza on Highway 1, a side road winds east to the village of Miramar, on the western slopes of the Cordillera Tilarán. Gold has been mined hereabouts since 1815; you can still visit **Las Minas de Montes de Oro,** where guests are taken inside the tunnels and shown the old-fashioned manner of sifting for gold. It has a functioning waterwheel.

The sole concession to visit the mine is owned by **Finca Daniel Adventure Park** (tel. 506/2639-8303, www.finca-daniel.com), a 27-hectare ranch and fruit farm in the hills four kilometers north of Miramar at Tajo Alto. It has horseback rides, ATV tours, and a rope-bridge treetop challenge course. A canopy tour has 11 cables, including a beginners' line that runs in front of the restaurant, permitting dad to wave to the kids as he passes; a second, more elaborate, zipline system has 25 cables. Alas, the horses looked malnourished at last visit.

The 2,400-hectare **Peñas Blancas Wildlife Refuge** (Refugio Silvestre de Peñas Blancas), 33 kilometers northeast of Puntarenas, protects the watersheds of the Ríos Barranca and Ciruelas, on the forested southern slopes of the Cordillera de Tilarán. The mountain slopes rise steeply from rolling plains carved with deep canyons to 1,400 meters atop Zapotal peak. Vegetation ranges from tropical dry forest in the southerly lower elevation to moist deciduous and premontane moist forest higher up. There are no visitor facilities and few visitors.

Orchid lovers should visit **Orquitur** (tel. 2639-1034, www.orchimex.com, 8 A.M.–4 P.M., $10), a huge orchid farm on Highway 1 about 20 kilometers north of Esparza. It breeds about 50 varieties, including hybrids, for export.

Accommodations and Food

Hotel Vista Golfo (tel. 506/2639-8303, www .finca-daniel.com, from $106 s, $162 d including breakfast, dinner, and one activity),

GUANACASTE

at Finca Daniel Adventure Park, has 10 rooms and apartments (one has a kitchenette) with modest decor and balconies. There's a swimming pool and a hot tub, plus a bar and restaurant, where you can dine beneath the shade of a huge spreading tree.

Far nicer, the German-run **Finca El Mirador B&B** (tel./fax 506/2639-8774, www.finca-mirador.com, $32–54 s/d low season, $35–60 high season) is an intimate red-tile-roofed mountainside home with two cabins with rich and inviting decor, terra-cotta floors, kitchenettes, and modern bathrooms. A smaller yet charming wooden cabin lacks a kitchenette. There's a swimming pool with great views. Monkeys abound on the forested property. It's two kilometers along a dirt road that begins about 600 meters before Finca Daniel.

Getting There
Buses depart Calle 12, Avenida 9 in San José for Miramar at 4:40 A.M., 5:30 A.M., 7:30 A.M., and 12:35 P.M., returning at 7 A.M., 12:30 P.M., 4:15 P.M., and 5:30 P.M. daily ($2). Direct buses depart Puntarenas for Miramar at 9:30 A.M. (at 10:30 A.M. on Sun.); return buses depart Miramar at 4:30 P.M. (at 5:45 P.M. on Sun.).

COSTA DE PÁJAROS
At San Gerardo, on the Pan-American Highway, 40 kilometers north of Puntarenas, a paved road leads west to Punta Morales and the Golfo de Nicoya. There's fabulous bird-watching among the mangroves that line the shore—known as the Costa de Pájaros—stretching north to **Manzanillo**, the estuary of the Río Abangaritos, and, beyond, to the estuary of the Río Tempisque. The mangroves are home to ibis, herons, pelicans, parrots, egrets, and caimans. You can follow this coast road through cattle country to Highway 18, five kilometers east of the Tempisque bridge.

La Enseñada National Wildlife Refuge (La Enseñada Refugio Nacional de Vida Silvestre) is near Abangaritos, two kilometers north of Manzanillo, 17 kilometers from the Pan-American Highway. The 380-hectare wildlife refuge is part of a family-run cattle *finca* and

salt farm, with nature trails and a lake replete with waterfowl and crocodiles. The lodge offers mangrove tours, boat trips to Palo Verde, a tractor tour of the *finca*, and horseback tours.

The **Birds Island Biological Reserve** (Isla Pájaros Reserva Biológica) is about 600 meters offshore from Punta Morales. The 3.8-hectare reserve protects a colony of brown pelicans and other seabirds. Access is restricted to biological researchers.

Parque MegaFauna Monteverde (tel. 506/2638-8229, 8 A.M.–5 P.M., $7 adults, $5 children), on the Pan-Am Highway at Chomes de Puntarenas, has recreations and exhibits relating to dinosaurs and other prehistoric animals. Kids might get a thrill from the rather crude life-size cement renditions along a 1.7-kilometer trail. At least there's a splendid restaurant adjoining, and frog, snake, and insect exhibits are to be added.

Accommodations
The **La Enseñada Lodge** (tel. 506/2289-6655, www.laensenada.net, $38 s or $46 d low season, $44 s or $55 d high season) enjoys a breezy location at the heart of La Ensenada Wildlife Refuge, with tremendous views down the bougainvillea-splashed lawns to the mangrove-lined gulf. It has 22 rustic yet spacious wooden *cabinas,* cross-ventilated by screened windows, with private baths with hot water and verandas with hammocks. It has a thatched restaurant, a tennis court, and a swimming pool.

Getting There
Buses depart Puntarenas for the Costa de Pájaros from Avenida Central, Calle 4 at 5:45 A.M., 10:45 A.M., 1:15 P.M., 4 P.M., and 5:15 P.M. daily.

LAS JUNTAS DE ABANGARES
Las Juntas, at the base of the Cordillera Tilarán about 50 kilometers north of Esparza and six kilometers east of Highway 1 (the turnoff is at Kilometer 164, about 12 kilometers north of the Río Lagarto and the turnoff for Monteverde), is splashed with colorful flowers and trim pastel-painted houses. A tree-lined main boulevard and streets paved with interlocking stones add to the

orderliness. Small it may be, but Las Juntas figures big in the region's history. When gold was discovered in the nearby mountains in 1884, it sparked a gold rush. Hungry prospectors came from all over the world to sift the earth for nuggets. Las Juntas was a Wild West town. Inflated gold prices have lured many *oreros* (miners) back to the old mines and streams (about 40 kilograms of gold a week are recovered).

The pint-size **locomotive**—the *María Cristina*—that sits in the town plaza once hauled ore for the Abangares Gold Fields Company and dates from 1904. The *oreros* are honored with a fine bronze **statue** in a triangular plaza on the northeast corner of town.

The road northeast from the triangular plaza leads into the Cordillera Tilarán via Candelaria and then (to the right) Monteverde or (to the left) Tilarán; a four-wheel-drive vehicle is recommended. In places the views are fantastic.

Centro Turístico Pueblo Antiguo

Pueblo Antiguo Tourist Center (tel. 506/2662-0033, www.puebloantiguo.com, 8 A.M.–10 P.M. daily, $5 admission), near the hamlet of La Sierra, three kilometers east of Las Juntas, enjoys a tremendous setting amid 60 forested hectares. This "touristic complex" has two hot thermal pools and a cold-water pool, plus a cavern-style stone-lined steam room and two whirlpool tubs. It has bars, a restaurant, and a lake stocked with trout and tilapia. Nature tours are offered, as is a "Gold Mine Adventure" down dank candlelit tunnels ($20, helmets and flashlights are provided). Farther downhill, and belonging to the Centro, is the **Ecomuseo Las Minas** (8 A.M.–5 P.M. Tues.–Fri.), displaying mining equipment at the entrance of an old mine. It is usually closed; call ahead.

Mina Tours (tel. 506/2662-0753, www.minatours.com), in Las Juntas, also offers tours of a miners' cooperative.

Accommodations and Food

Cabinas El Elcanto (tel. 506/2662-0677, $8 s or $14 d with fans, $10 s or $17 d with a/c), 100 meters northeast of the triangular plaza, has 14 clean, simple, modern rooms with fans, private baths, and cold water. Five additional rooms have air-conditioning and hot water. All have cable TV.

Centro Turístico Pueblo Antiguo (tel. 506/2662-1913, www.puebloantiguo.com, $62 s, $79 d) has 10 spacious wooden cabins for up to five people each. All have tile floors, fans, rattan sofas and chairs, two queen-size beds, basic kitchens with microwave, clean modern private bathroom with hot water, and verandas with rockers.

Getting There

Buses (tel. 506/2222-1867) depart San José for Las Juntas from Calle 12, Avenidas 7/9, at 8:40 A.M., 10:30 A.M., and 3 P.M. daily. Return buses to San José depart Las Juntas at 8:40 A.M., 10:30 A.M., and 3 P.M.

Monteverde and Vicinity

◖ MONTEVERDE, CERRO PLANO, AND SANTA ELENA

Monteverde, 35 kilometers north from the Pan-American Highway, means "Green Mountain," an appropriate name for one of the most idyllic pastoral settings in Costa Rica. Cows munch contentedly, and horse-drawn wagons loaded with milk cans still make the rounds in this world-famous community atop a secluded 1,400-meter-high plateau in the Cordillera de Tilarán. Monteverde is actually a sprawling agricultural community; the Monteverde Cloud Forest Biological Reserve, which is what most visitors come to see, is a few kilometers southeast and higher up. A growing number of attractions are found north of Santa Elena, which has its own cloud forest reserve. The two reserves are at different elevations and have different fauna and flora.

COSTA RICA'S QUAKER VILLAGE

Monteverde was founded in 1951 by a group of 44 North American Quakers – most from Fairhope, Alabama – who as a matter of conscience had refused to register for the draft. Led by John Campbell and Wilford "Wolf" Guindon, they chose Costa Rica for a new home because it had done away with its army. They built roads and cleared much of the virgin forest for dairy farming. They decided to make cheese because it was the only product that could be stored and moved to market without spoiling along a muddy oxcart trail. Cheese is still a mainstay of the local economy, and the Quaker organization is still active in Monteverde (it meets every Wednesday morning at the Friends' Meeting House; visitors are welcome).

Don't expect to find the Quakers walking down the road dressed like the chap off the oatmeal box. *Cuaquerismo* (Quakerism) in Monteverde is a low-key affair.

The reserves lie within the **Arenal-Monteverde Protection Zone.** Created in 1991, this protection zone encompasses more than 30,000 hectares extending down both the Caribbean and Pacific slopes of the Cordillera de Tilarán and encompassing eight distinct ecological zones, most notably cloud forest at higher elevations. Wind-battered elfin woods on exposed ridges are spectacularly dwarfed, whereas more protected areas have majestically tall trees festooned with orchids, bromeliads, ferns, and vines. Clouds sift through the forest primeval. February through May, quetzals are in the cloud forest. Later, they migrate downhill, where they can be seen around the hotels of Monteverde. Just after dawn is a good time to spot quetzals, which are particularly active in the early morning, especially April and May. Early morning and late afternoon are the best times to see birds.

The fame of the preserve has spawned an ever-increasing influx of tourists and an ever-increasing number of attractions, and the area is in danger of becoming overdeveloped and overpriced (visitation is up from a mere 3,257 in 1980 to more than 75,000 in 2008). The community spirit is being lost as locals put the pursuit of money above community interests.

Orientation

Monteverde is populated by North American Quakers. There is no concentrated village to speak of; most of the homes are hidden from view in the forest, accessible by foot trail and scattered along the dirt road that leads to Monteverde Cloud Forest Biological Reserve from the village of **Santa Elena.** Santa Elena, home to a community of Tico families, is distinct from Monteverde and is the center of things hereabouts: The bank, stores, bars (these being absent, of course, in a Quaker community), and other services are here. Separating the communities of Santa Elena and Monteverde is the region of **Cerro Plano,** where most accommodations concentrate.

Farm and Cultural Tours

Coffee is grown on the slopes just below Santa Elena and Monteverde; some three dozen small-scale coffee producers make up the Santa Elena cooperative. **Monteverde Coffee Tour** (tel. 506/2645-5006, www.monteverde-coffee.com, 8 A.M. and 1:30 P.M. by reservation, $30) has three-hour tours.

The **El Trapiche Tour** (tel. 506/2645-5834, www.eltrapichetour.com, 10 A.M. and 3 P.M. Mon.–Sat., and 3 P.M. Sun., $25 adults, $20 students, $10 children) offers a more rounded experience that teaches about production of a wide range of crops, from coffee to sugarcane.

For an idealistic take on Monteverde's history, check out the **História Monteverde** (tel. 506/2645-7097, www.historiamonteverde.com, $25 adults, $20 students, $10 children), a small museum (new in 2008) with eclectic exhibits of rusting farm equipment, plus an amphitheater and a giant scale-model of the area. Two-hour tours are given at 10 A.M., noon, 2 P.M., and 4 P.M. It's no prize-winner, but it helps pass time on rainy days.

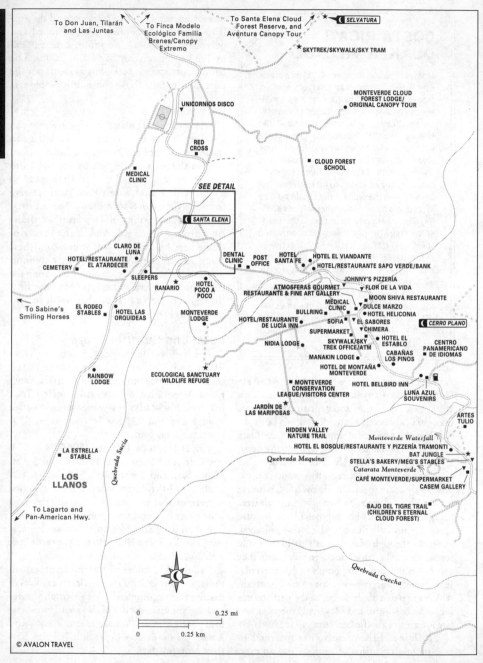

To Don Juan, Tilarán and Las Juntas

To Finca Modelo Ecológico Familia Brenes/Canopy Extremo

To Santa Elena Cloud Forest Reserve, and Aventura Canopy Tour

☾ SELVATURA

SKYTREK/SKYWALK/SKY TRAM

MONTEVERDE CLOUD FOREST LODGE/ ORIGINAL CANOPY TOUR

UNICORNIOS DISCO

RED CROSS

CLOUD FOREST SCHOOL

MEDICAL CLINIC

SEE DETAIL

☾ SANTA ELENA

CLARO DE LUNA

HOTEL/RESTAURANTE EL ATARDECER

CEMETERY

SLEEPERS

RANARIO

HOTEL POCO A POCO

DENTAL CLINIC

POST OFFICE

HOTEL SANTA FE

HOTEL EL VIANDANTE

HOTEL/RESTAURANTE SAPO VERDE/BANK

JOHNNY'S PIZZERÍA

ATMOSFERAS GOURMET RESTAURANTE & FINE ART GALLERY

FLOR DE LA VIDA

MOON SHIVA RESTAURANTE

DULCE MARZO

To Sabine's Smiling Horses

EL RODEO STABLES

HOTEL LAS ORQUIDEAS

MONTEVERDE LODGE

BULLRING

MEDICAL CLINIC

HOTEL HELICONIA

HOTEL/RESTAURANTE DE LUCÍA INN

SOFIA

EL SABORES

SUPERMARKET

CHIMERA

NIDIA LODGE

SKYWALK/SKY TREK OFFICE/ATM

HOTEL EL ESTABLO

CABAÑAS LOS PINOS

CERRO PLANO

CENTRO PANAMERICANO DE IDIOMAS

MANAKIN LODGE

HOTEL DE MONTAÑA MONTEVERDE

RAINBOW LODGE

ECOLOGICAL SANCTUARY WILDLIFE REFUGE

MONTEVERDE CONSERVATION LEAGUE/VISITORS CENTER

HOTEL BELLBIRD INN

LUNA AZUL SOUVENIRS

JARDÍN DE LAS MARIPOSAS

ARTES TULIO

HIDDEN VALLEY NATURE TRAIL

Monteverde Waterfall

HOTEL EL BOSQUE/RESTAURANTE Y PIZZERÍA TRAMONTI

Quebrada Maquina

STELLA'S BAKERY/MEG'S STABLES

BAT JUNGLE

Catarata Monteverde

LA ESTRELLA STABLE

CAFÉ MONTEVERDE/SUPERMARKET

CASEM GALLERY

LOS LLANOS

Quebrada Sucia

BAJO DEL TIGRE TRAIL (CHILDREN'S ETERNAL CLOUD FOREST)

To Lagarto and Pan-American Hwy.

Quebrada Cuecha

0   0.25 mi

0   0.25 km

© AVALON TRAVEL

MONTEVERDE AND VICINITY

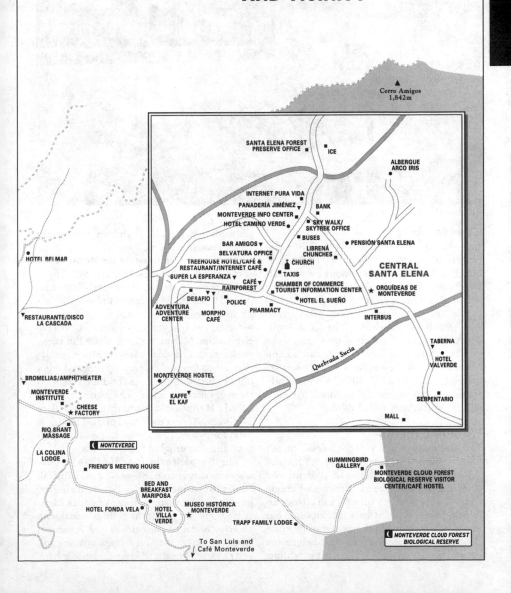

Cerro Amigos
1,842m

SANTA ELENA FOREST
PRESERVE OFFICE ■
ICE ■

ALBERGUE
ARCO IRIS ●

INTERNET PURA VIDA ■
PANADERÍA JIMÉNEZ ▼
MONTEVERDE INFO CENTER ■
HOTEL CAMINO VERDE ●

BANK ■
SKY WALK/
SKYTREK OFFICE ■
BUSES ■

PENSIÓN SANTA ELENA ●

BAR AMIGOS ▼
SELVATURA OFFICE ■
LIBRERÍA
CHUNCHES ■

HOTEL BELMAR ▼

TREEHOUSE HOTEL/CAFÉ &
RESTAURANT/INTERNET CAFÉ ●
SUPER LA ESPERANZA ▼

CHURCH ♦

TAXIS ■

CENTRAL
SANTA ELENA

CAFÉ ▼
RAINFOREST

CHAMBER OF COMMERCE
TOURIST INFORMATION CENTER ■
HOTEL EL SUEÑO ●

ORQUÍDEAS DE
MONTEVERDE ★

DESAFIO ▼ ▼
POLICE ■

ADVENTURA
ADVENTURE
CENTER ■
MORPHO
CAFÉ ▼

PHARMACY ■

INTERBUS ■

▼ RESTAURANTE/DISCO
LA CASCADA

TABERNA ▼
HOTEL
VALVERDE ■

Quebrada Sucia

BROMELIAS/AMPHITHEATER ▼

MONTEVERDE HOSTEL ■

MONTEVERDE
INSTITUTE ■
CHEESE
★ FACTORY

KAFFE ▼
EL KAF

SERPENTARIO ■

RIO SHANTI
MASSAGE ●

MALL ■

☾ MONTEVERDE

LA COLINA
LODGE ●

FRIEND'S MEETING HOUSE ■

HUMMINGBIRD
GALLERY ■
MONTEVERDE CLOUD FOREST
BIOLOGICAL RESERVE VISITOR
CENTER/CAFÉ HOSTEL ■

BED AND
BREAKFAST
MARIPOSA ■

HOTEL FONDA VELA ●
HOTEL
VILLA
VERDE ●

MUSEO HISTÓRICA
MONTEVERDE ★

TRAPP FAMILY LODGE ●

To San Luis and
Café Monteverde

☾ MONTEVERDE CLOUD FOREST
BIOLOGICAL RESERVE

© CHRISTOPHER P. BAKER

display at the Bat Jungle

Cheese Factory

La Lechería (tel. 506/2645-5436, 7:30 A.M.–5 P.M. Mon.–Sat., 7:30 A.M.–12:30 P.M. Sun.), in Monteverde, is famous for its quality cheeses. Production began in 1953 when the original Quaker settlers bought 50 Jersey cattle and began producing pasteurized Monteverde Gouda cheese. The factory produces 14 types of cheese—from parmesan and emmentaler to Danish-style dambo and Monte Rico, the best-seller. Guided tours are offered (tel. 506/2645-7090, www.crstudytours.com, 9 A.M. and 2 P.M. Mon.–Sat., $10 adults, $8 students and children).

Wildlife Exhibits

The Bat Jungle (tel. 506/2645-6566, http://paseodestella.googlepages.com, 9:30 A.M.–7:30 P.M. daily, $10 adults, $8 students and children), between the gas station and cheese factory, is the first in Costa Rica to provide an insight into the life of bats (Monteverde has at least 65 species). Eight species of live bats flit, feed, and mate within a sealed enclosure behind a wall of glass. Fascinating exhibits illuminate bat ecology, and an auditorium screens documentaries.

The impressive **Ranario de Monteverde** (Frog Pond of Monteverde, tel. 506/2645-6320, www.ranario.com, 9 A.M.–8:30 P.M. daily, $10 adults, $8 children/students) displays 28 species of frogs and amphibians, from the red-eyed tree frog and transparent frogs to the elephantine Marine toad, all housed in large, well-arranged display cases. It also has salamanders, a few snakes, plus termites and other bugs to be fed to the frogs. Evening is best, as the frogs become active. The owners recently added a **Mariposario** (butterfly garden, $10, or $16 if also visiting the Frog Pond). The cost is valid for two entries, so you can see both daytime and nocturnal species.

The **Serpentario** (tel. 506/2645-6002, www.snaketour.com, 8 A.M.–8 P.M. daily, $8 adults, $6 students, $5 children, including guide), on the eastern fringe of Santa Elena village, lets you get up close and personal with an array of coiled constrictors and venomous vipers, as well as their prey: frogs, chameleons, and the like. The dreaded fer-de-lance is here,

© CHRISTOPHER P. BAKER

ant colony display at Jardín de las Mariposas

along with 25 or so other species staring at you from behind thick panes of glass.

The **Jardín de las Mariposas** (Monteverde Butterfly Gardens, tel. 506/2645-5512, www.monteverdebutterflygarden.com, 9:30 A.M.–4 P.M. daily, $10 adults, $8 students, $4 children, including one-hour guided tour) features a nature center and three distinct habitats: a 450-square-meter netted butterfly flyway and two greenhouses representing lowland forest and mid-elevation forest habitats. Together, they are filled with native plant species and hundreds of tropical butterflies representing more than 40 species. Guided tours begin in the visitors center, where butterflies and other bugs are mounted for view and rhinoceros beetles, stick insects, and tarantulas crawl around inside display cases. There's a computer station with butterfly interactive software, plus an auditorium where videos are shown. A highlight is the three-camera "bug cam" that shows micro-detail, real-time insect life, including inside the leaf-cutter ant nest. Go mid-morning, when the butterflies become active (and most tourists are in the reserve).

Orquídeas de Monteverde (Monteverde Orchid Garden (tel. 506/2645-5308, www.monteverdeorchidgarden.com, 8 A.M.–5 P.M. daily, $10 adults, $7 students) took five years of arduous work to collate the results of the Monteverde Orchid Investigation Project, an ongoing effort to document and research local orchids. Short paths wind through the compact, displaying almost 450 species native to the region arranged in 22 groups ("subtribes"), each marked with an educational placard. Miniatures are preponderant, including the world's smallest flower, *Platystele jungermanniodes,* about the size of a pinhead (fortunately, you are handed a magnifying glass upon arrival).

◖ Monteverde Cloud Forest Biological Reserve

The 14,200-hectare Reserva Biológica Bosque Nuboso Monteverde (tel. 506/2645-5122, www.cct.or.cr, 7 A.M.–4 P.M. daily, $17 adults, $9 children and students), six kilometers east of Santa Elena, is owned and administered by the Tropical Science Center of Costa Rica. It

© CHRISTOPHER P. BAKER

clouds swirl around Monteverde

protects more than 100 species of mammals, more than 400 species of birds, and more than 1,200 species of amphibians and reptiles. It is one of the few remaining habitats of all six species of the cat family: jaguar, ocelot, puma, margay, oncilla, and jaguarundi. Bird species embrace black guan, emerald toucanet, the critically endangered three-wattled bellbird (whose metallic "BONK!" call carries for almost two miles), and 30 local hummingbird species. Hundreds of visitors arrive in hopes of seeing a resplendent quetzal (approximately 200 pairs nest in the reserve). Cognoscenti know that, ironically, the parking lot is perhaps the best place to see quetzals; go early in the morning.

The reserve has 13 kilometers of trails for day-visitors concentrated in an area called "The Triangle." Parts ooze with mud; other sections have been covered with raised wooden walkways. A maximum of 200 people are allowed on the trails at any one time. Access is first come, first served, except for those already booked on guided tours. See the website for a trail map.

Longer trails requiring an overnight lead down the Pacific slopes. **Sendero Valle** leads to La Cascada, a triple waterfall, and continues via the valley of the Río Peñas Blancas to Pocosol, about 20 kilometers south of La Fortuna. These are for experienced Indiana Jones–type hikers only. There are three basic backpacking shelters with bunks, showers, and hydroelectricity, plus propane stoves and pots and pans, but you'll need to bring food and sleeping bag (the shelters were closed at last visit for remodeling). Trail crews and researchers get priority. Rates are $3.50–5 nightly. Reservations are essential, since the huts are locked (you're told how to pick up the key after making your reservation). If you want to hike alone, buy your ticket the day before and set out before the crowds. You increase your chances of seeing wildlife if you hike with a guide; reservations are advisable (you can book online; from $7). Three-hour guided tours *(caminatas)* are also offered at 7:30 A.M., noon, and 1:30 P.M. daily (minimum three people, maximum nine people; $34 pp including entrance). A five-hour birding tour is offered at 6 A.M. ($64 pp including entrance).

THE DISAPPEARANCE OF THE GOLDEN TOAD

The Monteverde Cloud Forest Biological Reserve owes its existence in part to the discovery of a brilliant, neon orange arboreal toad – sapo dorado (Bufo periglenes) – discovered in 1964 and so stunning that one biologist harbored "a suspicion that someone had dipped the examples in enamel paint." The males are the orange ones; females, which are larger, are yellow and black with patches of scarlet. Monteverde is the only known home of this fabulous creature. But don't expect to see one – it may already be extinct. Although in 1986 it could be seen in large quantities, by 1988 very few remained. To my knowledge, no confirmed sightings have been made since 1996. These creatures may now exist only on the cover of tourist brochures, victims of a deadly fungus that has devastated the world's frog populations during the last decade.

A two-hour night hike is offered at 7:15 P.M. ($17, or $20 with hotel transfers).

Bring warm clothing and raingear. You can rent rubber boots in many hotels. The visitors center rents binoculars ($10 per day, plus deposit) and sells a self-guide pamphlet, trail map, and wildlife guides.

A café at the visitors center serves omelettes ($1.75), burgers, sandwiches, mochas ($1), and other fare. Also at the visitors center, there's dorm accommodation ($20 pp with shared bath, $30 pp private bath, including meals), with kitchens and hot water.

A bus (tel. 506/2645-6296) departs Santa Elena for the reserve at 6:15 A.M., 7:20 A.M., 9:20 A.M., 1:20 P.M., and 3 P.M. daily, returning at 6:45 A.M., 7:45 A.M., 11:30 A.M., 2 P.M., and 4 P.M. ($1 each way). Most hotels can arrange transportation. A taxi from Santa Elena should cost about $9 one-way, but there are reports of gouging. There's parking.

Santa Elena Cloud Forest Reserve

This 310-hectare cloud forest reserve (tel. 506/2645-5390, www.reservasantaelena.org, 7 A.M.–4 P.M. daily, $12 adults, $6 students and children) is five kilometers northeast of Santa Elena (4WD required). Owned by the Santa Elena community, it boasts all the species claimed by its eastern neighbor—plus spider monkeys, which are absent from the Monteverde reserve. It has four one-way trails (1.4–4.8 km) and an observation tower with views toward Volcán Arenal. At a higher elevation than Monteverde reserve, it tends to be cloudier and wetter.

The reserve is the site of the **Monteverde Cloud Forest Ecological Center,** a farm that educates youngsters and local farmers on forest ecology and conservation. There's also a visitors center. Guides are available, as are dormitory accommodations.

Guided three-hour hikes ($15) are offered at 7:30 A.M. and 11:30 A.M.; there is also a 90-minute night tour at 7 P.M. You can buy trail maps and a self-guided trail booklet and rent rubber boots ($1)—at the information center.

Shuttles for ticket-holders leave Santa Elena at 6:45 A.M., 11 A.M., and 2:30 P.M. A collective taxi leaves Santa Elena village at 6:45 A.M., 8 A.M., 10:30 A.M., 12:30 P.M., and 2 P.M., but you must book the day before ($2 per person). A regular taxi costs about $10 each way.

Children's Eternal Cloud Forest

Surrounding the Monteverde Cloud Forest Biological Reserve on three sides, the Bosque Eterno de Los Niños is the largest private reserve in Central America. It is administered by the Monteverde Conservation League (tel. 506/2645-5003, www.acmcr.org). The dream of a rainforest saved by children began in 1987 at a small primary school in rural Sweden. A study of tropical forests prompted nine-year-old Roland Teinsuu to ask what he could do to keep the rainforest and the animals that live in it safe from destruction. Young Roland's question launched a group campaign to raise money to help the League buy and save threatened rainforest in Costa Rica. Roland and his classmates raised enough money to buy six hectares of rainforest at a cost of $250 per hectare. Out of this initial success a group of children dedicated to saving the tropical rainforest formed Barnens Regnskog (Children's Rain Forest). The vision took hold, sweeping the globe, with contributions flocking in from the far corners. The original six-hectare preserve, established near Monteverde in 1988, has grown to more than 22,000 hectares.

It is accessed via the **Bajo del Tigre** (tel. 506/2645-5923,.7:30 A.M.–5:30 P.M., $5 admission), off the main road, just above the CASEM Gallery. This section of the reserve is at a lower elevation than the Monteverde Cloud Forest Biological Preserve and thus offers a different variety of plant and animal life. Quetzals are more easily seen here, for example, than higher up in the wetter, mistier cloud forest. Facilities include a Children's Nature Center, a self-guided interpretative trail, an arboretum, and a visitors center and library. Guided tours are offered at 7:30 A.M. and 1 P.M. Monday–Wednesday, plus a two-hour guided "Twilight Walk" (twilightwalk@racsa.co.cr, 5:30 P.M. Thursday–Sunday, $20 or $22 with transfer).

There are also two field stations: at Poco Sol, on the lower eastern slopes, with eight rooms (six with private bath) for 26 people and 10 kilometers of hiking trails; and San Gerardo, at 1,220 meters elevation, a 3.5-kilometer walk from the Santa Elena Cloud Forest Reserve, with accommodations for 26 people and six kilometers of trails. Guides are available by request.

Ecolodge San Luís

This ecolodge (tel. 506/2645-8049, www.uga .edu/costarica, $10 day visits, $6 students, $20 guided tour, $10 per hour horseback rides) is affiliated with the University of Georgia and doubles as an integrated tourism, research, and education project on a 70-hectare farm at San Luís eight kilometers southeast of Monteverde (the turnoff is immediately east of Hotel Fonda Vela on the road to the Monteverde reserve; it's

a steep descent). Resident biologists work with members of the San Luís community to develop a model for sustainable development.

The station offers a wide range of activities: horseback rides, bird-watching, cloud-forest hiking (plus a hike to the San Luís waterfall), night walks, and hands-on laboratory study. Open-air classes are given, including an intensive seven-day tropical biology course. And you can even help farm or participate in scientific research.

It has accommodations in a cozy wood-paneled bunkhouse with shared baths, a bungalow with private baths and verandas, and 12 *cabinas*.

A taxi from Monteverde costs about $10.

Private Wildlife Reserves

Ecological Sanctuary Wildlife Refuge (Finca Ecológica, tel./fax 506/2645-5869, www .ecologicalsanctuary.com, 7 A.M.–7:30 P.M. daily, $15 adults, $10 students, $5 children), on the same road as the Butterfly Garden, has six signed trails through the 48-hectare property, which has waterfalls. You have an excellent chance of seeing coatimundis, sloths, agoutis, porcupines, and white-faced monkeys, as well as butterflies and birds. It offers a twilight tour at 5:30 P.M. ($30 pp).

Sendero Tranquilo (Quiet Path Reserve, tel. 506/2645-5010, 7 A.M.–3 P.M. daily) has a three-hour guided tour beginning at the Hotel Sapo Dorado.

C Selvatura

Selvatura (tel. 506/2645-5929, www.selvatura .com, 7 A.M.–5 P.M. daily), two kilometers north of Sky Walk, offers a full-day's worth of things to see and do. A highlight is a canopy exploration along treetop walkways with three kilometers of suspended bridges ($25 adults, $20 students, $15 children) and via an 18-platform zipline canopy tour ($45 adults, $35 students, $30 children); tours are at 8.30 A.M., 11 A.M., 1 P.M. and 2:30 P.M. It also has a hummingbird garden ($5), a vast domed butterfly garden ($12), and a reptile exhibit ($12). Guided nature hikes are offered ($35).

The unique, not-to-be-missed highlight

JEWELS OF THE RAINFOREST

The Jewels of the Rainforest Bio-Art Exhibition ($12), at Selvatura, displays more than 50,000 insects from around the world, yet just a small fraction of Richard Whitten's (tel. 506/2645-5929, www.biophotos.com) findings from more than 50 years of collecting: the largest private collection of big, bizarre, and beautiful butterflies, beetles, and other bugs in the world. It surely is the most colorful – a veritable calliope of shimmering greens, neon blues, startling reds, silvers, and golds. Whitten began collecting "bugs" at a tender age; today his 1,900 boxes include more than one million specimens, many of them collected in Costa Rica. Part of the exhibit is dedicated to a collection of every species in the country. Some beetles are bigger than your fist; some moths outsize a salad plate. Other exhibits include shimmering beetles displayed against black velvet, like opal jewelry, and boxes of bugs majestically turned into caskets of gems.

Covering 232-square-meters, exhibits include a "Biodiversity Bank" with dozens of spectacular and informative displays; a wall of Neotropical Butterflies; a World of Beetles, from Tutankhamen scarabs to the giants of the beetle word; a Phasmid Room (stick insects and family); and a Silk Room, displaying elegant moths. Other special themes include paleontology and medical entomology. A 279-square-meter auditorium screens fascinating videos. "Stunning, educational, and fun!" says Smithsonian entomologist David Roubik.

The stunning, dynamic displays combine art, science, music, and video to entertain and educate about insect mimicry, protective coloration and other camouflage, prey-predator relationships, and more. The creativity is sheer choreography. Exhibits glitter against a background of opera and classical music, the climactic highs of the arias and ponderous lows of the cellos seemingly rising and falling to the drama of the displays, many of them re-creations of natural habitats under domed glass, the brilliant conception of Richard's wife, Margaret.

An unexpected treat may be an impromptu performance by Whitten (a former professional concert performer) displaying his talents on the glockenspiel, accordion, piano, or organ.

---

is the **Jewels of the Rainforest Bio-Art Exhibition,** the largest private collection of big, bizarre, and beautiful butterflies, beetles, and other bugs in the world.

Entertainment and Events

A **multimedia show**—*Sounds and Scenes of the Cloud Forest*—is offered nightly at 6:15 P.M. at the Monteverde Lodge ($5). And the Hotel Belmar has a slide show at 8 P.M. Saturday–Thursday ($5).

Bromelia's (tel. 506/2645-6272, 9 A.M.–5 P.M. daily) hosts live music and occasional theater in the Monteverde Amphitheater, an open-air performance space. Bring a cushion to soften the iron-hard seating.

Likewise, **Moon Shiva** (tel. 506/2645-6270, www.moonshiva.com), in Cerro Plano, has live music at 8 P.M., when it's *the* happenin' place in town, with acoustic rock on Wednesday, jazz Thursday–Friday, and *trova* on Saturday. For a similar Haight-Ashbury groove, check out **Kaffa el Café** (tel. 506/8829-5473, 11 A.M.– 11 P.M. daily), in Santa Elena. You can sit around on floor cushions imbibing cocktails or get wild on the impromptu dance floor.

For a taste of local working-class color, wet your whistle at **Bar Amigos** (506/2645-5071, noon–midnight), in Santa Elena, or at **Unicornios Disco** (tel. 506/2645-6282, noon–midnight), facing the soccer field north of the village. Both have pool tables.

The grooviest dance spot during midweek is **Taberna** (tel. 506/2645-5883), on the east side of Santa Elena, with a nightly disco (free entry). **La Cascada** (tel. 506/2645-5186, $5), a full-blown disco with flashing lights in Cerro Plano, is favored for Friday and Saturday nights. You can pick up some moves in advance with salsa lessons courtesy of Javier and Mia at

Dulce Marzo Bakery & Café (tel. 506/2645-6568, 7–11 P.M. every Thurs., $4).

Sports and Recreation
CANOPY TOURS
An intriguing way to explore the Santa Elena Cloud Forest Reserve is by ascending into the forest canopy on a guided **Sky Walk** (tel. 506/2645-5238, www.skywalk.co.cr), which offers a monkey's-eye view of things. You walk along five suspension bridges and platforms and 1,000 meters of pathways permitting viewing from ground level to the treetops, where you are right in there with the epiphytes. Two-hour tours depart at 8 A.M., 10 A.M., and 1 P.M. daily ($30 adults, $24 students, $19 children).

The same company offers a two-hour **SkyTrek** ($60 adults, $48 students, $38 children) for the more adventurous. You'll whiz through the canopy in a harness attached to a zipline that runs between three treetop canopies, spanning two kilometers. Tours are offered at 7:30 A.M., 9:30 A.M., 11:30 A.M., 1:30 P.M., and 2 P.M. daily. The tour starts with a ride on the **Sky Tram** cable car (which can only be taken in conjunction with the Sky Walk or Sky Trek).

Selvatura (tel. 506/2645-5929, www.selvatura.com) also has suspension bridges ($25 adults, $20 students, $15 children) and a zipline tour ($45 adults, $35 students, $30 children); tours are at 8.30 A.M., 11 A.M., 1 P.M. and 2:30 P.M.

The **Aventura Canopy Tour** (tel. 506/2645-6959, www.monteverdeadventure.com), on the road to the Sky Walk, has 16 zipline cables (tours at 8 A.M., 9 A.M., 9 A.M., 11 P.M. and 3 P.M., $40 adults, $30 students/children) and rappelling.

The canopy tour craze began at Monteverde Cloud Forest Lodge, where **The Original Canopy Tour** (tel. 506/2645-5243, www.canopy tour.com, $45 adults, $35 students, $25 children) was created. Zipline tours are offered at 7:30 A.M., 10:30 A.M., and 2:30 P.M. A thrilling beginning is the forest hike and a clamber up the interior of a hollow strangler fig to reach the first platform.

Extremo Canopy (tel. 506/2645-6058, www

.monteverdeextremo.com) opened in 2007 with a 16-cable zipline tour ($40 adults, $30 students, $25 children), a Tarzan swing, canyoning ($50), and horseback rides. And **Monteverde Waterfall** offers a wet clamber along ropes and rope-bridges; book through tour agencies in Santa Elena.

HORSEBACK RIDING
The following have stables and rent horses (usually about $10–15 per hour) and offer guided tours: **Meg's Stables** (tel. 506/2645-5560); **La Estrella** (tel. 506/2645-5075); **Sabine's Smiling Horses** (tel. 506/2645-6894, www.horseback-riding-tour.com); **Caballeriza El Rodeo** (tel. 506/2645-5764, elrodeo@racsa.co.cr); and **Terra Viva** (tel. 506/2645-5454, www.terravivacr.com), which gets good reviews from readers and also has an organic dairy farm and a private cloud forest reserve with trails.

I recommend **Desafío Adventure Company** (tel. 506/2645-5874, www.desafiocostarica .com) for horseback trips to La Fortuna ($65); the four-hour horseback ride from Monteverde to Río Chiquito is followed by a one-hour boat ride across Lake Arenal, then a 30-minute Jeep ride to La Fortuna.

Shopping
The **Artisans' Cooperative of Santa Elena and Monteverde** (CASEM, tel. 506/2645-5190, casemcr@yahoo.com, 8 A.M.–5 P.M. Mon.–Sat. and 10 A.M.–4 P.M. Sun.) features the handmade wares of 140 local artisans.

Monteverde boasts numerous excellent galleries. **Atmosfera Art Gallery** (tel. 506/2645-6555) has superb wood sculptures, as does **Artes Tulio** (tel. 506/2645-5567, www.artes tulio.com, 9 A.M.–6 P.M. daily), which sells the exquisite creations of gifted artist Marco Tulio Brenes. **Bromelia's** (tel. 506/2645-6272, 10 A.M.–5:30 P.M. daily, until 10 P.M. Thurs.) sells books and quality batiks, jewelry, and carvings. And the **Hummingbird Gallery** (tel. 506/2645-5030, 8:30 A.M.–4:30 P.M. daily), 100 meters below the entrance to the Monteverde Cloud Forest Biological Reserve, is well stocked with souvenirs, including the photographs of famed photographers (and nearby residents) Michael and Patricia Fogden.

In Santa Elena, **Librería Chunches** (tel./fax 506/2645-5147, 8 A.M.–6 P.M. Mon.–Sat.) sells English-language magazines and newspapers, plus natural history books and laminated *Costa Rican Field Guides.*

Accommodations

Monteverde is a popular destination, offering a varied choice of lodging. There are many more accommodations to choose from than presented here. Accommodations may be difficult to obtain in dry season, when tour companies block space. Book well ahead.

CAMPING

La Colina Lodge (tel. 506/2645-5009, www.lacolinalodge.com), in Cerro Plano, charges $5 pp for camping.

UNDER $25

Santa Elena: A popular offering among budget travelers is the (**Pensión Santa Elena** (tel. 506/2645-5051, www.pensionsantaelena.com, $5–7 pp dorm, $10 s or $14 d private room with shared bath, $17 s or $22 d private bath, $20–25 s or $30–35 d "suite"), owned by super-friendly Texan siblings, Randa and Shannon, who earn high marks from readers. It has 25 basic rooms of varying sizes (some dark). Some have private baths; all have hot water. A two-story annex with three rooms, bar, restaurant, and secure parking was being built at last visit. The hotel provides free use of kitchen, plus laundry service ($2), Internet access, and travel information.

Monteverde Backpackers (tel. 506/2645-5844, http://monteverdebackpackers.com, $10 pp dorm, $20 s or $30 d private rooms), in Santa Elena, is a splendid alternative. Rates include free breakfast, coffee, Internet, and lockers. And **Monteverde Information Center** (tel. 506/2645-6559, $6 pp dorm, $7 pp private room with shared bath, $10 pp with private bath) has basic but clean accommodation in the heart of Santa Elena.

Sleepers (tel. 506/2645-7133, www.sleepershostel.blogspot.com, $6 pp dorm, $15 s or $7 pp private room shared bath, $20 s or $12.50 pp private bath), at the southern entrance to Santa Elena, is a delightful new bargain-priced option, with colorful decor and a charming little café. It has nine well-lit rooms, including a co-ed dorm. All rates include breakfast, Internet access, and use of kitchen.

Cerro Plano/Monteverde: One of the nicest budget options, the **Manakin Lodge** (tel. 506/2645-5080, www.manakinlodge.com, $12 pp shared bath, $18 pp rooms with double bed and bunk plus private bath), is a cozy, albeit simple, bed-and-breakfast with 16 rooms with choice of bunk or double beds, and shared or private bathroom with hot water. Breakfast is served in the stone-and-timber lounge with fireplace. Land Rover tours are offered for groups, and it has a laundry.

The family-run **Hotel Bellbird** (tel. 506/2645-5026, www.hotelbellbird.com, $12 pp with breakfast) is a small wooden alpine lodge with nine minimally furnished rooms with hot water in clean, tiled, shared bathrooms. Some have bunks; others have a single and double bed. There's a simple restaurant.

Also to consider in this price bracket is **Hotel Santa Fe** (tel. 506/2645-5160, $10 pp upstairs, $20 s/d downstairs), in neoclassical Spanish style, enhanced by river-stone walls. It has four minimally furnished upstairs rooms with bunks or doubles.

A distinct advantage for early-birders keen to spot quetzals, the **Monteverde Cloud Forest Biological Reserve** (tel. 506/2645-5122, www.cct.or.cr, $20 pp with shared bath, $$30 pp private bath, including meals) visitors center has dormitory-style lodging and kitchens for up to 39 people. The dorms have shared baths with hot water. Scientists and students get priority.

$25-50

Santa Elena: The **Hotel El Sueño** (tel. 506/2645-5021, www.hotelelsuenocr.com, $15–25 s, $30–50 d), in the heart of town, has 15 basically furnished but cozy double rooms with private baths with hot water.

At the southern entrance to Santa Elena, **Rainbow Lodge** (tel. 506/2645-7015, www.monteverdecostarica.info, $25–40 s, $30–49 d), run by a pleasant Minnesotan, has two spacious, cross-lit, and cross-ventilated rooms in a lovely lodge with awesome views across the forested valley towards Monteverde. The lower of the two units has no valley views, but monkeys frolic in the treetops at fingertip distance. Readers rave about Rolf, the owner.

There are at least a dozen other options in this category on the hilly north side of Santa Elena, where I'm charmed by the cozy rusticity of the **Rustic Lodge** (tel. 506/2645-6256, www.monteverderusticlodge.com, $36 s, $50 d). The nicest newcomer in Santa Elena for 2008, it makes great use of natural woods, including cut tree trunks. Its 13 rooms are simple yet tastefully furnished.

Farther out, the hilltop **Sunset Hotel** (tel. 506/2645-7070, $30 s, $39 d), one kilometer northeast of Santa Elena (conveniently close to Selvatura), has 10 brightly lit, simply furnished wood-trimmed rooms with private baths. You have panoramic views from your veranda and the restaurant. Rates include tax and breakfast.

Cerro Plano/Monteverde: I love the dramatic frontage of the **La Colina Lodge** (tel. 506/2645-5009, www.lacolinalodge.com, $30 s/d shared bath, $38 private bath low season; $38 shared bath, $45 private bath high season), which has three wood-paneled rooms with private baths, plus nine rooms with shared bath with hot water. The rooms boast handcrafted furnishings and Guatemalan spreads. Some rooms are dark. There's a TV room and a charming alpine restaurant.

Lovingly run by a Italian/American couple, **Hotel El Viandante** (tel. 506/2645-6475, www.hotelelviandante.com, $30 s or $40 d low season, $45 s or $50 d high season) is a nice, no-frills, no-smoking newcomer with 12 brand new, simply appointed rooms with stone-lined walls, tile floors, orthopedic mattresses, and private bathrooms with hot water. Rooms have cable TV, free wireless Internet and most of the rooms have a view of Nicoya's gulf. Some

downstairs rooms lack windows; superiors, upstairs, are preferable. The owners specialize in mountain bike tours. There is a new spacious breakfast/dining room on the third floor with an amazing view of the gulf and the forest. The upstairs lounge has views and free Internet. Rates include breakfast and tax.

$50-100

Santa Elena: The **El Sol Retreat & Spa** (tel. 506/2645-5838, www.elsolnuestro.com, $60 s/d, or $80 s/d for larger cabin), five kilometers west of and below Santa Elena, is a calming holistic retreat run by a delightful and erudite German-Spanish couple, Elizabeth and Ignacio. Its two rustic Tom Sawyer–style log cabins boast awesome views over the plains of Guanacaste. Each features a tub-shower, king-size bed, kitchenette, and rough-hewn furniture and hammocks on decks. A third, larger cabin with parquet floors has a mezzanine bedroom and a lounge with deep-cushioned sofa bed. A Finnish sauna sits beside a fantastic landscaped swimming pool edged by a wooden sundeck. Guided horseback rides are offered ($10). Trails lead into the forest full of wildlife.

In Santa Elena proper, the splendid, German-owned **(Albergue Arco Iris** (tel. 506/2645-5067, www.arcoirislodge.com, $25 s or $35 d budget, $54–64 s or $59–128 d cabins, $171 honeymoon cabin low season; $30 s or $40 d budget, $54–64 s or $64–128 d cabins, $183 honeymoon cabin high season) is run with Teutonic efficiency. It has six "economic" bunkrooms, 11 standard rooms, and two handsome stone-and-hardwood *cabinas* amid a spacious garden with deck chairs on a hillside backed by a two-hectare forest reserve. They feature terra-cotta tile floors and orthopedic mattresses with Guatemalan spreads. Best of all is the fabulous honeymoon suite with kitchen, sexy tiger-print bedspread in the upstairs bedroom, and gorgeous black-stone walls and sea-blue tiles in the bathroom with his-and-hers whirlpool tub. A new airy restaurant offers breakfast only. Horses can be rented, and there's a library, laundry, and safe-deposit box.

Another romantic option, the **Treehouse Hotel** (tel. 506/2645-7475, www.treehouse.cr, $50 s, $65 d) offers a great bargain plus the advantage of its restaurant and Internet café. The seven spacious rooms have lively decor, modern bathrooms, and sliding glass doors onto balconies. Each room differs; one has a king-size bed.

The nonsmoking **Monteverde Cloud Forest Lodge** (tel. 506/2645-5058 or 877/623-3198, www.cloudforestlodge.com, $80 s, $90 d), northeast of Santa Elena, earns raves from readers. It is surrounded by gardens set on a 25-hectare private forest reserve. The 18 wood-and-stone *cabinas* are clean and spacious, with large clerestory windows, peaked ceilings, and large bathrooms. There's a large-screen TV and VCR. It has lawns, a duck pond, and five kilometers of trails into the nearby forests. There are views of Nicoya from the deck. A daunting circular staircase leads to the entrance to the Sky Walk, at Santa Elena Cloud Forest Reserve.

"High-rise" is creeping in, as at the contemporary-style, three-story **Hotel Poco a Poco** (tel. 506/2645-6000, www.hotelpoco apoco.com, $70 s or $80 d low season, $82 s or $92 d high season), about 500 meters outside the village center. It has 29 rooms with lively color schemes and modern fittings, including cable TV. It has a delightful restaurant and one of only two swimming pools in Monteverde, this one set in a flagstone sundeck with views.

One of the more exciting hotels, and an excellent bargain, is **Hotel Claro de Luna** (tel./fax 506/2645-5269, www.clarodelunahotel .com, $52 s or $61 d standard, $57 s or $68 d deluxe), on the southwest of the village. It resembles a Swiss cottage with cantilevered eaves and gingerbread trim. Its nine rooms draw heaps of light and have sponge-washed walls, polished hardwoods, and beautiful bathrooms with colonial tile. Breakfast is served in a gracious dining room, with a terrace overlooking the landscaped garden.

Cerro Plano/Monteverde: The **Hotel Finca Valverde** (tel. 506/2645-5157, www.monte verde.co.cr, $92 s/d standard, $11 s/d superior, including tax and breakfast), amid a setting of forest and pasture in Cerro Plano, about one kilometer east of Santa Elena and reached by a suspension bridge, has 18 standard eight rooms and four superiors. Ten have loft bedrooms and spacious bathrooms with tubs marvelous for soaking after a crisp hike. Its atmospheric alpine-style restaurant has plate-glass windows, and you can rent horses.

Nearby, I like the stone-and-timber **Nidia Lodge** (tel. 506/2645-5236, www.nidia lodge.com, $40 s or $55 d standard, $60 s or $75 d deluxe, $75 s or $95 d junior suite low season; $50 s or $65 d standard, $80 s or $85 d deluxe, $80 s or $100 d junior suite high season), with a two-story unit with four standards. Upstairs "deluxe" rooms and slightly more elegant junior suites have balconies, refrigerators, and tub-showers. It has a charmingly rustic restaurant, plus a small spa and an auditorium for slide shows.

The alpine-style **Cabañas Los Pinos** (tel. 506/2645-5252, www.lospinos.net, $65 s/d standard, $80 junior suite, $120 family cabin, including tax) has 12 *cabinas* in a lovely alpine setting with lots of cedars. Varying sizes sleep up to six people.

Hotel Villa Verde (tel. 506/2645-4697, www .villaverdehotel.com, $57 s or $75 d rooms, $94 s/d villas, including breakfast) has 16 cozy rooms with hardwood floors, while five rustic *cabinas* have roomy kitchenettes, a small lounge with fireplace, and large bedrooms with four beds (one double, three singles). Villa suites have fireplaces and tubs. Voluminous tiled bathrooms have hot water. The stone-and-timber lodge and atrium restaurant offer a homey atmosphere. It has a game room and offers horseback tours.

The family-run **Hotel Belmar** (tel. 506/2645-5201, www.hotelbelmar.net, $59 s or $69 d chalet, $79 s or $89 d standard low season; $69 s or $79 d chalet, $89 s or $99 d standard high season) is a beautiful, ivy-clad, Swiss-style hotel with chalets featuring 28 clean, comfortable rooms that are the prettiest in Monteverde. Four are family rooms. French doors in most rooms and lounges open

© CHRISTOPHER P. BAKER

Monteverde Lodge

onto balconies with views; a west-facing glass wall catches the sunset. Spacious, modestly elegant, wood-paneled rooms in a new addition offer large bathrooms with marble highlights. The large restaurant has views. The lounge in the older building is a quiet spot for reading and games and for slide shows on Fridays. A trail leads up to the mountain crest. Facilities include a whirlpool tub, volleyball court, pool table, and Internet. Rates include tax.

The more contemporary styled **Hotel de Montaña Monteverde** (tel. 506/2645-5046, www.monteverdemountainhotel.com, $71 s or $80 d standard, $138 s/d superior) is set on expansive grounds that include a lake and 15-hectare private reserve. Its wood-paneled rooms are modestly furnished and have cable TVs.

The **Trapp Family Lodge** (tel. 506/2645-5858, www.trappfam.com, $85 s/d rooms, $105 s/d suites) enjoys the advantage of being the hotel closest to the Monteverde Cloud Forest Biological Reserve, just one kilometer away. It has 20 spacious albeit modestly furnished rooms plus more gracious suites in a two-story all-wood structure enjoying a beautiful forested

locale. A large restaurant serves Italian meals, and there's a cozy TV lounge.

San Luís: The **Ecolodge San Luís** (tel. 506/2645-8049, www.uga.edu/costarica, $65 s or $120 d dorm, $85 s or $160 d cabin, including all meals and activities) has a cozy wood-paneled bunkhouse—a former milking shed—with 30 bunks and shared baths, and four rooms with 2–12 beds. It also has a four-room, 16-bed bungalow with private baths and verandas, plus 12 *cabinas* for three or four people each. Tico fare is cooked over a woodstove and served family-style.

$100-150

Cerro Plano/Monteverde: The modern, ecosensitive **⟨ Monteverde Lodge** (c/o Costa Rica Expeditions, tel. 506/2257-0766, www.costaricaexpeditions.com, $98 s/d garden room, $168 s/d standard year-round) is easily the best bargain in Monteverde. A cavernous entrance foyer leads up to a spacious open-plan dining room with a soaring beamed ceiling and a cozy bar with leather chairs around an open hearth. Chessboards and backgammon are at hand. The bar looks down on a large glass-enclosed whirlpool tub (open 24 hours). Wraparound windows offer wonderful views over the landscaped grounds and forested valley. Rooms are spacious and elegant, with large windows, two double beds, telephones, and well-lit solar-heated bathrooms. The lodge, set amid beautifully landscaped gardens, is operated by Costa Rica Expeditions and is popular with bird-watching and nature groups. Rates include taxes.

Another winner is ❰ **Sapo Dorado** (tel. 506/2645-5010, www.sapodorado.com, $88 s or $107 d low season, $103 s or $122 d high season). It has 30 handsome stone-and-timber cabins spread apart on the hillside, with great views. There are three types—older "classic suites" with fireplaces, and newer "fountain suites" and "sunset suites"—each with two queen-size beds, orthopedic mattresses, and balcony. Honeymooners should note that hotel rules prohibit the "moving of furniture or gymnastics after 9 P.M." The acclaimed restaurant is famous for its natural-food meals. Trails lead into forest.

Of similar standard and style, **Hotel Heliconia** (tel. 506/2645-5109, www.hotelheliconia.com, $104 s/d standard, $115 s/d junior suite, $140–149 s/d suites), in landscaped grounds at the foot of the private, 284-hectare Heliconia Cloud Forest Reserve, is an appealing Swiss-style chalet of lacquered cedar with lots of light. Home-style comforts include deep-cushioned sofas in the lobby, hand-painted curtains, and orthopedic mattresses in the 33 bedrooms in five types, from standards to master suites. Older units are simply furnished. Newer spa cabins in a two-story stone-and-hardwood structure offer a little more sophistication. It has an elegant restaurant, horse rides, and spa treatments.

Also consider the lovely, alpine-style **Hotel Fonda Vela** (tel. 506/2645-5125, www.fondavela.com, $99 s or $110 d standard, $110 s or $130 d junior suites), with 20 standard rooms and 18 junior suites in nine buildings, all with rich decor and hardwoods.

OVER $150

Cerro Plano/Monteverde: By far the most upscale (and the largest) place in Monteverde,

❰ **El Establo Hotel, Restaurant & Stable** (tel. 506/2645-5110 or 877/623-3198, www.hotelelestablo.com, $195 s/d deluxe, $158 s) offers 155 standard rooms and junior suites, all recently modernized with a stylish contemporary aesthetic. The original two-story wood-and-stone structure contains 20 standard rooms with cinderblock walls and wraparound windows; those on the ground floor open onto a wood-floored gallery lounge with deep-cushioned sofas and an open fireplace. A newer block on the hillside offers delightful junior suites with polished stone floors and exotic tiles, plus upper-story, carpeted suites with king-size beds in lofts (plus double beds downstairs), rattan furniture, and rockers on balconies. There's a TV lounge, new spa, a choice of two restaurants, a pool, and trails.

Food

For breakfast, try **Stella's Bakery** (tel. 506/2645-5560, 6 A.M.–6 P.M. daily), in Monteverde. It sells granola with homemade yogurt ($2), pancakes, omelettes, doughnuts, sandwiches, and killer milkshakes ($3).

Morpho Café (tel. 506/2645-5607, 11 A.M.–9:15 P.M. daily, $3–8), in Santa Elena, has tremendous decor, with rough-hewn furniture, natural stone and sponge-washed walls, and cool music. The menu includes salads, sandwiches, killer burgers, pastas, *casados* (set meals for $3), sweet-and-sour pork chops, and sea bass Dijon. Morpho's success was copied and improved on at the **Treehouse Café & Restaurant** (tel. 506/2645-5751, www.canopydining.com, 7 A.M.–10 P.M.), 50 meters away. Its menu ranges from burritos to fondues. My favorite? Chocolate fondue with cream and brandy ($28 for two people).

The simple **Moon Shiva Restaurante** (tel. 506/2645-6270, www.moonshiva.com, 11 A.M.–10 P.M. Mon.–Fri., until midnight Sat.–Sun.), in Cerro Plano, is known for its world music and lively atmosphere. Its simple "international fusion" menu includes moussaka ($10), chicken coconut curry ($9), and even filet mignon ($13.50).

For elegant dining, **Garden Restaurant**

(6–8:20 A.M., noon–2 P.M., and 6–8:30 P.M. daily), at Monteverde Lodge, offers excellent, inexpensive cuisine to all-comers. A typical dinner might include shredded duck *empanadas* ($6) and seared steak with sweet plantain ($15). It has a large wine list.

The finest dining in town is at **(Sofía** (tel. 506/2645-7017, knielsenmv@hotmail.com, 11:30 A.M.–9:30 P.M. daily). It serves gourmet nuevo Latino dishes. Chef-owner Karen Nielsen whips up mean appetizers, such as a roasted eggplant, tomato, and goat cheese quesadilla, and black bean soup. For a main course, try the seafood chimichanga $12) or plantain-crusted sea bass ($12). The bar serves killer mojitos, caipirinhas, and other cocktails ($5). It has wine tastings and occasionally hosts live music, from choral to jazz.

Karen also recently opened a gourmet tapas restaurant, **Chimera** (tel. 506/2645-7017, 11:30 A.M.–9:30 P.M. daily), with an open kitchen. Choice selections include cold roasted eggplant ($3.50), coconut shrimp lollipops with mango-ginger sauce ($7.50), and smoked provolone with sun-dried tomato sauce ($3.50).

Restaurante y Pizzería Tramonti (400 m uphill from the gas station in Monteverde, tel. 506/2645-6120, 11:30 A.M.–9:45 P.M. daily) offers good ambience along with carpaccio, lasagna, fried squid, and wood-fired pizzas. And **Johnny's Pizzería** (one km east of Santa Elena, tel. 506/2645-5066, 11:30 A.M.–9:30 P.M. daily), in Cerro Plano, is classy, with a wide-ranging pizza menu ($3.50–10, small–large), plus pastas and daily specials such as smoked salmon and capers. The **Restaurant de Lucía** (100 m south of the bullring in Cerro Plano, tel. 506/2645-5337, 11 A.M.–9 P.M. daily), is also genuinely Italian, with cappuccinos, lasagnas, and vegetarian dishes.

Vegetarians are served by **Flor de la Vida** (200 m east of Johnny's Pizzería, tel. 506/2645-6328, www.flordevida.net, 7 A.M.–10 P.M. Mon.–Sat.), a classy little place offering veggie burgers, veggie lasagna, veggie chili with salad, and the like.

The **(Restaurante Sapo Dorado** (in the Hotel Sapo Dorado, tel. 506/2645-5010, 6:30–9:30 A.M., noon–3 P.M. and 6–9:30 P.M., $5–20) is recommended for health-food dishes, including whole-grain pizza, banana bread, and tofu with vegetarian primavera; also try baked orange chicken with peppercorn, shrimp in sambuca mushroom sauce, and killer desserts.

Coffee Shops and Bakeries: The **Café Rainforest** (506/2645-7475, 7 A.M.–7 P.M. Mon.–Sat., 8 A.M.–7 P.M. Sun.), in Santa Elena, is a nice place to relax over cappuccino, a natural juice, or a shake. **Café Monteverde** (tel. 506/2645-5901, 7 A.M.–6 P.M. daily), opposite Stella's Bakery in Monteverde, serves cappuccinos and espressos, and you can taste and buy locally produced coffee ($4 per half pound). And **Dulce Marzo Bakery & Café** (tel. 506/2645-6568, 11 A.M.–7 P.M. daily), in Cerro Plano, is good for wraps, sandwiches, and cookies.

For a chocolaty treat, head to **Caburé Handmade Chocolatea** (tel. 506/2645-5020, 8 A.M.–8 P.M. Mon.–Sat.), at Paseo de Estella. Argentinian owner Susana Salas's eclectic menu offers chocolate-inspired dishes and drinks from around the world. Rum-flavored truffles? Mexican *mole?* She also serves salads and wraps and has Wi-Fi.

You can buy baked goods at **Musmanni,** next to La Esperanza, and **Panadería Jiménez** (4:30 A.M.–6 P.M. Mon.–Sat.).

Educational Courses

The **Centro Panamericano de Idiomas** (50 m west of the gas station in Monteverde, tel./fax 506/2645-5441, www.cpi-edu.com) offers Spanish-language courses at its impressive facility.

The **Monteverde Institute** (tel. 506/2645-5053, www.mvinstitute.org) hosts one-week arts workshops at the Monteverde Studios of the Arts (June–Aug.).

Information and Services

The best starting point for tourist information is the impartial **Chamber of Commerce**

BETWEEN MONTEVERDE AND LA FORTUNA

For many travelers in Monteverde, the next destination of choice is La Fortuna (or vice versa). There are several ways of getting between them. Most popular is a four-hour horseback ride from Monteverde to Río Chiquito, where you take a one-hour boat ride across Lake Arenal, then a 30-minute Jeep ride to La Fortuna. There are three different routes.

Several tour operators compete. Some have been accused of working their horses to death – literally – on the arduous San Gerardo trail, on which often poorly fed horses exhaust themselves thigh deep in mud on the steep hills during wet season. The Río Chiquito route can also be tough on horses in wet season. The Lake Trail is the easiest on the horses. Check to see that the horses are not used both ways on the same day.

Alternately, you can take a 90-minute Jeep ride to Río Chiquito, where you take a one-hour boat ride across Lake Arenal, then a 30-minute Jeep ride to La Fortuna.

(8 A.M.–8 P.M. daily) and, across the street, the **Monteverde Information Center** (tel. 506/2645-6559). **Desafío Tours** (tel. 506/2645-5874, www.monteverdetours.com), in Santa Elena, also books tours and offers tourist advice.

The **Monteverde Conservation League** (tel. 506/2645-5003, www.acmcr.org, 8 A.M.–5 P.M. Mon.–Fri., 8 A.M.–noon Sat.) is a great resource for information on ecological projects and the reserves.

The state-run **Centro Médico Monteverde** (tel. 506/2645-7080) is on the west side of Santa Elena. In Cerro Plano, the **Consultório Médico** (tel. 506/2645-7778, 24 hours) has an ambulance. And the **Red Cross** (tel. 128 or 506/645-6128) is on the north side of Santa Elena.

The **police** (Guardia Rural, tel. 911 or 506/2645-6248) faces Super La Esperanza, in Santa Elena.

The **Banco Nacional** (tel. 506/2645-5027), in Santa Elena, is open 8:30 A.M.–3:30 P.M., including weekdays. Super La Esperanza has an ATM.

The **post office** is on the east side of Santa Elena.

For Internet, head to **Treehouse Internet** (tel. 506/2645-5751, 6 A.M.–11 P.M. daily), or **Internet Pura Vida** (tel. 506/2645-5783, 9 A.M.–9 P.M. daily), which also has laundry. **Las Delicias Campesinas** (tel. 506/2645-7032), in Cerro Plano, has self-service laundry ($6 per load).

Getting There

Beware touts who intercept arriving buses and cars to direct you to properties or businesses at which they'll receive commissions.

Transportes Monteverde (tel. 506/2645-5159, in San José tel. 506/2222-3854) buses (four hours, $5) depart San José from Calle 12, Avenidas 7/9, at 6:30 A.M. and 2:30 P.M. daily; return buses depart Santa Elena at 6:30 A.M. and 2:30 P.M. The office in Santa Elena is open 5:45 A.M.–11:30 A.M. daily, as well as 1:30–5 P.M. Monday–Friday and until 3 P.M. Saturday–Sunday. Buy your return bus ticket as soon as you arrive in Santa Elena. Buses also depart Calles 2 and 4 in Puntarenas at 7:50 A.M., 1:50 P.M., and 2:15 P.M. daily (you can pick it up at the Río Lagarto turnoff for Monteverde on the Pan-American Highway) and depart Monteverde at 4:30 A.M., 6 A.M., and 3 P.M. A bus departs Tilarán for Monteverde at 12:30 P.M., returning from Monteverde at 7 A.M. daily.

Interbus (tel. 506/2282-5573, www.interbusonline.com) and **Grayline Costa Rica** (tel. 506/2220-2393, www.grayline costarica.com) operate shuttles between San José and Monteverde ($35) and key tourist destinations.

If driving, there are two turnoffs for Monteverde from Highway 1. The first is via Sardinal (the turnoff is at Rancho Grande, about 10 kilometers south of San Gerardo). The second is about seven kilometers north of San Gerardo (100 meters before the bridge over the Río Lagarto), 37 kilometers north of Esparza. The roads lead 35 kilometers uphill, a gut-jolting dirt road as famous as the place it leads to. The drive takes 1.5–2 hours.

Getting Around

There is no local bus service except to the Monterverde Cloud Forest Biological Reserve.

The gas station in Monterverde is open 5 A.M.–10 P.M. daily.

Tilarán and Vicinity

MONTEVERDE TO TILARÁN

A rough dirt road leads west from Santa Elena via Cabeceras and Quebrada Grande to Tilarán, gateway to Lake Arenal and La Fortuna. It's beautiful scenery all the way.

Cataratas de Viento Fresco (tel. 506/2661-8193, www.vientofresco.net, 7:30 A.M.–5 P.M. daily, entrance $15 adults, $12 students), 11 kilometers east of Tilarán and 25 kilometers west of Monteverde, has four 120-foot waterfalls, a waterslide, trails, and horseback riding ($55).

En route, you can stop at **Eco Coffee Tour** (tel. 506/2693-8220, www.coopeldos.com), a coffee-growers' cooperative, at El Dos de Tilarán; or the **Don Juan Coffee Tour** (tel. 506/2645-7100, www.donjuancoffee tour.com). And **Finca Agroturística Las Brisas** (tel. 506/2645-5937, fincalasbrisas@gmail.com, 8:30 A.M.–4:30 P.M. daily) has horseback riding tours.

Accommodations

Fabulous views of Arenal Volcano and Lake Arenal are enjoyed through picture windows in the 10 spacious all-wood rooms with private bathrooms and hot water at the **Vista Verde Lodge** (tel. 506/8380-1517, www.info -monteverde.com, $55 s or $68 d room, $57 s or $75 d junior suite low season; $75 s or $92 d room, $80 s or $99 d junior suite high season), four kilometers north of the Sky Walk, in the community of San Gerardo, on a steep and eroded dirt road that leads off the road to the Santa Elena Reserve. It has a restaurant, and hikes and horseback rides are offered.

One kilometer farther, and also offering fantastic views towards Arenal Volcano, is the rustic **Mirador Lodge San Gerardo** (tel.

506/2645-5354, www.miradorlodge.com, $69 s or $92 d low season, $80 s or $103 d high season, including breakfast and tax), a no-frills lodge with 15 simple yet cozy rooms with wood-burning stoves and basic but clean bathrooms with hot water. Two rooms are bunk-style with shared baths. It offers horseback rides.

TILARÁN

Tilarán, about 23 kilometers east of Cañas and the Pan-American Highway, is a spruce little highland town with a pretty square and a park with cedars and pines in front of the church. At this elevation (550 meters), the air is crisp and stirred by breezes working their way over the crest of the Cordillera de Tilarán from Lake Arenal, five kilometers to the northeast. The countryside hereabouts is reminiscent of the rolling hill country of England.

Local attractions include the **Vivero Popurrí** (tel. 506/2695-5047, 7:30 A.M.–6 P.M., $5), otherwise known as Teresa's Orchid Garden, run by an erudite and friendly Cuban woman. The garden, about two kilometers south of town, also has a small butterfly garden with about 22 species.

The last weekend in April, Tilarán hosts a rodeo and livestock show.

Accommodations and Food

Hotel y Restaurante Mary (tel. 506/2695-5479, $7 pp shared bath, $15 s, $25 d for TV and private bath), on the southeast side of the park, has 18 carpeted rooms with hot water.

A recommended bargain, **Hotel El Sueño** (tel. 506/2695-5347, $20 s or $30 d standard, $25 s or $35 d deluxe), one block north of the plaza, is one of the best hotels for its price in the country. Sixteen rooms, all with TVs, fans, and private baths with hot water, surround a sunlit second-floor courtyard with a fountain. Four newer, more deluxe rooms have refrigerators and somewhat more ostentatious furnishings. The friendly owners provide fruit and toiletry baskets. Downstairs the Restaurant El Parque has good seafood dishes. There is secure parking.

A similarly priced alternative is the ultraclean **Hotel Naralit** (tel. 506/2695-5393, fax 506/2695-6767), on the south side of the church.

Top choice in town, however, is **La Carreta Bed & Breakfast** (tel. 506/2695-6593, www.lacarretacr.com, $40 s, $50 d including full American breakfast), one block east of the church. This charming bed-and-breakfast has five simply yet pleasantly furnished rooms (several skylit), with hand-painted murals. Some have colonial tiles, lofty ceilings, and niches with pottery. Cable TVs, ceiling fans, and private bathrooms with hot water are standard. A suite features a ceramic beehive fireplace. Take one of the two rooms in the main house—they're the best. New U.S. owners, Ed and Rita, have revitalized this hotel after a few years in which it deteriorated. Although it no longer serves the pizza for which it was once famous, it now serves American fare, such as waffles, granola, sandwiches, and burgers, which can be enjoyed on the front patio with Wi-Fi.

For coffee and croissants, head to **Casa Antigua** (tel. 506/2695-6053, 7 A.M.–9:30 P.M. Mon.–Sat., 3–9:30 P.M. Sun.), two blocks

north of the plaza. This lovely old wooden house also serves Costa Rica dishes and milk shakes, and it has free Wi-Fi.

Information and Services

There are banks around the town square, which has public telephones. The **Red Cross** (tel. 506/2695-5256) is one block east of the church, and **Clínica Tilarín** (tel. 506/2695-5115) is open 24 hours. The **police station** (tel. 506/2695-5001) adjoins the bus station, 100 meters northwest of the plaza.

Getting There and Around

Auto Transportes Tilará buses (tel. 506/2222-3854) depart San José from Calle 12, Avenidas 7/9, at 7:30 A.M., 9:30 A.M., 12:45 P.M., 3:45 P.M., and 6:30 P.M. daily (four hours via Cañas, $3). The bus continues to Nuevo Arenal. Local buses depart Cañas for Tilarán at 5 A.M., 6 A.M., 9 A.M., 11 A.M., noon, and 1:45 P.M.; from Ciudad Quesada at 6 A.M. and 3 P.M. daily; from La Fortuna at 8 A.M. and 4:30 P.M.; and from Santa Elena (Monteverde) at 12:30 P.M.

Buses depart Tilarán for San José at 5 A.M., 7 A.M., 9:30 A.M., 2 P.M., and 5 P.M.; for Cañas at 5 A.M., 7 A.M., 8 A.M., 9 A.M., 10 A.M., 11:30 A.M., and 3:30 P.M.; for Ciudad Quesada at 7 A.M. and 12:30 P.M.; for La Fortuna at 7 A.M. and 12:30 P.M.; for Monteverde at 12:30 P.M.; for Nuevo Arenal at 10 A.M., 4 P.M., and 10 P.M.; and for Puntarenas at 6 A.M. and 1 P.M.

There's a gas station two blocks northeast of the plaza.

For taxis call Unidos Tilarán (tel. 506/2695-5324), or hail one on the west side of the plaza.

Cañas and Vicinity

The first impression as you continue northwest along Highway 1 from Cañas is of a vast barren plain, burning hot in dry season, with palms rising like tattered umbrellas over the scrubby landscape, flanked to the east by the steep-sided volcanoes of the Cordillera de Guanacaste, from which rivers feed the marshy wetlands of the Tempisque Basin. Away from the main highway, the villages of whitewashed houses are as welcoming as any in the country. For the traveler interested in history or architecture, there are some intriguing sights, and the area is charged with scenic beauty.

CAÑAS

Cañas is a modest-sized town and a pivotal point for exploring Palo Verde National Park (west) or Lake Arenal (east), and for rafting trips on the Río Corobicí. Named for the white-flowered wild cane that still grows in patches hereabouts, Cañas is indisputably a cowboy town, as the many tanned *sabaneros* riding horses and shaded by wide-brimmed hats attest. Note the church with its facade entirely inlaid with mosaic.

A paved road runs west from Cañas 14 kilometers to the village of **Bebedero,** a gateway to Palo Verde National Park; there's no bridge, but boats will take you across the wide Río Tenorio.

Seven kilometers north of Cañas (and one kilometer north of the Río Corobicí), a well-paved road (Hwy. 6) leads northeast 58 kilometers to Upala in the northern lowlands via the low-lying saddle of Tenorio and Miravalles Volcanoes.

(Centro de Rescate Las Pumas

Las Pumas Rescue Center (tel. 506/2669-6044, http://laspumas.org, 8 A.M.–5 P.M. daily, $10 adults, $5 children), five kilometers north of Cañas, was founded by the late Lilly Bodmer de Hagnauer, a Swiss-born environmentalist whose passion was saving and raising big cats: ocelots, jaguars, cougars, margays, jaguarundis, and "tiger" cats. All six species are housed in large chain-link cages, but beware: there are no guardrails (nor guards) and the temptation to reach out to stroke a cat through the mesh is tempting but stupid. These are not house cats! Most of the animals were either injured or orphaned and have been reared by Lily or her family, who still run the zoo.

Other species include deer, fox, monkeys, peccaries, macaws, toucans, and dozens of parrots and other birds. It also raises rabbits for sale. By selling only nonnative species, it hopes to help change the pet-keeping habits of Ticos. A new open-air exhibition area for big cats was in the works for 2009.

(Río Corobicí

Six kilometers north of Cañas, the Pan-American Highway crosses the Río Corobicí. The 40-kilometer-long river is fed by controlled runoff from Lake Arenal, providing water year-round, good for rafting. The trip is a relatively calm Class II run described as a "nature float." The river is lined with a riparian forest. Motmots, herons, crested caracaras, egrets, and toucans are common, as are howler monkeys, caimans, and iguanas basking on the riverbanks.

Safaris Corobicí (tel. 506/2669-6091, www.nicoya.com) has an office beside Highway 1, about 400 meters south of the river. It has guided floats on the river ($37–60), as does **Ríos Tropicales,** at Restaurante Rincón Corobicí (tel. 506/2669-6262, rincon@racsa.co.cr).

Accommodations

You can camp at **Hotel Capazauri** (tel. 506/2669-6280, capazuri@racsa.co.cr, $10 pp camping, $24 pp rooms), two kilometers north of town, on the east side of Highway 1. It has showers and toilets. The live-in owners have 19 rooms in two modern blocks. Rooms vary in size, but all are clean and meagerly furnished, with fans and private baths, all with hot water. It has a swimming pool and hosts a Friday and Saturday night dance popular with locals.

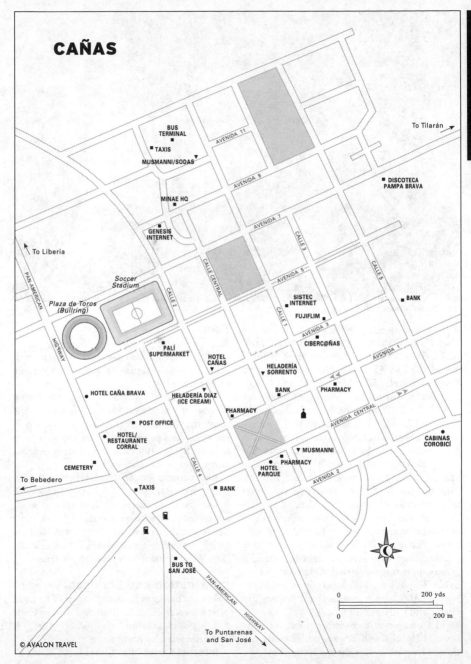

CAÑAS

To Tilarán

BUS TERMINAL

TAXIS

MUSMANNI/SODAS

AVENIDA 11

AVENIDA 9

DISCOTECA PAMPA BRAVA

MINAE HQ

AVENIDA 7

GENESIS INTERNET

To Liberia

CALLE 3

CALLE CENTRAL

AVENIDA 5

Soccer Stadium

Plaza de Toros (Bullring)

CALLE 2

SISTEC INTERNET

FUJIFLIM

CALLE 5

BANK

CALLE 1

PAN-AMERICAN

HIGHWAY

AVENIDA 3

CIBERC@ÑAS

AVENIDA 1

PALÍ SUPERMARKET

HOTEL CAÑAS

HELADERÍA SORRENTO

HOTEL CAÑA BRAVA

HELADERÍA DIAZ (ICE CREAM)

BANK

PHARMACY

PHARMACY

POST OFFICE

AVENIDA CENTRAL

HOTEL/ RESTAURANTE CORRAL

CABINAS COROBICÍ

CEMETERY

To Bebedero

MUSMANNI

PHARMACY

HOTEL PARQUE

CALLE 4

TAXIS

BANK

AVENIDA 2

BUS TO SAN JOSÉ

PAN-AMERICAN HIGHWAY

To Puntarenas and San José

0   200 yds

0   200 m

© AVALON TRAVEL

modernist church in Cañas

In town, merely adequate options are the **Hotel y Restaurante Corral** (tel. 506/2669-0622, $18 s, $35 d), at the junction of Avenida 3 and the Pan-American Highway; **Cabinas Corobicí** (tel. 506/2669-6921, $12 pp); and **Hotel Cañas** (tel. 506/2669-0039, fax 506/2669-1319, $15 s or $20 d without TV, $18 s or $22 with TV, $20 s or $30 d with a/c and TV), which has a good restaurant.

In 2007, the venerable **Hacienda La Pacífica** (tel. 506/2669-6050, www.pacifica cr.com, $65 s/d including breakfast), four kilometers north of town, reopened as a hotel after years as a private club. Part of a cattle and rice estate that also has an ecotourism and reforestation component, it has a delightfully rustic restaurant. The spacious rooms have high ceilings with aged wrought-iron candelabras, plus huge colonial-style oak closets, cable TV, Wi-Fi, and lovely modern bathrooms. Alas, the mattresses and pillows are cheap and truly awful!

The best place in town promises to be the upscale **Hotel Caña Brava,** under construction at last visit beside the main highway.

Food

The nicest place to eat is the modern air-conditioned restaurant in the **Hotel Cañas,** with dishes $3–10. It features cowboy paraphernalia on the walls.

The restaurant at **Hacienda La Pacífica** (7 A.M.–9 P.M. daily, $5–15) has an eclectic menu that includes cream of tomato soup, pastas, tenderloin pepper steak, and jumbo shrimp skewer. Most dishes are served with organic rice grown on the hacienda.

Restaurante Rincón Corobicí (tel. 506/2669-6262, rincon@racsa.co.cr, 8 A.M.–6 P.M. daily), beside the Pan-American Highway, is a pleasant place to eat, with good seafood dishes and a porch over the river where you can watch rafters go by. It prepares an excellent sea bass in garlic ($8). Wash it down with superb lemonade.

Information and Services

There are banks in the town center. The **post office** is on Avenida 3, 30 meters west of Calle 4. The **police station** (tel. 506/2669-0057) is two kilometers south of town.

Internet Ciberc@ñas (Avenida 3, Calles 1/3,

© CHRISTOPHER P. BAKER

traditional bar

tel. 506/2669-5232) is open 8:15 A.M.–9 P.M. Monday–Saturday, 2–9 P.M. Sunday. Or try **Genesis Internet** (tel. 506/2669-0810), catercorner to the **MINAE headquarters** (tel. 506/2669-0533) for the national park service.

Getting There

Auto Transportes Tilarán buses (tel. 506/2222-3854) depart San José for Cañas from Calle 16, Avenidas 1/3, at 5:30 A.M., 8:30 A.M., 11:50 A.M., 12:20 P.M., 1:45 P.M., 3:30 P.M., and 5 P.M. daily (three hours, $3). An express bus (tel. 506/2666-0138) departs Puntarenas for Liberia via Cañas at 5:30 P.M. (Empresa Arata).

Buses depart Cañas for San José from Calle 1, Avenidas 9/11, at 4 A.M., 4:50 A.M., 5:40 A.M., 6:30 A.M., 8:30 A.M., 11:20 A.M., and 1:30 P.M. Buses depart Cañas for destinations throughout Guanacaste from Calle 1, Avenidas 9/11.

Taxis Unidos de Cañas (tel. 506/2669-0898) has taxis on call.

BAGACES

The small, nondescript town of Bagaces is on Highway 1, about 22 kilometers north of Cañas. Several adobe-brick houses date back several centuries. Otherwise, even the most diligent search will not turn up anything more interesting than a bust of ex-president General Tomás Guardia on a pedestal in the park honoring the city's most illustrious child.

Bagaces is a gateway to Palo Verde National Park (west) and Miravalles Volcano (east). A regional office of **Area de Conservación Arenal-Tempisque** (ACT, tel. 506/2671-1290, www.acarenaltempisque.org, 8 A.M.–4 P.M. Mon.–Fri.), is opposite the junction for Palo Verde, next to the gas station on Highway 1.

Bagaces may soon get a Jack Nicklaus–designed golf course—the **Sabana Falls** project (http://sabanafallsgolf.com), expected to open in late 2010. It will also feature a luxury hotel, spa, and equestrian center.

Accommodations

There are a couple of budget options in town. For a little more sophistication, head north on the Pan-American Highway a short distance to **Hotel Laguna** (tel. 506/2671-8250, http:// losalcaravanes.com, $50 s, $60 d), a colorful,

GUANACASTE

© CHRISTOPHER P. BAKER

Miravalles Volcano

Italian-run hotel with 20 modestly furnished rooms, some with king-size beds. It has a lake with water sports, a large swimming pool, and an open-air bar and restaurant.

Information and Services
There's a **bank** facing the main square. The **police station** (Guardia Rural, tel. 506/2671-1173) is 50 meters east of Highway 1, on the road signed for Miravalles. The bus station is one block north of the main square.

Getting There
Buses (tel. 506/2221-3318) depart San José from Calle 12, Avenidas 3/5 at 5:30 A.M. and 2 P.M.

MIRAVALLES VOLCANO
Fabulously scenic Highway 164 leads northeast from Bagaces and climbs steadily up the western shoulder of Miravalles Volcano (2,028 meters), enshrined within the **Miravalles Protected Zone** (Zona Protectora Miravalles). The almost perfectly conical volcano is the highest in the Cordillera de Guanacaste. The western slopes are covered with savanna scrub; the northern

and eastern slopes are lush, fed by moist clouds that sweep in from the Caribbean. The southern slopes are cut with deep canyons and licked by ancient lava tongues, with fumaroles spouting and hissing like mini Old Faithfuls. The forests, replete with wildlife, are easily accessed from the road. However, there are no developed trails or facilities for tourists, and no ranger station.

Highway 164 runs via the village of **Guayabo,** 21 kilometers north of Bagaces (it has a bank and Internet café). It is paved as far as **Aguas Claras** and, beyond, the hamlet of San José in the northern lowlands. If souvenir shopping, call in at **Galería Tony Jiménez** (tel. 506/8821-83582, www.tonyjimenez.com), midway between Guayabo and Aguas Claras.

A loop road from Highway 164 leads east via the community of Fortuna and **Las Hornillas** (Little Ovens), an area of intense bubbling mud pots and fumaroles expelling foul gases and steam. Here the Costa Rican Institute of Electricity (ICE) harnesses geothermal energy for electric power, with two plants that tap the superheated vapor deep within the volcano's bowels. You can visit the main **Planta**

© CHRISTOPHER P. BAKER

hot mud baths at Las Hornillas in Miravalles

Miravalles geothermal plant (tel. 506/673-1111, ext. 232), about two kilometers north of Fortuna, by appointment.

The touristy **Centro Turístico Yökö** (tel. 506/2673-0410, www.yokotermales.com, $5 admission), is a recreation park amid lawns one kilometer west of Las Hornillas, with five clean thermal pools (ranging 30–50°C) set amid 13 hectares; one even has a waterslide and a man-made cave that serves as a sauna. Massage is offered, as are horseback rides ($15, four hours). Nearby, **Centro Turístico Termomanía** (tel. 506/2673-0233, $5) competes; the highlight is the *hornillas*—bubbling mud pools and fumaroles—immediately adjacent to the property. It's totally unguarded and very dangerous—*keep your distance!*

At Aguas Claras, you can turn west (4WD required) to visit **Finca La Anita** (tel. 506/8388-1775, www.fincalaanita.org) organic farm.

【 Las Hornillas Volcanic Activity Center

The prime spot to enjoy the volcanic activity is this mesmerizing facility (tel. 506/8839-9769, www.lashornillas.com, $20 entrance), a "walkable live crater" two kilometers southeast of the ICE geothermal plant. Here, boardwalks lead through the crater itself, with mud pools and fumaroles hissing and bubbling all around. You can walk around at will and even take a therapeutic bath in a warm mud bath, while a two-hour guided tour ($35) includes a horseback ride to waterfalls. Thermal swimming pools were being added at last visit. It has showers and toilets.

Sports and Recreation

There's a **Canopy Tour** (tel. 506/2673-0697, www.volcanoadventuretour.com, 8 A.M.–3 P.M. daily, $30) seven kilometers north of Guayabo. It has 11 ziplines and 14 platforms. The same owners operate **ATV Tours Miravalles** (tel. 506/2673-0585, $40 s, $60 d for two hours), one kilometer farther north.

Accommodations and Food

You can camp on the lovely grounds of the **Canopy Tour** (tel. 506/2673-0697, www.volcano adventuretour.com, $5 pp), seven kilometers

© CHRISTOPHER P. BAKER

waterslide at Centro Turístico Yökö in Miravalles

north of Guayabo, which also has four basic and overpriced cabins ($35) and a rustic restaurant. **Centro Turístico Yökö** (tel. 506/2673-0410, www.yokotermales.com, $30 s, $50 d) has 12 spacious cabins with verandas with volcano views, plus ceiling fans and large private bath and walk-in showers with thermal water. It has a restaurant with TV. Rates include breakfast and use of facilities.

A deluxe project, the **Ailanto Wellness Resort & Spa** (www.ailantoresort.com) was launched in 2008, to include a private gated community with private villas and condominiums, plus a 120-suite hotel and 30-hectare "adventure camp."

Information and Services

A good resource is the **Cámara de Turismo Tenorio-Miravalles** (tel. 506/2466-8221, tenorio-miravalles@hotmail.com, 9 A.M.–3 P.M. daily), the local Chamber of Tourism, on the south side of Bijagua.

Getting There

Buses (tel. 506/2221-3318) for Guayabo depart San José from Calle 12, Avenidas 3/5 at 5:30 A.M. and 2 P.M. and go via Bagaces.

⬛ PALO VERDE NATIONAL PARK

Parque Nacional Palo Verde ($10 admission), 28 kilometers south of Bagaces, protects 13,058 hectares of floodplain, marshes, and seasonal pools in the heart of the driest region of Costa Rica—the Tempisque basin, at the mouth of the Río Tempisque in the Gulf of Nicoya. The park, which derives its name from the *palo verde* (green tree) shrub that retains a bright green coloration year-round, is contiguous to the north with the remote 7,354-hectare Dr. Rafael Lucas Rodríguez Caballero Wildlife Refuge and, beyond that, the Lomas Barbudal Biological Reserve. The three have a similar variety of habitats, not least patches of dry forest that once extended along the entire Pacific coast of Mesoamerica. (The banks of the Tempisque, which are tidal, are also lined with archaeological sites.)

For half the year, from November to March, no rain relieves the heat of the Tempisque basin,

© CHRISTOPHER P. BAKER

crocodile at Palo Verde National Park

leaving plants and trees parched and withered. Rolling, rocky terrain spared Lomas Barbudal, in particular, from the changes wrought on the rest of Guanacaste Province by plows and cows. Here, the dry forest remains largely intact and several endangered tree species thrive: Panamá redwood, rosewood, sandbox, and the cannonball tree *(balas de cañón)*. A relative of the Brazil nut tree, the cannonball tree produces a pungent, nonedible fruit that grows to the size of a bowling ball and dangles from a long stem. Several evergreen tree species also line the banks of the waterways, creating riparian corridors inhabited by species not usually found in dry forests.

In all, there are 15 different habitats and a corresponding diversity of fauna. Plump crocodiles wallow on the muddy riverbanks, salivating, no doubt, at the sight of coatis, white-tailed deer, and other mammals that come down to the water to drink.

Corridors of swamp forest also link Palo Verde and Dr. Rafael Lucas Rodríguez Caballero with Lomas Barbudal. The mangroves are now protected within the **Cipancí**

National Wildlife Refuge along 3,500 square kilometers of riverside bordering the Tempisque and Bebedero Rivers.

Palo Verde National Park is best known as a bird-watchers' paradise. More than 300 bird species have been recorded, not least great curassows and the only permanent colony of scarlet macaws in the dry tropics. At least a quarter of a million wading birds and waterfowl flock here in fall and winter, when much of the arid alluvial plain swells into a lake. Isla de Pájaros, in the middle of the Río Tempisque, is replete with white ibis, roseate spoonbills, anhingas, wood storks, jabiru storks, and the nation's largest colony of black-crowned night herons.

Three well-maintained trails lead to lookout points over the lagoons; to limestone caves; and to water holes such as Laguna Bocana, gathering places for a diversity of birds and animals. Limestone cliffs rise behind the old Hacienda Palo Verde, now the **park headquarters** (tel./fax 506/2200-0125), eight kilometers south of the park entrance.

Lomas Barbudal Biological Reserve

© CHRISTOPHER P. BAKER

jabiru stork

(Reserva Biológica Lomas Barbudal, Bearded Hills, no tel., entrance by donation) is a 2,279-hectare biological reserve fed by protected river systems, some of which flow year-round. The Lomas Barbudal park office (Casa de Patrimonio) is on the banks of the Río Cabuyo. Trails span the park from here. It's open on a 10-days-on/four-days-off schedule.

Dry season is by far the best time to visit, although the Tempisque basin can get dizzyingly hot. Access is easier, and deciduous trees lose their leaves, making bird-watching easier. Wildlife gathers by the water holes. And there are far fewer mosquitoes and bugs. When the rains come, mosquitoes burst into action.

Hikes and Recreation

The **Organization of Tropical Studies** (tel. 506/2661-4717, www.ots.ac.cr) offers natural history visits by advance reservation (guided walks cost $25–70 depending on the number of people); it also has mountain bikes. The park rangers will take you out on their boat. Or you can hire boats in Puerto Humo or Bebedero. OTS also offers horseback tours ($6 per hour).

Accommodations

The Palo Verde National Park administration building has a run-down campsite ($2) beside the old Hacienda Palo Verde. Water, showers, and barbecue pits are available. There is also a campsite seven kilometers east near Laguna Coralillo (no facilities). However, no camping was being permitted at last visit in November 2008. You may be able to stay with rangers ($12) in basic accommodations with advance notice; for information call the **Tempisque Conservation Area** office (tel. 506/2695-5908, 8 A.M.–4 P.M. daily), in Tilarán. Spanish-speakers might try the ranger station radio telephone (tel. 506/2233-4160).

Visitors can also stay in a dormitory at the Organization of Tropical Studies' **Palo Verde Biological Research Station** (tel. 506/2661-4717, www.ots.ac.cr; for reservations, tel. 506/524-0628, reservas@ots.ac.cr, $65 pp adults, $34 children, including meals and guided walk) on a space-available basis. Eight rooms have shared bathrooms; five rooms have private bathrooms.

Lomas Barbudal has basic accommodations ($6 pp) and meals at the ranger station.

Getting There

The main entrance to Palo Verde National Park is 28 kilometers south of Bagaces, along a dirt road that begins opposite the gas station and Tempisque Conservation Area office on Highway 1. The route is signed; a four-wheel-drive vehicle is required, and high ground clearance is essential in wet season. No buses travel this route. A Jeep-taxi from Bagaces costs about $30 one-way.

Coming from the Nicoya Peninsula, a bus operates from the town of Nicoya to Puerto Humo, where you can hire a boat to take you three kilometers upriver to the Chamorro dock, the trailhead to park headquarters (it's a two-kilometer walk); it's muddy and swampy in wet season. Alternately, you can drive from Filadelfia or Santa Cruz (on the Nicoya Peninsula) to Hacienda El Viejo; the park is four kilometers east from El Viejo, and the Río Tempisque two kilometers farther. A local boatman will ferry you downriver to the Chamorro dock.

The unpaved access road for Lomas Barbudal Biological Reserve is off Highway 1, at the Kilometer 221 marker near Pijijes, about 10 kilometers north of Bagaces. A dirt road—4WD recommended—leads six kilometers to a lookout point then descends steeply from here to the park entrance. If conditions are particularly muddy you may park at the lookout point and hike to the ranger station rather than face not being able to return via the dauntingly steep ascent from the ranger station in your car. A Jeep-taxi from Bagaces will cost about $40 round-trip.

Palo Verde and Lomas Barbudal are also linked by a rough dirt road that is tough going in wet season.

Tour companies in San José and throughout Guanacaste offer river tours in Palo Verde, as do **Palo Verde Boat Tours** (tel. 506/2651-8001, www.paloverdeboattours.com), departing Filadelfia, in the Nicoya Peninsula. **CATA Tours** (tel. 506/2674-0180, $85 three hours, $150 full day including Isla Pajaros) and **Aventuras Arenal** (tel. 506/2479-9133) offer boat trips from Bebedero.

Liberia and Vicinity

LIBERIA

Liberia, 26 kilometers north of Bagaces, is the provincial capital. It is also one of the country's most intriguing historic cities, with charming aged structures made of blinding white ignimbrite, for which it is called the "White City." There's a rich simplicity, a purity to the surrounding landscape, to the craggy, penurious hills and the cubist houses sheathed in white light like a sort of celestial glow. Many old adobe homes still stand to the south of the landscaped central plaza, with high-ceilinged interiors and kitchens opening onto classical courtyards. Old corner houses have doors—*puertas del sol*—that open on two sides to catch both morning and afternoon sun. Many of the historic houses along **Calle Real** (Calle Central, between Avenidas Central/8) have been restored.

The leafy plaza hosts a modern white church—**Iglesia Imaculada Concepción de María**—and older town hall flying the Guanacastecan flag.

The town has a long history as a center for the local cattle industry. A **statue** honors the *sabaneros* (cowboys) in the central median along Avenida Central at Calle 10.

At the far end of Avenida Central, also known as Avenida 25 Julio, is **La Ermita La Agonía** (tel. 506/2666-0107, open 2:30–3:30 P.M. daily; at other times open by request) dating

from 1854 with a stuccoed adobe exterior, simple adornments, and a small **Religious Art Museum.** Behind the church is **Parque Rodolfo Salazar,** surrounded by old cottages. Finally, on the northwest corner of the main plaza is the old city jail, still in use, with barred windows and towers at each corner.

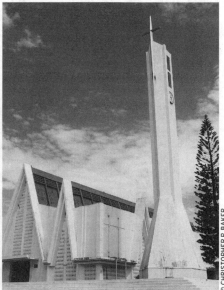

© CHRISTOPHER P. BAKER

Iglesia Imaculada Concepción de María

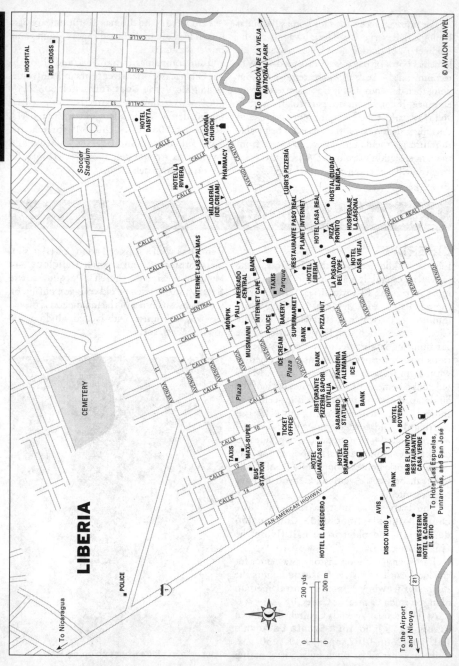

GUANACASTE

LIBERIA

To Nicaragua

POLICE

CEMETERY

Soccer Stadium

HOSPITAL
RED CROSS

HOTEL DAISYTA

HOTEL LA RIVIERA

LA AGONÍA CHURCH

HELADERIA (ICE CREAM)

PHARMACY

INTERNET LAS PALMAS

MONPIK

PALI

MUSMANNI

MERCADO CENTRAL

BANK

INTERNET CAFE

POLICE

TAXIS
Parque

BAKERY

SUPERMARKET

ICE CREAM
Plaza

Plaza

PIZZA HUT

BANK

BANK

RISTORANTE PIZZERIA SAPORI DI ITALIA

PANDERIA ALEMANIA

ICE

BANK

SABANERO STATUE

TAXIS

MAXI-SUPER

HOTEL GUANACASTE

HOTEL BRAMADERO

BUS STATION

TICKET OFFICE

HOTEL BOYEROS

BANK

B&B EL PUNTO/ RESTAURANTE CASA VERDE

PAN-AMERICAN HIGHWAY

DISCO KURÚ

AVIS

HOTEL EL ASSEDERO

BEST WESTERN HOTEL & CASINO EL SITIO

To Hotel Las Espuelas, Puntarenas, and San José

To the Airport and Nicoya

LUIGI'S PIZZERIA

RESTAURANTE PASO REAL

PLANET INTERNET

HOTEL CASA REAL

HOTEL LIBERIA

LA POSADA DEL TOPE

HOSTAL CIUDAD BLANCA

PIZZA PRONTO

HOSPEDAJE LA CASONA

HOTEL CASA VIEJA

CALLE REAL

To RINCÓN DE LA VIEJA NATIONAL PARK

© AVALON TRAVEL

200 yds
0
200 m
0

CALLE 17
CALLE 15
CALLE 13
CALLE 11
CALLE 9
CALLE 7
CALLE 5
CALLE 3
CALLE 1
AVENIDA CENTRAL
AVENIDA
CALLE CENTRAL
CALLE 2
CALLE 4
CALLE 6
CALLE 8
CALLE 10
CALLE 12
CALLE 14

La Chácara Hacienda & Fiesta Brava (tel. 506/8350-1527, www.haciendalachacara.com), 2.5 kilometers west of town, is a working cattle ranch with cowboy museum, horseback riding, plus trail rides. You can even help work the cattle. It has a traditional rodeo show at 5 P.M. Thursday.

Africa Mía

Guanacaste's savanna landscape is a perfect setting for My Africa (tel. 506/2666-1111, www.africamia.net, 8 A.M.–6 P.M. daily, $18 adults, $12 children), a private wildlife reserve at El Salto, nine kilometers south of Liberia. Elands, camels, ostriches, and zebras kick up dust alongside antelopes, giraffes, and warthogs; rhinos were to be introduced. You tour in an open-air safari Jeep; a special wildlife tour inside the fenced area costs $65 adults, $55 children. The facility includes a gorgeous waterfall, where a hotel was to be added.

Entertainment and Events

The best time to visit is July 25, **Día de Guanacaste,** when the town celebrates Guanacaste's 1812 secession from Nicaragua, with rodeos, bullfights, parades, marimba music, and firecrackers. A similar passion is stirred each first week of September for the Semana Cultural.

The Best Western Hotel & Casino El Sitio has a small **casino** (tel. 506/2666-1211, 4 P.M.–5 A.M. Mon.–Sat.). The **Disco Kurú** (tel. 506/2666-0769, $5 admission), across the street, pulses Thursday–Saturday and has karaoke Monday–Wednesday.

Multicines (tel. 506/2665-1515), in Plaza Liberia Shopping Center, one kilometer south of town, shows first-run Hollywood movies.

Accommodations

Liberia is crying out for a quality hotel, although there are plenty of budget and medium-priced options.

Several undistinguished options for barebones budget travelers line Calle Real. Expect basic rooms and minimal facilities. Consider **Hotel Liberia** (Calle Central, Avenida 2, tel./fax 506/2666-0161, hotelliberia@hotmail.com, $7 pp with shared bathroom, $10 pp with private bathroom); **La Posada del Tope** (Calle Central, Avenidas 2/4, tel./fax 506/2666-3876, $5 pp), where six basic rooms with fans share one bathroom; **Hotel Casa Real** (tel. 506/2666-3876, $15 s, $24 d with shared bath), across the street from La Posada del Tope and

---

COSTA RICAN RODEO

Fiestas populares (folk festivals), held throughout Guanacaste, keep alive a deep-rooted tradition of Costa Rican culture: *recorridos de toros* (bull riding), bronco riding, home-style Tico bullfighting, and *topes,* or demonstrations of the Costa Rican saddle horse. The bulls are enraged before being released into the ring, where *vaqueros* are on hand to distract the wild and dangerous animals if a rider is thrown or injured. (Their title comes from *vaqueta,* a piece of leather originally used by cowboys on haciendas to make stubborn bulls move in the direction desired, much as the red cape is used by Spanish matadors.)

Cowboys ride bareback and hang onto angry, jumping, twisting bulls with only one hand (or "freestyle" – with *no* hands), while the *vaqueta* has given way to red cloth (called a *capote* or *muleta*) or even the occasional clown. The *recorridos* also feature "best bull" competitions and incredible displays of skill – such as *sabaneros* (cowboys) who lasso bulls with their backs turned to the animals.

The events are a grand excuse for inebriation. As more and more beer is consumed, it fuels bravado, and scores of Ticos pour into the ring. A general melée ensues as Ticos try to prove their manhood by running past the bull, which is kept enraged with an occasional prod from an electric fork or a sharp instrument. The bull is never killed, but it's a pathetic sight nonetheless.

owned by the same owners; and **Hospedaje La Casona** (Calle Central, Avenidas 4/6, tel./fax 506/666-2971, casona@racsa.co.cr, $10 pp fan, $16 d, $24 d a/c).

The **Hotel Guanacaste** (tel. 506/2666-0085, www.higuanacaste.com, $11 s, $26 d, or 15 percent discount with IYH card) is affiliated with IYH. This popular option (many truckers use it) has 27 simple rooms with fans, some with private baths with cold water. Most are dorms with bunk beds. There's table tennis, a restaurant, TV lounge, Skype for free international calls, and secure parking. Camping ($5 pp) is available.

Of higher standard is **Hotel Daisyta** (Avenida 3, Calle 13, tel. 506/2666-0197, www.hoteldaisytaliberia.com, $48 s, $58 d rooms), with 23 air-conditioned rooms and seven villas, two small swimming pools, a bar and restaurant, plus secure parking and a laundry. Also of better quality is the venerable and popular **Hotel Bramadero** (Hwy. 1 at Avenida 1, tel. 506/2666-0371, www.hotelelbramadero.com, $32 s or $44 d low season, $40 s or $58 d high season), a motel-style hotel with 23 air-conditioned rooms with uninspired furniture and cable TV, plus a pool and atmospheric roadside restaurant.

Others in this price bracket to consider are *posada*-style **Hostal Ciudad Blanca** (Avenida 4, Calles 1/3, tel. 506/2666-3962, fax 506/2666-4382, $35 s, $55 d) in an atmospheric old wooden house with 12 modestly decorated, gloomy rooms; and the Spanish-style **Hotel Boyeros** (tel. 506/2666-0722, www.hotelboyeros.com, $56 s, $67 d), next to Highway 1 at Avenida 2, with 70 air-conditioned rooms with cable TV and telephones, plus a large pool in landscaped grounds.

The **Best Western Hotel & Casino El Sitio** (tel. 506/2666-1211 or U.S. tel. 800/780-7234, www.bestwestern.com, $60 s or $70 d low season, $75 s or $80 d high season), 150 meters west of Highway 1 on the road to Nicoya, is a modern motel-type lodging with 52 spacious and modestly furnished rooms with private baths. The hotel has atmospheric Guanacastecan trimmings:

red-tiled roofs, local landscape paintings, and wagon-wheel chandelier. There's a large swimming pool and sun deck, plus gift store and tour desk.

In similar vein, the **Best Western Hotel Las Espuelas** (tel. 506/2666-0144, www.bestwestern.com, $60 s or $75 d low season, $72 s or $84 d high season) is a modest hotel set amid tropical gardens facing Highway 1, two kilometers south of Liberia. The 44 spacious, modestly furnished air-conditioned rooms with cable TVs are supported by a country-style restaurant and poolside *palenque* bar with folkloric entertainment (for groups).

The most appealing place by far, done up in colorful minimalist Ikea style, is **《 Bed & Breakfast El Punto** (tel. 506/2665-2986, www.elpuntohotel.com, $58 s, $67 d), occupying a former school on the Pan-American Highway, 200 meters south of the main junction. Here, former classrooms have cleverly metamorphosed into six studio-style air-conditioned rooms with downstairs plus loft bedrooms with orthopedic mattresses, ceiling fans, and gorgeous private bathrooms with hot showers and organic toiletries. A common room has cable TV and Wi-Fi. The owner, Mariana Estreda, is an educated charmer and the adjoining restaurant is magnificent. A spa was to be added.

The brand new three-story **Hotel La Riviera** (Avenida 3, Calle 7, tel. 506/2666-1450), due to open at my last visit, also looks like it will be a classy winner.

Food

Liberia offers some tremendous options for dining. One such is **《 Panadería Alemania** (tel. 506/2665-2061, 7 A.M.–11 P.M. Mon.–Sat., 11 A.M.–11 P.M. Sun.), with elegant rattan furnishings and an open patio with a huge tree. Go for the bargain-priced *plato ejecutivo* lunch ($5), and $10 nightly specials (such as chicken salad, *dorado* with papaya sauce, and apple strudel with ice cream), and even sushi. It also has tremendous baked goods. Hans, the owner, also runs **Café Europa** (tel. 506/2668-1081, 6 A.M.–6 P.M. daily), a German bakery two kilometers west of the airport. Hans grinds his own flour to conjure succulent croissants, Danish pastries, pumpernickel breads, and much more.

For seafood, you can't beat **Restaurante Paso Real** (tel. 506/2666-3455, 11 A.M.–10 P.M. daily, $5–15), on the south side of the plaza, a modestly elegant seafood restaurant with options for indoor air-conditioning or patio dining with views over the square. It offers salads, soups, pastas, ceviche, and entrées such as fish with brandy sauce, squid and octopus with seafood sauce, and Mexican-style shrimp jalapeños, plus *casados.*

For pizza, head to **Luigi's Pizzería** (Avenida 2, Calles 3/5, tel. 506/2665-6909), with a delightful yesteryear ambience.

Taking Liberia into gourmet heights is **◖ Casa Verde Restaurant & Lounge Bar** (tel. 506/2665-2986, 11 A.M.–10 P.M. Tues.–Sun.), at Bed & Breakast El Punto. This stylish restaurant boasts walls of glass, chic black leather sofas, glazed concrete floors, and delicious fusion dishes. It hosts a five-course dinner with live music on Friday nights in the hotel's magnificent Casa Verde Restaurant & Lounge Bar.

You can stock up at the **Palí** (Avenida 3, Calle Central) supermarket. For baked goods, head to **Musmanni** (Avenida 3, Calle 2) or **Café Europa.**

Information and Services

The **Red Cross** adjoins the **hospital** (Avenida 4, Calles Central/2, tel. 506/2666-0011). The **police station** (tel. 506/2666-5656) is on Avenida 1, one block west of the plaza. The **post office** is at Calle 8, Avenida 3.

The icy **Planet Internet** (Calle Central, Avenida Central/2, cellular tel. 506/2666-3737, 8 A.M.–10 P.M. Mon.–Thurs., 8 A.M.–11 P.M. Fri.–Sat.) charges $1 per hour.

There's a **laundry** at Avenida Central, Calle 9.

Getting There

SANSA and **Nature Air** offer scheduled daily service between San José and **Daniel Oduber**

International Airport (tel. 506/2668-1032), 12 kilometers west of town. In addition to charter airlines, the following scheduled airlines serve the airport: Air Canada, American Airlines, Continental, Delta, Grupo Taca, United, and US Airways (twice weekly from Charlotte). The airport has a bank, and immigration (tel. 506/2668-1014) and customs (tel. 506/2668-1068).

Pulmitan buses (tel. 506/2222-1650) depart San José for Liberia from Calle 24, Avenidas 5/7, hourly 6 A.M.–6 P.M. and at 8 P.M. (four hours, $5). Buses (tel. 506/2663-1752) depart Puntarenas for Liberia from Avenida Central, Calle 4 nine times daily (2.5 hours, $2.25). Buses from Nicoya and Santa Cruz depart for Liberia hourly 5 A.M.–8 P.M.

Return Pulmitan buses (tel. 506/2666-0458) depart Liberia for San José from Avenida 9 and Calle 12 hourly 4 A.M.–8 P.M.

Buses for Nicaragua leave Liberia at 7 A.M. (Sirca), and 8 A.M. and noon (Transnica).

There are three gas stations at the junction of Highway 1 and Avenida Central.

Getting Around

For car rental, I recommend **U-Save Car Rental** (tel. 506/2667-0444 or 866/267-1070, www.usavecostarica.com), with an outlet near the airport. Several other car rental agencies are nearby.

Taxis (tel. 506/2666-3330) gather at the northwest corner of the plaza, by the bus station, and at the airport.

◖ RINCÓN DE LA VIEJA NATIONAL PARK

Rincón de la Vieja (1,895 meters), an active volcano in a period of relative calm, is the largest of five volcanoes that make up the Cordillera de Guanacaste. The volcano is composed of nine separate craters, with dormant Santa María (1,916 meters) the tallest; its crater harbors a forest-rimmed lake popular with tapirs. The main crater—Von Seebach—still steams; it features Linnet Bird Lagoon, to the southeast of the active volcano. Icy Lake Los Jilgueros lies between the two craters. The last serious

© CHRISTOPHER P. BAKER

Rincón de la Vieja National Park entrance at Las Pailas Ranger Station

eruption was in 1983, but the park has been temporarily closed as recently as 2006 due to volcanic activity. (In 2007, the national electricity company established a geothermal plant, **Planta Las Pailas,** just below the Las Pailas ranger station.)

The 14,083-hectare Parque Nacional Volcán Rincón de la Vieja extends from 650 to 1,965 meters in elevation on both the Caribbean and Pacific flanks of the *cordillera*. The Pacific side has a distinct dry season (if you want to climb to the craters, Feb.–Apr. is best); by contrast, the Caribbean side is lush and wet year-round, with as much as 500 centimeters of rainfall annually on higher slopes. The park is known for its profusion of orchid species. More than 300 species of birds include quetzals, toucanets, the elegant trogon, eagles, three-wattled bellbirds, and the curassow. Mammals include cougars; howler, spider, and white-faced monkeys; and kinkajous, sloths, tapirs, tayras, and even jaguars.

The lower slopes can be explored along relatively easy trails that begin at the two ranger stations. The **Sendero Encantado** leads through cloud forest full of *guaria morada* orchids (the national flower) and links with a 12-kilometer trail that continues to **Las Pailas** (Cauldrons), 50 hectares of bubbling mud volcanoes, boiling thermal waters, vapor geysers, and the so-called **Hornillas** (Ovens) geyser of sulfur dioxide and hydrogen sulfide. Be careful when walking around: It is possible to step through the crust and scald yourself, or worse.

Between the cloud forest and Las Pailas, a side trail (marked Aguas Thermales) leads to soothing hot-sulfur springs called **Los Azufrales** (Sulfurs). The thermal waters (42°C) form small pools where you may bathe and take advantage of their curative properties. Use the cold-water stream nearby for cooling off. Another trail leads to the **Hidden Waterfalls,** four continuous falls (three of which exceed 70 meters) in the Agria Ravine.

You're restricted to hiking one trail at a time, and must report to the ranger station before setting out on each subsequent trail. If you don't report, rangers set out to find you after a specified time.

Hiking to the Summit

The hike is relatively straightforward but challenging. You can do the round-trip to the summit and back in a day, two days from park headquarters. The trail begins at the **Santa María Ranger Station** (the 19th-century farmstead was once owned by former U.S. president Lyndon B. Johnson, who sold it to the park service), leads past Las Hornillas and the **Las Pailas Ranger Station** (the best place to start—it's four hours from here), and snakes up the steep, scrubby mountainside. En route, you cross a bleak expanse of purple lava fossilized by the blitz of the sun. Trails are marked by cairns, though it is easy to get lost if the clouds set in; consider hiring a local guide. The upper slopes are of loose scree and very demanding. Be particularly careful on your descent (three hours).

It can be cool up here, but the powerful view and the hard, windy silence make for a profound experience. From on high, you have a splendid view of the wide Guanacaste plain shimmering in the heat like a dream world between hallucination and reality, and, beyond, the mountains of Nicoya glistening like hammered gold from the sunlight slanting in from the south. On a clear day, you can see Lake Nicaragua. Magical! You have only the sighing of the wind for company.

It will probably be cloudy. Set off in early morning. Bring waterproof clothing and mosquito repellent. The grasses harbor ticks and other biting critters, so consider long pants. Fill up with water at the ranger station, which sells maps ($2).

Camping

Camping is not permitted, except at Santa María ranger station ($2 pp), which has bathroom and shower facilities; bring a sleeping bag and mosquito netting. You can buy groceries at a small store immediately below the ranger station at Las Pailes.

There are several nature lodges on the edge of the park located in the vicinity of Rincón de la Vieja.

Information and Services

The park is open 7 A.M.–5 P.M. Tues.–Sun. (last access is 3 P.M.). The headquarters is at **Hacienda Santa María** (tel. 506/2200-0296), about 27 kilometers northeast of Liberia. It contains an exhibition room. However, the main access point to the park is the **Las Pailas Ranger Station** (tel. 506/2200-0399), on the southwestern flank of the volcano. Admission costs $10; you need to give your passport number.

Getting There

The road to the Santa María Ranger Station begins from the Barrio Victoria suburb of Liberia (a sign on Hwy. 1 on the south side of Liberia points the way to Sector Santa María), where Avenida 6 leads east 25 kilometers past the ranger station entrance to the hamlets of San Jorge and Colonia Blanca (which can also be reached by a dirt road from Guayabo, north of Bagaces). The road is deeply rutted (and muddy in wet season); a four-wheel-drive vehicle is recommended. Santa María is linked to Las Pailas by a six-kilometer trail and, as of 2008, by a new road (it passes through private property; a $1.50 toll is charged).

Las Pailas is also reached off the Pan-American Highway via a dirt road from Curubandé. The turnoff is about six kilometers north of Liberia, from where the dirt road leads past the village of Curubandé (10 km) to the gates of Hacienda Guachipelín cattle ranch. The gates are open during daylight hours; you pay a $1.50 fee to use the private road, which leads three kilometers to Hacienda Lodge Guachipelín (the toll is reimbursed if you stay here) and, beyond, to Rincón de la Vieja Lodge and Las Pailas Ranger Station. A bus departs Liberia for Curubandé and Hacienda Lodge Guachipelín at 4:15 A.M., 12:45 P.M., and 4:15 P.M.

Lodges arrange transfers, and the Hotel Guanacaste in Liberia has transfers at 7 A.M. and 4 P.M. daily ($7 pp each way, three people minimum). A taxi from Liberia will cost about $30–40 each way.

VICINITY OF RINCÓN DE LA VIEJA

There are several haciendas and nature lodges on the lower slopes of Rincón de la Vieja. Together they offer a panoply of activities. All accept day visitors as well as offering accommodations.

Via Colonia Blanca

The **Rinconcito Canopy Tour** ($30), at Rinconcito Lodge (tel. 506/2200-0074 or 2666-2764, www.rinconcitolodge.com), has 10 platforms and seven cables. You can hike or ride a horse from the lodge.

Finca La Anita (tel. 506/8388-1775, www.fincalaanita.org), a macadamia, cacao, and organic fruit farm near Colonial Libertad, on the northeast side of the mountain, offers educational day tours ($50), including a rainforest hike, a cart-ride through the plantation, and a chocolate-making class. It is most easily reached via Aguas Claras.

Via Curubandé

Hacienda Lodge Guachipelín (tel. 506/2666-8075, www.guachipelin.com), a centenarian working cattle ranch east of Curubandé, 18 kilometers from Highway 1 and eight kilometers south of the Santa María Ranger Station, offers more than 1,000 hectares of terrain from dry forest to open savanna, plus a 1,200-hectare tree-reforestation project. Activities include guided horseback rides ($25–75 adult, $15–55 children) and a cattle round-up; volcano hikes ($60 adults, $50 children); river tubing ($50 adults, $40 students, $30 children); plus the **Cañon Canopy Tour** ($50 adults, $40 students, $30 children), where you can whiz across a canyon and between treetops from 10 platforms. A one-day "Adventure Pass" ($80 adults, $75 students, $70 children) lets you partake in all the fun. In 2008, the lodge opened the **Simbiosis Volcanic Mud Springs & Spa** (www.simbiosis-spa.com), close to the Las Pailes ranger station.

Rincón de la Vieja Mountain Lodge (tel. 506/2200-0238, www.rincondelavieja lodge.net), five kilometers beyond Hacienda Lodge Guachipelín and only one kilometer below the park near Las Pailas, is a superb base for exploring the park, with six types of tropical forest on its 900-acre private reserve. It, too, offers a zipline **canopy tour** ($35–55) with 21 platforms; also available are horse tours ($45–55) and hiking ($45).

White-water rafting, kayaking, rock-climbing, a canopy tour, rappelling, and horseback riding are also offered on the Río Colorado from the **Cañon de la Vieja Lodge** (tel. 506/2665-5912, www.canyonlodgegte.com), three kilometers along the Curubandé road.

Via Cañas Dulces

Beyond Cañas Dulces, four kilometers east of Highway 1 (the turnoff is 11 kilometers north of Liberia—don't mistake this for Cañas, farther south on Hwy. 1), the road turns to dirt and climbs uphill 13 kilometers to **Buena Vista Mountain Lodge & Adventure Center** (tel. 506/2665-7759, www.buenavistalodgecr.com), a 1,600-hectare ranch nestling high on the northwest flank of the mountain. The lodge offers a variety of guided hikes and horseback trips ($30–45). It has an 11-platform zipline canopy tour ($40); an aerial trail with 17 hanging bridges ($25); and a 420-meter water slide—like a toboggan run—ending with a plunge into a pool ($15). It also has frogs, snakes, and butterfly exhibits ($10), plus a spa.

One kilometer below Buena Vista Lodge, a side road leads three kilometers to **Hotel Borinquen Mountain Resort Thermae & Spa** (tel. 506/2690-1900, www.borinquen resort.com), an upscale mountain resort built around bubbling *pilas* (mud ponds) that feed the lovely **Amhra Sidae Spa,** which specializes in thermal treatments, including full-body mineral mud masks ($10). It has plunge pools (one hot, one tepid, one cold) and a beautiful landscaped swimming pool with whirlpool tub. Borinquen also offers guided hiking, horseback riding, a waterfall ride, various adventure tours, and a canopy adventure ($40 adults, $20 children). It is surrounded by primary forest accessed by trails. Day visits cost $70–90 including lunch, an adventure tour of your choosing, and use of the spa.

Buses depart Liberia for Cañas Dulces at 5:30 A.M., noon, and 5:30 P.M.

Accommodations and Food
NEAR SANTA MARÍA

The **Rinconcito Lodge** (tel. 506/2200-0074 or 2666-2764, www.rinconcitolodge.com, $40 s, $55 d including breakfast and tax), near San Jorge, has metamorphosed since 2006 from a working farm offering five rudimentary rooms in a cement-block house to a lovely hillside lodge with 14 spacious cabins with ceiling fans, simple hardwood furnishings, verandas, and modern bathrooms with spacious showers. Some overlook the old cattle corral. It specializes in horseback rides ($35–45) into the park and has its own zipline tour.

La Anita Rainforest Ranch (tel. 506/8388-1775, www.fincalaanita.org, $79 s/d low season, $99 s/d high season), at Finca Anita, on the northeast side of the mountain, offers a similar nature-oriented experience. It has six adorably cozy wooden cabins with ceiling fans, modern bathrooms with hot water showers, and verandas with hammocks and rockers for enjoying views of both Rincón de la Vieja and Miravalles volcanoes. Some have king-size beds; all have quality mattresses. It hosts yoga, birding, and other special-interest retreats, and gourmet meals are served.

NEAR CURUBANDÉ

My digs of choice is the Belgian-run 🍵 **Aroma de Campo** (tel. 506/2665-0008, www.aroma decampo.com, $47 s or $58 d low season, $49 s or $67 d high season including breakfast), a secluded hacienda-style bed-and-breakfast with four simple yet exquisitely romantic rooms, each in a rich, vibrant color scheme (avocado green, eggplant, papaya, or salmon), with gauzy drapes over the beds. It's a perfect combination of traditional architecture and a contemporary European aesthetic, such as glazed concrete floors. Quality meals are served family style in the open-air patio with hammocks, Adirondack chair, and lovely views.

A lesser alternative is the **Posada el Encuentro Inn** (tel./fax 506/8382-0815, $65

s/d rooms and cabins low season, $75 s/d room or $86 s/d cabin high season), about five kilometers east of the turnoff for Rincón via Curubandé. This private home, built of stone on a breeze-swept hilltop with views, has two *casitas* with two large bedrooms, private baths, and private terraces; there are three graciously appointed rooms in the house. It has a swimming pool and offers horseback rides.

Having evolved as an ecolodge that specializes in adventure tours, **Hacienda Lodge Guachipelín** (tel. 506/2666-8075, in North America tel. 877/998-7873, www.guachipelin .com, $89 s/d standard, $100 s/d superior year-round), on a working cattle ranch, boasts a gracious lobby with exquisite wrought-iron sofas, Internet, and a bar overlooking a kidney-shaped pool under shade trees. It has 34 small and simply appointed bedrooms, all with fans and wide verandas; 18 newer units are slightly more elegant. Four junior suites in the old *casona* overlook the corral, where you can watch cattle and horses being worked. The stone and timber bar-restaurant at the entrance to the hacienda is open to the public and offers rustic elegance, plus buffet dinners to the accompaniment of marimba players; open 6 A.M.–10 P.M. daily.

The simpler **Rincón de la Vieja Mountain Lodge** (tel. 506/2200-0238, www.rincondela viejalodge.net, $20 pp hostel year-round, $45 s or $65 d standard, $60 s or $75 d bungalow) offers nine no-frills dorm rooms with bunks and shared bath, 22 relatively spartan standard rooms with private bathrooms, and 11 Colorado-style log bungalows for six to eight people. All have verandas. There are two small pools in the lush gardens, and the restaurant serves hearty, simple fare. Students receive discounts. Rates include taxes.

In a similar vein are **Cañon de la Vieja Lodge** (tel. 506/2665-5912, www.canyonlodgegte .com) and the nearby **Rancho Curubandé Lodge** (tel. 506/2665-0375, www.rancho -curubande.com).

NEAR CAÑAS DULCES

The **Buena Vista Mountain Lodge & Adventure Center** (tel. 506/2665-7759, www.buenavistalodgecr.com, $60 s or $73 d room, $80–94 s/d cabins) has 77 rooms with private baths with hot water. The rustic and delightful cabins include some of stone and rough timbers, with pewter-washed floors and verandas looking down over lush lawns and, in some, a lake. You can admire the setting while soaking in a natural steam bath ringed by volcanic stone, and there's a bamboo sauna. It has transfers from Cañas Dulces. A rustic restaurant serves buffet meals. You can camp for $10.

The upscale **Hotel Borinquen Mountain Resort Thermae & Spa** (tel. 506/2690-1900, www.borinquenresort.com, $139–245 s, $155–273 d low season; $162–282 s, $180–314 d high season), in colonial hacienda style, has a classically aged feel. It offers 33 spacious air-conditioned rooms (including graciously appointed deluxe rooms and junior suites) in single and duplex red-tile-roofed villas and bungalows spaced apart on the grassy hills. They're well-lit and are graced by handmade furnishings, including wrought-iron candelabras and rustic country antiques (take your pick of decor: pre-Columbian or Spanish colonial). Guests move around on electric golf carts. Facilities include a tennis court, beauty salon, gym, spa, and a swimming pool with swim-up bar.

The Far North

QUEBRADA GRANDE

The village of Quebrada Grande, eight kilometers east of Highway 1—the turnoff is at Potrerillos, 23 kilometers north of Liberia (there's a Guardia Rural checkpoint at the junction)—sits on the lower saddle between Volcán Rincón de la Vieja to the southeast and Volcán Cacao to the northeast. It is surrounded by grasslands ranged by cattle. Several haciendas welcome visitors for horseback trail rides, including **Finca Nueva Zelandia** (c/o Curubanda Lodge, tel. 506/2691-8177, www.curubanda.com), a 500-hectare *finca* about 13 kilometers east of Quebrada Honda on the road to Upala, in the saddle between Rincón de la Vieja and the southeast side of Volcán Cacao. The *finca* includes a 200-hectare dairy farm and 250 hectares of tropical dry and humid forest abounding with wildlife.

Accommodations

Curubanda Lodge (tel. 506/2691-8177, www.curubanda.com, $50 pp low season, $55 high season), at Finca Nueva Zelandia, is a rustic but cozy lodge with a TV lounge and capacity for 15 people in four simply appointed but perfectly adequate and pleasing accommodations.

Getting There

A bus runs from Liberia to Quebrada Grande at 3 P.M. daily; a second bus departs Quebrada Grande at 4 P.M. daily for Nueva Zelandia. Group transfers from Daniel Oduber Airport cost $20 per person. The road turns to dirt about five kilometers east of Quebrada Grande.

⟨ SANTA ROSA NATIONAL PARK

Santa Rosa was founded in 1972 as the country's first national park. The 49,515-hectare park, which covers much of the Santa Elena peninsula, is part of a mosaic of ecologically interdependent parks and reserves—the 110,000-hectare Guanacaste Conservation Area (GCA) Parque Nacional. Santa Rosa is most famous for Hacienda Santa Rosa—better known as La Casona—the nation's most cherished historic monument. It was here in 1856 that the mercenary army of American adventurer William Walker was defeated by a ragamuffin army of Costa Rican volunteers.

The park is a mosaic of 10 distinct habitats, including mangrove swamp, savanna, and oak forest, which attract more than 250 bird species and 115 mammal species (half of them bats, including two vampire species), among them relatively easily seen animals such as white-tailed deer; coatimundis; howler, spider, and white-faced monkeys; and anteaters. In the wet season the land is as green as emeralds, and wildlife disperses. In dry season, however, wildlife congregates at watering holes and is easily spotted. Jaguars, margays, ocelots, pumas, and jaguarundis are here but are seldom seen. Santa Rosa is a vitally important nesting site for ridleys and other turtle species.

The park is divided into two sections: the more important and accessible Santa Rosa Sector to the south (the entrance is at Km 269 on Hwy. 1, about 37 km north of Liberia) and the Murciélago Sector (the turnoff from Hwy. 1 is 10 kilometers farther north, via Cuajiniquil), separated by a swath of privately owned land.

Santa Rosa Sector

On the right, one kilometer past the entrance gate, a rough dirt road leads to a rusting armored personnel carrier beside a memorial cross commemorating the Battle of 1955, when Somoza, the Nicaraguan strongman, made an ill-fated foray into Costa Rica. Six kilometers farther on the paved road is **La Casona,** a magnificent colonial homestead (actually, it's a replica, rebuilt in 2001 after arsonists burned down the original) overlooking a stone corral where the battle with William Walker was fought. Alas, the fire destroyed the antique furnishings and collection of photos, illustrations, carbines, and other military paraphernalia commemorating the battle of March 20, 1856. Battles were also fought here during the 1919 Sapoá Revolution and in 1955. The garden contains rocks with petroglyphs.

The **Naked Indian** loop trail (1.5 km) begins just before the house and leads through dry forest with streams and waterfalls and gumbo-limbo trees whose peeling red bark earned them the nickname "naked Indian trees." **Los Patos** trail has watering holes and is one of the best trails for spotting mammals.

The paved road ends just beyond the administration area. From here, a dirt road drops steeply to **Playa Naranjo,** 13 kilometers from La Casona. Negotiating this road takes good driving skills; a four-wheel-drive vehicle with high ground clearance is essential, but passage is never guaranteed, not least because the Río Nisperal can be impassable in wet season (the beach is usually off-limits Aug.–Nov.). Park officials sometimes close the road and will charge you a fee if you have to be hauled out. Playa Naranjo is a beautiful, kilometers-long, pale gray sand beach that is legendary in surfing lore for its steep, powerful, tubular waves and for **Witch's Rock** rising like a sentinel out of the water. The beach is bounded by craggy headlands and frequently visited by monkeys, iguanas, and other wildlife. Crocodiles lurk in the mangrove swamps at the southern end of the beach. At night, plankton light up with a brilliant phosphorescence as you walk the drying sand in the wake of high tide.

The deserted white-sand **Playa Nancite** (about a one-hour hike over a headland from Estero Real) is renowned as the site for *arribadas,* the mass nestings of olive ridley turtles that occur only here and at Ostional, farther south. More than 75,000 turtles will gather out at sea and come ashore over the space of a few days, with the possibility of up to 10,000 reptiles on the beach at any one time in September and October. You can usually see solitary turtles at other times August through December. Playa Nancite is a research site; access is restricted and permits are needed, though anyone can get one from the ranger station, or at the **Dry Tropical Forest Investigation Center** (Centro de los Investigaciones, tel. 506/2666-5051, ext. 233), next to the administrative center, which undertakes biological research. It is not open to visitors.

Playa Potrero Grande, north of Nancite, and other beaches on the central Santa Elena peninsula offer some of the best surf in the country. The makers of *Endless Summer II,* the sequel to the classic surfing movie, caught the Potrero Grande break perfectly. You can hire a boat at any of the fishing villages in the Golfo Santa Elena to take you to Potrero Grande or **Islas Murciélagos** (Bat Islands), off Cabo Santa Elena, the westernmost point

GUANACASTE

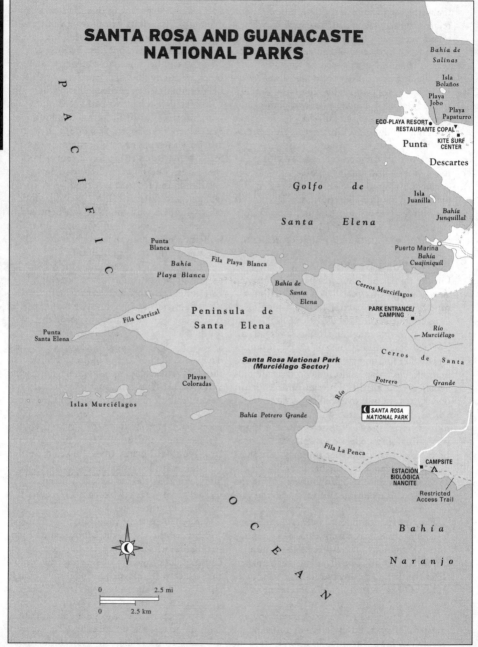

SANTA ROSA AND GUANACASTE NATIONAL PARKS

Bahía de Salinas

Isla Bolaños

Playa Jobo

Playa Papaturro

ECO-PLAYA RESORT
RESTAURANTE COPAL
KITE SURF CENTER

Punta

Descartes

P A C I F I C

Golfo de

Santa Elena

Isla Juanilla

Bahía Junquillal

Punta Blanca

Fila Playa Blanca

Puerto Marina
Bahía Cuajiniquil

Bahía Playa Blanca

Bahía de Santa Elena

Cerros Murciélagos

PARK ENTRANCE/ CAMPING

Fila Carrizal

Peninsula de Santa Elena

Punta Santa Elena

Río Murciélago

Cerros de Santa

Santa Rosa National Park (Murciélago Sector)

Potrero

Grande

Playas Coloradas

Río

Islas Murciélagos

Bahía Potrero Grande

SANTA ROSA NATIONAL PARK

Fila La Penca

CAMPSITE

ESTACIÓN BIOLÓGICA NANCITE

Restricted Access Trail

O C E A N

Bahía

Naranjo

0 ___ 2.5 mi

0 ___ 2.5 km

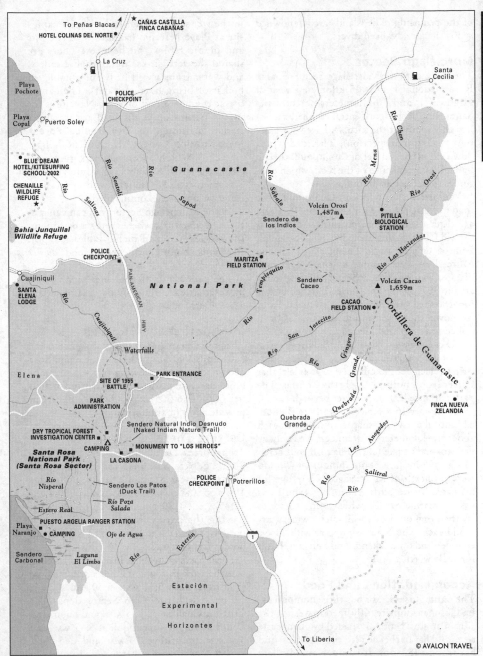

To Peñas Blacas
★ **CAÑAS CASTILLA**
   FINCA CABAÑAS
HOTEL COLINAS DEL NORTE

○ La Cruz

Santa
Cecilia ○

**POLICE
CHECKPOINT**

Playa
Pochote

Playa
Copal
○ Puerto Soley

Río Chon

G u a n a c a s t e

Río Sabalo

Río Orosí

Río Mena

● **BLUE DREAM
HOTEL/KITESURFING
SCHOOL 2002**

Río Sontoli

Río Salinas

Sapoá

Volcán Orosí
1,487m ▲

**PITILLA
BIOLOGICAL
STATION** ■

**CHENAILLE
WILDLIFE
REFUGE** ★

Sendero de
los Indios

*Bahía Junquillal
Wildlife Refuge*

Río Las Haciendas

**POLICE
CHECKPOINT**

**MARITZA
FIELD STATION** ●

Río Tempisquito

○ Cuajiniquil

● **SANTA
ELENA
LODGE**

N a t i o n a l   P a r k

Sendero
Cacao

Volcán Cacao
1,659m ▲

Río Cuajiniquil

**CACAO
FIELD STATION** ●

Cordillera de Guanacaste

Río San Josecito

Río Góngora

Waterfalls

Río Grande

E l e n a

PARK ENTRANCE ■

Río Quebrada

**FINCA NUEVA
ZELANDIA**

**SITE OF 1955
BATTLE** ■

**PARK
ADMINISTRATION** ■

Quebrada
Grande ●

Los Anagados

**DRY TROPICAL FOREST
INVESTIGATION CENTER** ■

Sendero Natural Indio Desnudo
(Naked Indian Nature Trail)

Río Salitral

△ **CAMPING**

● **MONUMENT TO "LOS HEROES"**

*Santa Rosa
National Park
(Santa Rosa Sector)*

■ **LA CASONA**

**POLICE
CHECKPOINT** ■ ○ Potrerillos

Río

*Río
Nisperal*

Sendero Los Patos
(Duck Trail)

*Río Poza
Salada*

Estero Real

PUESTO ARGELIA RANGER STATION ■

Playa
Naranjo ○

● **CAMPING**

Ojo de Agua

Río Estrón

① **1**

*Sendero
Carbonal*

*Laguna
El Limbo*

Río

E s t a c i ó n

E x p e r i m e n t a l

H o r i z o n t e s

To Liberia →

© AVALON TRAVEL

of the peninsula. The islands are a renowned scuba site for advanced divers.

Murciélago Sector

The entrance to the Murciélago Sector of Santa Rosa National Park is 15 kilometers west of Highway 1, and 10 kilometers north of the Santa Rosa Sector park entrance (there's a police checkpoint at the turnoff; have your passport ready for inspection). The road winds downhill to the hamlet of **Cuajiniquíl**, tucked half a kilometer south of the road, which continues to Bahía Cuajiniquíl.

You arrive at a Y-fork in Cuajiniquíl: the road to Murciélago (8 km) is to the left. There are three rivers to ford en route. You'll pass the old CIA training camp for the Nicaraguan Contras on your right. The place—Hacienda Murciélago—was owned by the Nicaraguan dictator Somoza's family before being expropriated in 1979, when the Murciélago Sector was incorporated into Santa Rosa National Park. It's now a training camp for the Costa Rican police force. Armed guards may stop you for an ID check as you pass. A few hundred meters farther, the road runs alongside the "secret" airstrip (hidden behind tall grass to your left) that Oliver North built to supply the Contras. The park entrance is 0.5 kilometer beyond.

It's another 16 kilometers to **Playa Blanca,** a beautiful horseshoe-shaped white-sand beach about five kilometers wide and enjoyed only by pelicans and frigate birds. The road ends here.

The 505-hectare **Bahía Junquillal Wildlife Refuge,** north of Murciélago, is a refuge for pelicans, frigate birds, and other seabirds, as well as marine turtles, which come ashore to lay their eggs on the two-kilometer-wide, gray-sand beach. The beach is popular with Ticos, who descend on weekends and holidays, but it is hardly worth a visit.

Accommodations and Food

The Santa Rosa Sector has three **campsites.** La Casona campsite, 400 meters west of the administrative center, is shaded by guanacaste trees and has barbecue pits, picnic tables, and bathrooms ($2 pp). It can get muddy here in the wet season. The shady Argelia campsite at Playa Naranjo has sites with fire pits and picnic tables and benches. There are shared showers, sinks, and outhouse toilets, and water from a well (it is not potable, so boil it or bring bottled water). The campsite at the north end of Playa Nancite is for use by permit only, obtained at the ranger station or through the **Dry Tropical Forest Investigation Center** (tel. 506/2666-5051, ext. 233), which accommodates guests on a space-available basis ($15 adult visitors, $10 scientists, $6 students and assistants). Reservations are recommended.

In the Murciélago Sector, you can camp at the ranger station, where there's a bathroom, showers, water, and picnic tables ($2 pp). Raccoons abound and scavenge food; *do not feed them!*

The park administration area serves meals by reservation only 6–7 A.M., 11:30 A.M.–12:30 P.M., and 5–6 P.M.

Information and Servcies

The park entrance station (8 A.M.–4 P.M. daily, $10 admission, $15 surfers) at the Santa Rosa Sector sells maps showing trails and campgrounds. The **park administration office** (tel. 506/2666-5051, fax 506/2666-5020) can provide additional information.

Getting There

Transportes Deldú buses (tel. 506/2256-9072) depart San José for La Cruz and Peñas Blancas from Calle 20, Avenidas 1/3, at 5 A.M., 7 A.M., 7:45 A.M., 9:30 A.M., 10:45 A.M., 1:20 P.M., and 4:10 P.M. daily, passing the park entrance—35 kilometers north of Liberia—en route to the Nicaraguan border (six hours, $5).

Local buses from Peñas Blancas and La Cruz pass the park en route to Liberia and San José eight times daily 5:30 A.M.–6:30 P.M.

Buses to Murciélago Sector depart La Cruz for Cuajiniquíl at 5 A.M. and noon, and from Liberia for Cuajiniquil at 5:45 A.M. and 3:30 P.M. (returning at 7 A.M. and 4:45 P.M.). You can catch the Liberia–Cuajiniquil–La

RESTORING THE DRY FOREST

Guanacaste National Park includes large expanses of eroded pasture that once were covered with native dry forest, which at the time of the Spaniards' colonization carpeted a greater area of Mesoamerica than did rainforests. It was also more vulnerable to encroaching civilization. After 400 years of burning, only 2 percent of Central America's dry forest remained. (Fires, set to clear pasture, often become free-running blazes that sweep across the landscape. If the fires can be quelled, trees can take root again.)

American biologist Daniel Janzen has for four decades led an attempt to restore Costa Rica's vanished dry forest to nearly 60,000 hectares of ranchland around a remnant 10,000-acre nucleus. Janzen, a professor of ecology at the University of Pennsylvania, has spent six months of every year for more than 30 years studying the intricate relationships between animals and plants in Guanacaste Province.

A key to success is to nurture a conservation ethic among the surrounding communities. Education for grade-school children is viewed as part of the ongoing management of the park; all fourth-, fifth-, and sixth-grade children in the region get an intense course in basic biology. And many of the farmers who formerly ranched land are being retrained as park guards, research assistants, and guides.

Another 2,400-hectare project is centered on Lomas Barbudal Biological Reserve in southern Guanacaste. Lomas Barbudal is one of the few remaining Pacific coast forests favored by the endangered scarlet macaw, which has a penchant for the seeds of the sandbox tree (the Spanish found the seed's hard casing perfect for storing sand, which was sprinkled on documents to absorb wet ink; hence its name).

Cruz bus from the Santa Rosa entrance at 4 P.M. From Cuajiniquil you may have to walk the eight kilometers to the park entrance.

GUANACASTE NATIONAL PARK

The Parque Nacional Guanacaste (tel. 506/2666-5051, $10 admission by reservation only) protects more than 84,000 hectares of savanna, dry forest, rainforest, and cloud forests extending east from Highway 1 to 1,659 meters atop Volcán Cacao. The park is contiguous with Santa Rosa National Park (to the west) and protects the migratory routes of myriad creatures, many of which move seasonally between the lowlands and the steep slopes of Volcán Cacao and the dramatically conical yet dormant Volcán Orosi (1,487 meters), whose rain-drenched eastern slopes contrast sharply with the dry plains.

It is one of the most closely monitored parks scientifically, with three permanent biological stations. The **Pitilla Biological Station** is at 600 meters elevation on the northeast side of Cacao amid the lush, rain-soaked forest. It is reached via a rough dirt road from Santa

Cecilia, 28 kilometers east of Highway 1. A four-wheel-drive vehicle is essential. It's a nine-kilometer drive via Esperanza. **Cacao Field Station** (also called Mengo) sits at the edge of a cloud forest at 1,100 meters on the southwestern slope of Volcán Cacao. You can get there by hiking or taking a horse 10 kilometers along a rough dirt trail from Quebrada Grande; the turnoff from Highway 1 is at Potrerillos, nine kilometers south of the Santa Rosa National Park turnoff. You'll see a sign for the station 500 meters beyond Dos Ríos (11 km beyond Quebrada Grande). The road—paved for the first four kilometers—deteriorates gradually. Four-wheel-drive vehicles can make it to within 300 meters of the station in dry season, with permission; in wet season you'll need to park at Gongora, about five kilometers before Cacao, and proceed on foot or horseback.

Maritza Field Station is farther north, at about 650 meters on the western side of the saddle between Cacao and Orosi Volcanoes. You get there from Highway 1 via a dirt road to the right at the Cuajiniquil crossroads. It's 15 kilometers. There are barbed-wire gates; simply close them behind you. Four-wheel drive is essential in wet season. The station has a research laboratory. From here you can hike to Cacao Biological Station. Another trail leads to **El Pedregal,** on the western slope of Orosi, where almost 100 petroglyphs representing a pantheon of chiseled supernatural beings lie half-buried in the luxurious undergrowth.

The park is administered from the Guanacaste Regional Conservation Area Headquarters at Santa Rosa.

Accommodations

You can camp at any of the field stations ($2 per day), which also provide spartan dormitory accommodations on a space-available basis; for reservations, contact the park headquarters in Santa Rosa National Park, which can also arrange transportation. **Cacao Field Station** has a lodge with five rustic dormitories for up to 30 people. It has water, but no towels or electricity. **Maritza Field Station** is less rustic and has beds for 32 people, with shared bath, water, electricity, and a dining hall. The **Pitilla Biological Station** has accommodations for 20 people, with electricity, water, CB radio, and basic meals. Students and researchers get priority. Rates are $15 adult visitors, $10 scientists, $6 students and assistants.

LA CRUZ

La Cruz—gateway to Nicaragua (19 kilometers north)—is dramatically situated atop an escarpment east of Bahía de Salinas. A good time to visit is May for its lively **Fiesta Cívica.**

There's a police checkpoint on Highway 1 at the junction for Cuanijiquil. Three kilometers south of La Cruz, Highway 4 runs east from the Pan-American Highway to Upala, in the northern lowlands. At **Santa Cecilia,** 27 kilometers east of Highway 1, a dirt road leads north seven kilometers to the hamlet of **La Virgen,** where you have stupendous vistas down over Lake Nicaragua.

Accommodations and Food

Hotel Bella Vista (tel. 506/2679-8060, $10 dorms, $13 pp rooms), one block west of the plaza in La Cruz, is run by a savvy Dutchman and has 36 simply furnished rooms plus backpackers' dorms in a two-story, wood-paneled structure that opens to an attractive sundeck and pool. Some have king-size beds; others have a double and bunk. The Bella Vista's open-air bar and restaurant (6 A.M.–10 P.M.) are the happening scene.

More upscale and intimate, the modern **Hotel La Mirada** (tel. 506/2679-9084, http://hotellamirada.com, $24 s or $30 d economy, $36 s or $42 d standard, $48 s or $54 d deluxe) is a lovely family-run option in colonial-Spanish vogue. It has 12 rooms in three types, plus secure parking.

My favorite hostelry in town is **Amalia Inn** (tel./fax 506/2679-9618, $20 pp), 100 meters south of the plaza. This charming place is operated by a friendly Tica, Amalia Bounds, and boasts a fabulous clifftop perch with views over Bahía Salinas and north along the Nicaraguan coast. Its eight rooms are large and cool, with tile floors, leather sofas, and striking paintings by Amalia's late husband, Lester. All have private bathrooms. A pool is handy for cooling off, though the inn's setting is breezy enough. Amalia will make breakfast, and you can prepare picnics in the kitchen.

North of town, try the German-run **Cañas Castilla Finca Cabañas** (tel. 506/8381-4030, www.canas-castilla.com, $30 s or $45 d low season, $35 s or $50 d high season), which has six delightfully rustic cabins and horseback rides on a 68-hectare farm.

Information and Services

There's a bank opposite the gas station on Highway 1 as you enter La Cruz. The **police** station (tel. 506/2679-9117), **Red Cross** (tel. 506/2679-9146), and **medical clinic** (tel. 506/2679-9116) are here, too.

Servicios Turísticas Integrales (tel. 506/2679-8190, 8 A.M.–7 P.M. Mon.–Sat.), 50 meters northeast of the plaza, is an Internet café and tourist information center.

Getting There

Transportes Deldú buses (tel. 506/2256-9072)

© CHRISTOPHER P. BAKER

Isla Bolaños, Bahía Salinas

depart San José for La Cruz and Peñas Blancas from Calle 20, Avenidas 1/3, at 5 A.M., 7 A.M., 7:45 A.M., 9.30 A.M., 10.45 A.M., 1:20 P.M., and 4:10 P.M. daily.

Local buses from Peñas Blancas and La Cruz to Liberia and San José leave eight times daily 5:30 A.M.–6:30 P.M.

Buses to Santa Rosa National Park's Murciélago Sector depart La Cruz for Cuajiniquil at 5 A.M. and noon, and from Liberia for Cuajiniquil at 5:45 A.M. and 3:30 P.M. (returning at 7 A.M. and 4:45 P.M.). You can catch the Liberia–Cuajiniquil–La Cruz bus from the Santa Rosa entrance of the national park at 4 P.M. Buses depart La Cruz for Santa Cecilia five times daily.

You can buy bus tickets from the *pulpería* (tel. 506/2679-9108), next to the bus station.

For a taxi, call **Taxi La Cruz** (tel. 506/2679-9112).

BAHÍA SALINAS

Immediately west of the plaza in La Cruz, a paved road drops to the flask-shaped Bahía Salinas, ringed by beaches backed by penurious coastal plains lined with salt pans and mangroves that attract wading birds and crocodiles. The beaches are of white sand fading to brown-gray along the shore of **Punta Descartes,** separating the bay from Bahía Junquillal to the south. High winds blow almost nonstop December–April, making this a prime spot for windsurfing.

The road, unpaved and in horrendous shape at last visit, leads past the hamlet of **Puerto Soley,** where the road splits. The right fork leads via **Playa Papaturro** to **Jobo,** a fishing village at the tip of Punta Descartes. Turn right in Jobo for **Playa Jobo** and **Playa La Coyotera.** The left fork leads to Bahía Junquillal; four-wheel drive is essential (this route was impassable in late 2008 due to mud and a washed out bridge). En route, you'll pass **Refugio de Vida Silvestre Chenailles,** a private wildlife refuge not currently open to the public.

Bolaños Island National Wildlife Refuge (Refugio Nacional de Vida Silvestre Isla Bolaños) is a wildlife refuge protecting one of only four nesting sites in Costa Rica for the

GUANACASTE

© CHRISTOPHER P. BAKER

stuck in mud near Bahía Junquillal

brown pelican, and the only known nesting site for the American oystercatcher. As many as 200 frigate birds also nest on the rugged, oval-shaped rocky crag, about half a kilometer east of Punta Descartes during the January–March mating season. Visitors are not allowed to set foot on the island, but you can hire a boat and guide in Puerto Soley or Jobo to take you within 50 meters.

Tours and Activities

Eco-Wind (tel. 506/2228-7146, www.eco playa.com, operates in high season only) surf center at Eco-Playa Resort and the **Kite Surf Center** (tel. 506/2826-5221, www.sun toursandfun.com), at Playa Papaturro, rent boards and offer classes and courses in windsurfing.

Accommodations and Food

The Dutch-owned **Eco-Playa Resort** (tel. 506/2679-9380 or 2228-7146, www.eco playa.com, $74 pp low season, $84 high season, two-night minimum required) is an attractive modern all-suite complex on Playa La

Coyotera, with landscaped lawns leading onto a thin and unappealing beach. The 36 spacious rooms feature open-plan lounges with terra-cotta floors, air-conditioning, ceiling fans, TVs, telephones, kitchenettes, and upscale, motel-style decor. The soaring *palenque* restaurant opens to a crescent-shaped pool and sun deck.

The modern, two-story **Blue Dream Hotel** (tel. 506/8826-5221, www.suntoursand fun.com, $33 s, $42 d), at Playa Papaturro, specializes in windsurfing and has 10 rooms with terra-cotta floors and sliding glass doors to terraces with views. The simple restaurant serves Italian fare.

For dinner, head to the hilltop **Restaurante Copal** (tel. 506/2676-1006, 7–9 P.M. daily), serving up Italian fare and gorgeous views.

Getting There

Buses (tel. 506/2659-8278) depart La Cruz daily at 5 A.M., 8:30 A.M., 11 A.M., 2 P.M., and 4:15 P.M. for Puerto Soley and Jobo. Return buses depart Jobo 90 minutes later. A taxi will cost about $3 one-way to Puerto Soley, $8 to Jobo.

PEÑAS BLANCAS: CROSSING INTO NICARAGUA

Peñas Blancas, 19 kilometers north of La Cruz, is the border post for Nicaragua. Be careful driving the Pan-American Highway, which hereabouts is dangerously potholed and chockablock with articulated trucks hurtling along.

The bus terminal contains the **Oficina de Migración** (immigration office, tel. 506/2679-9025), a bank, restaurant, and **Costa Rican Tourism Institute** (ICT, tel. 506/2677-0138).

Change money before crossing into Nicaragua (you get a better exchange rate on the Costa Rican side).

Transportes Deldú buses (tel. 506/2256-9072) depart San José for La Cruz and Peñas Blancas from Calle 20, Avenidas 1/3, at 5 A.M., 7 A.M., 7:45 A.M., 9:30 A.M., 10:45 A.M., 1:20 P.M., and 4:10 P.M. daily, en route to the Nicaraguan border (six hours, $5). Buses depart Peñas Blancas for San José at 5 A.M., 7:15 A.M., 10:30 A.M., 10:40 A.M., 1:30 P.M., 2:45 P.M., and 3:30 P.M.

THE NICOYA PENINSULA

Known for its magnificent beaches and a long dry season with sizzling sunshine, the Nicoya Peninsula is a broad, hooked protuberance—130 kilometers long and averaging 50 kilometers wide—separated from the Guanacaste plains by the Río Tempisque and Gulf of Nicoya. Most tourist activity is along the dramatically sculpted Pacific shoreline. Away from the coast, Nicoya is mostly mountainous.

More than three-quarters of Costa Rica's coastal resort infrastructure is in Nicoya, concentrated in northern Nicoya. Several deluxe hotels and a golf course are already in place, with more to follow, tilting the demographics away from eco-conscious travelers toward a more high-end crowd. The opening of the Daniel Oduber International Airport at Liberia in 1996 has significantly boosted arrivals. More

and more mega-resorts are going up. And all along the coast, residential condo complexes have sprouted like palm trees on a wet beach. Aquifers are being drained. Water pollution is rising. And wildlife is disappearing. In all, an ecological disaster is in the making, says alarmed environmentalists, not least thanks to government inaction in the face of developers who simply don't care. Finally, in April 2008, President Oscar Arias issued a temporary decree imposing new restrictions on coastal construction, and MINAE (the governmental environmental body) actually began tearing down offending buildings.

Though each beach community has its own distinct appeal, most remain barefoot and button-down, appealing to laid-back travelers who can hang with the locals and appreciate the

© CHRISTOPHER P. BAKER

HIGHLIGHTS

◖ **Guaitíl:** Ancient pottery traditions are kept alive at this charming village, where you can witness ceramics being crafted in age-old fashion (page 340).

◖ **Tempisque Safari Ecological Adventure:** Remote it may be, but this wildlife rescue center and zoo is one of the nation's finest. A visit includes a wildlife-filled boat tour on the Río Tempisque (page 341).

◖ **Marino Las Baulas National Park:** Here, surfers can enjoy consistent action while nature lovers can kayak or take boat trips in search of crocodiles, birds, and other wildlife in the reserve behind the beach. The highlight in season is a chance to witness giant leatherback turtles laying eggs (page 360).

◖ **Ostional National Wildlife Refuge:** Site of a unique mass turtle nesting, this remote reserve has few services, but the expe-rience of witnessing an *arribada* will sear your memory for the rest of your life (page 379).

◖ **Nosara:** Beautiful beaches, cracking surf, plentiful wildlife, and a broad choice of accom-modations combine to make Nosara a choice destination (page 382).

◖ **Isla Tortuga:** Stunning beaches, nature trails, warm turquoise waters, and plenty of water sports await passengers on day cruises to this gorgeous little isle off southeast Nicoya (page 404).

◖ **Cabo Blanco Absolute Wildlife Reserve:** This remote reserve is unrivaled locally for wildlife viewing, with all the main critters on show (page 411).

◖ **Santa Teresa and Malpaís:** These burgeoning yet offbeat communities are the gateway to Playa Santa Teresa, the perfect spot to bag some rays, ride the waves, and chill (page 412).

LOOK FOR ◖ TO FIND RECOMMENDED SIGHTS, ACTIVITIES, DINING, AND LODGING.

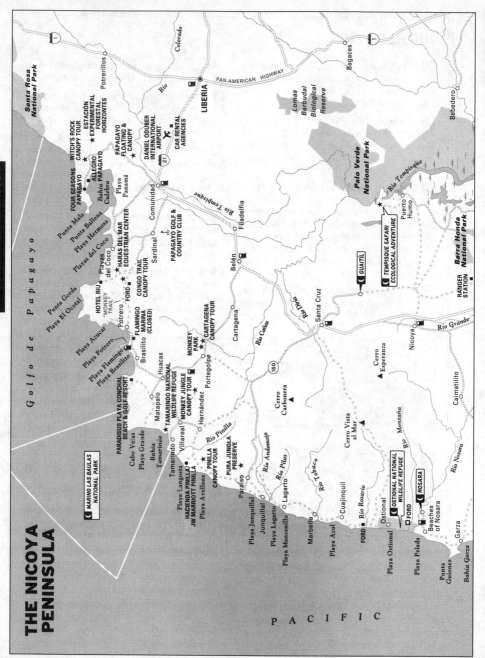

THE NICOYA PENINSULA

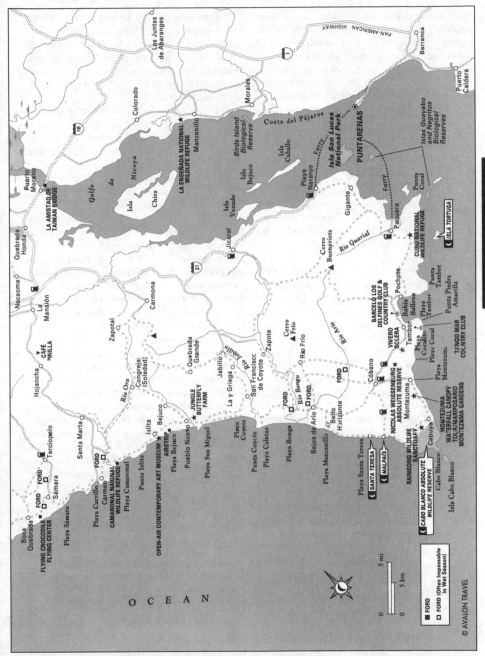

PAN-AMERICAN HIGHWAY

Las Juntas de Abaranges

Barranca

Puerto Caldera

1

Colorado

Moralea

Costa del Pájaros

Birds Island Biological Reserve

Isla San Lucas National Park

PUNTARENAS

Islas Guayabo and Negritos Biological Reserves

18

Puerto Moreno

LA ENSENADA NATIONAL WILDLIFE REFUGE

Manzanilla

Golfo de

Isla Nicoya

Isla Chira

Isla Bejuco

Isla Caballo

Playa Naranjo

Ferry

Ferry

Punta Coral

LA AMISTAD DE TAIWAN BRIDGE

Quebrada Honda

Isla Venado

Jicaral

Playa Gigante

Paquera

CURÚ NATIONAL WILDLIFE REFUGE

◀ ISLA TORTUGA

Niacaome

La Mansión

21

Cerro Buenavista

Río Guarial

Carmona

BARCELÓ LOS DELFINES GOLF & COUNTRY CLUB

Pochote

Punta Tambor

Zapotal

Cerro Frío ▲

Río Frío

Río Arío

Bahía Ballena

Playa Tambor

Punta Piedra Amarilla

Hojancha

CAFÉ PINILLA

Congreja (Soledad)

Quebrada Grande

Zapote

Cóbano

VIVERO SOLERA

Tambor

TANGO MAR COUNTRY CLUB

Río Ora

JUNGLE BUTTERFLY FARM

Jabillo

La y Griega

San Francisco de Coyote

Río Bongo

FORD

FORD

Playa Cocal

Playa Cocalito

Santa Marta

Terciopelo

Bejuco

Pueblo Nuevo

Playa Bejuco

Playa San Miguel

Playa Coyote

FORD

Bello Horizonte

Playa Montezuma

MONTEZUMA WATERFALL CANOPY TOUR/MARIPOSARIO MONTEZUMA GARDENS

FORD

FORD

Islita

Punta Islita

OPEN-AIR CONTEMPORARY ART MUSEUM ★

AIRSTRIP

Punta Coyote

Playa Caletas

Playa Bongo

Bajos de Arío

NICOLAS WEISSENBURG ABSOLUTE RESERVE

Montezuma

Boa Quebrada

FLYING CROCODILE FLYING CENTER

FORD

FORD

Carmen

Sámara

CAMARONAL NACIONAL/ WILDLIFE REFUGE

Playa Camaronal

Playa Manzanillo

RAINSONG WILDLIFE SANCTUARY

Cabuya

Playa Carrillo

Playa Sámara

◀ SANTA TERESA

◀ MALPAÍS

Cabo Blanco

◀ CABO BLANCO ABSOLUTE WILDLIFE RESERVE

Isla Cabo Blanco

Playa Santa Teresa

O C E A N

5 mi

5 km

0

0

FORD

FORD (Often Impassable in Wet Season)

© AVALON TRAVEL

wildlife that comes down to the shore. This is particularly so of the southern beaches. Waves pump ashore along much of the coastline, and many beaches have been discovered by surfers, who are opening up heretofore hidden sections of jungle-lined shore. Newly cut roads are linking the last pockets of the erstwhile inaccessible Pacific coast, though negotiating the dirt highways is always tricky—and part of the fun.

Predominantly dry to the north and progressively moist to the south, the peninsula offers a variety of ecosystems, with no shortage of opportunities for nature-viewing; monkeys, coatis, sloths, and other wildlife species inhabit the forests along the shore. Two of the premier nesting sites for marine turtles are here. The offshore waters are beloved of scuba divers and for sportfishing. And water sports are well developed.

The best time to visit is December–April, when rain is virtually unheard of (average annual rainfall is less than 150 centimeters in some areas). The rainy season generally arrives in May and lasts until November, turning dirt roads into muddy (and often impassable) quagmires sure to test your driving skills to the max. September and October are the wettest months. The so-called Papagayo winds— heavy northerlies *(nortes)*—blow strongly from January (sometimes earlier) through March and are felt mostly in northern Nicoya. Surfers rave about the rainy season (May–Nov.), when swells are consistent and waves—fast and tubular—can be 1.5 meters or more.

The downside—besides the immense overdevelopment of condominium projects—is the skyrocketing crime in Nicoya. In 2006 the police chief called it an emergency.

PLANNING YOUR TIME

Nicoya's beaches require a month to sample in earnest. One week to 10 days should be sufficient to sample two or three of the best beaches. In the north, Tamarindo makes a good base for exploring farther afield, but the poor state of coast roads is not conducive to round-trip travel. It's perhaps best to keep moving on, north or south.

If white-sand floats your boat, head to **Playa Flamingo** or nearby **Playa Conchal,** which is backed by the country's largest resort hotel, complete with golf course and water sports. **Montezuma,** a charming little community on the southern tip of Nicoya, also has a superb white-sand beach.

There's no shortage of options for accommodations for any budget, although reservations are highly recommended for holiday periods, when Ticos flock. The most complete services and range of accommodations are found at **Tamarindo,** a surfing center with a wide range of other activities, plus several fine restaurants. **Playas del Coco** and adjacent beach resorts of Ocotal and Hermosa, while less attractive than other beaches, are bases for sportfishing and scuba diving. Surfers can choose from dozens of beaches: the best begin at Playa Grande and extend south to **Malpaís** and **Playa Santa Teresa;** many are remote and have few, if any, facilities. **Playa Camaronal to Manzanillo,** with several superb and lonesome beaches—almost all favored by marine turtles for nesting— is a fabulous adventure by four-wheel drive.

Two nature experiences stand out: a visit to **Marino Las Baulas National Park** to see the leatherback turtles laying eggs, and the **Ostional National Wildlife Refuge** during its unique mass invasions of olive ridley turtles. These are, for me, the most momentous guaranteed wildlife encounters in Costa Rica. **Curú National Wildlife Refuge** and **Cabo Blanco Wildlife Refuge** offer their own nature highlights, as does **Nosara,** another prime surf destination.

Don't leave Nicoya without calling in at the village of **Guaitíl,** where Chorotega families make pottery in the same fashion their ancestors did one thousand years ago. Nearby, **Barra Honda National Park** is the nation's preeminent spelunking site.

Getting to the Coast

Driving from San José to the coast resorts takes a minimum of four or five hours. A single highway (Hwy. 21) runs north–south along the eastern plains of Nicoya, linking Liberia with the towns

FERRIES TO AND FROM NICOYA

Two car-and-passenger ferries and a passengers-only ferry cross the Río Tempisque and Gulf of Nicoya, shortening the driving distance to or from the Nicoya Peninsula. In high season and on weekends, lines can get long, and you should get there at least an hour before departure times, which change frequently. Check ahead!

PUNTARENAS TO PAQUERA

Ferry Naviera Tambor (tel. 506/2661-2084, ferrypeninsular@racsa.co.cr) ferries departs Avenida 3, Calles 33, in Puntarenas for Paquera daily every two or three hours 5 A.M.–9 P.M. Return ferries depart Paquera 5 A.M.–7 P.M. ($2 pedestrians, $9 car and passengers). Take this ferry to reach Montezuma and Malpaís.

A passengers-only *lancha* (water-taxi, tel. 506/2661-0515) departs Puntarenas for Paquera at 11:30 A.M. and 4 P.M. from Avenida 3, Calles 2/Central. Return ferries depart Paquera at 7:30 A.M. and 2 P.M. ($1.25 adults, $1 for bicycles and children).

Buses (tel. 506/642-0219) meet the ferries and depart Paquera for Cóbano at 6:15 A.M., 8:30 A.M., 10:30 A.M., noon, 2:30 P.M., 4:30 P.M., and 6:30 P.M.; and from Cóbano to Paquera at 3:45 A.M., 5:45 A.M., 8:30 A.M., 10:30 A.M., 12:15 P.M., 2:30 P.M., and 6:30 P.M.

PUNTARENAS TO NARANJO

Playa Naranjo is two-thirds of the way down the Nicoya Peninsula and makes a perfect landing stage if you're heading to Sámara or Nosara.

The **Coonatramar Ferry** (tel. 506/2661-1069, www.coonatramar.com) departs Puntarenas from Avenida 3, Calles 33/35, at 6:30 A.M., 10 A.M., 2:30 P.M., and 7:30 P.M. ($1.60 adult, $0.75 child, $3 motorcycle, $10.50 car). The return ferry departs Playa Naranjo at 8 A.M., 12:30 P.M., 5:30 P.M., and 9 P.M. Buy your ticket from a booth to the left of the gates at Naranjo, but be sure to park in line first.

Buses meet the ferry for Jicaral, Coyote, Bejuco, Carmona, and Nicoya.

---

of Filadelfia, Santa Cruz, and Nicoya, then south (deteriorating all the while) to Playa Naranjo, Paquera, Tambor, and Montezuma. Spur roads snake west over the mountains, connecting beach communities to civilization. Excepting a short section south of Sámara, no paved highway links the various beach resorts, which are connected by a network of dirt roads roughly paralleling the coast; at times you will need to head inland to connect with another access road. Plan accordingly, and allow much more time than may be obvious by looking at a map. Several sections require river fordings—no easy task in wet season, when many rivers are impassable (the section between Sámara and Malpaís is the most daunting and adventurous of wet season drives in the country). A four-wheel-drive vehicle is essential. It's wise to fill up wherever you find gas available (often it will be poured from a

can—and cost about double what it would at a true gas station). The roads are blanketed with choking dust in dry season, although every year sees more and more roads paved.

The Pan-American Highway (Hwy. 1) via Liberia gives relatively easy access to the northern Nicoya via Highway 21, which runs west for 20 kilometers to Comunidad, gateway to Bahía de Culebra, the Playas de Coco region, and Tamarindo.

The main access to central Nicoya from Highway 1 is via the Puente de Amistad con Taiwan (Friendship with Taiwan Bridge), about 27 kilometers west of Highway 1 (the turnoff is 2 kilometers north of Limonal). Highway 18 connects with Highway 21.

Daily car and passenger ferries also cross from Puntarenas to Naranjo (for central beaches) and Paquera (for Montezuma and Malpaís).

Highway 2 to Santa Cruz

The Río Tempisque is spanned by the **Puente de Amistad con Taiwan,** a suspension bridge whose construction was a gift from the Taiwanese government. On its west bank, Highway 18 continues 15 kilometers to a T-junction with Highway 21 at **Puerto Viejo;** the town of Nicoya, the regional capital, is 15 kilometers north of the junction (Highway 21 loops north via Santa Cruz and Filadelfia to reconnect with Highway 1 at Liberia).

Tempisque Eco-Adventures & Canopy Tour (tel. 506/2687-1212, ecoadventures@ racsa.co.cr), four kilometers west of the bridge, has a canopy tour ($40) and offers boat trips to Palo Verde National Park at 9:30 A.M. and 1 P.M. ($45).

BARRA HONDA NATIONAL PARK

The 2,295-hectare Parque Nacional Barra Honda (tel. 506/2659-1551 or 2659-1099, 8 A.M.–4 P.M., $10 admission), 13 kilometers west of the Río Tempisque, is a rugged upland area known for its limestone caverns dating back 70 million years (42 caverns have been discovered to date). Skeletons, utensils, and ornaments dating back to 300 B.C. have been discovered inside the Nicoya Cave. The deepest cavern thus far explored is the 240-meter-deep Santa Ana Cave, known for its Hall of Pearls, full of stalactites and stalagmites.

The only caverns open to the public are **Terciopelo Cave** (children must be 12 or over), with three chambers reached via an exciting 30-meter vertical ladder, then a sloping plane that leads to the bottom, 63 meters down; and **La Cuevita.** Within, Mushroom Hall is named for the shape of its calcareous formations; the Hall of the Caverns has large Medusa-like formations, including a figure resembling a lion's head. And columns in "The Organ" produce musical tones when struck.

Some of the caverns are frequented by bats, including the Pozo Hediondo (Fetid Pit) Cave, which is named for the quantity of excrement accumulated by its abundant bat population. Blind salamanders and endemic fish species have also evolved in the caves. Caverna Nicoya contains pre-Columbian petroglyphs.

Above ground, the hilly dry forest terrain is a refuge for howler monkeys, deer, agoutis, peccaries, kinkajous, anteaters, and many bird species, including scarlet macaws. The park tops out at Mount Barra Honda (442 m), which has intriguing rock formations and provides an excellent view of the Gulf of Nicoya. Las Cascadas are strange limestone formations formed by calcareous sedimentation along a riverbed.

Guides and Tours

Cave descents are allowed 7:30 A.M.–1 P.M. daily May–November, and until 2 P.M. December–April, except Holy Week ($36 s, $52 d four hours, including entrance, guide, and cave equipment; the price varies depending on number of participants). For cave descents, you must be accompanied by a guide from the **Asociación de Guías Ecologistas de Barra Honda,** which also has guided walks ($10 pp) plus nighttime tours ($7 pp, three person minimum) in dry season. Budget at least four hours to visit the caves. You can drive to about 1.5 kilometers beyond the park entrance, after which you're on foot: it's hot, steep, and there are mosquitoes.

Reservations are required for the Sendero Las Cascadas, which leads to waterfalls; guided tours only.

Accommodations

There's a campsite ($2 pp) at the ranger station, which also has simple cabins for volunteers willing to help with trail maintenance and other projects. It has basic showers and toilets plus picnic tables and water. At last visit, meal service was being planned.

One kilometer before the park entrance, **Hotel Barra Honda** (tel. 506/2659-1003, $15 s/d) is set in spacious tree-shaded grounds and has a simple open-air restaurant. It offers horseback rides. The 10 basic modern cabins have

THE NICOYA PENINSULA

© CHRISTOPHER P. BAKER

THE NICOYA PENINSULA

Parroquia San Blas church

fans and spacious modern bathrooms. Of similar standard, **Las Cavernas Tourist Lodge** (tel. 506/2659-1574, fax 506/2659-1573, $12 pp), 400 meters from the park entrance, has five bare-bones rooms with cold-water private bathrooms and a delightful cowboy-style restaurant and bar decorated with yokes and saddles. It has a small pool.

Getting There

The turnoff for the Nacaome (Barra Honda) ranger station is 1.5 kilometers east of Puerto Viejo and 15 kilometers west of the Tempisque Bridge. From here, an all-weather gravel road leads via Nacaome, all the while deteriorating (4WD recommended); signs point the way to the entrance, about six kilometers farther via Santa Ana.

A Tracopa-Alfaro (tel. 506/2222-2666) bus from San José to Nicoya will drop you at the turnoff for the park; Las Cavernas will send a pickup by prior arrangement. A bus departs Nicoya for Santa Ana and Nacaome at 12:30 P.M. daily, plus 4 P.M. on Monday, Wednesday, and Friday; you can walk to the park entrance. You can also enter the park from the east via a dirt road (from Quebrada Honda, off Highway 21 immediately east of Nicoya township.

NICOYA

Nicoya, about 78 kilometers south of Liberia, is Costa Rica's oldest colonial city. Today it bustles as the agricultural and administrative heart of the region. The town is named for the Chorotega chief who presented Spanish conquistador Gil González Dávila with gold. The native heritage is still apparent.

The only sight of interest is the **Parroquia San Blas** (tel. 506/2685-5109, 8 A.M.–4 P.M. Mon.–Fri., 8 A.M.–noon Sat.) church built in the 16th century, gleaming anew following a restoration and decorating the town's peaceful plaza. It contains a few pre-Columbian icons and religious antiques.

Accommodations

The **Hotel Venecia** (tel. 506/2685-5325, $15 pp with fan, $20 with a/c), on the north side of the plaza, has 37 clean but basic rooms. Newer, nicer units in a two-story unit are to the rear.

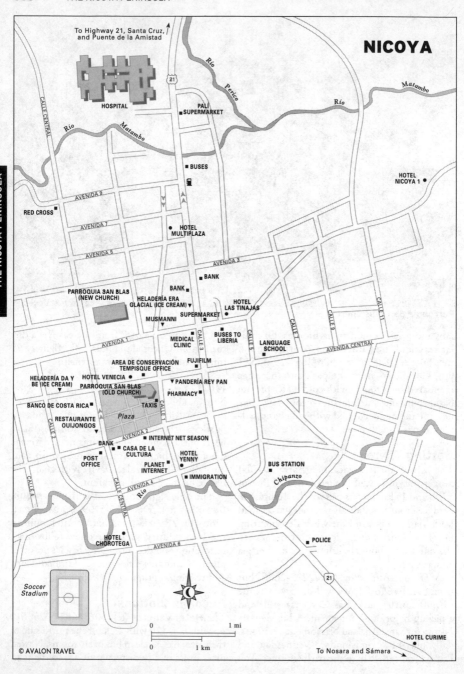

NICOYA

To Highway 21, Santa Cruz, and Puente de la Amistad

HOSPITAL

PALI SUPERMARKET

BUSES

HOTEL NICOYA 1

RED CROSS

HOTEL MULTIPLAZA

BANK

BANK

PARROQUIA SAN BLAS (NEW CHURCH)

HELADERÍA ERA GLACIAL (ICE CREAM)

HOTEL LAS TINAJAS

MUSMANNI

SUPERMARKET

MEDICAL CLINIC

BUSES TO LIBERIA

LANGUAGE SCHOOL

AREA DE CONSERVACIÓN TEMPISQUE OFFICE

FUJIFILM

HELADERÍA DA Y BE (ICE CREAM)

HOTEL VENECIA

PANDERÍA REY PAN

PARROQUIA SAN BLAS (OLD CHURCH)

PHARMACY

BANCO DE COSTA RICA

TAXIS

RESTAURANTE OUIJONGOS

Plaza

BANK

CASA DE LA CULTURA

INTERNET NET SEASON

HOTEL YENNY

POST OFFICE

PLANET INTERNET

IMMIGRATION

BUS STATION

Chipanzo

HOTEL CHOROTEGA

POLICE

Soccer Stadium

AVENIDA 9

AVENIDA 7

AVENIDA 5

AVENIDA 3

AVENIDA 1

AVENIDA CENTRAL

AVENIDA 2

AVENIDA 4

AVENIDA 6

CALLE CENTRAL

CALLE 2

CALLE 4

CALLE 3

CALLE 5

CALLE 7

CALLE 9

CALLE 11

Río Perico

Río Matambo

Río Matambo

Río

0   1 mi

0   1 km

© AVALON TRAVEL

To Nosara and Sámara →

HOTEL CURIME

FESTIVAL OF LA VIRGEN DE GUADALUPE

Try to visit Nicoya on December 12, when villagers carry a dark-skinned image of La Virgen de Guadalupe through the streets accompanied by flutes, drums, and dancers. The festival combines the Catholic celebration of the Virgin of Guadalupe with the traditions of the Chorotega legend of La Yequita (Little Mare), a mare that interceded to prevent twin brothers from fighting to the death for the love of a princess. The religious ceremony is a good excuse for bullfights, explosive fireworks (*bombas*), concerts, and general merriment. Many locals get sozzled on *chicha*, a heady brew made from fermented corn and sugar and drunk from hollow gourds.

There's a swimming pool and whirlpool tub in lush gardens.

Food

The best bet in town is **Restaurante Ouijongos** (tel. 506/2686-4748, 11 A.M.–10 P.M. daily) on the west side of the plaza. It serves excellent seafood, including ceviche ($5) and shrimp in oyster sauce ($12), plus meat dishes and *casados* (set lunches, $3).

There's a **Musmanni** bakery at Calle 1, Avenida 1. **Heladería Da y Be,** on the northwest side of the plaza, sells ice cream, as does **Heladería Era Glacial** (Calle 3, Avenida 1), a delightful coffee shop opposite **Super Compro** supermarket.

Information and Services

MINAE (tel. 506/2686-6760, fax 506/2685-5667, 8 A.M.–4 P.M. Mon.–Fri.), on the north side of the plaza, administers the Tempisque Conservation Area. It is not set up to serve tourists.

The **hospital** (tel. 506/2685-5066) is on the north side of town, and there are several medical clinics. The **post office** (Avenida 2, Calle Central) is open 7:30 A.M.–5:30 P.M. daily. The **police station** (tel. 506/2685-5559) is 500 meters south of the town center, on Calle 3, which has four banks. You can make international calls from **Planet Internet** (Avenida 4, Calle 1, tel. 506/2685-4281, 8 A.M.–8 P.M. Mon.–Sat.) or **Internet Net Season** (Avenida 2, Calles Central/1, tel. 506/2685-4045).

Inmigración (Avenida 4, Calle 1, tel. 506/2686-4155, 8 A.M.–4 P.M. Mon.–Fri.) can issue visa extensions.

Instituto Guanacasteco de Idiomas (tel. 506/2686-6948, www.spanishcostarica.com) offers Spanish-language instruction.

Getting There

Tracopa Alfaro buses (tel. 506/2222-2666) depart San José for Nicoya from Calle 14, Avenidas 3/5, at 5:30 A.M., 7:30 A.M., 10 A.M., noon, 1 P.M., 3 P.M., 5 P.M., and 6:30 P.M. daily ($5, six hours). Buses also serve Nicoya from Liberia every 30 minutes, 4:30 A.M.–8:20 P.M. daily; and from Santa Cruz hourly, 6 A.M.–9 P.M. daily.

It has secure parking. Budget options of similar standard include **Hotel Chorotega** (Calle Central, Avenida 6, tel. 506/2685-5245, $7 pp shared bath, $8 s or $12 d private bath, $14 s or $18 d with hot water and TV); and the similarly priced **Hotel Yenny** (Calle 1, Avenida 4, tel. 506/2685-5050); and **Hotel Las Tinajas** (Avenida 1, Calle 5, tel./fax 506/2685-5081).

The best bargain is **Hotel Multiplaza** (tel. 506/2685-3535, Calle 1, Avenidas 5/7, $15 pp), which has 25 dark but spacious air-conditioned rooms with fans, comfy mattresses, and cable TV, but cold water only. There's a small café outside. Slightly more upscale, the **Hotel Nicoya I** (tel. 506/2686-6331, $25 s, $30 d) has eight air-conditioned rooms with fan and private bathrooms with hot water.

The nicest place is **Hotel Río Tempisque de Lujo** (tel. 506/2686-6650, $40 s, $45 d), on Highway 21, 800 meters north of the junction for Nicoya township, with 30 well-lit, spacious, air-conditioned cabins in groomed gardens set back from the road for peace and quiet. Each has two double beds, cable TV, refrigerator, coffeemaker, microwave, and pleasing bathrooms with hair dryer and hot water.

Buses (tel. 506/2685-5032) depart Nicoya for San José from Avenida 4, Calle 3, at 3 A.M., 4:30 A.M., 5:15 A.M., 9:15 A.M., noon, 2:45 P.M., and 5 P.M. daily; for Playa Naranjo at 5:15 A.M. and 1 P.M. daily; for Sámara 13 times daily 5 A.M.–9:45 P.M.; and for Nosara at 5 A.M., 10 A.M., noon, and 3 P.M. daily. Buses also serve other towns throughout the peninsula.

SANTA CRUZ

This small town, 20 kilometers north of Nicoya, is the "National Folklore City" and a gateway to Playas Tamarindo and Junquillal, 30 kilometers to the west. Santa Cruz is renowned for its traditional music, food, and dance, which can be sampled during *fiestas cívicas* each January 15 and July 25.

The ruin of an old church (toppled by an earthquake in 1950) stands next to its modern replacement with a star-shaped roof and beautiful stained glass. The leafy plaza—**Parque Central**—boasts a Mayan-style cupola, lampshades with Mayan motifs, and monuments on each corner, including a "bucking bronco" (cowboy) on the northeast.

Diría National Park (Parque Nacional Diría, tel. 506/2680-1820, $10 entrance), covering 2,840 hectares of montane forests, including cloud forest, along the spine of the Nicoya mountains, lies 14 kilometers south of town. It has camping and trails.

Accommodations

A good deal is the motel-style **Hotel La Estancia** (tel./fax 506/2680-0476, $18 s or $25 d with fans, $23 s or $35 d with a/c), which has 15 pleasing modern units with fans, TVs, and private baths with hot water. Spacious family rooms have four beds. Some rooms are dark. There is secure parking.

Hotel La Rampa (tel. 506/2680-0586) competes and is similar.

Outshining all contenders is the **Hotel La Calle de Alcalá** (tel. 506/2680-0000, fax 506/2680-1633, $25 s, $40 d, $60 junior suite, $70 suite with whirlpool tub), one block south of Plaza de los Mangos. This Spanish-run hotel boasts a lively contempo decor and pleasing aesthetic. It has 29 air-conditioned rooms with cable TVs, bamboo furnishings, and pastels. They're set around an attractive swimming pool with swim-up bar. It has secure parking.

Food

For rustic ambience, try **Restaurante La Yunta** (tel. 506/2680-3031, 11 A.M.–11 P.M. Mon.–Sat., $2–10), facing Parque Ramos, in an old farmhouse-style building decorated in farm implements. It serves shrimp, lobster, octopus, and other seafood.

The most elegant restaurant in town is at **Hotel La Calle de Alcalá** (tel. 506/2680-0000, 7 A.M.–10 P.M.) serving *típico* dishes and seafood such as octopus in garlic ($8), plus filet mignon ($12). You'll also like **Casa Fonda** (tel. 506/2680-4949, 6 A.M.–10 P.M. Mon.–Sat., $2–10), facing Parque de los Mangos. Clean, modern, and open-air, this lovely spot serves ceviche ($3.50), soups, pastas, great seafood ($8), and even filet mignon ($9.50).

And the clean, modern **Ristorante Pizzería Da Giovanni** (tel. 2680-4128, 11 A.M.–10 P.M. Mon.–Sat.), on the main highway, will satisfy pizza cravings.

For baked goods, try **Musmanni,** 50 meters north of the main plaza.

Information and Services

MINAE (tel./fax 506/2680-1820 or 506/2680-1930, 8 A.M.–4 P.M. Mon.–Fri.) has a regional sub-office on the highway. However, it is not set up to assist tourists.

There are **banks** on Highway 21 at the entrance to town and on the north side of the main plaza. The **post office** is two blocks northeast of the main plaza.

The **Red Cross** is on the west side of the plaza. The **police station** (tel. 506/2680-0136) is on the northwest side of the bus station.

Cybermania (tel. 506/2680-4520, 8:30 A.M.–9:30 P.M. Mon.–Sat., 9 A.M.–8:30 P.M. Sun.), one block north of the main plaza, offers Internet service.

Getting There

Tracopa (tel. 506/2222-2666) buses depart

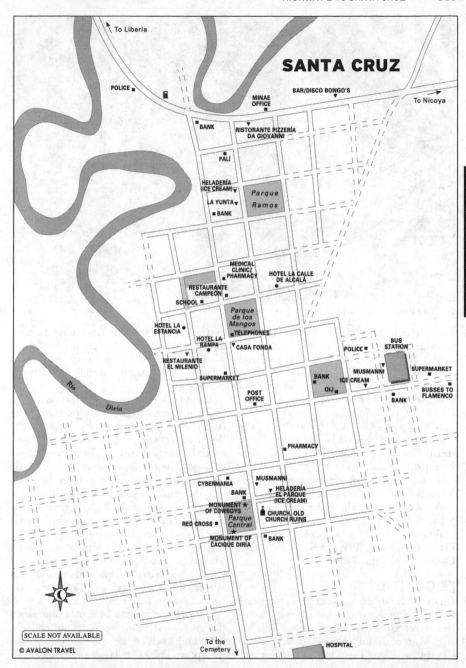

To Liberia

POLICE

SANTA CRUZ

MINAE OFFICE

BAR/DISCO BONGO'S

To Nicoya

BANK

RISTORANTE PIZZERÍA DA GIOVANNI

PALÍ

HELADERÍA (ICE CREAM)

LA YUNTA

BANK

Parque Ramos

MEDICAL CLINIC/ PHARMACY

HOTEL LA CALLE DE ALCALÁ

RESTAURANTE CAMPEÓN

SCHOOL

Parque de los Mangos

HOTEL LA ESTANCIA

HOTEL LA RAMPA

TELEPHONES

CASA FONDA

RESTAURANTE EL MILENIO

SUPERMARKET

POLICE

BUS STATION

SUPERMARKET

MUSMANNI ICE CREAM

BANK

OIJ

BANK

BUSSES TO FLAMENCO

POST OFFICE

Río Diría

PHARMACY

CYBERMANIA

BANK

MUSMANNI

HELADERÍA EL PARQUE (ICE CREAM)

MONUMENT OF COWBOYS ★

RED CROSS

Parque Central ★

CHURCH, OLD CHURCH RUINS

MONUMENT OF CACIQUE DIRÍA

BANK

SCALE NOT AVAILABLE

© AVALON TRAVEL

To the Cemetery

HOSPITAL

© CHRISTOPHER P. BAKER

crafting traditional pottery at the Oven Store, Guaitíl

San José for Santa Cruz from Calle 14, Avenida 5 at 6:30 A.M., 10 A.M., 1:30 P.M., 3 P.M., and 5 P.M. daily ($5). Tralapa buses (tel. 506/2223-5859) depart San José for Santa Cruz from Calle 20, Avenidas 3/5, at seven times daily. Buses (tel. 506/665-5891) for Santa Cruz depart Liberia every 30 minutes 4:30 A.M.–8:30 P.M. (returning at the same time); from Nicoya hourly 6 A.M.–9 P.M. (returning at the same time); and from Puntarenas at 6 A.M. and 4 P.M. daily.

Tracopa buses depart Santa Cruz for San José at 3 A.M., 5 A.M., 6:30 A.M., 10:30 A.M., and 1:30 P.M. daily; Tralapa buses depart at 4:30 A.M., 5 A.M., 8:30 A.M., 11:30 A.M., and 5 P.M. daily.

Buses also depart Santa Cruz for Puntarenas, Playa Junquillal, Playa Flamingo, Playa Ostional, and Tamarindo.

◖ GUAITÍL

Guaitíl, 12 kilometers east of Santa Cruz (the turnoff from the main highway is two kilometers east of Santa Cruz), is a tranquil little village. Many of the inhabitants—descendants of Chorotegas—have been making their unique pottery of red or black or ocher using the same methods for generations, turning the clay on wheels and polishing the pottery with small jadelike grinding stones taken from nearby archaeological sites.

There are several artists' families, including in the adjacent village of San Vicente. (Every family seems to be attended by the matriarch: Women run the businesses and sustain families and village structures.) The women happily take you to the back of the house to see the large open-hearth kilns where the pots are fired.

Unfortunately, tour operators all stop at **Willy's,** because of the high commissions it pays, to the detriment of other retailers. If your tour bus stops here, move on to give other retailers a chance! My favorite place is the **Oven Store** (tel. 506/2681-1696, sjchlv@hotmail .com), where friendly owners Susan and Jesús offer five-hour pottery classes; it's on the northwest side of the soccer field.

The **Ecomuseo de la Cerámica Chorotega** (tel. 506/2681-1214, www.ecomuseodesan vicente.org), behind the school in San Vicente, was opened in 2007 to honor the local culture.

THE NICOYA PENINSULA

© CHRISTOPHER P. BAKER

the author with a tapir at Tempisque Safari Ecological Adventure

Inspired by U.S. Peace Corps volunteers, it traces the ceramic tradition.

Getting There

Buses depart Santa Cruz for Guaitíl every two hours 7 A.M.–7 P.M. Mon.–Sat., 7 A.M.–2 P.M. Sunday. Hotels and tour companies throughout Nicoya also offer tours, as do some tour companies in San José.

PUERTO HUMO AND VICINITY

Puerto Humo is a small village on the west bank of the Río Tempisque, about 12 kilometers north of Barra Honda and most easily reached from the town of Nicoya (26 km). The bird-watching hereabouts is splendid. Puerto Humo is a gateway to Palo Verde National Park, across the river. **Aventuras Arenal** (tel. 506/2698-1142) offers boat trips ($45 pp with lunch).

The dirt road continues about five kilometers to the hamlet of Rosario, then peters out three kilometers farther along at the entrance (no facilities) to **Mata Redonda National Wildlife Refuge** (Refugio Nacional de Visa Silvestre Mata Redonda).

◖ Tempisque Safari Ecological Adventure

This fabulous facility (tel. 506/2698-1069, www.tempisquesafaricr.com, 10 A.M.–5 P.M. daily, $20 pp), hidden off the beaten track a kilometer beyond Rosario, is a total surprise and delight. Although part of a working cattle ranch, its highlight is the animal rescue and breeding center where snakes, monkeys, peccaries, tapirs, and cats such as the jaguarundi and margay are displayed in large cages. The crocodile lagoon is the real thing, and you'll be surprised to find yourself accompanied along the paths by free-strutting deer, rheas, and emus! There are even ostrich, capybara, and bison. A three-hour guided tour ($50 pp, minimum four people) is offered with a cart pulled by water buffalo, followed by a boat tour of the river. If the gates are closed, the *custodio* (guard) who lives opposite the entrance, will open up.

Getting There

A bus serves Puerto Humo twice daily, departing Nicoya township at 10 A.M., 3 P.M., and 6 P.M.

Playas del Coco and Vicinity

BAHÍA CULEBRA

Nicoya's most northerly beaches ring the horse-shoe-shaped Bahía Culebra (Snake Bay), enclosed to the north by the Nacascolo Peninsula, and to the south by the headland of Punta Ballena. The huge bay is a natural amphitheater rimmed by scarp cliffs cut with lonesome coves sheltering gray- and white-sand beaches and small mangrove swamps. There are remains of a pre-Columbian native settlement on the western shore of the bay at Nacascolo.

The north and south sides are approached separately by a pincer movement. The south side is reached via the road from Comunidad to Playa del Coco (the road divides two kilometers east of Playas del Coco; a turnoff leads three kilometers north to Playa Hermosa and, beyond Punta Ballena, to Playa Panamá). The north shore is reached from two kilometers north of Comunidad via a road immediately west of the Río Tempisque at Guardia. This road is a fast, sweeping, well-paved, lonesome beauty of a drive that dead-ends after 15 kilometers or so at the spectacular Four Seasons resort (no entry except to guests). En route you pass **Witch's Rock Canopy Tour** (tel. 506/2696-7101, http://witchsrockcanopytour.com, 8 A.M.–5 P.M. daily, last entry at 3:30 P.M.), 18 kilometers from Guardia. It has 23 platforms over a 2.5-kilometer course with four hanging bridges and even a tunnel ($55).

Marina Papagayo opened in December 2008 at Playa Manzanillo with 180 slips.

Playa Carbonal, immediately east of the bay, hosts the super-exclusive, members-only **Ellerstina Costa Rica Polo & Equestrian Beach Club** (tel. 506/2258-9219, http://ellerstinacr.com).

Accommodations

The **Occidental Allegro Papagayo** (tel. 506/2690-9900 or U.S. tel. 800/858-2258, www.occidental-hoteles.com, $286 s/d) overlooks Playa Manzanillo from a superb

---

THE GULF OF PAPAGAYO PROJECT

In 1993, the Costa Rican Tourism Institute (ICT) began to push roads into the hitherto inaccessible Nacascolo Peninsula. The government also leased 2,000 hectares surrounding the bay as part of the long-troubled Gulf of Papagayo Tourism Project of the ICT, begun in 1974 but left to languish until a few years ago, when development suddenly took off exponentially with the enthusiastic backing of the Rafael Calderón administration. The mini-Cancún that began to emerge was intended to push Costa Rica into the big leagues of resort tourism.

Headed by Grupo Papagayo, a conglomerate of independent companies headed by Mexico's Grupo Situr, the 88-kilometer-long coastal concession was planned as a 15-year development. Developers and environmentalists squared off over the project. An independent review panel expressed concern about illegal activities and environmental degradation. In March 1995, the former tourism minister and 12 other senior ICT officials were indicted as charges of corruption began to fly.

The Nacascolo Peninsula is an area of archaeological importance with many pre-Columbian sites. When it was discovered that the bulldozers were plowing heedlessly, the government issued an executive decree to declare the peninsula a place of historic importance. To improve its image, the Grupo changed the name of the project to Ecodesarollo Papagayo, or Papagayo Eco-Development. Then the company went bankrupt, bursting the Papagayo bubble. The bulldozers remained idle. In 1999, North American investors took over and more conscientious development resulted in the opening, in 2004, of the Four Seasons Papagayo resort. Development is ongoing.

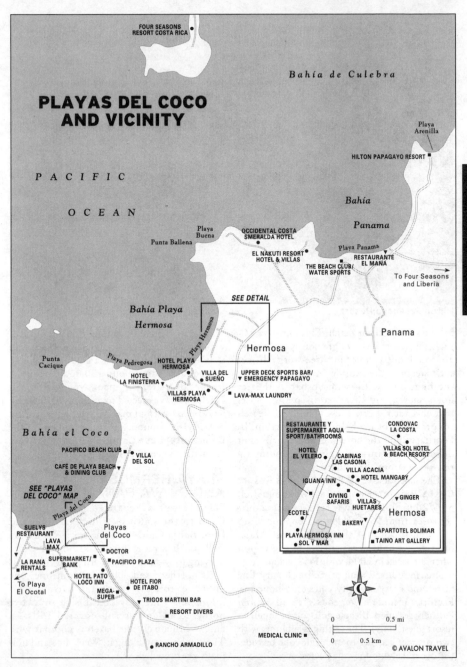

THE NICOYA PENINSULA

FOUR SEASONS
RESORT COSTA RICA

Bahía de Culebra

PLAYAS DEL COCO
AND VICINITY

Playa
Arenilla

HILTON PAPAGAYO RESORT

P A C I F I C

Bahía

O C E A N

Panama

Playa
Buena

OCCIDENTAL COSTA
SMERALDA HOTEL

Punta Ballena

Playa Panama

EL NAKUTI RESORT
HOTEL & VILLAS

RESTAURANTE
EL MANA

THE BEACH CLUB/
WATER SPORTS

To Four Seasons
and Liberia

Bahía Playa

SEE DETAIL

Hermosa

Playa Hermosa

Hermosa

Panama

Punta
Cacique

Playa Pedregosa

HOTEL PLAYA
HERMOSA

HOTEL
LA FINISTERRA

VILLA DEL
SUEÑO

UPPER DECK SPORTS BAR/
EMERGENCY PAPAGAYO

VILLAS PLAYA
HERMOSA

LAVA-MAX LAUNDRY

Bahía el Coco

PACIFICO BEACH CLUB

VILLA
DEL SOL

CAFÉ DE PLAYA BEACH
& DINING CLUB

SEE "PLAYAS
DEL COCO" MAP

Playa del Coco

SUELYS
RESTAURANT

LAVA
MAX

Playas
del Coco

DOCTOR

LA RANA
RENTALS

SUPERMARKET/
BANK

PACIFICO PLAZA

To Playa
El Ocotal

HOTEL PATO
LOCO INN

HOTEL FIOR
DE ITABO

MEGA-
SUPER

TRIGOS MARTINI BAR

RESORT DIVERS

MEDICAL CLINIC

RANCHO ARMADILLO

0   0.5 mi

0   0.5 km

© AVALON TRAVEL

Hermosa detail

RESTAURANTE Y
SUPERMARKET AQUA
SPORT/BATHROOMS

CONDOVAC
LA COSTA

HOTEL
EL VELERO

CABINAS
LAS CASONA

VILLAS SOL HOTEL
& BEACH RESORT

VILLA ACACIA

IGUANA INN

HOTEL MANGABY

DIVING
SAFARIS

VILLAS
HUETARES

GINGER

ECOTEL

Hermosa

BAKERY

PLAYA HERMOSA INN

APARTOTEL BOLIMAR

SOL Y MAR

TAINO ART GALLERY

© CHRISTOPHER P. BAKER

Hilton Papagayo Resort

breeze-swept hillside perch. This four-star, all-inclusive resort has 308 graciously appointed air-conditioned rooms in three-story edifices stair-stepping the hillside. Action centers on the huge pool with swim-up bar. A theater hosts shows, and there's a disco and sports bar, plus water sports and scuba. Alas, the paltry gray-sand beach holds little attraction. In February 2008 the hotel was temporarily shut down by the Ministry of Health for pumping raw sewage into the estuary.

The super-deluxe 《 **Four Seasons Resort Costa Rica at Peninsula Papagayo** (tel. 506/2696-0500, www.fourseasons.com/costarica, from $675 s/d low season, from $815 s/d high season), at the tip of Punta Mala, brought a whole new panache to the region when it opened in 2004, with 145 spacious guest rooms, including 25 suites, exuding luxury, fine taste, and every amenity you could hope for. Facilities include a gorgeous spa and Arnold Palmer–designed 18-hole golf course (open to resort guests only). The setting is sublime, with two distinct beaches to each side (one bayside, the other shelving into the Pacific ocean).

A super-deluxe **Fairmont** is also planned, with a marina and new golf course. **Mandarin Oriental** is slated to open a deluxe hotel, and the equally sumptuous 120-room **Regent Resort at La Punta Papagayo** (www.regent hotels.com) is expected to open by 2010 with a world-class spa and massive retail village. And at last visit, ground was to be broken on the **Condohotel Casa Conde del Mar** (www.casa condedelmar.com) at Playa Chorotega.

PLAYA HERMOSA AND PLAYA PANAMÁ

Playa Hermosa, separated from Playa del Coco to the south by Punta Cacique and from Bahía Culebra to the north by Punta Ballena, is a pleasant two-kilometer-wide, curving gray-sand beach with good tidepools at its northern end. The road continues one kilometer to Playa Panamá, a narrow, two-kilometers-wide gray-sand beach in a cove bordered by low, scrub-covered hills—a bay within a bay. The beach is popular with Ticos, who camp along it. Weekends and holidays get crowded.

The road dead-ends atop the headland overlooking **Playa Arenilla** and Bahía Culebra. The much-troubled **Cacique del Mar** residential project atop Punta Cacique has been resurrected and is slated to host two five-star boutique hotels.

Entertainment

Villas del Sueño has live bands three nights weekly in high season, plus guest appearances in low season. Sports fans might check out the charmless, overly air-conditioned **Upperdeck Bar** (tel. 506/2672-1276, 9 A.M.–2 A.M. daily).

Tours and Activities

Diving Safaris (tel. 506/2672-1259, www.costaricadiving.net) has daily two-tank dive trips ($65), night and Nitrox dives, and certification courses. Snorkelers can accompany dive boats ($30). **Resort Divers de Costa Rica** (tel. 506/2670-0421, www.resortdivers-cr.com) offers surfing trips and sportfishing as well as snorkeling and scuba trips.

Aqua Sport (tel. 506/2670-0050, samaci@racsa.co.cr) offers all manner of water sports, plus boat tours and fishing. And **Velas de Papagayo** (tel. 506/2223-2508, www.velasdepapagayo.com, $100 pp) has snorkeling, sunset, and nighttime sailing trips out of Playa Panamá, where **Water Sports** (tel. 506/2672-0012) has water-skiing and personal watercraft.

Accommodations

CAMPING
You can camp at **Restaurante El Mama**, 200 meters inland of the beach at Playa Panamá.

$25-50
The no-frills **Iguana Inn** (tel. 506/2672-0065, $20 s, $30 d), in the heart of Hermosa, is a popular surf camp with 10 simple rooms with private bathrooms in a two-story wooden lodge 100 meters from the beach. Its Jammin' Restaurant is a popular spot.

Nearby, backpackers might try the German-owned **Cabinas Las Casona** (tel. 506/2672-0025, $28 s/d low season, $38 s/d high season), an old wooden home that has eight simple but clean rooms with fans, small kitchenettes, and private baths with cold water.

$50-100
Nearby, the modern **Hotel ManGaby** (tel. 506/2672-0048, www.hotelmangaby.com, $72 s/d standard, $94 mini-suite, $172 suite low season; $102 s/d standard, $118 mini-suite, $197 suite high season) is a perfectly adequate option in the mid-price category, with pleasantly furnished rooms and a swimming pool.

Directly overlooking Playa Hermosa, **Hotel El Velero** (tel. 506/2672-1017, www.costaricahotel.net, $75 s/d low season, $89 high season) is an intimate Spanish colonial-style hostelry with 22 modestly appointed, air-conditioned rooms (some also have fans). The hotel has both upstairs and downstairs restaurants open to the breezes, plus a boutique and a small pool surrounded by shady palms. The hotel offers tours and scuba diving.

At the south end of Hermosa, you can't go wrong at the splendid Canadian-run **Villa del Sueño** (tel. 506/2672-0026 or U.S. tel. 800/378-8599, www.villadelsueno.com, $65 s/d standard, $89 superior, $109 junior suite low season; $75 s/d standard, $105 superior, $130 junior suite high season), an exquisite Spanish colonial-style building offering six air-conditioned rooms in the main house and eight rooms in two two-story, whitewashed stone buildings surrounding a lushly landscaped courtyard with a swimming pool. The rooms boast terra-cotta tiled floors, lofty hardwood ceilings with fans, large picture windows, contemporary artwork, beautiful batik fabrics, bamboo furniture, and pastels. The gourmet restaurant hosts live music.

Also to consider are the charming **Villa Acacia** (tel. 506/2672-1000, www.villacacia.com), with eight villas and a swimming pool; the upscale self-catering **Villas Playa Hermosa** (tel. 506/2672-1239, www.villasplayhermosa.com); the less impressive **Playa Hermosa Inn** (tel. 506/2672-0050, fax 506/2672-0060); and, if you're seeking a self-catering option, **Hotel & Villas Huetares** (tel. 506/2672-0052, www.villahuetares.com, $45 s/d room, $80 s/d villa low season; $80 s/d room, $135 s/d villa high season), an apartment-style complex of 15 two-bedroom bungalows in lush grounds.

The large-scale **Condovac La Costa** (tel. 506/2527-4000, www.condovac.com, from $75 s, $95 d, including breakfast) commands the hill at the northern end of the beach and appeals mainly to Ticos. It offers 101 air-conditioned villas, plus there's a selection of bars and restaurants, a full complement of tours, sportfishing, and scuba diving.

The former Costa Blanca del Pacifico is now the **Monarch Resort Hotel** (tel. 506/2672-1363, www.monarchresortonline.com, $109 s/d low season, $149 s/d high season), with suites furnished in elegant contemporary fashion. Its lofty perch atop the headland guarantees fine vistas.

$100-150

Another winner is the bargain-priced, Canadian-owned **Hotel La Finisterra** (tel. 506/2670-0227, www.lafinisterra.com, $90 s/d low season, $110 s/d high season), a handsome contemporary structure atop the breezy headland at the south end of the beach. What views! The 10 simply furnished yet delightful air-conditioned rooms boast fans, attractive bamboo furniture, and wide, screened windows; some have forest (not beach) views. The open-sided restaurant looks over a charming irregular-shaped swimming pool. The owners have a 38-foot sailboat ($60 for a full-day tour); sportfishing tours are arranged. Rates include full breakfast.

For an all-inclusive bargain consider **El Nakuti Resort Hotel & Villas** (tel. 506/2672-1212, www.nakutiresort.com, $75 s or $120 d low season, $95 s or $150 d high season), a handsome modern property with 97 rooms in thatched air-conditioned chalets arrayed in the style of an indigenous village in landscaped grounds. Sponge-washed walls in warm ocher shades enhance the mood. Each bungalow has a separate living room with kitchen. There's a large pool and kids' pool. It has sea kayaks, snorkeling, water-skiing, sunset cruises, plus mountain bike and ATV rentals. Rates include tax.

$150-200

Wearing an exciting new livery, **C Hotel Playa Hermosa** (tel./fax 506/2672-0046, www.hotelplayahermosa.com, $125 s/d junior suite, $150–175 suites low season; $175 s/d junior suite, $225–275 suites high season), at the southern end of the beach, has been turned into the class act in Playa Hermosa. Still in the works at last visit, the new twin-level suites are built around a gorgeous walk-in swimming pool and half-moon wooden sundeck shaded by a giant *guanacaste* tree. Designed with a graceful Balinese motif, the rooms have their own balconies overlooking the pool. It will have 38 junior suites when complete, and at last visit the old beachfront standard rooms were in the midst of being replaced by six smashing new rooms in a three-story tower with new restaurant and lounge-bar.

If all-inclusive resort elegance is your thing, **Villas Sol Hotel & Beach Resort** (tel. 506/2257-067, www.villassol.com, $574 standard, $828 one-bedroom villa for two nights minimum), next to Condovac La Costa, has 54 deluxe hotel rooms and 106 attractive villas (24 with private pools) recently refurbished in fashionably contemporary vogue, including flat-screen TVs, and modern amenities. There's a swimming pool, three restaurants, and a disco, and water sports and other activities are included.

OVER $200

At Playa Buena, the beautiful and expansive all-inclusive **Occidental Gran Papagayo** (tel. 506/2672-0193, www.occidental-hoteles.com, $392 s/d high season) draws a mostly Tico clientele. The 169 beautiful, air-conditioned bungalows (with seven types of rooms) stair-step down grassy lawns. Hardwoods and terra-cotta tiles abound. Plate-glass walls and doors proffer priceless vistas. Suites have mezzanine bedrooms and king-size beds, plus deep sea-green marble in the bathrooms, which have whirlpool tubs. It has two restaurants and a large pool set like a jewel on the slopes. There's a tennis court and shops, plus scuba diving and tours. Call for varying rates.

Sensational! That's the term for the marvelously situated **(Hilton Papagayo Resort** (tel. 506/2672-0000, www.hilton.com, from $369 s/d), a sprawling all-inclusive with 202 rooms, suites, and bungalows nestled on the scarp face overlooking Playa Arenilla, immediately north of Playa Panamá. This remarkable remake of the former Fiesta resort is stylish and sophisticated, beginning in the open-air lobby that offers tantalizing views over the bay. Its infinity pool and handsome use of thatch are pluses, as are the gorgeous bedrooms with sophisticated contemporary styling, quality linens, flat-screen TVs, in-room safes, and other modern conveniences. Three restaurants include an Italian open-air dining room under soaring thatch, the thatched beachfront grill, and the chic La Consecha, serving gourmet fusion fare. There's a great spa.

Westin plans to build a super-deluxe hotel. And the deluxe **Miraval Life in Balance** and **One and Only** boutique hotels are planned for Cacique del Mar.

Food

For simple surrounds on the sands, head to **Restaurant Valle's Mar** (tel. 506/8896-3694, 10 A.M.–9 P.M.). It serves hearty seafood dishes, such as ceviche, fried calamari ($8), and grilled mahimahi with garlic ($8).

The best food for miles is served at **(Ginger** (tel. 506/2672-0041, 5–10 P.M. Tues.–Sun., $5–20), beside the main road in the heart of Hermosa. This chic and contemporary tapas bar is run by Canadian chef Anne Hegney Frey. Striking for its minimalist design, with a trapezoidal bar, walls of glass, and cantilevered glass roof, it also delivers fantastic food. Try the ginger rolls, fried calamari, or superb ginger ahi tuna. Two-for-one sushi rolls are served 5–10 P.M. Friday. My martini was ridiculously small for the price, however.

I also recommend **Villas del Sueño** hotel restaurant (tel. 506/2672-0026), where the rotating daily menu may include scallopini parmesan, tenderloin with brandy and three-pepper sauce, mahimahi with shrimp and cream sauce ($15.50), and profiteroles ($5–13).

Elegant place settings, low lighting, and mellow music enhance the atmosphere. It does special dinners.

Similarly, **The Bistro** (tel. 506/2670-0227, 10 A.M.–10 P.M. daily), at Hotel Finisterra, is open to the public, with a creative French chef conjuring Caesar salad ($3.50), filet mignon with peppercorn sauce ($10), and daily pastas. Friday is sushi night. It earns rave reviews and draws diners from afar.

Restaurante Aqua Sport (tel. 506/2672-0050, 9 A.M.–9 P.M.) has a pleasing thatched beachfront restaurant at Playa Hermosa, with crepes, ceviche, salads, and a wide-ranging seafood menu.

Information and Services

Aqua Sport has a public telephone, souvenir shop, and general store (6 A.M.–9 P.M. daily). The **Emergencias Papagayo** (tel. 506/2670-0047) medical clinic is on the main road, alongside **Lavandería Lava Max** (tel. 506/2672-0136) laundry; and **Lavandería Bolimar** (8 A.M.–5 P.M. Mon.–Fri.) 100 meters farther north. Villa Acacia (tel. 506/2672-1000, www.villacacia.com) has an Internet café.

Getting There

A bus departs San José for Playa Hermosa and Panamá from Calle 20, Avenidas 1/3, daily at 3.25 P.M. (five hours). Buses depart Liberia for Playa Hermosa seven times daily, 5:30 A.M.–7:30 P.M. Buses depart Hermosa for San José at 5:10 A.M., and for Liberia seven times daily 6:10 A.M.–7:10 P.M.

A taxi from Coco will run about $5 one-way; from Liberia about $15.

PLAYAS DEL COCO

Playas del Coco, 35 kilometers west of Liberia, is one of the most accessible beach resorts in Guanacaste. The place can be crowded during weekends and holidays, when Josefinos flock. A two-kilometer-wide gray-sand beach (it is referred to in the plural—Playas del Coco) lines the horseshoe-shaped bay. Coco is still an active fishing village; the touristy area is to the east, and the laid-back fishing village is to the west.

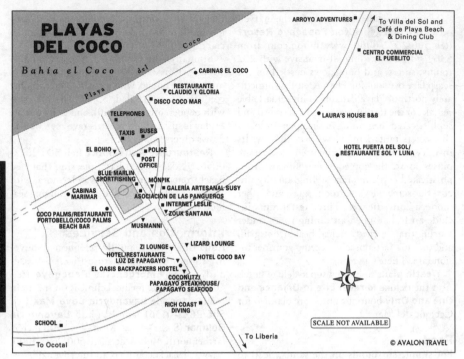

Playas del Coco is also a center for scuba diving.

The past few years have seen an incredible boom in real estate development. Meanwhile, in 2008 the local municipality bulldozed much of the shorefront property, which as a boon opened up more of the beach to view. At last visit, construction of the **Marina Punta Cacique** was slated to begin in 2009.

Entertainment and Events

Coco is a lively spot and hosts a five-day *fiesta cívica* in late January, with bullfights, rodeos, and folkloric dancing.

The most-fun spot is the open-air **Coconutz Sports Bar** (tel. 506/2670-1981, http://coconutz-cr.com), which shows alfresco movies on a big screen and has live music on Friday, Saturday, and Monday. It serves pizza and Tex-Mex.

The **Lizard Lounge** (tel. 506/2670-0307, www.lizardloungecr.com) has a pool table, plus a happy hour 5–7 P.M. daily. Wednesday is Italian night; Thursday is Ladies Night; and you're offered $2 shots Friday and Saturday.

The tiny, Italian-run **Zouk Santana** (tel. 506/2670-0191, www.zouksantana.com, 7:30 A.M.–11:30 A.M. daily) is a sophisticated spot for supping and enjoying a cigar, sold on-site. The same owners run the hip **Café de Playa** (tel. 506/2670-1621, www.cafedeplaya.com, 7 A.M.–midnight daily), a beach club where a DJs spin tunes and special theme parties are hosted.

The hip new **Tragos Martini Bar,** scheduled to open at last visit, also reflects the area's increasingly upscale trend. And the **Coco Palms Beach Bar** (2–9 P.M.), on the west side of the soccer field, is a nice spot for a quiet drink.

Later at night, the budget crowd and locals gravitate to the **Disco Coco Mar** (tel. 506/2670-0358), a no-frills disco on Saturday, and karaoke other nights.

Gamblers can try their hand with Lady Luck

at the small **casinos** in Hotel Flor de Itabo (506/2670-0290, 8 P.M.–2 A.M. daily).

Tours and Activities

The **Asociación de las Pangueros** (tel. 506/2670-0228, rocasurf@hotmail.com), the local fishermen's association, offers boats and guide services. **Rich Coast Diving** (tel./fax 506/2670-0176, www.richcoastdiving.com) has a full-service dive center, plus a 35-foot trimaran for charter. **Summer Salt Dive Center** (tel. 506/2670-0308, www.summer-salt.com) also has snorkel rental plus dive trips. **Coco Sea Sport** (tel. 506/2670-1514, www.cocoseasport.com) has personal watercraft rental, yacht charter, and snorkeling.

A fun day trip is to cruise the local beaches with **Arroyo Adventures** (tel. 506/2670-0239, www.grupomapache.com), which also offers sportfishing.

Hacienda Chapernal (tel. 506/2273-4545, www.elchapernal.com), four kilometers southeast of Sardinal, is a working cattle ranch offering horseback riding, plus folkloric music and dance.

Accommodations

UNDER $25

Backpackers give a thumbs up to **El Oasis Backpackers Hostel** (tel. 506/2670-0501, www.eloasiscostarica.com, $13 pp low season, $15 pp high season), new in 2008 and tucked behind Papagayo Steak House in a garden with hammocks beneath palms. It has three spacious air-conditioned dorms with ceiling fans and modern bathrooms. It has a communal kitchen, lockers, and a pleasant TV lounge with Internet, plus DVD library, a laundry, and bikes and snorkeling gear for rent.

The **Cabinas Marimar** (tel. 506/2670-1212, $15 pp), facing the beach, has 17 no-frills rooms with fans and private baths with cold water only.

$25-50

The ever-evolving **Coco Palms** (tel. 506/2670-0367, www.hotelcocopalms.com, $35–60 s/d rooms, $80–150 apartments low season; call for high season rates), on the west side of the soccer field, offers 48 spacious, adequately furnished air-conditioned rooms arrayed along an atrium corridor, all with fans, cable TV, and Wi-Fi. Some have whirlpool tubs and kitchens or kitchenettes. There's a lap pool and the delightful Restaurante Coco Sushi.

The pleasing, Italian-run **Hotel Pato Loco Inn** (tel./fax 506/670-0145, patoloco@racsa.co.cr, $35 s/d with fan, $45 with a/c low season; $40 s/d with fan, $50 with a/c high season), 800 meters inland on the main drag, has attractive rooms—three triples, one double, and two fully equipped apartments—with orthopedic mattresses, central air-conditioning, and modest furnishings with hardwood accents. There's a small but quality Italian restaurant.

New in 2008, and also to consider in this price bracket, is **Hotel Luz de Papagayo** (tel. 506/2670-0400, fax 506/2670-0319), with six nicely furnished upstairs rooms.

$50-100

The beachfront **Cabinas El Coco** (tel. 506/2670-0230, fax 506/2670-0276, cabinaselcoco@racsa.co.cr, $50 s/d low season, $100 s/d high season) has been remodeled but remains unimpressive and is now ridiculously overpriced.

Laura's House B&B (tel. 506/2670-0751, www.laurashousecr.net, $50 s, $60 d) is run by a delightful young Tica and offers seven lovely albeit simply furnished air-conditioned rooms in a two-story house, all with ceiling fans and clean private bathrooms. Downstairs rooms are pleasingly cool; some have bunks. There's a pool in the courtyard with hammocks, plus Wi-Fi and parking.

Farther east, the **Villa del Sol** (tel. 506/8301-8848, www.villadelsol.com, $45–50 s, $55–65 d low season; $50–65 s, $65–75 d high season), set amid lawns, is a homey bed-and-breakfast with an open atrium lounge. Seven air-conditioned rooms vary considerably, though all have ceiling fans and simple decor blessed with lively colors. Five have private bathrooms and balconies plus king-size bed. It also offers six new studio apartments.

There's a swimming pool and whirlpool tub. It has secure parking.

I love 【 **Hotel Puerta del Sol** (tel. 506/2670-0195, fax 506/2670-0650, no website, $45 s or $65 d standard, $85 suites low season; $55 s or $85 d standard, $110 suites high season), an intimate hotel with an Italian aesthetic. The 10 whitewashed air-conditioned rooms (with tropical pastels in counterpoint) feature soft-contoured walls enveloping king-size beds and melding into wraparound sofas built into the walls. All have ceiling fans, TVs, phones, safes, fridges, coffeemakers, and patios. Two are suites with refrigerators, and *casitas* have full kitchens. A small airy lounge has games and a TV, and there's a garden with a charming lap pool and gym. The restaurant excels. Free scuba lessons are offered in the pool. Rates include breakfast.

Sportfishing fans should head to **Hotel Flor de Itabo** (tel. 506/2670-0290, www.florde itabo.com, $55 s or $65 d standard, $85–105 s/d deluxe, $145 villas low season; $70 s or $85 d standard, $105–135 s/d deluxe, $145 villas high season), about one kilometer before Coco. It has 10 spacious standard rooms, seven deluxe rooms with whirlpool tubs, and eight bungalow apartments. The Sailfish Restaurant opens onto a pool in landscaped grounds full of parrots and macaws. There's also a casino. The hotel specializes in fishing trips.

For peaceful seclusion, I recommend **Rancho Armadillo** (tel. 506/2670-0108, www.ranchoarmadillo.com, $100–146 s/d low season, $145–200 high season). This beautiful Spanish-colonial-style hacienda, on a 10-hectare hillside *finca* 1.5 kilometers from the beach, has six spacious air-conditioned bungalows, including a two-bedroom suite. All have fans, magnificent hardwood furniture, wrought-iron balustrades, lofty wooden ceilings, hardwood floors, colorful Guatemalan bedspreads, stained-glass windows, "rainforest" showers, coffeemakers, refrigerators, and cable TV. There's also a house for families or groups, plus an open-air kitchen beside the swimming pool, a gym, a *mirador* lounge with hammocks and rockers, and a library. Meals are offered

by request. The estate is available for exclusive rental during peak season, with Rick, the owner, as chef (he was for years a professional chef). Rates include breakfast.

My favorite place to relax is the 【 **Café de Playa Beach & Dining Club** (tel. 506/2670-1621, www.cafedeplaya.com, $160 s/d low season, $200 s/d high season), a chic club with a circular swimming pool and "parachute" canopy over wooden sundeck and open-air sushi bar, plus lounge chairs on the beachfront lawn. It has a Hobie Cat and yacht. This hip conversion of the former Hotel Vista Mar has five totally remodeled rooms with a super contemporary aesthetic fitting for Manhattan or Beverly Hills. Each of the suites is distinct. And divine!

Food

Papagayo Steakhouse & Seafood (tel. 506/2670-0298, noon–10 P.M.) is a two-in-one restaurant: an open-air seafood restaurant downstairs and an air-conditioned one serving meats upstairs. The seafood menu includes sashimi and blackened Cajun-style catch of the day ($8–15). It also sells fresh fish at a streetside outlet.

Restaurante Coco Sushi (tel. 506/2670-0367, 11 A.M.–11 P.M. daily), on the west side of the soccer field, is a modestly elegant eatery with a creative menu featuring sautéed black tip shark, curry shrimp stir fry, and sushi and Japanese fare.

For prize Italian fare, head to **Restaurante Sol y Luna** (5–10 P.M. Wed.–Mon.) at Hotel Puerta del Sol; it serves homemade pastas ($5), cannelloni ($7.50), lasagna ($8), stuffed crepes, tiramisu, and daily specials, enjoyed amid exquisite Romanesque decor. It also serves cappuccinos and espressos, and has a large wine list and 15 types of beer.

If you want a truly classy ambience by the beach, check out **Café de Playa Beach & Dining Club** (tel. 506/2670-1621, www.cafede playa.com, 7 A.M.–midnight daily, $5–20). It serves great breakfasts and has a sushi bar, and the classy breeze-swept restaurant serves everything from salads and penne pastas to nouvelle seafood such as rum-sauce jumbo shrimp. In a similar vein, the beachfront **Restaurant Claudio y Gloria** (tel. 506/3670-1514, www.cocoseasport.com) competes with elegant place settings and an eclectic menu featuring ceviche, mahimahi with leek sauce ($13), and Peruvian dishes.

The tops in elegant dining, however, is the **Restaurant Pacifico Beach Club** (tel. 506/2670-2212, www.pacifico-costarica.com, 11 A.M.–3 P.M. daily, and 6–10 P.M. Fri.–Sun.), with a stately contemporary motif that includes an onyx-topped bar with flat-screen TVs. It serves tapas and Häagen-Daz ice cream.

Less pretentious, and my favorite place, is **Suely's Restaurant** (tel. 506/2670-1696, sti-costarica@hotmail.com, 11:30 A.M.–11 P.M. daily), one kilometer west of town. Run by two French sisters, it has a lovely ambience, with multitiered decks beneath shade trees. The changing menu might include tuna tartare ($5), gazpacho ($4), pan-seared brie ($6), crusted salmon ($7), and a seafood selection with jumbo shrimp, mussels, scallops and rice with saffron sauce on a bed of leek fondue. Leave room for the chocolate volcano.

Craving a cappuccino and a brownie sundae? Head to **Coco Coffee Co.** (tel. 506/2670-1055, 7 A.M.–4 P.M. Mon.–Sat.). It also has bagels, fruit plates, and salads.

Information and Services

The **post office** (8 A.M.–noon and 2–5:30 P.M. Mon.–Fri.) and **police station** (tel. 506/2670-0258) face the plaza, which has public telephones.

There's a **medical clinic** (tel. 506/2670-0047) about three kilometers east of town. The **Red Cross** (tel. 506/2670-0190) is in Sardinal, eight kilometers east of Playas del Coco.

For Internet, I use **Internet Leslie** (tel. 506/2670-0156, 8 A.M.–10 P.M. Mon.–Sat., 2–10 P.M. Sun.).

Lava Max (tel. 506/2670-1860, 8 A.M.–6 P.M. Mon.–Sat.) is the place to do laundry.

Getting There and Around

Pulmitan buses (tel. 506/2222-1650) depart San José for Playas del Coco from Avenida 5, Calles 24, daily at 8 A.M., 2 P.M., and 4 P.M. ($5.50, five hours), returning at 4 A.M., 8 A.M., and 2 P.M. Buses depart Liberia (Arata, tel. 506/2666-0138), for Coco eight times daily.

Interbus (tel. 506/2283-5573, www.inter busonline.com) operates minibus shuttles from San José ($35) and popular tourist destinations in Nicoya and Guanacaste.

Taxis (tel. 506/2670-0303) park by the plaza.

There's a gas station in Sardinal. **Adobe Rent-a-Car** (tel. 506/8811-4242, www.adobe car.com) has an office in Pacifico Plaza, and you can rent scooters at **La Rana Rentals** (tel. 506/2670-1312).

PLAYA EL OCOTAL

This secluded gray-sand beach is three kilometers southwest of Playa del Coco within the cusp of steep cliffs. It's smaller and more secluded than Coco, but it gets the overflow on busy weekends. The rocky headlands at each end have tidepools. Ocotal is a base for sportfishing and scuba diving. At Las Corridas, a dive spot only a kilometer from Ocotal, divers are sure of coming face-to-face with massive jewfish, which make this rock reef their home; black marlin are occasionally seen.

Ocotal Diving Safaris (tel. 506/2670-0321 ext. 120, www.ocotaldiving.com) rents equipment and offers various dive trips, including a free introductory dive daily, plus snorkeling. It also offers deep-sea fishing ($425 half day, $645 full day up to four people).

Accommodations

The bay is dominated by **El Ocotal Beach Resort & Marina** (tel. 506/2670-0321, www .ocotalresort.com, $120 s or $162 d standard, $241 s/d junior suite, $283 s/d suite low season; $157 s or $180 d standard, $278 s/d junior suite, $341 s/d suite high season), a gleaming whitewashed structure that stair-steps up the cliffs at the southern end of the beach. It has 71 attractive air-conditioned rooms with fans, freezers, two queen-size beds each, satellite TVs, direct-dial telephones, and ocean views. The original 12 rooms are in six duplex

© CHRISTOPHER P. BAKER

Playa el Ocotal

bungalows; newer rooms have their own whirl-pool tub, sunning area, and pool. Three small pools each have *ranchitos* for shade, and there are tennis courts and horseback riding, plus a fully equipped dive shop, sportfishing boats, and car rental.

Hotel Villa Casa Blanca (tel. 506/2670-448, www.hotelvillacasablanca.com, $85 s/d standard, $105 s/d suite low season; $195 s/d standard, $125 s/d suite high season) sets a standard for beachside bed-and-breakfasts, although at last visit the public structures were deteriorating. The upscale Spanish-style villa is set in a lush landscaped garden full of yuccas and bougainvillea. The small swimming pool has a swim-up bar and a sundeck with lounge chairs. Inside, the hotel epitomizes subdued elegance with its intimate allure: sponge-washed walls, four-poster beds (six rooms), stenciled murals, and massive bathrooms with deep tubs and wall-to-wall mirrors. The 14 rooms include four suites (two are honeymoon suites). You can relax in a whirlpool tub, and there's a patio restaurant and grill.

Food

The rustic and offbeat beachfront **【 Father Rooster Restaurant** (tel. 506/2670-1246, 11 A.M.–10 P.M. daily, $2–10) run by Steve, a friendly Floridian, is the hip, happening place to be. It serves seafood dishes, quesadillas, burgers, and Caesar salads, plus huge margaritas ($4.50). It has a sand volleyball court, pool table, darts, and occasional live music.

If you're feeling flush, try the cuisine at **El Ocotal Beach Resort** (tel. 506/2670-0321, www.ocotalresort.com), which one reader raves about.

Playa Flamingo and Vicinity

South of Playas del Coco are Playa Flamingo and a series of contiguous beaches accessed by paved road via the communities of **Portegolpe** and **Huacas** (reached from Hwy. 21 via Belén, 8 km south of Filadelfia). At Huacas, you turn right for Playas Brasilito, Flamingo, Potrero, Penca, and Azucar, where the road ends. If you don't turn right, the road keeps straight for **Matapalo,** where you turn right for Playa Conchal, and left for Playa Grande.

The "Monkey Trail"

A more direct route from Playas del Coco is via a dirt road—the "Monkey Trail"—that begins three kilometers east of Playa del Coco and one kilometer west of Sardinal and leads

PLAYA FLAMINGO AND VICINITY

PACIFIC OCEAN

Isla Plata

Playa Prieta
To Playa Azúcar
CATALINAS BEACH SUITES
PLAZA CAFÉ DEL SOL/INTERNET CAFÉ
Playa Penca
VILLAGIO FLOR DE PACÍFICO
Monkey Trail to Sardinal and Playas del Coco
To Tempate
BAHÍA ESMERALDA HOTEL & RESTAURANT
POTRERO
POLICE
BACK RD.
HOTEL ISOLINA
SUPER WENDY
CABINAS CRISTINA
BAHÍA DEL SOL
SURFSIDE
MAXWELL'S CAFÉ
Playa Potrero
MAYRA'S CAMPING & CABINAS
SODA RESTAURANTE PLEAMAR
FLAMINGO MARINA RESORT
Flamingo
DISCO AMBERES
CASA BELLA
BILLFISH SAFARIS
MARINER INN
ANGELINA'S/CENTRO COMERCIAL LA PLAZA/TOURIST INFORMATION
BANK/CLINIC/ PHARMACY
CENTRO PANAMERICANO DE IDIOMAS
MARIE'S
FLAMINGO BEACH RESORT
FLAMINGO
GRUPO BRINDISI
Mangrove Swamp
Playa Blanca
To Brasilito
SCALE NOT AVAILABLE
© AVALON TRAVEL

to Potrero. It can be rough going in wet season. About nine kilometers southwest from Sardinal is the **Congo Trail Canopy Tour** (tel. 506/2666-4422, congotrail@racsa.co.cr, 8 A.M.–5 P.M. daily), where for $35 you can whiz between treetop platforms on a zipline, granting a monkey's-eye view with the howler (congo) monkeys. It also has a butterfly farm, serpentarium, monkeys, and an aviary.

When passing through Portegolpe, consider a quick stop at the **Monkey Park** (tel. 506/2653-8060, www.monkey-park.org, 8 A.M.–4 P.M. Tues.–Sun., $5), an animal rescue center that takes in injured and confiscated monkeys that cannot survive in the wild. You'll also see peccaries, coati, deer, caimans, and lots of birds. It has a breeding program and accepts visitors for a one-hour guided tour ($15). Nearby, **Cartagena Canopy Tour** (tel. 506/2675-4501, www.canopytourcartagena.com, $35 pp) lets you whiz through the treetops. It has tours at 8 A.M., 11 A.M., 1 P.M., and 3 P.M. by reservation. Free hotel transfers are offered.

Horse-riding anyone? Head to **Haras del Mar Equestrian Center** (tel. 506/8820-0474, www.lomasdelmar.com), midway along the "Monkey Trail."

The Spanish RUI (www.riu.com) hotel group plans to build three luxury hotels totaling 2,000 rooms at Playa Matapalo. First up will be the 700-room **Hotel Riu Guanacaste,** Costa Rica's largest hotel to date, slated to open in November 2009 with a casino, spa, and conference center.

The following beaches are listed in north to south order, assuming access via the "Monkey Trail."

PLAYAS POTRERO AND AZÚCAR

The "Monkey Trail" emerges at Playa Potrero, about 16 kilometers southwest of Sardinal and immediately northeast of Playa Flamingo, from which it is separated by Bahía Potrero. The gray-sand beach curls southward for about three kilometers from the rustic and charming fishing hamlet of Potrero and is popular with campers during holidays.

North of Potrero, a dirt road leads to **Playa Penca,** a beautiful beach backed by a protected mangrove estuary—that of the Río Salinas—and rare saltwater forest replete with birdlife, including parrots, roseate spoonbills, and egrets. From Penca, the road snakes north three kilometers to Playa Azúcar (Sugar Beach), a narrow, 400-meter-wide spit of sun-drenched, coral-colored sand that just might have you dreaming of retiring here. There's good snorkeling offshore.

Accommodations

You can camp at **Mayra's Camping and Cabins** (tel. 506/2654-4213, $5 campsites, $20–35 cabins), a friendly beachfront spot with showers, toilets, and a small *soda* where Mayra makes *típico* and seafood dishes.

At **Cabinas Cristina** (tel. 506/2654-4006, www.cabinascristina.com, $50 s/d room, $60 mini-apartment) you have the benefit of a small pool. The six simple, all-wood, air-conditioned *cabinas* are set in shady albeit unkempt gardens and each sleeps four people, with private bathrooms and hot water, plus free Wi-Fi.

The Italian-run **Hotel Isolina** (tel. 506/2654-4333, www.isolinabeach.com, $45–55 s/d room, from $75 villa low season; $60–75 s/d room, from $90 villa high season), one kilometer south of Potrero, has 11 attractive if simple and somewhat dark air-conditioned cabins with cable TVs, and private bathrooms with hot water. It also has three villas and rooms in a twin-story hotel complex, plus a pool and restaurant in lush gardens.

Bahía Esmeralda Hotel and Restaurant (tel. 506/2654-4480, www.hotelbahiaesmeralda .com, $50 s or $60 d rooms, $70–116 apartments low season; $60 s or $70 d rooms, $93–142 apartments high season) is a modern, Italian-run hotel 200 meters on the southern edge of Potrero hamlet. The four simply furnished rooms, four houses, and eight apartments feature red-tile roofs and have all cable TV, lofty hardwood ceilings, double beds and bunks, and modern conveniences. Italian fare is served in an open-sided restaurant, and there's a swimming pool in lush gardens. Horseback tours and bike rental are available, as is a boat for turtle tours and fishing.

Villagio Flor de Pacífico (tel. 506/2654-4664, www.flordepacifico.com), on the "Monkey Trail" 400 meters inland of Potrero village and a 15-minute walk from the beach, is a modern Italian-run resort amid lush expansive gardens. Its 50 modestly furnished one- and two-bedroom villas get hot but have air-conditioning fans, lofty wooden ceilings, and cool tile floors, plus kitchens. Facilities include two pools, tennis, and an Italian restaurant. Call for rates.

The gorgeous **Hotel Bahía del Sol** (tel. 506/2654-4671, www.bahiadelsolhotel.com, $140 s/d standard, $175 s/d deluxe, $220–270 suites low season; $165 s/d standard, $190 s/d deluxe, $250–375 suites high season), at Playa Potrero, is a classy beach resort with colorful decor in its 13 rooms and 15 one- and two-bedroom suites, all with air-conditioning. Romantically lit at night, the resort has a gorgeous walk-in pool with swim-up bar plus handsome thatched open-air restaurant. The same owners operate the equally colorful **Catalinas Beach Suites** (tel. 506/2654-4671, fax 506/2654-5005, www.catalinasbeachsuites.com, $190–290 s/d low season, $240–360 s/d high season), with nicely furnished self-contained suites and a freeform pool.

I also recommend the gracious **Hotel Sugar Beach** (tel. 506/2654-4242, www.sugar-beach.com, $125–155 s/d standard, $155 s/d deluxe, $195–350 suites high season; 20 percent less in low season), offering the privacy of a secluded setting on a beachfront rise amid 10 hectares of lawns and forest full of wildlife. The hotel received an exciting contemporary livery in 2006, when a complete overhaul was completed. Choose from 16 new rooms in eight handsome Spanish colonial-style duplexes, or 10 units connected by stone pathways. Also available are a three-bedroom beach house and an apartment suite. A large open-air restaurant looks over the beach, and there's a small pool, horseback rides, and tours. Costa Rica Outriggers is based here.

New in 2009, the contemporary Mediterranean-themed **Hotel Mediterraneus** (tel. 506/2297-1029, www.hotelmediterraneus.com, rates vary monthly, from $160 s/d) will have 52 deluxe rooms, a spa, and extensive recreational facilities.

Rosewood Hotels & Resorts (www.rosewoodhotels.com) plans to build the super-deluxe resort **Rosewood Costa Carmel** at Playa Zapotal, north of Azúcar, due to open in 2012.

Food

A favorite of locals, **Maxwell's Café** (tel. 506/2645-4319, 8 A.M.–noon and 4 –10 P.M. daily), 300 meters inland of the beach, is an open-air bar and grill serving American fare. However, by far the best place is the open-air beachfront restaurant at **Bahía del Sol** (tel. 506/2654-4671, 6 A.M.–10 P.M. daily, $5–20), specializing in seafood and continental cuisine; it has a "*fiesta tropical*" on Friday night, and karaoke on Saturday.

Super Wendy (tel. 506/2654-4291), on the main road between Potrero and Flamingo, specializes in gourmet foodstuffs.

Information and Services

A **Welcome Center** (tel. 506/2654-5460) offers tourist information in the new Plaza Casa del Sol, to the northwest of the Potrero village soccer field; there's a **police station** on the south side of the soccer field.

PLAYA FLAMINGO

Playa Flamingo, immediately south of Potrero and facing it from the west side of the bay, is named for the two-kilometer-wide scimitar of white sand—one of the most magnificent beaches in Costa Rica—that lines the north end of Bahía Flamingo (there are no flamingos). The area is favored by wealthy Ticos and gringos (North Americans now own most of the land hereabouts), and expensive villas sit atop the headlands north and south of the beach, many with their own little coves as private as one's innermost thoughts.

The marina was closed by the government

© CHRISTOPHER P. BAKER

Playa Flamingo

for health reasons in 2006. It remained closed in late 2008 but was due to be rebuilt.

Entertainment and Events

The **Monkey Bar** at the Flamingo Marina Resort has a happy hour daily at 5:30 P.M. It has live music on Friday, barbecue on Saturday, ESPN with pizza on Sunday, and Monday night football (in season). The always-lively bar at the **Mariner Inn** (6 A.M.–10 P.M. daily) features cable TV and has live music at times.

Disco Amberes (tel. 506/2654-4001, 5 P.M.–2 A.M.), on the hill, has a spacious lounge bar, a lively disco, and a small casino that opens at 8 P.M. Live bands occasionally play starting at 9:30 P.M. Video slots and card tables are offered at **Flamingo Bay Resort** (tel. 506/2654-4444, 7 P.M.–3 A.M.).

Sports and Recreation

Costa Rica Diving (tel./fax 506/2654-4148, www.costarica-diving.com) offer diving to Islas Murciélagos, as does **Grupo Brindisi** (100 meters east of the marina, tel. 506/2654-4946, www.brindisicr.com), which also has kayak-snorkeling trips, ATV tours, and diving.

Billfish Safaris (tel. 506/2654-5244), next to the Mariner Inn, has sportfishing and ATV tours.

EcoTrans (tel. 506/2654-5151, www.ecotrans costarica.com), in Flamingo Marina Resort, offers tours to Palo Verde National Park, Guaitíl, and other destinations.

And **Flamingo Equestrian Center** (tel. 506/8846-7878, http://equestriancostarica .com) offers horse-riding instruction.

Accommodations

There are no budget properties. The least expensive option is the **Mariner Inn** (tel. 506/2654-4081, fax 506/2654-4024, marinerinn@ racsa.co.cr, $35 s/d standard, $48 with a/c and fridge, $70 suite year-round), a 12-room Spanish colonial-style hotel down by the marina. Dark hardwoods fill the air-conditioned rooms that feature color TVs, blue-and-white tile work, and terra-cotta tile floors. A suite has a mini-bar and kitchenette. There's a pool, and the bar gets lively.

The three-story, haphazardly arranged **Flamingo Marina Resort** (tel. 506/2654-4141 or U.S. tel. 800/276-7501, www.flamingo marina.com, $89 s/d room, $139–149 s/d suite, $169–210 apartments low season; $119 s/d room, $169–189 s/d suite, $209–280 apartments high season), on the hill overlooking the marina, has grand views toward Playa Potrero. It offers three types of accommodations in 123 spacious air-conditioned rooms with lively contempo decor. Suites have king-size beds, plus whirlpools on private terraces. And there are larger, beachfront, one- to three-bedroom apartments. The pleasant terrace restaurant opens onto a circular swimming pool with the thatched swim-up Monkey Bar. Tennis, a gift shop, tour office, and full-service dive shop are also offered. Rates include breakfast and tax.

Down by the beach, and a better bargain, is the **Flamingo Beach Resort** (tel. 506/2654-4444, www.resortflamingobeach.com, $118–131 s/d low season, $132–149 s/d high season), a large-scale complex centered on a voluminous pool with a swim-up bar. The 120 spacious air-conditioned rooms and suites in five types have finally been redone in a smart and colorful contemporary mode. All have fans and 29-inch flat-screen TVs plus free Internet access, minibars, and coffeemakers. Suites have kitchenettes and whirlpool tubs. There are three bars, two restaurants, tennis, large gym, Turkish bath, game room, beauty salon, souvenir shop, rental car agency, dive shop, and casino.

For your own luxurious hilltop villa, check into **Casa Bella** (tel. 919/820-6972, www .luxuryflamingovilla.com, $2,850 weekly), with five bedrooms and a pool.

Food
For unpretentious dining I like the thatched, breeze-swept **Soda Restaurante Pleamar** (tel. 506/2654-4521, 7 A.M.–4 P.M. Mon., 7 A.M.–9 P.M. Tues.–Sun., $5–15), with a splendid beachfront site 400 meters east of the Flamingo marina. It serves ceviche, burgers, lobster, and garlic fish, all for less than $10.

My favorite place is **Marie's Restaurant** (tel. 506/2654-4136, 6:30 A.M.–9:30 P.M. daily), now in ritzy new open-air digs under a huge thatched *palenque* in Centro Comercial La Plaza, 50 meters west of the marina. Aged terra-cotta floor tiles add to the ambience. It offers great breakfasts like granola and omelettes. Lunch and dinner brings fish and chips, chicken from the wood oven, rib eye steak ($14), barbecue pork ribs ($12), and a large selection of sandwiches, plus ice cream sundaes, cappuccinos, lattes, mochas, and espressos.

If chic 21st-century styling is your thing, opt for **◖ Angelina's** (tel. 506/2654-4839, no set hours), which opened in November 2008 upstairs in Centro Comercial La Plaza. It offers international fusion dishes, such as yellow-fin tuna poke starter ($7), and oven-roasted chicken topped with orange espresso glaze ($12). I love the decor! Imagine cowhide ceiling lamps, a bar made of a sliced tree trunk, leather sofas, and a slick lounge bar. Confirmation, indeed, that Flamingo now rocks!

Hitching Post Plaza, two kilometers south of Flamingo and mid-way to Brasilito, has three little gems. **Barnie's Smokehouse** (tel. 506/2654-5827, 9 A.M.–6:30 P.M. Tues.–Fri.) serves smoked chicken, ribs, and salads. Next door, **Cecile's** (tel. 506/2654-5449, 7 A.M.–7 P.M. Mon.–Sat.) serves fresh-baked goods, which you can enjoy at the adjoining **Café Crema** coffee shop, which has Wi-Fi.

Supermercado Flamingo is located at Plaza Que Pasa.

Information and Services
There's a **tourist information center** (tel. 506/2654-4021, www.infoflamingo.com) in Centro Comercial La Plaza; plus a bank, clinic, and pharmacy on the hill above the marina. For an **ambulance** call 506/2654-5523; for **police,** call 506/2654-5647.

Centro Panamericano de Idiomas (tel. 506/2654-5002, www.cpi-edu.com), 100 meters east of the marina, offers Spanish language courses.

Getting There
Tralapa buses (tel. 506/2221-7202) depart San José for Playa Portrero via Brasilito and Flamingo from Calles 20, Avenidas 3/5, daily at 8 A.M., 10:30 A.M., and 3 P.M. ($5.25, five hours), returning from Portrero at 2:45 A.M., 9 A.M., and 2 P.M. Buses (tel. 506/2680-0392) depart Santa Cruz for Playas Brasilito, Flamingo, and Potrero nine times daily 4 A.M.–5 P.M. Return buses depart for Santa Cruz 6 A.M.–8 P.M.

Grayline (tel. 506/2220-2126, www.grayline costarica.com) and **Interbus** (tel. 506/2283-5573, www.interbusonline.com) operate shuttles between Flamingo/Tamarindo and

San José ($35) plus key tourist destinations throughout Costa Rica.

To get to Flamingo from Playas Coco, Hermosa, or Panamá, take a bus to Comunidad, where you can catch a southbound bus for Santa Cruz or Nicoya; get off at Belén, and catch a bus for Flamingo.

PLAYA CONCHAL AND BRASILITO

The hamlet of Brasilito, about four kilometers south of Flamingo and three kilometers north of Huacas, draws an incongruous mix of offbeat budget travelers and the packaged all-inclusive resort set, drawn to the massive Paradisus Playa Conchal Beach & Golf Resort, a five-star hotel within the huge **Reserva Conchal** (tel. 506/2654-4000, www.reserva conchal.com) residential community.

The light-gray sand beach at Brasilito melds westward into Playa Conchal, one of Costa Rica's finest beaches. The beach lies in the cusp of a scalloped bay with turquoise waters, a rarity in Costa Rica. The beach is composed, uniquely, of zillions of tiny seashells that move with soft rustling sounds as you walk; the waters are of crystalline quality perfect for snorkeling. It's illegal to remove shells. Please leave them for future generations to enjoy.

Conchal can also be accessed by road from the west via the hamlet of **Matapalo,** three kilometers west of Huacas, where a rough dirt road leads from the northwest corner of the soccer field to the west end of Playa Conchal (4 km). A side road on the Matapalo-Conchal road leads west to **Playa Real,** a stunning little beauty of a beach nestled in a sculpted bay with a tiny tombolo leading to a rocky island. Venerable fishing boats make good resting spots for pelicans.

This region is booming! Roads have been cut to heretofore isolated beaches, such as **Playa Nombre de Jesús,** the setting for several new deluxe hotels in the works.

Sports and Recreation

Costa Rica Temptations (tel. 506/2654-4585, www.costarica4u.com, 8 A.M.–6 P.M. Mon.–Fri. and 8 A.M.–2 P.M. Sat.–Sun.), 100

angler with catch, Playa Nombre de Jesús

© CHRISTOPHER P. BAKER

meters south of the soccer field, offers tours throughout the region.

Santana Tours (tel. 506/2654-4359), opposite Hotel Conchal, offers ATV (all-terrain vehicle) tours, horseback rides, and scooter rental. And **Qcho's Shop** (tel. 506/2654-5704), nearby, specializes in surfing.

There are water sports concessions on Playa Conchal. You can buy day (8 A.M.–5 P.M.) and/ or night (6 P.M.–1 A.M.) passes ($65) that permit nonguests to use the Paradisus resort facilities. Its highlight is the **Garra de León Golf Club,** with an 18-hole golf course designed by the king of designers, Robert Trent Jones, Jr.; it is not open to walk-ins, but guests at local hotels can play by reservation.

Accommodations

You can camp under shade trees ($2 pp low season, $3 high season) behind the beach at **Brasilito Lodge** (tel./fax 506/2654-4452, www.brasilito-conchal.com), an otherwise unkempt place that also has seven motley cabins not worth recommending.

The **Cabinas Ojos Azules** (tel./fax 506/2654-4346, www.cabinasojosazules.com, from $10 pp.), 100 meters south of the soccer field, has 14 clean and neatly furnished yet basic cabins for up to eight people. Some have hot water. There's a laundry, a small plunge pool, and a *rancho* with hammocks.

The German-run **Hotel Brasilito** (tel. 506/2654-4237, www.brasilito.com, $29–60 s/d low season; $39–70 s/d high season), 50 meters from both the beach and soccer field, is a well-run hotel with 15 simple rooms (they vary greatly; some are air-conditioned) with fans and private baths with hot water, in a daffodil-yellow wooden home adorned with flowerboxes. It has an atmospheric restaurant.

My favorite place here is **Hotel Conchal** (tel. 506/2654-9125, http://conchalcr.com, $65 s, $85 d), 200 meters south of the soccer field. This charming Polynesian-style hotel is run by an English-Danish couple and has nine pretty, whitewashed, tile-floored air-conditioned rooms with wrought-iron beds (some are king-size), ceiling fans, TVs, halogen lighting, and river-stone exteriors. They face a landscaped garden full of bougainvillea. The Robinson Crusoe–style upstairs lounge is a delightful space. A dive school is on-site.

Next door, the new **Cabinas Diversion Tropical** (tel. 506/2654-5519, www.diversion tropical.com, $37 s/d, or $47 with kitchenette) has 12 clean, simply appointed rooms in a two-story unit.

Apartotel & Restaurant Nany (tel. 506/2654-4320, www.apartotelnany.com, $60–75 s/d low season, $93–110 s/d high season) has 11 uniquely designed, spacious, modern, air-conditioned two-bedroom "apartments" with kitchenettes and tall half-moon windows, ceiling fans, cable TV, security box, and private baths with hot water. It has an open-air restaurant and a plunge pool.

The U.S.–run **Condor Heights** (tel. 506/2653-8950, www.condorheights.com, $225 low season, $250 high season, three-night minimum), atop the hill 600 meters inland and south of Playa Conchal, rents fully furnished condominiums. The open-terrace dining room—offering spectacular views—is topped by a lofty lounge bar and casino. There's also a TV lounge and small library. A swimming pool with cascade is set on the lofty sundeck. A new alternative for the self-catering set is **Finca Buena Fuente Hotel** (tel. 506/8359-8183, www.buenafuente hotel.com, $60–150 s/d low season, $20 each additional person), combining traditional farm-style restaurant and bar with huge, modern apartment units furnished in spartan, uninspired fashion. Units differ; some have loft bedrooms. It's one kilometer from the beach.

For a more luxurious experience, check into the **Paradisus Playa Conchal Beach & Golf Resort** (tel. 506/2654-4123, www.solmelia.com, from $378 s/d), spanning 285 hectares and surrounded by rippling fairways. The resort has 308 open-plan junior suites and two master suites in 37 two-story units amid landscaped grounds behind the beach. They are beautiful, with exquisite marble bathrooms, mezzanine bedrooms supported by columns, and lounges with soft-cushioned sofas. The massive free-form swimming pool is a setting for noisy aerobics and games. It has three restaurants, two bars, a disco, a theater with nightly shows, tennis courts, plus the golf course. However, readers have complained that meals are mediocre and outrageously priced.

Playa Real is the setting for the Italian-run **Bahía de Las Piratas Resort** (tel. 506/2653-8951, www.bahiadelospiratas.com). Alas, this complex of 15 Spanish colonial-style condos and villas has deteriorated markedly and can no longer be recommended, despite its lovely location.

In 2007, ground was broken on the **Hyatt Regency Azulera** (www.hyatt.com), a 225-hectare resort with a 214-room hotel, 1,000 private residences, and a Greg Norman–designed golf course. In 2008 it fell afoul of environmental investigators, and at press time its future was uncertain.

Canyon Ranch Costa Rica, a deluxe spa resort, is planned for Playa Nombre de Jesús, with a Gary Player–designed golf course.

Food

Don't leave town without dining at the Hotel Brasilito's breezy, **Outback Jack's Australian Road Kill Grill** (tel. 506/2654-4596, 7 A.M.–11 P.M. daily), festooned with intriguing miscellany and serving killer breakfasts such as grilled croissants and eggs ranchero ($3). The wide-ranging lunch and dinner menu ranges from ceviche and shrimp on the barbie to lasagna and grilled pork loin. There's a large-screen TV for sports events.

Information and Services
The **police station** (tel. 506/2654-4425) is on the main road, facing the soccer field. The **Miracle Medical Center & Pharmacy** (tel. 506/2654-4996) is nearby, and there's a major medical center (tel. 506/2654-5440) in nearby Huacas.

Café Internet Nany is at Apartotel & Restaurant Nany (tel. 506/2654-4320, www .apartotelnany.com). **Books & More Books** (tel. 506/2653-7373), in Paseo del Mar Commercial Center, three kilometers south of Brasilito, sells guidebooks and novels in English.

Getting There and Around
The Flamingo-bound buses from San José and Santa Cruz stop in Matapalo and Brasilito.

For a taxi call 506/8836-1739. **Adobe Rent-a-Car** (tel. 506/8811-4242, www.adobecar .com) is in Conchal Commercial Center.

Tamarindo and Vicinity

Tamarindo, a former fishing village that has burgeoned into Guanacaste's most developed (some would say overdeveloped) resort, offers prime wildlife viewing, a scintillating beach, surfing action, and a choice of accommodations spanning shoestring to sophisticated.

Recent years have seen a growth in robberies against tourists. Rental car break-ins are common. Drugs and prostitution have also encroached, and hustlers can be a nuisance.

◖ MARINO LAS BAULAS NATIONAL PARK
Costa Rican beaches don't come more beautiful than **Playa Grande,** a seemingly endless curve of sand (varying from coral-white to gray) with water as blue as the summer sky. A beach trail to the north leads along the cape through dry forest and deposits you at **Playa Ventanas,** with tidepools for snorkeling and bathing. Surf pumps ashore at high tide. Surfing expert Mark Kelly rates Playa Grande as "maybe the best overall spot in the country."

The entire shoreline is protected within the 445-hectare Parque Nacional Marino Las Baulas (a.k.a. Playa Grande Marine Turtle National Park), which guards the prime nesting site of the leatherback turtle on the Pacific coast, including 22,000 hectares out to sea. The beach was incorporated into the national park system in May 1990 after a 15-year battle between developers and conservationists. The park is the result of efforts by Louis Wilson, owner of Hotel Las Tortugas, and his former wife, Marianel Pastor. The government agreed to support the couple's conservation efforts only if they could show that the site was economically viable as a tourist destination. The locals, who formerly harvested the turtles' eggs (as did a cookie company), have taken over all guiding (each guide is certified through an accredited course). However, much of the land backing the beach has recently been developed with condos, homes, and hotels. While MINAE officials contemplate tearing down some of these for violating environmental laws, other officials reportedly have recently granted permission for a Best Western Hotel to be built. And fishing boats continue to trawl illegally and unpoliced within the sanctuary with landlines, which snag turtles!

The beach sweeps south to the mouth of the Río Matapalo, which forms a 400-hectare mangrove estuary. This ecosystem is protected within **Tamarindo National Wildlife Refuge** (Refugio Nacional de Vida Silvestre Tamarindo, tel. 506/2296-7074) and features crocodiles, anteaters, deer, ocelots, and monkeys. Waterbirds and raptors gather, especially

THE LEATHERBACK TURTLE

The leatherback turtle (Dermochelys coriacea) is the world's largest reptile and a true relic from the age of the dinosaurs; fossils date back 100 million years. The average adult weighs about 455 kilograms and is two meters in length, though males have been known to attain a staggering 910 kilograms! It is found in all the world's oceans except the Arctic.

Though it nests on the warm beaches of Costa Rica, the baula (as it is locally known) has evolved as a deep-diving cold water critter; its great, near-cylindrical bulk retains body heat in cold waters (it can maintain a body temperature of 18°C in near-frigid water). The leatherback travels great distances, feeding in the open ocean as far afield as subarctic waters, where its black body helps absorb the sun's warming rays. Like seals, the leatherback has a thick oily layer of fat for insulation. Its preferred food is jellyfish.

The females – which reach reproductive age between 15 and 50 years – prefer to nest on steep beaches that have a deepwater approach, thus avoiding long-distance crawls. Nesting occurs during the middle hours of the night – the coolest hours. Leatherback eggs take longer to hatch – 70 days on average – than those of other sea turtles.

Whereas in other turtle species, the boney exterior carapace is formed by flattened, widened ribs that are fused and covered with corneous tissues resembling the human fingernail, the leatherback has an interior skeleton of narrow ribs linked by tiny bony plates all encased by a thick "shell" of leathery, cartilaginous skin. The leatherback's tapered body is streamlined for hydrodynamic efficiency, with seven longitudinal ridges that act like a boat's keel, and long, powerful flippers for maximum propulsion. Leatherbacks have been shown to dive deeper than 1,300 meters, where their small lungs, flexible frames, squishy bodies, and other specialist adaptations permit the animal to withstand well over 1,500 pounds of pressure per square inch.

The species is close to extinction. Contributions to help save leatherback turtles can be sent marked Programa de Tortugas Marinas to Karen and Scott Eckert, **Hubbs Sea World Research Institute** (2595 Ingraham St., San Diego, CA 92109, U.S. tel. 619/226-3870, www.hswri.org), or to the **Leatherback Trust** (161 Merion Av., Haddonfield, NJ 08033, U.S. tel. 215/895-2627, www.leatherback.org).

in dry season. The refuge's ranger station is about 500 meters upriver from the estuary.

The hamlet of **Comunidad Playa Grande** is on the main approach road, 600 meters inland from the beach. The sprawling woodsy community at the southern half of the beach is called Palm Beach Estates.

There's now guarded parking ($2) at the main beach entrance; elsewhere car break-ins are an everyday occurrence. *Don't leave anything in your vehicle.*

The El Mundo de la Tortuga (World of the Turtle museum) has closed.

Visiting the Turtles of Playa Grande

Turtles call at Playa Grande year-round. The nesting season for the giant leatherback is October–March, when females come ashore every night at high tide. Sometimes as many as 100 turtles might be seen in a single night. (Olive ridley turtles and Pacific green turtles can sometimes also be seen here, May–August.) Each female leatherback will nest as many as 12 times a season, every 10 days or so (usually at night to avoid dehydration). Most turtles prefer the center of the beach, just above the high-tide mark.

The beach is open to visitors by day at no cost, and by permit only with a guide at night in nesting season (6 P.M.–6 A.M., $10 entrance with guide; the fee is payable on *leaving* the beach if turtles have been seen); anyone found on the beach at night without a permit in

© CHRISTOPHER P. BAKER

Marino las Baulas National Park

nesting season faces a $1,000 fine (second offense; first offenders are escorted off the beach). Guides from the local community roam the beach and lead groups to nesting turtles; other guides spot for turtles and call in the location via walkie-talkies. Visitors are not allowed to walk the beach after dusk unescorted. Groups cannot exceed 15 people, and only 60 people are allowed onto the beach at night at each of two entry points (four groups per gate, with a maximum of eight groups nightly): one where the road meets the beach by the Hotel Las Tortugas, and the second at the southern end, by Villas Baulas. *Reservations are mandatory,* although entry without a reservation is possible if there's space in a group (don't count on it, as demand usually exceeds supply). You can make reservations up to eight days in advance, or 8 A.M.–5 P.M. for a same-day visit. At certain times the waiting time can be two hours before you are permitted onto the beach; each night differs.

Resist the temptation to follow the example of the many thoughtless visitors who get too close to the turtles, try to touch them,

ride their backs, or otherwise display a lack of common sense and respect. Flashlights and camera flashes are *not* permitted (professional photographers can apply in advance for permission to use a flash). And watch your step. Newborn turtles are difficult to see at night as they scurry down to the sea. Many are inadvertently crushed by tourists' feet.

The park headquarters (Centro Operaciones Parque Nacional Marina las Baulas, tel./fax 506/2653-0470) is 100 meters east of Hotel Las Tortugas. It features an auditorium on turtle ecology. *Viewing the film is obligatory for all people intending to witness the turtles nesting.*

Sports and Recreation

Hotels and tour companies in the area offer turtle-watching tours (about $25) and a "Jungle Boat Safari," aboard a 20-passenger pontoon boat that takes you into the mangrove-rich Tamarindo Wildlife Refuge ($30).

Hotel Las Tortugas (tel. 506/2653-0423, www.lastortugashotel.com) rents surfboards ($15–35) and boogie boards ($10 per day) and has canoe tours of the estuary ($30 solo, $55

© CHRISTOPHER P. BAKER

Playa Grande Surf Camp

guided). **Pura Vida Café** (tel. 506/2653-0835) offers surf lessons ($50), as does **Frijoles Locos** (tel. 506/2652-9235, www.frijoleslocos.com), at the entrance to Playa Grande; it's the best stocked surf store around. Next door, **El Frijol Feliz Day Spa** (tel. 506/2652-9236) can soothe weary muscles with a relaxing massage.

The **Hotel Bula Bula Beach Club** (tel. 506/2653-0975 or U.S. tel. 877/658-2880, www.hotelbulabula.com) at the south end of the beach, has funball, volleyball, ocean kayaks, boogie boards, and *boules.*

Accommodations

Camping is not allowed on the beach. You can camp at **Centro Vacacional Playa Grande** (tel./fax 506/2653-0834, $5 pp) at Comunidad Playa Grande; it has showers and toilets. It also has 12 two-bedroom *cabinas* with private bathrooms with cold water only; eight have kitchenettes ($15 pp fan, $20 pp a/c). There's a restaurant, pool, and free laundry.

For backpackers, I recommend **Playa Grande Surf Camp** (tel. 506/2653-1074, www.playagrandesurfcamp.com, $15 pp dorm,

$25 pp cabins). It has three small but delightful, air-conditioned, wood-and-thatch cabins on stilts, plus two A-frames, including a dorm with screened windows. The courtyard has a pool and thatched shade areas with hammocks, plus there's Wi-Fi, board rental, and surf lessons.

The **Playa Grande Inn** (tel./fax 506/2653-0719, www.playagrandeinn.com, $50 s/d room, $75 suite), a handsome surf camp with eight impeccably clean, simply appointed rooms in an all-wood two-story structure. There's a pool, whirlpool tub, and a lively bar. You can also rent an apartment.

There were two striking newcomers in 2008. First is the Italian-run **Sol y Luna Lodge** (tel. 506/8893-0198, www.solylunalodge.net, $30–40 pp), one kilometer inland of the beach. This lovely place has eight tree-shaded thatched cabins (for four or six people) with cable TVs, Indonesian batiks, ceiling fans, mosquito nets, verandas, and nice modern bathrooms with whirlpool tubs. A rustic restaurant was being added beside the landscaped pool with rock-wall hot tub and water cascade. Two smaller cabins are air-conditioned and have king-size beds. It has Wi-Fi.

And the **Playa Grande Surf Hotel** (tel. 506/2653-2656, www.playagrandesurfhotel .net, $75 standard, $95 deluxe, $175 suite low season, $125 standard, $150 deluxe, $275 suite high season) belies its name. This modern, two-story, Spanish colonial-style hotel is the most stylish around, with a hip contemporary aesthetic to its rooms and suites, all with flat-screen TVs, Wi-Fi, and air-conditioning. A sushi restaurant was to open in 2009.

Another excellent bet is the ecologically sound **Hotel Las Tortugas** (tel. 506/2653-0423, www.lastortugashotel.com, $35 s/d economy, $50–60 s/d standard, $85 suite low season; $50 economy, $80 standard, $120 suite high season), a comfortable ecolodge. The 12 rooms vary markedly, though all have air-conditioning, pewter-colored stone floors, orthopedic mattresses, cable TV, Wi-Fi, and private baths with hot water. A new suite and some standard rooms have lovely patios and hammocks. The hotel has a turtle-shaped swimming pool with sundeck, plus a large whirlpool tub and a quiet palm-shaded corner with hammocks. (Since newborn turtles are attracted to light and adults can be disoriented by it, there are no ocean views to the south, where the nesting beach is.) The restaurant is a highlight, with an outdoor patio and great food. The hotel rents surfboards and canoes for trips into the estuary ($55 half day) and has horseback riding ($40) and a mangrove boat tour ($25). Louis, the delightful owner, has added eight "student" rooms with bunk beds and shared hot-water shower facilities ($15 s, $20 d).

I like the aesthetic at the **RipJack Inn** (tel. 506/2653-0480, www.ripjackinn.com, $60 s/d standard, $80 s/d *cabina* low season, $80/100 high season), with eight simply appointed rooms graced by Guatemalan fabrics. The open-air restaurant, Upstairs @ the RipJack, serves nouvelle Costa Rican fare and has ocean views. Yoga fans will appreciate the yoga studio.

I adore the **(Hotel Bula Bula** (tel. 506/2653-0975 or U.S. tel. 877/658-2880, www.hotelbulabula.com, $95 s/d low season, $120 s/d high season), in lush gardens adjoining the mangrove estuary, two kilometers south of Las Tortugas. This attractive place is in the hands of two vivacious U.S. entrepreneurs, one a professional restaurateur. The 10 air-conditioned rooms are fabulous, with rich color schemes, king-size beds with orthopedic mattresses, batik wall hangings, plus fans, fresh-cut flower arrangements, batik sarongs for use by the pool, and a shady balcony. The rooms surround a pool in a landscaped garden. It has a stage for live music. The excellent restaurant and bar (with Wi-Fi and loaner laptops) are popular with locals. A free water-taxi to Tamarindo is available.

Playa Grande is a great place to kick back in your own home. The French-run **Hotel Manglar** (tel. 506/2653-0952, www.hotel-manglar .com) has 10 apartments that surround a lovely amoeba-shaped pool. However, in spring 2008, several private homes, most of which double as vacation rentals, were to be torn down as they lie within the 50-meter zone.

For greater intimacy, and great for families, try **Casa Verde** (tel. 506/2653-0481, casaverdecr@ yahoo.com, $135 room, or $285 entire house), a lovely modern home with pool. Three simply appointed, air-conditioned rooms with cable TV have glass sliding doors opening to broad eaves shading terra-cotta patios. One room has a king-size bed and kitchen.

Food

You don't have to leave the beach to eat. Just pop up to **Taco Star** (9 A.M.–sunset), a grill at the park entrance. Jay sells burgers and more. Here, too, the **Hotel Las Tortugas** has an airy restaurant (7:30 A.M.–9:30 P.M. daily) serving an eclectic menu; leave room for the apple pie and ice cream.

Inland, **Centro Vacacional Playa Grande** has an inexpensive *soda* selling *típico* dishes.

For true gourmet fare, head to the elegant **(Great Waltinis** (5:30–8:30 P.M. Tues.–Thurs., 5:30–9 P.M. Fri.–Sat.) restaurant at Hotel Bula Bula. It serves international cuisine, including quesadillas, chicken wings, shrimp and crab cakes, plus such superbly executed dishes as duckling with mango chutney ($14), filet mignon ($16), and filet of ahi tuna sautéed with white wine and garlic butter ($12). Leave room for the "Siberia" chocolate drink-dessert. Avoid the superb killer martinis if you're driving!

You can stock up at **Super Pura Vida,** in Comunidad Playa Grande, or at **Super Malinche** (tel. 506/2653-0236), which has a thatched seafood restaurant attached.

Getting There

From Flamingo, road access is via Matapalo, six kilometers east of Playa Grande (turn left at the soccer field in Matapolo). A rough dirt road also links Tamarindo and Playa Grande via Villareal. The Flamingo-bound buses from San José and Santa Cruz stop in Matapalo, where you can catch a taxi or the bus that departs Santa Cruz at 6 A.M. and 1 P.M.; the return bus departs Playa Grande at 7:15 A.M. and 3:15 P.M.

Tamarindo Shuttle (tel. 506/2653-2727) charges $24 for "door-to-door" service from Liberia airport; a taxi will cost about $80.

The **Asociación de Guías Locales** (tel. 506/2653-1687, 7 A.M.–4 P.M.) offers water-taxi between Tamarindo and a dock on the estuary near the Hotel Bula Bula every two hours ($3).

TAMARINDO

Playa Tamarindo, eight kilometers south of Huacas, is Nicoya's most developed beach resort and is especially popular with backpacking surfers. The gray-sand beach is about two kilometers wide, and very deep when the tide goes out—perfect for strolling and watching pelicans dive for fish. It has rocky outcrops, good for tidepooling. There's a smaller beach south of the main beach, with tidepools and relatively fewer people. Riptides are common, so ask locals in the know for the safest places to swim. The Río Matapalo washes onto the beach at its northern end, giving direct access to the Tamarindo Wildlife Refuge via the Estero Palo Seco; a boatman will ferry you for $0.50. You can also wade across at low tide, although crocodiles are sometimes present, as they are in the mangroves at the eastern end of Playa Tamarindo.

To the south, separated by a headland from Playa Tamarindo, is the rapidly evolving, more upscale **Playa Langosta,** a beautiful white-sand beach that stretches beyond the wide estuary of the Río Tamarindo for several kilometers.

Tamarindo has changed beyond recognition in the past decade, metamorphosing from a sleepy surfers' hangout to a full-blown resort, with uncontrolled development in the past few years. High-rise condominiums have arrived, as have shopping malls. But most roads remain unpaved—dusty as hell in dry season and deplorably potholed with vast pools of mud in wet season. Fecal contamination of the ocean has reached dangerous levels. And prostitutes, drug dealers, and a serious crime wave are now part of the scene.

Entertainment and Events

Costa Rica's annual **International Music Festival** is hosted in July and August at Hotel Cala Luna and Villa Alegre B&B.

The **Monkey Bar,** at Tamarindo Vista Villas (tel. 506/2653-0114), has Monday night football, with free shots at touchdowns; Wednesday is ladies' night, with free cocktails for the gals; Thursday is all-you-can-eat pasta; on Friday, the Monkey Bar is still popular for tequila shooters night.

At last visit the no-frills open-air **Pacifico Bar** (formerly Mambo) in the village center was a happening spot on Sunday for reggae night; it has a pool table and music but has had a history of drawing hookers, druggies, and a raffish crowd. **Babylon,** an outdoor bar, hops on Thursday (reggae night), although reportedly it can get violent after midnight! Less salacious, the **Rey Sol Disco Bar** (tel. 506/8301-3609, Fri.–Tues.) is the happening dance scene for the surf crowd; it recently added a huge video screen; Monday is ladies' night, Wednesday is martini night, and hip-hop fans should head there on Fridays. Across the street, the **Voodoo Lounge** (tel. 506/2653-0100, www.elvoodoo.com, 6 P.M.–1 A.M.) has Brazilian

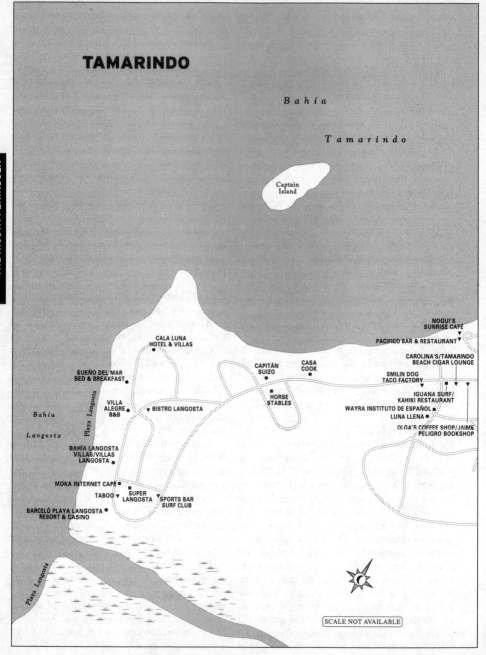

TAMARINDO

Bahía

Tamarindo

Captain
Island

NOGUI'S
SUNRISE CAFÉ

PACIFICO BAR & RESTAURANT

CALA LUNA
HOTEL & VILLAS

CAROLINA'S/TAMARINDO
BEACH CIGAR LOUNGE

CAPITÁN
SUIZO

CASA
COOK

SMILIN DOG
TACO FACTORY

SUEÑO DEL MAR
BED & BREAKFAST

IGUANA SURF/
KAHIKI RESTAURANT

VILLA
ALEGRE
B&B

BISTRO LANGOSTA

HORSE
STABLES

WAYRA INSTITUTO DE ESPAÑOL

LUNA LLENA

Bahía

Langosta

OLGA'S COFFEE SHOP/JAIME
PELIGRO BOOKSHOP

BAHÍA LANGOSTA
VILLAS/VILLAS
LANGOSTA

MOKA INTERNET CAFÉ

TABOO

SUPER
LANGOSTA

SPORTS BAR
SURF CLUB

BARCELÓ PLAYA LANGOSTA
RESORT & CASINO

Playa Langosta

Playa Langosta

SCALE NOT AVAILABLE

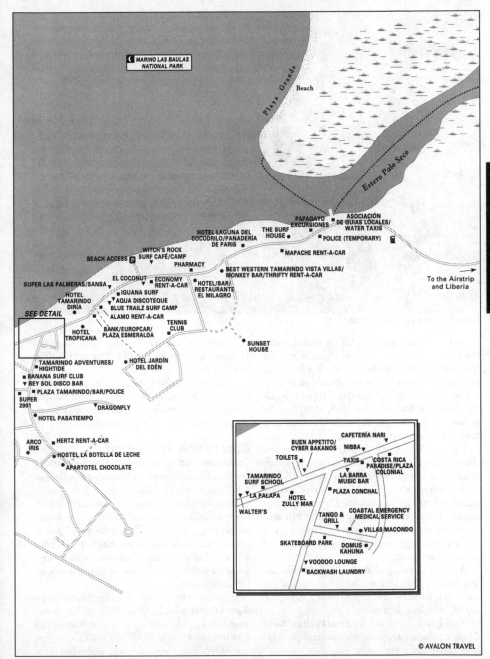

THE NICOYA PENINSULA

MARINO LAS BAULAS
NATIONAL PARK

Playa Grande

Beach

Estero Palo Seco

PAPAGAYO
EXCURSIONES

ASOCIACIÓN
DE GUIAS LOCALES/
WATER TAXIS

THE SURF
HOUSE

POLICE (TEMPORARY)

HOTEL LAGUNA DEL
COCODRILO/PANADERÍA
DE PARIS

MAPACHE RENT-A-CAR

WITCH'S ROCK
SURF CAFÉ/CAMP

BEACH ACCESS

PHARMACY

BEST WESTERN TAMARINDO VISTA VILLAS/
MONKEY BAR/THRIFTY RENT-A-CAR

EL COCONUT

ECONOMY
RENT-A-CAR

SUPER LAS PALMERAS/SANSA

HOTEL/BAR/
RESTAURANTE
EL MILAGRO

To the Airstrip
and Liberia

HOTEL
TAMARINDO
DIRÍA

IGUANA SURF

AQUA DISCOTEQUE

BLUE TRAILZ SURF CAMP

SEE DETAIL

ALAMO RENT-A-CAR

TENNIS
CLUB

HOTEL
TROPICANA

BANK/EUROPCAR/
PLAZA ESMERALDA

SUNSET
HOUSE

TAMARINDO ADVENTURES/
HIGHTIDE

HOTEL JARDÍN
DEL EDÉN

BANANA SURF CLUB

REY SOL DISCO BAR

PLAZA TAMARINDO/BAR/POLICE

SUPER
2001

DRAGONFLY

HOTEL PASATIEMPO

ARCO
IRIS

HERTZ RENT-A-CAR

HOSTEL LA BOTELLA DE LECHE

APARTOTEL CHOCOLATE

CAFETERÍA NARI

BUEN APPETITO/
CYBER BAKANOS

NIBBA

TOILETS

TAXIS

COSTA RICA
PARADISE/PLAZA
COLONIAL

TAMARINDO
SURF SCHOOL

LA BARRA
MUSIC BAR

PLAZA CONCHAL

LA PALAPA

HOTEL
ZULLY MAR

WALTER'S

TANGO &
GRILL

COASTAL EMERGENCY
MEDICAL SERVICE

VILLAS MACONDO

SKATEBOARD PARK

DOMUS
KAHUNA

VOODOO LOUNGE

BACKWASH LAUNDRY

© AVALON TRAVEL

beach massage, Tamarindo

acoustic and *carnavale* nights on Monday and Wednesday, respectively. And if you expect the **Copacabana Beach Bar** to have live Brazilian music, you won't be disappointed; go at sunset on Wednesday and Sunday. Meanwhile, **La Barra Music Bar** (tel. 506/2653-0342) hits the groove with Latin Night on Wednesday, and reggae and hip-hop on Saturday.

I expect **Bar 1** (tel. 506/2653-2586, www .bar1tamarindo.com, 6 P.M.–2 A.M.), which opened in November 2008 upstairs in Plaza Tamarindo, to rocket to popularity among martini-sipping city-slickers. Open-air, it has hip black-and-white New York styling. DJs spin on weekends, it shows movies on Tuesday, and it has ladies' night on Thursday. It was adding a sushi restaurant.

And the opening of **Aqua Discoteque** (tel. 506/2653-2782. 10 P.M.–2:30 A.M.) raised the bar with its sexy styling; Monday is ladies' night, with free drinks.

The best sports bar is **Sports Bar Surf Club,** in Playa Langosta, with several pool tables and a classy ambience.

There are **casinos** at the Barceló Playa Langosta (8 P.M.–3 A.M.) and Tamarindo Diría, in Plaza Colonial (6–11 P.M.).

You can surprise your significant other for his or her birthday by hiring any of several Nicaraguan mariachi trios that solicit customers on the beach and main boulevard.

Sports and Recreation

Tamarindo Adventures (tel. 506/2653-0108, www.tamarindoadventuras.com) specializes in ATV tours and kayaking.

Blue Dolphin Sailing (tel. 506/2653-0446, www.sailbluedolphin.com) offers day and sunset cruises, plus snorkeling aboard a 12-meter catamaran, as do **Mandingo Sailing** (tel. 506/ 2653-2323, www.tamarindosailing.com) and **Seabird Sailing** (tel. 506/8381-1060, www.sea birdsailng.com).

Fishing outfitters include **Tamarindo Sportfishing** (tel. 506/2653-0090, www .tamarindosportfishing.com) and **Papagayo Excursions** (tel. 506/2653-0227, www .papagayoexcursions.com), which also has ATV tours, horseback trips, kayak trips, windsurfing and scuba diving, plus surf tours.

A dozen or so other outlets cater to surfers. **Blue Trailz** (tel. 506/2653-1705, www .bluetrailz.com) is considered the best. **Iguana Surf** (tel. 506/2653-0148, www.iguana surf.net) rents surfboards, offers surf-taxi service to out-of-the-way surfing spots, and has surf lessons, as does **Witch's Rock Surf Camp** (tel. 506/2653-1262, www.witchsrocksurfcamp .com), which also offers weeklong and nine-day surf packages.

For diving, contact **Agua Rica Diving Center** (tel. 506/2653-0094, www.aguarica.net), which has dives and snorkeling from $50.

You can rent horses ($10 per hour) at Hotel Capitán Suizo, which offers guided rides, as does **Painted Pony Guest Ranch** (tel. 506/2653-8041, www.paintedponyguest ranch.com), at Portegolpe.

Off Road Adventures (tel. 506/2653-1968, www.offroadcostarica.com) offers day trips in open-air Toyota four-wheel-drive vehicles.

Tennis buffs can get in the swing at the **Tamarindo Tennis Club** (tel. 506/2653-0898, www.tamarindotennisclub.com, 7:30 A.M.–9 P.M. daily), which has lessons and clinics.

There's even a **skateboard park** now, opposite Villas Macondo.

Shopping

There's no shortage of boutiques and roadside stalls selling quality souvenirs. For something unique, check out **Tamarindo Beach Cigar Lounge** (tel. 506/2653-0862, where Nicaraguan rollers produce superb-quality cigars, including a robust "Espresso" brand, made of Cuban leaves aged with espresso beans, and "La Flor de Palmar," sold in a box in the form of a traditional Costa Rican oxcart ($178 for 25 Churchills). It has a smoking lounge.

Accommodations

Tamarindo has dozens of options; those listed here are recommended in their price bracket. There are many more hotels than can be listed here.

UNDER $25

Backpackers are spoiled for choice. My favorite place is **Hostel La Botella de Leche** (tel. 506/2653-2061, www.labotelladeleche.com, $10 pp dorm, $20 s, $35 d private room low season, $12 pp dorm, $30 s, $36 d high season), one of the most popular surfers' and backpackers' spots in the country. It is run to high standards by a delightful Argentinian woman, Mariana "Mama" Nogaro; her son Wences offers surfing tuition. The place (now in its third location) is painted like a Holstein cow! It has a laundry, a delightful lounge, a large common kitchen, plus surf rental, Internet and Wi-Fi, and lockers. It has three dorms, plus six private rooms for up to four people.

Another great bet is the beachfront **Witch's Rock Surf Camp** (tel. 506/2653-1262, www .witchsrocksurfcamp.com, from $1,100 for seven days), a lively place with great ambience. It has clean, colorful, nicely appointed oceanfront rooms, plus a swimming pool, game rooms, thatched restaurant, lockers, a surf shop, and surfing lessons. It specializes in one-week surf packages.

The equally impressive **Blue Trailz Surf Camp** (tel. 506/2653-1705, www.bluetrailz .com) and **Tamarindo Backpackers** (tel. 506/2653-2753, www.tamarindobackpackers .com) compete.

$25-50

Readers rave about **Villas Macondo** (tel. 506/2653-0812, www.villasmacondo.com, $25 s or $30 d with fan, $45 s or $50 d with a/c, $70–105 apartment low season; $35 s or $40 d with fan, $55 s or $65 d with a/c, $105–140 apartment high season), run by a German couple. This delightful spot has five colorful albeit simply appointed double rooms with ceiling fans. Four larger rooms have air-conditioning. Or, choose spacious, fully equipped, two-story one- or two-bedroom apartments. There's a community kitchen, and you can cool off in a kidney-shaped pool.

$50-100

French-run **La Laguna del Cocodrilo Hotel** (tel.

THE NICOYA PENINSULA

506/2653-0255, www.lalagunadelcocodrilo
.com, $45–90 s/d low season, $60–115 s/d
high season) has a unique location: the natural back garden merges into the adjacent
lagoon with crocodiles. The hotel remodeled and went more upscale in 2008 and has
added a restaurant and lounge. It has 12 air-
conditioned rooms and two ocean-view suites,
all with cable TV and minimalist but charming decor including terra-cotta tile floors,
batik wall hangings, ceiling fans, and beautiful glazed bathrooms with hot water. Some
rooms have stone terraces facing the beach.
It has a bakery.

In the center, **Hotel Zully Mar** (tel. 506/
2653-0140, http://zullymar.com, $41 s or $46
d low season, $56 s or $61 d high season) has
raised itself from shoestring status and is now
a well-run property with 27 clean rooms (eight
with a/c, refrigerator, and safe) with private
baths, though most still have cold water. The
old wing is still popular with backpackers (despite being overpriced), though a newer wing
has metamorphosed Zully Mar into a simple
albeit stylish hotel with a pool.

The attractive **Hotel/Bar/Restaurante El
Milagro** (tel. 506/2653-0043, www.elmilagro
.com, $67 s or $72 d low season, $87 s or $92 d
high season) has charm. The 32 modern conical *cabinas*—set in soothing, breezy, landscaped
grounds with a swimming pool—have air-
conditioning and private baths with hot water.
A restaurant serves seafood under the watchful guidance of European management. There's
also a kids' pool. Rates include breakfast.

Domus Kahuna (tel. 506/2653-0648,
www.domuskahuna.com, $50 s or $60 d
rooms, $75 one-bedroom apartments, $115
two-bedroom apartments low season; $60 s,
$75 d room, $115 one-bedroom apartments,
$155 two-bedroom apartments high season)
has three simply furnished one-bedroom and
three two-bedroom apartments in a landscaped
garden. Rough-hewn timbers add a nice note to
the earth-tone structures, with classic Central
American architectural hints. It has free Wi-Fi
and a swimming pool.

I like the new beachfront **La Palapa** (tel.

506/2653-0362, www.lapalapatamarindo.com,
$65 s, $75 d), tucked up to the beach in the
village center. Its compact loft bedrooms are
endearingly furnished and have cable TVs,
minibars, and safes. It has an enviable location,
and a pleasing restaurant with bar. Nice!

The exquisite, Italian-run, canary-yel-
low **Luna Llena** (tel. 506/2653-0082,
www.hotellunallena.com, $75 s/d stan-
dard, $89 bungalows low season; $90 standard, $109 bungalows high season) has
air-conditioned rooms and bungalows around
an alluring swimming pool with swim-up bar
and a raised wooden sundeck with a whirlpool tub. Stone pathways connect sponge-
washed conical bungalows done up in lively
Caribbean colors and tasteful decor, including
terra-cotta floors; a spiral staircase leads to a
loft bedroom, and the semicircular bathrooms
are marvelous. There's a small restaurant and
a laundry. Rates include tax and breakfast (the
seventh day is free).

Past guests who remember the old Cabinas
Arco Iris won't recognize the new **(Hotel
Arco Iris** (tel. 506/2653-0330, www.hotel
arcoiris.com, $79 s/d bungalows, $89 s/d deluxe rooms low season; $89 bungalows, $99 deluxe rooms high season) under its new owner.
The two highlights are the gorgeous wood-
and-stone pool deck with lounge chairs, pool,
and the superb Seasons Restaurant. Black stone
pathways link the five bungalows and four upstairs deluxe rooms in sepia-toned units with
timber supports. The lovely yet simple aesthetic combines chocolates and creams, and
all rooms have TV, refrigerator, and gorgeous
contemporary bathrooms with slate walls and
stylish fixtures.

$100-200

Down by the shores, **Hotel Tamarindo Diría**
(tel. 506/2653-0031, www.tamarindodiria
.com, $182–230 year-round) ranks in the top
tier with its quasi-Balinese motif and rich
color scheme, although locals complain that it
dumps waste matter directly into the sea. The
lobby, boasting Guanacastecan pieces and elegant rolled-arm chaise lounges, opens to an

exquisite horizon pool with fountains, with lawns and ocean beyond. It has 113 pleasantly furnished air-conditioned rooms (including 47 deluxe and 28 premium) with terra-cotta tile floors. Some have a whirlpool tub, and many are wheelchair accessible. A large and airy restaurant with a beautiful hardwood ceiling opens onto an expansive bar and outside cocktail terrace. It has a kids' pool, tennis courts, a small casino, golf driving range, and a boutique, plus sportfishing and tours.

The **Hotel Pasatiempo** (tel. 506/2653-0096, www.hotelpasatiempo.com, $89 s/d standard $109 deluxe, $119 suites low season; $109 s/d standard $119 deluxe, $139 suites high season) has 11 attractive, spacious, well-lit, thatched, air-conditioned cabins around a pool in pretty grounds full of bougainvillea, bananas, and palms. Note the beautiful hand-carved doors and hand-painted murals in each room. It has a book exchange, table games, and snorkeling gear. The Yucca Bar hosts live music.

The overpriced, hillside, all-suite **Tamarindo Vista Villas** (tel. 506/653-0114, fax 506/653-0115, www.tamarindovistavillas.com, $144–194 s/d low season, $159–209 s/d high season) offers 32 handsomely appointed, oceanview, air-conditioned one- to three-bedroom suites with full kitchens and spacious verandas. The property has a swimming pool with waterfall, swim-up bar, open-air poolside restaurant, and disco.

Wow! That was my first reaction to **15 Love Contemporary Bed & Breakfast** (tel. 506/2653-0898, www.15lovebedandbreakfast.com, $95 s/d room, $115 suite low season; $125 room, $155 suite high season), at the Tamarindo Tennis Club. Tucked in a courtyard with plunge pool, wooden deck, and sexily sinuous bar, this hip minimalist inspiration has just three rooms and a suite, each with lovely, clean, crisp, colorful, contemporary decor and orthopedic king-size beds, plus flat-screen TV and Wi-Fi. Stylish to the max! You can rent the entire place.

City-style sophistication is also a hallmark at **Hotel Jardín del Edén** (tel. 506/2653-0137, www.jardindeleden.com, $110–150 s/d rooms, $190 suite, $140–170 apartment), on a bluff overlooking Tamarindo. Truly a hillside "garden of Eden," it earns laurels for the chic and amorous tenor of its 34 rooms and two villas with gracious contemporary flair, and spacious terrace-porches offering ocean views. Rooms are themed on regional styles: Japan, Tunisia, Mexico. A stunning pool with swim-up bar, whirlpool tub, and a large sundeck with shady *ranchitos* are set in lush gardens floodlit at night in a quasi-*son et lumière*. The restaurant is one of the best in town. Rates include buffet breakfast.

Not quite as classy, but still a great bet, is the colorful **Cala Luna Hotel and Villas** (tel. 506/2653-0214 or 800/503-5202, www.cala luna.com, $170 s/d room, $345–465 villa low season; $205 s/d room, $410–520 villa high season), at Playa Langosta. Spanish tile and rough-hewn timbers add to the cozy New Mexico–Central American style. The 20 hotel rooms, 16 garden villas, and five master villas surround a pool in a small landscaped garden. King-size beds, cable TVs, and CD players are standard, and each villa has its own pool. There's a boutique and tour desk, pool bar, plus an evocative candlelit restaurant. Tours, horseback rides, and fishing trips are offered.

I love the **◖ Sueño del Mar Bed and Breakfast** (tel. 506/2653-0284, www.sueno-del-mar.com, $150–195 low season, $195–240 high season), a truly exquisite Spanish colonial house with four rooms cascading down a shaded alcove to a small landscaped garden that opens onto the beach. Each is cool and shaded, with rough-hewn timbers, white-washed stone walls, terra-cotta tile floors, security boxes, screened arched windows with shutters, and tasteful fabrics. Most have exquisite rainforest showers. The huge upstairs suite is a true gem, with all-around screened windows, mosquito net on the four-poster bed made of logs, and a Goldilocks'-cottage feel to the bathroom with rainforest shower with gorgeous tilework. It also has a *casita* for four people. A small landscaped pool and wooden sundeck has been added, along with thatched shade area with hammock, perfect for enjoying cocktails and *bocas*. Complimentary snorkel gear, boogie boards, and bikes are available. I also love **Villa Alegre** (tel. 506/2653-0270, www.villaalegrecostarica.com, $150–195 low season, $170–230 high season), a contemporary beachfront bed-and-breakfast run by gracious hosts Barry and Suzye Lawson from California, who specialize in wedding and honeymoon packages. The main house has lofty ceilings, tile floors, lots of hardwood hints, a magnificent lounge with library, and four air-conditioned bedrooms with French doors opening onto a private patio. Two *casitas*—one sleeping four people—each have a living room, bedroom, and small but fully equipped kitchen. The rooms are individually decorated with the globetrotting couple's collection of art, rugs, and miscellany. The Mexico and Russia rooms are wheelchair-accessible. A vast veranda overlooks a swimming pool, with a thatched bar serving *bocas*. Rates include breakfast.

If large-scale resorts are your thing, the handsome **Barceló Playa Langosta Resort & Casino** (tel. 506/2653-0363, www.barcelo .com, from $95 per person low season, from $130 high season), is Tamarindo's first megaresort. It sits above the river estuary. It has 240 rooms in three categories in nine two- and three-story blocks arrayed around a freeform pool, with a whirlpool for 30, set in lush landscaped grounds. It has a casino, boutique, tour desk, and tours. Rates include tax.

Seeking a self-catering rental? One of my favorites is **Casa Cook** (tel. 506/2653-0125, http://casacook.net, $150–250), about one kilometer west of town, with three one-bedroom *casitas* with a pool and patio. Other choices include two large bedrooms with private baths in the main house and an apartment added in 2007. Alternately, try **The Surf House** (tel. 506/2255-0448, www.thesurfhouse.com, from $140 per night) or look to **Vacation Rentals of Tamarindo** (www.vacationrental softamaraindo.com).

OVER $200

My preferred place to rest my head is the Swiss-run **❮ Capitán Suizo** (tel. 506/2653-0075, www.hotelcapitansuizo.com, $130–150 s/d rooms, $180–220 bungalow, $300–375 suite low season; $190–210 s/d rooms, $250–290 bungalow, $365–525 suite high season), a deserving member of the Small Distinctive Hotels of Costa Rica. Beach-loving cognoscenti will appreciate the resort's casual sophistication. Even the local howler monkeys have decided this is the place to be! Pathways coil sinuously through a botanical *Fantasia* to a wide sundeck and large amoeba-shaped pool with a faux beach shelving gently into the water. The lovely 22 rooms and eight bungalows (some lack air-conditioning) have natural gray-stone floors and deep-red hardwoods, halogen lamps, and soft-lit lanterns for a more romantic note. Spacious bungalows have mezzanine bedrooms with king-size bed and huge bathrooms with "rainforest" showers and whirlpool tubs. The wood-paneled Honeymoon Suite has a king size bed in its own loft. The bar and restaurant are among Tamarindo's finest. Capitán Suizo has its own horse stable ($20 first hour, $10 each extra hour), plus kayaks, boogie boards, and a game room.

Yoga anyone? **Panacea de la Montaña** (tel. 506/2653-8515, www.panaceacr.com, $160 s or $240 d low season, $188 s or $260 d high season, including all meals) is a holistic yoga and wellness retreat in the mountains outside Tamarindo, with delightful Tuscan-style cabins and gourmet fare.

Alternately, the supremely deluxe **❮ Los Altos de Eros** (tel. 560/8850-4222, www .losaltosdeeros.com, $395–495 s/d) graces an 11-hectare estate outside town. This Tuscanstyle villa boasts six gorgeous rooms (four poolside), including a two-bedroom suite; all are done up in pure white and are exquisitely romantic. Dinners are served twice weekly. The inn specializes in yoga in a thatched ashram, plus health and beauty treatments in a fullservice spa.

Food

Tamarindo is blessed with some of the most creative restaurateurs in the country, and the scene is ever-changing.

The French **Panadería La Laguna del Cocodrilo** (tel. 506/2653-0255, 6 A.M.–7 P.M. daily) offers an all-you-can-eat buffet breakfast in the garden ($5). It also sells delicious croissants, chocolate èclairs, fruit tarts, baguettes, and bread, plus enchiladas and *empanadas* at lunch. For hearty gringo breakfasts, you can't beat the beachfront **Nogui Bar/Sunrise Café** (tel. 506/2653-0029, 6 A.M.–9:30 P.M. daily).

The **Smilin' Dog Taco Factory** (tel. 506/2653-0658, 11 A.M.–10 P.M. Mon.–Sat.) sells tacos ($1.75), burritos ($3), veggie burritos, quesadillas, and soft drinks (no alcohol). Nearby, Iguana Surf's **Kahiki Restaurant** (tel. 506/2653-3816, 11 A.M.–2 P.M. and 5–10 P.M. Wed.–Mon.) has a great setting under thatch; it makes great burgers ($7) and offers Asian fusion cuisine, such as coconut ceviche ($5) and oven-roasted, herb-rubbed pork tenderloin ($12).

For a cool, unpretentious open-air beach option, try **Nibba** (tel. 506/2654-0447, 7:30 A.M.–10:30 P.M. daily), with an eclectic menu ranging from salads and seafood to pizza and pastas.

The hip **El Jardín del Edén** (noon–10 P.M. daily, lunch $6–13, dinner $15–60), at the hotel of that name, serves fusion dishes such as jumbo shrimp in whiskey and tenderloin in black truffle sauce. Its sophisticated decor is perfect for singles (at the bar) and couples (in romantic thatched mezzanines).

El Coconut (tel. 506/2653-0086, 5–10 P.M. Tues.–Sun.) offers open-air gourmet fusion dining in hip and elegant surrounds. Typical dishes include mussels in creamy brandy sauce ($29.50) and jumbo garlic shrimp ($32).

Another winner for nouvelle dining is **Capitán Suizo** (tel. 506/2653-0075, 7 A.M.–9:15 P.M. daily), where German chef Roland merges European influences into a tropical setting. The creative menu runs from a perfect tomato soup to tilapia with olives, fresh tomato sauce, and macadamia vegetables. I've also enjoyed a curried chicken ($6), corvina in mango sauce ($8), and tilapia in caper sauce ($10). The dinner menu changes daily.

The air-conditioned, glass-enclosed elegant **Carolina's Restaurant** (tel. 506/8379-6834, 6–11 P.M. Thurs.–Tues.) offers a similar variety of superb nouvelle dishes, such as papaya-curry soup ($7) and tuna filet in fresh green spicy sauce ($15). And Chef Tish Thalman's **Dragonfly** (tel. 506/2653-1506, www.dragonflybarandgrill.com, 5–11 P.M. Mon.–Sat.) delivers mouthwatering fusion dishes, such as Thai-style crispy fish cake with curried sweet corn. You dine beneath canvas, but the place exudes romantic elegance. It's open for dinner only, closes for the month of October, and accepts cash only.

Cordon Bleu-trained Israeli chef Shlomy Koren serves up delicious Mediterranean dishes at **Restaurante Seasons** (tel. 506/8368-6983, 6–10 P.M. Mon.–Sat.), at Hotel Arco Iris. How about stuffed rigatoni with shrimp in a light creamy tomato sauce ($7.50) as an appetizer? And Middle Eastern–style chicken marinated in red wine and spices ($13)? It has a great wine selection and friendly service.

My favorite coffee shop is **Olga's Coffee Shop** (tel. 506/8395-5838, 7 A.M.–7 P.M. Mon.–Sat., 8 A.M.–2 P.M. Sun.), named for the lively and erudite Russian owner. This modern café has walls of glass, free Wi-Fi, and World music. Olga serves granola with yogurt breakfasts, homemade sandwiches, banana bread, and organic salads. Another good bet is the elegant **Coffee Navi** (7 A.M.–10 P.M. daily), outside the Tamarindo Diría hotel, serving quiche, Caesar salad, panini, and cappuccinos. Somewhat simpler, and offering fabulous focaccia sandwiches is **Buon Appetito** (no tel., 6 A.M.–midnight daily).

For groceries, head to **Supermercado Tamarindo** (9 A.M.–5 P.M. daily) or **Super Las Palmeras,** 100 meters east of Hotel Tamarindo Diría.

Information and Services

For tourist information, head to the U.S.–run **Costa Rica Paradise Tour Information** (tel. 506/2653-2251, www.crparadise.com, 8 A.M.–6 P.M. daily), in Plaza Conchal.

Jaime Peligro Bookshop (tel. 506/8820-9004, 9 A.M.–7 P.M. Mon.–Sat., noon–5 P.M.

THE NICOYA PENINSULA

© CHRISTOPHER P. BAKER

a sign warns of crocodiles in Tamarindo

Sun.) sells used and new books and CDs and also has a book exchange.

In medical need? Call the **Coastal Emergency Medical Service** (tel. 506/2653-1974). There's a **pharmacy** (tel. 506/2653-0210) next to Hotel El Milagro.

The many Internet cafés include **Cyber Bakanos** (tel. 506/2653-0628, 9 A.M.–10 P.M. daily), which doubles as an international call center; and **ILACNET** (tel. 506/2653-1740, 8 A.M.–7 P.M. daily), in Plaza Conchal, which also hosts a bank, the post office, and public toilets.

The **police station** (tel. 506/2653-0283), near Tamarindo Vista Villas, was due to relocate to Plaza Tamarindo in 2009.

The **Wayra Instituto de Español** (tel. 506/2653-0359, www.spanish-wayra.co.cr) offers Spanish language tuition courses.

Getting There and Away

SANSA and **Nature Air** operate scheduled daily service between Tamarindo and San José. The SANSA office is on the main street. A $3 departure tax is collected at the airport.

Alfaro-Tracopa buses (tel. 506/2222-2666) depart San José from Calle 14, Avenidas 3/5, at 8:30 A.M., 11:30 A.M., and 3:30 P.M. ($5). Buses (tel. 506/665-5891) depart Liberia for Tamarindo six times daily 3:50 A.M.–4:10 P.M.; and from Santa Cruz at 4:20 A.M., 5:30 A.M., 8:30 A.M., 10:30 A.M., 1:30 P.M., 3:30 P.M., and 8 P.M.

Return buses depart Tamarindo for San José at 3:30 A.M., 5:45 A.M. (Sun.), and 2 P.M.; for Liberia six times 5:45 A.M.–6:30 P.M.; and for Santa Cruz at 6 A.M., 9 A.M., noon, 2:30 P.M., and 4:15 P.M.

Tamarindo Shuttle (tel. 506/2653-2727) charges $18 for "door-to-door" service from Liberia airport.

Grayline (tel. 506/2220-2126, www.grayline costarica.com) and **Interbus** (tel. 506/2653-4314,, www.interbusonline.com), in Plaza Conchal, offer shuttles.

There's no gas station, but the **Ferretería,** at the entrance to town, sells gas.

You can rent cars locally with **Hertz** (tel. 506/2653-1358) and **Mapache** (tel. 506/2653-6363).

Getting Around

Bahéa Tamarindo Tours (tel. 506/2653-1987) rents scooters ($39 per day) and mountain bikes ($13 per day).

South to Junquillal

PLAYA AVELLANAS

From Tamarindo, you must backtrack to Villarreal in order to continue southward via Hernández (three kilometers south of Villarreal). The narrow dirt coast road becomes impassable in sections in the wet season, when you may have better luck approaching Playa Avellanas and Lagartillo from the south via Paraíso, reached by paved road from Santa Cruz.

Between Tamarindo and Avellanas, most of the coastline backs onto **Hacienda Pinilla,** which covers 1,800 hectares. This former cattle ranch is one of the most upscale residential resort communities in the country, with a championship 18-hole golf course, trails through a nature reserve with lagoons, a stable for horse rides ($15–35), a small hotel, plus scores of villas and condos for rent. It was still a work in progress at last visit.

Beautiful coral-colored Playa Avellanas, 12 kilometers south of Tamarindo, is renowned for its barrel surf. You can rent surfboards at **Cabinas Las Olas** (tel. 506/2658-9315, www.cabinaslasolas.co.cr).

Avellanas Surf School (tel. 506/2652-9042, www.avellanasurfschool.com) rents surfboards and offers classes and clinics.

Theft and car break-ins are major problems at the beaches. Never leave items in your car!

Accommodations and Food

You can **camp** ($2 pp) under thatch at **Bar y Restaurante Gregorio's.** It also has three basic *cabinas* ($15 s, $20 d) with private baths and cold water. Nearby **Lola's on the Beach** (tel. 506/2658-8097), a rustic beachfront restaurant, is famous for its namesake giant pig and also for dishes such as Hawaiian rawfish salad.

There are several other basic options. The best bet for backpackers is **Blue Trailz** (tel./fax 506/2652-9153, $5 camping, $12 pp), with three bunkrooms and shared bathrooms. There's a bare-bones TV lounge, kitchen, barbecue, and hammocks under thatch, plus an Argentinian "gourmet" bistro. Surf packages are offered. It rents tents ($6.50).

Swiss-run **Cabinas Las Olas** (tel. 506/2658-8315, www.cabinaslasolas.co.cr, $60 s or $70 d low season; $70 s or $80 d high season) is an "upscale" surfers' place with 10 bungalows widely spaced amid the dry forest. Each has private bathroom, bidet, and hot water. A raised wooden walkway leads 300 meters across mangroves to the beach. The video-bar and restaurant have an appealing ambience. It has ping-pong and rents kayaks, boogie boards, snorkeling gear, mountain bikes, and surfboards.

If you like minimalist contemporary styling you'll like **Las Avellanas Villas** (tel. 506/2652-9212, www.lasavellanasvillas.com, $55 s/d low season, $65 s/d high season), 300 meters inland of the beach. The five self-contained cabins set amid spacious lawns have glazed concrete floors, slightly ascetic yet stylish furniture (including a double bed and bunk), small kitchens, and heaps of light through cross-ventilated French doors opening to wooden decks. A pool was planned. Next door, the six-room **Hotel Mauna Loa Surf Resort** (tel. 506/2652-9012, www.maunaloa.it, $70) offers a similar and perfectly appealing alternative. The impressive **Villas Kaiki** (tel. 506/2652-9060, www.villaskaiki.com, $55–65 low season, $75–85 high season) is a virtual carbon copy of Las Avellanas Villas, 400 meters away.

Hacienda Pinilla (tel. 506/2680-3000, www.haciendapinilla.com, from $120–140 rooms, $295 suites, $300 beach house low season; $145–175 rooms, $325 suites, $395 beach house high season) has a variety of deluxe accommodations, including Superior and Deluxe rooms in the La Posada Hotel, plus a large selection of beach houses and two-, three-, and four-bedroom villas. Here, too, is the lavish, beachfront **JW Marriott Guanacaste Resort & Spa** (tel. 506/2681-2000, www.marriott.com, $299–739 rooms, $999–2,199 suites), which opened in December 2008. It has 310 luxuriously appointed guest rooms, including 20 Junior Suites, all with Wi-Fi and lavish bathrooms. The most sumptuous rooms have their own plunge pools. Plus there's a full-service spa, a huge infinity pool, and four restaurants. The inspiration is old-world colonial, reborn in contemporary vogue.

PLAYAS LAGARTILLO AND NEGRA

Playa Lagartillo, beyond Punta Pargos, just south of Playa Avellanas, is another gray-sand beach with tidepools. Lagartillo is separated by Punta Pargos from Playa Negra, centered on the community of **Los Pargos.** It, too, is popular with the surfing crowd.

About five kilometers south of Los Pargos, the dirt road cuts inland about eight kilometers to the tiny hamlet of **Paraíso,** where another dirt road leads back to the coast and dead-ends at Playa Junquillal.

Pura Jungla Preserve (tel. 506/2652-9160, www.purajungla.com) is an eco-community in the hills one kilometer north of Paraíso. The brainchild of environmentalist Ray Beise, the 235-hectare nature preserve is designed to show that beautiful homes can be built in harmony with their natural surroundings. Ray has returned erstwhile cattle pasture to forest that now draws a plethora of wildlife, including monkeys and cats. There's an exotic fruit orchard, experimental tree farm, organic banana grove, and nature trails, one of which leads to a waterfall.

Accommodations

A delightful Peruvian couple run **Kontiki** (tel. 506/2652-9117, www.kontikiplayanegra.com, $10 s, $20 d, $25 quad), about three kilometers north of Los Pargos, between Lagartillo and Negra. This rustic and fairly basic farmhouse with a wonderful offbeat ambience has five thatched *cabinas* raised on stilts, with shared bath and cold water; one rates as a virtual treehouse and features two dorms with "Goldilocks and the Three Bears"–style bunks and a double bed (howler monkeys hang out in the treetops at eye level). The place abounds

with pre-Columbian figurines. Peruvian dishes are cooked in an outdoor oven, and it has Wi-Fi. Rates include breakfast.

The three-story, all-hardwood **Mono Congo Lodge** (tel. 506/2652-9261, www.monocongolodge.com, $65–95 s/d), about one kilometer north of Los Pargos, has lost its warm welcome of late. This Colorado-style lodge that has been described as "a mixture of Swiss Family Robinson tree house and Australian outback bed-and-breakfast" is hand-built of stone and hardwoods and has six simply furnished air-conditioned rooms with magnificent high beds boasting orthopedic mattresses, mosquito nets, and batik spreads, plus screened windows, TVs/DVDs, and exquisite tile work in the bathrooms (some have stone walls). A wraparound veranda has hammocks and leather lounge chairs. It's surrounded by fruit trees and dry forest. Horseback riding tours, boat charters, and massage can be arranged. Rates include breakfast.

Pablo's Picasso (tel. 506/2652-9158, $12.50 with fan, $15 with a/c), at Playa Negra, is legendary among surfers. This rustic hostelry and surfers' gathering spot is run by a friendly Yank named Paul. He offers four air-conditioned, spacious, and surprisingly elegant rooms with private baths with cold water (two with shared baths), and two air-conditioned *cabinas* with kitchens. You can camp for $4 per person, including toilets and showers. Hammocks are slung beneath the rustic bar, which has free Internet and a pool table.

For an alternative, consider **Pico Negro Surf Camp** (tel. 506/2652-9369, $10 pp), with four rooms in a two-story building facing the village soccer field. Each has shared stoned-lined showers with cold water only, and pizzas are served in a rustic restaurant.

By the sands at Playa Negra, **Hotel Playa Negra** (tel. 506/2652-9134, www.playanegra.com, $70 s or, $80 d low season; $77 s or $88 d high season) is designed like a South African kraal. The circular cabins are lovely, with simple yet colorful motifs. It has a simple restaurant and games room, plus a swimming pool and surf shop.

THE NICOYA PENINSULA

© CHRISTOPHER P. BAKER

"Burgers as Big as Your Head" at Pablo's Picasso in Playa Negra

My vote for best digs for miles goes to the Peruvian-run ⬅ **Café Playa Negra** (tel. 506/2652-9351, www.playanegracafe.com, $17–29 s, $30–42 d low season; $20–32 s, $36–48 d high season). This cozy option has expanded and now exudes tremendous ambience beyond the antique-style doors. It has six rooms (two with bunks) appointed with glazed concrete floors, plump sofas, mattresses atop poured concrete with Guatemalan spreads, sponge-washed walls, and hammocks on a broad veranda facing a gorgeous pool. Three rooms are air-conditioned; three have ceiling fans. It also has a full bar, board games, and Peruvian restaurant.

Food
Carlos at **Café Playa Negra** (7 A.M.–9 P.M. daily) conjures superb pancakes, French toast, quiches, sandwiches, ceviche, entrées such as mahi mahi with creamy seafood sauce with shrimp ($9), plus killer *batidos* (shakes). Friday is sushi night. The café also offers Internet connections ($2.50 per hour) and laundry service ($7.50 per load).

Paul, at **Pablo's Picasso** (11 A.M.–until the last guest leaves), serves "burgers as big as your head" ($4), plus pancakes ($3), sandwiches, and pastas.

PLAYA JUNQUILLAL
Playa Junquillal, four kilometers southwest of Paraíso and 31 kilometers west of Santa Cruz, is an attractive, four-kilometer-long, light-gray-sand beach with rock platforms and tidepools. Beware the high surf and strong riptides. The beachfront road dead-ends at the wide and deep Río Andumolo, whose mangrove estuary is home to birds and crocodiles.

Paradise Riding (tel. 506/2658-8162, www.paradiseriding.com) offers horse-riding trips.

Accommodations and Food
Accommodations in Junquillal struggle to draw a clientele, and the scene was fluid at last visit. There are more options than listed here.

Despite its fabulous clifftop perch, the **Iguanazul Beach Resort** (tel. 506/2658-8123, www.iguanazul.com) appeals mainly to Tico travelers, and at last visit the public areas remain in need of a total remake.

Villa Roberta B&B (tel. 506/2658-8127, www.junquillal.com, $35–50 low season, $50–75 high season) is a modern hilltop home about 400 meters inland of the beach. It rents two spacious rooms. One is a very attractive double room with a black stone floor and king-size bed, and a beautiful bathroom with stone floor, sink, and shower. The second is an air-conditioned apartment with lofty ceiling, small kitchen, and a tasteful bathroom with a bidet. Each has a pleasing motif with dark hardwood accents and sea-blue tiles. It has a deep kidney-shaped pool plus hammocks on verandas.

About 100 meters south, a German-Tico couple run **El Castillo Divertido** (tel./fax 506/2658-8428, castillodivertido@hotmail.com, $30 s, $42 d), a crenellated three-story structure with a breezy hillside setting 300 meters inland of the beach. It has six simply furnished rooms with large louvered-glass windows, private bath (three have hot water and ocean view). There's a rooftop sundeck.

The **Hibiscus Hotel** (tel./fax 506/2658-8437, $30 s, $40 d) is set amid landscaped grounds full of palms and plantains and run by a German couple. All five rooms—genteel and spotless—have fans and private baths with hot water, plus hammocks on terraces. Quality seafood is served in a pretty little dining area.

In the center of the beach, the German-run **Villa Serena** (tel./fax 506/2658-8430, www.land-ho.com, $65 s/d low season, $150 high season) has 10 modern bungalows. The spacious, light, and airy rooms—all with fans and private baths with hot water—are spread out among palms and surrounded by emerald-green grass and flowery gardens. The villa has a cozy lounge overlooking the beach, a library, and a swimming pool, and a hibiscus-encircled tennis court. Dinners are served on an elevated veranda overlooking the ocean. It offers spa treatments.

Prefer a bed-and-breakfast inn? **Hotelito Si Si Si** (tel. 506/2658-9021, www.hotelitosisisi.com, $79 s/d room, $99 casita) offers three rooms and a one-bedroom *casita* with king-size beds.

For self catering, try **Plumitas Pacífica** (tel. 506/2658-7125, www.plumitapacifica.com, $85 low season, $95 high season), with two spacious, simply furnished apartment units with full, marble-topped kitchens. They smelled of fresh concrete. It has a tremendous beachfront setting.

For the "The best fish sandwich in Central America," or an early morning espresso, head to **Rudy's** (no tel., 6:30 A.M.–10 P.M. daily), which doubles as the local grocery store. It has themed food nights.

Getting There

A bus (tel. 506/221-7202) departs San José for Junquillal from Avenida 3, Calle 20, daily at 2 P.M. ($5, five hours). Buses depart Santa Cruz at 5 A.M., 10 A.M., 2:30 P.M., and 5:30 P.M. Return buses depart for Santa Cruz at 6 A.M., 9 A.M., 12:30 P.M., and 4:30 P.M.; and for San José at 5 A.M.

Playa Lagarto to Ostional

PLAYA LAGARTO AND SOUTH

South of Junquillal, the dirt road leads along a lonesome stretch of coast to Nosara (35 km south of Junquillal). Fabulous beaches lie hidden along this route, albeit for most of the way out of sight of the road. Until recently, there were few hotels. Just forest, cattle pasture, lonesome rustic dwellings, and an occasional fishing village. Things are stirring here, finally, and several hotels have opened in the past two years.

If driving south from Tamarindo or west from Santa Cruz on the Santa Cruz–Junquillal road, you must turn south at Soda Las Lucas, four kilometers east of Paraíso—the turnoff is signed for Marbella (16 km) and Nosara. *There are several rivers to ford. A four-wheel-drive vehicle is essential.*

About six kilometers south of the junction, the road briefly hits the shore at **Lagarto** before curling inland to **Marbella,** from where a side road runs down to **Playa Lagarcito.** Four kilometers farther you'll pass black-sand **Playa Azul.** About eight kilometers farther south, a turnoff from the coast road leads to the fishing hamlet of **San Juanillo.** Ostional is five kilometers farther south.

Paski Adventures (tel. 506/2652-8086) offers sportfishing out of The Sanctuary resort (tel. 506/2682-8111, www.thesanctuaryresort.com).

Accommodations and Food

Casa Mango (tel. 506/2682-8032, donjim@racsa.co.cr, $12 pp), on a hillside three kilometers south of Marbella, has four handsome yet bare-bones wooden *cabinas* with fans, and shared bathrooms with cold water only; there is also a thatched *casa* with kitchen ($60 up to six people). It has a restaurant and bar with pool table and veranda with rockers.

Upscale travelers might check into **The Sanctuary** (tel. 506/2682-8111, www.the sanctuaryresort.com, $110 s/d rooms, $135–160 cottages low season; $140 s/d rooms, $175–210 cottages high season), a full-blown resort at Playa Azul. It has condos in a gracious contemporary take on colonial plantation style. There's a spa, tennis, swimming pool, and water sports. It no longer operates as an all-inclusive resort.

At San Juanillo, **Cabinas El Sueño** (tel. 506/2682-8074, $35 s/d low season, $40 high season) has 10 colorful, well-lit, simply furnished rooms.

For those who don't mind spartan accommodations, one of my all-time faves is **(Tree Tops Inn** (tel./fax 506/2682-1334, treetopscosta rica@gmail.com, $125–145 s/d), a secluded and rustic one-room bed-and-breakfast tucked above a cove at San Juanillo. This charming place is the home of former race-car champion Jack Hunter and his wife, Karen—delightful hosts who go out of their way to make you feel at home. You're the only guest. There's one basically furnished room with outdoor shower. As I said, spartan! You're here for the spectacular solitude and setting that includes a horseshoe reef with live coral that's great for snorkeling, and a private beach for an all-over tan.

Monkeys cavort in the treetops. The couple offers turtle safaris to Ostional, a swim-with-turtle excursion, plus sportfishing tours; if you catch your own fish, Karen will prepare sushi. She also fixes gourmet five-course dinners ($34 pp). Rates include a real English breakfast. Reservations are essential.

Another delight is the Swiss-run **Luna Azul** (tel. 506/2682-1400, fax 506/2682-1047, www .hotellunaazul.com, $80 s or $95 d low season, $110 s or $135 d high season), high on a hilltop between San Juanillo and Ostional. Its colorful contemporary aesthetic is appealing, and the views are killer from the mezzanine open-air restaurant overlooking a lovely infinity pool and sundeck. It has seven spacious, cross-ventilated cabins with garden showers. And health treatments are offered. A lovely place!

The hilltop **La Joya de Manzanillo** (tel. 506/8288-9843, www.lajoyademanzanillo .com), new for 2008 at Playa Manzanillo, has six cabins amid lawns on an old *finca*. A circular restaurant has all-around views. The rooms are nothing special, however, and have "suicide showers" (there is an electrical switch in the shower unit over your head). Somewhat more impressive is **Hotel Villa La Granadilla** (tel. 506/8810-8929, http://hotellagranadilla.com, $20 room, $30 suite, $40 apartment low season; $40 room, $50 suite, $60 apartment high season), two kilometers south of San Juanillo. This two-story Spanish colonial-style hotel has three suites, a one-bedroom apartment, and a suite. There's a pool and thatched restaurant.

Most impressive of the newcomers is **Hotel Punta India** (tel. 506/8815-8170, www.punta india.com, $100 s/d), with six self-contained, two-bedroom, two-story villas. The lovely layout includes poured concrete sofas with colorful cushions, and furnishings are comfortable and simple. I like the thatched open-air restaurant overlooking a pool.

(OSTIONAL NATIONAL WILDLIFE REFUGE

The 248-hectare Refugio Nacional Silvestre Vida Ostional begins at Punta India, about two kilometers south of San Juanillo, and extends

RESPITE FOR THE RIDLEY

Elsewhere in Costa Rica, harvesting turtle eggs is illegal and usually occurs only in the dead of night. At Ostional it occurs legally and by daylight. The seeming rape of the endangered ridley – called *lora* locally – is the pith of a bold conservation program that aims to help the turtles by allowing the local community to commercially harvest eggs in a rational manner.

Costa Rica outlawed the taking of turtle eggs nationwide in 1966. But egg poaching is a time-honored tradition. The coming of the first *arribada* to Ostional in 1961 was a bonanza to the people of Ostional. Their village became the major source of turtle eggs in Costa Rica. Coatis, coyotes, raccoons, and other egg-hungry marauders take a heavy toll on the tasty eggs, too. Ridley turtles have thus hit on a formula for outwitting their predators – or at least of surviving despite them: They deposit millions of eggs at a time (In any one season, 30 million eggs might be laid at Ostional). Ironically, the most efficient scourge are the turtles themselves. Since Ostional beach is literally covered with thousands of turtles, the eggs laid during the first days of an *arribada* are often dug up by turtles arriving later. Often before they can hatch, a second *arribada* occurs. Again the beach is covered with crawling reptiles. As the newcomers dig, many inadvertently excavate and destroy the eggs laid by their predecessors and the beach becomes strewn with rotting embryos. Even without human interference, only 1 percent to 8 percent of eggs in a given *arribada* will hatch. Meanwhile, tens of thousands of adult ridleys are killed at sea for meat and to make "shoes for Italian pimps," in the words of Archie Carr.

By the early 1970s, the turtle population seemed to be below the minimum required to maintain the species. After a decade of study, scientists concluded that uncontrolled poaching of eggs would ultimately exterminate the nesting colony. They also reasoned that a *controlled* harvest would actually rejuvenate the turtle population. Such a harvest during the first two nights of an *arribada* would *improve* hatch rates at Ostional by reducing the number of broken eggs and crowded conditions that together create a spawning ground for bacteria and fungi that prevent the development of embryos.

along 15 kilometers of shoreline to Punta Guiones, eight kilometers south of the village of Nosara. It incorporates the beaches of Playa Ostional, Playa Nosara, and Playa Guiones.

The village of **Ostional** is midway along **Playa Ostional,** which has some of the tallest breaking waves in the country. The refuge, one of the world's most important sea turtle hatcheries, was created to protect one of three vitally important nesting sites in Costa Rica for the *lora,* or olive ridley turtle (the others are Playa Camaronal, and Playa Nancite, in Santa Rosa National Park). A significant proportion of the world's Pacific ridley turtle population nests at Ostional, invading the beach en masse for up to one week at a time July–December (peak season is August and September, starting with the last quarter of the full moon), and singly or in small groups at other times during the year. Synchronized mass nestings are known to occur at only a dozen or so beaches worldwide (in Mexico, Nicaragua, Honduras, Surinam, Panama, Orissa in India, and Costa Rica).

Time your arrival correctly and out beyond the breakers you may see a vast flotilla of turtles massed shoulder to shoulder, waiting their turn to swarm ashore, dig a hole in the sand, and drop in the seeds for tomorrow's turtles. The legions pour out of the surf in endless waves. It's a stupendous sight, this *arribada* (arrival). Of the world's eight marine turtle species, only the females of the olive ridley and its Atlantic cousin, Kemp's ridley, stage *arribadas.* Ostional is the most important of these. So tightly packed is the horde that the turtles feverishly clamber over one another in their efforts to find an unoccupied nesting site. As they dig, sweeping their flippers back and forth, the petulant

In 1987, the Costa Rican Congress finally approved a management plan that would legalize egg harvesting at Ostional. The statute that universally prohibited egg harvesting was reformed to permit the residents of Ostional to take and sell turtle eggs. The unique legal right to harvest eggs is vested in members of the Asociación Desarrollo Integral de Ostional (ADIO). The University of Costa Rica, which has maintained a biological research station at Ostional since 1980, is legally responsible for management and review. A quota is established for each *arribada*. Sometimes, no eggs are harvested; in the dry season (Dec.-May), as many as 35 percent of eggs may be taken; when the beach is hotter than Hades, the embryos become dehydrated, and the hatching rate falls below 1 percent. The idea is to save eggs that would be broken anyway or that otherwise have a low expectation of hatching. By law, eggs may be taken only during the first 36 hours of an *arribada*. After that, the villagers protect the nests from poachers and the hatchlings from ravenous beasts.

The eggs are dealt to distributors, who sell on a smaller scale at a contract-fixed price to bakers (which favor turtle eggs over those of hens; turtle eggs give dough greater "lift") and bars, brothels, and street vendors who sell the eggs as aphrodisiacal *bocas* (snacks). Net revenues from the sale of eggs are divided between the community (80 percent) and the Ministry of Agriculture. ADIO distributes 70 percent of its share among association members as payment for their labors, and 30 percent to the Sea Turtle Project and communal projects. ADIO also pays the biologists' salaries. Profits have funded construction of a health center, a house for schoolteachers, the ADIO office, and a Sea Turtle Research Lab.

Scientists claim that the project also has the potential to stop the poaching of eggs on other beaches. It's a matter of economics: Poachers have been undercut by cheaper eggs from Ostional. Studies also show that the turtle population has stabilized. Recent *arribadas* have increased in size. And hatch rates are up dramatically.

Alas, illegal fishing within the marine park boundaries kills hundreds of turtles each year.

females scatter sand over one another and the air is filled with the slapping of flippers on shells. By the time the *arribada* is over, more than 150,000 turtles may have stormed this prodigal place and 15 million eggs may lie buried in the sand.

Leatherback turtles also come ashore to nest in smaller numbers October–January.

You can walk the entire length of the beach's 15-kilometer shoreline. Although turtles can handle the strong currents, humans have a harder time: swimming is not advised. Howler monkeys, coatimundis, and kinkajous frequent the forest inland from the beach. The mangrove swamp at the mouth of the Río Nosara is a nesting site for many of the 190 bird species hereabouts.

Turtle Viewing

You must check in with ADIO (Asociación Desarrollo Integral de Ostional, tel./fax 506/2682-0470, adiotort@racsa.co.cr) before exploring the beach; a guide is compulsory ($10) during arribadas, when an entry fee of $10 is payable at the *puesto* (ranger station) at the southern end of the village, where you check in; you watch a video before entering the beach as a group.

All vehicles arriving at night are requested to turn off their headlights when approaching the beach. Flashlights and flash photography are also forbidden. Personal contact with turtles is prohibited, as is disturbance of markers placed on the beach.

Accommodations and Food

Camping ($3) is allowed at **Soda La Plaza,** which has a portable toilet.

The refuge administrative office (tel. 506/ 2682-0428, $7 pp), at the south end of the village, has a clean modern dorm for volunteers with a two-week minimum stay.

Pacha Mama (tel. 506/2289-7081, www.pacha-mama.org) is a "spiritual-ecological village," or commune, on a hilltop near Limonal at the north end of Ostional, about three kilometers inland. Alas, this community has a long history of offending local sensibilities.

Cabinas Ostional (tel. 506/2682-0428, $12 pp), 50 meters south of the soccer field, has six clean, pleasing rooms sleeping three people, with fans and private baths with cold water. Two newer cabins have lofty thatched ceilings. About 100 meters south, the **Bar y Restaurante Las Guacamayas** (tel. 506/2682-0430, $10 pp) has four small but clean rooms with two single beds, fans, and shared bathroom with cold water only.

At the north end of Ostional is the Hungarian-owned **Hotel Rancho Brovilla** (tel. 506/8380-5639 or 2280-4919, www.brovilla.com, $33–45 s, $53–65 d room, $60–80 apartment, $125–200 casas), a hilltop retreat with a splendid setting offering views. It has 12 air-conditioned *cabinas,* each with fans, TV, and a private bath with hot water. It also has two two-bedroom *casas* and a two-bedroom apartment. There's a breezy terrace with a plunge pool and restaurant. Plans include tennis courts, horseback riding, fishing, and turtle tours. Rates include breakfast.

Information and Services

The **ADIO** (Asociación Desarrollo Integral de Ostional, tel./fax 506/2682-0470, adiotort@racsa.co.cr) office is beside the road, on the northwest corner of the soccer field. Rodrigo Morera, the community leader, is helpful. The **ranger booth** (tel. 506/2682-0400) is 200 meters south of the soccer field, behind the **Doug Robinson Marine Research Laboratory** (tel. 506/2682-0812).

The *pulpería* at the northern end of the soccer field has a **public telephone.** There's a **police station** (tel. 506/8828-2892).

Getting There

A bus departs Santa Cruz for Ostional at 12:30 P.M. (three hours, returning at 5 A.M.); it may not run in wet season. You can take a taxi (about $8) or walk to Ostional from Nosara.

The dirt road between Ostional and Nosara requires you to ford (*vanar* in Spanish) the Río Montaña (about 5 km south of Ostional), which can be impassable during wet season; sometimes a tractor will be there to pull you through for a fee. About one kilometer farther south the road divides: The fork to the left (east) fords the Río Nosara just before entering the village of Nosara and is impassable in all but the most favorable conditions; that to the right crosses the Río Nosara via a bridge and the community of **Santa Marta.**

Nosara and Vicinity

◖ NOSARA

Nosara boasts three of the best beaches in Nicoya, each with rocky tidepools where the seawater is heated by the sun—great for soaking. They are backed by hills smothered in moist tropical forest. **Playa Nosara** extends north from Punta Nosara and the river estuary to Ostional. It's backed by mangroves. *Arribadas* of olive Ridley turtles occasionally occur. More are expected. Tiny **Playa Pelada** is tucked in a cove south of Punta Nosara and has a blowhole at the south and a bat cave at the north end. **Playa Guiones,** separated from Playa Pelada by Punta Pelada, is a ruler-straight, five-kilometer-long expanse of white sand washed by surf and, hence, popular with surfers. *Beware strong riptides!*

The sleepy village of **Bocas de Nosara** is five kilometers inland from the coast, five kilometers south of Ostional, on the banks of the Río Nosara. It maintains a simple traditional Tico lifestyle but otherwise offers little of appeal. A large foreign community lives four kilometers south of the village, where about 200

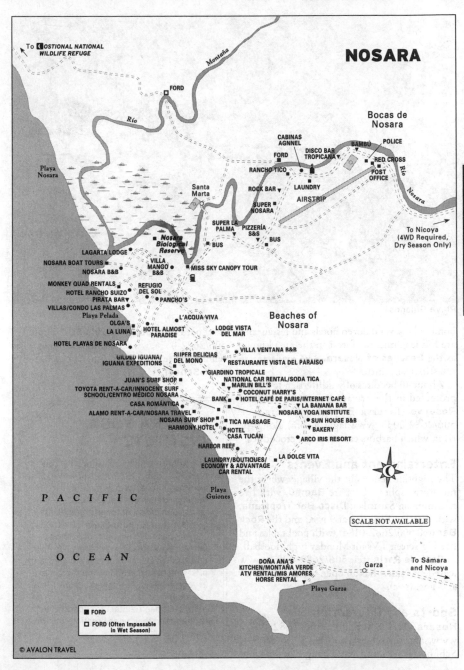

NOSARA

To Ostional National Wildlife Refuge

Montaña

Río

FORD

Río

Bocas de Nosara

Playa Nosara

CABINAS AGNNEL
POLICE
BAMBÚ
FORD
DISCO BAR TROPICANA
RED CROSS
RANCHO TICO
POST OFFICE

Santa Marta

ROCK BAR
LAUNDRY
AIRSTRIP
SUPER NOSARA

To Nicoya (4WD Required, Dry Season Only)

SUPER LA PALMA
PIZZERÍA S&S
BUS
BUS

Nosara Biological Reserve

Beaches of Nosara

LAGARTA LODGE
VILLA MANGO B&B
MISS SKY CANOPY TOUR
NOSARA BOAT TOURS
NOSARA B&B
REFUGIO DEL SOL
MONKEY QUAD RENTALS
HOTEL RANCHO SUIZO
PIRATA BAR
PANCHO'S
VILLAS/CONDO LAS PALMAS
Playa Pelada
OLGA'S
L'ACQUA VIVA
LA LUNA
HOTEL ALMOST PARADISE
LODGE VISTA DEL MAR
HOTEL PLAYAS DE NOSARA
VILLA VENTANA B&B
GILDED IGUANA/
SUPER DELICIAS DEL MONO
IGUANA EXPEDITIONS
RESTAURANTE VISTA DEL PARAISO
GIARDINO TROPICALE
JUAN'S SURF SHOP
NATIONAL CAR RENTAL/SODA TICA
MARLIN BILL'S
TOYOTA RENT-A-CAR/INNOCENT SURF
COCONUT HARRY'S
SCHOOL/CENTRO MÉDICO NOSARA
HOTEL CAFÉ DE PARIS/INTERNET CAFÉ
CASA ROMÁNTICA
BANK
LA BANANA BAR
ALAMO RENT-A-CAR/NOSARA TRAVEL
NOSARA YOGA INSTITUTE
NOSARA SURF SHOP
TICA MASSAGE
SUN HOUSE B&B
HARMONY HOTEL
HOTEL CASA TUCÁN
BAKERY
ARCO IRIS RESORT
HARBOR REEF
LA DOLCE VITA
LAUNDRY/BOUTIQUES/
ECONOMY & ADVANTAGE CAR RENTAL

Playa Guiones

SCALE NOT AVAILABLE

PACIFIC

OCEAN

DOÑA ANA'S KITCHEN/MONTAÑA VERDE
ATV RENTAL/MIS AMORES HORSE RENTAL
Garza
To Sámara and Nicoya

Playa Garza

FORD
FORD (Often Impassable in Wet Season)

© AVALON TRAVEL

THE NICOYA PENINSULA

© CHRISTOPHER P. BAKER

Playa Guiones

homes plus several dozen hotels and restaurants are hidden amid the forest in the area known as the **Beaches of Nosara**. The roads are an intestinal labyrinth.

About 40 hectares of wildlife-rich forest are protected in the private **Nosara Biological Reserve** (Reserva Biológica Nosara, tel. 506/2682-0035, www.lagarta.com) along the river, which harbors caimans and crocodiles.

Entertainment and Events

The nightlife centers in the village, where the most atmospheric bars are **Bambú,** with live marimba on Saturday; **Disco Bar Tropicana,** with disco on Saturday at 9 P.M.; and the **Rock Bar** (tel. 506/2682-0184), with pool tables and five big-screen TVs for Monday night football.

Café de Paris (tel. 506/2682-0087, www.cafedeparis.net) has an open-air movie Friday at 7 P.M. (free).

Sports and Recreation

Nosara Surf Shop (tel. 506/2682-0573, www.safarisurfschool.com) has a "Safari Surf School." It sells and rents boogie boards and surfboards. **Coconut Harry's Surf Shop** (tel. 506/2682-0574, www.coconutharrys.com) has rentals and surf tours, as does **Corky Carrol's Surf School** (U.S. tel. 714/969-3959, www

---

NOSARA YOGA INSTITUTE

This nonresidential yoga education center (tel. 506/2682-0071 or 866/439-4704, www.nosarayoga.com) is dedicated to professional training and advanced career development for teachers and practitioners in the field of yoga and bodywork. Perched in the hills behind Playa Guiones, it's the perfect place to relax and recharge. The institute specializes in advanced techniques and offers intensive one- to four-week programs in yoga, meditation, Pranassage (a private one-on-one yoga session, combining yoga assists and hand contact to support clients in deepening their yoga practice), plus nature and health programs.

© CHRISTOPHER P. BAKER

horseback riding at Playa Nosara

.surfschool.net) at Harbor Reef. **Innocent Surf School** (tel. 506/8810-4710, www.innocent surfschool.com) has lessons daily at 8 A.M., 10 A.M., and 2 P.M.

Iguana Expeditions (tel. 506/2682-0259), at the Gilded Iguana, offers sea kayaking and has a surf school. **Fishing Nosara** (tel. 904/591-2161, www.fishingnosara.com) offers sportfishing.

Inevitably, Nosara now has a canopy tour (where doesn't?) at **Miss Sky Canopy Tour** (tel. 506/2682-0969, www.missskycanopytour .com, $60 adults, $40 children), with 21 zipline runs. The longest is 750 meters. Fun! Tours leave at 8 A.M., 2 P.M., and 6 P.M.

Accommodations
UNDER $25
In the village, **Cabinas Agnnel** (tel. 506/2682-0142, $10 pp) offers simple rooms with private baths with cold water.

$25-50
The **Gilded Iguana Resort Hotel** (tel. 506/2682-0259, www.gildediguana.com, $30–65

s/d low season, $45–80 high season) has 12 spacious, cross-ventilated rooms and two-bedroom suites with fans, refrigerators, coffeemakers, toasters, and large walk-in showers with hot water. There's a pleasing bar-cum-restaurant with TV, and sea kayaking is offered.

For grandstand views of both jungle and coast, check into **Lodge Vista del Mar** (tel. 506/2682-0633, www.lodgevistadelmar.com, $36–48 s, $44–56 d), astride a ridge high in the hills overlooking Beaches of Nosara. This three-story modern structure has nine cross-ventilated rooms and one suite, all modestly furnished, with fans, cool limestone floors, and private bathroom with hot water. One has air-conditioning. It has an Olympic-length lap pool, laundry facilities, and a simple outdoor kitchen for guests. Rates include breakfast.

Two similarly priced options are **Harbor Reef Lodge** (tel. 506/2682-1000, www.harbor reef.com), which has four handsomely appointed air-conditioned suites with large sitting rooms and wet bars; and **Pancho's** (tel. 506/2682-0591, www.panchosresort.com), with six cross-ventilated bungalows and a duplex facing a magnificent circular pool. Opposite Pancho's, and a delightfully colorful option, is **Refugio del Sol** (tel./fax 506/2682-0287, www.refugiodelsol.com, $30 s, $40 d, $55 with kitchen), with four rooms and two apartments along a broad shady terrace with hammocks. The aesthetic is simple yet nice, with ocher and orange color schemes, brass-studded hardwood doors, orthopedic mattresses, ceiling fans, and small modern bathrooms.

Also to consider at Playa Guiones is the Swiss-run **Rancho Suizo Lodge** (tel. 506/2682-0057, www.nosara.ch, $34 s or $50 d low season, $45 s or $63 d high season), with 10 thatched *cabinas* with small but pleasant rooms and private baths with hot water; and **Nosara B&B** (tel. 506/2682-0209, www.nosarabandb.net, $29 s or $39 d low season, $39 s or $49 d high season), which has nice hosts but is a ho-hum property.

Readers continue to complain about the ongoing construction and lack of attention to guests at **Hotel Playas de Nosara,** which cannot be recommended.

$50-100

If setting is foremost in mind, check out **Lagarta Lodge** (tel. 506/2682-0035, www.lagarta.com, $45 s or $50 d low season, $65 s or $70 d high season), atop Punta Nosara and offering stupendous vistas north along Ostional. Four simple rooms are in a two-story house (the upper story reached by a spiral staircase), and three are in a smaller unit with whitewashed stone walls. The latter, with one entire wall a screened window, have mezzanine bedrooms overlooking voluminous open showers and bathrooms. Some have king-size beds. The lodge has a swimming pool and trails leading down to the river and the Reserva Biológica Nosara; boats and canoes are rented ($10). Readers have raved about the meals. Rates include tax and breakfast.

The beachfront **Casa Romántica** (tel./fax 506/2682-0272, www.casa-romantica.net, $60–70 s/d low season, $80–90 high season) appeals for its 10 rooms in beautiful two-story houses with gracious whites and earth tones. Upper rooms are cross-ventilated two-bedroom apartments with kitchens and a wide, shaded veranda. The landscaped grounds contain a pool, *ranchito* with hammocks, and restaurant. It has a tennis court, and you can rent surf and boogie boards. Rates include breakfast.

The attractive **Café de Paris** (tel. 506/2682-0087, www.cafedeparis.net, call for nightly rates) is run by a young French couple who continue to evolve their hotel. It has 12 modestly furnished air-conditioned rooms with ceiling fans, a slanted wooden ceiling with egress for the heat, and private bath with hot water. Rooms vary in size and include a two-bedroom "suite bungalow" with kitchen. There are also five bungalows plus two hilltop villa with suites: they offer fabulous views and each has a spiral staircase to two or three bedrooms. The restaurant is beneath a soaring *ranchito*. Facilities include a souvenir store, the splendid café, a lap pool, pool table, massage, and Internet café.

Run by a delightful French-Portuguese couple, **Villa Mango B&B** (tel. 506/2682-1168, www.villamangocr.com, $49 s or $59 d low season, $69 s or $79 d high season) is a bed-and-breakfast that enjoys views over Playa Guiones. It has four bedrooms with parquet floors, raised wooden ceilings, and large picture windows. It has a kidney-shaped pool (monkeys and coatis come to drink!), plus a delightfully rustic restaurant and sundeck with bamboo rockers and hammocks. It is "lifestyle-friendly." Rates include breakfast and tax.

Also to consider in this price bracket is the new, Mexican-style **Hotel El Ramal** (tel. 506/2682-1060, $40 s, $80 d), with 10 large, simply furnished rooms.

OVER $100

The environmentally sound **Harmony Hotel** (tel. 506/2682-4114, www.harmonynosara.com, $150 s/d rooms, $220–330 bungalows low season; $190 s/d rooms, $270–410 bungalows high season), within spitting distance of the beach, is one of the class acts in Nosara. It offers 24 rooms with king-size beds and simple yet edgily sexy furnishings, as well as 11 one- and two-bedroom bungalows with decks and rinse showers (plus private baths and hot water). Some units have air-conditioning; all have Wi-Fi. The landscaped grounds boast a curvaceous swimming pool, a tennis court, yoga dojo, plus a large bar and restaurant with rattans and bamboos. Rates include breakfast.

A cross-shaped pool highlights the new **Arco Iris Hotel & Resort** (tel. 506/2682-0615, www.samuelcarver.com/Arco Iris.html, $150 s/d), with 10 air-conditioned villas, Wi-Fi, and a Tuscan-style restaurant.

The sensational Balinese-inspired 【 **L'Acqua Viva Hotel & Spa** (tel. 506/2682-1087, fax 506/2682-0420, www.lacquaviva.com, $185 rooms, $300 suites, $450–600 villas low season; $190 rooms, $325 suites, $500–700 villas high season), which opened in December 2008, has raised the ante considerably at Playa Guiones. Let's start with the jaw-dropping lobby, with a peaked thatched roof and a brilliant contemporary design. Call it tropical post-modernism. Minimalist decor in the 35 spacious, peak-roofed, two-story guest quarters is tastefully contemporary, blending whites with dark Indonesian hardwood pieces, and bold salmons and stylish original art for color. Bathrooms have large walk-in showers. Sunlight pours in through shuttered windows and sliding glass doors, and sensuous bathrooms have coil-shaped showers. The huge trapezoidal pool begs lingering swims, and there's a whirlpool. The bar could well be the hippest west of San José. Lovely! The property is hilly but has ramps plus two units fitted for wheelchairs. There's Wi-Fi in the public areas.

Looking for self-catering? Bibi and Arne Bendixen (tel. 540/2297-8485, www.casa-banda.com) rent lovely apartments of various sizes as **Casa Banda.** And Tiffany Atkinson runs **Nosara Beach Rentals** (tel. 506/2682-0612, fax 506/2682-0153, www.nosara beachrentals.com).

Food

Marlin Bill's (tel. 506/2682-0458, 11 A.M.–2 P.M., and 6 P.M.–midnight daily, $3.50–13) offers great dining on a lofty, breeze-swept terrace with views. Lunch might include a blackened tuna salad or sandwich, French onion soup ($3.50), and brownie sundae or Key lime pie. Pork loin chops, New York strip steak, and eggplant parmesan typify the dinner menu. The bar has a TV. Next door, **Soda Tica** (tel. 506/2682-0728, 8 A.M.–3 P.M. Mon.–Sat.) is a charming little open-air *soda* serving hot *casados* for $3.

Olga's (no tel., 10 A.M.–10 P.M. daily), a rustic place fronting Playa Pelada, is recommended for seafood ($5 average). Tucked above the beach 50 meters to the south is **La Luna Bar and Grill** (tel. 506/2682-0122, 11 A.M.–10 P.M. daily, $5), an atmospheric place with cobblestone floor and bottle-green glass bricks, and a terrace for dining by sunset. It serves lentil soup, sushi rolls, carpaccio, and more and plays world music from Dylan to reggae.

Café de Paris (tel. 506/2682-0087, 7 A.M.–11 P.M. daily, $4–10) serves crepes, French toast, omelettes, sandwiches such as chicken curry or turkey, and entrées such as penne pasta with creamed pesto fish and duck breast in green pepper sauce, plus 12 types of pizza.

The **Gilded Iguana** (tel. 506/2682-0259, 7 A.M.–midnight daily, $2.50–8) is a favorite with locals and serves super tacos, stuffed jalapeños, tuna salad, seafood, and great shakes. It has live music Tuesday nights. And **Harmony Hotel** (7 –10:30 A.M., noon–3:30 P.M., and 6 –9 P.M., $5–15) is a winner for vegetarian cuisine and fusion cuisine such as coconut basil and ginger jumbo shrimp ($8), and a superb five-spice chicken risotto, although the sushi menu is disappointingly meager.

For Mexican food, head to **Pancho's** (tel. 506/2682-0591, noon–9:30 P.M. daily, high season only), serving all dishes under $8, plus killer margaritas under a thatch roof.

It's definitely worth the snaking drive into the hills to dine at **Restaurante Vista del Paraíso** (tel. 506/2682-0637, noon until the last guest leaves), where you can enjoy sensational views. Debbie, the Texan owner, is a French-trained chef who conjures up the likes of baked goat cheese salad ($8), filet mignon ($19), and Napoleon of beef tenderloin with layers of grilled pineapple and blue cheese ($18).

Information and Services

The Frog Pad (tel. 506/2682-4039, www
.thefrogpad.com), in Villa Tortuga, has a
book exchange.

Centro Médico Nosara (tel. 506/2682-
1212) is in the heart of Beaches of Nosara.
Plus, there's a **Red Cross** (tel. 506/2682-0175)
in Bocas de Nosara, and a clinic at the west
end of the village. The **police station** is on
the northeast side of the airstrip field and has
no telephone; call the public telephone (tel.
506/2682-1130) outside the station. The **post
office** (7:30–11:30 A.M. and 1:30–5:30 P.M.
Mon.–Fri.) is next door.

There's a bank next to Café de Paris, which
offers Internet service (7 A.M.–9 P.M. daily).

Getting There

SANSA and **Nature Air** have twice-daily service between San José and Nosara.

A Tracopa bus (tel. 506/2222-2666
or 506/2682-0297) departs San José for
Nosara from Calle 14, Avenidas 3/5, daily at
5:30 A.M. ($8); the return bus departs from
Bocas del Nosara at 12:30 P.M. Empresa
Rojas buses (tel. 506/2686-9089) depart
Nicoya for Nosara at 5 A.M., 10 A.M., noon,
and 3 P.M., returning at 5 A.M., 7 A.M., noon,
and 3 P.M.

Budget Rent-a-Car is located at Harmony
Hotel (tel. 506/2682-4114).

Interbus (tel. 506/2283-5573, www.inter
busonline.com) operates minibus shuttles from
San José ($45) and popular tourist destinations
in Nicoya and Guanacaste.

There is no direct road link between Nosara
and the town of Nicoya. You must drive south
15 kilometers to Barco Quebrado and turn inland; the dirt road meets the paved Nicoya–
Sámara road at Terciopelo.

Getting Around

The roads are all unpaved and distances are
long. You can rent an ATV for getting around
at **Monkey Quad Rentals** (tel. 506/2682-0027,
from $50 per day) and **Nosara Surf Shop** (tel.
506/2682-0573, www.safarisurfschool.com,
$50 daily).

BAHÍA GARZA TO SÁMARA

The dirt road from Nosara leads south to Playa
Sámara (26 km) via the horseshoe-shaped
Bahía Garza (8 km south of Nosara), rimmed
by a pebbly white-sand beach. Beyond Garza,
the road—four-wheel-drive vehicles essential—
cuts inland from the coast, which remains out
of view the rest of the way.

At **Barco Quebrado,** about 15 kilometers south of Nosara and 11 kilometers north
of Sámara, a road heads north uphill to
Terciopelo, on the paved Sámara–Nicoya road
(en route, you ford the Río Frío). Continuing
south from Barco Quebrado on the coast road,
you reach **Esterones,** where a side road leads
two kilometers to **Playa Buena Vista,** in
Bahía Montereyna. Meanwhile, the "main"
road divides, north for Terciopelo and south
for Sámara (the direct coast road to Sámara
requires fording the Río Buena Vista, which
isn't always possible; if impassable, take a one-
kilometer detour on the Terciopelo road then
turn right for Sámara). There are crocodiles in
the river estuary.

Sports and Recreation

Fancy a flight in an ultralight plane? Then
head to **Flying Crocodile Flying Center** (tel./
fax 506/2656-8048, www.flying-crocodile
.com, $75–100 for 20 minutes, $120–160 one
hour, $170–230 per hour instruction), where
Guido, a licensed commercial pilot, will take
you up in one of his state-of-the-art ultralights.
Highly recommended!

Mis Amores Horse Rental (tel. 506/8846-
3502, misamores@ice.co.cr), at La Cocina de
Doña Ana, offers horseback and ATV rides.

You can try your hand at catching the big
one with **Sport Fishing Center Hélios** (tel.
506/2656-8210, www.heliospeche.com), with
a fleet of seven boats.

Accommodations and Food

Budgeting backpackers gravitate to **El Castillo**
(tel. 506/8824-2822, $15 pp dorm, $20 s, $30
d rooms), at the river mouth at Playa Buena
Vista. This Moroccan-inspired freeform house
made of river stones has eight rooms with

private bathrooms. Campers share bathrooms and toilets in the garden. It has a communal kitchen and rainbow-hued bar.

Sportfishers may appreciate **Hotel Hélios** (tel. 506/2656-8210, www.heliospeche.com, call for rates), at Garza, with eight modern rooms opening onto a pool and lawns. It specializes in sportfishing packages.

You'll fall in love with the German-run ◖ **Flying Crocodile Lodge** (tel./fax 506/2656-8048, www.flying-crocodile.com, $35 s or $41 d "Pochote", $50 s or $60 d standard, $65 s or $75 d larger unit low season; $43 s or $49 d "Pochote", $60 s or $70 d standard, $80 s or $90 d larger unit high season), between Esterones and Playa Buena Vista. This marvelous spot is an artistic vision with eight exquisite and eclectic cabins spaced well apart in beautifully maintained grounds. Each boasts walls splashed with lively murals, plus hardwood floors, curving concrete bench seats with cushions, a soothing melange of Caribbean colors, and endearing bathrooms boasting black stone floors. The coup de grace is the Oriental Apartment, with a uniquely creative Moorish motif and an imaginative, skylit, freeform bathroom. It also has air-conditioned bungalows with kitchen. A pool has a water swing and slide, plus there are horses, mountain bikes, motorcycles, and 4WD vehicles. And the Flying Crocodile Flying Center is here.

Next door, **Paraíso del Cocodrilo** (tel./fax 506/2656-8055, www.travel-costarica.net) is a German-run hotel in Spanish neocolonial style and set in wide lawns. Rooms are uninspired but huge.

Perfect for yoga enthusiasts and "counter-culture" types, **Alegría** (tel. 506/8390-9026, www.alegria-cr.de, $25 s/d low season, $35 s/d high season), 400 meters toward the coast beyond Flying Crocodile, is a yoga retreat with eight cabin-tents made of bamboo, with woven palm floors, clear plastic A-frame roofs, and mosquito nets and mattresses. They're accessed by a steep trail. It has an open-air kitchen-bar and terrace with astounding views over Playa Esterones. Guests cook for each other and share outdoor "rainforest" showers. The Belgian owner also rents a beautiful wooden home ($60 s/d nightly, $250 per week) with wraparound veranda and gorgeous bathroom. Rates include breakfast and lunch.

La Cocina de Doña Ana (tel. 506/2656-8085, 8–10 A.M., noon 2 P.M. and 6–9 P.M. daily), atop Punta Garza, specializes in seafood; go for the fabulous setting between bays.

Playa Sámara to Carrillo

PLAYA SÁMARA

Playa Sámara, about 15 kilometers south of Garza, is a popular budget destination for Ticos, surfers, and travelers in search of the offbeat. The lure is its relative accessibility and attractive horseshoe-shaped bay with a light-gray beach.

Sámara can be reached directly from Nicoya by paved road (Hwy. 150) via Belén, and you can fly into nearby Playa Carrillo. The village is in the center of the beach. A cattle *finca* divides it from **Cangrejal,** a funky hamlet at the north end of the beach. Playa Sámara extends south about two kilometers to the small ramshackle fishing community of **Matapalo.**

Entertainment

The beachfront **Bar Las Olas,** at the west end of the village, is one of the livelier spots until after midnight, when the crowd gravitates to the no-frills **Tutti Frutti** disco at the Hotel Playa Sámara; the latter is a smoke-filled, sweatbox place and produces a fair share of local drunks, but it's the happenin' dance scene. A more mellow spot, favored by the local Rastafarian crowd, is the rustic yet always packed **La Gondola** (4 P.M.–2 A.M. daily), *the* bar of choice in town; it has darts, ping-pong, and pool. The open-air **La Vela Latina** video-music bar shows big games on a big screen.

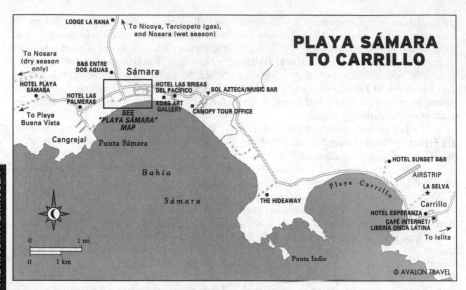

PLAYA SÁMARA TO CARRILLO

LODGE LA RANA
To Nicoya, Terciopelo (gas), and Nosara (wet season)
To Nosara (dry season only)
B&B ENTRE DOS AGUAS
Sámara
HOTEL PLAYA SÁMARA
HOTEL LAS PALMERAS
HOTEL LAS BRISAS DEL PACÍFICO
SOL AZTECA/MUSIC BAR
KOSS-ART GALLERY
CANOPY TOUR OFFICE
To Playa Buena Vista
SEE "PLAYA SÁMARA" MAP
Cangrejal   Punta Sámara
Bahía
Sámara
THE HIDEAWAY
HOTEL SUNSET B&B
AIRSTRIP
LA SELVA
Playa Carrillo
Carrillo
HOTEL ESPERANZA
CAFÉ INTERNET/ LIBRERÍA ONDA LATINA
To Islita
0   1 mi
0   1 km
Punta Indio
© AVALON TRAVEL

Sports and Recreation

Jesse's Surf School (tel. 506/8373-3006, www.samarasurfschool.com) rents surfboards and offers lessons, as does **C&C Surf School** (tel. 506/2656-0628). And **Pura Vida Dive** (tel. 506/2656-0643, www.puravidadive.com) offers dive trips.

Tio Tigre Tours (tel. 506/2656-0098, www.samarabeach.com/tiotigre) has sea kayaking, horseback rides, a dolphin spotting tour, and more, as does **Skynet Tours** (tel./fax 506/2656-0920, info@skynettours.com).

Wingnuts (tel. 506/2656-0153, www.samarabeach.com/wingnuts, $55 adults, $35 children) has a canopy tour.

Accommodations

CAMPING

The swampy **Bar Aloha Camping** (tel. 506/2656-0028, $5 pp) and **Camping Los Cocos** (tel. 506/2656-0496, www.samarabeach.com/campingcocos, $4 pp low season, $5 pp high season, $5 pp camper-van) both play second fiddle to the more appealing **Camping and Bar Olas** (tel. 506/2656-0187, $5 pp camping, $15 s or $25 d huts), with a lively beachside bar and restaurant with shaded campsites with lockers. It also has basic palm-thatch A-frame huts with loft bedrooms.

$25-50

The Italian-run **Cabinas Paraíso** (tel./fax 506/2656-0741, $25 s, $30 d) has four clean, simply furnished rooms with king-size beds, fans, verandas, and private baths with hot water. There's also a large unit that accommodates four people. It rents snorkeling gear and mountain bikes and has a simple open-air eatery. A lesser quality but similarly priced alternative is **Casa Valeria B&B** (tel. 506/2656-0511, fax 506/2656-0317, casavaleriaf@hotmail.com), with eight clean, simply furnished rooms plus four beachfront bungalows.

I like the bargain-priced **Tico Adventure Lodge** (tel. 506/2656-0628, www.ticoadventurelodge.com, $20 s or $30 d low season, $30 s or $50 d high season), made entirely of teak and offering nine rooms in a handsome, sepia-toned, two-story unit with glazed rough-hewn timbers. It also has an apartment and a villa for rent. The C&C Surf Camp is here.

A good bargain, the German-run **Hotel Belvedere** (tel./fax 506/2656-0213, www.belvederesamara.net, $45 s or $78 d room, $65

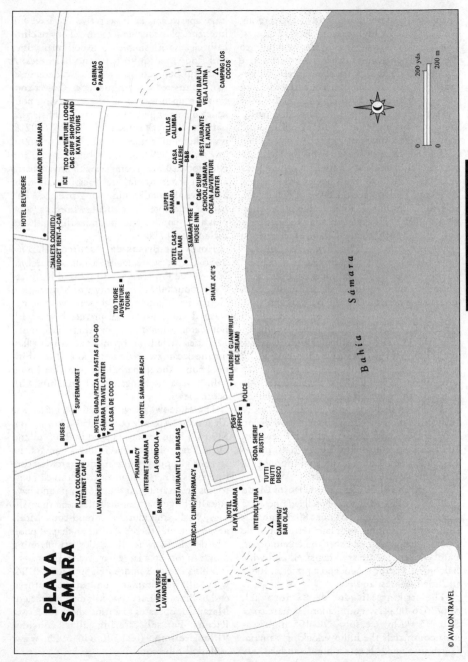

PLAYA SÁMARA

THE NICOYA PENINSULA

Bahía Sámara

- HOTEL BELVEDERE
- MIRADOR DE SÁMARA
- ICE
- CHALETS COQUITO/ BUDGET RENT-A-CAR
- TICO ADVENTURE LODGE/ C&C SURF SHOP/ISLAND KAYAK TOURS
- CABINAS PARAÍSO
- BEACH BAR LA VELA LATINA
- CAMPING LOS COCOS
- VILLAS CALIMBA
- CASA VALERIE B&B
- RESTAURANTE EL ANCLA
- SUPER SÁMARA
- C&C SURF SCHOOL/SÁMARA OCEAN ADVENTURE CENTER
- SÁMARA TREE HOUSE INN
- HOTEL CASA DEL MAR
- TÍO TIGRE ADVENTURE TOURS
- SHAKE JOE'S
- HELADERÍA G/JANIFRUIT (ICE CREAM)
- SUPERMARKET
- HOTEL GIADA/PIZZA & PASTAS / GO-GO
- SÁMARA TRAVEL CENTER
- LA CASA DE COCO
- HOTEL SÁMARA BEACH
- BUSES
- PLAZA COLONIAL/ INTERNET CAFÉ
- LAVANDERÍA SÁMARA
- PHARMACY
- INTERNET SÁMARA
- LA GONDOLA
- BANK
- RESTAURANTE LAS BRASAS
- MEDICAL CLINIC/PHARMACY
- POLICE
- POST OFFICE
- SODA SHERIF RUSTIC
- TUTTI FRUTTI DISCO
- HOTEL PLAYA SÁMARA
- INTERCULTURA
- CAMPING/ BAR OLAS
- LA VIDA VERDE LAVANDERÍA

200 yds
200 m
0
0

© AVALON TRAVEL

s/d apartment low season; $55 s or $90 d room, $75 apartment high season) has 12 pretty, Swiss-style chalets (ranging from doubles to two apartments with kitchens) with attractive bamboo furnishings, mosquito nets, whitewashed walls, fans, and private baths with hot water. Some rooms have king-size beds; some have air-conditioning. A stone-walled whirlpool tub sits amid lush gardens and a pool. Rates include breakfast and tax.

Another value-priced winner is the German-run **Bed & Breakfast Entre Dos Aguas** (tel./fax 506/2656-0998, www.hoteldosaguas.com, $40 s or $45 d low season, $45 s or $50 d high season), a charming tropical take on a stone-and-timber Swiss chalet set in a groomed hillside garden, 400 meters inland. It has seven pleasing rooms with rustic wooden furnishings, tile floors, fans, and circular private bathrooms with walls of river stones and hot water. There's a stone bar and a shaded patio. Rates include breakfast and tax. No credit cards.

$50-100

The **Hotel Casa del Mar** (tel. 506/2656-0264, www.casadelmarsamara.com, $30 s or $40 d shared bath year-round, $55 s/d private bath low season, $75 s or $85 d private bath high season), run by French-Canadians, is a relaxing and well-run bed-and-breakfast with 17 modestly furnished rooms with attractive decor, fans, private baths, hot water, and heaps of light through louvered windows (two rooms have a kitchenette). There's a whirlpool tub. Rates include breakfast and tax.

Charm and character pervade **Hotel Giada** (tel. 506/2656-0132, www.hotelgiada.net, $55 s or $65 d low season, $65 s or $80 d high season), with 13 rooms with faux terra-cotta tile floors, sponge-washed ocher and cream decor, bamboo beds (some are king-size), and wide balconies. There's a pool and a pizzeria. Rates include breakfast and tax.

The striking **Mirador de Sámara** (tel. 506/2656-0044, www.miradordesamara.com, $80–95 s/d low season, $90–105 high season) commands the hill overlooking Sámara. German-owned, it sets a high standard. Six

large apartments each sleep five and have full kitchens, plus four new rooms. They're clinically clean, with simple hardwood furnishings and floors, mosquito nets, and balconies. A beautiful pool fed by a water cascade is inset in a multitiered wooden sundeck. A tower contains an open-walled restaurant serving nouvelle cuisine. This property has lots of steps.

Hotel Sámara Beach (tel. 506/2656-0218, www.hotelsamarabeach.com, $55 s or $69 d low season, $89 s or $92 d high season) is a two-story, 20-room complex with private baths and hot water. Rooms are spacious and bright and have air-conditioning, king-size beds, and patios. The hotel has a small swimming pool, plus a bar-cum-restaurant under thatch. Rates include tax and breakfast.

Hotel Las Brisas del Pacífico (tel. 506/2656-0250, www.lasbrisascostarica.com, $65–90 s/d low season, $80–115 s/d high season), about 600 meters south of Sámara, is a German-run hotel with 38 rooms with whitewashed stone walls and private baths with hot water (some have a/c; others have fans). Facilities include an open-air restaurant facing the ocean, two swimming pools, two whirlpool tubs, and a shady lounging area under palms. Separate bungalows sit on a hill, with ocean views.

The Hideaway (tel. 506/2656-1145, www.thehideawaycostarica.com, $85 s/d low season, $100 s/d high season) opened in 2008 inland of the very southern end of Playa Sámara. Its stylish, gleaming white modern architecture impresses. The 12 huge air-conditioned guest rooms are in irregular fourplex units and have equally huge bathrooms, pleasant furnishings, Wi-Fi, and most other mod-cons. Meals are served, and there's a scimitar-shaped pool. The delightful owner, Rosy Rios, was planning movie nights on a large flat-screen TV.

Villas Playa Sámara (tel. 506/2656-0104, www.villasplayasamara.com), at the southern end of Playa Sámara, two kilometers south of Matapalo, operates as a time-share for Costa Ricans. For self-catering villas, consider **Villas Kalimba** (tel. 506/656-0929, www.villaskalimba.com).

$100-200

€ **Sámara Treehouse Inn** (tel. 506/2656-0733, www.samaratreehouse.com, $85–115 s/d low season, $95–125 s/d high season) is a thoughtful and irresistible addition, and the nicest place in town. Made entirely of glossy hardwoods, the four thatch-fringed tree-house units with open patios (with hammocks and lounge chairs) face the beach; each has terra-cotta floor, bamboo bed, and lively fabrics, plus TV, ceiling fan, delightful modern bathrooms faced with dark-blue tiles, and wall-of-glass oceanview windows. It offers secure parking and a lovely circular pool in the landscaped forecourt, plus a fully equipped, wheelchair-accessible ground-floor apartment.

Lodge Las Ranas (tel. 506/8859-0144, www.lodgelasranas.com, $75 s or $95 d low season, $95 s or $115 d high season), two ki-lometers east of town on the Terciopelo road, offers a lofty perch. Here, rustic furniture (in-cluding canopied log beds) and stylish contem-porary elements combine. A serpentine pool studs a hillside terrace.

Food

I breakfast at **La Casa de Coco** (tel. 506/2656-0665, 7 A.M.10 P.M. daily): it has huge omelettes and pancakes, plus lunchtime *casados,* sand-wiches, and even chicken curry ($6) at night.

Late risers might opt for breakfast at **Shake Joe's** (tel. 506/2656-0252, 11 A.M.–9 P.M. Tues.–Sun., $3–10), an offbeat hangout with oversize sofas with Guatemalan fabrics, plus rough-hewn tables and hammocks strewn around the gravel courtyard; it serves a French toast breakfast with tuna salad and eggs, plus smoked salmon, salade Niçoise, and ravioli.

The airy **Restaurante Las Brasas** (tel. 506/2656-0546, noon–10 P.M. daily) has heaps of ambience thanks to its effusive use of exotic logs. It serves Mediterranean fare, including gazpacho ($4) and paella ($9), plus surf-and-turf. Similarly, I like the creative menu at the no-frills, thatched, beachfront **Restaurante El Ancla** (10 A.M.–10 P.M. Fri.–Wed., $5–10), serving beef stroganoff, garlic sea bass, and calamari.

When things get too hot, head to **Heladería Era Glacial** (1 A.M.–7 P.M. daily), in Patio Colonial, for ice cream.

You can buy groceries at **Super La Sámara.**

Information and Services

Inter-Travel (tel. 506/2656-0302, 8 A.M.–8 P.M. daily), in Patio Colonial, is a tour infor-mation service that also sells Interbus tickets and has an Internet café. **Internet Sámara** is one block south.

The **post office** and **police** (tel. 506/2656-0436) are by the beach, near the soccer field.

A **medical clinic** (tel. 506/2656-0992) and **pharmacy** (tel. 506/2656-0123) adjoin each other on the north side of the soccer field.

Lavandería Sámara (tel. 506/8870-0448, 8:30 A.M.–5:30 P.M. Mon.–Sat.) offers same-day free delivery for laundry. **La Vida Verde** (tel. 506/2656-1051) competes, using biode-gradable soaps and detergents.

Sámara Language School (tel. 506/2656-0127, www.beachspanish.com) offers Spanish language courses.

Getting There

SANSA and **Nature Air** fly daily to Playa Carrillo.

Tracopa Alfaro buses (tel. 506/2222-2666 and 2685-5032) depart San José for Sámara from Calles 14, Avenidas 3/5, daily at noon and 6:30 P.M. ($6.50, five hours). Empresa Rojas buses (tel. 506/2685-5352) depart Nicoya for Sámara from three blocks east of the park 13 times daily 5 A.M.–9:45 P.M. ($1.75).

Buses depart Sámara for San José at 4 A.M. and 8 A.M.

Interbus (tel. 506/2283-5573, www.inter busonline.com) operates minibus shuttles from San José ($35) and popular tourist destinations in Nicoya and Guanacaste.

PLAYA CARRILLO

South of Sámara, the paved road continues over Punta Indio and drops down to coral-colored Playa Carrillo (5 km south of Sámara), one of the finest beaches in Costa Rica. An offshore reef protects the bay. The fishing hamlet of

© CHRISTOPHER P. BAKER

Playa Carrillo

Carrillo nestles around the estuary of the Río Sangrado at the southern end of the bay.

To check out native animal species that are hard to see in the wild, follow signs to **La Selva** (tel. 506/8305-1610, 9 A.M.–9 P.M. daily, $8 adults, $5 children), inland at the southern end of the beach. This wildlife refuge has coatis, tamanduas, peccaries, agoutis, monkeys, and even jaguarundis. Guided tours are offered at 9 A.M. and 5 P.M.

Café Internet Librería Onda Latina (tel. 506/2656-0434) has miniature golf.

Rick Ruhlow (tel./fax 506/2656-0091, www.costaricabillfishing.com) and **Costa Rica VIP Sportfishing** (tel. 506/2637-7262, www.vipsportfish.com/carrillo.htm) offer sportfishing.

Carrillo Tours (tel. 506/2656-0543, www.carrillotours.com) offers all manner of tours locally and far afield.

Accommodations and Food

I like the U.S.–run **Hotel Sunset B&B** (tel. 506/2656-0011, fax 506/2656-0009, puerto-carrillosunset@yahoo.com, $65 s/d), a beautiful hilltop property with a marvelous wooden deck inset with pool, and an open, thatched bar and restaurant with views. It has eight air-conditioned rooms with solar-heated hot-water showers. Rates include breakfast.

The hillside **Hotel Esperanza** (tel./fax 506/2656-0564, www.hotelesperanza.com, $88 s/d low season, $120 s/d high season, including breakfast) is a family-run bed-and-breakfast set in a delightful garden. Recently remodeled (the new exterior is ghastly), it has seven attractively furnished rooms—some larger than others—arrayed along an arcade. A restaurant, for guests only, specializes in seafood. A new level with five suites was to be added.

Carrillo has garnered several new hotels of late, including the Italian-run **Puerto Carrillo Hotel** (tel. 506/2656-1103, www.puertocarrillohotel.com, $50 s or $65 d low season, $60 s or $75 d high season), with eight air-conditioned rooms with pleasant contemporary furnishings, all with cable TV, and Wi-Fi.

At **Hotel Leyenda** (tel. 506/2656-0381, www.hotelleyenda.com, $105 s/d low season, $125 high season), two kilometers south of

Carrillo, a pleasant contemporary hotel enfolds a courtyard with pool. Decor is a bit uninspired, but standard rooms are spacious and have kitchenettes plus ceiling fan and air-conditioning. There's a "VIP House" ($420 low season, $500 high season) with its own pool. This hotel has come up with a fascinating concept: It provides shuttles to the beach, with mobile portable toilets and showers!

About three kilometers south of Carrillo, **El Sueño Tropical** (tel. 506/2656-0151, www.el suenotropical.com, $45–85 s/d low season, $95–195 s/d high season), now owned by a Tica-gringo couple, is a bargain, and I like the tropical motif throughout this lushly landscaped setting. It has 12 clean, simple, recently renovated air-conditioned bungalow rooms with terra-cotta tiles, queen- or king-size beds, direct-dial telephones, and free Wi-Fi; there is also a suite. The hilltop restaurant has a soaring *palenque* roof. There's a pool and a separate kids' pool. Howler monkeys abound in the surrounding forest. Rates include breakfast.

Getting There

The Nicoya–Sámara buses continue to Playa Carrillo. Or you can fly there daily on **SANSA** and **Nature Air.**

Playa Camaronal to Playa Manzanillo

The extreme southwest shore of the Nicoya Peninsula is one of the most remote coastal strips in Costa Rica. The beaches are beautiful and the scenery at times sublime.

South of Carrillo, the dirt road continues a few miles in good condition, then deteriorates to a mere trail in places. In the words of the old spiritual, there are many rivers to cross. The route can thwart even the hardiest four-wheel-drive vehicle in wet season, or after prolonged rains in dry season. For those who thrill to adventure, it's a helluva lot of fun.

Don't attempt the section south of Carrillo by ordinary sedan or at night, and especially not in wet season unless it's unusually dry—many tourists have had to have their vehicles hauled out of rivers that proved impossible to ford.

PLAYA CAMARONAL TO PUNTA BEJUCO

Playa Camaronal, beyond Punta El Roble about five kilometers south of Playa Carrillo, is a remote three-kilometer-long, gray-sand beach that is a popular nesting site for leatherback (Mar.–Apr.) and Pacific ridley turtles (year-round). It was recently earmarked as the **Camaronal Wildlife Refuge** (Refugio de Vida Silvestre Nacional Camaronal). An *arribada* (mass nesting of turtles) occurred here for the first time ever in November 2006. Officially, you are supposed to visit by night only with a MINAE guide ($4 pp). However, in 2008, when I arrived at the onset of an *arribada*, I was horrified to find hundreds of people being permitted on the beach uncontrolled. Children were touching and even sitting on the turtles, while ignorant adults looked on and laughed. I was even offered eggs for sale. *Don't molest the turtles!*

A dirt road leads south nine kilometers from Camaronal to **Playa Islita,** a pebbly black-sand beach squeezed between soaring headlands that will have your four-wheel drive wheezing in first gear. When heading south from Sámara, follow the signs for Hotel Punta Islita inland via Santa Marta (the road was graded and paved in 2008 and it's no longer a scramble over steep mountains). In dry season you may be able to shortcut the detour by fording the wide Río Ora, which is usually impassable in wet season.

The community of **Islita** is enlivened by the **Open-Air Contemporary Art Museum** (Museo de Arte Contemporáneo al Aire Libre), with houses, tree trunks, and even the police station throughout the village decorated in bright paints and mosaics.

South of the community of Islita, in the

© CHRISTOPHER P. BAKER

ridley turtles during an *arribada* at Playa Camaronal

valley bottom, the road climbs over Punta Barranquilla before dropping to **Playa Corazalito.** The dirt road then cuts inland to the village of **Corazalito** (with an airstrip) and continues parallel to and about two kilometers from the shore. The beach is backed by a large mangrove swamp replete with wildlife.

At the hamlet of **Quebrada Seca,** two kilometers south of Corazalito, a side road leads two kilometers to **Playa Bejuco,** a four-kilometer-long, gray-sand beach with a mangrove swamp at the southern end. The dirt road continues south from Quebrada Seca four kilometers to **Pueblo Nuevo,** where the road from Cangrejal connects with Carmona and Highway 21; a side road leads to the funky fishing community of **Puerto Bejuco,** great for birding. Pelicans, jabiru storks, and other wading birds are abundant, picking at the tidbits to be had as local fishermen cut up their catch. It's as colorful a taste of coastal life as you'll find in Costa Rica.

Less than one kilometer south of Pueblo Nuevo, **Jungle Butterfly Farm** (tel. 506/8822-5674, www.junglebutterfly.com, 9 A.M.–4 P.M.

daily, $10 adults, $6 children) offers a treat. Entomologist Michael Malliethas developed scenic trails through his 19-hectare forested mountainside property, which has a butterfly breeding facility. Monkeys and other critters abound. Night tours are offered by reservation.

Carrillo Tours (tel. 506/2656-0543, www .carrillotours.com) offers kayaking in the wetlands behind Bejuco beach ($45).

Accommodations and Food

Villas Malinche (tel. 506/2655-8044, $20 pp), in Pueblo Nuevo, has three nicely appointed, modern air-conditioned *cabinas* with ceiling fans, cable TV, kitchenettes, spacious private bathrooms with hot water, and wide terraces. There's a restaurant.

In 2008, Gwen and Edmund Rhodes opened **Rhodeside B&B and Café** (tel. 506/2655-8006, www.rhodesidecostarica .com, $45 s/d low season, $60 s/d high season), one kilometer south of Pueblo Nuevo. The tiny café (7 A.M.–7 P.M. daily) is a delightful spot to break your journey with a cappuccino and baked goodies, and yummy

THE NICOYA PENINSULA

© CHRISTOPHER P. BAKER

Hotel Punta Islita

natural breakfasts. The couple was also finishing off four spacious, cross-ventilated rooms with ceiling fans and private bathrooms; two rooms have outdoor showers. They share an upstairs kitchen with terrace and ocean views. There's a stable; guided horseback rides cost $35 per person.

One of Costa Rica's earliest deluxe hotels, ♦ **Hotel Punta Islita** (tel. 506/2290-4259, www.hotelpuntaislita.com, $360 s/d rooms, $360 junior suite, $425 casita low season; $275 s/d rooms, $395 junior suite, $450 casita high season) commands a hilltop above Playa Islita. The lobby lounge with thatched roof held aloft by massive tree trunks is open to three sides and looks over a sunken bar and horizon swimming pool melding into the endless blues of the Pacific. Rich color schemes are enhanced by terra-cotta tile floors and colorful tile work, and props from the movie *1492*—log canoes, old barrels, and a huge wrought-iron candelabra. The colony includes 20 luxuriously equipped hillside bungalows in Santa Fe style, eight junior suites (each with whirlpool spa on an oceanview

deck), and five two-bedroom *casitas*. In 2007 they were refurbished in stylish contemporary vogue, with flat-screen TVs, divinely comfortable beds and pillows, and luxury bathrooms. A three-bedroom casita sleeps six people. The elegant 1492 restaurant is acclaimed. A private forest reserve has trails, plus there's a canopy tour, gym, full-service spa, two tennis courts, beach club with water sports, and a nine-hole golf course. The restaurant (7–10:30 A.M., 12:30–3 P.M. and 6–9:30 P.M.) is open to the public (as is the beach club by request), serving such delights as bamboo-steamed mahimahi ($21) and tenderloin filet with gorgonzola au gratin ($28).

Bar Barranquilla (tel. 506/8368-2655, 11 A.M.–midnight daily low season, 8 A.M.–midnight daily high season, $2–12), atop Punta Barranquilla, offers spectacular vistas from its half-moon deck. It serves *comida típica* and seafood.

Information and Services
The **police station** (tel. 506/2656-2052) is beside the soccer field in Islita.

Playa San Miguel

Getting There

SANSA and **Nature Air** fly daily to Islita from San José.

ARZA buses (tel. 506/2258-3883 or 2650-0179) depart Calle 12, Avenidas 7/9, in San José at 6 A.M. and 3:30 P.M. (six hours, $5.30) and travel via the Puntarenas–Playa Naranjo ferry and Jicaral to Coyote, Bejuco, and Islita.

You can buy gas at the house of Ann Arias Chávez, on the southwest corner of the soccer field in Quebrada Seca.

PLAYA SAN MIGUEL TO PUNTA COYOTE

Crossing the Río Bejuco south of Pueblo Nuevo, you arrive at the hamlet of **San Miguel,** at the northern end of Playa San Miguel, reached by a side road. The silver-sand beach is a prime turtle-nesting site; there's a ranger station at the southern end of the beach, plus a turtle hatchery. The beach runs south into **Playa Coyote,** a lonesome six-kilometer-long stunner backed by a large mangrove swamp and steep cliffs. The beaches are separated by a river estuary. The wide Río

Jabillo pours into the sea at the south end of Playa Coyote, which, like Playa San Miguel, is reached by a side road that extends two kilometers north and south along the shore. The surfing is superb.

The Río Jabillo and marshy foreshore force the coast road inland for six kilometers to the village of **San Francisco de Coyote,** connected by road inland over the mountains with Highway 21. Turn right in San Francisco to continue south; fortunately, a bridge over the Río Jabillo now permits passage even in the wettest of wet seasons.

Accommodations and Food

San Miguel: The U.S.–run **Blue Pelican** (tel. 506/2655-8046, $35 s/d downstairs, $45 s/d upstairs), a three-story wooden house on Playa San Miguel, has six charming yet basic rooms with rough-hewn four-poster beds, ceiling fans, and shared bathrooms with cold water only. A large room upstairs sleeps five people; smaller rooms are downstairs, including dorm room. The rustic bar/restaurant (11 A.M.–10 P.M. daily low season, 7 A.M.–10 P.M. daily high season) serves inviting seafood such as Portuguese seafood stew ($9).

Also at Playa San Miguel the German-run **Restaurante Flying Scorpion** (tel. 506/2655-8080, www.vrbo.com/101715, 11 A.M.–10 P.M. daily, $2–12), serves pizzas, has a 42-inch flat-screen TV, and rents five *cabinas* ($45), a second-floor studio apartment ($75), and two houses ($100–250). Weimeraners abound underfoot! The owners make delicious homemade pastas, seafood dishes, and even ice cream.

Recently upgraded, **Hotel Arca de Noe** (tel./fax 506/2665-8065, www.hotelarcadenoe.com, $10 pp bunk, $60 s/d low season, $70 high season), one kilometer farther south on the main road inland of the shore, is an elegant, modern, Italian-run, hacienda-style property with lush landscaped grounds and a large swimming pool lined by mosaic tiles. It has five basically furnished bunk rooms with fans and clean, ample bathrooms (cold water only), plus 10 air-conditioned *cabinas* with lofty wooden ceilings, fans, verandas, louvered windows, exquisite fabrics, and private baths with hot water. A restaurant (8–10 A.M., noon–2 P.M., and 6–9 P.M. daily) is open to the public and serves Italian fare, including pizzas. It rents bicycles and horses and has kayak tours and massage. Rates include breakfast. It closes for the middle of low season.

The best place by far—and a great bargain—is 🌊 **Cristal Azul** (tel. 506/2655-8135 or U.S. tel. 800/377-9376, www.cristalazul.com, $145 low season, $175 high season, including breakfast), run by Henner and Zene—delightful hosts. The four thatched, glass-walled, air-conditioned rooms set amid hilltop lawns are gorgeous: charcoal-gray floors, white-and-blue decor, ceiling fans, fresh-cut flowers, handmade beds of glazed hardwood, and huge bathrooms with outdoor garden showers. There's an infinity swimming pool and open-air patio for enjoying hearty breakfasts with spectacular views. Henner is a professional skipper and offers sportfishing. A beach bar and a restaurant were to be added. A two-night minimum applies.

Coyote: In San Francisco de Coyote, **Cabinas Rey** (tel. 506/2655-1505, $8 s, $15 d) has simple rooms, plus a *soda* serving filling meals, and remarkably, a Wi-Fi hot spot!

Cabinas Coyote Lodge (tel. 506/2655-1162, fax 506/2655-0012, coyotelodge@gmail.com, $40 s/d low season, $60 s/d high season) has six simply furnished air-conditioned rooms around a courtyard with shady veranda. Each has cable TV.

The delightful ship-shaped, beachfront **Barco Nico** (tel. 506/2655-1205, www.barco-nico.com, 4–10 P.M. daily, $5–12), at Playa Coyote, offers gourmet fare, from fajitas and pineapple salad to curry chicken and jumbo shrimp in tequila.

You can drive south along the beach at low tide to reach **Restaurant Tanga** (tel. 506/2655-1107), 100 meters south of the Río Jabillo and tucked beneath shade trees beside the sands. It serves simple seafood and allows camping ($5 pp), with restrooms and showers.

Services
Coyote Online (tel. 506/2655-1007, 2–6 P.M. Mon., Tues., Thurs., and Fri.), in San Francisco de Coyote, has Internet service, including Wi-Fi.

Getting There
ARZA buses (tel. 506/2258-3883 or 2650-0179) depart Calle 12, Avenidas 7/9, in San José at 6 A.M. and 3:30 P.M. (six hours, $5.30) and travel via the Puntarenas–Playa Naranjo ferry and Jicaral to Coyote, Bejuco, and Islita. The San José–Islita buses pass through San Francisco de Coyote at about 11:30 A.M. and 10 P.M. and Playa San Miguel about 30 minutes later. Return buses depart Bejuco at 2:15 A.M. and 12:30 P.M., passing through Playa San Miguel around 3 A.M. and 1:15 P.M. and San Francisco de Coyote 30 minutes later.

PUNTA COYOTE TO MANZANILLO
Playa Caletas, immediately south of Punta Coyote and some five kilometers south of San Francisco de Coyote, can also be reached from Highway 21 (on the east side of the Nicoya Peninsula) via Jabillo and the community of La

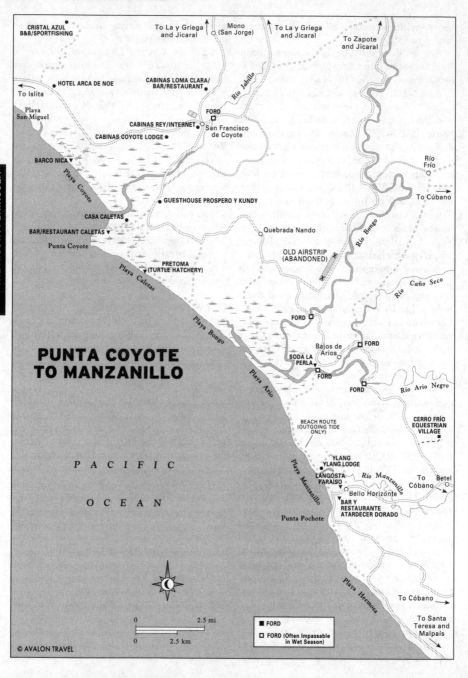

PUNTA COYOTE
TO MANZANILLO

CRISTAL AZUL
B&B/SPORTFISHING

To La y Griega
and Jicaral

Mono
(San Jorge)

To La y Griega
and Jicaral

To Zapote
and Jicaral

CABINAS LOMA CLARA/
BAR/RESTAURANT

Río Jabillo

HOTEL ARCA DE NOE

To Islita

Playa
San Miguel

FORD

CABINAS REY/INTERNET

CABINAS COYOTE LODGE

San Francisco
de Coyote

BARCO NICA

Playa Coyote

Río
Frío

GUESTHOUSE PROSPERO Y KUNDY

To Cúbano

CASA CALETAS

BAR/RESTAURANT CALETAS

Quebrada Nando

Río Bongo

Punta Coyote

Playa Caletas

PRETOMA
(TURTLE HATCHERY)

OLD AIRSTRIP
(ABANDONED)

Río Caño Seco

Playa Bongo

FORD

FORD

Bajos de
Arios

FORD

SODA LA
PERLA

FORD

Playa Ario

FORD

Río Ario Negro

BEACH ROUTE
(OUTGOING TIDE
ONLY)

CERRO FRÍO
EQUESTRIAN
VILLAGE

P A C I F I C

YLANG
YLANG LODGE

Playa Manzanillo

LANGOSTA
PARAISO

Río Manzanillo

To   Betel
Cóbano

O C E A N

Bello Horizonte

BAR Y
RESTAURANTE
ATARDECER DORADO

Punta Pochote

0   2.5 mi

0   2.5 km

■ FORD

□ FORD (Often Impassable
in Wet Season)

Playa Hermosa

To Cóbano

To Santa
Teresa and
Malpaís

© AVALON TRAVEL

y Griega. This miles-long, brown-sand beach has no settlements. Nothing! It's just you and the turtles that come ashore to lay eggs. The beach is considered the second most important nesting site for leatherback turtles in the eastern Pacific Ocean. **Programa Restauración de Tortugas Marinas** (PRETOMA, tel. 506/2241-5227, www.tortugamarina.org) has a turtle hatchery here and is pushing for creation of the **Playa Caletas-Ario National Wildlife Refuge** (alas, local landowners aren't sympathetic). Ridleys come ashore singly July–March; leatherbacks arrive December–March. Volunteers are needed.

Playa Caletas—a great surfing beach—extends southward into **Playa Bongo, Playa Ario,** and **Playa Manzanillo**—together forming a 12-kilometer-long expanse of sand broken by the estuaries of the Río Bongo and Río Ario, inhabited by crocodiles. Once while driving this road at night, I came around a bend to find a crocodile plodding across the road! Marshy shore flats force the coast road inland.

The route between Caletas and Manzanillo is a true adventure and a high-ground-clearance four-wheel-drive vehicle is absolutely essential in wet season, when the Bongo, Caño Seco, and Ario rivers are often impassable, forcing you over the mountains to Jicaral, on Highway 21 (and thence around the eastern seaboard of the Nicoya Peninsula via Paquera and Tambor) to reach Manzanillo—a five-hour journey! (A shorter, but still challenging route, is to head inland toward Jicaral but cut east to the hamlet of **Río Frío,** which is signed. From here, you can strike east for Cóbano, which is signed beside the soccer field in in Rio Frio. This route, however, may also be impassable, as you have to ford the Río Ario. A second, unsigned, route to Cóbano is signed in Río Frio for Bajo de Ario; after 1.5 kilometers, turn left off this road at a Y-fork, from where a really rugged, little-trafficked road leads to Cóbano and also involves fording the Río Ario.)

South of Caletas, keep straight via the hamlet of **Quebrada Nando** until you reach a major Y-fork by a field. Turn right (if you miss the junction you'll know it, as you'll soon come to

a 90-degree left turn, then run along a disused airstrip) for the Río Bongo. The river crossing is tricky, often with dangerously deep channels (they change yearly with each rainy season; floods in 2008 entirely rerouted the river). If the way across isn't clear, wait for a local to show you the way.

Once across, it's about two kilometers to Soda La Perla (a good place to check local conditions), where the dirt road veers left. About one kilometer along you must ford the Río Caño Seco, another challenge that requires scouting before crossing. Shortly beyond, you reach the 30-meter-wide Río Ario Negro. Again, you may need to wait for a local to arrive and show you the way.

About five or so kilometers farther, turn right at the only junction, just before the hamlet of **Betel.** The descent will deposit you by the shore at **Bello Horizonte,** a small fishing hamlet inland of Playa Manzanillo. South of Bello Horizonte, the tenuous coast road (a devil in wet season) leads over **Punta Pochote** and alongside **Playa Hermosa** to Playa Santa Teresa and Malpaís.

Alternately, from Soda La Perla you can follow a minor dirt road that leads down to Playa Ario; you'll have to ford the Río Ario en route. You can then drive four kilometers along the beach to Playa Manzanillo, where you meet the main road as it comes back to the coast. *Do not attempt to drive along Playa Ario except on an outgoing tide.*

A 1,114-hectare refuge, **Hacienda La Esperanza,** was being created in the Valle de Río Ario at last visit. It will include a butterfly garden, frog garden, and arboretum.

Accommodations and Food

In Bello Horizonte, several no-frills budget *cabinas* include **Bar y Restaurante Atardecer Dorado** (tel. 506/8360-9377), with two basic rooms with bed only (and funky outhouse toilets) for $12 per person. The bar (with TV and jukebox) is a lively center for locals. It serves filling meals; try the *filete al ajillo* (garlic fish, $6).

For comfort head to the Polynesian-style

Ylang Ylang Lodge (tel. 506/8359-2616, www.lodgeylangylang.com, $130 s or $150 d low season, $150 s or $170 d high season), run by a charming Italian woman. It has a TV lounge and small restaurant, a pool studs a huge wooden sundeck, and a suspension bridge leads to forest trails. The five breeze-swept, bi-level hilltop cabins are marvelous, with vast ocean views. Below, patios have swing seats and hammocks and huge walk-in showers; up-stairs the huge bedrooms have king-size beds and French doors open to large balconies. One cabin has a kitchen.

The gorgeous (**Casa Caletas** (tel. 506/ 2655-1271, www.casacaletas.com, $130–165 s/d low season, $165–200 high season) occupies a working cattle hacienda on the south bank of the Río Jabillo. The luxurious rooms fea-ture travertine floors and bathrooms, halogen lighting, rustic glazed hardwood king beds with high-thread-count linens and are cross-lit through sliding glass doors with river-mouth views. Some have loft bedrooms. An invitingly hip breeze-swept bar under thatch opens to the sundeck with kidney-shaped infinity pool, and the lounge with poured concrete sofas with classy fabrics is a delightful place to relax. It of-fers horseback rides and air-boat river trips.

For simple seafood at bargain prices, head to **Langosta Paraíso** (no tel., 11 A.M.–9 P.M.), a simple *soda* in Bello Horizonte, with fresh lob-ster for about $10.

Southeast Nicoya

HIGHWAY 21: CARMONA TO PLAYA NARANJO

Highway 21 winds south along the eastern shore of the Gulf of Nicoya via Jicaral to Playa Naranjo, beyond which it swings south around the Nicoya Peninsula bound for Paquera, Montezuma, and Malpaís. When I last drove it, the road was partially paved, with large sec-tions worn to the bone.

Playa Naranjo is one of two terminals for the Puntarenas ferry (Coonatramar Ferry, tel. 506/2661-1069, www.coonatramar.com); use the Naranjo ferry to access the beaches of northern and central Nicoya only. There's a gas station and supermarket here.

Inland of Jicaral, the **Karen Mogensen Wildlife Reserve** (tel. 506/2650-0607) pro-tects 730 hectares of tropical moist forest; to get there, turn off at Lepanto, 11 kilometers south of Jicaral. The **Costa Rican Association of Community-Based Rural Tourism** (ACTUAR, tel. 506/2248-9470, www.actuar costarica.com; two-day packages $68) arranges accommodation at Cerro Escondido, a lovely simple community lodge with four cabins, plus horseback rides, trails, an orchid garden, and small eco-museum.

Isla Chira

Costa Rica's second-largest island, Isla Chira floats below the mouth of the Río Tempisque, at the north end of the Gulf of Nicoya. It is sur-rounded by mangroves popular with pelicans and frigate birds, and uninhabited except for a few fishermen, farmers and others who eke out a living from *salinas* (salt pans). Roseate spoonbills and other wading birds pick among the pans.

Isla de Chira Amistad Lodge (tel./fax 506/2661-3261, or c/o Costa Rican Association of Community-Based Rural Tourism, tel. 506/2248-9470, www.actuarcostarica.com, $33–36 pp) offers a simple dorm and six quad rooms. ACTUAR offers packages with boat trips.

Isla San Lucas National Wildlife Refuge

Refugio Nacional de Via Silvestre Isla San Lucas (615 hectares), five kilometers offshore of Naranjo, seems a pleasant palm-fringed place where you might actually *wish* to be washed ashore and languish in splendid sun-washed isolation. Yet a visit to Isla San Lucas once amounted to an excursion to hell.

Until a few years ago, this was the site of the most dreaded prison in the Costa Rican penal system, with a legacy dating back 400 years. In the 16th century, the Spanish conquistador Gonzalo Fernandez Oviedo used San Lucas as a concentration camp for local Chara people, who were slaughtered on the site of their sacred burial grounds. The Costa Rican government turned it into a detention center for political prisoners in 1862. In 1991, it closed. There are still guards here, but today their role is to protect the island's resident wildlife from would-be poachers. It also has eight pre-Columbian sites.

In 2008, the prison was to be restored as a museum. Should you visit the grim bastion, the ghosts of murderers, miscreants, and maltreated innocents will be your guides. A cobbled pathway leads to the main prison building. The chapel has become a bat grotto, and only graffiti remains to tell of the horror and hopelessness, recorded by ex-convict José León Sánchez in his book, *La Isla de los Hombres Solos* (The Isle of the Lonely Men).

Coontramar (tel. 506/2661-1069, www .coonatramar.com/paq_sanluca_es.php, $60) offers tours from Puntarenas.

You can also rent motorboats through the Costa Rica Yacht Club (tel. 506/2661-0784), in Puntarenas, or Oasis del Pacífico (tel. 506/2641-8092) in Playa Naranjo.

Accommodations and Food

The nicest of several accommodations at Playa Naranjo is the modern, Italian-owned **Hotel El Ancla** (tel. 506/2641-3885, $40 s/d fan, $45 s/d a/c), just 200 meters from the ferry terminal, with nine brightly decorated, air-conditioned rooms fronted by a wide porch with hammocks. There's a pool and thatched bar and pizza restaurant where movies are shown at 8 P.M.

PAQUERA AND VICINITY

Paquera, 24 kilometers south of Playa Naranjo, is where the Paquera ferry (Ferry Naviera Tambor, tel. 506/2661-2084, ferrypeninsular@ racsa.co.cr) arrives and departs to/from Puntarenas. The ferry berth is three kilometers

northeast of Paquera. Paquera has banks and a gas station.

Note: If driving south from Playa Naranjo to Paquera, note that this unpaved section is very hilly, with tortuous switchbacks. It's a despairingly rugged ride: the 2009 national budget includes money to pave this section. No buses run this route. At least you get some marvelous views out over the Gulf of Nicoya—including toward Isla Guayabo, which comes into view about six kilometers south of Playa Naranjo, where the road briefly meets the coast at **Gigante,** at the north end of **Bahía Luminosa,** also called Bahía Gigante.

Offshore, **Islas Guayabo and Negritos Biological Reserves** protect nesting sites of the brown booby, frigate bird, pelican, and other seabirds, as well as the peregrine falcon. They are off-limits to visitors.

Dolphins and whales are often sighted offshore (January is the best month for whales).

Tiny **Isla Gitana,** in the middle of Bahía Luminosa, was once a burial site for local peoples (hence its other name, Isla Muertos— Island of the Dead—by which it is marked on maps). The undergrowth is wild, and cacti abound, so appropriate footwear is recommended. You can hire a boat on the mainland beach. You can also reach the island by sea kayak from Bahía Gigante, a 30-minute paddle journey.

Curú National Wildlife Refuge

The Curú Refugio Nacional de Vida Silvestre (tel. 506/2641-0100, www.curu.org, 7 A.M.–3 P.M. daily, $10 adults, $5 children) forms part of a 1,496-hectare cattle *finca,* two-thirds of which is preserved as primary forest. It is tucked in the fold of Golfo Curú, four kilometers south of Paquera, and is part privately owned. The reserve includes 4.5 kilometers of coastline with a series of tiny coves and three beautiful white-sand beaches—Playas Curú, Colorada, and Quesera—nestled beneath green slopes. Olive ridley and hawksbill turtles nest on the crystalline beaches. Mangrove swamps extend inland along the Río Curú, backed by forested hills. Monkeys are almost always playing in the treetops by the gift store, and agoutis, sloths, anteaters, and even ocelots are commonly seen. The facility has a macaw reintroduction program and a reproduction and rehabilitation program for endangered spider monkeys; you can spy them living freely behind an electrified fence (the trail to the enclosure is boggy, so bring appropriate footwear). Trails range from easy to difficult. You can rent horses ($10 per hour). Guided tours are offered (your tip is their pay). The bus between Paquera and Cóbano passes the unmarked gate. Ask the driver to let you off.

It has basic cabins ($8 pp) and serves meals. **Turismo Curú** (tel. 506/2641-0004, turismo curu@yahoo.com) offers snorkeling, kayaking, and scuba diving.

Accommodations

Cabinas y Restaurante Ginana (tel. 506/ 2641-0119, $33 s, $38 d), in Paquera, has 28 simply furnished rooms, some air-conditioned; all have private baths. The restaurant serves hearty local dishes.

You can also bunk in basic rooms with private cold water-only bathrooms at **Curú National Wildlife Refuge** ($35 pp, including meals). Bring a flashlight, as generator-powered electricity shuts down at night.

◖ ISLA TORTUGA

This stunningly beautiful, 320-hectare island lies three kilometers offshore of Curú. Tortuga is as close to an idyllic tropical isle as you'll find in Costa Rica. The main attraction is a magnificent white-sand beach lined with coconut palms. Tortuga is a favorite destination of excursion boats. Cruises depart Puntarenas and Los Sueños marina, at Playa Herradura, near Jacó. It's a 90-minute journey aboard any of a half dozen cruise boats. The cruise is superbly scenic, passing the isles of Negritos, San Lucas, Gitana, and Guayabo. En route you may spot manta rays or pilot whales in the warm waters. Even giant whale sharks have been seen basking off Isla Tortuga. You'll normally have about two hours on Isla Tortuga, with a buffet lunch served on the beach, plus options for sea

kayaking, snorkeling, volleyball, and hiking into the forested hills. It can get a bit cramped on weekends.

I recommend **Calypso Cruises** (tel. 506/ 2256-2727 or U.S. tel. 866/887-1969, www .calypsocruises.com), which runs daily trips from Puntarenas aboard the luxurious *Manta Raya* catamaran with full bar, a fishing platform, and two whirlpool tubs. Trips depart from Puntarenas ($109 low season, $119 high season, including transfer from San José).

The company also has cruises to **Punta Coral Private Reserve** (www.puntacoral .com), where snorkeling, sea kayaking, and other activities are offered, and monkeys and other animals abound in the adjacent forest, with trails. It offers "Paradise Weddings" in a South Seas setting.

Bay Island Cruises (tel. 506/2258-3536, www.bayislandcruises.com) offers cruises year-round aboard the *Bay Princess,* an ultramodern 16-meter cruise yacht with room for 70 passengers. The ship has a sundeck and music, and cocktails and snacks are served during the cruise. And 2008 saw the introduction of a sleek new 200-passenger catamaran with Jacuzzi. Trips depart Los Sueños marina, near Jacó.

TAMBOR

Tambor, 18 kilometers southwest of Paquera, is a small fishing village fronted by a gray-sand beach in **Bahía Ballena** (Whale Bay), a deep-pocket bay rimmed by **Playa Tambor** and backed by forested hills. I find the setting unappealing, but many readers report enjoying Tambor.

You can play a round of golf or tennis at the nine-hole **Tango Mar Golf Club** (tel. 506/2683-0001, www.tangomar.com). Play is free for guests; others pay a $25 greens fee ($15 club rental). Tango Mar also offers tours, sportfishing, and horseback riding.

Ultralight tours (tel. 506/2683-0480) from the Los Delfines airstrip give a fantastic bird's-eye view of the area.

Seascape Kayak Tours (tel. 506/2747-1884, www.seascapekayaktours.com) offers sea kayaking.

© CHRISTOPHER P. BAKER

Tambor ferry to Paquera, Puntarenas

Accommodations

Budget hounds might try **Cabinas y Restaurante Cristina** (tel. 506/2683-0028, eduardon@racsa.co.cr, $20 s/d with shared bath, $22 s or $27 d private bath, $35 *casita*), with nine simply furnished but clean and adequate rooms with fans and cold water only. It also has an air-conditioned *casita* with kitchen, sleeping four people.

I like the flame-orange **Hotel Costa Coral** (tel. 506/2683-0105, www.hotelcostacoral .com, $80 s/d weekdays, $95 s/d Fri.–Sat. low season; $105 Sun.–Thurs., $120 Fri.–Sat. high season), a colorful little beauty of a hotel on the main road in Tambor. It has six air-conditioned rooms in three two-story Spanish-colonial structures arrayed around an exquisite pool with whirlpool. The charming decor includes wrought iron, potted plants, climbing ivy, ceramic lamps, and a harmonious ocher-and-blue color scheme. The upstairs restaurant offers ambience and good cuisine, and its gift store is splendidly stocked.

Another lovely property is **Villas de la Bahía** (tel. 506/2683-0560, http://villasdelabahiacr

.com, $30–65 s/d), with two-story villas painted in tropical ice cream pastels.

The architecturally dramatic **Tambor Tropical** (tel. 506/2683-0011 or U.S. tel. 866/ 890-2537, www.tambortropical.com, $140–190 s/d year-round) is a perfect place to laze in the shade of a swaying palm. Ten hand-crafted two-story hexagonal *cabinas* (one unit upstairs, one unit down) face the beach amid lush landscaped grounds with an exquisite pool and whirlpool tub. The rooms are graced by voluminous bathrooms with deep-well showers, wraparound balconies, and fully equipped kitchens. Everything is handmade of native hardwoods, all of it lacquered to a nautical shine. A restaurant serves international cuisine. Snorkeling and horseback riding are offered. Rates include breakfast.

My favorite hostelry hereabouts is the Belgian-run **Tango Mar** (tel. 506/2683-0001, www.tangomar.com, $170 s/d room, $225 suite, $400–899 villas low season; $190 s/d room, $240 suite, $450–999 villas high season), five kilometers southwest of Tambor. It enjoys a beautiful beachfront setting backed by hectares of beautifully tended grounds splashed with bougainvillea and hibiscus. In 2007 rooms received a much needed and more stylish refurbishment, and in late 2008 the public spaces were being totally remade, and conference facilities and a spa were being added. It has 25 rooms, including five Polynesian-style thatched octagonal bamboo Tiki Suites raised on stilts, 18 spacious oceanfront rooms with large balconies, and 12 Tropical Suites with romantic four-poster beds with gauzy netting. You can also choose four- and five-person luxury villas ($400–900 low season, $450–999 high season). It has two swimming pools (one a lovely, freeform, multitiered complex), a nine-hole golf course, stables, water sports, Internet, plus massage and yoga. It rents 4WD vehicles. Rates include American breakfast.

If all-inclusive package resorts are your thing, consider the controversial **Barceló Playa Tambor Resort & Casino** (tel. 506/2683-0303, www.barcelo.com), with 402 rooms sprawling across a 2,400-hectare site. The sibling **Barceló Los Delfines Golf & Country Club** (same contact information), adjacent, comprises 64 Spanish-style, two-bedroom air-conditioned villas arrayed in military camp fashion around a nine-hole golf course.

Food
Restaurant Cristina (tel. 506/2683-0028, 8 A.M.–9 P.M. daily) proffers good seafood and pastas on a shady patio for those on a budget.

The **Restaurante Arrecife** (11 A.M.–2 P.M. and 6–10 P.M. daily low season, 11 A.M.–11 P.M. daily high season, $4–9), in the Hotel Costa Coral, is a charmer with its lively color scheme, and dishes such as ceviche, club sandwich, burgers, fettucine, chicken with orange sauce, and sea bass with heart-of-palm sauce. It has a large-screen TV and karaoke.

New in 2008, the roadside **Trattoria Mediterranea** (tel. 8821-7357, 5:30–10:30 P.M. Wed.–Sun.) has a special pizza Sunday.

The elegant new restaurant at **Tango Mar** (6:30–10 A.M., 11:30 A.M.–3:30 P.M., and 6:30–10 P.M. daily, $4.50–22), under construction at last visit, promises fine dining when completed.

Information and Services
Internet Kara (tel. 506/2683-0001) and a **pharmacy** (tel. 506/2683-0581) are above the roadside **Toucan Boutique.**

Budget Rent-a-Car (tel. 506/2683-0500) and **Tambor Adventures & Tours** (tel. 506/2683-0579) are here also.

Getting There
SANSA and **Nature Air** fly daily to Tambor from San José, with connecting service to other resorts.

Southern Nicoya

CÓBANO
Cóbano, a crossroads village 25 kilometers southwest of Paquera, is the gateway to Malpaís and to Montezuma (5 km) and Cabo Blanco Absolute Nature Reserve. Buses for Malpaís and the Paquera ferry depart from here.

The **police station** (tel. 506/2642-0770) and post office are 200 meters east of the bank; there are public telephones in front of the bank. The **medical clinic** (tel. 506/8380-4125) and **pharmacy** (tel. 506/2642-0685) are 100 meters south of the bank.

MONTEZUMA
Montezuma is a charming beachside retreat popular with budget-minded backpackers and counterculture travelers seeking an offbeat experience. Business owners are prone to shut up shop on a whim—sometimes for days at a time, or longer.

The fantastic beaches east of Montezuma are backed by forest-festooned cliffs from which streams tumble down to the sands. Monkeys frolic in the forests. *Beware riptides!* The **Nicolas Weissenburg Absolute Reserve**

Playa Montezuma

(Reserva Absoluta Nicolas Weissenburg) was created in 1998 to protect the shoreline and forested hills to the east of Montezuma. It's strictly off-limits, however.

The waterfall and swimming hole two kilometers southwest of town (the trail leads upstream from the Restaurante La Cascada) is dangerous. *Do not climb or jump from the top of the fall. Several lives have been lost this way.* The **Montezuma Butterfly Garden** (tel. 506/2642-1317, www.montezumagardens.com, 8 A.M.–4 P.M. daily, $8 entrance), west of the village, 0.5 kilometer above the Montezuma Waterfall Canopy del Pacífico tour, has a netted garden and breeds morphos and other butterflies species.

Entertainment and Events

Although hard to imagine, this tiny hamlet now hosts the **Montezuma International Film Festival** (www.montezumafilmfestival.com), created in 2007, each November.

El Sano Banano restaurant shows movies nightly at 7:30 P.M. (free with dinner or $6 minimum order).

Sports and Recreation

Montezuma Travel Adventures (tel. 506/2642-0808, www.montezumatraveladventures.com) offers all manner of activities, from ATV tours and horseback riding to its **Montezuma Waterfall Canopy del Pacífico,** which offers tours by zipline between the treetops at 8 A.M., 10 A.M., 1 P.M. and 3 P.M. ($35).

Montezuma Expeditions (tel. 506/2642-0919, www.montezumaexpeditions.com) similarly offers a wide range of tours and activities, as do **Montezuma Eco-Tours** (tel. 506/2642-0467, www.playamontezuma.net/ecotours.htm); **Zuma Tours** (tel. 506/2642-0024, www.zumatours.net); and **Chico's Tour** (tel. 506/2642-0556), which specializes in trips to Isla Tortuga ($40 pp).

Montezuma Yoga (tel. 506/2642-0076, www.montezumayoga.com) at Hotel Los Mangos offers yoga classes at 9:30 A.M. Sunday–Friday ($12).

For horse-riding, the best stable is at **Finca Los Caballos** (tel. 506/2642-0124, www.naturelodge.net, $20 pp per hour), which offers mountain and beach rides.

Accommodations

There are many more options than can be listed here.

CAMPING

You can camp at **Chinamo** (tel. 506/2642-1000, $5 pp), which rents tents and equipment.

UNDER $25

There's little to choose from between the mostly uninspired low-end properties, all with basic rooms with shared bathrooms with cold water for around $5 per person.

Budgeting backpackers should check in to **Mochila Inn** (tel. 506/2642-0030, mochila inn@hotmail.com, $11 pp dorm, $22 s/d room low season, $32 high season), an English-run hostel with shared kitchen, an upstairs dorm, one private room, and two cabins.

$25-50

The best bet for location in this price range is beachfront **Hotel Moctezuma** (tel./fax 506/2642-0058, $15 s or $20 d with fan, $30 s or $35 d with a/c and TV low season; $20 s or $30 d with fan, $30 s or $45 d with a/c and TV high season), with 28 spacious and clean rooms with fans. The main unit has a restaurant and bar directly over the beach.

The German/Tica-run **Cabinas El Pargo Feliz** (tel. 506/2642-0064, $25–30 s/d low season, $30–35 s/d high season) has eight spacious, clean, basically furnished modern *cabinas* with wooden floors, chipboard walls, fans, queen-size beds, tiled bathroom with cold water only, and hammocks on wide verandas. It has a rustic thatched restaurant.

Hotel L'Aurora (tel./fax 506/2642-0051, www.playamontezuma.net/aurora.htm, $22–50 s/d depending on room size), also run by a German-Tico couple, is a whitewashed house surrounded by lush gardens. It's recently been spruced up. The 18 rooms now have fans and air-conditioning, cable TV, and private baths with hot water. Upstairs is an airy lounge with bamboo and leather sofas, a small library, and hammocks. Rooms downstairs are dark.

$50-100

Hotel Playa Las Manchas (tel. 506/2642-0415, www.beach-hotel-manchas.com, $13 s, $25–50 d low season; $20 s, $40–75 d high season), nearby, has three lovely and distinct cabins in lush gardens. Los Colibris and Las Mariposa are two-bedroom bungalows; Casa Los Unicornos is a two-story house. They're simply furnished rooms and have large windows, a kitchen, and private bath and hot water. There's a disco.

I love the German-run **Hotel Horizontes de Montezuma** (tel. 506/2642-0534, www.horizontes-montezuma.com, $35 s, $45–55 d low season; $45 s, $55–65 d high season), midway between Cóbano and Montezuma. This Victorian-style home has seven rooms around a skylit atrium—saturating the hallway of black-and-white tile with magnesium light—and opening to a wraparound veranda with hammocks. The appealing rooms have white-washed wooden ceilings with fans, terra-cotta floors, sky-blue fabrics, and bathrooms done up in dark-blue tiles. Nice! A shady restaurant opens to the small pool. A solid bargain!

I like **Casacolores** (tel. 506/2642-0283, www.casacolores.com, $40–60 low season, $50–80 high season) for its four one-bedroom and one two-bedroom wooden cabins on stilts; each is painted a bright tropical color and has a kitchen. It has a swimming pool.

The **El Sano Banano Hotel** (tel. 506/2642-0636, www.ylangylangresort.com, $65 s/d low season, $75 s/d high season), above the restaurant in town, is a bed-and-breakfast with 11 air-conditioned rooms decorated in New Mexican style. They have satellite TV and hot-water showers.

With its landscaped pool and deck in lovely grounds, **Hotel El Jardín** (tel./fax 506/2642-0074, www.hoteleljardin.com, $65–75 s/d low season, $85–95 high season) is the best choice in the village itself. It offers 15 elegant hillside rooms with fans, hammocks on the veranda, refrigerators, and private baths (some with hot water). Each is individually styled in hardwoods and shaded by trees in landscaped grounds with pool and whirlpool tub. It also has two villas.

The relaxing **Hotel Amor de Mar** (tel./ fax 506/2642-0262, www.amordemar.com, $40–80 low season, $45–90 high season), 600 meters west of the village, enjoys a fabulous location on a sheltered headland, with a private tidepool and views along the coast in both directions. The hotel is set in pleasant landscaped lawns, with hammocks beneath shady palms. It has 11 rooms (all but two have private baths, some with hot water), each unique in size and decor and made entirely of hardwoods.

The **Luz de Mono Hotel** (tel. 506/2642-0090, www.luzdemono.com, $75 s/d standard, $140 casita low season; $100 standard, $175 casita high season) has improved and is now one of the better options in town, although readers complain of poor service. Centered on a lofty circular atrium with restaurant with conical roof and bamboo furnishings, it has 12 hotel rooms, plus eight stone *casitas* (some with whirlpool tubs). The Blue Congo Bar hosts stage shows and is the liveliest place around— noise can be a problem if you're trying to sleep. Rates include breakfast and tax.

$100-150

Out of town, I like **Nature Lodge Finca los Caballos** (tel./fax 506/2642-0124, www.nature lodge.net, $70–120 s/d low season, $86–138 high season, including taxes), on a 16-hectare ranch midway between Cóbano and Montezuma. Rooms here feature beautiful coral-stone floors and river-stone showers with poured-concrete sinks, tasteful contemporary furnishings that include Indian spreads on hardwood beds, and delightful patios with hammocks and rockers. Four new rooms have rattan or bamboo king-size beds and travertine balconies. A fan-shaped horizon swimming pool is inset in a multilevel wooden deck with poured-concrete, soft-cushioned sofas and lounge chairs for enjoying the fabulous forest and ocean views. There are trails and fantastic birding, as well as a stable. Meals include a full breakfast. A small spa has been added.

OVER $150

The nicest place is **(Ylang Ylang Beach**

Resort (tel. 506/2642-0636, www.ylangylang resort.com, $140 s/d tents, $190 rooms, $195 suites, $240–270 bungalows low season; $160 s/d tents, $195 rooms, $215 suites, $265–295 bungalows high season), a 10-minute walk along the beach 800 meters east of the village. Owners Lenny and Patricia Iacono have created a totally delightful property spread across eight hectares of beachfront that is a lush fantasia of ginger, pandanus, and riotous greens. It has three three-story suites (for up to four people) with kitchens; a three-bedroom apartment; and eight concrete and river-stone bungalows, all accessed by well-manicured paths lit at night. All have fans, private bath, fridge, coffeemaker, and Guatemalan bedspreads. French doors open to verandas within spitting distance of the ocean. The dome bungalows have private outdoor showers. And deluxe safari tents on decks have been added. The coup de grace is an exquisite freeform pool in a faux-natural setting of rocks with water cascading and foliage tumbling all around. Check in is at El Sano Banano café.

Food

For breakfast, head to the **Bakery Café** (tel. 506/2642-0458, 6 A.M.–6 P.M. Mon.–Sat.) for *gallo pinto,* banana bread, soy burgers, and tuna sandwiches served on a pleasant raised patio; or to **(El Sano Banano** (tel. 506/2642-0638, 7 A.M.–10 P.M. daily), where I recommend the scrambled tofu breakfast. This popular natural-food restaurant serves garlic bread, pasta, yogurt, veggie curry, and nightly dinner specials. It also has fresh-fruit thirst quenchers and ice cream and prepares lunches to go.

Tiny **Café Iguana** (6 A.M.–9:30 P.M. daily) is a great place to watch the street action in town. It serves waffles and muffins, sandwiches, scrumptious coconut cookies, cappuccinos, espressos, and natural juices.

Vegans will thrill to **Orgánico** (tel. 506/ 2642-1322, 8 A.M.–4 P.M. daily low season, 8 A.M.–6 P.M. daily high season), a bakery serving all-organic dishes, from a sushi bowl with tofu ($9) or stir fry rice and vegetables ($8) to brownies and ice cream. It has a pleasant, airy patio.

THE NICOYA PENINSULA

© CHRISTOPHER P. BAKER

Ocelots are only one of many animals found at Cabo Blanco.

For ocean views, head to **Restaurante Moctezuma** (tel. 506/2642-0058, 7:30 A.M.– 11 P.M. daily, $3–10), at Hotel Moctezuma; this atmospheric open-air eatery serves local fare and seafood, as does **Restaurant El Parque** (no tel., 7 A.M.–10 P.M. daily), on the village beach.

The best dining around is at **Ylang Ylang** (tel. 506/2642-0068, 7 A.M.–9:30 P.M. daily, $5–15), serving delicious fusion fare in romantic surrounds by the beach. The menu includes chilled gazpacho, fresh sushi, and Asian-inspired jumbo shrimp in pineapple and coconut sauce.

You can buy fresh produce at the organic fruit and vegetable market, held in the park every Saturday at 10 A.M.

Information and Services

Montezuma Sun Trails (tel. 506/2642-0808, 8 A.M.–8 P.M. daily), in the village center, has Internet service, but bring a sweater!

Librería Topsy (tel. 506/2642-0576, 8 A.M.– 1 P.M. Mon.–Fri., 8 A.M.–noon Sat.–Sun.) has heaps of used books, plus an amazingly large selection of international newspapers and magazines, from the *New York Times* to *The Economist*.

Getting There and Away

Buses (tel. 506/2642-0740) depart from Avenida 3, Calles 16/18 in San José at 7:30 A.M. and 2:30 P.M. daily; minibuses meet the bus in Cóbano. Return buses depart Montezuma at 6:15 A.M. and 3:30 P.M. Monday–Saturday (buses from Cóbano depart for San José 30 minutes later).

A bus for Cóbano and Montezuma ($4) meets the Paquera ferry. The bus for Paquera departs Montezuma at 5:30 A.M., 8:05 A.M., 10 A.M., noon, 2:15 P.M., and 4 P.M. and departs from Cóbano (from outside the Hotel Caoba) 15 minutes later.

Interbus (tel. 506/2283-5573, www.inter busonline.com) operates minibus shuttles from San José ($45), as does Montezuma Expeditions' **Tur Bus Shuttle.**

Most of the recreational tour companies offer water-taxis. For example, **Chico's Tour** (tel. 506/2642-0556) has a water-taxi to Jacó ($35 pp).

© CHRISTOPHER P. BAKER

sign in Cabo Blanco Absolute Wildlife Reserve

A taxi to Montezuma from Tambor airport costs about $25.

◖ CABO BLANCO ABSOLUTE WILDLIFE RESERVE

This jewel of nature at the very tip of the Nicoya Peninsula is where Costa Rica's quest to bank its natural resources for the future began. The 1,250-hectare Reserva Natural Absoluta Cabo Blanco (8 A.M.–4 P.M. Wed.–Sun., $10 admission)—the oldest protected area in the country—was created in October 1963 thanks to the tireless efforts of Nils Olof Wessberg, a Swedish immigrant commonly referred to as the father of Costa Rica's national park system (see David Rains Wallace's excellent book *The Quetzal and the Macaw: The Story of Costa Rica's National Parks*). Olof Wessberg was murdered in the Osa Peninsula in the summer of 1975 while campaigning to have that region declared a national park. A plaque near the Cabo Blanco ranger station stands in his honor.

The reserve, which includes 1,800 hectares out to sea, is named Cabo Blanco (White Cape) after the vertical-walled island at its tip, which owes its name to the accumulation of guano deposited by seabirds, including Costa Rica's largest community of brown boobies (some 500 breeding pairs). Two-thirds of the reserve is off-limits to visitors. One-third is accessible along hiking trails, some steep in parts. **Sendero Sueco** leads to the totally unspoiled white-sand beaches of Playa Balsita and Playa Cabo Blanco, which are separated by a headland (you can walk around it at low tide). A coastal trail, **Sendero El Barco,** leads west from Playa Balsita to the western boundary of the park. Check tide tables with the park rangers before setting off—otherwise you could get stuck. Torrential downpours are common April–December.

Isla Cabuya, about 200 meters offshore, has been used as a cemetery for the village of Cabuya. You can walk out to the island at low tide.

The gateway to the reserve is **Cabuya,** a tiny hamlet nine kilometers west of Montezuma. A rough rock-and-dirt track leads north over the mountains to Malpaís (seven kilometers; 4WD essential—and passable only in dry season). **Rainsong Wildlife Sanctuary** (tel. 506/2642-1265, www.rainsongsanctuary .com, 8–11 A.M. and 2–5 P.M. daily, $5 donation), one kilometer north of Cabuya, is a rescue center for animals such as monkeys, porcupines, raccoons, and kinkajous. They can be viewed in cages, and you can pet many of them; most were confiscated from illegal ownership or were injured and rescued in the wild. Its primary focus is education, as well as rehabilitation of animals on a 31-acre rainforest plot linked to Cabo Blanco. Volunteers are needed.

Information

The ranger station (tel./fax 506/2642-0093, cablanco@ns.minae.go.cr) has self-guided trail maps. Camping is not allowed, even at the ranger station.

Accommodations and Food

At Cabuya, **Jungalows El Ancla de Oro** (tel. 506/2642-0369, www.caboblancopark.com/ ancla.htm, $25 s/d rooms, $35–50 s/d bungalows low season; $27 s/d rooms, $40–55 bungalows high season) has camping for $5 per tent low season, $8 high season. It also has three delightful thatched hardwood A-frame cabins on tall stilts (one sleeps five). The restaurant serves tasty treats such as fish curry with coconut milk, shrimp curry, and garlic herb bread. The owners, Alex Villaloboso and his English wife, Fiona, rent horses ($20), mountain bikes ($10), and kayaks.

Getting There

A bus departs Montezuma for Cabuya and Cabo Blanco at 8:15 A.M., 10:15 A.M., 2:15 P.M., and 6:15 P.M. ($1 each way). The Cabuya–Montezuma bus departs at 7 A.M., 9 A.M., and 1 P.M.

Montezuma Travel Adventures (tel. 506/642-0802, www.montezumatravel adventures.com) offers transfers by reservation ($6 round-trip). Collective taxis depart Montezuma for Cabo at 7 and 9 A.M., returning at 3 and 4 P.M. ($1.50 pp). A private taxi costs about $12 one-way.

◖ SANTA TERESA AND MALPAÍS

The shoreline immediately north of Cabo Blanco is a lively surfers' paradise with some of the most splendid surfing beaches in the country. The past few years have seen a phenomenal tourist development, propelling Santa Teresa from offbeat obscurity to newfound popularity. Dozens of hotels and restaurants have popped up out of nowhere. Land prices have since skyrocketed, fueled in part by the fact that Mel Gibson, Drew Barrymore, and supermodel Giselle Bündchen are among the recent celebs to buy property here.

A road that leads west 10 kilometers from Cóbano hits the shore at the hamlet of **Carmen,** known in the surfing realm as Malpaís. The tiny fishing hamlet of Malpaís is actually three kilometers south of Carmen, but no matter; this dirt road dead-ends at the hamlet and turns inland briefly, ending at the northern entrance gate to Cabo Blanco Absolute Wildlife Reserve (there is no ranger station, hence no entrance fee). A rocky track that begins 800 meters north of the dead-end links Cabuya with Malpaís. Four-wheel drive is essential.

North from Carmen, the dirt road parallels **Playa Carmen** and **Playa Santa Teresa,** a seemingly endless beach with coral-colored sand, pumping surf, and dramatic rocky islets offshore. The community of Santa Teresa straggles along the road for several miles. The road continues to Manzanillo, where the going gets tougher and is a potholed bouillabaisse in wet season. The Malpaís–Santa Teresa community stretches along miles of shorefront, and local transport is minimal. Be prepared to walk if you don't have wheels.

Entertainment and Events

Malpaís Surf Camp has a lively bar that shows surf videos and has ping-pong, table soccer, a pool table, and (occasionally) a mechanical bull.

La Lora (tel. 506/2640-0132) is the in-vogue bar in Santa Teresa; it has a pool table and theme nights, including a house dance party

THE NICOYA PENINSULA

SANTA TERESA
AND MALPAÍS

AL CHILE VIOLA

To Manzanillo

THE RETREAT

FLORBLANCA RESORT

HOTEL RESTAURANTE MILAREPA

BLUE SURF SANCTUARY

Playa Hermosa

SUPER HACIENDA

HOTEL RAROTONGA

CUESTA ARRIBA B&B

CABINAS PLAYA SANTA TERESA

ESCENCIA
POINT BREAK HOTEL
PACIFIC SURF SCHOOL/
PACIFIC BURGER
LA LORA
CAMPING/
CABINAS ZENEIDA

SANTA TERESA

OTRO LADO LODGE
BARAKÁ CAFÉ
DON JON'S HOSTEL

FUNKY MONKEY LODGE

SANTA TERESA SURF CAMP/
INTERNET CAFÉ

SUPER OLAS/INTERNET GAVIOTA

BURGER RANCHO
INTERNET CAFÉ/
BAKERY/LAUNDRY

RESTAURANT BRISAS DEL MAR

WAVETROTTERS SURF HOSTEL

RANCHO ITAUNA
PLAZA ROYAL
CASA ZEN

CASA DEL MAR HOSTEL
SUPERMARKET RONNY
HOSTEL CHOPA CHUPA
RANCHO SANCHO

ZULA INN

LUZ DE VIDA
COSTA RICA MEDICAL RESPONSE

Playa Santa Teresa

Playa Carmen

TRÓPICO LATINO
ZULA
SUPERMARKET
HORIZON OCEAN VIEW HOTEL
TRANQUILO BACKPACKERS
SUPERMARKET

0   0.25 mi
0   0.25 km

MAP CONTINUED AT RIGHT

Carmén

To Cóbano

© AVALON TRAVEL

PHARMACY/BANK

HOWLING MONKEY SPORTS BAR
TITONET (INTERNET)
QUAD RENTAL/
TROPICAL TOURS
BUDGET & ALAMO RENT-A-CAR
HOTEL PLAYA CARMEN
To Cóbano
FRANK'S PLACE/
BANK/MEDICAL CLINIC
PLAZA CARMEN/
PHARMACY/BANK
Carmen
RITMO TROPICAL
THE PLACE

MALPAÍS SURF CAMP

BLUE JAY LODGE

ICE TOWER

VISTA LAS OLAS RESORT/THE WAVE
PACHAMAMA MALPAÍS

LA HACIENDA B&B

MOANA LODGE

BAR Y RESTAURANTE MAR AZUL
BEIJA FLOR

To Cabuya and Star Mountain Jungle Lodge

MALPAÍS
CEMETERY

CANOPY TOUR

FISHING BOATS

0   0.25 mi
0   0.25 km

Cabo Blanco Absolute Wildlife Refuge   ENTRANCE

Tuesday; reggae and hip hop on Thursday; and Latin night on Saturday.

Howlin Monkey Sports Bar & Grill (tel. 506/2640-0007) has sporting events on the big screen.

The most upscale and happening place at last visit was **D&N Day & Night Beach Club** (tel. 506/2640-0353, 9 A.M.–2:30 A.M. daily), with live DJs.

Sports and Recreation

Canopy del Pacífico (tel. 506/2640-0360, www.canopydelpacifico.com) offers tours by zipline between the treetops at 9 A.M. and 2 P.M. by reservation ($49).

There are a dozen or more surf shops, several offering tours, including **Adrenalina Surf & Kite School** (tel. 506/8324-8671, laurent_trinci@hotmail.com). **Malpaís Surf Camp** (tel. 506/2642-0031, www.malpais surfcamp.com) and **Santa Teresa Surf Camp** (tel. 506/2640-0049, surf@expreso .co.cr) also rent boards and offer surf lessons. **Malpaís Quad Tours** (tel. 506/2640-0178) and **Santa Teresa Sunset** (tel. 506/2640-0315, www.santateresasunset.com) rent ATVs and offers tours.

Malpaís Bike Tours (tel. 506/2640-0550, info@malpaisbiketours.com) has bicycling tours.

After all your activities, relax with a massage at **Sonja Spa** (tel. 506/2640-1060, jenifer106@ hotmail.com), in Plaza Carmen.

Accommodations

There are many more options than can be listed here.

CAMPING

In Santa Teresa, **Camping y Cabinas Zeneida** (tel. 506/2640-0118) is tucked amid shade trees (with hammocks) beside the beach. It charges $3 pp for camping, including toilets and showers. It also has two A-frame cabins with loft bedrooms and toilets and kitchenettes, plus a thatched cabin ($5 pp). The owners will cook meals.

You can also camp at **Tranquilo Backpackers**

(tel. 506/2640-0589, www.tranquiloback packers.com, $7 pp), and at **Malpaís Surf Camp and Resort** (tel. 506/2642-0031, www .malpaissurfcamp.com, $7 pp). Both have showers and toilets.

UNDER $25

An in spot with budgeting backpackers is **Tranquilo Backpackers** (tel. 506/2640-0589, www.tranquilobackpackers.com, $11 pp dorms, $13 pp loft, $35 s/d private). Rooms are in a two-story New Mexican–style building with dangerously open rails on the balcony—take care up there! It has seven dorms with lofts and bunks, plus clean, airy, spacious private rooms with bathrooms. There's an open-air lounge with hammocks, plus a kitchen, Internet café, and parking.

The well-run **Malpaís Surf Camp and Resort** (tel. 506/2642-0031, www.malpais surfcamp.com, $15 pp camp beds, $35 s/d cabins with shared bath, $95 d casita), 200 meters south of the junction, has a panoply of accommodations set in eight hectares of grounds. An oceanview *rancho* has "semi-private" camp beds beneath a tin roof with shared baths. There are also *cabinas* with shared bath with cold water, and poolside *casitas* with stone floors, tall louvered screened windows, and beautiful tile bathrooms with hot water. There's a lively bar, a pool, and horse and surfboard rentals.

My fave backpackers' hostel, though, is **Wavetrotters Surf Hostel** (tel. 506/2640-0805, www.wavetrotterhostel.com, $12 pp), new in 2007. This Italian-run winner is basically an atrium lodge with an open downstairs lounge with soaring ceiling and four all-wooden upstairs dorms with lockers. They open to a common terrace, and you can descend to the lounge via a firepole! Plus there's a private room downstairs ($30 s/d low season, $35 s/d high season). It rents surfboards.

For a great bargain, choose **Casa Zen** (tel. 506/2640-0523, www.zencostarica.com, $12 pp dorm, $24 s/d room, $135 apartment), with an Indian motif, colorful cushions, chessboards, free movies by night, a great Thai restaurant, and four simply furnished sponge-washed rooms (including two dorms) with batiks, ceiling fans, and shared bathrooms. Casa Zen also has an upstairs three-room apartment with a huge terrace with hammocks. It recently added a spa.

$25-50

Once a backpackers' place, **Frank's Place** (tel./fax 506/2640-0096, www.franksplacecr.com, $28 s/d shared bathroom, $30–95 private bathroom), at the junction for Cóbano, has grown beyond recognition and now offers 33 rooms and bungalows in various styles. Alas, the upper-end rooms are overpriced.

I like **Ritmo Tropical** (tel. 506/2640-0174, www.nicoyapeninsula.com/malpais/ritmo tropical, $40 s/d low season, $50 high season), 400 meters south of Frank's Place, with seven modern, cross-ventilated, well-lit cabins in a landscaped complex, each for four people and each with fans, modest furnishings, and nice private bathroom with hot water. It has secure parking, plus an Italian restaurant (Thurs.–Tues.).

Ingo offers eight rooms at **Cabinas Playa Santa Teresa** (tel./fax 2640-0137, $20 s/d, $25 with kitchen low season; $30 s/d, $35 kitchen high season), built around a massive strangler fig favored by howler monkeys. Three have kitchens; all have two double beds and private baths with cold water. It has hammocks under shade, plus parking.

The well-maintained, U.S.–run **Santa Teresa Surf Camp** (tel. 506/2640-0049, surf@expreso.co.cr, $8 hammock, $12 pp shared bath, $48 s/d cabin low season; $10 hammock, $15 pp shared bath, $67 s/d cabin high season) offers wonderful *cabinas* with beautiful color schemes. It has one spacious cabin with sloping tin roof, ceiling fans, cement tile floors, and kitchenette with large fridge; large louvered windows open to a terrace. Four other cabins have clean, shared outside bathrooms with cold-water showers. It also has a beach-front, two-bedroom, air-conditioned house with cable TV, colorful walk-in showers, large kitchen, and wraparound veranda.

$50-100

The lovely **Rancho Itauna** (tel./fax 506/2640-0095, www.ranchos-itauna.com, $70 without kitchen, $80 with kitchen low season; $80 without kitchen, $90 with kitchen high season), in Santa Teresa, is run by a charming Austrian-Brazilian couple and offers four rooms in two octagonal two-story buildings. Each room has a fan, refrigerator, double bed plus bunk, and private bathroom with hot water. Two rooms have a kitchen. The pleasing restaurant serves international cuisine. Rates include tax.

The **Star Mountain Jungle Lodge** (tel. 506/2640-0101, www.starmountaineco.com, $50 s, $65 d), two kilometers northeast of Malpaís, on the track to Cabuya, is a gem tucked in the hills amid an 80-hectare private forest reserve, with trails (the turnoff is 400 meters north of the soccer field in Malpaís). The four charming, cross-ventilated *cabinas* are simply yet tastefully decorated and have Sarchí rockers on the veranda. A *casita* bunkhouse sleeps up to nine people. There's a pool, and guided horseback rides are offered. Grilled meats and fish are prepared in a huge open oven. It offers horseback rides ($30 two hours).

Also a delight, **The Place** (tel. 506/2640-0001, www.theplacemalpais.com, $60–80 s/d room, $120 s/d bungalow low season; $70–90 s/d room, $140 s/d bungalow low season) is a romantic delight. The high point is a lovely jade-colored pool and adjoining open-air lounge with rattan pieces with leopard-skin prints. Rooms are simply furnished and dark but have earth tones, yellows, and graceful batiks. Far nicer are the bungalows, with trendy cement floors, all-around floor-to-ceiling louvered French doors, and pink spreads enlivening whitewashed wooden walls. Each bungalow has its own style—I like the African villa.

Another winner is **Luz de Vida** (tel. 506/2640-0568, www.luzdevida-resort.com, $65 s/d room, $80 s/d bungalow low season; $80 s/d room, $95 s/d bungalow high season), with delightfully decorated split-level bungalows surrounded by forest, plus a splendid colorful restaurant overlooking a handsome pool, gorgeously floodlit at night.

Worthy alternatives include **Pachamama** (tel. 506/2640-0195, www.pacha-malpais.com); **Funky Monkey Lodge** (tel. 506/2640-0272, www.funky-monkey-lodge.com), with some of the loveliest rooms and dorms around; and **Tropical Surf House** (tel. 506/8345-7746, www.tropicalpasta.com).

$100-150

A tasteful newcomer, the Argentinian-run **Blue Surf Sanctuary** (tel. 506/2640-1001, www.bluesurfsanctuary.com, $110–135 s, $125–150 d) is a delight. It has an open kitchen-lounge with hammocks and sofas, plus four individually themed and raised villas with pendulous open-air queen-size lounge beds slung beneath. Lovely furnishings include dark contemporary hardwoods, ethnic pieces and fabrics, and gorgeous albeit small bathrooms with mosaic tiles and large walk-in showers. It has a plunge pool and surf school.

The delightful **Trópico Látino Lodge** (tel. 506/2640-0062, www.hoteltropicolatino.com, $77–120 s/d low season, $103–155 s/d high season), at Playa Santa Teresa, backs a rocky foreshore with hammocks under shade trees. There's a pool and whirlpool tub, and a breezy bar and restaurant (serving excellent cuisine) by the shore. It has 10 high-ceilinged, simply furnished wooden bungalows amid lawns; each has wide shady verandas, a king-size bed and a sofa bed, mosquito nets, fans, and a private bath with hot water. Two newer cabins have ocean views. It arranges fishing, horseback rides, and tours. Rates include tax.

The best hotel in this price bracket is the gorgeous, African-themed 〖 **Moana Lodge** (tel. 506/2640-0230, www.moanalodge.com, $95 s/d standard, $125 deluxe, $165–265 suite low season; $115 s/d standard, $140 deluxe, $195–295 suite high season), with seven rooms, some in huge colonial-style wooden cabins, featuring four-poster beds with cowhide drapes, zebra (fake) skins, leopard-print cushions, free Wi-Fi, and large well-lit bathrooms with huge showers. An open-air rancho with poured concrete sofa overlooks a large whirlpool tub and freeform pool in a stone-faced sundeck. Nice! And a bargain!

A newcomer, the Asian-inspired **Beija Flor** (tel. 506/2640-1007, www.beijaflorresort.com, $85–105 s/d rooms, $120 s/d bungalows, $135 s/d suite, $185 villa) specializes in yoga and wellness retreats. The air-conditioned guest quarters have a stylish contemporary motif of whites and taupes, and most have Wi-Fi.

The **Hotel Playa Carmen** (tel. 506/2640-0404, www.playacarmenhotel.com, $90 s/d room, $125–250 suite low season; $140 s/d room, $195–275 suite high season), at Plaza Carmen, has clean contemporary lines. Although guest rooms are dark, they have ceiling fans and bathrooms with glass walls and travertine, and they open to a lovely courtyard with pool, hot tub, and a circular thatched bar.

Also new in 2008, the Israeli-run **Zula Inn Aparthotel** (tel. 506/2640-0940, www.zulainn.com, $90 s/d low season, $110 high season), at Playa Santa Teresita, is another lovely hotel worth considering.

OVER $150

The French-owned **Hotel Restaurante Milarepa** (tel. 506/2640-0023, www.milarepahotel.com, $170–200 low season, $194–224 high season), at the north end of Playa Santa Teresa, exemplifies tasteful simplicity and has four cabins, spaced apart amid lawns inset with a lap pool. Two cabins are literally on the beach. They're made of bamboo and rise from a cement base: exquisite albeit sparse appointments invoke a Japanese motif, and there are four-poster beds in the center of the room, with mosquito drapes, plus open-air bathroom-showers in their own patio gardens. One wall folds back entirely to offer ocean vistas. It has a splendid restaurant.

Then there's the **Otro Lado Lodge** (tel. 506/2640-1941, www.otroladolodge.com, $100 s/d low season, $120 s/d high season), another lovely contemporary-style newcomer with a crisp aesthetic, combing gleaming whites with colorful tropical highlights. The restaurant here is a winner.

Yoga fans might check out **Horizon Ocean View Hotel** (tel. 506/2640-0524, www.horizon-yogahotel.com, $80–150 low season,

© CHRISTOPHER P. BAKER

La Reserva

$100–180 high season), a dedicated hilltop yoga center with simply appointed cabins.

"Stunning" and "serene" are fitting descriptions for (**Florblanca Resort** (tel. 506/2640-0232, www.florblanca.com, $475–850 s/d), perhaps the finest boutique beach resort in the country. This gem enjoys an advantageous beachfront position at the north end of Santa Teresa. Imbued with a calming Asiatic influence (Tibetan prayer flags flutter over the entrance), it offers 10 luxury oceanside villas stairstepping down to the beach. Fragrant plumeria and namesake *flor-blanca* trees drop petals at your feet as you walk stone pathways that curl down through an Asian garden. The motif is Santa Fe–meets–Bali in ochers, soft creams, and yellows. The villas are furnished with silent air-conditioning, large wall safes, quality rattan furnishings, tasteful art pieces, and exquisite furnishings, from lamps of tethered bamboo stalks to king-size beds on raised hardwood pedestals. Each has a kitchenette, a vast lounge, and stone-floored "rainforest" bathroom with lush gardens, and separate showers and oversize tub. Resort facilities

include a TV lounge, quality souvenir store, and a walk-in landscaped horizon pool fed by a waterfall with swim-up bar. The superb oceanfront restaurant and sushi bar is worth a visit in its own right. New owner, Rusty Carter, from Carolina, was adding a deluxe spa and a sumptuous bi-level honeymoon suite at last visit. Tours, including horseback riding at the cattle roundup at Hacienda Ario ($60 three hours), plus yoga, kickboxing, and dance classes in a world-class dojo are all available. Pricing here has been fickle, as guests stayed away when Rusty raised the rates a tad too much.

In 2008, Rusty opened (**La Reserva** (tel. 506/2640-0232, www.florblanca.com, call for rates), a super and super-exclusive adjunct (formerly Latitude 10) with three junior suites, two master suites, and a deluxe room (actually, they're all private villas) hidden within its own forest garden. With its pampering personalized service, this is the ultimate in deluxe, private lodgings in Nicoya. Villas are infused with Asian influences, including dark colonial plantation furnishings, glassless windows and French doors, king-size beds a mile off the

nouvelle cuisine at Néctar, Florblanca Resort

floor, and fabulous open-air bathrooms with rainforest showers. A highlight is the guest-only restaurant. Imagine coconut-carrot-ginger soup ($10), pan-seared snook with black Thai rice, and butter-poached asparagus and jalapeño beurre blanc ($26).

Care to splash out big money for a private villa? Try **The Red Palm Villas** (tel. 506/2640-0447, www.redpalmvillas.com, $105–185 s/d apartments, $350–675 s/d villas), next to Florblanca, with gorgeous wooden beachfront villas seemingly inspired by Frank Lloyd Wright. I also love **Casa Pura Vida Beachfront Luxury Villas** (tel. 506/2640-0511, www.casaspuravida.com), with three gorgeous villas, "each quite different in style," in Santa Teresa.

Food

Malpaís Surf Camp (7 A.M.–10 P.M. daily) serves American breakfasts (from $5), plus lunch and dinner. And I like **Casa Zen** (tel. 506/2640-0523, 7 A.M.–10 P.M. daily), a marvelous Thai restaurant by night, but serving American-style breakfasts ($4) such as veggie scramble and pancakes and lunches that include BLTs and tuna sandwiches. For dinner ($8), try the seared yellowfin tuna or red coconut curry.

Jungle Juice (tel. 506/2640-0279) serves health foods like pancakes, veggie burgers, quesadillas, and fresh juices. And for a great option for burgers, veggie dishes, kabobs, and slow-cooked chicken, try **Burger Rancho** (tel. 506/2640-0583, 8 A.M.–midnight daily), a tiny little spot that gets packed, despite the road dust.

The restaurant at **Rancho Itauna** (506/2640-0095, 7:30–9:30 A.M. and 6:30–9 P.M. daily, high season only) specializes in Brazilian seafood dishes but also has a barbecue on Thursday.

The open-air **Restaurante Soma** (tel. 506/2640-0023, 7–10 A.M., 11:30 A.M.–2:30 P.M., and 6–9 P.M. daily) at the Hotel Milarepa specializes in Pacific Rim fusion cuisine. Reservations are recommended.

Despite its simple thatched ambience, **Restaurant Brisas del Mar** (tel. 506/2640-0941, 5–10 P.M. does a mean job of nouvelle

© CHRISTOPHER P. BAKER

fusion dishes, such as lemon rosemary chicken with herbed yogurt ($11.50); seared tuna with red wine, capers, and anchovy ($12.50); and self-described "sinfully wicked desserts."

The best cuisine by far is at **Néctar** (7 A.M.–3 P.M. daily café only, 3–6 P.M. daily sushi only, 6–9 P.M. daily full menu) at Florblanca, where Chef Spencer Graves conjures up fabulous Asian-Pacific-Latin fusion creations, including smoked trout, cream cheese, and scallion maki roll appetizers ($7), and salmon, scallion, and caviar jumbo roll ($9). Entrées include Chinese five-spice marinated duck breast with caramelized red onion latkes and butter-wilted spinach ($20). The raised hemispheric bar is a good place to enjoy top-quality sushi (don't fail to order the caterpillar rolls). A chef's five-course tasting menu is offered with 24 hours' notice. It plays cool music, from jazz to classical.

The past few years have seen an explosion of sushi restaurants that include **Omi Sushi,** in Plaza Carmen; **Sushi Ukiy** (tel. 506/2640-0690, 6–10 P.M. Thurs.–Sun.); and **Cameleon Restaurant & Sushi Bar** (tel. 506/2640-0949, 6–10:30 P.M. Mon.–Sat.).

In Plaza Carmen, **Artemis Café** (tel. 506/2640-0561, 7 A.M.–midnight daily) is clean and modern and has Wi-Fi plus an outdoor courtyard. The wide-ranging menu includes paninis, salads, smoked salmon appetizer ($8), and dinners such as spinach ravioli ($7.50), as well as cookies.

Across the way, the **Azucar Restaurant** (tel. 506/2640-0071, www.azucar-restaurant.com, 8 A.M.–9:30 P.M. daily) opened at Frank's Place in 2007; it's run by a French-Cuban couple. Norbis is the Cuban (yet London-trained) chef at the helm delivering delicious nouvelle tropical cuisine, such as seared ahi tuna with ginger ($12), and mahimahi with basil mashed potatoes with tomato and parsley sauce ($10). It's a great spot to try *ropa vieja* or a burger, then a chocolate tart with ice cream before bedding down poolside for a snooze.

You can buy fresh produce at the organic fruit and vegetable market, held in Santa Teresa every Saturday at 3 P.M.

Information and Services

There's a **bank** at Plaza Carmen, where **Carmen Connections** (tel. 506/8823-8600) is a tour information center.

There's a **medical clinic** (tel. 800/367-2000) with ambulance service next to Frank's Place, and a **pharmacy** across the street in Plaza Carmen, which has a bank. **Costa Rica Medical Response** (tel. 506/2665-2626) also has 24/7 ambulance service. Teeth trouble? Head to **Sunny Smile Dental Clinic** (tel. 506/2640-0660), in Plaza Royal.

There are half-a-dozen or so Internet cafés, including **Frank's Internet Café,** at the Carmén junction, and **Cyber-Phone Santa Teresa** (tel. 506/2640-0996).

The **Santa Teresa Surf Camp** doubles as a Spanish-language school.

You can buy gasoline at a *pulpería* 0.5 kilometer north of the soccer field.

Getting There and Away

Buses depart Cóbano for Malpaís at 10:30 A.M. and 2:30 P.M. Return departures are at 7 A.M. and noon, connecting with onward buses to San José.

Montezuma Expeditions (tel. 506/2642-0919, www.montezumaexpeditions.com) has a daily minibus shuttle from San José ($40), as does **Interbus** (tel. 506/2283-5573, www.interbusonline.com, $45).

You can rent an ATV (a virtual necessity in wet season) from **Malpaís Quad Tours** (tel. 506/2640-0178) and **Santa Teresa Sunset** (tel. 506/2640-0315, www.santateresasunset.com). And **Alamo Rent-a-Car** (tel. 506/2640-0526) and **Budget** (tel. 506/2640-0500, www.budget.co.cr) have offices at Carmen.

Taíno Gas (tel. 506/2640-0009), in Santa Teresa, is open 7 A.M.–6 P.M. daily.

CENTRAL PACIFIC

The Central Pacific region comprises a thin coastal plain narrowing to the southeast and backed by steep-sided mountains cloaked in dense forest. The coast is lined by long gray-sand beaches renowned for fantastic surf. It is distinguished from more northerly shores by its wetter climate. The region becomes gradually humid southward, with the vegetation growing ever more luxuriant. No surprise then that this region has some of the nation's prime national parks, where visitors are virtually guaranteed to see scarlet macaws screeching overhead and rare spider monkeys swinging from treetop to treetop.

Rivers cascade down from the precipitous mountains, providing opportunities to hike to the base of spectacular waterfalls. The rivers slow to a crawl amid extensive mangrove swamps separated by miles-long sandy swaths interspersed with craggy headlands. Several of these estuarine systems are home to thriving populations of crocodiles, easily seen. The resort town of Jacó, the sportfishing town of Quepos, and more relaxed Manuel Antonio are in the throes of rampant development (in 2006, for example, Starwood Resorts announced it would build a super-deluxe St. Regis resort at Playa Coyol).

South of Jacó, vast groves of African palms smother the coastal plains. Interspersed among them are quaint workers' villages, with gaily painted plantation houses raised on stilts.

Highway 34 (the Costanera Sur) runs the length of the coast, linking the region with Puntarenas and Guanacaste to the north and Golfo Dulce and Osa southward. It is paved almost the entire

© CHRISTOPHER P. BAKER

HIGHLIGHTS

《 Jungle Crocodile Safari: You're sure to see crocs close up on a riverboat cruise up the Río Tárcoles, with fabulous birding to boot. Your guide may even get out onto the muddy bank to feed a croc (page 426).

《 Carara National Park: This reserve at the meeting point of moist and dry tropical ecosystems is easily accessed. Monkeys, sloths, and macaws are virtually guaranteed (page 426).

《 Rainmaker Conservation Project: Boardwalks in the sky? Yes, elevated walkways lead you through the forest canopy at this private reserve in the mountains (page 441).

《 Manuel Antonio National Park: Popular and heavily visited, this small rainforest preserve offers diverse wildlife, good nature trails, beautiful beaches, and a small coral reef ideal for snorkeling (page 459).

《 Hacienda Barú National Wildlife Refuge: Wildlife abounds in this small reserve, which spans numerous ecosystems, from mangroves to montane rainforest (page 466).

《 Parque Reptilandia: Dozens of snake species from around the world are displayed at this well-run reptile zoo, which even has a komodo dragon (page 467).

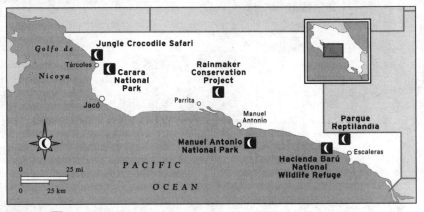

LOOK FOR **《** TO FIND RECOMMENDED SIGHTS, ACTIVITIES, DINING, AND LODGING.

way and at last visit was being widened and tarred with the intent that Highway 34 will become the new Pan-American Highway, linking Nicaragua and Panamá (doing away with the need to head up over Cerro de la Muerte and shortening the route considerably). For now the road south of Quepos is still an unpaved adventure, and parts of this region are still being opened up, luring offbeat travelers in search of tomorrow's find.

PLANNING YOUR TIME

The Central Pacific zone is predominantly a beach destination, particularly favored by surfers: **Playa Hermosa** and **Dominical** are their favored haunts. The area is easily explored along the coast highway, with dead-end side roads branching off to specific attractions. Allocate a week minimum to explore the entire region north to south, although three days is sufficient if you wish to concentrate on Manuel Antonio, Jacó, or Dominical.

The most developed of the beach resorts is **Jacó,** long a staple of Canadian package charter groups but recently, having spruced itself up, an in-vogue destination for surfers and Tico youth. If you like an active nightlife, this is also for you,

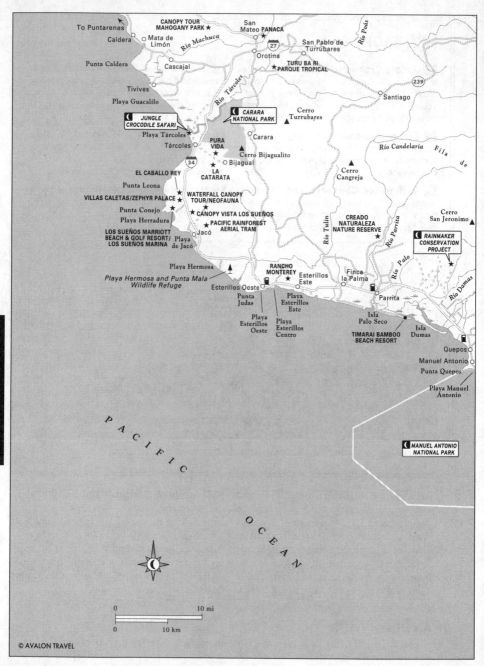

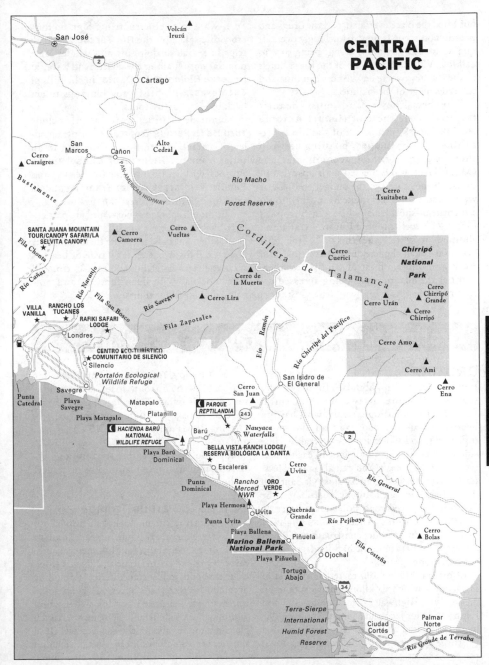

CENTRAL PACIFIC

San José

Volcán Iruzú ▲

2

Cartago ○

San Marcos

Cañon

Cerro Caraigres ▲

Alto Cedral ▲

Bustamente

PAN-AMERICAN HIGHWAY

Río Macho

Forest Reserve

Cerro Tsuitabeta ▲

Cerro Camorra ▲

Cerro Vueltas ▲

SANTA JUANA MOUNTAIN TOUR/CANOPY SAFARI/LA SELVITA CANOPY ★

Fila Chonta

Río Cañas

C o r d i l l e r a   d e   T a l a m a n c a

Cerro Cuerici ▲

Chirripó National Park

Cerro de la Muerta ▲

Cerro Chirripó Grande ▲

Cerro Urán ▲

Cerro Chirripó ▲

Río Naranjo

Fila San Bosco

Río Savegre

Cerro Lira ▲

VILLA VANILLA ★

RANCHO LOS TUCANES ★

RAFIKI SAFARI LODGE ★

Londres ○

Fila Zapotales

Río Ramón

Río Chirripó del Pacífico

Cerro Amo ▲

Cerro Ami ▲

CENTRO ECO-TURÍSTICO COMUNITARIO DE SILENCIO ★

Silencio

Portalón Ecological Wildlife Refuge

Savegre

Cerro Ena ▲

San Isidro de El General ○

Punta Catedral

Playa Savegre

Matapalo ○

Playa Matapalo

Platanillo ○

Cerro San Juan ▲

(*PARQUE REPTILANDIA* ★

243

Barú ○

Nauyaca Waterfalls

[*HACIENDA BARÚ NATIONAL WILDLIFE REFUGE* ▲

Playa Barú

Dominical ○

BELLA VISTA RANCH LODGE/ RESERVA BIOLÓGICA LA DANTA ★

Escaleras ○

Cerro Uvita ▲

2

Punta Dominical

Rancho Merced NWR

ORO VERDE ★

Playa Hermosa

Uvita ○

Punta Uvita

Quebrada Grande ▲

Río General

Río Pejibaye

Cerro Bolas ▲

Piñuela ○

Fila Costeña

Playa Ballena

Marino Ballena National Park

Playa Piñuela

Ojochal ○

Tortuga Abajo

34

Terra-Sierpe International Humid Forest Reserve

Ciudad Cortés ○

Palmar Norte ○

Río Grande de Terraba

but I find the place overrated, and the drugs and prostitution scene is now disturbingly overt. If quality is your gig, move along, being sure to call in at **Villa Caletas,** one of the finest hotels in the country, where day visitors can dine and take advantage of the facilities.

The best-known and most beautiful beaches are those of **Manuel Antonio National Park,** just south of the hip sportfishing town of **Quepos,** boasting between them a wide array of accommodations (Manuel Antonio is blessed with upscale options; Quepos caters to the budget end). Clear waters and a coral reef make Manuel Antonio a favorite of snorkelers, while a lush tropical forest with well-groomed nature trails and abundant wildlife makes this one of the most visited parks in the nation. **Carara National Park** also offers a feast of wildlife wonders and has the advantage of being accessed direct from the coast highway (the Costanera Sur). Want to go croc-spotting? Sign up for a crocodile safari on the **Río Tárcoles.** Kayak trips in search of dolphins and whales are a popular option along the coast. And a stay at **Reserva Biológica La Danta,** in the hills of **Escaleras,** will satisfy any longings to get back to your earthy roots.

Manmade facilities worth a call include **Turu Ba Ri Parque Tropical,** offering a medley of attractions from a petting zoo to an aerial tramway; **Rainmaker Conservation Project** with its boardwalks in the sky; and **Pacific Rainforest Aerial Tram,** a gondola ride through the rainforest canopy.

The months of December–April are particularly busy anywhere along the central Pacific coast, when Costa Ricans take their "summer" holidays. This is particularly true of beaches such as Playas Esterillos Oeste, Centro, and Este, popular with Tico families and now being developed for tourists.

Orotina to Playa Herradura

OROTINA

From the central highlands, Highway 3 descends to Orotina, gateway to the Central Pacific. The road drops steeply, with hairpin bends, washed-out sections of road, slow-moving trucks, and Costa Ricans overtaking like suicidal maniacs. It's single-lane in each direction. *Drive cautiously!* You can also take a less-trafficked route west from San José via Santiago de Puriscal and San Pablo de Turrubares; the deteriorated paved road sidles magnificently downhill to Orotina, where it joins Highway 3. (A new highway under construction will link directly with Escazú in the highlands; expect it to open around 2010.)

Orotina is hidden 400 meters northwest of Highway 3, which six kilometers west of town merges with Highway 27 (for Puntarenas) and Highway 34 for Jacó and Manuel Antonio. The town is centered on an attractive plaza shaded by palms and has a railway track running down the main street.

The **Canopy Tour Mahogany Park** (tel. 506/2291-4465 in San José, www.canopy tour.com) is on a 120-hectare forest reserve at Jesús María, 11 kilometers northwest of Orotina. It has tours at 8 A.M., 10 A.M., noon, and 2:30 P.M. ($45 adult, $35 student, $25 child). You'll ascend to the treetops and traverse from platform to platform using pulleys on horizontal cables.

Turu Ba Ri Parque Tropical

This adventure theme park (tel. 506/2250-0705, www.turubari.com), at San Juan de Mata, in the mountains four kilometers southeast of Orotina, claims to be the biggest tropical theme park in Central America. Extending over 200 hectares, it is accessed via an aerial tramway with enclosed gondolas that whisk you on a "sky ride tour" ($15) down from a plateau into the valley of the Río Tárcoles (land shuttles are also offered). Highlights include a 16-platform canopy zipline ($20, two hours;

© CHRISTOPHER P. BAKER

guide with goat at Panaca

offered at 9 A.M., 11:30 A.M., and 2 P.M.), plus guided horseback rides ($10–20), trails, a petting zoo, and tropical gardens with a butterfly garden and theme gardens dedicated to palms, orchids, and bamboos. Kids can have fun in two mazes, and a Finca Campesina replicates life of yore on a typical country farm. The full Tropical Park tour starts at $55.

Frog and snake exhibits, rock climbing, and Tarzan swings were being added at last visit.

Panaca

Want to ride a water buffalo? Or milk a cow? Or see a zebroid (half zebra, half horse)? Then head to this international farm-focused theme park (tel. 506/2427-9485, www.panacacostarica .com, 8:30 A.M.–6 P.M. daily), at San Mateo de Alajuela, about five kilometers northeast of Orotina. The splendidly conceived, sprawling facility features six themed stations (equestrian, hogs, cattle, etc.) and has more than 2,000 animals, including African watusi cattle, the giant French Percheron draft horse (among 32 equine species), and even 150 breeds of dogs. Kids from seven to 70 will love the horse-drawn carriage rides, the parade of oxcarts, equestrian shows, and even a dog show.

TÁRCOLES

Twenty-five kilometers south of Orotina, Highway 34 crosses the **Río Tárcoles.** The bridge over the river is the easiest place in the country for spotting crocodiles, which bask on the mud banks below the bridge: Don't lean over too far. *Several tourists have been victims of armed robberies here.* There is now a police post, but caution is still required.

Crocodiles gather in even greater numbers at the river mouth, near the fishing village of Tárcoles (the turnoff is signed 5 km south of the bridge). The estuary is also fantastic for bird-watching: More than 400 species have been identified. Frigate birds wheel overhead, while cormorants and kingfishers fish in the lagoons. Roseate spoonbills add a splash of color. And scarlet macaws fly overhead on their way to and from roosts in the mangrove swamps that extend 15 kilometers northward.

Mangrove Birding Tours (tel. 506/2637-0472) offers exactly that.

At the turnoff for Tárcoles from Highway 34, a dirt road leads east and climbs steeply to the hamlet of **Bijagual**. About two kilometers above the road is the **SkyWay** (tel. 506/2637-0232, www.villalapas.com, $20 adults, $10 children), a canopy tour with bridges and fantastic views down over the coast. You must buy tickets at the Villa Lapas Hotel, which also operates a zipline **Canopy Tour** ($35 adult, $17 children). Continuing uphill, about five kilometers from Highway 34 you pass the trailhead to **Catarata Manantial de Agua Viva** (tel. 506/2645-1215, 8 A.M.–3 P.M., $20 admission), a spectacular 183-meter-high waterfall, also known as the Bijagua Waterfall. Best time is rainy season, when the falls are going full tilt. They don't cascade in one great plume but rather tumble down the rock face to natural pools good for swimming. There are scarlet macaw nesting sites, and poison-dart frogs hop along the paths. The trail is a stiff two-hour hike each way (take lots of water).

Another two kilometers brings you to **Pura Vida Botanical Garden** (tel. 506/2645-1001, www.puravidagarden.com, 7:30 A.M.–5 P.M., $20), a delight for the botanical minded. Manicured gravel trails through the gardens offer dramatic views over mountain ridges toward the Manantial de Agua Viva waterfall and the coast. A self-guided tour takes about one hour. It has a delightful restaurant and a gift store. A bus (tel. 506/8831-2930) departs Orotina for Bijagual at 11 A.M. (returns from Bijagual at 5:30 A.M.) and will drop you at the front gate.

(Jungle Crocodile Safari

Jungle Crocodile Safari (tel./fax 506/2637-0338, www.junglecrocodilesafari.com) offers a two-hour croc-spotting trip upriver aboard a pontoon boat ($25). It has an office in the village. What a fantastic experience! You'll see all manner of birds, such as roseate spoonbills, whistling ducks, jabiru storks, even scarlet macaws as you sidle upriver, spotting for crocodiles. The three largest—"Mike Tyson," "Fidel Castro," and "Osama Bin Laden"—are five meters long and guard their turf and harems at recognized holes. Your guide will probably step

ashore into the gooey mud and draw one of these giants up onto the bank to snatch chicken from his hand! Morning is best.

Competing are **Crocodile Man Tours** (tel./fax 506/2637-0771, crocodilemantour@hotmail.com) and **J.D.'s Watersports** (tel. 506/2290-1560, www.jdwatersports.com).

Accommodations and Food

Restaurante y Cabinas El Cocodrilo (tel. 506/2661-8261, $25 s/d), on the north side of the bridge of the Río Tarcoles, has eight basic *cabinas* with fans and shared baths with cold water. There's a kids' playground, a souvenir store, and an atmospheric restaurant serving *típico* dishes and *casados* (set meals, $4).

The **Casa del Café** (tel. 506/2449-5152, 7 A.M.–5 P.M. daily), across the road, is a delightful coffee shop serving espressos and cappuccinos.

Hotel Villa Lapas (tel. 506/2637-0232, www.villalapas.com, $116 pp low season, $126 pp high season, all-inclusive), on the road to Manatial waterfall, is set amid beautifully landscaped grounds on the edge of Carara Reserve. It has 55 comfortable (albeit dingy) air-conditioned rooms aligned along the river with simple yet attractive decor, fan, and large bathrooms. Facilities include an elegant, hacienda-style restaurant/bar with a deck over the river (alas, food is mediocre at best), plus a swimming pool, whirlpools, miniature golf, volleyball, and nature trails. There's a netted butterfly garden. Birding and nature walks are offered.

(CARARA NATIONAL PARK

Rainforest exploration doesn't come any easier than at Carara, 20 kilometers south of Orotina and beginning immediately south of the Tárcoles bridge. Carara is unique in that it lies at the apex of the Amazonian and Mesoamerican ecosystems—a climatological zone of transition from the dry of the Pacific north to the very humid southern coast—and is a meeting place for species from both. The 5,242-hectare park borders the Pan-American Highway, so you can literally step from your car and enter the primary forest.

Carara protects evergreen forest of great complexity and density; the diversity of trees is among the highest in the world. Some of the most spectacular animals of tropical America are here: American crocodiles, great anteaters, ocelots, spider monkeys, and poison-dart frogs. Carara is also one of the best bird-watching locales in all Costa Rica. Fiery-billed aracari and toucans are common. So, too, are boat-billed herons. And around dawn and dusk, scarlet macaws—there are at least 400—can be seen in flight as they migrate daily between the wet forest interior and the coastal mangrove swamps (a macaw protection and reintroduction program has been very successful). The bridge over the Río Tárcoles is a good place to spot them as they fly over. Carara also has numerous pre-Columbian archaeological sites.

Information and Services

The **Visitors Center** (Centro de Visitantes, tel. 506/2637-1054, 7 A.M.–4 P.M. daily; last entrance at 3 P.M., $10 admission) sits beside the coastal highway, three kilometers south of the Río Tárcoles. Here begins the Las Araceas Nature Trail, a one-kilometer loop; and a handicapped-accessible trail that links to the Quebrada Bonita Trail. The 4.5-kilometer Laguna Meandrica Trail begins beside the highway and follows an old road paralleling the Río Tárcoles; the entrance gate, however, is usually locked. The rest of Carara is off-limits. Camping is not allowed. You can rent rubber boots ($2), and the **Asociación de Guías del Pacífico Central** (tel. 506/826-7438, asoguipace@yahoo.com) hires out guides for $20 per person.

Most tour operators based in San José arrange tours to Carara. Even if you want to explore on your own, it pays to have a guide, which can be booked through Costa Rica Expeditions (tel. 506/2257-0766, www.costaricaexpeditions.com), or other tour operators.

Robberies have occurred. Avoid parking by the Laguna Meandrica Trail; park by the visitors center and ask rangers about current conditions. The ranger station has secure lockers ($1).

Getting There

All buses traveling between San José or Puntarenas and Jacó and Quepos pass by the reserve.

PLAYA HERRADURA

A series of coves and beaches lines the coast south of Tárcoles, beginning with **Playa Malo,** a scenic bay fringed by a scalloped, 800-meter-wide, white-sand beach. Fishing boats bob at anchor and are roosts for pelicans. At the south end rises the headland of Punta Leona, smothered with forest protected in a 300-hectare private nature reserve—part of a self-contained resort called Punta Leona.

About seven kilometers from both Tárcoles and Jacó, just south of the Río Caña Blanca, is a turnoff for Playa Herradura, which gained attention a few years ago as a film set for the movie *1492.* The long gray-sand beach is swarmed by Ticos on weekends and holidays. Playa Herradura hit the big time in 1999 with the opening of the mammoth **Los Sueños Marriott Beach & Golf Resort** and **Los Sueños Marina.** The **Marina Carara Bay,** to be built at Punta Leona, will add 260 slips. Meanwhile, since 2006, Playa Herradura has exploded with real estate development.

South of Punta Leona the road climbs steeply before dropping down to Playa Herradura. At the crest of the rise is the entrance to **Villa Caletas,** a fabulous resort hotel atop a 500-meter headland with staggering views. You owe it to yourself to visit for lunch or dinner or for a massage or treatment at the Serenity Spa.

Entertainment and Events

Villa Caletas has monthly music concerts, particularly jazz and New Age, in a Greek amphitheater tucked into a cliff face. Costa Rica's annual International Music Festival is hosted here each July and August.

Stellaris Casino (tel. 506/2630-9000), at Los Sueños Marriott Beach & Golf Resort, is open 6 P.M.–2 A.M.

The best show for miles is **El Caballo Rey** (tel. 506/8824-3360, info@equisa.biz), at Quebrada Ganado de Jacó, near Punta Leona. It offers a thrilling two-hour Andalusian horse show with gourmet dinner at 7 P.M. Thursday and Saturday in high season (Saturday only low season, $55). The horses even parade through the restaurant! Reservations are needed. A cabaret and Arabian-themed shows were to be added. You can also watch horses being trained on Tuesday and Wednesday.

Sports and Recreation

Costa Rica Dreams Sportfishing (tel. 506/2643-8942 or U.S. tel. 732/901-8625, www.costaricadreams.com) offer half- and full-day sportfishing charters out of Los Sueños Marina.

Herradura Divers (tel. 506/2637-7123, www.herraduradivers.com) offers scuba trips.

A round of golf at Los Sueño's **Los Iguanas Golf Resort** (tel. 506/2630-9000 ext. 372, www.golflaiguana.com) costs $95 for guests, $140 nonguests, including cart. Club rental costs $35.

Inevitably, there's a canopy tour: **Canopy Vista Los Sueños** (tel. 506/8342-3683, www.canopyvistalossuenos.com, $60), with 15

platforms and 14 zipline cables. And you can take ATV and "Rhino" (small off-road vehicles) tours with **Ricaventura** (tel. 506/2643-5720, www.ricaventura.com), which also rents motorcycles.

The **Jacó Equestrian Center** (tel. 506/2643-1569) offers rides.

Accommodations

If you like planned resorts, consider **Punta Leona Beach Hotel** (tel. 506/2661-2414 or 506/2231-3131, www.hotelpuntaleona.com, call for rates), a time-share that packs in the Tico crowds and has a canopy tour.

The swank **Los Sueños Marriott Beach & Golf Resort** (tel. 506/2630-9000 or U.S. tel. 888/223-2427, www.lossuenosresort.com, $175–295 s/d low season, $339–441 s/d high season) mega-resort and residential complex is centered on a championship golf course and draws a predominantly Yankee clientele. At its heart is a four-story hotel in Spanish-colonial style—lots of red tile, natural stone, and wrought iron—but nonetheless with an

breakfast at Hotel Villa Caletas

© CHRISTOPHER P. BAKER

"Anywhere, USA" feel. Its 201 regally appointed air-conditioned rooms have all the expected amenities, and the resort boasts six restaurants, a casino, and a wide range of sports, shopping, and services. Suspended walkways lead through the forest canopy, and Costa Rica's largest marina is here.

You can also rent the deluxe three-bedroom villas at Los Sueños Resort & Marina from **Costa Rica Luxury Rentals** (tel. 506/2637-7105, www.crluxury.com).

To feel like royalty or a Hollywood star, head to the palatial **(Hotel Villa Caletas** (tel. 506/2637-0505, www.villacaletas.com, $180–460 s/d low season, $207–547 high season), a member of the Small Distinctive Hotels of Costa Rica and perhaps the finest boutique hotel in Costa Rica. Imagine a French colonial–style gingerbread villa—reached by a winding hillcrest driveway lined with Roman urns—and self-contained matching *casitas* overlooking the sea. Surround each with sensuous, tropical greenery, then add sublime decor and stunning museum pieces, such as

tasteful paintings, Renaissance antiques, giant clam shells, and Oriental rugs. You'll think you've entered the Louvre! It has 35 luxurious air-conditioned accommodations in eight categories, including eight bedrooms in the main house. Each is done up in warm tropical colors, with antique-style beds, Japanese-style lampshades, floor-to-ceiling, silk French curtains and Indian bedspreads, cable TVs, minibar, and (in most) verandas opening onto stunning ocean vistas. Suites have outside spas, and self-contained master-suite villas in their own private gardens have private parking and entrance, whirlpool tubs with wraparound windows, horizon swimming pools, and bedrooms mirrored wall to wall for the ultimate romantic experience. Some are a hefty hike up and down stone-walled pathways. Eight sumptuous and huge "Junior Superior Suites" were added for 2008, and all other rooms were being remodeled for 2009. A shuttle runs down to the beach, with decks and bar. Guests get golf privileges at the nearby Los Sueños Resort.

In 2007, Villas Caletas's French owner,

Imperial Suite at Zephyr Palace, Playa Herradura

Denis Roy, opened the adjoining 【 **Zephyr Palace** (www.zephyrpalace.com, $450–1,500 s/d, $7,500 daily for the entire place), indisputably the most extravagant and deluxe hotel in the country. Inspired by Imperial Rome and truly palatial, it has just seven individually themed suites, including an Imperial Suite with its own mirrored gymnasium and Turkish sauna. As the website reads: "Relax with the comforts of an emperor." Other suites transport you allegorically to Africa, Egypt, the Orient, and, dare I say, Heaven! They reflect a genius of interior design. It has spectacular salons and state-of-the-art meeting rooms, plus a gorgeous infinity-edge pool, its own small private disco, and a boardroom and art gallery with a secret tunnel that leads to the Imperial Suite!

Food

Steve N' Lisa's Paradise Cove (tel. 506/2637-0594, 7 A.M.–10 P.M. daily, $2–20), on the main highway, offers breezy patio dining overlooking the beach. It serves burgers, grilled chicken, tuna melt sandwiches, and the like.

For a beachfront porch, head to **El Pelícano** (tel. 506/2637-8910, noon–10 P.M. daily), serving seafood.

【 **Restaurante Mirador** (Fri.–Sun. only during low season) at Villa Caletas offers a sublime setting in which to enjoy Chef Miguel Bolaños's gourmet nouvelle cuisine ($10 breakfast, $22 lunch, $35 or $45 three-course dinner, or $65 seven-course gastronomic menu), such as appetizer of veggie moussaka with spinach coulis ($8); and for entrées, duet of tuna and scallops with jasmine rice and lentils ($27), or roasted lamb tenderloin with sautéed mangoes and coriander sauce ($29). The Mirador is a tad formal and aloof (waitstaff seem to walk on eggshells), but more informal is the **Antifeatro Sunset Restaurant,** beneath the Mirador. Breakfast on the mountaintop with New Age music playing softly is a sublime way to start the day. Each July and August, it hosts a Gastronomic Festival with a different national theme each week.

Opened in 2008, the Plaza Herradura (beside Highway 34) features an **Inka Grill** (for Peruvian fare), the **Samurai Fusion** (for Japanese and sushi), and a branch of **Spoon** (tel. 2637-8086), a great place for inexpensive sandwiches and hot plates.

Information and Services

Plaza Herradura has a bank and pharmacy, as does the marina. Ocean Plaza, one kilometer inland of the beach, also has a bank, plus **Lava Max** (tel. 506/2637-8737) laundry. The **police station** is next to the gas station on Highway 34.

The marina has an **internet café** (tel. 506/2637-8476, 9 A.M.–9 P.M. daily).

Getting There and Around

Los Sueños Marina (tel. 506/2643-4000) has a state-of-the-art dock with 200 slips.

National Rent-a-Car (tel. 506/2242-7878 in San José) has an outlet at the marina.

Jacó and Vicinity

Jacó was the country's first developed beach resort, when it was put on the map by wintering Canadian charter groups. Jacó faded from the spotlight for a few years but has bounced back with vigor. The past few years have seen an explosion of high-rise development. The snowbird scene has been diluted by Ticos, as it's the closest beach resort to San José and therefore popular with Josefinos (a mix of families and young adults on a fling). It also draws backpackers, surfers, the young offbeat party crowd, Europeans (especially Italians, bringing a nascent sophistication), and more recently, middle-aged North American fishermen trawling for prostitutes, thus evoking a response among more righteous expats: *"Ah, yes, Jacó. Drugs, sex,*

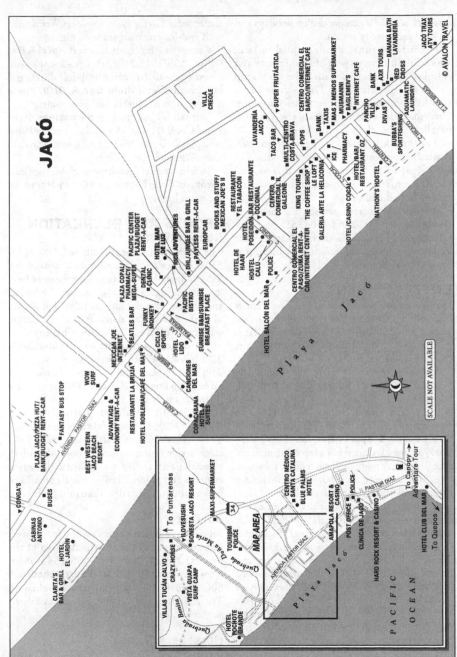

JACÓ

SCALE NOT AVAILABLE

CENTRAL PACIFIC

and rock 'n' roll!" It gets packed on holidays and on weekends in dry season.

Highway 34 runs inland, parallel to Jacó, which lies 400 meters west of the highway and is linked by four access roads. The main strip in town—Avenida Pastro Díaz—runs south two kilometers to the suburb of Garabito. Everything lines the single main street, which parallels the beach for its full length.

The three-kilometer-long beach is not particularly appealing, and swimming is discouraged (signs warn of dangerous rip currents, and the river estuaries at each end of the beach are said to be polluted).

If frogs and snakes interest you, check out **Neofauna** (tel. 506/2643-1904, $15 pp), outside the entrance to the Waterfalls Canopy four kilometers northeast of Jacó. It has educational tours of its exhibits.

ENTERTAINMENT

Jacó has no shortage of bar action. The scene is ever shifting. **Beatles Bar** (www.beatlebarjaco .com, 6 P.M.–2:30 A.M. daily) has pool tables, darts, table football, TV, and classic music, although its clientele includes a posse of sex workers.

My favorite bar for early evening is the beachfront **Clarita's Sports Bar & Grill** (tel. 506/2643-2615, 7 A.M.–10 P.M. daily), popular with the expat crowd, not least for its Hooters-style bartenders. The Blind Pigs perform. And **Sky Lounge & Sports Bar** (tel. 506/2643-1642) at Hotel Poseidon has a revolving menu of events: Monday night football, tequila Tuesdays, two-for-one beers on Thursday, movies on Friday. I enjoyed a mean martini here!

In 2008, Jacó got its first real upscale, live music lounge-bar, **Le Loft** (tel. 506/2643-5846, www.leloftcr.com, 9 P.M.–4 A.M.). Pick up a flyer locally for half-price entry before midnight. Thursday is Ladies' Night, with free entry and drinks all night. Le Loft was swiftly followed by **Conga's** (tel. 506/8350-0808, www.congas jacobeach.com), operated by Cuban-born jazz artist Tomasito Cruz. And the **Funky Monkey** (tel. 506/2643-2357) reopened in 2009 after being refitted as a more upscale lounge bar with DJs and live music, including VIP rooms with leather sofas. Go for 1980s music on Wednesday, with two-for-one margaritas all night.

Competing for football fans is **Hotel & Bar Oz** (tel. 506/2643-2162, 11 A.M.–3 A.M.), with a vast open-air bar offering pool, darts, and big-screen TV. **Jungle Bar & Grill,** above Subway, also has fusbol and pool tables.

You can try your luck in the **casinos** of the Hotel Cocal (11 A.M.–3 A.M. daily) or the Hotel Amapola (tel. 506/2693-2316, www.casinojazz .com, 7 P.M.–3 A.M. daily).

Jacó has several "gentlemen's clubs," not least **Divas,** on Calle Hicaco, and **Crazy Horse,** on the main highway.

SPORTS AND RECREATION

Canopy Tours

The **Waterfalls Canopy Tour** (tel. 506/2643-3322, www.waterfallscanopy.com, $60 adults, $45 children), four kilometers northeast of Jacó, has 14 platforms, a waterslide, suspension bridge, and 80-foot rappel; tours are offered at 8 A.M., 11 A.M., and 2 P.M. daily. It also has nature walks, and a "Jungle Adventure Challenge."

The **Canopy Adventure** (tel./fax 506/2643-3271, www.adventurecanopy.com, 8 A.M.–4 P.M. daily) has 13 platforms and three kilometers of cable, including an "X-cable" (i.e. X-treme) for "extreme adventure."

The **Pacific Rainforest Aerial Tram** (tel. 506/2257-5961, www.rainforestram.com, 9 A.M.–4 P.M. Mon., 6 A.M.–4 P.M. Tues.–Sun.) offers a ride into the forest canopy aboard 18 wheelchair-accessible gondolas (with canvas awnings and guides). It also has a herbarium, snake exhibit, and trails. Take rain gear.

Surfing

More than a dozen outlets on the main street cater to surfers. Take your pick! Two of the best are **W.O.W. Surf** (tel. 506/2643-3844, www.wowsurf.net) and **Jaco Surf School** (tel. 506/2643-1905, www.jacosurfschool.com). There is also good surfing, as well as related services, in nearby Playa Hermosa.

Horseback Riding

Discover Costa Rica (tel. 506/2637-0586, www

.crocodilecostarica.com) offers a horseback ride along the Río Tárcoles.

Tours

Several tour companies along the main strip offer a similar menu of canopy tours, kayaking, crocodile tours, and trips farther afield. **Kayak Jacó** (tel. 506/2643-1233, www.kayakjaco.com) offers outrigger canoe and kayak trips, including inflatable kayaks on the Río Dulce.

ATV tours are a gas! Check with **Paradise Adventure Travel & ATV Tours** (tel. 506/8849-5892, www.paraisocostarica.com); **Jaguariders** (tel. 506/2643-0180, www.jaguariders.com); **Jacó Trax ATV Tours** (tel. 506/2643-3970); or **AXR Tours** (tel. 506/8810-7271, www.axrjaco.com), which has one-hour ($65 pp) to full-day ($180 pp) tours in ATVs and French-made AXR off-road vehicles. Lots of fun!

King Tours (tel. 506/2643-2441, www.kingtours.com) specializes in sportfishing.

You can fly like a bird with **HangGlide Costa Rica** (tel. 506/8353-5514, www.hangglidecostarica.com), which has tandem tours ($99).

Solutions Tourism & Services (tel. 506/2643-3485, www.solutionscr.com), in Multi-Centro Costa Brava, is a full-service travel agency.

SHOPPING

There are a score of boutiques along the main drag. One of the largest souvenir selections is at **ILoveSushi** (tel. 506/2643-3083), which also has a humidor stocked with Cuban cigars. **Galeria Arte La Heliconia** is a trendy art gallery. **Books & Stuff** (tel. 506/2643-2508, 9 A.M.–9 P.M. daily), on the drag, sells magazines and used and new books.

ACCOMMODATIONS

There are many more hotels than can be recommended here.

Under $25

A *real* surfers' hostel, **Nathon's Hostel** (Calle Central, tel. 506/8835-4359, www.nathonshostel.com, $10 pp dorm, $25 s/d private room) has an air-conditioned dorm with 12 beds, plus five private rooms with shared bath and cable

TV. There's laundry, lockers, a communal kitchen, and a bar with live music.

At the north end, **Cabinas Antonio** (tel. 506/2643-3043, $14 s or $22 d low season, $15 pp high season) is a popular bargain for budget travelers, with 13 rooms offering fans and private baths with hot water.

Other backpackers' hostels to consider include **Hotel De Haan** (tel. 506/2643-1795, www.hoteldehaan.com) and, next door, **Hostel Calú** (tel. 506/2643-1107, www.hostelcalu.com), both with private rooms and bunks.

$25-50

Danny, at **Sunrise B&B** (tel. 506/2643-3361, $15 s, $25 d), has simple rooms above the eponymous café on the main drag. The rooms have fans but not air-conditioning.

The prices are right at the **Blue Palms Hotel** (tel. 506/2643-0099, www.bphotel.net, $30–40 s/d depending on room size and day of the week), a two-story modern hotel new in 2006. Its 14 clean rooms vary; avoid west-facing rooms, which get hot in late afternoon. Also in this price range, I like **Hotel Roblemar** (tel./fax 506/2643-2444), with 15 huge air conditioned rooms.

$50-100

Villa Creole (tel. 506/2643-3298, www.hotelvillacreole.com, $60 s/d low season, $75 s/d high season) offers nine elegant, well-lit, air-conditioned rooms around a large pool with water cascade and an orchid garden. The rooms have orthopedic mattresses, Guatemalan fabrics, kitchenettes, security boxes, patios, and stone-walled private baths with hot water. A minibus is on hand for tours, a *rancho* restaurant (open high season only) serves gourmet French creole cuisine. Rates include tax.

One of the best beachfront options is **Clarita's Hotel** (tel. 506/2643-2615, www.claritashotel.com, $40 s/d with fan, $60 s/d with a/c), with 16 rooms and one apartment with ceiling fans. Rooms get lots of light, and the batik fabrics are a nice touch. Its bar/restaurant is a winner.

The German-run **Hotel Pochote Grande**

(tel. 506/2643-3236, www.hotelpochotegrande .net, $65 s/d low season, $80 s/d high season), on the north bank of the river, has 24 attractive beachfront rooms in shaded grounds with a pool. The clean, modern, modestly furnished rooms have private baths with hot water; four have air-conditioning.

Two separate readers recommend the Canadian-run **Vista Pacífico Aparthotel** (tel. 506/2643-3261, www.vistapacifico.com, $50–120 s/d low season, $65–140 s/d high season), perched on a hill outside town and run with loving concern by Greg and Jan Bertrand. The cozy rooms, studios, and one- and two-bedroom units have kitchens or kitchenettes, plus cable TV and hot water. A poolside deck with barbecue is a lovely setting for enjoying the sublime views. It has Wi-Fi, plus a pet-friendly room.

The Dutch-run **Hotel Mar de Luz** (tel./fax 506/2643-3000, www.mardeluz.com, $63 s or $65 d low season, $81 s or $83 d high season), across the street, has modestly furnished air-conditioned apartments arrayed around a lush garden with a lap pool, kiddies' pool, and solar-heated whirlpool tub. Some units are lined appealingly with river stones and have mezzanine bedrooms. Junior suites in a two-story structure have nicer furnishings. There's a barbecue, laundry service, and games.

The contemporary beachfront **The Copacabana Hotel & Suites** (tel. 506/2643-1005, www.copacabanahotel.com, call for pricing) offers pleasantly furnished air-conditioned standards, studios, suites, and junior suites. It has a charming garden eatery and a sports bar, plus a swim-up bar in the pool in the rear garden. A cigar lounge is a cozy place to puff away, and there's live music on Saturday nights.

Competing for the same market, but less inspired, is **Hotel Oz** (tel. 506/2643-2162, www.costaricanet.net/oz, $55 s or $65 d low season, $75 s or $95 d high season), inland of the beach. It has 13 well-lit, air-conditioned rooms with fans, cable TV, and colorful furnishings.

The **Vista Guapa Surf Camp** (tel. 506/2643-2830 www.vistaguapa.com, packages from $600 including two nights, transfers,

surfing, and meals), 400 kilometers inland of the beach north of town, is owned by former Costa Rican surf champion Alvaro Solano. A thoroughly modern surprise, its raised-ceiling clubhouse has walls of glass, a spacious TV lounge, and huge cut-log table and chairs where meals are served, plus a large wooden deck with hammocks. There's a small pool. It offers six air-conditioned rooms on a ridge (a steep hike); all are spacious, with heaps of light, terra-cotta floors, security boxes, tall wooden "Goldilocks and the Three Bears"–style beds, modern tiled bathrooms, and glass French doors opening to wooden decks with hammocks. It specializes in surfers' packages. Free shuttles to and from San José are offered on Saturday.

The French/Swiss-owned **Hotel Poseidon** (tel. 506/2643-1642 or 888/643-1242, www.hotel-poseidon.com, $75 s/d standard, $85 s/d premium low season; $105 standard, $115 premium high season) boasts a stunning frontispiece with carved wooden columns bearing Poseidon motifs and Persian throw rugs. There's a tiny pool with whirlpool and swim-up bar. The 15 large rooms are delightfully furnished, and bathrooms have large mosaic-tiled showers. Upstairs air-conditioned rooms get the light; downstairs rooms (fans only) are a bit dingy.

The contemporary, beachfront **Hotel Balcón del Mar** (tel./fax 506/2643-3251, www.hotel balcondelmar.com, $95 s/d standard, $150 suite low season; $110 s/d standard, $190 suite high season) has remodeled and gone upscale, with 47 modestly furnished air-conditioned rooms in a five-story unit, each with refrigerator, private bath and hot water, plus balcony. There's an elegant Mediterranean-style restaurant serving seafood, plus a small pool and Internet access.

With its own beachfront pool and lawns, the low-rise **Hotel Tangeri** (tel. 506/2643-3001, www.hoteltangeri.com, $105 s/d low season, $130 high season) offers 14 pleasantly furnished rooms plus villas. It also has its own sportfishing boat.

Hotel Canciones del Mar (www.canciones delmar.com, $85–180 s/d low season, $115–225 high season) offers heaps of personality in its design, and the 11 one- and two-bedroom suites have lovely tropical furnishings. It's known for its live music bar and lovely little courtyard pool and sundeck. Wi-Fi is available here.

The U.S.–owned **Hotel Cocal and Casino** (tel. 506/2643-3067 or U.S. tel. 800/732-9266, www.hotelcocalandcasino.com, $75–90 rooms, $120 suite low season; $120–140 rooms, $150 suite high season) is also elegant and appealing. The hacienda-style hotel is popular with charter groups. Arched porticos grace 43 spacious air-conditioned rooms surrounding a courtyard with two pools and a bar. An upstairs restaurant overlooks the beach, and there's a small casino. No children are permitted.

If a large-scale hotel is your thing, consider the **Best Western Jacó Beach Resort** (tel. 506/2643-1000 or U.S. tel. 800/780-7234, www.bestwestern.com, $84–99 s/d low season, $89–105 s/d high season), at the north end of the drag. It has 130 air-conditioned rooms, all with pool or garden exposures. Amenities include a discotheque, car rental, swimming pool, floodlit tennis court, volleyball court, and water sports.

$100-150

Elegant and contemporary, the **Hotel Club del Mar** (tel. 506/2643-3194, www.clubdelmarcostarica.com, $128 s/d rooms, $192–280 condos low season; $153 d rooms, $224–330 condos high season) nestles beneath the cliffs at the southern end of Jacó. It has eight hotel rooms, 22 one- and two-bedroom condos, and a penthouse suite. The spacious, conservatively furnished condos have huge lounges with green tile floors with throw rugs, rich hardwoods, king-size beds, twin bathrooms, and full kitchens. The suite has a quasi-Asiatic motif. Three rooms are wheelchair accessible. There's a pool and kids' pool in lush grounds, plus a sunken horseshoe-shaped tapas bar and a Serenity Spa.

The upscale **Amapola & Casino** (tel. 506/2643-2255, www.hotelamapola.com, $110 s/d standard, $160 junior suite, $240 villa low season; $130 standard, $185 junior suite, $260 villa high season) is an all-inclusive hotel with two-story condo-style units in beautifully landscaped grounds some distance from the beach. It has 44 standard rooms, six suites, and three fully equipped villas. Facilities include two swimming pools, a pool bar, and a whirlpool tub, plus a casino and a disco. Nearby, the 80-room **Hard Rock Hotel & Casino** (tel. 506/2643-3147, www.hardrockresortcasino.cr), formerly the Jacó Fiesta Hotel, is a similar alternative with a beachfront advantage and an all-inclusive option.

I like **Docelunas Hotel Restaurant & Spa** (tel. 506/2643-2211, www.docelunas.com, $130 s/d deluxe, $150 junior suite low season; $140 deluxe, $160 junior suite high season), a two-tier hotel with 20 spacious, elegantly furnished rooms (all with free Wi-Fi), spa, yoga studio, and open-air thatched gourmet restaurant facing an exquisitely landscaped pool complex.

The sensational 13-story **Sonesta Jacó Resort** (tel. 506/2208-6000, www.sonesta.com) was due to open by 2010, bringing the first real luxury accommodations to town. The condo-hotel offers 190 suites, all with flat-screen TVs, pillow-top mattresses, individual climate control, whirlpools, and gourmet kitchens. Other draws include three restaurants, a full-service spa, beach club, free transfers, and a butterfly farm. A casino was to be added.

The **Wyndham Jacó Beach** (tel. 506/2643-5097, www.wyndhamjacobeach.com) also promises a new level of luxe when it opens, probably in 2010.

FOOD

The place for breakfast is the **Sunrise Breakfast Place** (tel. 506/2643-3361, 6 A.M.–12:30 P.M. daily), serving waffles, eggs Benedict ($5), omelettes, and more; and **The Coffee Shop** (tel. 506/2643-3240, 7:30 A.M.–2 P.M. Mon.–Fri.), also with omelettes and pancakes. And you can't go wrong at **Clarita's Sports Bar & Grill** (tel. 506/2643-2615, 7 A.M.–10 P.M. daily) for its omelettes, burgers, burritos, and entrées ranging from teriyaki mahimahi ($8) to filet mignon ($12).

My favorite lunch spot is the ◖ **Taco Bar** (tel. 506/2643-0222, http://tacobar.info, 7 A.M.–10 P.M. daily), a delightful open-air Japanese-style restaurant with a great buffet, gourmet fish tacos, sashimi ($7), and a citrus-teriyaki chicken ($8) on the menu.

You can't go wrong, either, at the elegant, open-air **Bar Restaurante Colonial** (tel. 506/2643-3326, 10 A.M.–midnight daily, $4.50–12), centered on an octagonal bar under a skylight. Its wide-ranging menu includes burgers, onion rings, chowders, ceviche, chicken in honey, and mussels in garlic and olive oil.

For sushi, head to the small, clean, air-conditioned **Tsunami** (tel. 506/2643-3678, 5–11 P.M. daily), in Mall Il Galeone; or to **ILoveSushi** (tel. 506/2643-3083, noon–10 P.M. daily), beside Highway 34 and offering two-for-one sushi during happy hour (5–6 P.M.).

The best dining in town is at ◖ **Pacific Bistro** (tel. 506/2643-3771, 6–10 P.M. Wed.–Sun.), where Californian chef Kent Green conjures up Pacific Rim dishes using fresh ingredients. The revolving menu includes shiitake mushroom–topped salmon with *beurre blanc* ($10), filet mignon ($12), and spicy Indonesian shrimp noodles, served in large portions (half-portions are offered).

For delicious seafood, head to the upscale, beachfront **Restaurant Hicacos** (tel. 506/2643-3226, www.elhicaco.net, 11 A.M.–10 P.M. daily), which has an all-you-can-eat lobster feast 6–10 P.M. every Wednesday.

Another of my favorites is the elegant **Hotel Poseidon Restaurant** (tel. 506/2643-1642, 7 A.M.–2 P.M. and 6–10 P.M. daily), with consistently good dishes such as marlin ceviche, a fabulous seared ahi tuna with mashed potatoes and crisp veggies, or filet mignon with béarnaise-jalapeño sauce ($15). Breakfasts include biscuits with gravy ($5) and bagel and eggs ($5).

The elegant **Pancho Villa** (tel. 506/2643-3571, 24 hours, $5–15) serves surf and turf, but also has Mexican fare, sushi, seafood fettuccine, and such specialties as vinaigrette chicken with honey.

For baked goods, try **Panadería Tosso,** 100 meters east of Avenida Pastor Díaz;

Musmanni, on the main drag; or **Pachispan L** (tel. 506/2643-1153, 6 A.M.–10 P.M. daily).

Super Frutástica has a fresh produce market. **Max X Menos,** 50 meters south of Banco Nacional, is the town's largest supermarket.

INFORMATION AND SERVICES

The private, 24-hour **Centro Médico Santa Catalina** (tel. 506/2643-5059) is 400 meters east of the drag in the center of town. The government's **Clínica de Jacó** (tel. 506/2643-3667) is behind the police station at the south end of town. The **Red Cross** (tel. 506/2643-3090) has ambulance service; as does **Emergencias 2000** (tel. 506/8380-4125), on Highway 21 midway between Herradura and Jacó. **Farmacia Fischel** (tel. 506/2643-2705), in Centro Comercial Il Galeone, is open 8 A.M.–10:30 P.M. daily. **Dr. Darío Chaves** (tel. 506/2643-3221) has a dental clinic; also try **VitalDent** (tel. 506/2643-4039), upstairs in Plaza Il Galeone.

There's a **police station** (tel. 506/2643-3011) on the beach, next to Hotel Balcón del Mar, and another (same tel.) in Garabito, adjoining the OIJ (Costa Rica's equivalent of the FBI or CID, tel. 506/2643-1723). The **Tourist Police** were setting up an office on Calle Ancha at last visit.

The **post office** adjoins the police station in Garabito.

International Central (tel. 506/2643-2601, 7:30 A.M.–9 P.M. daily), in Centro Comercial El Paso, is an international call center; as is **Mexican Joe's** (tel. 506/2643-0017, 9 A.M.–midnight daily), the most prominent of several internet cafés.

Dirty laundry? Clean up at **Aquamatic** (tel. 506/2643-2083, 7 A.M.–5 P.M. Mon.–Sat.) or **Banana Bath Lavandería** (tel. 506/2643-1153), both at the south end of town.

GETTING THERE AND AWAY

Transportes Jacó buses (tel. 506/2223-1109 or 2643-3135) depart San José from Calle 16, Avenida 3, at 6 A.M. then every two hours 7 A.M.–7 P.M. (2.5 hours, $2.75). Buses between San José and Quepos and Manuel Antonio also stop in Jacó.

Return buses depart Jacó for San José every two hours 5 A.M.–5 P.M., and for Puntarenas at 6 A.M., 9 A.M., noon, 2 P.M., and 4:30 P.M., from the Supermercado, picking up at the north end of town also.

From Puntarenas, buses to Jacó depart from near the train station at 6 A.M., 9:30 A.M., 12:30 P.M., 4 P.M., and 6 P.M. Buses depart Quepos for Jacó at 6 A.M., 9 A.M., noon, 2 P.M., and 4:30 P.M.; and depart Jacó for Quepos at 6:30 A.M., 9:30 A.M., 12:30 P.M., 4 P.M., and 6 P.M.

Interbus (tel. 506/2283-5573, www.inter busonline.com) and **Grayline** (tel. 506/2220-2126, www.graylinecostarica.com) operate minibus shuttles from San José ($35) and popular tourist destinations.

Kevin's Transfers (tel. 506/2643-2604, www .kevinstransfers.com) and **CR VIP Transfers** (tel. 506/2643-6011, www.costaricaholiday rentals.com) offer personalized transfers.

Zuma Tours (tel. 506/8849-8569, www .zumatours.net) offers water-taxis from Montezuma at 9:30 A.M. and to Montezuma at 10:45 A.M. ($40 adult, $30 child one-way).

GETTING AROUND

Car rental companies in Jacó include **Europcar** (tel. 506/2643-2049); **Budget** (tel. 506/2643-2665), in Plaza de Jacó; and **Economy** (tel./ fax 506/2643-1719), toward the north end of town.

You can rent bicycles at **Ciclo-Sport** (tel. 506/8838-9178). Companies renting ATVs, motorcycles, and scooters include **AXR Tours** (tel. 506/643-3130, www.axrider.com).

For taxis, call **Taxi Jacó** (tel. 506/2643-3009).

PLAYA HERMOSA

Highway 34 south from Jacó crests a steep headland, beyond which Playa Hermosa (not to be confused with Playa Hermosa in Nicoya) comes into sight—there's a *mirador* for enjoying the incredible view. The beach is 10 kilometers long and arrow-straight, with waves pummeling ashore, drawing surfers.

Beginning some two kilometers south of the village, the **Playa Hermosa and Punta Mala Wildlife Refuge** (Refugio de Vida Silvestre Playa Hermosa y Punta Mala) protects the nesting grounds of four species of marine turtles. It is off-limits to visitors. The sandy beach road ends at the ranger station, which has a turtle hatchery.

Sports and Recreation

Discovery Horseback Tours (tel. 506/8838-7550, www.horseridecostarica.com) has guided tours, and **Motoworld** (tel. 506/2643-7111), at Marea Brava Beachfront Suites & Villas, has motorcycle and ATV tours.

Las Olas Hotel (tel./fax 506/2643-7021, www.lasolashotel.com) offers tours and rents surfboards, snorkeling gear, and mountain bikes. **Loma Del Mar Surf Camp** (tel. 506/2643-2313, www.rovercam.com) offers surf classes and board rental. Surf camps include **Waves Costa Rica** (tel. 506/2643-7025, www.wavescr.com) and **Jim Hogan Surf Camp** (jimhogansurfcamp.com). **Del Mar All Girls Surf Camp** (tel. 506/2643-3197, www.costarica surfingchicas.com) serves the ladies.

Chiclets Tree Tour (tel. 506/2643-1880, www.jacowave.com) has a canopy tour that includes a daunting tree climb. Trips are offered at 7 A.M., 9 A.M., 1 P.M., and 3:30 P.M.

Accommodations
$25-50

The snazzy **Marea Brava** (tel. 506/2643-7043, www.mareabravacostarica.com) has a rustic and atmospheric, air-conditioned, co-ed surfers rancho with bunks.

The Argentinian-run **Posada Playa Hermosa** (tel. 506/2643-2640, www.fbsurf boards.com/surfcamp, $40 s/d low season, $50 high season) has five simply furnished, ocher-painted, log-beamed cabins in a delightful Robinson Crusoe kind of place. Each has private bathroom with hot water. There's a communal kitchen. Fischer Bros. surfboard rental and repair is here.

My budget pick, beloved of surfers, is the offbeat **Cabinas Las Arenas** (tel. 506/2643-7013, www.cabinaslasarenas.com, $33 s, $42

© CHRISTOPHER P. BAKER

turtle hatchery at Playa Hermosa and Punta Mala Wildlife Refuge

d), well run by a Yorkshire-Canadian transplant. The seven rooms are in a two-story unit, each with refrigerator, fan, stove, and private bath with hot water; some have cable TV and refrigerators. It has a simple, attractive bar-restaurant, and a river-stone courtyard over the beach. You can camp ($12 per tent).

Surfer dudes Jason and Jonathan run **Las Olas Hotel** (tel./fax 506/2643-7021, www.las olashotel.com, $45–75 room, $100 cabin), a modern three-story structure with eight nicely kept rooms with kitchenettes and patios. There are also three two-story cabins, each with three bunks below and a double and single in the loft. There's a pool and a restaurant beachside. A similar alternative, run by U.S. surfer dudes Tobik and Dennis, is **Cabinas Brisa del Mar** (tel. 506/2643-7078, www.ranchocoral.com/page4.html, $35 s, $40 d year-round) with a community kitchen, basketball court, and ping-pong.

$50-100

The once-budget **Ola Bonita** (tel. 506/2643-7090, www.olabonitacr.com, $75 s/d) is refurbished and now offers seven cross-ventilated, air-conditioned rooms with cable TV, kitchens, and walls of whitewashed stone. Downstairs rooms are dark. It has a small pool.

I like the **Sandpiper Inn** (tel. 506/2643-7042, www.sandpipercostarica.com, $80–130 s/d), with eight spacious, air-conditioned rooms in landscaped grounds with a tiny pool fed by a water cascade emanating from a whirlpool. Rooms have cable TV and high-speed Wi-Fi. A shady restaurant offers meals.

For intimacy, opt for the modern **Hotel Fuego del Sol** (tel. 506/2643-6060, www.fuego delsolhotel.com, $74 s or $86 d room, $124 junior suite, $143 master suite low season; $86 s or $98 d room, $161 junior suite, $182 master suite high season), a handsome two-story colonial-style structure in landscaped grounds. It has 17 spacious air-conditioned rooms and two suites, with cool tiles painted in tropical motifs, plus a pool with swim-up bar, gym, and beachfront restaurant. It has a one-week surf camp.

$100-150

A tad overpriced, the new **Marea Brava** (tel. 506/2643-7043, www.mareabravacosta

rica.com, $107–185 s/d low season, $133–266 high season), next to Fuego del Sol, has a range of accommodations, from simply appointed rooms to suites with kitchenettes to more elegantly furnished suites and villas, all air-conditioned and with ceiling fans and furnished decks. It has a lovely pool complex with thatched restaurant.

The standout property, at the extreme north end of the beach, is **Terraza del Pacífico** (tel. 506/2643-6852, www.terrazadelpacifico.com, $97 s/d rooms, $158 junior suite low season; $112 rooms, $189 junior suite high season), a modern complex that caters to the more upscale surf crowd. This contemporary Spanish colonial–style property has a superb beachfront location and 43 well-appointed, air-conditioned rooms. The landscaped grounds boast a circular pool with a swim-up bar. There's a casino, restaurant, and bar. Rates include breakfast and tax.

Meanwhile, 2008 saw the opening of several new hotels, including **The Plaza Resort** (tel. 506/2643-7223, http://the plazadehermosa.com, $150–200 low season, $150–250 high season), with beautifully furnished luxury condos in a three-story beachfront tower. Adjoining, the new **Tortuga del Mar** (tel. 506/2643-7132, www.tortugadel mar.net, $75 s/d standard, $85 s/d studio low season; $88 standard, $98 studio high season) has eight pleasing and spacious rooms, including studios, in a two-story unit. The new bunch also includes the three-story **Hermosa Beach House** (tel. 506/2643-7178, www.hbhcr.com, $54–159 s/d low season, $64–179 high season), with a variety of rooms and suites, and which throws a swimming pool into the mix.

My favorite newbie is **The Backyard** (tel. 506/2643-7041, www.backyardhotel.com, $125 room, $175 suite low season; $150 room, $200 suite high season), with modestly stylish furniture, including king-size beds, in its "deluxe" rooms and suites, all with cable TV and a full roster of mod-cons. The main draw here, though, is the happening restaurant and bar.

Hermosa Bungalows (tel. 506/2643-7190, www.beachlifemgmt.com), all on its lonesome two kilometers along the dirt beach road, offers colonial-style bungalows on stilts.

Yoga fans will want to check into **Vida Asana Retreat Center** (tel. 506/2643-7108, www.vidaasana.com), in the hills inland of Playa Hermosa. It has a gorgeous tropical aesthetic. It offers surf and yoga packages.

Food

For a quick bite, the roadside **Jungle Surf Café** (tel. 506/2643-1495, 7 A.M.–9 P.M., $2–10) satisfies with Tex-Mex, "killer omelettes," burgers, barbecued chicken, and filet mignon. Surf movies play on the TV at the bar.

Steeped in ambience, the rough-hewn, Rastafarian-themed **Jammin Café** (tel. 506/2643-1853, 7 A.M.–9 P.M. daily, $4), at Cabinas Las Arenas, serves pancakes and omelettes for breakfast, plus nachos, chicken quesadillas, ceviche, and vegetarian Rasta pasta in Caribbean sauce.

The center of action is the **Backyard Bar,** at the Backyard Hotel, with a large international menu, including tapas, burgers, seafood, and steaks. It draws a crowd for live music and barbecue on weekends (4–8 P.M.), a nightly sunset happy hour (4:30–7:30 P.M.), and free drinks for ladies on Friday (5–8 P.M.).

PLAYAS ESTERILLOS

The Playas Esterillos extend for miles south of Hermosa. Craggy Punta Judas separates Hermosa from **Playa Esterillos Oeste,** a favorite with surfers, and with littering Ticos on weekends. The seven-kilometer-long beach has tidepools at its northern end, where a **sculpture of a mermaid** sits atop the rocks and mollusk fossils are embedded in the rock strata.

Farther south, **Esterillos Centro** is accessed by a separate road signed off Highway 34.

Playa Esterillos Este, separated by a river from Esterillos Centro, is identical to its northerly siblings: kilometers long, ruler-straight, with gray sand cleansed by high surf. The **Emi-Waves Surf School** is here, at La Puesta del Sol B&B.

Del Pacífico (tel. 506/2778-7080, www.del pacifico.net) is a deluxe residential resort development with a stable offering horseback rides, wrangler programs, and other ranch activities. The southern end of the beach is known as **Playa Bejuco,** reached via a separate access road. Farther south, about four kilometers north of Parrita, a dirt road leads west from the coast road and zigzags through African palm plantations until you emerge at **Playa Palma,** separated from Bejuco by yet another river mouth.

Accommodations

Esterillos Oeste: Several uninspired options at the extreme north of the beach serve budget travelers; they mostly attract Ticos and can get noisy on weekends. The nicest place is **Cabinas y Apartamento Maliye** (tel. 506/2778-7085, $25 s, $30 d), with simply appointed air-conditioned units that opened in 2008.

Esterillos Centro: The place of choice is the French Canadian–run **Casa Amarilla** (tel. 506/2778-8408 or in North America 905/731-6501, www.vrbo.com/59476, $90 nightly, $590 weekly low season; $125 nightly, $850 weekly high season), a beautiful two-story home with kidney-shaped pool. It has two rooms with full kitchens and spacious lounge/dining rooms and lovely modern bathrooms. Here, too, the French Canadian–run **La Felicidad Country Inn** (tel./fax 506/2778-6824, www.lafelicidad .com, $40–65 low season, $55–80 high season) is a simple wooden home with nine unremarkable rooms.

I much prefer the beachfront **Hotel Monterey del Mar** (tel. 506/2778-8686, www.monterey delmar.com, $100–180 s/d low season, $125–220 s/d high season) for its luxe and romantic aesthetic in public arenas. The 27 spacious rooms and suites have pleasant albeit uninspired decor and all modern conveniences.

Opened in 2008, the lovely **Mirador del Mar Luxury Suites and Retreat** (tel. 506/2778-7150, www.miradordelmarcr.com, $90 s/d low season, $110 s/d high season) is set on a hilltop beside Highway 34 and offers coastal views. The rooms are elegantly furnished and have

king-size beds with orthopedic mattresses, satellite TV, and free Wi-Fi. The freeform horizon pool is inviting, and the restaurant serves organic fare.

Esterillos Este: The venerable **Pélican Hotel** (tel. 506/2778-8105, www.pelicanhotel cr.com, $40–70 s/d low season, $45–80 s/d high season), now under new owners, has eight colorful but simply appointed air-conditioned rooms (two are accessible for wheelchairs) with fans in a two-story house, plus two rooms in a separate *casita.* Upper-story rooms have heaps of light and are breezy and have huge walk-in showers. Rooms 4 and 5 have outside oceanview bathrooms. There are hammocks beneath shady palms, plus a barbecue pit, a small pool, and a lively bar/restaurant with pool table. Come for the friendly ambience. Rates include breakfast.

Visually more appealing, the French-run **La Puesta del Sol B&B** (tel. 506/2778-8070, www.emi-waves.com, $70 s/d) has four nicely furnished apartments with batik spreads and balconies overlooking a circular pool. It specializes in surfing and offers surf lessons.

Encantada Ocean Cottages (tel. 506/2778-7048, www.encantadacostarica.com, $35–40 rooms, $55–75 cabins low season; $40 rooms, $65–85 cabins high season) offers a pleasant, no-frills mid-priced alternative.

Meanwhile, Esterillos Este has hit the big time with the opening of **《 Xandari by the Pacific** (tel. 506/2778-7070, www.xandari .com, $210–345 s/d low season, $235–370 high season), a spectacular and sophisticated addition that opened in 2006. The second of Sherrill and Charlene Brody's magnificent creations (they also run Xandari Plantation, near Alajuela), this stunner is a colorful boutique beachfront hotel set in gorgeous grounds that are themselves a work of art. The hotel is a mini-museum of contemporary art. The vast villas are highlighted by signature waveform wooden ceilings, huge poured-concrete sofas with leather cushions, and gorgeous bathrooms with colorful mosaic showers facing private patio gardens through walls of glass. All the accoutrements you could wish for are there, including thoughtful magazines, umbrellas, flashlights, and kitchenettes. The restaurant serves gourmet health-conscious fare, and the pool is inviting. An outright winner!

Playa Bejuco: New in 2008 and 100 meters inland of the beach, the Dutch-owned **Hotel Playa Bejuco** (tel. 506/2778-8181, www.hotel playabejuco.com, $150 s/d) is a lovely addition making handsome use of river stone and timber. The 20 air-conditioned rooms on two levels (upper level rooms are preferable for their sleeping lofts) boast pleasant furnishings, plus cable TVs, phones, coffeemakers, safes, and terraces, but are overpriced. It has a swimming pool and airy restaurant.

The far more modest and unassuming **Delfin Beachfront Resort** (tel. 506/2778-8054, www.delfinbeachfront.com, $90 s/d low season, $110 s/d high season) offers a beachfront alternative.

Food

The place to hang at Esterillos Oeste is the thatched **Lowtide Lounge** (www.my space.com/lowtidelounge, 9 A.M.–9 P.M. daily) seafood restaurant.

At Esterillo Este, the rustic yet colorful **Arena Fuego** (tel. 506/2778-7278, 7 A.M.–4 P.M. Tues.–Thurs. and Sunday, 7 A.M.–10 P.M. Fri.–Sat.), 400 meters south of Xandari, serves breakfast burritos and omelettes in the morning, quesadillas and burgers for lunch, and Chicago-style pizza by night.

For gourmet and health-conscious fare, head for the open-air thatched restaurant at **Xandari by the Pacific** (tel. 506/2778-7070, www .xandari.com, 6:30 A.M.–10 P.M. daily), which uses organic products grown in its own garden.

PARRITA

This small town, 45 kilometers south of Jacó, is a center for the 1,700-hectare African oil palm ranch. A dirt road immediately south of Parrita leads eight kilometers to **Playa Palo Seco,** a black-sand beach backed by the mangrove swamps and braided channels of the Palo Seco and Damas. The Damas estuary mangrove forest is home to crocodiles, monkeys, pumas, coatimundis, and wading and water

birds by the thousands. **Isla Damas** lies across the 400-meter-wide estuary and is reached by boat ($4 each way) from the dock one kilometer southwest of **Damas,** 12 kilometers south of Parrita on Highway 34.

Iguana Tours (tel. 506/2777-2052, www .iguanatours.com) and **EcoTropical Tours** (tel. 506/2777-3557, www.ecotropicaltours.com) offer guided boat tours of the estuary.

Rainmaker Conservation Project

Rainmaker (tel. 506/2777-3565, www.rain makercostarica.com, closed Sun.) is a 540-hectare private reserve on the forested slopes of the Fila Chonta mountains, near the village of Pocares, southeast of Parrita and seven kilometers inland of Highway 21. The main draw is a treetop trail formed by six suspension bridges to form a 250-meter aerial walkway through the rainforest canopy ($70 half day, including hotel transfers). Far below, a wooden boardwalk and other bridges lead you through a river canyon, with cool pools for bathing. It's a stiff climb up several hundred steps to reach the first platform. Tours are offered at 8:45 A.M., 10:45 A.M., and 12:45 P.M. A birding tour is offered at 5:30 A.M. ($90) and a night tour at 7 P.M. ($60). Reservations are a must! Tour operators in Quepos and Manuel Antonio offer excursions. There's a restaurant and interpretive center.

Sports and Recreation

Sky Mountain (tel. 506/2770-8325, www .canopycostarica.com), at La Chirraca, in the mountains about 20 kilometers north of Parrita, lets you whiz by zipline across a mountain gorge; it has 2,195 meters of zipline ($65). The views over the coast are stunning. It's within Reserva Ecológico Creando Naturaleza, with a stable for horseback rides ($50).

Nexteam Action Sports, at Timarai Bamboo Beach Resort & Spa (tel./fax 506/2770-8360, www.timaraibambooresort .net), at Isla Playa Seco, offers paramotor tandem flights, boat tours of the mangroves, and other adventures.

CENTRAL PACIFIC

Accommodations and Food

At Playa Palo Seco, the beachfront **Beso del Viento** (tel. 506/2779-9674, bdviento@ racsa.co.cr, $82–87 s/d rooms, $112–132 apartments) offers six rooms in the main house and three apartments of varying sizes with kitchens. The French owners arrange horse rides, and a sportfishing boat is available for charters and tours. Rates include breakfast. It was for sale at last visit.

The rather soulless but perfectly adequate **Pueblo Real** (tel. 506/2777-1403 or 908/708-4676, www.costaricamycondo.com, call for rates), near the dock one kilometer southwest of Damas, spreads across 120 hectares on the banks of the river. It features 28 fully furnished Spanish-style condos, and facilities include two tennis courts, a pool, and marina.

Nestled between beach and lagoon at the very end of Playa Palo Seco, the **Cabinas La Tranquilidad** (tel. 506/8836-7775, www.cabinaslatranquilidad.com, $80 cabin, $110 house low season; $100 cabin, $130 house high season) is well named. Behind its white picket fence are three cabins and a four-person house. Although modestly furnished, they're handsome enough, and the grounds include a shaded bar and restaurant, plus hammocks, a pool, and various games for relaxation.

Next door, the **Timarai Bamboo Beach Resort & Spa** (tel./fax 506/2770-8360, www.timaraibambooresort.net, call for rates) is constructed of natural materials throughout. The 22 circular, tree house–style loft rooms and suites are made of bamboo and have a lovely, somewhat rustic aesthetic graced by floral displays. It has lots of high-adrenaline activities. The dramatic **Kanbambú Restaurant** (7 A.M.–10 P.M.), made of cantilevered bamboo poles, serves Mediterranean dishes, salads, and creole chicken.

At Damas, **Hotel Kayak Inn** (tel. 506/2777-6620, www.kayak-inn.com, $60 s, $70 d) has an unsalubrious location abutting the mangroves but is great for folks wishing to explore the mangroves.

Babilon, where the access road meets Playa Palo Seco, is a rustic yet groovy place for seafood and a beer.

Quepos and Manuel Antonio

QUEPOS

The small yet booming port town of Quepos (pop. 11,000) is the gateway for travelers heading to Manuel Antonio National Park, seven kilometers south over a sinuous mountain road lined with hotels, restaurants, and bars. Banana plantations were established in the nearby flatlands in the 1930s, and Quepos rose to prominence as a banana-exporting port. The plantations were blighted by disease in the 1950s, and the bananas were replaced by African palms, which produce oil for food, cosmetics, and machines. The trees stretch in neatly ordered rows for miles north and south of Quepos.

Quepos is sportfishing central! Half a dozen sportfishing outfits are based here. In late 2008, work was almost complete on the 196-slip **Marina Pez Vela** (tel. 506/2777-9069, www.marinapezvela.com), which promises to launch Quepos into the big time.

The waters off Quepos's El Cocal beach are contaminated—avoid swimming!

There's little of interest to see in town, except perhaps the dilapidated fishing village of **Boca Vieja,** with rickety plank walkways extending over a muddy beach; and the old residential compounds of the Standard Fruit Company in the hills south of town.

Río Naranjo

Rancho Los Tucanes (tel. 506/2777-0775, www.rancholostucanes.com), near Londres on the banks of the Río Naranjo, offers ATV tours and horseback rides to the 90-meter Los Tucanos waterfall in a private wildlife reserve.

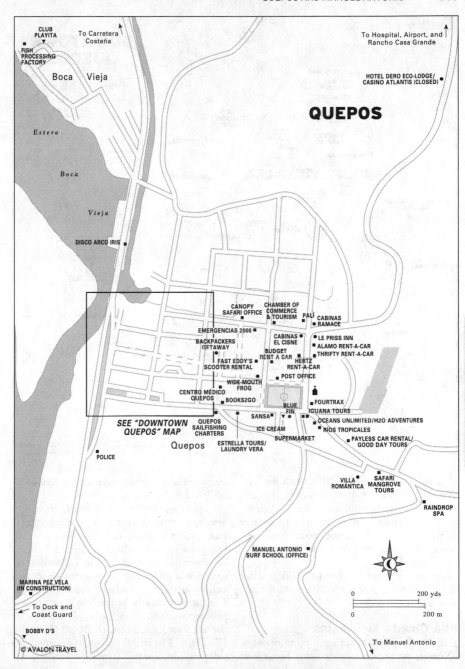

CLUB PLAYITA
To Carretera Costeña
FISH PROCESSING FACTORY

To Hospital, Airport, and Rancho Casa Grande

HOTEL DERO ECO-LODGE/ CASINO ATLANTIS (CLOSED)

Boca Vieja

QUEPOS

Estero

Boca

Vieja

DISCO ARCO IRIS

CANOPY SAFARI OFFICE
CHAMBER OF COMMERCE & TOURISM
PALÍ
CABINAS RAMACE

EMERGENCIAS 2000
CABINAS EL CISNE
LE PRISS INN
ALAMO RENT-A-CAR
THRIFTY RENT-A-CAR

BACKPACKERS GETAWAY
BUDGET RENT A CAR
HERTZ RENT-A-CAR

FAST EDDY'S SCOOTER RENTAL

POST OFFICE

WIDE-MOUTH FROG

CENTRO MÉDICO QUEPOS
BOOKS2GO

BLUE FIN
FOURTRAX
IGUANA TOURS

SANSA
OCEANS UNLIMITED/H2O ADVENTURES

SEE "DOWNTOWN QUEPOS" MAP

QUEPOS SAILFISHING CHARTERS
ICE CREAM
RÍOS TROPICALES

Quepos
ESTRELLA TOURS/ LAUNDRY VERA
SUPERMARKET
PAYLESS CAR RENTAL/ GOOD DAY TOURS

POLICE

VILLA ROMÁNTICA
SAFARI MANGROVE TOURS

RAINDROP SPA

MANUEL ANTONIO SURF SCHOOL (OFFICE)

MARINA PEZ VELA (IN CONSTRUCTION)

To Dock and Coast Guard

BOBBY D'S

© AVALON TRAVEL

0   200 yds
0   200 m

To Manuel Antonio

CENTRAL PACIFIC

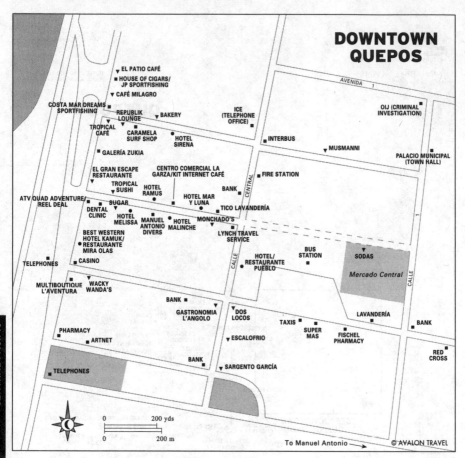

DOWNTOWN QUEPOS

EL PATIO CAFÉ
HOUSE OF CIGARS/ JP SPORTFISHING
CAFÉ MILAGRO
AVENIDA 1
COSTA MAR DREAMS SPORTFISHING
ICE (TELEPHONE OFFICE)
OIJ (CRIMINAL INVESTIGATION)
REPUBLIK LOUNGE   BAKERY
TROPICAL CAFÉ
CARAMELA SURF SHOP   HOTEL SIRENA
INTERBUS
MUSMANNI
GALERÍA ZUKIA
PALACIO MUNICIPAL (TOWN HALL)
EL GRAN ESCAPE RESTAURANTE
CENTRO COMERCIAL LA GARZA/KIT INTERNET CAFÉ
FIRE STATION
TROPICAL SUSHI   HOTEL RAMUS
BANK
ATV QUAD ADVENTURE/ REEL DEAL
SUGAR
HOTEL MAR Y LUNA
TICO LAVANDERÍA
DENTAL CLINIC   HOTEL MELISSA   MANUEL ANTONIO DIVERS   HOTEL MALINCHE   MONCHADO'S
BEST WESTERN HOTEL KAMUK/ RESTAURANTE MIRA OLAS
LYNCH TRAVEL SERVICE
TELEPHONES   CASINO
HOTEL/ RESTAURANTE PUEBLO
BUS STATION
SODAS
Mercado Central
MULTIBOUTIQUE L'AVENTURA   WACKY WANDA'S
BANK
GASTRONOMIA L'ANGOLO   DOS LOCOS
TAXIS
LAVANDERÍA
BANK
PHARMACY   ARTNET
ESCALOFRIO
SUPER MAS   FISCHEL PHARMACY
RED CROSS
TELEPHONES
BANK
SARGENTO GARCÍA

0   200 yds
0   200 m

To Manuel Antonio →   © AVALON TRAVEL

En route you'll pass **Villa Vanilla** (tel. 506/2779-1155, www.rainforestspices.com), at Buena Vista, 10 kilometers east of Quepos, an organic spice farm with three kilometers of trails. It has fascinating educational two-hour tours that include a hike to a massive ceiba tree ($20).

Buses run from Quepos to Londres daily at 4:30 A.M., 7 A.M., 9 A.M., noon, 4 P.M., and 6 P.M.

Fila Chonta Mountains

Deep in the Fila Chonta mountains inland of Quepos, the community of Santa Juana is at the center of an ambitious ecological project established by Jim Damalas, owner of the Hotel Si Como No, in Manuel Antonio. Community members are being engaged in ecotourism projects, such as breeding butterflies, reforestation, and growing and making products for use in local hotels. Meanwhile, the 1,000-hectare terrain is a pristine mountain sanctuary with trails, waterfalls, and natural swimming pools. The **Santa Juana Mountain Tour** (www .sicomono.com/tours/santa_juana.php, or contact EcoQuest Tours, tel. 506/2777-0850, $75 adult, $30 child) grants access and provides an educational "farm experience" (such as picking coffee or citrus) that includes a *campesino* lunch.

Entertainment and Events

Quepos's three-week **Carnivale** (mid-Feb. to early Mar.) offers plenty of entertainment. The unpretentious **Wacky Wanda's Bar** (506/2777-2245, 3 P.M.–1 A.M. Thurs.–Tues.) and **Los Pescadores Bar** (tel. 506/2777-1827), next door, are Key West kind of places for seafarers and working girls. For live music and impromptu dancing, try **El Gran Escape** (tel. 506/2777-0395, 8 A.M.–midnight daily).

For dancing, locals gravitate to **Arco Iris** (tel. 506/2777-0449, $5), an air-conditioned disco on a barge north of the bridge in town; don't even think of getting here before midnight. The DJ spins everything from reggae to salsa. To learn some moves in advance, head to **Sargento García** (tel. 506/2777-2960, 10 A.M.–9 P.M. daily), which has salsa lessons Tuesday and Friday at 8 P.M.

Hotel Kamuk (tel. 506/2777-0811, noon–3 A.M. daily) has a 24-hour casino.

Quepos was due to get its first upscale New York–style lounge bar—**Republik Lounge**—in 2009.

Sports and Recreation

Lynch Travel Service (tel. 506/2777-1170, www.lynchtravel.com) offers a full range of local tours.

CANOPY TOURS

If you care to whiz through the treetops on a zipline, three canopy tours compete: **Canopy Safari** (tel. 506/2777-0100, www.canopy safari.com); **Titi Canopy Tour** (tel. 506/2777-3130, www.titicanopytours.com), at Hotel Rancho Casa Grande; and **Dream Forest Canopy** (tel. 506/2777-4567, www.dreamforest canopy.com).

KAYAKING, RAFTING, AND WATER SPORTS

Amigos Del Río (tel. 506/2777-0082, www .amigosdelrio.net) and **Iguana Tours** (tel. 506/2777-2052, www.iguanatours.com) offer sea-kayaking trips, boat tours of the mangroves, river-rafting trips, and horseback rides. **H2O Adventures** (tel. 506/2777-4092, www.hzocr.com) has similar tours; and **Safari Mangrove Tours** (tel. 506/2777-3557, www .safarimangrove.com) specializes in kayak trips to Damas. **Quepoa Expeditions** (tel. 506/2777-0058, www.quepoaexpeditions.com) has inflatable kayak ("rubber duckies") trips.

SPORTFISHING

The Quepos region offers outstanding sportfishing for marlin and sailfish, December through August, while the inshore reefs are home to snapper, amberjack, wahoo, and tuna. The many operators in Qupeos include **Dream Charter** (tel. 506/2777-0593, www.costamarsportfishing .com); **Sportfishing Quepos** (www.sportfishing quepos.com); **J.P. Sportfishing Tours** (tel. 506/2777-1613, www.jpsportfishing.com); **Reel Deal Sportfishing** (tel. 506/2777-0007, www.reeldeal1.com); **Good Day Team** (tel. 506/2777-3537, www.gooddayteam.com); **Luna Tours Sportfishing** (tel. 506/2777-0725, www.lunatours.net); and **Bluefin Sportfishing** (tel. 506/2777-2222, www .bluefinsportfishing.com).

OTHER RECREATION

For guided horseback tours, try **Finca Valmy Tours** (tel. 506/2779-1118, www.valmy tours.com).

Fourtrax Adventures (tel. 506/2777-1829, www.fourtraxadventure.com); **ATC Quad Adventures** (tel. 506/2777-7500, www.atvquad adventures.com); and **Adrenaline Tours** (tel. 506/2777-0117, www.adrenalinetours.com) specialize in ATV tours—Adrenaline even has its own nearly three-hectare motocross park with huge mud bog!

Planet Dolphin (tel. 506/2777-1647, www.planetdolphin.com) has a boat tour in search of whales and dolphins ($65, with snorkeling), plus a catamaran adventure to Manuel Antonio National Park ($65). And **Sunset Sails Tours** (tel. 506/2777-1304, www.sunset sailstours.com) offers sailing excursions.

For diving, contact **Oceans Unlimited** (tel.

506/2777-3171, www.oceansunlimitedcr.com) or **Manuel Antonio Divers** (tel. 506/2777-3483, www.manuelantoniodivers.com).

The pink-painted twin-deck **Pink Panther Boat** (tel. 506/2777-0792) operates sunset and dolphin-watch cruises.

Shopping

Zoíla, a delightful Cuban, rolls excellent quality cigars at **House of Cuban Cigars** (tel. 506/2777-2208, 7 A.M.–6 P.M. Mon.–Sat.).

Accommodations

Hotels in town are about a 30-minute bus or taxi ride from Manuel Antonio park; the mountain road over the hill to the park is lined with more upscale hotels, plus a sprinkling of budget options. Staying in town is cheaper and offers the benefit of services close at hand but is invariably noisy. There are many more options than can be recommended here.

UNDER $25

In the budget category try the spic-and-span, family-run **Hotel Mar y Luna** (tel. 506/2777-0394, $12 pp shared bath, $20–30 s/d private bath), with 17 small, basic upper-floor rooms with fans and shared baths; ground-floor rooms have private baths (some with hot water) but no windows.

Who could resist a place called **Wide Mouth Frog** (tel. 506/2777-2798, www.wide mouthfrog.org, $11 pp dorm, $30 s/d room with shared bath, $40 s/d private bath), two blocks east of the bus station. Actually, this clean backpackers' haven—run by a Kiwi and a Brit—is a hip option, with pool, kitchen, games, parking, and more. It has two dorms and 22 private rooms, all with beautiful tiled showers; four more rooms were to be added. It charges $10 extra for air-conditioning. There's a TV room, Internet, laundry, and peaceful gardens. No credit cards are accepted.

Hotel Ramus (tel. 506/2777-0245), and, opposite, **Hotel Melissa** (tel. 506/2777-0025) both have clean rooms with ceiling fans and private baths with hot water for about $10 pp, and the latter has secure parking. Handy for

an early morning bus, the uninspired **Hotel Pueblo** (tel. 506/2777-1003, $10 pp with fans, $34 s/d with a/c and TV), on the north side of the bus station, has eight simple but adequate rooms with private bath.

$25–50

Cabinas El Cisne (tel. 506/2777-0719, $25 s or $35 d with fan, $35 s or $45 d with a/c), with secure parking, has 12 cabins with fans, private baths, and hot water; plus 12 newer, more spacious air-conditioned rooms in a three-story unit. The same owner operates the identical **Le Priss Inn** (tel. 506/2777-0719, www.lepriss .com) across the street.

Almost identical, and catercorner to El Cisne, **Cabinas Ramace** (tel. 506/2777-0590) offers an alternative.

$50–100

The two-story, white-and-blue **Hotel Sirena** (tel. 506/2777-0572 or 800/493-8426, www .lasirenahotel.com, $55 s or $65 d low season, $59 s or $90 d high season) has 10 double rooms (most with a/c) with fans and private baths and hot water. They have whitewashed walls but are sparsely furnished, and street noise is a problem. The courtyard dining area has a sundeck and pool. With a bit of creativity and money, this could be a lovely property.

A more tranquil alternative is the **Hotel Villa Romántica** (tel. 506/2777-0037 or 888/790-5264, www.villaromantica.com, $59 s or $74 d low season, $69 s or $94 d high season), on the southeast edge of town. This two-tiered Mediterranean-style building is set in landscaped grounds. Sixteen simply but nicely appointed rooms have spacious bathrooms and heaps of light, plus fans (some have a/c), and balconies overlooking a swimming pool.

The best bargain in town, and the classiest lodging, is the **Best Western Hotel Kamuk** (tel. 506/2777-0811, www.kamuk.co.cr, $50–100 s/d low season, $90–125 high season). It has 44 spacious and elegant, nicely furnished air-conditioned rooms, some with balconies, all with TVs and telephones, all beautifully decorated in light pastels. The Miraolas Bar and

Restaurant on the third floor has vistas. There's a small boutique, a pool, a classy bar, and small casino. Rates include continental breakfast.

Nature-lovers might consider **Hotel Rancho Casa Grande** (tel. 506/2777-3130, www.ranchocasagrande.com, $80 s/d rooms, $85 one-room bungalow, $95 two-room bungalow low season; $95 rooms, $110 one-room bungalow, $125 two-room bungalow high season), about four kilometers northeast from town on the road to the Quepos airport. Set in 73 hectares, it has 14 modestly furnished air-conditioned rooms and 10 fully equipped bungalows (with king-size beds) amid sprawling lawns. Highlights include a pool, whirlpool tub, horseback riding, and nature trails.

Food

Quepos is blessed with excellent options for dining.

The place to start your day is **El Patio Café** (tel. 506/2777-4982, 6 A.M.–10 P.M. daily), serving *gallo pinto,* granola with fruit and yogurt ($4), ice cream sundaes, homemade baked goods, sandwiches, raspberry iced mochas, lattes, espressos, and an inspired Nuevo Latino dinner menu. Next door, the same owners have **Café Milagro** (tel. 506/2777-1707, www.cafemilagro.com, 9 A.M.–5 P.M. Mon.–Sat. low season, 6 A.M.–10 P.M. high season), which roasts its coffee fresh and sells iced coffee, espresso, and cappuccino to be enjoyed in a delightful airy space.

The *mercado central,* by the bus station, has budget *sodas* serving local dishes.

My favorite restaurant is 🄒 **El Gran Escape Restaurante** (tel. 506/2777-0395, 6 A.M.–11 P.M. Wed.–Mon., $5–20), serving salads, seafood, surf and turf, tuna melts, enchiladas, killer burgers, and coconut curry chicken, with large portions at bargain prices.

Adjoining El Gran Escape, tiny **Tropical Sushi** (tel. 506/2777-1710, 4:30–11 P.M.) serves quality sashimi and sushi. All-you-can-eat sushi is served 5–7 P.M.

Grilled cheese sandwiches? Hot dogs? Head to the U.S.–run **Sargento García** (tel. 506/2777-

2960, 10 A.M.–9 P.M. daily, $2–10), a little piece of the Midwest. For Mexican fare, head to **Dos Locos** (tel. 506/2777-1526, 8 A.M.–11 P.M. Mon.–Sat., 11 A.M.–8 P.M. Sun., $3–15), offering breakfast omelettes, plus chimichangas and chili con carne; my *burrito gigante* was superb. It has live music on Wednesday evening and Saturday afternoon. **Monchado's** (tel. 506/2777-1972), one block north and east, competes and has an excellent tongue in *salsa* ($5.50), plus live music in high season.

Locals head to **Bobby D's** (tel. 506/2777-3202, noon–11 P.M. daily), in the former Club Americano in the hills west of town, for its American classics, from burgers to pizzas. It has a bowling alley too!

Hugely popular, **Escalofrio** (tel. 506/2777-0833, 2:30–10 P.M. Tues.–Sun.) is an atmospheric Italian spot open to the street and serving spaghetti and pizza. You can also gorge on banana splits and shakes at this "Italian ice cream factory."

You'll think you're in New York when you pop into **Gastronomia L'Angolo** (tel. 506/2777-4129, 8 A.M.–8 P.M. Mon.–Sat.), a *real* Italian deli with hams, cheeses, and the like.

For baked goods, head to **Musmanni,** one block north of the bus station, or **Sugar** (tel. 506/2777-0478, 7 A.M.–5 P.M. Tues.–Sat.), a delightful space to use free Wi-Fi while munching on omelettes, pancakes, soups, salads, or delicious pastries and cheesecakes. It even has barbecue chicken and filet mignon ($12).

Information and Services

The **Cámara de Comercio y Turismo** (tel. 506/2777-0749, www.visitmanuelantonio.com) represents local tourism companies and can provide information.

Hospital Dr. Max Teran V (tel. 506/2777-0020) is three kilometers south of town on the Costanera Sur. The **Red Cross** is one block east of the bus station. For an ambulance, call **Emergencias 2000** (tel. 506/8380-4125 or 800-EMS-2000). **Farmacia Quepos** (tel. 506/2777-0038) is open 8 A.M.–9 P.M. There's a **dental clinic** (tel. 506/2777-0522,

9 A.M.–9 P.M. Mon.–Sat.) catercorner to El Gran Escape restaurant.

The **police station** (tel. 506/2777-2117) is 100 meters south of the town center, en route to the dock; the OIJ (tel. 506/2777-0511), or FBI equivalent, is two blocks northeast of the bus station.

The **post office** is on the north side of the soccer field. For Internet, head to **Artenet Internet** (tel. 506/2777-3447), which has Skype; or **KIT Internet** (tel. 506/2777-7575) in Centro Comercial La Garza.

There's no bookstore, but **Books 2 Go** (tel. 506/2777-1754, 9 A.M.–5 P.M. Mon.–Sat.) has a book exchange.

There are three laundries: **Lavandería Casa Tica** (tel. 506/2777-2533, 8 A.M.–5 P.M. Mon.–Sat.), adjoining the bus station; **Tico Lavandería** (tel. 506/2777-1484), in the center; and **Laundry Vera** (8 A.M.–5 P.M. Mon.–Sat.), on the south side of town.

Getting There

Both **SANSA** and **Nature Air** have scheduled daily service to Quepos. Lynch Travel Service (tel. 506/2777-1170, www.lynchtravel.com) can make reservations. SANSA offers hotel/airport transfers ($5 pp).

Transportes Delio Morales buses (tel. 506/2223-5567, in Manuel Antonio, tel. 506/2777-0318) depart San José for Quepos from Calle 16, Avenida 3, at 6 A.M., 9 A.M., noon, 2:30 P.M., 6 P.M., and 7:30 P.M. (3.5 hours, $5). Buses for Quepos depart Puntarenas daily at 4:30 A.M., 7:30 A.M., 10:30 A.M., 12:30 P.M., 3 P.M., and 5:30 P.M., returning at 5 A.M., 8 A.M., 11 A.M., 12:30 P.M., 2:30 P.M., and 4:30 P.M.; from San Isidro at 7 A.M., 9 A.M., 1:30 P.M., and 4 P.M.

Return buses depart Quepos for San José at 6 A.M., 9 A.M., noon, 2 P.M., and 5 P.M.; for Puntarenas at 4:30 A.M., 7:30 A.M., 10:30 A.M., 12:30 P.M., and 3 P.M.; and for San Isidro at 6:30 A.M., 7:30 A.M., 2:45 P.M., and 3:30 P.M. The ticket office in Quepos is open 7–11 A.M. and 1–5 P.M. Monday–Saturday, 7 A.M.–2 P.M. Sunday.

Interbus (tel. 506/2283-5573 or 506/2777-7866, www.interbusonline.com) has shuttles between Quepos and San José, as well as to other major tourist destinations.

Getting Around

For taxis, call **Quepos Taxi** (tel. 506/2777-0425).

Rental car agencies in town include: **Alamo Rent-a-Car** (tel. 506/2242-7733), **Budget** (tel. 506/2436-2000), **Hertz** (tel. 506/2777-3365), **Payless** (tel. 506/2257-0026), and **Thrifty** (tel. 506/2777-3334). **Fast Eddie's** (tel. 506/2777-4127) rents scooters.

QUEPOS TO MANUEL ANTONIO

Immediately southeast of Quepos, a road climbs sharply over the forested headland of Punta Quepos and snakes, dips, and rises south along a ridge for seven kilometers before dropping down to the evolving beachfront community of Manuel Antonio, consisting of a handful of hotels and restaurants catering to the visitors descending on Manuel Antonio National Park, immediately south. The beachfront by the park gets jam-packed!

Manuel Antonio is fringed by **Playa Espadilla,** a two-kilometer-long scimitar of gray sand. Crocodiles are said to inhabit the lagoon at the north end of Playa Espadilla, beyond which lies **Playita** (a.k.a. Playa Dulce Vida), a small beach cusped by tall headlands; it was once favored by gays but is now co-ed since the Hotel Arenas del Mar opened here. Other beaches are tucked into tiny coves, but the only one accessible to the public is **Playa Biesanz,** facing north towards Quepos.

Beware of riptides! There are lifeguards.

Fincas Naturales Butterfly Garden

This 16-hectare nature refuge (tel. 506/2777-0850, www.butterflygardens.co.cr, $15 adults, $8 children) is a project of Hotel Si Como No and features multilevel trails that wind through a netted butterfly garden, a snake pit, and crocodile and caiman lagoon. The forested reserve is excellent for sighting monkeys

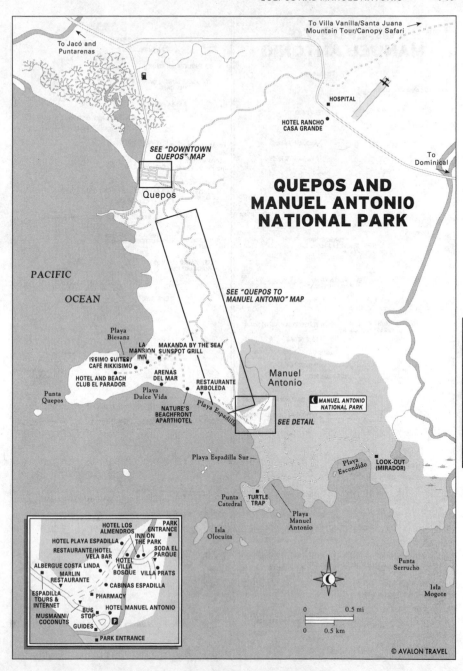

To Villa Vanilla/Santa Juana
Mountain Tour/Canopy Safari

To Jacó and
Puntarenas

HOSPITAL

HOTEL RANCHO
CASA GRANDE

To
Dominical

SEE "DOWNTOWN
QUEPOS" MAP

Quepos

QUEPOS AND MANUEL ANTONIO NATIONAL PARK

PACIFIC

OCEAN

SEE "QUEPOS TO
MANUEL ANTONIO" MAP

Playa
Biesanz

LA MANSION
INN

MAKANDA BY THE SEA/
SUNSPOT GRILL

ISSIMO SUITES/
CAFÉ RIKKISIMO

ARENAS
DEL MAR

HOTEL AND BEACH
CLUB EL PARADOR

Playa
Dulce Vida

RESTAURANTE
ARBOLEDA

Manuel
Antonio

MANUEL ANTONIO
NATIONAL PARK

Punta
Quepos

NATURE'S
BEACHFRONT
APARTHOTEL

Playa Espadilla

SEE DETAIL

Playa Espadilla Sur

Playa
Escondido

LOOK-OUT
(MIRADOR)

Punta
Catedral

TURTLE
TRAP

Playa
Manuel
Antonio

Isla
Olocuita

Punta
Serrucho

Isla
Mogote

HOTEL LOS
ALMENDROS

PARK
ENTRANCE

HOTEL PLAYA ESPADILLA

INN ON
THE PARK

RESTAURANTE/HOTEL
VELA BAR

SODA EL
PARQUE

HOTEL
VILLA
BOSQUE

ALBERGUE COSTA LINDA

MARLIN
RESTAURANTE

VILLA PRATS

CABINAS ESPADILLA

ESPADILLA
TOURS &
INTERNET

PHARMACY

MUSMANNI/
COCONUTS

BUS
STOP

HOTEL MANUEL ANTONIO

GUIDES

PARK ENTRANCE

0   0.5 mi

0   0.5 km

© AVALON TRAVEL

CENTRAL PACIFIC

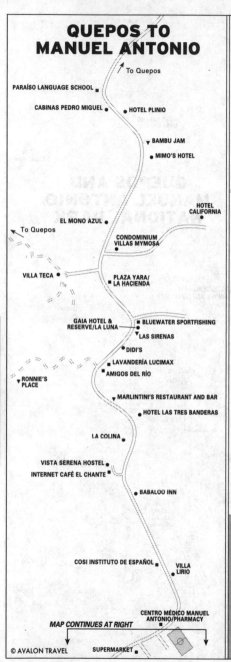

QUEPOS TO MANUEL ANTONIO

↑ To Quepos

PARAÍSO LANGUAGE SCHOOL

CABINAS PEDRO MIGUEL ● HOTEL PLINIO

■ BAMBU JAM

■ MIMO'S HOTEL

HOTEL CALIFORNIA

EL MONO AZUL ●

← To Quepos

CONDOMINIUM VILLAS MYMOSA

VILLA TECA ●

PLAZA YARA/ LA HACIENDA

GAIA HOTEL & RESERVE/LA LUNA
■ BLUEWATER SPORTFISHING

▼ LAS SIRENAS

● DIDI'S

■ LAVANDERÍA LUCIMAX

■ AMIGOS DEL RÍO

▼ RONNIE'S PLACE

▼ MARLINTINI'S RESTAURANT AND BAR

● HOTEL LAS TRES BANDERAS

LA COLINA ●

VISTA SERENA HOSTEL ●
INTERNET CAFÉ EL CHANTE ■

● BABALOO INN

COSI INSTITUTO DE ESPAÑOL ■
● VILLA LIRIO

CENTRO MÉDICO MANUEL ANTONIO/PHARMACY

MAP CONTINUES AT RIGHT
↓

© AVALON TRAVEL   SUPERMARKET ■

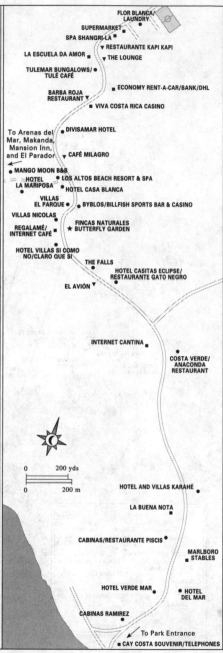

FLOR BLANCA/ LAUNDRY

SUPERMARKET ■
SPA SHANGRI-LA ■
▼ RESTAURANTE KAPI KAPI
LA ESCUELA DA AMOR ■ ▼ THE LOUNGE

TULEMAR BUNGALOWS/ TULÉ CAFÉ ●

BARBA ROJA RESTAURANT ▼   ■ ECONOMY RENT-A-CAR/BANK/DHL

■ VIVA COSTA RICA CASINO

● DIVISAMAR HOTEL

To Arenas del Mar, Makanda, Mansion Inn, and El Parador
▼ CAFÉ MILAGRO

● MANGO MOON B&B
HOTEL ● LOS ALTOS BEACH RESORT & SPA
LA MARIPOSA ● HOTEL CASA BLANCA

VILLAS EL PARQUE ● ● BYBLOS/BILLFISH SPORTS BAR & CASINO

VILLAS NICOLAS ●

REGALAMÉ/ INTERNET CAFÉ
FINCAS NATURALES
★ BUTTERFLY GARDEN

HOTEL VILLAS SI COMO NO/CLARO QUE SI ■
THE FALLS ●
HOTEL CASITAS ECLIPSE/ RESTAURANTE GATO NEGRO

EL AVIÓN ▼

INTERNET CANTINA ■

COSTA VERDE/ ANACONDA RESTAURANT

0   200 yds
0   200 m

HOTEL AND VILLAS KARAHÉ ●

LA BUENA NOTA ■

CABINAS/RESTAURANTE PISCIS ●

MARLBORO ■ STABLES

HOTEL VERDE MAR ●   ● HOTEL DEL MAR

CABINAS RAMIREZ ■

To Park Entrance
■ CAY COSTA SOUVENIR/TELEPHONES

and other endangered wildlife. Five different tours are offered, including a nocturnal "Jungle Night Walk" (5:30 P.M., $35)—the trails have ultraviolet lighting to show off insect markings normally visible by night to other insects with ultraviolet vision! It has guided birding tours by reservation at 4 P.M. and 6 P.M. Monday–Saturday high season only ($25), as well as hourly guided nature walks Monday–Saturday ($25).

Entertainment

I like the **El Avión** (tel. 506/2777-3378, 2–10 P.M. daily), a Fairchild C-123 transport plane turned into a bar. It has live music Monday–Saturday. The aircraft-turned-bar, opposite Casitas Eclipse, dates from 1954 and was used by the CIA to run arms to the contras in Nicaragua and, according to the posted spiel, when shot down by the Sandinistas was responsible for "breaking open the 'contra affair' that exposed the story and the Reagan administration's illegal and secret scheme."

The **Bat Cave** (tel. 506/2777-3489, 7 P.M.–midnight daily) at La Mansion Inn is a piece of Tolkien fantasy, not least because it is entered by a Lilliputian door. This limestone cave-turned-bar has fish tanks inset in the walls, and a stupendous polished hardwood bartop.

Coconuts (tel. 506/2777-2382, 9 P.M. until the last guest leaves, daily), in Manuel Antonio villa, has a fabulous vibe and packs in the party crowd. Ladies get in free on Friday and Saturday.

For jam sessions, head to **Bambu Jam** (tel. 506/2777-3369, 6–10 P.M. daily), which has live music Tuesday–Friday, including flamenco. And **The Lounge** (tel. 506/2777-5143) is a hip open-air space that draws the sophisticated dance crowd who prefer martinis to Budweiser. Ladies get free drinks Tuesday and Thursday. Reggae fans should check it out on Monday nights.

New in 2008, **Marlintinis** (tel. 506/2777-7474, www.manuel-antonio-restaurants.com, 11 A.M.–1 A.M.) is the happening spot at last visit. It has large-screen TVs, live music, and DJs, and killer cocktails.

Football fans should head to **Billfish Sportbar & Grill** (tel. 506/2777-0411) at the Byblos Hotel, which screens football games on Monday nights.

How about a movie in a surround-sound theater? Then head to **Si Como No** (tel. 506/2777-0777) for dinner, which grants you free entrance to the nightly movie at 8:30 P.M.

Manuel Antonio even has a "gentlemen's club," **Las Sirenas.**

Sports and Recreation

Marlboro Stables (tel. 506/2777-1108), 200 meters before Playa Espadilla, offers guided horseback rides.

Manuel Antonio Surf School (tel. 506/2777-4842, www.masurfschool.com) offers surf lessons; it has a beach outlet.

Scuba divers should sign up with **Manuel Antonio Divers** (tel. 506/2777-3483, www.manuelantoniodivers.com).

For a relaxing massage or health treatment, check into the **Raindrop Spa** (tel. 506/2777-2880, www.raindropspa.com); or **Serenity Spa** (tel. 506/2777-0777 ext. 220) at Hotel Si Como No.

Shopping

La Buena Nota (tel. 506/2777-1002, buena nota@racsa.co.cr), 800 meters uphill from the beach, sells beachwear, handicrafts, postcards, maps, and international magazines, plus a large stock of used books upstairs. For quality art, head to **Regalame** (tel. 506/2777-0777, www.regalameart.com), at Hotel Si Como No; or **Galería** (tel. 506/2777-0846), in Plaza Yara.

Accommodations

Budget hotels are mostly found down near the beach. More expensive hotels have loftier, breezy perches. Many hotels that advertise as being in "Manuel Antonio" are actually on this road. There are many more options than recommended here.

CAMPING

You can camp near the park entrance under shade trees on lawns at the back of the Hotel

Manuel Antonio ($5 pp; showers cost $1); it will supply tents ($6).

UNDER $25

Quepos-Manuel Antonio: The ridge-top **Vista Serena Hostel** (tel. 506/2777-5162, www.vistaserena.com, $6–9 pp dorm, $30 s/d room low season; $10–15 pp dorm, $50 s/d room high season) is a hostel with a view, deservedly beloved of backpackers for the loving care and all-in-the-family feel infused by owner Conrad and his mum. There's a cozy TV lounge, and a broad veranda has table soccer (foosball), hammocks, and a barbecue where communal pig-outs draw out "community" in the very best sense of the word. Dorms and almost luxurious apartment-style private rooms are super clean and inviting. It has an Internet café.

Playa Espadilla: By the beach, the best budget option is **Backpackers Paradise** (formerly Albergue Costa Linda, tel. 506/2777-0304, $10 pp room, $40 s/d apartments), 200 meters inland of Playa Espadilla. It has 22 basic rooms with shared and uninspiring outside toilets and showers, plus apartments with private bath. The handsome frontage belies the dour interior, though the restaurant is attractive.

$25-50

Quepos-Manuel Antonio: About one kilometer south of Quepos, **El Mono Azul** (tel. 506/2777-2572, www.hotelmonoazul.com, $40–60 s/d low season, $40–65 s/d high season) has 20 clean and comfortable rooms in handsome condo-style units facing a small and pretty oval pool. Some have fans only; others are air-conditioned; all have cable TV. There's a small gym, Internet café, game room, and art gallery, and movies are shown free in the highly rated restaurant.

$50-100

Quepos-Manuel Antonio: The **Hotel Plinio** (tel. 506/2777-0055, www.hotelplinio.com, $30 s or $40 d standard, $50 s/d with a/c low season; $55 s or $65 d standard, $75 s/d with a/c high season) has an open restaurant serving

hotels on Manuel Antonio

GAY MANUEL ANTONIO

Manuel Antonio is popular with a gay and lesbian clientele, drawn to the several hotels that cater to them. The following places accept a gay and lesbian clientele only:
Hotel Casa Blanca (tel./fax 506/2777-0253, www.hotelcasablanca.com, $60 s/d rooms, $90 apartments, $130 suites low season; $100 s/d rooms, $140 apartments, $220 suites high season) is run by Americans Don and Jack. It has four standard rooms, two two-bedroom suites, four apartments, and a home. There are two pools set in tropical gardens, plus a bar.
Villa La Roca (tel./fax 506/2777-1349, www.villaroca.com, $49–110 low season, $95–1905 high season) offers 11 rooms and three apartments.
La Plantación (alias Big Ruby's) has gone straight under new owners.

Asian-influenced cuisine, and bar resembling a rambling East African tree house. The 13 rooms (three with a/c) are dark but clean and have hot water. There's an attractive swimming pool. A nature trail leads uphill through 10 hectares of primary forest to a wooden *mirador* that proffers a 360-degree vista.

Recently revamped by new owners, **Hotel La Colina** (tel. 506/2777-0231, www.lacolina.com, $45 s/d standard, $85 s/d suite, $70 s/d casita, $80 s/d casa low season; $65 standard, $105 suite, $90 casita, $100 casa high season), about two kilometers south of Quepos, has rooms in a two-story *ranchito*-style house with black-and-white checkered floors. The modestly furnished rooms are dark but pleasant enough, and have air-conditioning and cable TV. Six suites are more upscale, with lots of light, plus views from balconies. It also has two *casitas*. There's a small two-tier pool with cascade, and a nice *rancho* restaurant.

Playa Espadilla: The **Restaurante/Hotel Vela Bar** (tel. 506/2777-0413, www.velabar.com, $40 s or $45 d low season, $40 s or

$52 d high season), near the main park entrance, has 13 air-conditioned *cabinas* with fans and private baths with hot water, plus a house and two small apartments with kitchen. It has a popular thatched restaurant and bar.

The delightful **Cabinas Espadilla** (tel. 506/2777-2113, www.espadilla.com, $52 s/d family, $64 s/d standard low season; $79 family, $84 standard high season) has modestly furnished units a short stroll from the beach. There's a swimming pool in beautifully landscaped grounds, plus secure parking.

Offering one of the Costa Rica's premier beachfront vistas, the Canadian-run **Nature's Beachfront Aparthotel** (tel. 506/2777-1473, www.maqbeach.com/natures.html, $45 s or $49 d small studio, $89 s/d luxury studio, $120 s/d villa, $159 s/d penthouse low season; $49 s or $54 d small studio, $99 s/d luxury studio, $140 s/d villa, $189 s/d penthouse high season), sits beachside at the bottom of a dirt road far from the main highway (you'll need wheels). Recently refurbished, it has four self-catering units, including three studios and a backpackers' studio. An upstairs penthouse sleeps eight people and has a wraparound wall of glass, cable TV, and huge terrace. And it has added a villa.

Just steps from the main park entrance, the three-story **Hotel Villa Prats** (tel. 506/2777-5391, www.villapratscr.com, $40–50 low season, $50–60 high season) has charmingly furnished air-conditioned rooms with ceiling fans, TVs, and Wi-Fi; some have kitchenettes. It has a plunge pool with waterslide. Nearby, **Hotel Los Almendros** (tel. 506/2777-0225, http://hotellosalmendroscr.com, rates upon request) also has comfy, spacious rooms and a restaurant.

The closest hotel to the southern park entrance, **Hotel Manuel Antonio** (tel. 506/2777-1237, hotelmanuelantonio@racsa.co.cr, $55 s or $75 d low season, $69 s or $85 d high season) offers 26 spacious air-conditioned rooms in a modern two-story unit in Spanish colonial style; all have ceiling fans, security boxes, and private bathrooms with hot water. There's a swimming pool and a simple restaurant.

CENTRAL PACIFIC

The lovely **Hotel Verde Mar** (tel. 506/2777-2122, www.verdemar.com, $60–90 s/d low season, $90–120 high season), has 20 air-conditioned rooms in a two-story structure with balconies supported on rough-hewn logs. Each room is painted in soft pastels and has a queen-size bed, ceiling fan, and kitchenette; eight suites have two queens and a kitchen. There's a pool, and a raised walkway ("77 steps") leads to the beach.

$100-150

Quepos-Manuel Antonio: The French Canadian–run **Condominium Villas Mymosa** (tel. 506/2777-1254, www.villasmymosa.com, $70–100 s/d low season, $112–152 high season) is a splendid option with 10 large, tastefully furnished, air-conditioned villas in three types, each with a king-size and queen-size bed, kitchen, and exquisite bathrooms. There's a pool and restaurant.

   Villa Teca (tel. 506/2777-1117, www.villatecahotel.com, $80 s/d standard, $115 s/d superior, $190 s/d suite year-round) is an exquisite, aesthetically appealing modern property with daffodil-yellow, red-tile-roofed villas scattered throughout the lushly vegetated hillside. There are 40 rooms in 20 air-conditioned bungalows with beautiful tropical floral spreads and a terrace. Highlights include an attractive pool and sundeck, thatched restaurant, and a free beach shuttle. Rates include tax.

   I like **Hotel Las Tres Banderas** (tel. 506/2777-1871, www.hoteltresbanderas.com, $45 s/d standard, $70 s/d deluxe, $90 s/d suite low season; $70 standard, $90 deluxe, $100 suite high season) for its friendly Polish owner Andrzej Nowacki. This handsome two-story Spanish colonial–style property has 14 spacious air-conditioned rooms in three types, including three suites with glossy hardwoods and exquisite bathrooms. Balconies open to both pool (front) and forest (rear). Suites have minibars and small refrigerators. Two deluxe rooms with king-size beds and a fully equipped apartment were added in 2007, and Wi-Fi was planned. There's also a self-contained, stone-walled cabin apartment ($200 low season,

$250 high season). Meals are prepared at an outside grill and served on the patio beside the pool and large whirlpool tub. Trails lead into the forest. There's a game room and a TV in the bar, where live music is hosted on Sunday afternoons in high season.

   Villas El Parque (tel. 506/2777-0096, www.hotelvillaselparque.com, $70–100 s/d suites, $140–170 s/d villas low season; $100–130 suites, $200–220 suites high season) has 17 standard rooms, 16 villas (no kitchens), and 18 suites with kitchens, in handsome Mediterranean style, all with large balconies with hammocks and views out over the park. Delightful decor includes lively Guatemalan bedspreads. Suites can be combined with standard rooms to form bi-level villas. One suite is wheelchair-accessible. There's a restaurant and a triple-level swimming pool. Monkeys visit the property every afternoon at "monkey hour." It has sportfishing packages. A similar and similarly priced entity is **Villas Nicolas** (tel. 506/2777-0481, www.villasnicolas.com), with 12 privately owned, pleasantly furnished, one- and two-bedroom villa suites (in six types), all with private oceanview verandas overlooking lush grounds.

   The intimate **Hotel Casitas Eclipse** (tel./fax 506/2777-0408, www.casitaseclipse.org, $95 s/d standard, $120 suite, $200 casita low season; $125 standard, $170 suite, $300 casita high season) is a lovely property offering 30 rooms in nine beautiful, well-lit, two-story, air-conditioned villas. The brightly decorated, whitewashed Mediterranean-style accommodations are set in a hollow around three swimming pools with sun terraces and bougainvillea cascading over white walls. You can rent the entire villa or one floor only. Some rooms have full kitchens. The effect is marvelous, although one reader complains about upkeep. Rates include breakfast.

   Also to consider in this price bracket are the **Costa Verde** (tel. 506/2777-0584, www.hotelcostaverde.com), a three-story modern unit offering efficiencies, studios, studio apartments, and a penthouse; **Byblos** (tel. 506/2777-0411, www.bybloshotelcostarica.com), a stylish quasi-Swiss lodge with seven bungalows and nine rooms in lush landscaped grounds; and **Casa Roland's Villas Lirio** (tel. 506/2777-0403, www.rolandhotels.com), which has a lovely ambience that recalls a Spanish hacienda of old.

The former La Plantacion, catering mostly to gays, has metamorphosed as the gorgeous all-suite **◖ The Falls** (tel. 506/2777-1332, www.fallsresortcr.com, $70–95 s/d low season, $149–220 high season), named for the cascades in lush gardens. Luxuriously appointed with quality linens and tasteful white-and-chocolate color schemes, the rooms have king-size beds, flat-screen cable TVs, DVD players, and terraces. Three luxury tree houses were to be added, connected by hanging bridges and served by their own infinity pool. Low season rates are a steal.

Playa Espadilla: The **Hotel Villa Bosque** (tel. 506/2777-0463, www.hotelvillabosque.com, $80 s or $100 d low season, $114 s or $134 d high season), close to the main park entrance, is a Spanish-colonial remake with 17 pleasant, atmospheric air-conditioned rooms that each sleep three people; rooms have fans, cable TV, security boxes, and private baths with hot water, as well as verandas with chairs. It has a restaurant serving surf and turf, and a pool on the raised terrace. Potted plants abound.

OVER $150
On the Road to Manuel Antonio: The nicely refurbished ridgetop **Hotel California** (tel. 506/2777-1234, www.hotel-california.com, $90 s/d standard, $105 s/d deluxe low season; $160 standard, $175 deluxe high season) is now under U.S. owners. The three-story hotel with the name you'll never forget has terra-cotta tile throughout, plus 28 graciously appointed rooms with marvelous views from the balconies overlooking a pool with wooden deck. It's a tad overpriced, though, given the competitive standards hereabouts.

The ever-expanding **Hotel La Mariposa** (tel. 506/2777-0355 or U.S. tel. 800/572-6440, www.hotelmariposa.com, $140–315 s/d low season, $205–440 high season) is dramatically

perched on cliffs above the sea, with magnificent views over Manuel Antonio National Park. It has 66 air-conditioned rooms. Eight vast (but overpriced) standard rooms in the main house offer garden views from lower stories, and fabulous coastal views from upper rooms, enjoyed through picture windows and wraparound balconies, but I don't like their frumpy decor or the access by a frail metal spiral staircase that can induce vertigo in the weak-hearted. Ten split-level Mediterranean-style cottage-villas nestle on the hillcrest; each has a deck—with outside whirlpools in the junior suites—and a sky-lit bathroom. Deluxe units have beam ceilings with fans and whirlpool bathtubs. Fifteen premier suites and a penthouse with walls of glass have striking contemporary furnishings. The restaurant serves French-inspired fare. It has two swimming pools (one a brand new infinity pool) with swim-up bars, a massage room, and gift store. A trail leads to the beach.

For intimacy, I would opt for **Mango Moon B&B** (tel. 506/2777-5323, www.mangomoon.net, $110–185 low season, $150–250 high season), a Spanish colonial–style mansion with eight romantically furnished rooms. A shady terrace overlooks a kidney-shaped pool surrounded by forest, but with ocean views.

Readers report favorably on **Tulemar Bungalows** (tel. 506/2777-0580, www.tulemar.com, $128–550 s/d low season, $220–700 high season), which claims its "own exclusive beach" (with free kayaks and snorkeling) and forest reserve. Tulemar's loftily perched, oceanview, air-conditioned bungalows in various types are surrounded by trees and lawns. All have beautiful interiors highlighted by 180-degree windows and bulbous skylights. There's a small horizon swimming pool with a bar, plus a shop and snack bar. Choose from one-bedroom units or multi-bedroom units on two levels accessed by a bridged walkway. Tulemar also has three gorgeous houses for rent, including Casa de Frutas, a Balinese-inspired beauty with its own infinity plunge pool.

A delightful alternative, **Makanda by the Sea** (tel. 506/2777-0442 or 888/625-2632, www.makanda.com, $200–300 s/d low season, $265–400 high season) is blessed by an enviable setting. Eleven elegant, individually styled, timber-beamed villas and studios line walkways that weave through a series of Japanese gardens designed into the hillside. All have king-size beds, vaulted ceilings, polished hardwoods, and minimalist decor that melds Milan with Kyoto. Wall-to-wall French doors open to wraparound verandas. The aesthetic vision extends to a pool suspended on the hillside, with a whirlpool tub and the exceptional Sunsport Poolside Bar and Grill. A complimentary breakfast is delivered to your door each morning. It's a long hike to the private beach, which lacks facilities. Readers have complained about customer service and plumbing.

The luxurious **La Mansion Inn** (tel. 506/2777-3489 or 800/360-2071, www.lamansion inn.com, $125–750 s/d low season; $195–850 s/d high season) is a boutique hotel with a contemporary Spanish colonial theme. It boasts original artwork and tremendous views. Each of the 20 perfumed, air-conditioned rooms and five suites comes with a fruit basket and wine bottle. Rooms feature French drapes, handmade Italian furnishings (including gracious king-size wrought-iron beds), large walk-in showers, and luxurious fittings. The huge one-, two-, and three-bedroom suites have marble bathrooms, en-suite whirlpool tubs, and 24-carat gold faucets! A freeform pool complex is fed by a water cascade from a whirlpool tub. The on-site Bat Cave bar is one of a kind. It also has a billiards room, massage, and a new air-conditioned dining room.

Hotel and Beach Club El Parador (tel. 506/2777-1414, www.hotelparador.com, $135–300 s/d low season, $150–300 s/d high season) stands atop the tip of Punta Quepos, with fine beach views. This flashback to the romantic *posadas* of Spain is adorned with a suit of armor, hefty oak beams, antique wrought-iron chandeliers, tapestries, antiques, and historic artifacts, and thick-timbered wooden doors and shuttered windows from Spanish castles. The 25 motel-style standard rooms (which disappoint), 20 deluxe rooms, and 15 suites (complete with whirlpool tub), however, are

furnished in contemporary vogue. Facilities include a huge terrace bar, stone-lined wine-tasting room-cum-casino, miniature golf course, two swimming pools, hair salon, health spa, and business center.

(**Issimo Suites** (tel. 506/2777-4410 or in North America 888/400-1985, www.issimo suites.com, $215–650 s/d low season, $290–760 s/d high season) enjoys an enviable position with fantastic views. I love its contemporary vogue. Clad with coral stone floors, the nine suites are gorgeous and have leopard-print spreads, wraparound sofas, and heaps of light pouring in through walls of glass opening to stone-paved balconies (the Presidential suite even has its own patio pool). The restaurant has fabulous views, the lounge bar boasts a large-screen TV, and there's a deluxe spa plus a plunge pool used for dive training.

Nearby, the deluxe, eco-friendly **Arenas del Mar** (tel. 506/2777-2777, www.arenasdel mar.com, $220–340 low season, $260–430 high season) was opened in 2008 by the owners of Finca Rosa Blanca Coffee Plantation & Inn, near Heredia, and is the sole hotel with both a forested hillside perch and direct beach access. The sensational Asian-inspired lobby has a huge open-air bar and stylish restaurant (serving contemporary Costa Rican cuisine) opening to a freeform pool with a deck having views over Playa Espadilla, silvered by sunlight through the trees. The 38 one- and two-bedroom, air-conditioned suites in seven three-story blocks have a stylish contemporary aesthetic, divinely comfortable beds, flat-screen TVs, Wi-Fi, recessed ceilings studded with halogens, and whirlpools inset in balconies—many with beach views. Families might opt for huge two-bedroom apartments. Its position overlooking *both* Playa Espadilla and Playa Dulce Vida is unbeatable. Golf carts ferry you up and down from the parking lot and to the hotel's beach club at Playitas, where some of the guest rooms are located. One thing I love here—you sleep to the sound of the waves crashing ashore below.

My favorite hotel remains (**Hotel Villas Si Como No** (tel. 506/2777-0777 or

© CHRISTOPHER P. BAKER

Arenas del Mar

in North America tel. 888/742-6667, www .sicomono.com, $185 s/d standard, $215 s/d superior, $240 s/d deluxe, $285–320 suites low season; $210 standard, $250 superior, $265 deluxe, $305–340 suites high season). It has 58 spacious and elegant suites with terra-cotta floors, tropical prints, queen- or king-size beds of rustic teak, mosquito nets, halogen reading lamps, bathrooms with bench seats and glass-brick walls, and French doors opening to balconies with views. It also has apartment units. The original units received a total face-lift in 2007, with high-thread-count sheets, travertine bathrooms, and poured-concrete sofas with rich red fabrics. Even better are the 18 deluxe, wheelchair-accessible units, which have a classy contemporary aesthetic, with king-size beds, oversize sofas, flat-screen TVs, and fabulous bathrooms with huge walk-in showers. Three honeymoon suites have garden whirlpool tubs, and there's a three-bedroom Penthouse Suite. The ecologically state-of-the-art hotel is only one of four hotels in the country that has earned five leaves in the Certified Sustainable Tourism campaign. A pool and sundeck feature a water slide, cascades, whirlpool, and swim-up bar. A second pool is for adults only. The two restaurants are among Manuel Antonio's finest. There's also a state-of-the-art movie theater, conference center, and upscale spa.

Gaia Hotel and Reserve (tel. 506/2777-9797, www.gaiahr.com, $220–760 s/d low season, $260–920 s/d high season), three kilometers south of Quepos, is one of chicest places around. Opened in 2006, this hip, angular, postmodern hotel makes good use of brushed steel and the classiest 21st-century decor, with not a hint of the tropics. Sumptuous suites boat flat-screen TVs, surround-sound music systems, portable phones, home entertainment units, and clinically white decor against rattan and dark hardwood furnishings. The mattresses are divinely comfortable. Get the picture? Guests even get private butlers. The spa is top-class, and there's a triple-tiered horizon pool, a 12-acre nature reserve with trails, and La Luna Restaurant, one of the best in town (not least for the panoramic views).

For better or worse, Manuel Antonio has finally got its first high-rise complex with the opening in 2009 of **Los Altos Beach Resort & Spa** (tel. 506/2777-1197, www.losaltoscr.com), with luxury suites, many to be made available for rent.

Meanwhile, lovers of contemporary architecture may thrill to rent out **Casa Elsa** (tel. www.casaelsa.net, $4,500–14,000 weekly), a chic four-bedroom hillside villa.

Opened in 2009, **The Ocean Boutique Resort & Spa** (www.theocean.com, $300 s/d superior, $350 s/d deluxe, $400 s/d junior suites, $500 s/d suites low season; $350 superior, $400 deluxe, $450 junior suites, $550 suites high season) competes for the luxury stakes with its sumptuous rooms suspended above Playa Biesanz. The architecture is Spanish colonial but the decor, which varies according to room type, ranges from Laura Ashley to Tommy Bahama. Its Antonio's Restaurant promises new levels of gourmet dining hereabouts. Other highlights include the Nirvana champagne-and-caviar bar and a deluxe spa.

Playa Espadilla: The well-kept but overpriced **Hotel Playa Espadilla** (tel. 506/2777-0903, www.hotelespadilla.com, $125 s/d standard, $142 s/d efficiency, $176 s/d junior suite low season; $163 standard $184 efficiency $209 junior suite high season), 200 meters inland, has 16 large units in two-story blocks set in attractive grounds with nine hectares of private reserve accessed by trails. All have air-conditioning, refrigerators, fans, cable TV, security box, and large private bathroom with hot water (four have kitchenettes). There's a thatched restaurant, swimming pool, tennis court, bar, and secure parking. Rates include breakfast and tax.

Food

The following recommendations are the best of many possibilities.

The place for breakfast is **Café Milagro** (tel. 506/2777-0794, www.cafemilagro.com, 6 A.M.–6 P.M. daily low season, 6 A.M.–10 P.M. daily high season), opposite Hotel Casa Blanca, with a full array of coffee drinks, pastries, and sandwiches to be enjoyed on a tree-shaded patio.

Down by the beach, the simple **Marlin Restaurante** (tel. 506/2777-1134, $2–12) offers seafood and steaks in a two-story structure with options for open-air dining. It serves killer margaritas and piña coladas and has happy hour 4:30–6:30 P.M. daily.

The budget-priced **Soda El Parque** (7 A.M.–10 P.M., daily), outside the northern park entrance, has simple patio dining and serves a special seafood dinner nightly.

Worth the journey, **Ronnie's Place** (tel. 506/2777-5120, milugar@racsa.co.cr, noon–10 P.M. daily, $2–10) is *the* place to enjoy simple but tasty local fare, including seafood. Try the caramelized pumpkin in cane juice, best washed down with a piña colada served in a pineapple.

Down on Playa Espadilla is **Restaurant Terraza del Sol** (tel. 506/2777-1015, 7 A.M.–8 P.M., closed Tuesday in low season), a delightful open-air place in colonial style at Hotel Arboleda. Choose from American or Bavarian breakfasts ($8) and a wide-ranging dinner menu—from pastas and chicken wok to cordon bleu ($10).

The rustic but hip *palenque* at **Bambu Jam** (tel. 506/2777-3369, 6–10 P.M., daily) is a fabulous venue. The French-run restaurant serves the likes of beef stuffed with gorgonzola ($15) and mahimahi with almonds and lime ($12). Leave room for the profiteroles ($5).

For romantic elegance *and* tremendous nouvelle cuisine, head to the elegant open-air (**Claro Que Si** (tel. 506/2777-0777, 6:30–10:30 P.M. daily) at Hotel Si Como No. I enjoyed fried squid ($6), roasted bell peppers, olives and avocado salad ($7), stuffed ravioli with seafood and spinach ($10), and chocolate ice cream pie.

Equally romantic by night is the (**Sunspot Grill** (tel. 506/2777-0442, 11 A.M.–10 P.M. daily, closed in October), at Makanda. This classy spot serves *bocas* such as calamari, mussels in Chardonnay broth ($7–9), quesadillas, sandwiches, and huge salads for lunch. Dinner is a romantic, candlelit, gourmet affair; the menu includes gourmet pizzas, scallops with blackberry and balsamic reduction ($20), and divine foccacia with homemade herb butter. The extensive wine list includes many California reserves.

La Lima (tel. 506/2777-9797, 7 A.M.–10 P.M.) at Gaia Hotel & Reserve, offers world-class service as well as mouthwatering dishes. For a starter I recommend the gorgonzola and sun-dried tomato tart ($6) followed by tequila-lime scallops ($25) or pan-seared tuna ($20). A lobster will set you back $45. Sorbets are served between courses.

For fine fusion dining, I also like **Restaurante Kapi Kapi** (tel. 506/2777-5049, www.kapi kapirestaurante.com, 4–10 P.M. daily), where a starter of Thai chicken lettuce wrap might be followed by sugarcane skewered prawns with coconut, tamarind, and rum glaze.

Gato Negro (tel. 506/2777-1728, 6:30–10 A.M., noon–6 P.M., and 6:30–10 P.M.), at Hotel Eclipse, has a warm ambience, conscientious service, and superb Mediterranean cuisine, such as tagliatelle and salad Niçoise, carpaccio, and pastas.

La Hacienda (tel. 506/2777-3473, www.la haciendacr.com, 10:30 A.M.–10 P.M. Mon.–Sat., 4–10 P.M. Sun., $5–25), at Plaza Yara, is a lovely, contemporary themed open-air space serving Mediterranean fusion cuisine, such as grilled marinated pork tenderloin with vanilla port and dried sherry sauce ($7.50). And the elegant and rather formal **Jacques Cousteau Restaurant** at La Mansion Inn (tel. 506/2777-3489 or 800/360-2071, www.lamansion inn.com) is another option for fine dining.

Marlintinis (tel. 506/2777-7474, http://manuel-antonio-restaurants.com, 11 A.M.–10 P.M. daily) made a splash when it opened in 2008. This open-air restaurant serves seafood, including fresh lobster and USDA rib eye and New York sirloin steaks.

You can buy baked goods at **Musmanni** (tel. 506/777-5286, 6:30 A.M.–9 P.M. daily), on the beachfront road.

Information and Services

The **Internet Café El Chante** (tel. 506/2777-9224, 9 A.M.–10 P.M. Mon.–Sat. and 2–10 P.M. Sun. low season, until 10 P.M. daily high season) is the best Internet option and offers international online calling. **Regalame** (tel. 506/2777-0777, 7:15 A.M.–10 P.M. daily), next

to Hotel Si Como No, and **Espadilla Tours & Internet** (tel. 506/2777-5334), by the beach, also have Internet service.

Lavandería Lucimax (tel. 506/2777-2164) has a public laundry.

La Escuela de Idiomas D'Amore (tel. 506/2777-0233, www.acadamiadamore.com), about three kilometers south of Quepos, and **El Paraíso Spanish Language School** (tel. 506/2777-4681, www.elparaisoschool.com) have Spanish-language programs.

Farmacia La Económica (tel. 506/2777-2130, 8 A.M.–8 P.M. daily) and **Centro Médico Manuel Antonio** (tel. 506/2777-2422, emergencies 506/367-7256, 9 A.M.–9 P.M. daily) adjoin each other midway between Quepos and the beach, where there's another pharmacy.

Getting There

Public buses depart Quepos for Manuel Antonio every 30 minutes 7 A.M.–7 P.M. ($0.25) and will pick you up (and drop you off) along the road if you flag them down.

A metered taxi from Quepos to Manuel Antonio will cost about $6.

◖ MANUEL ANTONIO NATIONAL PARK

Tiny it may be, but this 682-hectare national park epitomizes everything tourists flock to Costa Rica to see: stunning beaches, a magnificent setting with islands offshore, lush rainforest laced with a network of trails, and wildlife galore.

Despite its diminutive size, Manuel Antonio is one of the country's most popular parks. In 1994, the Park Service began limiting the numbers of visitors to 600 per day (800 on Sat. and Sun.), and the park is now closed on Monday. Consider visiting in the "green" or wet season. Pack out what you pack in.

Howler monkeys move from branch to branch, iguanas shimmy up trunks, and toucans and scarlet macaws flap by. About 350 squirrel monkeys live in the park, another 500 on its outer boundaries. And capuchin (white-faced) monkeys welcome you at tree-top height on the beaches, where they will steal

© CHRISTOPHER P. BAKER

Playa Espadilla Sur

your belongings given half a chance. Some of them have become aggressive in recent years, and attacks on humans have been reported. *It is illegal to feed the monkeys.* If you're caught, you may be ejected from the park. Studies have found an increase in heart disease and heart failure among the monkey population, attributed to human foods.

Beaches and Trails

The park has four lovely beaches: **Espadilla Sur, Manuel Antonio, Escondido,** and **Playita.** The prettiest is Playa Manuel Antonio, a small scimitar of coral-white sand with a small coral reef. It's separated from Playa Espadilla Sur by a *tombolo*—a natural land bridge formed over eons through the accumulation of sand—tipped by **Punta Catedral,** an erstwhile island now linked to the mainland. Playa Espadilla Sur (also known as the Second Beach) and Playa Manuel Antonio offer tidepools brimming with minnows and crayfish, plus good snorkeling, especially during dry season when the water is generally clear.

At the far south on Playa Manuel Antonio,

you can see ancient turtle traps dug out of the rocks by pre-Columbian Quepoas. Female sea turtles would swim over the rocks to the beach on the high tide. The tidal variation at this point is as much as three meters; the turtles would be caught in the carved-out traps on the return journey as the tide level dropped. Olive ridley and green turtles still occasionally come ashore at Playa Manuel Antonio.

Between bouts of beaching, you can explore the park's network of wide trails, which lead into humid tropical forest. Manuel Antonio's treetop carnival is best experienced by following the **Perezoso Trail,** named after the sloths that favor the secondary growth along the trail.

Hire a guide. The **Asociación de Guías Naturalistas** (c/o Amigos del Parque tel. 506/8894-1358) offers licensed guides by the two park entrances ($20 pp for 2–5 hours). A guide, such as Leo Goding (tel. 506/8821-7532), can spot (and inform you about) wildlife you're not likely to see without assistance, such as the superbly camoflaged and unusually immobile sloths. They'll also show you interesting tree species—among them,

© CHRISTOPHER P. BAKER

Sea Voyager at Manuel Antonio

the manchineel tree *(manzanillo)*, or "beach apple," common along the beaches. The manchineel is highly toxic and possesses a sap that irritates the skin; its tempting apple-like fruits are also poisonous. Avoid touching any part of the tree.

Theft is a major problem on the beaches, not least by the monkeys. Don't leave your things unguarded while you swim. There's parking by the creek near the park entrance ($2.50), but security is an issue. Don't leave anything in your vehicle.

Information and Services
The park is open 7 A.M.–4 P.M. Tuesday–Sunday ($10). There are now two separate entrances, linked by a trail. The main entrance is 600 meters inland of Playa Espadilla, in the village. The second entrance is at the southern end of Playa Espadilla, where you wade across the shallow Río Camaronera; rowboats are on hand at high tide ($0.50), when you may otherwise be waist-deep.

Park headquarters (tel. 506/2777-5185) is within the park.

Camping is not allowed in the park. There are no accommodations or snack bars, but there are showers by the beach.

Getting There
Public buses depart Quepos for Manuel Antonio every 30 minutes 7 A.M.–7 P.M. ($0.25) and will pick you up (and drop you off) along the road if you flag them down.

A metered taxi from Quepos to Manuel Antonio will cost about $6.

Savegre to Dominical

South of Quepos, unpaved Highway 34 leads, almost ruler-straight, 45 kilometers southeast to Dominical. Expect a bone-jarring dirt road. The first few miles south of town pass a sea of African palms. In 2009, the government finally approved funds for completion of the highway, which will become the new Pan-American Highway; expect truck traffic to increase substantially.

SAVEGRE

Twenty-five kilometers southeast of Quepos, at the hamlet of Savegre, a dirt road leads inland six kilometers up the valley of the Río Savegre to the community of **El Silencio**, at the base of the mountains. Here, the local farmers' cooperative operates the **Centro Eco-Turístico Comunitario de Silencio** (tel./fax 506/2779-9554, www.turismoruralcr.com). It's a great spot for lunch and has a butterfly garden, well-marked trails, horseback rides ($20, three hours), and rafting trips.

The **Río Naranjo** and **Río Savegre** flow down from the rainforest-clad mountains and eventually fan out into an estuary in Manuel Antonio National Park. In wet season both offer Class II–V white-water action, fabulous for kayaking. Tour operators in Quepos and San José offer trips, as does **Rafiki Safari Lodge** (tel. 506/2777-2250, www.rafikisafari.com), 16 kilometers beyond El Silencio and 19 kilometers from Highway 21. Rafiki also offers a full-day white-water special ($85 including breakfast and lunch), as well as horseback rides, guided hikes, and kayak rentals. Indiana Jones–types can sign up for the arduous "Bushmaster" hike-and-raft trip into the upper Savegre valley. It also has a tapir breeding and reintroduction program in the works; the tapirs will be released in a controlled environment that includes the lake beside the lodge, as in an African safari game park. You'll need a four-wheel-drive vehicle to get there.

Reserva Los Campesinos, near the hamlet of Quebrada Arroyo, is a 33-hectare reserve with a canopy walkway and trails that lead to Los Chorros waterfall. Guided hikes, horseback rides, plus accommodation at a delightful albeit simple lodge are offered through **Costa Rican Association of Community-based Rural Tourism** (ACTUAR, tel. 506/2248-9470, www.actuarcostarica.com).

Accommodations and Food

Albergue El Silencio ($30 students, $40 s, $47 d) is a rustic lodge nestled on a breezy hill above Silencio village, with views down over a sea of palms. There are nine thatch-and-wood cabins (some with bunks) with lofts with two single beds, screened windows, and tiled private baths with cold water. Rates include breakfast.

You'll love ◖ **Rafiki Safari Lodge** (tel. 506/2777-2250, www.rafikisafari.com, $144 s or $229 d low season, $175 s or $300 d high season including all meals), run by a hospitable South African family. It offers 10 genuine luxury African-safari four-person tents on stilts, with rough-hewn timber beds, gracious fabrics, wooden floors, huge skylit bathrooms with fire-heated hot water showers, and large wooden decks. One is wheelchair accessible; another is a Honeymoon Suite with stone-lined outside whirlpool tub. Quality international dining at the thatched Lekker Bar includes meats from a South Africa *braai* (barbecue). It has a water slide into a spring water pool, and a lagoon great for birding. Dinners for nonguests are offered by reservation (7–9 P.M.).

PLAYA MATAPALO

Playa Matapalo, five kilometers south of Savegre, is a beautiful gray-sand beach two kilometers east of the coast road: the turnoff is in the hamlet of Matapalo. The surf kicks in here (swimmers should beware riptides), and fishing from the beach is guaranteed to deliver a snapper or snook. The beach track leads into

© CHRISTOPHER P. BAKER

Rafiki Safari Lodge

the **Portalon Ecological Wildlife Refuge** (Refugio de Vida Silvestre Ecológico Portalon), where there's a marine turtle protection project (ASVO, tel. 506/2258-4430, http://asvocr.org) that welcomes volunteers.

South of Matapalo, habitation is sparse and the lonesome road is rutted all the way to Dominical, a few kilometers before which you cross the Río Hatillo Viejo; you can hike or take horseback rides up the valley to the **Terciopelo Waterfalls,** a three-tiered cascade tumbling 120 feet into pools good for swimming.

The **Pulpería del Mar,** in the village, offers Internet service.

Accommodations and Food

There are numerous budget and mid-priced accommodations. Surfers gravitate to **Cabinas El Mar** (tel. 506/2787-5278, $10 pp), with simple rooms. It has a tiny open-air restaurant, laundry, and a supermarket.

Bahari Beach (tel. 506/2787-5014, www.baharibeach.com, $45 s/d rooms, $70 s/d tents low season; $55 s/d rooms, $105 s/d

tents high season) offers tastefully furnished safari-style tent-bungalows atop platforms, with tile floors, full bathrooms, and canopied patios looking over lovely garden, exquisite pool, and beach. It also has air-conditioned rooms in the main building. The restaurant is equally airy and serves European classics plus seafood.

Long-time Matapalo resident Charlie Berghammer has lovely accommodations at **Jungle House** (tel. 506/2787-5005, http://junglehouse.com, $65–80 s/d), with six bedrooms in a wooden lodge, plus a bungalow with outdoor kitchen, and the exquisitely rustic "Cane House."

In the hills, **El Castillo B&B** (tel. 506/8836-8059, www.elcastillo.net, $75 s/d low season, $95 s/d high season), two kilometers inland, is a beautiful two-story modern house with a huge, columned atrium TV lounge with half-moon sofa with views through the arcing doorway. It has four bedrooms modestly furnished in rattan, with raised, beamed ceilings. They open to a wraparound veranda. There's a spring-fed plunge pool. The turnoff is 0.5

kilometer north of Matapalo; you'll need a 4WD. Rates include breakfast.

Another hillside delight, **La Palapa Resort** (tel. 506/2787-5050, www.lapalapahotel.com, $40 s or $60 d room, $90 s/d bungalow), inland of Portalon, has delightfully furnished rooms and spacious bungalows with kitchens set in landscaped grounds with a pool and open-air, thatched Peruvian restaurant.

For something more rustic, from Portalon head into the mountains and the Río División valley, where **Finca Tres Semillas** (tel. 506/8371-5869, www.finca3semillas.com, $60 pp, $25 students, $20 volunteers including meals), an ecolodge with eight simple but spotless rooms. Run by Tamara Newton and Gerardo Saenz, it adjoins the Los Santos Forest Reserve, perfect for nature hikes.

Farther south, **Albergue Alma de Hatillo B&B** (tel. 506/8850-9034, www.cabinas alma.com, $45 s/d low season, $60 s/d high season), in Hatillo, is a pleasant option run by a personable Polish woman, Sabina. It has eight simple rooms in three cabins furnished with custom-made bamboo furniture and original artwork, ceiling fans, coffeemakers, minifridges, and hot showers.

The **Hotel E Coquito** (www.elcoquito.com) has metamorphosed from eight *cabinas* into an upscale condo-hotel project with 22 villas. It was a work in progress at last visit.

My favorite place to eat is **Soda Chasa** (no tel., 8 A.M.–6 P.M.), a rustic open-air restaurant on the main road. Here Miguel and his grandmother serve typical Costa Rica dishes at bargain prices.

Getting There

A bus departs San José daily for Dominical and Uvita at 3 P.M. via Quepos (departing Quepos at 7 P.M.) and passing Matapalo at 8:30 A.M. Another bus departs weekends at 5 A.M. (departing Quepos at 9:15 A.M.) and passes Matapalo at 10:45 A.M. The northbound bus departs Uvita at 4:30 A.M. and Dominical at 6 A.M., passing Matapalo at 6:30 A.M. On weekends, a second bus departs Uvita at 12:30 P.M. and Dominical at 1:15 P.M., passing Matapalo at 2:30 P.M.

Costa Ballena

Completion of the Costanera Sur Highway in recent years has opened up one of Costa Rica's most inaccessible regions: the lush, once untrammeled section of coastline south of Dominical. The paved highway slices south along the forested coast past long beaches with pummeling surf and estuaries full of wildlife. The pencil-thin coastal plain is backed by steep mountains perfect for hiking and horseback trips.

The region is a new frontier of quickening development. Alas, the boom in construction in the coastal mountains is threatening the coral reefs and Terraba-Sierpe mangroves with sediment and untreated waste, causing algal blooms.

The **Cámara de Turismo de Costa Ballena** (Costa Ballena Chamber of Tourism, www.costa ballenacr.com) is a good resource.

DOMINICAL AND VICINITY

Dominical, 45 kilometers southeast of Quepos, is a tiny, laid-back "resort" favored by surfers, backpackers, and the college-age crowd. The four-kilometer-long beach is beautiful albeit pebbly, and the warm waters attract whales and dolphins close to shore. Río Barú supposedly empties polluted waters into the sea near the beach north of the village. The beach extends south five kilometers from Dominical to **Dominicalito,** a little fishing village in the lee of Punta Dominical.

Swimming is dangerous because of riptides. **Dominical Lifeguards** (tel. 506/2787-0210) are on duty 8 A.M.–5 P.M.

If you overdose on the sun, sand, and surf, head into the lush mountains inland of Dominicalito, where a series of dirt roads lead steeply uphill to **Escaleras** (Staircases), a

DOMINICAL AND VICINITY

To San Isidro de El General

To Quepos

Barú

(243)

HACIENDA BARÚ

HACIENDA BARÚ NATIONAL WILDLIFE REFUGE

Río Barú

CASCADAS FARALLAS

Platanillo

PARQUE REPTILANDIA

PARAÍSO TROPICAL HOTEL

DON LULO'S (NAUYACA WATERFALLS)

POLICE CHECKPOINT

VILLAS RÍO MAR RESORT

Playa Barú

Dominical

Fila Cariblanco

Río Diamante

PLAZA SUITES

SEE DETAIL

HOTEL/BAR/ RESTAURANTE ROCA VERDE

VILLA AMBIENTE

COSTA PARAÍSO LODGE

COCONUT GROVE

FORD

Escaleras

RESERVA BIOLÓGICA/ LA DANTA

Playa Dominical

NECOCHEA INN

BELLA VISTA RANCH LODGE

Punta Dominical

PACIFIC EDGE

VILLAS ESCALERAS

CUNA DEL ÁNGEL

CLÍNICA GONZÁLEZ/PHARMACY/ SOLID CAR RENTAL

SOUTHERN EXPEDITIONS/ LAVANDERÍA LAS OLAS

ADVENTURE EDUCATION CENTER

PUEBLO DEL RÍO PLAZA

FRUTERÍA

BLOWFISH SURF SHOP/CHAPYS

BAR MARACATÚ

ATV TOURS

DOMINICAL SURF ADVENTURES

HOTEL RÍO LINDO/ CAFÉ DELICIAS

POSADA DEL SOL

COMPLEJO ARENA Y SOL

PLAZA PACÍFICA/ BANK/ SUPERMARKET

DOMINICAL BACKPAKERS HOSTEL

SUNDANCE

SAN CLEMENTE BAR & GRILL/ POST OFFICE/INTERNET CAFÉ

CABINAS SAN CLEMENTE

SUPERMARKET

COSTA RICA DIVE & SURF

CAMPING ANTORCHAS

DIUWAK HOTEL

ICE

PINEAPPLE SURF SHOP

POLICE

TORTILLA FLATS

SOUTH WAVE SURF SHOP

THRUSTERS

RESTAURANTE COCO

HOTEL DOMILOCOS/ CONFUSIONES

PIRANYS

CAFÉ DEL SUEÑO

PACIFIC

0   2 mi

0   2 km

OCEAN

© AVALON TRAVEL

CENTRAL PACIFIC

forest-clad region fantastic for horseback rides. Alternately, head east on a paved road that leads to San Isidro, winding up through the valley of the Río Barú into the Fila Costanera mountains, where the climate cools and you may find yourself amid swirling clouds.

Reserva Biológica La Danta

Whenever I research Costa Rica, I delight in visiting this rustic, secluded, 10-hectare, economically sustainable fruit farm (Apdo. 2-8000, San Isidro de El General, cellular tel. 506/8396-6206 or 506/2787-8141), formerly called Finca Brian y Emilia, in Escaleras. It's run by Missouri transplant Brian, with his charming and artistic daughter, Emilia. Brian has about 100 species of fruit trees in production (many of them unusual species such as the mangosteen, lanson, rambutan, and the deliciously sweet but foul-smelling durian, as well as nuts and spices and a collection of local orchids. Brian sees his *finca* as a key to conservation with his unique method of soil improvement through subsistence permaculture. Ecological investors are also needed to amplify the land area of the farm so as to perpetually conserve this unique spot as an important link in the Paso de la Danta biological corridor.

© CHRISTOPHER P. BAKER

chillin' at Dominical

Brian will share his knowledge on a fascinating tour of the mountainside orchard. He also guides visitors on hikes, including a ridge-top trail that leads to a Yosemite-like setting and connects with the Santo Cristo waterfall. The wildlife viewing and birding is fantastic. Ocelots and even pumas are sometimes sighted but more often heard or smelled. Rare chestnut-mandibled toucans and great curassows are common. A three-day minimum is required for the Santo Cristo trek, including an unforgettable overnight with a peasant family.

A day visit (minimum four people) includes lunch, farm and forest tour, and a soak in a streamside rock-walled pool heated by a wood-fired oven ($30 adults, $15 for children under 15).

Volunteers are sought to assist with harvesting fruit and other farm tasks. Volunteers work 40–80 hours in a two-week minimum stay and pay a fee according to the work elected.

A four-wheel-drive vehicle is recommended for the steep 2.5-kilometer climb from the school in Dominicalito. Brian will pick up visitors arriving in Dominical by bus at no charge.

◖ Hacienda Barú National Wildlife Refuge

This national wildlife refuge, one kilometer north of Dominical, was created from a 330-hectare private preserve at Hacienda Barú (tel. 506/2787-0003, www.haciendabaru.com). It protects three kilometers of beach plus mangrove swamp and at least 40 hectares of primary rainforest: a safe haven for anteaters, ocelots, kinkajous, tayras, capuchin monkeys, and jaguarundis. More than 310 bird species have been recorded, from roseate spoonbills to curassows and owls. Olive ridley and hawksbill turtles come ashore to nest at Playa Barú. Seven kilometers of trails ($6 pp) lead through pasture, fruit orchards, cacao plantations, and forest. Petroglyphs carved onto large rocks are the most obvious remains of what may be an ancient ceremonial site. Other highlights include a birding tower, orchid garden, butterfly garden, and turtle hatchery.

There's a canopy observation platform suspended 30 meters up, and guided tree-climbing is offered. You can rent horses. A series of guided hikes include early-morning birding

($35 including breakfast), and "A Night in the Jungle" that ends at a fully equipped jungle tent camp ($60).

◀ Parque Reptilandia

Well worth the drive, Reptile Park (tel. 506/2787-8007, www.crreptiles.com, 9 A.M.–4:30 P.M. daily, $10 adults, $1 children), near Platanillo, about 10 kilometers east of Dominical, is one of the best-laid-out animal parks in the country. Large cages and tanks display turtles, crocodiles, snakes (including 16 species of vipers, not least the dreaded fer-de-lance, plus sea snakes), lizards, and poison-dart frogs from throughout Latin America. It even has a komodo dragon from Indonesia. Night tours are offered by appointment. Friday is feeding day.

Don Lulo's Nauyaca Waterfalls

Near Platanillo, signs point the way east to these magnificent waterfalls, tumbling 70 meters in two cascades that plunge into deep pools good for swimming. They're surrounded by tropical moist forest full of wildlife accessed by trails. The falls, which are six kilometers east of the road, also go by other names: Don Lulo's and Santo Cristo. You can reach them on horseback from Escaleras or from **Don Lulo's** (tel. 506/2787-8013, www.cataratasnauyaca.com), at Platanillo, where a trail leads via the hamlet of Libano. Guided horseback tours leave at 8 A.M. and 2 P.M. ($45, reservations essential). Don Lulo also has a mini zoo with macaws, toucans, and *tepezcuintles*. Tour companies in Dominical offer trips to the falls.

Entertainment

San Clemente Bar & Grill (tel. 506/2787-0055) has a pool table, table football, darts, ping-pong, and a large TV showing videos and sports events.

Thrusters (tel. 506/2787-0127, 10 A.M.–2 A.M. daily) is a stone-and-thatch bar with pool tables, and a disco on weekend. And at **Maracatú** (tel. 506/2787-0091, 11 A.M.–midnight), a rasta DJ named Ranks plays reggae on Thursday nights, while Wednesday is ladies'

night. The happening scene, however, is **Roca Verde** (7 A.M.–2 A.M.) bar (with large-screen TV) one kilometer south of Dominical; live music is offered on Sunday afternoon, and the Saturday night disco is legendary ($3).

At **Confusione** (tel. 506/2787-0244, 7 A.M.–11:30 P.M. daily), accomplished classical guitarists perform during dinner—reason enough to eat there.

And **Cuna del Angel** (tel. 506/2222-0704, www.cunadelangel.com), nine kilometers south of Dominical, has live classical music at 8 P.M. each third Saturday of the month ($25, or $45 with dinner).

Sports and Recreation

Surfing is the name of the game, and outfits offering board rentals and gear include **South Wave** (tel. 506/2787-0260), **Pineapple Surf Shop** (tel. 506/2787-0302), **Blowfish** (tel. 506/2787-0420), and **Dominical Surf & Adventures** (tel. 506/2787-0431, www.dominicalsurfadventures.com), which has tours. **Costa Rica Dive & Surf** (tel. 506/8319-5392, www.costaricadiveandsurf.com) has surf and dive tours plus PADI certification.

Southern Expeditions (tel. 506/2787-0100, www.southernexpeditionscr.com) offers all manner of active excursions, from a crocodile night safari to scuba diving.

Tree of Life Tours (tel. 506/2787-8133, www.treeoflifetours.com) offers guided hikes, rappelling, and horseback trips. **Rancho Savegre** (tel. 506/8834-8687, www.costaricahorsevacation.com) has beach and mountain horseback rides at 7:30 A.M. and 1:30 P.M. ($58).

Adventure Aviation (tel. 506/2787-8266, adventure_aviation@gmail.com) will take you up in ultralight aircraft.

Accommodations

CAMPING AND BACKPACKERS' DORMS

Theft is a major problem, and tents on the beach are routinely burglarized! Stick to **Camping Antorchas** (tel. 506/2787-0307, $5 pp camping, $10 pp dorm), with two-story shade platforms for tents and hammocks. It also has a dorm room, and three private rooms with

lifeguards at Dominical

© CHRISTOPHER P. BAKER

double beds and shared bathrooms, plus a communal kitchen, laundry, parking, and cold-water showers. You can rent tents ($5 pp).

You can also camp at the following hostels: **Dominical Backpackers Hostel** (c/o Cabinas San Clemente, tel. 506/2787-0026, fax 506/2787-0055, snclemte@racsa.co.cr, $8 pp low season, $10 pp high season) with a female dorm, three mixed dorms, and two private rooms, all with shared bathrooms. At the south end of Dominical, the rough-around-the-edges **Piranys** (tel. 506/2787-0196, piranys@hotmail.com, $10 private room) has colorful offbeat rooms with ceiling fans, mosquito nets, and shared bath.

Green Iguana Surf Camp (tel. 506/8825-1381, www.greeniguanasurfcamp.com) looks like a winning option, but I haven't had a chance to visit.

UNDER $25

The **Posada Del Sol** (tel./fax 506/2787-0085, posadadelsol@racsa.co.cr, $20 s or $30 d low season, $25 s or $40 d high season) has five pleasant rooms with safes and private bathrooms with hot water.

Surfers gravitate to **Tortilla Flats** (tel. 506/2787-0033, www.tortillaflatsdominical .com, $20 s/d with fan, $25 s/d with a/c, $60 s/d suite low season; $25 fan, $35 a/c, $110 suite high season), with 19 modest beachside cabins and rooms—some in a two-story unit—with fans, hammocks on the patios, and private baths with hot water. An upstairs suite has a balcony. Nice! The restaurant is a great breakfast and lunch spot for pancakes with bananas ($3), BLT sandwiches, and other fare.

Cabinas San Clemente (tel. 506/2787-0026, fax 506/2787-0055, snclemte@ racsa.co.cr, from $15 with fan, $30 with a/c low season; from $20 fan, $40 a/c high season) offers 12 large airy rooms in a two-story beachfront unit with a bamboo roof, natural stone, and thatched veranda; some have air-conditioning and hot water. It also has two fully furnished houses for up to eight people.

$25-50

I recommend the ever-improving **Complejo Arena y Sol** (tel. 506/2787-0140, www .arenaysol.com, $20 s or $30 d dorm, $30 s or $45 d standard low season; $30 s or $45 d dorm, $35 s or $55 d standard high season), with cable TV in air-conditioned rooms; some are a tad small and dark, despite soothing tropical color schemes. It has a pool, Internet café, popular restaurant, and a supermarket.

No frills but perfectly adequate, **Hotel Río Lindo** (tel. 506/2787-0028, fax 506/2787-0078, riolindo@baslink.com, $30 s/d with fan, $40 s/d with a/c low season; $40 fan, $50 a/c high season), at the northern entrance to Dominical, has five standard rooms with fans and five deluxe air-conditioned rooms downstairs.

$50-100

The **Villas Río Mar Jungle & Beach Resort** (tel. 506/2787-0052, www.villasriomar.com) recently refurbished its bungalows, which have a lovely aesthetic. But upkeep here continues to be an issue and the overall mood is ho-hum. The mediocre **DiuWak Hotel** (tel. 506/2787-0087, www.diuwak.com, $65 fan, $70 a/c standard, $85 deluxe, $125–135 suites low season; $75 fan, $90 a/c standard, $105 deluxe, $135–160 suites high season) is now vastly overpriced. And despite its superb restaurant, the spartan rooms at Italian-run **Hotel Domilocos** (tel. 506/2787-0244, www.domilocos.net, $35 s/d low season, $50 high season) are a huge disappointment, not least the awful mattresses.

I like the hip **Hotel Roca Verde** (tel. 506/2787-0036, www.rocaverde.net, $75 s/d low season, $85 high season), a colorful place offering 10 air-conditioned rooms in a two-story unit. Ochers predominate (including the sponge-washed cement floor with pebble inlay around the edges), hardwoods abound, and wall murals, glass brick, and tile mosaics highlight the bathrooms. The action revolves around a chic, breeze-swept bar; there's also a pool and sundeck.

Two kilometers south of Dominical, the appealing U.S.–run **Coconut Grove** (tel./fax 506/2787-0130, www.coconutgrovecosta rica.com, $65–110 low season, $75–135 high season) sits in a cove and is a hidden charmer. It has two houses and four bungalows (with kitchenettes), all with air-conditioning, cool tile floors, wooden ceilings with fans, orthopedic mattresses, simple but pleasant furnishings, and verandas with rockers. The owners have lots of Great Danes. There's a small pool and bar with hammocks.

Appealing to birders and nature lovers, **Hacienda Barú** (tel. 506/2787-0003, www.haciendabaru.com, $40–50 s/d low season, $69–70 s/d high season) has six two-bedroom cabins in a grassy clearing backed by forest; each has two doubles and one single bed, fans, hot water, refrigerator, and cooking facilities, plus a patio. There's a moderately priced, thatch-fringed restaurant and a swimming pool.

$100-150

The cozy and attractive **Costa Paraíso Lodge** (tel. 506/2787-0025, www.costa-paraiso.com, $110–140 s/d), two kilometers south of Dominical, enjoys a fabulous location over a rocky inlet. This beautiful, secluded property offers two fully furnished, cross-ventilated guesthouses with lofty wooden ceilings, kitchens, ceiling fans, and bamboo furniture. It also has four two-bedroom *casitas* (two with kitchenettes, two with kitchens). They're set in lush lawns falling down to the shore. It's reached via a steep trail that leads to a beautiful rocky shore.

Promising to be the first deluxe digs in town, **The Villas at Dominical** (tel. 506/2258-0150, www.kiana-dominical.com) had been scheduled to open in 2009 with a deluxe spa and gourmet restaurant. It fell afoul of authorities, however, and at press time its future was uncertain.

Meanwhile, for a truly Zen-like experience, lay your head at ◖ **Cascadas Farallas** (tel. 506/2787-8378, www.waterfallvillas.com, $120–165 suites, $230–275 villas low season; $135–185 suites, $260–310 villas high season), in a forested riverside setting near Platanillo. Run by a delightful Tico-Californian couple, it has a lovely Balinese-inspired aesthetic that makes bold use of lava rock, river stones, and bamboo and has a feng shui layout tiered up the hillside. Three villas each have two huge, individually decorated suites with stone-lined bathrooms. All have forest-view balconies and

CENTRAL PACIFIC

gardens; two rooms have king-size canopied bamboo beds. An open lounge with huge bamboo sofas puts you up close and personal with the forest. Vegan meals are served. It's popular with yoga groups.

Another great bet for yoga enthusiasts is **Bamboo Dancer** (tel. 506/8841-7954, www.bamboodancer.com), a dedicated yoga retreat in Dominical.

IN ESCALERAS

For a totally rustic escape, head to **Reserva Biológica La Danta** (tel. 506/8396-6206 or 506/2787-8141, $75 pp), where guests can find harmony with nature. Your home away from home is a cozy albeit spartan cabin—"Ocelot House"—with private bath and a solar-heated shower. It sleeps three; a folding cot on the balcony can accommodate a fourth person. At night, after Costa Rican–style all-natural meals, you can soak by starlight in the rock-walled hot tub. Advance reservations and a two-night minimum stay are required. Rates include meals, snacks, hot tub, and tour (children under 15 pay $25).

The **Bella Vista Ranch Lodge** (tel. 506/2787-8069 or U.S. tel. 877/268-2916, www.bellavistalodge.com, $45 s/d room, $65 cabin low season; $45 room, $75 cabin high season) is a rustic Colorado-style ranch perched loftily on a plateau with sweeping coastal vistas. The converted farmhouse has four simple but comfortable rooms with shared bath and solar-heated water. There are also spacious two-bedroom cabins with all-around screened windows and verandas. The lodge specializes in horseback tours.

For something more exquisite, try **The Necochea Inn** (tel. 506/2787-0155, www.thenecocheainn.com, $65–100 low season, $75–125 high season), a luxuriously appointed hideaway with four rooms with individual and eclectic decor, including hardwood floors and private balconies. Two rooms (one with king-size bed) share a bathroom with whirlpool tub and double sinks. A master suite also has a king-size bed, whirlpool tub, glass shower, and wraparound deck with ocean views. The

inn has a game room, library, and full bar, plus a pool with sundeck that stair-steps to natural springs. Rates include gourmet breakfast.

Another of my favorites, **Pacific Edge** (tel. 506/2787-8010, www.pacificedge.info, $50 s/d standard, $60 s/d deluxe, $75 s/d bungalow), reached via its own steep dirt road at Kilometer 148 off the highway, has four cabins stair-stepping down the lower mountain slopes. The coast vistas are awesome and can be best enjoyed from a purpose-built lookout! One is a two-bedroom, two-bath bungalow with living room and kitchen. Each cabin has a "half-kitchenette." And there's an exquisite freeform pool and deck with views. It's run by an amiable Californian, Susie, and her affable Limey husband, George Atkinson. Susie whips up mean cuisine spanning the globe in her bamboo restaurant.

Self-catering? A marvelous deluxe option is **Villa Escaleras** (in North America tel. 630/456-4229 or 866/658-7796, www.vrbo.com/52302, from $240), one kilometer south of Bella Vista, with staggering views. It offers four deluxe, vaulted-ceiling bedrooms boasting an exquisite aesthetic. The 4,000-square-foot villa has a bar and library, and swimming pool and terrace. Several other deluxe rental villas are represented by **Luna Roja Rentals** (tel. 506/8821-4047, http://lunarojarentals.com).

SOUTH OF DOMINICAL

The **Cuna del Ángel** (tel. 506/2222-0704, www.cunadelangel.com, $79 s/d standard, $134 s or $143 d deluxe low season; $97 s/d standard, $170 s or $178 d deluxe high season), nine kilometers south of Dominical, combines classical and contemporary themes. In 2008 it became a member of the prestigious Small Distinctive Hotels of Costa Rica group (www.distinctivehotels.com). Personally, the overly colorful decor doesn't turn me on. Japanese-style fabrics and terra-cotta floors highlight the 16 air-conditioned rooms with ceiling fans, Wi-Fi, minibars, safes, and hair dryers. There's a full spa, an infinity pool, and a splendid bar, and the circular upstairs restaurant has views. It specializes in sportfishing (www.sportfishingdominical.com).

Food

For breakfast I gravitate to **Roca Verde** (tel. 506/2787-0036, 7 A.M. until the last guest leaves, daily), serving excellent, filling *gallo pinto* or granola, fruit, and yogurt. For lunch or dinner my choice is **San Clemente Bar & Grill** (tel. 506/2787-0055, 7 A.M.–10 P.M. daily, $2–8), with a shaded open-air bar serving hearty breakfasts (including a filling "Starving Surfers Special"), plus burgers, Tex-Mex and Cajun dishes (nachos and blackened chicken sandwiches), and a killer tuna melt. And imagine grilled mahimahi with honey, rosemary, and orange sauce served with fresh vegetables!

Another great breakfast spot, the casual **Complejo Arena y Sol** (tel. 506/2787-0140, 7 A.M.–10 P.M. daily) also does a mean *gallo pinto,* plus ceviche, burgers, and even lasagna.

Serving great Thai food, **Coconut Spice** (tel. 506/2787-0073, from 5 P.M. Tues.–Sun.) offers a romantic ambience. I recommend the spicy fish cake ($5) or Chiang Mai noodle soup ($9) appetizers, followed by prawns in coconut and pineapple sauce ($15).

Caribbean-themed **Bar/Restaurante Maracatu** (tel. 506/2787-0091, 10 A.M.–10 P.M.) nearby specializes in seafood but also has veggie burgers, and all-you-can-eat pasta on Thursday nights.

Sushi has even arrived at **Sushi** (tel. 506/8826-7946, 5–10 P.M.), at Thrusters Bar.

For fine dining, head to Hotel Domilocos, where **C Confusione** (7 A.M.–11:30 P.M. daily) combines elegance with mouthwatering dishes at fair prices. I enjoyed *funghi* á la gorgonzola ($6) and an exceptional penne with shrimp and capers in a white vodka sauce ($8.50). It also has seafood and steaks in a thousand variations! A classical guitarist plays on Friday and Sunday nights, and a violinist on Thursday and Saturday.

The Italian-run **Café del Sueño** (tel. 506/2787-0029), next door, serves mochas, cappuccinos, and the like, although I prefer **Café Delicias** (tel. 506/2787-0097, 7 A.M.–6 P.M. Wed.–Sun.), where pastries, cakes, cappuccinos, and sandwiches can be enjoyed in a lovely airy space.

Chapy's (tel. 506/2787-0283) can help you beat the heat with ice cream and smoothies.

Information and Services

San Clemente Bar & Grill hosts a post office, DHL, and the **Dominical Internet Café** (tel. 506/2787-0191, 8:30 A.M.–8 P.M. daily). An alternative is **Emanuel Internet** (tel. 506/2787-4022, 8 A.M.–8 P.M. daily), in Pueblo del Río.

The **police station** (tel. 506/2787-0011) is at the southern end of the village; the **tourist police** (tel. 506/2787-0369) is also here. **Clínica González Arellano** (tel. 506/8358-9701) and **Farmacia Dominical** (tel. 506/2787-0197) adjoin each other in the Pueblo del Río complex, and the **Centro Médico** (tel. 506/2787-0326), with a 24-hour ambulance, is 50 meters to the south.

Lavandería Las Olas (tel. 506/2787-0105) is open 7 A.M.–9 P.M. daily.

Adventure Education Center (tel. 506/2787-0023, www.adventurespanishschool.com) offers Spanish-language instruction.

Getting There and Away

Transportes Blanco buses (tel. 506/2771-4744) depart San Isidro de El General for Dominical at 7 A.M., 9 A.M., 1:30 P.M., and 4 P.M. Southbound buses from Quepos depart at 5 A.M., 9:30 A.M., 1:30 P.M., 4 P.M., and 7 P.M. Buses also serve Dominical from Ciudad Neilly at 6 A.M. and 3:30 P.M.

Buses depart Dominical for San José at 5:45 A.M. and 1:45 P.M.; for Quepos at 8:30 A.M. and 3 P.M.; for San Isidro at 6:45 A.M., 7:15 A.M., 2:30 P.M., and 3:30 P.M.; for Dominical and Uvita at 10:30 A.M. and 5:30 P.M.; and for Ciudad Neilly at 10:30 A.M. and 3:30 P.M.

The gas station is about one kilometer north of Dominical.

You can rent cars with **Solid Car Rental** (tel. 506/2787-0422, www.solidcarrental.com).

UVITA

South of Dominicalito, seemingly endless **Playa Hermosa** extends south to the headland of **Punta Uvita,** a *tombolo* (a narrow sandbar connecting an island to the mainland), jutting

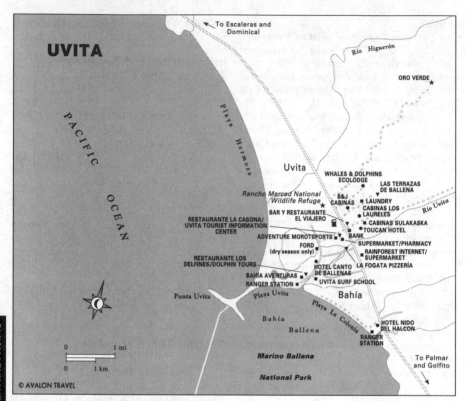

out west of the blossoming hamlet of Uvita, 16 kilometers south of Dominical. The Río Uvita pours into the sea south of Punta Uvita at **Bahía,** one kilometer east of the Costanera Sur and one kilometer south of Uvita; Bahía is an entry point to the northern end of Marino Ballena National Park.

Crocodiles abound. A great place to see them is **Rancho Merced National Wildlife Refuge** (tel. 506/2771-4582 or 8861-5147, www .ranchomerced.com), a 1,369-hectare biological reserve on a cattle ranch that includes mangrove wetlands good for spotting all manner of wildlife. It offers horseback riding (8 A.M. and 1:30 P.M., $35), self-guided hikes ($6), and birding ($35), and you can even play "Cowboy for a Day" ($35 half day, $60 full day).

An alternative is **Oro Verde Biological Reserve** (tel./fax 506/2743-8072, www.costa

rica-birding-oroverde.com), a rustic *finca* in the valley of the Río Uvita, three kilometers inland of Uvita. It boasts 300 hectares of primary forest with trails good for birding. It has birding tours (6 A.M. and 2 P.M., $30) and hiking and horseback trips (7 A.M. and 3 P.M., $15–35). A four-wheel-drive vehicle is recommended.

Entertainment
Las Terrazas de Ballena (tel. 506/2743-8034, www.terrazasdeballena.com) hotel hosts free movies each Thursday at 3 P.M.

Sports and Recreation
Costa Canyoning (tel. 506/2787-0033, www .costacanyoning.com, $75) offers waterfall rappelling.

Skyline (tel. 506/2743-8037, www.flyultra-light.com, from $95) offers flights by ultralight planes. **Dolphin Tour** (tel. 506/2743-8013, delfintour@yahoo.com) offers kayak, boat, and snorkel trips, as does **Bahía Aventuras** (tel. 506/8846-6576, www.bahiaaventuras.com), specializing in whale and dolphin trips. **Uvita Surf School** (tel. 506/2743-8022, uvita surfschool@hotmail.com) speaks for itself.

You can buzz around on an ATV with **Adventure Motorsports** (tel. 506/2743-8281, www.jungleatv.com).

Accommodations

You can camp for $6 pp at **Toucan Hotel** (tel. 506/2743-8140, www.tucanhotel.com, $10 pp dorm room, $26–30 s/d with a/c). This well-run place operated by a friendly Yankee named Steven is also the first choice for backpackers. You can sleep in a hammock ($6 pp). Three dorm rooms (each different) share a bathroom. Seven air-conditioned rooms have private bathrooms. Guests have free Internet access, laundry, a Sony PlayStation, TV/VCR, and DVD player. There's a communal kitchen, plus a restaurant and bar with Caribbean-themed menu.

You can also camp at the rustic **Cabinas Los Laureles** (tel. 506/2743-8008, www.cabinas loslaureles.com, $10 pp camping, $30–50 room s/d), in Uvita, set amid a grove of laurel trees. Four rooms have private baths and cold water. There are also four twin-story, pitched-roofed *cabinas* with timber beams and private baths, plus parking and porch. Congenial owner Victor Pérez offers horseback trips ($10 per hour) or boat rides to Marino Ballena National Park.

Cabinas Sulakaska (tel. 506/2743-8998), near Toucan Hotel, is an uninspired also-ran budget option if all else fails.

There are about one dozen modest budget options in Bahía, including **Hotel Canto de Ballenas** (tel. 506/2743-8085 or 506/2248-2538, www.turismoruralcr.com, $43 s or $54 d low season, $58 s or $72 d high season), run by the rural cooperative Coopeuvita. It has 12 spacious, rustic, cross-ventilated rooms in wooden huts. Four are handicapped-equipped. Rates include breakfast. Competing in the same price range: **Cabinas Hegalva** (tel. 506/2743-8016).

Despite its fabulous hilltop location overlooking Playa Ballena, the architecturally misguided and overpriced **Whales & Dolphins Ecolodge** (tel. 506/2743-8150, www.whalesand dolphins.net, $104–115 s, $126–143 d low season; $143–170 s, $181–203 d high season) fails to inspire and is far from an "ecolodge," although the open-air restaurant and bar with views are delightful. It's also a tough haul requiring a four-wheel drive car to get up the hill.

My favorite place hereabouts is **◖ Las Terrazas de Ballena** (tel. 506/2743-8034, www.terrazasdeballena.com, $120–150 s/d low season; $150–170 s/d high season), in the hills one kilometer inland of Uvita. Formerly Balcón de Uvita, this charming enclave around an old wooden home has been expanded and stylishly upgraded with a gorgeous Balinese aesthetic under new owners. It has three well-ventilated, stone-walled, thatched cabins with screened windows, orthopedic mattresses, huge walk-in showers with solar-heated water, and broad balconies with vast views; two have king-size beds. There's a marvelous candlelit restaurant, the exotic Buddha bar, and sumptuous open-air lounge with hip rattan furniture and Wi-Fi. A guitar-shaped pool is inset in the stone sundeck. A four-wheel drive vehicle is required. Rates include tax.

Makara Resort & Spa (tel. 506/2786-5318, http://makararesorts.com) promises to set a new standard of luxury if and when it opens, perhaps in 2010.

Food

The best place for miles is **◖ Las Terrazas de Ballena** (tel. 506/2743-8034, www.terrazasde ballena.com), serving comfort food such as burgers and grilled cheese sandwiches, plus gourmet fusion fare like tuna carpaccio, or jumbo shrimp marinated in orange juice, ginger, and honey and rolled in shaved coconut and served with sweet chili sauce ($19.50). *Yum!*

La Fogata Pizzería (tel. 506/2743-8284, 5–9 P.M. Monday and Wed.–Fri., noon–9 P.M. Sat.–Sun., $5–10), roadside in Uvita, has a delightfully rustic ambience and serves pizza from a wood oven.

© CHRISTOPHER P. BAKER

Las Terrazas de Ballena, Uvita

In the mood for sushi? Head to **Cristal Ballena,** which has sushi nights on Thursday at 6 P.M.

For a cappuccino and baked goods, opt for the airy **Kasa Tuya Bakery** (tel. 506/2743-8060), in the heart of Uvita.

Information and Services

Toucan Hotel has Internet service, as does **Online Uvita** (tel. 506/2743-8489, www .onlineuvita.com). The **Consultorio Médico** (tel. 506/2743-8310), next door, has a pharmacy. You can pick up the local scoop at **Uvita Tourist Information Center** (tel. 506/2743-8072 or 506/8843-7142, www.uvita.info), also at the junction.

There's a **police station** on the highway in Uvita; it has no telephone (call the grocery next door, tel. 506/2743-8043).

Getting There

Transportes Blanco buses (tel. 506/2771-4744) for Uvita depart San Isidro from Calle 1, Avenidas 4/6, at 9 A.M. and 4 P.M. ($1.50); return buses depart Bahía at 6 A.M. and 1:45 P.M.

Two buses also serve Uvita from Dominical at 10 A.M. and 5 P.M. ($0.75).

MARINO BALLENA NATIONAL PARK

Parque Nacional Ballena Marino (6 A.M.–6 P.M. daily, $6 entrance, Mon. free) was created in February 1990 to protect the shoreline of Bahía de Coronado and 4,500 hectares of water surrounding Isla Ballena. The park extends south for 15 kilometers from Uvita to Punta Piñuela, and about 15 kilometers out to sea. The park harbors within its relatively small area important mangroves and a large coral reef. Green marine iguanas live on algae in the saltwater pools. They litter the golden-sand beaches like prehistoric jetsam, their bodies angled at 90 degrees to catch the sun's rays most directly. Once they reach 37°C, they pop down to the sea for a bite to eat. Olive ridley and hawksbill turtles come ashore May–November to lay their eggs (September and October are the best months to visit). Dolphins frolic offshore. And the bay is the southernmost mating site for the humpback whale, which migrates

chilling at Playa Piñuela

from Alaska, Baja California, and Hawaii (December–April).

Snorkeling is good close to shore during low tides (although sedimentation resulting from local construction has killed off much of the coral reef) and there are caves worth exploring. Isla Ballena and the rocks known as Las Tres Hermanas (The Three Sisters) are havens for pelicans, frigate birds, and boobies. At the southern end, Playa Ventanas has caves accessible by kayak.

There are rangers stations at Uvita (Bahía), La Colonia, Playa Ballena, and Piñuela. Park headquarters (tel. 506/2786-5392) is at Playa Ballena, but the park is administered by MINAE (tel. 506/2786-7161) in Palmar Norte.

Accommodations and Food

All the ranger stations except Bahía permit camping and have showers and toilets; La Colonia has by far the nicest beach and gets packed on weekends.

At La Colonia, the overpriced **Hotel Nido del Halcon** (tel. 506/2743-8298, www.hotel nidodelhalcon.com, $70 s/d low season, $108 s/d high season) is 400 meters from the beach. It offers 14 modestly furnished air-conditioned rooms, a pool, and restaurant.

A far better deal, the nonsmoking **Mar y Selva**

THE GREAT WHALE PARADE

During summer and winter, you can count on humpbacks playing up and down the Pacific coast of the Americas. Increasingly, they're showing up off the coast of Costa Rica. Until recently, scientists believed that North Pacific humpbacks limited their breeding to the waters off Japan, Hawaii, and Mexico's Sea of Cortez. New findings, however, suggest that whales may get amorous off the coast of Costa Rica, too. Whales seen December–March migrate from Californian waters, while those seen July–October come from Antarctica. Thus, two distinct populations of humpbacks exist here.

Ecolodge (tel. 506/2786-5670, www.mary
selva.com, $85–95 s/d low season, $112–122
s/d high season) has lovely digs in the forested
hills inland of Playa Ballena. Ten air-conditioned
bungalows feature king-size beds, satellite TV,
fans, and heaps of light. There's a large swimming pool. Wi-fi is available for a fee.

OJOCHAL AND VICINITY

South of Piñuela and Whale Marine National
Park, Playa Tortuga sweeps south to the mouth
of the Río Terraba and the vast wildlife-rich
mangrove swamps of the Delta del Terraba; the
estuary of the Río Terraba is awesome for fishing for snapper, catfish, and snook. One kilometer south of **Tortuga Abajo,** and stretching
inland from the highway, Ojochal has a large
community of French-Canadians and some of
the best dining on the Pacific coast.

The Costanera Sur continues south to
Palmar Norte, gateway to the Golfo Dulce
and Osa region.

Sports and Recreation

Crocodive (tel. 506/2786-5417, www.crocodive
.com), in Ojochal, offers dive trips, snorkeling,
and fishing, as does **Mystic Dive Center** (fax
506/2786-5217, www.mysticdivecenter.com),
in the Centro Comercial Los Delphines, at
Tortuga Abajo. **Tres Tucanes** (tel. 506/2786-
5214, www.trestucanes.com) has ATV tours
and airboat tours of the Terraba-Sierpe
mangroves.

Villas Gaia offers excursions and activities
from sea kayaking to sportfishing, and diving.

Accommodations

TORTUGA ABAJO

I'm enamored of **La Cusinga** (tel. 506/2770-
2549, www.lacusingalodge.com, $73–136
s/d room, $160 s/d suite), about five kilome-
ters south of Uvita at Finca Tres Hermanas, a
farm involved in reforestation and sustainable
agriculture. It has huge and delightful albeit
modestly appointed all-wood cabins with terra-
cotta and river-stone floors, screened glassless
windows, and exquisite stone-faced bathrooms.
The restaurant is fabulous, with staggering

views, and trails lead through 250 hectares of
primary forest ($5 to day visitors).

I also like the German-run **Finca Bavaria**
(tel. 506/8355-4465, www.finca-bavaria.de, $57
s or $64 d standard, $74 s or $87 d superior), in
the hills one kilometer inland of Playa Ballena
and 0.5 kilometer south of La Cusinga. It offers
five bungalows with a beautiful aesthetic that
includes louvered glass windows, raised wooden
ceilings, bamboo and rattan furnishings, halogen lamps, mosquito nets over the beds, and hot
water in clinically clean bathrooms with glass-
brick showers. Trails lead through the forested
15-hectare property. Filling and delicious meals
are served, washed down with chilled German
beer served in steins (dinners are offered for
nonguests by reservation). There's a swimming
pool in the landscaped garden.

Another adorable option here is the **The
Lookout** (tel. 506/2786-5074, www.hotelcosta
rica.com, $74 s/d standard, $84 s/d superior
low season; $89 s/d standard, $95 s/d superior
high season). This hilltop hotel exudes a bold
and beautiful contemporary aesthetic. Paths
weave through lush landscaped gardens to
12 bungalows with delightfully bright color
schemes (such as fresh lime or turquoise and
mint, with crisp white linens), cool tile floors,
raised wooden ceilings with fans, huge louvered
glass windows, and terraces with hammocks. A
mirador offers fantastic views over both beach
and jungle. Gourmet meals are prepared by a
professional chef. And there's a spa.

The Swiss-run **Cristal Ballena Hotel
Resort** (tel. 506/2786-5354, www.cristal-bal-
lena.com, $74 s/d cabins, $159–174 suites low
season; $80 cabins, $207–223 suites high season) is a Mediterranean-style two-story hotel
in 12 hectares of lovely grounds. It has 19 junior suites and suites and four simpler "adventure lodges," all colorfully furnished with
four-poster beds, ceiling fans, air-conditioning,
and TVs. The lovely open-air restaurant looks
over the ocean, and there's a vast pool.

The delightful Dutch-owned **Villas Gaia**
(tel. 506/2786-5044 www.villasgaia.com, $70
s/d with fan only, $80 s/d air-conditioned) is
another good option. The 14 colorful wooden

cabinas dot the forested hillside; they feature muted pastel decor and minimalist furnishings, a double and single bed with orthopedic mattresses, and solar hot water. One cabin is wheelchair-accessible. A sundeck and open-sided thatched bar overhanging the pool boast views down over the forest and mangroves. The restaurant is recommended, and boat tours, snorkeling, fishing, hiking, bird-watching, horseback riding, diving, and excursions are offered.

OJOCHAL

Several options for budget travelers include **Rancho Soluna** (tel./fax 506/2788-8210, soluna cr@yahoo.com, $20 s or $25 d low season, $25 s or $30 d high season), which has two simple rooms and two cabins with private bathrooms. It has a small pool in the garden; camping is permitted. Sitting in beautiful gardens, the French-Canadian **Hacienda de los Sueños** (tel. 506/678-9720, hacienda_suenos@hotmail.com, http://suenos .netfirms.com, $40 s/d) has two rooms in a two-story house, with bamboo and plastic furnishings, ceiling fans, and a simple kitchen. There's a pool, and trails lead into the forest.

The Dutch-run **Hotel El Mono Feliz** (tel. 506/2786-5146, www.elmonofeliz.com, $45–60 s/d room, $75–90 s/d cabins), in the heart of Ojochal, is a fairly simple charmer with choice of no-frills but perfectly adequate rooms and self-contained wooden cabins (two of which share a bathroom). It has a swimming pool.

The best bet here by far is **Diquis el Sur** (tel. 506/2786-5012, www.diquiscostarica.com, $50–90 s/d), enjoying a breeze-swept hillside setting. This is another French Canadian–run option. The two twin-bedroom cabins amid tree-shaded lawns and lovely gardens are cross-lit through huge louvered windows and feature handsome fabrics and modern bathrooms. Meals are served under a lofty *palenque*. And there's a nice pool and sundeck, plus Internet with library.

For self-catering villas, check out **Shelter From the Storm** (tel. 506/2787-8262, www.shelter-from-the-storm.net), or the dramatic Spanish-colonial-themed **El Castillo** (tel. 506/2786-5543, http://elcastillodelsur.com).

Food

A laid-back favorite of local expats, **Ron & Adie's Soda** (tel. 506/2786-5259, 8 A.M.–8 P.M. daily) has all-day breakfast, burgers, fish and chips, and chicken wings spiced up with their own "Jungle Heat" sauce. On Saturday, everyone congregates at **Gringo Mike's Bakery & Pizzería** (tel. 506/2786-5200, 6:30–9 P.M.) for a pizza buffet.

Villas Gaia's elegant roadside restaurant (tel. 506/2786-5044 www.villasgaia.com, 7 A.M.–9 P.M. daily, $2–20) serves filling breakfasts, plus creative sandwiches, excellent *casados* (set meals), and international fare such as superb Thai curry and macadamia-crusted fish fillet. Friday is tapas night.

Belying its boondocks locale, the open-air **[Restaurante Exótica** (tel. 506/2786-5050, 8 A.M.–3 P.M. and 5–9 P.M. Mon.–Sat., $3–22), at Ojochal, is a hole-in-the-wall with world-class cuisine. You dine by candlelight at tables of hewn tree trunks. I enjoyed a green salad with raspberry vinaigrette, Tahitian fish carpaccio, fish filet with banana curry sauce, and shrimps with Pernod Ricard and garlic sauce. It has Wi-Fi.

In 2008, Exótica's founder opened another surefire winner: **[Citrus** (tel. 506/2786-5175, restocitrus@yahoo.ca, 11 A.M.–10 P.M. Tues.–Sat.), setting a new standard for sophisticated dining beyond San José. In fact, it's sublime! Take the stylish contemporary themed lounge with Balinese elements, and rattan chairs beneath wrought-iron chandeliers. I salivated over a gazpacho ($7), Indian chicken curry ($14), and to-die-for *torta de la pasión* dessert. The wine list impressed equally. It holds monthly special events, including belly dancers, tango and flamenco, and sexy Cuban-style cabarets. Congratulations to Belgian owner-chef Marcella Marciano and business partner/spouse Sylvain Fillion.

Information and Services

The **police station** (tel. 506/2786-5661) is opposite Crocodive, in Ojochal.

CENTRAL PACIFIC

GOLFO DULCE AND THE OSA PENINSULA

Costa Rica's southwesternmost region is a distinct oblong landmass, framed on its east side by the Fila Costeña mountain chain and indented in the center by a vast gulf called Golfo Dulce. Curling around the gulf to the north is the mountainous, hook-shaped Peninsula de Osa and, to the south, the pendulous Peninsula de Burica. North and south of the gulf are two broad fertile plains smothered by banana plantations—the Valle de Diquis, to the northwest, separating the region from the central Pacific by a large mangrove ecosystem fed by the Río Grande de Terraba; and the Valle de Coto Colorado, extending south to the border with Panamá.

Nature lovers with a taste for the remote and rugged will find themselves in their element. A seamless expanse of rainforest enfolds the few towns and scattered settlements, many of them small beach communities beloved by diehard surfers. Star billing goes to the Osa Peninsula, smothered in a vast wilderness filled with the stentorian roar of howler monkeys, the screeches of scarlet macaws, and the constant dripping of water. Much of the jungle— a repository for some of the nation's greatest wildlife treasures—is protected within a series of contiguous parks and reserves served by remote jungle lodges.

The region is the largest gold source in the country, as it has been since pre-Columbian times. In the early 1980s, gold fever destroyed thousands of hectares of the Osa forests: The physical devastation was a deciding factor in the creation of Corcovado National Park. Rivers such as the Tigre and Claro still produce

© CHRISTOPHER P. BAKER

HIGHLIGHTS

◖ Terraba-Sierpe Wetland Reserve: This vast mangrove ecosystem teeming with wildlife can be explored by boat from Sierpe and Ojochal (page 483).

◖ Drake Bay: A dramatic setting close to Corcovado and Caño Island adds to the appeal of this hidden corner, where nature lodges specialize in sportfishing and diving. A nighttime insect tour is guaranteed to be fascinating and educational. It's now accessible by an improved road, but you'll still need to ford three rivers (page 485).

◖ Corcovado National Park: Jaguars, tapirs, crocodiles, colorful snakes, and monkeys and scarlet macaws galore are among the easily seen wildlife in this rugged rainforest reserve. Numerous lodges and tent-camps nearby grant access (page 501).

◖ Playa Zancudo: A magnificent beach and dramatic setting combine with low-key accommodations to provide a lazy, laid-back retreat where all you need is a hammock and swimwear (page 512).

◖ Pavones: This surfers' paradise has it all: great waves, stupendous palm-shaded beaches, and plenty of budget options for eats and places to rest your head. Tiskita Lodge is a rustic delight for nature lovers (page 515).

◖ Isla de Cocos National Park: This remote isle is off-limits to all but experienced scuba divers, who come to commune with pelagic creatures, including whale sharks, rays, and hammerhead sharks (page 518).

◖ Paradise Garden: You'll learn fascinating lore about plants, including their medicinal qualities, at this tropical garden lovingly tended by its North American creator and owner (page 519).

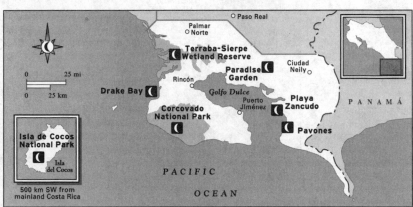

LOOK FOR ◖ TO FIND RECOMMENDED SIGHTS, ACTIVITIES, DINING, AND LODGING.

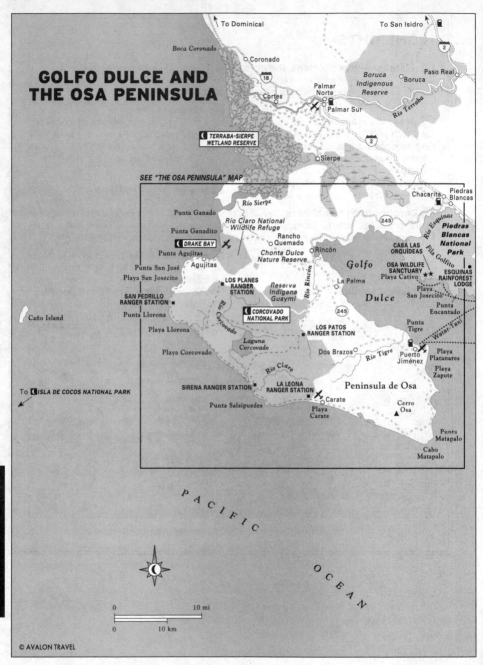

© AVALON TRAVEL

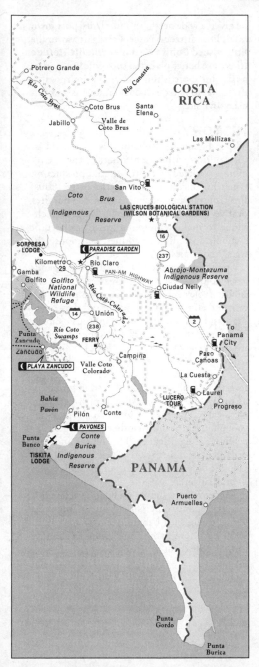

sizeable nuggets; former gold miners have turned to ecotourism and today lead visitors on gold-mining forays.

The waters of the Golfo Dulce are rich in game fish, and the area is popular for sport-fishing. Whales occasionally call in, and three species of dolphin—bottle-nosed, black spotted, and spinner—frolic in the gulf, which is charged by luminescent microbes after sunset. Though the gulf is protected and relatively calm, surfers flock for the ripping waves that wash the southeast tip of the Osa Peninsula and push onto the beaches of the Burica Peninsula, where indigenous communities exist in isolation within the mountains. Offshore to the southwest is craggy, desolate Cocos Island.

This is one of Costa Rica's wettest regions. Be prepared for rain and a lingering wet season: the area receives 4–8 meters of rain annually! Violent thunderstorms move in October–December.

The government plans to build an international airport in the region.

PLANNING YOUR TIME

Many visitors come to visit Corcovado National Park—the main draw—or Drake Bay, and fly out after a brief two- or three-day stay. You'll shortchange yourself with such a strict regimen. Allow at least a week.

Scheduled air service is offered to Ciudad Neily, Drake Bay, Palmar, and Puerto Jiménez (you can also charter flights to Corcovado), and Jeep-taxis and local tour operators offer connecting service to almost anywhere you may then wish to journey. If you're driving yourself, a four-wheel drive is mandatory to negotiate the at-times-appalling dirt roads of the Osa and Burica Peninsulas. In wet season, the road to Corcovado can prove impassable to even the largest 4WD vehicles.

Accommodations tend to cater to nature lovers: take your pick from safari-style tent-camps to deluxe ecolodges. Dozens of nature lodges line the western shores of the Osa Peninsula and the contiguous Piedras Blancas, while beach options that primarily draw surfers and the student crowd tend toward the budget end of the spectrum.

GOLFO DULCE

Highway 2 (the Pan-American Highway) cuts a more or less ruler-straight line along the base of the Fila Costeña mountains, connecting the towns of Palmar (to the north) with Ciudad Neily and Paso Canoas (to the south), on the border with Panamá. The towns offer no interest to travelers, other than as way-stops in times of need.

Sierpe, a port hamlet in the midst of banana plantations, is starting point for boat forays into the **Terraba-Sierpe Wetland Reserve** and to **Drake Bay,** the only community on the western side of the Osa Peninsula. Drake Bay has some splendid accommodations for every budget and particularly caters to sportfishers and divers. If you're planning on visiting **Caño Island,** you'll typically do so from here. A coast trail grants access to **Corcovado National Park,** which offers some of the finest wildlife viewing in Costa Rica. Tapirs are relatively easily seen, and jaguar sightings—while rare—are as likely here as anywhere else in the country.

The main gateway to Corcovado is **Puerto Jiménez,** until recently catering exclusively to the surfing and backpacking crowd, but broadening its appeal with the addition of sportfishing lodges and delightful accommodations at nearby **Playa Platanares.** This beach has an enviable setting adjacent to a mangrove ecosystem harboring crocodiles and all manner of wildlife. Centrally located Puerto Jiménez makes an ideal base for exploring the region; water-taxis connect with the laid-back surfers' beach communities of **Zancudo** and **Pavones,** and the otherwise hard-to-reach beaches of Golfo Dulce, where the **Casa de Orquideas** and **Osa Wildlife Sanctuary** are must-visits.

Though it is pulling itself up by its bootstraps, **Golfito,** the only town of any size, can be given a wide berth; this unsavory port town holds little attraction except as a gateway to the little-visited **Golfito National Wildlife Refuge** (there are better places to spot wildlife) and as a base for sportfishing forays and journeys by dive-boat to **Isla de Cocos,** famous as a world-class dive site.

HISTORY

The indigenous peoples of this zone had historical links with South America, and the region was already a center of gold production when Europeans arrived in the early 1500s. Pre-Columbian goldsmiths pounded out decorative ornaments and used a lost-wax technique to make representations of important symbols, including crocodiles, scorpions, jaguars, and eagles.

Spaniards searched in vain for the legendary gold of Veragua and thereafter forsook the inhospitable region for the more temperate terrain and climate of Guanacaste and the central highlands. A unique and ubiquitous element of the region is the perfectly spherical granite balls (*bolas* or *esferas de piedra*) that range from a few centimeters to three meters across and weigh as much as 16 tons. They litter the forest floors and have been found in groups of as many as 25. No one is certain when they were carved or how, or for what purpose, although it is probable that they had religious or ceremonial significance. The spheres and gold ornaments dating back to A.D. 400–1400 provide the only physical legacy of the indigenous Diquis culture.

Most towns in the region were born late this century, spawned by United Fruit Company, which established banana plantations here in 1938 and dominated the regional economy until it pulled out in 1985.

Valle de Diquis

PALMAR

The small town of Palmar is a service center for the banana plantations of the Valle de Diquis and a major crossroads at the junction of the highways to/from Dominical and the central Pacific coast (north), Golfito and the Osa Peninsula (south), and San Isidro and Valle de El General (east).

The town is divided into Palmar Norte and Palmar Sur by the Río Terraba. **Palmar Norte** is the main center, but there is nothing here of tourist appeal. **Palmar Sur,** southwest of the bridge over the river, displays pre-Columbian granite spheres in the plaza alongside a venerable steam locomotive that once hauled bananas. They're now preserved in the **Parque Temático y Museo de las Esferas de Piedra** (The Stone Sphere Museum & Theme Park, tel. 506/2786-7433).

Accommodations

Cabinas Ticos Alemán (tel. 506/2786-6232, $15 s/d, $22 pp with a/c and TV), on the Pan-American Highway, has 25 basic but well-lit motel-style rooms with private bath; some have a/c, TV, and hot water, while others have cold water only. It has secure parking.

Hotel y Cabinas Casa Amarilla (tel. 506/ 2786-6251, $8 pp shared bath, $15 s, $22 d private bath) has 19 clean but basic rooms in an old wooden home, with shared bath and cold water only. The 16 slightly better rooms in a modern motel-style unit to the rear have private bath with cold water only. There's a TV in the lounge.

The nicest place in town is the new **Brunka Lodge** (tel. 506/2786-7489, www.brunkalodge .com, $35 s, $46 d), 75 meters south of Banco Nacional. It has nicely furnished, well-lit rooms with modern bathrooms, cable TV, refrigerator, and Wi-Fi. There's secure parking.

Information and Services

There are two banks, a **post office** (Palmar Norte), and a **police station** (tel. 506/2786-

6320, Palmar Sur). The regional hospital (tel. 506/2788-8148) is in Cortés, an administrative town seven kilometers north of Palmar.

Café Internet B&F (tel. 506/2787-6167), in Palmar Norte, is open 8 A.M.–8 P.M. Monday–Saturday.

Getting There

SANSA and **Nature Air** both fly daily to Palmar.

Tracopa buses (tel. 506/2222-2666) depart San José for Palmar from Calle 5, Avenidas 18/20, at 8:30 A.M. and 2:30 P.M. daily (five hours, $5). Return buses depart Palmar Norte at 5 A.M. and 7:30 A.M. daily.

Buses for Sierpe leave from Supermercado Térraba in Palmar five times daily ($0.50).

SIERPE

The end-of-the-road village of Sierpe, 15 kilometers due south of Palmar, is a hamlet on the banks of the Río Sierpe, trapped forlornly between banana plantations and swamp. Sierpe serves as departure point for boats to Drake Bay and for exploring the Delta de Terraba.

◖ Terraba-Sierpe Wetland Reserve

The 22,000-hectare Reserva Forestal del Humedad Internacional Terraba-Sierpe is a vast network of mangrove swamps fed by the waters of the Ríos Terraba (to the north) and Sierpe (to the south), which near the sea form an intricate lacework of channels and tidal *esteros* (estuaries) punctuated by islets anchored by *manglares* (mangroves). The delta, which extends along 40 kilometers of shoreline, is home to crocodiles, caimans, and myriad birds.

Sports and Recreation

Tour Gaviotas de Osa (tel. 506/2788-1212, www.tourcorcovado.com), **Aldea del Río Sportfishing** (tel. 506/2788-1157, www.al-deadelrio.com), and **Southern Expeditions** (tel. 506/2787-0100, www.southernexpeditions.com)

GOLFO DULCE

all have mangrove and crocodile tours (by day and night), plus fishing and hiking trips. All three companies are dockside in Sierpe.

Accommodations and Food

Cabinas Las Gaviota de Osa (tel. 506/2788-1212, www.tourcorcovado.com, $12 pp) has six *cabinas* with fans and private bath with cold water only. Nearby, newer, and nicer, **Cabinas Sofia** (tel. 506/2788-1299, cabinassofia@gmail.com, $20 s/d) has simple air-conditioned riverside rooms, plus Internet.

No frills, but with a good riverside restaurant, secure parking, and a handy locale next to the dock, **Hotel Oleaje Sereno** (tel. 506/2788-1111, www.hoteloleajesereno.com, $45 s, $70 d) is overpriced for its simply appointed rooms.

On the east side of the bridge, the charming ◖ **Veragua River House** (tel. 506/788-1460, www.hotelveragua.com, $50 s/d) has reopened. The artist owner, Benedetto, has turned this old two-story riverside house into a splendid lodge. Inside is like a piece of Sienna transplanted, simply yet tastefully furnished with sponge-washed walls, old wicker and antiques, aging sofas, and Oriental throw rugs on the terra-cotta floors. There's a pool table in the parlor. The upper floor has a library-lounge. Three rooms in the house share a Victorian-style bathroom with clawfoot tub, louvered windows, and a rocker. One of the rooms is in the loft, with dormer windows and a honeymoon feel. Four cabins in the garden are simpler yet still romantic; some have iron-frame beds. Guests share the kitchen and outside rotisserie oven in a stone courtyard. Tours are offered. It also has a beach house ($120 up to five people).

Run by Gary, a friendly gringo, the riverside **Estero Azul Lodge** (tel. 506/2788-1422, www.samplecostarica.com, $90 pp including meals) is a peaceful place with monkeys in the treetops. The eight spacious, simply furnished all-wood cabins have cross-ventilated screened windows and enclosed porches. Some have canopied beds with net drapes. The upstairs restaurant with river views is nicely furnished and includes such gourmet treats as chicken breast flambéed in amaretto. Gary rents boats, kayaks, and Jet Skis, and he offers sportfishing packages.

Ecolodges accessed solely by boat include **Río Sierpe Lodge** (tel. 506/2253-5203 or 8995-5770, www.riosierpelodge.com, see website for package rates), 25 kilometers downriver from Sierpe near the river's mouth. It specializes in fishing and diving excursions. The 11 wood-paneled rooms are rustic but large, and each has a private bathroom with solar-heated water. Six additional rooms have lofts. There's a dining and recreational area with a library. The lodge also has trails into the nearby rainforests and offers hiking, horseback trips, kayaking, and excursions. It specializes in multi-day packages.

An almost identical alternative is **Sabalo Lodge** (tel. 506/8866-9082, www.sabalolodge.com, see website for package rates), a family-run ecolodge midway between Sierpe and Drake Bay. It offers elegant rusticity and close-up access to the mangroves and rainforest. Rooms and cabins are solar-powered and modestly but charmingly appointed. Home-cooked meals are served, and tours and fishing trips are offered. It specializes in multi-day packages.

Getting There

Buses and taxis (about $20) operate from Palmar Norte. Cabinas La Gaviota de Osa has water-taxi service to Drake Bay, Corcovado, and Caño Island.

The Osa Peninsula

CHACARITA TO RINCÓN

Access to the Osa Peninsula is via a single road that runs along the east coast to Puerto Jiménez (the only town of significance) and Cabo Matapalo before curling west to dead-end at Carate, on the border with Corcovado National Park. The turnoff from the Pan-American Highway (Hwy. 2) is at **Chacarita,** about 32 kilometers southeast of Palmar and 26 kilometers northwest of Río Claro. There's a gas station at the junction.

The road to Puerto Jiménez is paved as far as **Rincón,** 42 kilometers south of Chacarita (beyond Rincón the road is badly potholed and either hellaciously muddy or dusty, depending on the weather). Here you begin to get your first sense of the cathedral-like immensity of the rainforests of the Osa Peninsula.

The **Neotropic Foundation Tropical Center** (tel. 506/2253-2130, www.neotropica.org) at Agua Buena de Rincón has forest trails and guided hikes, including a "Night Walk" at Los Patos, plus kayaking.

Accommodations and Food

The **Cabinas Golfo Dulce** (tel. 506/2775-0244, $20 s, $25 d), in Rincón, has seven basically furnished rooms with verandas in a two-story lodge. Five rooms have shared bath; the rest have private bath but cold water only. It offers boat tours.

Run by a delightful Tico family, **El Mirador Osa** (tel. 506/8823-6861, www.elmirado-rosa.com, $30 pp including breakfast and tax), midway between Chacarita and Rincón, straddles a ridge with glorious views over both the gulf and the forested Osa Peninsula. Five cozy, charming if simple wooden cabins with kitchenettes, and meals (for hotel guests only) served in a homey family setting make this a winner. It has Internet and a small pool, and it offers tours.

I also recommend the Swiss- and Tico-run **Suital Lodge** (tel. 506/8826-0342, www.suital.com, $38 s or $56 d low season, $44 s or $62 d high season), between Chacarita and Rincón. This simple but pleasing wooden lodge has hillside vistas over the gulf. Its three spacious, cross-ventilated wooden cabins sit on stilts and have ceiling fans, mosquito nets, small terraces with rockers, and hot-water showers. Meals are served, and box lunches are prepared. There are four kilometers of trails, including to the beach.

The **Neotropic Foundation** (tel. 506/2253-2130, www.neotropica.org) has a lodge with 14 clean private rooms plus a restaurant at Agua Buena de Rincón. Trails lead into the forest.

❰ **Villa Corcovado** (tel. 506/8817-6969, www.villacorcovado.com, $290 s or $390 d low season, $390 s or $540 d high season, including meals), at Rincón, is gorgeous! The eight luxurious villas stair-stepping a hillside boast sumptuous furnishings in a combination of hardwoods, rattans, and rich, tropical colors, plus precious views from the verandas overlooking a pool sensuously floodlit at night. The gourmet restaurant utilizes fresh produce from the organic garden, and gourmet picnic baskets are prepared.

❰ DRAKE BAY

This lovely bay (pronounced "DRA-cay" locally), on the north side of the Osa Peninsula, lies between the mouth of the river Sierpe and the vastness of Corcovado National Park. It is a good base for sportfishing and scuba diving, and for hikes into several wildlife refuges plus the national park. The bay is named for Sir Francis Drake, who supposedly anchored the *Golden Hind* in the tranquil bay in March 1579.

Most people fly in, or take a boat from Sierpe. You can also drive via a challenging dirt road requiring three river crossings that begins about one kilometer south of Rincón and leads via the community of **Rancho Quemado.** The **Laguna Chocuarco,** near Rancho Quemado, is good for spotting crocodiles and tapirs (the Corcovado Agroecotourism Association, on the western side of Rancho Quemado, offers canoe trips).

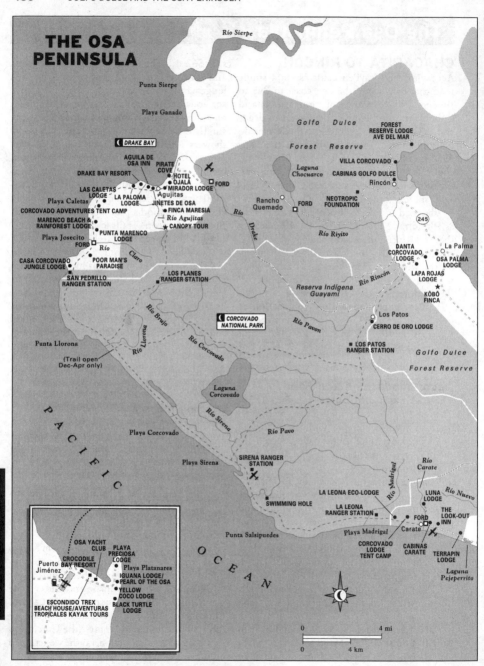

THE OSA PENINSULA

Río Sierpe

Punta Sierpe

Playa Ganado

Golfo   Dulce

Forest   Reserve

FOREST RESERVE LODGE
AVE DEL MAR

☾ DRAKE BAY

AGUILA DE OSA INN
PIRATE COVE
DRAKE BAY RESORT
HOTEL OJALÁ
MIRADOR LODGE
FORD
VILLA CORCOVADO
CABINAS GOLFO DULCE
Rincón
Laguna Chocuarco
NEOTROPIC FOUNDATION

LAS CALETAS LODGE
LA PALOMA LODGE
Aguijitas
JINETES DE OSA
Playa Caletas
CORCOVADO ADVENTURES TENT CAMP
FINCA MARESIA
Río Aguijitas
CANOPY TOUR
Rancho Quemado
FORD

MARENCO BEACH & RAINFOREST LODGE
PUNTA MARENCO LODGE
Río Riyito

Playa Josecito
FORD
Río Claro
POOR MAN'S PARADISE
DANTA CORCOVADO LODGE
La Palma
OSA PALMA LODGE

CASA CORCOVADO JUNGLE LODGE
SAN PEDRILLO RANGER STATION
LOS PLANES RANGER STATION
LAPA ROJAS LODGE

KOBO FINCA

Reserva Indígena Guaymí
Río Rincón

Río Brujo
☾ CORCOVADO NATIONAL PARK
Río Pavon
Los Patos
CERRO DE ORO LODGE

Río Llorona
Río Corcovado
LOS PATOS RANGER STATION

Punta Llorona
(Trail open Dec-Apr only)
Golfo Dulce
Forest Reserve

P A C I F I C

Laguna Corcovado

Río Sirena
Playa Corcovado
Río Pavo

Playa Sirena
SIRENA RANGER STATION

Río Madrigal
Río Carate

LA LEONA ECO-LODGE
Río Nuevo
LUNA LODGE

SWIMMING HOLE
LA LEONA RANGER STATION
FORD
THE LOOK-OUT INN

Punta Salsipuedes
Playa Madrigal
Carate
CORCOVADO LODGE TENT CAMP
CABINAS CARATE
TERRAPIN LODGE
Laguna Pejeperrito

O C E A N

OSA YACHT CLUB
PLAYA PRECIOSA LODGE
CROCODILE BAY RESORT
Puerto Jiménez
Playa Platanares
IGUANA LODGE/ PEARL OF THE OSA
YELLOW COCO LODGE
ESCONDIDO TREX BEACH HOUSE/AVENTURAS TROPICALES KAYAK TOURS
BLACK TURTLE LODGE

0   4 mi
0   4 km

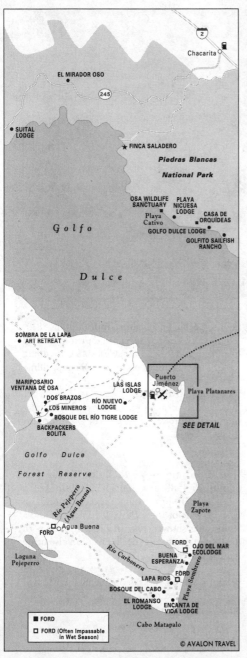

Hotels concentrate around **Agujitas,** a hamlet at the southern end of the bay. Caño Island dominates the view out to sea.

Marine turtles come ashore to nest, and whales pass by close to shore. There's good snorkeling at the southern end of the bay, where a coastal trail leads to the mouth of the Río Agujitas, good for exploration by canoe. You can follow a coast trail south via **Playa Cocalito** (immediately south) and **Playa Caletas** (4 km), and a paternoster of golden sand beaches, ending at **Playa Josecito** on the edge of Corcovado National Park (13 kilometers). There are lodgings along the route; however, hiking all the way is often impossible, as the Río Claro is sometimes impassable, especially in wet season.

The 500-hectare **Punta Río Claro National Wildlife Refuge** sits above and behind Playa Caletas and Punta Marenco. The reserve forms a buffer zone for Corcovado National Park and is home to all four monkey species and other wildlife species common to Corcovado. The area's 400-plus bird species include the scarlet macaw. The Punta Marenco Lodge (tel. 506/8877-3535, www.puntamarenco.com) serves as a center for scientific research and welcomes ecotourists. Resident biologists lead nature hikes ($35).

Farther south, **Proyecto Campanario** (tel. 506/2258-5778, www.campanario.org), bordering Parque Nacional Corcovado, protects 100 hectares of rainforest and has trails. The Campanario Biological Station operates principally as a "university in the field" and offers courses in neotropical ecology and has four-day/three-night "eco-camps" and "conservation camps" for environmentally minded travelers. Accommodations are offered in a field station with bunkrooms and in a simple tent camp. There' only ephemeral electricity. Access is by boat or hiking in.

Nighttime Insect Tour

Professional entomologist Tracie Stice—The "Bug Lady"—and Costa Rican naturalist Gianfranco Gomez run a marvelously educational nocturnal bug-hunt (tel. 506/8867-6143,

GOLFO DULCE

© CHRISTOPHER P. BAKER

Playa Caletas

www.thenighttour.com, 7:30 P.M. nightly, $35). The 2.5-hour tour is fascinating and fun, made more so by Tracie's wit and enthralling anecdotes on such themes as six-legged sex and eight-eyed erotica. Reservations are strongly recommended and can be made through individual lodges.

Sports and Recreation
Costa Rica Adventure Divers (tel. 506/2231-5806 or U.S. tel. 866/553-7070, www.costaricadiving.com) is based at Jinetes de Osa hotel and has dive trips to Isla Caño. **Pirate Cove** (tel. 506/2234-6154 or 506/8393-9449, www.piratecovecostarica.com) also specializes in diving.

The Hotel Ojalá (tel. 506/8868-7385, www.hotelojala.com) and Aguila de Osa Inn (tel. 506/2296-2190 or 8840-2929, www.aguiladeosainn.com) specialize in sportfishing.

Corcovado Expeditions (tel. 506/8833-2384, www.corcovadoexpeditions.net), in Agujitas, offers tours to Corcovado, Isla Caño, and the Terraba mangroves, as well as dolphin-spotting tours, mountain biking, and kayaking, among other options.

The **Corcovado Canopy Tour** (tel. 506/8810-8908, www.corcovadocanopytour.com) has 13 platforms and 11 zipline cables. **Osa Canyoning** (tel. 506/8875-0696) offers waterfall rappelling.

Accommodations
Most lodges deal in multi-day packages; one-night stays are rare because the bay is so difficult to reach.

CAMPING
You can camp at **Vista Bahía Drake** (tel. 506/8845-1588, fax 506/2732-2696, $18 pp with bed, $10 pp with own tent) atop a hill on the east side of the village. It has toilets and a cold-water shower, plus five roomy tents with beds or mattresses on decks. You can also bring your own tent.

You can camp on lawns by the beach at **Playa Caletas** (no telephone, $10 with own tent, $15 rented tent), with bathrooms. Meals are made by request.

UNDER $25
Around Agujitas: If you can't get through to

Drake Bay by land, the nearest lodging is at Rancho Quemado, where **Laguna del Valle,** beside the soccer field, has cabins.

On the north side of Agujitas, budget hounds have **Cabinas Manolo** (tel. 506/8885-9114, www.cabinasmanolo.com, $10 s/d shared bathroom, $15 s/d private bathroom low season; $15 shared, $20 private bath high season), with four small and basic yet clean rooms with ceiling fans and porches with hammocks. Modern bathrooms have cold water only. Next door, seven bare-bones cabins at **Bambu Sol** (tel. 506/8387-9138, $9 pp) are the cheapest around; it has a small *soda* attached.

The **Río Drake Lodge** (tel. 506/8830-9911, $25 pp) is close to the airport north of Drake Bay and has decks for pitching tents ($6 pp), plus simply furnished wooden cabins.

And **Cabinas Murillo** (tel. 506/8892-7702, $15 pp) offers seven simple roadside rooms in Agujitas.

Between Agujitas and Corcovado: It's too steep and demanding a climb to reach the **Cabinas Vista del Mar** to recommend this disappointing budget option, five kilometers south of Agujitas.

$50-100

Around Agujitas: The hilltop **Cabinas Jade Mar** (tel. 506/8384-6681, www.drakebayjademar.com, $45 s/d room, $55 s/d cabin) can be recommended for the views, although the seven wooden cabins are simple yet clean. Rooms vary in size.

I like the simple charm of the no-frills **Hotel Ojalá** (tel. 506/8868-7385, www.hotelojala.com, $67 s/d standard, $79 s/d deluxe, including meals), one kilometer north of Agujitas. This two-story wooden structure has three rooms downstairs, with lofty ceilings, tile floors, air-conditioning and fans, and private bathrooms with hot water. A deluxe hilltop cabin offers views and has a four-poster king-size bed. It specializes in sportfishing and has a restaurant and a whirlpool. Rates include all meals.

The charmingly rustic **Mirador Lodge** (tel. 506/8356-4758, www.miradordrakebay.com,

$45 pp including meals and tax), atop a hill about two miles north of Agujitas, offers great views. It has 13 simple but pleasing rooms in wooden stilt units with bamboo walls; baths have cold water (both shared and private baths are available). There's a deck, and meals are served using veggies from the organic garden; hot meals are cooked in the wood-burning oven. Rates include meals.

Inland, two kilometers along the road to Los Patos, **◖ Finca Maresia** (tel. 506/8332-6730, www.fincamaresia.com, $18 pp dorm, $25 s or $36 d room, $55–75 s/d cabin, including breakfast and tax) opened in 2008 and set a new standard for mid-priced properties with its contemporary minimalist vogue. Run by a Spanish couple, and set on three hectares, it has seven wooden cabins (three types), all with walls of glass, mosquito nets and Guatemalan spreads, and open bathrooms with stylish accoutrements. Larger cabins are Japanese-style and have wrap-around balconies. There's also a dorm.

Between Agujitas and Corcovado: Nature lovers will like the bargain-priced **Marenco Beach & Rainforest Lodge** (tel. 506/2258-1919 or 506/2770-8002, or U.S. tel. 800/2278-6223, www.marencolodge.com, $53–78 s/d), a hilltop lodge set in beautiful gardens at Punta Río Claro National Wildlife Refuge. It has 17 rustic yet romantically adorned thatched bamboo-and-wood cabins, each with a terrace offering panoramic views. Meals are served family-style in a large dining hall.

$100-150

Around Agujitas: Enjoying a splendid waterfront setting, **Jinetes de Osa** (tel. 506/2231-5806, www.costaricadiving.com, $55 s or $66 d standard, $77 s or $105 d superior low season; $66 s or $77 d standard, $88 s or $115 d superior high season), at the southern edge of Agujitas, is a dedicated dive resort with nine rooms, each sleeping three people, with fans, cool tile floors, screened glassless windows, Guatemalan spreads, and spacious bathrooms with hot water.

Also specializing in diving, **Pirate Cove** (tel. 506/2234-6154 or 506/8393-9449,

Corcovado Adventures Tent Camp, Playa Caletas

www.piratecovecostarica.com, $90 s or $140 d bungalow, $70 pp cabin low season; $120 s or $180 d bungalow, $90 pp cabin high season), overlooking the mouth of the Río Drake, north of Agujitas, has a delightful ambience. The lodge has eight elegant wooden cabins set amid landscaped grounds and connected by wooden walkways. It also has simpler yet cozy "bungalows." Each has two beds with orthopedic mattresses, mosquito netting, and deck with hammock. Dining is family-style on a shaded deck. Contact the lodge for rates.

Rancho Corcovado (tel. 506/8889-3221, www.ranchocorcovado.com, $99 s/d standard, $111 s/d superior low season; $105 s/d standard, $116 s/d superior high season), on the beach about one mile north of Agujitas, is of a similar style and standard to Pirate Cove and specializes in multi-day nature packages.

Between Agujitas and Corcovado: I really like the rustic yet Swiss-clean (and Swiss-Tico run) **Las Caletas Lodge** (tel. 506/8826-1460, www.caletas.co.cr, $70–80 pp including meals and taxes), at Playa Las Caletas. The lodge opens to three sides, with open-air family dining and lovely views beyond the manicured lawns. The five simply appointed one- or two-story cabins are cross-ventilated with screened windows and have tiled hot-water bathrooms and hammocks on balconies. The lodge is closed in September and October. Competing hotels may tell you that Las Caletas Lodge has closed; it was not so at my recent visit in January 2009.

At Playa San Josecito, a Tico named Pincho Amaya and his gringa wife, Jenny, run **Poor Man's Paradise** (tel. 506/2771-4582, www.my-poormansparadise.com, from $315 pp three-day packages, including meals, boat transfers, and tours). They have two rooms, plus 12 tent-cabins, all with shared baths. You can also camp ($10 pp, meals cost extra). Meals are served in an airy *rancho*. Electricity shuts off at 9 P.M. Pincho offers sportfishing and tours.

At Playa Caletas, **Corcovado Adventures Tent Camp** (tel. 506/8384-1679, www.corcovado.com, $80 pp) has two-person tents pitched on wooden platforms, protected by thatched tarps. Each has a closet, wooden beds made up with cotton sheets, and two armchairs. It

GOLFO DULCE

has communal washrooms, and hearty meals are served. Guided hikes and horseback rides are offered, and you can rent sea kayaks. Rates include meals.

$150-250

Around Agujitas: Enjoying a marvelous shorefront location on the south side of the mouth of the Río Agujitas, **Drake Bay Resort** (tel./ fax 506/2770-8012, www.drakebay.com, $585–1,020 pp three-night package) is good for multi-day package deals. It has 20 two- and four-person *cabinas* with ceiling fans, tile floors, oceanview patios, and modern bathrooms with solar-heated showers. Some are tiny "economy" cabins, perfect for budget travelers. Four rooms are more upscale; one is misleadingly named a "honeymoon suite." There's a charmingly rustic dining room, open-air bar, saltwater pool, and free laundry. It offers three-night special-interest packages, such as fishing and kayaking.

Between Agujitas and Corcovado: The beautiful **Punta Marenco Lodge** (tel. 506/8877-3535, www.puntamarenco.com, from $339 pp two-night package including meals), at Marenco, has rustic hilltop *cabinas* with cold-water private bathrooms, plus terraces with fabulous views. Family-style meals are served.

OVER $250

Around Agujitas: The class act in Aguitas is the American-run **Aguila de Osa Inn** (tel. 506/2296-2190 or 8840-2929, www.aguiladeosainn.com, from $531 s, $900 d two-night package), at the mouth of the Río Agujitas. The 11 stone-faced deluxe rooms and two suites are spacious and have cathedral ceilings with fans, screened glassless windows, bamboo beds with Guatemalan spreads, and exquisite bathrooms with huge walk-in showers with piping hot water. Junior suites, farther up the hill, have magnificent views and wraparound verandas with hammocks. The focal point is the circular open-air restaurant and bar-lounge. It specializes in diving and sportfishing.

A delightful, serenely landscaped alternative is **Villas La Paloma Lodge** (tel. 506/2293-7502, www.lapalomalodge.com, from $1,155 pp three-night package), which perches atop a cliff overlooking Playa Cocalito and offers a superb view of Caño Island. Seven spacious bungalows—simply furnished with hammocks on the balcony—and five more attractively furnished and comfortable cabins perched on stilts have ceiling fans, orthopedic mattresses, private baths with solar-heated water, and balconies. The clubhouse is a perfect spot for family-style dining. There's a small pool with bar. Hikes and horseback rides are offered, as are boat trips to Caño Island and sportfishing, and there's a fully stocked dive shop. Two beach villas were being added. Rates include meals.

For a private house rental, check out **Drake Bay Beach House** (http://drakesbaybeachhouse.com).

Between Agujitas and Corcovado: Perfect for honeymooners and others seeking solitude is the **(Drake Bay Rainforest Chalet** (tel. 506/8867-6143, www.drakebayholiday.com, from $1,150 pp three-night package, including round-trip airfare), up the Río Agujitas, a 20-minute walk from Playa Cocalito. This open-plan mahogany chalet with full kitchen and full entertainment system (including satellite TV) has vast picture windows and a gracious aesthetic, including rattan furniture and romantic mosquito netting over the king-size bed.

By far the most luxurious place in the region is **(Casa Corcovado Jungle Lodge** (tel. 506/2256-3181 or U.S. tel. 888/896-6097, www.casacorcovado.com, from $995 s, $1,750 d three-night package), run by Chicago expat Steven Lill, who has conjured a wonderful hilltop resort from a defunct cacao plantation. There are 14 thatched, conical *cabinas* (including two "honeymoon" units) with hardwood four-poster beds and mosquito nets, ceiling fans, twin-level ceilings, and huge showers with hot water and designer fixtures. There's a lounge and library, plus a *mirador* bar. Trails lace the 120-hectare property. A small spring-fed pool provides cooling dips. It has guided hikes, sea kayaking, and scuba diving. The restaurant serves gourmet cuisine, family-style.

GOLFO DULCE

Food

The two recommended stand-outs in Aguitas are the hotel restaurants at **Jinetes de Osa** (tel. 506/2231-5806, www.costaricadiving.com), with a rustic but attractive open-air bar that serves Costa Rican cuisine as well as great burgers and hot dogs; and **Aguila de Osa Inn** (tel. 506/2296-2190 or 8840-2929, www.aguiladeosainn.com, 7 A.M.–9 P.M., $5–18), where meals include treats such as sashimi with ginger and horseradish sauce.

Locals gravitate to **Bar y Restaurante Jade Mar** (tel. 506/8822-8595, 6 A.M.–1 A.M. daily), a modern open-air eatery with tin roof and slippery tile floor, atop a hill on the east side of the village. The menu runs from *gallo pinto* ($3) to filet mignon ($10). I enjoyed chicken in mushroom sauce ($5). Food service stops at 10 P.M. It has a large-screen TV and hosts a weekend disco.

Information and Services

In Aguijitas, the *pulpería* (tel. 506/2771-2336) has a public telephone. **Corcovado Expeditions** (tel. 506/8833-2384), in the village, has an Internet café (9–11:30 A.M. and 1–7 P.M. Mon.–Sat. and 1–6 P.M. Sun.). The **Hospital Clínica Bíblica** is by the beach in Aguijitas.

Getting There

Both **SANSA** and **Nature Air** provide scheduled air service to Aguijitas.

A bus for Aguijitas departs Rincón at 11 A.M. daily, and from Aguijitas for Rincón at 3:45 A.M. daily.

A water-taxi departs Sierpe for Drake Bay at about 10 A.M. daily, and from Aguijitas for Sierpe at 7 A.M. daily. The trip takes two hours down the jungle-draped Río Sierpe ($25 pp). Lodges arrange transfers for guests.

The dirt road from Rincon to Aguijitas requires several river fordings; a four-wheel-drive vehicle is essential, not least to tackle the steep and muddy sections in wet season, when you'll want a high-ground-clearance vehicle; you'd be wise to wade the rivers to check the depth and shallowest route across, especially the wide Río Drake.

RINCÓN TO PUERTO JIMÉNEZ

At **La Palma,** 11 kilometers south of Rincón, turn left for Puerto Jiménez. To the right, the gravel and mud road leads 12 kilometers up the Valle del Río Rincón to the Estación Los Patos ranger station, easternmost entry point to Corcovado National Park. Eventually you find yourself driving along a riverbed to reach the park; not possible in wet season! En route, you'll pass the 2,713-hectare **Reserva Indígena Guaymí,** with a primary rainforest reserve.

CoopeUnioro (c/o Cooprena, tel. 506/2290-8646, www.turismoruralcr.com), at Los Patos, is a local cooperative of ex-gold miners who offer guided tours. Pre-Columbian peoples sifted gold from the streams of the Osa millennia ago. But it wasn't until the 1980s that gold fever struck. After gold panners—*oreros*—found some major nuggets, prospectors poured into the region. At the boom's heyday, at least 3,000 miners were entrenched in Corcovado National Park. Because of the devastation they wrought—dynamiting riverbeds, polluting rivers, and felling trees—the Park Service and Civil Guard ousted the miners in 1986. Most *oreros* have turned to other ventures—not least ecotourism—but it is not unusual to bump into a lucky (or luckless) *orero* celebrating (or commiserating) over a beer in a bar.

Back on the road to Puerto Jiménez, **Finca Köbö** (tel. 506/8398-7604, www.fincakobo.com), four kilometers south of La Palma, is worth a visit. This self-sufficient organic farm grows cacao, plus fruits and vegetables, and has trails through regenerated forest and 30 hectares of primary rainforest. A chocolate tour is offered ($28), as is kayaking and even a night tour in the forest.

About 25 kilometers southeast of La Palma, four kilometers before Puerto Jiménez, a turn-off to the right follows the Río Tigre 14 kilometers west to **Dos Brazos,** the old center of gold mining, one kilometer from the eastern border of Corcovado National Park.

Accommodations and Food

Tucked in forest, the charming **Danta Corcovado**

Lodge (tel. 506/2735-1111, www.dantacorcovado.net, $35 pp), about two kilometers west of La Palma on the Los Patos road, is a "Goldilocks and the Three Bears"–style lodge of rough-hewn timbers and cut logs. It has exquisite, albeit simply appointed, rooms in the lodge, plus two tin-roofed, cement-floor cabins in the 12-hectare private forest; the latter have super outside showers and modern toilets. A lagoon contains caimans. Horseback, birding, and hiking tours are offered. Bring insect repellent.

The nicest place around is **Finca Köbö** (tel. 506/8398-7604, www.fincakobo.com, $33 s, $60 d), with a lovely upscale rustic ambience. It manages a gracious aesthetic despite the simple furniture. Six bedrooms are above the lounge and have fans, mosquito nets, and hot water, plus hammocks on the veranda. It serves hearty meals using products from the organic garden.

The rustic **Cerro de Oro Lodge** (tel. 506/2290-8646, www.turismoruralcr.com, $30 s or $35 d low season, $35 s or $40 d high season), 1.6 kilometers beyond Los Patos, is run by the CoopeUnioro cooperative. The six rooms have shared baths with cold water and solar electricity. There are also two three-room cabins. Host Ricardo and his sons, Gabriel and Jordy, conjure tasty meals, served in a rancho-style dining room, using herbs from their own garden. The lodge offers guided hikes and horseback trips. Rates include breakfast.

At Dos Brazos, the rustic yet pleasant wood-and-stone, tin-roofed **Bosque del Río Tigre Sanctuary & Lodge** (tel. 506/8824-1372 or 506/8383-3905, www.osaadventures.com, $116 s, $232 d including meals) adjoins a 31-acre private nature reserve and has four bedrooms, plus a cabin with private bath. It has airy open spaces with Adirondack chairs, plus a library. Birding is a specialty of the owners, who keep the place spic-and-span. A night frog walk, mangrove kayaking, and other activities are offered, as are package rates. Turn left at the school as you enter Dos Brazos; the lodge is 400 meters up the valley, surrounded by forest. You need to ford the river, which can be impassable in wet season.

A basic alternative is **Backpackers Bolita** (tel.

506/8877-7334, $5 pp camping, $8 pp dorm), which rents foam mattresses to campers and has dorms and solar-heated showers. It's a tough 700-meter hike from the end of the road, and you have to cross the river. If you don't want to tackle the river, **Los Mineros Guesthouse** (tel. 506/8835-6258 or 506/2735-5531, www.losmineroscr.blogspot.com, $12 pp shared bath, $15 pp private bath), on the north side of Dos Brazos, has three basic A-frame huts with shared bathroom, plus four no-frills rooms with private bath. Meals are served, and guests get kitchen use. This place once served as the community's brothel. Your room can tell some tales!

House rentals don't get much better than at **❰ Sombra de la Lapa Art Retreat** (tel. 506/2714-0622, www.costaricaartretreat.com), at Agujas; the turnoff from the La Palma–Puerto Jiménez road is about four kilometers west of the Dos Brazos turnoff. This property offers retreats ($2,585 nine days). The gorgeous three-bedroom home surrounded by forest rents for $1,800 weekly low season, $2,200 high season. It's part Gaudi, part Tolkien in inspiration and makes fabulous use of natural timbers and river stone, with open walls and a pool.

Getting There and Away

Puerto Jiménez–bound buses pass through La Palma. Buses serve Dos Brazos from Super 96 in Puerto Jiménez at 5:45 A.M., 11 A.M., and 4 P.M. daily.

PUERTO JIMÉNEZ

This small, laid-back town is popular with the backpacking crowd and surfers. Locals have colorful tales to tell of gambling and general debauchery during the gold-boom days in the 1980s, when the town briefly flourished, prostitutes charged by the ounce, and miners bought bottles of whiskey just to throw at the walls.

A mangrove estuary lies northeast of town, fed by the **Río Platanares.** You stand a superb chance of seeing caimans, white-faced monkeys, freshwater turtles, rays, even river otters and crocodiles—and scarlet macaws can be seen and heard squawking in the treetops and flying overhead. The mangroves extend east

PUERTO JIMÉNEZ

Golfo

Dulce

CABINAS JIMÉNEZ

To Rincón

CABINAS IGUANA IGUANA

THE PALMS

CABINAS AGUA LUNA

RESTAURANTE AGUA LUNA

PARROT BAY VILLAGE

POST OFFICE

RED CROSS

BUS STATION

MEDICAL CLINIC

POLICE

Estero and Mangroves

BAKERY

CAFENET EL SOL

COLECTIVO BUS TO CARATE

SUPER 96

JUANITAS MEXICAN BAR AND GRILL

CABINAS THE CORNER

CABINAS/RESTAURANTE CAROLINA/ESCONDIDO TREX

PHARMACY

RÍO NUEVO ECO-ADVENTURES

OSA PARADISE

RESTAURANTE EL DELFIN BLANCO

SODA Y HELADERÍA KANDY (ICE CREAM)

SURFDOG TOURS

CABINAS/ RESTAURANTE ORO VERDE

CORCOVADO NATIONAL PARK HEADQUARTERS/ VISITORS' CENTER

AIRSTRIP

LAUNDRY

CAFÉ INTERNET OSA CORCOVADO

CABINAS MARCELINA

SANSA

BANK

LAPA RÍOS OFFICE

ALFA ROMEO AERO TAXI

NATURE AIR

BANK

FRIENDS OF THE OSA (OFFICE)

CAFÉ LA ONDA

LA CHOZA DEL MANGLAR

To Corcovado

SUPERMARKET

SOLID CAR RENTAL

To Crocodile Bay Lodge, Osa Yacht Club, and Playa Platanares

BAKERY

CABINAS EYLIN

0   100 yds

0   100 m

© AVALON TRAVEL

to **Playa Platanares** (a.k.a. Playa Preciosa), a gorgeous miles-long swath of sand about five kilometers east of town. A reef lies offshore in jade-colored waters, the forest behind the beach abounds with monkeys and other wildlife (even a jaguar has been sighted on the beach), and the views across the gulf are fantastic. Five species of marine turtles come ashore to lay eggs on the beach, notably May–December. There's a **turtle *vivero*** (hatchery) at Playa Platanares; nocturnal turtle tours can be arranged (no flashlights are permitted).

Jardín Botánico Herrera (tel. 506/2735-5210, $5 self-guided, $15 two-hour guided tours), opposite Crocodile Bay Lodge, is a 103-hectare botanical garden and swatch of rainforest with trails good for birding and animal spotting. The garden part is actually a mosaic, with individual sections given to specific botanical themes. Tour operators in town arrange visits.

Entertainment

The hot spot in town is the open-air bar at **Cabinas Iguana Iguana** (tel. 506/2735-5158, 4 P.M.–2 A.M. daily), where backpackers gravitate to watch surf videos and play foosball and pool. **Juanita's** (tel. 506/735-5056), one block south of the soccer field, has a lively bar and has happy hour 4–6 P.M. daily, plus live music on Fridays and Saturdays.

On Friday nights head out to **Pearl of the Osa** (tel. 506/8848-0752, www.iguanalodge.com), at the Iguana Lodge, at Playa Platanares. Bring your dance shoes for sexy salsa, merengue, and cumbia dancing, fueled by a live band and killer cocktails.

Sports and Recreation

Escondido Trex (tel./fax 506/2735-5210, www.escondidotrex.com), inside Soda Cantina, and Osa Travel (tel. 506/8850-9596, www.osa travel.com) offer active adventures, from snorkeling and sea kayaking to waterfall rappelling and gold-mining trips.

Osa Discoveries (tel. 506/2735-5260, www.osadiscoveries.com) specializes in ATV tours. And **Osa Paradiso** (tel. 506/2755-5857) specializes in surfing trips.

Crocodile Bay Lodge (tel. 506/2735-5631 or U.S. tel. 800/733-1115, www.crocodile-bay.com), **Osa Yacht Club** (tel. 506/2735-5920 or 888/OSA-YACHT, www.osayachtclub.com), and **La Islas Lodge** (tel. 506/2735-5242, www.lasislaslodge.com) specialize in sportfishing, as does **Mar Huron Sportfishing** (tel. 506/2735-5889, www.marhuron.com).

Surfdog Tours (tel. 506/2735-5825) can reserve the above tours, plus waterfall rappelling ($75), tree climbing ($55), and a zipline canopy tour ($75). And **Toucan Travel** (tel. 506/2735-5826, www.toucan-travel.com) has some intriguing tours that include mangrove kayaking ($30).

Accommodations
UNDER $25
Backpackers rave about **The Corner** (tel. 506/2735-5328, www.jimenezhotels.com/cabinasthecorner, $8 s cold water, $12 s or $18 d with hot water), with secure and super clean digs that include a dorm and five rooms, all with fans and private bathrooms. It has laundry and rents tents ($8) and bikes ($1.50).

$25-50
The nicest *cabinas* in town are at the well-run **Cabinas Jiménez** (tel. 506/2735-5090, www.cabinasjimenez.com, $35–65 s, $$50–80 d), offering bay vistas. Kept spic and span, these lovely air-conditioned cabins in various types all come with fans, mini-fridge, safes, lively Guatemalan bedspreads, and porches with chairs for enjoying the views.

Cabinas Marcelina (tel. 506/2735-5286, fax 506/2735-5007, cabmarce@hotmail.com, $40 s/d with fan, $50 s/d air-conditioned), 200 meters south of the soccer field, has upgraded and offers six simply furnished, clean, and charming rooms with private baths and fans. It can arrange fishing trips, horseback rides, and even gold-panning expeditions.

Cabinas Carolina (tel. 506/2735-5969, $35 s/d with fan, $40 s/d with a/c and cable TV), in the heart of town, is associated with the popular restaurant. Rooms here are spacious and have private baths, but many lack windows and are therefore overpriced.

Although pricey for what you get, the beachfront **Agua Luna Restaurant and Cabinas** (tel. 506/2735-5393, www.jimenezhotels.com/cabinasagualuna. $45 s, $65 d) is one of the nicer places and has clean, simply furnished, air-conditioned rooms with large windows, TVs, and private baths; six rooms have hot water.

Alas, **The Palms** (tel. 506/2735-5012, www.thepalmscostarica.com) had deteriorated markedly at last visit and can no longer be recommended.

$50-100
If you're a group (minimum 11 people) looking to rent an entire hotel for five days minimum, I'm pleased to report that **La Choza del Manglar** (tel. 506/2735-5002, www.manglares.com) has done up its previously gloomy and spartan rooms, which can now be recommended. It has eight rooms, two cabins, and a duplex. It has Wi-Fi. Nature lovers will appreciate being amid lush gardens that merge into mangroves, and all manner of wildlife (from monkeys to olingos) can be spotted while you sip a cocktail in the lounge bar. But don't feed the animals!

$100-150

New in 2008, **La Islas Lodge** (tel. 506/2735-5242, www.lasislaslodge.com, $60–75 s, $70–85 d low season; $130–150 s, $140–165 d high season, including breakfast and tax), about two kilometers west of town, has four rooms and four cabins, all pleasantly furnished and with lots of light. It specializes in sportfishing packages.

I like **Parrot Bay Village** (tel. 506/2735-5180 or U.S. tel. 866/551-2003, www.parrotbayvillage.com), on the oceanfront northeast of the airstrip. It has three two-story cabins, plus four octagonal wood-and-thatch cabins, all attractively furnished with wooden ceilings, fans, and kitchenettes. There's a handsome open-air restaurant and bar. It has turned its attention to sportfishers of late. *At last visit, this property was being leased for private use but planned to reopen in 2010.*

The inviting **Crocodile Bay Resort** (tel. 506/2735-5631 or U.S. tel. 800/733-1115, www.crocodilebay.com, see website for rates), about one kilometer east of town, specializes in sportfishing and has 20 spacious, graciously furnished air-conditioned rooms in two-story fourplex units; 12 rooms have whirlpool tubs. It has a slightly austere air-conditioned bar and restaurant, but the beautiful freeform pool fed by a water cascade, a butterfly garden, and a deluxe full-service spa make amends. It offers multi-day packages only.

Competition for Crocodile Bay arrived in 2008 in the form of **Osa Yacht Club** (tel. 506/2735-5920 or 888/OSA-YACHT, www.osayachtclub.com, see the website for pricing), about one kilometer east of town. This compact place has quaint wooden cabins tucked in a secure courtyard. However, the website is misleading: Dining, for example, is listed as being at the defunct Jade Luna restaurant.

PLAYA PLATANARES

I love the beachfront **◖ Iguana Lodge** (tel./fax 506/8848-0752, www.iguanalodge.com, $105 low season, $120 high season Club Room including breakfast; $125 pp low season, $155 pp high season casitas including breakfast and dinner), which boasts a breezy setting and a luxurious aesthetic. This is the finest digs for miles! It's run by Loran and Toby Cleaver from Colorado, who gave it all up to live in harmony with nature. There's a frog garden, and trails lead into the adjacent forest, and Loran was creating a flower garden at last visit. It has two types of accommodation. First, to one side, four hardwood "casitas" raised on stilts amid the forest have louvered windows on all sides, plus broad verandas. Shared showers and bathrooms (candlelit at night) are located nearby. Newer, more luxurious cabins have private bathrooms. To the other side, a lime-green wooden lodge has eight upstairs "Iguana Club Rooms" done up in sumptuous albeit simple tropical fashion, divinely comfy king-size beds, ceiling fans, inset ceiling halogens, and gorgeous modern bathrooms with travertine walls and huge walk-in showers. And a simply furnished three-bedroom house—"Villa Villa Kula"—includes master suite with its own wraparound veranda ($350 low season, $450 high season, minimum three nights). Two deluxe cabins were being added in 2009, along with a Balinese-inspired spa. Gourmet meals (the breakfasts astound!) are served family-style on a wide veranda in the main lodge, which has a Gaudí-esque feel in its curvaceous layout; there's also a more simple restaurant and bar.

The **Black Turtle Lodge** (tel. 506/2735-5005, www.blackturtlelodge.com, $85–1055 s, $140–170 d low season; $95–120 s, $150–190 d high season, including breakfast and dinner) is a more rustic virtual carbon copy of Iguana Lodge. It is now run by California siblings Nico and Meggie Zimmerman, who specialize in yoga retreats. They have two tree-house *cabinas* and two *cabinettas* amid the jungle. Family dining is offered by candlelight.

Another perfectly adequate option is the **Yellow Coco Lodge** (tel. 506/8811-4934 or in North America tel. 941/376-0910, www.yellowcocolodge.com, from $170 s/d), between Iguana Lodge and Black Turtle Lodge. It has graciously appointed bungalows and a lovely beach house (three nights minimum).

© CHRISTOPHER P. BAKER

Iguana Lodge, Playa Platanares

FARTHER AFIELD

Looking for a true nature experience? **Río Nuevo Lodge** (tel. 506/2735-5095, www.rionuevolodge.com, $65 s, $100 d with meals), about five kilometers west of town, offers safari-style tents atop wooden platforms. Surrounded by rainforest, it's a fabulous base for hiking.

Food

The breakfast spot of choice, **Restaurante Carolina** (tel./fax 506/2735-5185, 7 A.M.–10 P.M. daily, $2–10) serves a good granola with fruit and yogurt, plus other American-style breakfasts. It has cheap *casados* for lunch, and the inexpensive menu ranges to chicken cordon bleu and fettucine alfredo.

Juanita's Mexican Bar & Grill (tel. 506/2735-5056, 6 A.M.–midnight daily, below $8), run by a real Mexican lady, serves hearty fare in atmospheric surrounds. The menu includes fish and chips and burgers.

Worth the drive to Playa Platanares is **(Pearl of the Osa** (11 A.M.–9 A.M. daily $2–15) at Iguana Lodge, with a beautiful hardwood bar and spacious shaded patio with hammocks. It serves ceviche, chicken fingers, burritos, burgers, tuna melts, *casados* (set lunches), and seafood dishes. Nonguests can also make reservations for gourmet family-style dinners at Iguana Lodge, with its revolving menu of regional specials. Friday night is pasta night, with live music and dancing.

There's a bakery (*panadería*) 50 meters south of the soccer field. **Café la Onda** (tel. 506/8335-9441, closed Oct.–Dec.) is a quaint little café.

Information and Services

Escondido Trex (tel./fax 506/2735-5210, www.escondidotrex.com), **Osa Travel** (tel. 506/2735-5649, www.osatravel.com), and **Cafenet el Sol** (tel. 506/2735-5719, 7 A.M.–11 P.M. daily) offer tourist information service. The **Osa Conservation Area headquarters** (tel. 506/2735-5580, fax 506/2735-5681, corcovado@minae.go.cr, 7:30 A.M.–noon and 1–5 P.M. Mon.–Fri.), beside the airstrip, has a tourist information office; you must register here if visiting Corcovado on your own.

There's a **medical clinic** (tel. 506/2735-5203) and a **Red Cross** (tel. 506/2735-5109).

GOLFO DULCE

The **police station** (tel. 506/2735-5114) is 50 meters south of the soccer field.

The **Banco Nacional** is at the south end of town. The **post office** is on the west side of the soccer field. **Cafenet el Sol** charges $2 per hour of Internet time; better bets are **Surfdog Tours** (tel. 506/2735-5825) and **Café Internet Osa** (tel. 506/2735-5757), both with high-speed Internet and Wi-Fi.

Dirty laundry? Head to **Lavandería Kandy** (tel. 506/2735-5345, 8 A.M.–6 P.M. Mon.–Sat.).

Getting There and Around

SANSA and **Nature Air** have scheduled daily flights. **Alfa Romeo Aero Taxi** (tel. 506/2735-5353, aerocorcovado@racsa.co.cr) has an office at the airstrip.

Transportes Blanco-Robo buses (tel. 506/2771-4744) depart San José for Puerto Jiménez from Calle 12, Avenidas 7/9, at noon daily (8 hours, $7); from San Isidro de El General at 6 A.M. daily; and Ciudad Neily at 7 A.M. and 2 P.M. daily ($2.50). Buses depart Puerto Jiménez for San José at 5 A.M. daily; for Ciudad Neily at 5:30 A.M. and 2 P.M., and for San Isidro at 1 P.M. daily.

Water-taxis, or *lanchas,* run daily from the *muelle* (dock) in Golfito at 6 A.M., 11 A.M. and 3 P.M., and return at 6 A.M., 8:45 A.M., 11 A.M. and 2 P.M. (tel. 506/2775-0472 or 506/8896-7519, $6, 90-minute journey). Private boats can be hired for the journey ($8).

Taxis await customers on the main street.

PUERTO JIMÉNEZ TO CARATE

The southeast shores of Osa are lined with hidden beaches—**Playa Tamales, Playa Sombrero**—in the lee of craggy headlands, notably **Cabo Matapalo** at the southeast tip of the Osa Peninsula about 18 kilometers south of Puerto Jiménez. This section of coast is popular with surfers, who come for the powerful six-foot waves, especially in summer. At Matapalo, a side road leads through an arched "gate" and winds three kilometers to the beach at Cabo Matapalo.

The rough dirt road peters out at **Carate,** 43 kilometers from Puerto Jiménez, consisting

of an airstrip and a small *pulpería* (grocery). About three kilometers east of Carate, you pass **Laguna Pejeperrito,** good for spotting crocodiles, caimans, and waterfowl. The road to Carate takes about two hours under good conditions. It gets gradually narrower and bumpier and muddier. *There are several rivers to ford, and they may be impassable in wet season.* A high-clearance, four-wheel-drive vehicle is essential, but no guarantee of passage. The Río Agua Buena is the real challenge, but even the narrow and seemingly innocuous Río Carbonera has washed vehicles downriver after torrential rains.

Sports and Recreation

Everyday Adventures (tel. 506/8353-8619, www.psychotours.com) offers adrenaline-charged hikes ($45) that involve wading rivers. You can also thrill to a rope climb up a giant strangler fig ($55), then leap (if you choose!) from a platform 20 meters above the ground. And the waterfall rappels will have your heart racing ($85).

Aventuras Bosque Mar (tel. 506/2735-5752), eight kilometers south of Puerto Jiménez, has a five-platform zipline.

Accommodations

You can camp at Carate in front of the *pulpería,* which has bathrooms, showers, and a water faucet. It also has five basic *cabinas* without fans, and with cold water only ($10 pp).

$25-50

At Carbonera, the eclectic **Buena Esperanza** (tel. 506/2735-5531, martinatica@hotmail .com, $25 pp), alias Martina's, is beloved by surfers and backpackers for its colorful Moroccan-style decor and unique arrangement—its windowless, open-sided *cabinas* have low cement walls with wrap-around sofas with batiks and Army-fatigue cushions, sponge-washed concrete floors, and rough-hewn beds with mosquito nets. Shared outdoor showers and toilets have cold water only. Its offbeat bar-restaurant is a popular hangout. Rates include breakfast.

$50-100

Seeking a safari-style experience? The overpriced **La Leona Ecolodge** (tel. 506/2735-5704, www.laleonaecolodge.com, $35 s or $60 d shared bath, $50–55 s, $90–100 d private bath), just 200 meters from the La Leona ranger station, is a simple tent camp with 17 tent-cabins on wooden platforms, each with two small mattress-beds. They share a bathhouse with four bathrooms and showers.

$100-150

I like the offbeat, German-run **Ojo del Mar B&B** (tel. 506/2735-5531, www.ojodelmar.com, $60 s, $100 d cabin low season, $65 s, $110 d high season), enjoying a secluded forest setting at Carbonera. It has two open-sided bamboo cabins with "rainforest" showers, plus two double beds with batiks and mosquito nets (one cabin has a loft bedroom). They share a clean outdoor bathroom. Meals are served in a charming Robinson Crusoe–style dining area. It has no electricity. Rates include breakfast.

The **Terrapin Lodge** (tel. 506/2735-5211 or 831/278-1003, www.terrapinlodge.com, $90 s, $150 d including meals), about 400 meters inland of the beach one kilometer east of Carate, offers five simply appointed all-wood cabins in the forest; all have private bathrooms with cold water only. Meals are served in a charming skylit restaurant on stilts, with hammocks. It has a pool.

Meanwhile, also at Carate, **Finca Exotica** (satellite tel. 1-416/628-9855, www.fincaexotica.com, $70–80 pp tent, $95 pp cabin, including all meals) offers lovely A-frame safari-style open-air thatched cabins plus safari-style tents (most with private outdoor shower). Plus there's a fully equipped two-story cabin for rent. The owners pay special attention to serving healthy gourmet meals. Tours here include hikes in the private rainforest refuge. The lodge itself is a delightful place to relax, and a yoga platform is being added. You get real value for money here.

$150-250

Encanta la Vida (tel. 506/2735-5670, www.encantalavida.com, $85 pp suite, $99 pp honeymoon suite), in the gated community of Matapalo, is a three-story wooden lodge, handsomely decorated and fringed by wide verandas with hammocks and rockers with views over both ocean and jungle. It has two beautiful suites plus a honeymoon suite, all with mosquito nets over four-poster rough-hewn beds and huge walk-in showers. It requires a two-day minimum stay. Rates include meals.

The **Lookout Inn** (tel./fax 506/2735-5431, www.lookout-inn.com, $105–140 pp including meals) sits on the hillside one kilometer east of Carate. Terry and Wendy, from New Mexico, are live-in owners of this three-story house with seven tall-ceilinged, tastefully decorated bedrooms. Sponge-washed walls merge with bamboo furnishings and tropical hardwood accents, not least bed frames made from tree trunks. A lounge has a small library. A spiral staircase opens onto a *mirador* with hammocks, a telescope, and fabulous vistas. A swimming pool and deck are inset in the garden below, and a pond draws poison-dart frogs. Guests get free use of kayaks, canoes, mountain bikes, and boogie boards.

OVER $250

Another winner is the calming **Luna Lodge** (tel. 506/8380-5036, or U.S. tel. 888/409-8448, www.lunalodge.com, $105 s or $190 d tent, $135 s or $240 d room, $195 s or $290 d cabin low season; $115 s or $190 d tent, $165 s or $270 d room, $240 s or $350 d cabin high season including taxes, meals, and tour), nestling in the hills above Carate amid primary rainforest and centered on a massive thatched rancho reception lounge/restaurant with deck offering fabulous views. Eight circular bungalows are simply yet delightfully furnished; they stair-step the hill, reached via paths of black slate. Exquisite "rainforest" bathrooms have shower-tubs enclosed by a stone wall with garden. There are also five safari-style budget tents reached by a stiff uphill climb. The bar and restaurant serves international cuisine. A wellness center offers yoga, tai chi, and massage, plus there's a lovely solar-heated pool. To get there, you have to crisscross the Río Carate several

GOLFO DULCE

times; the river is often impassable! Fortunately, once across, the steep hill is paved.

The **Corcovado Lodge Tent Camp** (c/o Costa Rica Expeditions, tel. 506/2257-0766, www.costaricaexpeditions.com), 1.5 kilometers west of Carate, was closed at last visit for a total remake that will take this safari-style lodge upscale. It will be all-inclusive.

The Spanish- and German-run **El Remanso Lodge** (tel./fax 506/2735-5569, www.elremanso.com, $160–205 s, $250–330 d low season; $180–225 s, $290–370 d high season, including meals), atop Cabo Matapalo, is an ecofriendly entity running entirely on its own hydro-electric power. It offers seven spacious and airy cabins, with sponge-washed concrete floors and a gorgeous, simple aesthetic that includes soft-contoured concrete bed bases, batik covers, hammocks, and wall-to-wall louvered windows to three sides. It also has a two-story group cabin for four people, plus a six-bedroom house with king-size beds and glazed concrete floors and handsome dark-stone tubs. It has a beautiful restaurant, a deck with plunge pool, and a zipline. An open-air restaurant has stylish rattan lounge chairs.

A deluxe gem, **◖ Bosque del Cabo** (tel./fax 506/2735-5206, www.bosquedelcabo.com, $140–195 s, $220–320 d cabins, low season; $165–195 s, $250–390 d high season) nestles atop the 180-meter cliff of Cabo Matapalo and part of a 250-hectare forest reserve. It has recently upgraded with a stylish new *palenque* restaurant and lounge-bar with poured-concrete sofas with Guatemalan cushions. Nice! Set in landscaped grounds are seven thatched clifftop *cabinas* with superb ocean views. Screened open-air showers have their own little gardens; verandas have hammocks. Three splendid deluxe cabins each have terra-cotta floors, king-size bed with mosquito net, chic decor, and lofty rough-hewn stable doors that open to a wraparound veranda with sublime ocean vistas. Then there's the Casa Blanca and Casa Miramar, exquisitely decorated two-bedroom villas. And budget travelers get two much simpler cabins, new for 2008 and accessed by a muddy forest trail and suspension bridge. Lanterns light the place at night. There's a cooling-off pool fed by spring waters, a sundeck, and a yoga platform. It offers hikes and horseback rides, and there's a zipline canopy tour.

The world-renowned **◖ Lapa Ríos** (tel. 506/2735-5130, www.laparios.com, $350 s or $490 d low season, $460 s or $650 d high season, including meals) is an exquisite, eco-conscious resort with a great location atop a ridge overlooking Cabo Matapalo. Sixteen romantic, luxuriously appointed bungalows reached by wooden walkways feature gleaming hardwood floors, screened windows, gorgeous stone-lined bathrooms, a patio garden complete with outdoor shower, and louvered French doors opening to a private terrace. The thatched lodge has a spiral staircase augering up from the restaurant to a *mirador* (lookout platform). There's a small pool with sundeck and bar. The property is backed by a 400-hectare private reserve. Walks in the rainforest, kayaking, horseback rides, and a full-day Corcovado tour with air transfers to/from Sirena are offered. Despite being overpriced, this place fills up. It's one of only four hotels in the country with five leaves in the Certified Sustainable Tourism program.

Food

At Carbonera, the **Buena Esperanza** (tel. 506/2735-5531, 9 A.M.–midnight daily) draws surfers for its tremendous offbeat ambience and international cuisine (such as Thai and Mexican) at budget prices. It's the only bar hereabouts and gets lively with a mix of foreigners and locals.

Lapa Ríos offers superb gourmet dishes in its **Restaurante Brisas Azul** (7 A.M.–8:30 A.M. daily, $5–25). It's worth the drive just for the carrot cake! Come on Wednesday or Saturday for the tortilla-making class.

Getting There

You can charter an airplane to Carate, but the airstrip sometimes floods in wet season.

A *colectivo* truck (tel. 506/2837-3120) runs daily from Puerto Jiménez at 6 A.M. and 1:30 P.M., departing Carate for Puerto

© CHRISTOPHER P. BAKER

Please Don't Feed the Wildlife

Jiménez at 8:30 A.M. and 4 P.M. ($7). It stops at Matapalo ($4).

You can also rent a Jeep-taxi ($80–100 per carload).

◖ CORCOVADO NATIONAL PARK

Parque Nacional Corcovado—the Amazon of Costa Rica—is the largest stronghold of Pacific coastline primary forest, which has been all but destroyed from Mexico to South America. Its 41,788 hectares encompass eight habitats, from mangrove swamp and jolillo palm grove to montane forest. The park protects more than 400 species of birds (20 are endemic), 116 of amphibians and reptiles, and 139 of mammals—representing 10 percent of the mammals in the Americas on only 0.000101777 percent of the landmass.

Its healthy population of scarlet macaws (about 1,200 birds) is the largest concentration in Central America. Corcovado is also a good place to spot the red-eyed tree frog and enamel-bright poison-dart frogs. Corcovado is one of very few places in the country

harboring squirrel monkeys. It's also one of the last strands in the world for the harpy eagle. Four species of sea turtles—green, Pacific ridley, hawksbill, and leatherback—nest on the park's beaches. And the park supports a healthy population of tapirs and big cats, which like to hang around the periphery of the Corcovado Lagoon. Corcovado also has a large population of peccaries, a massive-necked razor-backed hog that grows to the size of a large hound. (The park's mammal population—notably peccaries—is under intense pressure from illegal hunters.)

The Osa Peninsula bears the brunt of torrential rains April–December. It receives up to 400 centimeters per year. The driest months, January–April, are the best times to visit.

Hiking Trails

Corcovado has a well-developed trail system, though the trails are primitive and poorly marked. Several short trails make for rewarding half- or full-day hikes. Longer trails grant an in-depth backpacking experience in the rainforest. Allow three days to hike from one

GOLFO DULCE

ABUSING THE OSA

The Osa region has had a tormented history in recent decades at the hands of gold miners, hunters, and loggers (half of the land that now forms Corcovado National Park, for example, was obtained in a land trade from a logging company).

The opening of a road linking Rincón with Bahía Drake in 1997 resulted in a cutting frenzy within the forest reserves (it is claimed that the road was put in against the wishes of local inhabitants following lobbying by the loggers). In November 1997, a moratorium *(veda)* on logging in Osa was issued following a grassroots campaign by local residents, but laws go unenforced. The loggers are accused of being a *mafiosi* who pay locals to allow illegal logging on their land, while people who speak out against them often end up being intimidated into silence or even killed.

Hunting by Ticos of tapir, jaguars, peccaries, and other big mammals continues under the nose of – and even in collusion with – park staff. *Oreros* occasionally show up in Puerto Jiménez with ocelot skins and other poached animals for sale. Scarlet macaw nests are routinely poached. The turtle population continues to be devastated by the local populace, who poach the nests simply because there is nobody to stop them. Poison is being used to harvest fish from

coastal breeding lagoons such as Peje Perro and Peje Perrito. And the system of issuing wildlife permits is routinely abused by people who obtain a permit for "rescuing" a specific animal, then use the permit to trade other animals. It's a lucrative trade. Local expats claim that some of the money finds its way to park rangers, who routinely turn a blind eye. In any event, the rangers are not equipped to fight fire with fire. "They're ticket sellers!" says a prominent expat.

The Osa Peninsula was even slated to get Central America's largest woodchip mill, courtesy of Ston Forestal, a Costa Rican subsidiary of the paper giant Stone Container Corporation of Chicago. The chip mill would have dramatically increased truck traffic and caused excessive pollution that would have threatened the marinelife of the Golfo Dulce. Community efforts to fight the project forced Ston Forestal to shelve its project.

COVIRENA (tel. 506/2283-4746, fax 506/2283-5148), a branch of the park service, exists to combat logging and poaching. **Fundación Corcovado** (tel. 506/2297-3013, www.corcovadofoundation.org), **Friends of the Osa** (tel. 506/2735-5756, www.osaconservation.org), and **Osa Campaign** (tel. 506/2234-3360, www.osacampaign.org) also work to save Corcovado's wildlife.

end of the park to the other, which can be done in dry season only.

From La Leona: It's 15 kilometers to Sirena, following the beach for most of the way. Allow up to eight hours. Beyond Salsipuedes Point, the trail cuts inland through the rainforest. Don't try this at high or waning tide: You must cross some rocky points that are cut off by high tide. Don't trust the ranger's statements—consult a tide table before you arrive. The hike from La Leona to the Madrigal waterfall is recommended.

From Sirena: A trail leads northeast to Los Patos via Corcovado Lagoon. Another trail—only possible at low tide (not least because sharks like to come up the mouths of rivers in the hours immediately before and after

high tide)—leads to the San Pedrillo Ranger Station (23 kilometers). There are three rivers to wade. The trick is to reach the Río Sirena and slightly shallower Río Llorona before the water is thigh-deep. Here, watch the crocodiles. Don't let me put you off; dozens of hikers follow the trail each week. Halfway, the trail winds steeply into the rainforest and is often slippery. The last three kilometers are along the beach. The full-day hike takes you past La Llorona, a 30-meter-high waterfall that cascades spectacularly onto the beach. Tapirs are said to come down to the beach around sunrise, but you must remain silent at all times, as the animals are timid and easily scared away.

From Los Patos: The trail south climbs

steeply for six kilometers before flattening out for the final 14 kilometers to the Sirena Research Station. The trail is well marked but narrow, overgrown in parts, and has several river crossings where it is easy to lose the trail on the other side. You must wade. Be especially careful in rainy season, when you may find yourself hip-deep. There are three small shelters en route. A side trail will take you to Corcovado Lagoon. Allow up to eight hours. Another trail leads from Los Patos to Los Planes.

Accommodations

A basic bunkhouse with foam mattresses (but no sleeping bags or linens) is available at **Sirena** ($8 pp), which have showers and water; reservations are essential via the Corcovado park headquarters in Puerto Jiménez. Rangers will cook meals by prior arrangement ($5 breakfast, $7 lunch and dinner), but you have to supply your own food.

Camping is allowed only at ranger stations ($4 pp). Rangers can radio ahead to the various stations within the park and book you in for dinner and a tent spot. No-see-ums (pesky microscopic flies you'll not forget in a hurry) infest the beaches and come out to find you at dusk. Take a watertight tent, a mosquito net, and plenty of insect repellent. You can rent tents and stoves in Puerto Jiménez from Escondido Trex.

Reservations are required for overnight (30 days' notice is recommended due to limited space); prepayment is required through Banco Nacional.

Information and Services

The park has four entry points: **La Leona,** on the southeast corner near Carate (the ranger station is about two kilometers from Carate); **Los Patos,** on the northern perimeter; **San Pedrillo,** at the northwest corner, 18 kilometers south of Drake Bay; and **Los Planes,** on the northern border midway between San Pedrillo and Los Patos. You can also fly into the park headquarters at **Sirena,** midway between La Leona and San Pedrillo. All are linked by trails. Entrance costs $10 (maximum four nights). The park is administered through the Osa

Conservation Area headquarters in Puerto Jiménez (tel. 506/2735-5580, fax 506/2735-5581, pncorcovado@gmail.com).

Getting There

You can charter an air-taxi to fly you to Sirena from Puerto Jiménez with **Alfa Romeo Aero Taxi** ($500 up to five people). Otherwise you'll have to hike in from Carate or one of the other access points.

Boats from Marenco and Drake Bay will take you to either San Pedrillo or Sirena.

CAÑO ISLAND BIOLOGICAL RESERVE

Caño Island ($10 admission) is 17 kilometers off the western tip of the Osa Peninsula, directly west of Drake Bay. It is of interest primarily for its importance as a pre-Columbian cemetery. Many tombs and artifacts—pestles, corn-grinding tables, and granite spheres *(bolas)*—are gathering moss in the rainforest undergrowth (Caño Island gets struck by lightning more often than any other part of Central America, and for that reason was considered

---

THE MARCH OF THE SOLDIER CRABS

If you think you see the beach moving, it's not the heat nor last night's excess of *guaro* messing with your mind. Daily, whole columns of seashells – little whelks and conchs of green and blue and russet – come marching down from the roots of the mangroves onto the sand. Scavengers only an inch long, soldier crabs are born and grow up without protective shells. For self-preservation they move – "lock, stock, and abdomen," says one writer – into empty seashells they find cast up on the beach. Although they grow, their seashell houses do not; thus whole battalions of crabs continually seek newer and larger quarters. When threatened, a soldier crab pulls back into its shell, totally blocking the entrance with one big claw.

sacred by pre-Columbian peoples, who used it as a burial ground). The 300-hectare island is ringed with secluded white-sand beaches that attract olive ridley turtles. Among its residents are boa constrictors (the only venomous snakes here are sea snakes), giant frogs, a variety of hummingbirds, and three mammal species: a marsupial, the paca (which was introduced), and a bat. Surprisingly, only 13 terrestrial bird species are found here. Snorkelers can see brilliant tropical fish and moray eels among the coral beds. Offshore waters teem with dolphins and whales.

A wide and well-maintained trail leads steeply uphill from the ranger station. Contact the Osa Conservation Area headquarters for information (tel. 506/2735-5580, fax 506/2735-5581, pncorcovado@gmail.com).

Most lodges in the region offer day trips. It is forbidden to overnight.

Golfito and Golfo Dulce

The Golfo Dulce region fringes the huge bay of the same name, framed by the Osa Peninsula to the west and the Fila Costeña mountains to the north. The region is centered on the town of Golfito, on the north shore of the gulf. The bay is rimmed by swamp, lonesome beaches, and remote tracts of rainforest accessible only by boat. Humpback whales and dolphins are frequently seen in the bay.

Río Claro, 64 kilometers southeast of Palmar and about 15 kilometers west of Ciudad Neily, is a major junction at the turnoff for Golfito from Highway 2. It's about 23 kilometers to Golfito from here. Río Claro has restaurants, a gas station, and taxi service.

PIEDRAS BLANCAS NATIONAL PARK

Centered on the village of **La Gamba,** this rainforest zone was split from Corcovado National Park in 1999 and named a national park in its own right. Land within its bounds is still in private ownership, and logging permits issued before 1991 apparently remain valid. The Austrian government underwrites local efforts to save the forest. A cooperative provides income for local families whose members are employed at Esquinas Rainforest Lodge (which has miles of forest trails) and on fruit farms and a botanical garden; it also has a tepezcuintle breeding program. Guides ($15) can be hired for hiking. The "Rainforest of the Austrians" also operates **La Gamba** Biological Station in conjunction with the University of Vienna.

The turnoff from the Pan-American Highway is at Kilometer 37, midway between Piedras Blancas and Río Claro (Gamba is 6 km from the highway; 4WD not required). You can also get there via a very rough dirt road that leads north from Golfito (4WD required).

Playa San Josecito, about 10 kilometers northwest and a 25-minute boat ride from Golfito, is a wide, lonesome, pebbly, brown-sand beach. The jungle sweeps right down to the shore, as it does a few kilometers north at **Playa Cativo.** The beaches can be accessed by boat and are popular day trips from Golfito.

Casa de Orquídeas (tel. 506/8829-1247, $5 admission, $8 with guided tour, 8 A.M.–5 A.M. Sat.–Thurs.) has nearly five hectares of private botanical gardens at the northwest end of Playa San Josecito. This labor of love culminates the 20-odd-year efforts of Ron and Trudy MacAllister. Ornamental plants, not least of them 100 species of orchids, attract zillions of birds. Two-hour guided tours are offered at 8:30 A.M. Thursday and Sunday. Tour operators throughout Golfo Dulce offer tours to the garden; otherwise take a water-taxi from Golfito or any of the local lodges. Call ahead.

Osa Wildlife Sanctuary (Fundación Sanctuario Silvestre de Osa, tel. 506/8861-1309, www.osawildlife.org, closed May–Nov.), at Playa Cativo, is a nonprofit animal rescue shelter run by Earl and Carol Crews and spanning 304

Casa de Orquídeas

hectares. You're welcomed by howler and spider monkeys, scarlet macaws flap and squawk in the treetops, and don't be surprised if a baby tamandua climbs up your leg and onto your shoulders. Tours are given at 9:30 A.M., 11:30 A.M., and 1:30 P.M. daily. A full-day advance notice is required; children under five are not permitted. Interns are sought.

Avellan Trails & Waterfalls (tel. 506/2789-9359, http://avellancr.com, $5 entrance adults, $3 children), at La Gamba, has trails to waterfalls in the midst of the forest. You can whiz past the cascades on a zipline cable ($20 adults, $15 children and students), and plunge through the water on a rappel. Horseback rides cost $20.

The **Original Canopy Tour** (www.canopytour.com) company was planning a facility here.

Accommodations

Avellan Trails & Waterfalls (tel. 506/2789-9359, http://avellancr.com) has camping as well as simple cabins, plus a rustic restaurant.

The reclusive stone-and-timber **Esquinas Rainforest Lodge** (tel. 506/2741-8001, www.esquinaslodge.com, $125 s, $190 d low

season; $145 s, $230 d high season, including three meals and taxes) is a great base for exploring the forest. Its five duplex cabins are connected by a covered walkway to the main lodge, which features an open-walled lounge with forest views. Guest rooms have rattan furniture and lively decor, screened glass-less windows, and porches with rockers and hammocks. Facilities include a bar, gift shop, library, and thatched dining room plus naturally filtered swimming pool. Excursions are offered. Simple bunks at **La Gamba Biological Station** (c/o Esquinas Rainforest Lodge, $8 pp) accommodate eight people in a small, self-contained farmhouse.

Anglers are catered to at **Golfito Sailfish Rancho** (U.S. tel. 813/249-9908 or 877/726-2468, www.golfitosailfishrancho.com), at Punta Encantado. This modern sportfishing lodge offers 10 spacious, pleasingly decorated rooms with ceiling fans, two double beds, safe, and walk-in showers with hot water. Most folks come in to fish on multi-day packages; contact the resort for rates.

The Swiss-run **Golfo Dulce Lodge** (tel. 506/8821-5398, www.golfodulcelodge.com,

GOLFO DULCE

© CHRISTOPHER P. BAKER

fishing boats in Golfito

three-night packages cost $315–345 s, $510–570 d low season; $345–405 s, $570–670 d high season, including transfers, meals, and taxes), surrounded by 275 hectares of forest at Playa San Josecito, has five handsome wooden bungalows plus a brick cabin with bamboo furnishings, large veranda with hammocks and rockers, and tiled bathrooms. There are also three rooms with verandas. There's a small swimming pool and a *rancho*-style restaurant and bar. Sea kayaking, horseback riding, hikes, and excursions are offered. Electricity is supplied by a Pelton wheel, water is recycled, and sewage is treated in septic tanks.

Fronted by a beach and coral reef (good for snorkeling) and backed by a mountain with trails leading into a 77-hectare private reserve (a former cacao plantation that is being reforested), the splendid **C** **Playa Nicuesa Rainforest Lodge** (tel. 506/2222-0704 or in North America tel. 866/504-8116, www.nicuesalodge.com, $185–205 s, $300–340 d low season; $215–235 s, $360–400 d high season) is a perfect base for adventures. Crafted entirely of multi-hued hardwoods, the two-story, open-atrium ecolodge is a stunner. Four hexagonal cabins and a four-room guesthouse spread throughout the forested grounds all feature a quasi-Japanese motif, canopied beds, ceiling fans in open-beam roofs, and full-length, wraparound louvered doors, plus open bathrooms with outdoor showers. The open-air upstairs lounge–cum–dining room looks over the lush grounds, candlelit at night; the lodges grows most of its own organic produce. It has family programs, and yoga is offered on the beachfront deck. River otters and caimans frequent the lagoon accessed by kayaks, and animals have been known to pay visits into the cabins. How exciting: "An ocelot slept here!" Closed October–mid-November.

Nearby, and similar, the former **Rainbow Adventures Lodge** was being refurbished to reopen under new owners at my last visit.

New in 2008, **Finca Saladero** (tel. 506/2735-5062, www.fincasaladero.com, $85 tree house, $125 beach house), aims to compete. It permits camping on manicured lawns and offers a fully screened tree house and a two-story beach house. It also has its own rainforest reserve.

Also new in 2008, **Agua Dulce Lodge & Resort** (tel. 506/2723-0766, www.aguadulcelodge.com, contact the lodge for rates) opened at Playa Preciosa with 21 air-conditioned two-bedroom cabins. It specializes in sportfishing packages.

GOLFITO

Golfito, a sportfishing center and the most important town in the Pacific southwest, is for travelers who love forlorn ports. This one is a muggy, funky, semi-down-at-the-heels place born in 1938, when the United Fruit Company moved its headquarters here after shutting down operations on the Caribbean coast. By 1955, more than 90 percent of the nation's banana exports were shipped from Golfito. The United Fruit Company pulled out in 1985 after a series of crippling labor strikes.

The town, which is today popular as a sportfishing center, sprawls for several kilometers along a single road on the estuary of the Río Golfito. First entered, to the southeast, is the **Pueblo Civil,** the run-down working-class section full of tumbledown houses (many hanging on stilts over the water). The Pueblo Civil extends northwest to the compact town center, a quarter of cheap bar life, with an uninspired plaza. Nearby, the Hotel Centro Turístico Samoa has a small **Museo Marino** displaying a large collection of seashells and coral. About two kilometers farther is the **Muelle de Golfito,** the banana-loading dock (also called Muelle Bananero) at the southern end of the **Zona Americana,** a more tranquil and orderly quarter where the administrative staff of United Fruit used to live in brightly painted, two-story wooden houses raised on stilts set in manicured gardens shaded by tall trees hung with epiphytes and lianas. Here, too, is the **Depósito Libre,** a duty-free shopping compound that lures Ticos in droves on weekends, when the town's dozens of cheap *cabinas* fill up. (Golfito was declared a duty-free port in 1990—an attempt to offset the economic decline that followed United Fruit's strategic retreat.)

The vision of Golfito improves dramatically from across the bay at **Playa Cacao,** literally at the end of the road, five kilometers southwest of Golfito. Popeye the Sailor would have felt at home here. Funky charm was never funkier or more charming. The road from Golfito winds around the shore and spills steeply down to the shingly, brown-sand beach (the narrow dirt road can be a harpy in wet season).

The 1,309-hectare **Golfito National Wildlife Refuge,** created to protect the city's watershed, is formed of primary rainforest covering the steep mountains immediately east of town. Trails connect northward with Piedras Blancas National Park. A sign across from the Plaza Deportes soccer field in the Pueblo Civil points the way along a dirt road that leads about nine kilometers uphill to Las Torres radio station. You can also hike a steep trail from opposite Hotel Centro Turístico Samoa. A third option is the road that parallels the airstrip; it leads past the Hotel Sierra and, deteriorating all the while, deposits you three kilometers farther at a sign for Senderos Naturales (Nature Trails). Lastly, you can take the dirt road beyond the Depósito Libre that leads through the reserve to Esquinas.

The 216-slip **Marina Bahía Escondida & Yacht Club** (www.crmarinavillage.com), with a luxury residential complex, was under construction at last visit, and promises to bring a new luster to town.

Entertainment

On the waterfront in the center of Golfito, **Centro Turística Samoa** (tel. 506/2775-0233, www.samoadelsur.com, 10 A.M.–2 A.M. daily) has a dartboard (a darts club meets on Monday nights), table soccer, and a pool table, plus music at a bar that is shaped like a sailing ship with a busty mermaid prow. **Bar La Bomba,** upstairs opposite the gas station, is another lively, colorful bar with karaoke. Expatriate gringos gravitate toward **Latitude Bar 8,** opposite Hotel Costa Surf. **Hotel Roland** (tel. 506/2775-0180), by the Depósito Libre, offers a snazzier alternative. Nearby, the **Casino Golfito** (tel. 506/775-0666), is open 6 P.M.–2 A.M. daily.

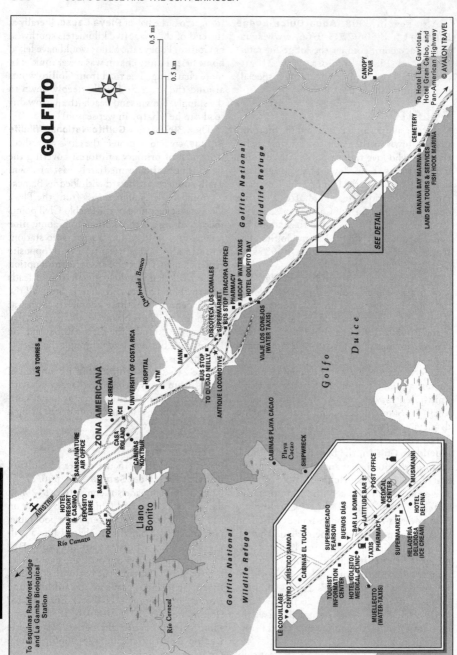

GOLFO DULCE

CHRISTOPHER P. BAKER

squirrel monkeys near Golfito

Sports and Recreation

Prime season for sailfish is December–May; for marlin, June–September; and for snook, May–September.

Banana Bay Marina (tel. 506/2775-0838) and **Fish Hook Marina** (tel. 506/2775-1624) offer sportfishing packages and charters, as does **Capt. Bobby McGuinness** (tel. 506/2775-0664, bobbymcguinness@racsa.co.cr).

Accommodations

UNDER $25

The town is awash in budget—and often grim—accommodations not worth recommending. Some are quasi-brothels.

You can camp at **Camping Rancho Atlantis** (tel./fax 506/2775-0373, $3 pp, $5 pp under thatch), at Playa Cacao. It rents canoes and catamarans.

In the town center, **Cabinas El Tucán** (tel. 506/2775-0553, $10 pp cold water and fan, $30 s/d with hot water and a/c), opposite Centro Turístico Samoa, has 16 small, simple rooms with fans and private bathrooms with cold water only. Twelve new rooms have air-conditioning, TVs, refrigerators, and hot water.

The most atmospheric of several budget places at the north end of town is **Cabinas Koktsur** (tel. 506/2775-1191, $15 s/d), with eight simple, clean rooms in a well-kept old wooden home. Each has a fan and local TV, plus a private bath with cold water. **Hotel Golfito Bay** (tel. 506/2775-0006, golfitobay@hotmail.com) is a similar priced alternative.

$25-50

The **Hotel y Restaurante el Gran Ceibo** (tel./fax 506/2775-0403, www.hotel-elgran-ceibo.com, $20–50 s/d), where the road meets the shore at the entrance to Golfito, has 27 simple rooms in modern two-story and one-story units. All have cool tile floors, TV, and clean bathrooms. There's a good restaurant and a nice poolside breakfast area, plus a swimming pool and kids' pool. Road noise is a problem. The lively bar draws a young crowd.

Nearby, **Las Gaviotas** (tel. 506/2775-0062, fax 506/2775-0544, $45 s/d with fan, $58 with a/c and kitchenette, $90 a/c bungalows) has 21 modestly furnished rooms with cable TV, refrigerators, private porches, and spacious tiled bathrooms with large showers. The outdoor restaurant overlooks the gulf and serves seafood. There's a pool and free Internet.

GOLFO DULCE

Your best bet in this price range is **Hotel Centro Turístico Samoa** (tel. 506/2775-0233, www.samoadelsur.com, $40–45 up to four people low season, $55 high season), on the waterfront in the center of Golfito. It has 17 well-kept *cabinas* with fans and TVs. There's an excellent restaurant, the liveliest bar in town, and a pool. It also accepts RV campers for $15 per vehicle in a guarded parking lot with gleaming showers and toilets.

At Playa Cacao, **Cabinas Playa Cacao** (c/o tel. 506/2221-1169, www.kapsplace.com/EN/other/, $30 s/d low season, $50 s/d high season) is an eccentric charmer with six African-style thatch-roofed, tile-floored cottages. Each has two beds, fan, refrigerator, and private bathroom with hot water; three have kitchens. It has a small restaurant, laundry, and swimming pool fed by a multi-tiered cascade falling from a whirlpool set in the hillside. It can be tough to get to by road in wet season, but you can take a water-taxi. It's most appropriate for self-sufficient folks.

The Swiss-run **La Purruja Lodge** (tel. 506/2775-1054, www.purruja.com, $30 s, $40 d), four kilometers east of Golfito, has five *cabinas* with spartan furnishings. They're set amid landscaped lawns on a hill overlooking a forested valley, with trails. However, until this place stops feeding local *titi* monkeys for guests' amusement, it cannot be recommended!

$50-100

Serving the serious shopping and gambling crowd is the **Hotel Sierra Resort & Casino** (tel. 506/2775-0666, www.hotelsierra.com, $70 s or $80 d low season, $80 s or $90 d high season), between the airport and the duty-free zone. Although soulless, it has 72 well-lit, nicely furnished air-conditioned rooms, plus a pool with wet bar, a children's pool, restaurant, bar, disco, and casino. I find the similarly priced **Sirena** (tel. 506/2775-9191), formerly Big Thunder B&B, on the hillside north of the airstrip, to have more intimacy.

My favorite place in town is the contemporary **Banana Bay Marina** (tel. 506/2775-0838, www.bananabaymarina.com, $85 s/d rooms, $135 s/d suite), with three standard air-conditioned rooms and a gorgeous master suite, all with gracious mint and sea-green decor, ceiling fans, and large bathrooms with walk-in showers. The master suite has its own computer, cable TV, and sofa set. It has a lively bar and restaurant, Internet café, and the best sportfishing marina in town.

OVER $100

The **Fish Hook Marina & Lodge** (tel. 506/2775-1624, www.fishhookmarina.com, $120–135 low season, $130–145 high season), formerly King & Bartlett, competes with Banana Bay Marina (next door) but is less appealing. Its spacious rooms are sumptuous enough, with a surfeit of glossy hardwoods, but they're dark. It has a bar-restaurant.

Outside town, **Calathea Lodge** (tel. 506/2789-7869, www.calathealodge.com, contact the hotel for rates) is a delightfully rustic nature lodge between Río Claro (on Highway 2) and Únion, about 23 kilometers east of Golfito. It doubles as a small farmstead and has forest trails for hiking and horseback rides, plus an alfresco hot tub. Traditional Costa Rican dishes are served. Albeit simply appointed, the cabins are cozy, clean, and have hot water showers.

Casa Roland Marina Resort (tel. 506/2775-0180, www.fishingmarinaresort.com, $125–165 rooms, $215–260 suites), in the Zona Americana, opened in 2008 to much acclaim. It's by far the classiest act in town, beginning with the marble-clad reception lounge and lavish bar with rust-red leather chairs. The hotel is festooned tip to toe with contemporary art. And the three types of air-conditioned rooms are graciously furnished and have ceiling fans and mod-cons such as flat-screen TVs. But what on earth was the architect (and owner) thinking? The place is virtually devoid of natural light: Bedrooms have only tiny windows, labyrinthine hallways are gloomy and claustrophobic, and the restaurant has no windows at all. It has a movie theater, and a spa, tennis courts, conference center, and swimming pool were being added at last visit. It's landlocked, not a marina.

The deluxe **Bahía Escondida** (tel. 866/502-2442) was set to open in 2009 with a swimming pool, luxury villas, tennis courts, and huge marina. A casino will follow.

Land-Sea Services (tel./fax 506/2775-1614, www.marinaservices-yachtdelivery.com) offers vacation rentals, including furnished waterfront villas and apartments.

Food

Latitude Bar 8 (tel. 506/2775-0235), in the town center is a meeting spot for expats eager to start their day with omelettes, pancakes, and other hearty breakfasts. Nearby, the super-clean, air-conditioned **Buenos Días** (tel. 506/2775-1124, 6 A.M.–10 P.M. daily), on the main road, serves U.S.–style breakfasts, green salads, and local lunches at bargain prices.

For elegance and variety head to **Banana Bay Marina** (tel. 506/2775-0838, 6 A.M.–10 P.M. daily, $5–15), where the menu includes spicy Louisiana gumbo, and pork loin with mushroom pasta and veggies. Or try the chic **Casa Roland Marina Resort** (tel. 506/2775-0180, 7–10 A.M. and noon–10 P.M. daily) restaurant, serving such nouvelle delights as jumbo shrimp with whiskey and honey mustard ($20) or beef tenderloin over portobello mushroom and goat cheese ($22).

For inexpensive seafood, I opt for the open-air **Le Coquillage** (6 A.M.–11:30 P.M.) at Centro Turística Samoa, which also offers a wide menu, from burgers and pizzas to paella. Portions are filling, and the *corvina al ajillo* (garlic sea bass, $6) is splendid.

Musmanni, 200 meters south of the gas station, sells baked goods.

Information and Services

Land-Sea Services (tel./fax 506/2775-1614, www.marinaservices-yachtdelivery.com, 7:30 A.M.–5 P.M. Mon.–Fri.), on the waterfront at Kilometer 2, is a one-stop, full-service tourist information and reservation center, with laundry, Internet, book exchange, and international call service. The **ICT Tourist Information Center** (tel. 506/2775-1820, 8 A.M.–noon and 1–4 P.M. Mon.–Fri.), by the dock, has an Internet café, as does **Banana Bay Marina** (tel. 506/2775-0838, 6 A.M.–10 P.M. daily).

The **Hospital de Golfito** (tel. 506/2775-0011) is in the Zona Americana; the **Consultório Médico** (tel. 506/8832-5800) is by the soccer field.

The **police station** (tel. 506/2775-1022) is in front of the Depósito Libre. There are three banks in the Depósito Libre, and a Banco Nacional in the Zona Americana. The **post office** is on the northwest side of the soccer field, in Pueblo Civil.

The **immigration office** (tel. 506/2775-0487, 7–11 A.M. and 12:30–4 P.M. Mon.–Fri.) is beside the Muelle.

Getting There and Away

Both **SANSA** and **Nature Air** operate scheduled flights to Golfito.

Tracopa buses (tel. 506/2222-2666 and 506/2775-0365) depart San José from Calle 5, Avenidas 18/20, at 7 A.M., 3 P.M., 6 P.M., and 10:15 P.M. daily (eight hours, $5). The return bus departs Golfito at 5 A.M. and 1 P.M.

Buses depart for Ciudad Neily hourly, and to Zancudo from the Muellecito (the little dock immediately north of the gas station in the center of Golfito) at 1:30 P.M.; and for Puerto Jiménez from the Muelle at 11 A.M.

The **Association ABOCOP** (tel. 506/2775-0712) operates water-taxis *(lanchas)* from the main dock to Puerto Jiménez ($5–12 pp each way depending on the boat), Playa Cacao ($1 pp each way), Playa Zancudo ($5 pp each way), as well as Playa San Josecito and other destinations. **Viajes Los Conejos** (tel. 506/2775-2329) operates similar water-taxis from near the commercial dock.

You can rent cars with **Solid Car Rental** (tel. 506/2775-3333 or 506/2775-0666, www.solidcarrental.com), in the Hotel Sierra.

Getting Around

Buses run between the two ends of town. *Colectivos* (shared taxis) also cruise up and down and will run you anywhere in town for $1–2, picking up and dropping off passengers along the way. You can call for a taxi (tel. 506/2775-2242).

GOLFO DULCE

The Burica Peninsula

The rugged Peninsula de Burica, on the east side of Golfo Dulce, forms the southernmost tip of Costa Rica. Its dramatically beautiful coast is washed by surf. To the northeast, the Valle de Coto Colorado is planted with banana trees stretching to the border with Panamá.

◀ PLAYA ZANCUDO

Playa Zancudo, 10 kilometers from Golfito as the crow flies, strung below the estuary of the Río Coto Colorado, is one of my favorite spots, exuding a South Seas feel. The ruler-straight gray-sand beach (littered with coconuts and flotsam) stretches about six kilometers along a slender spit backed by the eerie mangroves of the **Río Coto Swamps,** fed by the estuarine waters of the Río Coto Colorado. Waterfowl are plentiful. And with luck you may see river otters, and crocodiles and caimans basking on the riverbanks. The fishing is good in the fresh water (there are several docks on the estuary side) and in the surf at the wide river mouth. The waves are good for surfing and windsurfing. At dusk and during full moon the no-see-ums are voracious.

The hamlet of **Zancudo** is near the river mouth at the north end of the spit, reached along a sandy roller-coaster of a track.

Entertainment

The bar at **Cabinas Sol y Mar** (tel. 506/2776-0014, www.zancudo.com) is a local meeting spot and hosts live music (Tues.), NFL and BBQ (Thurs.), volleyball (Sat.), and horseshoes (Sun.). Rough-around-the-edges **El Coquito,** in the village, is favored by locals for dancing, while unpretentious **Bar Sussy** is the place of choice for a tipple.

Sports and Recreation

Sportfishing Unlimited (tel./fax 506/2776-0036) is just south of the Zancudo Lodge.

Zancudo Boat Tours at Cabinas Los Cocos (tel./fax 506/2776-0012, www.loscocos.com)

rents pedal boats and snorkeling equipment, and has kayak trips and boat trips up the Río Coto.

Accommodations

Accommodations are strung out along the five-kilometer-long spit; there are more than listed here.

I like **Coloso del Mar** (tel. 506/2776-0050, www.coloso-del-mar.com, $25–30 s/d low season, $40–45 d high season), 200 meters north of Tranquilo, for its four rustic, simply furnished, yet lovely palm-shaded wooden cabins with ceiling fans, firm mattresses, screened windows, porches, safes, and hot-water showers. It has a quaint wooden restaurant, plus a gift shop and Internet café. Boat trips and water-taxi service are offered.

About two kilometers further is **Cabinas Sol y Mar** (tel. 506/2776-0014, www.zancudo.com, $25–45 s/d), with a pleasant casual ambience and landscaped grounds. The five simple *cabinas* are tastefully furnished with ceiling fans, and private skylit bathrooms. It also has a thatched three-story house designed without dividing walls for free air-flow ($800 monthly). There's volleyball and other games at the delightful thatched bar, plus great food. You can camp ($3 pp).

Competing for price and pleasantly simple ambience, **Restaurante Iguana Verde** (tel. 506/2776-0902, www.iguanaverde.net, $40 s/d low season, $60 high season), run by Andrew, from Chicago, has a breeze-swept bar and restaurant under a huge *palenque.* Three spacious, cross-lit, air-conditioned cabins (and a three-bedroom house) with tile floors, cable TV, and clean modern bathrooms are available. Next door, the French-run **Au Coeur du Soleil** (no tel., www.aucoeurdusoleil.com) is a similar alternative.

Cabinas Los Cocos (tel./fax 506/2776-0012, www.loscocos.com, $50 s/d low season, $70 high season), about 600 meters north of Sol y Mar, has four attractive, self-catering oceanfront units tucked amid landscaped

Playa Zancudo

grounds. One is a thatched, hardwood unit with a double bed downstairs and another in the loft; two others are venerable refurbished banana-company properties shipped from Palmar. Each has a kitchenette, mosquito nets, both inside and outside showers, and a veranda with hammocks. The place is run by a delightful couple: Susan (a gringa) and Andrew (a Brit) Robertson.

El Oasis (tel. 506/2776-0087, www.oasis-onthebeach.com, $45–60 s/d low season, $55–75 high season), run by Yankee transplants Gary and Debbie Walsh, is a laid-back place popular with surfers. It has five cabins of varnished hardwoods on stilts, all with orthopedic mattresses, microwaves, coffeemakers, and solar-heated water. It has a restaurant. Reports suggest it might have gone downhill.

The class act in Zancudo is **(Oceano** (tel. 506/776-0921, www.oceanocabinas.com, $59 s/d low season, $69 s/d high season), which opened in 2006. The two tiled air-conditioned rooms with ceiling fans have simple yet adorable decor and furnishings, including mosquito nets over the beds, plus cable TV. Umbrellas,

flashlights, and toiletries are among the thoughtful extras provided by gracious Canadian owners, Stephanie and Mark Homer. Nice! Free Internet, bicycle use, and breakfast are included. And the restaurant is cool!

In 2008, **Zancudo Lodge** (tel. 506/2776-0008 or U.S. tel. 800/854-8791, fax 506/776-0011, www.thezancudolodge.com, see the website for package rates), at the far north end of Zancudo, received a total remake and shifted from a sportfishing lodge to an upscale hotel, although sportfishing is still a forté. Its 19 rooms (most in a two-story unit set around lawns with palms and a swimming pool) have metamorphosed as junior suites with beautiful hardwood floors, glossy hardwood furnishings, and Wi-Fi throughout. Two oceanfront suites were being added. There's a beachfront restaurant and bar.

Competing for the upscale market, **Playa Zancudo B&B** (tel. 506/2776-0006, www.playazancudobedandbreakfast.com, $80 s, $90 d) is a handsome ranch-style wooden home raised on stilts at the north end of Zancudo. It has just two bedrooms, each with

GOLFO DULCE

© CHRISTOPHER P. BAKER

© CHRISTOPHER P. BAKER

Oceano restaurant, Zancudo

satellite TV, quality linens, and gracious furnishings. Reservations are required.

Food

For the best dining around, head to **Oceano** (tel. 506/776-0921, www.oceanocabinas.com, 11 A.M. until the last guest leaves; closed Mon. in low season), where you eat at tree-trunk tables under thatch. Huevos rancheros, waffles, omelettes ($2.50–4), salads, burgers, soups, filet mignon with béarnaise ($9), and a shrimp dinner made to order ($13) are all featured. *Do* try the awesome brownie sundae! It has Mexican night on Wednesdays, plus Sunday brunch (9 A.M.–3 P.M.), and a separate ice cream stand to help beat the heat. Oh, and there's Wi-Fi.

The breakfast menu at **Cabinas Sol y Mar** (7 A.M.–9 P.M. daily, $3–13) includes omelettes, French toast, home fries, home-baked breads and muffins, and coffee from a real espresso machine. The lunch and dinner menu features Thai dishes and barbecue. The nightly special when I visited was tuna with capers, rice, choyote squash, and green beans with roasted pepper sauce ($6).

Coloso del Mar (tel. 506/2776-0203, 4:30–9 P.M. Sun.–Fri.) is good for international fare. The open-air **Restaurante Puerta Negra** serving Italian cuisine such as gnocchi and tortellini, is also a good bet.

For sunsets, many locals head inland to **Hollywood** (tel. 506/8889-0821, noon–2 P.M.), between Conté and Zancudo (the turnoff is signed in La Virgen de Pavones). The lively restaurant-bar has a jukebox and pinball and hosts karaoke on Saturday. It serves *casados* ($5), jumbo shrimp ($12), and even chop sucy. It also has spacious rooms and apartments.

Information and Services

The **police station** (tel. 506/2776-0212) is on the north side of Zancudo village.

Getting There and Around

A bus departs from the municipal dock in Golfito for Zancudo at 2 P.M. daily and travels via Paso Canoas and Laurel ($2). The return bus departs Zancudo at 5:30 A.M.

The paved road to Zancudo begins about eight kilometers south of the Pan-American

Highway, midway along the road to Golfito; the turn is signed at Únion. An aging ferry will transport you across the Río Coto, 18 kilometers beyond El Rodeo; the ferry operates daily 5 A.M.–8 P.M. ($1 per car, $0.20 pedestrians), except in extreme wet season (or when it breaks down, which is often), when you're forced to drive all the way around via Paso Canoas and Laurel (fortunately, this road is paved). On the south bank, the intermittently paved road runs five kilometers to a Y-junction (La Cruce) at Pueblo Nuevo; turn right for Zancudo and Pavones and continue about 10 kilometers to a T-junction at Conte. Turn right here: Zancudo (18 km) and Pavones (22 km) are signed. This road divides one kilometer along; take the right-hand fork for Zancudo, and the left for Pavones.

The **Mini-Super Tres Amigos** (closed Sun.) and **Super Bella Vista** (tel. 506/2776-0101), in Zancudo, sell gas.

A *lancha* (water-taxi) departs Golfito's *muellecito* (dock) for Zancudo at noon daily, returning from Zancudo at 7 A.M. ($5 pp, or $50 charter up to six passengers). Call the Asociación de Boteros (tel. 506/2775-0357). **Zancudo Boat Tours** at Cabinas Los Cocos also has water-taxi service ($20 pp to Golfito or Puerto Jiménez; $50 minimum, two passengers).

Super Bella Vista has taxi service.

◖ PAVONES

From Conte, a bumpy potholed road clambers over the hills south of Zancudo and drops to Punta Pilón and the fishing hamlet of Pavones, a legend in the surfing world for possessing one of the longest waves in the world—more than a kilometer on a good day. The waves are at their best May–November, during rainy season, when surfers flock for the legendary very fast and very hollow tubular left. Riptides are common and swimmers should beware.

South from Pavones, the dirt road crosses the Río Claro and follows the dramatically scenic and rocky coast about five kilometers to the tiny community of **Punta Banco**. About two kilometers south of Punta Banco you reach the end

of the road. From here, the Peninsula de Burica sweeps southeast 50 kilometers to Punta Burica along a lonesome stretch of coast within the mountainous **Reserva Indígena Guaymí.**

Martial arts enthusiasts can sign up for workshops and summer retreats with **Tai Chi Vacations** (tel. 305/751-6221, http://taichivacations.com), which has a retreat at Pavones. And **The Yoga Farm** (no tel., www.yogafarmcostarica.org), above Punta Banco on the rough dirt road to the Guaymí reserve, offers yoga retreats.

Tiskita Lodge

Farm. Nature lodge. Exotic-fruit station. Biological reserve. Seaside retreat. Tiskita Lodge (c/o Costa Rica Sun Tours, tel. 506/2296-8125 or in North America tel. 786/664-4443, www.tiskita-lodge.co.cr) is all these and more. Overlooking Punta Banco, one kilometer north of the village, Tiskita offers sweeping panoramas. The rustic old lodge is surrounded by 150 hectares of virgin rainforest laced by trails; one leads sharply uphill to a series of cascades and pools. Wildlife abounds. Owner Peter Aspinall's pride and joy is his tropical-fruit farm, which contains the most extensive collection of tropical fruits in Costa Rica. Peter is also involved in a scarlet macaw release program. Guided nature walks and birding hikes are offered. Horse rides cost $35 for a half day.

Punta Banco Sea Turtle Restoration Project

Endangered ridley turtles (plus hawksbill and green turtles in lesser numbers) lay their eggs along these shores, predominantly August–December. The locals long considered them a resource to be harvested for eggs and meat. In 1996, the **Programa Restauración de Tortugas Marinas** (PRETOMA, tel. 506/2241-5227, www.tortugamarina.org) began a program to instill a conservation ethic in the community. It initiated a program to collect and hatch turtle eggs, and release hatchlings directly into the ocean, dramatically increasing their chances of survival. Poaching of nests has been reduced from 100 percent of nests in 1995 to less than 20 percent, and the hatcheries now achieve a better than 80 percent hatching rate for translocated eggs.

Sports and Recreation

Sea Kings Surf Shop (tel. 506/2776-2015, www.surfpavones.com) rents boards. **Shooting Star Studio** (tel. 506/8393-6982, www.shootingstarstudio.org) and **Venus Surf Adventures** (tel. 506/2776-2014, http://venus-surfadventures.com) also rent boards, offer surf lessons, and have yoga.

Accommodations

In Pavones, there are six or so budget options on the north side of the soccer field, including **Cabinas Maureen** (tel. 506/2746-2002, $15 pp with fan and shared bathroom, $50 s/d with a/c and private bathroom), with six small but high-ceilinged hardwood rooms in a two-story unit (each sleeps four people). And **Cabinas Carol** (tel. 506/8310-7507, $10 pp), with eight charming cabins in an enclosed garden (some have shared baths) also appeals.

There are half a dozen other budget accommodations of a similar standard within shouting distance, including **Café de la Suerte** (tel. 506/2776-2388, www.cafedelasuerte.com, $45 s/d low season, $60 s/d high season), which has one lovely, colorful room behind the café in the heart of Pavones. It has a double bed and bunk with Guatemalan spreads, tatami rugs, a bamboo ceiling with fan, and a delightful bathroom plus a garden with hammock.

The Italian-run **Soda/Restaurant La Piña** (no tel., $10 pp room, $20 pp cabin, $50–60 s/d duplex), 400 meters north of the soccer field, permits camping and has one basic room with private bathroom, a more substantial cabin with tiled private bathroom, and a two-story duplex of timber and river stone. The restaurant serves Italian dishes, including wood-oven pizza, and the owners rent surfboards and kayaks.

The nicest place in Pavones village is **Hotel La Perla** (tel. 506/8347-1020, $60 s/d), a modern-two-story structure with six pleasant air-conditioned rooms and lovely bathrooms.

A popular budget option at the end of the road in Punta Banco, the Dutch-run **Rancho Burica** (no tel., www.ranchoburica.com, $12.50 pp dorm, $30–40 s/d room including breakfast and dinner) offers a great bargain. Set in trim gardens, the seven simple cabins have huge cold-water showers and large porches, and there's a dorm in a circular *rancho,* plus a new "boathouse" room sleeping three people. Barbecues are made on the grill, guests have kitchen privileges, and there's a fishing boat for trips.

La Ponderosa Beach & Jungle Resort (tel. 506/8824-4145 or U.S. tel. 954/771-9166, www.laponderosapavones.com, $60–200 s/d) is a surfers' lodge run by Angela and Marshall McCarthy. It's set in lush gardens and offers six handsome two-story cabins with varnished hardwoods, fans, large screened windows, and private baths with hot water; four have air-conditioning and two are suites. A dining room serves everything from burgers and tuna melts to seafood. It has a lounge with bar, TV/VCR, sand volleyball court, and swimming pool. It also rents a two-bedroom house with king-size bed and kitchen. Trails lead into a forest with a waterfall. No credit cards are accepted.

The American-run **Cabinas Mira Olas** (tel. 506/2776-2006, www.miraolas.com, $30–45 s/d) has four beautifully decorated log *cabinas* with fans, and outdoor showers with warm water. One is rustic; the others are "jungle deluxe." They're set amid lush lawns.

I also recommend **Riviera Villas** (tel. 506/2776-2396, http://pavonesriviera.com, $80 s, $90 d), with three simply yet charmingly furnished self-contained cabins.

"Eclectic" and "Tolkienian" perfectly describe **Castillo de Pavones** (tel. 506/9396-6409, www.castillodepavones.com, $85–150 s/d including breakfast), in the hills above Pavones. This three-story, stone-and-timber lodge has four huge suites with king-size beds hewn of lofty tree trunks, and quaint blackstone-lined bathrooms with waterfall sinks, Jacuzzi tubs, and homemade organic toiletries. The bi-level restaurant is a winner.

I adore the gorgeous ◖ **Casa Siempre**

Domingo Bed and Breakfast (tel./fax 506/ 8820-4709, www.casa-domingo.com, $100 s/d), a deluxe, breeze-brushed Colorado-style lodge nestled on the hillside 400 meters inland, 1.5 kilometers south of the Río Claro. Owned and run by East Coasters Greg and Heidi, this beautiful lodge is set amid hibiscus-tinged lawns surrounded by six hectares of jungle-clad slopes. A mammoth cathedral ceiling soars over the lounge and dining room done up in evocative tropical style, with plentiful bamboo and jungle prints. The four rooms have two double beds or a double and single, ceramic tile floors, plus walk-in closets. The restaurant serves hearty fare. You'll enjoy dramatic ocean vistas from the sprawling deck. Rates include breakfast.

I also like the rustic, American-run **Sotavento** (tel. 506/8308-7484, www.sotaventoplantanal.com, $60 Casa Poinsietta, $80 Casa Vista Grande), which offers two simple two-bedroom wooden houses with tremendous views. The first, in a two-story unit, has a TV lounge, kitchen, mosquito nets, old wooden trunks for seats, and a large walk-in shower. The second has a massive dining table in the open kitchen. You can rent horses and surfboards, and boogie boards and fishing poles come free.

In late 2008, Joseph Robertson and his girlfriend Shirley were putting finishing touches to **Rancho Cannatella** (tel. 506/8393-2659, www.ranchocannatella.com), two kilometers south of Pavones. This lovely four-bedroom villa with wings flanking a freeform pool can be rented in entirety, but the air-conditioned rooms (which vary) are also rented individually; one has a king-size bed and rainforest shower. There's also a simple wooden cabin.

Everyone loves ☾ **Tiskita Lodge** (tel. 506/2664-4443, www.tiskita-lodge.co.cr, $155 s, $272 d, including all meals and a guided hike), centered on a charming old farmhouse that serves as lounge and dining room. There are 16 spacious rooms in nine rustic, sparsely furnished, but huge and comfortable wooden cabins in a combination of double, twin, and bunk beds (with rather soft mattresses). Each cabin has screened windows, wide veranda with hammock and Adirondack chair, plus a stone-lined outdoor bathroom with shower and solar-heated water. "Country-style" meals are served family-style at set times (don't be late), and packed lunches are provided for hikers. It has a small swimming pool and a rustic bar. It closes mid-September–mid-October. Two- to seven-day packages are offered.

Food

The best place to start your day is **Café de la Suerte** (tel. 506/2776-2388, www.cafedelasuerte.com, 7:30 A.M.–5:30 P.M. daily, $3) on the plaza in Pavones. This simple open-air eatery serves granola with yogurt and fruit, plus sandwiches, hummus, omelettes, cappuccinos, and fruit shakes.

La Manta Club (www.la-manta.com, noon–10 P.M. daily, $2–12), in Pavones, sells falafel, hummus, shish kabob, ice cream, iced tea, and iced coffee drinks, to be enjoyed in a splendid thatched bar (until 1 A.M. daily) with hammocks. Movies are shown on a big screen at 6 P.M.

The beachfront **Restaurante Esquina del Mar** (no tel., 6:30 A.M.–9 P.M. daily, $2–10), in Pavones, has simple breakfasts, plus *casados* and burgers. However, readers write to say that at night it draws prostitutes and roughnecks and reportedly occasionally turns violent. Far better is to head to the hills and the **Blue Morpho Grill and Lounge** (6–10 P.M. nightly), at Castillo de Pavones. Hewn of sturdy timbers and natural stone floors, this bi-level restaurant-bar serves California fusion cuisine and seafood, such as ahi tuni and filet mignon on skewers. Look for the occasional Brazilian-style all-you-can-eat buffets ($15).

Restaurante La Pina (no tel., noon–10 P.M. daily, $5–15), betwixt Pavones and Punta Banco, is an exquisite open-air Italian restaurant serving the expected fare (gnocchi, lasagna, and the like) of high quality.

Information and Services

The public telephone (tel. 506/2770-8221) is at Soda La Plaza, beside the soccer field in Pavones. Nearby, **Clear River Sports & Adventure** (tel. 506/2776-2016) has an Internet café with Skype.

GOLFO DULCE

There's a **police station** (no tel.) on the north side of the soccer field in Pavones.

Getting There

A private airstrip allows direct access to Tiskita by chartered plane (55 minutes from San José). Buses depart Golfito for Pavones and Punta Banco at 10:30 A.M. (Pavones only) and 3 P.M., returning at 5:30 A.M. (from Rancho Burica) and 12:30 P.M. (from Pavones only).

The coast road that leads south from Pavones ends at the mouth of the Río Claro, one kilometer south of the village. To cross it and continue to Punta Banco, back up and turn inland at Escuela Las Gemelas, then right at Super Mares; you'll cross a bridge, then drop back down to the coast.

A private water-taxi charter from Golfito will cost about $65 one-way. A Jeep taxi from Golfito to Pavones will cost about $75.

◖ ISLA DE COCOS NATIONAL PARK

The only true oceanic island off Central America, Isla de Cocos—500 kilometers southwest of Costa Rica—is a 52-square-kilometer mountainous chunk of land that rises to 634 meters at Iglesias Peak. Declared a UNESCO World Heritage Site in 1997, the island is the northernmost and oldest of a chain of volcanoes, mostly submarine, stretching south along the Cocos Ridge to the equator, where several come to the surface as the Galápagos Islands. These islands were formed by a hot spot, which pushes up volcanic material from beneath the earth's crust. The hot spot deep inside the earth remains stationary while the sea floor moves over it. Over time, the volcanic cone is transported away from the hot spot and a new volcano arises in the same place.

Cliffs reach higher than 100 meters around almost the entire island, and dramatic waterfalls cascade onto the beach.

Cocos's forested hills supposedly harbor gold doubloons. More than 500 expeditions have sought in vain to find the Lima Booty—gold and silver ingots that mysteriously disappeared while en route to Spain under the care of Captain James Thompson. The pirate William Davies supposedly hid his treasure here in 1684, as did Portuguese buccaneer Benito "Bloody Sword" Bonito in 1889. The government has placed a "virtual moratorium" on treasure hunts, although the Ministry of Natural Resources sanctioned a hunt in January 1992.

It is inhabited only by national park guards who patrol the park equipped with small Zodiacs. The only safe anchorage for entry is at Chatham Bay, on the northeast corner, where scores of rocks are etched with the names and dates of ships dating back to the 17th century.

There are no native mammals. The surrounding waters, however, are home to four unique species of marine mollusks. The island has one butterfly and two lizard species to call its own. And three species of birds are endemic: the Cocos Island finch, Cocos Island cuckoo, and the Ridgeway or Cocos flycatcher. Three species of boobies—red-footed, masked, and brown—live here, too. Isla de Cocos is also a popular spot for frigate birds to roost and mate, and white terns may hover above your head. Feral pigs, introduced in the 18th century by passing sailors, today number about 5,000 and have caused substantial erosion.

Access to the island is restricted. **Friends of Cocos Island** (FAICO, tel. 506/2256-7476, www.cocosisland.org) works to protect the area from illegal fishing.

Diving

The island is one of the world's best diving spots, famous for its massive schools of white-tipped and hammerhead sharks, eerie manta rays, pilot whales, whale sharks, and sailfish. *Cocos is for experienced divers only:* Dropoffs are deep, currents are continually changing, and beginning divers would freak at the huge shark populations. (In fact, converging ocean currents stir up such a wealth of nutrients that the sharks have a surfeit of fish to feed on, and taking a chunk out of divers is probably the last thing on their minds.) Snorkelers swimming closer to the surface can revel in moray eels and colorful reef fish.

Two dive vessels operate out of Los Sueños Marina. The **Okeanos Aggressor** (U.S. tel. 866/348-2628, www.aggressor.com) is a 34-meter, fully air-conditioned, 10-stateroom ship with complete facilities for 21 divers. It offers eight- and 10-day trips from $2,495 per person all-inclusive (the $35 per day park fee is extra). **Undersea Hunter** (tel. 506/2228-6613, or U.S. tel. 800/203-2120, www.underseahunter.com) operates 10- and 12-day Isla de Cocos trips using the 18-passenger MV *Sea Hunter,* which features a three-passenger submarine, and 14-passenger MV *Undersea Hunter.*

Information and Services

For information, contact the National Parks Service (tel. 506/2283-0022 or tel./fax 506/2258-7350, islacoco@ns.minae.co.cr), or the **ranger station** (satellite tel. 0087-468712-0010). There are no accommodations, and camping is not allowed.

Ciudad Neily and Vicinity

CIUDAD NEILY

Ciudad Neily squats at the base of the Fila Costeña mountains, beside the Pan-American Highway, 18 kilometers northwest of Panamá and 15 kilometers east of the town of **Río Claro** and the turnoff for Golfito. Ciudad Neily is surrounded by banana plantations and functions as the node for plantation operations. There is nothing to hold your interest, though you are likely to see indigenous women in colorful traditional dress, usually begging for a meager living.

North from Ciudad Neily, a road switchbacks steeply uphill to San Vito (31 kilometers). South from town, a road leads through a sea of African palm plantations to the airstrip at **Coto 47.**

◖ Paradise Garden

A decade of labor and love has gone into creating this gem of a botanical garden (tel. 506/2789-8746, rbeatham@hotmail.com, 6 A.M.–5 P.M. daily), immediately west of Río Claro (the ill-marked turnoff is on the west side of the Río Lagarto bridge, opposite the Arrocera El Ceibo rice factory; the garden is 200 meters north from the turnoff). Owner Robert Beatham, from Maine, started the garden as a hobby; today he produces 16 tons of African palm fruits per month. But it's the heliconias, gingers, and dozens of other species that delight, while Robert's immense knowledge keeps you wide-eyed in awe. Lunch is served as Robert expounds about the various fruits, seeds, and nuts used in the meal and introduces you to local remedies (such as "wandering jew," good for treating diabetes).

Accommodations

There's no shortage of budget hotels. One of the best bets is **Cabinas Heileen** (tel. 506/2783-3080, $12 pp, $16 pp with TVs), in a nicely kept home festooned with epiphytes. Its 10 simple but clean rooms have fans and private baths with cold water (one room has hot water). Five rooms have TVs.

The nicest place in town is **Hotel Andrea** (tel. 506/2783-3784, elhotelandrea@hotmail.com, $28 s or $34 d with fans, $35 s or $41 d with a/c), with 35 rooms in a handsome two-story colonial-style property festooned with hanging plants, 50 meters west of the bus station. Rooms are clean, with tile floors and modest furnishings. All have TV and hot water, and 14 have air-conditioning. It has secure parking and an appealing open-air restaurant and bar.

Two kilometers west, the Belgian-run **Hospedaje Eurotica** (tel. 506/2783-3756, http://xref.ws/Euro-Tica, $30 s or $40 d low season, $35 s or $45 d high season) is a nice option, with simply furnished rooms in a garden. And the views from **Hotel El Mirador** (tel. 506/8841-2935, $18 s, $26 d), 600 meters

GOLFO DULCE

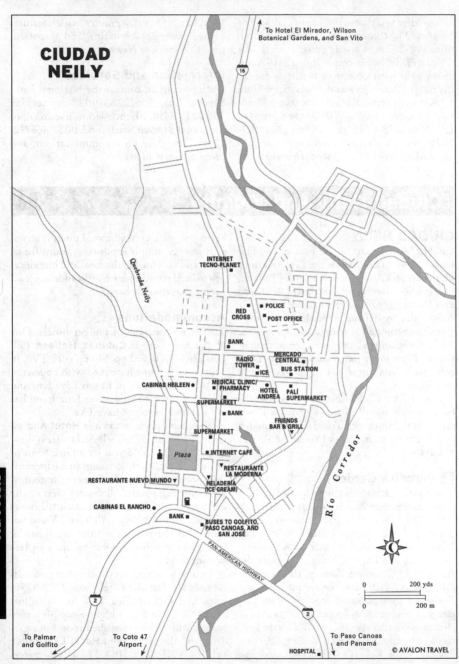

CIUDAD NEILY

To Hotel El Mirador, Wilson Botanical Gardens, and San Vito

Quebrada Neily

INTERNET TECNO-PLANET

RED CROSS

POLICE

POST OFFICE

BANK

RADIO TOWER

ICE

MERCADO CENTRAL

BUS STATION

CABINAS HEILEEN

MEDICAL CLINIC/ PHARMACY

HOTEL ANDREA

PALÍ SUPERMARKET

SUPERMARKET

BANK

SUPERMARKET

FRIENDS BAR & GRILL

Plaza

INTERNET CAFÉ

RESTAURANTE LA MODERNA

RESTAURANTE NUEVO MUNDO

HELADERÍA (ICE CREAM)

CABINAS EL RANCHO

BANK

BUSES TO GOLFITO, PASO CANOAS, AND SAN JOSÉ

Río Corredor

PAN-AMERICAN HIGHWAY

To Palmar and Golfito

To Coto 47 Airport

To Paso Canoas and Panamá

HOSPITAL

0   200 yds

0   200 m

© AVALON TRAVEL

GOLFO DULCE

Robert Beatham with fan palm, Paradise Garden

above town on the snaking road to San Vito, make a stay here worthwhile, despite simply furnished rooms. It has a nice restaurant, but it also serves as a love motel!

At Río Claro, 1.5 kilometers north of the Pan-American Highway, the German-run **Hotel Palmeral Dorima** (tel. 506/8315-1966, www.palmeraldorima.com, $52 s or $58 d low season, $64 s or $69 d high season) offers fabulous views from its mountainside perch. Set in a tropical garden, this rather rough-hewn place has 16 air-conditioned rooms in eight duplex bungalows; all have king-size beds with mosquito nets, solar-heated showers, satellite TV, telephone, in-room safe, refrigerator, and a private terrace with lounge chairs for soaking in the views. There's a pool and hot tub.

Food

Hotel Andrea (6 A.M.–10:30 P.M. daily, $1.50– 15) has the most elegant eatery in town. The menu includes pancakes and honey, huevos rancheros, omelettes, onion soup, shrimp salad, pastas, and filet mignon.

The clean, modern **Restaurante La Moderna** (tel. 506/2783-3097, $2–12), on the main street, one block east of the plaza, has an eclectic menu ranging from burgers and pizza to ceviche and *típico* dishes.

Information and Services

The hospital is 1.5 kilometers southeast of town on Highway 2. **Consultório Médico** (tel. 506/2783-3840, 8 A.M.–8 P.M. Mon.–Sat.) and **Pharmacy Kayros** adjoin each other on the main street. The **Red Cross** (tel. 506/2783-3757) is on the northeast side of town, opposite the **police station** (tel. 506/2783-3388).

There are three banks in the center. The post office is on the northeast side of town. **Tecno-Planet Internet** (tel. 506/2783-4744, 8 A.M.–9 P.M. Mon.–Fri., 8 A.M.–10 P.M. Sat.) is on the main drag, at the north end of town.

Getting There

The airport is four kilometers south of town, at Coto 47. **SANSA** and **Nature Air** both have scheduled service to Coto 47.

Tracopa buses (tel. 506/2222-2666) depart San José for Ciudad Neily from Calle 5, Avenidas

GOLFO DULCE

18/20, at 5 A.M., 10 A.M., 1 P.M., 4:30 P.M., and 6 P.M. daily (eight hours). Buses depart Ciudad Neily for San José at 4:30 A.M., 9 A.M., 11:30 A.M., and 3 P.M. daily; for Dominical at 6 A.M. and 2:30 P.M. daily; for Paso Canoas hourly 6 A.M.–6 P.M. daily; for Puerto Jiménez at 7 A.M. and 2 P.M. daily; for San Vito at 6 A.M., 11 A.M., 1 P.M., and 3 P.M. daily; and for Cortes at 4:45 A.M., 6 A.M., 9:15 A.M., noon, 2:30 P.M., 4:30 P.M., and 5:45 P.M. daily.

For taxis call **Taxi Ciudad Neily** (tel. 506/783-3374).

PASO CANOAS AND VICINITY

There's absolutely no reason to visit ugly Paso Canoas unless you intend to cross into Panamá. Endless stalls and shops selling duty-free goods are strung out along the road paralleling the border (there's no barrier separating the well-paved Panamanian highway and the potholed Costa Rican highway, so be careful that you don't cross into Panama unexpectedly, which is easily done). Avoid Easter week and the months before Christmas, when Paso Canoas is a zoo.

The border road runs south to the town of **Laurel**, a regional center for the banana industry with lots of old wooden plantation homes, and thence to Conte. **Lucero Tours** (Edificio Téllez, Paso Canoas, tel. 506/2732-3118, grupolucerodelsur@racsa.co.cr) offers "Banana Tours" that include Panamá and the Coopetrabasur (www.coopetrabasur.com) plantation and packing plant at Lucero, five kilometers south of Laurel.

Accommodations and Food

There are lots of accommodation choices.

One of the best is the modern, motel-style **Cabinas Alpina** (tel. 506/2732-2612, $8 pp for basic rooms, $20 s/d for nicer a/c rooms upstairs), two blocks south of the bus terminal, offering rooms away from the bustle. It also has secure parking. Opposite, the salmon-pink **Hotel Azteca** (tel. 506/2732-2217) offers similar standards and prices, as does **Hotel Real Victoria** (tel. 506/2732-2586, fax 506/2732-2762), nearby.

The most upscale option is **Hotel Los Higueros** (tel. 506/2732-2157, $36 s, $42 d), a classical-themed hotel that opened in 2008 with 28 air-conditioned rooms in secure landscaped grounds on the south side of town.

Information and Services

There's a **bank** 20 meters west of the border post. The **police station** (tel. 506/2732-2106) is 100 meters west of the border post. **Customs and immigration** (tel. 506/2732-2150) are opposite the bus terminal 100 meters west of the border post. **PC Doctor Café Internet** (tel. 506/2732-3509) is 400 meters south of the border post.

Getting There

Tracopa buses (tel. 506/2222-2666 or 2732-2119) depart San José for Paso Canoas from Calle 5, Avenidas 18/20, daily at 5 A.M., 7:30 A.M., 11 A.M., 1 P.M., 4:30 P.M., and 6 P.M. (eight hours, approximately $12). Buses leave Paso Canoas for San José at 4 A.M., 7:30 A.M., 9 A.M., and 3 P.M. Buses also run frequently from Ciudad Neily to the border (about $0.25), and from Golfito almost hourly 5:15 A.M.–6:30 A.M. Weekend buses to and from Paso Canoas fill up early; reservations are recommended. Local buses depart for Neily every hour.

Taxis (tel. 506/2727-6334) wait in front of the border crossing.

Lucero Tours (tel. 506/2732-3118, grupolucerodelsur@rasca.co.cr) rents cars.

SOUTH-CENTRAL COSTA RICA

The south-central region is the Cinderella of Costa Rican tourism. A larger proportion of the region is protected as national park or forest reserve than in any other part of the country. Much remains inaccessible and unexplored. Herein lies the beauty: Huge regions such as Chirripó National Park and La Amistad International Peace Park harbor incredibly diverse populations of Central American flora and fauna.

The region is dominated to the east by the massive and daunting Talamanca massif. Slanting southeast and paralleling the Talamancas to the west is a range of lower-elevation mountains called the Fila Costeña. Between the two lies the 100-kilometer-long by 30-kilometer-wide Valle de El General, extending into the Valle de Coto Brus to the south. The valley is a center of agriculture, with pineapples covering the flatlands of the Río General, and coffee smothering the slopes of Coto Brus (alas, much of the coffee plants have been removed in recent years). The rivers that drain the valley merge to form the Río Grande de Terraba, which slices west through the Fila Costeña to reach the sea.

The region is home to the nation's largest concentration of indigenous people. In the remote highland reaches, and occasionally in towns, you'll see indigenous Guaymi and Boruca women dressed in traditional colorful garb, often walking barefoot, their small frames laden with babies or bulging bags.

The regional climate varies with topography. Clouds moving in from the Pacific dump most of their rain on the western slopes of the Fila

© CHRISTOPHER P. BAKER

HIGHLIGHTS

◖ Los Cusingos Bird Sanctuary: Birders should make haste to this fabulous birding site, where visitors can thrill to sightings of more than 300 species (page 527).

◖ Río Chirripó Valley: Tucked into a fold of the Talamanca mountains, this splendidly scenic valley is gateway to Chirripó National Park. Its fabulous opportunities for birding and hiking culminate in the two-day hike to the summit of Chirripó (page 531).

◖ Chirripó National Park: Hiking to the summit of Costa Rica's highest mountain requires no more than stamina and offers the reward of sensational views as you pass through a wide range of habitats (page 536).

◖ Durika Biological Reserve: High on the mountain slopes abutting La Amistad International Peace Park, this eco-sensitive

commune provides a unique experience for travelers seeking to participate in a rustic communal lifestyle. Hikes are offered into the park (page 540).

◖ Las Cruces Biological Station/ Wilson Botanical Garden: This reserve and research station has miles of nature trails through humid montane ecosystems, offering magnificent wildlife viewing. The highlight is the Wilson Botanical Garden, a jewel among tropical botanical gardens (page 542).

◖ La Amistad Friendship Park – South: This park, shared with Panama, is the ultimate in rugged, remote mountain terrain. It's most easily accessed from the south; here, trails lead into a private cloud-forest reserve with rustic accommodation at La Amistad Lodge, above San Vito (page 545).

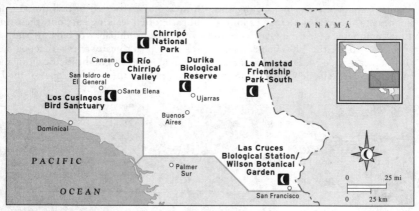

LOOK FOR ◖ TO FIND RECOMMENDED SIGHTS, ACTIVITIES, DINING, AND LODGING.

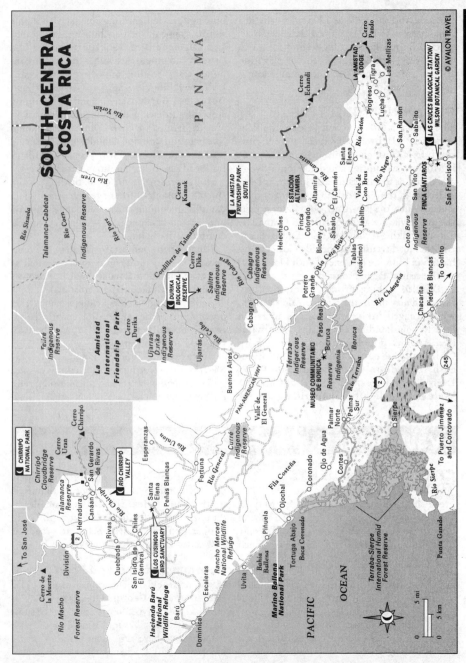

© AVALON TRAVEL

Costeña, and the Valle de El General sits in a rain shadow. To the east, the Talamanca massif is rain-drenched and fog-bound for much of the year. Temperatures drop as elevation climbs, and atop the Talamancas temperatures approach freezing.

PLANNING YOUR TIME

The region is linked to San José by the Pan-American Highway (Hwy. 2), which runs south from Cartago, climbs over the Cerro de la Muerte—a daunting and dangerous drive—and descends to San Isidro (also known as Pérez Zeledón) in the Valle de El General. South of Buenos Aires, the Pan-American Highway exits the valley via the gorge of the Río Grande de Terraba, linking it with the Golfo Dulce region. Another road transcends the Fila Costeña and links San Isidro de El General with Dominical on the central Pacific coast.

Travelers seeking virtually unexplored terrain find nirvana in the remote **Talamancas,** where rugged hiking trails grant access to lightly populated areas teeming with wildlife. Another popular option is the trek up Chirripó, the nation's highest mountain, enshrined within **Chirripó National Park.** Even for non-trekkers, the **Río Chirripó Valley** is a delightful Shangri-la good for birding, and invigorating for its crisp alpine setting. Some of the best birding is at nearby **Los Cusingos Bird Sanctuary,** and at **Las Cruces Biological Station,** with well-maintained trails, rivaling anywhere in the country for wildlife-viewing. Las Cruces' **Wilson Botanical Garden** is a superlative among tropical gardens, a tonic for your spirits in even the rainiest weather. Both the **Talamanca Reserve** and **Chirripó Cloudbridge Reserve,** near the entrance to Chirripó National Park trailhead, are other fabulous nature reserves with opportunities for great birding, while **Durika Biological Reserve**—accessed via a daunting mountain drive—will appeal to anyone seeking to experience life on a ecological commune firsthand.

Much of the mountain fastness is incorporated within indigenous reserves, such as **Reserva Indígena Boruca,** which welcomes visitors. Tourist facilities are minimal.

As yet, the region lacks a canopy tour. Other organized activities are minimal, with the exception of **white-water rafting** on the Ríos Chirripó and General.

Selva Mar (tel. 506/771-4582, fax 506/771-8841, www.exploringcostarica.com) acts as a tour information center and reservation service for the region.

Valle de El General

CERRO DE LA MUERTE TO SAN ISIDRO

From the 3,491-meter summit of Cerro de la Muerte, about 100 kilometers south of San José, the Pan-American Highway drops steeply to San Isidro, in the Valle de El General. When the clouds part, you are rewarded with a fabulous vista, the whole Valle de El General spread out before you. The route is often fog-bound and there are many large trucks (some without lights). Frequent landslides, fathoms-deep potholes, and too many accidents for comfort are among the dangers—take extreme care. *Avoid this road at night!*

A statue of Christ balances precariously on the cliff face above the highway two kilometers north of **San Rafael** (Km 104). A small, traditional *trapiche* (ox-driven sugar mill) is still in operation immediately below at a roadside *soda* called **El Trapiche de Nayo.**

Accommodations and Food

If you're stuck on the mountain, **Hotel/ Restaurant Las Georgina** (tel./fax 506/2770-8043, $25 s/d), five kilometers below the summit at Villa Mills, has four simple rooms with hot water; two have bunks, one has a TV. It also has a cabin with kitchen, fireplace, and views.

The huge buffet is a treat (6 A.M.–8 P.M.), and the views as you dine at 3,100 meters are awesome when the clouds clear!

At Kilometer 119 is **Mirador Vista del Valle** (tel./fax 506/8384-4685, $25 s/d), a delightfully rustic restaurant named for its stunning view. It has eight simple wooden *cabinas* with modern bathrooms, and bird-watching and fishing are offered.

A Canadian/German couple, Lisa and Rolf Zersch, lovingly tend their bed-and-breakfast home, **Bosque del Tolomuco** (tel. 506/8847-7207, www.bosquedeltolomuco.com, $70 s/d including breakfast and taxes), at Kilometer 118. Their charming inn, set in lush landscaped gardens, has three cozy wooden cabins with modern bathrooms. The simply appointed lounge is heated by a roaring wood-burning stove. Dinners are served by appointment. There's a heated swimming pool, and trails lead into a private forest, good for spotting wildlife and birds. Day visitors are welcome ($2 pp). What a thrill to awaken to sunrise views towards Chirripó, and you can see as far as the Osa Peninsula on a clear day from atop the mountain.

SAN ISIDRO DE EL GENERAL

San Isidro, regional capital of the Valle de El General, is an agricultural market town, gateway to Chirripó National Park and Dominical, and a base for white-water rafting.

There is little to see in town. The small **Southern Regional Museum** (Calle 2, Avenida 1, tel. 506/2771-5273, 8 A.M.–noon and 1–4:30 P.M. Mon.–Fri., free admission) tells the story of the local indigenous peoples. More impressive, the Modernist concrete **cathedral** on the east side of the plaza has lovely stained-glass windows.

La Ribera Centro Ecológico (tel. 506/2737-0004, www.lariberaecoturismo.com), at Mollejones de Plantaneres, 22 kilometers south of San Isidro, on the road to Pejibaye, has waterfalls, tropical forest, natural swimming holes as well as man-made swimming pools, and a restaurant. It is a popular weekend destination for locals.

modernist cathedral in San Isidro de El General

© CHRISTOPHER P. BAKER

Finca Ipe (www.fincaipe.com) is a self-supporting commune on a 12-hectare farm, 20 kilometers west of San Isidro. You can volunteer (a two-month minimum is required; from $300 for 30 nights); five hours of labor a day is expected. Free time grants a chance for hiking, horseback riding, or yoga.

La Gran Vista Agro-ecological Farm (tel. 506/2357-9688, www.lagranvista.com), at El Peje de Repunta, 15 kilometers south of San Isidro, teaches sustainable agricultural practices to local farmers. It relies on travelers for volunteer labor. Accommodation is in dorms ($20 per person, including all meals) with hot showers. A minimum weeklong stay is recommended.

◖ Los Cusingos Bird Sanctuary

This 142-hectare bird sanctuary, in Quizarrá de Pérez Zeledón, on the lower slopes of Chirripó, near the small community of Santa Elena, 15 kilometers southeast of San Isidro, is the former home of the late Dr. Alexander Skutch (co-author with Gary Stiles of *Birds of Costa Rica*); it now lies with the Alexander Skutch Biological

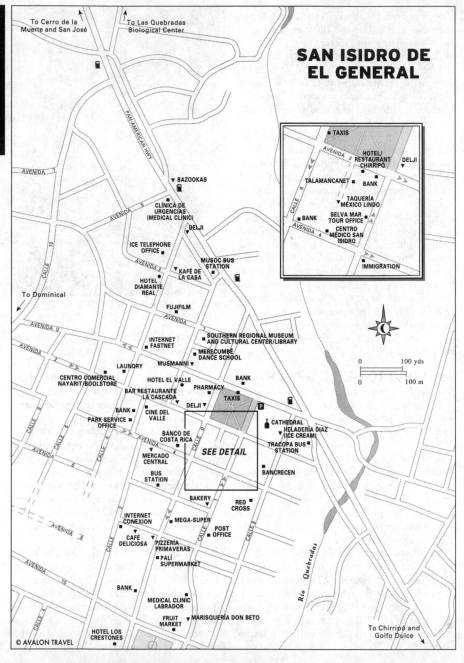

SAN ISIDRO DE EL GENERAL

To Cerro de la Muerte and San José

To Las Quebradas Biological Center

PAN-AMERICAN HWY

AVENIDA 1

AVENIDA 5

CALLE 10

To Dominical

TAXIS

AVENIDA 2

HOTEL/ RESTAURANT CHIRRIPÓ

DELJI

TALAMANCANET

BANK

CALLE 0

TAQUERÍA MÉXICO LINDO

BANK

SELVA MAR TOUR OFFICE

AVENIDA 4

CENTRO MÉDICO SAN ISIDRO

IMMIGRATION

BAZOOKAS

CLÍNICA DE URGENCIAS (MEDICAL CLINIC)

DELJI

ICE TELEPHONE OFFICE

MUSOC BUS STATION

AVENIDA 3

KAFÉ DE LA CASA

HOTEL DIAMANTE REAL

FUJIFILM

AVENIDA

AVENIDA 0

INTERNET FASTNET

SOUTHERN REGIONAL MUSEUM AND CULTURAL CENTER/LIBRARY

MERECUMBÉ DANCE SCHOOL

AVENIDA 2

LAUNDRY

MUSMANNI

CENTRO COMERCIAL NAYARIT/BOOLSTORE

HOTEL EL VALLE

PHARMACY

BANK

BAR RESTAURANTE LA CASCADA

TAXIS

P

CALLE 8

BANK

CINE DEL VALLE

DELJI

PARK SERVICE OFFICE

CALLE 6

CATHEDRAL

HELADERÍA DIAZ (ICE CREAM)

AVENIDA

BANCO DE COSTA RICA

TRACOPA BUS STATION

AVENIDA 8

MERCADO CENTRAL

SEE DETAIL

BUS STATION

BANCRECEN

AVENIDA 8

BAKERY

RED CROSS

INTERNET CONEXION

MEGA-SUPER

CALLE 5

CAFÉ DELICIOSA

POST OFFICE

CALLE 3

PIZZERÍA PRIMAVERAS

PALÍ SUPERMARKET

AVENIDA 10

Río Quebradas

BANK

MEDICAL CLINIC LABRADOR

CALLE 4

FRUIT MARKET

MARISQUERÍA DON BETO

To Chirripó and Golfo Dulce

© AVALON TRAVEL

HOTEL LOS CRESTONES

0   100 yds

0   100 m

© CHRISTOPHER P. BAKER

Los Cusingos Bird Sanctuary

Corridor. Run by the Tropical Science Center, the reserve is surrounded by primary forest, home to more than 300 bird species.

You get there via General Viejo (5 km east of San Isidro from the San Gerardo de Rivas road, then south for Peñas Blanca) or from Highway 2 via Peñas Blancas (then north for General Viejo). Turn east for Quizarrá–Santa Elena, two kilometers north of Peñas Blanca, then follow the signes of Quizarrá.

Visits are by appointment only and limited to researchers, students, naturalists, and bird-watchers (contact the Tropical Science Center, tel. 506/2200-5472, cusingosreservation@cct.or.cr, www.cct.or.cr, 7 A.M.–4 P.M. Mon.–Sat., 7 A.M.–1 P.M. Sunday, $10 entrance).

Entertainment and Events

The town comes alive late January and early February for its **Fiesta Cívica,** when agricultural fairs, bullfights, and general festivities occur. The best time to visit, however, is May 15, for the **Día del Boyero,** featuring a colorful oxcart parade.

The upstairs, open-air **Bar La Cascada** is the local gathering spot of choice. Hotel del Sur Country Club (tel. 506/771-3033, fax 506/771-0527) has a **casino.**

Accommodations

In town, the best option for budget hounds is the **Hotel/Restaurante Chirripó** (tel. 506/2771-0529, fax 506/2771-0410, $10 s or $15 d shared bath, $15 s or $22 d private bath and TV), on the southwest side of the square, offering 41 rooms with hot water and a pleasing outdoor restaurant. The **Hotel El Valle** (Calle 2, Avenida 0, tel. 506/771-0246) is a similarly priced alternative.

A better bet is the modern **Hotel y Restaurante San Isidro** (tel. 506/2770-3444, fax 506/2770-3673, $18 s, $30 d), two kilometers south of town. Centered on a two-story atrium, it has 40 smallish air-conditioned rooms modestly furnished with contemporary decor, fans, cable TV, and clean bathrooms with hot water. It has an Internet café and secure parking.

The bargain-priced class act in town is the **Hotel Diamante Real** (Calle 4, Avenida 3, tel. 506/2770-6230, www.hoteldiamantereal.com,

$40 s/d standard, $50 suite, $60 deluxe), which offers elegant art deco furniture and beautiful bathrooms, some with whirlpool tubs. Its restaurant is San Isidro's finest.

If the Diamante Real is full, consider **Hotel Los Crestones** (Calle Central, Avenidas 10/12, tel. 506/2770-1200, www.hotelloscrestones.com, $35 s or $45 d with fan, $45 s or $50 d with a/c), a tranquil three-story property done up in a complementary cream-and-green color scheme, with tasteful rattan furniture. It has 17 rooms with cable TV, balconies festooned with climbing plants, and modern bathrooms.

The other hotel in this price bracket—**Hotel del Sur Country Club & Casino** (tel. 506/771-3033, fax 506/771-0527), six kilometers south of San Isidro—is popular with businessfolk but is less appealing, despite having a pool, tennis, and a casino.

Looking for an organic farm in the mountains? Then consider **Finca Tres Semillas Mountain Inn** (tel. 506/8371-5869, http://finca3semillas.com, $60 pp including meals, $25 students, $20 volunteers), about 35 kilometers northwest of town. Here, Tamara Newton and Geraldo Saenz welcome guests seeking a genuine Costa Rican experience. This is simple living and simple accommodations, *campesino* (country farmer) style. You can hike and go horseback riding.

Food

You can eat cheaply at *sodas* at the **Mercado Central,** adjoining the bus station.

The **Restaurant Chirripó** (tel. 506/2771-0529, 7 A.M.–10 P.M.), on the south side of the plaza, is recommended for breakfast and *casados* (set lunches). For lunch, I gravitate next door to ◖ **Taquería México Lindo** (tel. 506/2771-8222, 9:30 A.M.–8 P.M. Mon.–Sat., $2–10), where a Mexican cook produces the real enchilada, plus burritos and other dishes. Be sure to try the coconut and vanilla flans.

The always packed and lively **Bar Restaurante La Cascada** (Avenida 2, Calle 2, tel. 506/2771-6479, 11 A.M.–midnight daily), with an open-air terrace, has a reasonably priced international menu.

For seafood, locals beeline to **Marisquería Don Beto** (Calle 1, Avenida 10, tel. 506/2771-7000, 8 A.M.–10 P.M. daily), where a *casado* costs $4.

Delji (tel. 506/2771-7070), a U.S.–style diner serving roast chicken, has three outlets.

Pizzería Primaveras (Avenida 8, Calles 0/2, tel. 506/2772-1975, 10:30 A.M.–10:30 P.M. Thurs.–Tues.) serves tasty pizzas. Next door, **Café Deliciosa** (tel. 506/2771-0476, 8 A.M.–7 P.M. Mon.–Sat.) has a patio good for enjoying baked goods, cappuccinos, and espressos. For a bohemian ambience, I prefer **Kafé de la Casa** (Avenida 3 at Calle 4, tel. 506/2770-4816, 6 A.M.–9 P.M. Mon.–Fri., 6 A.M.–7 P.M. Sat., 8 A.M.–5 P.M. Sun.), housed in a charming wooden colonial home. And **Musmanni** bakery has outlets three blocks southwest of the plaza and at Avenida 0, Calles 0/2.

Information and Services

Selva Mar (Calle 1, Avenidas 2/4, tel. 506/2771-4582, www.exploringcostarica.com) offers tourist information and acts as a reservation service.

The **hospital** (tel. 506/2771-3122) is on the southwest side of town. Medical centers include **Centro Médico San Isidro** (Avenida 4, Calles Central/1, tel. 506/2771-4467); **Hospital Clínica Labrador** (Calle 1, Avenidas 8/10, tel. 506/2771-7115); and **Clínica de Urgencias** (Highway 1, Avenida 5, tel. 506/2772-7070), with a 24-hour pharmacy.

The **post office** (tel. 506/2770-1669) is three blocks south of the plaza, on Calle 1. The town has a dozen Internet cafés.

Getting There

Musoc buses (tel. 506/2222-2422) depart Calle Central, Avenida 22, in San José hourly 5:30 A.M.–6:30 P.M., plus express service at 1 P.M. and 4 P.M. Return buses (in San Isidro, tel. 506/771-0414) depart from Highway 2 at the junction of Avenida 0 in San Isidro at 5 A.M. and 5:30 A.M. then hourly 5:30 A.M.–5:30 P.M.

Tracopa (tel. 506/2222-2666) buses depart Calle 5, Avenidas 18/20 in San José hourly 5 A.M.–6 P.M.; returning hourly 5:30 P.M.–9:30 P.M.

The regional bus station in San Isidro is at Calle Central and Avenidas 4/6. Transportes Blanco (tel. 506/2771-2550) buses depart for San Isidro from both Quepos and Dominical five times daily; from Puerto Jímenez at 1 P.M.; from San Vito four times daily; and from Uvita at 6 A.M. and 1:45 P.M.

Buses depart San Isidro for Dominical at 7 A.M., 9 A.M., 1:30 P.M., and 4 P.M.; for Puerto Jiménez at 6:30 A.M.; for Quepos at 7 A.M., 9 A.M., 1:30 P.M., and 4 P.M.; for San Gerardo de Rivas at 5:30 A.M. and 4:30 P.M.; for San Vito at 5:45 A.M., 8:15 A.M., 11:30 A.M., and 2:45 P.M.; and for Uvita at 9 A.M. and 4 P.M.

Chirripó and Vicinity

◖ RÍO CHIRRIPÓ VALLEY

The Valle del Río Chirripó cuts deeply into the Talamancas northeast of San Isidro, fed by waters cascading down from Cerro Chirripó (3,819 m), Costa Rica's highest mountain. The river is favored for trout fishing, and for kayaking and rafting, with enormous volumes of water. Contact **Costa Rica Expeditions** (tel. 506/2257-0766, www.costaricaexpeditions.com) for rafting tours and trips. The drive offers spectacular scenery.

Rivas, a little village six kilometers east of San Isidro, is famous for the roadside **"Rock of the Indian,"** carved with pre-Columbian motifs (but defaced by vandals' graffiti) 100 meters north of **Rancho La Botija** (tel./fax 506/2770-2146, www.rancholabotija.com, 9 A.M.–5 P.M. Tues.–Sun., $5 adults, $3 children). This coffee and fruit *finca* has a 150-year-old *trapiche,* or sugar mill, trails, a lake with tilapia, an atmospheric café, and a swimming pool. It has trail tours at 9 A.M. Tuesday–Sunday ($5).

Passing through the hamlet of **Canáan,** 18 kilometers northeast of San Isidro, you arrive at **San Gerardo de Rivas.** This quaint village, on the southwest flank of Chirripó at 1,300 meters, is the gateway to Chirripó National Park. The setting is alpine, the air crisp. The scent of pines and the burbling of rushing streams fill the air. And the locale is perfect for hiking and birding.

A side road in San Gerardo follows the Río Blanco upstream three kilometers to the hamlet of **Herradura,** from where begins a more arduous trail to Cerro Chirripó and Cerro Urán. In late 2008, floods wiped out the bridge, and at last visit the hamlet was accessible solely by a makeshift footbridge. En route you'll pass the **Aguas Termales** (tel. 506/2742-5210, 7 A.M.–6 P.M. daily), a peaceful spot with landscape hot spring pools, hugely popular with locals on weekends. And horticulturalists on a busman's holiday will appreciate **Jardín Secreto** (8 A.M.–5 P.M., $3), a lovely little garden with orchids, heliconias, and bromeliads on display.

The **Cámara de Turismo** (Chamber of Tourism, tel. 506/2742-5050, www.sangerardocostarica.com) is a good resource.

Museo el Pelicano

This small "museum" (tel. 506/2742-5050, 8 A.M.–8 P.M. Tues.–Sat., free) on a coffee *finca* between Canáan and San Gerardo displays the eclectic and unique works of local artist Rafael Elizondo Basulta. Crafted from stones and natural timbers, the exhibits include a five-meter snake hewn from a branch. My favorite is a half-scale motorbike made from 1,000 twigs and other pieces of wood. Rafael's stone sculptures are displayed in the beautifully landscaped garden. With luck you may be invited into his charming house to see the tree trunks hewn magically into a storage cupboard and even a wooden fridge. It also has a swimming pool ($3).

Private Reserves

About 800 kilometers above the soccer field in San Gerardo, the dirt road divides: To the right, it clambers steeply for about one kilometer to the trailhead to Chirripó National Park.

En route, you'll pass **Talamanca Reserve** (tel. 506/2742-5080, www.talamancareserve.com), a

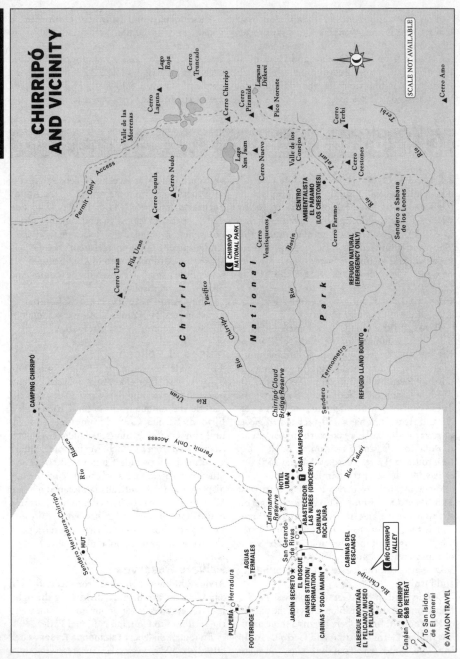

CHIRRIPÓ AND VICINITY

SCALE NOT AVAILABLE

© AVALON TRAVEL

SOUTH-CENTRAL COSTA RICA

© CHRISTOPHER P. BAKER

trail sign at Talamanca Reserve, San Gerardo de Rivas

2,000-hectare reserve that has miles of trails—some for hikers (but steep), others for ATVs ($50 two hours, with guide). One follows a river to a cascade and swimming holes. Horseback rides and guided walks ($15–45) from two to six hours are offered. Overnight guests here use the facility for free. Trails here offer the best views of Chirripó, with Los Crestones clearly visible on a fine day.

The dirt road continues in deteriorating condition past the Chirripó National Park trailhead, 1.5 kilometers to **Chirripó Cloudbridge Reserve** (www.cloudbridge.org), a private reserve and reforestation project with 12 kilometers of trails and more than a dozen waterfalls, plus a meditation garden. Entry is by donation; simply sign in and set off.

Accommodations

Many lodgings offer meals; some shutter up in low season.

Midway between San Isidro and San Gerardo is the calming **Talari Mountain Lodge** (tel./fax 506/2771-0341, talaripz@racsa.co.cr, $39 s or $59 d low season, $42 s or $62 d high season),

a small resort nestled over the Río Chirripó on an eight-hectare property good for birding. Much of the balance is made up of orchards. The eight soulless but adequate rooms have terraces proffering grand vistas. There's a swimming pool and a little restaurant where Jan, the Dutch owner, plays jazz on the piano. Guided hiking and birding are offered. It was severely damaged by the floods of 2008.

Also below San Gerardo, **Rancho la Botija** (tel. 506/2770-2147, www.rancholabotija.com, $52 s/d) has four simple yet beautiful little cabins with wooden walls, bamboo ceilings, and romantic charm. Eight newer cabins are more spacious; four have TV and two cater to handicapped travelers. Rates include breakfast.

An outstanding recommendation, **Río Chirripó B&B and Retreat** (tel. 506/2742-5109, www.riochirripo.com, $80 pp), one kilometer above Canáan, enjoys an exquisite setting in a ravine beneath huge granite boulders. This charmer (run by American expat Frank Faiella and his Costa Rican girlfriend, Oriana) is one of the most appealing mountain lodges in Costa Rica, not least thanks to

Aguas Termales, Herradura

its Santa Fe aesthetic. Its heart is a huge lounge in a circular *ranchito* with soaring *palenque* roof, Aztec motifs, New Mexican throw rugs, Guatemalan wall hangings, sofa seats with batik cushions arcing around a raised brick fireplace, and open walls with mountain vistas. A delightful dining area is swarmed by bougainvillea; Oriana makes fabulous meals! Eight small, rustic wooden cabins hanging over the river boast soothing earth-tone color schemes, wooden beds with Guatemalan bedspreads, cross-ventilation, balconies, and walk-in showers with hot water. Trails lead down to a swimming pool, sundeck, and a heated riverside whirlpool tub, and there's a yoga *dojo*.

Albergue Montaña El Pelicano (tel./fax 506/2742-5050, www.hotelpelicano.net, $15 pp low season, $18 pp high season, $35 s/d cabin, $65 large cabin), 800 meters above Canáan, is another splendid option on the mountainside coffee *finca* of Rafael Elizondo. The focal point is a large alpine-style wooden lodge with 10 skylit and bare-bones hostel-type upstairs rooms sharing four spic-and-span toilets and tiled showers with hot water. Walls do not reach the ceiling, so no romantic antics please. There's also a charming cabin. It has a restaurant, swimming pool, and trails.

In San Gerardo, the **Cabinas y Soda Marín** (tel. 506/2742-5091, $10 pp shared bath, $25 pp private bath), next to the ranger station below San Gerardo, has eight simple but clean cabins with hot water. You can camp here for $10 per person, with tent and sleeping bag provided). A budget alternative is **Bar/Restaurant El Bosque** (c/o tel. 506/2771-4129); it permits camping ($5 pp).

I prefer **Cabinas del Descanso** (tel. 506/2742-5061, www.sangerardocostarica.com, $5 pp camping, $12 pp in dorms, $15 pp in *cabinas*), 200 meters uphill from the ranger station. It has a tiny dorm with bunks and shared baths, plus nine relatively salubrious *cabinas* with double beds and hot water (two rooms have private baths). It also permits camping (there are cold-water showers) and has Internet and laundry. And a rustic restaurant serves filling *típico* meals. The Elizondo family leads treks (including birding), offers trout fishing, and will drive you to the park entrance.

© CHRISTOPHER P. BAKER

Restaurante Talamanca Reserve, San Gerardo de Rivas

A similar and basic alternative is **Cabinas Roca Dura** (tel. 506/2742-5071, $5 camping, $10 s or $15 with shared bath, $25 s or $35 d private bath), with eight rooms built into the rock face, like little caves.

Above the village, **Hotel Urán** (tel. 506/2742-5004, www.hoteluran.com, $11 pp small room, $22, s or $32 d larger room), 100 meters below the Chirripó trailhead, enjoys a pleasant hillside setting gaily planted with ornamentals. It offers 10 simple but well-kept rooms, barracks-style, in a modern wooden two-story structure with tin roof and shared bathrooms with hot water. It has a *pulpería* (grocery), and clean, airy restaurant (4:30 A.M.–8 P.M.). A larger room has four beds and a private bathroom.

Next door, **Casa Mariposa** (tel. 506/2742-5037, www.hotelcasamariposa.net, $12 pp dorm, $16 s or $28 d rooms) offers fabulous ambience for budget digs. This wooden backpackers' hostel run by a live-in family (John from Virginia, Jana a Czech) is built into the boulders. It has five rooms and a dorm, plus laundry, Internet, storage, and a fabulous soaking tub built into the rocks (as is the dorm's outdoor communal toilet and shower). John leads birding tours.

Set in lush landscaped gardens, **Talamanca Reserve** (tel. 506/2742-5080, www.talamancareserve.com, $69 s/d standard, $79 s/d junior suite, $150 cabin suite) causes a double-take. Built in dramatic contemporary style, it has modestly furnished rooms with firm mattresses and lovely sunlit bathrooms; junior suites are preferable, again highlighted by tasteful bathrooms. It serves the best gourmet food for miles and has an Internet café.

Food

Cabinas y Soda Marín and **Bar/Restaurant El Bosque** (c/o tel. 506/2771-4129) each has a basic restaurant and *pulpería* (general store) where you can buy food for the hike up Chirripó. For rustic charm, try the restaurant at **Cabinas Roca Dura** (7 A.M.–10 P.M.), built atop boulders; it serves typical Costa Rican dishes, plus burgers and sandwiches.

The **Talamanca Reserve** café-restaurant (8 A.M.–10 P.M.) is the place for everything from pancakes, omelettes, and eggs and smoked ham breakfasts to bowls of chili, chicken fingers, and triple-decker sandwiches. Dinner leans towards gourmet. I enjoyed a steaming bowl of garbanzos and a superb dish of sautéed liver with onion and green peppers with mashed potato. It also sells ice creams and cappuccinos.

Information and Services

Talamanca Reserve has an Internet café (8 A.M.–10 P.M.) and a book exchange.

Getting There

Buses (tel. 506/2742-5083) depart San Isidro for San Gerardo de Rivas at 5 A.M. and 2 P.M., returning at 7 A.M. and 4:30 P.M. Be sure to specify San Gerardo de Rivas, not San Gerardo de Dota.

If driving, the unsigned turnoff for Rivas and San Gerardo is one kilometer south of San Isidro. A four-wheel-drive taxi from San Isidro will cost about $20.

◖ CHIRRIPÓ NATIONAL PARK

Parque Nacional Chirripó ($15 admission two days, $10 each extra day) protects 50,150 hectares of high-elevation terrain surrounding Cerro Chirripó (3,819 m), Costa Rica's highest peak. The park is contiguous with La Amistad International Peace Park to the south; together they form the Amistad-Talamanca Regional Conservation Unit. Flora and fauna thrive here relatively unmolested by humans. One remote section of the park is called Savannah of the Lions, after its large population of pumas. Tapirs and jaguars are common, though rarely seen. And the forests protect several hundred bird species. Cloud forest, above 2,500 meters, covers almost half the park, which features three distinct life zones; the park is topped off by subalpine rainy *páramo,* marked by contorted dwarf trees and marshy grasses.

Cerro Chirripó was held sacred by pre-Columbian peoples. Tribal leaders and shamans performed rituals atop the lofty shrine; lesser mortals who ventured up Chirripó were killed.

Just as Sir Edmund Hillary climbed Everest "because it was there," so Chirripó lures the intrepid who seek the satisfaction of reaching the summit. Many Ticos choose to hike the mountain during the week preceding Easter, when the weather is usually dry. Avoid holidays, when the huts may be full. The hike from San Gerardo ascends 2,500 meters and is no Sunday picnic but requires no technical expertise. The trails are well marked but steep and slippery.

The park service is pushing the lesser-known Herradura Trail (minimum three days/two nights), via Paso de los Indios, with the first night atop Cerro Urán.

The weather is unpredictable—dress accordingly. When the bitterly cold wind kicks in, the humidity and wind-chill factor can drop temperatures to freezing. Rain is always a possibility, even in "dry season," and a short downpour usually occurs mid-afternoon. Fog is almost a daily occurrence at higher elevations, often forming in midmorning. And temperatures can fall below freezing at night. February and March are the driest months.

The mountain plays host to the annual **Carrera Internacional Campo Traviesa de Chirripó,** a rugged race to the top and back!

Guides and Equipment

No guides are required for hiking the Termometro trail, but they are compulsory for the Herradura trail. The communities of San Gerardo and Herradura run an association of guides and porters (*arrieros,* tel. 506/2742-5225). Prices are fixed at $30–50 per day, with a 35-pound limit per porter. If you want to attempt the Herradura Trail, check with the *pulpería* (tel. 506/742-5066) in Herradura.

You can rent tents, stoves, sleeping bags, and other equipment at Roca Dura and Cabinas del Descanso; stoves are permitted only within the "Los Crestones hut."

Accommodations

There's a cave refuge halfway up the mountain, and an open-air hut, **Refugio Llano Bonito,** with a one-night limit ($5). The main lodge—**Centro Ambientalista El Páramo** (tel. 506/2770-8040), "Los Crestones"—is 14 kilometers from the trailhead and has four bunks (with foam pads) to each of 15 rooms,

CLIMBING CHIRRIPÓ

You can do the 16-kilometer hike to the summit in a day, but it normally takes two days (three days round-trip). Call the National Parks Service three days in advance to register and pay your deposit; if you arrive without reservations, pay your fee at the ranger station at San Gerardo. There are distance markers every two kilometers. *Pack out all your trash and bury human waste.*

DAY 1

Today is 14 kilometers, mostly steeply uphill. Less fit hikers should begin not long after dawn, as it can take 12 hours or even longer in bad conditions (fitter hikers should be able to hike this section in 6–7 hours). You can hire local porters to carry your packs to base camp.

From the soccer field in San Gerardo, walk uphill about 600 meters to the Y-fork; turn right, cross the bridge, and follow the rocky track one kilometer uphill. The trailhead is well signed on the right, 100 meters above Albergue Urán (you can drive up to this point with a four-wheel-drive vehicle; several homesteads advertise parking for a small fee). There's a stream 0.5 kilometer beyond Refugio Llano Bonito, beyond which you begin a grueling uphill stretch called La Cuesta del Agua; allow at least two hours for this section. The climb crests at Monte Sin Fé

(Faithless Mountain). You'll see a rudimentary wooden shelter at the halfway point, beyond which you pass into dwarf cloud forest adorned with old man's beard.

About six kilometers below the summit is a cave large enough to sleep five or six people, if rains dictate. From here a two-kilometer final climb – La Cuesta de los Arrepentidos (Repentants' Hill) – takes you to Centro Ambientalista El Páramo lodge, beside the Río Talari beneath an intriguing rock formation called Los Crestones. It has heating, but be prepared for a cold night anyway.

DAY 2

Today, up and onto the trail by dawn to make the summit before the fog rolls in. It's about a 90-minute hike from the hut via the Valle de los Conejos (Rabbits' Valley). On clear days the view is awesome! With luck, you'll be able to see both the Pacific and the Caribbean.

You can head back to San Gerardo the same day, or contemplate a round-trip hike to Cerro Ventisqueros, the second-highest mountain in Costa Rica (by permit only); the trail begins below the Valle de los Conejos. Another trail through the Valle de las Morenas, on the northern side of Chirripó, is off-limits without a permit, as is the Camino de los Indios, a trail that passes over Cerro Urán and the far northern Talamancas.

and shared bathrooms with lukewarm showers, a communal kitchen, and solar-powered electricity 6–8 P.M. You can reserve meals; otherwise, you need to cook for yourself. Rates are $10 per person per night.

Camping is *not* permitted except at **Camping Chirripó,** 10 kilometers from the trailhead on the Herradura trail (eight people maximum; reservations are required).

What to Take

- Warm clothes—preferably layered clothing for varying temperatures and humidity. A polypropylene jacket remains warm when wet.
- Raingear. A poncho is best.
- Sturdy hiking boots.
- Warm sleeping bag—good to 0°C.
- Flashlight with spare batteries.
- A compass and map.
- Water. There is no water supply for the first half of the hike.
- Food, including snacks. Dried bananas and peanuts are good energy boosters.
- Bag for litter/garbage.
- Wind/sun protection.

Information and Services

The **ranger station** (tel. 506/2742-5083, parquechirripo@racsa.co.cr, 6:30 A.M.–4:30 P.M.) in San Gerardo de Rivas has toilets. It sells a *Visitors Guide* ($0.75) and map ($0.75) showing trails to the summit; the station does not sell the 1:50,000 topographical survey (sections 3444 II San Isidro and 3544 III Durika; if you plan on hiking to nearby peaks, you may also need sections 3544 IV Fila Norte and 3444 I Cuerici), available from the Instituto Geográfico Nacional in San José.

Only 40 visitors are allowed within the park at any one time. Only 10 spaces daily are available for people arriving without reservations; the other 30 spaces are for people with reservations. Reservations are accepted Monday–Friday only and require a $10 deposit to be prepaid via the Banco Nacional. Experienced hikers recommend showing up anyway, as there are usually some no-shows.

Costa Rica Trekking Adventure (tel. 506/2771-4582, www.chirripo.com), in San Isidro, offers guided treks.

La Amistad Friendship Park and Vicinity

The 193,929-hectare International Friendship Park is shared with neighboring Panamá. Together with the adjacent Chirripó National Park, the Hitoy-Cerere Biological Reserve, Tapantí National Park, Las Tablas and Barbilla Protective Zones, Las Cruces Biological Station, and a handful of Indian reservations, it forms the 600,000-hectare Amistad Biosphere Reserve, a UNESCO World Heritage Site also known as the Amistad-Talamanca Regional Conservation Unit.

The park transcends the Cordillera Talamanca ranges, rising from 150 meters above sea level on the Caribbean side to 3,819 meters atop Cerro Chirripó. The Talamancas are made up of separate mountain chains with only a limited history of volcanic activity; none of the mountains is considered a volcano. La Amistad's eight life zones form habitats for flora and fauna representing at least 60 percent of the nation's various species, including no fewer than 450 bird species (not least the country's largest population of resplendent quetzals and 49 endemic species), as well as the country's largest density of tapirs, jaguars, harpy eagles, ocelots, and many other endangered species. Cloud forests extend to 2,800 meters, with alpine *páramo* vegetation in the upper reaches.

Most of this massive park remains unexplored. It has few facilities, and trails are unmarked and often barely discernible. Don't even think about hiking into the park without a guide.

The park, which extends the entire length of the South Central region, has five official entry points, one accessed via **Buenos Aires,** one via **Helechales,** one via **Altamira,** and two via **San Vito.** Admission costs $6.

BUENOS AIRES

About 40 kilometers south of San Isidro the air becomes redolent of sweet-smelling pineapples, the economic mainstay of the Valle de El General, which is centered on Buenos Aires, a small agricultural town in the midst of an endless-green ocean of spiky *piñas*. The nondescript town, 63 kilometers south of San Isidro de El General, is the main base for exploring La Amistad International Peace Park.

Southeast from Buenos Aires, the Pan-American Highway follows the Río General 25 kilometers to its confluence with the Río Coto Brus at Paso Real.

Accommodations and Food

Cabinas Fabi (tel. 506/2730-1110, $11 s, $15 d), 50 meters west of the bus station, has six spacious, modern cabins with private bath and cold water. There's secure parking.

The nicest digs is **Cabinas Kamarachi** (tel. 506/2730-5222, $20 s, $30 d), one kilometer off Highway 2 on the road into town. It has

modernist church in Buenos Aires

20 air-conditioned rooms in a two-story block with cable TV, and secure parking.

Information and Services

There are two banks on the plaza. The **police station** (tel. 117 or 506/2730-0103) is one block northeast of the plaza; the **Red Cross** (tel. 506/2730-0078) is at the entrance to town.

Getting There

Tracopa buses (tel. 506/2222-2666) to Buenos Aires depart San José from Calle 5, Avenidas 18/20 at 5 A.M., 7 A.M., 8:30 A.M., 10 A.M., 1 P.M., 2:30 P.M., and 6 P.M. Buses (tel. 506/2742-5083) depart San Isidro for San Gerardo de Rivas at 5 A.M. and 2 P.M., returning at 7 A.M. and 4:30 P.M. Be sure to specify San Gerardo de Rivas, not San Gerardo de Dota.

LA AMISTAD FRIENDSHIP PARK–NORTH

Buenos Aires is a gateway to La Amistad International Friendship Park, which provides superb wildlife-viewing, particularly of animals such as pumas and jaguars. The mountains around Buenos Aires are home to several indigenous tribes.

A dirt road that begins in Buenos Aires leads north 10 kilometers to the hamlet of **Ujarrás,** beyond which the boulder-strewn dirt road continues four kilometers to **Balneario de Aguas Termales** (a.k.a. Rocas Calientes), where thermal waters pour forth amid a rock landscape; the rickety suspension bridge the width of your outstretched arms was washed out in late 2008, when only a tentative footbridge remained.

Ujarrás is also a gateway to La Amistad International Friendship Park. A trail from Ujarrás crosses the Talamancas via Cerro Abolado and the valley of the Río Taparí, ending in the Hitoy-Cerere Biological Reserve on the Caribbean side. It's a strenuous, multi-day endeavor. *Do not attempt this hike without an indigenous guide.* The **Talamanca Association of Ecotourism and Conservation** (ATEC, tel./fax 506/2750-0191 www.greencoast.com/atec.htm), based in Puerto Limón, on the Caribbean coast, offers 6- to 15-day guided "Transcontinental Hikes" ($750) from Ujarrás to the Caribbean side or vice versa.

Another dirt road that begins at the gas station at **Brujo**, 10 kilometers southeast of Buenos Aires, leads north to the **Reserva Indígena Cabagra** (Cabagra Indigenous Reserve). The gas station's **Restaurante Brujo** (tel. 506/2730-1645) serves an excellent buffet.

DURIKA BIOLOGICAL RESERVE

Founded in 1989 as Finca Anael, this 700-hectare farm reserve (tel./fax 506/2730-0657, www.durika.org), operated by the Fundación Durika, is the outgrowth of a self-sufficient agricultural community of 100 or so members who work on behalf of conservation, protecting and reforesting a mountain reserve encompassing various forest types, including cloud forest. The community operates an authentic ecotourism project that welcomes visitors. A guide is assigned to you. Besides the opportunity to milk the goats, make yogurt and cheese, try your hand at carpentry, and participate in organic farming, you can attend classes in martial arts, meditation, and art. Guided hikes, including one to an indigenous village, plus a five-day camping trip to the summit of Cerro Durika are available.

To get there from Buenos Aires, follow the Ujarrás signs to Rancho Cabecar restaurant, then take the right at the Y-fork (Durika is signed) and continue uphill 15 kilometers until you see the entrance for the farm. *This drive is not for the faint-hearted! The first 12 or so kilometers are a breeze, then suddenly the narrow, rocky, muddy track plunges into a canyon and begins a long, dauntingly steep, snaking ascent that requires you to floor the gas at all times, come what may! It could well be the single most challenging drive in the nation.* Jeep-taxis operate from Buenos Aires.

Accommodations and Food

Alberque de Montaña Angeles de Paraíso (tel. 506/2730-0034, $5 pp camping, $6 pp dorm), on the southern edge of Ujarrás, is a delightful spot with a basic backpackers' dorm with shared outside toilets. Three small swimming pools were a bit grungy at last visit. Set amid a fruit orchard, it has a soccer pitch, thatched shade areas with hammocks, and a rustic restaurant serving local fare. Two cabins were to be added.

Durika Biological Reserve (tel./fax 506/2730-0657, www.durika.org, $12 pp dorm, $45 s or $75 d cabins) has a basic dorm hut, but you'll need to bring your own sleeping bag. It also has three simple, candlelit cabins with fantastic views; one has two beds and a private bathroom, while the others each have four beds and share a bathroom. Rates include meals and transfers.

Getting There

Buses depart Buenos Aires for Potrero Grande at 6:30 A.M. and noon; you can get a Jeep-taxi from here. Buses also serve Ujarrás from Buenos Aires.

RÍO GRANDE DE TERRABA VALLEY AND VALLE DE COTO BRUS

Southwest of Buenos Aires, at **Paso Real** (there is no community as such), the Río El General and Río Coto Brus merge to form the Río Grande de Terraba, which swings west and runs through a ravine in the Fila Costeña mountains, connecting the Valle de El General to Palmar and the Golfo Dulce region; the Pan-American Highway follows the river.

South of the junction of the two rivers, the Valle de Coto Brus is drained by the Río Coto Brus and its tributaries. Once a center for coffee production, the industry has declined in recent years. The summits of Cerro Kamuk (3,549 m) and Cerro Fabrega (3,336 m) loom massively overhead. The Río Terraba is spanned by a bridge one kilometer south of Paso Real. From here, Highway 237 leads to San Vito, the regional capital on a ridge at the head of the valley. It's one of the most scenic drives in the country.

Boruca

About 10 kilometers south of Paso Real, a dirt road leads sharply uphill and runs along a ridge (offering fantastic views) to **Reserva Indígena Boruca**, in the Fila Sinancra, comprising a series of Indian villages scattered throughout the mountains. The main village is **Boruca**,

FIESTA DE LOS DIABLITOS

Every year on December 30, a conch shell sounds at midnight across the dark hills of the Fila Sinancra. Men disguised as devils burst from the hills into Boruca and go from house to house, performing skits and receiving rewards of tamales and *chicha*, the traditional corn liquor. Drums and flutes play while villagers dressed in burlap sacks and traditional balsa-wood masks perform the Fiesta de los Diablitos. Another dresses as a bull. Plied with *chicha*, the *diablitos* chase, prod, and taunt the bull. Three days of celebrations and performances end with the symbolic killing of the bull, which is then reduced to ashes on a pyre. The festival re-enacts the battles between native forebears and Spanish conquistadors with a dramatic twist: The native people win.

a slow-paced hamlet set in a verdant valley in the heart of the reserve. There's a tiny **Museo Comunitario Boruca** honoring the local culture, but it's usually locked and not worth the drive. It's funded by the sale of beautiful carved balsa-wood masks, weavings, and other crafts. Some 35 local artisans have a cooperative centered on the home of Marina Lazaro Morales, fronting the plaza. Try to visit for the Festival de los Diablitos on December 30.

The **Bar, Soda y Cabinas Boruca** (no tel., $10 s/d), in Boruca, has five basic rooms with private bathrooms with cold water. You can also stay with local families by prior arrangement; call the public administrator for information (tel. 506/2730-1673).

A bus departs Buenos Aires for Boruca at 11:30 A.M. and 3:30 P.M. (two hours). The return bus departs Boruca at 6:30 A.M. and 1 P.M.

LA AMISTAD FRIENDSHIP PARK–CENTRAL

Three kilometers southeast of the bridge over the Río Terraba, a dirt road off Highway 237 leads north five kilometers to **Potrero Grande** and thence 12 kilometers to **Helechales** and the **Estación Tres Colinas** ranger station for La Amistad International Peace Park—four-wheel drive required. *Tough going!*

Another rough dirt road begins at Guácimo (also known as Las Tablas) on Highway 237 about three kilometers north of Jabillo and about 18 kilometers southeast of the Terraba River; it leads 21 kilometers via the communities of **El Carmén** and **Altamira** to the La Amistad International Friendship Park headquarters at **Estación Altamira** (tel. 506/2730-0846 or 506/2200-5355 in Buenos Aires), on the edge of the cloud forest. *This is the main access point to the park.* Neither the road nor Altamira are marked on most road maps (turn left about three kilometers above El Carmén; it's easy going to Altamira, beyond which it's signed via a steep and rugged two-kilometer 4WD climb). The Altamira ranger station has a small ecology museum. Trails include Sendero Valle del Silencio, a six-hour, 20-kilometer hike into the cloud forest good for spotting quetzals. There's a basic three-room dorm; reservations are required.

The dirt road that begins at Guácimo divides after three kilometers: take the right fork for El Carmén; the left fork leads 14 kilometers to the village of **Biolley** (again, 4WD is essential), a center of coffee-production (in winter picking season, Guaymí laborers flock in from Panamá, brightening the scene with their gaily colored dresses). Two trails into La Amistad Park begin about two kilometers above Biolley, where **Finca Palo Alto** (tel. 506/2743-1063, www.hotelfincapaloalto.com) is a farm with cattle, horses, and goats. The charming owner hosts educational day visits and leads guided horseback and hiking trips to high-altitude waterfalls.

Accommodations

Estación Atlamira has a camping area with toilets and showers, drinking water, and a picnic area for $5 per person (you'll need to bring stoves and food). There's even a TV lounge with sofas.

In El Carmén, Marialeno Garbanzo Camacho

© CHRISTOPHER P. BAKER

San Vito

is the gracious owner of **Soda y Cabinas La Amistad** (tel. 506/2743-1080, $8 pp), next to the police station. She has eight simple, clean rooms with fans and shared outside bathrooms with hot water. The *soda* (6 A.M.–10 P.M.) serves filling *casados* (set lunches).

At Biolley, **Finca Palo Alto** (tel. 506/2743-1063, www.hotelfincapaloalto.com, $6 pp dorm, $25–30 pp room, including all meals) has six wooden, basically furnished cabins with modern bathrooms and TV. It also has male and female dorms with narrow bunks for 26 people. This place has a real *campesino* ambience, and filling meals are served in the country-style outdoor restaurant.

Getting There
Tracopa buses (tel. 506/2771-3297) depart Buenos Aires for San Vito via El Carmén and Biolley at 11:30 A.M.; the Buenos Aires–bound bus departs San Vito at noon.

SAN VITO
San Vito is a pleasant hill town that nestles on the east-facing flank of the Fila Costeña,

overlooking the Valle de Coto Brus, at 990 meters above sea level. The town was founded by Italian immigrants in the early 1850s. The tiny park at the top of the hill as you enter town from Buenos Aires or Ciudad Neily has a life-size statue of two children under an umbrella dedicated to "La Fraternidad Italo-Costarricense."

Finca Cántaros (tel./fax 506/2773-3760, 8:30 A.M.–4 P.M. Sat.–Sun., $2 admission), a 9.5-hectare reserve three kilometers southeast of San Vito, is centered on a beautifully restored farmhouse converted into a gallery with beautiful indigenous crafts, and a children's library and education center that teaches local ecology and culture. Trails lead to **Laguna Julia,** which attracts waterfowl, and into forest good for spotting such rare endemics as the collared trogon, orange-collared manakin, and streaked saltator. Rest spots offer lovely views over San Vito.

⟨ Las Cruces Biological Station/ Wilson Botanical Garden
This biological research station (tel. 506/2773-4004, www.ots.ac.cr), six kilometers south of San Vito, is a botanist's delight. The center, in

© CHRISTOPHER P. BAKER

Laguna Julia at Finca Cántaros, San Vito

the midst of a 290-hectareforest reserve, is run by the Organization of Tropical Studies (OTS). New plants are propagated for horticulture, and species threatened with habitat loss and extinction are maintained for future reforestation efforts. Maintaining the reserve—proclaimed part of La Amistad Biosphere Reserve—is the cornerstone of a larger effort to save the watershed of the Río Java; you can donate to its "Adopt a Pasture Program."

The reserve is in mid-elevation tropical rainforest along a ridge of the Fila Zapote. During the wet season, heavy fog and afternoon clouds spill over the ridge, nourishing a rich epiphytic flora of orchids, bromeliads, ferns, and aeroids. The forest is a vital habitat for pacas, anteaters, opossums, kinkajous, porcupines, armadillos, sloths, tayras, monkeys, deer, small cats, more than 45 species of bats, and some 800 species of butterflies. Bird-watching at Las Cruces is especially rewarding: More than 400 species have been recorded.

The spectacular highlight is the 12-hectare Wilson Botanical Garden (8 A.M.–5 P.M. daily, $8 admission adult, free for children half day;

$24 adult, $14 children full day) established in 1963 by Robert and Catherine Wilson, former owners of Fantastic Gardens in Miami. Both are now buried on the grounds. The garden was inspired by the famous Brazilian gardener Roberto Burle-Marx, who designed much of the garden following his vision of parterres as a palette. Approximately 10 kilometers of well-maintained trails (and many more in the forest reserve) meander through the Fern Grove, Orchid Grotto, the largest palm collection in the world, heliconia groves, and other locales. The garden also has a new open-air cacti exhibit, plus greenhouses of anthuriums, ferns, elkhorns, and more.

Guided walks ($18/24 half-/full-day, $30/38 half-/full-day) and meals are available by reservation; and you can buy self-guided tour booklets in the well-stocked gift store.

Accommodations and Food

Finca Cántaros has camping ($6 pp), with showers, toilets, and use of a simple outdoor grill and kitchen converted from cattle stalls.

Several budget options in town include **Hotel**

Wilson Botanical Garden, San Vito

Rino (tel. 506/2773-3071, fax 506/2773-4214, $11 s or $20 d with fan, $15 pp with cable TV, $20 s or $30 d with bathtub), on the main street, with 13 simple but adequate rooms with private bathrooms and hot-water showers.

The nicest place in town is **Hotel El Ceibo** (tel./fax 506/2773-3025, $35 s, $45 d), with 40 modern air-conditioned rooms with fans and private baths with hot water, a large restaurant, a lounge with TV, and a small bar. The hotel's restaurant (7 A.M.–10 P.M.) serves the likes of cannelloni, lemon scallopini, and fresh tuna spaghetti.

Outside town, I recommend **Hotel Cuenca de Oro** (tel. 506/2773-4420, www.hotelcuencadeoro.com, $35 s or $50 d low season, $45 s or $60 d high season), a lovely nature lodge five kilometers northwest of town. It has six simply appointed but cozy hilltop cabins. It has tours to caverns and hot springs, as well as the Guaymí reserve. However, the food is said to be disappointing.

Las Cruces (reservations c/o tel. 506/2524-0628, fax 506/2524-0629, nat-hist@ots.ac.cr, $88 s, $164 d including meals, taxes, and guided

walk) will accept drop-by overnighters on a space-available basis. It's advisable to reserve c/o OTS (tel. 506/2773-4004, www.ots.ac.cr). It has 12 spacious and cozy rooms with picture windows opening to verandas with views, and Wi-Fi throughout. Dining is family-style at set hours. Discount rates apply for researchers, volunteers, and students. Three researchers' cabins were being added for 2009. Walk-in backpackers can bunk in well-run dorms with plenty of modern showers and toilets, plus Internet.

Pizzería Lilliana (tel. 506/2773-3080, 10 A.M.–10 P.M.), 50 meters west of the plaza, is recommended for Italian fare; I had a tasty pizza served on the patio.

Information and Services

The **hospital** (tel. 506/2773-3103) is two kilometers south of town, on the road to Ciudad Neily. The **Red Cross** (tel. 506/2773-3196) is on the northwest side of town.

There are two **banks** on the main street. **Cybershop** (tel. 506/2773-3521, 8 A.M.–noon and 1–8 P.M. Mon.–Sat.), 60 meters west of the gas station, charges $2 per hour.

The **post office** and **police station** (tel. 506/2773-3225) adjoin each other, 200 meters up the hill north of the main bus station.

Getting There

Tracopa buses (tel. 506/2222-2666, tel. 506/2773-3410 in San Vito) depart San José from Calle 5, Avenidas 18/20 at 6 A.M., 8 A.M., noon, and 4 P.M.; and depart San Vito for San José at 5 A.M., 7 A.M., 10 A.M., and 3 P.M. Buses from San Isidro depart for San Vito five times daily.

Buses depart Terminal Cepul for Ciudad Neily, Las Mellizas, and Las Tablas.

Local buses will drop you off at Las Cruces Biological Station; they operate from San Vito at 7:30 A.M., 9 A.M., 9:30 A.M., 11 A.M., 2 P.M., 3 P.M., 4 P.M., and 6 P.M.; and from the garden gate to San Vito at 6 A.M., 9 A.M., 12:30 P.M., 1:45 P.M., and 4:30 P.M. Buses depart Ciudad Neily for the gardens at 6 A.M., 9 A.M., 1:30 P.M., and 5:30 P.M. Tracopa buses from San José pass Las Cruces four times daily.

◖ LA AMISTAD FRIENDSHIP PARK–SOUTH

Northeast of San Vito, the Talamancas are protected within La Amistad, which provides splendid options for spotting quetzals, pumas, and other rare wildlife. The **Estación Pittier** (tel./fax 506/2773-4060), at Progreso, about 30 kilometers northeast of San Vito, has an exhibition room and a *mirador,* plus basic facilities.

At Sabalito, six kilometers east of San Vito, turn left at the gas station, and left again at Centro Social El Nicoyano, at La Trucha. There are no signs, so ask. You can also continue straight past Centro Social El Nicoyano until you reach the police station at Las Mellizas; here, turn left for **La Amistad Lodge** (tel. 506/2289-7667, www.laamistad.com), on a 1,215-hectare coffee farm within Las Tablas Protective Zone, a private wildlife reserve adjoining La Amistad International Friendship Park (4WD is required

for the rocky skunk of a road). Horseback rides and guided hiking are offered.

From La Amistad Lodge, a trail leads to the remote **Estación Las Tablas.** It's a rugged 10-kilometer hike or four-wheel drive (conditions permitting); continue uphill from the lodge and take the right fork beyond the gates.

You can also enter La Amistad International Friendship Park via the equally remote **Estación La Escuadra** ranger station, at Agua Caliente, in the Cotón valley some 30 kilometers northeast of San Vito and reached via the communities of Juntas, Poma, and Santa Elena; a four-wheel-drive vehicle is required.

Accommodations

You can camp at **Estación Las Tablas,** which has no facilities, for $2 per person.

The three-story, Swiss-style, all-wood **La Amistad Lodge** (tel. 506/2289-7667, www.laamistad.com, $100 s, $175 d including all meals and guided tour), run by the amiable Montero family, has seven simple yet adequate rooms with large tiled bathrooms. The lodge boasts a stone fireplace and a restaurant serving meals family-style. There are also three *cabinas* with verandas with rockers. La Amistad Lodge also has four high-mountain camps, each with a dining room and flush toilets but no electricity: Cotoncito Station, at 1,600 meters, is set amid premontane forests; Cotobrus Station (2,000 m) is surrounded by montane oak forest; Punta Mira Camp (1,950 m) offers spectacular views; and **Las Juntas Station** (1,400 m) opened in 2007 and overlooks a river. Rates ($65) include meals.

Getting There

Buses depart San Vito for Cotón at 3 P.M., for Progreso and Las Mellizas at 9:30 A.M. and 2 P.M., for Las Tablas at 10:30 A.M. and 3 P.M., and for Santa Elena at 10 A.M. and 4 P.M. Jeep-taxis will run you there in dry season from San Vito (about $75 round-trip).

BACKGROUND

The Land

Travelers moving south overland through Central America gradually have their choice of routes whittled away until they finally reach the end of the road in the swamps and forests of Darien, in Panamá, where the tenuous land bridge separating the two great American continents is almost pinched out and the Pacific Ocean and the Caribbean Sea almost meet. Costa Rica lies at the northern point of this apex—a pivotal region separating two oceans and two continents vastly different in character.

The region is a crucible. There are few places in the world where the forces of nature so actively interplay. Distinct climatic patterns clash and merge; the great landmasses riding atop the Cocos and Caribbean plates jostle and shove one another, triggering earthquakes and spawning volcanic eruptions; and the flora and fauna of the North and South American realms—as well as those of the Caribbean and the Pacific—come together and play Russian roulette with the forces of evolution. The result is an incredible diversity of terrain, biota, and weather concentrated in a country barely bigger than the state of New Hampshire.

Lying between 8 and 11 degrees north of the equator, Costa Rica (50,895 sq km) sits wholly within the tropics, a fact quickly confirmed in

© CHRISTOPHER P. BAKER

PLATE TECTONICS

Until the 1960s, when the theory of plate tectonics revolutionized the earth sciences, geologists trying to explain the distribution of earthquakes and volcanoes were at a loss. When earthquakes and volcanoes were plotted on a map, geologists realized that the planet is a puzzle – literally. The pieces of the terrestrial jigsaw are some 25 tectonic plates, interconnected pieces of the earth's crust (the lithosphere), 40-95 miles thick. Seven major plates carry the continents and ocean basins on their backs.

These plates are in continual motion, ponderously inching along on endless journeys across the surface of the earth, powered by forces originating deep within the earth. They ride on a viscous layer called the aesthenosphere, with a molten component welling up to the earth's surface on great convection currents fueled by heat from the core of our planet.

As the plates move, they pull apart or collide, unleashing titanic geological forces. When two plates slide past each other or converge – as off the Pacific coast of Central America – the geological forces generally drive one plate beneath the other, causing earthquakes. The friction created by one plate grinding beneath another melts part of both crusts, forming magma – molten rock – which wells up under pressure, erupting to form a chain of volcanoes.

---

the middle of a rainy afternoon in the middle of the rainy season in the middle of the Caribbean lowlands or Osa Peninsula. Elevation and extremes of relief, however, temper the stereotypical tropical climate. In fact, the nation boasts more than a dozen distinct climatic zones.

A Backbone of Mountains

Costa Rica sits astride a jagged series of volcanoes and mountains, part of the great Andean–Sierra Madre chain that runs the length of the western littoral of the Americas. The mountains rise in the nation's northwestern corner as a low, narrow band of hills. They grow steeper and broader and ever more rugged until they gird Costa Rica coast to coast at the Panamanian border, where they separate the Caribbean and Pacific from one another as surely as if these were the Himalayas.

Volcanic activity has fractured this mountainous backbone into distinct cordilleras. In the northwest, the Cordillera de Guanacaste rises in a leapfrogging series of volcanoes, including Rincón de la Vieja and Miravalles, whose steaming vents have been harnessed to provide geothermal energy. To the southeast is the Cordillera de Tilarán, dominated by Arenal, one of the world's most active volcanoes. To the east is the Cordillera Central, with four great volcanoes—Poás, Barva, Irazú, and Turrialba—within whose cusp lies the Meseta Central, an elevated plateau ranging in height from 900 to 1,787 meters. To the south of the valley rises the Cordillera Talamanca, an uplifted mountain region that tops out at the summit of Cerro Chirripó (3,819 m), Costa Rica's highest peak.

Meseta Central

The Meseta Central, the heart of the nation, comprises a rich agricultural valley cradled by the flanks of the Cordillera Talamanca to the south, and by the fickle volcanoes of the Cordillera Central to the north and east. San José, the capital, lies at its center, at an elevation of 1,150 meters, San José enjoys a springlike climate year-round.

The Meseta Central measures about 40 kilometers north to south and 80 kilometers east to west and is divided from a smaller valley by the low-lying Cerros de la Carpintera that rise a few miles east of San José. Beyond lies the somewhat smaller Cartago Valley, at a slightly higher elevation. To the east the turbulent Reventazón—a favorite of white-water enthusiasts—tumbles to the Caribbean lowlands. The Río Virilla exits more leisurely, draining the San José Valley to the west.

Northern Zone and Caribbean Coast

The broad, wedge-shaped northern lowlands are cut off from the more densely populated Meseta Central by the Cordillera Central. The plains or *llanuras* extend along the entire length of the Río San Juan, whose course demarcates the Nicaraguan border. Farther south the plains narrow to a funnel along the Caribbean coast, framed by the steep eastern slopes of the central mountains, which run along a northwest–southeast axis. Numerous rivers drop quickly from the mountains to the plains. Beautiful beaches line the Caribbean coast, which sidles gently south.

Pacific Coast

Beaches are a major calling card of Costa Rica's Pacific coast, which is deeply indented by two large gulfs—the Golfo de Nicoya (in the north) and Golfo Dulce (in the south), enfolded by the hilly, hook-nosed peninsulas of Nicoya and Osa, respectively. Mountains tilt precipitously toward the Pacific, and the slender coastal plain is only a few kilometers wide. North of the Golfo de Nicoya, the coastal strip widens to form a broad lowland belt of savanna—the Tempisque Basin. The basin is drained by the Río Tempisque and narrows northward until hemmed in near the Nicaraguan border by the juncture of the Cordillera de Guanacaste and rolling, often steep, coastal hills that follow the arc of the Nicoya Peninsula.

A narrow, 64-kilometer-long intermontane basin known as the Valle de El General nestles comfortably between the Cordillera Talamanca and the coastal mountains—*Fila Costeña*—of the Pacific southwest.

AN UNSTABLE LAND

Costa Rica lies at the boundary where the Pacific's Cocos Plate—a piece of the earth's crust some 510 kilometers wide—meets the crustal plate underlying the Caribbean. The two are converging as the Cocos Plate moves east at a rate of about 10 centimeters a year. It is a classic subduction zone in which the Caribbean Plate is forced under the Cocos.

Central America has been an isthmus, a peninsula, and even an archipelago in the not-so-distant geological past. Costa Rica has one of the youngest surface areas in the Americas—only three million years old—for the volatile region has only recently been thrust from beneath the sea.

In its travels eastward, the Cocos Plate gradually broke into seven fragments, which today move forward at varying depths and angles. This fracturing and competitive movement causes the frequent earthquakes with which Costa Ricans contend.

The most devastating earthquakes generally occur in subduction zones, when one tectonic plate plunges beneath another. Ocean trench quakes off the coast of Costa Rica have been recorded at 8.9 on the Richter scale and are among history's most awesome, heaving the sea floor sometimes scores of feet. This is what happened when the powerful 7.4 earthquake struck Costa Rica on April 22, 1991. That massive quake, which originated near the Caribbean town of Pandora, caused the Atlantic coastline to rise permanently—in parts by as much as 1.5 meters, thrusting coral reefs above the ocean surface and reducing them to bleached skeletons. And a 6.2 earthquake that struck near Poás volcano on January 8, 2009, triggered massive landslides that killed dozens of people.

Volcanoes

Costa Rica lies at the heart of one of the most active volcanic regions on earth. Costa Rica is home to seven of the isthmus's 42 active volcanoes, plus 60 dormant or extinct ones. Some have the look classically associated with volcanoes—a graceful, symmetrical cone rising to a single crater. Others are sprawling, weathered mountains whose once-noble summits have collapsed into huge depressions called calderas (from the Portuguese word for "cauldron").

In 1963, Irazú (3,412 m) broke a 20-year silence, disgorging great clouds of smoke and ash. The eruptions triggered a bizarre storm that showered San José with 13 centimeters of muddy ash, snuffing out the 1964 coffee crop but enriching the Meseta Central for years to come. The binge lasted for two years, then abruptly ceased.

Poás (2,692 m) has been particularly violent during the past 30 years. In the 1950s, the restless 6.5-kilometer-wide giant awoke with a roar after a 60-year snooze, and it has been huffing and puffing ever since. Eruptions then kicked up a new cone about 100 meters tall. Two of Poás's craters now slumber under blankets of vegetation (one even cradles a lake), but the third crater belches and bubbles persistently.

Arenal (1,624 m) gives a more spectacular light-and-sound show. After a four-century-long Rip van Winkle–like dormancy, this 4,000-year-young juvenile began spouting in 1968, when it laid waste to a 10-square-kilometer area. Arenal's activity, sometimes minor and sometimes not, continues unabated; it erupted spectacularly in August 2000, killing two people. Though more placid, Miravalles, Turrialba, and Rincón de la Vieja, among Costa Rica's coterie of coquettish volcanoes, also occasionally fling fiery fountains of lava and breccia into the air.

Several national parks have been created around active volcanoes. Atop Poás's crater rim, for example, you can gape down into the great well-like vent and see pools of molten lava bubbling menacingly, giving off diabolical fumes and emitting explosive cracks, like the sound of distant artillery.

CLIMATE

When talk turns to Costa Rica's climate, hyperbole flows as thick and as fast as the waterfalls that cascade in ribbons of quicksilver down through the forest-clad mountains. English 19th-century novelist Anthony Trollope was among the first to wax lyrical: "No climate can, I imagine, be more favorable to fertility and to man's comfort at the same time than that of the interior of Costa Rica."

The country lies wholly within the tropics, yet boasts at least a dozen climatic zones and is markedly diverse in local microclimates. Most regions have a rainy season (May–Nov.) and a dry season (Dec.–Apr.). Rainfall almost everywhere follows a predictable schedule. In general, highland ridges are wet, and windward sides always the wettest.

The terms "summer" *(verano)* and "winter" *(invierno)* are used by Ticos to designate their dry and wet seasons, respectively. Since the Tican "summer" occurs in what are winter months elsewhere in the Northern Hemisphere (and vice versa), it can be confusing.

Temperatures

Temperatures, dictated more by elevation and location than by season, range from tropical on the coastal plains to temperate in the interior highlands. Mean temperatures average 27°C at sea level on the Caribbean coast and 32°C on the Pacific lowlands. In the highlands, the weather is refreshingly clear and invigorating. San José's daily temperatures are in the low 20s Celsius almost year-round, with little monthly variation, and there's never a need for air-conditioning. A heat wave is when the mercury reaches above 27°C. Nights are usually 16–21°C year-round, so bring a sweater.

Temperatures fall steadily as elevation climbs (about one degree for every 100-meter gain). They rarely exceed a mean of 10°C atop Chirripó (at 3,819 m, the highest mountain), where frost is frequent and enveloping clouds drift dark and ominous among the mountain passes.

Sunrise is around 6 A.M. and sunset about 6 P.M. throughout the year, and the sun's path is never far from overhead, so seasonal variations in temperatures rarely exceed five degrees in any given location.

Everywhere, March to May are the hottest months, with September and October not far behind. Cool winds bearing down from northern latitudes lower temperatures during December, January, and February, particularly on the northern Pacific coast, where certain days during summer (dry season) months can be surprisingly cool. The most extreme daily fluctuations occur during the dry season, when clear skies at night allow maximum heat loss through radiation. In the wet season, nights are generally warmer, as the heat built up during the day is trapped by clouds.

flooding in November 2008 near Rincón, Osa Peninsula

© CHRISTOPHER P. BAKER

Rainfall

Rain is a fact of life in Costa Rica. Annual precipitation averages 250 centimeters nationwide. Depending on the region, the majority of this may fall in relatively few days. The Tempisque Basin in Guanacaste, for example, receives as little as 48 centimeters, mostly in a few torrential downpours. The mountains, by contrast, often exceed 385 centimeters per year, sometimes as much as 7.6 meters on the more exposed easterly facing slopes.

Generally, rains occur in the early afternoons in the highlands, mid-afternoons in the Pacific lowlands, and late afternoons (and commonly during the night) in the Atlantic lowlands. Sometimes it falls in sudden torrents called *aguaceros,* sometimes it falls hard and steady, and sometimes it sheets down without letup for several days and nights.

Dry season on the Meseta Central and throughout the western regions is December through April. In Guanacaste, the dry season

usually lingers slightly longer; the northwest coast (the driest part of the country) often has few rainy days even during wet season. On the Atlantic coast, the so-called dry season starts in January and runs through April.

Be prepared: 23 hours of a given day may be dry and pleasant; during the 24th, the rain can come down with the force of a waterfall. The sudden onset of a relatively dry period, called *veranillo* (little summer), sometimes occurs in July and August or August and September, particularly along the Pacific coast.

Seasonal patterns can vary, especially in years when the occasional weather phenomenon known as El Niño sets in. For example, 2008 was the wettest year ever on record—torrential rainfall struck the entire country, causing horrendous flooding and landslides. Rarely do hurricanes strike Costa Rica, although Hurricane Cesár came ashore on July 27, 1996, killing 41 people and trashing the Pacific southwest.

Flora

In 1947, biologist L. H. Holdridge introduced a system of classifying vegetation types or "zones" according to a matrix based on combinations of temperature, rainfall, and seasonality. Each zone has a distinct natural vegetation and ecosystem. Costa Rica has 12 such zones, ranging from tidal mangrove swamps to sub-alpine *paramó* with stunted dwarf plants atop the high mountains.

Costa Rica's tropical situation, in combination with its remarkable diversity of local relief and climates, has resulted in the evolution of a stupendously rich biota. Some habitats, such as the mangrove swamps, are relatively simple. Others, particularly the ecosystem of the tropical rainforests of the Caribbean lowlands and the Osa Peninsula, are among the most complex on the planet.

The lowland rainforests have strong affinities with the *selva* (jungle) of South America and form a distinctive assemblage of species in which the large number of palms, tree ferns, lianas, and epiphytes attest to the constant heat and humidity of the region. The impressive tropical rainforest of eastern Costa Rica and the Osa Peninsula gives way on the central Pacific to a dry evergreen forest at lower elevations and dry deciduous forest farther north. Above about 1,000 meters, the species are fewer and the affinities with North America are stronger. In the Cordillera Talamanca, conifers of South American provenance are joined by North American oaks. Above the tree line (approximately 3,000 m), hikers familiar with the mid-elevation flora of the high Andes of Peru and Ecuador will find many similarities in the shrubby open landscape of Costa Rica's cordillera.

The forests and grasslands flare with color. Begonias, anthuriums, and blood of Christ, named for the red splotches on the underside of its leaves, are common. My favorite plant is the "hot lips" *(labios ardientes),* sometimes called "hooker's lips" *(labios de puta),* whose bright red bracts remind me of Mick Jagger's famous pout. The vermilion *poró* tree (the bright flame-of-the-forest), pink-and-white meadow oak, purple jacaranda, and the almost fluorescent-yellow *corteza amarilla* all add their seasonal bouquets to the landscape. And the morning glory spreads its thick lavender carpets across lowland pastures, joined by carnal red passionflowers (their unromantically foul smell is a crafty device to enlist the help of flies in pollination).

Costa Rica offers an extraordinary abundance of flora, including more than 9,000 species of higher plants, and no less than 2,000 species of bromeliads. Of heliconias (members of the banana family) there are some 30 species. It has many more species of ferns—about 800—than the whole of North America, including Mexico. It is a nation of green upon green upon green. Ferns are light-gap pioneers found from sea level to the highest elevations. The big tree ferns are relics from the age of the dinosaurs, sometimes four meters tall,

© CHRISTOPHER P. BAKER

walking pandanus palm

ORCHIDS

It's appropriate that the orchid is the national flower of Costa Rica: The country has more than 1,400 identified species. Countless others await discovery. At any time of year you're sure to find dozens of species in bloom, from sea level to the highest, subfreezing reaches of Chirripó. There is no best time for viewing orchids, although the beginning of both the dry season and the wet season are said to be particularly favorable. Orchid lovers should head for the cloud forests; there the greatest diversity exists in humid mid-elevation environments where they are abundant as epiphytes (constituting 88 percent of orchid species).

Orchids are not only the largest family of flowering plants, they're also the most diverse – poke around with magnifying glass in hand and you'll come across species with flowers less than one millimeter across. Others, like the native *Phragmipedium caudatum*, have pendulant petals that can reach more than half a meter. Some flower for only one day; others last several weeks.

Orchids have evolved a remarkable array of ingenious pollination techniques. Some species attract insects by sexual impersonation. One species, for example, produces a flower that closely resembles the form of a female wasp – complete with eyes, antennae, and wings. It even gives off the odor of a female wasp in mating condition. Male wasps, deceived, attempt to copulate with it. In their vigor, they deposit pollen within the orchid flower and immediately afterward receive a fresh batch to carry to the next false female. Male bees and other insects are known to use the pollen of orchids as a perfume to attract females.

Guile seems to be the forte of orchids. One species drugs its visitors. Bees clamber into its throat and sip a nectar so intoxicating that they become inebriated, lose their footing, and slip into a small bucket. Escape is offered up a spout – the proverbial light at the end of the tunnel. As the drunken insect totters up, it has to wriggle beneath an overhanging rod, which showers its back with pollen.

An annual orchid show is held each March at Instituto Nacional de Biodiversidad (INBio), near San José.

Gardens dedicated to orchids include the **Botanical Orchid Garden** (La Garita, tel. 506/2487-8095, www.orchidgardencr.com, 8:30 A.M.-4:30 P.M. Tue.-Sun., $12 adults, $6 children) and **Jardín de la Guaría** (Palmares, tel. 506/2452-0091, 7 A.M.-6 P.M., $4, May-June by donation).

Orquídeas del Bosque (tel. 506/2232-1466, www.costaricanorchids.com) sells orchids for export.

---

with fiddleheads large enough to grace a cello. Others are epiphytes (arboreal "nesters" that take root on plants but that are not parasitic).

The epiphytic environment is extremely poor in mineral nutrients. The bromeliads—brilliantly flowering, spiky-leafed "air" plants—have developed tanks or cisterns that hold rainwater and decaying detritus in the whorled bases of their tightly overlapping stiff leaves. The plants gain nourishment from dissolved nutrients in the cisterns. Known as tank epiphytes, they provide trysting places and homes for tiny aquatic animals high above the ground.

All plants depend on light to power the chemical process by which they synthesize their body substances from simple elements. Height is therefore of utmost importance. When an old tree falls, the strong, unaccustomed light triggers seeds that have lain dormant, and banana palms and ginger plants, heliconias and cecropias—all plants that live in the sunshine on riverbanks or in forest clearings—burst into life and put out big broad leaves to soak up the sun. Another prominent plant is the poor man's umbrella (*sombrilla de pobre*), whose giant leaves make excellent impromptu shelters.

TROPICAL RAINFOREST

Once upon a time, before the freezing embraces of the Ice Age, thick evergreen forests

heliconia at Paradise Garden

easy to move about in. (The plants array their leaves to avoid leaf shade; others are shaded purple underneath to help reflect back the light passing through the leaf; the "walking palm" literally walks across the forest floor in search of light on its stiltlike roots.)

The stagnant air is loaded with moisture. To a visitor, the tropical rainforest seems always the same: uniform heat and stifling 90 percent humidity. But this is true only near the ground. High in the tops of the trees, where the sun comes and goes, breezes blow, and moisture has a chance to be carried away, the swings in temperature between day and night are as much as 15 degrees, and the humidity may drop from 95 percent, its fairly constant nighttime level, to as low as 60 percent as the sun rises and warms the forest. Thus, within 30 vertical meters, two distinctly different climates prevail. Tropical rainforests are places of peace and renewal, like a vast vaulted cathedral—mysterious, strangely silent, and of majestic proportions.

Botanists have distinguished among 30 or so different types of rainforest. Tropical evergreen rainforest exists in areas of high rainfall (at least 200 cm) and regular high temperatures averaging no less than 25°C. In Costa Rica, the lush tropical evergreen rainforest of the Caribbean lowlands gives way on the Pacific side to a seasonally dry evergreen forest in the well-watered south.

While in temperate forests distinct species of flora congregate neatly into distinctive plant "neighborhoods" with few other species interspersed, in the rainforest you may pass one example of a particular tree species, then not see another for half a mile. In between, however, are hundreds of other species. In the rainforest, too, life is piled upon life—literally. The firm and unyielding forest floor is a "dark factory of decomposition," where bacteria, mold, and insects work unceasingly, degrading the constant rain of leaf litter and dislodged fruits into nutrient molecules.

Fungi proliferate, too. They are key to providing the nourishment vital to the jungle's life cycle. While a fallen leaf from a North American

blanketed much of the world's warm, humid surface. Today's tropical rainforests—the densest and richest proliferation of plants ever known—are the survivors of these primeval jungles of ages past.

These forests, the largest of which is Brazil's Amazon jungle, are found in a narrow belt that girdles the earth at the equator. In the tropics, constant sunlight, endless rains, and high temperatures year-round spell life. The steamy atmosphere and fast nutrient turnover have promoted favorable growth conditions and intense competition, allowing the forest flora to evolve into an extraordinary multitude of different species, exploiting to the full every conceivable niche. Tropical rainforests contain more than half of all living things known to man.

Only superficially does the rainforest resemble the fictional jungles of Tarzan. Yes, the foliage can indeed be so dense that you cannot move without a machete. But since only about 10 percent of the total sunlight manages to penetrate through the forest canopy, the undergrowth is generally correspondingly sparse, and the forest floor surprisingly open and relatively

RECYCLING NUTRIENTS IN THE RAINFOREST

One of the most important differences between tropical and temperate environments is what biologists call "species richness." A natural forest patch of a few hundred acres in Michigan, for example, might contain 25–30 species of trees; an equivalent tract of Costa Rican rainforest might contain more than 400. Ohio, at twice Costa's Rica geographical size, has only about 10 species of bats; Costa Rica has more than 100.

Why such complexity, such stupefying abundance of species in the neotropics – the tropics of the New World? It all has to do with the rapid pace of nutrient recycling and the way the natural world competes most effectively for nourishment.

In the temperate world, with the warm days and sunlight of spring, plants burst forth with protein-rich buds, shoots, and young leaves, which appear simultaneously in a protein "pulse." Animals bring forth their young during this period of protein abundance: Birds return from over-wintering areas to lay eggs and raise their broods, insect eggs hatch, frogs and toads crawl out of hibernation to reproduce. Come autumn, the same plants produce a second protein glut as tender berries, seeds, and nuts, which critters pack in to sustain themselves through the hardships of impending winter. The synchronized budding and fruiting of foliage is so great that all the hungry mouths gobbling protein hardly threaten a plant species' survival.

In the tropics, by contrast, the seasonal cycle is far less pronounced: Sunlight, rain, and warm temperatures are constant, and plants germinate, grow, flower, and seed year-round. Hence, there is no distinct protein surplus. Leaf-fall, too, occurs continuously and slowly in the tropical rainforest, unlike the autumnal drops of temperate deciduous forests, and the same tropical conditions of heat and moisture that fuel year-round growth also sponsor fast decomposition of dead leaves. The humus that enriches the soils of more temperate latitudes doesn't have a chance to accumulate in the tropics. Thus, soils are thin and, after millions of years of daily rainfall and constant heat, leached of their nutrient content.

Result? The ecosystem of a tropical rainforest is upside-down when compared to forests in the temperate zone, where nutrients

---

oak may take a year to decompose, a leaf in the tropical rainforest will fully decay within a month. The trees suck up the minerals and nutrients through a thick mat of rootlets that grow close to the surface of the inordinately thin soil. To counteract their inherent instability, many species grow side buttresses: wafer-thin flanges that radiate in a ring around the base of the tree like the tail fins of rockets.

For every tree in the jungle, there is a clinging vine fighting for a glimpse of the sun. Instead of using up valuable time and energy in building their own supports, these clutching vines and lianas rely on the straight, limbless trunks typical of rainforest tree species to provide a support in their quest for sunlight. They ride piggyback to the canopy, where they continue to snake through the treetops, sometimes reaching lengths of 300 meters. One species spirals around its host like a corkscrew; another cements itself to a tree with three-pronged tendrils.

The bully of the forest, however, is the strangler fig, which isn't content to merely coexist. While most lianas and vines take root in the ground and grow upward, the strangler figs do the opposite. After sprouting in the forest canopy from seeds dropped by birds and bats, the strangler fig sends roots to the ground, where they dig into the soil and provide a boost of sustenance. Slowly but surely—it may take a full century—the roots grow and envelop the host tree, choking it until it dies and rots away, leaving a hollow, trellised, freestanding cylinder.

The vigorous competition for light and space has promoted the evolution of long, slender, branchless trunks, many well over 35 meters tall, and flat-topped crowns with foliage so dense that rainwater from driving tropical downpours are stored in the soil. In the tropics they're stored overhead in the densely leafed canopy. Leaves and young shoots represent a major investment of scarce nutrients, which plants cannot afford to have gobbled up by hungry multitudes of animals, insects, and birds. Hence, says one biologist, "It might be said that the plants want to be different from one another in order to avoid being devoured." Intense competition has pressured tropical plants to diversify greatly, to disperse, and to develop defense mechanisms, such as thorns or sickening toxins. Other species stagger their production of shoots and new leaves throughout the year so that they never expose too much new growth to predation at any one time.

Because plant protein is scarce at any given time, and because plants have evolved stratagems to guard it, animals have been forced to compete fiercely. They've diversified like the plants, and competition has resulted in examples of specialization, with individual species staking claims to a narrow ecological niche in which other creatures can't compete.

Through these intricate associations, specific plants and predators become totally dependent on one another. A perfect example is the ant acacia, a tree common along the Pacific coast. The plant is weak and defenseless, a poor competitor in the upward race for sunlight and easily overshadowed by faster-growing neighbors. Its tiny nectaries (glands that exude sugar) and leaf-tip swellings filled with proteins and vitamins are tempting morsels for hungry insects and birds. None, however, dares steal a nibble, for a species of tiny yet aggressive ants acts as the acacia's praetorian guard. In exchange for the honey-like food that they love, the ants defend their plant fiercely. Any predator foolish enough to touch the acacia is attacked; if a vine threatens to envelop the tree, the ants cut the vine down. If the branches of a neighboring plant threaten to steal the acacia's sunlight, the ants will prune the interloper; if a neighbor's seeds fall to the ground beneath the acacia, the insects will cart them off before they can germinate. If the ants were to become extinct, the plant would never survive. If the plant disappeared, the ants would starve. Each is inextricably in the debt of the other.

often may not reach the ground for 10 minutes. This great vaulted canopy—the clerestory of the rainforest cathedral—is the jungle's powerhouse, where more than 90 percent of photosynthesis takes place. Above this dense carpet of greenery rise a few scattered giants towering to heights of 70 meters or more.

The scaffolding of massive boughs is colonized at all levels by a riot of bromeliads, ferns, and other epiphytes. As they die and decay, they form compost on the branch capable of supporting larger plants that feed on the leaf mold and draw moisture by dangling their roots into the humid air. Soon every available surface is a great hanging gallery of giant elkhorns and ferns, often reaching such weights that whole tree limbs are torn away and crash down to join the decaying litter on the forest floor.

Sit still awhile and the unseen beasts and birds will get used to your presence and emerge from the shadows. Enormous morpho butterflies float by, flashing like bright neon signs. Is that vine really moving? More likely it's a brilliantly costumed tree eyelash viper, so green it is almost iridescent, draped in sensuous coils on a branch.

Scarlet macaws and lesser parrots plunge and sway in the high branches, announcing their playacting with an outburst of shrieks. Arboreal rodents leap and run along the branches, searching for nectar and insects, while insectivorous birds watch from their vantage points for any movement that will betray a stick insect or leaf-green tree frog to scoop up for lunch. Legions of monkeys, sloths, and fruit- and leaf-eating mammals also live in the green world of the canopy. Larger hunters live up there, too. In addition to the great eagles plunging through the canopy to grab monkeys, there are also tree-dwelling cats. These superbly athletic climbers are quite capable of catching monkeys and squirrels as they leap from branch to branch and race up trunks. There are also snakes here, some twig-thin, such as the chunk-headed snake with catlike eyes, which feasts on frogs and lizards and nestling birds.

Come twilight, the forest soaks in a brief moment of silence. Slowly, the lisping of insects begins. There is a faint rustle as nocturnal rodents come out to forage in the ground litter. All around, myriad beetles and moths take wing in the moist velvet blanket of the tropical night.

TROPICAL DRY FOREST

Before the arrival of the Spanish in the early 16th century, dry forests blanketed the Pacific coastal lowlands from Panamá to Mexico. Fires set by the Spanish and by generations of farmers and ranchers thereafter spread savannas across the province. Three decades ago, the dry forests had dwindled to some 2 percent of their former range—a mere 520 square kilometers of Costa Rica in scattered patches centered on the lower Río Tempisque of Guanacaste. Far rarer than rainforests, they are significantly more endangered, especially by fires, which eviscerate whole forest patches, opening holes in which weeds and other ecological opportunists rush in. Eventually savanna comes to replace the forest. (The fate of even the preserved dry-forest parcels hinges on the success of two ambitious conservation projects that are exemplars of forest restoration: one focusing on educating children and former farmers about the value of the dry forest, one studying and promoting the scarlet macaw, vital to the survival of the sandbox tree.)

Unlike Costa Rica's rainforests, the rare tropical dry forest is relatively sparsely vegetated, with far fewer tree species and only two strata. Canopy trees have short, stout trunks with large, flat-topped crowns, rarely more than 15 meters above the ground. Beneath is an understory with small, open-top crowns, and a layer of shrubs with vicious spines and thorns. Missing are the great profusion of epiphytes and the year-round lush evergreens of the rainforest.

From November through March, no rain relieves the parching heat. Then, the deciduous dry forests undergo a dramatic seasonal transformation, the purple jacaranda, pink-and-white meadow oak, yellow *corteza amarilla*, scarlet *poró*, and the bright orange flame-of-the-forest exploding in Monet colors in the midst of drought.

MANGROVE ESTUARIES

Costa Rica's shorelines are home to five species of mangroves. These pioneer land builders thrive at the interface of land and sea, forming a stabilizing tangle that fights tidal erosion and reclaims land from the water.

Mangroves are what botanists call halophytes, plants that thrive in salty conditions. Costa Rica's rivers deposit silt and volcanic ash onto the coastal alluvial plains. The nutrient-rich mud generates algae and other small organisms that form the base of the marine food chain. Their sustained health is vital to the health of other marine ecosystems.

The nutrients the mangroves seek lie near the surface of the acid mud, deposited by the tides. There is no oxygen to be had in the mud. Hence, there is no point in the mangroves sending down deep roots. Instead, they send out aerial roots, maintaining a hold on the glutinous mud and giving the mangroves the appearance of walking on water. They draw oxygen from the air through small patches of spongy tissue on their bark.

The irrepressible, reddish-barked, shrubby mangroves rise from the dark water on interlocking stilt roots. Brackish streams and labyrinthine creeks wind among them like snakes, sometimes interconnecting, sometimes petering out in narrow cul-de-sacs, sometimes opening suddenly into broad lagoons.

Mangrove swamps are esteemed as nurseries of marinelife and as havens for waterbirds—cormorants, frigate birds, pelicans, herons, and egrets—which feed and nest here by the thousands, producing guano that makes the mangroves grow faster.

A look down into the water reveals luxuriant life: oysters and sponges attached to the roots, small stingrays flapping slowly over the bottom, and tiny fish in schools of tens of thousands. Baby black-tipped sharks and other juvenile fish, too, spend much of their early lives among mangrove roots, shielded by the root maze that keeps out large predators. Raccoons, snakes, and arboreal creatures also inhabit the mangroves. There is even an arboreal mangrove tree crab *(Aratus pisonii),* which eats mangrove leaves and is restricted to the very crowns of the trees by the predatory activities of another arboreal crab, *Goniopsis pulchra.*

Mangroves are aggressive colonizers, thanks to one of nature's most remarkable seedlings. The heavy, fleshy mangrove seeds, shaped like plumb bobs, germinate while still on the tree.

The flowers bloom for a few weeks in the spring and then fall off, making way for a fruit. A seedling shoot soon sprouts from each fruit and grows to a length of 15–30 centimeters before dropping from the tree. Falling like darts, at low tide they land in the mud and put down roots immediately. Otherwise, seaborne seedlings may drift for hundreds of miles. Eventually, it touches the muddy floor and anchors. By its third year a young tree starts to sprout its own forest of arching prop roots; in about 10 years it has fostered a thriving colony of mangroves, which edge ever out to sea, forming a great swampy forest. As silt builds up among the roots, land is gradually reclaimed from the sea. Mangroves build up the soil until they strand themselves high and dry. In the end they die on the land they have created.

Fauna

Anyone who has traveled in the tropics in search of wildlife can tell you that disappointment comes easy. But Costa Rica is one place that lives up to its reputation. Costa Rica is nature's live theater—and the actors aren't shy. The scarlet macaws are like rainbows, the toucans and hummingbirds like the green flash of sunset. The tiny poison-dart frogs are bright enough to scare away even the most dimwitted predator. And the electric-blue morphos, the neon narcissi of the butterfly world, make even the most unmoved of viewers gape in awe.

Then there are all the creatures that mimic other things and are harder to spot: insects that look like rotting leaves, moths that look like wasps, the mottled, bark-colored *machaca* (lantern fly), and the giant *Caligo memnon* (cream owl) butterfly, whose huge open wings resemble the wide-eyed face of an owl.

Much of the wildlife is glimpsed only as shadows. Well-known animals that you are *not* likely to see are the cats—pumas, jaguars, margays, and ocelots—and tapirs and white-lipped peccaries. With patience, however, you can usually spot monkeys galore, as well as iguanas, quetzals, and sloths that get most of their aerobic exercise by scratching their bellies and look, as someone has said, like "long-armed tree-dwelling Muppets."

Identifying the species is a prodigious task, which every day turns up something new. Insects, for example, make up about half of the estimated 500,000 to one million plant and animal species in Costa Rica. The country is home seasonally to more than 850 bird species—10 percent of all known bird species (the U.S. and Canada combined have less than half that number). There are 5,000 different species of grasshoppers, 160 known amphibians, 220 reptiles, and 10 percent of all known butterflies (Corcovado National Park alone has at least 220 different species).

Early Migrations

About three million years ago, the Central American isthmus began to rise from the sea to form the first tentative link between the two Americas. Going from island to island, birds, insects, reptiles, and the first mammals began to move back and forth between the continents.

During this period, rodents of North America reached the southern continent, and so did the monkeys, which found the tropical climate to their liking.

In due course, South America connected with North America. Down this corridor came the placental mammals to dispute the possession of South America with the marsupial residents. Creatures poured across the bridge in both directions. The equids used it to enter South America, the opossums to invade North America. Only a few South American mammals, notably armadillos, ground sloths, and porcupines, managed to establish themselves successfully in the north. The greatest migration was in the other direction. The mammals soon came to dominate the environment, diversifying into forms more appropriate to the tropics. In the course of this rivalry, many marsupial species disappeared, leaving only the tough, opportunistic opossums.

The isthmus has thus served as a "filter bridge" for the intermingling of species and the evolution of modern, distinctive Costa Rican biota, resulting in a proliferation of species that is vastly richer than the biota of either North or South America.

MAMMALS

Given the rich diversity of Costa Rica's ecosystems, it may come as a surprise that only 200 mammal species—half of which are bats—live here. Several species of dolphins and seven species of whales are common in Costa Rican waters, but there are no seals. And the only endemic marine mammal species of any significance is the endangered manatee.

Before man hunted them to extinction, there were many more mammal species. Even today all large—and many small—mammal populations are subject to extreme pressure from hunting or habitat destruction.

Anteaters

Anteaters are common in lowland and middle-elevation habitats throughout Costa Rica. Anteaters are purists and subsist solely on a diet of ants and termites, plus a few unavoidable bits of dirt. There is no doubt about what the best tool is for the job—a long tongue with thousands of microscopic spines. The anteater's toothless jaw is one long tube. When it feeds, using its powerful forearms and claws to rip open ant and termite nests, its thong of a tongue flicks in and out of its tiny mouth, running deep into the galleries. Each time it withdraws, it brings with it a load of ants, which are scraped off inside the tunnel of its mouth and swallowed, ground down by small quantities of sand and gravel in its stomach.

The most commonly seen of Costa Rica's three anteater species is the tree-dwelling **lesser anteater** (or *tamandua* locally), a beautiful creature with a prehensile tail and the gold-and-black coloration of a panda bear. It can grow to 1.5 meters and weigh up to eight kilograms.

The critically endangered **giant anteater,** with its huge, bushy tail and astonishingly long proboscis, is now restricted to the Osa Peninsula. It can grow to two meters long and when threatened rears itself on its hind legs and slashes wildly with its claws.

At night you may, with luck, see the strictly arboreal, cat-sized **silky anteater,** which can hang from its strong prehensile tail.

Bats

The most numerous mammals by far are the bats (109 species). You may come across them slumbering by day halfway up a tree or roosting in a shed or beneath the eaves of your lodgings. In true Dracula fashion, most bats are lunarphobic: They avoid the bright light. They suspend foraging completely while the moon is at its peak, probably for fear of owls.

Many bat species—like the giant **Jamaican fruit bat** *(murciélago frútero),* with a wingspan of more than 50 centimeters—are frugivores (fruit eaters) or insectivores. Quite harmless, they play a vital role in pollination, seed dispersal, and mosquito control.

The three species of **vampire bats** (Ticos call them *vampiros*)—which belong to the neotropics, not Transylvania—are a different matter: They inflict an estimated $100 million of damage on domestic farm animals throughout

Central and South America by transmitting rabies and other diseases. Two species feed on birds; the third on mammals, with a modus operandi almost as frightening as the stuff of Bram Stoker's *Dracula*. It lands on or close to a sleeping mammal, such as a cow. Using its two razor-sharp incisors, it punctures the unsuspecting beast and, with the aid of an anticoagulant saliva, merrily squats beside the wound and laps up the blood while it flows.

The most interesting of bats, however, and one easily seen in Tortuguero, is the **fishing bulldog bat** *(murciélago pescador)*, with its huge wingspan (up to 60 cm across) and great gaff-shaped claws with which it hooks fish.

Cats

Costa Rica boasts six endangered members of the cat family. All are active by day and night, but are rarely seen. Cats are primarily solitary and nocturnal and spend the greater part of the day sleeping or hidden in dense vegetation. Although they are legally protected, hunting of cats still occurs in Costa Rica. However, the main threat to the remaining populations is deforestation.

One of the most abundant of cats is the **jaguarundi** (called *león breñero* locally), a spotless dark-brown or tawny critter about the size of a large house cat. It has a long, slender body, short stocky legs (its hind legs are taller than its forelegs), long tail, and a venal face with yellow eyes suggesting a nasty temperament. It is more diurnal than its cousins and is sometimes seen hunting in pairs, preferring lowland habitats.

Pumas *(león)* also inhabit a variety of terrains, though they are rarely seen. This large cat—also called the "mountain lion"—is generally dun-colored, though coloration varies markedly among individuals and from region to region.

The spotted cats include the cute-looking, house-cat-sized **margay** *(caucel)* and its smaller cousin, the **oncilla.** Both wear an ocher coat spotted with black and brown spots, like tiny leopards. Their chests are white. The solitary and strongly nocturnal margay, which can weight up to six kilograms, has a very long tail in relation to its body size, which, combined with its ability to turn its hind feet by

180 degrees, provides monkey-like climbing abilities. It is found only in primary or very little-disturbed forests. The oncilla or tiger cat has black ears and is distinguished from the margay by its face (closely resembling that of a domestic cat), its shorter tail, and more slender body shape. This solitary animal prefers montane cloud forest.

The most commonly seen cat is the **ocelot** *(manigordo),* which is well distributed throughout the country and among various habitats. The ocelot is the biggest (males can weigh up to 15 kg; the females up to 11 kg) of Costa Rica's "small" cats and has short, dense fur with brown spots and rosettes with black edges, arranged in parallel rows along its body length, with a background of grayish-yellow. It has a characteristic white spot on each ear, and black stripes on both cheeks and forehead.

Worshiped as a god in pre-Columbian civilizations, the **jaguar** is the symbol of the Central American jungle. *Panthera onca* (or *tigre* to locals) was once abundant throughout Central America. Today this magnificent and noble beast is an endangered species, rare except in parts of the larger reserves: Santa Rosa, Tortuguero, and Corcovado National Parks, and the Cordillera Talamanca. When roads penetrate the primeval forest, the jaguar is among the first large mammals to disappear. While a few of the famous black "panther" variety exist, most Central American jaguars are a rich yellow, spotted with large black rosettes. Jaguars are the largest and most powerful of the American members of the cat family— a mature jaguar measures over two meters, stands 60 centimeters at the shoulders, and weighs up to 90 kilograms. The animal's head and shoulders are massive, the legs relatively short and thick. An adept climber and swimmer, the beast is a versatile hunter, at home in trees, on the ground, and even in water. Like all wild cats, jaguars are extremely shy and attack humans very rarely.

Deer

Costa Rica has two species of deer: the **red brocket deer** (called *cabro de monte*), which favors the rainforests, and the larger, more commonly seen **white-tailed deer** (*venado*), widely dispersed in habitats throughout the country, but especially Guanacaste. The former is slightly hump-backed and bronze. The latter varies from gray to red, normally with a white belly and a white dappled throat and face.

Manatees

Anyone venturing to Tortuguero National Park or Gandoca-Manzanillo National Park will no doubt hope to see a West Indian manatee (*manati*). This herbivorous marine mammal looks like a tuskless walrus, with small round eyes, fleshy lips that hang over the sides of its mouth, and no hind limbs, just a large, flat, spatulate tail. The animals, sometimes called sea cows, can grow to four meters long and weigh as much as a ton. Now endangered throughout their former range, these creatures once inhabited brackish rivers and lagoons along the whole coast of Central America's Caribbean shoreline. Today, only a few remain in the most southerly waters of the United States and isolated pockets of Central America and the Caribbean Isles. Tortuguero, where the animals are legally protected, has one of the few significant populations.

They are not easy to spot, for they lie submerged with only nostrils showing. Watch for rising bubbles in the water: Manatees suffer from flatulence, a result of eating up to 45 kilograms of water hyacinths and other aquatic flora daily.

Monkeys

Costa Rica has four species of monkeys: the white-faced (or capuchin), howler, spider, and squirrel. Along with approximately 50 other species, they belong to a group called New World monkeys. They inhabit a wide range of habitats, from the rainforest canopy to the scrubby undergrowth of the dry forests, though each species occupies its own niche and the species seldom meet. Together, they are the liveliest and most vocal jungle tenants. Beyond the reach of most predators, they have little inhibition in announcing their presence

© CHRISTOPHER P. BAKER

squirrel monkey

© CHRISTOPHER P. BAKER

howler monkey with baby

with their roughhousing and howls, chatterings, and screeches.

The distinctive-looking **capuchin,** or white-faced monkey *(mono cara blanca),* is the smartest and most inquisitive of Central American simians. It derives its name from its black body and monklike white cowl. They're the little guys favored by organ grinders worldwide. Capuchins range widely throughout the wet lowland forests and the deciduous dry forests of the northwest Pacific below 1,500 meters. Two excellent places to see them are Santa Rosa and Manuel Antonio National Parks, where family troops are constantly on the prowl.

These opportunistic feeders are fun to watch as they search under logs and leaves or tear off bark as they seek out insects and small lizards. Capuchins also steal birds' eggs and nestlings. While their taste is eclectic, they *are* fussy eaters: They'll meticulously pick out grubs from fruit, which they test for ripeness by smelling and squeezing.

The **howler** *(mono congo)* is the most abundant as well as the largest of Central American monkeys (it can weigh up to 5 kg). It inhabits both lowland and montane forests throughout Costa Rica and can be found clinging precariously to existence in many relic patches of forest.

The stentorian males greet each new day with reveille calls that seem more like the explosive roars of lions than those of small arboreal leaf-eaters. The hair-raising vocalizations can carry for almost a mile in even the densest of jungle. The males sing in chorus again at dusk (or whenever trespassers get too close) as a spacing mechanism to keep rivals at a safe distance. Their Pavarotti-like vocal abilities are due to unusually large larynxes and throats that inflate into resonating balloons. Females generally content themselves with loud wails and groans—usually to signal distress or call a straying infant. This noisy yet sedentary canopy browser feeds on leaves and fruit.

The smallest and most endangered Costa Rican primate, the **squirrel monkey** *(mono titi)* grows to 25–35 centimeters, plus a tail up to 45 centimeters. Fewer than 2,000 individuals are

DON'T FEED THE ANIMALS!

It's amazing how many visitors to Costa Rica display the most appalling behavior in their interactions with wildlife. I know, those cuddly coatimundis begging for tidbits roadside sure are cute, and it's oh-so-tempting to snap a photo of your girlfriend feeding the critters. So why not "reward" them with a handout?

Feeding wild animals is harmful to them and can kill them. Here's why:

- Feeding wild animals draws them into high-traffic areas, such as roads, where they are subject to accidents.

- Feeding wild animals changes their behavior – often they become more aggressive towards humans – and interferes with their natural habitat.

- Contrary to myth, bananas are not a natural part of most monkeys' diets (squirrel monkeys are omnivores that feed on insects, fruits, seeds, and lizards). Feeding them bananas upsets their digestive system and changes their dietary pattern.

- Pregnant females fed bananas and other human foods do not give birth to healthy babies.

- Feeding wild animals increases their dependence on humans and decreases their natural feeding instincts.

- Animals need to roam their natural territories to maintain their vigor. When fed by humans, they stay in that particular spot and become inactive.

- Increased human contact facilitates poaching for illegal animal trafficking.

- Wild animals are susceptible to human diseases that you may carry on your hands.

---

thought to exist. It is restricted to the rainforests of the southern Pacific lowlands. Always on the go, day and night, they scurry about in the jungle understory and forest floor on all fours. Squirrels are more gregarious than most other monkeys; bands of 40 individuals or more are not uncommon. The golden-orange titi (with its face of white and black) is the arboreal goat of the forest. It will eat almost anything: fruit, insects, small lizards. The titi is well on its way to extinction.

The large, loose-limbed **spider monkey** (*mono colorado*)—the supreme acrobat of the forest—was once the most widespread of the Central American monkeys. The last few decades have brought significant destruction of spider monkey habitats, and land clearance and hunting have greatly reduced spider monkey populations throughout much of their former range.

These copper-colored acrobats can attain a length of 1.5 meters. They have evolved extreme specialization for a highly mobile arboreal lifestyle. Long slender limbs allow spider monkeys to make spectacular leaps. But the spider's greatest secret is its extraordinary prehensile tail, which is longer than the combined length of its head and body. The underside is ridged like a human fingertip for added grip at the end of treetop leaps (it is even sensitive enough for probing and picking). You might see individuals hanging like ripe fruit by their tails.

Gregarious by night (they often bed down in heaps), by day they are among the most solitary of primates. The males stay aloof from the females. While the latter tend to their young, which they carry on their backs, the males are busy marking their territory with secretions from their chest glands.

Peccaries

These myopic, sharp-toothed wild pigs are potentially aggressive creatures whose presence in the rainforest may be betrayed by their pungent, musky odor and by the churned-up ground from their grubbing. Gregarious beasts, they forage in herds and make a fearsome noise if frightened or disturbed. Like most animals, they prefer to flee from human presence. Occasionally, however, an aggressive male may show his bravado by threatening to have a go at you, usually in a bluff charge. Attacks by groups of a dozen or more peccaries sometimes occur. Rangers advise that if attacked, you should climb a tree or stand absolutely still. Don't try to frighten them away—that's a sure way to get gored.

The more common **collared peccary** *(saíno)* is marked by an ocher-colored band of hair running from its shoulders down to its nose; the rest of its body is dark brown. The larger **white-lipped peccary** *(cariblanco)*, which can grow to one meter long, is all black, or brown, with a white mustache or "beard."

Raccoons

Raccoons, familiar to North Americans, are present throughout Costa Rica, where they are frequently seen begging tidbits from diners at hotel restaurants. The **northern raccoon** *(mapache* to Ticos) is a smaller but otherwise identical cousin of the North American raccoon and can be found widely in Costa Rica's lowlands, predominantly in moist areas. Its cousin, the darker-colored **crab-eating raccoon,** is found only along the Pacific coast.

A relative, the long-nosed **coatimundi** (called *pizote* locally), is found throughout the country. Coatis wear many coats, from yellow to deepest brown, though all are distinguished by faintly ringed tails, white-tipped black snouts, and panda-like eye rings. They are gregarious critters and often seen in packs.

Another raccoon family member is the small and totally nocturnal **kinkajou** (known to Ticos as the *martilla*), with its large limpid eyes and velvet-soft coat of golden brown. It's a superb climber (it can hang by its prehensile tail) and spends most of its life feeding on fruit, honey, and insects in the treetops. Its smaller cousin is the much rarer, grayish, bug-eyed **olingo** *(cacomistle)*, with panda-like white spectacled eyes and a bushy white tail ringed with black hoops.

Rodents

The **agouti** *(guatusa* to Ticos) is a brown, cat-size rodent related to the guinea pig. It inhabits the forests up to 1,980 meters elevation and is often seen by day feeding on the forest floor on fruits and nuts (the wet-forest agoutis are darker than their chestnut-colored dry-forest cousins). It looks like a giant tailless squirrel with the thin legs and tiptoeing gait of a deer, but it sounds like a small dog. They are solitary critters yet form monogamous pairs.

Agoutis have long been favored for their meat and are voraciously hunted by humans. Their nocturnal cousin, the **paca** (called *tepezcuintle* by locals), also makes good eating. It can grow to a meter long and weigh 10 kilograms, three times larger than the agouti; it is favored by a wide variety of predators. It is brown with rows of white spots along its side. Both are easily captured because of the strong anal musks they use to scent their territories and because of their habit of running in circles. If you disturb one in the forest, you may hear its high-pitched alarm bark before you see it.

Costa Rica also has five squirrel species and about 40 species of rats, mice, and gophers.

Sloths

Ask anyone to compile a list of the world's strangest creatures, and the sloth (locally called *perezoso,* which means "lazy"), a creature that moves with the grace and deliberation of a tai chi master, would be right up there with the duck-billed platypus. The sloth, which grows to the size of a medium-size dog, has a small head and flat face with snub nose, beady eyes, and seemingly rudimentary ears (its reputation for poor hearing is entirely incorrect). Its long, bony arms are well developed, with curving claws that hook over and grasp the branches from which it spends almost its entire life suspended upside down. The creature spends up to 18 hours daily sleeping curled up with its feet drawn close together and its head tucked between the forelimbs.

Its shaggy fur harbors an algae, unique to the beast, that makes the sloth greenly inconspicuous—wonderful camouflage from prowling jaguars and keen-eyed eagles, its chief

coatis near Lake Arenal

predators. Communities of moths live in the depths of its fur and feed on the algae as well.

Costa Rica has two species of sloths: the **three-fingered sloth** *(perezoso de tres dedos)* and the nocturnal, relatively omnivorous **Hoffman's two-fingered sloth** *(perezoso de dos dedos)*. You're more likely to see the three-fingered sloth, which is active by day. The animals are commonly called "three-toed" and "two-toed." In fact, both species have three toes.

In fact, there's a very good reason sloths move at a rate barely distinguishable from rigor mortis. A sloth's digestion works as slowly as its other bodily functions, and food remains in its stomach for up to a week. Hence, it has evolved a large ruminant-like stomach and intestinal tract to process large quantities of relatively indigestible food. To compensate, it has sacrificed heavy muscle mass—and, hence, mobility—to maximize body size in proportion to weight. Sloths need warm weather to synthesize food. During long spells of cold weather, the animals may literally starve to death.

Sloths live up to 20 years or longer and reach sexual maturity at three years. Females screech to draw males, which have a bare orange patch on their back with unique sexual markings. Females give birth once a year and spend half their adult lives pregnant. When the juvenile reaches six months of age, the mother simply turns tail on her youngster, which inherits her home range of trees.

An easy way to find sloths is to look up into the green foliage of cecropia trees, which form one of the sloth's favorite food staples. The sight of a sloth languishing in open cecropia crowns is a heavenly vision to harpy eagles, which swoop in to snatch the torpid creature like plucking fruit.

Tapirs

Another symbol of the New World tropics is the strange-looking **Baird's tapir** *(danta* locally), a solitary, ground-living, plant-eating, forest-dwelling, ungainly mixture of elephant, rhinoceros, pig, and horse. The tapir uses its short, highly mobile proboscis—an evolutionary forerunner to the trunk of the elephant—for plucking leaves and shoveling them into its mouth. Tapirs live in dense forests and swamps and rely on concealment for defense. They are generally found wallowing up to their knees in swampy waters, to which they rush precipitously at the first sign of danger. This endangered species is the largest indigenous terrestrial mammal in Central America. Like its natural predator the jaguar, the tapir has suffered severely at the hands of humans. The animal was once common in Costa Rica and ranged far and wide in the lowland swamps and forests. Hunters have brought it to the edge of extinction. Today, tapirs are found only in national parks and reserves where hunting is restricted, with the greatest density in Corcovado National Park.

Weasels

Costa Rica boasts seven members of the weasel family. The most ubiquitous is the **skunk** (*zorro* in local parlance), one of the most commonly seen mammal species, of which Costa Rica has three species. The black **striped hog-nosed skunk**, with its bushy white tail and white stripe along its rump, will be familiar to North Americans. The smaller **spotted skunk** and **hooded skunk** are more rarely seen. Their defense is a disgusting scent sprayed at predators from an anal gland.

Costa Rica is also home to the badger-like **grison,** another member of the weasel family that can weigh three kilograms and is often seen hunting alone or in groups in lowland rainforest during the day. The grison is gray, with a white stripe running across its forehead and ears, white eye patches, and a black nose, chest, and legs. Meter-long **otters** (*perro de agua,* or water dog, to locals) are commonly seen in lowland rivers, especially in Tortuguero.

A cousin, the sleek, long-haired, chocolate-brown **tayra** (locals call it *tolumuco*)—a meter-long giant of the weasel family—resembles a mix of grison and otter. It is often seen in highland habitats throughout Costa Rica.

Other Mammals

The mostly nocturnal and near-blind **nine-banded armadillo** (*cusuco*), will be familiar to anyone from Texas. The animal can grow to almost one meter long. They are terrestrial dwellers that grub about on the forest floor, feeding on insects and fungi. The female lays a single egg that, remarkably, divides to produce identical triplets. Its smaller cousin, the **naked-tailed armadillo,** is far less frequently seen.

The dog family is represented by the brown-gray **coyote** and nocturnal **gray fox,** both found mostly in the dry northwest.

The marsupials—mammals whose embryonic offspring crawl from the birth canal and are reared in an external pouch—are represented by nine species of **opossums.**

The blunt-nosed, short-spined, **prehensile-tailed porcupine** (*puerco espín*) is nocturnal and arboreal and rarely seen. There are also two species of **rabbits** (*conejos*).

SEALIFE

Costa Rica is as renowned for its marinelife as for its terrestrial and avian fauna—most famously, perhaps, for the billfish (marlin and sailfish) that cruise the deep blue waters offshore, and for tarpon and snook, feisty estuarine and wetland game fish. The former swim seasonally in the warm waters off the Golfo de Papagayo and Golfo Dulce; the latter are concentrated in the waters of the Río Colorado and Caño Negro.

Sharks are forever present in Costa Rican waters. They seem particularly to favor waters in which marine turtles swim. Isla Cocos is renowned for its schools of hammerhead sharks, as well as giant whale sharks (the world's largest fish), which can also be found hanging out with giant grouper, jewfish, and manta rays in the waters around the Islas Murciélagos, off the Santa Elena Peninsula of Guanacaste.

Whales—notably humpbacks—can be seen predictably along the west coast of Costa Rica December–October, when they migrate from both Antarctic and northern Pacific waters to mate and give birth in the warm waters off the Costa Ballena.

BIRDS

With approximately 850 recorded bird species, the country boasts one-tenth of the world's total. More than 630 are resident species; the

fiery-billed aracari

others are travelers who fly in for the winter. Birds that have all but disappeared in other areas still find tenuous safety in protected lands in Costa Rica, though many species face extinction from deforestation.

It may surprise you to learn that in a land with so many exotic species the national bird is the relatively drab *yiquirro,* or clay-colored **robin,** a brown-and-buff bird with brick-red eyes. You may hear the male singing during the March–May breeding season when, according to *campesino* folklore, he is "calling the rains."

The four major "avifaunal zones" roughly correspond to the major geographic subdivisions of the country: the northern Pacific lowlands, the southern Pacific lowlands, the Caribbean lowlands, and the interior highlands. Guanacaste's dry habitats (northern Pacific lowlands) share relatively few species with other parts of the country. This is a superlative place, however, for waterfowl: the estuaries, swamps, and lagoons that make up the Tempisque Basin support the richest freshwater avifauna in all Central America, and Palo Verde National Park, at the mouth of the Tempisque, is a bird-watcher's mecca. The southern Pacific lowland region is home to many South American neotropical species, such as jacamars, antbirds, and, of course, parrots.

Depending on season, location, and luck, you can expect to see many dozens of species on any one day. Many tour companies offer guided bird-study tours, and the country is well set up with lodges that specialize in birdwatching programs. But the deep heart of the jungle is not the best place to look for birds: you cannot see well amid the complex, disorganized patterns cast by shadow and light. For best results, find a large clearing on the fringe of the forest, or a watercourse where birds are sure to be found in abundance.

Anhingas and Cormorants

The anhinga (*pato aguja* to locals) and its close cousin, the olivaceous cormorant *(cormorán),* are sleek, long-necked, stump-tailed waterbirds with the pointy profile of a Concorde. Though they dive for fish in the lagoons and rivers of the lowlands and are superb swimmers, their feathers lack the waterproof oils of other birds. You can thus often see them after a dousing, perched on a branch, sunning themselves in a vertical position with widespread wings. These birds have kinked necks because they spear fish using the kink as a trigger.

Aracaris and Toucans

The bright-billed toucans—"flying bananas"—are a particular delight to watch as they pick fruit with their long beaks, throw it in the air, and catch it at the back of their throats. Costa Rica's six toucan species are among the most flamboyant of all Central American birds.

The gregarious **keel-billed toucan** (*tucan pico iris*) inhabits lowland and mid-elevation forests throughout the country except the Pacific southwest. This colorful stunner has a jet-black body, blue feet, a bright yellow chest and face, beady black eyes ringed by green feathers, and a rainbow-hued beak tipped by scarlet. Its similarly colored cousin, Swainson's or **chestnut-mandibled toucan** (Ticos call it *dios tedé*, for the onomatopoeic sound it makes), is the largest of the group—it grows to 60 centimeters long and has a two-tone yellow-and-brown beak. It is found in moist forests below 610 meters, notably along the coastal zones, including the Pacific southwest.

There are also two species of toucanets, smaller cousins of the toucan: the green **emerald toucanet,** a highland bird with a red tail; and the black **yellow-eared toucanet,** found in the Caribbean lowlands.

Aracaris (*tucancillos*) are smaller and sleeker relatives, with more slender beaks. Both the **collared aracari** (a Caribbean bird) and **fiery-billed aracari** (its southern Pacific cousin) boast olive-black bodies, faces, and chests, with a dark band across their rust-yellow underbellies. The former has a two-tone yellow-and-black beak; the latter's beak is black and fiery orange.

Birds of Prey

Costa Rica has some 50 raptor species: birds that hunt down live prey and seize it with their talons. The various species have evolved adaptations to specific habitats. For example, the large **common black hawk** (*gavilán cangrejero*, or "crab-hunting hawk" to Ticos) snacks on crabs

and other marine morsels. And the **osprey** is known as *agula pescadora* (fishing eagle) locally for scooping fish while on the wing.

That lunatic laughter that goes on compulsively at dusk in lowland jungles is the **laughing falcon** (*guaco*).

The endangered neotropical **harpy eagle** (*águila arpía*), at one meter long the largest of all eagles, is renowned for twisting and diving through the treetops in pursuit of sloths and monkeys. Sightings in Costa Rica—where in recent years it has been relegated to the Osa Peninsula and more remote ranges of the Talamancas—are extremely rare.

Costa Rica's two species of caracaras—the **crested caracara** and **yellow-headed caracara**—are close cousins to the eagles, though like vultures they also eat carrion. You'll often see these large, fearsomely beaked, goose-stepping, long-legged birds picking at roadkill.

Costa Rica also has eight species of hawks, which are physically robust, with broad wings and short, wide tails, compared to the sleeker kites, which have longer, slender tails and wings. The most ubiquitous hawk is the small, gray-brown **roadside hawk** (*gavilán chapulínero*).

Doves and Pigeons

Doves and pigeons—*palomas*—are numerous (Costa Rica has at least 25 species, including endemic neotropical species and migratory visitors familiar to North Americans).

Many neotropical species are far more colorful than their northern counterparts. The large **band-tailed pigeon,** for example, though predominantly gray, has a green nape with white band, blue wings tipped by brown, a yellow bill, and mauve chest and belly. The mauve-gray **red-billed pigeon** has a red nape, bright red feet and forewings, and pale-blue rear quarters fading to a black-and-gray tail.

Egrets, Herons, and Relatives

Some 25 or so stilt-legged, long-necked wading birds are found in Costa Rica. Most common is the snowy white **cattle egret.** It favors cattle pastures and can often be seen hitching a ride on the back of cattle, which are happy to have it pick off fleas and ticks. The males have head plumes, which, along with the back and chest, turn tawny in breeding season. The species is easily mistaken for the **snowy egret,** a larger though more slender bird wearing "golden slippers" (yellow feet) on its black legs. Largest of the white egrets is the **great egret,** which grows to one meter tall.

There are three species of brown herons—called "tiger herons" *(garza tigre)*—in Costa Rica, most notably the **bare-throated tiger heron.** The **little blue heron,** commonly seen foraging alongside lowland watercourses, is a handsome blue-gray with purplish head plumage (the female is white, with wings tipped in gray). The northern lowlands are also a good place to spot the relatively small **green-backed heron.** The dun-colored **yellow-crowned night heron** is diurnal, not nocturnal as its name suggests. It is unmistakable, with its black-and-white head crowned with a swept-back yellow plume. Another instantly identifiable bird is the stocky gray **boat-billed heron,** named for the keel shape of its abnormally wide, thick bill.

Storks—notable for their fearsomely heavy, slightly upturned bills—also inhabit the lowland wetlands, notably in Caño Negro and Palo Verde National Parks, where the endangered **jabiru** can be seen. This massive bird (it grows to over one meter tall) wears snow-bright plumage, with a charcoal head, and a red scarf around its neck. Its relative, the **wood stork,** is also white, but with black flight feathers and featherless black head.

The **roseate spoonbill** *(espátula rosada)* is the most dramatic of the waders, thanks to its shocking-pink plumage and spatulate bill. Costa Rica also has three species of **ibis.**

Hummingbirds

Of all the exotically named bird species in Costa Rica, the hummingbirds beat all contenders. Their names are poetry: the **green-crowned brilliant, purple-throated mountain-gem, Buffon's plummeteer,** and the bold and strikingly beautiful **fiery-throated hummingbird.** More than 300 species of New World hummingbirds constitute the family Trochilidae (Costa Rica has 51). The fiery-throated hummingbird is a glossy green, shimmering iridescent at close range, with dark blue tail, violet-blue chest, glittering coppery orange throat, and a brilliant blue crown set off by velvety black on the sides and back of the head. Some males take their exotic plumage one step further and are bedecked with long streamer tails and iridescent mustaches, beards, and visors.

These tiny high-speed machines are named because of the hum made by the beat of their wings. At up to 100 beats per second, the hummingbirds' wings move so rapidly that the naked eye cannot detect them. They are often seen hovering at flowers, from which they extract nectar (and often insects) with their long, hollow, and extensile tongues forked at the tip. Alone among birds, they can generate power on both the forward and backward wing strokes, a distinction that allows them to also fly backward. Nests are often no larger than a thimble and eggs no larger than coffee beans.

Motmots

The motmot is a sickle-billed bird that makes its home in a hole in the ground. Motmots have a pendulous twin-feathered tail with the barbs missing three-quarters of the way down, leaving two bare feather shafts with disc-shaped tips. (According to Bribrí legend, the god Sibö asked all the creatures to help him make the world. They all chipped in gladly except the motmot, who hid in a hole. Unfortunately, the bird left his tail hanging out. When the other birds saw this they picked the feathers from the motmot's tail but left the feathers at the tip. When the world was complete, Sibö gave all the tired animals a rest. Soon the motmot appeared and began boasting about how hard he had labored. But the lazy bird's tail gave the game away, so Sibö, who guessed what had happened, admonished the motmot and banished him to living in a hole in the ground.)

Of nine species of motmot in tropical America, six live in Costa Rica. You'll find them from humid coastal southwest plains to

© CHRISTOPHER P. BAKER

blue-crowned motmot

the cool highland zone and dry Guanacaste region. Two commonly seen species are the **blue-crowned motmot** and **turquoise-bowed motmot**.

Owls

Costa Rica's 17 species of owls are nocturnal hunters, more often heard than seen. An exception is the large dark-brown **spectacled owl** (*bujo de anteojos*), which also hunts by day.

Parrots

If ever there were an avian symbol of the neotropics, it must be the parrot. This family of birds is marked by savvy intelligence, an ability to mimic the human voice, and uniformly short, hooked bills hinged to provide the immense power required for cracking seeds and nuts. Costa Rica claims 16 of the world's 330 or so species, including six species of parakeets and two species of macaws, the giants of the parrot kingdom. The parrots are predominantly green, with short, truncated tails (parakeets and macaws, however, have long tails), and varying degrees of colored markings. All are voluble, screeching raucously as they barrel overhead.

Although **macaw** is the common name for any of 15 species of these large, long-tailed birds found throughout Central and South America, only two species inhabit Costa Rica: the scarlet macaw (*lapa roja*) and the great green or Buffon's macaw (*lapa verde*). Both bird populations are losing their homes to deforestation and poaching.

The largest of the neotropical parrots, macaws have harsh, raucous voices that are filled with authority. They are gregarious and rarely seen alone. They are usually paired male and female—they're monogamous for life—often sitting side by side, grooming and preening each other, and conversing in rasping loving tones, or flying two by two.

Macaws usually nest in softwood trees, where termites have hollowed out holes. They rarely eat fruit, but prefer seeds and nuts, which they extract with a hooked nutcracker of such strength that it can split the Brazil nut—or a human finger.

SAVING THE MACAW

Several conservation groups are working to stabilize and reestablish the scarlet macaw population.

Zoo Ave (tel. 506/2433-8989, www. zooave.org), at La Garita, west of Alajuela, has an extensive macaw breeding program, and as of 2008 had released almost 100 macaws to Piedras Blancas National Park.

Amigos de las Aves (tel./fax 506/2441-2658, www.hatchedtoflyfree.com; in the U.S., SJO 465, P.O. Box 025216, Miami, FL 33102) is a macaw-breeding program on a three-hectare estate – Flor de Mayo – in Río Segundo de Alajuela. Here, Richard Frisius and his staff raise baby macaws using special techniques and cages. The first macaws were released in January 1999 at a private reserve in Nicoya. Dozens of macaws have since been released in pairs. Donations are needed, as are volunteer workers.

The **scarlet macaw** can grow to 85 centimeters in length. It wears a dazzling, rainbow-colored jacket of bright yellow and blue, green, or scarlet. Though the scarlet macaw ranges from Mexico to central South America and was once abundant on both coasts of Costa Rica, today it is found only in a few parks on the Pacific shore, and rarely on the Caribbean side. Until recently only three wild populations of scarlet macaws in Central America were thought to have a long-term chance of survival—at Carara National Park and Corcovado National Park in Costa Rica, and Coiba Island in Panamá. The bird can also be seen with regularity at Palo Verde National Park, Manuel Antonio National Park, and Santa Rosa National Park, though these populations were below the minimum critical size. An estimated 400 scarlets live at Carara and 2,500 at Corcovado. Following a decade of reintroduction of human-bred scarlet macaws to the wild, populations are rebounding throughout their range.

The **Buffon's macaw,** or great green macaw, is slightly smaller than the scarlet. It has a pea-green body, a white face splotched with red, blue wingtips, and a red tail. A few more than 50 breeding pairs of Buffon's macaw are thought to exist in the wild, exclusively in the Caribbean and northern lowlands. The bird relies on the almendro tree—a heavily logged species—for nest sites, and calls have gone out for a ban on logging almendros. Its population is increasing due to environmental efforts.

Seabirds and Shorebirds

Costa Rica has almost 100 species of seabirds and shorebirds, including a wide variety of gulls, with the most common being the **laughing gull** (gaviota reidora). Many are migratory visitors, more abundant in winter months, including the **sanderling,** a small light-gray shorebird.

The large, pouch-billed **brown pelican** (pelicano) can be seen up and down the Pacific coast (and, in lesser numbers, on the Caribbean). **Boobies** inhabit several islands off Nicoya, as do **storm petrels, jaegers,** and the beautiful red-billed, fork-tailed **royal tern,** as well as a variety of other seabirds. **Oystercatchers, whimbrels, sandpipers** (often seen in vast flocks), and other shoreline waders frequent the coastal margins.

Frigate birds, with their long scimitar wings and forked tails, hang like kites in the wind all along the Costa Rican coast. Despite the sinister look imparted by its long hooked beak, the frigate bird is quite beautiful. The adult male is all black with a lustrous faint purplish-green sheen on its back (especially during the courtship season). The female, the much larger of the two, is easily distinguished by the white feathers that extend up her abdomen and breast, and the ring of blue around her eyes. Superb stunt flyers, frigate birds often bully other birds on the wing, pulling at the tails of their victims until the latter release or regurgitate a freshly caught meal (bird-watchers have a name for such thievery: kleptoparasitism). Frigate birds also catch much of their food themselves. You may see them skimming the water and snapping up squid, flying fish, and other morsels off the water's surface. (They must keep themselves dry, as they have only a small preen gland, insufficient to oil their feathers; if they get too wet they become waterlogged and drown.)

Tanagers and Other Passerines

Costa Rica boasts 50 species of tanagers—small, exorbitantly colored birds that favor dark tropical forests. The tanagers' short stubby wings enable them to swerve and dodge through the undergrowth as they chase after insects.

Among the most astonishing is the **summer tanager,** flame-red from tip to tail. The black male **scarlet-rumped tanager** also has a startlingly flame-red rump (his mate is orange and olive-gray). The exotically plumed **blue-gray tanager** is as variegated in turquoise and teal as a Bahamian sea, while the **silver-throated tanager** is lemon yellow.

Tanagers belong to the order Passerines—"perching birds"—that includes about half of all Costa Rica's bird species. It is a taxonomically challenging group, with members characterized by certain anatomical features: notably, three toes pointing forward and a longer toe pointing back. **Sparrows, robins,** and **finches** are Passerines, as are **antbirds** (30 species), **blackbirds** (20 species), **flycatchers** (78 species), **warblers** (52 species), and **wrens** (22 species).

Trogons

Costa Rica has 10 of the 40 species of trogons: brightly colored, long-tailed, short-beaked, pigeon-sized, forest-dwelling tropical birds. Most trogons combine bodies of two primary colors—red and blue, blue and yellow, or green and some other color—with a black-and-white striped tail. The **orange-bellied trogon,** for example, is green, with a bright orange belly beneath a sash of white.

Many bird-watchers travel to Costa Rica simply to catch sight of the **quetzal,** or resplendent trogon. What this bird lacks in physical stature it makes up for in audacious plumage: vivid, shimmering green that ignites in the sunshine, flashing emerald to golden and back to iridescent green. The male sports a fuzzy punk hairdo, a scintillating crimson belly, and two brilliant green tail plumes up to 60 centimeters long, sinuous as feather boas. The female lacks the elaborate plumage.

Early Maya and Aztecs worshiped a god called Quetzalcoatl, the Plumed Serpent that bestowed corn on humans, and depicted him with a headdress of quetzal feathers. The bird's name is derived from *quetzalli,* an Aztec word meaning "precious" or "beautiful." The Maya considered the male's iridescent green tail feathers worth more than gold. Quetzal plumes and jade, which were traded throughout Mesoamerica, were the Mayas' most precious objects. It became a symbol of authority vested in a theocratic elite, much as only Roman nobility was allowed to wear purple silks. Its beauty was so fabled and the bird so elusive and shy that early European naturalists believed the quetzal was a fabrication of Central American natives.

The male proclaims its territory each dawn through midmorning and again at dusk with a telltale melodious whistle—a hollow, high-pitched call of two notes, one ascending steeply, the other descending—repeated every 8–10 minutes. Narcissistic males show off their tail plumes in undulating flight, with spiraling skyward flights presaging a plummeting dive with their tail feathers rippling behind, all part of the courtship ritual.

Nest holes (often hollowed out by woodpeckers) are generally about 10 meters from the ground. By day, the male incubates the eggs while his tail feathers (0.6 m) hang out of the nest. At night, the female takes over.

The movement of quetzals follows the seasonal fruiting of different laurel species. Everywhere throughout its 1,600-kilometer range (from southern Mexico to western Panamá), the quetzal is endangered by loss of its cloud-forest habitat.

Waterfowl

Costa Rica lies directly beneath a migratory corridor between North and South America, and in the northern lowland wetlands, the air is always full of **blue-winged teals, shoveler ducks,** and other waterfowl settling and taking off. Most duck species are winter migrants from North America. Neotropical species include **black-bellied whistling ducks** and **Muscovy ducks.**

The wetlands are also inhabited by 18 species of the order Gruiformes: rails, bitterns, and their relatives, with their large, wide-splayed feet good for wading and running across lily- and grass-choked watercourses. Many are brightly colored, including the **purple gallinule,** liveried in vivid violet and green, with a yellow-tipped red bill. The black-and-brown, yellow-beaked **northern jacana** is easy to see, especially in the canals of Tortuguero, hopping about atop water lilies thanks to its long, slender toes—hence its nickname, the "lily-trotter." The female jacana is promiscuous, mating with many males, who take on the task of nest-building and brooding eggs that may have been fertilized by a rival. Tortuguero is also a good place to spot the **sungrebe,** a furtive, brown waterbird with black-and-white striped neck and head and red beak. Males carry young chicks in a fold of skin under their wings.

Vultures

Costa Rica has four species of vultures (*zopilotes*). You can't help but be unnerved at the first sight of scrawny black vultures swirling overhead on the thermals as if waiting for your car to break down. They look quite ominous in their undertaker's plumage, with bald heads and hunched shoulders.

The red-headed **turkey vulture** is common in all parts of Costa Rica below 2,000 meters, noticeably so in moister coastal areas where it hops about on the streets of forlorn towns such as Golfito. The stockier **black vulture** has a black head. Both are otherwise charcoal colored.

Count yourself lucky to spot the rarer **lesser yellow-headed vulture,** with its namesake yellow head; or the mighty **king vulture,** which wears a handsome white coat with black wing feathers and tail, and a wattled head variegated in vermilion and yellow.

Other Notable Birds

The **three-wattled bellbird,** which inhabits the cloud forests, is rarely spotted in the mist-shrouded treetops, though the male's eerie call, like a hammer clanging on an anvil, haunts the forest as long as the sun is up. It is named for the strange wattles that dangle from its bill. Its population is declining alarmingly.

In the moist Caribbean lowlands (and occasionally elsewhere) you may spot the telltale pendulous woven nests—often one meter long—of **Montezuma oropendolas,** a large bronze-colored bird with a black neck, head, and belly, a blue-and-orange bill, and bright yellow outer tail feathers. The birds nest in colonies. The **chestnut-headed oropendola** is less commonly seen.

The great **curassow,** growing as tall as one meter, is almost too big for flight and tends to run through the undergrowth if disturbed. You're most likely to see this endangered bird in Corcovado or Santa Rosa National Parks.

All four New World species of kingfishers inhabit Costa Rica: the large red-breasted; the slate-blue **ringed kingfisher,** which can grow to 40 centimeters; its smaller cousin, the **belted kingfisher;** and the **Amazon kingfisher** and smaller **green kingfisher,** both green with white and red underparts.

The **common pauraque** (or *cuyeo*) is a member of the nightjar family—nocturnal birds that in flight are easily mistaken for bats. They like to sit on the dusty roads at night, where they are well camouflaged, causing you a heck of a scare as they lift off.

Another neotropical nightjar is the odd-looking **great potoo** *(nictibio grande),* a superbly camouflaged bird that perches upright on tree stumps and holds its head haughtily aloft. Its squat cousin, the **common potoo,** resembles an owl.

REPTILES

Costa Rica is home to more than 200 species of reptiles, half of them snakes.

full-grown male crocodile, Río Tárcoles

Crocodiles and Caimans

Many travelers visit Costa Rica in the hope of seeing American crocodiles and caimans, the croc's diminutive cousins. Both species are easily seen in the wet lowlands. They are superbly adapted for water. Their eyes and nostrils are atop their heads for easy breathing and vision while otherwise entirely submerged, and their thick, muscular tails provide tremendous propulsion.

The American crocodile—one of four species of New World crocodiles—can easily be seen in dozens of rivers throughout the lowlands and estuaries along the Pacific coastline. Sections of the Tárcoles River have as many as 240 crocodiles per mile, far higher than anywhere else in Costa Rica. The creatures, which can live 80 years or more and reach six meters in length, spend much of their days basking on mudbanks, maintaining an even body temperature, which they regulate by opening their gaping mouths. To the crocodile (*cocodrilo*), home is a "gator hole" or pond, a system of trails, and a cavelike den linked by a tunnel to the hole. The croc helps maintain the health of aquatic water systems by weaning out weak and large predatory fish. Mating season begins in December. For all their beastly behavior, crocodiles are devoted parents. Eggs are laid March–May, during dry season. The mother will guard the nest and keep it moist for several months after laying. When they are ready to hatch, the hatchlings pipe squeakily and she uncovers the eggs and takes the babies into a special pouch inside her mouth. She then swims away, with the youngsters peering out between a palisade of teeth. The male assists, and soon the young crocs are feeding and playing in a special nursery, guarded by the two watchful parents (only 10 percent of newborn hatchlings survive).

Despite being relics from the age of the dinosaurs, croc brains are far more complex than those of other reptiles. They are sharp learners (in the Tempisque basin, crocs have been seen whacking tree trunks with their tails to dislodge chicks from their nests). They also have an amazing immune system that can even defeat gangrene.

At night, they sink down into the warm waters of the river for the hunt. The American

© CHRISTOPHER P. BAKER

spiny-tailed iguana

crocodile is generally a fish-eater, but adults are known to vary their diet with meat, even taking cattle carelessly taking a drink at the river's edge…so watch out! Crocs cannot chew. They simply snap, tear, and swallow. Powerful stomach acids dissolve everything, including bones. A horrible way to go!

No more than two meters long, the speckled caiman (*guajipal* locally) is still relatively common in parts of wet lowland Costa Rica on both the Atlantic and Pacific coasts. Palo Verde and Tortuguero are both good places to spot them in small creeks, *playas,* and brackish mangrove swamps, or basking on the banks of streams and ponds.

Caiman or croc? It's easy to tell. The former is dark brown with darker bands around its tail and holds its head high when sunning. The much-larger crocodile is an olive color with black spots on its tail.

Iguanas and Lizards

The most common reptile you'll see is the dragonlike, tree-dwelling iguana, which can grow to a meter in length. You'll spot them in all kinds of forest habitats, but particularly in drier areas below 760 meters elevation. There's no mistaking this reptile for any other lizard. Its head is crested with a frightening wig of leathery spines, its heavy body encased in a scaly hide, deeply wrinkled around the sockets of its muscular legs. Despite its menacing *One Million Years B.C.* appearance, it is a nonbelligerent vegetarian.

There are two species in Costa Rica: the green and the spiny-tailed iguana. The **green iguana** (Iguana iguana), which is a dull to bright green, with a black-banded tail, can grow to two meters long. The males turn a bright orange when they get ready to mate in November or December and choose a lofty perch from which to advertise their prowess as potential lovers. Females nest in holes in the ground, then abandon their eggs. Male iguanas are territorial and defend their turf aggressively against competitors. *Campesinos,* for reasons you may not wish to know, call the green iguana the "tree chicken."

The smaller, gray or tan-colored **spiny-tailed iguana,** also called the **ctenosaur** *(Iguana*

vine snake

negra)—known locally as the *garrobo*—has a tail banded with rings of hard spines that it uses to guard against predators by blocking the entrance to holes in trees or the ground.

Another miniature dinosaur is *Basilicus basilicus,* or **Jesus Christ lizard,** a Pacific lowland dweller common in Santa Rosa, Palo Verde, and Corcovado National Parks. These use water as their means of escape, running across it on hind legs (hence their name).

To learn more, visit the website of the Green Iguana Foundation (www.iguanaverde.com).

Snakes

The 138 species of snakes make up more than half of all reptile species in the nation. Wherever you are in the country, snakes are sure to be about. They are reclusive, however, and it is a fortunate traveler indeed who gets to see in the wild the fantastically elongated **chunk-headed snake,** with its catlike elliptical eyes, or the slender, beak-nosed, bright green **vine snake.**

Among the more common snake species you are likely to see are the wide-ranging and relatively benign **boas.** Boas are aggressive when confronted: though not venomous, they are quite capable of inflicting serious damage with their large teeth.

Only 18 species of snakes in Costa Rica are venomous (nine are *very* venomous).

The **coffee palm viper** is a heat-seeking missile that can detect differences of 0.0003°C per meter! And *zopilota* eats only other snakes and prefers the fearsome **fer-de-lance** (locally called *terciopelo,* Spanish for "velvet"), which is much feared for its aggressiveness—it accounts for 80 percent of all snakebites in Costa Rica—and lethal venom. One of several Central American pit vipers—another is the sheepish, albeit three-meter-long and deadly **bushmaster**—the fer-de-lance can grow to a length of three meters and is abundant throughout the country except Nicoya, particularly in overgrown fields and river courses in drier lowland regions. Tiny juvenile fer-de-lance are just as deadly and are almost impossible to see as they rest in loose coils of black and brown on the forest floor. Give the fer-de-lance a wide berth! Unlike other vipers, which usually slither away at the approach of humans, the fer-de-lance stands its ground and will bite with little provocation. The snake's powerful venom dissolves nerve tissue and destroys blood cells and artery walls; those fortunate enough to survive may suffer paralysis or tissue damage so massive as to require amputation of the bitten limb.

The small (yet potentially deadly) **eyelash vipers** are also superbly camouflaged—yellow, green, mottled brown, gray, or chocolate to suit their environment—and often remain immobile for days on end, awaiting passing prey.

Among the more colorful snakes are the four species of **coral snakes,** with small heads, blunt tails, and bright bands of red, black, and yellow or white. These highly venomous snakes (often fatal to humans) exhibit a spectacular defensive display: They flatten their bodies and snap back and forth while swinging their heads side to side and coiling and waving their tails.

In the Pacific Ocean, you may sometimes encounter venomous pelagic **sea snakes,** yellow-bellied and black-backed serpents closely related to terrestrial cobras and coral snakes. This gregarious snake has developed an oarlike tail to paddle its way through the ocean. Its venom is among the most deadly toxins known to man, but they are known to have bitten humans only rarely.

Turtles

Six of the world's eight species of marine turtles nest on Costa Rica's beaches, and you can see turtles laying eggs somewhere in Costa Rica virtually any time of year.

Tortuguero National Park, in northeastern Costa Rica, is one of fewer than 30 places in the world that the **green turtle** considers clean enough and safe enough to lay its eggs. Although green turtles were once abundant throughout the Caribbean, today there are only three major sites in the region where they nest: one on Aves Island, 62 kilometers west of Montserrat, a second at Gandoca-Manzanillo, and the third on the endless beach between Pacuare and Tortuguero.

On the Pacific coast, the most spectacular nestings are at Playa Nancite, in Santa Rosa National Park, and Ostional Wildlife Refuge,

and recently at Playa Camaronal, where tens of thousands of **olive ridley turtles** (*lora*) come ashore July–December in synchronized mass nestings known as *arribadas.* Giant **leatherback turtles** (*baula*) nest at Playa Grande, near Tamarindo, October–April and in lesser numbers at several other beaches. Hawksbills, ridleys, leatherbacks, Pacific greens, and occasionally loggerheads (primarily Caribbean nesters) appear in lesser numbers at other beaches along the Pacific coast.

Most of the important nesting sites in Costa Rica are now protected, and access to some is restricted. Turtle populations continue to decline because of illegal harvesting and environmental pressure, and all species are now critically endangered. Despite legislation outlawing the taking of turtle eggs or disturbing nesting turtles, nest sites continue to be raided by humans (encouraged by an ancient Mayan legend that says the eggs are aphrodisiacs). Mother Nature, too, poses her own challenges. Coatis, dogs, raccoons, and peccaries dig up nest sites to get at the tasty eggs. Gulls and vultures pace the beach hungrily awaiting the hatchlings; crabs lie in wait for the tardy; and hungry jacks, barracudas, and sharks come close to shore for the feast. Of the hundreds of eggs laid by a female in one season, only a handful will survive to reach maturity.

Turtles have hit on a formula for outwitting their predators, or at least for surviving despite them. Each female turtle normally comes ashore two to six times each season and lays an average of 100 eggs on each occasion.

Most females make their clumsy climb up the beach and lay their eggs under the cover and cool of darkness (loggerheads and ridleys often nest in the daytime). They normally time their arrival to coincide with high tide, when they do not have to drag themselves puffing and panting across a wide expanse of beach. Some turtles even die of heart attacks brought on by the exertions of digging and laying.

Once she settles on a comfortable spot above the high-tide mark, the female scoops out a large body pit with her front flippers. Then her dexterous hind flippers go to work hollowing

© CHRISTOPHER P. BAKER

ridley turtle coming ashore to lay eggs at Playa Camaronal

out a small egg chamber below her tail and into which white, spongy, golf-ball-size spheres fall every few seconds. After shoveling the sand back into place and flinging sand wildly about to hide her precious treasure, she makes her way back to sea.

The eggs normally take six to eight weeks to hatch, incubated by the warm sand. Some marvelous internal clock arranges for most eggs to hatch at night when hatchlings can make their frantic rush for the sea concealed by darkness. Often, baby turtles will emerge from the eggs during the day and wait beneath the surface of the beach until nightfall. They are programmed to travel fast across the beach to escape the hungry mouths. Even after reaching the sea they continue to swim frantically for several days— flippers paddling furiously—like clockwork toys. No one knows where baby turtles go. They swim off and generally are not seen again until they appear years later as adults.

Turtles are great travelers capable of amazing feats of navigation. Greens, for example, navigate across up to 2,400 kilometers of open sea to return, like salmon, to the same nest site, guided presumably by stars and currents and their own internal compass.

When near nesting sites, respect the turtles' need for peace and quiet. Nesting turtles are very timid and extremely sensitive to flashlights, sudden movements, and noise, which will send a female turtle in hasty retreat to the sea without laying her eggs. Sometimes she will drop her eggs on the sand in desperation, without digging a proper nest.

Freshwater turtles *(jicoteas)* are also common in Costa Rica, particularly in the Caribbean lowlands.

INSECTS

Butterflies, moths, ants, termites, wasps, bees, and other tropical insects have evolved in astounding profusion. There are so many species, no one knows the true numbers.

Ants

Ants, which number several thousand species, are the most abundant insects (one hectare of rainforest contains an average of nine million ants). Though related to bees and wasps, like butterflies they pass through four life stages: egg, larva, pupae, and adult. They are entirely social creatures, each ant entirely dependent upon its siblings so that the colony acts as a single organism. They are also almost entirely blind and rely for communication upon the chemicals—pheromones—that they release to alert each other to danger and food sources.

Each colony is dependent on the queen ant, whose sole task is to produce eggs (thus, most colonies die when the queen, which can live up to 20 years, dies). Only the queen, who may boast a thousand times the body weight of a minor worker, is fertile. Once a year, usually at the beginning of rainy season (around May and June), the queen produces a unique brood of about 50,000 eggs; the approximately one-fifth that are fertilized will become new queens, and the others will become males. The entire colony doubles its efforts to care for and feed the large larva. Upon maturity, males and queens develop wings and, upon a particular weather cue, set out to form a new colony. Males exist only to fertilize the queen and then die.

Army ants march through the forest with the sole intent of turning small creatures into skeletons in a few minutes. They're like a wolf pack, but with tens of thousands of miniature beasts of prey that merge and unite to form one great living creature. While the ants advance across the forest floor driving small creatures in front of them, humans and other large creatures can simply step aside and watch the column pass by—this can take several hours. Even when the ants raid human habitations, people can simply clear out with their food stock while the ants clean out the cockroaches and other vermin.

The army ants' jaws are so powerful that indigenous people used them to suture wounds: the tenacious insect is held over a wound and its body squeezed so that its jaws instinctively clamp shut, drawing the flesh back together. The body is then pinched off.

The most noticeable ant is the **leafcutter ant** (*Atta cephalotes*), a mushroom-farming insect that carries upright in its jaws a circular green shard scissored from the leaves of a plant. They are found in forests throughout Costa Rica. At some stage in your travels you're bound to come across a troop of workers hauling their cargo along jungle pathways as immaculately cleaned of debris as any swept doorstep. The nests are built below ground, sometimes extending over an area of 200 square meters, with galleries to a depth of six meters. The largest nests provide homes for single colonies of up to five million insects. Trails span out from the nests, often for 100 meters or more. The worker ants set off from their nests day and night in long columns to demolish trees, removing every shoot, leaf, and stem section by tiny section and transporting them back to their underground chambers (about 15 percent of total leaf harvesting in Costa Rica is the work of leafcutter ants).

They don't eat this material. Instead, they chew it up to form a compost on which they cultivate a nutritional breadlike fungus whose tiny white fruiting bodies provide them with food. So evolved has this symbiosis become that the fungus has lost its reproductive ability (it no longer produces sexual spores) and relies exclusively on the ants for propagation. When a new queen leaves her parent colony, she carries a piece of fungus with her with which to start a new garden. The cutting and carrying are performed by intermediate-size workers (*"medias"*) guarded by ferocious-looking "majors," or soldier ants, about two centimeters long and with disproportionately large heads and jaws that they use to protect the workers—usually fighting to the death—from even the largest marauder. They also work to keep the trails clear. Beneath ground, tiny "minors" (*"minimas"*) tend the nest and mulch the leaves to feed the fungus gardens.

Butterflies

With nearly 1,000 identified species (approximately 10 percent of the world total), Costa Rica is a lepidopterist's paradise. You can barely stand still for one minute without checking off a dozen dazzling species: metallic gold riondinidae; delicate black-winged heliconius splashed with bright red and yellow; orange-striped paracaidas; and the deep neon-blue flash of morphos fluttering and diving in a ballet of subaqueous color.

Some butterflies are ornately colored to keep predators at bay. The bright white stripes against black on the **zebra butterfly** (like other members of the Heliconid family), for example, tell birds that the butterfly tastes acrid. There are even perfectly tasty butterfly species that mimic the heliconid's colors, tricking predators into disdain. Others use their colors as camouflage so that at rest they blend in with the green or brown leaves or look like the scaly bark of a tree. Among the most intriguing are the **owl-eye butterflies,** with their 13-centimeter wingspans and startling eye spots. The blue-gray *Caligo memnon,* the cream owl butterfly, is the most spectacular of the owl eyes: the undersides of its wings are mottled to look like feathers and two large yellow-and-black "eyes" on the hind wing, which it displays when disturbed, give it an uncanny owl's face appearance.

The Narcissus of the Costa Rican butterfly kingdom is the famous **blue morpho.** There are about 50 species of morphos, all in Central and South America, where they are called *celeste común.* The males of most species are bright neon blue, with iridescent wings that flash like mirrors in the sun. This magnificent oversized butterfly grows to 13–20 centimeters. The morpho is a modest, nondescript brown when sitting quietly with wings closed. But when a predator gets too close, it flies off, startling its foe with a flash of its beautiful electric blue wings. The subspecies differ in color: In the Atlantic lowlands, the morpho is almost completely iridescent blue; one population in the Meseta Central is almost completely brown, with only a faint hint of electric blue. One species, commonly seen gliding about in the forest canopy, is red on the underside and gray on top. Showmen have always used mirrors to produce glitter and illusion. The morpho is no exception. Look through a morpho butterfly's wing toward a strong light and you will see only brown. This is because the scales *are* brown. The fiery blue is produced by structure, not by pigment. Tiny scales on the upper side of the wing are laid in rows that overlap much like roof shingles. These scales are ridged with minute layers that, together with the air spaces between them, refract and reflect light beams, absorbing all the colors except blue.

The best time to see butterflies is in the morning, when most species are active. A few are active at dawn and dusk. In general, butterfly populations are most dense in June and July, corresponding with the onset of the rainy season on the Pacific side. Like birds, higher-elevation species migrate up and down the mountains with changes in local weather. The most amazing migration—unsurpassed by any other insect in the neotropics—is that of the black and iridescent green uranidae, in which millions of individuals pass through Costa Rica heading south from Honduras to Colombia.

AMPHIBIANS

Costa Rica hosts approximately 160 species of amphibians, primarily represented by the dozens of species of frogs and toads. That catlike meow? That's Boulenger's hyla, one of Costa Rica's more than 20 kinds of toxic frogs. That insectlike buzz is probably two bright-red poison-dart frogs wrestling belly-to-belly for the sake of a few square meters of turf. And the deafening choruses of long loud whoops that resound through the night in Nicoya and the adjacent lowlands of Guanacaste? That's an orgiastic band of orange and purple-black Mexican burrowing toads getting it on.

Of all Central America's exotic species, none are more colorful than the **poison-dart frogs,** from which indigenous people extract deadly poisons to tip their arrows. Frogs are tasty little fellows to carnivorous amphibians, reptiles, and birds. Hence, in many species, the mucous glands common in all amphibians have evolved to produce a bitter-tasting poison. In Central and South America at least 20 kinds of frogs have developed this defense still further: Their alkaloid poisons are so toxic that they can paralyze a large bird or small monkey immediately. Several species—the dendrobatids—produce among the most potent toxins known. Some species' eggs and tadpoles even produce toxins, making them unpalatable, like bad caviar!

Of course, it's no value to an individual frog if its attacker dies *after* devouring the victim. Hence poison-dart frogs have developed conspicuous, striking colors—bright yellow, scarlet, purple, and blue, the colors of poison recognized throughout the animal world—and sometimes "flash colors" (concealed when at rest but flashed at appropriate times to startle predators) that announce, "Beware!" These confident critters don't act like other frogs either. They're active by day, moving boldly around the forest floor,

"confident and secure," says one writer, "in their brilliant livery."

In April and May, toads go looking for love in the rain pools of scarlet bromeliads that festoon the high branches. Here, high in the trees, tadpoles of arboreal frogs wriggle about. Many species, particularly the 39 species of hylids, spend their entire lives in the tree canopies, where they breed in holes and bromeliads. (The hylids have enlarged suction-cup pads on their toes. They often catch their prey in mid-air leaps, and the suction discs guarantee sure-footed landings.) Others deposit their eggs on vegetation over streams; the tadpoles fall when hatched. Others construct frothy foam nests, which they float on pools, dutifully guarded by the watchful male.

Environmental Issues

DEFORESTATION

One hundred years ago, rainforests covered two billion hectares, 14 percent of the earth's land surface. Now less than half remains, and the rate of destruction is increasing: an area larger than the U.S. state of Florida is lost every year. If the destruction continues apace, the world's rainforests will vanish within 40 years. Today, the rainforests resound with the carnivorous buzz of chain saws.

It is a story that's been repeated again and again during the past 400 years. Logging, ranching, and the development of large-scale commercial agriculture have transformed much of Costa Rica's wildest terrain. Cattle ranching has been particularly wasteful. Large tracts of virgin forest were felled in the 1930s through 1960s to make way for cattle, stimulated by millions of dollars of loans provided by U.S. banks and businesses promoting the beef industry to feed the North American market.

Throughout the 1980s, Costa Rica's tropical forest was disappearing at a rate of at least 520 square kilometers a year—faster than anywhere else in the Western Hemisphere and, as

a percentage of national land area, reportedly nine times faster than the rainforests of Brazil. By 1990, less than 1.5 million hectares of primal forest remained (about 20 percent of its original habitat).

By anyone's standards, Costa Rica has since led the way in moving Central America away from the soil-leaching deforestation that plagues the isthmus (when humans cut the forest down, the organic-poor soils are exposed to the elements and arc rapidly washed away by the intense rains, and the ground is baked by the blazing sun to leave an infertile wasteland). The country has one of the world's best conservation records: about one-third of the country is under some form of official protection. The nation has attempted to protect large areas of natural habitat and to preserve most of its singularly rich biota. But it is a policy marked by the paradox of good intent and poor application.

Many reserves and refuges are poorly managed, and the Forestry Directorate, the government office in charge of managing the country's forest resources, has been accused of failing to fulfill its duties. In the 1970s, the

CONSERVATION ORGANIZATIONS

The following organizations are active in conservation efforts in Costa Rica.

The Association for the Conservation of the Mono Titi (tel. 506/2777-2306, www.ascomoti.com) works to protect the endangered squirrel monkey.

The Caribbean Conservation Corps (CCC, 4424 NW 13th St. Suite #A1, Gainesville, FL 32609, U.S. tel. 352/373-6441 or 800/678-7853, www.cccturtle.org) works to protect turtle populations and accepts donations and volunteers.

Conservation International (2011 Crystal Dr., Suite 500, Arlington, VA 22202, U.S. tel. 703/341-2400 or 800/429-5660, www.conservation.org) supports conservation projects worldwide.

The Monteverde Conservation League (tel. 506/2645-5003, www.acmcr.org) promotes reforestation projects and works to assist farmers of the Monteverde region to increase productivity in a sustainable manner.

Nature Conservancy (4245 N. Fairfax Drive, Suite 100, Arlington, VA 22203-1606, U.S. tel. 703/841-5300 or 800/628-6860, http://nature.org) identifies species in need of protection and acquires land to protect them.

The Neotropic Foundation, or Fundación Neotrópica (tel. 506/2253-2130, www.neotropica.org), promotes sustainable development and conservation among local communities.

Organization for Tropical Studies (OTS, tel. 506/2524-0607, www.ots.ac.cr) is dedicated to biological research. It offers Rainforest Ecology Workshops in Costa Rica, where it has research facilities and lodges open to the public.

ProParques (tel./fax 506/2263-4162, www.proparques.org) works to improve national park facilities, increase resources, foster a professional Park Rangers corps, and implement other changes that contribute to the park system's economic viability.

The Rainforest Alliance (665 Broadway, Suite 500, New York, NY 10012, U.S. tel. 212/941-1900 or 888/693-2786, www.rainforest-alliance.org) works to save rainforests worldwide.

The World Wildlife Fund (1250 24th St. N.W., Washington, DC 20037, U.S. tel. 202/293-4800, www.wwf.org) works to protect endangered wildlife worldwide.

Costa Rican government banned export of more than 60 diminishing tree species, and national law proscribes cutting timber without proper permits. It happens anyway, much of it illegally, with logs reportedly trucked into San José and the coastal ports at night. Wherever new roads are built, the first vehicles in are usually logging trucks.

It's a daunting battle. Every year Costa Rica's population grows by 2.5 percent, increasing pressure on land and forcing squatters onto virgin land, where they continue to deplete the forests that once covered 80 percent of Costa Rica. Fires set by ranchers lap at the borders of Santa Rosa National Park. And oil-palm plantations squeeze Manuel Antonio against the Pacific. In 2000 the Ángel Rodríguez administration even authorized oil exploration within an indigenous reserve and adjacent to two national parks; while MINAE (the ministry responsible for land welfare and use) proposed a plan to open protected areas for mining and agriculture.

REFORESTATION AND PROTECTION

Part of the government's answer to deforestation has been to promote reforestation, mostly through a series of tax breaks, leading to tree farms predominantly planted in nonnative species such as teak. These efforts, however, do little to replace the precious native hardwoods or to restore the complex natural ecosystems, which take generations to reestablish. Nonetheless, dozens of dedicated individuals and organizations are determined to preserve and replenish core habitats. Privately owned forests constitute the majority of unprotected primary forest remaining in Costa Rica outside the national parks. Scores of private reserves

CONSERVATION AREAS AND NATIONAL PARKS

Costa Rica has 11 Regional Conservation Areas (RCAs); more information can be found at www.sinac.go.cr.

AMISTAD CARIBBEAN CONSERVATION AREA

The country's least accessible protected area encompasses rugged, mountainous terrain in southeastern Costa Rica, plus parks of the southern Caribbean littoral. It incorporates several indigenous reserves, plus Las Cruces Biological Station as well as the following:

- Barbilla National Park

- Cahuita National Park

- Gandoca-Manzanillo National Wildlife Refuge

- Hitoy-Cerere Biological Reserve

AMISTAD PACIFIC CONSERVATION AREA

Costa Rica's largest protected zone is also among its more inaccessible and rugged, and includes:

- Chirripó National Park

- La Amistad International Friendship Park

- Los Quetzales National Park

- Tapantí Macizo de la Muerte National Park

ARENAL-TILARÁN CONSERVATION AREA

This conservation area encompasses wildlife-rich environments of the Cordillera de Tilarán,

including three private cloud forest reserves, Monteverde Cloud Forest Biological Reserve, the Children's Eternal Forest, and the Santa Elena Cloud Forest Reserve, plus:

- Arenal Volcano National Park

- Diría National Park

- Miravalles Volcano National Park

- Tenorio Volcano National Park

CENTRAL VOLCANIC RANGE CONSERVATION AREA

Dramatic topography and a wide range of montane and humid tropical forest types characterize this area flanking the Central Valley. Includes:

- Braulio Carrillo National Park

- Guayabo National Monument

- Irazú Volcano National Park

- Poás Volcano National Park

- Turrialba Volcano National Park

GUANACASTE CONSERVATION AREA

Protects diverse ecosystems in Guanacaste, from shoreline to mountaintop, including:

- Bahía Junquillal Wildlife Refuge

- Guanacaste National Park

- Rincón de la Vieja National Park

- Santa Rosa National Park

---

have been created to prove that rainforests can produce more income from ecotourism than if cleared for cattle. As a result of all these efforts, forest cover increased to 51 percent of the nation in 2005, up from only 21 percent in 1987, according to MINAE, while illegal logging is down significantly.

A conservationist ethic is extremely weak among Costa Ricans, relatively few of whom display a respect for nature. The vast majority of ecological efforts, including that which resulted in creation of the national park system, are the result of initiatives by foreign residents.

President Oscar Arias wants Costa Rica to become the first carbon-neutral country in the world by 2021. In 2007 his administration began more aggressively enforcing environmental regulations against hotel and other property

ISLA DEL COCO MARINE CONSERVATION AREA

Protects the waters surrounding Cocos Island, incorporated within:

- Isla de Cocos National Park

NORTHERN HUETAR CONSERVATION AREA

Covering the northern lowlands, this newly created entity includes:

- Caño Negro National Wildlife Refuge

- Frontier Corridor National Wildlife Refuge

- Juan Castro Blanco National Park

OSA CONSERVATION AREA

This humid region, in the Pacific southwest, comprises some of the largest stands of rainforest in Central America and includes:

- Caño Island Biological Reserve

- Corcovado National Park

- Marino Ballena National Park

- Piedras Blancas National Park

- Terraba-Sierpe International Humid Forest Reserve

PACIFIC CENTRAL CONSERVATION AREA

Incorporates the central coast and coastal mountain ranges, plus offshore waters, and includes:

- Carara National Park

- El Rodeo Protected Zone

- La Cangreja National Park

- Manuel Antonio National Park

- Playa Hermosa Wildlife Refuge

- Tivives Wildlife Refuge

TEMPISQUE CONSERVATION AREA

This conservation area unites varied ecosystems protected in:

- Barra Honda National Park

- Cabo Blanco Absolute Nature Reserve

- Camaronal Wildlife Refuge

- Curú National Wildlife Refuge

- Lomas Barbudal Biological Reserve

- Marino Las Baulas National Park

- Nicolas Weissenburg Absolute Reserve

- Ostional National Wildlife Refuge

- Palo Verde National Park

- Tamarindo Wildlife Refuge

TORTUGUERO CONSERVATION AREA

Combines vast wetland and forest regions of the northeast Caribbean, most significantly:

- Barra del Colorado National Wildlife Refuge

- Tortuguero National Park

---

developers along the coast. And none too soon! Fecal contamination in the waters around Tamarindo was far above levels considered unsafe by the United States' Environmental Protection Agency (an alarming 97 percent of the nation's sewage flows untreated into rivers and/or the ocean). Illegal well drilling is draining precious aquifers. And much of the fauna of Nicoya (and other regions) is fast disappearing following a construction boom that has seen a 600 percent increase in the land area developed during the past decade.

National Parks

While much of Costa Rica has been stripped of its forests, the country has managed to protect a larger proportion of its land than any other country in the world in national parks. In 1970

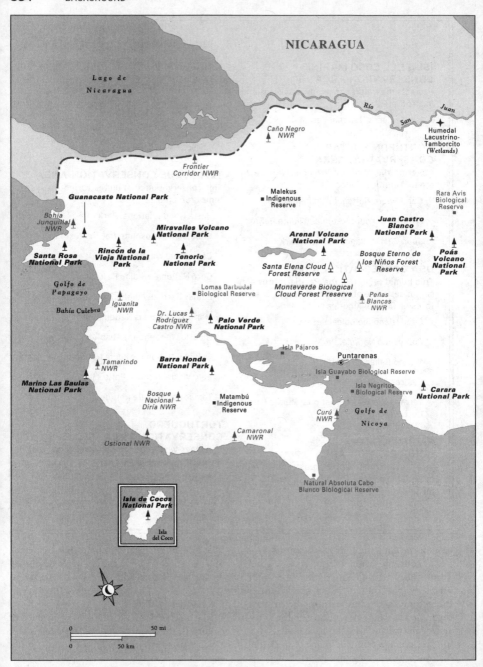

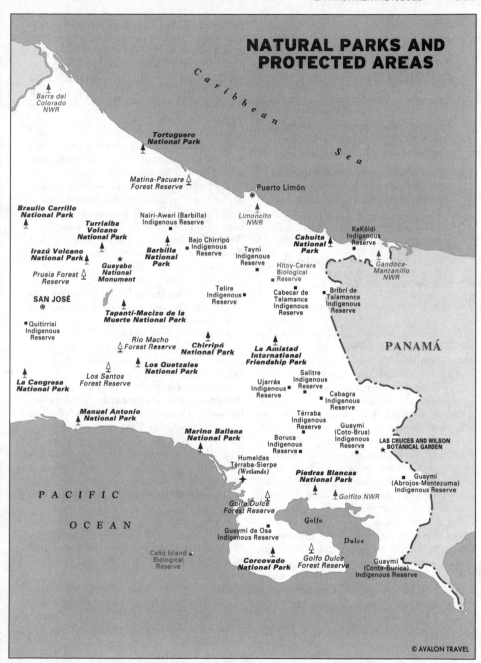

NATURAL PARKS AND PROTECTED AREAS

Caribbean Sea

Barra del Colorado NWR

Tortuguero National Park

Matina-Pacuare Forest Reserve

Puerto Limón

Braulio Carrillo National Park

Nairi-Awari (Barbilla) Indigenous Reserve

Limoncito NWR

Turrialba Volcano National Park

Irazú Volcano National Park

Barbilla National Park

Bajo Chirripó Indigenous Reserve

Tayni Indigenous Reserve

Cahuita National Park

KeKöldi Indigenous Reserve

Prusia Forest Reserve

Guayabo National Monument

Hitoy-Cerere Biological Reserve

Gandoca-Manzanillo NWR

SAN JOSÉ

Telire Indigenous Reserve

Cabecar de Talamanca Indigenous Reserve

Bribrí de Talamanca Indigenous Reserve

Quitirrisi Indigenous Reserve

Tapantí-Macizo de la Muerte National Park

PANAMÁ

Río Macho Forest Reserve

Chirripó National Park

La Amistad International Friendship Park

La Cangresa National Park

Los Santos Forest Reserve

Los Quetzales National Park

Ujarrás Indigenous Reserve

Salitre Indigenous Reserve

Cabagra Indigenous Reserve

Manuel Antonio National Park

Térraba Indigenous Reserve

Guaymi (Coto-Brus) Indigenous Reserve

LAS CRUCES AND WILSON BOTANICAL GARDEN

Marino Ballena National Park

Boruca Indigenous Reserve

Humeldas Térraba-Sierpe (Wetlands)

Piedras Blancas National Park

Guaymi (Abrojos-Montezuma) Indigenous Reserve

PACIFIC

Golfo Dulce Forest Reserve

Golfito NWR

OCEAN

Golfo

Guaymi de Osa Indigenous Reserve

Dulce

Caño Island Biological Reserve

Corcovado National Park

Golfo Dulce Forest Reserve

Guaymi (Conte-Burica) Indigenous Reserve

© AVALON TRAVEL

ANIMAL PROTECTION AGENCIES

If you wish to report abuse of animals, contact the following organizations:

- **Animal Shelter Costa Rica** (AHPPA, tel. 506/2267-7158, www.animalsheltercostarica.com)

- **Asociación Nacional Protectora de Animales** (ANPA, tel. 506/2235-3757, www.adoptame.org)

- **Asociación Unidad Especial de Protección y Rescate Animal** (UESPRA, tel. 506/2236-7516, www.mordisquitos.or)

- **Oficina del Controlar Ambiental** (tel. 192 or 506/2258-3353, controlariaambiental@minae.go.cr, www.minae.go.cr)

there came a growing acknowledgment that something unique and lovely was vanishing, and a systematic effort was begun to save what was left of the wilderness. That year, the Costa Ricans formed a national park system that has won worldwide admiration. Costa Rican law declared inviolate 10.27 percent of land; an additional 20 percent or so is legally set aside as forest reserves, "buffer zones," wildlife refuges, and indigenous reserves. Throughout the country representative sections of all the major habitats and ecosystems are protected for tomorrow's generations. The National Conservation Areas System (SINAC) protects more than 190 areas—including 34 national parks, eight biological reserves, 13 forest reserves, 56 wildlife refuges, 32 protected zones, and 14 wetlands—in 11 conservation areas.

However, the National Parks Service remains severely hampered by underfunding. The government has also found it impossible to pay for land set aside as national parks (15 percent of national parks, 46 percent of biological and nature reserves, and 75 percent of forest reserves are private property with payments

outstanding). And budgetary constraints prohibit the severely understaffed Parks Service from hiring more people (there are only eight park officials to patrol Corcovado's 25,000 hectares). Thus, poaching continues inside national parks, often with the connivance of rangers and corrupt NPS officials who receive shares of the booty.

Much of the praise heaped on the National Parks Service actually belongs to individuals (preponderantly foreigners), private groups, and local communities whose efforts—often in the face of bureaucratic opposition—have resulted in creation of many of the wildlife refuges and parks for which the NPS takes credit. (The creation of the National Parks Service itself was the product of lobbying by a foreigner, Olaf Wessberg, as related in David Rains Wallace's *The Quetzal and the Macaw*.)

The current focus is on turning poorly managed forest reserves and wildlife refuges into national parks, and integrating adjacent national parks, reserves, and national forests into Regional Conservation Areas (RCAs) to create corridors where wildlife can move with greater freedom over much larger areas. Each unit is characterized by its unique ecology.

National parks are under the jurisdiction of the **Sistema Nacional Areas de Conservación** (SINAC, Calle 25, Avenidas 8/10, San José, tel. 506/2248-2451, www.sinac.go.cr, 7 A.M.–3 P.M. Mon.–Fri.), which is responsible to the Ministerio de Ambiente y Energia (Ministry of the Environment and Energy, or MINAE, www.minae.go.cr). Alternately, visit the **Fundación de Parques Nacionales** (tel. 506/2257-2239, www.fpncostarica.org).

If you need specialized information on scientific aspects of the parks, contact the Conservation Data Center, **Instituto Nacional de Biodiversidad** (INBio, tel. 506/2507-8100, www.inbio.ac.cr).

Entrance for walk-in visitors varies from $10 to $15, valid for 24 hours only. No permits are required. You will need permits for a few of the biological reserves; these can be obtained in advance from SINAC. You can buy a "Friends of the National Parks" passport good for unlimited park entry from **ProParques** (tel./fax 506/2263-4162, www.proparques.org), a private foundation that works to support and strengthen operation of the national park system.

International Parks

Wildlife doesn't observe political borders. Birds migrate. Plants grow on each side. "It's not enough to draw lines on a map and call it a park," says Alvaro Ugalde, the former National Parks Service director. Park management increasingly requires international cooperation through the creation of transnational park networks, with neighboring countries viewing the rivers and rainforests along their borders not as dividing lines but as rich tropical ecosystems that they share.

The idea fruited in Central America as the Paseo Pantera, dedicated to preserving biodiversity through the creation of a contiguous chain of protected areas from Mexico to Colombia. This cooperative effort has since evolved into the multinational Mesoamerican Biological Corridor project. The intent is for the isthmus to once again be a bridge between continents for migrating species.

The most advanced of the transfrontier parks is the La Amistad International Peace Park, created in 1982 when Costa Rica and Panamá signed a pact to join two adjacent protected areas—one in each country—to create one of the richest ecological biospheres in Central America. UNESCO cemented the union by recognizing the binational zone as a biosphere reserve.

History

EARLY HISTORY

When Spanish explorers arrived in what is now Costa Rica at the dawn of the 16th century, they found the region populated by several poorly organized, autonomous tribes living relatively prosperously, if wanton at war, in a land of lush abundance. In all, there were probably no more than 200,000 indigenous people on September 18, 1502, when Columbus put ashore near current-day Puerto Limón. Although human habitation can be traced back at least 10,000 years, the region had remained a sparsely populated backwater separating the two areas of high civilization: Mesoamerica and the Andes. Though these tribes were advanced in ceramics, metalwork, and weaving, there are few signs of large complex communities, little monumental stone architecture lying half-buried in the luxurious undergrowth, and no planned ceremonial centers of comparable significance to those located elsewhere in the isthmus.

The region was a potpourri of distinct cultures divided into chiefdoms. In the east along the Caribbean seaboard and along the southern Pacific shores, the peoples shared distinctly South American cultural traits. These groups—the Caribs on the Caribbean and the Borucas, Chibchas, and Diquis in the southwest—were semi-nomadic hunters and anglers who raised yucca, squash, *pejibaye* (bright orange palm fruits), and tubers supplemented by crustaceans, shrimp, lobster, and game. They chewed coca and lived in communal village huts surrounded by fortified palisades. The matriarchal Chibchas and Diquis had a highly developed slave system and were accomplished goldsmiths. They were also responsible for the perfectly spherical granite balls *(bolas)* of unknown purpose found in large numbers at burial sites in the Río Terraba valley, Caño Island, and the Golfito region. The people had no written language, and their names are of Spanish origin—bestowed by colonists, often reflecting the names of tribal chiefs.

The most advanced tribes lived in the Central Highlands. The tribes here were the Corobicís, and the Nahuatl, who had recently arrived from Mexico at the time that Columbus stepped ashore. The largest and most significant of Costa Rica's archaeological sites found to date is here, at Guayabo, on the slopes of Turrialba.

Perhaps more important (little architectural study has been completed) was the Nicoya Peninsula in northwest Costa Rica. In late prehistoric times, trade in pottery from the Nicoya Peninsula brought this area into the Mesoamerican cultural sphere, and a culture developed among the Chorotegas that in many ways resembled the more advanced cultures farther north. The Chorotegas were heavily influenced by the Olmec culture and may have even originated in southern Mexico before settling in Nicoya early in the 14th century (their name means Fleeing People). They developed towns with central plazas; brought with them an accomplished agricultural system based on beans, corn, squash, and gourds; had a calendar; wrote books on deerskin parchment; and produced highly developed ceramics and stylized jade figures depicting animals, humanlike effigies, and men and women with oversized genitals, often making the most of their sexual apparati. Like the Olmecs, they filed their teeth; like the Mayans and Aztecs, the militaristic Chorotegas kept slaves and maintained a rigid class hierarchy dominated by high priests and nobles. Human sacrifice was a cultural mainstay. Little is known of their belief system, though the potency and ubiquity of phallic imagery hints at a fertility-rite religion. Shamans, too, were an important part of each tribal political system.

Alas, the pre-Columbian cultures were quickly choked by the stern hand of gold-thirsty colonial rule—and condemned, too, that Jehovah might triumph over local idols.

COLONIALISM
The First Arrivals

When Columbus anchored his storm-damaged vessels—*Captiana, Gallega, Viscaína,* and *Santiago de Palos*—in the Bay of Cariari, off the Caribbean coast on his fourth voyage to the New World in 1502, he was welcomed and treated with great hospitality by indigenous peoples who had never seen white men before.

The tribal dignitaries appeared wearing much gold, which they gave Columbus. "I saw more signs of gold in the first two days than I saw in Española during four years," his journal records. He called the region La Huerta (The Garden). The great navigator struggled home to Spain in worm-eaten ships (he was stranded for one whole year in Jamaica) and never returned. The prospect of vast loot, however, drew adventurers whose numbers were reinforced after Vasco Nuñez de Balboa's discovery of the Pacific in 1513. To these explorers the name Costa Rica would have seemed a cruel hoax. Floods, swamps, and tropical diseases stalked them in the sweltering lowlands. And fierce, elusive Indians harassed them maddeningly.

In 1506, Ferdinand of Spain sent a governor, Diego de Nicuesa, to colonize the Atlantic coast of the isthmus he called "Veragua." He ran aground off the coast of Panamá and was forced to march north. Antagonized indigenous bands used guerrilla tactics to slay the strangers and willingly burned their own crops to deny them food. Nicuesa set the tone for future expeditions by foreshortening his own cultural lessons with the musket ball. Things seemed more promising when an expedition under Gil González Davila set off from Panamá in 1522 to settle the region. It was Davila's expedition—which reaped quantities of gold—that won the land its nickname of Costa Rica, the "Rich Coast." Alas, the local peoples never revealed the whereabouts of the fabled mines of Veragua (most likely it was placer gold found in the gold-rich rivers of the Osa Peninsula).

Later colonizing expeditions on the Caribbean failed as miserably as Davila's. When two years later Francisco Fernández de Córdova founded the first Spanish settlement on the Pacific at Bruselas, near present-day Puntarenas, its inhabitants all died within three years.

For the next four decades Costa Rica was virtually left alone. The conquest of Peru by Pizarro in 1532 and the first of the great silver strikes in Mexico in the 1540s turned eyes away from southern Central America. Guatemala became the administrative center for the Spanish Main in 1543, when the captaincy-general of Guatemala, answerable to the viceroy of New Spain (Mexico), was created with jurisdiction from the Isthmus of Tehuantepec to the neglected lands of Costa Rica and Panamá.

Prompted by an edict of 1559 issued by Philip II of Spain, the representatives in Guatemala thought it time to settle Costa Rica and Christianize the natives. Alas, barbaric treatment and European epidemics—opthalmia, smallpox, and tuberculosis—had already reaped the indigenous people like a scythe and had so antagonized the survivors that they took to the forests and eventually found refuge amid the remote valleys of the Cordillera Talamanca. Only in the Nicoya Peninsula did there remain any significant indigenous population, the Chorotegas, who soon found themselves chattel on Spanish land under the *encomienda* (serfdom) system.

Settlement

In 1562, Juan Vásquez de Coronado—the true conquistador of Costa Rica—arrived as governor. He treated the surviving indigenous people more humanely and moved the few existing Spanish settlers into the Meseta Central, where the temperate climate and rich volcanic soils offered the promise of crop cultivation. Cartago was established as the national capital in 1563.

After the initial impetus given by its discovery, Costa Rica lapsed into a lowly Cinderella of the Spanish empire. Land was readily available, but there was no indigenous labor to work it. The colonists were forced to work the land themselves (even the governor, it is commonly claimed, had to work his own plot of land to survive). Without gold or export crops, trade with other colonies was infrequent at best. The Spanish found themselves impoverished in a subsistence economy. Money became so scarce that the settlers eventually reverted to the indigenous method of using cacao beans as currency. A full century after its founding, Cartago could boast little more than a few score adobe houses and a single church, which all perished when Volcán Irazú erupted in 1723.

Gradually, however, towns took shape. Heredia (Cubujuquie) was founded in 1717, San José (Villaneuva de la Boca del Monte) in 1737, and Alajuela (Villa Hermosa) in 1782.

Later, exports of wheat and tobacco placed the colonial economy on a sounder economic basis and encouraged the intensive settlement that characterizes the Meseta Central today.

In other colonies, Spaniard married native and a distinct class system arose, but mixed-bloods *(mestizos)* represent a much smaller element in Costa Rica than they do elsewhere on the isthmus. All this had a leveling effect on colonial society. As the population grew, so did the number of poor families who had never benefited from the labor of *encomienda* indigenous people or suffered the despotic arrogance of *criollo* (Creole) landowners. Costa Rica, in the traditional view, became a "rural democracy," with no oppressed mestizo class resentful of the maltreatment and scorn of the Creoles. Removed from the mainstream of Spanish culture, the Costa Ricans became individualistic and egalitarian.

Not all areas of the country, however, fit the model of rural democracy. Nicoya and Guanacaste on the Pacific side were administered quite separately in colonial times from the rest of Costa Rica. They fell within the Nicaraguan sphere of influence, and large cattle ranches or haciendas arose. The cattle-ranching economy and the more traditional class-based society that arose persist today. On the Caribbean of Costa Rica, cacao plantations became well established. Eventually large-scale cacao production gave way to small-scale sharecropping, and then to tobacco as the cacao industry went into decline. Spain closed the Costa Rican ports in 1665 in response to English piracy, thereby cutting off seaborne sources of legal trade. Smuggling flourished, however, for the largely unincorporated Caribbean coast provided a safe haven to buccaneers and smugglers, whose strongholds became 18th-century shipping points for logwood and mahogany.

EMERGENCE OF A NATION
Independence

Independence of Central America from Spain came on September 15, 1821. Independence had little immediate effect, however, for Costa

THE WILLIAM WALKER SAGA

Born in Nashville in 1824, William Walker graduated from the University of Pennsylvania with an M.D. at the age of 19. He tried his hand unsuccessfully as a doctor, lawyer, and writer, and even joined the miners and panners in the California Gold Rush. Somewhere along the line, he became filled with grandiose schemes of adventure and an arrogant belief in America's "manifest destiny" to control other nations.

He dreamed of extending the glory of slavery and forming a confederacy of southern American states to include the Spanish-speaking nations. To wet his feet, he invaded Baja California in 1853 with a few hundred cronies bankrolled by a pro-slavery group called the Knights of the Golden Circle. Forced back north of the border by the Mexican army, Walker found himself behind bars for breaking the Neutrality Act. Acquitted and famous, he attracted a following of kindred spirits to his next wild cause.

During the feverish California Gold Rush, eager fortune hunters sailed down the East Coast to Nicaragua, traveled up the Río San Juan and across Lake Nicaragua, and thence were carried by mule the last 19 kilometers to the Pacific, where with luck a San Francisco-bound ship would be waiting. In those days, before the Panamá Canal, wealthy North Americans were eyeing southern Nicaragua as the perfect spot to build a passage linking the Pacific Ocean and the Caribbean Sea. The government of Nicaragua wanted a hefty fee.

Backed by North American capitalists and the tacit sanction of President James Buchanan, Walker landed in Nicaragua in June 1855 with a group of mercenaries and the ostensible goal of molding a new government that would be more accommodating to U.S. business interests. But Walker, it seems, had secret ambitions – he dreamed of making the five Central American countries a federated state with himself as emperor. After subduing the Nicaraguans, he had himself "elected" president of Nicaragua and promptly legalized slavery there. Next, Walker looked south to Costa Rica. In March 1856, he invaded Guanacaste. President Mora called up an army of 9,000. Armed with machetes and rusty rifles, they marched for Guanacaste and routed Walker and his cronies, who retreated pell-mell. Eventually, the Costa Rican army cornered Walker's forces in a wooden fort at Rivas, in Nicaragua. A drummer boy named Juan Santamaría bravely volunteered to torch the fort, successfully flushing Walker out into the open. (His bravery cost Santamaría his life; he is now a national hero and a symbol of resistance to foreign interference.)

With his forces defeated, Walker's ambitions were temporarily scuttled. He was eventually rescued by the U.S. Navy and taken to New York, only to return in 1857 with even more troops. The Nicaraguan army defeated him again, and Walker was imprisoned. Released three years later and unrepentant, he seized a Honduran customs house. In yet another bid to escape, he surrendered to an English frigate captain who turned him over to the Honduran army, which promptly shot him, thereby bringing to an end the pathetic saga.

Rica had required only minimal government during the colonial era. In fact, the country was so out of touch that the news that independence had been granted reached Costa Rica a full month after the event. In 1823, the other Central American nations proclaimed the United Provinces of Central America, with their capital in Guatemala City. A Costa Rican provincial council, however, voted for accession to Mexico.

The four leading cities of Costa Rica felt as independent as had the city-states of ancient Greece, and the conservative and aristocratic leaders of Cartago and Heredia soon found themselves at odds with the more progressive republican leaders of San José and Alajuela. The local quarrels quickly developed into civic unrest and, in 1823, to civil war. After a brief battle in the Ochomogo Hills, the republican forces of San José were victorious. They rejected Mexico, and Costa Rica joined the federation with full autonomy for its own affairs. Guanacaste voted to secede from Nicaragua and join Costa Rica the following year.

From this moment on, liberalism in Costa Rica had the upper hand. Elsewhere in Central America, conservative groups tied to the church and the erstwhile colonial bureaucracy spent generations at war with anticlerical and laissez-faire liberals, and a cycle of civil wars came to dominate the region. By contrast, in Costa Rica colonial institutions had been relatively weak, and early modernization of the economy propelled the nation out of poverty and laid the foundations of democracy far earlier than elsewhere in the isthmus. While other countries turned to repression to deal with social tensions, Costa Rica turned toward reform.

Juan Mora Fernández, elected the federalist nation's first chief of state in 1824, set the tone by ushering in a nine-year period of progressive stability. He established a sound judicial system, founded the nation's first newspaper, and expanded public education. He also encouraged coffee cultivation. The nation, however, was still riven by rivalry, and in September 1835 the War of the League broke out when San José was attacked by the three other towns. They were unsuccessful, and the national flag was planted firmly in San José.

Braulio Carrillo, who seized power as a benevolent dictator in 1835, established an orderly public administration and new legal codes to replace colonial Spanish law. In 1838, he withdrew Costa Rica from the Central American federation and proclaimed independence. The Honduran general Francisco Morazán invaded and toppled Carrillo in 1842. Morazán's extra-national ambitions and the military draft and direct taxes he imposed soon inspired his overthrow. He was executed within the year.

Coffee is King

The reins of power were taken up by a nouveau elite, the *cafetaleros* (coffee barons) who in 1849 announced their ascendancy by conspiring to overthrow the nation's enlightened president, José María Castro. They chose as Castro's successor Juan Rafael Mora, a powerful *cafetalero*. Mora is remembered for the remarkable economic growth that marked his first term and for "saving" the nation from the imperial ambitions of the American adventurer William Walker during his second term. Still, his countryfolk ousted him from power in 1859. After failing in his own coup against his successor, he was executed—a prelude to a second cycle of militarism.

The Guardia Legacy

The 1860s were marred by power struggles among the coffee elite, supported by their respective military cronies. General Tomás Guardia, however, was his own man. In April 1870, he overthrew the government and ruled for 12 years as an iron-willed military strongman backed by a powerful centralized government of his own making.

True to Costa Rican tradition, Guardia proved himself a progressive thinker and a benefactor of the people. His towering reign set in motion forces that shaped the modern liberal-democratic state. Hardly characteristic of 19th-century despots, he abolished capital punishment, managed to curb the power of the coffee barons, and, ironically, tamed the use of the army for political means. He used coffee earnings and taxation to finance roads and public buildings. And in a landmark revision to the Constitution in 1869, he made "primary education for both sexes obligatory, free, and at the cost of the Nation."

During the course of the next two generations, militarism gave way to peaceful transitions to power. In 1917, democracy faced its first major challenge. At that time, the state collected the majority of its revenue from the less wealthy. Flores's bill to establish direct, progressive taxation based on income and his espousal of state involvement in the economy had earned the wrath of the elites. They decreed his removal. Minister of War Federico Tinoco Granados seized power. Tinoco ruled as an iron-fisted dictator, but Costa Ricans were no longer prepared to acquiesce in oligarchic restrictions. Women and high-school

MINOR KEITH AND THE ATLANTIC RAILROAD

Costa Rica became the first Central American country to grow coffee when seeds were introduced from Jamaica in 1808. Coffee flourished and transformed the nation. It was eminently suited to the climate (the dry season made harvest and transportation easy) and volcanic soils of the central highlands. There were no rival products to compete for investments, land, or labor. And the coffee bean – *grano d'oro* – was exempt from taxes. Soon, peasant settlements spread up the slopes of the volcanoes and down the slopes toward the coast.

By 1829, coffee had become the nation's most important product. Foreign money was pouring in. The coffee elite owed its wealth to its control of processing and trade rather than to direct control of land. Small farmers dominated actual production. Thus, no sector of society failed to advance. The coffee bean pulled the country out of its miserable economic quagmire and placed it squarely on a pedestal as the most prosperous nation in Central America. Nonetheless, in 1871, when President Guardia decided to build a railroad to the Atlantic, coffee for export was still being sent via mule and oxcart 100 kilometers from the Meseta Central to the Pacific port of Puntarenas, then shipped (via a circuitous, three-month voyage) around the southern tip of South America and up the Atlantic to Europe.

Enter Minor Keith. In 1871 at the age of 23, Minor came to Costa Rica at the behest of his brother Henry, who had been commissioned by his uncle, Henry Meiggs, to oversee the construction of the Atlantic Railroad linking the coastal port of Limón with the coffee-producing Meseta Central. By 1873, when the railway should have been completed, only a third had been built and money for the project had run out. Henry Keith promptly packed his bags and went home.

The younger brother, who had been running the commissary for railroad workers in Puerto Limón, picked up the standard and for the next 15 years applied unflagging dedication to achieve the enterprise his brother had botched. He renegotiated the loans and raised new money. He hired workers from Jamaica and China, and drove them – and himself – like beasts of burden.

The workers had to bore tunnels through mountains, bridge rivers, hack through jungles, and drain the Caribbean marshlands. During the rainy season, mudslides would wash away bridges. And malaria, dysentery, and yellow fever plagued the workers (the project eventually claimed more than 4,000 lives). In December 1890, a bridge high over the turbulent waters of the Birris River finally brought the tracks from Alajuela and Puerto Limón together.

For Keith, the endeavor paid off handsomely. He had wrangled from the Costa Rican government a concession of 800,000 acres of land (nearly seven percent of the national territory) along the railway track and coastal plain, plus a 90-year lease on the completed railroad. And the profits from his endeavors were to be tax-free for 20 years.

Keith planted his lands with bananas, and Costa Rica became the first Central American country to grow them. Like coffee, the fruit flourished. Exports increased from 100,000 stems in 1883 to more than a million in 1890, when the railroad was completed. By 1899 Keith, who went on to marry the daughter of the Costa Rican president, had become the "Banana King" and Costa Rica the world's leading banana producer.

Along the way, the savvy entrepreneur had wisely entered into a partnership with the Boston Fruit Company, the leading importer of tropical fruits for the U.S. market. Thus was born the United Fruit Company, which during the first half of the 20th century was to become the driving force and overlord of the economies of countries the length and breadth of Latin America.

students led a demonstration calling for his ouster, and Tinoco fled to Europe.

There followed a series of unmemorable administrations. The apparent tranquility was shattered by the Depression and the social unrest it engendered. Old-fashioned paternalistic liberalism had failed to resolve social ills such as malnutrition, unemployment, low pay, and poor working conditions. The Depression distilled all these issues. Calls grew shrill for reforms.

CIVIL WAR
Calderón

The decade of the 1940s and its climax, the civil war, marked a turning point in Costa Rican history: from paternalistic government by traditional rural elites to modern, urban-focused statecraft controlled by bureaucrats, professionals, and small entrepreneurs. The dawn of the new era was spawned by Rafael Angel Calderón Guardia, a profoundly religious physician and a president (1940–1944) with a social conscience. In a period when neighboring Central American nations were under the yoke of tyrannical dictators, Calderón promulgated a series of farsighted reforms, including founding the University of Costa Rica.

Calderón's social agenda was hailed by the urban poor and leftists and despised by the upper classes, his original base of support. His early declaration of war on Germany, seizure of German property, and imprisonment of Germans further upset his conservative patrons, many of whom were of German descent. World War II stalled economic growth at a time when Calderón's social programs called for vastly increased public spending. The result was rampant inflation, which eroded his support among the middle and working classes. Abandoned, Calderón crawled into bed with two unlikely partners: the Catholic Church and the communists (Popular Vanguard Party). Together they formed the United Social Christian Party.

The Prelude to Civil War

In 1944, Calderón was replaced by his puppet, Teodoro Picado Michalsky, in an election widely regarded as fraudulent. Picado's uninspired administration failed to address rising discontent throughout the nation. Intellectuals, distrustful of Calderón's "unholy" alliance, joined with businessmen, *campesinos,* and labor activists and formed the Social Democratic Party, dominated by the emergent professional middle classes allied with the traditional oligarchic elite. The country was thus polarized. Tensions mounted.

Street violence finally erupted in the run-up to the 1948 election, with Calderón on the ballot for a second presidential term. When he lost to his opponent Otilio Ulate (the representative of *Acción Democrática,* a coalition of anticalderonistas), the government claimed fraud. The next day, the building holding many of the ballot papers went up in flames, and the calderonista-dominated legislature annulled the election results.

Don Pepe: "Savior of the Nation"

Popular myth suggests that José María ("Don Pepe") Figueres Ferrer—42-year-old coffee farmer, engineer, economist, and philosopher—raised a "ragtag army of university students and intellectuals" and stepped forward to topple the government that had refused to step aside for its democratically elected successor. In actuality, Don Pepe's "revolution" had been long in the planning; the 1948 election merely provided a good excuse.

Don Pepe, an ambitious and outspoken firebrand, had been exiled to Mexico in 1942. Figueres returned to Costa Rica in 1944, began calling for an armed uprising, and arranged for foreign arms to be airlifted in to groups trained by Guatemalan military advisors. In 1946, he participated with a youthful Fidel Castro in an aborted attempt to depose General Trujillo of the Dominican Republic.

In 1948, back in Costa Rica, Figueres formed the National Liberation Armed Forces. On March 10, 1948, he made his move and plunged Costa Rica into civil war: the "War of National Liberation." Supported by the governments of Guatemala and Cuba, Don Pepe's insurrectionists captured the cities of Cartago and Puerto Limón from calderonistas (the government's army at the time numbered only about 500 men) and were poised to pounce on San José when Calderón surrendered. The 40-day civil war claimed more than 2,000 lives, mostly civilians.

CONTEMPORARY TIMES
Foundation of the Modern State

Don Pepe became head of the Founding Junta of the Second Republic of Costa Rica. He consolidated Calderón's progressive social reform program and added his own landmark reforms: He banned the press and Communist Party, introduced suffrage for women and full citizenship for blacks, revised the Constitution to outlaw a standing army, established a presidential term limit, and created an independent Electoral Tribunal to oversee future elections.

On a darker note, Calderón and many of his followers were exiled to Mexico, special tribunals confiscated their property, and, in a sordid episode, many prominent left-wing officials and activists were abducted and murdered. (Supported by Nicaragua, Calderón twice attempted to invade Costa Rica and topple his nemesis but was each time repelled. Eventually he was allowed to return and even ran for president unsuccessfully in 1962.)

Then, Figueres returned the reins of power to Otilio Ulate, the actual winner of the 1948 election. Costa Ricans later rewarded Figueres with two terms as president, 1953–1957 and 1970–1974. Figueres dominated politics for the next two decades. A socialist, he founded the Partido de Liberación Nacional (PLN), which became the principal advocate of state-sponsored development and reform. He died on June 8, 1990, a national hero.

The Contemporary Scene

Social and economic progress since 1948 have helped return the country to stability, and though post–civil war politics have reflected the play of old loyalties and antagonisms, elections have been free and fair. The country has ritualistically alternated its presidents between the PLN and the opposition Social Christians.

Successive PLN governments have built on the reforms of the calderonista era, and the 1950s and 1960s saw a substantial expansion of the welfare state. The intervening conservative governments have encouraged private enterprise and economic self-reliance.

By 1980, the bubble had burst. Costa Rica was mired in an economic crisis: epidemic inflation; crippling currency devaluation; soaring oil bills and social welfare costs; plummeting coffee, banana, and sugar prices; and disruptions to trade caused by the Nicaraguan war.

On July 19, 1979, the leftist Sandinistas toppled Nicaragua's Somoza regime. Thousands of Nicaraguan National Guardsmen and rightwing sympathizers fled to Costa Rica, where they were warmly welcomed by wealthy ranchers sympathetic to the right-wing cause. By the summer of 1981, the anti-Sandinistas had been cobbled into the Nicaraguan Democratic Front (FDN), headquartered in Costa Rica, and the CIA was beginning to take charge of events. Costa Rica's foreign policy underwent a dramatic reversal as the former champion of the Sandinista cause found itself embroiled in the Reagan administration's vendetta to oust the Sandinista regime.

In May 1984, events took a tragic turn at a press conference on the banks of the Río San Juan held by Edén Pastora, the U.S.–backed leader of the contras. A bomb exploded, killing foreign journalists (Pastora escaped). A general consensus is that the bomb was meant to be blamed on the Sandinistas; the CIA has been implicated.

In February 1986, Costa Ricans elected as their president a relatively young sociologist and economist-lawyer, Oscar Arias Sánchez. Arias' electoral promise had been to work for peace. Immediately, he put his energies into resolving Central America's regional conflicts. Arias' tireless efforts were rewarded in 1987, when his peace plan was signed by the five Central American presidents—an achievement that earned Arias the 1987 Nobel Peace Prize.

In February 1990, Rafael Angel Calderón Fournier, a conservative lawyer, won a narrow victory. He was inaugurated 50 years to the day after his father, the great reformer, was named president. Restoring Costa Rica's economy to sound health was Calderón's paramount goal. Under pressure from the World Bank and International Monetary Fund, Calderón initiated a series of austerity measures aimed at redressing the country's huge deficit and national debt.

In March 1994, in an intriguing historical quirk, Calderón, son of the president ousted by Don Pepe Figueres in 1948, was replaced by Don Pepe's youthful son, José María Figueres, a graduate of West Point and Harvard. The Figueres administration (1994–1998), however, was bedeviled by problems, including the collapse of the Banco Anglo Costarricense in 1994, followed in 1995 by inflation, a massive teachers' strike, and antigovernment demonstrations. A slump in tourism and Hurricane César, which ripped through the Pacific southwest in July 1996 causing $100 million in damage, worsened the country's plight. Ticos took some solace in the gold medal—the first ever for the country—won at the 1996 Olympics by Costa Rican swimmer Claudia Poll. And President Clinton's visit to Costa Rica in May 1997 during a summit of Central American leaders heralded a new era of free trade.

In April 2000, a series of strikes by government employees erupted into the worst civil unrest since the 1970s, as an attempt by the government to break up the country's 50-year-old power and telecommunications monopoly resulted in nationwide street protests that brought the country to a halt.

In April 2002, voters elected a folksy poet and TV personality, Abel Pachecho (Social Christian Unity Party), as president. He pledged to dedicate himself to the poor and disadvantaged. His administration found it difficult to get traction and was beset by a series of ministerial resignations. Meanwhile, former presidents Miguel Angel Rodríguez, Rafael Angel Calderón, and José Figueres were all caught in corruption scandals.

In April 2003, the Supreme Court voted to reverse the 1969 law barring presidents from running for office again within an eight-year period following the end of their single term. In spring 2006, the nation reelected former president Oscar Arias as president. His administration is considered less corrupt by far than predecessors, and perhaps more effective. Arias' campaign in favor of the CAFTA treaty paid off when voters approved it in 2007. That year, MINAE, the environmental watchdog agency, began forcefully applying the nation's maritime laws.

The lingering 2008 rainy season was the wettest ever recorded, resulting in extensive flooding and landslides nationwide. When a moderate 6.2 Richter-scale earthquake shook the Poís volcano region on January 8, 2009, saturated hillsides gave way, destroying the village of Cinchona and killing dozens of people.

Government

Costa Rica is a democratic republic, as defined by the 1949 Constitution. As in the United States, the government is divided into independent executive, legislative, and judicial branches, with separation of powers.

The executive branch comprises the president, two vice presidents, and a cabinet of 17 members called the Council of Government (*Consejo de Gobierno*). Legislative power is vested in the Legislative Assembly, a unicameral body composed of 57 members. *Diputados* are elected for a four-year term, to a maximum of two terms. The Assembly can override presidential decisions by a two-thirds majority vote. The power of the legislature to go against the president's wishes is a cause of constant friction, and presidents have not been cowardly in using executive decrees.

The Legislative Assembly also appoints Supreme Court judges for minimum terms of eight years. Twenty-four judges now serve on the Supreme Court. These judges, in turn,

Costa Rican flag at Parroquia San Blas church, Nicoya

© CHRISTOPHER P. BAKER

select judges for the civil and penal courts. The courts also appoint the three "permanent" magistrates of the Special Electoral Tribunal, an independent body that oversees each election and is given far-reaching powers. Control of the police force reverts to the Supreme Electoral Tribunal during election campaigns to help ensure constitutional guarantees.

The nation is divided into seven provinces—Alajuela, Cartago, Guanacaste, Heredia, Limón, Puntarenas, and San José—each ruled by a governor appointed by the president. The provinces are subdivided into 81 *cantones* (counties), which, in turn, are divided into a total of 421 *distritos* (districts) ruled by municipal councils.

POLITICAL PARTIES

The largest party is the National Liberation Party (Partido de Liberación Nacional, or PLN), founded by the statesman-hero of the Civil War, "Don Pepe" Figueres. The PLN, which roughly equates with European social democracy and American-style welfare-state

liberalism, has traditionally enjoyed a majority in the legislature, even when an opposition president has been in power. Its support

COSTA RICA'S VITAL STATISTICS

Area: 50,664 square kilometers (19,561 square miles)
Population: 4,196,000 (July 2008 est.)
Annual Population Growth: 1.39 percent
Annual Birth Rate: 17.71 per 1,000
Mortality Rate: 4.31 per 1,000
Infant Mortality Rate: 9.01 per 1,000
Life Expectancy: 77.4 years
Literacy: 95 percent
Highest Point: Cerro Chirripó, 3810 meters (12,500 feet)
Religion: 73.6 percent Roman Catholic
GDP Per Capita: $10,300
Population Below Poverty Line: 16 percent

is traditionally drawn from among the middle-class professionals, entrepreneurs, and small farmers. PLN's archrival, the Social Christian Unity Party (Partido de Unidad Social Cristiana, or PUSC), formed in 1982, represents more conservative interests.

In addition, a number of less influential parties represent all facets of the political spectrum, notably the Citizen Action Party (PAC), formed in 2002 by former Justice Minister José Miguel Villalobos, who resigned from the Abel Pacheco government to protest corruption. Most minor parties form around a candidate and represent personal ambitions rather than strong political convictions.

A small number of families are immensely powerful, regardless of which party is in power, and it is said that they pull the strings behind the scenes.

ELECTIONS

Costa Rica's national elections, held every four years (on the first Sunday of February), reaffirm the pride Ticos feel for their democratic system. In the rest of Central America, says travel writer Paul Theroux, "an election can be a harrowing piece of criminality; in Costa Rica [it is] something of a fiesta." Schoolchildren decked out in party colors usher voters to the voting booths. The streets are crisscrossed with flags, and everyone drives around honking their horns, throwing confetti, and holding up their purple-stained thumbs to show that they voted. (Cynics point out that most of the hoopla is because political favors are dispensed on a massive scale by the victorious party, and that it pays to demonstrate fealty.)

Costa Rican citizens enjoy universal suffrage, and citizens are automatically registered to vote on their 18th birthdays. Since 1959, voting has ostensibly been compulsory for all citizens under 70 years of age.

All parties are granted equal airtime on radio and television, and campaign costs are largely drawn from the public purse: Any party with 5 percent or more of the vote in the prior election can apply for a proportionate share of the official campaign fund, equal to 0.5 percent of the national budget.

Don't expect to buy a drink in the immediate run-up to an election: Liquor and beer sales are banned for the preceding three days.

BUREAUCRACY

Little Costa Rica is big on government. Building on the reforms of the calderonista era, successive administrations have created an impressive array of health, education, and social-welfare programs while steadily expanding state enterprises and regulatory bodies, all of which spell a massive expansion of the government bureaucracy that pays the salaries of approximately one in four employed people.

Costa Rica's government employees have nurtured bureaucratic formality to the level of art. The problem has given rise to *despachantes,* people who for a fee will wait in line and gather the necessary documents on your behalf.

ARMED FORCES AND POLICE

Costa Rica has no army, navy, or air force. The nation disbanded its military forces in 1949, when it declared itself neutral. Nonetheless, Costa Rica's police force has various powerfully armed branches with a military capability. In 2000, the Central American Commission on Human Rights published a report castigating the nation for increased police corruption. The government has made serious efforts in recent years to purge the force of its cancer. Major investment, including new cars and equipment and better training, has resulted in a noticeably more professional police force in recent years, notably in the tourist and transit divisions. However, the local constabulary is underpaid and little educated.

CORRUPTION AND CRONYISM

Despite the popular image as a beacon of democracy, nepotism and cronyism are entrenched in the Costa Rican political system, and corruption is part of the way things work. The political system is too weak to resist the "bite," or bribery, locally called *chorizo* (a poor grade of bacon). Corruption is so endemic that a board game, suitably called *Chorizo,* was launched in 2000.

Abel Pacheco's much-troubled government witnessed the resignation of 13 ministers, some allegedly due to financial irregularities, and three of Costa Rica's past four presidents have been indicted on corruption charges since leaving office.

Economy

Costa Rica's economy this century has, in many ways, been a model for developing nations. Highly efficient coffee and banana industries have drawn in vast export earnings, and manufacturing has grown modestly under the protection of external tariffs and the expanding purchasing power of the domestic market. Since the late 1970s, Costa Rica has moved progressively toward a more diversified trading economy (coffee, bananas, sugar, and beef, which together represented almost 80 percent of exports in 1980, earn less than 40 percent today). Tourism is the number one income earner, followed by technology, then agriculture.

GDP grew 3.5 percent in 2008, with growth primarily in telecommunications, electronics, real estate, and service industries. Nonetheless, the country faces a huge trade deficit and high inflation (14 percent in 2009). Moreover, the colón has continued to decline in value, and real wages remain stagnant. One in six of the nation's families are officially below the poverty line, with seven percent in "extreme poverty."

AGRICULTURE

Everywhere you go in the Central Highlands, a remarkable feature of the land is almost complete cultivation, no matter how steep the slope. Nationwide, some 11 percent of the land area is planted in crops; 46 percent is given to pasture. Agriculture's share of the economy, however, continues to slip.

Despite Costa Rica's reputation as a country of yeoman farmers, land ownership has always been highly concentrated, and there are parts, such as Guanacaste, where rural income distribution resembles the inimical patterns of Guatemala and El Salvador. The top one percent of farm owners own more than one-quarter of the agricultural land.

The mist-shrouded slopes of the Meseta Central and southern highlands are adorned with green undulating carpets of coffee—the *grano d'oro,* or golden bean—the most important crop in the highlands. In the higher, more temperate areas flowers grow under acres of plastic sheeting, and dairy farming is becoming more important in a mixed-farming economy that has been a feature of the Meseta since the end of the 19th century.

Vast banana plantations swathe the Caribbean plains and Golfo Dulce region. Cacao, once vital to the 18th-century economy, is on the rise again in the Caribbean. And pineapples are important throughout the Northern Zone and Valle de El General (Costa Rica is the world's leading pineapple exporter). Cassava, papaya, camote (sweet potato), melons, strawberries, chayote (vegetable pear), eggplant, *curraré* (plantain bananas), pimiento, macadamia nuts, ornamental plants, and cut flowers are all important export items.

Bananas

Bananas have been a part of the Caribbean landscape since 1870, when American entrepreneur Minor Keith shipped his first fruit stems to New Orleans. In 1899, his Tropical Trading & Transport Co. merged with the Boston Fruit Co. to form the United Fruit Co., which soon became the overlord of the political economies of the "banana republics." By the 1920s, much of the jungle south of Puerto Limón had been transformed into a vast sea of bananas. The banana industry continues to expand to meet the demand of a growing international market, and plantations now cover about 50,000

man pulling bananas at a plantation near Siquirres

hectares; Costa Rica exported US$659 million of bananas in 2007 (up from US$473 million in 2005), representing 7.1 percent of national export earnings.

Then, as now in some areas, working conditions were appalling, and strikes were so frequent that when Panamá disease and then *sigatoka* (leaf-spot) disease swept the region in the 1930s and 1940s, United Fruit took the opportunity to abandon its Atlantic holdings and move to the Pacific coast. Violent clashes with the banana workers' unions continued to be the company's nemesis. In 1985, after a 72-day strike, United Fruit closed its operations in southwestern Costa Rica. Many of the plantations have been replaced by stands of African palms (used in cooking oil, margarine, and soap); others are leased to independent growers and farmers' cooperatives that sell to Standard Fruit. Labor problems still flare—a telling tale of continued abuse by the banana companies.

The Standard Fruit Co. began production in the Atlantic lowlands in 1956. Alongside ASBANA (Asociación de Bananeros), a government-sponsored private association, Standard Fruit helped revive the Atlantic coast banana industry (at the expense of thousands of acres of virgin jungle). The banana companies have cut back production in recent years due to overproduction (the country is still the second-biggest exporter of bananas in the world, behind Ecuador). Alas, it has been the independent growers (many of whom were encouraged to expand their acreage by the large banana companies) who have suffered, as the banana conglomerates have cut back on buying from outside growers.

Cattle

By far the largest share of agricultural land (70 percent) is given over to cattle pasture. Costa Rica is today Latin America's leading beef exporter. Guanacaste remains essentially what it has been since midcolonial times—cattle country—and three-quarters of Costa Rica's 2.2 million head of cattle are found here. They are mostly humpbacked zebu. Low-interest loans in the 1960s and 1970s encouraged a rush into cattle farming for the export market, prompting rapid expansion into new areas such as the Valle de El General and more recently the Atlantic lowlands.

The highland slopes are munched upon by herds of Charolais, Hereford, Holstein, and Jersey cattle, raised for the dairy industry.

Coffee

Costa Rica, 13th among world producers, produces two percent of the world's coffee, which represents 15 percent of the country's exports. Beans grown here are ranked among the best in the world. Costa Rica's highlands possess ideal conditions for coffee production. The coffee plant loves a seasonal, almost monsoonal climate with a distinct dry season; it grows best in well-drained, fertile soils at elevations between 800 and 1,500 meters with a narrow annual temperature range—natural conditions provided by much of the country. The best coffee is grown near the plant's uppermost altitudinal limits, where the bean takes longer to mature.

The first coffee beans were brought from Jamaica in 1779. Within 50 years coffee had become firmly established; by the 1830s it was the country's prime export earner, a position it occupied until 1991, when coffee plunged to third place in the wake of a precipitous 50 percent fall in world coffee prices and the onset of the tourism boom.

The plants are grown in nurseries for their first year before being planted in long rows that ramble invitingly down the steep hillsides, their paths coiling and uncoiling like garden snakes. After four years they fruit. In April, with the first rains, small white blossoms burst forth and the air is laced with perfume not unlike jasmine. By November, the glossy green bushes are plump with shiny red berries—the coffee beans—and the seasonal labor is called into action.

The hand-picked berries are trucked to *beneficios* (processing plants), where they are machine-scrubbed and washed to remove the fruity outer layer and dissolve the gummy substance surrounding the bean (the pulp is returned to the slopes as fertilizer). The moist beans are then blow-dried or laid out to dry in the sun in the traditional manner. The leather skin of the bean is then removed by machine, and the beans are sorted according to size and shape before being vacuum-sealed to retain the fragrance and slight touch of acidity characteristic of the great vintages of Costa Rica.

INDUSTRY

Manufacturing accounts for about 40 percent of GNP. This is due almost entirely to Costa Rica's newfound favor as a darling of high-tech industries. The arrival of Intel, the computer chip manufacturer, in 1997 presaged the evolution of a "Silicon Valley South." Motorola, 3COM, and Abbott Laboratories have since built assembly plants. The nation has also staked a claim as a world center for the Internet gaming industry (online casinos).

Local industrial raw materials are restricted to agricultural products, wood, and a small output of mineral ores. Manufacturing is still largely concerned with food processing, although pharmaceutical and textile exports have risen dramatically in recent years. Major industrial projects also include aluminum processing, cement production, and an oil refinery at Puerto Limón.

The state has a monopoly in key economic sectors such as energy, telecommunications, and insurance.

TOURISM

In 1993, tourism overtook the banana industry to become the nation's prime income earner. In 2008, more than 2 million visitors came, generating about $2.2 billion, and an increase of 7 percent over 2007. More than 50 percent of visitors originate in the United States. About 100,000 workers are directly employed in tourism-related activities; another 400,000 are indirectly employed.

The majority of tourists cite natural beauty as one of their main motivations for visiting Costa Rica, and one-third specifically cite ecotourism. Costa Rica practically invented the term—defined as responsible travel that contributes to conservation of natural environments and sustains the wellbeing of local people by promoting rural economic development. The government has since positioned Costa Rica as a comprehensive destination for the whole family. Surfers and others seeking active adventures (including ziplines, ATV tours, and kayaking) have also flocked in recent years, as have North Americans traveling in search of real estate investments, fostering an explosion in condominium construction along the Nicoya coast. And in 2008, the government announced plans to promote medical tourism (cosmetic surgery and yoga, for example).

The nation has lacked any sort of coherent tourism development plan to control growth, and zoning regulations have traditionally not been enforced. Consequently, developers large and small were pushing up hotels and condominiums along Costa Rica's coastline in total disregard of environmental laws. Investors have also pushed the price of land beyond reach of the local population. More than 50 percent of Costa Rica's habitable coastline is now owned by North Americans and Europeans. Ecotour operators have warned that without a conscientious national development plan, the government could kill the goose that lays the golden egg. Defenders of large-scale resorts point out that surging tourism and investment dollars can pull the country out of debt. And the employment opportunities are huge. In 2008, President Oscar Arias issued several presidential decrees to regulate new construction along the coast in an effort to get a grip on development that has already spiraled out of control; as a result, MINAE actually began shutting down, and even pulling down, some hotels and businesses.

The People

Costa Rica has a population of about 4,075,000, more than half of whom live in the Meseta Central. Approximately 350,000 live in the capital city of San José (about three times that number live in the metropolitan region). Sixty percent of the nation's population is classed as urban.

DEMOGRAPHY

Costa Rica is the most homogeneous of Central American nations in race as well as social class. The census classifies 94 percent of the population as "white" or "mestizo" and less than three percent as "black" or "Indian." Exceptions are Guanacaste, where almost half the population is visibly mestizo, a legacy of the more pervasive unions between Spanish colonists and Chorotega Indians through several generations; and the population of the Atlantic coast province of Puerto Limón, which is one-third black, with a distinct culture that reflects its West Indian origins.

Afro-Caribbean People

Costa Rica's approximately 40,000 black people are the nation's largest minority. For many years they were the target of racist laws that restricted them to the Caribbean coast (only as late as 1949, when the new Constitution abrogated apartheid on the Atlantic Railroad, were black people allowed to travel beyond Siquirres and enter the highlands). Hence, they remained isolated from national culture. Most black Costa Ricans trace their ancestry back to the 10,000 or so Jamaicans hired by Minor Keith to build the Atlantic Railroad, and to later waves of immigrants who came to work the banana plantations in the late 19th century.

In the 1930s, when "white" highlanders began pouring into the lowlands, black people were quickly dispossessed of land and the best-paying jobs. Late that decade, when the banana blight forced the banana companies to abandon their Caribbean plantations and move to the Pacific, "white" Ticos successfully lobbied for laws forbidding the employment of *gente de color* in other provinces, one of several circumstances that kept blacks dependent on the United Fruit Company, whose labor policies were often abhorrent. Many converted their subsistence plots into commercial cacao farms and reaped large profits during the 1950s and 1960s from the rise of world cacao prices.

West Indian immigrants played a substantial role in the early years of labor organization, and their early strikes were often violently suppressed. Many black workers, too, joined hands with Figueres in the 1948 civil war. Their reward? Citizenship and full guarantees under the 1949 Constitution, which ended apartheid. Many black Costa Ricans are now found in leading professions throughout the nation. Race relations are relatively harmonious, and black people are more readily accepted as equals by Ticos than in years past. On the Caribbean coast, they have retained much of their traditional culture, including religious practices rooted in African belief about transcendence through spiritual possession (obeah), their cuisine (such as, "rundown"), the rhythmic lilt of their slightly antiquated English, and the deeply syncopated funk of their music.

Indigenous People

Costa Rica's indigenous peoples have suffered abysmally. Today, approximately 20,000 peoples of the Bribrí, Boruca, and Cabecar tribes manage to eke out a living in remote valleys in the Cordillera Talamanca of southern Costa Rica, where their ancestors had sought refuge from Spanish muskets and dogs. Twenty-four national indigenous communities and eight ethnic groups live on 22 Indian reserves.

In December 1977 a law was passed prohibiting non-Indians from buying, leasing, or renting land within the reserves. Although various agencies continue to work to promote education, health, and community development, the indigenous people's standard of living is appallingly low, alcoholism is endemic, and they remain subject to constant exploitation. Many indigenous people have been tricked into selling their allotments or otherwise forced off their lands. Banana companies have gradually encroached, pushing campesinos onto marginal land. And mining companies are infiltrating the reserves along newly built roads. The National Commission for Indigenous Affairs (CONAI) has proved ineffective in enforcing protections.

The Borucas, who inhabit scattered villages in tight-knit patches of the Pacific southwest, have been most adept at conserving their own language and civilization, including matriarchy, communal land ownership, and traditional weaving. For most other groups, only a few elders still speak the languages. Virtually all groups have adopted elements of Catholicism along with their traditional animistic religions, and Spanish is today the predominant tongue.

The past decade has seen a resurgence of cultural pride, assisted by tourism efforts that are opening the reserves to respectful visitation and an interest in traditional crafts.

Other Ethnic Groups

Immigrants from many nations have been made welcome over the years (between 1870 and 1920, almost 25 percent of Costa Rica's population growth was due to immigration). Jews are prominent in the liberal professions. A Quaker community of several hundred people centers on Monteverde. Germans settled a century ago as coffee farmers. Italians gathered in the town of San Vito. Many Chinese are descended from approximately 600 Asians who were brought in as contract laborers to work on the Atlantic Railroad; chinos and arc now conspicuously successful in the hotel, restaurant, and bar trade, and in Limón as middlemen controlling the trade in bananas and cacao.

More recently, Costa Rica has become a favorite home away from home for a new influx of North Americans, Europeans, and (notably in recent years) Israelis—including a large percentage of misfits and miscreants evading the law (Costa Rica has been called the "land of the wanted and the unwanted"). In addition, tens of thousands of Central American immigrants from El Salvador, Guatemala, and Nicaragua provide cheap labor for the coffee fields. The largest group of recent immigrants are Nicas (Nicaraguans), with as many as 450,000—one seventh of the Costa Rican population—the majority of whom are considered "illegals" not protected by law.

WAY OF LIFE

Most Costa Ricans—Los Costarricense, or Ticos—insist that their country is a "class-less democracy." There is considerable social mobility, and no race problem. A so-called middle-class mentality runs deep, including a belief in the Costa Rican equivalent of "the American Dream"—a conviction that through individual effort and sacrifice and a faith in schooling, every Costa Rican can climb the social ladder and better himself or herself. Still, despite the high value Ticos place on equality and democracy, their society contains all kinds of inequities.

Despite its relative urban sophistication, Costa Rica remains a predominantly agrarian society. Urbanites, like city dwellers worldwide, condescendingly chuckle at rural "hicks." And the upwardly mobile "elite," who consider menial labor demeaning, prefer to indulge in conspicuous spending and, sometimes, in snobbish behavior.

Though comparatively wealthy compared to most Latin American countries, by developed-world standards most Costa Ricans are poor; the average income in the northern lowlands is barely one-seventh of that in San José. Many rural families still live in simple huts of adobe or wood; at least one-fifth of the population are *marginados* who live in poverty. More than half of rural homes lack clean drinking water, while almost one-third of urban homes lack clean water. Child labor exploitation is also a major issue, as is sexual crime against minors.

However, that all paints far too gloomy a picture. In a region where millions starve, the Costa Ricans are comparatively well-to-do. Most Costa Ricans keep their proud little bungalows tidy and bordered by flowers, and even the poorest are generally well groomed and neatly dressed.

Costa Rica is a class-conscious society. Nonetheless, overt class distinctions are kept within bounds by a delicate balance between "elitism" and egalitarianism unique in the isthmus: Aristocratic airs are frowned on and blatant pride in blue blood is ridiculed; even the president is inclined to mingle in public in casual clothing and is commonly addressed in general conversation by his first name or nickname.

The Tican Identity

Costa Ricans' unique traits derive from a profoundly conscious self-image, which orients much of their behavior as both individuals and as a nation. The Ticos—the name is said to stem from the colonial saying "we are all *hermaniticos*" (little brothers)—feel distinct from their neighbors by their "whiteness" and relative lack of indigenous culture. Above all, the behavior and comments of most Ticos are dictated by *quedar bien,* a desire to leave a good impression. Like the English, they're terribly frightened of embarrassing themselves and of appearing rude or vulgar. They often prefer to lie in lieu of telling you an unpleasant truth, which is considered rude and to be avoided.

Ticos are also hard to excite. They lack the volatility, ultranationalism, and deep-seated political divisions of their Latin American brethren. It is almost impossible to draw a Tico into a spirited debate or argument. They are loath to express or defend a position and simply walk away from arguments. Former president Figueres once accused Ticos of being as domesticated as sheep; they are not easily aroused to passionate defense of a position or cause. (As such, resentments fester and sneaky retributions—such as arson—are common.) The *notion* of democracy and the ideals of personal liberty are strongly cherished. Costa Ricans are intensely proud of their accomplishments in this arena and gloss over endemic theft, corruption, and fraud.

There is only a limited sense of personal responsibility among Ticos, who display an equally limited regard for the law. Their Bud Light culture has been called the "white bread" of Latin America. Many North American and European hoteliers and residents bemoan the general passivity that often translates into a lack of initiative. Nonetheless, they are savvy businessfolk with a bent for entrepreneurship.

The cornerstone of society is the family

and the village community. Social life still centers on the home. Nepotism—using family ties and connections for gain—is the way things get done in business and government. But traditional values are severely challenged. Drunkenness among the working classes is common. Drug abuse has intruded (Costa Rica has become a major trading zone for cocaine traffic). And though many Ticos display a genuine concern for conservation, the ethic is still tentative among the population as a whole.

Machismo and the Status of Women

By the standards of many Latin American countries, the nation is progressive and successful in advancing the equal rights of women. Women outnumber men in many occupations, notably in university faculties, and the nation has had several female vice-presidents, including both vice-presidents in the 1998–2001 Ángel Rodríguez administration. Nonetheless, low-level occupations especially reflect wide discrepancies in wage levels for men and women. The greater percentage of lower-class women remains chained to the kitchen sink and the rearing of children. And gender relationships, particularly in rural villages, remain dominated to a greater or lesser degree by machismo and *marianismo,* its female equivalent. Women are supposed to be bastions of moral and spiritual integrity while accepting of men's infidelities.

Legacies of the Spanish Catholic sense of "proper" gender roles are twined like tangled threads through the national fabric. The Latin male expresses his masculinity in amorous conquests, and the faithful husband and male celibate is suspect in the eyes of his friends. But it always takes two to tango. Hip urban Ticas have forsaken old-fashioned romanticism for a latter-day liberalism. Even in the most isolated rural towns, dating in the Western fashion has displaced the *retreta*—the circling of the central plaza by men and women on weekend evenings—and chaperones, once common, are now virtually unknown.

In fact, almost 10 percent of all Costa Rican adults live together in "free unions," one-quarter

of all children are *hijos naturales* (born out of wedlock), and one in five households is headed by a single mother. *Compañeras,* women in consensual relationships, enjoy the same legal rights as wives. Many rural households are so-called queen-bee (all-female) families headed by an elderly matriarch who looks after her grandchildren while the daughters work. Divorce is common and easily obtained under the Family Code of 1974, although desertion remains as it has for centuries "the poor man's divorce."

Religion

More than 90 percent of the population is Roman Catholic, the official state religion, but Protestant missionaries have begun to make a dent in Costa Rica, notably among the indigenous community. Nonetheless, the country has always been relatively secular, and the church has not attained undue political power. Every village has its own saint's day, and every taxi, bus, government office, and home has its token religious icons. Holy Week (the week before Easter) is a national holiday, and communities throughout Costa Rica organize processions.

Resignation to the imagined will of God is tinged with fatalism. In a crisis Ticos will turn to a favorite saint to request a miracle. And folkloric belief in witchcraft is still common (Escazú is renowned as a center for *brujos,* or witches). Superstitions abound in all segments of society, such as the belief that if you climb a tree on Good Friday, you'll grow a tail; and single men refuse to carry the Saint John icon during the procession of the Holy Burial due to the belief that they will never marry.

Education

Costa Ricans are a relatively highly educated people: The country boasts 95 percent literacy, the most literate populace in Central America (in 1869, the country became one of the first in the world to make education both obligatory and free).

Nonetheless, according to United Nations statistics, about 40 percent of Costa Rican teenagers drop out of school by the sixth grade or never gain access to secondary education (Panamá and

El Salvador both outperform Costa Rica in secondary education). Almost 1,000 schools have only one teacher, often a partially trained *aspirante* (candidate teacher) lacking certification. And many rural schools are underfunded and lacking in basic facilities.

Costa Rica has four state-funded schools of higher learning, and opportunities abound for adults to earn the primary or secondary diplomas they failed to gain as children. The University of Costa Rica (UCR), the largest and oldest university, enrolls some 35,000 students, mostly on scholarships. The State Correspondence University is modeled after the United Kingdom's Open University and has 32 regional centers offering 15 degree courses in health, education, business administration, and the liberal arts. In addition, there are also scores of private "universities," though the term is applied to even the most marginal cubbyhole college.

Health

Perhaps the most impressive impact of Costa Rica's modern welfare state has been the truly dramatic improvements in national health. Infant mortality has plummeted from 25.6 percent in 1920 to only 9 percent in 2008. And the average Costa Rican today can expect to live to a ripe 77.4 years—about as long as the average U.S.–born citizen.

One key to the nation's success was the creation of the Program for Rural Health in 1970 to ensure that basic health care would reach the furthest backwaters. Costa Rica assigns about 10 percent of its GNP to health care, provided free of cost to all citizens. In fact, in some arenas (notably within the private field) the health-care system isn't far behind that of the United States in terms of the latest medical technology, at least in San José, where transplant surgery is now performed. Many North Americans fly here for surgery, including dental work and cosmetic surgery.

Language

The Costa Ricans speak Spanish, and do so with a clear, concise dialect littered with phraseology unique to the nation. The most common Costa Rican phrase is *¡pura vida!*, a popular saying literally meaning "pure life" but used in various contexts, including as a greeting and to express a positive attitude.

Arts and Culture

Historically, Costa Rica has been relatively impoverished in the area of native arts and crafts. The country, with its relatively small and heterogeneous pre-Columbian population, had no unique cultural legacy that could spark a creative synthesis where the modern and the traditional might merge. And social tensions (often catalysts to artistic expression) felt elsewhere in the isthmus were lacking.

In recent years, however, artists across the spectrum have found a new confidence. The performing arts are flourishing, amply demonstrated by the introduction of an International Art and Music Festival in 1992 (tel. 506/233-6441).

Costa Rica has a strong *peña* tradition, introduced by Chilean and Argentinian exiles.

Literally "circle of friends," *peñas* are bohemian gatherings where moving songs are shared and wine and tears flow.

ART

Santa Ana and neighboring Escazú, immediately southwest of San José, have long been magnets for artists. Escazú in particular is home to many contemporary artists: Christina Fournier; the brothers Jorge, Manuel, Javier, and Carlos Mena; and Dinorah Bolandi, who was awarded the nation's top cultural prize. Here, in the late 1920s, Teodorico Quiros and a group of contemporaries provided the nation with its own identifiable art style—the Costa Rican "Landscape" movement—which expressed in stylized forms the personality of little mountain towns with

© CHRISTOPHER P. BAKER

traditional pottery at Guaitíl

their cobblestone streets and adobe houses backdropped by volcanoes. Quiros had been influenced by the French impressionists. The group also included Luisa Gonzales de Saenz, whose paintings evoke the style of Magritte; the expressionist Manuel de la Cruz, the "Costa Rican Picasso"; as well as Enrique Echandi, who expressed a Teutonic sensibility following studies in Germany. One of the finest examples of sculpture from this period, the chiseled stone image of a child suckling his mother's breast, can be seen outside the Maternidad Carit maternity clinic in southern San José. Its creator, Francisco Zuñigo (Costa Rica's most acclaimed sculptor), left for Mexico in a fit of artistic pique in 1936 when the sculpture, titled *Maternity,* was lampooned by local critics.

By the late 1950s, many local artists looked down on the work of the prior generation as the art of *casitas* (little houses) and were indulging in more abstract styles. Today, Costa Rica's homegrown art is world-class.

Isidro Con Wong, a once-poor farmer from Puntarenas, is known for a style redolent of magic realism and has works in permanent collections

in several U.S. and French museums. Roberto Lizano collides Delacroix with Picasso and likes to train his eye on the pomposity of ecclesiastics. Alajuelan artist Gwen Barry is acclaimed for her "Movable Murals"—painted screens populated by characters from Shakespeare and the Renaissance. The works of Rodolfo Stanley seemingly combine those of Toulouse-Lautrec with Gauguin. Rolando Castellón, who was a director of the Museum of Modern Art in New York before returning to Costa Rica in 1993, translates elements of indigenous life into three-dimensional art. Escazú artist Katya de Luisa is known for stunning photo collages. And a Cuban aesthetic finds its way into the works of Limonese artist Edgar León, who was influenced by travels in Cuba and Mexico.

Costa Rica Art Tours (www.costaricaart-tour.com) offers day-long visits to various leading artists' studios, including that of Rodolfo Stanley.

CRAFTS

The tourist dollar has spawned a renaissance in crafts. The Boruca peoples are known for

THE OXCARTS OF SARCHÍ

Sarchí is famous as the home of gaily decorated wooden *carretas* (oxcarts), the internationally recognized symbol of Costa Rica. The carts, which once dominated the rural landscape of the central highlands, date back only to the end of the 19th century.

At the height of the coffee boom and before the construction of the Atlantic Railroad, oxcarts were used to transport coffee beans to Puntarenas, on the Pacific coast. In the rainy season, the oxcart trail became a quagmire. Costa Ricans thus forged their own spokeless wheel to cut through the mud without becoming bogged down. In their heyday, some 10,000 cumbersome, squeaking *carretas* had a dynamic impact on the local economy, spawning highway guards, smithies, inns, teamsters, and crews to maintain the roads.

Today's *carretas* bear little resemblance to the original rough-hewn, cane-framed vehicles. Even then, though, the compact wheels — about 120-150 centimeters in diameter — were natural canvases awaiting an artist. Enter the wife of Fructuoso Barrantes, a cart maker in San Ramón with a paintbrush and a novel idea.

She enlivened her husband's cart wheels with a geometric starburst design in bright colors set off by black and white. Soon every farmer in the district had given his aged *carreta* a lively new image.

By 1915, flowers had bloomed beside the pointed stars. Faces and even miniature landscapes soon appeared. And annual contests (still held today) were arranged to reward the most creative artists. The *carretas* had ceased to be purely functional. Each cart was also designed to make its own "song," a chime produced by a metal ring striking the hubnut of the wheel as the cart bumped along. Once the oxcart had become a source of individual pride, greater care was taken in their construction, and the best-quality woods were selected to make the best sounds.

The *carretas*, forced from the fields by the advent of tractors and trucks, are almost purely decorative now, but the craft and the art form live on in Sarchí, where artisans still apply their masterly touch at two *fábricas de carretas* (workshops), which are open to view. A finely made reproduction oxcart can cost up to $5,000.

their devil masks, and balsa ornamental masks featuring colorful wildlife and Indian faces. At Guaitíl, in Nicoya, the Chorotega tradition of pottery is booming, flooding souvenir stores nationwide with quintessential Costa Rica pieces. Santa Ana, in the Highlands, is also famous for its ceramics. In Escazú, master craftsman Barry Biesanz crafts subtle, delicate bowls and decorative boxes with tight dovetailed corners from carefully chosen blocks of lignum vitae (ironwood), *narareno* (purple heart), rosewood, and other tropical hardwoods.

Many of the best crafts in Costa Rica come from Sarchí, known most notably for its *carretas* (oxcarts) and rockers. Although full-size oxcarts are still made, today most of the *carretas* are folding miniature trolleys that serve as liquor bars or indoor tables, and half-size carts used as garden ornaments or simply to accent a corner of a home. The carts are decorated with geometric mandala designs and floral patterns that have found their way, too, onto wall plaques, kitchen trays, and other craft items.

LITERATURE

In literature, Costa Rica has never fielded figures of the stature of Latin American writers such as Gabriel García Márquez, Pablo Neruda, or Jorge Luís Borges. Indeed, the Ticos are not at all well read and lack a passionate interest in literature. Only a handful of writers make a living from writing, and Costa Rican literature is often belittled as the most prosaic and anemic in Latin America. Lacking great goals and struggles, Costa Rica was never a breeding ground for the passions and dialectics that spawned the literary geniuses of Argentina, Brazil, Mexico, Cuba, and Chile.

© CHRISTOPHER P. BAKER

ox-drawn cart

Costa Rica's early literary figures were mostly essayists and poets: Roberto Brenes Mesen and Joaquín García Monge are the most noteworthy. Even the writing of the 1930s and 1940s, whose universal theme was a plea for social progress, lacked the verisimilitude and rich literary delights of other Latin American authors. Carlos Luis Fallas's *Mamita Yunai,* which depicts the plight of banana workers, is the best and best-known example of this genre. Modern literature still draws largely from the local setting, and though the theme of class struggle has given way to a lighter, more novelistic approach it still largely lacks the depth and subtlety of the best of Brazilian, Argentinean, and Colombian literature. An outstanding exception is Julieta Pinto's *El Eco de los Pasos,* a striking novel about the 1948 civil war.

MUSIC AND DANCE

The country is one of the southernmost of the "marimba culture" countries using the African-derived marimba (xylophone). The guitar, too, is a popular instrument, especially as an accompaniment to folk dances such as the *punto guanacasteco,* a heel-and-toe stomping dance for couples, officially decreed the national dance.

Says *National Geographic:* "To watch the viselike clutching of Ticos and Ticas dancing, whether at a San José discotheque or a crossroads cantina, is to marvel that the birthrate in this predominantly Roman Catholic nation is among Central America's lowest." When it comes to dancing, Ticos prefer the hypnotic Latin and rhythmic Caribbean beat and bewildering cadences of cumbia, lambada, merengue, salsa, and soca, danced with sure-footed erotic grace. The Caribbean coast is the domain of calypso and reggae.

Folkloric Dancing

Guanacaste is the heartland of Costa Rican folkloric music and dancing. Here, even such pre-Columbian instruments as the *chirimía* (oboe) and *quijongo* (a single-string bow with gourd resonator) popularized by the Chorotega are still used. Dances usually deal with the issues of enchanted lovers (usually legendary coffee pickers) and are based on the Spanish *paseo,* with pretty maidens in frilly satin skirts

dancers in traditional costume

and white bodices circled by men in white suits and cowboy hats, accompanied by tossing of scarves, a fanning of hats, and loud lusty yelps from the men.

Vestiges of the indigenous folk dancing tradition linger (barely) elsewhere in the nation. The Borucas still perform their Danza de los Diablitos, and the Talamancas their Danza de los Huelos. But the drums and flutes, including the curious *dru mugata,* an ocarina (a small potato-shaped instrument with a mouthpiece and finger holes which yields soft, sonorous notes), are being replaced by guitars and accordions.

On the Caribbean, the *cuadrille* is a maypole dance in which each dancer holds one of many ribbons tied to the top of a pole: As they dance they braid their brightly colored ribbons.

Classical Music

Costa Rica stepped onto the world stage in classical music with the formation in 1970 of the National Symphony Orchestra under the baton of an American, Gerald Brown. The orchestra, which performs in the Teatro Nacional, often features world-renowned guest soloists and conductors, such as violinist José Castillo and classical guitarist Pablo Ortíz, who often play together. Its season is April–November. Costa Rica also claims a state-subsidized youth orchestra.

THEATER

A nation of avid theater lovers, Costa Rica supports a thriving acting community. In fact, Costa Rica supposedly has more theater companies per capita than any other country in the world. The streets of San José are lined with tiny theaters—everything from comedy to drama, avant-garde, theater-in-the-round, mime, and even puppet theater. Crowds flock every night Tuesday–Sunday. Performances are predominantly in Spanish. The English-speaking Little Theater Group is Costa Rica's oldest theatrical troupe; it performs in its own theater in Escazú.

Recreation and Tours

Costa Rica has scores of tour operators offering a complete range of options, to all the major points of attraction. The nation also boasts scores of bilingual naturalist guides.

I highly recommend **Costa Rica Expeditions** (tel. 506/2257-0766, www.costaricaexpeditions.com), a pioneer in natural history and adventure travel in Costa Rica; it has a complete range of tour packages nationwide, including from its acclaimed Monteverde Lodge, Tortuga Lodge, and Corcovado Tent Camp. Its website offers a unique homepage that helps direct you to identify an itinerary that perfectly matches your dreams and desires.

Other recommended tour operators include **Costa Rica Sun Tours** (tel. 506/2296-7757, www.crsuntours.com); **Horizontes Nature Tours** (tel. 506/2222-2022, www.horizontes.com); and **Swiss Travel Service** (tel. 506/2282-4898, www.swisstravelcr.com).

Ecole Travel (tel. 506/2253-8884, www.ecoletravel.com) specializes in budget travel but offers a full tour-planning service for all budgets.

CRUISES/YACHTING

Half- and full-day excursions and sunset cruises are offered from dozens of beaches along the Pacific coast. By far the most popular trip is to Isla Tortuga, in the Gulf of Nicoya. Several companies offer daylong excursions from Puntarenas and Los Sueños, near Jacó (the cruises are also offered as excursions from San José).

Natural History Cruise Touring

Natural-history cruise touring is a splendid way to explore Costa Rica's more remote wilderness sites. Normally you'll cruise at night so that each morning when you awake, you're already anchored in a new location. You spend a large part of each day ashore on guided natural-history hikes or recreational-cultural excursions. Most vessels cruise the Pacific coast.

The longest-established operator, locally based, is **Cruise West** (tel. 888/851-8133, www.cruisewest.com), which operates out of Los Sueños Marina, at Playa Herradura, year-round. Its Costa Rican–staffed *Pacific Explorer* comfortably accommodates up to 100 passengers on eight- and 10-day itineraries combining Costa Rica and Panamá.

Lindblad Expeditions (tel. 212/765-7740 or 800/397-3348, www.expeditions.com) offers 8-, 11-, and 15-day itineraries combining Costa Rica and Panamá aboard the 64-passenger *Sea Voyager*. I escort trips for **National Geographic Expeditions** (tel. 888/966-8687, wwww.nationalgeographicexpeditions.com) aboard the *Sea Voyager*. Join me!

Windstar Cruises (tel. 206/281-3535 or 877/827-7245, www.windstarcruises.com) uses its luxurious 148-passenger *Wind Song* for nine-day itineraries, December–March, down the Pacific Coast and combining Panamá.

CANOPY TOURS

Hardly a month goes by without *another* "canopy tour" opening in Costa Rica (at least 40 existed at last visit). No experience is necessary for most such treetop explorations, which usually consist of a system of treetop platforms linked by horizontal transverse ziplines (cables) that permit you to "fly" through the treetops.

The originator of the concept, the **Original Canopy Tour** (tel. 506/2291-4465, www.canopytour.com) has four facilities, at Monteverde, Liverpool (near Limón), Drake Bay, and Mahogany Park (near Orotina).

There is no government regulation, and not all operators use safe practices. Several people have been killed or seriously injured. We cannot guarantee the safety of any particular operation, and we recommend you attempt to find out the level of safety at any specific operation. If you have doubts, pass!

BIRD-WATCHING

Few places in the world can boast so many different bird species in such a small area. However, birding requires some knowledge of where you are going, what you're looking for, and the best season. No self-respecting

© CHRISTOPHER P. BAKER

ATVs near Manuel Antonio

ornithologist would be caught in the field without his copy of *A Guide to the Birds of Costa Rica* by F. Gary Stiles and Alexander Skutch; *Birds of the Rainforest: Costa Rica* by Carmen Hidalgo; or *A Travel and Site Guide to Birds of Costa Rica* by Aaron Sekerak. Even with these in hand, your best bet is to hire a qualified guide or to join a bird-watching tour.

In Costa Rica, dozens of companies offer birding tours, including **Horizontes** (tel. 506/2222-2022, www.horizontes.com).

In North America, **Cheeseman's Ecology Safaris** (20800 Kittredge Rd., Saratoga, CA 95070, tel. 408/741-5330 or 800/527-5330, www.cheesemans.com); **Field Guides** (9433 Bee Cave Road, Bldg., 1, Suite 150, Austin, TX 78733, tel. 512/263-7295 or 800/728-4953, www.fieldguides.com); and **Holbrook Travel** (3540 N.W. 13th St., Gainesville, FL 32609, tel. 800/451-7111, www.holbrooktravel.com) offer birding tours to Costa Rica.

In Europe, **Journey Latin America** (12 Heathfield Terrace, Chiswick, London W4 4JE, tel. 020/8747-8315, www.journeylatinamerica.co.uk) offers a 16-day bird-watching tour.

Among the many fine independent guides specializing in birding, a stand-out is eagle-eyed Pietra Westra (tel. 506/2574-2319, www.aratinga-tours.com). He leads birding tours in fluent English (or Dutch, or Spanish), and his website provides an excellent primer on birds.

SCUBA DIVING

Costa Rica's diving is for pelagics. If you're looking for coral, you'll be happier in Belize or the Bay Islands of Honduras. Visibility, unfortunately, ranges only 6–24 meters, but water temperatures are a steady 24–29°C or higher.

The **National Association of Underwater Instructors** (NAUI, www.naui.org) and the **Professional Association of Diving Instructors** (PADI, www.padi.com) are handy resources.

Scuba outfitters are located at the principal beaches. In San José, **Mundo Aquático** (tel. 506/2224-9729, mundoac@racsa.co.cr), 25 meters north of Mas X Menos, in San Pedro, rents and sells scuba gear.

The only hyperbaric chamber is at Cuajiniquíl, in Guanacaste.

Pacific Coast

Most dive-site development has been along the Pacific coast. You'll see little live coral and few reefs. In their place, divers find an astounding variety and number of fish, soft corals, and invertebrates. Most diving is around rock formations. Visibility can often be obscured (particularly in rainy season, May–Nov.), but on calm days you may be rewarded with densities of marinelife that cannot be found anywhere in the Caribbean.

Favored dive destinations in the Pacific northwest include Islas Murciélagos and the Catalinas. Both locations teem with grouper, snapper, jacks, sharks, and giant mantas, as well as indigenous tropical species. Dozens of morays peer out from beneath rocky ledges. And schools of tang, Cortez angelfish, bright yellow butterflies, hogfish, parrot fish, giant jewfish, turtles, and eagle rays are common. Great bull sharks congregate at a place called "Big Scare." The two island chains are challenging because of their strong currents and surges.

Punta Gorda dive site, six kilometers west of Playa Ocotal, is known for thousands of eagle rays and whale sharks. Divers also report seeing black marlin cruising gracefully around pinnacle rocks. At Las Corridas, only one kilometer from El Ocotal, you're sure to come face to face with one of the 180-kilogram jewfish that dwell here. Bahía Herradura has an area known as El Jardín, famed for its formations of soft coral and sea fans.

Uvita, midway down the Pacific coast, has a small coral reef, as does Caño Island, just off the Osa Peninsula. About two kilometers out from Caño is a near-vertical wall and parades of pelagic fish, including manta rays. The island is serviced by dive boats out of Drake Bay and Golfito. Charters can also be arranged out of Quepos.

Cocos Island is the Mount Everest of dive experiences in Costa Rica. Its reputation for big-animal encounters—whale sharks, hammerheads (sometimes schooling 500 at a time), and mantas—have made it renowned. Cocos is 550 kilometers southwest of Costa Rica, necessitating a long sea journey aboard live-aboard dive vessels.

Caribbean Coast

The Caribbean coast has yet to develop a serious infrastructure catering to sport divers. At Isla Uvita, just offshore from Limón, are tropical fish, sea fans, and a coral reef, plus the wreck of the *Fenix,* a cargo ship that sank within a kilometer of the island years ago.

Farther south, at Cahuita, is Costa Rica's most beautiful—but much damaged—coral reef, extending 500 meters out from Cahuita Point. The fan-shaped reef covers 593 hectares and has 35 species of coral, including the giant elkhorn. Two old shipwrecks—replete with cannons—lie on the Cahuita reef, seven meters down.

The Gandoca-Manzanillo Wildlife Refuge protects a southern extension of the Cahuita reef, and one in better condition. If undersea caverns are your thing, check out Puerto Viejo, 20 kilometers south of Cahuita. The best time for diving is during the dry season (Feb.–Apr.), when visibility is at its best. Check with park rangers for conditions, as the area is known for dangerous tides.

FISHING

Fishing expert Jerry Ruhlow (tel. 800/308-3394, www.costaricaoutdoors.com) has a column on fishing in the weekly *Tico Times* and also publishes *Costa Rica Outdoors,* a bimonthly dedicated to fishing and outdoor sports.

Carlos Barrantes has a tackle shop, **La Casa del Pescador** (Calle 2, Avenidas 18/20, San José, tel. 506/2222-1470).

In North America, **Rod & Reel Adventures** (tel. 800/356-6982, www.rodreeladventures.com) and **Sportfishing Worldwide** (tel. 513/984-8611 or 800/638-7405, www.sfww.com) offer fishing packages to Costa Rica.

Deep-Sea Fishing

When your fishing-loving friend tells you all about the big one that got away in Costa Rica, don't believe it. Yes, the fish come big in Costa Rica. But hooking trophy contenders comes easy; the fish almost seem to line up to get a bite on the hook. The country is the world's undisputed sailfish capital on the Pacific, the tarpon capital on the Caribbean. Fishing varies from season to season, but hardly a month goes by without some International Game Fish Association record broken. No place in the world has posted more "super grand slams"—all three species of marlin and one or more sailfish on the same day—than the Pacific coastal waters of Costa Rica, where it's not unusual to raise 25 or more sailfish in a single day.

Boat charters run around $250–400 a half day, and $350–650 for a full day for up to four people, with lunch and beverage included.

The hard-fighting blue marlin swims in these waters year-round, although this "bull of the ocean" is most abundant in June and July, when large schools of tuna also come close to shore. June–October is best for dorado. Then, too, yellowfin tuna weighing up to 90 kilograms offer a rod-bending challenge. Wahoo are also prominent, though less dependable. Generally, summer months are the best in the north; winter months are best in the south.

Flamingo and Tamarindo are the two most prominent fishing centers in the northern Pacific (although the Flamingo marina remained closed down in 2009 for an indefinite period). However, northern Guanacaste is largely unfishable December–March because of heavy winds (boat operators at Flamingo and Tamarindo move boats south to Los Sueños and Quepos during the windy season, when the Central Pacific posts its best scores). Quepos is a year-round sportfishing center. Many operators offer multi-day trips from Quepos to the waters off Drake Bay and Caño Island. Golfito is the base for another popular fishing paradise, the Golfo Dulce.

Inland and Coastal Fishing

Part of the beauty of fishing Costa Rica, says one fisherman, is that "you can fish the Caribbean at dawn, try the Pacific in the afternoon, and still have time to watch a sunset from a mountain stream." Forget the sunset—there are fish in those mountains. More than a dozen inland rivers provide action on rainbow trout, *machaca* (Central America's answer to American shad), drum, *guapote, mojarra* (Costa Rica's bluegill

with teeth), and *bobo* (a moss-eating mullet). A good bet is the Río Savegre and other streams around San Gerardo de Dota, Copey, and Cañon. Caño Negro Lagoon and the waters of the Río San Juan present fabulous potential for snook and tarpon. Lake Arenal is famed for its feisty rainbow bass *(guapote),* running 3.5 kilograms or more. A freshwater fishing license is mandatory; the limit is a maximum of five specimens (of any one species) per angler per day. The closed season runs September–December. Lodges and outfitters provide the permit (license, not fish), as does the Banco Nacional de Costa Rica (Avenida 1, Calle 2/4, San José).

Costa Rica's northeastern shores, lowland lagoons, and coastal rivers offer the world's hottest tarpon for the light-tackle enthusiast. At prime fishing spots, tarpon average 35 kilograms (sometimes reaching up to 70 kg). These silver rockets are caught in the jungle rivers and backwater lagoons, and ocean tarpon fishing just past the breakers is always dependable. When you tire of wrestling these snappy fighters, you can take on snook—another worthy opponent. Fall is the best time to get a shot at the trophy snook that return to the beaches around the river mouths to spawn. The all-tackle IGFA record came from Costa Rica, which regularly delivers 14-kilogram fish. Tarpon are caught year-round. Snook season runs from late August into January, with a peak August–November. November–January the area enjoys a run of *calba,* the local name for small snook that average two kilograms and are exceptional sport on light tackle. Jacks are also common year-round in Caribbean waters.

KAYAKING AND CANOEING

Sea kayaking is quickly catching on in Costa Rica, and no wonder. The sea kayak's ability to move silently means you can travel unobtrusively, sneaking close up to wildlife without freaking it out. Dolphins and even turtles have been known to surface alongside to check out kayakers. The one- and two-person craft are remarkably stable and ideally suited for investigating narrow coastal inlets and flat-water rivers larger vessels cannot reach.

Anyone planning on kayaking rivers should refer to *The Rivers of Costa Rica: A Canoeing, Kayaking, and Rafting Guide* by Michael W. Mayfield and Rafael E. Gallo, which provides detailed maps plus a technical description of the entire river system.

In San José, you can rent kayaks, canoes, and camping equipment from **Mundo Aventura** (tel. 506/2221-6934, www.maventura.com).

Ríos Tropicales (tel. 506/233-6455, or U.S. tel. 866/722-8273, www.riostropicales.com), **Kayak Jacó** (tel. 506/2643-1233, www.kay-akjaco.com), and **Serendipity Adventures** (tel. 506/2558-1000, www.serendipityadven-tures.com) offer kayaking trips.

In North America, **BattenKill Canoe** (tel. 802/362-2800 or 800/421-5268, www.batten-kill.com) offers canoeing trips to Costa Rica, as do **Canoe Costa Rica** (tel. 506/2282-3579; in the U.S., tel./fax 732/736-6586, www.canoeco-starica.com); and **Gulf Islands Kayaking** (S-24, C-34, Galiano Island, BC, Canada V0N 1PO, tel./fax 250/539-2442, www.seakayak.ca).

WHITE-WATER RAFTING

White-water rafting is the ultimate combi-nation of beauty and thrill—an ideal way to savor Costa Rica's natural splendor and exotic wildlife. Because the land is so steep, streams pass through hugely varied landscapes within relatively short distances. Rainforest lines the riverbanks. You'll tumble through a tropical *Fantasia* of feathery bamboo, ferns, and palms, a roller-coaster ride amid glistening jungle. Everything is as silent as a graveyard, except for the chattering of monkeys and birds.

Rafters are required to wear helmets and life jackets, which are provided by tour opera-tors. Generally, all you need to bring is a swim-suit, a T-shirt, and tennis shoes or sneakers. Sunscreen is a good idea, as you are not only in the open all day, but also exposed to reflec-tions off the water. You'll also need an extra set of clothing, and perhaps a sweater or jacket, as you can easily get chilled if a breeze kicks up when you're wet. And you *will* get wet. Most operators provide a special waterproof bag for cameras. One-day trips start at about $75.

When and Where

Generally, May–June and September–October are the best times for high water. Rivers are rated from Class I to VI in degree of difficulty, with V considered for true experts only.

The **Río Chirripó** (Class III–IV) runs down the slopes of the southwest Pacific and is rec-ommended for two- to four-day trips. The river, which tumbles from its source on Mount Chirripó, has been compared to California's Tuolomne River and Idaho's Middle Fork of the Salmon, with massive volumes of water and giant waves.

The **Río Corobicí** (Class II) provides more of a float trip and makes an ideal half-day trip for families, with superb wildlife viewing and calm waters the whole way. The river flows westward through Guanacaste into the Gulf of Nicoya. It is runnable year-round.

The high-volume **Río General** is famous for its dramatic gorges, challenging rapids, and big waves ideal for surfing.

Río Naranjo and **Río Savegre,** in the mountains above Manuel Antonio on the cen-tral Pacific coast, are real corkers in high water, with swirling Class IV action. However, they're inconsistent, with dramatic changes in water level. The upper sections run through rain-forest; lower down, they slow through ranch land before winding through Manuel Antonio National Park and exiting into the Pacific.

For an in-depth immersion in nature, the **Río Pacuaré** (Class III–IV) is the best choice as it slices through virgin rainforest, plung-ing through mountain gorges to spill onto the Caribbean plains near Siquirres. Toucans, monkeys, and other animals galore make this journey unforgettable. Overhead loom cliffs from which waterfalls drop right into the river. Black tongues of lava stick out into the river, creating large, technically demanding rapids and making great lunch beaches. And steep drops produce big waves. The best months are June and October.

The **Río Reventazón** (Class II–V) tum-bles out of Lake Angostura and cascades to the Caribbean lowlands in an exciting series of rapids. Beginners can savor Class II and III rapids on the "mid-section," the most popular run for one-day trips. The Guayabo section offers Class V runs. Constant rainfall allows operators to offer trips year-round; June and July are the best months.

The **Río Sarapiquí** (Class III) runs along the eastern flank of the Cordillera Central and drops to the Caribbean lowlands. It is noted for its crystal-clear water, variable terrain, and exciting rapids. Trips are offered May–December.

Tour Companies

In Costa Rica, I recommend **Costa Rica Expeditions** (tel. 506/2257-0766, www.costaricaexpeditions.com), which offers one-day and multi-day trips on most major rivers. The other preeminent operator is **Ríos Tropicales** (tel. 506/233-6455, fax 506/2255-4354, www.riostropicales.com), which runs the Corobicí, Sarapiquí, Reventazón, General, and Pacuaré rivers. Numerous smaller companies also offer white-water trips.

WINDSURFING

Strong winds sweep the coast of the Pacific northwest in summer; Bahía Salinas is recommended and has two windsurfing centers. Inland, Lake Arenal is paradise, with 23–35 kph easterly winds funneling through a mountain corridor year-round. Strong winds rarely cease during the dry season (Dec.–Apr.). The lake is one of the best all-year freshwater windsurfing spots in the world, with two dedicated windsurfing centers.

HIKING

Hiking tours with a professional guide can be arranged through nature lodges or local tour operators. Most reserves and national parks maintain marked trails. The hardy and adventurous might try a strenuous hike to the peak of Chirripó, Costa Rica's tallest mountain. Hiking in the more remote parks may require a high degree of self-sufficiency, and, says one writer, "a guide so comfortable with a machete he can pick your teeth with it." If you plan on hiking in the Talamancas or other high mountain areas, you're advised to obtain topographical maps from the **Instituto Geográfica Nacional** (National Geographic Institute, Avenida 20, Calles 9/11, tel. 506/2523-2630, www.mopt.go.cr/ign, 7 A.M.–noon and 12:45–3:30 P.M. Mon.–Fri.). Raingear and a warm sweater or jacket are essential for hiking at higher elevations.

Coast to Coast Adventures (tel. 506/2280-8054, www.ctocadventures.com) specializes in hiking trips.

In North America, **Backroads** (tel. 510/527-1555 or 800/462-2848, www.backroads.com); **Mountain Travel-Sobek** (tel. 510/594-6000 or 888/831-2576, www.mtsobek.com); and **Wildland Adventures** (tel. 206/365-0686 or 800/345-4453, www.wildland.com) all offer hiking programs in Costa Rica.

For the truly hardy, **Outward Bound** (tel. 506/2278-6059 or 800/676-2018, www.crrobs.org) offers courses, not "trips," that include a hike up Chirripó and have been described by participants as having "fistfuls of experience mashed in your face."

HORSEBACK RIDING

Horseback riding is very popular in Costa Rica, where the *campesino* culture depends on the horse for mobility. Wherever you are, horses are sure to be available for rent. (The native horse of Costa Rica is the *crillo,* a small, big-chested creature of good temperament.)

In Santa Ana (about 9 km west of San José), **Club Hípico la Caraña** (tel. 506/2282-6106, fax 506/2282-6754) provides riding instruction.

Scores of ranches nationwide offer trail rides, notably in Guanacaste, where city slickers longing to be the Marlboro Man can pay perfectly good money to get coated with dust and manure alongside workaday cowboys.

Equitour (tel. 307/455-3363 or 800/545-0019, www.ridingtours.com) has eight- to 11-day riding adventures in Costa Rica.

BICYCLING

The occasional sweat and effort make Costa Rica's spectacular landscapes and abiding serenity all the more rewarding from a bicycle saddle. Sure, you'll work for your reward. But you'd never get so close to so much beauty in a car. Away from the main highways, roads are little traveled. However, there are no bike lanes, potholes are a persistent problem, and traffic can be hazardous on the steep and windy mountain roads. Leave your touring bike at home: Bring a mountain bike or rent one once you arrive. A helmet is essential.

Costa Ricans are fond of cycling (both road racing and mountain biking), and bicycle racing is a major Costa Rican sport, culminating each November in the grueling **La Ruta de los Conquistadores** (tel. 506/2225-8295, www.adventurerace.com), which crosses the mountain chain from sea level to over 3,000 meters.

Airlines generally allow bicycles to be checked free (properly packaged) with one piece of luggage. **Taca** (www.taca.com), for example, still permits free transport of bicycles.

The following Costa Rican Tour companies are recommended: **Aventuras Naturales** (tel. 506/2225-3939, or in North America tel. 800/321-8410, www.adventurecostarica.com); **Bike Arenal** (tel. 506/2479-7150, or in North America tel. 866/465-4114, www.bikearenal.com); **Coast to Coast Adventures** (tel. 506/2280-8054, www.ctocadventures.com); **Costa Rica Biking Adventure** (tel. 506/2225-6591 or 888/862-2424, www.bikingcostarica.com); and **Lava Tours** (tel. 506/2281-2458 or 888/862-2424, www.lava-tours.com). And **Railbike Adventures** (tel. 506/2233-3300, www.railbike.com) offers trips along old railway tracks using "rail-bikes."

In North America, **Backroads** (tel. 510/527-1555 or 800/462-2848, www.backroads.com) and **Experience Plus!** (tel. 970/484-8489 or 800/685-4565, www.experienceplus.com) also have guided tours.

MOTORCYCLE TOURING

Motorbike enthusiasts haven't been left out of the two-wheel touring business. **Wild Rider** (tel. 506/2258-4604, www.wild-rider.com) uses scramblers for its tours. **Tour's María Alexandra** (tel. 506/2289-5552, www.costaricamotorcycles.com) offers one- to eight-day

trips using Harley-Davidsons, as does **Harley Rentals** (tel. 506/2288-6362, www.harley-tourscostarica.com).

In North America, **Moto-Discovery Tours** (tel. 830/438-7744 or 800/233-0564, www.motodiscovery.com) runs eight-day guided tours in Costa Rica and four- to 11-day "El Vagabundo" tours, a go-as-you-please program. **MotoAdventures** (tel. 506/2228-8494, in North America tel. 440/256-8508, www.motoadventuring.com); **Costarica-Moto** (tel. 506/2533-1564. www.costarica-moto.com); and **Moto Tours Costa Rica** (tel. 540/980-7675, www.mototourscostarica.com) also offer organized tours, the latter using scrambler bikes.

GOLFING

Before 1995, the country had just two courses: the championship course at Meliá Cariari and Country Club outside San José, and the nine-hole Hotel Tango Mar, overlooking the Gulf of Nicoya on the Pacific coast. However, the country is in the midst of a course-building binge and now claims half a dozen championship courses, with more coming. The prime courses include a Robert Trent Jones, Jr. stunner at the Paradisus Playa Conchal, at Playa Conchal, in Nicoya; the Marriott Los Sueños course at Playa Herradura, in the Central Pacific; Los Delfines Golf & Country Club, at Playa Tambor, in Nicoya; Parque Valle del Sol, at Santa Ana, west of San José; the Arnold Palmer–designed course at Four Seasons, at Bahía Culebra, in Nicoya; and the new course at Hacienda Pinilla, also in Nicoya. Contact the **Costa Rica National Golf Association** (tel. 506/2296-5772, www.anagolf.com) for information.

There are also numerous nine-hole courses.

HANG-GLIDING AND AERIAL TOURS

Ballooning is offered by **Serendipity Adventures** (tel. 506/2558-1000 or U.S. tel. 800/635-2325, www.serendipityadventures.com).

Helitours by AeroDiva (tel. 506/2296-7241, www.aerodiva.com) offers helicopter tours.

And ultralight flights are offered at Flying

Crocodile Lodge, in Playa Sámara, at Bahía (near Uvita), and at Timarai, near Parrita.

SURFING

Prime surfing is one of Costa Rica's main assets, drawing tens of thousands of eager boarders each year. Long stretches of oceanfront provide thousands of beach breaks. Numerous rivers offer quality sandbar river-mouth breaks, particularly on the Pacific coast. The coral reefs on the Caribbean coast, says Costa Rican surf expert Peter Brennan, "take the speed limit to the max." And there are plenty of surf camps.

If the surf blows out or goes flat before you are ready to pack it in for the day, you can simply jump over to the other coast, or—on the Pacific—head north or south. If one break isn't working, another is sure to be cooking. You rarely see monster-size, Hawaiian-type waves, but they're nicely shaped, long, and tubular, and in places never-ending—often nearly a kilometer! All the major surf beaches have surf shops

where board sales and rentals are offered. Many hotels and car rental companies offer discounts to surfers.

Generally, your double board bag flies free (or for a small fee) as a second piece of checked luggage on international airlines. Airlines require that you pack your board in a board bag. (Within Costa Rica, Nature Air permits short boards, but not long boards, for a $40 fee.) **Costa Rican Surf Report** (www.crsurf .com) is a great information source, as are **Surf Costa Rica** (www.surfcostarica.com); the **Costa Rica Surfing Guide** (www.costarica-surfguide.com); and *H2O Surf Travel Guide: Costa Rica* (http://h2osurftravel.com). In Costa Rica, look for *Surfos,* a slick bi-annual magazine available free.

Board rentals and repair, plus surfing tuition, are available at all the main surfing beaches. The main Costa Rican player is **Alacran Surf Tours** (tel. 506/2280-7328 or 888/751-0135, www.alacransurf.com).

ESSENTIALS

Getting There

BY AIR

About 20 international airlines provide regular service to Costa Rica. Most flights land at **Juan Santamaría International Airport** at Alajuela (19 km northwest, and 20 minutes by taxi, from San José). An increasing number of flights land at **Daniel Oduber International Airport,** 12 kilometers west of Liberia in Guanacaste. **Tobías Bolaños Airport,** 6.5 kilometers southwest of San José, is for domestic flights only.

Reservations and Fares

To get the cheapest fares, make your reservations as early as possible (several months is ideal),

especially during peak season, as flights often sell out. Central American carriers are usually slightly cheaper than their American counterparts but often stop over at more cities en route. Low-season and midweek travel is often cheaper, as are stays of more than 30 days. Travel during Christmas, New Year, and Easter usually costs more. Buy your return segment before arriving in Costa Rica, as tickets bought in the country are heavily taxed.

Compare any restrictions on tickets, and check to see what penalties may apply for changes to your ticket. "Open-jaw" tickets permit you to arrive in one city and depart from

another; however, they cost considerably more. Always reconfirm your reservation within 72 hours of your departure (reservations are frequently cancelled if not reconfirmed, especially during December–January holidays).

You can buy tickets online through **Expedia** (www.expedia.com), **Orbitz** (www.orbitz.com), **Priceline** (www.priceline.com), **Travelocity** (www.travelocity.com), or similar discount travel websites. Compare quotes at different sites, as they vary, even for the same flight.

Alternately, use a Costa Rica travel specialist, such as **Tico Travel** (tel. 800/493-8426, www.ticotravel.com) or **Costa Rica Experts** (tel. 800/827-9046, www.costaricaexperts.com).

International specialists in low fares include **STA Travel** (tel. 800/781-4040, www.sta-travel.com), which has offices worldwide.

Most airlines have recently imposed high excess baggage charges, including for surfboards.

From the United States

U.S. flights are either direct or have stopovers in Central America. Fares typically range about $400–800 depending on season and city of origin. **American Airlines** (tel. 800/433-7300, www.aa.com) flies direct to San José daily from Miami, Dallas, and Los Angeles, and to Liberia from Dallas and Miami. **Continental** (tel. 800/523-3273, www.continental.com) flies direct to San José daily from Houston and Newark, and to Liberia daily from Houston and weekly from Newark. **Delta** (tel. 800/221-1212, www.delta.com) flies direct to Liberia and San José daily from Atlanta. **JetBlue** (tel. 800/539-2583, www.jetblue.com) initiated daily nonstop service between Orlando and San José in March 2009. **Spirit Air** (tel. 800/772-7117, www.spiritair.com) flies to San José from Fort Lauderdale. **United Airlines** (tel. 800/864-8331, www.united.com) serves San José daily from Chicago and Los Angeles, and six times weekly from Washington DC. **U.S. Airways** (tel. 800/428-4322, www.usairways.com) has direct flights to San José from Charlotte, Fort Lauderdale, and Philadelphia. **TACA** (tel. 800/400-8222, www.taca.com), a consortium of Central American carriers (including Costa Rica's LACSA) offers daily flights from Dallas, Los Angeles, Miami, New York (JFK), Orlando, and San Francisco. Some flights are nonstop; others make stops in Central America.

Charters are usually priced for stays of one or two weeks; longer stays usually cost considerably more. "Open-jaw" tickets are not usually permitted. Charters have an added disadvantage of often leaving at ungodly hours. Departure dates cannot be changed, and heavy cancellation penalties usually apply. Remember to calculate the cost of any savings for accommodations, airport transfers, meals, and other services that may be included in the cost of an air-hotel package.

Apple Vacations (tel. 800/517-2000, www.applevacations.com) and **Funjet Vacations** (tel. 888/558-6654, www.funjet.com) offer charter packages.

Martinair (tel. 800/627-8462, www.martinairusa.com) flies from Orlando three times weekly and from Miami four times weekly in high season.

From Canada

TACA (tel. 800/400-8222, www.taca.com) flies between Toronto and San José three times weekly. **Air Canada** (tel. 888/247-2262, www.aircanada.com) also flies four times weekly from Toronto to San José.

Charters may need to be booked through a travel agent. **Signature Vacations** (tel. 866/324-2883, www.signature.ca) flies to Liberia once weekly from Calgary, Toronto, and Vancouver (Dec.–Apr.) using **Skyservice** (tel. 800/701-9448, www.skyserviceairlines.com). **Air Transat** (tel. 866/847-1112, www.airtransat.com) flies weekly to San José from Toronto and Montreal.

Canadian Universities Travel Service (Travel Cuts, tel. 866/246-9762, www.travelcuts.com) sells discount airfares and has offices throughout Canada.

From Latin America and the Caribbean

Mexicana (tel. 59/9848-5998 or 800/801-2010 or U.S. tel. 800/531-7921, www.mexicana.com)

flies between Mexico City and San José daily, and Guatemala City and San José twice weekly. **TACA** (tel. 800/400-8222, www.taca.com) serves Costa Rica from all the Central American nations.

TACA flies between Costa Rica and Argentina, Brazil, Chile, Ecuador, Peru, and Venezuela. Aviateca flies from Colombia; Ladeco links Costa Rica and Chile. And American Airlines, Continental, and United Airlines flights all connect Costa Rica with destinations throughout South America.

Cubana (tel. 506/2221-7625, www.cubana.co.cu) and TACA offer regular scheduled service between San José and Havana.

From the United Kingdom

Costa Rica is served by **British Airways** (tel. 0844/493-0787, www.british-airways.co.uk) from London. American Airlines, British Airways, Continental, United Airlines, USAirways, and Virgin Atlantic fly from London to Miami (or New York), where you can connect with an airline serving Costa Rica. **Go,** British Airways' budget wing, connects to European destinations.

Typical APEX fares (advance purchase, discounted international fares) between London and Costa Rica begin at about £700 via the United States for stays of less than 30 days. However, you can buy reduced-rate fares on scheduled carriers from "bucket shops" (discount ticket agencies), which advertise in leading magazines and Sunday newspapers. One of the most reputable is **Trailfinders** (tel. 0845/058-5858, www.trailfinders.com), with offices throughout Britain. **STA Travel** (tel. 0871/230-0040, www.statravel.co.uk), also with offices throughout the U.K., specializes in student fares. And **Journey Latin America** (tel. 020/8747-3108, www.journeylatinamerica.co.uk) specializes in cheap fares and tour packages.

Good online resources for discount tickets include www.flightline.co.uk and www.cheapflights.co.uk; for charter flights, resources include **Charter Flight Centre** (tel. 0845/045-0153, www.charterflights.co.uk) and **Dial a Flight** (tel. 0870/333-4488, www.dialaflight.co.uk).

From Continental Europe

Air France (tel. 09-69-39-02-15, www.airfrance.fr) flies to San José from Paris. **Air Caraibes** (www.aircaraibes.com) flies from France. From **Germany,** charter carrier **Condor** (tel. 0/180-570-7202, www.condor.com) flies direct from Dusseldorf and Munich in high season. From the **Netherlands,** Costa Rica is served by **Martinair** (tel. 1805/100-211 www.martinair.com) from Amsterdam via Miami and Orlando. From **Russia, Aeroflot** (tel. 095/753-5555 in Moscow, tel. 812/118-5555 in St. Petersburg, www.aeroflot.ru) flies between Moscow and San José via Miami. From **Spain,** Costa Rica is served by **Iberia** (tel. 902/400-500, www.iberia.com) direct from Madrid from about €988 in high season.

From Australia and New Zealand

The best bet is to fly either to Los Angeles or San Francisco and then to Costa Rica. **Air New Zealand** (in Australia tel. 13-24-76, in New Zealand tel. 0800/737-000, www.airnewzealand.com), **Qantas** (tel. 13-13-13, in New Zealand tel. 0800/808-767, www.qantas.com.au), and **United Airlines** (tel. 131-777, in New Zealand tel. 0800/747-400) offer direct service between Australia, New Zealand, and North America. Roundtrip fares from Sydney typically begin at around US$700. A route via Buenos Aires or Santiago de Chile and then to Costa Rica is also possible.

Specialists in discount fares include **STA Travel** (in Sydney, tel. 134-782, www.statravel.com.au, in Auckland, tel. 0800/474-400, www.statravel.co.nz), which has offices throughout Australia and New Zealand.

A good online resource for discount airfares is **Flight Centre** (tel. 133-133, www.flightcentre.com.au).

From Asia

Asian travelers fly via Europe or the United States. Flying nonstop to Los Angeles is perhaps the easiest route. Alternately, fly United or Malaysia Airlines to Mexico City. From Macau, you can fly with **Iberia** nonstop to Madrid and then on to Costa Rica.

STA Travel is a good resource for tickets and has branches throughout Asia.

BY LAND
By Bus
The overland route from North America is an attractive alternative for travelers for whom time is no object. Allow at least one week. Obtain all necessary visas and documentation in advance. You can travel from San Diego or Texas to Costa Rica by bus for as little as $100 (with hotels and food, however, the cost can add up to more than flying direct). Book as far ahead as you can—the buses often sell out well in advance. You will need to provide a passport and visas when buying your ticket.

Buses serve Mexico City from the U.S. border points at Mexicali, Ciudad Juárez, and Laredo. From Nicaragua, cross-border buses ($0.75) depart from Peñas Blancas every hour for Rivas, a small town about 40 kilometers north of the border. From Panamá, buses leave from David for Panamá City.

By Car
Many people drive to Costa Rica from the United States via Mexico, Guatemala, Honduras, and Nicaragua. It's a long haul, but you can follow the Pan-American Highway all the way from the United States to San José. It's 3,700 kilometers minimum, depending on your starting point. Experienced travelers recommend skirting El Salvador and the Guatemalan highlands in favor of the coast road. Allow three weeks at a leisurely pace. Make sure that your vehicle is in tip-top mechanical condition. You should plan your itinerary to be at each day's destination before nightfall (80 percent of insurance claims are a result of nighttime accidents).

You'll need a passport, visas, driver's license, and vehicle registration. It's also advisable to obtain tourist cards (good for 90 days) from the consulate of each country before departing. A U.S. driver's license is good throughout Central America, although an International Driving Permit—issued through AAA—can be handy, too. You'll need to arrange a transit visa for Mexico in advance, plus car entry

permits for each country. AAA can provide advice on *carnets* (international travel permits).

A separate vehicle liability insurance policy is required for each country. Most U.S. firms will not underwrite insurance south of the border. (Insurance sold by AAA covers Mexico only, not Central America.) **Sanborn's** (tel. 800/222-0158, www.sanbornsinsurance.com) specializes in insurance coverage for travel in Mexico and Central America. It publishes a booklet, *Overland Travel,* full of practical information, as well as regional guides.

Upon arrival in Costa Rica, foreign drivers must buy insurance stamps for a minimum of three months (approximately $15). There's also a $10 road tax (good for three months) payable upon arrival in Costa Rica. Vehicle permits are issued at the border for stays up to 30 days. You can extend this to six months at the Instituto Costarricense de Turismo.

BY SEA
Costa Rica appears on the itineraries of several cruise ships. However, stops are usually no more than one day, so don't expect more than a cursory glimpse of the country. Cruises from Florida usually stop off at various Caribbean islands and/or Cozumel before calling in at Puerto Limón. Cruises from San Diego or Los Angeles normally stop off in Puerto Caldera or Puntarenas.

Contact the **Cruise Line International Association** (CLIA, tel. 754/224-2200, www.cruising.org) for a list of companies that include Costa Rica on their itineraries.

Private yachters can berth at an ever-increasing number of marinas on the Pacific coast. As of 2009, 16 new marinas were in the works with the potential to host about 5,000 boats.

Natural History Cruise Tours are offered throughout Costa Rica by the following companies: **Cruise West** (tel. 888/851-8133, www.cruisewest.com); **Lindblad Expeditions** (tel. 212/765-7740 or 800/397-3348, www.expeditions.com); **National Geographic Expeditions** (tel. 888/966-8687, wwww.nationalgeographicexpeditions.com); and **Windstar Cruises** (tel. 206/281-3535 or 877/827-7245, www.windstarcruises.com).

Getting Around

BY AIR

Traveling by air in Costa Rica is easy and economical, a quick and comfortable alternative to often long and bumpy road travel. Flights to airstrips around the country are rarely more than 40 minutes from San José. Book well in advance.

The government-subsidized domestic airline **SANSA** (tel. 506/2229-4100, or in North America tel. 877/767-2672, www.flysansa.com) uses 22- to 35-passenger Cessnas. Reservations have to be paid in full and are nonrefundable. You can check in at the airport or SANSA's San José office in the basement of Centro Colón (Paseo Colón, Calle 24), which provides a free minibus transfer to Juan Santamaría Airport. SANSA baggage allowance is 11 kilograms. Schedules change frequently, especially between seasons.

The privately owned **Nature Air** (tel. 506/2299-6000, U.S. tel. 800/235-9272, www.natureair.com) flies to 14 destinations (including Nicaragua and Panamá) from Tobías Bolaños Airport, three kilometers west of downtown San José. Its rates are higher than SANSA's, but the airline is somewhat more reliable. Baggage limit is 12 kilograms.

Charters

You can charter small planes to fly you to airstrips throughout the country. The going rate is about $300–500 per hour per planeload (usually for up to 4–6 people). You'll have to pay for the return flight, too, if there are no passengers returning from your destination. Luggage space is limited.

Aerobell (tel. 506/2290-0000, www.aerobell.com) is recommended for small plane charter, as is **Paradise Air** (tel. 506/2231-0938, www.flywithparadise.com).

Aerodiva (tel. 506/2296-7241, www.aerodiva.com) offers helicopter tours and charter.

BY BUS

Buses serve even the most remote towns: Generally, if there's a road, there's a bus. Popular destinations are served by both fast buses (*directo*) and slower buses (*normal* or *corriente*), which make stops en route. Most buses serving major towns from San José use modern air-conditioned buses with toilets and sometimes even movies. In the boondocks, local buses are usually old U.S. high-school buses with arse-numbing seats. You can travel to most parts of the country for less than $10.

Buy tickets (*boletos*) in advance for long-distance travel (for local buses, you'll have to pay when getting aboard). Get there at least an hour before departure or your reservation may not be honored. Long-distance buses have storage below; local buses do not. Travel light; a soft duffel is preferable, so you can tuck it under your seat or carry it on your lap.

Bus stops (*paradas*) nationwide are plain to see; most have shelters. Elsewhere, you can usually flag down rural buses anywhere along their routes. Long-distance buses don't always stop when waved down. To get off, shout "*¡Pare!*" (pa-reh).

Many buses don't run on Thursday and Friday during Easter week.

You can check schedules online at http://thebusschedule.com.

Tourist Buses

Interbus (tel. 506/2283-5573, www.interbusonline.com) operates door-to-door shuttles between major tourist destinations. Complete listings of routes, schedules, and fares are available online. **Grayline Fantasy Bus** (tel. 506/2220-2126, www.graylinecostarica.com) offers a similar service to destinations throughout Costa Rica.

Costa Rica Shuttle (tel. 506/2289-9509, or U.S. tel. 305/720-2787, www.costaricashuttle.com) and **Coach Costa Rica** (tel. 506/2229-4192, www.coachcostarica.com) offer customized shuttle service nationwide using minivans, as does **Transport Costa Rica Monteverde** (tel. 506/2645-6768, www.transportcostarica.net).

© CHRISTOPHER P. BAKER

Interbus shuttle near Monteverde

BY CAR AND MOTORCYCLE

Rent a car if you want total freedom of movement. Costa Rica has some 30,000 kilometers of highway (20 percent paved). The MOPT (Ministry of Public Transport) has invested considerably in road improvements in recent years, particularly in the highlands. However, beyond the Central Highlands, roads generally deteriorate with distance and can shake both a car and its occupants until their doors and teeth rattle. Parts of the country are often impenetrable by road during the rainy season, when flooding and landslides are common and roads get washed out.

Traffic Regulations

You must be at least 21 years old and hold a passport to drive in Costa Rica. Foreign driver's licenses are valid for three months upon arrival. For longer, you'll need a Costa Rican driver's license. Apply at Avenida 20, Calle 11 in San José (tel. 506/2523-2000). The speed limit on highways is 80 kilometers per hour, and 60 kilometers per hour on secondary roads. Speed limits are vigorously enforced, although the number of traffic police is relatively few. (Costa Rican drivers typically flash their high beams at other drivers to warn of traffic police ahead.)

Seat belt use is mandatory, and motorcyclists must wear helmets. Insurance—a state monopoly—is also mandatory; car rental companies sell insurance with rentals.

It is illegal to:

- enter an intersection unless you can exit

- make a right turn on a red light unless indicated by a white arrow

- overtake on the right—you may pass only on the left.

- Cars coming uphill have the right of way.

Driving Safety

Tico males display unbelievable recklessness, often driving at warp speed, flouting traffic laws, holding traffic lights in disdain, crawling up your tailpipe at 100 kilometers per hour, and overtaking on blind corners with a total disregard for anyone else's safety. Costa Rica's fatality statistics are sobering!

© CHRISTOPHER P. BAKER

car being towed out of a river on the Osa Peninsula

Roads usually lack sidewalks, so pedestrians—and even livestock—walk the road. Be particularly wary at night. And treat mountain roads with extra caution: they're often blocked by thick fog, floods, and landslides. The two roads from San José to Puntarenas; the road linking San José to Limón; and the Pan-American Highway between the Nicaraguan border and Panamá are notoriously dangerous.

Potholes are a particular problem. Hit a big one and you may damage a tire or even destroy a wheel. Vehicles often swerve into your path to avoid potholes. And slower-moving vehicles ahead of you often turn on their left-turn indicator to signal that you can overtake—a dangerous practice that is the cause of many accidents with vehicles that really are turning left!

Consider driving with your lights on at *all times* to ensure being seen.

Accidents and Breakdowns

The law states that you must carry fluorescent triangles in case of breakdown. Locals, however, generally pile leaves, rocks, or small branches in the road or at the roadside to warn approaching drivers of a car in trouble. If your car is rented, call the rental agency: It will arrange a tow. Otherwise call 800/800-8001 for roadside assistance.

After an accident, *never* move the vehicles until the police arrive. Get the names, license plate numbers, and *cedulas* (legal identification numbers) of any witnesses. Make a sketch of the accident. And call the traffic police *(tráfico)* (tel. 117 or 800/872-6748).

Do *not* offer statements to anyone other than the police. In case of injury, call the Red Cross (tel. 128 or 911 or 506/2221-5818). Try not to leave the accident scene, or at least keep an eye on your car: the other party may tamper with the evidence. And don't let honking traffic—there'll be plenty!—pressure you into moving the cars.

Show the *tráfico* your license and vehicle registration. Make sure you get them back: He is not allowed to keep any documents unless you've been drinking (if you suspect the other driver has been drinking, ask the *tráfico* to administer a Breathalyzer test, or *alcolemia*). Nor can the *tráfico* assess a fine. The police will

RIVER FORDINGS

Every year, more bridges are built over rivers that once had to be forded (*varear* in Spanish), but in certain parts of the country – notably southwest Nicoya and the Osa Peninsula – there are still enough rivers without bridges to add spice to your driving adventure. Usually these are no problem in dry season. But wet season is another matter. Many unwary foreigners misjudge the crossing, swamp the engine, and have to be towed out. Do not expect the car rental agency to be sympathetic; you will have to pay for the damage. It is not unknown for cars to be washed away!

If the river is murky, wade across on foot first to gauge the depth and force of the river, which may be strong enough to whip your wheels from under you. Check for the engine's air filter placement to ensure that it won't swamp. Even if the engine won't swamp, you need to check the height of the door sills. Sure, your car might make it across without stalling, but do you really want six inches of muddy water inside the car? Keep the windows down and the doors unlocked.

Look for the tire tracks of other vehicles. It usually pays to follow them. Sometimes you may need to run *along* the riverbed to find the exit, rather than it being a straight-across route. It's often best to wait for a local to arrive and show the way. Be patient!

OK, ready to go? There's a technique to fording rivers successfully. Firstly, *enter the river slowly!* Many drivers charge at the river, causing a huge wave that rides over the hood and drowns the engine. It pays to inch across gently, not least because a shallow crossing often betrays a hidden channel (usually near the bank) where the water runs deep and into which it is easy to plunge nose-first just as you think you've made it across. Still, once you enter the water, keep your foot on the gas.

---

issue you a green ticket or "summons." You must present this to the nearest municipal office *(alcaldía)* or traffic court *(tribunal de tránsito)* within eight days to make your *declaración* about the accident. Wait a few days so that the police report is on record. Don't skip this! The driver who doesn't show is often found at blame by default. Then take your driver's license, insurance policy, and a police report to the **INS** (Avenida 7, Calles 9/11, San José, tel. 506/2287-6000 or 800/800-8000, ext 1, www.ins.go.cr), the state insurance monopoly, to process your claim. Car rental companies will take care of this if your car is rented.

Hitchhiking

Hitchhiking is far from safe and I do not endorse it. Women should never hitchhike alone.

Car Rentals

The leading U.S. car rental companies have franchises in Costa Rica, though not always as reliable as their U.S. parents. There are many local rental companies (some reputable, some not), with slightly cheaper rates. Several agencies have offices at or near Juan Santamaría Airport, plus representatives in popular resort towns.

I highly recommend **U-Save** (tel. 560/2430-4647, in North America tel. 866/267-1070, www.usavecostarica.com). The staff and service proved consistently professional when I used this company in 2008, and its vehicles have always been in good repair.

Other agencies include **Alamo** (tel. 506/2233-7733, www.alamocostarica.com), **Budget** (tel. 506/2436-2000, www.budget.co.cr), **Europcar** (tel. 506/2440-9990, www.europcar.co.cr), **Hertz** (tel. 506/2221-1818, www.costaricarentacar.net) and **National** (tel. 506/2290-8787, www.natcar.com).

Regardless of where you plan to go, rent a four-wheel-drive vehicle! If you don't, you'll regret it the first time you hit one of Costa Rica's infamous dirt and/or potholed roads. Four-wheel-drives are essential for off-the-beaten-path destinations. Many rental agencies will insist you rent a four-wheel drive for specific regions, especially in rainy season.

Minimum age for drivers ranges 21–25, depending on the agency. You'll need a valid driver's license plus a credit card. Without a credit card you'll have to pay a hefty cash deposit. Most agencies offer discounts during the low season (May–Oct.) and for making your reservations from abroad before departure. Stick shift is the norm; you'll pay extra for automatic.

Reserve as far in advance as possible, especially in dry season and for Christmas and holidays. Make sure you clarify any one-way drop-off fees, late return penalties, and other charges. Take a copy of your reservation with you. And be prepared to defend against mysterious new charges that may be tagged on in Costa Rica. You must rent for a minimum of three days to qualify for unlimited mileage.

Economy cars such as the Toyota Yaris begin at about $40 daily, $250 weekly low season; $50 daily, $290 weekly in high season with unlimited mileage. Compact (midsize) cars such as the Toyota Corolla cost about $52 daily, $300 weekly low season; $55 daily, $320 weekly high season with unlimited mileage. Smaller 4WD models such as the Suzuki Sidekick begin at about $65 daily, $380 weekly with unlimited mileage. A midsize 4WD such as the Toyota RAV-4 will cost $75 daily, $400 weekly low season; $80 daily, $480 weekly high season. A full-size 4WD such as the Toyota 4-Runner will cost about $90 daily, $460 weekly low season; $115 daily, $700 weekly high season.

Readers constantly write to report of scams pulled by unscrupulous agencies. Always leave one person with the car when you return it to the car rental office, especially if unforeseen billing problems arise (there are numerous examples of renters having their belongings stolen from the vehicle while their attention is distracted). And thieves have been known to slash tires, or deflate them, while you're picking up or dropping off your car; while you're occupied changing the tire, the thieves pounce and strip your vehicle of its contents, then drive off! If you experience a flat, be suspicious; drive to the nearest secure public place.

Fly-Drive Packages

Discover Costa Rica (tel. 506/2293-8109, www.allcostaricadestinations.com) is an "open voucher" package that includes hotel, breakfast, and 4WD car rental for $38 per person per day.

Motorcycles

María Alexandra Tours (tel. 506/2289-5552, www.costaricamotorcycles.com) rents Harley-Davidsons (from $90 per day, $540 per week). A valid motorcycle license is required, and you must be 25 years old. **Wild Rider Motorcycles** (tel. 506/258-4604, www.wild-rider.com) rents five types of motorcycles.

Motorcycling in Costa Rica is not recommended except for experienced riders, as road conditions can be challenging. Organized tours are another option, offered by the following companies: **Wild Rider** (tel. 506/2258-4604, www.wild-rider.com); **Tour's María Alexandra** (tel. 506/2289-5552, www.costaricamotorcycles.com); **Harley Rentals** (tel. 506/2288-6362, www.harleytourscostarica.com); **Moto-Discovery Tours** (tel. 830/438-7744 or 800/233-0564, www.motodiscovery.com); **MotoAdventures** (tel. 506/2228-8494, in North America tel. 440/256-8508, www.motoadventuring.com); **Costarica-Moto** (tel. 506/2533-1564. www.costarica-moto.com); and **Moto Tours Costa Rica** (tel. 540/980-7675, www.mototourscostarica.com).

Insurance

Insurance is mandatory and you will need to accept the obligatory collision damage waiver (CDW) charged by car rental companies. If you make a reservation through a rental agency abroad and are told the rate includes insurance, or that one of your existing policies will cover it, *get it in writing!* Otherwise, once you arrive in Costa Rica, you may find that you have to pay the mandatory insurance fee on top of your quoted rate. The insurance does not cover your car's contents or personal possessions, nor a deductible. Each company determines its own deductible—ranging $500–1,000—even though the INS sets this at 20 percent of damages.

Rates range from $12 per day for smaller vehicles to $15 daily for larger vehicles.

Inspect your vehicle for damage before departing. Note even the smallest nick and dent on the diagram you'll be presented to sign. Don't forget the inside, as well as the radio antenna, and check that all the switches and buttons function. Don't assume the rental agency has taken care of oil, water, brakes, fluids, or tire pressure: check them yourself before setting off. Most agencies provide 24-hour road service.

Gasoline

Unleaded gasoline is called Super and is universally available. Many service stations *(bombas* or *gasolineras)* are open 24 hours; in rural areas they're usually open dawn to dusk only, and they're often far apart. Gasoline cost about $3.50 per gallon (470 colones a liter) in early 2009. In the boondocks, there's sure to be someone nearby selling from their backyard stock at a premium.

Maps and Directions

The past few years have seen signposts erected in major cities and along major highways, but don't count on a sign being there when you need it. In towns, many signs point the wrong way: they were placed by crews who hadn't the foggiest idea which street was a Calle and which an Avenida. Ticos often use left-pointing arrows to indicate straight ahead.

You'll need the best road map you can obtain. I recommend the *Costa Rica Nature Atlas-Guidebook,* which has detailed 1:200,000 road maps that are mostly accurate, but not entirely.

You can rent GPS from most car rental agencies, and from **506 Travel GPS & Cell Rental** (tel. 506/2440-2740, www.506travelcell.com).

Traffic Police

Traffic police patrol the highways. In the past they've been fond of rental cars (the TUR on rental car license plates gives the game away) in the hope of extorting bribes, although such instances now seem rare. If you're stopped, the police will request to see your license, passport, and rental contract. *Transitos* use radar guns, and you will get no special treatment as a tourist if you're caught speeding. Speeding fines are paid at a bank; the ticket provides instructions. Don't think you can get away with not paying a fine. Delinquent fines are reported to the immigration authorities, and people have been refused exit from the country. Normally, the car rental agency will handle the tickets, although you pay the fine.

Never pay a fine to police on the road. The police cannot legally request payment on-site. If he (I've never seen a female traffic cop) demands payment, note the policeman's name and number from his MOPT badge (he is legally required to show his *carnet* upon request). Report the incident to the **Office for the Reception of Complaints** (Oficina de Recepción de Denuncias, tel. 506/2295-3272 or 506/2295-3273, 24 hours).

Oncoming vehicles will often flash their lights at you to warn you of traffic police—or an accident or disabled vehicle—ahead.

BY RAIL

Railway lines, run from San José to Puntarenas on the Pacific and Puerto Limón on the Caribbean. The **Tico Train Company** (tel. 506/2233-3300, www.ticotraintour.com) offers a four-hour (each way) train ride from San José to Calderas, on the Pacific, departing at 6 A.M. and returning at 3 P.M. and traveling via San Antonio de Belén, Atenas, and Orotina ($25).

TAXIS

Taxis are inexpensive by U.S. standards, so much so that they are a viable means of touring for short trips, especially if you're traveling with two or three others. A white triangle on the front door contains the taxi's license plate number. Taxi drivers are required by law to use their meters *(marías).* Many drivers don't use them. Insist on it being used, as Costa Rican taxi drivers are notorious for overcharging. Don't be afraid to bargain.

Outside San José, you'll usually find taxis around the main square of small towns. Generally, taxis will go wherever a road leads. Most taxis are radio dispatched. Jeep-taxis are common in more remote areas. Outside cities, few taxis are metered and taxi drivers are allowed to negotiate their fare for any journey over 15 kilometers. Check rates in advance with your hotel concierge.

At press time, the government-established fares were 405 colones (about $0.80) for the first kilometer and 380 colones (about $0.75) for each additional kilometer in the metropolitan area and 350 for every kilometer in rural areas. Rates are periodically adjusted and apply 24 hours. You do not have to tip taxi drivers.

FERRIES
Car/passenger ferries link Puntarenas to both Playa Naranjo and Paquera, on the southeastern corner of the Nicoya Peninsula. Water-taxis operate between key destinations within Golfo Dulce.

Visas and Officialdom

DOCUMENTS AND REQUIREMENTS
Passports, Visas, and Tourist Cards
All citizens of the United States, Canada, Western European nations, plus Australia and New Zealand need a valid passport to enter Costa Rica. No visas are required. Tourist cards are issued during your flight or at the immigration desk upon arrival and permit stays of 90 days. Citizens of China and most Asian, Middle Eastern, and African countries are either limited to entry for up to 30 days or need a visa (see www.migracion.go.cr/visas/directrices.doc).

The law requires that you carry your passport or tourist card with you at all times during your stay. Make photocopies of all documentation and keep them with you, separate from the originals. (A recent attempt to crack down on illegal immigration has resulted in many innocent tourists being carted off to jail to face a bureaucratic minefield.)

You can request a **tourist card extension** (*prórroga de turismo*) monthly for up to 60 days ($3) from the immigration office (Migración, tel. 506/2299-8026, www.migracion.go.cr), near Hospital Mexico, in La Uruca (open 8:30 A.M.–3:30 P.M. weekdays) and regional immigration offices around the country. You'll need three passport-size photos, a certified copy of your outbound ticket, a certified copy of *all* pages in your passport, and a written statement of the reason for your extension.

Be sure to begin the process *before* your 30 or 90 days are up. Since you'll need to allow three days minimum—plus an additional four days or more if you are asked to submit to a blood test for AIDS—it may be just as easy to travel to Nicaragua or Panamá for 72 hours and then re-enter with a new visa or tourist card.

If you extend your stay illegally beyond the authorized time, you may be deported (deportees are not allowed back in for 10 years). You will also not be allowed to leave without first obtaining an exit visa ($50), which means a trip back to the immigration office, plus a visit to the Tribunales de Justicia for a document stating you aren't abandoning any offspring or dependents in Costa Rica. Exit visas take 48 hours or more to process; a reputable attorney or tour operator can usually obtain what you need for a small fee.

Immunizations
If you plan on staying beyond the 30 or 90 days, you may be required to show proof of being free from AIDS or its precursor, HIV. The Ministerio de Salud, Ministry of Health, Calle 16, Avenidas 6/8, can oblige.

EMBASSIES
The following embassies are located in San José: **United States** (Blvd. Rohrmoser, tel. 506/2519-2000 ext. 4 or 506/2220-3127 for after-hours emergencies, http://sanjose.usembassy.gov), **Canada** (Oficentro Ejecutivo La Sabana, Edificio 5, Sabana Sur, tel. 506/2242-4400, fax

© CHRISTOPHER P. BAKER

Fuerza publica police

506/2242-4410), and **United Kingdom** (Centro Colón, Paseo Colón, Calles 38/40, tel. 506/2258-2025 or 2225-4049 bccpcr, fax 506/2233-9938, www.britishembassycr.com). Australia and New Zealand have no embassies.

CUSTOMS AND DEPARTURE TAXES

Travelers arriving in Costa Rica are allowed 500 cigarettes or 500 grams of tobacco, plus three liters of wine or spirits. You can also bring in two cameras, binoculars, a personal computer, electrical and video equipment, camping, scuba, and other sporting equipment duty-free.

Travelers exiting Costa Rica by air are charged $26 (or its equivalent in colones), including for residents (no tax is imposed for transit stays of less than 12 hours).

Costa Rica prohibits the export of pre-Columbian artifacts.

Returning Home

U.S. citizens can bring in $600 of purchases duty-free. You may also bring in one quart of spirits plus 200 cigarettes (one carton). Live animals, plants, and products made from endangered species will be confiscated by U.S. Customs. Tissue-cultured orchids and other plants in sealed vials are OK.

Canadian citizens are allowed an "exemption" of C$300 annually (or C$100 per quarter) for goods purchased abroad, plus 1.1 liters of spirits and 200 cigarettes.

U.K. citizens are permitted to import goods worth up to £200, plus 200 cigarettes, 50 cigars, and two liters of spirits.

Australian citizens may import A$400 of goods, plus 250 cigarettes or 50 cigars, and 1.125 liters of spirits. New Zealand citizens can import NZ$700 worth of goods, 200 cigarettes or 50 cigars, and 1.125 liters of spirits.

Drugs

Trying to smuggle drugs through customs is not only illegal, it's stupid. Trained dogs are employed to sniff out contraband at U.S. airports as well as at Juan Santamaría Airport.

CROSSING INTO NICARAGUA AND PANAMÁ

You cannot cross into Nicaragua or Panamá with a rental car. You can only do so with your own vehicle. If it has Costa Rican plates, you'll need a special permit from the **Registro Nacional** (tel. 506/2202-0800, www.registronacional.go.cr). It's good for 15 days and must be obtained in person from the main office in Curridabat, San José (there's also a Registro Nacional in Liberia).

Visa requirements are always in flux, so check in advance with the Nicaraguan or Panamanian embassy.

Nicaragua
OFFICIALDOM

Citizens of Canada, the United States, and most European and Central and South American nations do not need visas to enter Nicaragua. A **tourist visa** is issued at the border ($10 weekdays, $11 weekends, good for three months).

You can cross into Nicaragua for 72 hours and renew your 30- or 90-day Costa Rican visa if you want to return to Costa Rica and stay longer. A 72-hour transit visa for Nicaragua costs $1.

BORDER CROSSINGS

Peñas Blancas: Most people arriving from Nicaragua do so at Peñas Blancas, in northwest Costa Rica. This is a border post, not a town. The Costa Rican and Nicaraguan posts are contiguous. The border (Costa Rican Immigration, tel. 506/677-0064) is open 6 A.M.–8 P.M. daily. There are no signs telling you how to negotiate the complicated procedures; hence touts will rush up to you offering assistance when you arrive at Peñas Blancas. First you must get an exit form, which you complete and return with your passport. Then walk 600 meters to the border, where your passport will be validated (it must have at least six months remaining before it expires). On the Nicaraguan side, go to the immigration building, where you'll pay $7 for a 30-day tourist visa, plus $1 municipal stamp (plus $22 for your car, if driving). Then complete a customs declaration sheet, present it with your passport, and proceed to the customs inspection (next building along). Then take your papers to the gate for final inspection.

The wait in line can be several hours. Count on at least an hour for the formalities, and be sure to have *all* required documents in order or you may as well get back on the bus to San José.

Cross-border buses ($0.75) depart from here every hour for Rivas, a small town about 40 kilometers north of the border. *Colectivo* (shared) taxis also run regularly between the border and Rivas, the nearest Nicaraguan town with accommodations. Buses fill fast—get there early.

The bus terminal contains the **Oficina de Migración** (immigration office, tel. 506/2679-9025), a bank, restaurant, and **Costa Rican Tourism Institute** (ICT, tel. 506/2677-0138). Change money before crossing into Nicaragua (you get a better exchange rate on the Costa Rican side).

Transportes Deldú buses (tel. 506/2256-9072) depart San José for La Cruz and Peñas Blancas from Calle 20, Avenidas 1/3, at 5 A.M., 7 A.M., 7:45 A.M., 9:30 A.M., 10:45 A.M., 1:20 P.M., and 4:10 P.M. daily, en route to the Nicaraguan border (six hours, $5). Buses depart Peñas Blancas for San José at 5 A.M., 7:15 A.M., 10:30 A.M., 10:40 A.M., 1:30 P.M., 2:45 P.M., and 3:30 P.M.

Southbound, you may be required to pay an exit fee ($2) leaving Nicaragua, plus $1 stamp (the Costa Rica tourist card is free). If you're asked for proof of onward ticket when entering Costa Rica, you can buy a bus ticket—valid for 12 months—back to Nicaragua at the bus station at Peñas Blancas. If driving south, your car will be fumigated upon entering Costa Rica ($4).

Los Chiles: In late 2008, plans were announced for a border crossing to be established at Tablillas, seven kilometers north of Los Chiles, where there's an immigration office (by the wharf, tel. 506/2471-1233, 8 A.M.–6 P.M. daily). Meanwhile, foreigners can cross into Nicaragua by a *colectivo* (shared water-taxi) that departs Los Chiles for San Carlos de Nicaragua at 11 A.M. (it departs when full, which often isn't until 1:30 P.M.) and 2:30 P.M. daily ($10 pp).

BUSES

Northbound, **Ticabus** (Avenida 3, Calles 26/28, tel. 506/2248-9636 reservations, tel. 506/2223-8680 terminal, www.ticabus.com) has express service from San José to Nicaragua ($32) and El Salvador ($58) at 3 A.M.; and "regular" service for Nicaragua ($21), El Salvador ($53), and Guatemala ($74) at 6 A.M., 7:30 A.M., and 12 P.M. **Transnica** (Calle 22, Avenidas 3/5, tel. 506/2223-4242, www.transnica.com) has express service from San José to Nicaragua ($40) daily at noon and for El Salvador ($80) at 4 A.M., plus regular service for Nicaragua ($20) at 4 A.M., 5:30 A.M., 7 A.M., and 9 A.M.

Southbound, **Ticabus** (tel. 505/222-6094) buses depart Managua daily at 6 A.M., 7 A.M., and noon (regular); and **Transnica Bus** departs Managua daily at 5:30 A.M., 7 A.M., 10 A.M., and 3 P.M. (regular), plus noon (express).

Panamá

OFFICIALDOM

Citizens of Canada, the United States, and most European and Central and South American nations do not need visas to enter Panamá. A **tourist visa** is issued at the border ($5, good for 30 days).

BORDER CROSSINGS

Paso Canoas: The main crossing point is on the Pan-American Highway. The border posts have been open 24 hours, but are subject to change (at press time, they were open 6 A.M.–10 P.M.). If you don't have a ticket out of the country, you can buy a Tracopa bus ticket in David to Paso Canoas and back. A bus terminal on the Panamanian side offers service to David, the nearest town (90 minutes), every hour or two until 7 P.M. Buses leave from David for Panamá City (last bus 5 P.M.; seven hours). Panamanian border guards may require proof that you have a ticket out of the country; there have been reports of disreputable guards at Paso Canoas causing problems for tourists. It's best to buy your return ticket in advance in Costa Rica.

First, get a Costa Rica exit visa from *migración* (tel. 506/2732-2150) by the Tracopa bus terminal 400 meters west of the border post, where you can buy your Panama tourist card. No rental vehicles are permitted, and private cars are usually fumigated ($4). Still, it's very easy to accidentally drive through this border post without realizing it. The post is crowded, confusing, and has no barriers. I've done it twice, and no one stopped me. Simply turn around and drive back!

Sixaola: This rather squalid village on the Caribbean coast sits on the north bank of the Río Sixaola. Its counterpart is Guabito, on the Panamanian side of the river. The two are linked by a bridge. The Costa Rican Customs and Immigration offices (tel. 506/2754-2044; open 7 A.M.–5 P.M.) are on the west end of the bridge. Panamá is one hour ahead. Hence, the Panamanian office (tel. 507/759-7952), on the east end of the bridge, is open 8 A.M.–6 P.M.

Minibuses operate a regular schedule from Guabito to Changuinola (16 km) and Almirante (30 km). Taxis are available at all hours to Changuinola ($5), from where you can take a water-taxi to Bocas del Toro ($5) or fly or catch a bus onward to the rest of Panama.

Río Sereno: There's another crossing between Costa Rica and Panamá, at the remote mountain border post of Río Sereno east of San Vito, in the Pacific southwest. The Costa Rican Immigration (tel. 506/2784-0130) and Panamanian Immigration (tel. 507/722-8054) are 50 meters apart and open 8 A.M.–5 P.M. daily.

BUSES

Southbound, **Tracopa** (tel. 506/2221-4214, www.tracopacr.com) express buses from Avenida 5, Calle 14 in San José for Paso Canoas at 5 A.M., 1 P.M., and 6:30 P.M., and for David in Panamá at 7:30 A.M. ($9, eight hours). Northbound, **Tracopa** express buses depart David at 8:30 A.M.

Ticabus (tel. 506/2248-9636 reservations, tel. 506/2223-8680 terminal, www.ticabus.com) buses depart Avenida 4, Calles 9/11 in San José for Panamá City daily at 11 P.M. (executive,

$37) and noon (regular, $26). Return buses (tel. 507/314-6385) depart Panamá City at 11 A.M. (executive) and 11 P.M. (regular).

Transporte Mepe (tel. 506/2257-8129) buses depart the Gran Caribe terminal in San José for Sixaola and to Changuinola daily at 10 A.M. ($10, eight hours). Return buses depart Changuinola at 10 A.M.

Conduct and Customs

It is a rare visitor to the country who returns home unimpressed by the Costa Ricans' cordial warmth and hospitality. However, Ticos have a hard time speaking forthrightly. They can't say "no!" They'd prefer to tell you what they think you might want to hear, rather than the truth. Thus, when a Tico makes a promise, don't expect him or her to come through, to show up for a date or appointment, or even to return a call. And don't expect an apology! You usually receive an excuse. Ticos have been called icebergs, for their tendency to conceal the real meaning of what they say or feel below the surface.

Nor should you count on a Tico's punctuality. Most businesses are efficient and operate *hora americana,* punctually, but many other Ticos, particularly in government institutions, still tick along on turtle-paced *hora tica.* "*¿Quien sabe?*" ("Who knows?") is an oft-repeated phrase. So too "*¡Tal vez!*" ("Perhaps!") and, of course, "*¡Mañana!*" ("Tomorrow!").

Making friends with Ticos usually takes considerably longer than it does in North America or the U.K., for example. Family bonds are so strong that foreigners often find making intimate friendships a challenge.

Young female travelers should be prepared to receive *piropos*—effulgent, romantic, but often vulgar, compliments. Dressing conservatively can help thwart unwanted advances. Since 2005, it has been illegal for men to pay unwelcome compliments to women on the street.

FESTIVALS, EVENTS, AND HOLIDAYS

Local fiestas called *turnos* are found nationwide, notably in Guanacaste and Nicoya, highlighted by rodeos, fireworks, and firecrackers *(bombetas).* Individual towns also celebrate their patron saint's day: Highlights usually include a procession, benign bullfights, rodeos, dancing, and parades. The *Tico Times* (www.ticotimes.net) provides weekly listings of festivals and events nationwide. The website www.whereincostarica.com is another excellent resource.

Costa Rica is a Catholic country, and its holidays *(feriados)* are mostly religious. Most businesses, including banks, close on official holidays. The country closes down entirely during the biggest holiday time, Easter Holy Week *(semana santa),* Wednesday through Sunday—a good time to see colorful religious processions. Buses don't run on Holy Thursday or Good Friday. Banks and offices are closed. And hotels and rental cars are booked solid months in advance as everyone heads for the beach. Avoid the popular beaches during Easter week. Most Ticos now take the whole Christmas *(navidad)* holiday week through New Year as an unofficial holiday.

Official Holidays

January 1	New Year's Day
March/April	Easter Week
April 11	Juan Santamaría Day
May 1	Labor Day
May 29	Corpus Christi Day
July 25	Annexation of Guanacaste Day
August 15	Mother's Day
September 15	Independence Day
November 2	All Soul's Day
December 25	Christmas Day

Festivals and Events
JANUARY
Alajuelita: **Fiesta Patronales.** Parade and pilgrimage (week of January 15).

ETHICAL TOURISM

- Travel with a spirit of humility and a genuine desire to meet and talk with local people.

- Be aware of the feelings of others. Act respectfully and avoid offensive behavior.

- Cultivate the habit of actively listening and observing rather than merely hearing and seeing. Avoid the temptation to "know all the answers."

- Realize that others may have concepts of time, and attitudes that are different – not inferior – to those you inherited from your own culture.

- Instead of looking only for the exotic, discover the richness of another culture and way of life.

- Learn local customs and respect them.

- Remember that you are only one of many visitors. Do not expect special privileges.

- When bargaining with merchants don't take advantage of the poor. Pay a fair price.

- Keep your promises to people you meet. If you cannot, do not make the promise.

- Spend time each day reflecting on your experiences in order to deepen your understanding. Is your interaction beneficial for all involved?

- Be aware of why you are traveling in the first place. If you truly want a "home away from home," why travel?

Palmares: Folk dances, music, rodeos (early January).

Santa Cruz: **Fiestas de Santa Cruz.** Folk dances, music, rodeos, bullfights (week of January 15).

FEBRUARY

Puntarenas: **Carnival.** Parade floats, music, and dancing (first two weeks).

San Isidro de El General: Agricultural fair, bullfights, floral exhibits.

MARCH

Escazú: **Día del Boyeros.** Oxcart parade with music, dancing, and competitions (second Sunday).

Cartago: Holy pilgrimage to Ujarrás (mid-month).

Playa Chiquita: **Caribbean Music Festival.**

San José: **National Orchid Show.**

APRIL

Alajuela: **Juan Santamaría Day.** Parade with marching bands (April 11).

San José: **University Week.** Concerts, exhibits, parades (final week).

San José: **Festival de Salsa.** Concerts, dance parties.

MAY

Puerto Limón: **May Day.** Cricket matches, music, and dancing (May 1).

Zarcero: **Tourist Fair** (mid-month).

JUNE

Monteverde: **Tourist Fair** (late June).

JULY

Liberia and Santa Cruz: **Guanacaste Day.** Folkloric dancing, music, rodeos, and bullfights (July 25).

Puntarenas: **Virgin of the Sea Festival.** Boat regatta, parades, music, fireworks (Saturday closest to July 16).

AUGUST

Cartago: **Día del Virgén de los Angeles.** Religious processions (August 2).

Nationwide: **International Music Festival.** Concerts ranging from classical to jazz.

Turrialba: **National Adventure Tourism Festival.** Competitions and demonstrations of kayaking, rafting, mountain biking (end of month).

Puerto Limón: **Festival Afrocultural.** Celebration of Afro-Caribbean culture.

SEPTEMBER

Nationwide: **Día de Independencia.** Parades, marching bands, music and dance (September 15).

OCTOBER

Puerto Limón: **Carnival.** Music, dancing, parades (mid-month).

Upala: **Fiesta del Maíz.** Parades and music in celebration of corn (maize).

San José: **Feria Indígena.** Celebration of indigenous culture.

NOVEMBER

Nationwide: **All Soul's Day.** Church processions (November 2).

San José: **International Festival of the Arts.** Dance troupes, theater, experimental music, puppets, jazz, folklore, and classical music.

San José: **Oxcart Parade.** *Boyeros* camp and hold a song festival in Parque La Sabana, followed by a parade down Paseo Colón (last Sunday).

Nationwide: **Encuentro Nacional de la Mascarada Tradicional.** Clowns and masks.

DECEMBER

Boruca: **Fiesta de los Negritos.** Costumed dancing (December 8).

Nationwide: **Immaculate Conception.** Fireworks (December 8).

San José: **Festival of Lights.** Parade with floats adorned with lights, plus fireworks (second week).

Nicoya: **Fiesta de la Yegüita.** Processions, bullfights, fireworks, and concerts (December 12).

Nationwide: **Los Posadas.** Caroling house to house (December 15 onwards).

Nationwide: **Topes Caballos.** Horse parades, including downtown San José (December 26).

Boruca: **Fiesta de los Diablitos.** Indian festival, masked dancing, fireworks (December 30).

Accommodations

Accommodations run the gamut from cheap *pensiones,* beachside *cabinas,* and self-catering *apartotels* to rustic jungle lodges, swank mountain lodges, and glitzy resort hotels with casinos. (The term *cabina*—literally, cabin—is a loose term used throughout Costa Rica to designate accommodations, and as often as not refers to hotel rooms as well as true cabins.)

Far too many Costa Rican hoteliers fail to rectify faults with their hotels. Guests who complain about very real problems are often treated with disdain, and many readers have written to complain about threatening behavior by hotel owners or their staff. Failure to honor reservations is another common complaint. If you make a reservation by phone, be sure to follow up by fax (or email), as you may need that paper trail. Discounts or refunds are rarely offered, regardless of circumstances. The

problem spans all price levels, although foreign-owned properties have a better record.

Most hotels supply towels and soap, but unless you're staying in the upscale hotels, you may need to bring your own shampoos, washcloths, and even a sink plug. The cheapest accommodations usually have communal bathrooms and, especially in hot lowland areas, cold-water showers only; often shower units are powered by electric heating elements, which you switch on for the duration of your shower (don't expect steaming-hot water, however). *Beware!* It's easy to give yourself a shock from any metal object nearby—hence the nickname "suicide showers." Where trying to flush your waste paper down the toilet may cause a blockage, waste receptacles are provided for toilet paper. Unhygienic, yes, but use the basket unless you fancy a smelly back-up.

Finca Rosa Blanca Coffee Plantation & Inn, Santa Barbara de Heredia

Rooms in any one hotel can vary dramatically. Don't be afraid of looking at several rooms in a hotel (particularly in budget hotels) before making your decision—this is quite normal and accepted. Ensure that the door is secure and that your room can't be entered through the window.

Reservations

Reservations are strongly advised for dry-season months (Dec.–Apr.). Christmas, Easter week, and weekends are particularly busy. Don't rely on mail to make reservations; it could take several months to confirm. Instead, book online, call direct, send a fax, email, or have your travel agent make reservations for you. It may be necessary to send a deposit, without which your space may be released to someone else. Take a copy of your reservation with you, and reconfirm a few days before arrival.

Rates

Many hotels have separate rates for low ("green") season (May–Oct.) and high season (Nov.–Apr.), often with premium rates during Christmas, New Year, and Easter. Couples requesting a *casa matrimonial* (i.e., wishing to sleep in one bed) will often receive a discount off the normal double rate. A 16.3 percent tax is added to your room bill at most hotels. Some hotels charge extra (as much as 6 percent) for paying by credit card.

Rates are subject to fluctuation. Every attempt has been made to ensure that prices given here are accurate at press time.

ACCOMMODATION TYPES
Apartotels and Villas

A hybrid of hotels and apartment buildings, *apartotels* resemble motels on the European and Australian model and offer rooms with kitchens or kitchenettes (pots and pans and cutlery are provided) and sometimes small suites furnished with sofas and tables and chairs. Weekly and monthly rates are offered. Apartotels are popular with families and Ticos.

Scores of private homes and villas are available for rent nationwide. A good resource is **Escape Villas** (tel. 506/777-5258 or 877/533-8988, www.villascostarica.com).

CERTIFICATE FOR SUSTAINABLE TOURISM

The Certificate for Sustainable Tourism (CST, tel. 506/2299-5800, www.turismo-sostenible.co.cr) seeks to categorize and certify hotels and other tourism entities according to the degree to which they comply to a model of sustainability. Hotels are graded according to environmental, socioeconomic, and other attributes, with 150 variables judged by independent investigators on a level of one to five. Entities are then awarded one to five "leaves" according to the total score. Only five hotels in the country have received the maximum five leaves. Hoteliers have been provided a real incentive to improve their practices, with an eye to earning the maximum leaves and therefore a competitive advantage.

Homestays and Bed-and-Breakfasts

Many Costa Rican families welcome foreign travelers into their homes as paying guests—an ideal way to experience Tico hospitality and to bone up on your Spanish. "Guesthouse" refers to a bed-and-breakfast hotel in a family-run home where you are made to feel like part of the family, as opposed to hotels that include breakfasts in their room rates. Many local hosts advertise in the *Tico Times*.

Bell's Home Hospitality (tel. 506/2225-4752, www.homestay.thebells.org; in the U.S., Dept. 1432, P.O. Box 025216, Miami, FL 33102) lists more than 70 host homes in the residential suburbs of San José, plus a few in outlying towns. Rates are from $30 s, $45 d (dinners $7 per person). The company will match you with an English-speaking family if you wish.

Hotels

Costa Rica's hotels run the gamut from beach resorts, mountain lodges, and haciendas-turned-hotels to San José's plusher options. Many upper-end hotels can hold their own on the international hotel scene. Others can't justify their price: Where this is the case, I've said so.

Small Distinctive Hotels of Costa Rica (tel. 506/2258-0150, www.distinctivehotels.com) is an association of eight of the finest hotels in the country. **Small Unique Hotels** (www.costa-rica-unique-hotels.com), comprising less stupendous but still worthy hotels, attempts to compete. The **Charming Nature Hotels Group** (www.charminghotels.net) is a consortium of small German- and Swiss-owned properties.

Motels

As throughout Latin America, "motels" are explicitly for lovers. Rooms are rented out by the hour. If mirrors over the bed and adult videos are your thing, fine!

Nature Lodges

Costa Rica is richly endowed with mountain and jungle lodges, many in private reserves. Most have naturalist guides and arrange nature hikes, horseback riding, and other activities. Some are relatively luxurious; others are basic.

Cooprena (tel. 506/2290-8646, www.turismoruralcr.com) is a cooperative of rural community organizations that promotes 10 rustic ecolodges. The **Costa Rican Association of Community-Based Rural Tourism** (ACTUAR, tel. 506/2248-9470, www.actuarcostarica.com) is a similar organization representing 27 community groups, most with lodgings.

Hostels

Many backpackers' hostels have opened in recent years; San José has at least one dozen great options, including several super options in converted mansions and 1960s modernist homes.

Hostelling International (the U.S. affiliate of the International Youth Hostel Federation, or IYHF) is represented in Costa Rica by the **Hostel Casa Yoses** (Avenida 8, Calle 41, San José, tel. 506/2234-5486, www.hihostels.com/dba/country-CR.en.htm).

© CHRISTOPHER P. BAKER

The Twentieth Years Suite at Zephyr Palace

CAMPING

Several national parks have basic camping facilities, as do several commercial spots at popular beach sites. Camping is discouraged, and even illegal, on beaches, although that doesn't stop the locals, for whom camping on the beach during national holidays is a tradition.

You'll need a warm sleeping bag and a waterproof tent for camping in the mountains, where you may need permission from local landowners or park rangers before pitching your tent. You'll also need a mosquito net and plenty of bug repellent. Avoid grassy pastures: They harbor chiggers and ticks. And don't camp near riverbanks, where snakes congregate and flash floods may occur.

Theft is a problem. If possible, camp with a group of people so one person can guard the gear.

Food and Drink

COSTA RICAN CUISINE

Costa Rican cuisine is simple and spices are shunned. *Comida típica,* or native cuisine, relies heavily on rice and beans, and "homestyle" cooking predominates. *Gallo pinto,* the national dish of fried rice and black beans, is ubiquitous, including as a breakfast *(desayuno)* staple. Many meals are derivatives, including *arroz con pollo* (rice and chicken) or *arroz con tuna.* At lunch, *gallo pinto* becomes

the *casado* (literally "married"), a cheap set lunch plate of rice and beans supplemented with cabbage-and-tomato salad, fried plantains, and meat. Vegetables do not form a large part of the diet, and when they do, they are usually overcooked.

Food staples include *carne* (beef, sometimes called *bistec*), *pollo* (chicken), and *pescado* (fish). Beef and steaks are quite lean—Costa Rican cattle is grass-fed and flavorful. Still, don't

EATING COSTA RICAN: SOME SPECIALTIES

arreglados – sandwiches or tiny puff pastry stuffed with beef, cheese, or chicken. Greasy!

arroz con pollo – a basic dish of chicken and rice.

casado – set lunch, usually consisting of *arroz* (rice), frijoles (black beans), *carne* (beef), *repollo* (cabbage), and *plátano* (plantain). Avocado *(aguacates)* or egg may also be included.

ceviche – marinated seafood, often chilled, made of *corvina* (sea bass), *camarones* (shrimp), or *conchas* (shellfish). Normally served with lemon, chopped onion, garlic, and sweet red peppers.

chorreados – corn pancakes, often served with sour cream *(natilla)*

elote – corn on the cob, either boiled *(elote cocinado)* or roasted *(elote asado)*

empanadas – turnovers stuffed with beans, cheese, meat, or potatoes

enchiladas – pastries stuffed with cheese and potatoes and occasionally meat

gallo – tortilla sandwiches stuffed with beans, cheese, or meat

gallo pinto – the national dish (literally "spotted rooster"), made of lightly spiced rice and black beans. Traditional breakfast *(desayuno)* or lunch dish. Sometimes includes *huevos fritos* (fried eggs).

olla de carne – soup made of squash, corn, yuca (a local tuber), *chayote* (a local pear-shaped vegetable), *ayote* (a pumpkinlike vegetable), and potatoes

palmitos – succulent hearts of palm, common in salads

patacones – thin slices of deep-fried plantain, a popular Caribbean dish.

pescado ahumado – smoked fish

picadillo – a side dish of ground meat

sopa de mondongo – soup made from tripe

sopa negra – a creamy soup, often with a hard-boiled egg and vegetables soaking in the bean broth

tamales – steamed cornmeal pastries stuffed with corn, chicken, or pork, and wrapped in a banana or corn leaf. A popular Christmas dish.

tortillas – Mexican-style corn pancakes or omelettes

DESSERTS AND SWEETS (*POSTRES Y DULCES*)

cono capuchino – an ice-cream cone topped with chocolate

dulce de leche – a syrup of boiled milk and sugar, also thicker, fudgelike *cajeta* – delicious!

flan – cold caramel custard

mazamorra – cornstarch pudding

melcocha – candy made from raw sugar

milanes – chocolate candies

pan de maíz – sweet cornbread

queque seco – pound cake

torta chilena – multilayered cake filled with *dulce de leche*

---

expect your tenderloin steak *(lomito)* to match its North American counterpart.

Seafood is popular—especially sea bass *(corvina),* mahimahi, shrimp *(camarones),* and lobster *(langosta).* Light and flavorful tilapia (African bass) is increasingly popular, especially served with garlic *(al ajillo).* Marlin and sailfish are regional specialties at local restaurants. They are particularly delicious when prepared with a marinated base of fresh herbs and olive oil, and seared over an open grill to retain the moist flavor. Ceviche is also favored, using the white meat of *corvina* steeped in lemon juice mixed with dill or cilantro and finely cut red peppers. Guanacaste province is particularly noted for its local specialties, such as *sopa de albondigas* (spicy meatball soup, with chopped eggs) and *pedre* (carob beans, pork, chicken, onions, sweet peppers, salt, and mint), plus foods based on corn, such as tortillas.

Sodas, open-air lunch counters, serve inexpensive snacks and meals.

Eating in Costa Rica doesn't present the health problems that plague the unwary traveler elsewhere in Central America, but you need to be cautious. *Always* wash vegetables in water known to be safe. And ensure that you personally peel any fruits you eat; you never know where someone else's hands have been. Otherwise, stick to staples such as bananas and oranges.

In San José, restaurants serve the gamut of international cuisine at reasonable prices. And hoteliers and gourmet chefs are opening restaurants worthy of note in even the most secluded backwaters. On the Caribbean coast, for example, the local cuisine reflects its Jamaican heritage with mouthwatering specialties such as johnnycakes, curried goat, curried shrimp, and pepperpot soup.

Many bars in Costa Rica serve *bocas*—savory tidbits ranging from ceviche to *tortillas con queso* (tortillas with cheese)—with drinks. Some provide them free, as long as you're drinking. Others apply a small charge. Turtle *(tortuga)* eggs are a popular dish in many working-class bars.

Most towns have Saturday-morning street markets *(ferias de agricultor)*. Even the smallest hamlet has its *pulpería* or *abastacedor*—local grocery store.

FRUIT

Costa Rica grows many exotic fruits. The bunches of bright vermilion fruits on the stem found at roadside stalls nationwide are *pejibayes*. You scoop out the boiled avocado-like flesh; its taste is commonly described as falling between that of a chestnut and a pumpkin. The *pejibaye* palm (not to be confused with the *pejibaye*) produces the *palmito* (heart of palm), used in salads. *Guayabas* (guavas) come into season September–November; their pink fruit is used for jams and jellies. The *marañón*, the fruit of the cashew, is also commonly used in *refrescos*. *Mamones* are little green spheres containing grapelike pulp. And those yellow-red, egg-size fruits are *granadillas* (passion fruit). One of my favorites—it comes both sweet and sour—is the star fruit, or *carambeloa*, with the flesh of a grape and the taste of an orange.

Sweet and succulent *sandías* (watermelons) should not be confused with the lookalike *chiverre*, whose "fruit" resembles spaghetti! *Piña* (pineapple) is common. So too are *mélon* (cantaloupe) and mangos. Papayas come in two forms: the round, yellow-orange *amarilla* and the elongated, red-orange *cacho*. *Moras* (blackberries) are most commonly used for fruit sodas.

DRINK

Costa Rica has no national drink, perhaps with the exception of *horchata,* a cinnamon-flavored cornmeal drink. Coffee, of course, is Costa Rica's *grano de oro* (grain of gold). Most of the best coffee is exported. Coffee is traditionally served very strong and mixed with hot milk. When you order coffee with milk *(café con leche),* you'll generally get half coffee, half milk. If you want it black, you want *café sin leche* or *café negro.*

The more popular North American soda pops, such as Pepsi and Coca-Cola, as well as sparkling water (called *agua mineral* or *soda*) are popular and also widely available, as are their Tico equivalents. *Refrescos* refers to energizing fruit sodas and colas. *Batidos* are fruit shakes served with water *(con agua)* or milk *(con leche).*

Sugar finds its way into all kinds of drinks, even water: *agua dulce* is boiled water with brown sugar—energy for field workers. Roadside stalls also sell *pipas*, green coconuts with the tops chopped off. You drink the refreshing cool milk from a straw.

Imported alcohol is expensive in Costa Rica, so stick with the local drinks. Lovers of beer *(cerveza)* are served locally brewed pilsners and lagers that reflect an early German presence in Costa Rica. Imperial and Bavaria are the two most popular brews. Tropical is a low-calorie light beer. Heineken is also brewed here under license. Bavaria makes a flavorful dark beer *(negra)*. Even the poorest *campesino* can afford the native red-eye, *guaro,* a harsh, clear spirit distilled from fermented sugarcane. My favorite drink? *Guaro* mixed with Café Rica, a potent coffee liqueur. The national liquor monopoly also produces vodka and gin (both recommended), rum (so-so), and whiskey (not recommended). Imported whiskeys—Johnnie Walker is popular—are less expensive than other imported liquors, which are expensive.

© CHRISTOPHER P. BAKER

coffee liqueur

Costa Rica even makes its own (unremarkable) wines, sold under the *La Casa Tebar* label, and grown at La Garita by the Vicosa company, which also makes a sparkling wine. Chilean and Argentinian vintages are widely available and inexpensive.

Tips for Travelers

ACCESS FOR TRAVELERS WITH DISABILITIES

Few allowances have been made in infrastructure for travelers with disabilities, although wheelchair ramps are now appearing on sidewalks, and an increasing number of hotels are provisioning rooms and facilities for the physically challenged.

In the U.S., the **Society for Accessible Travel & Hospitality** (347 5th Ave. #610, New York, NY 10016, tel. 212/447-7284, www.sath.org); and the **American Foundation for the Blind** (11 Penn Plaza No 300, New York, NY 10001, tel. 212/502-7600 or 800/232-5463, www.afb.org) are good resources.

Flying Wheels Travel (143 W. Bridge St., Owatanna, MN 55060, tel. 507/451-5005 or 877/451-5006, www.flyingwheelstravel.com) is a travel agency for the physically challenged.

In Costa Rica, **Vaya con Silla de Ruedas** (Go with Wheelchairs; tel./fax 506/2452-2810, www.gowithwheelchairs.com) is a specialized transport service for the ambulatory disabled. It operates a specially outfitted vehicle with three wheelchair stations, has 24-hour service, and offers overnight and multi-day tours. And **The Association of Costa Rican Special Taxis** (tel. 506/2296-6443) operates taxis and vans equipped for the disabled.

TRAVELING WITH CHILDREN

Generally, travel with children poses no special problems, and virtually everything you'll need for children is readily available. There are

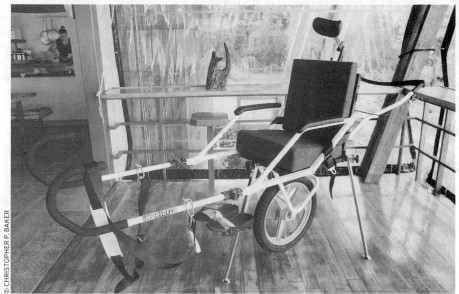

© CHRISTOPHER P. BAKER

handicapped trail-chair at Celeste Mountain Lodge, Tenorio

few sanitary or health problems to worry about. However, ensure that your child has vaccinations against measles and rubella (German measles), as well as any other inoculations your doctor advises. Bring cotton swabs, adhesive bandages, and a small first-aid kit with any necessary medicines for your child. The **Hospital Nacional de Niños** (Children's Hospital, tel. 506/2222-0122), is at Paseo Colón, Calle 14, in San José.

Children under two travel free on airlines; children ages 2–12 are offered discounts (check with individual airlines). Children are also charged half the adult rate at many hotels; others permit free stays when kids are sharing parents' rooms. Baby foods and milk are readily available. Disposable diapers, however, are expensive (consider bringing cloth diapers; they're ecologically more acceptable). If you plan on driving around, bring your child's car seat—they're not offered for rental cars.

Single parents traveling alone with children need a notarized letter of permission from the other parent, otherwise you may not be allowed onto your departing flight.

The **Playa Nicuesa Lodge** (tel. 506/2222-0704 or U.S. tel. 866/504-8116, www.playa-nicuesa.com) specializes in family adventure packages.

Family Friendly Tour Companies

Rascals in Paradise (U.S. tel. 415/921-7000, www.rascalsinparadise.com); **Wildland Adventures** (U.S. tel. 206/365-0686 or 800/345-4453, www.wildland.com); and **Country Walkers** (U.S. tel. 800/464-9255, www.country-walkers.com) offer family trips to Costa Rica.

WOMEN TRAVELING ALONE

Most women enjoy traveling in Costa Rica. The majority of Tico men treat foreign women with great respect. Still, Costa Rica *is a machismo* society and you may experience certain hassles. The art of gentle seduction is to Ticos a kind of national pastime: a sport and a trial of manhood. Men might hiss in appreciation from a distance like serpents, and call out epithets such as *"guapa"* ("pretty one"), *"machita"* (for blondes), or *"mi amor."* Be aware that many Ticos think a gringa is an "easy" *conquista*. The wolf-whistles can grate but, fortunately, sexual assault of female tourists is rare—though it *does* happen.

If you welcome the amorous attentions of men, take effusions of love with a grain of salt; while swearing eternal devotion, your Don Juan may conveniently forget to mention he's married. And when he suggests a nightcap at some romantic locale, he may mean one of San José's love motels. On the Caribbean coast, "Rent-a-Rastas" earn their living giving pleasure to women looking for love beneath the palms. Come prepared! Carry condoms; don't rely on the man.

If you're not interested in love in the tropics, unwanted attention can be a hassle. Pretend not to notice. Avoid eye contact. An insistent stare—*dando cuervo* (making eyes)—is part of their game. You can help prevent these overtures by dressing modestly. There have been reports of a few taxi drivers coming on to women passengers. Though this is the exception, where possible take a hotel taxi rather than a street cab. And beware illegal unmarked "taxis" that may be cruising for single women. Avoid deserted beaches, especially at night.

Women Travel: Adventures, Advice, and Experience, by Niktania Jansz and Miranda Davies (Rough Guides), offers practical advice for women travelers, as does *Gutsy Women,* by Marybeth Bond (Travelers' Tales).

Mariah Wilderness Expeditions (tel. 530/626-6049 or 800/462-7424, fax 530/626-4305, www.mariahwe.com) specializes in trips to Costa Rica for women.

In Costa Rica, **CEFEMINA** (Centro Feminista de Información y Acción, tel. 506/2224-3986, www.cefemina.org) is a feminist organization that can provide assistance to women travelers. The **Women's Club of Costa Rica** (tel. 506/2282-6801, www.wccr.org), an English-speaking social forum, is a good resource, as is the **National Institute of Women** (Instituto Nacional de Las Mujeres, tel. 506/2253-8066, www.inamu.go.cr).

The **Feminist International Radio Network** (FIRE, tel. 506/2249-1319, www.fire.or.cr) broadcasts online at its website.

GAY AND LESBIAN TRAVELERS

On the books, Costa Rica is tolerant of homosexuality and has laws to protect gays from discrimination; despite being a Roman Catholic nation, homosexual intercourse is legal. Still Costa Rica remains a *machismo* society, and 1999 witnessed violently anti-gay demonstrations. That said, things have progressed markedly and there is a general tolerance among educated urbanites. Nonetheless, many gay Costa Ricans prefer to remain in the closet. There is even less tolerance of lesbians.

One of the best resources is www.gaycostarica.com. *Gente 10* (www.gente10.com) is a gay magazine published in Costa Rica.

The destinations most welcoming of gays and lesbians are San José and Manuel Antonio.

Organizations

Useful resources include the **International Gay and Lesbian Association** (tel. 212/620-7310 or 800/421-1220, www.gaycenter.org) and the **International Gay & Lesbian Travel Association** (tel. 954/630-1637, www.iglta.org).

Tours

Colours Destinations (tel. 954/241-7472 or 866/517-4390, www.colours.net) offers tours to Costa Rica. **Journeywoman** (tel. 416/929-7654, www.journeywoman.com) serves the lesbian community.

Odysseus: The International Gay Travel Planner lists worldwide hotels and tours and publishes travel guides for gays and lesbians.

In Costa Rica, try **Gay Travel Costa Rica** (tel. 506/2219-8722, www.costaricagaytraveler.com) and **Gaytours Costa Rica** (tel. 506/8305-8044, www.gaytourscr.com).

STUDENTS AND YOUTHS
Student Cards

An **International Student Identity Card** issued by the International Student Travel Federation (www.istc.org) entitles students

LANGUAGE STUDY

Costa Rica has dozens of language schools. Most programs include homestays with Costa Rican families – a tremendous (and fun) way to boost your language skills and learn the local idioms. Many also feature workshops on Costa Rican culture, dance lessons, and excursions. Courses run an average of 2-4 weeks.

The following language schools are recommended:

Centro Panamericano de Idiomas (tel. 506/2265-6306 or 877/373-3116, www.cpi-edu.com).

Costa Rica Language Academy (tel. 506/2280-1685 or U.S. tel. 866/230-6361, www.spanishandmore.com).

Institute for Central American Development Studies (tel. 506/2225-0508, www.icads.org). Weds Spanish tuition to learning about the politics, social conditions, environmental issues, and politics.

Intensa (tel. 506/2281-1818 or 866/277-1352, www.intensa.com).

Spanish Abroad (tel. 602/778-6791 or 888/722-7623, www.spanishabroad.com). The largest language school in Costa Rica, with nine locals nationwide and classes starting every Monday year-round.

Speak Spanish like a Costa Rican, by Christopher Howard, is a book and 90-minute cassette.

---

12 years and older to discounts on transportation, entrances to museums, and other savings. When purchased in the United States ($20), ISIC even includes $3,000 in emergency medical coverage, limited hospital coverage, and access to a 24 hour, toll-free emergency hotline. Students (and educators under 26) can obtain ISICs at any student union. Alternately, contact the **Council on International Educational Exchange** (tel. 207/553-4000 or 800/40-STUDY, www.ciee.org), which issues ISICs and also arranges study vacations in Costa Rica. In Canada, cards can be obtained from **Travel Cuts** (tel. 416/614-2887 or 866/246-9762, www.travelcuts.com). In the United Kingdom, students can obtain an ISIC from any student union office.

Travel and Work Study

The **University of Costa Rica** offers special *cursos libres* (free courses) during winter break (Dec.–Mar.). It also grants "special student" status to foreigners. Contact the Oficina de Asuntos Internacionales (tel. 506/2207-5080, www.ucr.ac.cr). The **University for Peace** (tel. 506/2205-9000, www.upeace.org), and **Organization for Tropical Studies** (tel. 506/2524-0607, in the U.S., tel. 919/684-5774,

fax 919/684-5661, www.ots.duke.edu) also sponsor study courses. **EcoTeach** (tel. 800/626-8992, www.ecoteach.com) places students on environmental projects in Costa Rica.

Work abroad programs are also offered through **CIEE's Work Abroad Department** (tel. 888/268-6245, www.ciee.org) which publishes *Work, Study, Travel Abroad* and *The High School Student's Guide to Study, Travel, and Adventure Abroad.*

Holbrook Travel (tel. 800/451-7111, www.holbrooktravel.com) offers an eight-day "Tropical Education Program" in Costa Rica for students and teachers. The **School for Field Studies** (tel. 978/741-3567 or 800/989-4418, www.fieldstudies.org) has summer courses in sustainable development.

Transitions Abroad (tel./fax 802/442-4827, www.transitionsabroad.com) provides information for students wishing to study abroad; as does **Studyabroad.com** (tel. 484/766-2920, www.studyabroad.com).

SENIOR TRAVELERS

Useful resources include the **American Association of Retired Persons** (AARP, 888/687-2277, www.aarp.org), whose benefits include a "Purchase Privilege Program" offering discounts on airfares, hotels, car rentals, and more. The AARP also offers group tours for seniors.

Canadian company **ElderTreks** (tel. 416/588-5000 or 800/741-7956, www.eldertreks.com) and **Elderhostel** (tel. 800/454-5768, www.elderhostel.org) offers educational tours to Costa Rica for seniors, including ecological tours in which participants contribute to the welfare of Mother Nature.

Thinking of retiring in Costa Rica? I recommend the "Live or Retire in Paradise Tour" offered by Christopher Howard (tel. 800/365-2342, www.liveincostarica.com), author of *The New Golden Door to Retirement and Living in Costa Rica;* and *Living Abroad in Costa Rica,* by Erin Van Rheenen (www.moon.com/books/living-abroad). The **Association of Residents of Costa Rica** (tel. 506/2233-8068, www.arcr.net) serves the interests of foreign residents as well as those considering living in Costa Rica.

Health and Safety

Sanitary standards in Costa Rica are high, and the chances of succumbing to a serious disease are rare. As long as you take appropriate precautions and use common sense, you're not likely to incur serious illness. If you do, you have the benefit of knowing that the nation has a good health-care system. There are English-speaking doctors in most cities.

BEFORE YOU GO

Dental and medical checkups may be advisable before departing home, particularly if you have an existing medical problem. Take along any medications, including prescriptions for glasses and contact lenses; keep prescription drugs in their original bottles to avoid suspicion at Customs. If you suffer from a debilitating health problem, wear a medical alert bracelet. A basic health kit is a good idea. Pack the following (as a minimum) in a small plastic container: alcohol swabs and medicinal alcohol, antiseptic cream, adhesive bandages, aspirin or painkillers, diarrhea medication, sunburn remedy, antifungal foot powder, calamine, antihistamine, water-purification tablets, surgical tape, bandages and gauze, and scissors.

The U.S. **Centers for Disease Control and Prevention** (tel. 800/232-4636, www.cdc.gov) issues the latest health information and advisories by region. Information on health concerns can be answered by the **Department of State Citizens Emergency Center** (tel. 202/501-4444 or 888/407-4747, http://travel.state.gov),

and the **International Association for Medical Assistance to Travellers** (tel. 716/754-4883, www.iamat.org). In the U.K., you can get information, inoculations, and medical supplies from the **MASTA Travel Clinics** (www.masta-travel-health.com).

An indispensable pocket-sized book is *Staying Healthy in Asia, Africa, and Latin America,* by Dirk G. Schroeder (Avalon Travel Publishing), which is packed with first-aid and basic medical information.

Medical Insurance

Travel insurance is highly recommended. Travel agencies can sell you traveler's health and baggage insurance, as well as insurance against cancellation of a prepaid tour. Travelers should check to see if their health insurance or other policies cover medical expenses while abroad.

The following U.S. companies are recommended for travel insurance: **Travelers** (tel. 888/695-4625, www.travelers.com) and **TravelGuard International** (tel. 800/826-4919, www.travelguard.com). The **Council on International Education Exchange** (CIEE, www.ciee.org) offers insurance to students.

In the U.K., the **Association of British Insurers** (tel. 020/7600-3333, www.abi.org.uk) provides advice for obtaining travel insurance. Inexpensive insurance is offered through **Endsleigh Insurance** (tel. 0800/028-3571, www.endsleigh.co.uk) and **STA Travel** (tel. 0871/230-0400, www.sta.com).

In Australia, **AFTA** (tel. 02/9264-3299, www .afta.com.au) and **Travel Insurance on the Net** (tel. 800/1900-89, www.travelinsurance .com.au) are good resources.

Costa Rica's social security system (Instituto Nacional de Seguros, or INS; also called the Caja) has a Traveler's Insurance program specifically for foreigners. As well as loss or theft of possessions, it covers emergency medical treatment (hospitalization and surgery, plus emergency dental treatment are covered; services for pre-existing conditions are not), plus repatriation of a body. You can choose coverage between 500,000 and 10 million *colones* for up to 12 weeks. You can buy coverage at travel agencies or the Instituto Nacional de Seguros (tel. 506/2287-6000, www.ins.go.cr).

Vaccinations

No vaccinations are required to enter Costa Rica. Epidemic diseases have mostly been eradicated throughout the country. Consult your physician for recommended vaccinations. Travelers planning to rough it should consider vaccinations against tetanus, typhoid, and infectious hepatitis.

MEDICAL SERVICES

In **emergencies,** call 911. Alternately, call 128 for the Red Cross, which provides ambulance service nationwide.

The state-run Social Security system (INS, or the Caja) operates full-service hospitals and clinics nationwide. Foreigners receive the same emergency service as Costa Ricans in public hospitals, and no one is turned away in an emergency (however, a $39 fee applies; a typical overnight with care costs about $350).

Private hospitals offer faster and superior treatment than public hospitals (a large deposit may be requested on admittance). Private doctor visits usually cost $25–50. Hospitals and clinics accept credit card payment. U.S. insurance is not normally accepted, but you can send your bill to your insurance company for reimbursement.

Pharmacies (*farmacias*) are well stocked. Every community has at least one pharmacy (*farmacia* or *botica*).

Medical Evacuation

Traveler's Emergency Network (tel. 800/275-4836, www.tenweb.com) and **International SOS Assistance** (tel. 713/521-7611 or 800/523-8930, www.internationalsos.com) provide worldwide ground and air evacuation and medical assistance, plus access to medical facilities around the world. Swiss-based **Assist-Card** (in the U.S. tel. 305/381-9959 or 800/874-2223, www.assist-card.com), with offices worldwide, provides emergency services, including arranging doctor's visits to your hotel and even emergency evacuation.

Many medical and travel insurance companies also provide emergency evacuation coverage.

HEALTH PROBLEMS
Infection

Even the slightest scratch can fester quickly in the tropics. Treat cuts promptly and regularly with antiseptic and keep the wound clean.

Hepatitis is epidemic throughout Central America, although only infrequently reported in Costa Rica. Main symptoms are stomach pains, loss of appetite, yellowing skin and eyes, and extreme tiredness. Hepatitis A is contracted through unhygienic foods or contaminated water (salads and unpeeled fruits are major culprits). A gamma globulin vaccination is recommended. The much rarer hepatitis B is usually contracted through unclean needles, blood transfusions, or unprotected sex.

Intestinal Problems

Water is safe to drink almost everywhere, although more remote rural areas, as well as Escazú, Santa Ana, Puntarenas, and Puerto Limón, are suspect. To play it safe, drink bottled mineral water (*agua mineral* or *soda*). Remember, ice cubes are water, too. And don't brush your teeth using suspect water.

Food hygiene standards in Costa Rica are generally high. However, the change in diet— which may alter the bacteria that are normal and necessary in the bowel—may cause temporary **diarrhea** or **constipation.** Most cases of diarrhea are caused by microbial bowel infections resulting from contaminated food.

Common-sense precautions include not eating uncooked fish or shellfish, uncooked vegetables, unwashed salads, or unpeeled fruit.

Diarrhea is usually temporary and many doctors recommend letting it run its course. Personally, I like to plug myself up straightaway with Lomotil. Treat diarrhea with rest and lots of liquid to replace the water and salts lost. Avoid alcohol and milk products. If conditions persist, seek medical help.

Diarrhea accompanied by severe abdominal pain, blood in your stool, and fever is a sign of **dysentery.** Seek immediate medical diagnosis. Tetracycline or ampicillin is normally used to cure bacillary dysentery. More complex professional treatment is required for amoebic dysentery. The symptoms of both are similar. **Giardiasis,** acquired from infected water, causes diarrhea, bloating, persistent indigestion, and weight loss. Again, seek medical advice. **Intestinal worms** can be contracted by walking barefoot on infested beaches, grass, or earth.

Sunburn and Skin Problems

Don't underestimate the tropical sun! It's intense and can burn you through light clothing or while you're lying in the shade. *Use a sunscreen or sunblock*—at least SPF 15 or higher. Zinc oxide provides almost 100 percent protection. Use an aloe gel after sunbathing. Calamine lotion and aloe gel will soothe light burns; for more serious lobster-pink burns, use steroid creams.

Sun glare—especially prevalent if you're on water—can cause **conjunctivitis** (eye infection). Sunglasses will protect against this. **Prickly heat** is an itchy rash, normally caused by clothing that is too tight and/or in need of washing. This, and **athlete's foot,** are best treated by airing out the body and washing your clothes.

Drink plenty of water to avoid dehydration. Leg cramps, exhaustion, and headaches are possible signs of dehydration.

Snakebite

Snakes are common in Costa Rica. Fewer than 500 snakebites are reported each year, and less than 3 percent of these are fatal. The majority of bites occur from people stepping on snakes. Always watch where you're treading or putting your hands. Never reach into holes or under rocks, debris, or forest-floor leaf litter without first checking with a stick to see what might be slumbering there. Be particularly wary in long grass. Avoid streams at night. Many snakes are well-camouflaged arboreal creatures that snooze on branches, so never reach for a branch without looking. If you spot a snake, keep a safe distance, and give the highly aggressive fer-de-lance a very wide berth.

If bitten, seek medical attention without delay. Rural health posts and most national park rangers have antivenin kits on-site. Commercial snakebite kits are normally good only for the specific species for which they were designed, so it will help if you can definitively identify the critter. But don't endanger yourself further trying to catch it.

If the bite is to a limb, immobilize the limb and apply a tight bandage between the bite and body. Release it for 90 seconds every 15 minutes. Ensure you can slide a finger under the bandage; too tight and you risk further damage. Do *not* cut the bite area in an attempt to suck out the poison. Recommendations to use electric shock as snakebite treatment have gained popular favor recently in Costa Rica; do *not* follow this medically discredited advice.

Insects and Arachnids

Spiders, scorpions, no-see-ums... It's enough to give you the willies! Check your bedding before crawling into bed, which you should move away from the wall if possible. Always shake out your shoes and clothing before putting them on. Repellent sprays and lotions are a must, especially in jungle, marshy areas, and coastal lowlands.

Bites can easily become infected in the tropics, so avoid scratching. A baking soda bath can help relieve itching if you're badly bitten, as can antihistamine tablets, hydrocortisone, and calamine lotion. Long-sleeved clothing and full-length pants help keep insects at bay.

Chiggers *(coloradillas)* inhabit grasslands,

particularly in Guanacaste. Their bites itch like hell. Mosquito repellent won't deter them. Dust your shoes, socks, and ankles with sulphur powder. Sucking sulphur tablets *(azufre sublimado)* apparently gives your sweat a smell that chiggers find obnoxious. Nail polish apparently works, too (on the bites, not the nails) by suffocating the beasts.

Ticks *(garrapatas)* hang out near livestock. They bury their heads into your skin. Remove them immediately with tweezers—grasp the tick's head parts as close to your skin as possible and pull gently but steadily.

Tiny, irritating **no-see-ums** (sandflies about the size of a pinpoint, and known locally as *purrujas*) inhabit many beaches and marshy coastal areas: avoid beaches around dusk. They're not fazed by bug repellent with DEET, but Avon's Skin-So-Soft works a treat. Sandflies on the Atlantic coast can pass on leishmaniasis, a debilitating disease: Seek urgent treatment for non-healing sores.

If stung by a **scorpion** *(alacrán)*—not normally as bad as it sounds—take plenty of liquids and rest. If you're unfortunate enough to contract **scabies** (a microscopic mite) or **lice,** which is possible if you're staying in unhygienic conditions or sleeping with unhygienic bedfellows, use a body shampoo containing gamma benzene hexachloride. You should also wash all clothing and bedding in very hot water, and toss out your underwear. The severe itching caused by scabies infestation appears after three or four weeks (it appears as little dots, often in lines, ending in blisters, especially around the genitals, elbows, wrists, lower abdomen, and nipples).

Avoid **bees'** nests. Africanized bees have infiltrated Costa Rica. They're very aggressive and will attack with little provocation.

Many bugs are local. The bite of a rare kind of insect found along the southern Caribbean coast and locally called *papalamoya* produces a deep and horrible infection that can even threaten a limb. It may be best to have such infections treated locally (and certainly promptly); doctors back home (or even in San José) might take forever to diagnose and treat the condition.

AIDS and Sexually Transmitted Diseases

AIDS is on the rise throughout Central America. Avoidance of casual sexual contact and/or use of condoms are the best prevention against contracting sexually transmitted diseases.

Malaria

Malaria is a limited risk in the lowlands, although an increase in the incidence of malaria has been reported in the Caribbean lowlands, south of Cahuita (the majority of cases are among banana plantation workers). Consult your physician for the best type of antimalarial medication. Begin taking your tablets a few days (or weeks, depending on the prescription) before arriving in an infected zone, and continue taking the tablets for several weeks after leaving the malarial zone. Malaria symptoms include high fever, shivering, headache, and sometimes diarrhea.

Chloroquine (called Alaren in Costa Rica) and Fansidar are both used for short-term protection. Chloroquine reportedly is still good for Costa Rica, although Panamanian mosquitoes have built up a resistance to the drug. Fansidar may be a safer bet for travel south of Puerto Limón. Fansidar can cause severe skin reactions and is dangerous for people with a history of sulfonamide intolerance.

Avon Skin-So-Soft oil is such an effective bug repellent that U.S. Marines use it by the truckload ("Gee, private, you sure smell nice, and your skin's so soft!"). The best mosquito repellents contain DEET (diethylmetatoluamide). Use mosquito netting at night in the lowlands; you can obtain good hammocks and "no-see-um" nets in the U.S. from **Campmor** (tel. 800/226-7667, www.campmor.com). A fan over your bed and mosquito coils *(espirales)* also help keep mosquitoes at bay. Coils are available from *pulperías* and supermarkets (don't forget the metal stand—*soporte*—for them).

Other Problems

Occasional and serious outbreaks of **dengue fever** have occurred in recent years, notably around Puntarenas and along the Caribbean coast and the Golfito region. Transmitted by mosquitoes, the illness can be fatal (death usually results from internal hemorrhaging). Its symptoms are similar to malaria, with additional severe pain in the joints and bones (it is sometimes called "breaking bones disease") but, unlike malaria, is not recurring.

Rabies, though rare, can be contracted through the bite of an infected dog or other animal. It is always fatal unless treated. If you're sleeping in the open (or with an unscreened window open) in areas with vampire bat, don't leave your flesh exposed. Their bite, containing both anesthetic and anticoagulant, is painless.

SAFETY CONCERNS

With common sense, you are no more likely to run into problems in Costa Rica than you are in your own backyard. The vast majority of Costa Ricans are honest and friendly. However, burglary is rampant and crimes against tourists have risen alarmingly in recent years; although most take place in and around San José, violent crimes against tourists are increasingly occurring in major tourist destinations. *Passport theft is also a serious problem;* more U.S. passports were stolen in Costa Rica in 2005—some 783 between January and June—than anywhere else in the world. Car break-ins have become a pandemic along the Nicoya shoreline, particularly at the most popular surf beaches. And one-third of thefts reported by tourists occurred on public transportation.

In San José, use common big-city sense. In addition, don't ride buses at night, be careful in parks, and watch for traffic at all times. Outside the city, you need to be savvy to some basic precautions. Hikers straying off trails can easily lose their way amid the rainforests. And don't approach too close to an active volcano, such as Arenal, which may suddenly explode. Atop mountains, sunny weather can turn cold and rainy in seconds, so dress accordingly. And be extra cautious when crossing rivers; a rainstorm upstream can turn the river downstream into a raging torrent without any warning.

If Things Go Wrong

The **Fuerza Pública** (uniformed police), based in most communities, provide patrols and detention. The **Organismo de Investigación Judicial** (OIJ, Judicial Investigative Agency) investigates crime.

In an emergency, call 911 for an English-speaking operator, or:

Police, tel. 506/2222-1365

Fire, tel. 118

Ambulance, tel. 119

If things go wrong, contact the **Victims Assistance Office** (tel. 506/2295-3271 or 506/2295-3643, 7:30 A.M.–noon and 1–4 P.M. Mon.–Fri.), in the OIJ building, Avenidas 4/6, Calles 15/17, in San José You might also contact your embassy or consulate. Consulate officials can't get you out of jail, but they can help you locate a lawyer, alleviate unhealthy conditions, or arrange for funds to be wired if you run short of money. They can even authorize a reimbursable loan—the U.S. Department of State hates to admit it—while you arrange for cash to be forwarded, or even lend you money to get home. Don't expect the U.S. embassy to bend over backward; it's notoriously unhelpful. The *Handbook of Consular Services* (Public Affairs Staff, Bureau of Consular Affairs, U.S. Department of State, Washington, D.C. 20520) provides details of such assistance. Friends and family can also call the Department of State's **Overseas Citizen Service** (tel. 888/407-4747, from overseas tel. 202/501-4444, www.travel.state.gov) to check on you if things go awry. The **U.S. State Department** (www.state.gov) also publishes travel advisories warning U.S. citizens of trouble spots. The **British Foreign & Commonwealth Office** (tel. 020/7008-1500, www.fco.gov.uk) has a similar service.

To report issues relating to drugs, contact the **Policía de Control de Drogas** (tel. 800/376-4266, www.msp.go.cr/pcdold). Report theft or demands for money by traffic police to the **Ministry of Public Works and Transportation** (Ministerio de Obras Públicas y Transportes, Calle 9, Avenidas 20/22, tel. 506/2227-2188 or 2523-3000). For complaints about the police,

PROSTITUTION

Prostitution is legal in Costa Rica, drawing male tourists whose presence has earned Costa Rica a controversial reputation. Many Costa Rican men use prostitutes as a matter of course, and almost every town and village has a brothel – San José has dozens. The government issues licenses for brothels and prostitutes. Statistics suggest that most of the estimated 15,000 prostitutes who work nationwide are not registered. Many fall into the profession after a childhood of trauma and sexual abuse – a widespread problem within Costa Rican society (as many as 30 percent of female students at the University of Costa Rica say they were sexually abused as children).

Sex is legal at the age of 16 in Costa Rica but prostitution under 18 is not, and under Costa Rican and international law, foreigners can be prosecuted for having sex with anyone under 18. The issue hit the fan in December 2000 after ABC's *20/20* television program ran an exposé claiming that Costa Rica had an epidemic of child-sex tourism (estimates suggest that as many as 3,000 prostitutes nationwide may be underage). Several foreigners have been jailed for operating brothels or Internet prostitution rings involving minors.

The Costa Rican government has launched a major campaign to eradicate child prostitution and to prosecute foreigners having sexual relations with minors. The **Patronato Nacional de la Infancia** (tel. 506/2523-0700, www.pani.go.cr) is a government-sponsored organization to fight sexual exploitation of children. **Fundación Paniamor** (tel. 506/2234-2993, www.paniamor.or.cr) is a tourism community organization that works to eradicate sex with minors.

Casa Luz (tel. 506/2255-3322, in the U.S., c/o Samaritan's Purse, tel. 800/665-2843, www.casaluz.org) is a home for young mothers who have been physically and/or sexually abused and are at high social risk. By providing shelter, emotional support, educational and vocational development, parental skills, and spiritual counseling, the goal is for the young mothers and their children to be able to live socially healthy lives. It is run by a nonprofit association operated by the owners of the Hotel Grano de Oro, San José. Donations are requested.

If you know of anyone who is traveling to Costa Rica with the intent of sexually abusing minors, contact **Interpol** (children@interpol.int, www.interpol.int); the **Task Force for the Protection of Children from Sexual Exploitation in Tourism** (www.world-tourism.org); or the **U.S. Customs Service's International Child Pornography Investigation and Coordination Center** (tel. 800/843-5678, www.cybertipline.com).

---

contact the **Office for the Reception of Complaints** (tel. 506/2295-3643, 24 hours).

Theft

Costa Rica's many charms can lull visitors into a false sense of security. Like anywhere else, the country has its share of social ills, with rising street crime among them. An economic crisis and influx of impoverished refugees has spawned a growing band of petty thieves and purse-slashers. Violent crime, including armed holdups and muggings, is on the rise. Still, most crime is opportunistic, and thieves seek easy targets. Don't become paranoid, but a few common-sense precautions are in order.

The Instituto Costarricense de Turismo publishes a leaflet—*Let's Travel Safe*—listing precautions and a selection of emergency phone numbers. It's given out free at airport immigration counters. The ICT operates a 24-hour toll-free tourist information line (tel. 800/012-3456) for emergencies.

Make photocopies of all important documents: your passport, airline ticket, credit cards, insurance policy, driver's license. Carry the photocopies with you, and leave the originals in the hotel safe if possible. If this isn't possible, carry the originals with you in a secure inside pocket. Don't put all your eggs in one basket! Prepare an "emergency kit," to include photocopies of your documents and an adequate sum of money in case your wallet gets stolen. If you're robbed, immediately file a police report. You'll need this to make an insurance claim.

Don't wear jewelry, chains, or expensive watches. They mark you as a wealthy tourist. Wear an inexpensive digital watch. Never carry more cash than you need for the day. The rest should be kept in the hotel safe. For credit card security, insist that imprints are made in your presence. Make sure any incorrectly completed imprints are torn up. Destroy the carbons yourself. Don't let store merchants or anyone else walk off with your card. Keep it in sight!

Never leave your purse, camera, or luggage unattended in public places. Always keep a wary eye on your luggage. And never carry your wallet in your back pocket. Carry your bills in your front pocket beneath a handkerchief. Carry any other money in a money belt, inside pocket, a "secret" pocket sewn into your pants or jacket, or in a body pouch or an elastic wallet below the knee. Spread your money around your person.

Don't carry more luggage than you can adequately manage. Limit your baggage to one suitcase or duffel. And have a lock for each luggage item. Purses should have a short strap (ideally, one with metal woven in) that fits tightly against the body and snaps closed or has a zipper. Always keep purses fully zipped and luggage locked.

Don't trust locals to handle your money. And don't exchange money before receiving the services or goods you're paying for.

Be particularly wary after cashing money at a bank. And be cautious at night, particularly if you intend to walk on beaches or park trails, which you should do with someone trusted wherever possible. Stick to well-lit main streets in towns.

Don't leave anything of value within reach of an open window. Make sure you have bars on the window and that your room is otherwise secure (bringing your own lock for the door is a good idea). And don't leave anything of value in your car. Don't leave tents or cars unguarded. Be especially cautious if you have a flat tire, as many robberies involve unsuspecting tourists who are robbed while changing a tire by the roadside. The ICT advises driving to the nearest gas station or other secure site to change the tire. And never permit a Costa Rican male to sit in the back seat of a taxi while you're in the front; there have been several reports of robberies in taxis in which the driver has worked in cahoots with an accomplice, who strangles the victim from behind.

A few uniformed policemen are less than honest, and tourists occasionally get shaken down for money. *Never* pay money to a police officer. If you are stopped by one who wants to see your passport or search you, insist on a neutral witness—"*solamente con testigos.*" Be wary, too, of "plainclothes policemen." Ask to see identification, and never relinquish your documentation. And be especially wary if he asks a third party to verify his own credentials; they could be in league.

Many men are robbed by prostitutes or amorous encounters. Be suspicious of drinks offered by strangers; the beverage may be laced with a knockout drug.

Never allow yourself to be drawn into arguments (Costa Ricans are usually so placid that anyone with a temper is immediately to be suspected). And don't be distracted by people spilling things on you. These are ruses meant to distract you while an accomplice steals your valuables. Remain alert to the dark side of self-proclaimed good Samaritans.

Drugs

Drug trafficking and laundering of drug money has increased markedly since the ouster of Manuel Noriega from Panamá. And traffickers have been able to entice impoverished farmers into growing marijuana and cocaine, notably in the Talamancas of southern Puntarenas.

The Costa Rican government and U.S. Drug Enforcement Agency (DEA) has an ongoing anti-narcotics campaign. Penalties for possession or dealing are stiff. Article 14 of the Drug Law stipulates: "A jail sentence of eight to 20 years shall be imposed upon anyone who

© CHRISTOPHER P. BAKER

sign warning of riptides

participates in any way in international drug dealing." You will receive no special favors because you're foreign.

Riptides

Riptides cause the deaths by drowning of dozens of people every year in Costa Rica. Tides change from extremely low to extremely high, and the volume of water pouring onto or off the beach can be immense. Riptides are channels of water pulling out to sea at high speed. The period two hours before and two hours after low tide are most dangerous. Riptides are often identifiable by their still surface where surf is otherwise coming ashore. If you get caught in one, swim *parallel* to the shore; if you try to swim directly back to shore you will be unsuccessful, and you'll tire yourself out and possibly drown.

Currency

Costa Rica's currency is the colón (colones plural), which is written ¢ and sometimes colloquially called a peso. Notes are issued in the following denominations: 1,000 (red; called a *rojo*), 2,000 (called *dos rojos*), 5,000 (blue; called a *tucán*), and 10,000 (called a *jaguar*) colones; coins come in five, 10, 25, 50, and 100 colones (new coins are gold in color; old coins are silver in color). You may hear cash referred to colloquially as *efectivo* or *plata. Menudo* is loose change.

Most businesses accept payment in U.S. dollars, as do taxis. Other international currencies are generally not accepted. Many shopkeepers won't accept notes that are torn, however minute the tear, but will dispense such notes to you without guilt.

The value of the colón has fallen steadily against the U.S. dollar over the past few years. At press time the official exchange rate was approximately 570 colones to the dollar. All prices in this book are quoted in U.S. dollars unless otherwise indicated.

CHANGING MONEY

You can change money at Juan Santamaría Airport upon arrival; the bank is inside the departures terminal. Travel with small bills. Legally, money may be changed only at a bank or hotel cash desk. You are allowed to convert only $50 in colones to dollars when departing, so spend all your local currency before leaving.

Banks are normally open 9 A.M.–4 P.M., but hours vary. Foreign-exchange departments are often open longer. Don't expect fast service. At some banks you may have to stand in two lines: one to process the transaction, the other to receive your cash. It can sometimes take more than an hour. Ask to make sure you're in the correct line. Banks close during Easter, Christmas, New Year's, and other holidays.

Most hotels will exchange dollars for colones for guests; some will do so even for nonguests. Hotels offer similar exchange rates to banks.

Many hustlers offer money exchange on the street, although this is strictly illegal and dangerous (the Judicial Police say they receive between 10 and 15 complaints a day from tourists who've been ripped off while changing money on the street).

TRAVELERS CHECKS

Most businesses are reluctant to take travelers checks. You'll usually need your passport. You'll receive one or two colones less per dollar than if changing cash. Take small-denomination checks, and stick to the well-known international brands, such as **American Express** (www.americanexpress.com), **Citibank** (www.citibank.com), **Barclays** (www.barclays.com), or **Thomas Cook Currency Services** (www.thomascook.co.uk).

CREDIT CARDS

Most larger hotels, car rental companies, and travel suppliers, as well as larger restaurants and stores, will accept credit card payment. Visa is the most widely accepted, followed by MasterCard. Conversion is normally at the official exchange rate, although a 6 percent service charge may be added. You can also use your credit cards to get cash advances at banks (minimum $50); some banks will pay cash advances in colones only. Most banks accept Visa; very few accept MasterCard.

At least one bank in every major town now has 24-hour ATM (*cajero automatico*) for automatic credit. You'll need your PIN number. Stick to regular banking hours if possible in case of problems (such as the *cajero* not returning your card).

The **American Express** Express Cash system (tel. 800/528-4800, www.americanexpress.com) links your AmEx card to your U.S. checking account. You can withdraw up to $1,000 in a 21-day period; a $2 fee is charged for each transaction.

You can reach the major credit card companies from within Costa Rica by calling the following numbers:

- American Express, tel. 0800/012-3211
- MasterCard, tel. 0800/011-0184
- Visa International, tel. 0800/011-0030

The Credomatic office (Calle Central, Avenidas 3/5, tel. 506/2295-9898, 8 A.M.–7 P.M. Mon.–Fri., 9 A.M.–1 P.M. Sat.) is authorized to assist with American Express, Visa, and MasterCard replacement.

MONEY TRANSFERS

You can arrange wire transfers through **Western Union** (tel. 506/2283-6336 or 800/777-7777, www.westernunion.com), which has agencies throughout the country. **MoneyGram** (tel. 506/2295-9595 or 800/328-5678) provides similar service. In either case, funds are transferred almost immediately to be retrieved by the beneficiary with photo ID at any location. You'll be charged a hefty commission.

Major banks will arrange cash transfers from the United States for a small commission fee. Ask your bank for details of a "correspondent" bank in San José.

COSTS

Budget travelers should be able to get by on as little as $30 a day. Backpackers hotels will cost

$5–15 per night. A breakfast or lunch of *gallo pinto* will cost $2–4, and a dinner with beer at an *soda* (lunch-counter) should cost no more than $5. At the other end of the spectrum, the most expensive restaurants might run you $40 or more per head, and $300-a-night accommodation is available.

Your mode of transportation will make a difference. You can fly anywhere in the country for $50 or so, or travel by bus for less than $12. Renting a car will send your costs skyrocketing—a minimum of $45 a day, plus insurance ($15 per day minimum) and gas.

Haggling over prices is *not* a tradition in Costa Rica, except at street-side crafts stalls.

Restaurants (but not snack bars, or *sodas*), and most service businesses add a 13 percent sales tax. Tourist hotels add a 13 percent tax.

Tipping

Taxi drivers do not normally receive tips. Nor is tipping in restaurants the norm—restaurants automatically add both a 13 percent sales tax and a 10 percent service charge to your bill. Add an additional tip as a reward for exceptional service. Bellboys in classy hotels should receive $0.25–0.50 per bag, and chambermaids should get $1 per day. Tour guides normally are tipped $1–2 per person per day for large groups, and much more, at your discretion, for small, personalized tours. Again, don't tip if you had lousy service.

Maps and Tourist Information

TOURIST INFORMATION OFFICES

The **Costa Rican Tourism Institute** (Instituto Costarricense de Turismo, or ICT, www.visit-costarica.com) has a 24-hour toll-free tourist information line (tel. 800/343-6332) in the United States. You can request brochures. There are no ICT offices abroad. The ICT head office (tel. 506/2299-5800, fax 506/2291-5645) is on the north side of the General Cañas highway, in San José.

MAPS

The best all-round map is the 1:350,000 scale *National Geographic Adventure Map* (published by the National Geographic Society). Another good road map is a topographical 1:500,000 sheet published by **ITMB Publishing** (tel. 604/273-1400, www.itmb.com). And the **Neotropic Foundation** (tel. 506/2253-2130, www.neotropica.org) publishes a superb topographical map with nature reserves and parks emphasized. All are sold at gift stores throughout Costa Rica, as is the *Costa Rica Nature Atlas* (San José: Editorial Incafo), with detailed 1:200,000 scale maps and accounts of national parks and other sites.

In the U.S., **Omni Resources** (tel. 800/742-2677, www.omnimap.com) and **Treaty Oak** (tel. 512/326-4141, www.treatyoak.com) sell these maps.

In the U.K., try **Stanford's** (12-14 Long Acre, London WC2E 9LP, tel. 020/7836-1321, www.stanfords.co.uk). In Australia, try **The Map Shop** (6-10 Peel St., Adelaide, SA 5000, tel. 08/8231-2033, www.mapshop.net.au); in New Zealand, try **Auckland Map Centre** (Shop 3, 209 Queen St., National Bank Centre, Auckland, tel. 9/309-7725, www.aucklandmapcentre.co.nz).

The best commercial resource in Costa Rica is **Jiménez & Tanzi, Ltda.** (tel. 506/2233-8033, www.jitan.co.cr), with stores in major cities. Topographic maps and detailed city maps can be bought from the **Instituto Geográfica Nacional** (National Geographic Institute, Avenida 20, Calles 9/11, tel. 506/2523-2630, www.mopt.go.cr/ign, 7 A.M.–noon and 12:45–3:30 P.M. Mon.–Fri.).

OTHER SOURCES

The **National Archives** (tel. 506/2234-7223, www.archivocanioncal.go.cr, 8 A.M.–3 P.M. Mon.–Fri.), in San José's Barrio Zapote, nine blocks south and one block east of Plaza del Sol, has thousands of documents, maps, and photos dating back to 1539.

You can rent GPS from **Rutas Satelitales** (Calle 34, Avenidas 1/3, tel. 506/2256-1762, www.rsgps.net).

Film and Photography

EQUIPMENT
Digital cameras do away with the hassle of film and have the advantage of being more versatile in high-contrast lighting. Not least, you can change the ASA setting at whim according to changing light conditions: in the dark conditions of the gloomy rainforest, for example, you may want to set your ASA to a higher speed (say ASA400 or higher).

Bring extra batteries for light meters and flashes. Protect your lenses with a UV or skylight filter, and consider buying "warming," neutral-density, and/or polarizing filters, which can dramatically improve results. Keep your lenses clean and dry when not in use (believe it or not, there's even a tropical mildew that attacks coated lenses). Silica gel packs are essential to help protect your camera gear from moisture; use them if you carry your camera equipment inside a plastic bag.

SHOOTING TIPS
Midday is the worst time for photography. Early morning and late afternoon provide the best light; the wildlife is more active then, too. Use hoods on all your lenses to screen out ambient light. Don't underestimate the intensity of light when photographing in bright sunlight. In the forest, you'll need as much light as possible. Use a tripod, slow shutter speed, wide-open aperture, and higher ASA. Use a flash in daytime to "fill in" shaded subjects or dark objects surrounded by bright sunlight, such as people's faces.

Photo Etiquette
Ticos enjoy being photographed and will generally cooperate willingly, except in the Caribbean, where many people have a surly response to being photographed. Never assume an automatic right to take a personal photograph, however. Ask permission as appropriate. And respect an individual's right to refuse.

Communications and Media

POSTAL SERVICES
Correos de Costa Rica (tel. 800/900-2000, www.correos.go.cr), the nation's mail service, has been privatized and has improved markedly, although there is a long way to go. The situation is exacerbated by the lack of street addresses nationwide. There is a post office in every town and most villages (typically open Mon.–Fri. 6 A.M.–5 P.M.).

Airmail *(correo aereo)* to/from North America averages two weeks. To/from Europe, anticipate a minimum of three weeks; sea mail *(marítimo)* takes anywhere from six weeks to three months. Postcards cost 95 colones (approximately $0.25) to North America, and 115 colones to Europe; letters cost 155 colones (about $0.30) to North America, and 180 colones to Europe. Express mail costs about 400 colones more, and certified mail costs 500 colones, to North America. Operating hours vary; most post offices are open 7 A.M.–6 P.M. Monday–Friday and 7 A.M.–noon Saturday.

Mailing packages overseas is expensive. *Don't* seal your package. You must first take any package over two kilograms to the central post office for customs inspection. The *correo* courier service is most economical up to 20 kilograms (international service is said to now be efficient), after which it is best to use UPS or another private courier service.

Receiving Mail

Most people rent a post office box (*apartado*—abbreviated Apdo.—but increasingly written as "P.O. Box"). Costa Rican postal codes sometimes appear before the name of the town, or even after the *apartado* number (e.g., Apdo. 890-1000, San José, instead of Apdo. 890, San José 1000).

You can receive international mail c/o "Lista de Correos" at the central post office in San José (Lista de Correos, Correos Central, San José 1000), or any other large town. Each item costs $0.15. You must pick up your mail in person at window 17 in the hall at the southern end of the building on Calle 2. You need to show your passport. Mail is held for one month.

Incoming letters are filed alphabetically. Tell anyone you expect to write to you to *print* your surname legibly and to include the words "Central America." Also tell them not to send money or anything else of monetary value, nor to mail parcels larger than a magazine size envelope. For mail weighing more than two kilos, you'll need to make two or more visits to the Aduana (Customs) in Zapote, on the outskirts of San José; one visit to declare the contents, the second to pay duty.

Private Courier Services

The incidence of mail theft has spawned many private mail services. FedEx and DHL have offices in San José and a few other towns.

TELEPHONES

Costa Rica has an efficient direct-dial telephone system under the control of ICE, which has offices in most towns. ICE offers a far-from-comprehensive telephone directory online at www.amarillasdelice.com.

In March 2008 the country changed to an eight-digit system by adding "2" to the front of all existing numbers (but "8" for cellular numbers).

Public Phones

Public phone booths are found throughout the nation. In more remote spots, the public phone is usually at the village *pulpería,* or store. Most public phone booths now use phone cards, not coins. Coin phones accept only 5-, 10-, and 20-colones coins (only the old silver coins work). Wait for the dial tone (similar to that of U.S. phones) before inserting your coin. The coin will drop when your call is connected. Have subsequent coins ready to insert immediately when the beep indicating "time up" sounds, or you'll be cut off.

With phone cards, the cost of your call is automatically deducted from the value of the card. You buy them at ICE telephone agencies, banks, calling card vending machines, and stores. **CHIP cards** (1,000 and 2,000 colones) can be used in public phones by inserting in the slot and following the English-language instructions. **Viajera 199** cards ($10, $20, and 3,000 colones) are for touch-tone phones; dial 199, then 2 for instructions in English; then dial the card number, then 00, the country code, area code, and telephone number. **Colibri 197** cards (500 and 1,000 colones) are for in-country calls only. With 199 and 197 cards, you enter the code on the back of the card.

Local Calls

Local telephone calls within Costa Rica cost 4.10 colones per minute Monday–Friday and 2 colonies Saturday–Sunday, regardless of distance. Calls from your hotel room are considerably more expensive (and the more expensive the hotel, the more they jack up the fee). There are no area or city codes; simply dial the eight-digit number.

International Calls

The Costa Rica country code is 506. When calling Costa Rica from North America, dial 011 (the international code), then 506, followed by the eight-digit local number. For outbound calls from Costa Rica, dial 00, then the country code and local number. For an English-speaking international operator, dial 116, as well as to make collect calls (reverse the charges) or to charge to a credit card. Hotel operators can also connect you, although charges for calling from hotels are high. The easiest and least costly way to make direct calls is to bill to your credit card or phone card by calling one of the calling assistance operators.

You can direct dial to U.S. operators via AT&T (tel. 0800/011-4114), MCI (tel. 162 or 0800/012-2222), Sprint (tel. 163 or 0800/013-0123), or Worldcom (tel. 0800/014-4444), and to Canada (tel. 161 or 0800/015-1161) and the United Kingdom (tel. 167 or 0800/044-1044).

AT&T Language Line (tel. 0800/011-4114 in Costa Rica) will connect you with an interpreter. USADirect phones, found at key tourist locations, automatically link you with an AT&T operator.

Direct-dial international calls to North America cost $0.23 cents per minute; calls to the U.K., Europe and Australia cost $0.90 per minute. Cheaper rates apply between 8 P.M. and 7 A.M. and on weekends. However, those are from personal phones. Hotels add their own, often exorbitant, charges, plus government tax.

Cellular Phones

Costa Rica employs both GSM and TDMA systems, but the latter is not compatible with TDMA systems (such as Verizon in the U.S.) elsewhere. Any number of companies offer cellular phone rentals. Look in the Yellow Pages (Pápinas Amarillas) under "Telefonia Celular."

FAX

Most tourist hotels will permit you to use their fax for a small fee, as do most post offices. You can also send and receive faxes via **Radiográfica Costarricense** (RACSA, www.racsa.co.cr) or ICE (Insituto Costarricense de Electricidad. Most towns have one. Fax transmissions cost $7 per page to Europe, $5 to the United States.

INTERNET ACCESS

Costa Rica has scores of inexpensive cyber-cafés nationwide; rates vary. Many upscale hotels have telephone jacks for laptop plug-in (calls aren't cheap, however, as most hotels add a huge markup), and many hotels and other outlets have Wi-Fi (wireless fidelity) access for travelers with their own laptops with Wi-Fi capability.

Most post offices nationwide are equipped with Internet-connected computers available to the public. Radiográfica Costarricense (RACSA) and ICE (the Costa Rican Electricity Institute) operate the major website servers through a closely guarded monopoly. The service is inefficient, unreliable, and slow, especially in early evening.

KitCom (tel. 506/2234-65813, www.kitcom.net) is recommended for online services.

PUBLICATIONS
Local Publications

Costa Rica has three major dailies. *La Nación* (www.nacion.co.cr) is an excellent newspaper, up to international standards, with broad-based coverage of national and international affairs. *La República* and *La Prensa Libre* are lesser alternatives. *El Día* and the mass-market *Diario Extra* are sensationalist rags serving the lumpenproletariat with reports on sex, mayhem, and gore.

The weekly English-language *Tico Times* (tel. 506/2258-1558, www.ticotimes.net) is more analytical than its Costa Rican peers and diligently covers environmental issues, tourism, and cultural events. It's sold at newsstands and in hotels nationwide ($1). *Costa Rica Traveler* (tel. 506/2280-1837, www.cr-traveler.com) is a glossy bimonthly focused on tourism. And the bimonthly *Costa Rica Outdoors* (tel. 506/2231-0306, www.costaricaoutdoors.com) is dedicated to fishing and outdoor sports. And *Nature Landings,* the in-flight magazine of Nature Air, is full of fascinating articles.

International Publications

International newspapers and magazines are available at a few newsstands, bookstores, and upscale hotels. The *Miami Herald's* Latin American edition is printed in Costa Rica as an English daily. Away from large towns you'll be hard-pressed to find magazines and newspapers, Spanish-language or otherwise.

BROADCASTING

Costa Rica has more than a dozen TV stations. Satellite coverage from the United States is widely available and many hotels provide North American and European programming.

There are about 120 radio stations. The vast majority play Costa Rican music, and finding Western music isn't easy. One of my favorite stations is **Eco 95.7 FM,** which plays oldies and jazz and has world news and discussions. **Radio Dos,** 99.5 FM, plays "lovers' rock" and all-time classics and has news and traffic reports in English. Classical music fans are served by **Radio Universidad,** 870 AM and 96.7 FM (which also plays jazz). Jazz lovers should tune to **95.5 FM Jazz.**

Weights, Measures, and Time

WEIGHTS AND MEASURES

Costa Rica operates on the metric system. Liquids are sold in liters, fruits and vegetables by the kilo. Some of the old Spanish measurements still survive in vernacular usage. Street directions, for example, are often given as 100 *varas* (the Spanish "yard," equal to 33 inches) to indicate a city block. See the chart at the back of this book for metric conversions.

TIME

Costa Rica time is equivalent to U.S. Central Standard Time (six hours behind Greenwich mean time, one hour behind New York, two hours ahead of California). Costa Rica has no daylight saving time, during which time it is *seven* hours behind Greenwich and *two* hours behind New York. There is little seasonal variation in dawn (approximately 6 A.M.) and dusk (6 P.M.).

BUSINESS HOURS

Businesses are usually open 8 A.M.–5 P.M. Monday–Friday. A few also open Saturday morning. Lunch breaks are often two hours; businesses and government offices may close 11:30 A.M.–1:30 P.M. Bank hours vary widely, but in general are open from between 8:15 A.M. or 9 A.M. and 3 P.M. to 3:45 P.M. Most shops open 8 A.M.–6 P.M. Monday–Saturday. Some restaurants close Sunday and Monday. Most businesses also close on holidays.

ELECTRICITY

Costa Rica operates on 110-volts AC (60-cycle) nationwide. Some remote lodges are not connected to the national grid and generate their own power. Check in advance to see if they run on direct current (DC) or a nonstandard voltage. Two types of U.S. plugs are used: flat, parallel two-pins and three rectangular pins. A two-prong adapter is a good idea (most hardware stores in Costa Rica—*ferreterías*—can supply them).

Power surges are common. If you plan on using a laptop computer, use a surge protector. Take a flashlight and spare batteries. A couple of long-lasting candles are also a good idea. Don't forget the matches or a lighter.

RESOURCES

Glossary

abastacedor small grocery

alacrán scorpion

a la leña oven-roasted

albergue hostel

almuerzo ejecutivo business lunch (set menu)

apartado post office box (written Apdo.)

apartotel self-catering hotel with kitchen units

arribada mass arrival of marine turtles

arroz con pollo rice with chicken

autopista freeway

avenida avenue

balneario swimming pool

barrio district

batido milk shake

beneficio coffee-processing factory

biblioteca library

boca bar snack

bola ball (refers to the large granite balls from Golfo Dulce)

boyero oxcart driver

cabina refers to any budget accommodation

cafetalero coffee baron

calle street

campesino small-scale farmer or peasant

campo countryside

canton county

carreta traditional oxcart

carretera road

casado set lunch (literally "married")

casita small house, cottage

cayuco canoe

cerveza beer

chorizo corruption, bribery, a poor grade of bacon

circunvalación ring-road

cocodrilo crocodile

colón local currency

comida típica local food

cordillera mountain chain

costeños coastal people

danta tapir

empanada stuffed turnover

encomienda feudal servitude

estero estuary

fiesta party

fiesta cívica civic fiesta

finca farm

gallo pinto rice, beans, and fried egg

gasolinera gas station

grano de oro coffee bean

guaro a cheap liquor

guayaba guava

hacienda large farmstead, cattle ranch

helado ice cream

hornilla geysers

hospedaje lodging

invierno "winter" (refers to summer wet season)

lancha motorized boat, ferry

lapa roja scarlet macaw

lapa verde green macaw

lavandería laundry

manglar mangrove

manigordo ocelot

manzanillo manchineel tree

mapache northern raccoon

marisquería seafood restaurant or outlet

mercado market

mirador lookout point

mola stitched appliqué fabric

mono carablanca capuchin monkey
mono colorado spider monkey
mono congo howler monkey
mono titi squirrel monkey
murciélago bat
museo museum
orero gold-miner
palenque thatched roof
palmito heart of palm
panga small motorized boat
parada bus stop
páramo high-altitude savanna
pastelería bakery
pejibaye bright orange palm fruit
peña an intellectual soirée where poems are read, music played, and bonhomie shared
pensionado pensioner
perezoso sloth
pila mud pond
pizote coatimundi

plato fuerte main dish
playa beach
pulpería small grocery
purruja no-see-um, tiny insect
ranchito open-sided thatched structure
refresco soda pop or fruit juice
sabanero cowboy
selva jungle
soda simple eatery, usually open to the street
tamandua lesser anteater
tepezcuintle a large rodent, also called a *paca*
terciopelo fer-de-lance – a fearsome snake
Tica female Costa Rican
Tico male Costa Rican
topes equestrian show
tráfico traffic police
trapiche ox-driven sugar mill
venado deer
verano "summer" (refers to winter dry season)
vivero hatchery or nursery

Spanish Phrasebook

PRONUNCIATION GUIDE
Consonants
c as 'c' in "cat," before 'a,' 'o,' or 'u'; like 's' before 'e' or 'i'
d as 'd' in "dog," except between vowels, then like 'th' in "that"
g before 'e' or 'i,' like the 'ch' in Scottish "loch"; elsewhere like 'g' in "get"
h always silent
j like the English 'h' in "hotel," but stronger
ll like the 'y' in "yellow"
ñ like the 'ni' in "onion"
r always pronounced as strong 'r'
rr trilled 'r'
v similar to the 'b' in "boy" (not as English 'v')
y similar to English, but with a slight "j" sound. When y stands alone it is pronounced like the 'e' in "me."
z like 's' in "same"
b, f, k, l, m, n, p, q, s, t, w, x, z as in English

Vowels
a as in "father," but shorter
e as in "hen"
i as in "machine"
o as in "phone"
u usually as in "rule"; when it follows a 'q' the 'u' is silent; when it follows an 'h' or 'g' it's pronounced like 'w,' except when it comes between 'g' and 'e' or 'i,' when it's also silent

NUMBERS
0 *cero*
1 *uno* (masculine), *una* (feminine)
2 *dos*
3 *tres*
4 *cuatro*
5 *cinco*
6 *seis*
7 *siete*
8 *ocho*
9 *nueve*
10 *diez*
11 *once*
12 *doce*
13 *trece*

14 *catorce*
15 *quince*
16 *dieciseis*
17 *diecisiete*
18 *dieciocho*
19 *diecinueve*
20 *veinte*
21 *vientiuno*
30 *treinta*
40 *cuarenta*
50 *cincuenta*
60 *sesenta*
70 *setenta*
80 *ochenta*
90 *noventa*
100 *cien*
101 *cientouno*
200 *doscientos*
1,000 *mil*
10,000 *diez mil*

DAYS OF THE WEEK

Sunday *domingo*
Monday *lunes*
Tuesday *martes*
Wednesday *miércoles*
Thursday *jueves*
Friday *viernes*
Saturday *sábado*

TIME

What time is it? *¿Qué hora es?*
one o'clock *la una*
two o'clock *las dos*
at two o'clock *a las dos*
ten past three *las tres y diez*
six A.M. *las seis de la mañana*
six P.M. *las seis de la tarde*
today *hoy*
tomorrow, morning *mañana, la mañana*
yesterday *ayer*
week *semana*
month *mes*
year *año*
last night *la noche pasada* or *anoche*
next day *el próximo día* or *al día siguiente*

USEFUL WORDS AND PHRASES

Hello. *Hola.*
Good morning. *Buenos días.*
Good afternoon. *Buenas tardes.*
Good evening. *Buenas noches.*
How are you? *¿Cómo está?*
Fine. *Muy bien.*
And you? *¿Y usted?* (formal) or *¿Y tú?* (familiar)
So-so. *Así así.*
Thank you. *Gracias.*
Thank you very much. *Muchas gracias.*
You're very kind. *Usted es muy amable.*
You're welcome; literally, "It's nothing." *De nada.*
yes *sí*
no *no*
I don't know. *no sé* or *no lo sé*
It's fine; okay *está bien*
good; okay *bueno*
please *por favor*
Pleased to meet you. *Mucho gusto.*
Excuse me. (physical) *perdóneme*
Excuse me. (speech) *discúlpeme*
I'm sorry. *Lo siento.*
Goodbye. *Adiós.*
See you later; literally, "until later" *hasta luego*
more *más*
less *menos*
better *mejor*
much *mucho*
a little *un poco*
large *grande*
small *pequeño*
quick *rápido*
slowly *despacio*
bad *malo*
difficult *difícil*
easy *fácil*
He/She/It is gone; as in "She left," "He's gone" *Ya se fue.*
I don't speak Spanish well. *No hablo bien español.*
I don't understand. *No entiendo.*
How do you say . . . in Spanish? *¿Cómo se dice . . . en español?*

Do you understand English? *¿Entiende el inglés?*
Is English spoken here? (Does anyone here speak English?) *¿Se habla inglés aquí?*

TERMS OF ADDRESS

I *yo*
you (formal) *usted*
you (familiar) *tú*
he/him *él*
she/her *ella*
we/us *nosotros*
you (plural) *ustedes*
they/them (all males or mixed gender) *ellos*
they/them (all females) *ellas*
Mr., sir *señor*
Mrs., madam *señora*
Miss, young lady *señorita*
wife *esposa*
husband *marido or esposo*
friend *amigo* (male), *amiga* (female)
sweetheart *novio* (male), *novia* (female)
son, daughter *hijo, hija*
brother, sister *hermano, hermana*
father, mother *padre, madre*

GETTING AROUND

Where is . . . ? *¿Dónde está . . . ?*
How far is it to . . . ? *¿Qué tan lejos está a . . . ?*
from . . . to . . . *de . . . a . . .*
highway *la carretera*
road *el camino*
street *la calle*
block *la cuadra*
kilometer *kilómetro*
north *el norte*
south *el sur*
west *el oeste*
east *el este*
straight ahead *al derecho or adelante*
to the right *a la derecha*
to the left *a la izquierda*

ACCOMMODATIONS

Can I (we) see a room? *¿Puedo (podemos) ver una habitación?*

What is the rate? *¿Cuál es el precio?*
a single room *una habitación sencilla*
a double room *una habitación doble*
key *llave*
bathroom *retrete or lavabo*
bath *baño*
hot water *agua caliente*
cold water *agua fría*
towel *toalla*
soap *jabón*
toilet paper *papel sanitario*
air conditioning *aire acondicionado*
fan *abanico, ventilador*
blanket *cubierta or manta*

PUBLIC TRANSPORT

bus stop *la parada de la guagua*
main bus terminal *la central camionera*
airport *el aeropuerto*
ferry terminal *la terminal del transbordador*
I want a ticket to . . . *Quiero un tiqué a . . .*
I want to get off at . . . *Quiero bajar en . . .*
Here, please. *Aquí, por favor.*
Where is this bus going? *¿Dónde va este guagua?*
round-trip *ida y vuelta*
What do I owe? *¿Cuánto le debo?*

FOOD

menu *carta, menú*
glass *taza*
fork *tenedor*
knife *cuchillo*
spoon *cuchara, cucharita*
napkin *servilleta*
soft drink *refresco*
coffee, cream *café, crema*
tea *té*
sugar *azúcar*
drinking water *agua pura, agua potable*
bottled carbonated water *club soda*
bottled uncarbonated water *agua sin gas*
beer *cerveza*
wine *vino*
milk *leche*
juice *jugo*
eggs *huevos*
bread *pan*

watermelon *patilla*
banana *plátano*
apple *manzana*
orange *naranja*
meat (without) *carne (sin)*
beef *carne de res*
chicken *pollo*
fish *pescado*
shellfish *camarones, mariscos*
fried *frito*
roasted *asado*
barbecue, barbecued *barbacoa, al carbón, or a la parilla*
breakfast *desayuno*
lunch *almuerzo*
dinner (often eaten in late afternoon) *comida*
dinner, or a late night snack *cena*
the check *la cuenta*

MAKING PURCHASES
I need . . . *Necesito . . .*
I want . . . *Deseo . . . or Quiero . . .*
I would like...(more polite) *Quisiera . . .*

How much does it cost? *¿Cuánto cuesta?*
What's the exchange rate? *¿Cuál es el tipo de cambio?*
Can I see . . . ? *¿Puedo ver . . . ?*
this one *ésta/ésto*
expensive *caro*
cheap *barato*
cheaper *más barato*
too much *demasiado*

HEALTH
Help me please. *Ayúdeme por favor.*
I am ill. *Estoy enfermo.*
pain *dolor*
fever *fiebre*
stomachache *dolor de estómago*
vomiting *vomitar*
diarrhea *diarrea*
drugstore *farmacia*
medicine *medicina*
pill, tablet *pastilla*
birth control pills *pastillas anticonceptivas*
condoms *condomes, gomas*

Suggested Reading

GENERAL INFORMATION
Koutnik, Jane. *Costa Rica: A Quick Guide to Customs & Etiquette.* Portland, OR: Graphic Arts Books, 2005. Concise yet detailed insight into the local culture.

Ras, Barbara, ed. *Costa Rica: A Traveler's Literary Companion.* San Francisco: Whereabouts Press, 1994. Twenty-six stories by Costa Rican writers that reflect the ethos of the country.

NATURE AND WILDLIFE
Allen, William. *Green Phoenix: Restoring the Tropical Forests of Guanacaste.* Oxford: Oxford University Press, 2006. A wonderful read, this powerfully engaging book tells the story of the remarkable, and successful, efforts to resurrecting Costa Rica's ravaged dry forests.

Beletsky, Les. *The Ecotravellers' Wildlife Guide to Costa Rica.* San Diego: Academia Press, 2002. A superbly illustrated volume for nature lovers.

Boza, Mario, and A. Bonilla. *The National Parks of Costa Rica.* Madrid: INCAFO, 1999. Available in both hardbound coffee-table and less bulky softbound versions, as well as in a handy pocket-size edition. Lots of superb photos. Highly readable, too.

Carr, Archie F. *The Windward Road.* Gainesville: University of Florida Press, 1955. A sympathetic book about the sea turtles of Central America.

DeVries, Philip J. *The Butterflies of Costa Rica and Their Natural History.* Princeton, NJ:

Princeton University Press, 1987. A well-illustrated and thorough lepidopterist's guide.

Emmons, Louise H. *Neotropical Rainforest Mammals—A Field Guide*. Chicago: University of Chicago Press, 1997. A thorough yet compact book detailing mammal species throughout the neotropics.

Fogden, Michael and Patricia. *Hummingbirds of Costa Rica*. Richmond Hill, Canada: Firefly Books, 2006. Lavishly illustrated coffee-table book.

Fogden, Michael and Susan. *Photographic Field Guide to the Birds of Costa Rica*. Sanibel Island, FL: Ralph Curtis Publishing, 2005. Superbly illustrated, pocket-sized guide.

Garigues, Richard & Robert Dean. *The Birds of Costa Rica: A Field Guide*. Ithaca, NY: Cornell University Press, 2007. A splendidly illustrated guide written by one of Costa Rica's foremost ornithologists.

Henderson, Carrol L. *Field Guide to the Wildlife of Costa Rica*. Austin: University of Texas Press, 2002. This weighty tome provides a thorough layman's treatment of individual wildlife species, but it's a bit too bulky for the road. Most species are shown in color photographs.

Herrera, Wilberth. *Costa Rica Nature Atlas-Guidebook*. San José: Editorial Incafo, 1992. A very useful and readable guide to parks, reserves, and other areas of interest. Text is supported by stunning photos and detailed maps showing roads and gas stations.

INBio. *Colección Guías de Campo de Costa Rica*. San José: Instituto Nacional de Biodiversidad (INBio). This series of beautifully illustrated pocket-size nature guides offers 10 titles, including *Mammals of Costa Rica, Birds of Costa Rica,* and *Snakes of Costa Rica*. plus separate titles on arboreal ferns; bees, wasps, and ants; beetles; bromeliads; flying insects; mushrooms and fungi; scorpions; and ornamental plants.

Janzen, Daniel, ed. *Costa Rican Natural History*. Chicago: University of Chicago Press, 1983. Weighty, large-format, it's the bible for scientific insight into individual species of flora and fauna. With 174 contributors.

Perry, Donald. *Life Above the Jungle Floor*. New York: Simon & Schuster, 1986. A fascinating account of life in the forest canopy, relating Perry's scientific studies at Rara Avis.

Savage, Jay M. *The Amphibians and Reptiles of Costa Rica*. Chicago: University of Chicago Press, 2005. The most comprehensive treatment of amphibian and reptile ecology, with in-depth information on 396 species.

Stiles, F. Gary, and Alexander Skutch. *A Guide to the Birds of Costa Rica*. Ithaca, NY: Cornell University Press, 1989. A superbly illustrated compendium for serious birders.

Wainwright, Mark. *The Natural History of Costa Rica: Mammals*. San José: Zona Tropical, 2003. A splendid companion for naturalists, with identifying charts and lots of esoteric information.

Wallace, David R. *The Quetzal and the Macaw: The Story of Costa Rica's National Parks*. San Francisco: Sierra Club Books, 1992. An entertaining history of the formation of Costa Rica's national park system.

Zuckowski, Willow. *A Guide to Tropical Plants of Costa Rica*. San José, Costa Rica: Zona Tropical, 2006. Beautifully illustrated field guide.

Zuckowski, Willow and Turid Forsyth. *Tropical Plants of Costa Rica: A Guide to Native and Exotic Flora*. Ithaca, NY: Cornell University Press, 2007. More than 500 photographs.

HISTORY, POLITICS, AND SOCIAL STRUCTURE

Biesanz, Richard, et al. *The Ticos: Culture and Social Change in Costa Rica*. Boulder, CO: Lynne Reinner, 1999. This essential work for understanding Tico culture is an updated version of its popular forerunner, *The Costa Ricans*.

Booth, Thomas. *Costa Rica: Quest for Democracy*. Boulder CO, Westview Press, 1999. The story of how the fight to establish and sustain democracy in Costa Rica.

Daling, Tjabel. *Costa Rica In Focus: A Guide to the People, Politics, and Culture*. Northampton, MA: Interlink, 2001. A general and insightful review of national culture.

Molina Jiménez, Ivan (ed) and Steven Palmer (ed). *The Costa Rica Reader: History, Culture, Politics*. Durham, NC: Duke University Press, 2004. Essential background reading and the most thoughtful and readable academic account of the nation.

Wallerstein, Claire. *Culture Shock! Costa Rica*. Portland, OR: Graphic Arts, 2003. Insights into what makes Ticos tick.

TRAVEL GUIDES

Aritio, Luis Blas, ed. *Costa Rica National Parks Guide*. San José: INCAFO, 2003. Compact and lavishly illustrated pocket guide provides succinct and detailed information on the national parks.

Eudy, Lee. *Chasing Jaguars: The Complete Guide to Costa Rican Whitewater*. Chapel Hill, NC: Earthbound Sports, 2003. This is a comprehensive profile on 40 of the country's best white-water runs, with maps.

Mead, Rowland. *Travel Atlas: Costa Rica*. London, UK: New Holland Publishers, 2007. Illustrated with color photographs, with 86 maps to the country.

Pariser, Mike. *The Surfer's Guide to Costa Rica*. San José, Costa Rica: Surf Press, 2005. Well-rounded guidebook for the wave-seeking set.

LIVING IN COSTA RICA

Howard, Christopher. *The New Golden Door to Retirement and Living in Costa Rica*, 14th ed. San José: C.R. Books, 2005. A splendid comprehensive guide to making the break.

Van Rheenen, Erin. *Moon Living Abroad in Costa Rica*. Emeryville, CA: Avalon Travel, 2007. The definitive guide to living in Costa Rica also includes highly useful information for travelers passing through.

Internet Resources

TRAVEL

www.centralamerica.com
CentralAmerica.com is one of the largest and best Central America-related travel sites on the Net and is categorized into sections for maps, national parks, recommended hotels, day tours, transportation, activities, etc. It offers online booking.

www.crexpeditions.com
Website of Costa Rica Expeditions, one of the leading travel operators specializing in nature adventures.

www.distinctivehotels.com
For travelers with a taste for elegance, this site represents eight of the most endearing hotels in the country, marketed under the umbrella of Small Distinctive Hotels of Costa Rica.

www.flysansa.com
Costa Rica's state-owned regional airline.

Online reservations. Also linked to the websites of affiliate Central American airlines.

www.natureair.com
Website of privately owned Nature Air, serving Costa Rica and Panamá.

www.visitcostarica.com
The official website of the Costa Rican Tourism Boards offers search capability plus online reservations.

ACTIVITIES
www.costaricaoutdoors.com
The first-stop site for anglers and active travelers.

ECOTOURISM
www.ecotourism.org
The website of the International Ecotourism Society serves anyone interested in responsible travel.

www.turismo-sostenible.co.cr
Overseen by the Costa Rican Tourism Institute (ICT), this site lets you differentiate tourism sector businesses based on the degree to which they comply with a sustainable model of natural, cultural, and social resource management. It has a search tool for finding individual hotels.

GENERAL INFORMATION
www.costarica.com
This broad-ranging site offers something for everyone, from classifieds and culture to real estate and retirement living.

www.costarica.net
Spans the spectrum of possibilities, from real estate to a language translator. Includes a large travel section.

www.infocostarica.com
One of the most comprehensive sites, provides links that will meet most needs of travelers, businessfolk, and anyone else with a lay interest.

www.insidecostarica.com
Excellent English-language news source, with sections on travel and real estate.

www.sinaccr.net
Website of the Sistema Nacional de Áreas de Conservación, with information on individual national parks and wildlife reserves. Solely in Spanish at press time.

GOVERNMENT
www.casapres.go.cr
The official site of the Costa Rican President, with links to all of the government ministries, national institutions, and government-owned banks.

NEWS AND PUBLICATIONS
www.amcostarica.com
The website of A.M. Costa Rica, a daily English-language news source for issues relating to Costa Rica. It also has a classified ad section, job listings, restaurant reviews, and an entertainment section.

www.nacion.com/ln_ee/english
The website of the nation's foremost newspaper, *La Nación,* is the best source by which to catch up on daily events in Costa Rica.

www.ticotimes.net
The online edition of *The Tico Times,* the excellent English-language daily published in Costa Rica provides a brief capsule of stories appearing every Friday in the print edition.

TELEPHONE DIRECTORIES
www.ice.co.cr
Website of ICE (Costa Rica Institute of Electricity), the nation's telephone company. It has both white- and yellow-page online directories, although they feature only a small percentage of actual numbers.

Index

List of Maps